# EDUCATIONAL PSYCHOLOGY

WOOLFOLK
WINNE
PERRY

SIXTH CANADIAN EDITION

PEARSON

Toronto

To William James, who wisely said in *Talks to Teachers* (1899),

"Psychology is a science, and teaching is an art; and sciences never generate arts directly out of themselves. An intermediary inventive mind must make the application, by using its originality."

and also

To all the inventive minds reading this book whose originality will prove James right.

—A.W.

In memory of missed parents, Bill Perry and Jean and Hawley Winne, and to family, friends, and students who continue to teach us the joys of life and learning.

—P.H.W.
—N.E.P.

Vice-President, CMPS: Gary Bennett
Editorial Director: Claudine O'Donnell
Executive Acquisitions Editor: Kimberley Veevers
Marketing Manager: Michelle Bish
Program Manager: John Polanszky
Project Manager: Susan Johnson
Team Lead, Development:
    Suzanne Schaan
Senior Developmental Editor: Lise Dupont
Media Editor: Lila Campbell
Media Producer: Bogdan Kosenko

Production Services: Yasmita Hota,
    Cenveo® Publisher Services
Permissions Project Manager: Erica Mojzes
Photo Permissions Research: James Fortney,
    Lumina Datamatics
Text Permissions Research: Jamey O'Quinn,
    Lumina Datamatics
Cover Designer: Alex Li
Interior Designer: Jerilyn Brockorick,
    Cenveo Publisher Services
Cover Image: John Foxx Collection/Imagestate

Credits and acknowledgments for material borrowed from other sources and reproduced, with permission, in this textbook appear on the appropriate page within the text.

Original edition published by Pearson Education, Inc., Upper Saddle River, New Jersey, USA. Copyright © 2013 Pearson Education, Inc. This edition is authorized for sale only in Canada.

If you purchased this book outside the United States or Canada, you should be aware that it has been imported without the approval of the publisher or the author.

**Library and Archives Canada Cataloguing in Publication**

Woolfolk, Anita, author
    Educational psychology / Woolfolk, Winne, Perry.—Sixth Canadian edition.

Includes bibliographical references and index.
ISBN 978-0-13-310529-2 (paperback).—ISBN 978-0-13-428360-9 (paperback)

    1. Educational psychology—Textbooks.  I. Winne, Philip H., author
II. Perry, Nancy E. (Nancy Ellen), 1962-, author III. Title.

LB1051.W73 2015                 370.15            C2015-900043-2

ISBN: 978-0-13-428360-9

# ABOUT THE AUTHORS

So you will know the authors a bit better, here is some information.

**Anita Woolfolk Hoy** was born in Fort Worth, Texas, where her mother taught child development at Texas Christian University and her father was an early worker in the computer industry. She is a Texas Longhorn—all her degrees are from the University of Texas, Austin, the last one a Ph.D. After graduating, she was a psychologist working with children in elementary and secondary schools in 15 counties of central Texas. She began her career in higher education as a professor of educational psychology at Rutgers University, and then moved to The Ohio State University in 1994. Anita's research focuses on motivation and cognition, specifically students' and teachers' sense of efficacy and teachers' beliefs about education. She is the editor of *Theory Into Practice,* a journal that brings the best ideas from research to practicing educators. With students and colleagues, she has published over 80 books, book chapters, and research articles. Anita has served as Vice-President for Division K (Teaching & Teacher Education) of the American Educational Research Association and President of Division 15 (Educational Psychology) of the American Psychological Association. Just before completing this twelfth edition of *Educational Psychology,* she collaborated with Nancy Perry, of the University of British Columbia, to write the second edition of *Child and Adolescent Development* (Pearson, 2015), a book for all those who work with and love children. Her next project is the fourth edition of *Instructional Leadership: A Research-Based Guide to Learning in School* (Pearson), written with her husband, Wayne K. Hoy, the Novice Fawcett Chair of Educational Administration at The Ohio State University.

**Philip H. Winne** received his Ph.D. from Stanford University, accepted a position at Simon Fraser University in 1975, and has happily worked there his entire career. At SFU, he is Professor and Associate Dean for Graduate Studies and Research in the Faculty of Education. His research accomplishments earned him a Tier I Canada Research Chair in Self-Regulated Learning & Learning Technologies and election as a Fellow of the American Educational Research Association, the American Psychological Association, the Association for Psychological Science, and the Canadian Psychological Association. His research interests include self-regulated learning, metacognition, motivation, study tactics and learning strategies, adaptive software for research, and promoting self-regulated learning. To pursue these topics, he leads a team developing state-of-the-art software called nStudy. As students use nStudy to study online, it collects extensive and detailed data about how they study. He has published more than 150 scholarly works and served as President of the Canadian Educational Researchers' Association, the Canadian Association for Educational Psychology, and Division 15–Educational Psychology of the American Psychological Association. With Patricia Alexander, he co-edited the *Handbook of Educational Psychology* (second edition) as well as the field-leading journal *Educational Psychologist (*2001–2005), co-edited with Lyn Corno. He has served as Associate Editor of the *British Journal of Educational Psychology* for 16 years, and currently is a member of the editorial board of nine other leading journals in the field.

**Nancy Perry** worked as a classroom and resource teacher in school districts in British Columbia, Canada, before obtaining her Ph.D. from the University of Michigan in 1996. Today, she is Professor of Educational and Counselling Psychology, and Special Education at the University of British Columbia (UBC). There, she teaches graduate courses in two program areas—Human Development, Learning, and Culture; and Special Education—as well as teaching students in a B.Ed. cohort that focuses on self-regulated learning (SRL). She is a recipient of UBC's Killam Teaching Prize and holds the UBC-endowed Professorship for the Faculty of Education's Struggling Youth Initiative. Her research examines the role of tasks, instructional practices, and interpersonal relationships in promoting motivation and self-regulation in school. Related projects are profiled at her website: "Seeding Success through Motivation and Self-Regulation in Schools," http://self-regulationinschool.research.educ.ubc.ca. In addition to these teaching and research activities, Nancy is Associate Editor for the *Journal of Learning and Instruction* and President Elect of Division 15, Educational Psychology, of the American Psychological Association. She is a Past President of the Canadian Association for Educational Psychology and has served on the Executive Boards of the Canadian Association for Studies in Education and, previously, Division 15, Educational Psychology, of APA as Member at Large.

# PREFACE

Many of you reading this book are enrolled in an educational psychology course as part of your professional preparation for teaching, counselling, speech therapy, nursing, or psychology. The material in this text should be of interest to everyone who is concerned about education and learning, from the Kindergarten volunteer to the instructor in a community program for adults with disabilities. No background in psychology or education is necessary to understand this material. It is as free of jargon and technical language as possible, and many people have worked to make this edition clear, relevant, and interesting.

Since the first edition of *Educational Psychology* appeared, there have been many exciting developments in the field. The sixth Canadian edition continues to emphasize the educational implications and applications of research on child development, cognitive science, learning, motivation, teaching, and assessment. Theory and practice are not separated in the text, but are considered together. The book is written to show how information and ideas drawn from research in educational psychology can be applied to solve the everyday problems of teaching. To help you explore the connections between research and practice, you will find in these pages a wealth of examples, lesson segments, case studies, guidelines, and even practical tips from experienced teachers. As you read this book, we believe you will see the immense value and usefulness of educational psychology. The field offers unique and crucial knowledge to any who dare to teach and to all who love to learn.

## NEW CONTENT IN THE SIXTH CANADIAN EDITION

Across the book, there is increased coverage of a number of important topics. The key content revisions are described below:

### Chapter 1: Learning, Teaching, and Educational Psychology

- A new section is introduced called **Differentiated Instruction**, which includes:
  - A **Stop & Think** box, which describes the scenario where a teacher gives a practice test and finds that the lesson plans he/she prepared are not fitted to the students
  - A new section called **Why Do We Need Differentiated Instruction?**, which sets up the factors that lead to diversity in classrooms
- The section called **Elements of Differentiation** sets up differentiation in curriculum and instruction.

### Chapter 2: Cognitive Development

- The section called **Adolescent Development and the Brain** discusses how the teenage brain is not fully developed and how teachers can help students navigate risks and decision making. New research is used to discuss how sleep patterns of teenagers can affect their performance.
- The section called **Putting It All Together: How the Brain Works** uses new research to discuss how our cultural differences affect our brains and information processing.
- A new section called **Neuroscience, Learning, and Teaching** incorporates the following:
  - **Instruction and Brain Development** describes current research, which demonstrates how teaching instruction affects brain activity.
  - A **Stop & Think** box questions how teachers can be aware of neuroscience.

- Point/Counterpoint box: **Brain-Based Education** debates the question "Are there clear educational implications from the neuroscience research on the brain?" using up-to-date research from 1999–2013.
- **Lessons for Teachers: General Principles** is a list of implications drawn from four researchers about neuroscience and teaching.
- New research from Kurt Fischer (2009), under the subhead **Information Processing and Neo-Piagetian Views of Cognitive Development**, explains that while different skills are developed separately, there are predictable levels of development and no development stage occurs in isolation.
- New sections called **Technical Tools in a Digital Age** and **Psychological Tools** make a case for tools that allow for higher mental processing, like the calculator, and recent research expands on developing a cultural toolkit.

## Chapter 3: Self and Social and Moral Development

- The section called **The Adolescent Years** has been expanded to discuss early development, popularity, and feeling normal.
- A new Guidelines box appears: **Supporting Positive Body Images**.
- A **Society and Media** section discusses how heavily students use technology and social media to connect with friends and how this is distracting in a classroom.
- An **Identity and Technology** section explores how identity develops when parents are constantly connected to others (e.g., to their parents via cellphones) and how people can maintain multiple identities online.

## Chapter 4: Learner Differences and Learning Needs

- The section called **Possible Biases in the Application of Labels** explains the likely causes of over- and underrepresentations.
- **Multiple Intelligences: Lessons for Teachers** showcases Gardner's two lessons for teachers.
- The **Neuroscience and Learning Challenges** section discusses current research on how injury or disease can lead to learning disabilities.
- The section called **Characteristics of Students With Hyperactivity and Attention Disorders** is updated with the latest research.

## Chapter 5: Language Development, Language Diversity, and Immigrant Education

- Content on language development and learning has been consolidated and expanded in a new chapter, including discussions of diversity in language development and bilingualism, dialects in the classroom, teaching immigrant students, and the special challenges in teaching English Language Learners who have learning disabilities or special gifts.

## Chapter 6: Culture and Diversity

- Research is updated in the **Poverty and School Achievement** section to reflect current statistics on poverty and single-parent homes.
- New Guidelines box: **Teaching Students Who Live in Poverty**.
- The section called **Ethnicity and Race Differences in Teaching and Learning** offers updated 2013 Statistics Canada data on diversity in Canada.

## Chapter 7: Behavioural Views of Learning

- New table appears titled **A Simple Structured Observation Guide for Functional Behavioural Analysis Using the ABC Frame**.

## Chapter 8: Cognitive Views of Learning

- A new section called **Attention and Multitasking** appears.
- New content in the section called **Working Memory** focuses on the research of Alan Baddeley and colleagues, who developed the model of working memory.
- New table appears called **Three Kinds of Cognitive Load**.
- New Guidelines box: **Organizing Learning**.
- New section appears called **Individual Differences and Long-Term Memory**.

## Chapter 9: Complex Cognitive Process

- **Lessons for Teachers: Developing Metacognition** explores research with younger, secondary, and university students.
- The **Reaching Every Student** section is reframed from Students with Learning Disabilities to **Learning Strategies for Struggling Students.** The writing strategy called DEFENDS has been replaced with up-to-date research and a new strategy called LINCS Vocabulary Strategy.
- New table: **What Is a Critical Thinker?**
- **Argumentation** section discusses how the skills of argumentation take time and instruction to learn.

## Chapter 10: The Learning Sciences and Constructivism

- New section appears called **Embodied Cognition**.
- Point/Counterpoint box added: **Are Inquiry and Problem-Based Learning Effective Teaching Approaches?**
- The section called **Preparing Students for Cooperative Learning** now reflects data from 2009.
- Several new sections discuss the impact of technology. See **Learning Environments and Technology, Virtual Learning Environments, Developmentally Appropriate Computer Activities for Young Children,** and **Computers and Older Students**.
- Seven new terms introduced: **cloud computing, virtual learning environments (VLEs), learning management system (LMS), personal learning environment (PLE), personal learning network (PLN), immersive virtual learning environment (IVLE),** and **massive multi-player online games (MMOGs)**.

## Chapter 11: Social Cognitive Views of Learning and Motivation

- **Stop & Think** box: **Elements of Observational Learning** explains who a teacher's role model is.
- New sections appear devoted to the topics of **Attention, Retention, Production,** and **Motivation and Reinforcement**.
- New section is introduced called **Development of Self-Regulation**.
- The **Emotional Self-Regulation** section is now based on the Collaborative for Academic, Social, and Emotional Learning (CASEL), five core social and emotional skills and competencies.

## Chapter 12: Motivation in Learning and Teaching

- New table: **Building a Concept of Motivation to Learn**.
- New table: **Strategies That Support and Undermine Motivation in the Classroom**.

## Chapter 13: Creating Learning Environments

- The **Bullying and Cyberbullying** section is updated throughout with current research and new examples based on real events that have happened in the past few years.
- New section called **Victims**.

### Chapter 14: Teaching Every Student

- Section on **Teachers' Knowledge** has been expanded with recent research and discusses whether a teacher's expertise in a subject influences student performance.
- New section appears called **Recent Research on Teaching**.
- New section, **An Example of Standards: Technology**, introduces two sets of standards from the International Society for Technology in Education and the Partnership for 21st Century Skills.
- **The Cognitive Domain** section describes the first major revision of the Bloom's taxonomy (2001).
- New sections have been added: **Fitting Teaching to Your Goals, Adaptive Teaching,** and **Mentoring Students as a Way of Differentiating Teaching**.
- New guidelines box: **Teachers as Mentors**.

### Chapter 15: Classroom Assessment, Grading, and Testing

- New Guidelines box: **Writing Objective Test Items**.
- Section on **Evaluating Essays** has been rewritten based on new research by Gronlund and Waugh (2009).
- New section called **Standardized Testing** covers the following:
  - **Types of Scores for Commercially Developed Tests**
  - **Accountability and High-Stakes Testing**
  - **Reaching Every Student: Helping Students With Disabilities Prepare for High-Stakes Tests**
  - **Lessons for Teachers: Quality Assessment**
- New Guidelines box: **Conferences and Explaining Test Results**.
- New Table has been added called **Inappropriate Uses for High-Stakes Test Results**.
- New Guidelines box: **Preparing Yourself and Your Students for Testing**.

## A CRYSTAL-CLEAR PICTURE OF THE FIELD AND WHERE IT IS HEADED

The sixth Canadian edition maintains the lucid writing style for which the book is renowned. The text provides accurate, up-to-date coverage of the foundational areas within educational psychology: learning, development, motivation, teaching, and assessment, combined with intelligent examination of emerging trends in the field and society that affect student learning, such as student diversity, inclusion of students with special learning needs, education and neuroscience, and technology.

### Important New Content in Learning and Development

Some of the most significant changes in the new edition involve a reorganization and expansion of the learning and development content.

- The new edition includes expanded coverage of cognitive science, self-regulated learning, and argumentation as well as a new chapter devoted to *language development, language diversity, and immigrant education* (Chapter 5).
- You will find significantly increased coverage of the brain and neuroscience in Chapter 2 and integrated into five chapters—Chapters 3, 6, 7, 8, and 12.
- Increased coverage of technology can be found in Chapters 3, 4, 10, and 13.

## SUPPLEMENTS

**PEARSON eTEXT** Pearson eText gives students access to the text whenever and wherever they have access to the Internet. eText pages look exactly like the printed text, offering powerful new functionality for students and instructors. Users can create notes, highlight text in different colours, create bookmarks, zoom, click hyperlinked words and phrases to view definitions, and view in single-page or two-page view. Pearson eText allows for quick navigation to key parts of the eText using a table of contents, and provides full-text search. The eText may also offer links to associated media files, enabling users to access videos, animations, or other activities as they read the text.

**COURSESMART FOR STUDENTS**    CourseSmart goes beyond traditional expectations—providing instant, online access to the textbooks and course materials you need at an average savings of 60%. With instant access from any computer and the ability to search your text, you'll find the content you need quickly, no matter where you are. And with online tools like highlighting and note-taking, you can save time and study efficiently. See all the benefits at www.coursesmart.com/students.

**FOR INSTRUCTORS**    The following instructor's supplements are available for downloading from a password-protected section of Pearson Education Canada's online catalogue: www.pearsoncanada.ca/highered. Navigate to your book's catalogue page to view a list of those supplements that are available. See your local sales representative for details and access.

- **Instructor's Manual**    The **Instructor's Manual** includes a wealth of resources designed to help instructors teach the course from a variety of perspectives. Activities in the Instructor's Manual cover using the chapter case, cooperative activities, research activities, using technology, field experiences and other teaching activities.
- **PowerPoint Presentation**    Ideal for instructors to use for lecture presentations or student handouts, the PowerPoint presentation provides dozens of ready-to-use graphic and text images tied to the text.
- **Computerized Test Bank**    Pearson's computerized test banks allow instructors to filter and select questions to create quizzes, tests or homework. Instructors can revise questions or add their own, and may be able to choose print or online options. These questions are also available in Microsoft Word format.

**COURSESMART FOR INSTRUCTORS**    CourseSmart goes beyond traditional expectations—providing instant, online access to the textbooks and course materials you need at a lower cost for students. And even as students save money, you can save time and hassle with a digital eTextbook that allows you to search for the most relevant content at the very moment you need it. Whether it's evaluating textbooks or creating lecture notes to help students with difficult concepts, CourseSmart can make life a little easier. See how when you visit www.coursesmart.com/instructors.

**PEARSON CUSTOM LIBRARY**    For enrollments of at least 25 students, you can create your own textbook by choosing the chapters that best suit your own course needs. To begin building your custom text, visit www.pearsoncustomlibrary.com. You may also work with a dedicated Pearson Custom editor to create your ideal text—publishing your own original content or mixing and matching Pearson content. Contact your local Pearson Representative to get started.

**LEARNING SOLUTIONS MANAGERS**    Pearson's Learning Solutions Managers work with faculty and campus course designers to ensure that Pearson technology products, assessment tools, and online course materials are tailored to meet your specific needs. This highly qualified team is dedicated to helping schools take full advantage of a wide range of educational resources, by assisting in the integration of a variety of instructional materials and media formats. Your local Pearson Education sales representative can provide you with more details on this service program.

# Acknowledgments

During the years we have worked on this book, from initial draft to this most recent revision, many people have supported the project. Without their help, this text simply could not have been written.

Many educators contributed to this and previous editions. For their revision reviews, thanks to:

Rob McTavish, Simon Fraser University
Gene Ouellette, Mount Allison University
Ajit Bedi, Memorial University of Newfoundland
Scott Conrod, McGill University
Sonja Grover, Lakehead University

For revision reviews in connection with the fifth and fourth Canadian editions, thanks to:

Jill Singleton-Jackson, University of Windsor
Carlin J. Miller, University of Windsor
Anne MacGregor, Douglas College
John C. Nesbit, Simon Fraser University
Kenneth A. Pudlas, Trinity Western University
Jeff St. Pierre, University of Western Ontario
Noella Piquette-Tomei, University of Lethbridge
Irina Tzoneva, University of Fraser Valley

Connie Edwards, University of Toronto
Michael Harrison, University of Ottawa
Linda Lysynchuck, Laurentian University
Marlene Maldonado-Esteban, University of Windsor
Krista Pierce, Red Deer College
Noella Piquette-Tomei, University of Lethbridge
Jennifer A. Vadeboncoeur, University of British Columbia
David Young, University of Western Ontario

—PHIL WINNE AND NANCY PERRY

# BRIEF CONTENTS

# CONTENTS

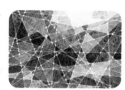

# CHAPTER 4

# LEARNER DIFFERENCES AND LEARNING NEEDS   106

# CHAPTER 5

# LANGUAGE DEVELOPMENT, LANGUAGE DIVERSITY, AND IMMIGRANT EDUCATION   155

# CHAPTER 6

## CULTURE AND DIVERSITY  189

# PART II  LEARNING AND MOTIVATION

# CHAPTER 7

## BEHAVIOURAL VIEWS OF LEARNING  225

CHAPTER 8

# COGNITIVE VIEWS OF LEARNING    258

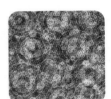

CHAPTER 9

# COMPLEX COGNITIVE PROCESSES    292

## CHAPTER 10

# THE LEARNING SCIENCES AND CONSTRUCTIVISM    328

## CHAPTER 11

# SOCIAL COGNITIVE VIEWS OF LEARNING AND MOTIVATION    367

# CHAPTER 12

# MOTIVATION IN LEARNING AND TEACHING 398

# PART III TEACHING AND ASSESSING

# CHAPTER 13

# CREATING LEARNING ENVIRONMENTS 437

## CHAPTER 14
## TEACHING EVERY STUDENT 473

## CHAPTER 15
## CLASSROOM ASSESSMENT, GRADING, AND TESTING 510

# SPECIAL FEATURES

# LEARNING, TEACHING, AND EDUCATIONAL PSYCHOLOGY

Irina_QQQ/Shutterstock

▶ **TEACHERS' CASEBOOK:** What Is an Effective Teacher?

It is your second year as a teacher at John A. Macdonald Public School (kindergarten–grade 8). One of your colleagues has been nominated for a Prime Minister's Award for Teaching Excellence. This person has been a role model to you in your first two years as a teacher, providing advice and encouragement. You would like to support her by writing a letter of recommendation to the Prime Minister's Office highlighting her exemplary teaching practices, commitment, and leadership. The deadline for submissions is a week away. How will you prepare to write the letter?

## CRITICAL THINKING

- What do you need to know about teaching to complete this task?
- What are some indicators of excellent teaching?
- Do different philosophies of teaching provide different answers to this question?
- What points will you make in your letter, and how will you back them up?

## OVERVIEW AND OBJECTIVES

If you are like many students, you begin this course with a mixture of anticipation and wariness. Perhaps you are required to take educational psychology as part of a program in teacher education, speech therapy, nursing, or counselling. Or you may have chosen this class as an elective because you are interested in education or psychology. Whatever your reason for enrolling, you probably have questions about teaching, schools, students—or even about yourself—that you hope this course may answer. This sixth Canadian edition of *Educational Psychology* has been written with questions such as these in mind.

In this first chapter, we begin not with the concept of educational psychology but rather with education—more specifically, with what it is like to be a teacher in Canada's diverse classrooms today. Teachers have been both criticized as ineffective and lauded as the best hope for young people. Do teachers make a difference in students' learning? What characterizes good teaching? Only when you are aware of the challenges teachers face can you appreciate the contributions of educational psychology.

After a brief introduction to the world of the teacher, we turn to a discussion of educational psychology itself. How can principles identified by educational psychologists benefit teachers, therapists, parents, and others who are interested in teaching and learning? What exactly is the content associated with the field of educational psychology, and where does this information come from?

By the time you have completed this chapter, you should be able to:

1.1   Explain how teaching matters.
1.2   Define the essential characteristics of effective teaching.
1.3   Describe the knowledge that expert teachers draw on.
1.4   Explain the value of studying educational psychology.
1.5   Describe the roles that theory and research play in this field.
1.6   List the greatest concerns of beginning teachers.

> Look for the **Explore, Watch, Practise,** and **Listen** icons throughout this chapter . . . these symbols lead you to online content that will enhance and complement your text experience.

## LEARNING AND TEACHING TODAY

Welcome to one of our favourite topics—educational psychology—the study of development, learning, and motivation that takes place in and out of schools. We believe this is the most important course you will take to prepare for your future as an educator, whether your "students" are children or adults learning in classrooms or in environments that are outside schools. In fact, there is evidence that new teachers who have completed coursework in development and learning are twice as likely to stay in teaching (National Commission on Teaching and America's Future, 2003). This may be a required course for you, so let us make the case for educational psychology, first by introducing you to classrooms today.

### What Are Classrooms Like Today? Dramatically Diverse

Who are the students in Canadian classrooms today? Where do they come from? Here are a few facts (taken from Campaign 2000, 2013; Canadian Teachers Federation, 2009; Statistics Canada, 2010d; Statistics Canada, 2013):

- By 2031, projections indicate Canada's foreign-born population will increase from 20% to 25%–28%, and 55% of these immigrants will come from Asian countries.
- Between 29% and 32% of the population will be members of visible minority groups, nearly twice this population's size in the 2006 census.
- Diversity is most concentrated in our largest cities. For example, visible minorities will comprise more than half the population in Toronto and Vancouver, but no more than 5% of the population in St. John's, Trois-Rivières, or Saguenay.
- Currently, there are classrooms in Vancouver where more than 80% of children are English language learners.
- Similarly, children come from a wide range of religious communities. Participation in religions other than Christianity has doubled since 2006 (from 6% to 14%), and approximately 50% of people with a religious affiliation other than Christian identify themselves as Muslim.
- Currently, approximately one in seven children in Canada lives in poverty. Children represent 36% of regular users of food banks. Particularly disturbing is the fact that four in 10 of Canada's Indigenous children are poor.
- Children in classrooms have diverse abilities and disabilities. Our inclusive policies mean that children with disabilities spend the majority of their school day in general education classrooms.
- Children are surviving diseases as serious as cancer and returning to school, but sometimes with late effects related to the treatment they underwent that have implications for learning (Daly, Kral, & Brown, 2008).
- Finally, children's families are diverse. Some children live with a mom and dad, but many live with a mom or dad, and some live with two moms or two dads, or with grandparents, or with aunts and uncles.

**TEACHER EFFICACY** Teachers' personal sense of efficacy is related to a school atmosphere of high expectations for teachers and students, administrative support, and real success with students.

Zurijeta/Shutterstock

Dealing with such diversity in the classroom can be daunting. It presents unique challenges to schools and communities, but it presents opportunities, too. These statistics are dramatic, but a bit impersonal. As a teacher, counsellor, recreational worker, speech therapist, or family member, you will encounter real children. You will meet many individual children in this text, too. Even though students in classrooms are increasingly diverse in race, ethnicity, language, and economic level, the teaching force remains very homogeneous. Clearly, it is important for all teachers to understand and work effectively with all their students. Several chapters in this text are devoted to understanding students. In addition, we will explore the concepts of student diversity and inclusion through research, cases, and practical applications within each chapter.

## Confidence in Every Context

Schools are about teaching and learning; all other activities are secondary to these basic goals. But teaching and learning in the contexts described above can be challenging for both teachers and students. This text is about understanding the complex processes of development, learning, motivation, teaching, and assessment so that you can become a capable and confident teacher.

Much of Anita Woolfolk's research has focused on **teachers' sense of efficacy**, defined as a teacher's belief that he or she can reach even difficult students to help them learn. This confident belief appears to be one of the few personal characteristics of teachers that predict student achievement (Tschannen-Moran & Woolfolk Hoy, 2001; Tschannen-Moran, Woolfolk Hoy, & Hoy, 1998; Woolfolk & Hoy, 1990; Woolfolk Hoy, Hoy, & Davis, 2009).

Teachers' sense of efficacy A teacher's belief that he or she can reach even difficult students to help them learn.

Teachers with a high sense of efficacy work harder and persist longer even when students are difficult to teach, in part because these teachers believe in themselves and in their students. Also, teachers are less likely to experience burnout and more likely to be satisfied with their jobs (Fives, Hamman, & Olivarez, 2005; Klassen & Chiu, 2010).

Anita Woolfolk (and other researchers) have found that prospective teachers tend to increase their personal sense of efficacy as a consequence of completing student teaching, but sense of efficacy may decline after the first year as a teacher, perhaps because the support that was available during student teaching is gone (Woolfolk Hoy & Burke-Spero, 2005). Teachers' sense of efficacy is higher in schools when the other teachers and administrators have high expectations for students and the teachers receive help from their principals in solving instructional and management problems (Capa, 2005; Hoy & Woolfolk, 1993). Another important conclusion from our research is that efficacy grows from real success with students, not just from the moral support or cheerleading of professors and colleagues. Any experience or training that helps you succeed in the day-to-day tasks of teaching will provide a foundation for developing a sense of efficacy in your career. This text aims to provide the knowledge and skills that form a solid foundation for an authentic sense of efficacy in teaching.

**Listen**
Do Teachers Make
a Difference?

## Do Teachers Make a Difference?

For a while, some researchers reported findings suggesting that wealth and social status, not teaching, were the major factors determining who learned in schools (e.g., Coleman, 1966). In fact, much of the early research on teaching was conducted by educational psychologists who refused to accept these claims that teachers were powerless in the face of poverty and other societal problems among students (Wittrock, 1986).

How could you decide if teaching makes a difference in the lives of students? You could look to your own experience. Did you have teachers who had an impact on your life? Perhaps one of your teachers even influenced your decision to become an educator. That said, one of the purposes of educational psychology is to go beyond individual experiences and testimonies, powerful as they are, to systematically examine the impact of teaching on the lives of students by using carefully designed research studies. Several such studies are described below.

TEACHER–STUDENT RELATIONSHIPS.   Bridget Hamre and Robert Pianta (2001) followed 179 children in a small school district from the time they entered kindergarten through to the end of grade 8. The researchers concluded that the quality of the teacher–student relationship in kindergarten (defined in terms of level of conflict with the child, the child's dependency on the teacher, and the teacher's affection for the child) predicted a number of academic and behavioural outcomes through grade 8, particularly for students with high levels of behavioural problems. Even when the gender, ethnicity, cognitive ability, and behaviour ratings of the student were accounted for, the relationship with the teacher still predicted aspects of school success.

In a more recent study that followed children from grade 3 through grade 5, Pianta and his colleagues found that two factors helped children with lower skills in mathematics begin to close the achievement gap. The factors were higher-level (not just basic skills) instruction and positive relationships with teachers (Crosnoe et al., 2010). Evidence is mounting for a strong association between the quality of teacher–child relationships and school performance. Also, students with significant behavioural problems in the early years are less likely to have problems later in school if their first teachers are sensitive to their needs and provide frequent, consistent feedback.

RELATIONSHIPS MATTER Research has shown that the quality of the teacher–student relationship in kindergarten predicts a number of academic and behavioural outcomes, particularly for students with behavioural problems, who are less likely to have problems later in school if their teachers are sensitive to their needs and provide frequent, consistent feedback.

TEACHER PREPARATION AND QUALITY.   Linda Darling-Hammond (2000), a researcher at Stanford University, examined the ways in which teacher qualifications are related to student

TABLE 1.1 • Correlations Between Teacher Quality Variables and Student Achievement, United States

| | GRADE 4 MATH, 1992 | GRADE 4 MATH, 1996 | GRADE 8 MATH, 1996 | GRADE 4 READING, 1992 | GRADE 4 READING, 1994 |
|---|---|---|---|---|---|
| Percentage of teachers well-qualified (with full certification and a major in their field) | .71** | .61** | .67** | .80** | .75** |
| Percentage of teachers out of field (with less than a minor in the field they teach) | −.48* | −.44* | −.42* | −.56* | −.33 |

*p , .05; **p , .01
Source: Darling-Hammond, L. (2000). Teacher quality and student achievement: A review of state policy evidence. Educational Policy Analysis Archives, 8, pp. 1–48. Retrieved January 27, 2005, from http://epaa.asu.edu/epaa/v8n1. Copyright © Educational Policy Analysis Archives. Adapted with permission of the EPAA.

achievement using data from several U.S.-based sources, including a survey of policies in the 50 states, case study analyses, the 1993–1994 *Schools and Staffing Surveys*, and the *National Assessment of Educational Progress* (NAEP). Her findings indicated that the quality of teachers—as measured by whether the teachers were fully certified and earned a major in their teaching field—was related to student performance. In fact, measures of teacher preparation and certification were by far the strongest predictors of student achievement in reading and mathematics, both before and after controlling for student poverty and English language proficiency. For example, look at Table 1.1. In the first row, all the correlations are positive and significant. This means that the higher the percentage of teachers who earned full certification and a major in their teaching field, the higher their students' achievement in math and in reading. All but one of the correlations in the second row are negative and significant. This indicates that the higher the percentage of teachers who are teaching outside their field, the lower their students' achievement tends to be. So there is evidence that more qualified teachers make a difference in student learning. (Later in the chapter, we will look closely at how to interpret these statistics.)

Setting standards for teacher qualification is controversial, however. The *Point/ Counterpoint* box examines issues in the debate about whether or not to set teaching standards.

Effective teachers who establish positive relationships with their students appear to be a powerful force in those students' lives. Students who have problems seem to benefit the most from good teaching. What makes a teacher effective? What is good teaching? We consider those points next.

# WHAT IS GOOD TEACHING?

Educators, psychologists, philosophers, novelists, journalists, filmmakers, mathematicians, scientists, historians, policy-makers, and parents, to name only a few groups, have examined the question "what is good teaching?" There are hundreds of answers. And good teaching is not confined to classrooms—it occurs in homes and hospitals, in museums and sales meetings, and in therapists' offices and summer camps. In this text we are primarily concerned with teaching in classrooms, but much of what you will learn applies to teaching in other settings as well.

## Inside Three Classrooms

To begin our examination of good teaching, let's step inside the classrooms of several outstanding teachers. All the situations that follow reflect the conditions in real classrooms today.

A MULTILINGUAL GRADE 1 CLASS.  Anne Lee-Hawman teaches grade 1 in Mississauga, Ontario. Of the 22 children in her classroom, half are English (or additional language) learners. As is true for most linguistically diverse students in Canada, they spend 100% of

## POINT/COUNTERPOINT  Standards for Teachers

Research has revealed many teaching practices that are highly effective. Some educators argue that all teachers should demonstrate a "standard" of performance relating to these practices to earn their teaching certificates. Other educators believe that excellent teachers don't just implement a set of standard practices; excellent teachers are reflective—thoughtful and inventive—about teaching. Teaching standards have been developed and used as measures of teaching quality in several provinces across Canada (e.g., in British Columbia, Alberta, Ontario, Quebec), in the United States, and around the world (e.g., in New Zealand, the United Kingdom). Is this how we should evaluate teaching quality? Should teachers demonstrate performance to a set of standards in order to be certified?

### POINT

▶ **School renewal depends on what teachers know and can do to enhance their students' learning.** Advocates of the teaching standards movement claim that teaching standards honour and advance the profession by highlighting the complex and varied nature of educators' work (BC College of Teachers, 2008). Furthermore, proponents of teaching standards argue that the role of standards is to articulate the knowledge, skills, and attitudes that professional educators should possess and to outline the responsibilities that accrue to them as professionals who hold the public trust. The proponents believe that professional standards will contribute to a safe and high-quality learning environment for students.

Many educators are welcoming teaching standards as a basis for educational reform, believing that such standards will lead to higher status and to greater autonomy for the teaching profession (Beck, Hart, & Kosnik, 2002). Teachers' talents and effectiveness often are underestimated by the public and in the media. Standards can lift the morale of teachers by informing others about their skills and accomplishments. Standards can also clarify how teachers contribute to the lives of students through caring, reflective, and innovative practices.

In the past, standards movements have tended to focus on knowledge and skills that students need to acquire, assuming that once educators know *what* students need to learn, getting them to learn it will be relatively easy. There is widespread agreement among teaching experts, however, that teaching and learning are complex processes and that some pedagogical approaches are more effective than others for supporting learning. Shouldn't all teachers be required to learn and effectively implement these approaches?

### COUNTERPOINT

▶ **The teaching standards movement has more to do with punishing teachers than with enhancing their professionalism.** Those who oppose the teaching standards movement are concerned about how standards will be used in practice. Will they become the basis for disciplining teachers? Will they drive the curricula in teacher education programs, just as high-stakes assessments of students have led to a narrowing of curricula in kindergarten through grade 12? Who will set the standards? How specific will they be?

One of the *Standards for Education, Competence and Professional Conduct of Educators in BC* indicates that teachers should have "a broad knowledge base and understand the subject areas they teach" (BC College of Teachers, 2008). Most teachers agree that this is ideal. However, many teachers are assigned to teach classes or topics for which they have no expertise, often as a result of conditions that exist within a school or district and that are beyond the teachers' control (e.g., budget cutbacks, shortage of teachers with particular qualifications). The BC Teachers' Federation argues that it is unfair to create standards as a set of responsibilities for teachers without also acknowledging the responsibility of employers (i.e., school and district administrators, governments) to ensure that conditions are met that enable teachers to meet the standards (BCTF, 2003).

In the United Kingdom, the government's standards for teaching imposed a very narrow definition of both professionalism and failure to meet these standards, which resulted in funding sanctions. A similar model is reflected in the *No Child Left Behind* legislation in the United States. These outcomes reinforce the skepticism of opponents of the teaching standards movement.

It appears that many educators welcome standards that elevate the teaching profession and articulate what effective teachers know and do with respect to instruction. Concern arises from the potential for governments to use standards that create a high-stakes and punitive environment for teachers that could end up having a negative impact on students' ability to learn.

*Sources: BC College of Teachers. (2014). Standards for the competence, professional conduct and ethical behaviour of educators in British Columbia. Retrieved June 2, 2014 from http://www.bcteacherregulation.ca/Standards/StandardsDevelopment.aspx; BCTF. (2003). Summary analysis of the BC College of Teachers' standards for the education competence and professional conduct of educators in BC. Retrieved from http://www.bctf.ca.*

their school day using English as opposed to their native language. This immersion, or submersion, approach to second-language learning contrasts with the bilingual approaches to language learning used in many American states.

An English language teacher helps Anne to integrate these students by working in Anne's classroom each day. Together Anne and the English language teacher support students in small groups and make modifications to the curriculum to enable students who are English language learners to participate in all the activities of the classroom. One strategy the two teachers have found useful is to make information available through visual materials (e.g., pictures, diagrams, word or concept maps). Anne also makes use of peer tutors and, whenever possible, offers one-on-one instruction to students who need it.

In addition to supporting students' acquisition of English, Anne encourages students and their parents to continue talking, reading, and writing in their first language at home. As well, she fosters an appreciation for diverse languages and cultures in her classroom by celebrating a wide range of cultural holidays and by having students compare and contrast their home or community experiences and practices during classroom discussions and sharing times.

Anne makes a point of learning as much as she can about her students' linguistic and cultural heritages. She recognizes how important it is for teachers to understand how issues of language and culture influence children's learning, so that they don't misinterpret children's motivation and behaviour. This year, five languages are represented in Anne's classroom: English, Hindi, Punjabi, Chinese, and Malaysian. She has a lot of learning to do.

**A SUBURBAN GRADE 6 CLASS.** Ken teaches grade 6 in a suburban elementary school in Richmond, BC. Students in the class have varying racial, ethnic, family income, and language backgrounds. Ken emphasizes "process writing." His students complete first drafts, discuss them with others in the class, revise, edit, and "publish" their work. The students also keep daily journals and often use these to share personal concerns with Ken. They tell him of problems at home, fights, and fears; he always takes the time to respond in writing. The study of science is also placed in the context of the real world. The students use a National Geographic Society computer network to link with other schools in order to identify acid rain patterns around the world. For social studies, the class plays simulation games; for example, in two games that focused on the first half of the 1800s, the students "lived" as trappers collecting animal skins and as pioneers heading west.

Throughout the year, Ken is very interested in the social and emotional development of his students—he wants them to learn about responsibility and fairness as well as science and social studies. This concern is evident in the way he develops his class rules at the beginning of the year. Rather than specifying dos and don'ts, Ken and his students generate a list of rights and responsibilities for their class. This list covers most of the situations that might need a "rule."

**AN ADVANCED MATH CLASS.** Hilda Borko and Carol Livingston (1989) describe how Randy, an expert secondary school mathematics teacher, worked with his students' confusion to construct a review lesson about strategies for doing integrals. When one student said that a particular section in the book seemed "haphazard," Randy led the class through a process of organizing the material. He asked the class for general statements about useful strategies for doing integrals. He clarified their suggestions, elaborated on some, and helped students improve others. He asked the students to relate their ideas to passages in the text. Even though he accepted all reasonable suggestions, he listed only the key strategies on the board. By the end of the period, the students had transformed the disorganized material from the book into an ordered and useful outline to guide their learning. They also had a better idea about how to read and understand difficult material.

One thing that's noticeable in all three of these classrooms is the teachers' commitment to their students. These teachers must deal with a wide range of student abilities and challenges: different languages, different home situations, and different abilities and disabilities. They must adapt instruction and assessment to students' needs. They must make the most abstract concepts, such as integrals, real and understandable for their particular students. Then there is the challenge of how to use new technologies and techniques. The teachers must use them appropriately to accomplish important goals, not just to entertain the students. And the whole time these experts are navigating through the academic material, they are also taking care of the emotional needs of their students, propping up sagging self-esteem and encouraging responsibility. If we followed these individuals from the first day of class, we would see that they carefully plan and teach the basic procedures for living and learning in their classes. These teachers can efficiently collect and correct homework, regroup students, give directions, distribute materials, collect lunch money, and deal with disruptions—and they can do all this while also making a mental note to find out why one of their students is so tired. Finally, these teachers are also **reflective**—they constantly think back over situations to analyze what they did and why, and to consider how they might improve learning for their students.

**SO, WHAT IS GOOD TEACHING?**   Is good teaching science or art, the application of research-based theories or the creative invention of specific practices? Is a good teacher an expert explainer––"a sage on the stage"—or a great coach––"a guide by the side"? These debates have raged for years. In your other education classes, you probably will encounter criticisms of the scientific, teacher-centered sages. You will be encouraged to be inventive, student-centred guides. *But beware of either/or choices.* Teachers must be both knowledgeable and inventive. They must be able to use a range of strategies, and they must also be able to invent new strategies. They must have some basic research-based routines for managing classes, but they must also be willing and able to break from the routine when the situation calls for change. They must know the research on student development, "patterns common to particular ages, culture, social class, geography, and gender" (Ball, 1997, p. 773), and they also need to know their own particular students, who are unique combinations of culture, gender, and geography. Personally, we hope you all become teachers who are both "sages" and "guides," wherever you stand.

Anne, Ken, and Randy are examples of expert teachers, but they have been teaching for a long time. What about you? Let's look at what it's like to be a new teacher.

## Differentiated Instruction

**STOP & THINK** You are preparing a unit on habitats for your students. You decide to do as your educational psychology professor recommended and give an alternate form of the final unit test as a pretest to find out what the students already know about the subject. After you reassure them that the test won't be graded—you just want an idea about where to go in developing the lesson—the students settle in and seem to take the task seriously. Looking over the papers that night, you are dismayed. A quarter of the students make over 90% on the "final." Quite a few get around half of the questions right, but the rest of the class is clueless. The next day, when you ask Shanequa why she did so well on the test, she explains that in science class last year her group (and several others) chose habitats as the focus of their special project work. You stare at your lesson plans and realize that they fit practically no one in this class. What will you do? What would expert teachers such as Anne, Ken, or Randy do? •

**Reflective** Thoughtful and inventive. Reflective teachers think back over situations to analyze what they did and why, and to consider how they might improve learning for their students.

**WHY DO WE NEED DIFFERENTIATED INSTRUCTION?**   As you will see throughout this text, today's classrooms are diverse. Students differ in knowledge of the subjects being taught, language, socioeconomic status (SES), culture, race, and ethnicity. They bring different strengths, abilities, and challenges to the task of learning. Many educators believe that "classes should include students of diverse needs, achievement levels, interests, and learning styles, and instruction should be differentiated to take advantage of the diversity, not ignore it" (Jackson & Davis, 2000, p. 23). **Differentiated instruction** (Tomlinson, 2005b) is one way of going beyond accommodating these learner differences to seeing diversity as an array of strengths on which to build. The basic idea of differentiated instruction is that teachers must take into account not only the subjects they are teaching but also the students. In differentiated classrooms, students work at different paces, sometimes exercising varied learning options, and they are assessed using indicators that fit their interests and needs (George, 2005).

ELEMENTS OF DIFFERENTIATION.   Differentiated instruction conceives of all students as seeking purpose, challenge, affirmation, power, and the chance to contribute. The confident teacher views these different student needs as opportunities, not problems, and responds with invitation, investment, persistence, opportunity, and reflection. The teacher works to create curriculum and instruction for each student that is focused, engaging, demanding, important, and scaffolded. Carol Ann Tomlinson (2003) describes these characteristics as the *cogs of differentiation*. They are called *cogs* because they are interdependent and interlocking, like the inner workings of a clock. Each student's needs interact and connect with the differentiated curriculum and instruction created by the teacher for that student.

What are some examples of differentiation in curriculum and instruction? Consider teaching a unit on mammals to a class of grade 2 and 3 students. Allowing students to choose which mammal to study and how to represent their learning (e.g., through writing, drawing, diagrams, models) can help to address their diverse interests and abilities. Similarly, making sure students can access a wide range of material and people resources to help them do their research and writing can enable students who may struggle with standard grade level texts to participate. A great benefit of differentiating instruction is that, more often than not, it enables all learners in the classroom to participate in the same activity, which makes planning and teaching so much more manageable for teachers.

Is all this talk about expert teachers, science, art, and differentiated instruction making you a little nervous? Anne, Ken, and Randy are experts at the science, art, and differentiating of teaching, but they have years of experience. What about you?

## What Are the Concerns of Beginning Teachers?

STOP & THINK Imagine walking into class on your first day of teaching. List the concerns, fears, and worries you have. What assets do you bring to the job? •

Beginning teachers everywhere share many concerns, including how to maintain classroom discipline, motivate students, accommodate differences among students, evaluate students' work, deal with parents, and get along with other teachers (Conway & Clark, 2003; Melnick & Meister, 2008; Veenman, 1984). Many teachers also experience what has been called "reality shock" when they take their first job because they really cannot ease into their responsibilities. On the first day of their first job, beginning teachers face the same tasks as teachers with years of experience. Student teaching, while a critical element of becoming a good teacher, does not really prepare prospective teachers for starting off a school year with a new class.

With experience, hard work, and good support, seasoned teachers can focus on students' needs and judge their teaching success by the accomplishments of their students (Fuller, 1969; Pigge & Marso, 1997). Here's how one experienced teacher described the shift from concerns about yourself to concerns about your students: "The difference

**Differentiated instruction** Teaching that takes into account students' abilities, prior knowledge, and challenges so that instruction matches not only the subject being taught but also students' needs.

TABLE 1.2 • **Advice for Student Teachers from Their Students**

The students in Ms. Amato's elementary school class gave this advice as a gift to their student teacher on her last day.

1. Teach us as much as you can.
2. Give us homework.
3. Help us when we have problems with our work.
4. Help us to do the right thing.
5. Help us make a family in school.
6. Read books to us.
7. Teach us to read.
8. Help us write about faraway places.
9. Give us lots of compliments, like "Oh, that's so beautiful."
10. Smile at us.
11. Take us for walks and on trips.
12. Respect us.
13. Help us get our education.

*Source: From Nieto, S. Affirming Diversity: The Sociopolitical Context of Multicultural Education, 4e. Published by Allyn and Bacon, Boston, MA. Copyright © 2004 by Pearson Education. Reprinted by permission of the publisher.*

between a beginning teacher and an experienced one is that the beginning teacher asks, 'How am I doing?' and the experienced teacher asks, 'How are the children doing?'" (Codell, 2001, p. 191).

Our goal in writing this text is to give you the foundation to become an expert as you gain experience. One thing experts do is listen to their students. Table 1.2 shows some advice students in a grade 1 class gave to their student teacher: It looks like the students know about good teaching, too.

We began this chapter claiming that educational psychology is the most important course you will take. Okay, maybe we are a bit biased—we have been teaching the subject for decades! So let us now turn to our favourite topic.

# THE ROLE OF EDUCATIONAL PSYCHOLOGY

For as long as the field of **educational psychology** has existed—about 100 years—there have been debates about what it really is. Some people believe educational psychology is simply knowledge gained from psychology and applied to the activities of the classroom. Others believe it involves applying the methods of psychology to study classroom and school life (Brophy, 2003; Wittrock, 1992). A look at history shows the close connections between educational psychology and teaching.

## In the Beginning: Linking Educational Psychology and Teaching

In one sense, educational psychology is very old. Topics that Plato and Aristotle discussed—the role of the teacher, the relationship between teacher and student, methods of teaching, the nature and order of learning, the role of affect in learning— are still studied by educational psychologists today. From its beginning, psychology in North America was linked to teaching. In 1890, William James officially founded the field of psychology and developed a lecture series for teachers entitled *Talks to Teachers on Psychology*. These lectures were given in summer schools for teachers and then published in 1899. James's student, G. Stanley Hall, founded the American Psychological Association. His dissertation was about children's understandings of the world; teachers helped him collect data. Hall encouraged teachers to make detailed observations to study their students' development—as his mother had done when she was a teacher. Hall's student, John Dewey, founded the Laboratory School at the University of Chicago and is considered the father of the progressive education

**Educational psychology** The discipline concerned with teaching and learning processes; it applies the methods and theories of psychology and has its own as well.

movement (Berliner, 2006; Hilgard, 1996; Pajares, 2003). Another of William James's students, E. L. Thorndike, wrote the first educational psychology text in 1903, and founded the *Journal of Educational Psychology* in 1910.

In the 1940s and 1950s, the study of educational psychology concentrated on individual differences, assessment, and learning behaviours. In the 1960s and 1970s, the focus of research shifted to the study of cognitive development and learning, with attention to how students learn concepts and remember. More recently, educational psychologists have investigated how culture and social factors affect learning and development (Pressley & Roehrig, 2003).

## Educational Psychology Today

What is educational psychology today? The view generally accepted is that educational psychology is a distinct discipline with its own theories, research methods, problems, and techniques. Both in the past and today, educational psychologists study learning and teaching and, at the same time, strive to improve educational practice (Pintrich, 2000). In order to understand as much as possible about learning and teaching, educational psychologists examine what happens when *someone* (a teacher or parent) or *something* (a computer) teaches *something* (math or weaving or dancing) to *someone else* (a student or co-worker or team) in some *setting* (a classroom or theatre or gym) (Berliner, 2006; Schwab, 1973). So educational psychologists study child and adolescent development; learning and motivation, including how people learn different academic subjects such as reading or mathematics; social and cultural influences on learning; teaching and teachers; and assessment including testing (Alexander & Winne, 2006).

But even with this long history of interest in teaching and learning, are the findings of educational psychologists really that helpful for teachers? After all, most teaching is just common sense, isn't it? Let's take a few minutes to examine these questions.

## Is It Just Common Sense?

In many cases, the principles set forth by educational psychologists—after spending much thought, research, and money—sound pathetically obvious. People are tempted to say, and usually do say, "Everyone knows that!" Consider these examples:

TAKING TURNS.    What method should a teacher use in selecting students to participate in a primary-grade reading class?

**Common-Sense Answer.**    Teachers should call on students randomly so that everyone will have to follow the lesson carefully. If a teacher were to use the same order every time, the students would know when their turn was coming up.

**Answer Based on Research.**    Research by Ogden, Brophy, and Evertson (1977) indicates that the answer to this question is not so simple. In grade 1 reading classes, for example, going around the circle in order and giving each child a chance to read led to better overall achievement than calling on students randomly. The critical factor in going around the circle may be that each child has a chance to participate. Without a system for calling on everyone, many students can be overlooked or skipped. Research suggests there are better alternatives for teaching reading than going around the circle, but if teachers choose one of these alternatives, they should make sure that everyone has the chance for practice and feedback (Tierney, Readence, & Dishner, 1990).

HELPING STUDENTS.    When should teachers provide help for lower-achieving students as they do class work?

**Commonsense Answer.**    Teachers should offer help often. After all, these lower-achieving students may not know when they need help or they may be too embarrassed to ask for help.

**RESEARCH MATTERS** These students are participating in true "hands-on" cooperative learning. Will their knowledge of science improve using this approach? Are there better ways to learn this subject? Educational research should shed light on questions like these.

Jim West/PhotoEdit

**Answer Based on Research.** Sandra Graham (1996) found that when teachers provide help before students ask, the students and others watching are more likely to conclude that the helped student does not have the ability to succeed. The student is more likely to attribute failures to lack of ability instead of lack of effort, so motivation suffers.

SKIPPING GRADES. Should a school encourage exceptionally bright students to skip grades or to enter university or college early?

**Common-Sense Answer.** No! Very intelligent students who are a year or two younger than their classmates are likely to be social misfits. They are neither physically nor emotionally ready for dealing with older students and would be miserable in the social situations that are so important in school, especially in the later grades.

**Answer Based on Research.** Maybe. In *A Nation Deceived: How Schools Hold Back America's Brightest Children* (2004), Nicholas Colangelo, Susan Assouline, and Miraca Gross list the 20 most important points from their report. The first two are: (1) Acceleration is the most effective curriculum intervention for gifted children, and (2) for bright students, acceleration has long-term beneficial effects, both academically and socially. Whether acceleration is the best solution for a student depends on many specific individual characteristics, including the intelligence and maturity of the student as well as the other available options. For some students, moving quickly through the material and working in advanced courses with older students is a very good idea. See Chapter 4 for more on adapting teaching to students' abilities.

OBVIOUS ANSWERS? Lily Wong (1987) demonstrated that just seeing research results in writing can make them seem obvious. She selected 12 findings from research on teaching; one of them was the "taking turns" result noted above. She presented six of the findings in their correct form and six in *exactly the opposite form* to university students and to experienced teachers. Both the college students and teachers rated about half of the *wrong* findings as "obviously" correct. In a follow-up study, other participants were shown the 12 findings and their opposites and were asked to pick which ones were correct. For 8 of the 12 findings, the participants chose the wrong result more often than the right one.

You may have thought that educational psychologists spend their time discovering the obvious, but the preceding examples point out the danger of this kind of thinking. When a principle is stated in simple terms, it can sound simplistic. A similar phenomenon takes place when we see a gifted dancer or athlete perform; the well-trained performer makes it look easy. But we see only the results of the training, not all the work that went into mastering the individual movements. And bear in mind that any research finding—or its opposite—may sound like common sense. The issue is not what *sounds* sensible, but what is demonstrated when the principle is put to the test (Gage, 1991).

## Using Research to Understand and Improve Learning

STOP & THINK Quickly, list all the different research methods you can name. •

Educational psychologists design and conduct many different kinds of research studies. Some of these are "descriptive"—that is, their purpose is simply to describe events in a particular class or several classes.

DESCRIPTIVE STUDIES.     Reports of **descriptive studies** often include survey results, interview responses, samples of actual classroom dialogue, or observations of class activities. One descriptive approach, classroom **ethnography**, is borrowed from anthropology. Ethnographic methods involve studying naturally occurring events in the life of a group and trying to understand the meaning of these events to the people involved. For example, the description of an expert high school mathematics teacher that appears earlier in this chapter was taken from an ethnographic study Hilda Borko and Carol Livingston (1989) conducted. The researchers made detailed in-class observations and analyzed these observations, along with audio recordings and information from interviews with the teachers, in order to describe differences between novice and expert teachers. In some descriptive research, researchers carefully analyze videos of classes to identify recurring patterns of teacher and student behaviour. In other studies, the researcher uses **participant observation** and works within the class or school to understand the actions from the perspectives of the teacher and the students. Researchers also may employ case studies. A **case study** investigates in depth how a teacher plans courses, for example, or how a student tries to learn specific material.

CORRELATIONAL STUDIES.     Often the results of descriptive studies include reports of correlations. We will take a minute to examine this concept, because you will encounter many correlations in the coming chapters. A **correlation** is a number that indicates both the strength and the direction of a relationship between two events or measurements. Correlations range from 1.00 to –1.00. The closer the correlation is to either 1.00 or –1.00, the stronger the relationship. For example, the correlation between height and weight is about .70 (a strong relationship); the correlation between height and number of languages spoken is about .00 (no relationship at all).

The sign of the correlation tells the direction of the relationship. A **positive correlation** indicates that the two factors increase or decrease together. As one gets larger, so does the other. Height and weight are positively correlated because greater height tends to be associated with greater weight. A **negative correlation** means that increases in one factor are related to decreases in the other. For example, the less you pay for a theatre or concert ticket, the greater your distance from the stage. It is important to note that correlations do not prove cause and effect (see Figure 1.1). Height and weight are correlated—taller people tend to weigh more than shorter people. But gaining weight obviously does not cause you to grow taller. Knowing a person's height simply allows you to make a general prediction about that person's weight. Educational psychologists identify correlations so that they can make predictions about important events in the classroom.

**Descriptive studies** Studies that collect detailed information about specific situations, often using observation, surveys, interviews, recordings, or a combination of these methods.

**Ethnography** A descriptive approach to research that focuses on life within a group and tries to understand the meaning of events to the people involved.

**Participant observation** A method for conducting descriptive research in which the researcher becomes a participant in the situation in order to better understand life in that group.

**Case study** Intensive study of one person or one situation.

**Correlation** Statistical description of how closely two variables are related.

**Positive correlation** A relationship between two variables in which the two increase or decrease together. Example: calorie intake and weight gain.

**Negative correlation** A relationship between two variables in which a high value on one is associated with a low value on the other. Example: height and distance from top of head to the ceiling.

**FIGURE 1.1**

### CORRELATIONS DO NOT SHOW CAUSATION

When research shows that broken homes and crime are correlated, it does not show causation. Poverty, a third variable, may be the cause of both crime and broken homes.

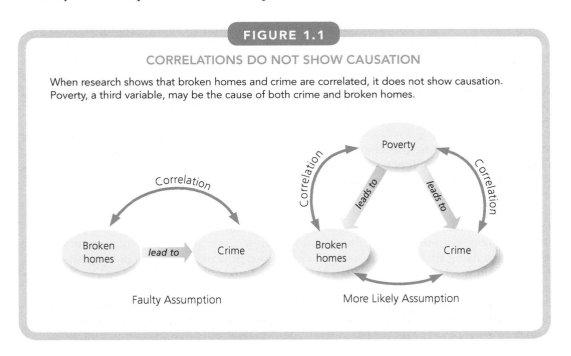

EXPERIMENTAL STUDIES.    A second type of research—**experimentation**—allows educational psychologists to go beyond predictions and actually study cause and effect. Instead of just observing and describing an existing situation, the investigators introduce changes and note the results. First, a number of comparable groups of subjects are created. In psychological research, the term **participants** (also called **subjects**) generally refers to the people being studied—such as teachers or grade 8 students—not to subjects such as math or science. One common way to make sure that groups of subjects are essentially the same is to assign each subject to a group using a random procedure. **Random** means that each subject has an equal chance to be in any group. **Quasi-experimental studies** meet most of the criteria for true experiments, with the important exception that the participants are not assigned to groups at random. Instead, existing groups such as classes or schools participate in the experiments.

In experiments or quasi-experiments, for one or more of the groups studied, the experimenters change some aspect of the situation to see if this change or "treatment" has an expected effect. The results in each group are then compared. Usually, statistical tests are conducted. When differences are described as **statistically significant**, it means that they probably did not happen simply by chance. For example, if you see $p < .05$ in a study, this indicates that the result reported could happen by chance less than 5 times out of 100, and $p < .01$ means less than 1 time in 100.

A number of the studies we will examine attempt to identify cause-and-effect relationships by asking questions such as this: If some teachers receive training in how to teach spelling using morphology, the study of the smallest parts of words that contain meaning such as "s" or "ies" for making words plural (*cause*), will the trained teachers' students become better spellers than students whose teachers did not receive training in morphology (*effect*)? This actually was a *field experiment* because it took place in real classrooms and not a simulated laboratory situation. In addition, it was a *quasi-experiment* because the students were in existing classes and had not been randomly assigned to teachers, so we cannot be certain the experimental and control groups were the same before the teachers received their training. The researchers handled this by looking at improvement in spelling, not just final achievement level (Hurry et al., 2005).

In many cases, both descriptive and experimental research occur together. The study by Ogden, Brophy, and Evertson (1977) described earlier in this section is a good example. To answer questions about the relationship between how students are selected to read in a primary-grade class and their achievement in reading, these investigators first observed students and teachers in a number of classrooms and then measured the reading achievement of the students. The researchers found that having students read in a predictable order was associated, or correlated, with gains in reading scores. With a simple correlation such as this, however, the researchers could not be sure that the strategy was actually causing the effect. In the second part of the study, Ogden and her colleagues asked several teachers to call on each student in turn. They then compared reading achievement in these groups with achievement in groups where teachers used other strategies. This second part of the research was thus an experimental study.

SINGLE-SUBJECT EXPERIMENTAL STUDIES.    The goal of **single-subject experimental studies** is to determine the effects of a therapy, teaching method, or other intervention. One common approach is to observe an individual for a baseline period (A) and assess the behaviour of interest; then try an intervention (B) and note the results; then remove the intervention and go back to baseline conditions (A); and finally reinstate the intervention (B). This form of single-subject design is called an ABAB experiment. For example, a teacher might record how much time students are out of their seats without permission during a week-long baseline period (A), and then try ignoring those who are out of their seats but praising those who are seated, and record how many are wandering out of their seats for the week (B). Next, the teacher returns to baseline conditions (A) and records results, and then reinstates the praise-and-ignore strategy (B) (Landrum & Kauffman, 2006). When this intervention was first tested, the praise-and-ignore strategy proved effective in increasing the time students spent in their seats (Madsen, Becker, Thomas, Koser, & Plager, 1968).

**Experimentation** Research method in which variables are manipulated and the effects recorded.

**Participants/subjects** People or animals being studied.

**Random** Without any definite pattern; following no rule.

**Quasi-experimental studies** Studies that fit most of the criteria for true experiments, with the important exception that the participants are not assigned to groups at random. Instead, existing groups such as classes or schools participate in the experiments.

**Statistically significant** Not likely to be a chance occurrence.

**Single-subject experimental studies** Systematic interventions to study effects with one person, often by applying and then withdrawing a treatment.

**MICROGENETIC STUDIES.** The goal of **microgenetic studies** is to intensively study cognitive processes in the midst of change—as the change is actually happening. For example, researchers might analyze how children learn a particular strategy for adding two-digit numbers over the course of several weeks. The microgenetic approach has three basic characteristics: the researchers (a) observe the entire period of the change—from when it starts to the time it is relatively stable; (b) make many observations, often using videotape recordings, interviews, and transcriptions of the exact words of the individuals being studied; (c) put the observed behaviour "under a microscope;" that is, examined moment by moment or trial by trial. The goal is to explain the underlying mechanisms of change—for example, what new knowledge or skills are developing to allow change to take place (Siegler & Crowley, 1991). This kind of research is expensive and time-consuming, so often only one or a few children are studied.

**THE ROLE OF TIME IN RESEARCH.** Another distinction is useful in understanding research—a distinction based on time. Many things that psychologists want to study, such as cognitive development, happen over several months or years. Ideally, researchers would study the development by observing their subjects over many years as changes occur. These are called **longitudinal studies**. They are informative, but time-consuming, expensive, and not always practical—keeping up with subjects over years as they grow up and move can be impossible. So instead, much research involves **cross-sectional studies**, which focus on groups of children at different ages. For example, to study how children's conceptions of "alive" change from ages 3 to 16, researchers can interview children of several different ages rather than following the same children for 14 years.

**TEACHERS AS RESEARCHERS.** Research can also be a way to improve teaching in one classroom or one school. The same kind of careful observation, intervention, data gathering, and analysis that occurs in large research projects can be applied in any classroom to answer questions such as: Which writing prompts seem to encourage the best descriptive writing in my class? When does Kenyon seem to have the greatest difficulty concentrating on academic tasks? Would assigning task roles in science groups lead to more equitable participation of girls and boys in the work? This kind of problem-solving investigation is called **action research** (or teacher research, or teacher inquiry). By focusing on a specific problem and making careful observations, teachers can learn a great deal about both their teaching and their students.

You can find reports of the findings from all types of studies in journals that are referenced in this text. Table 1.3 provides a list of some of the major journals that publish work in educational and developmental psychology. As authors, we have published articles in many of these journals and also have reviewed manuscripts to decide what will be published. For many years, Anita was the editor of the *Theory Into Practice* journal, and Nancy sat on the Editorial Board. The goal of that journal is just what the title says—to bring the most useful theories into educational practice and also to bring the wisdom of practice back to researchers who study education. *Theory Into Practice* is a great journal to inspire and guide action research in classrooms.

## Theories for Teaching

As we saw earlier, the major goal of educational psychology is to understand what happens when someone teaches something to someone else in some setting (Berliner, 2006; Schwab, 1973). Reaching this goal is a slow process. There are very few landmark studies that answer a question once and for all. There are so many different kinds of students, teachers, tasks, and settings; and besides, human beings are pretty complicated. To deal with this complexity, research in educational psychology examines limited aspects of a situation—perhaps a few variables at a time or life in one or two classrooms. If enough studies are completed in a certain area and findings repeatedly point to the same conclusions, we eventually arrive at a **principle**. This is the term for an established relationship between two or more factors—between a certain teaching strategy, for example, and student achievement.

**Microgenetic studies** Detailed observation and analysis of changes in a cognitive process as the process unfolds over several days or weeks.

**Longitudinal studies** Studies that document changes that occur in subjects over time, often many years.

**Cross-sectional studies** Studies that focus on groups of subjects at different ages rather than following the same group for many years.

**Action research** Systematic observations or tests of methods that teachers or schools conduct to improve teaching and learning for their students.

**Principle** Established relationship between factors.

TABLE 1.3 • **Examples of Journals in Educational Psychology and Child Development**

| JOURNAL | ORGANIZATION/PUBLISHER | WEBSITE |
|---|---|---|
| *Alberta Journal of Educational Research* | Faculty of Education, University of Alberta | www.ajer.ca |
| *Canadian Journal of Behavioural Science* | Canadian Psychological Association | www.apa.org/pubs/journals/cbs |
| *Canadian Journal of Experimental Psychology* | Canadian Psychological Association | www.apa.org/pubs/journals/cep |
| *Canadian Psychology* | Canadian Psychological Association | www.apa.org/pubs/journals/cap |
| *Child Development* | Society for Research in Child Development | www.srcd.org |
| *Cognitive Development* | Jean Piaget Society | www.piaget.org |
| *Contemporary Educational Psychology* | Elsevier | www.elsevier.com |
| *Developmental Psychology* | American Psychological Association | www.apa.org/journals/dev |
| *Developmental Review* | Thompson Scientific | www.journals.elsevier.com/developmental-review |
| *Early Childhood Research Quarterly* | National Association for the Education of Young Children (NAEYC) | www.naeyc.org |
| *Educational Psychologist* | The Division of Educational Psychology (15) of the American Psychological Association | www.tandf.co.uk/journals |
| *Educational Psychology Review* | Springer | www.springer.com |
| *Exceptionality Education International* | Faculty of Education, University of Western Ontario | ir.lib.uwo.ca/eei |
| *Journal of Applied Developmental Psychology* | Elsevier | www.elsevier.com |
| *Journal of Educational Psychology* | American Psychological Association | www.apa.org/pubs/journals/edu/index.aspx |
| *Learning and Instruction* | European Association for Research on Learning and Instruction (EARLI) | www.elsevier.com |
| *Merrill Palmer Quarterly* | Wayne State University | muse.jhu.edu/journals/merrill-palmer_quarterly |
| *Theory Into Practice* | Taylor Francis and The Ohio State University | www.tandfonline.com/loi/htip20#.U--hG0iazAQ |
| *Psychology in the Schools* | Wiley | www.wiley.com/WileyCDA |
| *School Psychology Quarterly* | American Psychological Association | www.apa.org/journals/spq |
| *Teaching and Teacher Education* | Elsevier | www.elsevier.com |
| *The British Journal of Educational Psychology* | British Psychological Society | onlinelibrary.wiley.com/journal/10.1111/(ISSN)2044-8279 |
| *The Elementary School Journal* | University of Chicago Press | www.journals.uchicago.edu |

Another tool for building a better understanding of the teaching and learning processes is *theory*. The commonsense notion of theory (as in "Oh well, it was only a theory") is "a guess or hunch." But the scientific meaning of *theory* is quite different. "A **theory** in science is an interrelated set of concepts that is used to explain a body of data and to make predictions about the results of future experiments" (Stanovich, 1992, p. 21). Given a number of established principles, educational psychologists have developed explanations for the relationships among many variables and even whole systems of relationships. There are theories to explain how language develops, how differences in intelligence occur, and, as noted earlier, how people learn.

You will encounter many theories of development, learning, and motivation in this text. Theories are based on systematic research and they are the beginning and ending points of the research cycle. In the beginning, theories provide the research *hypotheses* to be tested or the questions examined. A **hypothesis** is a prediction of what will happen in a research study based on theory and previous research. For example, two different theories might suggest two competing predictions that could be tested. Piaget's theory might suggest that instruction cannot teach young children to think more abstractly, whereas Vygotsky's theory might suggest that this is possible. Of course, at times, psychologists don't know enough to make predictions, so they just ask *research questions*. An example question might be: "Is there a difference in internet usage by male and female adolescents from different ethnic groups?"

Research is a continuing cycle that involves:

- clear specification of hypotheses or questions based on current understandings or theories;
- systematic gathering and analyzing of all kinds of information (data) about the questions from well-chosen research participants;
- modification and improvement of explanatory theories based on the results of those analyses; and
- formulation of new and better questions based on the improved theories . . . and on and on.

This empirical process of collecting data to test and improve theories is repeated over and over, as you can see in Figure 1.2. **Empirical** means "based on data." When researchers

**Theory** Integrated statement of principles that attempts to explain a phenomenon and make predictions.

**Hypothesis** A prediction of what will happen in a research study based on theory and previous research.

**Empirical** Based on systematically collected data.

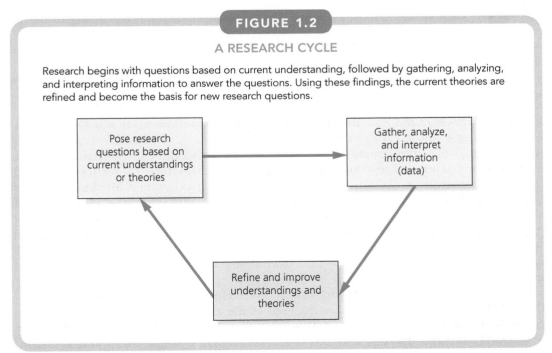

## FIGURE 1.2

### A RESEARCH CYCLE

Research begins with questions based on current understanding, followed by gathering, analyzing, and interpreting information to answer the questions. Using these findings, the current theories are refined and become the basis for new research questions.

Pose research questions based on current understandings or theories

Gather, analyze, and interpret information (data)

Refine and improve understandings and theories

*Source: Woolfolk, A; Perry, N. E. (2002). Child and Adolescent Development, 1st Edition. Reprinted by permission of Pearson Education, Inc., Upper Saddle River, NJ.*

say that identifying an effective antibiotic or choosing a successful way to teach reading is an "empirical question," they mean that you need data and evidence to make the call. Constructing decisions from empirical analyses protects psychologists from developing theories based on personal biases, rumours, fears, faulty information, or preferences (Mertler & Charles, 2005). Answering questions with carefully gathered data means that science is self-correcting. If predictions do not play out or if answers to carefully formulated questions do not support current best understandings (theories), then the theories have to be changed. You can use the same kind of systematic and self-correcting thinking in your work with students.

Few theories explain and predict perfectly. In this text, you will see many examples of educational psychologists taking different theoretical positions and disagreeing on the overall explanations of such issues as learning and motivation. Since no one theory offers all the answers, it makes sense to consider what each has to offer.

So why, you may ask, is it necessary to deal with theories? Why not just stick to principles? The answer is that both are useful. Principles of classroom management, for example, will give you help with specific problems. A good theory of classroom management, on the other hand, will give you a new way of thinking about discipline problems; it will give you tools for creating solutions to many different problems and for predicting what might work in new situations. A major goal of this text is to provide you with the best and the most useful theories for teaching—those that have solid evidence behind them. Although you may prefer some theories over others, consider them all as ways to understand the challenges teachers face.

The theories you encounter in this text should be used as cognitive tools to help you examine, inspect, and interpret the claims you will hear and read throughout your career (Leinhardt, 2001). No matter which theories or research methods we explore, education and psychology have had a long relationship. Educational psychology stands with a foot in two worlds: scholarship and practice. Merle Wittrock (1992, p. 138) sums it up well, saying that educational psychology focuses on "the psychological study of the everyday problems of education, from which one derives principles, models, theories, teaching procedures, and practical methods of instruction and evaluation, as well as research methods, statistical analyses, and measurement and assessment procedures appropriate for studying the thinking and affective processes of learners and the socially and culturally complex processes of schools." That about covers it.

We began this chapter by asserting that educational psychology is our favourite topic, as well as a key source of knowledge and skills for teaching. We end this chapter with one more bit of evidence for our enthusiasm. Educational psychology will help you support student learning, which is the goal of all teaching.

## Supporting Student Learning

In a recent article in the *Educational Psychologist*, a major journal in our field, Jihyun Lee and Valerie Shute (2010) sifted through thousands of studies of student learning conducted over the course of 60 years, seeking to identify those that had direct measures of student achievement in reading and mathematics. Then they narrowed their focus to studies with strong effects. About 150 studies met all their rigorous criteria. Using the results from these studies, Lee and Shute identified about a dozen variables that were directly linked to K–12 students' achievement. The researchers grouped these factors into two categories: *student/personal factors* and *school and social-contextual factors*. These are shown in Table 1.4. It doesn't surprise us that educational psychology provides a base for developing knowledge and skills in virtually every area.

As you can see in Table 1.4, this text should help you become a capable and confident teacher who can get students engaged in the classroom learning community—a community that respects its members. This text will guide you toward becoming a teacher who helps students develop into interested, motivated, self-regulated, and confident learners. As a consequence, you will be able to set high expectations for your students, rally the support of parents, and build your own sense of efficacy as a teacher.

TABLE 1.4 • **Research-Based Personal and Social-Contextual Factors That Support Student Achievement in K–12 Classrooms**

| STUDENT PERSONAL FACTORS | EXAMPLES | WHERE IN THIS TEXT |
|---|---|---|
| *Student Engagement* | | |
| Engaging Students' Behaviour | Make sure students attend classes, follow rules, participate in school activities. | Chapters 5, 6, 7, 13 |
| Engaging Students' Minds and Motivations | Design challenging tasks, tap intrinsic motivation, support student investment in learning, nurture student self-efficacy and other positive academic beliefs. | Chapters 2, 3, 10, 12 |
| Engaging Students' Emotions | Connect to student interest, pique curiosity, foster a sense of belonging and class connections, diminish anxiety, and increase enjoyment in learning. | Chapters 3, 5, 6, 10, 12 |
| *Learning Strategies* | | |
| Cognitive Strategies | Directly teach knowledge and skills that support student learning and deep processing of valuable information (e.g., summarizing, inferring, applying, reasoning). | Chapters 7, 8, 9, 14 |
| Metacognitive Strategies | Directly teach students to monitor, regulate, and evaluate their own cognitive processes, strengths, and weaknesses as learners; teach them about when, where, why, and how to use specific strategies. | Chapters 7, 8, 9, 11 |
| Behavioural Strategies | Directly teach students strategies and tactics for managing, monitoring, and evaluating their action, motivation, affect, and environment, such as skills in:<br>• time management<br>• test taking<br>• help seeking<br>• note taking<br>• homework management | Chapters 7, 8, 9, 10, 11, 12, 13, 14 |
| SOCIAL-CONTEXTUAL FACTORS | EXAMPLES | WHERE IN THIS TEXT |
| *School Climate* | | |
| Academic Emphasis | Set high expectations for your students and encourage the whole school to do the same; emphasize positive relations with the school community. | Chapters 11, 12, 13 |
| Teacher Variables | If possible, teach in a school with the positive qualities of collective efficacy, teacher empowerment, sense of affiliation. | Chapters 1, 11, 13 |
| Principal Leadership | If possible, teach in a school with the positive qualities of collegiality, high morale, and clearly conveyed goals. | See Woolfolk, Hoy & Hoy (2009) |
| *Social-Familial Influences* | | |
| Parental Involvement | Support parents in supporting their children's learning. | Chapters 3, 4, 6, 12 |
| Peer Influences | Create class and school norms that honour achievement, encourage peer support, and discourage peer conflict. | Chapters 10, 13, 15 |

*Source: Based on Lee, J., & Shute, V. J. (2010). Personal and social-contextual factors in K–12 academic performance: An integrative perspective on student learning. Educational Psychologist, 45, 185–202.*

# ▼ SUMMARY

Irina_QQQ/Shutterstock

### Learning and Teaching Today (pp. 2–5)

**What are classrooms like today?** Projections indicate that 25%–28% of Canada's population will be foreign-born by the year 2031, and 29%–32% will be members of visible minorities. Diversity continues to be concentrated in our largest cities (Toronto, Montreal, and Vancouver), and schools in these areas can have a majority of children who are English language learners. Too many children (one in seven) live in poverty, and these figures are higher for Aboriginal and immigrant populations. Classrooms include children with a wide range of abilities and disabilities. These statistics represent a challenge and an opportunity for Canada's teaching force, which is very homogeneous. The overarching goal of this text is to help you understand the complex processes of development, learning, motivation, teaching, and assessment so that you can become a capable and confident teacher.

**What evidence is there that teachers make a difference?** We cited several studies that speak to the power of teachers in the lives of students. The first found that the quality of the teacher–student relationship in kindergarten predicted several aspects of school success through grade 8. The second study examined mathematics achievement for students in two large school districts as they moved through grades 3, 4, and 5. Again, the quality of the teacher made a difference—students who had three high-quality teachers in a row were way ahead of students who spent one or more years with less competent teachers. In the study that followed children from grades 3 through 5, two factors helped children with lower skills in mathematics begin to close the achievement gap: higher-level (not just basic skills) instruction and positive relationships with teachers.

### What Is Good Teaching? (pp. 5–10)

**What is good teaching?** Good teachers are committed to their students. They must deal with a wide range of student abilities and challenges: different languages, different home situations, and different abilities and disabilities. They must adapt instruction and assessment to students' needs. The whole time that these experts are navigating through the academic material, they also are taking care of the emotional needs of their students, propping up sagging self-esteem, and encouraging responsibility. From the first day of class, they carefully plan and teach the basic procedures for living and learning in their classes.

**How does differentiated instruction help?** Differentiated instruction is one way of going beyond accommodating learner differences to viewing diversity as an array of strengths on which to build. The basic idea of differentiated instruction is that teachers must take into account not only the subjects they are teaching but also the students. In differentiated classrooms, students work at different paces, sometimes exercising varied learning options, and they are assessed using indicators that fit their interests and needs. Differentiated instruction conceives of all students as seeking purpose, challenge, affirmation, power, and the chance to contribute. The confident teacher sees these different student needs as opportunities, not problems, and responds with invitation, investment, persistence, challenge, and reflection.

**What are the concerns of beginning teachers?** Learning to teach is a gradual process. The concerns and problems of teachers change as they progress through their careers and grow in their ability. During the beginning years, attention tends to be focused on maintaining discipline, motivating students, accommodating differences among students, evaluating students' work, dealing with parents, and getting along with other teachers. Even with these concerns, many beginning teachers bring creativity and energy to their teaching and improve every year. The more experienced teacher can move on to concerns about professional growth and effectiveness in teaching a wide range of students.

**Good teachers are reflective, thoughtful, and inventive.** Reflective teachers think back over situations to analyze what they did and why, and to consider how they might improve learning for their students.

### The Role of Educational Psychology (pp. 10–19)

**What is educational psychology?** Educational psychology has been linked to teaching since the field was established over a century ago. The goals of educational psychology are to understand and to improve the teaching and learning processes. Educational psychologists develop knowledge and methods; they also use the knowledge and methods of psychology and other related disciplines to study learning and teaching in everyday situations. Educational psychologists examine what happens when *someone* (a teacher or parent) teaches *something* (math or weaving or dancing) to *someone else* (a student or co-worker or team) in some *setting* (a classroom or theatre or gym).

**What are descriptive studies?** Reports of descriptive studies often include survey results, interview responses, samples of actual classroom dialogue, or records of the class activities. Ethnographic methods involve studying the naturally occurring events in the life of a group and trying to understand the meaning of these events to the people involved. A case study investigates in depth how a teacher plans courses, for example, or how a student tries to learn specific material.

**What are correlational, experimental, and quasi-experimental studies?** A correlation is a number that indicates both the strength and the direction of a relationship between two events or measurements. The closer the correlation is to either 1.00 or −1.00, the stronger the relationship. Experimental studies can indicate cause-and-effect relationships and should help teachers implement useful changes. Instead of just observing and describing an existing situation, the investigators introduce changes and note the results. Quasi-experimental studies meet most of the criteria for true experiments, with the important exception being that the participants are not assigned to groups at random. Instead, existing groups such as classes or schools participate in the experiments.

**What are single-subject and microgenetic studies?** In single-subject experimental studies, researchers examine the effects of treatments on one person, often by using a baseline/intervention/baseline/intervention, or ABAB, approach. Microgenetic studies take many detailed observations of subjects to track the progression of change from the very beginning until a process becomes stable.

**What is action research?** When teachers or schools make systematic observations or test out methods to improve teaching and learning for their students, they are conducting action research. *Teacher research* and *teacher inquiry* are also used to describe these activities.

**What is the difference between principles and theories?** A principle is an established relationship between two or more factors—between a certain teaching strategy, for example, and student achievement. A theory is an interrelated set of concepts that is used to explain a body of data and to make predictions about the results of future experiments. The principles from research offer a number of possible answers to specific problems, and the theories offer perspectives for analyzing almost any situation that may arise. Research is a continuing cycle that involves clear specification of hypotheses or questions based on good theory, systematic gathering and analyzing of data, modification and improvement of explanatory theories based on the results, and the formulation of new, better questions based on the improved theories.

**What key factors support student learning?** A synthesis of about 150 studies of student learning found two broad categories of influence: *student personal factors* and *school and social-contextual factors*. When you read this article, you'll see that what might be your favourite subject, educational psychology, provides a base for developing knowledge and skills in virtually every area except principal leadership.

## ▼ WHAT WOULD THEY DO?

## TEACHERS' CASEBOOK: What Is an Effective Teacher?

Here is how two practising teachers responded to the teaching situation described on the first page of this chapter.

### SALLY BENDER
George Fitton School, Brandon, MB

While, individually, we have our ideas about what an exemplary teacher is and should be, it is important to look at what the profession is saying about the same issue. Taking time to read the professional journals and other literature would help in determining what a letter describing a colleague's performance should include. The granting of such a prestigious award could well depend on your words.

To prepare for writing the letter, I would list qualities describing my colleague's commitment to the profession and to the children whose lives are touched by excellent teaching practice. The list would include the following:

- builds close relationships with students and the school community through respect and example;
- creates a classroom that encourages and honours diversity in thinking and response;
- provides ongoing opportunities for children to take responsibility and ownership for what happens in the classroom and beyond;
- knows about child growth and development and uses that knowledge to drive the teaching and learning that occur in the classroom;
- manages the classroom with respect for the rights of the children and encourages them to take responsibility for their own actions at all times;
- is flexible enough to respond to "teachable moments" by giving up the "teaching" agenda for the "learning" one;
- models patience, tolerance, and respect for all;
- shares learning and teaching practice with colleagues;
- works as a team member and shares responsibility;
- is enthusiastic, challenging, and responsive to all students and colleagues;
- has consistent expectations and evaluates regularly the learning that is taking place for all students;
- provides a positive and encouraging atmosphere where children are free to take risks while learning and to learn from and through their mistakes;
- sees learning as a process that results in better performance;
- is knowledgeable about learning styles and uses that knowledge when planning lessons and learning experiences for all children;
- provides opportunities for learning that begin with the child's experiences and develop from the child's perspective;
- plans activities where cooperation is a necessity, for it is a life skill;
- ensures a classroom environment that is rich in print and language-stimulating possibilities;
- provides a balance between teacher-directed and child-initiated experiences;
- encourages parent support through regular communication.

By determining the qualities that you value in your colleague, you will be better prepared to write the letter of recommendation to accompany the nomination for such a prestigious award.

### JOCELYN SCHMIDT
Robert Munsch Public School, Mount Albert, ON

The definition of an "effective teacher" in the classroom is subject to interpretation on many levels, dependent on one's own experiences and knowledge of "good pedagogy," as well as one's familiarity with the research and literature that supports student development and curriculum practice. As a way of preparing a letter of recommendation for this colleague, whom I look up to, I would describe not only the specific qualities and skills that she brings into her classroom each day, but also the powerful and positive impact she has made on myself, her students, the school, and the community that has been touched by her teaching. By generating a list of key points based on my observations, interactions, and conversations with her, I would be able to make visible firsthand the depth and breadth of her commitment, leadership, and exemplary teaching practices within the profession. The list of strengths I would include in the letter appears below.

- Her passion drives her practice in a way that allows every student, teacher, and parent who enters her classroom to feel valued, respected, loved, cared for, and inspired to love learning.
- She views every child as a capable, competent, and creative thinker. As a result, she puts the essence of the "whole child" at the centre of her teaching and is responsive to students' interests, strengths, needs, and learning styles. Moreover, she ensures every child is motivated, challenged, and celebrated in diverse ways. She takes the time to differentiate tasks, entry points, and assessment to ensure every child can feel successful in their learning.
- She believes in the nature of "collaborative culture." She takes the time to get to know her students and their families and treats them as "partners" in their child's educational journey. She makes her learning and that of her students transparent and extends her knowledge to build positive relationships with community partners.
- She is a passionate risk-taker and reflective practitioner who creates a positive climate for learning whereby flexibility, differentiation, possibility, and encouragement are at the forefront of her teaching and of the relationships she creates with students, staff, and families.
- She has a "growth mindset" whereby, as a professional, she instils a level of self-motivation to always be a lifelong learner, which inspires her students and colleagues to strive to be the best they can be. As a result, she builds capacity within our school through the lens of professional development and student initiatives.

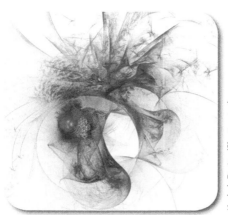

# COGNITIVE DEVELOPMENT

▶ **TEACHERS' CASEBOOK:** Symbols and Cymbals

The provincial curriculum guide calls for a unit on poetry, including lessons on *symbolism* in poems. You are concerned that many of your grade 5 students may not be ready to understand this abstract concept. To test the waters, you ask a few students to describe a symbol.

"It's sorta like a big metal thing that you bang together." Tracy waves her hands like a drum major.

"Yeah," Sean adds, "my sister plays one in the high school band."

You realize they are on the wrong track here, so you try again. "I was thinking of a different kind of symbol, like a ring as a symbol of marriage or a heart as a symbol of love, or . . ."

You are met with blank stares.

Trevor ventures, "You mean like the Olympic torch?"

"And what does that symbolize, Trevor?" you ask.

"Like I said, a torch." Trevor wonders how you could be so dense.

**CRITICAL THINKING**

- What do these students' reactions tell you about children's thinking?

- How would you approach this unit?

- What would you do to "listen" to your students' thinking so that you could match your teaching to their level of thinking?

- How would you give your students concrete experience with the concept of symbolism?

- How will you decide if the students are not developmentally ready for this material?

## OVERVIEW AND OBJECTIVES

What is going on with Trevor? In this chapter, you will find out. We begin with a definition of development and three questions that have intrigued psychologists who study it: nature versus nurture, continuity versus discontinuity, and critical versus sensitive periods for development. Next we look at general principles of human development that most psychologists affirm. To understand cognitive development, we begin by studying how the brain works, and then we explore the ideas of two of the most influential cognitive developmental theorists, Jean Piaget and Lev Vygotsky. Piaget's ideas have implications for teachers about how their students think and what they can learn. We will consider criticisms of his ideas as well. The work of Lev Vygotsky, a Russian psychologist, highlights the important role teachers and parents play in the cognitive development of the child. Vygotsky's theory is becoming more and more influential in the field of child development. By the time you have completed this chapter, you should be able to:

2.1 Provide a definition of development that takes into account three agreed-upon principles.

2.2 Discuss three ongoing debates about development, along with current consensus on these questions.

2.3 Summarize some current research on the physical development of the brain and possible implications for teaching.

2.4 Explain how the principles and stages presented in Piaget's theory of cognitive development influence current educational research and practice.

2.5 Explain how the principles presented in Vygotsky's theory of development influence current educational research and practice.

Look for the **Explore, Watch, Practise,** and **Listen** icons throughout this chapter . . . these symbols lead you to online content that will enhance and complement your textbook experience.

# A DEFINITION OF DEVELOPMENT

In the next few chapters, we will explore how students develop, and we will encounter some surprising situations. In this chapter, you will learn why the following children behave in peculiar ways:

- Leah, a 5-year-old, is certain that rolling out a ball of clay into a snake makes more clay.
- A 9-year-old child in Geneva, Switzerland, firmly believes that it is impossible to be Swiss and Genevan at the same time, insisting, "I'm already Swiss, I can't also be Genevan."
- Jamal, a very bright elementary school student, cannot answer the question, "How would life be different if people did not have to sleep?" because he insists, "People *have* to sleep!"
- A young girl who once said her *feet* hurt suddenly begins to refer to her *foots* hurting, then describes her *footses*, before she finally returns to talking about her *feet*.
- A 2-year-old brings his own mother to comfort a friend who is crying, even though the friend's mother is available, too.

What explains these interesting events? You will soon find out, because you are entering the world of child and adolescent development.

The term **development** in its most general psychological sense refers to certain changes that occur in human beings (or animals) between conception and death. The term is not applied to all changes, but rather to those that appear in orderly ways and remain for a reasonably long period of time. A temporary change caused by a brief illness, for example, is not considered a part of development.

Human development can be divided into a number of different aspects. **Physical development**, as you might guess, deals with changes in the body. **Personal development** is the term generally used for changes in an individual's personality. **Social development** refers to changes in the way an individual relates to others. And **cognitive development** refers to changes in thinking, reasoning, and decision making.

Many changes that occur during development are simply matters of growth and maturation. **Maturation** refers to changes that occur naturally and spontaneously, and that are, to a large extent, genetically programmed. Such changes emerge over time and are relatively unaffected by environment, except in cases of malnutrition or severe illness. Much of a person's physical development falls into this category. Other changes are brought about through learning, as individuals interact with their environment. Such changes make up a large part of a person's social development. What about the development of thinking and personality? Most psychologists agree that in these areas, both maturation and interaction with the environment (or nature and nurture, as they are sometimes called) are important, although they may disagree about the amount of emphasis to place on each. Nature versus nurture is one of three continuing discussions in theories of development.

## Three Questions Across the Theories

Because there are many different approaches to research and theory, as you saw in Chapter 1, there are some continuing debates about key questions surrounding development.

WHAT IS THE SOURCE OF DEVELOPMENT? NATURE VERSUS NURTURE.  Which is more important in development, the "nature" of an individual (heredity, genes, biological processes, maturation, etc.) or the "nurture" of environmental contexts (education, parenting, culture, social policies, etc.)? This debate has raged for at least 2000 years, and has had many labels along the way, including "heredity versus environment," "biology versus culture," "maturation versus learning," and "innate versus acquired abilities." In earlier centuries, philosophers, poets, religious leaders, and politicians argued the question. Today scientists bring new tools to the discussion as they can map genes or trace the effects of drugs on brain activity, for example (Gottlieb, Wahlsten, & Lickliter, 2006). Even in scientific explanations, the pendulum has swung back and forth between nature and nurture (Cairns & Cairns, 2006; Overton, 2006).

Today the environment is seen as critical, but so are biological factors and individual differences. In fact, some psychologists assert that behaviours are determined 100% by *biology* and 100% by environment—they can't be separated (Miller, 2002). Current views emphasize complex **coactions** (joint actions) of nature and nurture. For example, a child born with a very easygoing, calm disposition will likely elicit different reactions from parents, playmates, and teachers compared to a child who is often upset and difficult to soothe; this shows that individuals are active in constructing their own environments. But environments shape individuals as well—if not, what good would education be? So today, the either/or debates about nature and nurture are of less interest to educational and developmental psychologists. As a pioneering developmental psychologist said over 100 years ago, the more exciting questions involve understanding how "both causes work together" (Baldwin, 1895, p. 77).

WHAT IS THE SHAPE OF DEVELOPMENT? CONTINUITY VERSUS DISCONTINUITY.  Is human development a continuous process of adding to and increasing abilities, or are there leaps or moves to new stages when abilities actually change? A continuous process would be like gradual improvement in your running endurance through systematic exercise. A discontinuous change (also called *qualitative*) would be like many of the changes that occur

**Development** Orderly, adaptive changes that humans (or animals) go through from conception to death.

**Physical development** Changes in body structure that take place as one grows.

**Personal development** Changes in personality that take place as one grows.

**Social development** Changes over time in the ways in which one relates to others.

**Cognitive development** Gradual, orderly changes by which mental processes become more complex and sophisticated.

**Maturation** Genetically programmed, naturally occurring changes over time.

**Coactions** Joint actions of individual biology and environment—each shapes and influences the other.

in humans during puberty, such as the ability to reproduce—an entirely different ability. Qualitative changes are contrasted with purely *quantitative* change, such as an adolescent growing taller.

You can think of continuous or quantitative change like walking up a ramp to go higher and higher. Progress is steady. A discontinuous or qualitative change is more like walking up stairs—there are level periods, then you move up to the next step all at once. Piaget's theory of cognitive development, described in the next section, is an example of qualitative, discontinuous change in children's thinking abilities. But other explanations of cognitive development based on learning theories emphasize gradual, continuous quantitative change.

TIMING: IS IT TOO LATE? CRITICAL PERIODS AND EARLIER VERSUS LATER EXPERIENCES.   Are there critical periods when certain abilities, such as language, need to develop? If those opportunities are missed, can the child still "catch up"? These are questions about timing and development. Many earlier psychologists, particularly those influenced by Freud, believed that early childhood experiences were critical, especially for emotional/social and cognitive development. Does early toilet training really set all of us on a particular life path? Probably not. More recent research shows that later experiences are powerful, too, and can change the direction of development (Kagan & Herschkowitz, 2005). Most psychologists today talk about **sensitive periods**, not critical periods. There are times when a person is especially ready for or responsive to certain experiences. Also, early experiences, particularly those that have an adverse impact, have long-term consequences for development.

BEWARE OF EITHER/OR.   As you might imagine, the debates above proved too complicated to be settled by splitting alternatives into either/or possibilities (Griffins & Gray, 2005). Today, most psychologists see human development, learning, and motivation as a set of interacting and coacting contexts, from the inner biological structures and processes that influence development, such as genes, cells, nutrition, and disease, to the external factors of families, neighbourhoods, social relationships, educational and health institutions, public policies, time periods, historical events, and so on. So the effects of a childhood disease on the cognitive development of a child born in the sixteenth century to a poor family and treated by bloodletting or leeches will be quite different from the effect of the same disease on a child born in 2014 to a wealthy family and given the best treatment available for that time period. Throughout the rest of this text, we will try to make sense of development, learning, motivation, and teaching without falling into the *either/or trap*.

## General Principles of Development

Although there is disagreement about what is involved in development and about the way it takes place, there are a few general principles that almost all theorists would support.

1. *People develop at different rates.* In your own classroom, you will have a whole range of examples of different developmental rates. Some students will be larger, better coordinated, or more mature in their thinking and social relationships. Others will be much slower to mature in these areas. Except in rare cases of very rapid or very slow development, such differences are normal, and are to be expected in any large group of students.

2. *Development is relatively orderly.* People develop certain abilities before others. In infancy, they sit before they walk, babble before they talk, and see the world through their own eyes before they can begin to imagine how others see it. In school, they master addition before algebra, Harry Potter before Shakespeare, and so on. But "orderly" does not necessarily mean linear or predictable—people might advance, stay the same for a period of time, or even go backward.

3. *Development takes place gradually.* Very rarely do changes appear overnight. A student who cannot manipulate a pencil or answer a hypothetical question may well develop this ability, but the change is likely to take time.

**Sensitive periods** Times when a person is especially ready for or responsive to certain experiences.

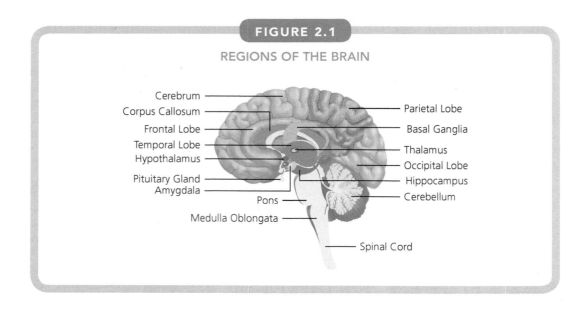

**FIGURE 2.1**

REGIONS OF THE BRAIN

Cerebrum — Parietal Lobe
Corpus Callosum — Basal Ganglia
Frontal Lobe — Thalamus
Temporal Lobe — Occipital Lobe
Hypothalamus — Hippocampus
Pituitary Gland — Cerebellum
Amygdala
Pons
Medulla Oblongata
Spinal Cord

# THE BRAIN AND COGNITIVE DEVELOPMENT

If you have taken an introductory psychology class, you have read about the brain and nervous system. You probably remember that there are several different areas of the brain, and that certain areas are involved in particular functions. For example, the feathery looking *cerebellum* coordinates and orchestrates balance and smooth, skilled movements—from the graceful gestures of a dancer to the everyday action of eating without stabbing yourself in the nose with a fork. The cerebellum may also play a role in higher cognitive functions such as learning. The *hippocampus* is critical in recalling new information and recent experiences, while the *amygdala* directs emotions. The *thalamus* is involved in our ability to learn new information, particularly if it is verbal. Figure 2.1 shows the various regions of the brain.

Advances in brain imaging techniques have allowed scientists remarkable access to the functioning brain. For example, **functional magnetic resonance imaging (fMRI)** shows how blood flows within the brain when children or adults do different cognitive tasks. **Event-related potential (ERP)** measurements assess electrical activity of the brain through the skull or scalp as people perform activities such as reading or learning vocabulary words. **Positron emission tomography (PET)** scans can track brain activity under different conditions.

Let's begin our look at the brain by examining its tiny components—neurons, synapses, and glial cells.

## The Developing Brain: Neurons

A newborn baby's brain weighs about one pound, or 454 grams, barely one-third of the weight of an adult brain. But this infant brain has billions of **neurons**, the specialized nerve cells that accumulate and transmit information (in the form of electrical activity) in the brain and other parts of the nervous system. Neurons are a greyish colour, so they sometimes are called the *grey matter* of the brain. One neuron has the information processing capacity of a small computer. That means the processing power of one 3-pound (1.4-kilogram) human brain is likely greater than all the computers in the world. Of course, computers do many things, like calculate square roots of large numbers, much faster than humans can (Anderson, 2010). These incredibly important neuron cells are tiny—about 30 000 could fit on the head of a pin (Sprenger, 2010). Scientists once believed that all the neurons a person would ever have were present at birth, but now we know that the production of new neurons, **neurogenesis**, continues into adulthood (Johnson, 2003).

**Functional magnetic resonance imaging (fMRI)** An MRI is an imaging technique that uses a magnetic field along with radio waves and a computer to create detailed pictures of the inside of the body. A functional MRI uses the MRI to measure the tiny changes that take place in the brain during brain activity.

**Event-related potential (ERP)** Measurements that assess electrical activity of the brain through the skull or scalp.

**Positron emission tomography (PET)** A method of localizing and measuring brain activity using computer-assisted motion pictures of the brain.

**Neurons** Nerve cells that store and transfer information.

**Neurogenesis** The production of new neurons.

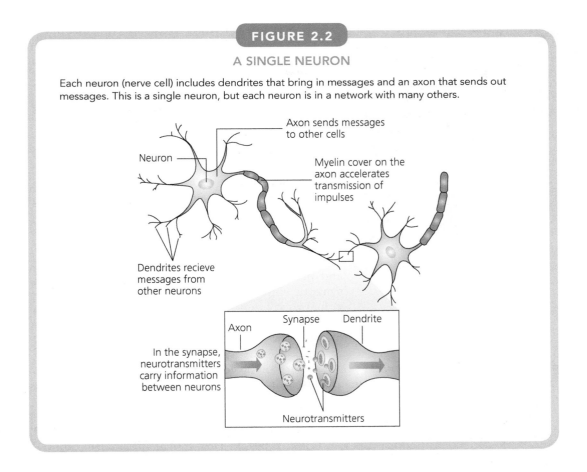

**FIGURE 2.2**

A SINGLE NEURON

Each neuron (nerve cell) includes dendrites that bring in messages and an axon that sends out messages. This is a single neuron, but each neuron is in a network with many others.

Axon sends messages to other cells

Neuron

Myelin cover on the axon accelerates transmission of impulses

Dendrites recieve messages from other neurons

Axon     Synapse     Dendrite

In the synapse, neurotransmitters carry information between neurons

Neurotransmitters

Neuron cells send out long arm- and branch-like fibres called *axons* and *dendrites* to connect with other neuron cells. The fibre ends from different neurons don't actually touch—there are tiny spaces between them, about one billionth of a metre in length, called **synapses**. Neurons share information by releasing chemicals that jump across the synapses. Axons transmit information out to muscles, glands, or other neurons; dendrites receive information and transmit it to the neuron cells themselves. Figure 2.2 shows these components of the neuron system (Anderson, 2010).

At birth, each of the child's 100 to 200 billion neurons has about 2500 synapses. However, the fibres that reach out from the neurons and the synapses between the fibre ends increase during the first years of life, perhaps into adolescence or longer. By ages 2 to 3, each neuron has around 15 000 synapses. Children this age have many more synapses than they will have as adults. In fact, they are *oversupplied* with the neurons and synapses that they will need to adapt to their environments. However, only those neurons that are used will survive. Unused neurons will be "pruned." This pruning is necessary and supports cognitive development. Researchers have found that some developmental disabilities are associated with a gene defect that interferes with pruning (Bransford, Brown, & Cocking, 2000; Cook & Cook, 2009).

Two kinds of overproduction and pruning processes take place. One is called *experience-expectant* because synapses are overproduced in certain parts of the brain during specific developmental periods, awaiting (expecting) stimulation. For example, during the first months of life, the brain expects visual and auditory stimulation. If a normal range of sights and sounds occurs, then the visual and auditory areas of the brain develop. But children who are born completely deaf receive no auditory stimulation and, as a result, the auditory processing area of their brains becomes devoted to processing visual information. Similarly, the visual processing area of the brain for children blind from birth becomes devoted to auditory processing (Nelson, 2001; Neville, 2007).

**Synapses** The tiny space between neurons; chemical messages are sent across these gaps.

**SUPPORTING BRAIN DEVELOPMENT** Studies of the brain indicate that stimulating environments and meaningful interactions with parents and teachers likely support better brain development.

Stephen McBrady/PhotoEdit

Experience-expectant overproduction and pruning processes are responsible for general development in large areas of the brain, and may explain why adults have difficulty with pronunciations that are not part of their native language. The neurons and synapses that are not involved in recognizing native language sounds may have been "pruned." For example, the distinction between the sounds of *r* and *l* is important in English but not in Japanese, so by about 10 months, Japanese infants lose the ability to discriminate between *r* and *l*—*those neurons are pruned away*. As a result, Japanese adults learning these sounds require intense instruction and practice (Bransford, Brown, & Cocking, 2000; Hinton, Miyamoto, & Della-Chiesa, 2008).

The second kind of synaptic overproduction and pruning is called *experience-dependent*. Here, synaptic connections are formed based on the individual's experiences. New synapses are formed in response to neural activity in very localized areas of the brain when the individual is not successful in processing information. Again, more synapses are produced than will be kept after "pruning." Experience-dependent processes are involved in individual learning, such as mastering unfamiliar sound pronunciations in a second language you are studying, or developing an ear for music.

Stimulating environments may help in the pruning process in early life (experience-expectant period) and also may support increased synapse development in adulthood (experience-dependent period) (Cook & Cook, 2009). In fact, animal studies have shown that rats raised in stimulating environments (with toys, tasks for learning, other rats, and human handling) develop and retain 25% more synapses than rats that are raised with little stimulation. Even though the research with rats may not apply directly to humans, it is clear that extreme deprivation can have negative effects on human brain development. Perhaps the best examples of this come from studies of children raised in institutions/orphanages (Nelson, Zeanah, Fox, Marshall, Smyke, & Guthrie, 2007; Twardosz, 2012). In these contexts, where infants and children receive very basic physical care, very little in the way of sensory or social stimulation, and very limited opportunities to develop meaningful relationships with caregivers, studies find evidence of *cortical hypoarousal*, or diminished electrical activity in the brain, as well as problems with attachment, attention, and emotion control, and delays in cognitive and language development (Chugani, Behen, Muzik, Juhasz, Nagy, & Chugani, 2001; Smyke, Zeanah, Fox, Nelson, & Guthrie, 2010; Windsor, Glaze, Koga, & BEIP Core Group, 2007). But extra stimulation will not necessarily improve development for young children who are getting adequate or typical amounts (Byrnes & Fox, 1998; Kolb & Whishaw, 1998). So spending money on expensive toys or baby education programs probably offers more stimulation than is necessary. Pots and pans, blocks and books, sand and water all provide excellent stimulation—especially if accompanied by caring conversations with parents or teachers.

**Glial cells** The white matter of the brain. These cells greatly outnumber neurons and appear to have many functions, such as fighting infections, controlling blood flow and communication among neurons, and providing the myelin coating around axon fibres.

**Myelination** The process by which neural fibres are coated with a fatty sheath called myelin that makes message transfer more efficient.

In Figure 2.2, it appears that there is nothing between the neurons but air. Actually, the spaces are filled with **glial cells**, the *white matter* of the brain. There are trillions of these cells—they greatly outnumber neurons. Glial cells appear to have many functions, such as fighting infections, controlling blood flow and communication among neurons, and providing the *myelin* coating (see Figure 2.2) around axon fibres (Ormrod, 2012). **Myelination**, the coating of axon neuron fibres with an insulating fatty glial covering, influences thinking and learning. This process is something like coating bare electrical wires with rubber or plastic. This myelin coating makes message transmission faster and more efficient. Myelination happens quickly in the early years, but continues gradually into adolescence, with the child's brain doubling in volume in the first year of life and doubling again around puberty (Anderson, 2010).

**FIGURE 2.3**

### A VIEW OF THE CEREBRAL CORTEX

This is a simple representation of the left side of the human brain, showing the cerebral cortex. The cortex is divided into different areas, or lobes, each having a variety of regions with different functions. A few of the major functions are indicated here.

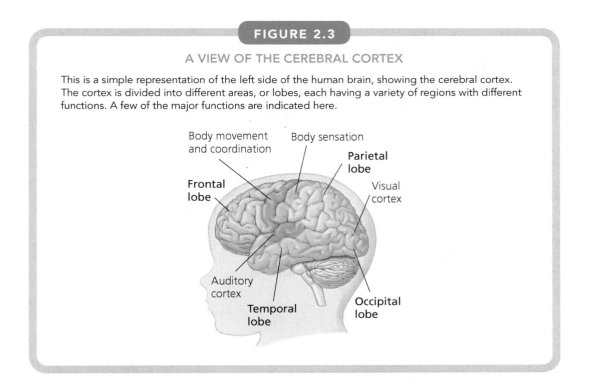

## The Developing Brain: Cerebral Cortex

Let's move from the neuron level to the brain itself. The outer 1/8-inch-thick (3.18-millimetre) covering is the cerebral cortex—the largest area of the brain. It is a thin sheet of neurons, but it is almost 3 square feet (0.28 square metres) in area for adults. To get all that area in your head, the sheet is crumpled together with many folds and wrinkles (Anderson, 2010). In humans, this area of the brain is much larger than it is in lower animals. The cerebral cortex accounts for about 85% of the brain's weight in adulthood and contains the greatest number of neurons. The cerebral cortex allows the greatest human accomplishments, such as complex problem solving and language.

The cortex is the last part of the brain to develop, so it is believed to be more susceptible to environmental influences than other areas of the brain (Gluck, Mercado, & Myers, 2008; Schacter, Gilbert, & Wenger, 2009). Parts of the cortex mature at different rates. The region of the cortex that controls physical motor movement matures first, then the areas that control complex senses such as vision and hearing, and last, the frontal lobe that controls higher-order thinking processes. The temporal lobes of the cortex that play major roles in emotions, judgment, and language do not develop fully until the high school years and maybe later.

Different areas of the cortex seem to have distinct functions, as shown in Figure 2.3. Even though different functions are found in particular areas of the brain, these specialized functions are quite specific and elementary. To accomplish more complex functions such as speaking or reading, the various areas of the cortex must communicate and work together (Anderson, 2010; Byrnes & Fox, 1998).

Another aspect of brain functioning that has implications for cognitive development is **lateralization**, or the specialization of the two hemispheres of the brain. We know that each half of the brain controls the opposite side of the body. Damage to the right side of the brain will affect movement of the left side of the body and vice versa. In addition, certain areas of the brain affect particular behaviours. For most of us, the left hemisphere of the brain is a major factor in language processing, and the right hemisphere handles much of our spatial-visual information and emotions (nonverbal information). For some left-handed people, the relationship may be reversed, but for most left-handers, and for females on average, there is less hemispheric specialization altogether (Anderson, 2010;

**Lateralization** The specialization of the two hemispheres (sides) of the brain cortex.

O'Boyle & Gill, 1998). The brains of young children show more **plasticity** (adaptability) because they are not as specialized or lateralized as the brains of older children and adults. Young children with damage to the left side of the brain are somewhat able to overcome the damage, which allows language development to proceed. Different areas of the brain take over the functions of the damaged area. But in older children and adults, this compensation is less likely to occur after damage to the left brain hemisphere.

These differences in performance by the brain's hemispheres, however, are more relative than absolute; one hemisphere is just more efficient than the other in performing certain functions. The left and right hemispheres process language "differently, but simultaneously" (Alferink & Farmer-Dougan, 2010, p. 44). Nearly any task, particularly the complex skills and abilities that concern teachers, requires simultaneous participation of many different areas of the brain in constant communication with each other. For example, the right side of the brain is better at figuring out the meaning of a story, but the left side is where grammar and syntax are understood, so both sides of the brain have to work together in reading. Remember, no mental activity is exclusively the work of a single part of the brain—so there is no such thing as a "right-brained student" unless that individual has had the left hemisphere removed—a rare and radical treatment for some forms of epilepsy.

## Adolescent Development and the Brain

The brain continues to develop throughout childhood and adolescence. During adolescence, changes in the brain increase individuals' abilities to control their behaviour in both low-stress and high-stress situations, to be more purposeful and organized, and to inhibit impulsive behaviour (Wigfield, Byrnes, & Eccles, 2006). But these abilities are not fully developed until the early 20s, so adolescents may "seem" like adults, at least in low-stress situations, but their brains are not fully developed. They often have trouble avoiding risks and controlling impulses. This is why adolescents' brains have been described as having "high horsepower, poor steering" (Organisation for Economic Co-operation and Development [OECD], 2007, p. 6). One explanation looks to differences in the pace of development for two key systems involved in making sound decisions about risky behaviours and controlling impulsive behaviour—the limbic system and the prefrontal cortex of the brain (Casey, Getz, & Galvan, 2008). The limbic system develops earlier; it is involved with emotions and reward-seeking/novelty/risk-taking/sensation-seeking behaviours. The prefrontal lobe takes more time to develop; it is involved with judgment and decision making.

As the limbic system matures, adolescents become more responsive to pleasure seeking and emotional stimulation. In fact, adolescents appear to need more intense emotional stimulation than either children or adults, so these young people are set up for taking risks and seeking thrills. Risk taking and novelty seeking can be positive factors for adolescent development as young people courageously try new ideas and behaviours—and learning is stimulated (McAnarney, 2008). But their less mature prefrontal lobe is not yet good at saying, "Whoa—that thrill is too risky!" So in emotional situations, thrill seeking wins out over caution, at least until the prefrontal lobe catches up and becomes more integrated with the limbic system toward the end of adolescence. Then risks can be evaluated in terms of long-term consequences, not immediate thrills (Casey, Getz, & Galvan, 2008; Steinberg, 2008). In addition, there are individual differences: Some adolescents are more prone than others to engage in risky behaviours.

Teachers can take advantage of their adolescent students' intensity by helping them devote their energy and passion to areas such as politics, the environment, or social causes (Price, 2005) or by guiding them to explore emotional connections with characters in history or literature. Connections to family, school, community, and positive belief systems help adolescents "put the brakes" on reckless and dangerous behaviours (McAnarney, 2008).

Other changes in the neurological system during adolescence affect sleep. Teenagers are notorious for staying up late and wanting to sleep late. It turns out there may be a brain-based biological explanation for this (Mayo Clinic Staff, 2013). We all have an

**Plasticity** The brain's tendency to remain somewhat adaptable or flexible.

internal clock that influences sleep cycles among other things. Before puberty this internal clock is set such that most children naturally fall asleep around 8 or 9 p.m. During puberty, it appears this clock is reset, delaying the time at which teens feel tired and making it difficult for them to get to sleep early. Teenagers need about nine hours of sleep per night, but according a study published in the *Journal of School Health* (Noland, Price, Dake, & Telljohann, 2009) most adolescents (more than 90%) report they get less than that (10% reported getting less than six hours of sleep on school nights). Over time, this sleep deprivation can have serious consequences for teens. They may experience difficulties concentrating and learning, experience mood swings and behaviour problems, and "drowsy driving" could lead to serious accidents. Some parents and other advocates argue high school should begin later in the day to be more in synch with teenagers' internal clocks. Other strategies include establishing a schedule that has teens going to bed and getting up at the same time each day, even on weekends; curbing daytime naps and caffeinated drinks; winding down in the evening—limit socializing and "unplug" as bedtime approaches (Mayo Clinic Staff, 2013).

## Putting It All Altogether: How the Brain Works

What is your conception of the brain? Is the brain a culture-free container that holds knowledge the same way for everyone? Is the brain like a library of facts or a computer filled with information? Do you wake up in the morning, download what you need for the day, and then go merrily on your way? Is the brain like a pipe that transfers information from one person to another—a teacher to a student, for example? Kurt Fischer (2009) offers a different view, based on neuroscience research. Knowing is actively constructing understandings and actions. Knowledge is based in our activities:

> When animals and people do things in their worlds, they shape their behavior. Based on brain research, we know that likewise they literally shape the anatomy and physiology of their brains (and bodies). When we actively control our experience, that experience sculpts the way that our brains work, changing neurons, synapses, and brain activity. (p. 5)

Cultural differences in brain activity provide examples of how interactions in the world shape the brain. For example, in one study, when Chinese speakers added and compared Arabic numbers, they showed brain activity in the motor (movement) areas of their brains, whereas English speakers performing the same tasks had activity in the language areas of their brains (Tang et al., 2006). One explanation is that Chinese children are taught arithmetic using an abacus—a calculation tool that involves movement and spatial positions. As adults, these children retain a kind of visual-motor sense of numbers (Varma, McCandliss, & Schwartz, 2008). There also are cultural differences in how languages affect reading. For example, when they read, native Chinese speakers activate additional parts of their brain associated with spatial information processing, probably because the characters used in written Chinese are pictures. But Chinese speakers also activate these spatial areas of the brain when they read English, demonstrating that reading proficiency can be reached through different neural pathways (Hinton, Miyamoto, & Della-Chiesa, 2008).

So the brain is ever changing, shaped by activity, culture, and context. We build knowledge as we do things, as we manipulate objects and ideas mentally and physically. What are the implications of this for teaching? Many publications for parents and teachers have useful ideas about the brain and education, but beware of suggestions that oversimplify. As you will see next, the jury still is out on many of these "brain-based" programs.

## Neuroscience, Learning, and Teaching

There are many popular neuromyths about the brain, as you can see in Table 2.1. We have to be careful about what we encounter in the media.

We know teaching can change the organization and structure of the brain. For example, individuals who are deaf and use sign language have different patterns of electrical

TABLE 2.1 • **Myths About the Brain**

| COMMON MYTHS | TRUTH |
| --- | --- |
| 1. You use only 10% of your brain. | 1. You use all of your brain. That is why strokes are so devastating. |
| 2. Listening to Mozart will make children smarter. | 2. Listening won't, but learning to play a musical instrument is associated with increased cognitive achievement. |
| 3. Some people are more "right brained," and others are more "left brained." | 3. It takes both sides of your brain to do most things. |
| 4. A young child's brain can only manage to learn one language at a time. | 4. Children all over the world can and do learn two (or more) languages at once. |
| 5. You can't change your brain. | 5. Our brains are changing all the time. |
| 6. Damage to the brain is permanent. | 6. Most people recover well from minor brain injuries. |
| 7. Playing games like Sudoku keeps your brain from aging. | 7. Playing Sudoku makes you better at playing Sudoku and similar games. Physical exercise is a better bet to prevent decline. |
| 8. The human brain is the biggest brain. | 8. Sperm whales have brains five times heavier than those of humans. |
| 9. Alcoholic beverages kill brain cells. | 9. Heavy drinking does not kill brain cells but it can damage the nerve ends called dentrites, and this causes problems with communicating messages in the brain. This damage is mostly reversible. |
| 10. The adolescent's brain is the same as that of an adult. | 10. There are critical differences between adolescents' and adults' brains: Adolescents' brains have "high horsepower, but poor steering" (Fischer, 2009). |

*Source: Adapted from Aamodt, S., & Wang, S. (2008). Welcome to your brain: Why you lose your car keys but never forget how to drive and other puzzles of everyday life. New York, NY: Bloomsbury; Fischer, K. W. (2009). Mind, brain, and education: Building a scientific groundwork for learning and teaching. Mind, Brain, and Education, 3, 2–16; Freeman, S. (2011). Top 10 Myths About the Brain, How Stuff Works. Available online at http://health.howstuffworks.com/human-body/systems/nervous-system/10-brain-myths.htm; OECD (2007).*

activity in their brains than people who are deaf and do not use sign language (Varma, McCandliss, & Schwartz, 2008).

**INSTRUCTION AND BRAIN DEVELOPMENT.**   Several studies have shown differences in brain activity associated with instruction. For example, the intensive instruction and practice provided to rehabilitate stroke victims can help them regain functioning by forming new connections and using new areas of the brain (Bransford, Brown, & Cocking, 2000; McKinley, 2011). In another example, Margarete Delazer and her colleagues (2005) compared students' brain activity as they learned new arithmetic operations, either by just memorizing the answers or by learning an algorithm strategy. Using functional magnetic resonance imaging (fMRI), the researchers found that students who simply memorized answers showed greater activity in the area of the brain that specializes in retrieving verbal information, whereas the students who used a strategy showed greater activity in the visual-spatial processing portion of the brain.

Bennett Shaywitz and his colleagues (2004) reported a dramatic demonstration of brain changes in children following instruction. The researchers studied 28 children ages 6 to 9 who were good readers and 49 children who were poor readers. Again, fMRIs showed differences in the brain activity of the two groups. The poor readers underused parts of their brains' left hemispheres and sometimes overused their right hemispheres. After over 100 hours of intensive instruction in letter–sound combinations, reading ability improved; the brains of the poor readers started to function more like those of the good readers and continued this functioning a year later. Poor readers who received the standard school remediation did not show the brain function changes.

In another dramatic example of how teaching can affect brain development, Fischer (2009) describes two children who each had one brain hemisphere removed as a treatment for severe epilepsy. Nico's right hemisphere was removed when he was 3, and his parents were told he would never have good visual-spatial skills. With strong and constant support and teaching, Nico grew up to be a skilled artist! Brooke's left hemisphere was removed when he was 11. His parents were told he would lose his ability to talk. Again, with strong support, he regained enough speaking and reading ability to finish high school and attend community college.

THE BRAIN AND LEARNING TO READ. Brain imaging research is revealing interesting differences among skilled and less skilled readers as they learn new vocabulary. For example, one imaging study showed that less skilled readers had trouble establishing high-quality representations of new vocabulary words in their brains, as indicated by *event-related potential (ERP)* measurements of electrical activity of the brain. When they encountered the new word later, less skilled readers' brains often didn't recognize that they had seen the word before, even though they had learned the words in an earlier lesson. If words you have learned seem unfamiliar later, you can see how it would be hard to understand what you read (Balass, Nelson, & Perfetti, 2010).

**BRAIN RESEARCH AND READING** Brain research may help us understand why strategies for teaching reading are or are not effective.

Digital Vision/Thinkstock/Getty Images

Reading is not innate or automatic—every brain has to be taught to read (Frey & Fisher, 2010). Reading is a complex integration of the systems in the brain that recognize sounds, written symbols, meanings, and sequences, and then connect with what the reader already knows. This has to happen quickly and automatically (Wolf et al., 2009). Will brain research help us teach reading more effectively? Judith Willis (2009), a neurobiologist who became a science teacher, cautions that neuroimaging and the other brain monitoring systems used for reading research offer *suggestive* rather than directive evidence.

Although the strategies for teaching reading that are consistent with brain research are not completely new, the research may help us understand *why* these strategies work. What are some strategies suggested? Use multiple approaches that teach sounds, spelling, meanings, sequencing, and vocabulary through reading, writing, discussing, explaining, drawing, and modelling. Different students may learn in different ways, but all need practice in literacy.

EMOTIONS, LEARNING, AND THE BRAIN. Finally, another clear connection between the brain and classroom learning is in the area of emotions and stress. For an example, let's step inside a high school math classroom Hinton, Miyamoto, and Della-Chiesa (2008, p. 91) described.

> Patricia, a high school student, struggles with mathematics. The last few times she answered a mathematics question she got it wrong and felt terribly embarrassed, which formed an association between mathematics . . . and negative emotions. . . . Her teacher had just asked her to come to the blackboard to solve a problem. This caused an immediate transfer of this emotionally-charged association to the amygdala, which elicits fear. Meanwhile, a slower, cortically-driven cognitive appraisal of the situation is occurring: she remembers her difficulty completing her mathematics homework last night, notices the problem on the board contains complicated graphs, and realizes that the boy she has a crush on is watching her from a front-row seat. These various thoughts converge to a cognitive confirmation that this is a threatening situation, which reinforces her progressing fear response and disrupts her ability to concentrate on solving the mathematics problem.

# POINT/COUNTERPOINT Brain-Based Education

Educators are hearing more and more about brain-based education, the importance of early stimulation for brain development, the "Mozart effect," and right- and left-brain activities. In fact, based on some research findings that listening to 10 minutes of Mozart can briefly improve spatial reasoning (Rauscher & Shaw, 1998; Steele, Bass, & Crook, 1999), a former governor of Georgia established a program to give a Mozart CD to every newborn. The scientists who had done the work couldn't believe how their research had been "applied" (Katzir & Pare-Blagoev, 2006). In fact, the governor apparently had confused experiments on infant brain development with studies of adults (Pinker, 2002). Are there clear educational implications from the neuroscience research on the brain?

**POINT** ▶ **No, the implications are not clear.** Catherine and Miriam Beauchamp (2013) note that the application of neuroscience to education actually has been plagued by misapplications because the findings have been treated in isolation, without attention to knowledge from other disciplines such as cognitive science or educational psychology that place the findings in context. To further complicate the problem of misapplication, educators and neuroscience researchers have different meanings for "learning," and don't have an appreciation for each other's reality—neuroscientists don't understand schools, and educators don't have a background in neurobiology.

John Bruer, president of the James S. McDonnell Foundation, has written articles that are critical of the brain-based education craze (Bruer, 1999, 2002). He notes that many so-called applications of brain research begin with solid science, but then move to unwarranted speculation, and end in a sort of appealing folk tale about the brain and learning. He suggests that for each claim, the educator should ask, "Where does the science end and the speculation begin?" For example, one claim that Bruer questions is the notion of right-brain, left-brain learning.

*"Right brain versus left brain" is one of those popular ideas that will not die. Speculations about the educational significance of brain laterality have been circulating in the education literature for 30 years. Although repeatedly criticized and dismissed by psychologists and brain scientists, the speculation continues. David Sousa devotes a chapter of How the Brain Learns to explaining brain laterality and presents classroom strategies that teachers might use to ensure that both hemispheres are involved in learning. . . . Now let's consider the brain sciences and* how or whether they offer support for some of the particular teaching strategies Sousa recommends. To involve the right hemisphere in learning, Sousa writes, teachers should encourage students to generate and use mental imagery. . . . What brain scientists currently know about spatial reasoning and mental imagery provides counter examples to such simplistic claims as these. Such claims arise out of a folk theory about brain laterality, not a neuroscientific one. . . . Different brain areas are specialized for different tasks, but that specialization occurs at a finer level of analysis than "using visual imagery." Using visual imagery may be a useful learning strategy, but if it is useful it is not because it involves an otherwise underutilized right hemisphere in learning. (Bruer, 1999, pp. 653–654)

Ten years later, Kurt Fischer (2009), president of the International Mind, Brain, and Education Society, lamented

*Expectations for neuroscience and genetics to shape educational practice and policy have exploded far beyond what is merited by the state of the emerging field of MBE [mind body education] and the level of knowledge about how brains and genetics function ... Many neuromyths "have entered popular discourse—beliefs about how the brain and body work that are widely accepted but blatantly wrong" (OECD, 2007b). Most of what is put forward as "brain-based education" builds on these scientifically inaccurate myths: The one small way that neuroscience relates to most brain-based education is that the students have brains. There is no grounding for these claims in the young field of neuroscience.*

No teacher doubts that the brain is important in learning. As Steven Pinker (2002), professor of psychology at Harvard

---

In Chapter 7 you will learn about how emotions can become paired with particular situations; in Chapter 11, you will see that anxiety interferes with learning, whereas challenge, interest, and curiosity can support learning. If students feel unsafe and anxious, they are not likely to be able to focus attention on academics (Sylvester, 2003). But if students are not challenged or interested, learning suffers, too. Keeping the level of challenge and support "just right" is a challenge for teachers. And helping students learn to regulate their own emotions and motivation is an important goal for education (see Chapter 10).

Simply put, learning will be more effective "if educators help to minimize stress and fear at school, teach students emotional regulation strategies, and provide a positive learning environment that is motivating to students" (Hinton, Miyamoto, & Della-Chiesa, 2008).

University, observed, does anyone really think learning takes place somewhere else, like the pancreas? But knowing that learning affects the brain does not tell us how to teach. All learning affects the brain: ". . . this should be obvious, but nowadays any banality about learning can be dressed up in neurospeak and treated like a great revelation of science" (2002, p. 86). Virtually all of the so-called best practices for brain-based education are simple restatements of good teaching based on understandings of how people learn, not how their brains work. For example, we have known for over 100 years that it is more effective to learn in many shorter practice sessions as opposed to one long cramming session. To tie that fact to building more dendrites does not give teachers new strategies (Alferink & Farmer-Dougan, 2010). Finally, Richard Haier and Rex Jung (2008) look to the future: "Someday, we believe that our educational system will be informed by neuroscience knowledge, especially concerning intelligence, but how we get from here to there remains unclear" (p. 177).

▶ **Yes, teaching should be brain-based.** Articles in popular magazines such as *Newsweek* assert, " . . . it's naive to say that brain discoveries have no consequences for understanding how humans learn" (Begley, 2007). Do scientists agree? In their article "Applying Cognitive Neuroscience Research to Education" in *Educational Psychologist*, Tami Katzir and Juliana Paré-Blagoev (2006) conclude, "When applied correctly, brain science may serve as a vehicle for advancing the application of our understanding of learning and development. . . . Brain research can challenge common-sense views about teaching and learning by suggesting additional systems that are involved in particular tasks and activities" (p. 70). If we are to guard against overstating the links between brain research and education, then we should not ask *if*, but instead "how best to teach neuroscience concepts to preservice teachers" (Dubinsky et al., 2013, p. 325). A number of universities, including Harvard, Cambridge, Dartmouth, the University of Texas at Arlington, the University of Southern California, Beijing Normal University, Southeast University in Nanjing, and Johns Hopkins, have established training programs for educators in brain-education studies (Dubinsky et al., 2013; Fischer, 2009; Wolfe, 2010). Other educational

psychologists have called for a new professional specialty—neuro-educators (Beauchamp & Beauchamp, 2013).

Brain research is leading to much better understandings about learning disabilities. For example, neuroscience studies of people with reading disabilities have found that these individuals may have trouble with sounds and sound patterns or with retrieving the names of very familiar letters, so there may be different bases for the reading disabilities (Katzir & Paré-Blagoev, 2006).

There are examples of applying knowledge of brain research to education. A reading improvement product called FastForword was developed by two neuroscientists, Dr. Michael Merzenich and Dr. Paula Tallal, and is in use today in classrooms around the country (see http://www.scilearn.com/results/success-stories/index.php). It specifically uses discoveries in neural plasticity to change the brain's ability to read the printed word (Tallal & Miller, 2003).

In his presidential address for the First Conference of the International Mind, Brain, and Education Society, Kurt Fischer, a developmental psychologist and Harvard professor, noted,

*The primary goal of the emerging field of Mind, Brain, and Education is to join biology, cognitive science, development, and education in order to create a sound grounding of education in research. The growing, worldwide movement needs to avoid the myths and distortions of popular conceptions of brain and genetics and build on the best integration of research with practice, creating a strong infrastructure that joins scientists with educators to study effective learning and teaching in educational settings. (2009, pp. 3–16)*

Fischer makes the point that we can go from understanding how the brain works to understanding cognitive processes, and then to developing educational practices. But jumping directly from knowledge about the brain to educational practices probably involves too much speculation.

**Beware of Either/Or.** Schools should not be run on curriculums based solely on the biology of the brain. However, to ignore what we do know about the brain would be equally irresponsible. Brain-based learning offers some direction for educators who want more purposeful, informed teaching. At the very least, the neuroscience research is helping us to understand why effective teaching strategies, such as distributed practice, work.

*Resources: Podcast on understanding the brain: http://www.oecd.org/document/60/0,3343,en_2649_35845581_38811388_1_1_1_1,00.html.*

As you can imagine, based on these and other amazing research results, educators have looked for applications of neuroscience research for their instruction. This has led to vigorous debate between the enthusiastic educational advocates of brain-based education and the skeptical neuroscience researchers who caution that studies of the brain do not really address major educational questions. See the *Point/Counterpoint* for a slice of this debate.

**STOP & THINK** As a teacher, you don't want to fall for overly simplistic "brain-based" teaching slogans. But obviously the brain and learning are intimately related—this is not a surprise. So how can you be savvy about neuroscience as a teacher (Murphy & Benton, 2010)? •

**Listen**
Neuroscience, Learning,
and Teaching

## Lessons for Teachers: General Principles

What can we learn from neuroscience? Here are some general teaching implications drawn from Driscoll (2005), Murphy and Benton (2010), Sprenger (2010), and Wolfe (2010):

1. The brain can place some limits on learning in the form of brain anomalies in neural wiring or structure, but learning can occur through alternate pathways in the brain (as Nico and Brooke demonstrate). Thus, there are multiple ways both to teach and to learn a skill, depending on the student.
2. Many cognitive functions are differentiated—they are associated with different parts of the brain. Thus, learners are likely to have preferred modes of processing (visual or verbal, for example) as well as varying capabilities in these modes. Using a range of modalities for instruction and activities that draw on different senses may support learning—for example, using maps and songs to teach geography. Assessment should be differentiated, too.
3. The brain is relatively plastic, so enriched, active environments and flexible instructional strategies are likely to support cognitive development in young children and learning in adults.
4. Some learning disorders may have a neurological basis; neurological testing may assist in diagnosing and treating these disorders, as well as in evaluating the effects of various treatments.
5. The brain can change, but it takes time, so teachers must be consistent, patient, and compassionate in teaching and reteaching in different ways, as Nico's and Brooke's parents and teachers could tell you.
6. Learning from real life problems and concrete experiences helps students construct knowledge and also gives them multiple pathways for learning and retrieving information.
7. The brain seeks meaningful patterns and connections with existing networks, so teachers should tie new information to what students already understand, and help them form new connections. Information that is not linked to existing knowledge will be easily forgotten.
8. It takes a long time to build and consolidate knowledge. Numerous visits in different contexts over time (not all at once) help to form strong, multiple connections.
9. Large, general concepts should be emphasized over small specific facts so students can build enduring, useful knowledge categories and associations that are not constantly changing.
10. Stories should be used in teaching. Stories engage many areas of the brain—memories, experiences, feelings, and beliefs. Stories also are organized and have a sequence—beginning, middle, end—so they are easier to remember than unrelated or unorganized information.

For the rest of the chapter, we turn from the brain and cognitive development to examine several major theories of cognitive development, the first offered by a biologist turned psychologist, Jean Piaget.

## PIAGET'S THEORY OF COGNITIVE DEVELOPMENT

Swiss psychologist Jean Piaget was a real prodigy. In fact, in his teens, he published so many scientific papers on molluscs (marine animals such as oysters, clams, octopuses, snails, and squid) that he was offered a job as the curator of the mollusc collection at the Museum of Natural History in Geneva. He told the museum officials that he wanted to finish high school first. For a while, Piaget worked in Alfred Binet's laboratory in Paris developing intelligence tests for children. The reasons children gave for their wrong answers fascinated him, and this prompted him to study the thinking behind their answers—this question intrigued him for the rest of his life (Green & Piel, 2010). He continued to write until his death at the age of 84 (Miller, 2011).

During his long career, Piaget devised a model describing how humans go about making sense of their world by gathering and organizing information (Piaget, 1954, 1963,

1970a, 1970b). We will examine Piaget's ideas closely because they provide an explanation of the development of thinking from infancy to adulthood.

------------------------------------------------

**STOP & THINK** Can you be in Montreal, Quebec, and Canada at the same time? Is this a difficult question for you? How long did it take you to answer? •

------------------------------------------------

According to Piaget (1954), certain ways of thinking that are quite simple for an adult, such as the Montreal question above, are not so simple for a child. For example, do you remember the 9-year-old child at the beginning of the chapter who was asked if he could be Genevan? He answered, "No, that's not possible. I'm already Swiss, I can't also be Genevan" (Piaget, 1965/1995, p. 252). Imagine teaching this student geography. The student has trouble with classifying one concept (Geneva) as a subset of another (Switzerland). There are other differences between adult and child thinking. Children's concepts of time may be different from your own. They may think, for example, that they will some-day catch up to a sibling in age, or they may confuse the past and the future. Let's examine why.

**STUDYING CHILDREN'S THINKING** Jean Piaget was a Swiss psychologist whose insightful descriptions of children's thinking changed the way we understand cognitive development.

*Source: Bill Anderson/Photo Researchers, Inc.*

## Influences on Development

Cognitive development is much more than the addition of new facts and ideas to an existing store of information. According to Piaget, our thinking processes change radically, though slowly, from birth to maturity because we constantly strive to make sense of the world. Piaget identified four factors—biological maturation, activity, social experiences, and equilibration—that interact to influence changes in thinking (Piaget, 1970a). Let's briefly examine the first three factors. We'll return to a discussion of equilibration in the next section.

One of the most important influences on the way we make sense of the world is *maturation*, the unfolding of the biological changes that are genetically programmed. Parents and teachers have little impact on this aspect of cognitive development, except to ensure that children get the nourishment and care they need to be healthy.

*Activity* is another influence on cognitive development. With physical maturation comes the increasing ability to act on the environment and learn from it. When a young child's coordination is reasonably developed, for example, the child may discover principles about balance by experimenting with a seesaw. Thus, as we act on the environment—as we explore, test, observe, and eventually organize information—we are likely to alter our thinking processes at the same time.

As we develop, we also interact with the people around us. According to Piaget, our cognitive development is influenced by *social transmission*, or learning from others. Without social transmission, we would need to reinvent all the knowledge already offered by our culture. The amount people can learn from social transmission varies according to their stage of cognitive development.

Maturation, activity, and social transmission all work together to influence cognitive development. How do we respond to these influences?

## Basic Tendencies in Thinking

As a result of his early research in biology, Piaget concluded that all species inherit two basic instincts, or "invariant functions." The first of these tendencies is toward **organization**—the combining, arranging, recombining, and rearranging of behaviour and thoughts into coherent systems. The second tendency is toward **adaptation**, or adjusting to the environment.

**ORGANIZATION.**   People are born with a tendency to organize their thinking and knowledge into psychological structures or schemes. These psychological structures are our systems for understanding and interacting with the world. Simple structures are

**Organization** Ongoing process of arranging information and experience into mental systems or categories.

**Adaptation** Adjustment to the environment.

continually combined and coordinated to become more sophisticated and thus more effective. Very young infants, for example, can either look at an object or grasp it when it comes in contact with their hands. They cannot coordinate looking and grasping at the same time. As they develop, however, infants organize these two separate behavioural structures into a coordinated higher-level structure of looking at, reaching for, and grasping the object. They can, of course, still use each structure separately (Ginsburg & Opper, 1988; Miller, 2002).

Piaget gave a special name to these structures: **schemes**. In his theory, schemes are the basic building blocks of thinking. They are organized systems of actions or thought that allow us to mentally represent or "think about" the objects and events in our world. Schemes may be very small and specific—for example, the sucking-through-a-straw scheme or the recognizing-a-rose scheme. Or they may be more general—the drinking scheme or the categorizing-plants scheme. As a person's thinking processes become more organized and new schemes develop, behaviour also becomes more sophisticated and better suited to the environment.

● **Watch**
Four Stages of Cognitive Development

ADAPTATION.   In addition to the tendency to organize their psychological structures, people also inherit the tendency to adapt to their environment. Two basic processes are involved in adaptation: assimilation and accommodation.

**Assimilation** takes place when people use their existing schemes to make sense of events in our world. Assimilation involves trying to understand something new by fitting it into what we already know. At times, we may have to distort the new information to make it fit. For example, the first time many children see a raccoon, they call it a "kitty." They try to match the new experience with an existing scheme for identifying animals.

**Accommodation** occurs when a person must change existing schemes to respond to a new situation. If data cannot be made to fit any existing schemes, more appropriate structures must be developed. We adjust our thinking to fit the new information, instead of adjusting the information to fit our thinking. Children demonstrate accommodation when they add the scheme for recognizing skunks to their other systems for identifying animals.

People adapt to their increasingly complex environments by using existing schemes whenever these schemes work (assimilation) and by modifying and adding to their schemes when something new is needed (accommodation). In fact, both processes are required most of the time. Even using an established pattern, such as sucking through a straw, may require some accommodation, if you are used to a straw of a different size or length. If you have tried drinking juice from box packages, you know that you have to add a new skill to your sucking scheme—don't squeeze the box or you will shoot juice through the straw, straight up into the air, and into your lap. Whenever new experiences are assimilated into an existing scheme, the scheme is enlarged and changed somewhat, so assimilation involves some accommodation (Mascolo & Fischer, 2005).

There are also times when neither assimilation nor accommodation is used. If people encounter something that is too unfamiliar, they may ignore it. Experience is filtered to fit the kind of thinking a person is doing at a given time. For example, if you overhear a conversation in a foreign language, you probably will not try to make sense of the exchange unless you have some knowledge of the language.

**Schemes** Mental systems or categories of perception and experience.

**Assimilation** Fitting new information into existing schemes.

**Accommodation** Altering existing schemes or creating new ones in response to new information.

**Equilibration** Search for mental balance between cognitive schemes and information from the environment.

**Disequilibrium** In Piaget's theory, the "out-of-balance" state that occurs when a person realizes that his or her current ways of thinking are not working to solve a problem or understand a situation.

EQUILIBRATION.   According to Piaget, organizing, assimilating, and accommodating can be seen as a kind of complex balancing act. In his theory, the actual changes in thinking take place through the process of **equilibration**—the act of searching for a balance. Piaget assumed that people continually test the adequacy of their thinking processes in order to achieve that balance. Briefly, the process of equilibration works as follows. If we apply a particular scheme to an event or situation and the scheme works, equilibrium exists. If the scheme does not produce a satisfying result, **disequilibrium** exists, and we become uncomfortable. This motivates us to keep searching for a solution through assimilation and accommodation, and thus our thinking changes and moves ahead. Of course, the level of disequilibrium must be just right or optimal—too little and we aren't interested in changing, too much and we may be discouraged or anxious and not change.

TABLE 2.2 • Piaget's Stages of Cognitive Development

| STAGE | APPROXIMATE AGE | CHARACTERISTICS |
|---|---|---|
| Sensorimotor | 0–2 years | Learns through reflexes, senses, and movement—actions on the environment. Begins to imitate others and remember events; shifts to symbolic thinking. Comes to understand that objects do not cease to exist when they are out of sight—object permanence. Moves from reflexive actions to intentional activity. |
| Preoperational | Begins about the time the child starts talking, to about 7 years old | Develops language and begins to use symbols to represent objects. Has difficulty with past and future—thinks in the present. Can think through operations logically in one direction. Has difficulties understanding the point of view of another person. |
| Concrete operational | Begins about grade 1, to early adolescence, around 11 years old | Can think logically about concrete (hands-on) problems. Understands conservation and organizes things into categories and in series. Can reverse thinking to mentally "undo" actions. Understands past, present, and future. |
| Formal operational | Adolescence to adulthood | Can think hypothetically and deductively. Thinking becomes more scientific. Solves abstract problems in logical fashion. Can consider multiple perspectives, and develops concerns about social issues, personal identity, and justice. |

## Four Stages of Cognitive Development

Now we turn to the actual differences that Piaget hypothesized for children as they grow. Piaget believed that all people pass through the same four stages in exactly the same order. These stages are generally associated with specific ages, as shown in Table 2.2, but these are only general guidelines, not labels for all children of a certain age. Piaget noted that individuals may go through long periods of transition between stages and that a person may show characteristics of one stage in one situation, but characteristics of a higher or lower stage in other situations. Therefore, knowing a student's age is never a guarantee of knowing his or her level of cognitive development (Orlando & Machado, 1996).

INFANCY: THE SENSORIMOTOR STAGE.    The earliest period is called the **sensorimotor** stage, because the child's thinking involves the major senses of seeing, hearing, moving, touching, and tasting. During this period, the infant develops **object permanence**, the understanding that objects in the environment exist whether they perceive them or not. This is the beginning of the important ability to construct a mental representation. As most parents discover, before infants develop object permanence, it is relatively easy to take something away from them. The trick is to distract them and remove the object while they are not looking—"out of sight, out of mind." The older infant who searches for the ball that has rolled out of sight is indicating an understanding that objects still exist even when they are not in view (Moore & Meltzoff, 2004). Some researchers suggest that infants as young as 3 to 4 months may know that an object still exists, but they do not have either the memory skills to "hold on" to the location of the object or the motor skills to coordinate a search (Baillargeon, 1999; Flavell, Miller, & Miller, 2002).

A second major accomplishment in the sensorimotor period is the beginning of logical, **goal-directed actions**. Think of the familiar container toy for babies. It is usually plastic, has a lid, and contains several colourful items that can be dumped out and replaced.

Sensorimotor Involving the senses and motor activity.

Object permanence The understanding that objects have a separate, permanent existence.

Goal-directed actions Deliberate actions toward a goal.

"I can't tell you 'cause I'm wearin' my mittens."

Source: Family Circus © 2002 Bil Keane, Inc. King Features Syndicate

A 6-month-old baby is likely to become frustrated trying to get to the toys inside. An older child who has mastered the basics of the sensorimotor stage will probably be able to deal with the toys in an orderly fashion. Through trial and error, the child will slowly build a "container toy" scheme: (1) get the lid off; (2) turn the container upside down; (3) shake if the items jam; (4) watch the items fall. Separate lower-level schemes have been organized into a higher-level scheme to achieve a goal.

The child is soon able to reverse this action by refilling the container. Learning to reverse actions is a basic accomplishment of the sensorimotor stage. As we will soon see, however, learning to reverse thinking—that is, learning to imagine the reverse of a sequence of actions—takes much longer.

### EARLY CHILDHOOD TO THE EARLY ELEMENTARY YEARS: THE PREOPERATIONAL STAGE.

By the end of the sensorimotor stage, the child can use many action schemes. However, as long as these schemes remain tied to physical actions, they are of no use in recalling the past, keeping track of information, or planning. For this, children need what Piaget called **operations**, or actions that are carried out and reversed mentally rather than physically. At the **preoperational** stage the child has not yet mastered these mental operations but is moving toward mastery (so thinking is *pre*operational).

According to Piaget, the first type of thinking that is separate from action involves making action schemes symbolic. The ability to form and use symbols—words, gestures, signs, images, and so on—is thus a major accomplishment of the preoperational period and moves children closer to mastering the mental operations of the next stage. This ability to work with symbols, such as using the word *horse* or a picture of a horse or even pretending to ride a horse to represent a real horse that is not actually present, is called the **semiotic function**. In fact, the child's earliest use of symbols occurs during pretending. Children who are not yet able to talk will often use action symbols—pretending to drink from an empty cup or touching a comb to their hair, showing that they know what each object is for. This behaviour also shows that their schemes are becoming more general and less tied to specific actions. The eating scheme, for example, can be used in playing house. During the preoperational stage, there is also rapid development of that very important symbol system, language. Between the ages of 2 and 4, most children enlarge their vocabulary from about 200 to 2000 words.

As the child moves through the preoperational stage, the developing ability to think about objects in symbolic form remains somewhat limited to thinking in one direction only, or using one-way *logic*. It is very difficult for the child to "think backward," or imagine how to reverse the steps in a task. **Reversible thinking** is involved in many tasks that are difficult for the preoperational child, such as the conservation of matter.

**Conservation** is the principle that the amount or number of something remains the same even if the arrangement or appearance is changed, as long as nothing is added and nothing is taken away. You know that if you tear a piece of paper into several pieces, you will still have the same amount of paper. To prove this, you know that you can reverse the process by taping the pieces back together. Here is a classic example of difficulty with the principle of conservation. Leah, a 5-year-old, is shown two identical glasses, both short and wide in shape. Both have exactly the same amount of coloured water in them. She agrees that the amounts are "the same." The experimenter then pours the water from one of the glasses into a taller, narrower glass and asks, "Now, does one glass have more water, or are they the same?" Leah responds that the tall glass has more because "It goes up more here" (she points to the higher level on the taller glass).

Piaget's explanation for Leah's answer is that she is focusing, or *centring*, attention on the dimension of height. She has difficulty considering more than one aspect of the situation at a time, or **decentring**. The preoperational child cannot understand that increased diameter compensates for decreased height, since this would require taking into account two dimensions at once. Thus, children at the preoperational stage have trouble freeing themselves from their own perceptions of how the world appears.

This brings us to another important characteristic of the preoperational stage. Preoperational children, according to Piaget, are very **egocentric**; they tend to see the

**Operations** Actions that a person carries out by thinking them through instead of literally performing them.

**Preoperational** The stage of development before a child masters logical mental operations.

**Semiotic function** The ability to use symbols—language, pictures, signs, or gestures—to represent actions or objects mentally.

**Reversible thinking** Thinking backward, from the end to the beginning.

**Conservation** Principle that some characteristics of an object remain the same despite changes in appearance.

**Decentring** Focusing on more than one aspect at a time.

**Egocentric** Assuming that others experience the world the way you do.

world and the experiences of others from their own viewpoints. Egocentric, as Piaget intended it, does not mean selfish; it simply means that children often assume that everyone else shares their feelings, reactions, and perspectives. For example, if a little girl at this stage is afraid of dogs, she may assume that all children share this fear. The 2-year-old at the beginning of this chapter who brought his own mother to comfort a friend who was crying, even though the friend's mother was available, was simply seeing the situation through his own eyes. Very young children centre on their own perceptions and on the way the situation appears to them. This is one reason it is difficult for these children to understand that your right hand is not on the same side as theirs when you are facing them.

Research has shown that young children are not totally egocentric in every situation, however. Even at age 2, children will describe more details about a situation to a parent who was not present than they will provide to a parent who experienced the situation with them. So young children do seem quite able to take the needs and different perspectives of others into account, at least in certain situations (Flavell, Miller, & Miller, 2002). And in fairness to young children, even adults can make assumptions that others feel or think as they do. For example, have you ever received a gift that the giver loved but was clearly inappropriate for you? The *Family and Community Partnerships Guidelines* provide ideas for how to work with preoperational thinkers in the classroom.

**LATER ELEMENTARY TO THE MIDDLE SCHOOL YEARS: THE CONCRETE OPERATIONAL STAGE.** Piaget coined the term **concrete operations** to describe this stage of "hands-on" thinking. The basic characteristics of the stage are the recognition of the logical stability of the physical world; the realization that elements can be changed or transformed and still conserve many of their original characteristics; and the understanding that these changes can be reversed.

> **Concrete operations** Mental tasks tied to concrete objects and situations.

---

## GUIDELINES — FAMILY AND COMMUNITY PARTNERSHIPS

### Teaching the Preoperational Child

**Use concrete props and visual aids whenever possible.**
*Examples*
1. When you discuss concepts such as "part," "whole," or "one-half," use shapes on a felt board or cardboard "pizzas" to demonstrate.
2. Let children add and subtract with sticks, rocks, or coloured chips.

**Make instructions relatively short—not too many steps at once. Use actions as well as words.**
*Examples*
1. When giving instructions about how to feed a pet, first model the process, then ask the child to try it.
2. Explain a game by acting out one of the parts.

**Help children develop their ability to see the world from someone else's point of view.**
*Examples*
1. Ask children to imagine "how your sister felt when you broke her toy."

2. Be clear about rules for sharing or use of material. Help children understand the value of the rules, and develop empathy in children by asking them to think about how they would like to be treated. Avoid giving long lectures on "sharing" or being "nice."

**Give children a great deal of hands-on practice with the skills that serve as building blocks for more complex skills such as reading comprehension.**
*Examples*
1. Provide cut-out letters to build words.
2. Do activities that require measuring and simple calculations—cooking, dividing a batch of popcorn equally.

**Provide a wide range of experiences in order to build a foundation for concept learning and language.**
*Examples*
1. Take field trips to zoos, gardens, theatres, and concerts; encourage storytelling.
2. Give children words to describe what they are doing, hearing, seeing, touching, tasting, and smelling.

FIGURE 2.4

SOME PIAGETIAN CONSERVATION TASKS

In addition to the tasks shown here, other tasks involve the conservation of number, length, weight, and volume. These tasks are all achieved over the concrete-operational period.

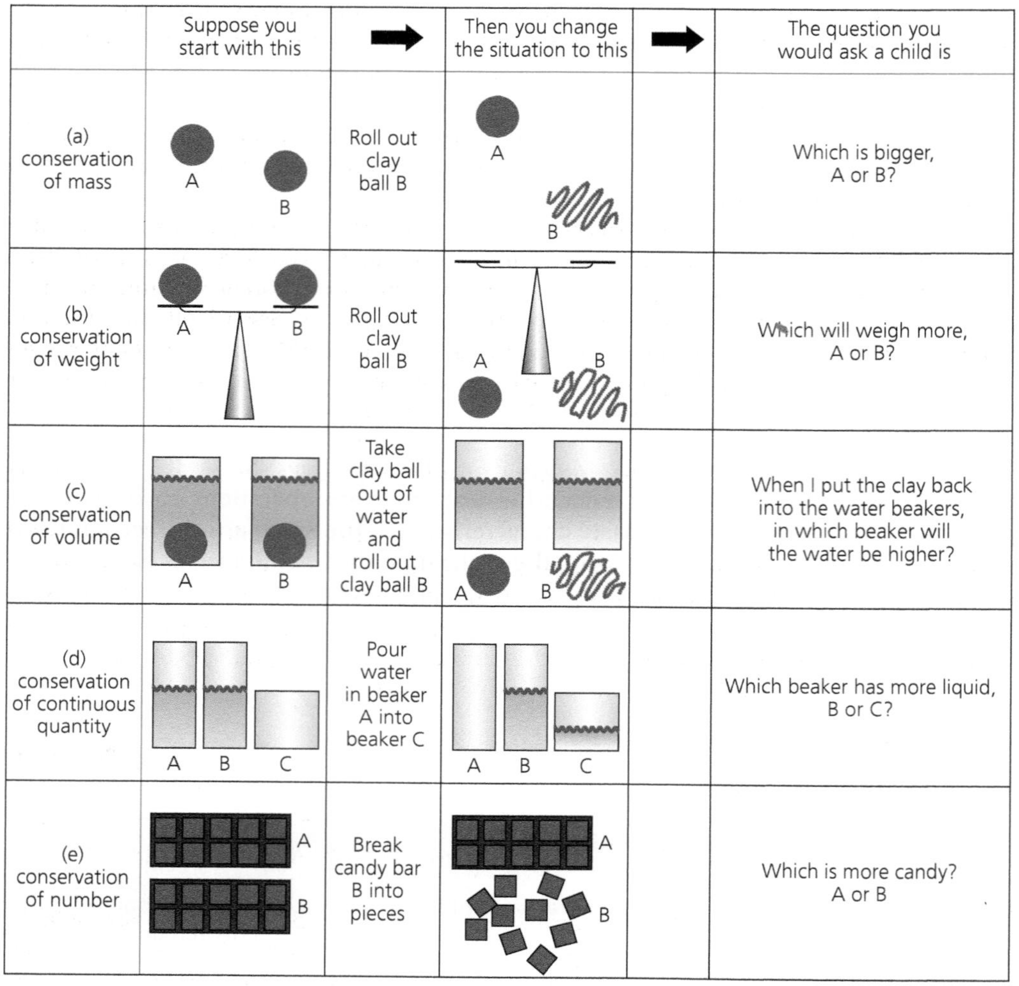
Suppose you start with this
Then you change the situation to this
The question you would ask a child is
(a) conservation of mass
A
B
Roll out clay ball B
A
B
Which is bigger, A or B?
(b) conservation of weight
A
B
Roll out clay ball B
A
B
Which will weigh more, A or B?
(c) conservation of volume
A
B
Take clay ball out of water and roll out clay ball B
A
B
When I put the clay back into the water beakers, in which beaker will the water be higher?
(d) conservation of continuous quantity
A B C
Pour water in beaker A into beaker C
A B C
Which beaker has more liquid, B or C?
(e) conservation of number
A
B
Break candy bar B into pieces
A
B
Which is more candy? A or B

*Source:* Woolfolk, A., & Perry, N. E. (2012). *Child Development.* Pearson Education, Inc. *Reproduced by permission of Pearson Education, Inc. All rights reserved.*

**Identity** The principle that a person or object remains the same over time.

**Compensation** The principle that changes in one dimension can be offset by changes in another dimension.

**Reversibility** A characteristic of Piagetian logical operations—the ability to think through a series of steps, then mentally reverse the steps and return to the starting point; also called *reversible thinking*.

**Classification** Grouping objects into categories.

Look at Figure 2.4, which shows examples of the different tasks given to children to assess conservation and the approximate age ranges when most children can solve these problems. According to Piaget, a student's ability to solve conservation problems depends on an understanding of three basic aspects of reasoning: identity, compensation, and reversibility. With a complete mastery of **identity**, the student knows that if nothing is added or taken away, the material remains the same. With an understanding of **compensation**, the student knows that an apparent change in one direction can be compensated for by a change in another direction. That is, if the liquid rises higher in the glass, the glass must be narrower. And with an understanding of **reversibility**, the student can mentally cancel out the change that has been made. Leah apparently knew it was the same water (identity), but lacked compensation and reversibility, so she was still moving toward conservation.

Another important operation mastered at this stage is **classification**. Classification depends on a student's abilities to focus on a single characteristic of objects in a set (for example, colour) and group the objects according to that characteristic. More advanced classification at this stage involves recognizing that one class fits into another. A city can be in a particular province and also in Canada. As children apply this advanced classification to locations, they often become fascinated with "complete" addresses, such as this one: Lee Jary, 5116 Forest Hill Drive, Richmond Hill, Ontario, Canada, North America, Northern Hemisphere, Earth, Solar System, Milky Way, Universe.

Classification is also related to reversibility. The ability to reverse a process mentally now allows the concrete-operational student to see that there is more than one way to classify a group of objects. The student understands, for example, that buttons can be classified by colour and then reclassified by size or by the number of holes they have.

**Seriation** is the process of making an orderly arrangement from large to small or vice versa. This understanding of sequential relationships permits a student to construct a logical series in which A < B < C (A is less than B is less than C) and so on. Unlike the preoperational child, the concrete-operational child can grasp the notion that B can be larger than A but smaller than C.

**Watch**
Conservation

With the abilities to handle operations such as conservation, classification, and seriation, the student at the concrete-operational stage has finally developed a complete and very logical system of thinking. However, this system of thinking is still tied to physical reality. The logic is based on concrete situations that can be organized, classified, or manipulated. Thus, children at this stage can imagine several different arrangements for the furniture in their rooms. They do not have to solve the problem strictly through trial and error by actually moving the furniture. However, the concrete-operational child is not yet able to reason about hypothetical, abstract problems that involve the coordination of many factors at once. This kind of coordination is part of Piaget's next and final stage of cognitive development.

In any grade you teach, knowledge of concrete-operational thinking will be helpful. In the early grades, the students are moving toward this logical system of thought. In the middle grades, it is in full flower, ready to be applied and extended by your teaching. Students in high school and even adults still commonly use concrete-operational thinking, especially in areas that are new or unfamiliar. The *Guidelines* should give you ideas for how to teach children who can apply concrete operations.

**HIGH SCHOOL AND UNIVERSITY: THE FORMAL-OPERATIONAL STAGE.**   Some students remain at the concrete-operational stage throughout their school years, even throughout life. However, new experiences, usually those that take place in school, eventually present most students with problems that they cannot solve using concrete operations.

**STOP & THINK** You are packing for a long trip, but you want to pack light. How many different three-piece outfits (pants, shirt, jacket) will you have if you include three shirts, three pants, and three jackets (assuming of course that they all go together in fashion perfection)? Time yourself to see how long it takes to arrive at the answer. •

What happens when a number of variables interact, as in a laboratory experiment or the problem just posed in the Stop & Think feature? Then a mental system for controlling sets of variables and working through a set of possibilities is needed. These are the abilities that Piaget called **formal operations**.

At the level of formal operations, the focus of thinking can shift from what *is* to what *might be*. Situations do not have to be experienced to be imagined. You met Jamal at the beginning of this chapter. Even though he is a bright elementary school student, he could not answer the question, "How would life be different if people did not have to sleep?" because he insisted, "People *have to sleep*!" In contrast, the adolescent who has mastered formal operations can consider contrary-to-fact questions. In answering, the adolescent demonstrates the hallmark of formal operations—**hypothetico-deductive reasoning**. The formal thinker can consider a hypothetical situation (people do not have to sleep) and reason deductively (from the general assumption to specific implications, such as longer workdays, more money spent on lighting, or new entertainment industries). Formal operations also include inductive reasoning, or using specific observations to identify general principles. For example, the economist observes many specific changes in the stock market and attempts to identify general principles about economic cycles from this information.

**Seriation** Arrangement of objects in sequential order according to one aspect, such as size, weight, or volume.

**Formal operations** Mental tasks involving abstract thinking and coordination of a number of variables.

**Hypothetico-deductive reasoning** A formal-operations problem-solving strategy in which an individual begins by identifying all the factors that might affect a problem and then deduces and systematically evaluates specific solutions.

## GUIDELINES

## Teaching the Concrete-Operational Child

**Continue to use concrete props and visual aids, especially when dealing with sophisticated material.**
*Examples*

1. Use timelines in history lessons and three-dimensional models in science lessons.
2. Use diagrams to illustrate hierarchical relationships, such as branches of government and the agencies under each branch.

**Continue to give students a chance to manipulate and test objects.**
*Examples*

1. Set up simple scientific experiments like the following involving the relationship between fire and oxygen. What happens to a flame when you blow on it from a distance? (If you don't blow it out, the flame gets larger briefly, because it has more oxygen to burn.) What happens when you cover the flame with a jar?
2. Have students make candles by dipping wicks in wax, weave cloth on a simple loom, bake bread, set type by hand, or do other craftwork that illustrates the daily occupations of people during the pioneer period.

**Make sure that presentations and readings are brief and well organized.**
*Examples*

1. Assign stories or books with short, logical chapters, moving to longer reading assignments only when students are ready.
2. Break up a presentation, giving students an opportunity to practise the first steps before introducing the next steps.

**Use familiar examples to explain more complex ideas.**
*Examples*

1. Compare students' lives with those of characters in a story. For example, after reading *Island of the Blue Dolphins* (the true story of a girl who grew up alone on a deserted island), ask, "Have you ever had to stay alone for a long time? How did you feel?"
2. Teach the concept of area by having students measure two rooms in the school that are different sizes.

**Give opportunities to classify and group objects and ideas on increasingly complex levels.**
*Examples*

1. Give students slips of paper that each have one sentence written on them and ask the students to group the sentences into paragraphs.
2. Compare the systems of the human body to other kinds of systems: the brain to a computer, the heart to a pump. Break down stories into components, from the broad to the specific: author; story; characters, plot, theme; place, time.

**Present problems that require logical, analytical thinking.**
*Examples*

1. Discuss open-ended questions that stimulate thinking, such as "Are the brain and the mind the same thing?" "How should the city deal with stray animals?" "What is the largest number?"
2. Use sports photos or pictures of crisis situations (Red Cross helping in disasters, victims of poverty or war, senior citizens who need assistance) to stimulate problem-solving discussions.

---

Abstract formal-operational thinking is necessary for success in many advanced high school and college courses (Meece & Daniels, 2008). For example, most math is concerned with hypothetical situations, assumptions, and givens: "Let $x = 10$," or "Assume $x^2 + y^2 = z^2$," or "Given two sides and an adjacent angle . . ." Work in social studies and literature requires abstract thinking, too: "What did Woodrow Wilson mean when he called the First World War the 'war to end all wars'?" "What are some metaphors for hope and despair in Shakespeare's sonnets?" "What symbols of old age does T. S. Eliot use in *The Waste Land*?" "How do animals symbolize human character traits in Aesop's fables?"

The organized, scientific thinking of formal operations requires that students systematically generate different possibilities for a given situation. For example, if asked, "How many different shirt/pants/jacket outfits can you make using three of each kind of clothing?" the child using formal operations can systematically identify the 27 possible combinations. (Did you get it right?) A concrete-operational thinker might name just a few combinations, using each piece of clothing only once. The underlying system of combinations is not yet available to the concrete thinker.

Another characteristic of this stage is **adolescent egocentrism**. Unlike egocentric young children, adolescents do not deny that other people may have different perceptions and beliefs; the adolescents just become very focused on their own ideas. They spend much time examining their own beliefs and attitudes. This can lead to what Elkind (1981) calls the sense of an *imaginary audience*—the feeling that everyone is watching. Thus, adolescents

**Adolescent egocentrism** Assumption that everyone else is interested in one's thoughts, feelings, and concerns.

believe that others are analyzing them (e.g., "Everyone noticed that I wore this shirt twice this week." "The whole class thought my answer was dumb!"). You can see that social blunders or imperfections in appearance can be devastating to an adolescent if he or she believes that "everybody is watching." In fact, Kimberly Schonert-Reichl (1994) at the University of British Columbia linked adolescent egocentrism with adolescent depression. In particular, her study found that girls from high-socioeconomic-status (SES) families tended to be overly self-conscious and more at risk for depression. In contrast, boys from high-SES families reported a heightened sense of omnipotence, uniqueness, and invulnerability. Luckily, this feeling of being "on stage" seems to peak in early adolescence, by age 14 or 15.

The ability to think hypothetically, consider alternatives, identify all possible combinations, and analyze their own thinking has some interesting consequences for adolescents. Since they can think about worlds that do not exist, they often become interested in science fiction. Because they can reason from general principles to specific actions, they are often critical of people whose actions seem to contradict their principles. Adolescents can deduce the set of "best" possibilities and imagine ideal worlds (or ideal parents and teachers, for that matter). This explains why many students at this age develop interests in utopias, political causes, and social issues. They want to design better worlds, and their thinking allows them to do so. Adolescents can also imagine many possible futures for themselves and may try to decide which is best. Feelings about any of these ideals may be strong.

**Do We All Reach the Fourth Stage?**    Most psychologists agree that there is a level of thinking more sophisticated than concrete operations. But the question of how universal formal-operational thinking actually is, even among adults, is a matter of debate. The first three stages of Piaget's theory are forced on most people by physical realities. Objects really are permanent. The amount of water doesn't change when it is poured into another glass. Formal operations, however, are not so closely tied to the physical environment. Being able to use formal operations may be the result of practice in solving hypothetical problems and using formal scientific reasoning—abilities that are valued and taught in literate cultures, particularly in college and university. Even so, only about 30%–40% of high school students can perform Piaget's formal-operational tasks (Meece & Daniels, 2008). The *Guidelines* will help you support the development of formal operations in your students.

## GUIDELINES

## Helping Students to Use Formal Operations

**Continue to use concrete-operational teaching strategies and materials.**
*Examples*
1. Use visual aids, such as charts and illustrations, as well as somewhat more sophisticated graphs and diagrams, especially when the material being covered is new.
2. Compare the experiences of characters in stories to students' experiences.

**Give students the opportunity to explore many hypothetical questions.**
*Examples*
1. Have students write position papers, then exchange their papers with students who embraced the opposing side of the issue, and debate topical social issues, such as the environment, the economy, national unity.
2. Ask students to write about their personal vision of a utopia, a description of a universe that has no sex differences, a description of Earth after humans are extinct, and so forth.

**Give students opportunities to solve problems and to reason scientifically.**
*Examples*
1. Set up group discussions in which students design experiments to answer questions.
2. Ask students to justify two different positions on animal rights, with logical arguments for each position.

**Whenever possible, teach broad concepts, not just facts, using materials and ideas relevant to students' lives (Delpit, 1995).**
*Examples*
1. When discussing Native land claims, consider other issues that have divided Canadians (e.g., Quebec separation).
2. When teaching about poetry, let students find lyrics from popular songs that illustrate poetic devices, and talk about how these devices do or don't work well to communicate the meanings and feelings the songwriters intended.

Piaget himself (1974) suggested that most adults may be able to use formal-operational thought in a few areas where they have the greatest experience or interest. Taking a college or university class fosters formal-operational abilities in that subject, but not necessarily in others (Lehman & Nisbett, 1990). So expect many students in your middle school or high school class to have trouble thinking hypothetically, especially when they are learning something new. Sometimes, students find shortcuts for dealing with problems that are beyond their grasp; they may memorize formulas or lists of steps. These systems may be helpful for passing tests, but real understanding will take place only if students are able to go beyond this superficial use of memorization.

## Information Processing and Neo-Piagetian Views of Cognitive Development

As you will see in Chapter 8, there are explanations for why children have trouble with conservation and other Piagetian tasks. These explanations focus on the child's developing information processing skills, such as attention, memory capacity, and learning strategies. As children mature and their brains develop, they are better able to focus their attention, process information more quickly, hold more information in memory, and use thinking strategies more easily and flexibly. Siegler (2000) proposed that as children grow older, they develop progressively better rules and strategies for solving problems and thinking logically. Teachers can help students to develop their capacities for formal thinking by putting the students in situations that challenge their thinking and reveal the shortcomings of their logic. Siegler's approach is called *rule assessment* because it focuses on understanding, challenging, and changing the rules that students use for thinking.

Some developmental psychologists have formulated **neo-Piagetian theories** that retain Piaget's insights about children's construction of knowledge and the general trends in children's thinking, but add findings from information processing about the role of attention, memory, and strategies. For example, Robbie Case (1992, 1998), who was a professor at both Stanford University and the Ontario Institute for Studies in Education of the University of Toronto before his untimely death in 2000, devised an explanation of cognitive development suggesting that children develop in stages within specific domains such as numerical concepts, spatial concepts, social tasks, storytelling, reasoning about physical objects, and motor development. As children practise using the schemes in a particular domain (for example, using counting schemes in the number concept area), accomplishing the schemes takes less attention. The schemes become more automatic because the child does not have to "think so hard" about it. This frees up mental resources and memory to do more. The child now can combine simple schemes into more complex ones and invent new schemes when needed (assimilation and accommodation in action).

Kurt Fischer (2009) connected cognitive development in different domains to research on the brain. He also examined development in different domains such as reading or math. You may remember Nico and Brooke, the remarkable children we met earlier in the chapter who each had one side of their brain removed to treat severe epilepsy, yet both still developed other pathways in their brains to recover lost spatial and verbal abilities. We have seen that one of the implications of research on the brain is that there are multiple pathways for learning.

Fischer has found, however, that even though their brains follow different pathways as they master skills in speaking, reading, and mathematics, children's growth patterns show a similar series of spurts, and they go through predictable levels of development. When learning a new skill, children move through three tiers—from *actions* to *representations* to *abstractions*. Within each tier, the pattern is moving from accomplishing a single action to mapping or coordinating two actions together, creating whole systems of understanding—such as coordinating addition and multiplication in math. At the level of abstractions, they finally move to constructing explanatory principles. This may remind you of sensorimotor, concrete operations, and formal operations in Piaget's

**Neo-Piagetian theories** More recent theories that integrate findings about attention, memory, and strategy use with Piaget's insights about children's thinking and the construction of knowledge.

TABLE 2.3 • **A Pattern of Cognitive Development over 30 Years**

As children develop skills in speaking, reading, and mathematics, their growth patterns show a similar series of spurts. In learning a new skill, children move from actions to representations to abstractions.

| TIERS | LEVELS | AGE OF EMERGENCE OF OPTIMAL LEVEL | AGE OF FUNCTIONAL LEVEL |
| --- | --- | --- | --- |
| | | 23–25 yrs | 30–45 yrs |
| Abstraction | Ab4. Principles | 18–20 | 23–40 |
| | Ab3. Systems | | |
| | Ab2. Mappings | 14–16 | 17–30 |
| | Rp4./Ab1. Single Abstraction | 10–12 | 13–20 |
| Representations | Rp3. Systems | 6–7 | 7–12 |
| | Rp2. Mappings | 3½–4½ | 4–8 |
| | Sm4./Rp1. Single Representations | 2 | 2–5 |
| Actions | Sm3. Systems | 11–13 mos | 11–24 mos |
| | Sm2. Mappings | 7–8 | 7–13 |
| | Sm1. Single Actions | | |
| | | 3–4 | 3–9 |

*Source: Fischer, K. W. (2009). Mind, brain, and education: Building a scientific groundwork for learning and teaching. Mind, Brain, and Education, 3, 2–16.*

theory. Look at Table 2.3, which shows the movement through the tiers of *actions* to *representations* to *abstractions*.

For each skill level, the brain reorganizes itself, too. Table 2.3 shows this progression between birth and 30 years old for the skill of arithmetic operations: addition, subtraction, multiplication, and division. Notice the column that says "emergence of optimal level."

This column shows the ages at which the skills will develop if the individuals have *quality support* and *the chance to practice*. The age the skill emerges without support and practice is shown in the last column. Support and practice are keys in another explanation of cognitive development we will discuss soon—Vygotsky's theory.

## Limitations of Piaget's Theory

Although most psychologists agree with Piaget's insightful descriptions of *how* children think, many disagree with his explanations of *why* thinking develops as it does.

THE TROUBLE WITH STAGES.   Some psychologists have questioned the existence of four separate stages of thinking, even though they agree that children do go through the changes that Piaget described (Mascolo & Fischer, 2005; Miller, 2011). One problem with the stage model is the lack of consistency in children's thinking. For example, children can conserve number (the number of blocks does not change when they are rearranged) a year or two before they can conserve weight (the weight of a ball of clay does not change when you flatten it). Why can't they use conservation consistently in every situation? In fairness, we should note that in his later work, even Piaget put less emphasis on stages of cognitive development and gave more attention to how thinking *changes* through equilibration (Miller, 2011).

Another problem with the idea of separate stages is that the processes may be more continuous than they seem. Changes may seem like discontinuous, qualitative leaps when we look across longer time periods. The 3-year-old persistently searching for a lost toy seems qualitatively different from the infant who doesn't seem to miss a toy or to search when the toy rolls under a sofa. But if we watched a developing child very closely and observed moment-to-moment or hour-to-hour changes, we might see that indeed there are gradual, continuous changes. Rather than appearing all at once, the knowledge that a hidden toy still exists may be a product of the older child's more fully developed memory: He knows that the toy is under the sofa because he remembers seeing it roll there, whereas for the infant the toy is "out of sight, out of mind." The longer you require children to wait before searching—the longer you make them remember the object—the older they have to be to succeed (Siegler & Alibali, 2005).

Change can be both continuous and discontinuous, as described by a branch of mathematics called *catastrophe theory*. Changes that appear suddenly, like the collapse of a bridge, are preceded by many slowly developing changes such as gradual, continuous corrosion of the metal structures. Similarly, gradually developing changes in children can lead to large changes in abilities that seem abrupt (Dawson-Tunik, Fischer, & Stein, 2004; Siegler & Alibali, 2005).

UNDERESTIMATING CHILDREN'S ABILITIES.   It now appears that Piaget underestimated the cognitive abilities of children, particularly younger ones. The problems he gave young children may have been too difficult and the directions too confusing. His subjects may have understood more than they could show on these problems. For example, work by Gelman and her colleagues (Gelman, 2000; Gelman & Cordes, 2001) shows that preschool children know much more about the concept of number than Piaget thought, even if they sometimes make mistakes or get confused. As long as preschoolers work with only three or four objects at a time, they can tell that the number remains the same, even if the objects are spread far apart or clumped close together. Mirjam Ebersbach (2009) demonstrated that most of the German kindergartners in her study considered all three dimensions—width, height, and length—when they estimated the volume of a wooden block (actually, how many small cubes it would take to make bigger blocks of different sizes). In other words, we may be born with a greater store of cognitive tools than Piaget suggested. Some basic understandings or core knowledge, such as the permanence of objects or the sense of number, may be part of our evolutionary equipment, ready for use in our cognitive development (Geary & Bjorklund, 2000; Woodward & Needham, 2009).

Elena Rooraid/PhotoEdit

**CHILD EXPERTS** One limitation of Piaget's theory appears to be the underestimation of young children's cognitive abilities. For instance, his theory does not explain how these young girls can play chess at the same level as many adults could.

Piaget's theory also does not explain how even young children can perform at an advanced level in certain areas where they have highly developed knowledge and expertise. For example, Marion Porath (1996), a former student of Robbie Case, found the drawings of artistically gifted children and the story plots of verbally gifted children to be far more elaborate than those of children in a same-age control group. Similarly, an expert 9-year-old chess player can think abstractly about chess moves, whereas a novice 20-year-old player may have to resort to more concrete strategies to plan and remember moves (Siegler, 1998).

Finally, Piaget argued that the development of cognitive operations such as conservation or abstract thinking cannot be accelerated. He believed that children had to be developmentally ready to learn. Quite a bit of research, however, has shown that children can learn to perform cognitive operations such as conservation with effective instruction. They do not have to naturally discover these ways of thinking on their own. Knowledge and experience in a situation affect the kind of thinking that students can do (Brainerd, 2003).

COGNITIVE DEVELOPMENT AND CULTURE.   One final criticism of Piaget's theory is that it overlooks the important effects of the child's cultural and social group. Research across different cultures has generally confirmed that Piaget was accurate about the sequence of the stages in children's thinking he described, but age ranges for the stages vary. Children living in Western countries typically move to the next stage about two to three years earlier than their peers in non-Western societies. But careful research has shown that these differences across cultures depend on the subject or domain tested and whether the culture values and teaches knowledge in that domain. For example, children in Brazil who sell candy in the streets instead of attending school appear to fail a certain kind of Piagetian task—class inclusion (e.g., "Are there more daisies, more tulips, or more flowers in the picture?"). But when the tasks are phrased in concepts they understand—selling candy—then these children perform better than Brazilian children the same age who attend school (Saxe, 1999). When a culture or context emphasizes a cognitive ability, children growing up in that culture tend to acquire that ability sooner. In a study that compared Chinese students in grades 1, 3, and 5 to same grade North American peers, the Chinese students mastered a Piagetian task that involved distance, time, and speed relationships about two years ahead of the North American students, most likely because the Chinese education system puts more emphasis on math and science in the early grades (Zhou, Peverly, Beohm, & Chongde, 2001).

Even concrete operations such as classification may not be so basic to people of other cultures. For example, when individuals from the Kpelle people of Africa were asked to sort 20 objects, they created groups that made sense to them—a hoe with a potato, a knife with an orange. The experimenter could not get the Kpelle to change their categories; they said this is how a wise man would do it. Finally, the experimenter asked in desperation, "Well, how would a fool do it?" Then the subjects promptly created the four neat classification piles the experimenter had expected—food, tools, and so on (Rogoff & Morelli, 1989).

Lev Vygotsky proposed another increasingly influential view of cognitive development. His theory ties cognitive development to culture.

# Vygotsky's Sociocultural Perspective

Psychologists today recognize that the child's culture shapes cognitive development by determining what and how the child will learn about the world. For example, young Zinacanteco Indian girls of southern Mexico learn complicated ways of weaving cloth through informal instruction by adults in their communities. Cultures that prize cooperation and sharing teach these skills early, whereas cultures that encourage competition nurture competitive abilities in their children (Bakerman, Adamson, Koner, & Barr, 1990; Ceci & Roazzi, 1994). The stages observed by Piaget are not necessarily "natural"

**SOCIOCULTURAL THEORY** Lev Vygotsky elaborated the sociocultural theory of development. His ideas about language, culture, and cognitive development have become major influences in the fields of psychology and education.

Felicia Martinez/PhotoEdit

for all children because to some extent they reflect the expectations and activities of the children's culture (Kozulin, 2003; Rogoff, 2003).

Lev Semenovich Vygotsky, a Russian psychologist who died more than 70 years ago, was major spokesperson for this **sociocultural theory** (also called *sociohistoric theory*). He was only 38 when he died of tuberculosis, but during his life he produced more than 100 books and articles. Some of his translations are now available (Vygotsky, 1978, 1986, 1987a, 1987b, 1993, 1997). Vygotsky's work began when he was studying learning and development to improve his own teaching (Wink & Putney, 2002). He wrote about language and thought, the psychology of art, learning and development, and educating students with special needs. His work was banned in Russia for many years because he referenced Western psychologists. But in the past 40 years, with the rediscovery of his work, Vygotsky's ideas about language, culture, and cognitive development have become major influences in psychology and education and have provided alternatives to many of Piaget's theories (Kozulin, 2003; Van Der Veer, 2007; Wink & Putney, 2002).

Vygotsky believed that human activities take place in cultural settings and cannot be understood apart from the settings. One of his key ideas was that our specific mental structures and processes can be traced to our interactions with others. These social interactions are more than simple influences on cognitive development—they actually create our cognitive structures and thinking processes (Palincsar, 1998). In fact, "Vygotsky conceptualized development as the transformation of socially shared activities into internalized processes" (John-Steiner & Mahn, 1996, p. 192). We will examine two themes in Vygotsky's writings that explain how social processes form learning and thinking: the social sources of individual thinking and the role of tools in learning and development, especially the tool of language (Driscoll, 2005; Wertsch & Tulviste, 1992).

## The Social Sources of Individual Thinking

Vygotsky assumed that

> Every function in a child's cultural development appears twice: first on the social level and later on the individual level; first between people (interpsychological) and then inside the child (intrapsychological). This applies equally to voluntary attention, to logical memory, and to the formation of concepts. All the higher functions originate as actual relations between human individuals. (1978, p. 57)

In other words, higher mental processes, such as directing your own attention and thinking through problems, first are **co-constructed** during shared activities between the child and another person. Then the processes are internalized by the child and become part of that child's cognitive development (Gredler, 2007). For example, children first use language in activities with others, to regulate the behaviour of the others ("No nap!" or "I wanna cookie"). Later, however, children can regulate their own behaviour using private speech ("Don't spill"), as you will see in a later section. So, for Vygotsky, social interaction was more than influence—it was the origin of higher mental processes such as problem solving. Consider this example:

> A six-year-old has lost a toy and asks her father for help. The father asks her where she last saw the toy; the child says, "I can't remember." He asks a series of questions—did you have it in your room? Outside? Next door? To each question, the child answers, "no." When he says "in the car?" she says "I think so" and goes to retrieve the toy. (Tharp & Gallimore, 1988, p. 14)

Who remembered? The answer is really neither the father nor the daughter, but the two together. The remembering and problem solving was co-constructed—between people—in the interaction. But the child may have internalized strategies to use next time something is lost. At some point, the child will be able to function independently to solve this kind of problem. So, as the strategy for finding the toy indicates, higher functions appear first between a child and a "teacher" before they exist within the individual child (Kozulin, 1990, 2003).

**Sociocultural theory** Theory that emphasizes the role in development of cooperative dialogues between children and more knowledgeable members of society; children learn the culture of their community (ways of thinking and behaving) through these interactions.

**Co-constructed** Constructed through a social process in which people interact and negotiate (usually verbally) to create an understanding or to solve a problem; the final product is shaped by all participants.

Here is another example of the social sources of individual thinking. Richard Anderson and his colleagues (Anderson & Krathwohl, 2001) studied how grade 4 students in small-group classroom discussions *appropriate* (take for themselves and use) argument stratagems that occur in the discussions. An argument stratagem is a particular form such as "I think [POSITION] because [REASON]," where the student fills in the position and the reason. For example, a student might say, "I think that the wolves should be left alone because they are not hurting anyone." Another strategy form is "If [ACTION], then [BAD CONSEQUENCE]," as in "If they don't trap the wolves, then the wolves will eat the cows." Other forms manage participation, for example, "What do you think, [NAME]?" or "Let [NAME] talk."

Anderson's research identified 13 forms of talk and argument that helped to manage the discussions, to get everyone to participate and present and defend positions, and to handle confusion. The researchers found that the use of these different forms of talking and thinking *snowballed*—once a useful argument was employed by one student, it spread to other students, and the argument stratagem form appeared more and more in the discussions. Open discussions—students asking and answering each other's questions—were better than teacher-dominated discussion for the development of these argument forms. Over time, these ways of presenting, attacking, and defending positions could be internalized as mental reasoning and decision making for the individual students.

Both Piaget and Vygotsky emphasized the importance of social interactions in cognitive development, but Piaget saw a different role for interaction. He believed that interaction encouraged development by creating disequilibrium—cognitive conflict—that motivated change. Thus, Piaget believed that the most helpful interactions were between peers because peers are on an equal basis and can challenge each other's thinking. Vygotsky, on the other hand, suggested that children's cognitive development is fostered by interactions with people who are more capable or advanced in their thinking—people such as parents and teachers (Moshman, 1997; Palincsar, 1998). Of course, students can learn from both adults and peers, and today, computers can play a role in supporting communication across distances or in different languages.

## Cultural Tools and Cognitive Development

Vygotsky believed that **cultural tools** play very important roles in cognitive development. Cultural tools include real tools (in Vygotsky's day, these might include pens and pencils, printing presses, rulers, the abacus; today, we would add mobile devices, computers, the internet, real-time translators for mobile devices and chat tools, digital organizers and calendars, and assistive technologies for students with learning challenges) and psychological tools (sign and symbol systems such as numbers and mathematical systems, maps, works of art, signs, codes such as Braille, language, and sign language). For example, as long as the culture provides only Roman numerals for representing quantity, certain ways of thinking mathematically—from long division to calculus—are difficult or impossible. But with a number system that has a zero, fractions, positive and negative values, and an infinite quantity of numbers, much more is possible. The number system is a cultural tool that supports thinking, learning, and cognitive development. This symbol system is passed from adult to child and from child to child through formal and informal interactions and teachings.

TECHNICAL TOOLS IN A DIGITAL AGE.   The use of technical tools such as calculators and spell checkers has been somewhat controversial in education. Technology is increasingly "checking up" on us. You may rely on the spell checker in your word processing program to protect yourself from embarrassment. But you might also have read papers with spelling replacements that must have come from decisions made by the word processing program—without a "sense check" by the writer. Is student learning harmed or helped by these technology supports? Just because students learned mathematics in the past with paper-and-pencil procedures and practice does not mean

**Cultural tools** The real tools (computers, scales, etc.) and symbol systems (numbers, language, graphs, etc.) that allow people in a society to communicate, think, solve problems, and create knowledge.

that this is the best way to learn. For example, in the Third International Mathematics and Science Study (TIMSS, 1998), on every test at the advanced level, students who said that they used calculators in their daily math coursework performed much better than students who rarely or never used calculators. In fact, the research on calculators over the past decade has found that rather than eroding basic skills, calculator use has positive effects on students' problem-solving skills and attitudes toward math (Waits & Demana, 2000).

PSYCHOLOGICAL TOOLS.  Vygotsky believed psychological tools *mediate* (help to accomplish) all higher-order mental processes, such as reasoning and problem solving. These tools allow children to transform their thinking by enabling them to gain greater and greater mastery of their own cognitive processes; thus they advance their own development as they use the tools. In fact, Vygotsky believed the essence of cognitive development is mastering the use of psychological tools such as language to accomplish the kind of advanced thinking and problem solving that could not be accomplished without those tools (Gredler, 2009; Karpov & Haywood, 1998). The process goes something like this: As children engage in activities with adults or more capable peers, they exchange ideas and ways of thinking about or representing concepts—drawing maps, for example, as a way to represent spaces and places. Children internalize these co-created ideas. Thus, children's knowledge, ideas, attitudes, and values develop through appropriating or "taking for themselves" the ways of acting and thinking provided by their culture and by the more capable members of their group (Wertsch, 2007).

In this exchange of signs and symbols and explanations, children begin to develop a "cultural tool kit" to make sense of and learn about their world (Wertsch, 1991). The kit is filled with physical tools such as pencils or paintbrushes directed toward the external world and with psychological tools such as learning and problem solving or memory strategies for acting mentally. Children do not just receive the tools transmitted to them by others, however. Children transform the tools as they construct their own representations, symbols, patterns, and understandings. As we learned from Piaget, children's constructions of meaning are not the same as those of adults. In the exchange of signs and symbols such as number systems, children create their own understandings (a raccoon is a "kitty"). These understandings are gradually change (a raccoon is a raccoon) as the children continue to engage in social activities and try to make sense of their world (John-Steiner & Mahn, 1996; Wertsch, 1991). In Vygotsky's theory, language is the most important symbol system in the tool kit, and it is the one that helps fill the kit with other tools.

## The Role of Language and Private Speech

Language is critical for cognitive development. It provides a means for expressing ideas and asking questions, the categories and concepts for thinking, and the links between the past and the future (Das, 1995; Driscoll, 2005). When we consider a problem, we generally think in words and partial sentences. Vygotsky thought that

> The specifically human capacity for language enables children to provide for auxiliary tools in the solution of difficult tasks, to overcome impulsive action, to plan a solution to a problem prior to its execution, and to master their own behavior. (Vygotsky, 1978, p. 28)

Vygotsky placed more emphasis than Piaget on the role of learning and language in cognitive development. He believed that "thinking deepends on speech, on the means of thinking, and on the child's socio-cultural experience" (Vygotsky, 1987a, p. 120). In fact, Vygotsky believed that language in the form of *private speech* (talking to yourself) guides cognitive development.

PRIVATE SPEECH: VYGOTSKY'S AND PIAGET'S VIEWS COMPARED.  If you have spent much time around young children, you know that they often talk to themselves as they play. This can happen when the child is alone or, even more often, in a group of children—each child talks enthusiastically, without any real interaction or conversation. Piaget called this the **collective monologue**, and he called all of the children's self-directed talk "egocentric speech." He assumed that this egocentric speech is another indication that young children can't see the world through the eyes of others. They talk about what matters to them, without taking into account the needs or interests of their listeners. As they mature, and especially as they have disagreements with peers, Piaget believed, children develop socialized speech. They learn to listen and exchange (or argue) ideas.

Vygotsky had very different ideas about young children's **private speech**. He suggested that, rather than being a sign of cognitive immaturity, these mutterings play an important role in cognitive development because they move children toward self-regulation—the ability to plan, monitor, and guide one's own thinking and problem solving (see Chapter 10 for a detailed description of this highly effective form of learning). First, the child's behaviour is regulated by others, usually parents, using language and other signs such as gestures. For example, the parent says "No!" when the child reaches toward a candle flame. Next, the child learns to regulate the behaviour of others using the same language tools. The child says "No!" to another child who is trying to take away a toy, often even imitating the parent's voice tone. The child also begins to use private speech to regulate her own behaviour, saying "no" quietly to herself as she is tempted to touch the flame. Finally, the child learns to regulate her own behaviour by using silent inner speech (Karpov & Haywood, 1998).

In any preschool room, you might hear 4- or 5-year-olds saying, "No, it won't fit. Try it here. Turn. Turn. Maybe this one!" while they do puzzles. As these children mature, their self-directed speech goes underground, changing from spoken to whispered speech and then to silent lip movements. Finally, the children just "think" the guiding words. The use of private speech peaks at around age 9, although one study found that some students from ages 11 to 17 still spontaneously muttered to themselves during problem solving (McCafferty, 2004; Winsler, Carlton, & Barry, 2000; Winsler & Naglieri, 2003). Vygotsky called this inner speech "an internal plane of verbal thinking" (Vygotsky, 1934/1987c, p. 279)—a critical accomplishment on the road to higher-order thinking.

This series of steps, from spoken words to silent inner speech, is another example of how higher mental functions appear first between people as they communicate and regulate each other's behaviour—what McCaslin and Good (1996) refer to as co-regulating learning—and then appear again within the individual as a cognitive process. Through this fundamental process, the child is using language to accomplish important cognitive activities such as directing attention, solving problems, planning, forming concepts, and gaining self-control. Research supports Vygotsky's ideas (Berk & Spuhl, 1995; Emerson & Miyake, 2003). Children and adults tend to use more private speech when they are confused, having difficulties, or making mistakes (Duncan & Cheyne, 1999). Have you ever thought to yourself something like, "Let's see, the first step is …" or "Where did I use my glasses last?" or "If I work to the end of this page, then I can …"? You were using inner speech to remind, cue, encourage, or guide yourself.

This internal verbal thinking is not stable until about age 12, so children in elementary school may need to continue talking through problems and explaining their reasoning in order to develop their abilities to control their thinking (Gredler, 2009). Because private speech helps students to regulate their thinking, it makes sense to allow, and even encourage, students to use private speech in school. Teachers' insisting on total silence when young students are working on difficult problems may make the work even harder for them. Note when muttering increases in your class—this could be a sign that students need help.

Table 2.4 contrasts Piaget's and Vygotsky's theories of private speech. We should note that Piaget accepted many of Vygotsky's arguments and came to agree that language could be used in both egocentric and problem-solving ways (Piaget, 1962).

**Collective monologue** Form of speech in which children in a group talk but do not really interact or communicate.

**Private speech** Children's self-talk, which guides their thinking and action; eventually, these verbalizations are internalized as silent inner speech.

TABLE 2.4 ● **Differences Between Piaget's and Vygotsky's Theories of Egocentric or Private Speech**

|  | PIAGET | VYGOTSKY |
|---|---|---|
| **Developmental significance** | Represents an inability to take the perspective of another and engage in reciprocal communication | Represents externalized thought; its function is to communicate with the self for the purpose of self-guidance and self-direction |
| **Course of development** | Declines with age | Increases at younger ages and then gradually loses its audible quality to become internal verbal thought |
| **Relationship to social speech** | Negative; least socially and cognitively mature children use more egocentric speech | Positive; private speech develops out of social interaction with others |
| **Relationship to environmental contexts** | — | Increases with task difficulty; private speech serves a helpful self-guiding function in situations where more cognitive effort is needed to reach a solution |

Source: *From Berk, L. E., & Garvin, R. A. (1984). Development of private speech among low-income Appalachian children. Developmental Psychology, 20, 272.* Copyright © 1984 by the American Psychological Association. Adapted by permission.

**Watch**
The Zone of Proximal Development

## The Zone of Proximal Development

According to Vygotsky, at any given point in development, there are certain problems that a child is on the verge of being able to solve. The child just needs some structure, clues, reminders, help with remembering details or steps, encouragement to keep trying, and so on. Some problems, of course, are beyond the child's capabilities, even if every step is explained clearly. The **zone of proximal development (ZPD)** is the area between the child's current developmental level "as determined by independent problem solving" and the level of development that the child could achieve "through adult guidance or in collaboration with more peers" (Vygotsky, 1978, p. 86). It is a dynamic and changing space as student and teacher interact and understandings are exchanged. This is the area where instruction can succeed. Kathleen Berger (2012) called this area the "magic middle"—somewhere between what the student already knows and what the student isn't ready to learn.

PRIVATE SPEECH AND THE ZONE.   We can see how Vygotsky's beliefs about the role of private speech in cognitive development fit with the notion of the zone of proximal development. Often, an adult helps a child to solve a problem or accomplish a task using verbal prompts and structuring. We will see later that this type of support has been called *scaffolding*. This support can be gradually reduced as the child takes over the guidance, perhaps first by giving the prompts as private speech and finally as inner speech. Let's move forward to a future day in the life of the girl in the earlier example who had lost her toy and *listen to* her thoughts when she realizes that a school book is missing. They might sound something like this:

> "Where's my math book? Used it in class. Thought I put it in my book bag after class. Dropped my bag on the bus. That dope Larry kicked my stuff, so maybe . . ."

The girl can now systematically search for ideas about the lost book without help from anyone else.

THE ROLE OF LEARNING AND DEVELOPMENT.   Piaget defined *development* as the active construction of knowledge, and learning as the passive formation of associations (Siegler, 2000). He was interested in knowledge construction and believed that cognitive development has to come before learning—the child has to be cognitively "ready" to learn. He said that "learning is subordinated to development and not vice-versa" (Piaget, 1964, p. 17). Students can memorize, for example, that Geneva is in Switzerland but still insist that

**Zone of proximal development (ZPD)** Phase at which a child can master a task if given appropriate help and support.

they cannot be Genevan and Swiss at the same time. True understanding will happen only when the child has developed the operation of *class inclusion*—the idea that one category can be included in another. But as we saw earlier, research has not supported Piaget's position on the need for cognitive development to precede learning (Brainerd, 2003).

In contrast, Vygotsky believed that learning is an active process that does not have to wait for readiness. In fact, "properly organized learning results in mental development and sets in motion a variety of developmental processes that would be impossible apart from learning" (Vygotsky, 1978, p. 90). He saw learning as a tool in development—learning pulls development up to higher levels, and social interaction is a key in learning (Glassman, 2001; Wink & Putney, 2002). Vygotsky's belief that learning pulls development to higher levels means that other people, including teachers, play a significant role in cognitive development.

### Limitations of Vygotsky's Theory

Vygotsky's theory added important considerations by highlighting the role of culture and social processes in cognitive development, but he may have gone too far. As we have seen in this chapter, we may be born with a greater store of cognitive tools than either Piaget or Vygotsky suggested. Some basic understandings, such as the idea that adding increases quantity, may be part of our biological predispositions, ready for use to guide our cognitive development. Young children appear to figure out much about the world before they have the chance to learn from either their culture or teachers (Schunk, 2008). Also, Vygotsky did not detail the cognitive processes underlying developmental changes—which cognitive processes allow students to engage in more advanced and independent participation in social activities? The major limitation of Vygotsky's theory, however, is that it consists mostly of general ideas; Vygotsky died before he could expand and elaborate on his ideas and pursue his research. His students continued to investigate his ideas, but much of that work was suppressed until the 1950s and 1960s by Stalin's regime (Gredler, 2005; Kozulin, 1990, 2003). A final limitation might be that Vygotsky did not have time to detail the applications of his theories for teaching, even though he was very interested in instruction. So most applications of Vygotsky's theory described today have been created by others—we don't even know if he would agree with them.

## IMPLICATIONS OF PIAGET'S AND VYGOTSKY'S THEORIES FOR TEACHERS

Piaget did not make specific educational recommendations, and Vygotsky did not have time to make a complete set of applications, but we can still glean some guidance from them.

### Piaget: What Can We Learn?

Piaget was more interested in understanding children's thinking than in guiding teachers. He did express some general ideas about educational philosophy, however. He believed that the main goal of education should be to help children learn how to learn, and that education should "form not furnish" the minds of students (Piaget, 1969, p. 70). Piaget taught us that we can learn a great deal about how children think by listening carefully and by paying close attention to their ways of solving problems. If we understand children's thinking, we will be better able to match teaching methods to children's abilities; in other words, we will be better able to differentiate instruction.

Even though Piaget did not design programs of education based on his ideas, his influence on twentieth-century education is huge (Hindi & Perry, 2007). For example, the National Association for the Education of Young Children has guidelines for developmentally appropriate practice (DAP) that incorporate Piaget's findings (Bredekamp & Copple, 1997).

UNDERSTANDING AND BUILDING ON STUDENTS' THINKING.   The students in any class will vary greatly both in their level of cognitive development and in their academic knowledge. As a teacher, how can you determine whether students are having trouble

**ACTIVE LEARNING** The ability to manipulate concrete objects helps children understand abstract relationships such as the connection between symbols and quantity.

Dibyangshu Sarkar/AFP/Getty Images

because they lack the necessary thinking abilities or because they simply have not learned the basic facts? To do this, Robbie Case (1985b) suggested that you observe your students carefully as they try to solve the problems you have presented. What kind of logic do they use? Do they focus on only one aspect of the situation? Are they fooled by appearances? Do they suggest solutions systematically or by guessing and forgetting what they have already tried? Ask your students how they tried to solve the problem. Listen to their strategies. What kind of thinking is behind repeated mistakes or problems? Students are the best sources of information about their own thinking abilities (Confrey, 1990a).

An important implication of Piaget's theory for teaching is what J. M. Hunt (1961) years ago called the "problem of the match." Students must be neither bored by work that is too simple nor left behind by teaching they cannot understand. According to Hunt, disequilibrium must be kept "just right" to encourage growth. Setting up situations that lead to errors can help create an appropriate level of disequilibrium. When students experience some conflict between what they think should happen (a piece of wood should sink because it is big) and what actually happens (it floats!), they may rethink their understanding, and new knowledge may develop.

Many materials and lessons can be understood at several levels and can be "just right" for a range of cognitive abilities. Classics such as *Alice in Wonderland,* myths, and fairy tales can be enjoyed at both concrete and symbolic levels. It is also possible for a group of students to be introduced to a topic together and then work individually on follow-up activities matched to their learning needs and interests. Using multi-level lessons is called *differentiated instruction* (Hipsky, 2011; Tomlinson, 2005b). We encountered this idea in Chapter 1, and will look at it more closely in Chapter 14.

**ACTIVITY AND CONSTRUCTING KNOWLEDGE.**  Piaget's fundamental insight was that individuals *construct* their own understanding; learning is a constructive process. At every level of cognitive development, you will also want to see that students are actively engaged in the learning process. In his words:

> Knowledge is not a copy of reality. To know an object, to know an event, is not simply to look at it and make a mental copy or image of it. To know an object is to act on it. To know is to modify, to transform the object, and to understand the process of this transformation, and as a consequence to understand the way the object is constructed. (Piaget, 1964, p. 8)

This active experience, even at the earliest school levels, should not be limited to the physical manipulation of objects. It should also include mental manipulation of ideas that arise out of class projects or experiments (Gredler, 2005; 2009). For example, after a social studies lesson on different jobs, a primary-grade teacher might show the students a picture of a woman and ask, "What could this person be?" After answers such as "teacher," "doctor," "secretary," "lawyer," "saleswoman," and so on, the teacher could suggest, "How about a daughter?" Answers such as "sister," "mother," "aunt," and "granddaughter" may follow. This should help the children switch dimensions in their classification and centre on another aspect of the situation. Next, the teacher might suggest "Canadian," "jogger," or "blonde." With older children, hierarchical classification might be involved: "It is a picture of a woman, who is a human being; a human being is a primate, which is a mammal, which is an animal, which is a life form."

All students need to interact with teachers and peers in order to test their thinking, to be challenged, to receive feedback, and to watch how others work out problems. Disequilibrium is often set in motion quite naturally when the teacher or another student suggests a new way of thinking about something. As a general rule, students should act, manipulate, observe, and then talk and/or write (to the teacher and each other) about what they have experienced. Concrete experiences provide the raw materials for thinking. Communicating with others makes students use, test, and sometimes change their thinking strategies.

THE VALUE OF PLAY.    Maria Montessori once noted, and Piaget would agree, that "play is children's work." We saw that the brain develops with stimulation, and that play provides some of that stimulation at every age. Babies in the sensorimotor stage learn by exploring, sucking, pounding, shaking, throwing—acting on their environments. Preoperational preschoolers love pretend play, and through pretending they form symbols, use language, and interact with others. They are beginning to play simple games with predictable rules. During their elementary school years, children also like fantasy, but they are beginning to play more complex games and sports and thus learn cooperation, fairness, negotiation, winning, and losing, as well as developing language. As children grow into adolescents, play continues to be part of their physical and social development (Meece, 2002).

Piaget taught us that children do not think like adults, but discussions about the implications of Piaget's theory often centre on the question of whether cognitive development can be accelerated. This issue is at the heart of many discussions about the nature of programming in preschool and kindergarten. Many provinces across Canada have implemented, or are in the process of implementing, full-day kindergarten, including British Columbia, Ontario, Quebec, Nova Scotia, and New Brunswick. Some provinces have begun a targeted implementation, focusing on particular groups of children who are believed to be disadvantaged in terms of their readiness for school (e.g., Aboriginal children, immigrant children, children with disabilities). Others, like British Columbia and Ontario, are quickly moving to universal programs (universally available, although not universally required). These provinces are promoting a play-based approach to instruction, emphasizing that through play children can develop language and literacy, math and science skills, and social competence (BC Ministry of Education, n.d.; Elementary Teachers' Federation of Ontario, 2008).

## Vygotsky: What Can We Learn?

Like Piaget, Vygotsky believed that the main goal of education was the development of higher mental functions, not simply filling students' memories with facts. So Vygotsky probably would oppose educational curricula that are an inch deep and a mile wide or seem like "trivial pursuit." As an example of this trivial pursuit curriculum, Margaret Gredler (2009) described a set of materials for a nine-week science unit that had 61 glossary terms such as *aqueous solution, hydrogen bonding,* and *fractional crystallization*—many terms described with only one or two sentences.

There are at least three ways that higher mental functions can be developed through cultural tools and passed from one individual to another: *imitative* learning (where one person tries to imitate the other), *instructed* learning (where learners internalize the instructions of the teacher and use these instructions to self-regulate), and *collaborative* learning (where a group of peers strives to understand each other and learning occurs in the process) (Tomasello, Kruger, & Ratner, 1993). Vygotsky was most concerned with the second type, *instructed* learning through direct teaching or by structuring experiences that encourage another's learning, but his theory supports learning through *imitation* or *collaboration* as well. Thus, Vygotsky's ideas are relevant for educators who teach directly, intentionally use modelling to teach, or create collaborative learning environments (Das, 1995; Wink & Putney, 2002). That pretty much includes all of us.

**SCAFFOLDING LEARNING** According to Vygotsky, much of children's learning is assisted or mediated by teachers or parents and tools in their environment, and most of this guidance is communicated through language.

John Birdsall/The Image Works

**THE ROLE OF ADULTS AND PEERS.**   Vygotsky believed that the child is not alone in the world "discovering" the cognitive operations of conservation or classification. This discovery is *assisted* or *mediated* by family members, teachers, peers, and even software (Puntambekar & Hubscher, 2005). Most of this guidance is communicated through language, at least in Western cultures. In some cultures, observing a skilled performance, not talking about it, guides the child's learning (Rogoff, 1990). Some people have called this adult assistance scaffolding, taken from Wood, Bruner, and Ross (1976). The idea is that children use the help for support while they build a firm understanding that will eventually allow them to solve the problems on their own. Actually, when Wood and his colleagues introduced the term **scaffolding**, they were talking about how teachers set up or structure learning environments, but Vygotsky's theory implies more dynamic exchanges between students and teachers that allow teachers to support students in the parts of a task they cannot do alone. In the section below, we offer an example of how one teacher scaffolds her students' learning about math concepts and problem solving.

**Watch**
Assisted Learning

**ASSISTED LEARNING.**   Vygotsky's theory suggests that teachers need to do more than just arrange the environment so that students can discover on their own. He believed that children cannot and should not be expected to reinvent or rediscover knowledge already available in their cultures. Rather, they should be guided and assisted in their learning—so, Vygotsky saw teachers, parents, and other adults as central to the child's learning and development (Karpov & Haywood, 1998).

**Assisted learning**, or guided participation in the classroom, requires scaffolding—it requires first learning from the student what is needed; then giving information, prompts, reminders, and encouragement at the right time and in the right amounts; and gradually allowing the students to do more and more on their own. Teachers can assist learning by adapting materials or problems to students' current levels; demonstrating skills or thought processes; walking students through the steps of a complicated problem; doing part of the problem (for example, in algebra, the students set up the equation and the teacher does the calculations or vice versa); giving detailed feedback and allowing revisions; or asking questions that refocus students' attention (Rosenshine & Meister, 1992). Cognitive apprenticeships, reciprocal teaching, and instructional conversations (described in Chapter 10) are other examples. Table 2.5 gives examples of assisted learning strategies that can be used in any lesson.

**Scaffolding** Support for learning and problem solving; the support could be clues, reminders, encouragement, breaking the problem down into steps, providing an example, or anything else that allows the student to grow in independence as a learner.

**Assisted learning** Learning by having strategic help provided in the initial stages; the help gradually diminishes as students gain independence.

## Reaching Every Student: Teaching in the "Magic Middle"

Both Piaget and Vygotsky probably would agree that students need to be taught in the magic middle (Berger, 2006) or the place of the "match" (Hunt, 1961)—where they are neither bored nor frustrated. Students should be put in situations where they have to

TABLE 2.5 • **Strategies to Provide Scaffolding**

- Model the thought process for the students: Think out loud as you solve the problem or outline an essay, for example.
- Provide organizers or starters such as *who, what, why, how, what next?*
- Do part of the problem.
- Give hints and cues.
- Encourage students to set short-term goals and take small steps.
- Connect new learning to students' interests or prior learning.
- Use graphic organizers: timelines, charts, tables, categories, checklists, and graphs.
- Simplify the task, clarify the purpose, and give clear directions.
- Teach key vocabulary and provide examples.

*Sources: Adapted from http://projects.coe.uga.edu/epltt/index.php?title=Scaffolding#Sharing_a_Specific_Goal; http://condor.admin.ccny.cuny.edu/~group4, http://k6educators.about.com/od/helpfornewteachers/a/scaffoldingtech.htm.*

## GUIDELINES

### Applying Vygotsky's Ideas to Teaching

**Tailor scaffolding to the needs of students.**
*Examples*

1. When students are beginning new tasks or topics, provide models, prompts, sentence starters, coaching, and feedback. As the students grow in competence, give less support and more opportunities for independent work.

2. Give students choices about the level of difficulty or degree of independence in projects; encourage them to challenge themselves but to seek help when they are really stuck.

**Make sure that students have access to powerful tools that support thinking.**
*Examples*

1. Teach students to use learning and organizational strategies, research tools, language tools (dictionaries or computer searches), spreadsheets, and word-processing programs.

2. Model the use of tools; show students how you use an appointment book or electronic notebook to make plans and manage time, for example.

**Build on the students' cultural funds of knowledge (Gonzalezs, Moll, & Amanti, 2005; Moll, Amanti, Neff, & Gonzales, 1992).**
*Examples*

1. Identify family knowledge by having students interview each other's families about their work and home knowledge (agriculture, economics, manufacturing, household management, medicine and illness, religion, child care, cooking, etc.).

2. Tie assignments to these funds of knowledge and use community experts to evaluate assignments.

**Capitalize on dialogue and group learning.**
*Examples*

1. Experiment with peer tutoring; teach students how to ask good questions and how to give helpful explanations.

2. Experiment with cooperative learning strategies, described in Chapters 9 and 11, including using the internet to create communities of learners.

*For more information about Vygotsky and his theories, see http://tip. psychology.org/vygotsky.html.*

---

reach to understand, but where support from other students or the teacher is also available. Sometimes the best teacher is another student who has just figured out how to solve the problem, because this student is probably operating in the learner's *zone of proximal development*. When a student works with another student who is a bit better at the activity, both students benefit in the exchange of explanations, elaborations, and questions. In addition, students should be encouraged to use language to organize their thinking and to talk about what they are trying to accomplish. Dialogue and discussion are important avenues to learning (Karpov & Bransford, 1995; Kozulin & Presseisen, 1995; Wink & Putney, 2002). The *Guidelines* box gives more ideas for how to apply Vygotsky's ideas in the classroom.

## Cognitive Development: Lessons for Teachers

In spite of cross-cultural differences in cognitive development and the different theories of development, there are some convergences. Piaget, Vygotsky, and more recent researchers studying cognitive development and the brain probably would agree with the following big ideas:

1. Cognitive development requires both physical and social stimulation.
2. To develop thinking, children have to be mentally, physically, and linguistically active. They need to experiment, talk, describe, reflect, write, and solve problems. But they also benefit from teaching, guidance, questions, explanations, demonstrations, and challenges to their thinking.
3. Teaching students what they already know is boring. Trying to teach what the student isn't ready to learn is frustrating and ineffective.
4. Challenge with support will keep students engaged but not fearful.

# ▼ SUMMARY

## A Definition of Development (pp. 23–26)

**What are the different kinds of development?** Human development can be divided into physical development (changes in the body), personal development (changes in an individual's personality), social development (changes in the way an individual relates to others), and cognitive development (changes in thinking).

**What are three questions about development and three general principles?** For decades, psychologists and the public have debated whether development is shaped more by nature or nurture, whether change is a continuous process or involves qualitative differences or stages, and whether there are critical times for the development of certain abilities. We know today that these simple either/or distinctions cannot capture the complexities of human development, where coactions and interactions are the rule. Theorists generally agree that people develop at different rates, that development is an orderly process, and that development takes place gradually.

## The Brain and Cognitive Development (pp. 26–36)

**What part of the brain is associated with higher mental functions?** The cortex is a crumpled sheet of neurons that serves three major functions: receiving signals from sense organs (such as visual or auditory signals), controlling voluntary movement, and forming associations. The part of the cortex that controls physical motor movement develops or matures first, followed by the areas that control complex senses such as vision and hearing, and then the frontal lobe, which controls higher-order thinking processes.

**What is lateralization and why is it important?** Lateralization is the specialization of the two sides, or hemispheres, of the brain. For most people, the left hemisphere is the major factor in language, and the right hemisphere is prominent in spatial and visual processing. Even though certain functions are associated with certain parts of the brain, the various parts and systems of the brain work together to learn and perform complex activities such as reading and to construct understanding.

**What are some implications for teachers?** Recent advances in both methods and findings in the neurosciences provide exciting information about brain activity during learning and brain activity differences among people with varying abilities and challenges and from different cultures. There are some basic implications for teaching based on these findings, but many of the strategies offered by "brain-based" advocates are simply good teaching. Perhaps we now know more about why these strategies work.

## Piaget's Theory of Cognitive Development (pp. 36–49)

**What are the main influences on cognitive development?** Piaget's theory of cognitive development is based on the assumption that people try to make sense of the world and actively create knowledge through direct experience with objects, people, and ideas. Maturation, activity, social transmission, and the need for equilibrium all influence the way thinking processes and knowledge develop. In response to these influences, thinking processes and knowledge develop through changes in the organization of thought (the development of schemes) and through adaptation—including the complementary processes of assimilation (incorporating new information into existing schemes) and accommodation (changing existing schemes).

**What is a scheme?** Schemes are the basic building blocks of thinking. They are organized systems of actions or thought that allow us to mentally represent or "think about" the objects and events in our world. Schemes may be very small and specific (grasping, recognizing a square), or they may be larger and more general (using a map in a new city). People adapt to their environment as they increase and organize their schemes.

**As children move from sensorimotor to formal-operational thinking, what are the major changes?** Piaget believed that young people pass through four stages as they develop: sensorimotor, preoperational, concrete operational, and formal operational. In the sensorimotor stage, infants explore the world through their senses and motor activity and work toward mastering object permanence and performing goal-directed activities. In the preoperational stage, symbolic thinking and logical operations begin. Children in the stage of concrete operations can think logically about tangible situations and can demonstrate conservation, reversibility, classification, and seriation. The ability to perform hypothetico-deductive reasoning, coordinate a set of variables, and imagine other worlds marks the stage of formal operations.

**How do neo-Piagetian and information processing views explain changes in children's thinking over time?** Information processing theories focus on attention, memory capacity, learning strategies, and other processing skills to explain how children develop rules and strategies for making sense of the world and solving problems. Neo-Piagetian approaches also look at attention, memory, and strategies and at how thinking develops in different domains such as numbers or spatial relations. Research in neuroscience suggests that when learning a new skill, children move through three tiers—*from actions to representations to abstractions*. Within each tier, the pattern is moving from accomplishing a single action to mapping or coordinating two actions together such as coordinating addition and multiplication in math, to creating whole systems of understanding.

**What are some limitations of Piaget's theory?** Piaget's theory has been criticized because children and adults often think in ways that are inconsistent with the notion of invariant stages. It also appears that Piaget underestimated children's cognitive abilities; he insisted that children could not be taught the operations of the next stage, but had to develop them on their own. Alternative explanations place greater emphasis on students' developing information processing skills and ways teachers can enhance their development. Piaget's work is also criticized for overlooking cultural factors in child development.

## Vygotsky's Sociocultural Perspective (pp. 49–55)

**According to Vygotsky, what are three main influences on cognitive development?** Vygotsky believed that human activities must be understood in their cultural settings. He believed that our specific mental structures and processes can be traced to our interactions with others; that the tools of the culture, especially the tool of language, are key factors in development; and that the zone of proximal development is the area where learning and development are possible.

**What are psychological tools and why are they important?** Psychological tools are signs and symbol systems such as numbers and mathematical systems, codes, and language that support learning and cognitive development—they change the thinking process by enabling and shaping thinking. Many of these tools are passed from adult to child through formal and informal interactions and teachings.

**Explain how interpsychological development becomes intrapsychological development.** Higher mental processes appear first between people as they are co-constructed during shared activities. As children engage in activities with adults or more capable peers, they exchange ideas and ways of thinking about or representing concepts. Children internalize these co-created ideas. Thus children's knowledge, ideas, attitudes, and values develop through appropriating, or "taking for themselves," the ways of acting and thinking provided by their culture and by the more capable members of their group.

**What are the differences between Piaget's and Vygotsky's perspectives on private speech and its role in development?** Vygotsky's sociocultural view asserts that cognitive development hinges on social interaction and the development of language. As an example, Vygotsky described the role of children's self-directed talk in guiding and monitoring thinking and problem solving, while Piaget suggested that private speech was an indication of the child's egocentrism. Vygotsky, more than Piaget, emphasized the significant role played by adults and more able peers in children's learning. This adult assistance provides early support while students build the understanding necessary to solve problems on their own.

**What is a student's zone of proximal development?** At any given point in development, there are certain problems that a child is on the verge of being able to solve and others that are beyond the child's capabilities. The zone of proximal development is the area where the child cannot solve a problem alone, but can be successful under adult guidance or in collaboration with a more advanced peer.

**What are two criticisms or limitations of Vygotsky's theory?** Vygotsky may have overemphasized the role of social interaction in cognitive development—children figure out quite a bit on their own. Also, because he died so young, Vygotsky was not able to develop and elaborate on his theories. His students and others since have taken up that work.

### Implications of Piaget's and Vygotsky's Theories for Teachers (pp. 55–59)

**What is the "problem of the match" described by Hunt?** The "problem of the match" is that students must be neither bored by work that is too simple nor left behind by teaching they cannot understand. According to Hunt, disequilibrium must be carefully balanced to encourage growth. Situations that lead to errors can help create an appropriate level of disequilibrium.

**What is active learning? Why is Piaget's theory of cognitive development consistent with active learning?** Piaget's fundamental insight was that individuals construct their own understanding; learning is a constructive process. At every level of cognitive development, students must be able to incorporate information into their own schemes. To do this, they must act on the information in some way. This active experience, even at the earliest school levels, should include both physical manipulation of objects and mental manipulation of ideas. As a general rule, students should act, manipulate, observe, and then talk and/or write about what they have experienced. Concrete experiences provide the raw materials for thinking. Communicating with others makes students use, test, and sometimes change their thinking abilities.

**What is assisted learning, and what role does scaffolding play?** Assisted learning, or guided participation in the classroom, requires scaffolding—understanding students' needs; giving information, prompts, reminders, and encouragement at the right time and in the right amounts; and then gradually allowing the students to do more and more on their own. Teachers can assist learning by adapting materials or problems to students' current levels, demonstrating skills or thought processes, walking students through the steps of a complicated problem, doing part of the problem, giving detailed feedback and allowing revisions, or asking questions that refocus students' attention.

## ▼ WHAT WOULD THEY DO?

# TEACHERS' CASEBOOK: Symbols and Cymbals

Here is how two practising teachers responded to the teaching situation described on the first page of this chapter.

### JANET E. GETTINGS
Willoughby Elementary School, Langley, BC Faculty Adviser and Sessional Instructor, University of British Columbia

The students of the class have indicated a need for scaffolded learning to enhance their understanding of the concept of symbolism.

To introduce the concept, I would build on the children's prior knowledge of homonyms by doing a quick review of commonly used word pairs, such as bear/bare, stare/stair, I/eye, pair/pear, two/to/too, followed by cymbal/symbol. With the latter example, I would explain that Tracy had defined "cymbal." I would then invite suggestions for "symbol," summarizing with a formal definition, such as "something that stands for or represents something else."

I would follow the discussion with a "Think, Pair, Share" activity. Students would be asked to think about symbols independently, and then pair with a partner to share ideas. Next, the partners would be invited to go on a "detective search" of the room and their desks for symbols they could share with the class. For example, when I hang an umbrella on the door, students know they can stay in the classroom at lunch.

Another follow-up activity would be a modified game of Pictionary. The class would be divided into teams of five or six and take turns being artists. Each team would send a student to the teacher to view a phrase, which the student then has to represent pictorially. Sample phrases might include "the house had not been lived in for a long time" or "her face reflected pain and sadness."

At this stage, the students might be ready to move to usage of symbolism in written language. Sections of a familiar novel that includes symbolic phrases to describe feelings and emotions could be shared. For example, the phrase "thunderclouds passed over her face" describes the feelings of a character in a story in language that students understand easily. I would engage the class in a discussion to share the author's message and intent.

Reading aloud humorous poetry, such as that of Jack Prelutsky, might be used to move toward the final goal of identifying the use of symbolism in poetry. Students could demonstrate their understanding by researching the use of symbolic language in the genre of poetry and by writing their own poems, incorporating symbolism into their products.

### MARY LIGHTLY

Terry Fox Secondary School, Port Coquitlam, BC

In planning activities for the classroom, I try to be mindful of research on effective teaching. In particular, I draw on the work of Anita Archer at the University of Oregon and Barrie Bennet at the University of Toronto. Both these researchers have written texts that summarize current research, and both relate that research to actual classroom situations.

To develop the concept of symbol, I would first design activities in which students could engage independently or in small groups. For example, I might engage students in a matching activity that requires them to identify the symbolic meaning of concrete, or real-life, objects. I might create a worksheet that includes two lists: one list would include real-world objects, such as a dove or a heart (this list might be presented as pictures); the second list would include descriptions of the symbolic meaning for each object. Students would match the picture of the dove with peace, and the picture of the heart with love. I might ask students to generate their own symbols. For example, a red rose could symbolize passion, a sword could symbolize war. Students could colour their images and display them in the classroom as a reminder of how real-life objects can have symbolic meaning.

After introducing the concept in this manner, I would take the class through one or two concept attainment lessons, a strategy in which students are presented with "yes" and "no" examples of a concept, in this case examples and nonexamples of symbols and/or symbolism. I would begin with very clear and simple examples and then increase the level of difficulty as students become more confident and skilled at recognizing symbols and symbolism.

It might take many trials and a variety of strategies, but eventually students would be ready to look for symbolic meaning in literature.

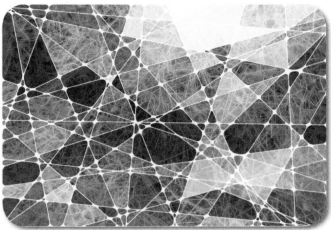

Color Symphony/Shutterstock

# SELF AND SOCIAL AND MORAL DEVELOPMENT

## TEACHERS' CASEBOOK: Mean Girls

You have seen it before, but this year the situation in your middle-school classroom seems especially vicious. A clique of popular girls has made life miserable for one of their former friends, Stephanie, who is now rejected. Stephanie committed the social sin of not fitting in—wearing the wrong clothes or not being pretty enough or not being interested in boys yet. To keep the status distinctions clear between themselves and Stephanie, the popular girls spread gossip about their former friend, often disclosing the intimate secrets revealed when Stephanie was still considered a close friend, which was only a few months ago. However, these girls are not using traditional methods of spreading gossip: Instead of passing notes or whispering in the hallways, they are using the internet to humiliate Stephanie. First they forwarded a long, heart-baring email from Stephanie to her former best friend, Alison, to the entire school. More recently, one of them used a cell phone to take a picture of Stephanie while she was changing after gym class and then posted it on her Facebook page so anyone could see. Stephanie has been absent from school for three days since this latest incident.

### CRITICAL THINKING

- How would you respond to the girls?
- Would you say anything to your other students? If so, what would you say?
- In your teaching, are there ways you can address the issues raised by this situation?
- Reflecting on your years in school, were your experiences more like those of Alison or Stephanie?

## OVERVIEW AND OBJECTIVES

Schooling involves more than cognitive development. As you remember your years in school, what stands out—memories of academic knowledge or memories of feelings, friendships, and fears? In this chapter, we examine personal, social, and moral development.

We begin by looking at a basic aspect of development that affects all the others—physical changes as students mature. Then we explore Urie Bronfenbrenner's bioecological theory and use it as a framework for examining the three major influences on children's personal and social development: families, peers, and teachers. Families today have gone through many transitions, and these changes affect the roles of teachers. Next, we explore ideas about how we come to understand ourselves by looking at self-concept and identity, including racial-ethnic identity. Erikson's theory of psychosocial development provides a lens for viewing these developments. Finally, we look at moral development. What factors determine our views about morality? What can teachers do to foster such personal qualities as honesty and cooperation? Why do students cheat in their academic work, and what can be done about it?

By the time you have completed this chapter, you should be able to:

3.1   Describe general trends and group differences in physical development through childhood and adolescence.

3.2   Discuss how the components of Bronfenbrenner's bioecological model influence development.

3.3   Discuss the relationship between parenting styles and children's development.

3.4   Describe general trends and group differences in the development of self-concept and identity.

3.5   Explain how positive peer relations (friendships) and negative peer relations (aggression) affect children's social development.

3.6   Explain current theories of moral development.

> Look for the **Explore, Watch, Practise**, and **Listen** icons throughout this chapter . . . these symbols lead you to online content that will enhance and complement your text experience.

# PHYSICAL DEVELOPMENT

This chapter is about personal and social development, but we begin with a kind of development that is a basic concern of all individuals and families—physical development.

**STOP & THINK** How tall are you? What grade were you in when you reached that height? Were you one of the tallest or shortest students in your middle or high school, or were you about average? Did you know students who were teased because of something about their physical appearance? How important was your physical development to your feelings about yourself? •

## Physical and Motor Development

For most children, at least in the early years, growing up means getting bigger, stronger, and more coordinated. It also can be a frightening, disappointing, exciting, and puzzling time.

**YOUNG CHILDREN.**    Preschool children are very active. Their *gross motor* (large muscle) skills improve greatly during these early years. Between ages 2 and about 4 or 5, preschoolers' muscles grow stronger and their brains develop to better integrate information about movements. Their balance improves, and their centre of gravity moves lower, so they are able to run, jump, climb, and hop. By age 2, most children stop "toddling." Their awkward, wide-legged gait becomes smooth and rhythmic—they have perfected walking. During their third year, most children learn to run, throw, and jump, but these activities are not well controlled until age 4 or 5. Most of these movements develop naturally if the child has normal physical abilities and the opportunity to play. Children with physical problems, however, may need special training to develop these skills. For young children, as for many adolescents and adults, physical activity can be an end in itself. It is fun just to improve. Because they can't always judge when to stop, preschoolers may need interludes of rest scheduled after periods of physical exertion (Darcey & Travers, 2006; Thomas & Thomas, 2008).

*Fine motor* skills such as tying shoes or fastening buttons, which require the coordination of small movements, also improve greatly during the preschool years. Children should be given the chance to work with large paintbrushes, fat pencils and crayons, large pieces of drawing paper, large Lego blocks, and soft clay or playdough to accommodate their developing skills. During this time, most children will begin to develop a lifelong preference for their right or left hand. By age 5, about 90% of students prefer their right hand for most skilled work, and 10% or so prefer their left hand, with more boys than girls being left-handed (Feldman, 2004). A small but indeterminate number of individuals are ambidextrous (estimates are approximately 1%)—their hand preference often depends on what task they need to complete, or they may switch hands while they complete the same task (Porac, Coren, & Searleman, 1986). Handedness is a genetically based preference, so don't force children to choose or switch.

**ELEMENTARY SCHOOL YEARS.**    During the elementary school years, physical development is fairly steady for most children. They become taller, leaner, and stronger, so they are better able to master sports and games. There is tremendous variation, however. A particular child can be much larger or smaller than average and still be perfectly healthy. Because children at this age are very aware of physical differences but are not the most tactful people, you may hear comments such as, "You're too little to be in grade 5. What's wrong with you?" or "How come you're so fat?"

Throughout elementary school, many of the girls are likely to be as large as or larger than the boys in their classes. Between the ages of 11 and 14, girls are, on average, taller and heavier than boys of the same age. The size discrepancy can give the girls an advantage in physical activities, although some girls may feel conflict over this and, as a result, downplay their physical abilities (Woolfolk & Perry, 2015).

**THE ADOLESCENT YEARS.**    **Puberty** marks the beginning of sexual maturity. It is not a single event, but rather a series of changes involving almost every part of the body. The sex differences in physical development observed during the later elementary years become even more pronounced at the beginning of puberty. But these changes take time. The earliest visible signs of puberty in girls are the growth of nipples and budding of their breasts at around age 10 for European, American, and Canadian adolescents. At about the same time, boys' testes and scrotum begin to grow larger. On average, between ages 12 and 13, girls have their first menstrual period (called **menarche**) and boys have their first sperm ejaculation (called **spermarche**). Boys develop facial hair over the next several years, reaching their final beard potential by about age 18 or 19—with some exceptions who take longer to develop their final facial hair. Less welcome changes in puberty are increases in skin oiliness, skin acne, and body odour.

Girls reach their final height by age 15 or 16, several years ahead of boys, so there is a time in middle school, as in late elementary school, when many girls are taller than their male classmates. Most boys continue growing until about age 19, but both boys and girls can continue to grow slightly until about age 25 (Thomas & Thomas, 2008; Wigfield, Byrnes, & Eccles, 2006). Some ethnic groups reach their maximum heights sooner than

**Puberty** The physiological changes during adolescence that lead to the ability to reproduce.

**Menarche** The first menstrual period in girls.

**Spermarche** The first sperm ejaculation for boys.

STUDENTS COME IN ALL SIZES The physical changes of adolescence have significant effects on the individual's identity. Psychologists have been particularly interested in the academic, social, and emotional differences they have found between adolescents who mature early and those who mature later.

Jeff Greenberg/The Image Works

**Watch**
The Adolescent Years

others. For example, the ages for reaching maximum height are a bit younger for African American and Latino adolescents and a bit older for Asian adolescents.

Psychologists have been particularly interested in the academic, social, and emotional differences they have found between adolescents who mature early and those who mature later. For girls, maturing way ahead of classmates can be a definite disadvantage. Being larger and more "developed" than everyone else your age is not a valued characteristic for girls in many cultures (Jones, 2004). Early maturation is associated with emotional difficulties such as depression, anxiety, and eating disorders, especially in societies that define thinness as attractive (Steinberg, 2005). Other problems for early maturing girls are lower achievement in school, drug and alcohol abuse, unplanned pregnancy, suicide, and greater risk of breast cancer in later life. Around the world, early menarche has been related to bulimia and alcohol use in Finland, suicide and alcohol use in Norway, and depression and anxiety in Australia (Mendle, Turkheimer, & Emery, 2007). In addition, researchers have found a correlation between age at menarche and adult **body mass index (BMI**, a measure of body fat); the younger the girl was when she had her first period, the greater her adult BMI, on average (Harris, Prior, & Koehoom, 2008). Later-maturing girls seem to have fewer problems, but they may worry that something is wrong with them, so adult reassurance and support is important.

Early maturity in males is associated with popularity. The early maturer's taller, broad-shouldered body type fits the cultural stereotype for the male ideal; late-maturing boys may experience lower self-esteem because they are smaller and less muscular than the "ideal" for men. In fact, there is some evidence that the standards regarding physical appearance have increased (Harter, 2006). Even so, recent research points to more disadvantages than advantages for early maturation in boys (Westling, Andrews, Hampson, & Peterson, 2008). Early maturing boys tend to engage in more delinquent behaviour. They also appear to be at greater risk for depression and for abusing alcohol and cigarettes (Westling, Andrews, Hampson, & Peterson, 2008).

Boys who mature late may have a more difficult time initially. However, some studies show that in adulthood, males who matured later tend to be more creative, tolerant, and perceptive. Perhaps the trials and anxieties of maturing late teach some boys to be better problem solvers (Brooks-Gunn, 1988; Steinberg, 2005). All adolescents can benefit from knowing that there is a very wide range for timing and rates in "normal" maturation and that there are advantages for both early and late maturers. The *Guidelines* give ideas for dealing with physical differences in the classroom.

## Play, Recess, and Physical Activity

Maria Montessori once noted, "Play is children's work," and Piaget and Vygotsky would agree. More recently, the American Academy of Pediatrics stated, "Play is essential to development because it contributes to the cognitive, physical, social, and emotional well-being of children and youth" (Ginsburg, 2007, p. 182). The brain develops with stimulation, and play provides some of that stimulation at every age. In fact, some neuroscientists suggest that play might help in the important process of pruning brain synapses during childhood (Pellis, 2006). Other psychologists believe play allows children to experiment safely as they learn about their environment, try out new behaviours, solve problems, and adapt to new situations (Pellegrini, Dupuis, & Smith, 2007). Babies in the sensorimotor stage learn by exploring, sucking, pounding, shaking, and throwing—acting on

Body mass index (BMI) A measure of body fat that evaluates weight in relation to height.

## GUIDELINES

## Dealing With Physical Differences in the Classroom

**Address students' physical differences in ways that do not call unnecessary attention to the variations.**
*Examples*
1. Try to seat smaller students so they can see and participate in class activities, but avoid seating arrangements that are obviously based on height.
2. Balance sports and games that rely on size and strength with games that reflect cognitive, artistic, social, or musical abilities, such as charades or drawing games.
3. Don't use or allow students to use nicknames based on physical traits.
4. Make sure there is a good supply of left-handed scissors for preschool classes.

**Help students obtain factual information about differences in physical development.**
*Examples*
1. Assign science projects that explore sex differences in growth rates.
2. Have readings available that focus on differences between early and late maturers. Make sure that you present the positives and the negatives of each.

3. Find out the school policy on sex education and on informal guidance for students. Some schools, for example, encourage teachers to talk to girls who are upset about their first menstrual period, while other schools expect teachers to send the girls to talk to the school nurse (if your school still has one—budget cuts have eliminated many).
4. Give the students models in literature or in their community of accomplished and caring individuals who do not fit the culture's ideal physical stereotypes.

**Accept that concerns about appearance and the opposite sex will occupy much time and energy for adolescents.**
*Examples*
1. Allow some time at the end of class for socializing.
2. Deal with issues related to physical differences in curriculum-related materials.

---

*For more information about accommodations for physical differences in your classroom, see www.extension.org/pages/61358/adapting-the-child-care-environment-for-children-with-special-needs#.Vld2IL6sqE4.*

---

their environments. Preoperational preschoolers love pretend play and use pretending to form symbols, use language, and interact with others. They are beginning to play simple games with predictable rules. Elementary-school-age children also like fantasy, but begin to play more complex games and sports, and thus learn cooperation, fairness, negotiation, and winning and losing as well as develop more sophisticated language. As children grow into adolescents, play continues to be part of their physical and social development (Meece & Daniels, 2008).

PHYSICAL EXERCISE AND RECESS.   There are good, academic reasons for encouraging children to exercise. Phillip Tomporowski and his colleagues (2008) reviewed the research on physical activity and cognitive development and concluded that "systematic exercise programs may actually enhance the development of specific types of mental processing known to be important for meeting challenges encountered both in academics and throughout the lifespan" (p. 127). Other researchers note that students in Asian countries, who consistently outperform U.S. students on international reading, science, and mathematics tests, have more frequent recess breaks throughout the school day. One study of 11 000 students who were 8 and 9 years old found that students who had daily recess of 15 minutes or longer every day were better behaved in class than students who had little or no recess. This was true even after controlling for student gender and ethnicity, public or private school setting, and class size (Barros, Silver, & Stein, 2009). These recess breaks may be especially important for students with attention-deficit hyperactive disorders (ADHD). In fact, if more breaks were provided, there might be fewer students, especially boys, diagnosed with ADHD (Pellegrini & Bohn, 2005).

Schools have a role in promoting physical activity. This can be especially important for students living in poverty and for children with disabilities. In Canada, the federal government has recognized the value of physical activity and recommends that children

**Watch**
Physical Activity

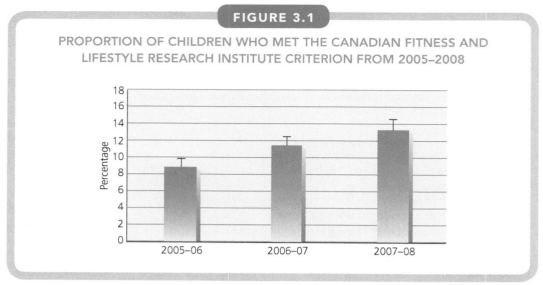

**FIGURE 3.1**

PROPORTION OF CHILDREN WHO MET THE CANADIAN FITNESS AND
LIFESTYLE RESEARCH INSTITUTE CRITERION FROM 2005–2008

Source: Canadian Fitness and Lifestyle Research Institute. (2008). Kids can play! Encouraging children to be active at home, at school, and in their communities. Retrieved August 26, 2010, from www.cflri.ca/eng/provincial_data/ canplay_bulletins/canplay_canada.php.

engage in 90 minutes of moderate to vigorous physical activity every day. However, the Canadian Fitness and Lifestyle Research Institute (CFLRI, 2008) reports that only about 23% of Canadian children reach this benchmark. From 2005 through 2008, the institute studied more than 10 000 children (ages 5–19) using pedometers to count their daily steps. A goal was set for children to take 16 500 steps each day, which translates roughly to 90 minutes of physical activity over and above that required for incidental daily living. Figure 3.1 shows the proportion of children who reached this criterion in each period of the study. On average, boys took more steps than girls, and children aged 5–10 were almost twice as likely to meet the criterion as those aged 15–19. Differences across regions of the country also were found. The amount of physical activity increased from east to west, and children in higher socioeconomic status (SES) communities engaged in more physical activity than children living in low SES communities. One reason for concern about physical activity for children is the increase in childhood obesity, as you will see in the next section.

## Challenges in Physical Development

Physical development is public—everyone sees how tall, short, heavy, thin, muscular, or coordinated you are. As students move into adolescence, they feel as if they are "on stage" (i.e., as if everyone is evaluating them); physical development is part of what is evaluated. So there are psychological consequences to physical development, too (Thomas & Thomas, 2008).

OBESITY.   If you have seen the news lately, you know that obesity is a growing problem in North America, especially for children. In fact, in Canada, the rate of obesity in teenagers has tripled in the past 25 years, and current estimates are that 32% of children and youth are overweight or obese (Canadian Obesity Foundation, 2014; Statistics Canada, 2012). Childhood obesity usually is defined in terms of body mass index, or BMI, which calculates weight in relation to height. Children with BMIs between the 85th and 95th percentiles (i.e., 85% of children the same age and sex weigh less than they do) are considered overweight, and children with BMIs above the 95th percentile are considered obese. Although the BMI provides a good screening tool for identifying overweight and obese children, children with BMIs at the 85th percentile or higher should be assessed by a health care professional who will consider other factors, such as diet, physical activity, and family history, to determine whether excess fat is a problem.

The consequences of obesity are serious for children and adolescents: diabetes, strain on bones and joints, respiratory problems, and greater chance of heart problems as adults. Playing with friends or participating in sports can be affected negatively. In addition, children with obesity often are the targets of cruel teasing. Like everything involving children's development, there probably are many interacting causes for this increase in obesity rates, including poor diet, genetic factors, increased hours in front of the television and video games, and lack of exercise (Woolfolk & Perry, 2015). Programs that address this problem emphasize healthy eating, increased physical activity, and decreased television viewing.

There is another challenge in physical development for many children that involves not too much weight, but too little.

EATING DISORDERS.    Adolescents experiencing the changes of puberty are very concerned about their bodies. This has always been true, but today, the emphasis on fitness and appearance makes adolescents even more likely to worry about how their bodies "measure up." Both boys and girls can become dissatisfied with their bodies during adolescence because they do not match the cultural ideals in magazines and films. For girls, it also appears that conversations with friends about appearance can make dissatisfactions worse (Jones, 2004). For some, the concern becomes excessive. One consequence is eating disorders such as **bulimia** (binge eating) and **anorexia nervosa** (self-starvation), both of which are more common in females than in males. People who are bulimic often binge, eating a huge carton of ice cream or a whole cake. Then, to avoid gaining weight, they force themselves to vomit, or they use strong laxatives, to purge themselves of the extra calories. Bulimics tend to maintain a normal weight, but the purging can permanently damage their digestive systems.

Anorexia is an even more dangerous disorder—people who are anorexic either refuse to eat

**DON'T TURN AWAY FROM ME** Students with anorexia usually require professional help—don't ignore the warning signs. A teacher may be the person who begins the chain of help for students with these tragic disorders.

Angela Hampton Picture Library/Alamy

or eat practically nothing while often exercising obsessively. In the process, they may lose 20%–25% of their body weight, and some (about 20%) literally starve themselves to death. Individuals who are anorexic become very thin, and may appear pale, have brittle fingernails, and develop fine dark hairs all over their bodies. They are easily chilled because they have so little fat to insulate their bodies. They are often depressed, insecure, moody, and lonely. Girls may stop having their menstrual period. These eating disorders often begin in adolescence and are becoming more common—about 1% of adolescents (mostly, but not all, girls) become anorexic (Rice & Dolgin, 2002). These students usually require professional help. Don't ignore the warning signs—less than one-third of people with eating disorders actually receive treatment (Stice & Shaw, 2004). A teacher may be the person who begins the chain of help for students with these tragic problems. The *Guidelines* give a few ideas for supporting positive body images in adolescents.

**Bulimia** Eating disorder characterized by overeating, then getting rid of the food by self-induced vomiting or use of laxatives.

**Anorexia nervosa** Eating disorder characterized by very limited food intake.

## Supporting Positive Body Images

**Listen to adolescents talk about their health.**
*Examples*
1. If they mention wanting to lose weight, seize the opportunity to talk about healthy weight, body image, and cultural influences on youth.
2. It they mention diets they or their friends are trying, provide them with nutritionally sound information about myths, misinformation, and dangers related to fad diets.
3. In general, be attentive. An adolescent may make a brief comment that could serve as a terrific entrance into a valuable conversation about body image.

**Ask questions.**
*Examples*
1. Are you concerned about your weight (or shape or size) at all? Do you think your friends are concerned about their weight? Do you or your friends talk a lot about your weight?
2. Do you know that diets are the worst way to lose or maintain weight? Have you ever dieted? Why?

3. Do you know that eating only low-fat or fat-free foods is *not* healthy eating? Do you know that you need fat in your diet, and that without it you can have all kinds of health problems?

**Make resources available for adolescents who have body image issues.**
*Examples*
1. Have accurate, youth-oriented resources available to read, look up on the internet, or find in a library.
2. Encourage youth to continue conversations about these issues with you, their parents, a health professional, a trusted teacher, or a caring, knowledgeable adult.
3. Deal with some of these issues in curriculum-related materials.

---

*For more information about adolescents and body image, see http://www.epi.umn.edu/let/pubs/img/adol_ch13.pdf.*

*Source: Adapted from Story, M., & Stang, J. (2005). Nutrition needs of adolescents. In J. S. M. Story (Ed.), Guidelines for adolescent nutritional services. Minneapolis, MN: University of Minnesota, pp. 158–159.*

# BRONFENBRENNER: THE SOCIAL CONTEXT FOR DEVELOPMENT

We put the developing person in context by exploring the work of Urie Bronfenbrenner (1917–2005), who was born in Moscow, Russia, but moved with his family to the United States when he was 6. Bronfenbrenner completed a double major in psychology and music at Cornell in 1938 and a Ph.D. in psychology from the University of Michigan in 1942. Over his long career in psychology he worked as a clinical psychologist in the U.S. Army and as a professor at the University of Michigan and at Cornell. He also helped to found the Head Start early childhood program.

Educational and developmental psychologists are increasingly interested in the role of **context**, which refers to the total situation that surrounds and interacts with an individual's thoughts, feelings, and actions and shapes development and learning. There are contextual effects on learning and motivation that are both internal and external to the developing individual. For example, hormone levels within the body are contexts for developing organs, including the brain, as well as for adolescents' self-concepts during puberty. In this text, however, we focus on the contexts outside the person. Children grow up in families and are members of particular ethnic, religious, economic, and language communities. They live in neighbourhoods, attend schools, and are members of classes, teams, or choirs. The social and educational programs and policies of governments affect their lives. These contexts influence the development of behaviours, beliefs, and knowledge by providing resources, supports, incentives and punishments, expectations, teachers, models, and tools—all the building blocks of learning and development (Dodge, 2011; Lerner, Theokas, & Bobek, 2005).

Contexts also affect how actions are interpreted. For example, when a stranger approaches a 7-month-old infant, the baby is likely to cry if the setting is unfamiliar, but not cry when the stranger approaches in the baby's home. Adults are more likely to help a stranger in need in small towns as opposed to larger cities (Kagan & Herschkowitz, 2005). Think about a ringing telephone. Is it 3:00 in the afternoon or 3:00 a.m.? Did you just call

**Context** The total setting or situation that surrounds and interacts with a person or event. It includes internal and external circumstances and situations that interact with the individual's thoughts, feelings, and actions to shape development and learning.

**FIGURE 3.2**

### URIE BRONFENBRENNER'S BIOECOLOGICAL MODEL OF HUMAN DEVELOPMENT

Every person develops within a *microsystem* (family, friends, school activities, teacher, etc.) inside a *mesosystem* (the interactions among all the microsystem elements), embedded in an *exosystem* (social settings that affect the child, even though the child is not a direct member—community resources, parents' workplace, etc.); all are part of the *macrosystem* (the larger society with its laws, customs, values, etc.). All development occurs in and is influenced by the time period—the *chronosystem*.

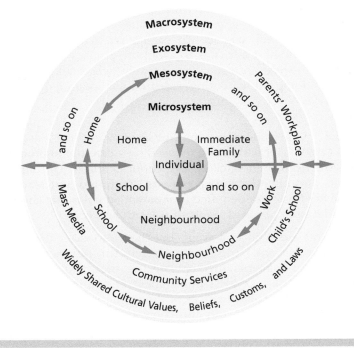

someone and leave a message asking for a return call? Has the phone been ringing off the hook, or is this the first call in days? Did you just sit down to dinner? The meaning of the ring and the feelings you have about it will vary, depending on the context.

Urie Bronfenbrenner's **bioecological model** of development (Bronfenbrenner, 1989; Bronfenbrenner & Morris, 2006) recognizes that the physical and social contexts in which we develop are ecosystems because they are in constant interaction and influence each other. Look at Figure 3.2. Every person lives within a *microsystem,* inside a *mesosystem,* embedded in an *exosystem,* all of which are a part of the *macrosystem*—like a set of Russian painted dolls, nested one inside the other. In addition, all development occurs in and is influenced by the time period—the chronosystem.

In the microsystem are the person's immediate relationships and activities. For a child, the microsystem might be the immediate family, friends, or teachers and the activities of play and school. Relationships in the microsystem are reciprocal—they flow in both directions. The child affects the parent, and the parent influences the child, for example. The mesosystem is the set of interactions and relationships among all the elements of the microsystem—the family members interacting with each other or with the teacher. Again, all relationships are reciprocal—the teacher influences the parents and the parents affect the teacher, and these interactions affect the child. The exosystem includes all the social settings that affect the child, even though the child is not a direct member of the systems. Examples are the teachers' relations with administrators and the school board; parents' jobs; the community resources for health, employment, or recreation; or the family's religious affiliation. The macrosystem is the larger society—its values, laws, conventions, and traditions.

**Bioecological model** Bronfenbrenner's theory describing the nested social and cultural contexts that shape development. Every person develops within a *microsystem,* inside a *mesosystem,* embedded in an *exosystem,* all of which are a part of the *macrosystem* of the culture.

## Families

The first context for child development is the mother's womb. Scientists are learning more about the effects of this first environment—the role of the expectant mother's level of stress, nutrition, smoking, alcohol and drug intake, exercise, and general health in her infant's development. Clearly, the influence of the family begins before birth, but many new influences follow (Woolfolk & Perry, 2015).

The most appropriate expectation to have about your students' families is no expectation at all. Increasingly, children today may be part of **blended families**, with stepbrothers or stepsisters who move in and out of their lives. Some of your students may live with an aunt, with grandparents, with one parent, in foster or adoptive homes, or with an older brother or sister. In some cultures (e.g., Asian, Latin American, African), children are more likely to grow up in **extended families**, with grandparents, aunts, uncles, and cousins living in the same household or at least in daily contact with each other. In addition, some children have two moms or two dads. The best advice is to avoid the phrases "your parents" and "your mother and father" and to speak instead of "your family" when talking to students.

No matter who is doing the parenting, research has identified characteristic differences in parenting styles.

PARENTING STYLES.    One well-known description of parenting is based on the research of Diane Baumrind (1991). Her early work focused on a careful longitudinal study of 100 (mostly European American, middle-class) preschool children. Through observation of children and parents and interviews with parents, Baumrind and Maccoby and Martin (1983), who built on her findings, identified four **parenting styles** that characterize parents' interactions with children in terms of levels of warmth and control:

- *Authoritative* parents are high in warmth but they also exert firm control. They set clear limits, enforce rules, and expect mature behaviour. But they are warm with their children. They listen to concerns, give reasons for rules, and allow more democratic decision making. There is less strict punishment and more guidance. Parents help children think through the consequences of their actions (Hoffman, 2001).
- *Authoritarian* parents can seem cold and controlling in their interactions with their children. The children are expected to be mature and to do what the parent says, "Because I said so!" There is not much talk about emotions. Punishments are strict, but not abusive. The parents love their children, but they are not openly affectionate.
- *Permissive* parents are warm but have little control. They have few rules or consequences for their children and expect little in the way of mature behaviour because "they're just kids." Rather than actively trying to shape their children's behaviour, these parents view themselves as resources for their children to use as they wish.
- *Rejecting/neglecting* parents are low in warmth and control. Maccoby and Martin (1983) referred to these parents as "uninvolved." They put little effort into parenting and, often, are more focused on their own needs than the needs of their children. They may fail to set schedules for sleeping and eating, and react harshly to children's advances or requests for attention. Often these parents have significant problems of their own that limit or inhibit their ability to meet the needs of their children. Parents who are depressed or who have drug or alcohol problems may become neglecting or rejecting.

In broad strokes, there are different outcomes for children associated with the four parenting styles. At least in North American, middle-class families, children of authoritative parents are more likely to be happy with themselves and to relate well to others. They do well in school and maintain positive relationships with parents. On average, children of authoritarian parents perform less well in school, are more hostile and less popular with peers, and have lower levels of self-control than children raised by authoritative parents (Baumrind, 1971; Thompson, Hollis, & Richards, 2003).

Children raised by permissive parents tend to be immature and demanding. Also, they tend to be more impulsive, rebellious, and aggressive than children raised by authoritative parents, and less socially competent and confident (Baumrind, 1971; Parke & Buriel, 2006). Of course, the extreme of permissiveness becomes indulgence. Indulgent parents cater to their children's every whim—perhaps it is easier than being the adult who must make unpopular

**Blended families** Parents, children, and stepchildren merged into families through remarriages.

**Extended families** Parents, children, grandparents, aunts, uncles, and cousins living in the same household or in close proximity so they can have daily contact with one another.

**Parenting styles** The ways of interacting with and disciplining children.

decisions. Both indulgent and rejecting/neglecting parenting styles are harmful, but children of rejecting/neglecting parents fare worst of all. They tend to be insecure in their relationships, noncompliant, aggressive, and withdrawn (Baumrind, 1991; Parke & Buriel, 2006). In adolescence, these children are more likely to engage in risky and delinquent behaviour, suffer disruptions in social and cognitive development, and perform poorly in school.

Research on parenting styles is extensive and appeals to North American and Western European cultures. However, it is important to note that most of this research is correlational—we cannot claim that parenting styles cause the observed outcomes for children. Also, the differences observed among parenting styles, although statistically reliable, are generally small. The largest effects are observed between authoritative and rejecting/neglecting parents (Lamborn, Mounts, Steinberg, & Dornbusch, 1991). Finally, research findings about parenting styles are not universal. Outcomes for children raised by authoritarian parents have been found to differ across cultural and socioeconomic status, and across religious communities.

CULTURE AND PARENTING.   Research indicates that higher control and more authoritarian parenting are linked to better grades for African American and some Asian students (Leung, Lau, & Lam, 1998; Spera, 2005). Parenting that is strict and directive, with clear rules and consequences, combined with high levels of warmth and emotional support, is associated with higher academic achievement and greater emotional maturity for inner-city children (Garner & Spears, 2000; Jarrett, 1995). Differences in cultural values and in the danger level of some urban neighbourhoods may make tighter parental control appropriate, and even necessary (Smetana, 2000). In addition, in cultures that have a greater respect for elders and a more group-centred rather than individualist philosophy, it may be a misreading of the parents' actions to perceive their demand for obedience as "authoritarian" (Lamb & Lewis, 2005; Nucci, 2001). Ruth Chao (Chao, 2001; Chao & Tseng, 2002) has challenged Baumrind's conclusions for Asian families. Chao finds that an alternative parenting style of *chiao shun* (a Chinese term that Chao translates to mean "training") better characterizes parenting in Asian and Asian American families.

Whatever the structure of the families you work with, here are some *Family and Community Partnership Guidelines* for making connections.

**STUDYING CULTURAL DIFFERENCES IN PARENTING** The results of Ruth Chao's studies of Asian American parenting styles have challenged models of parenting based on European American parents and children. She is also studying whether serving as a translator or "language broker" for parents who do not speak English has an impact on the child's psychological well-being and relationship with the parents.

Courtesy of Ruth Chao

## GUIDELINES — FAMILY AND COMMUNITY PARTNERSHIPS

### Connecting With Families

1. Work with families to co-create methods for family involvement. Offer a range of possible participation methods. Make sure the plans are realistic and fit the lives of the families you are dealing with.

2. Remember that some students' families have had negative experiences with schools or may fear or mistrust schools and teachers. Find other places to collaborate: before or after extracurricular activities, or at a local church or recreation centre. Go where families go; don't always expect them to come to school.

3. Maintain regular home–school contact through telephone calls or notes. If a family has no telephone, identify a contact person (relative or friend) who can take messages. If literacy is a problem, use pictures, symbols, and codes for written communication.

4. Make all communications positive, emphasizing growth, progress, and accomplishments.

5. With the families, design family–student celebrations of the student's efforts and successes (a movie, special meal, trip to the park or library, or going out for ice cream or pizza).

6. On a regular basis, send home a note in word or picture form that describes the student's progress. Ask families to indicate how they celebrated the success and to return the note.

7. Follow up with a telephone call to discuss progress, answer questions, solicit family suggestions, and express appreciation for the families' contributions.

8. Make sure families feel welcome if they visit the classroom.

*For more information on family school partnerships, see www.psychologytoday.com/blog/the-moment-youth/201108/family-school-partnerships-the-21st-century.*

*Source: From "Effects of Parent Involvement in Isolation or in Combination with Peer Tutoring on Student Self-Concept and Mathematics Achievement," by J. Fantuzzo, G. Davis, and M. Ginsburg, Journal of Educational Psychology, 87, pp. 272–281. Copyright © 1995 by the American Psychological Association. Adapted with permission of the APA.*

ATTACHMENT AND PARENTING STYLES.   The emotional bond that forms between people is called **attachment**. The first attachment is between the child and parents or other caregivers. The quality of this bond appears to have implications for forming relationships throughout life (Thompson & Raikes, 2003). Children who form what are called *secure attachments* with caregivers receive comfort when needed and are more confident to explore their world, perhaps because they know they can count on the caregiver. Children who form insecure or disorganized attachments can be fearful, sad, anxious, clinging, rejecting, or angry in interactions with the caregivers. Some research indicates that authoritarian parenting styles are related to forming insecure attachments, but as we saw earlier, many factors influence the effects of parenting styles (Roeser, Peck, & Nasir, 2006).

The quality of attachment children experience has implications for teachers. For example, in preschools, children who have formed secure attachments with parents are less dependent on teachers and interact with other children appropriately. Secure attachment is positively related to achievement test scores, teacher assessments of social competence throughout the school years, and even to lower dropout rates (Roeser, Peck, & Nasir, 2006). We will see later in this chapter, and in Chapter 13, how researchers are currently examining students' attachment to teachers and schools as a positive force in their lives.

DIVORCE.   According to 2004 census data, approximately 38% of marriages in Canada in any given year will end in divorce before the couple's thirtieth anniversary (Institute of Marriage and Family Canada, 2010). The risk of divorce decreases the longer couples remain married, and the divorce rate for first marriages is lower than for second and subsequent marriages (first-time marriages have a 67% chance of lasting a lifetime). As many of us know from experiences in our own families, separation and divorce are stressful events for all participants, even under the best circumstances. The actual separation of the parents may have been preceded by years of conflict in the home or may come as a shock to all, including friends and children. During the divorce itself, conflict may increase as property and custody rights are being decided.

After the divorce, more changes may disrupt the children's lives. Today, as in the past, the mother is most often the custodial parent, even though the number of households headed by fathers has been increasing, to about 20% by 2006 (Statistics Canada, 2010b). The parent who has custody may have to move to a less-expensive home, find new sources of income, go to work for the first time, or work longer hours. For the child, this can mean leaving behind important friendships in the old neighbourhood or school, just when support is needed the most. Even in cases where few conflicts arise, when ample resources are available, and when the continuing support of friends and extended family is present, divorce is never easy for anyone, though it can be a better alternative for children than growing up in a home filled with conflict and discord: "Destructive conflict in any type of family undermines the well-being of parents and children" (Hetherington, 2006, p. 232).

The first two years after a divorce seem to be the most difficult period for both boys and girls. Recent research also indicates that divorce is harder on boys than girls, maybe because mothers still tend to get custody of children, which leaves boys without a male role model in the house (Fuller-Thomson & Dalton, 2011). Children may have problems in school or just skip school, lose or gain an unusual amount of weight, have trouble sleeping, or experience other difficulties. However, adjustment to divorce is an individual matter; some children respond with increased responsibility, maturity, and coping skills (Amato, 2006; Amato, Loomis, & Booth, 1995). Over time, about 75%–80% of children in divorced families adapt and become reasonably well adjusted (Hetherington & Kelly, 2002). See the *Guidelines* for ideas about how to help students who are dealing with divorce.

### Peers

Children also develop within peer groups. Rubin and his colleagues (2005) distinguish between two kinds of peer groups: cliques and crowds. *Cliques* are relatively small friendship-based groups (typically between three and a dozen members). Cliques are more evident in middle childhood. *Crowds* are less intimate, more loosely organized groups in which members may or may not interact with one another.

**Attachment** Forming an emotional bond with another person, initially a parent or family member.

## GUIDELINES

### Helping Children of Divorce

**Take note of any sudden changes in behaviour that might indicate problems at home.**
*Examples*

1. Be alert to physical symptoms such as repeated headaches or stomach pains, rapid weight gain or loss, fatigue, or excess energy.
2. Be aware of signs of emotional distress, including moodiness, temper tantrums, and difficulty in paying attention or concentrating.
3. Let parents know about the students' signs of stress.

**Talk individually to students about their attitude or behaviour changes. This gives you a chance to find out about unusual stress such as divorce.**
*Examples*

1. Be a good listener. Students may have no other adult willing to hear their concerns.
2. Let students know you are available to talk, and then let students who approach you set the agenda.

**Watch your language to make sure you avoid stereotypes about "happy" (two-parent) homes.**
*Examples*

1. Simply say "your families" instead of "your mothers and fathers" when addressing the class.
2. Avoid statements such as "We need volunteers for room mother" or "Your father can help you."

**Help students maintain self-esteem.**
*Examples*

1. Recognize a job well done.
2. Make sure the student understands the assignment and can handle the workload. This is not the time to pile on new and very difficult work.

3. The student may be angry at his or her parents but may direct the anger at teachers. Don't take the student's anger personally.

**Find out what resources are available at your school.**
*Examples*

1. Talk to the school psychologist, guidance counsellor, social worker, or principal about students who seem to need outside help.
2. Consider establishing a discussion group, led by a trained adult, for students going through a divorce.

**Be sensitive to both parents' rights to information.**
*Examples*

1. When parents have joint custody, both are entitled to receive information and attend parent–teacher conferences.
2. The noncustodial parent may still be concerned about the child's school progress. Check with your principal about provincial laws regarding the noncustodial parent's rights.

**Be aware of long-term problems for students moving between two households.**
*Examples*

1. Books, assignments, and gym clothes may be left at one parent's house when the student is currently on visitation with the other parent.
2. Parents may not show up for their turn to pick up their child at school or may miss a parent–teacher conference because the note about the conference never made it home.

---

*For ideas about how to help children understand divorce, see www.helpguide.org/articles/family-divorce/children-and-divorce.htm.*

**STOP & THINK** Think back to high school—did you have friends in any of these groups: normals, populars, brains, jocks, partyers, druggies, others? What were the main "crowds" at your school? How did your friends influence you? •

**CROWDS.** Adolescents are more likely to affiliate with larger crowds that provide them with an identity (e.g., Terrice is a jock, Lou's a brain, Olivia is a druggie). Laurence Steinberg is an authority on children's and youth's relationships with parents, peers, friends. He and his colleagues have identified peer groups or crowds such as "jocks," "brains," "populars," and "druggies" that share common behaviours and attitudes (Durbin, Darling, Steinberg, & Brown, 1993; Steinberg, 1996, 1998). Based on a three-year study that surveyed 20 000 students in nine high schools in Wisconsin and California, Steinberg found that peers provide incentives for certain activities and ridicule others, which creates a school culture that affects the way the teachers behave. One in every five students Steinberg studied said

that their friends made fun of people who tried to do well in school. Steinberg concluded that about 40% of the students were just going through the motions of learning. About 90% had copied someone else's homework, and 66% had cheated on a test within the past year. Steinberg claims that this lack of investment is due in part to peer pressure, because for many adolescents, "peers—not parents—are the chief determinants of how intensely they are invested in school and how much effort they devote to their education" (1998, p. 331). Let's look more closely at these powerful peer influences.

**PEER CULTURES.** Different groups of students who have a set of "rules"—how to dress, talk, style their hair, and interact with others—are called **peer cultures**. The group determines which activities, music, or other students are in or out of favour. For example, when Jessica, a popular high school student, was asked to explain the rules that her group lives by, she had no trouble:

> OK. No. 1: clothes. You cannot wear jeans any day but Friday, and you cannot wear a ponytail or sneakers more than once a week. Monday is fancy day—like black pants or maybe you bust out with a skirt. You have to remind people how cute you are in case they forgot over the weekend. No. 2: parties. Of course we sit down and discuss which ones we're going to because there is no point in getting all dressed up for a party that's going to be lame. (Talbot, 2002, p. 28)

These peer cultures encourage conformity to the group rules. When another girl in Jessica's group wore jeans on Monday, Jessica confronted her: "Why are you wearing jeans today? Did you forget it was Monday?" (Talbot, 2002, p. 28). Jessica explained that the group had to suspend this "rebel" several times, not allowing her to sit with them at lunch.

To understand the power of peers, we have to look at situations where the values and interests of parents clash with those of peers, and then see whose influence dominates. In these comparisons, peers usually win in matters of of style and socializing. Parents and teachers still are influential in matters of morality, career choice, and religion (Harris, 1998). Also, not all aspects of peer cultures are bad or cruel. The norms in some groups are positive and support achievement in school.

**CLIQUES AND FRIENDSHIPS.** Friendships are central to students' lives. When there has been a falling-out or an argument, when rumours are started and pacts are made to ostracize someone (as with Alison and Stephanie at the beginning of the chapter), the results can be devastating. Beyond the immediate trauma of being "in" or "out" of the clique, peer relationships influence students' motivation and achievement in school (A. Ryan, 2001). In one study, grade 6 students without friends showed lower levels of academic achievement and fewer positive social behaviours and were more emotionally distressed, even two years later, than students with at least one friend (Wentzel, Barry, & Caldwell, 2004). The characteristics of friends and the quality of the friendships matter too. Having stable, supportive relationships with friends who are socially competent and mature enhances social development, especially during difficult times such as parents' divorce or transition to new schools (Hartup & Stevens, 1999). Children who are rejected by their peers are less likely to participate in classroom learning activities, so their achievement suffers; they are more likely to drop out of school as adolescents and may even evidence more problems as adults. For example, rejected aggressive students are more likely to commit crimes as they grow older (Buhs, Ladd, & Herald, 2006; Coie & Dodge, 1998; Fredricks, Blumenfeld, & Paris, 2004).

**POPULARITY.** What does it mean to be popular? We could answer this question by observing students or by using ratings from parents or teachers. But the most common

**DRESS CODES AND MORE** Peer cultures may set "rules" for how to dress and behave and in so doing determine which activities, music, or other students are in or out of favour.

Bubbles Photolibrary/Alamy

👁 **Watch**
Cliques and Friendships

Peer cultures Groups of children or adolescents with their own rules and norms, particularly about such things as dress, appearance, music, language, social values, and behaviour.

TABLE 3.1 • **What Does It Take to Be Popular?**

| POPULAR CHILDREN |
| --- |
| *Popular prosocial children:* These children are both academically and socially competent. They do well in school and communicate well with peers. When they disagree with other children, they respond appropriately and have effective strategies for working things out.<br>*Popular antisocial children:* This subgroup of children often includes boys who are aggressive. They may be athletic, and other children tend to think they are "cool" in the ways they bully other children and defy adult authority. |
| **REJECTED CHILDREN** |
| *Rejected aggressive children:* High rates of conflict and hyperactivity/impulsivity characterize the behaviours of this subgroup. These children have poor perspective-taking skills and self-control. They often misunderstand the intentions of others, assign blame, and act aggressively on their angry or hurt feelings.<br>*Rejected withdrawn children:* These children are timid and withdrawn, often the targets of bullies. They are often socially awkward and withdraw from social interactions to avoid being scorned or attacked. |
| **CONTROVERSIAL CHILDREN** |
| As the descriptor implies, these children have both positive and negative social qualities and, as a result, their social status can change over time. They can be hostile and disruptive in some situations and then engage in positive prosocial behaviours in others. These children have friends and are generally happy with their peer relationships. |
| **NEGLECTED CHILDREN** |
| Perhaps surprisingly, most of these children are well adjusted and they are not less socially competent than other children. Peers tend to view them as shy, but they don't report being lonely or unhappy about their social lives. Apparently they don't experience the extreme social anxiety and wariness that withdrawn children do. |

*Source: Woolfolk, A., & Perry, N. E. (2012). Child and adolescent development. Columbus, OH: Pearson, p. 416.*

way to assess popularity is to ask the students themselves two questions: Is this child liked? and What is this child like? Based on answers to these questions, we can identify four categories of children (see Table 3.1).

As you can see in Table 3.1, *popular* (highly rated) children may behave in positive or negative ways. *Rejected* children probably merit their low ratings because they are aggressive, immature, socially unskilled, or withdrawn. *Controversial* children get mixed reviews; they display both positive and negative social behaviours. Finally, *neglected* children are almost invisible—their peers simply do not mention them—but there is no consistent evidence that neglected children are anxious or withdrawn (Rubin, Coplan, Chen, Buskirk, & Wojslawowicz, 2005).

WHO IS LIKELY TO HAVE PROBLEMS WITH PEERS?    Children and adolescents are not always tolerant of differences. New students who are physically, intellectually, ethnically, racially, economically, or linguistically different may be rejected in classes with established peer groups. Students who are aggressive, withdrawn, and inattentive–hyperactive are also more likely to be rejected. But classroom context matters, too, especially for aggressive or withdrawn students. In classrooms where the general level of aggression is high, being aggressive is less likely to lead to peer rejection. And in classrooms where solitary play and work are more common, being withdrawn is not as likely to lead to rejection. Thus, being rejected is often linked to being just too different from the norm. At the same time we are revising this text, there is a news report about an 11-year-old boy experiencing racism and bullying because he is the only African American boy in a school in Westport, Newfoundland (a community with population 200; CBC, 2014). Apparently the threats from his classmates are so serious, the school has arranged for this child to use a separate washroom, and he is under constant supervision at school.

Prosocial behaviours such as sharing, cooperating, and friendly interactions are associated with peer acceptance, no matter what the classroom context. But many aggressive and withdrawn students lack these social skills; inattentive-hyperactive students often misread social cues or have trouble controlling impulses, so their social skills suffer, too (Coplan, Prakash, O'Neil, & Armer, 2004; Stormshak, Bierman, Bruschi, Dodge, & Coie, 1999). A teacher should be aware of how each student gets along with the group. Are there outcasts? Do some students play the bully role? Careful adult intervention can often correct such problems, especially when students are at the late elementary and middle school levels (Pearl, Leung, Acker, Farmer, & Rodkin, 2007). We discuss the seriousness of bullying and aggressive behaviour later in this chapter when we talk about moral development.

## Reaching Every Student: Teacher Support

Because they are the main adults in students' lives for many hours each week, teachers have the opportunity to play a significant role in students' personal and social development. For students facing emotional or interpersonal problems, teachers are sometimes the best source of help. When students have chaotic and unpredictable home lives, they need a caring, firm structure in school. They need teachers who set clear limits, are consistent, enforce rules firmly but not punitively, respect students, and show genuine concern. Being liked by teachers can offset the negative effects of peer rejection in middle school. And students who have few friends, but are not rejected—simply ignored by other students—can remain well adjusted academically and socially when they are liked and supported by teachers.

As a teacher, you can be available to your students if they want to talk about their personal problems without requiring them to do so. One of Anita's student teachers gave a boy in her class a journal entitled "Very Hard Thoughts" so that he could write about his parents' divorce. Sometimes he talked to her about the journal entries, but at other times, he just recorded his feelings. The student teacher was very careful to respect the boy's privacy about his writings.

ACADEMIC AND PERSONAL CARING. When researchers ask students to describe a "good teacher," three qualities are at the centre of their descriptions. First, good teachers have positive interpersonal relationships—they care about their students. Second, good teachers can keep the classroom organized and maintain authority without being rigid or "mean." Finally, good teachers are good motivators—they can make learning fun by being creative and innovative so students learn something. It appears that authoritative teaching strategies, like authoritative approaches to parenting, lead to positive relationships with students and enhance motivation for learning (Noguera, 2005; Woolfolk Hoy & Weinstein, 2006). We will look at motivation in Chapter 11 and management in Chapter 12, so for now let's focus on caring and teaching.

For nearly two decades, research has documented the value and importance of positive relationships with teachers for students at every grade level (Davis, 2003). Teachers' behaviours that communicate liking and respect, such as eye contact, relaxed body posture, and smiling, are associated with students' liking of teachers, interest in courses, and motivation to achieve (Woolfolk & Perry, 2015). For example, one of Anita's doctoral graduates studied middle-school mathematics classes and found that students' perceptions of their teachers' affective support and caring were related to the effort they invested in learning math (Sakiz, Pape, & Woolfolk Hoy, 2008). Tamera Murdock and Angela Miller (2003) found that grade 8 students' perceptions that their teachers cared about them were significantly related to the students' academic motivation, even after taking into account the motivational influences of parents and peers.

Students define caring in two ways. One is *academic caring*—setting high but reasonable expectations and helping students to reach those goals. The second is *personal caring*—being patient, respectful, humorous, willing to listen, and interested in students' issues and personal problems. For higher-achieving students, academic caring is especially important, but for students who are at risk of experiencing academic, social, or behavioural difficulties and who often are alienated from school, personal caring is critical (Cothran & Ennis, 2000; Woolfolk Hoy & Weinstein, 2006). In fact, in one study of a Texas high school, the Mexican and Mexican American students saw teacher caring as a prerequisite for their own caring about school; in other words, they needed to be *cared for* before they could *care about* school (Valenzuela, 1999). Unfortunately, in the same school, the mostly non-Latino teachers expected the students to care about school before they would invest their caring in the students. And for many teachers, caring about school meant behaving in more "middle-class" ways.

These contrasting student and teacher views can lead to a downward spiral of mistrust. Students withhold their cooperation until teachers "earn it" with their authentic caring. Teachers withhold caring until students "earn it" with respect for authority and cooperation. Marginalized students expect unfair treatment and behave defensively when they sense any unfairness. Teachers get tough and punish. Students feel correct in mistrusting, and become more guarded and defiant. Teachers feel correct in mistrusting and become more controlling and punitive, and so it goes (Woolfolk Hoy & Weinstein, 2006).

Of course, students need both academic and personal caring. Katz (1999) interviewed eight immigrant students in a middle school and concluded the following:

> High expectations without caring can result in setting goals that are impossible for the student to reach without adult support and assistance. On the other hand, caring without high expectations can turn dangerously into paternalism in which teachers feel sorry for "underprivileged" youth but never challenge them academically. High expectations and caring in tandem, however, can make a powerful difference in students' lives. (p. 814)

In short, caring means not giving up on students as well as demonstrating and teaching kindness in the classroom (Davis, 2003).

## Teachers and Child Abuse

Certainly, one critical way to care about students is to protect their welfare and intervene in cases of abuse. Accurate information about the number of abused children in Canada is difficult to find because many cases go unreported. That said, an estimated 235 842 child maltreatment investigations were conducted in Canada in 2008 (Public Health Agency of Canada, 2008). In more than one-third of these investigations (36%, or 85 440 cases), the maltreatment allegations were substantiated. Aboriginal children are a focal group in these investigations due to concerns about their overrepresentation in foster care. The incidence of substantiated maltreatment investigations for this group was four times higher than it was for non-Aboriginal children and youth. Parents are the most likely perpetrators in familial physical and sexual abuse cases, but parents are not the only people who abuse children. Siblings, other relatives, and even teachers have been responsible for the physical and sexual abuse of children. And today, children's activities on the internet need to be carefully monitored, as the content they view and the relationships they form in that context can lead to abuse.

There are five types of child maltreatment. These are defined with examples in Table 3.2 (Government of Canada, 2006). As a teacher, you must alert your principal, a school counsellor, or a school social worker if you suspect a child is being abused or neglected. Child protection is a provincial responsibility, so be sure you understand the laws in your province concerning this important role. In British Columbia, the *Child, Family, and Community Service Act* clearly states that *anyone* who has reason to believe that a child (defined as any individual under the age of 19) has been or is likely to be physically or sexually abused, exploited, or neglected has a legal responsibility to report the matter to a child-protection social worker (British Columbia Ministry for Children and Families, 2013). Sometimes, people don't report their suspicions because they think they need proof. This is not true. All that is required is a reasonable belief

TABLE 3.2 • **Types of Child Maltreatment and Examples of Abusive Behaviours**

| CATEGORY | DEFINITION | EXAMPLES OF ABUSIVE BEHAVIOURS |
|---|---|---|
| 1. Physical abuse (assault) | The application of unreasonable force by an adult or youth to any part of a child's body | Harsh physical discipline, forceful shaking, pushing, grabbing, throwing, hitting with a hand, punching, kicking, biting, hitting with an object, choking, strangling, stabbing, burning, shooting, poisoning, and the excessive use of restraints |
| 2. Sexual abuse | Involvement of a child, by an adult or youth, in an act of sexual gratification, or exposure of a child to sexual contact, activity, or behaviour | Penetration, attempted penetration, oral sex, fondling, sex talk, voyeurism, and sexual exploitation |
| 3. Neglect | Failure by a parent or caregiver to provide the physical or psychological necessities of life to a child | Failure to supervise, leading to physical harm or to sexual harm; permitting criminal behaviour; physical neglect; medical neglect; failure to provide psychological treatment; abandonment; and educational neglect |
| 4. Emotional harm | Adult behaviour that harms a child psychologically, emotionally, or spiritually | Hostile or unreasonable and abusive treatment, frequent or extreme verbal abuse (that may include threatening and demeaning or insulting behaviours), causing nonorganic failure to thrive*, emotional neglect, and direct exposure to violence between adults other than primary caregivers |
| 5. Exposure to family violence | Circumstances that allow a child to be aware of violence occurring between a caregiver and his/her partner or between other family members | Allowing a child to see, hear, or otherwise be exposed to signs of the violence (e.g., to see bruises or physical injuries on the caregiver or to overhear violent episodes) |

* *"Nonorganic failure to thrive" is a diagnostic term applied in cases of children less than three years of age who have suffered a slowing or cessation of growth for which no physical or physiological causes can be identified.*

*Source: Government of Canada. (2006).* Child maltreatment in Canada: Overview paper. *Table 1. Prepared by Susan Jack et al. Ottawa: Public Health Agency of Canada.*

that a child is in emotional or physical danger. What should you look for as signs of abuse? Table 3.3 lists some indicators.

## Society and Media

All of the students you will teach grew up in a world of media, mobility, and machines. An astounding percentage, over 70% in 2010, had a television in their own bedroom. Many had computers and cell phones, even from early ages (Rideout, Foehr, & Roberts, 2010; Turkle, 2011). Each year their use of technology increases (Nielsen, 2010). In 2010, 75% of children aged 12–17 had cell phones. Figure 3.3 shows the different technologies that 12- and 17-year-olds use daily to keep in touch with friends.

A recent Nielsen Report documented that teens are sending or receiving an average of 3339 text messages per month—over 100 per day (Nielsen, 2010). When do they have time for anything else? And these texts demand immediate attention. One high school sophomore told Sherry Turkle (2011) that within his circle of friends, texts had to be answered as soon as possible, within 10 minutes, maximum. As he noted, "Texting is pressure" (p. 266). This pressure means that peers and even parents are always present—their messages demanding a response, even if the student is in class and must text in secret under the desk or with hands inside a backpack. Students and adults are spending more time with technology and less with each other. But these instant, superficial communications via cell phones, computers, iPads, and other electronic communication devices are not necessarily ties that bind students in deep relationships; instead, they are ties that preoccupy and distract (Turkle, 2011). What will it be like to teach students who send and receive over 100 text messages a day, and who can't focus on your class when a Facebook posting appears? These are questions you will have to answer when you step into a classroom.

TABLE 3.3 • **Indicators of Child Abuse**

The following are some of the signs of abuse. Not every child who exhibits these signs is abused, but these indicators should be investigated.

|  | PHYSICAL INDICATORS | BEHAVIOURAL INDICATORS |
|---|---|---|
| **Physical Abuse** | • Unexplained bruises and welts (in various stages of healing), marks in the shape of belt buckles or electrical cords, human bite marks, puncture marks, bald spots, regularly appearing after absences or weekends<br>• Unexplained burns, especially cigarette burns, burns in the shape of irons, rope burns, or immersion-burns (sock-like or glove-like)<br>• Unexplained fractures, lacerations, or abrasions in various stages of healing<br>• Injuries attributed to the child being "clumsy" or "accident-prone" | • Moves awkwardly, complains of soreness<br>• Self-destructive<br>• Withdrawn and aggressive—behavioural extremes<br>• Uncomfortable with physical contact<br>• Arrives at school early or stays late, as if afraid<br>• Chronic runaway (adolescents)<br>• Wears high-neck, long-sleeved clothing, not matching weather, to cover body<br>• Frequent absences |
| **Physical Neglect** | • Abandonment<br>• Unattended physical problems or medical needs<br>• Constant fatigue, lack of energy<br>• Little or no supervision<br>• Often hungry, dressed inappropriately for weather, poor hygiene<br>• Lice, distended stomach, emaciation | • Falls asleep in class<br>• Steals food, begs from classmates<br>• Reports that no caretaker is at home<br>• Frequently absent or tardy, or stays as long as possible at school<br>• Self-destructive<br>• Trouble with the law |
| **Sexual Abuse** | • Difficulty walking or sitting<br>• Pain or itching in genital area<br>• Torn, stained, or bloodied underclothing<br>• Bruises or bleeding in external genitalia<br>• Venereal disease, especially in preteens<br>• Frequent urinary or yeast infections<br>• Pregnancy | • Doesn't want to change for gym, PE<br>• Withdrawn, chronic depression<br>• Role reversal, overly concerned for siblings<br>• Promiscuity, excessive seductiveness<br>• Peer problems, lack of involvement<br>• Massive weight change<br>• Suicide attempts (especially adolescents)<br>• Inappropriate sex play or premature understanding of sex, frequent masturbation, sexual play with dolls or stuffed animals<br>• Sudden school difficulties |

*Sources: Adapted from several state and national child abuse prevention websites: U.S. Department of Health and Human Services:*
*http://www.childwelfare.gov/pubs/usermanuals/sexabuse/sexabusec.cfm;*
*Pennsylvania: http://www.pa-fsa.org/about_child_abuse__neglect/indicators_of_child_abuse.aspx;*
*New Jersey: http://www.state.nj.us/dcf/abuse/indicators.*

**FIGURE 3.3**

TECHNOLOGY AND KEEPING IN TOUCH WITH FRIENDS

Here are the percentages of 12-, 14-, and 17-year-olds who contact their friends *daily* using different media. When do they study?

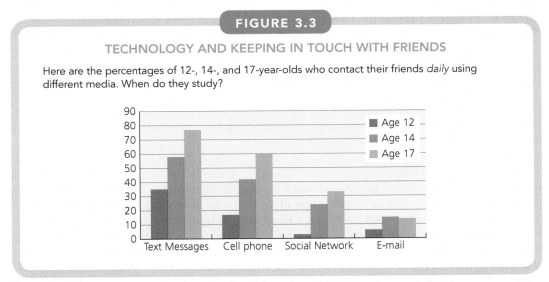

*Source: Based on data from Lenhart, A. (2010). Teens, cell phones and texting: Text messages become the centerpiece communication. Washington, D.C.: Pew Research Center.*

# IDENTITY AND SELF-CONCEPT

What is identity? Is identity different from self-concept or self-esteem? How do we come to understand other people and ourselves? In this section we look at the individual's sense of self and how that understanding develops. You will see patterns similar to those noted in Chapter 2 for cognitive development. Children's understandings of themselves are concrete at first. Early views of self and friends are based on immediate behaviours and appearances. Children assume that others share their feelings and perceptions. Their thinking about themselves and others is simple, segmented, and rule-bound, not flexible or integrated into organized systems. In time, children are able to think abstractly about internal processes—beliefs, intentions, values, and motivations. With these developments in abstract thinking, knowledge of self, others, and situations can incorporate more abstract qualities (Harter, 2003; Woolfolk & Perry, 2015).

In this section you will encounter the term *identity* along with several *self*-terms: self-concept, self-esteem, and self-worth. The distinctions among these terms are not always sharp, and there is disagreement even among psychologists about what each term means (Roeser, Peck, & Nasir, 2006). In general, identity is a broader concept than the other self-terms. Identity includes people's general sense of themselves with all their beliefs and attitudes about themselves. Identity integrates all the different aspects and roles of the self (Wigfield, Byrnes, & Eccles, 2006). But it is common for researchers to use self-concept and identity interchangeably. To make matters easier, we will, too. We begin our consideration of self-concept/identity within the framework of Erik Erikson.

**PSYCHOSOCIAL THEORY** Erik Erikson proposed a theory of psychosocial development that describes tasks to be accomplished at different stages of life.

Ted Streshinsky/Corbis

## Erikson: Stages of Individual Development

Like Piaget, Erik Erikson did not start his career as a psychologist. He skipped university, travelled around Europe, and ended up teaching in Vienna, where he studied psychoanalysis with Anna Freud, the daughter of Sigmund Freud. Soon after completing his training, he had to flee from the Nazis. He was denied citizenship in Denmark, so he moved to his second choice—New York City. Even though he had never attended university, on the basis of his groundbreaking work he became a distinguished university professor at Harvard. Later in his career he worked with the original Dr. Spock—Benjamin Spock, the widely read paediatrician whose books guided many baby boomers' parents (Green & Piel, 2010; Miller, 2011).

Erikson offered a basic framework for understanding the needs of young people in relation to the society in which they grow, learn, and ultimately make their contributions. Erikson's **psychosocial** theory emphasized the emergence of the self, the search for identity, the individual's relationships with others, and the role of culture throughout life.

Like Piaget, Erikson regarded development as a passage through an interdependent series of stages, each with its particular goals, concerns, accomplishments, and dangers, as shown in Table 3.4. At each stage, Erikson suggests, the individual faces a **developmental crisis**—a conflict between a positive alternative and a potentially unhealthy alternative. The way in which the individual resolves each crisis has a lasting effect on that person's self-image and view of society. We will look briefly at all eight stages in Erikson's theory—or, as he called them, the "eight ages of man."

**Psychosocial** Describing the relation of the individual's emotional needs to the social environment.

**Developmental crisis** A specific conflict whose resolution prepares the way for the next stage.

**THE PRESCHOOL YEARS: TRUST, AUTONOMY, AND INITIATIVE.**    Erikson identifies *trust versus mistrust* as the basic conflict of infancy. According to Erikson, the infant will develop a sense of trust if its needs for food and care are met with comforting regularity and responsiveness from caregivers. In this first year, infants are in Piaget's sensorimotor stage and are just beginning to learn that they are separate from the world around them. This realization is part of what makes trust so important: Infants must trust the aspects of their world that are beyond their control (Miller, 2011; Posada et al., 2002). Having a secure attachment (described earlier in this chapter) helps young children

TABLE 3.4 • **Erikson's Eight Stages of Psychosocial Development**

| STAGE | APPROXIMATE AGE | IMPORTANT EVENT | DESCRIPTION |
|---|---|---|---|
| 1. Basic trust versus basic mistrust | Birth to 12–18 months | Feeding | The infant must first form a loving, trusting relationship with the caregiver or develop a sense of mistrust. |
| 2. Autonomy versus shame and doubt | 18 months to 3 years | Toilet training | The child's energies are directed toward the development of physical skills, including walking, grasping, controlling the sphincter. The child learns control but may develop shame and doubt if not handled well. |
| 3. Initiative versus guilt | 3 to 6 years | Independence | The child continues to become more assertive and to take more initiative but may be too forceful, which can lead to feelings of guilt. |
| 4. Industry versus inferiority | 6 to 12 years | School | The child must deal with demands to learn new skills or risk a sense of inferiority, failure, or incompetence. |
| 5. Identity versus role confusion | Adolescence | Peer relationships | The teenager must achieve identity in occupation, gender roles, politics, and religion. |
| 6. Intimacy versus isolation | Young adulthood | Love relationships | The young adult must develop intimate relationships or suffer feelings of isolation. |
| 7. Generativity versus stagnation | Middle adulthood | Parenting/ mentoring | Each adult must find some way to satisfy and support the next generation. |
| 8. Ego integrity versus despair | Late adulthood | Reflection on and acceptance of one's life | The culmination is a sense of acceptance of oneself as one is and a sense of fulfillment. |

*Source: Lefton, L. A. (1994). Psychology, 5th Edition. Reprinted by permission of Pearson Education, Inc. Upper Saddle River, NJ.*

develop trust and also learn when mistrust is appropriate—either extreme of complete trust or mistrust is dysfunctional.

Erikson's second stage, **autonomy** *versus shame and doubt*, marks the beginning of self-control and self-confidence as young children begin to assume responsibilities for self-care such as feeding, going to the toilet, and dressing. During this period parents must tread a fine line; they must be protective—but not overprotective. If parents do not reinforce their children's efforts to master basic motor and cognitive skills, children may begin to feel shame; they may learn to doubt their abilities to manage the world. Erikson believes that children who experience too much doubt at this stage will lack confidence in their own abilities throughout life. Of course, some doubt is appropriate if the task is too difficult or dangerous—again the need for balance.

For Erikson, the next stage of **initiative** *versus guilt* ". . . adds to autonomy the quality of undertaking, planning, and attacking a task for the sake of being active and on the move" (Erikson, 1963, p. 255). The challenge of this period is to maintain a zest for activity

**Autonomy** Self-control and self-confidence.

**Initiative** Willingness to begin new activities and explore new directions.

and at the same time understand that not every impulse can be acted on. Again, adults must tread a fine line, this time in providing supervision without interference. If children are not allowed to do things on their own, a sense of guilt may develop; they may come to believe that what they want to do is always "wrong." The *Guidelines* suggests ways of encouraging initiative in your students.

ELEMENTARY AND MIDDLE SCHOOL YEARS: INDUSTRY VERSUS INFERIORITY.   Let's set the stage for the next phase. Between the ages of 5 and 7, when most children start school, cognitive development proceeds rapidly. Children can process more information faster and their memory spans are increasing. They are moving from preoperational to concrete operational thinking. As these internal changes progress, the children spend hours every weekday in the new physical and social world of school. They must now re-establish Erikson's stages of psychosocial development in the unfamiliar school setting. They must learn to trust new adults, to act autonomously in this more complex situation, and to initiate actions in ways that fit the new rules of school.

## GUIDELINES

## Encouraging Initiative and Industry

**Encourage children to make and to act on choices.**
*Examples*

1. Have a free-choice time when children can select an activity or game.
2. Try to avoid interrupting children who are very involved in what they are doing.
3. When children suggest an activity, try to follow their suggestions or incorporate their ideas into ongoing activities.
4. Offer positive choices: Instead of saying, "You can't have the cookies now," ask, "Would you like the cookies after lunch or after naptime?"

**Make sure that each child has a chance to experience success.**
*Examples*

1. When introducing a new game or skill, teach it in small steps.
2. Avoid competitive games that highlight differences in children's abilities.

**Encourage make-believe with a wide variety of roles.**
*Examples*

1. Have costumes and props that go along with stories the children enjoy. Encourage the children to act out the stories or make up new adventures for favourite characters.
2. Monitor the children's play to be sure no one monopolizes playing "teacher," "Mommy," "Daddy," or other heroes.

**Be tolerant of accidents and mistakes, especially when children are attempting to do something on their own.**
*Examples*

1. Use cups and pitchers that make it easy to pour and hard to spill.
2. Recognize the attempt, even if the result is unsatisfactory.
3. If mistakes are made, show children how to clean up, repair, or redo.

4. Most important, help children to view errors as opportunities to learn and let them know that everyone makes mistakes (even adults, even you).
5. If a student consistently behaves in ways that are highly unusual or unacceptable, seek guidance from the school counsellor or psychologist. The best time to help children deal with psychosocial problems is at an early age.

**Make sure that students have opportunities to set and work toward realistic goals.**
*Examples*

1. Begin with short assignments, then move on to longer ones. Monitor student progress by setting up progress checkpoints.
2. Teach students to set reasonable goals. Write down goals, and have students keep a journal of progress toward these goals.

**Give students a chance to show their independence and responsibility.**
*Examples*

1. Tolerate honest mistakes.
2. Delegate to students tasks such as watering class plants, collecting and distributing materials, monitoring the computer lab, grading homework, keeping records of forms returned, and so on.

**Provide support to students who seem discouraged.**
*Examples*

1. Use individual charts and contracts that show student progress.
2. Keep samples of earlier work so students can see their improvements.
3. Have awards for most improved, most helpful, most hardworking.

The new psychosocial challenge for the school years is what Erikson calls **industry** *versus inferiority*. In this stage, students are beginning to see the relationship between perseverance and the pleasure of a job completed. In modern societies, children's ability to move between the worlds of home, neighbourhood, and school and to cope with academics, group activities, and friends will lead to a growing sense of competence. Difficulty with these challenges can result in feelings of inferiority. Children must master new skills and work toward new goals while being compared with others and risking failure.

The skills and concepts children learn in preschool and the early grades are critical. They set students on pathways toward achievement or failure in the rest of their school years (Paris, Morrison, & Miller, 2006). In fact, Entwisle and Alexander (1998) claim, "How well students do in the primary grades matters more for their future success than does their school performance at any other time" (p. 354). Because schools tend to reflect middle-class values and norms, making the transition to school and meeting the challenge of *industry versus inferiority* may be especially difficult for children who differ economically or culturally. See the *Guidelines* for ideas about how to encourage industry in the classroom.

In the transition from elementary to middle school, students confront an increased focus on grades and performance as well as more competition on all fronts—academic, social, and athletic. Just when they are eager to make decisions and assume more independence, these developing minds encounter more rules, required courses, and assignments. Students change from having a close connection with one teacher all year to having more impersonal relations with many teachers in many different subjects across the year. They also go from being regarded as the most mature and highest-status students in a small, familiar elementary school to being regarded as the "babies" in what may seem like a large, impersonal middle or high school (Murdock, Hale, & Weber, 2001; Rudolph, Lambert, Clark, & Kurlakowsky, 2001; Wigfield, Eccles, MacIver, Rueman, & Midgley, 1991). In the midst of this demanding context, students face the next challenge—the search for identity.

**DEVELOPING INITIATIVE** Children need opportunities to learn things for themselves in order to develop a sense of initiative.

Ryan McVay/Photodisc/Thinkstock/Getty Images

**ADOLESCENCE: THE SEARCH FOR IDENTITY.** As students move into adolescence, they develop capabilities for abstract thinking and understanding the perspectives of others. Even greater physical changes are taking place as students approach puberty. So, with developing minds and bodies, young adolescents must confront the central issue of constructing an identity that will provide a firm basis for adulthood. The individual has been developing a sense of self since infancy. But adolescence marks the first time that a conscious effort is made to answer the now-pressing question, "Who am I?" The conflict defining this stage is *identity versus role confusion*. **Identity** refers to the organization of the individual's drives, abilities, beliefs, and history into a consistent image of self. It involves deliberate choices and decisions, particularly about work, values, ideology, and commitments to people and ideas (Miller, 2011; Penuel & Wertsch, 1995). If adolescents fail to integrate all these aspects and choices, or if they feel unable to choose at all, they may experience role confusion.

**Industry** Eagerness to engage in productive work.

**Identity** The principle that a person or object remains the same over time.

**Exploration** In Marcia's theory of identity statuses, the process by which adolescents consider and try out alternative beliefs, values, and behaviours in an effort to determine which will give them the most satisfaction.

**STOP & THINK** Have you decided on your career? What alternatives did you consider? Who or what was influential in shaping your decision? •

James Marcia (1991, 1994, 1999) expanded on Erikson's theory of identity formation. Specifically, he focused on two essential processes in achieving a mature identity: exploration and commitment. **Exploration** refers to the process by which adolescents consider and

Marc Dolphin/Getty Images

**CONSTRUCTING AN IDENTITY** With developing minds and bodies, young adolescents must confront the central issue of developing an identity that will provide a firm basis for adulthood. With adolescence comes a pressing question: "Who am I?"

try out alternative beliefs, values, and behaviours in an effort to determine which will give them the most satisfaction. **Commitment** refers to individuals' choices concerning political and religious beliefs, for example, usually as a consequence of exploring the options. Then, Marcia identified four categories of identity status that arise from four patterns of exploration and commitment.

The first, **identity achievement** , means that after *exploring* the realistic options, the individual has made choices and is *committed* to pursuing them. It appears that few students achieve this status by the end of high school; students who attend university may take even longer to decide. It is not uncommon for the explorations to continue into the early twenties. About 80% of students change their majors at least once. And some adults may achieve a firm identity at one period in their lives, only to reject that identity and achieve a new one later. So identity, once achieved, may not be unchanging for everyone (Adams, Berzonsky, & Keating, 2006; Kroger, 2000; Nurmi, 2004).

Adolescents in the midst of struggling with choices are experiencing what Erikson called a **moratorium**. Erikson used the term *moratorium* to describe exploration with a delay in commitment to personal and occupational choices. This delay is very common, and probably healthy, for modern adolescents. Erikson believed that adolescents in complex societies have an identity crisis during moratorium. Today, the period is no longer referred to as a *crisis* because, for most people, the experience is a gradual exploration rather than a traumatic upheaval (Grotevant, 1998; Wigfield, Byrnes, & Eccles, 2006). Both identity-achieved and moratorium statuses are considered healthy.

**Identity foreclosure** is commitment without exploration. Foreclosed adolescents have not experimented with different identities or explored a range of options, but simply have committed themselves to the goals, values, and lifestyles of others—usually their parents, but sometimes cults or extremist groups. Foreclosed adolescents tend to be rigid, intolerant, dogmatic, and defensive (Frank, Pirsch, & Wright, 1990).

**Identity diffusion** occurs when individuals do not explore any options or commit to any actions. They reach no conclusions about who they are or what they want to do with their lives. Adolescents experiencing identity diffusion may be apathetic and withdrawn, with little hope for the future, or they may be openly rebellious. These adolescents often go along with the crowd, so they are more likely to abuse drugs (Archer & Waterman, 1990; Kroger, 2000).

Schools that give adolescents experiences with community service, real-world work, internships, and mentoring help to foster identity formation (Cooper, 1998). See the *Guidelines* for other ideas about how to support identity formation in your students.

IDENTITY AND TECHNOLOGY.   Some scholars of technology have speculated that establishing a separate identity is complicated for adolescents today because they are constantly connected to others. Parents often give a cell phone to their children somewhere between the ages of 9 and 13, or even earlier, with the specific requirement that the children always answer a call from the parent. Sherry Turkle (2011) calls this happy recipient of a new cell phone a "tethered child," now able to participate in activities such as spending time at a mall or on the beach that would not have been allowed without the safety tether of the phone. But the price paid is that these children never navigate social and physical landscapes completely alone—parents and friends always are a speed dial away. The chance to solve problems, experience autonomy, and handle situations on your own is the basis for achieving identity and mature judgment. The tethered child is never alone. Texting means the tether is even shorter. The high school students Turkle

**Commitment** In Marcia's theory of identity statuses, individuals' choices concerning political and religious beliefs, for example, usually as a consequence of exploring the options.

**Identity achievement** Strong sense of commitment to life choices after free consideration of alternatives.

**Moratorium** Identity crisis; suspension of choices because of struggle.

**Identity foreclosure** Acceptance of parental life choices without consideration of options.

**Identity diffusion** Uncentredness; confusion about who one is and what one wants.

## GUIDELINES

## Supporting Identity Formation

**Give students many models for career choices and other adult roles.**
*Examples*

1. Point out models from literature and history. Have a calendar with the birthdays of eminent women, minority leaders, or people who made a little-known contribution to the subject you are teaching. Briefly discuss the person's accomplishments on her or his birthday.

2. Invite guest speakers to describe how and why they chose their professions. Make sure all kinds of work and workers are represented.

**Help students find resources for working out personal problems.**
*Examples*

1. Encourage students to talk to school counsellors.

2. Discuss potential services available outside the school setting.

**Be tolerant of teenage fads as long as they don't offend others or interfere with learning.**
*Examples*

1. Discuss the fads of earlier eras (e.g., neon hair, powdered wigs, love beads).

2. Don't impose strict dress or hair codes.

**Give students realistic feedback about themselves.**
*Examples*

1. When students misbehave or perform poorly, make sure they understand the consequences of their behaviour—the effects on themselves and others.

2. Give students model answers or show them other students' completed projects so that they can compare their work with good examples.

3. Never use a student's work as a "bad" example. Create negative examples from multiple sources including mistakes you have made.

4. Because students are "trying on" roles, keep the roles separate from the person. You can criticize behaviour without criticizing the student.

---

interviewed talked about the "big mistake" of teaching their parents to text or IM. A physician at a university health centre describes undergraduate patients who respond to her question, "What are your health concerns today?" with the answer, "My mom is on the phone—she'll tell you" and then the college student hands a cell phone to the doctor. Constant connectivity complicates achieving a separate identity and autonomy.

Connectivity also "offers new possibilities for experimenting with identity, particularly in adolescence, the sense of a free space, what Eric Erikson called the *moratorium* " (Turkle, 2011, p. 152). On Second Life or The Sims Online or other life simulations sites, adolescents can create whole new identities and keep multiple personalities "alive." Some people even talk about their "life mix," a mash up of what they live online and what they live in real life. For some adolescents, the boundaries may be unclear and easily crossed. Is the profile adolescents create on Facebook the "real" person, or, as one high school senior described, the identity that you "mould" to present to the world? But with worldwide access to the self-presentation, a critical question arises, "How will the self I present be judged by others?" For connected and tethered adolescents today, Elkind's imaginary audience (discussed in Chapter 2) is now a real online audience. The consequences are not all positive, as another grade 12 student agonized:

> You have to know that everything you put up will be perused very carefully. And that makes it necessary for you to obsess over what you do put up and how you portray yourself. . . And when you have to think about what you come across as, that's just another way that. . . . you are thinking of yourself in a bad way. (Turkle, 2011, p. 184)

**BEYOND THE SCHOOL YEARS.** The crises of Erikson's stages of adulthood all involve the quality of human relations. **Intimacy** *versus isolation* refers to a willingness to relate to another person on a deep level, to have a relationship based on more than mutual

Intimacy Forming close, enduring relationships with others.

need. Someone who has not achieved a sufficiently strong sense of identity tends to fear being overwhelmed or swallowed up by another person and may retreat into isolation. **Generativity** *versus stagnation* extends the ability to care for another person and involves concern and guidance for both the next generation and future generations. Productivity and creativity are essential features. Finally, achieving **integrity** *versus despair* means consolidating your sense of self and fully accepting its unique and now unalterable history.

Erikson's work helped start the lifespan development approach, and his theories have been especially useful in understanding adolescence and developing concepts of self. But feminists have criticized his notion that identity precedes intimacy, because their research indicates that for women, identity achievement is fused with achieving intimacy (Miller, 2002). And, as you will see next, recent research has focused on identity issues Erikson didn't fully explore—ethnic and racial identity.

## Ethnic and Racial Identity

As early as 1903, W. E. B. DuBois wrote about the "double consciousness" of African Americans. He argued they, like other ethnic or racial groups, are conscious of their ethnic identity as they negotiate being members of the larger culture as well. Ethnic minority students have to "sift through two sets of cultural values and identity options" to achieve a firm identity, so they may need more time to explore possibilities—a longer *moratorium* in Erikson's terms (Markstrom-Adams, 1992, p. 177). But the exploration is important; some psychologists consider ethnic identity a "master status," one that dominates all other identity concerns when judging the self (Charmaraman & Grossman, 2010; Herman, 2004).

ETHNIC IDENTITIES: OUTCOME AND PROCESS.    Jean Phinney (1990, 2003) describes four outcomes for ethnic minority youth in their search for identity. They can try *assimilation,* fully adopting the values and behaviours of the majority culture and rejecting their ethnic culture. At the opposite end, they can be *separated,* associating only with members of their ethnic culture. A third possibility is *marginality,* living in the majority culture, but feeling alienated and uncomfortable in it and disconnected from the minority culture as well. The final alternative is *biculturalism* (sometimes called integration), maintaining ties to both cultures. And there are at least three ways to be bicultural. Minority youth can alternate between the two cultures, being fully "majority" in their behaviour in one situation and fully "minority" in other situation. Or they can blend the two cultures by finding values and behaviours that are common to both and acting on them. Finally, minority youth can fuse the two cultures by truly merging them into a new and complete whole (Phinney & Devich-Nevarro, 1997).

No matter what your identity outcome is, having strong positive feelings about your own ethnic group seems to be important for good mental health (Steinberg, 2005). In fact, Amy Marks and her colleagues (2011) determined that bicultural adolescents who form strong, positive multiethnic identities have higher self-esteem, fewer mental health problems, and higher academic achievement than peers with a single ethnic identity or an undeveloped multiethnic identity.

Some psychologists have used James Marcia's identity statuses to understand the process of forming an ethnic identity. Children may begin with an unexamined ethnic identity, either because they have not explored at all (diffusion) or because they have accepted the identity encouraged by others (foreclosure). Many European American adolescents could fit the unexamined category. A period of ethnic identity exploration (moratorium) might be followed by a resolution of the conflict (identity achieved).

RACIAL AND ETHNIC PRIDE.    For all students, pride in family and community is part of the foundation for a stable identity. Special efforts to encourage **racial and ethnic pride** are particularly important, so that students examining their identities do not get the message that differences are deficits (Spencer & Markstrom-Adams, 1990). Schools should make special efforts to foster ethnic pride by, for example, displaying bilingual and multilingual signs, providing opportunities for students to use their first languages, and arranging for parents and community members who represent ethnic minorities to be involved in school events (Cummins, 1989).

**Generativity** Sense of concern for future generations.

**Integrity** Sense of self-acceptance and fulfillment.

**Racial and ethnic pride** A positive self-concept about one's racial or ethnic heritage.

Each of us has an ethnic heritage. Janet Helms (1995) has written about stages in white identity development. Richard Milner (2003) has pointed to the importance of racial identity development and awareness, especially in teaching. When majority adolescents are knowledgeable and secure about their own heritage, they are also more respectful of the heritage of others. Thus, exploring the racial and ethnic roots of all students should foster both pride in self and acceptance of others (Rotherham-Borus, 1994).

In the next sections we move from overarching considerations of identity to the more specific conception of self. In educational psychology, much research is focused on self-concept and self-esteem.

**KNOWING YOURSELF** When majority adolescents are knowledgeable and secure about their own heritage, they are also more respectful of the heritage of others.

## Self-Concept

The term *self-concept* is part of our everyday conversation. We talk about people who have a "low" self-concept or individuals whose self-concept is not "strong," as if the notion of self-concept were like fluid levels in a car or a muscle to be developed. These are actually misuses of the term. In psychology, **self-concept** generally refers to individuals' knowledge and beliefs about themselves—their ideas, feelings, attitudes, and expectations (Harter, 2006; Pajares & Schunk, 2001). We could consider self-concept to be our attempt to explain ourselves to ourselves, to build a scheme (in Piaget's terms) that organizes our impressions, feelings, and attitudes about ourselves. But this model or scheme is not permanent, unified, or unchanging. Our perceptions of ourselves vary from situation to situation and from one phase of our lives to another.

**Listen**
Self-Concept

**THE STRUCTURE OF SELF-CONCEPT.** A student's overall self-concept is based on other, more specific concepts, including academic and nonacademic self-concepts. Herbert Marsh and his colleagues (2006) have identified up to 17 different self-concepts in nonacademic areas (e g., physical appearance, popularity, trustworthiness, relations with parents, emotional stability) and academic areas (verbal, mathematics, problem solving, art, computers). For adolescents, both their overall academic self-concept (how quickly they learn or how well they do in school in general) and their subject-specific self-concept (how good they are in math) may influence their actions and motivation. For example, Martin Brunner and his colleagues (2010) suggest "students' educational aspirations (e.g., whether to go on to higher education) are driven by general academic self-concept, whereas the training program or university major chosen is influenced by the profile of subject-specific academic self-concepts" (p. 977). For adults, however, the separate, specific self-concepts are not necessarily integrated into an overall self-concept, so self-concept probably is more situation-specific in adults (Marsh & Ayotte, 2003; Marsh, Craven, & Martin, 2006; Schunk, Pintrich, & Meece, 2008).

**HOW SELF-CONCEPT DEVELOPS.** The self-concept evolves through constant self-evaluation in different situations. Children and adolescents are continually asking themselves, in effect, "How am I doing?" They gauge the verbal and nonverbal reactions of significant people—parents and other family members in the early years and friends, schoolmates, and teachers later—to make judgments (Harter, 1998).

Younger children tend to have positive and optimistic views of themselves. In one study, over 80% of grade 1 students surveyed thought they were the best students in class (Stipek, 1981). With more experience in school, children make self-concept appraisals based on their own improvement. For example, researchers in New Zealand followed 60 students from the time they started school until the middle of their third year

**Self-concept** Individuals' knowledge and beliefs about themselves—their ideas, feelings, attitudes, and expectations.

(Chapman, Tunmer, & Prochnow, 2000). In the first two months of school, differences in reading self-concept began to develop, based on the ease or difficulty students had learning to read. Students who entered school with good knowledge about sounds and letters learned to read more easily and developed more positive reading self-concepts. Over time, differences in the reading performance of students with high and low reading self-concepts grew even greater. Thus, the early experiences with the important school task of reading had strong impact on reading self-concept.

As they mature, students become more realistic, but many are not accurate judges of their own abilities (Paris & Cunningham, 1996). In fact, some students suffer from "illusions of incompetence"—they seriously underestimate their own competence (Phillips & Zimmerman, 1990). As we have seen, during the middle-school years, students grow more self-conscious. At this age, self-concepts are tied to physical appearance and social acceptance as well as school achievement, so these years can be exceedingly difficult for students such as Stephanie, described at the opening of this chapter (Shapka & Keating, 2005; Wigfield, Eccles, & Pintrich, 1996).

Both self and other comparisons shape self-concepts, at least in Western cultures. Students' self-concepts in math are shaped by how their math performance compares to their performance history. They also compare themselves to other math students (Altermatt, Pomerantz, Ruble, Frey, & Greulich, 2002; Schunk, Pintrich, & Meece, 2008). Students who are strong in math in an average school feel better about their math skills than do students of equal ability in high-achieving schools. Marsh (1990; Marsh et al., 2008) calls this the "Big-Fish-Little-Pond Effect (BFLP)." Research that surveyed 265 180 15-year-old students in 10 221 schools across 41 countries around the world found the BFLP effect in every one of these countries (Seaton, Marsh, & Craven, 2009). Participation in a gifted and talented program seems to have a "Little-Fish-in-a-Big-Pond" effect:

> Students who participate in gifted programs, compared to similar students who remain in regular classes, tend to show declines in academic self-concepts over time, but no changes in nonacademic self-concepts (Marsh & Craven, 2002; Preckel, Goetz, & Frenzel, 2010).

**SELF-CONCEPT AND ACHIEVEMENT.** Many psychologists consider self-concept to be the foundation of both social and emotional development. Research has linked self-concept to a wide range of accomplishments—from performance in competitive sports to job satisfaction to pride, enjoyment, and achievement in school (Byrne, 2002; Marsh & Hau, 2003; Shapka & Keating, 2003; Goetz, Cronjaeger, Frenzel, Ludtke, & Hall, 2010; Möller & Pohlmann, 2010). Some evidence for the link between self-concept and school achievement is that performance in academic subjects is correlated with specific self-concepts in those areas, but not with social or physical self-concepts. For example, in one study, math self-concept correlated .77 with math test scores, .59 with grades, and .51 with coursework selection (Marsh, Craven, & Martin, 2006; O'Mara, Marsh, Craven, & Debus, 2006).

That last correlation of math self-concept with course selection points to an important way that self-concept affects learning in school. Think back to high school. When you had a chance to choose courses, did you pick your worst subjects—those where you felt least capable? Probably not. Herbert Marsh and Alexander Yeung (1997) examined how 246 boys in early high school in Sydney, Australia, chose their courses. Academic self-concept for a particular subject (mathematics, science, etc.) was the most important predictor of course selection—more important than previous grades in the subject or overall self-concept. The courses selected in high school put students on a path toward the future, so self-concepts about particular academic subjects can be life-changing influences. Canadian researcher Jennifer Shapka also has found that self-concept is one of the biggest predictors of post-secondary enrolment, particularly in the areas of math and science (Shapka & Keating, 2003).

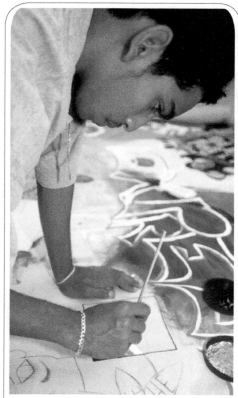

**CHOICES SHAPE FUTURES** The courses selected in high school put students on a path toward the future, so self-concepts about particular academic subjects can be life-changing influences.

Jeff Greenberg/PhotoEdit

## Self-Esteem

**STOP & THINK** How strongly do you agree or disagree with these statements?

On the whole, I am satisfied with myself.

I feel that I have a number of good qualities.

I wish I could have more respect for myself.

At times, I think that I am no good at all.

I certainly feel useless at times.

I take a positive attitude toward myself. •

These *Stop & Think* questions are taken from a widely used measure of self-esteem (Rosenberg, 1979; Hagborg, 1993). **Self-esteem** is an affective reaction—an overall judgment of self-worth that includes feeling confident and proud of yourself as a person. If people judge themselves positively—if they "like what they see"—we say that they have high self-esteem (Schunk, Pintrich, & Meece, 2008). Can you see the judgments of self-worth in the *Stop & Think* questions?

*Self-concept* and *self-esteem* are often used interchangeably, even though they have distinct meanings. Self-concept is a cognitive structure—a belief about who you are. Self-esteem is an overall, general feeling of self-worth that incorporates your self-concepts in all areas of your life, so it is the "summary judgment" about your worth as a person (O'Mara, Marsh, Craven, & Debus, 2006). You can see in the *Stop & Think* items above that the questions are pretty general; no specific areas such as academics or appearance are targeted. Self-esteem is influenced by whether the culture around you values your particular characteristics and capabilities (Bandura, 1997; Schunk, Pintrich, & Meece, 2008). So, although some writers use self-concept and self-esteem interchangeably, a conceptual difference between these terms exists—thinking versus feeling about yourself.

Do schools affect self-esteem? Is school important? As you can see from the *Point/Counterpoint* box, the school's role in student self-esteem has been hotly debated.

More than 100 years ago, William James (1890) suggested that self-esteem is determined by how successful we are in accomplishing tasks or reaching goals we value. If a skill or accomplishment is not important, incompetence in that area doesn't threaten self-esteem. Students must have legitimate success with tasks that matter to them. The reasons individuals give for their successes or failures also are important. In order to build self-esteem, students must attribute their successes to their own actions, not to luck or to special assistance.

## Sex Differences in Self-Concept and Self-Esteem

Do girls and boys differ in their self-concepts? A recent study followed 761 middle-class, primarily European American students from grade 1 through high school (Jacobs, Lanza, Osgood, Eccles, & Wigfield, 2002). It is difficult to obtain longitudinal data, so this is a valuable study. In grade 1, girls and boys had comparable perceptions of their own abilities in language arts, but boys felt significantly more competent in math and sports. Competence beliefs declined for both boys and girls across the grades, but boys fell faster in math so that by high school, math competence beliefs were about the same for boys and girls. In language arts, boys' competence ratings fell more sharply than those of girls after grade 1, but both levelled off during high school. In sports, competence ratings for both boys and girls dropped, but boys remained significantly more confident in their competence in sports throughout the entire 12 years.

Other studies have also found that girls tend to see themselves as more able than boys in reading and developing close friendships, and that boys are more confident about their abilities in math and athletics. Of course, some of these differences in self-confidence may reflect actual differences in achievement—girls tend to be better readers than boys, for example. It is likely that confidence and achievement are reciprocally related—it is quite likely that each affects the other (Eccles, Wigfield, & Schiefele, 1998; Pinxten, De Fraine, Van Damme, & D'Haenens, 2010; Shapka & Keating, 2005). When these results are

**Self-esteem** The value each of us places on our own characteristics, abilities, and behaviours.

## POINT/COUNTERPOINT  What Should Schools Do to Encourage Students' Self-Esteem?

More than 2000 books about how to increase self-esteem have been published. Schools and mental-health facilities continue to develop self-esteem programs (Slater, 2002). The attempts to improve students' self-esteem have taken three main forms: personal development activities such as sensitivity training; self-esteem programs where the curriculum focuses directly on improving self-esteem; and structural changes in schools that place greater emphasis on cooperation, student participation, community involvement, and ethnic pride. Are these efforts valuable?

**POINT**

▶ **The self-esteem movement has problems.** Some people have accused schools of developing programs where the main objective is "to dole out a huge heaping of praise, regardless of actual accomplishments" (Slater, 2002, p. 45). But Erik Erikson (1980) warned years ago: "Children cannot be fooled by empty praise and condescending encouragement. They may have to accept artificial bolstering of their self-esteem in lieu of something better. . . ." Erikson went on to explain that a strong and positive identity comes only from "wholehearted and consistent recognition of real accomplishment, that is, achievement that has meaning in their culture" (p. 95).

Frank Pajares and Dale Schunk (2002) point to another problem. "[W]hen what is communicated to children from an early age is that nothing matters quite as much as how they feel or how confident they should be, one can rest assured that the world will sooner or later teach a lesson in humility that may not easily be learned. An obsession with one's sense of self is responsible for an alarming increase in depression and other mental difficulties" (p. 16). Sensitivity training and self-esteem courses assume that we encourage self-esteem by changing the individual's beliefs, making the young person work harder against the odds. But what if the student's environment is truly unsafe, debilitating, and unsupportive? Some people have overcome tremendous problems, but to expect everyone to do so "ignores the fact that having positive self-esteem is almost impossible for many young people, given the deplorable conditions under which they are forced to live by the inequities in our society" (Beane, 1991, p. 27).

Worse yet, some psychologists are now contending that low self-esteem is not a problem, whereas high self-esteem may be. For example, they contend, people with high self-esteem are more willing to inflict pain and punishment on others (Baumeister, Campbell, Krueger, & Vohs, 2003; Slater, 2002). In addition, high self-esteem does not seem to predict academic learning. In a large study of adolescents, global self-esteem did not correlate with any of the nine academic outcomes measured (Marsh, Seaton, Trautwein, Ludtke, Hau, O'Mara, & Craven, 2008). And when people set self-esteem as a main goal, they may pursue that goal in ways that are harmful over the long run. They may, for example, avoid constructive criticisms or challenging tasks (Crocker & Park, 2004). Psychologist Lauren Slater (2002), in her article titled "The Trouble with Self-Esteem," suggests that we rethink self-esteem and move toward honest self-appraisal that will lead to

self-control. She suggests, "Maybe self-control should replace self-esteem as a primary peg to reach for" (p. 47).

**COUNTERPOINT**

▶ **The self-esteem movement has promise.** A study that followed 322 grade 6 students for two years found that students' satisfaction with school, their sense that classes were interesting and teachers cared, and teacher feedback and evaluations influenced students' self-esteem. In physical education, teachers' opinions were especially powerful in shaping students' conceptions of their athletic abilities (Hoge, Smit, & Hanson, 1990). Being placed in a low-ability group or being held back in school seems to have a negative impact on students' self-esteem, but learning in collaborative and cooperative settings seems to have a positive effect (Covington, 1992; Deci & Ryan, 1985). Interestingly, special programs such as "Student of the Month" or admission to advanced math classes had little effect on self-esteem. (Relate the latter to the "Big-Fish-Little-Pond Effect.")

Beyond the "feel-good psychology" of some aspects of the self-esteem movement is a basic truth: Self-esteem is a basic right of all humans. We deserve to respect ourselves, and schools should not undermine this right (Beane, 1991). If we view self-esteem accurately as a product of our thinking and our actions—our values, ideas, and beliefs as well as our interactions with others—then we see a significant role for the school. Practices that allow authentic participation, cooperation, problem solving, and accomplishment should replace policies that damage self-esteem, such as tracking and competitive grading.

**Beyond Either/Or.** Another possibility is to refocus on more specific self-concepts, because self-concepts in specific areas such as math are related to learning in math (O'Mara, Marsh, Craven, & Debus, 2006). Because self-concept and achievement probably affect each other, Marsh and colleagues (2006) concluded:

*In summary, whereas the optimal way to improve self-concept over the short term is to focus interventions directly on self-concept enhancement, interventions that combine direct self-concept enhancement in concert with performance enhancement, coupled with appropriate feedback and praise, are likely to be advantageous when the goals of the intervention are to improve both self-concept and performance (p. 198).*

examined together with Marsh and Yeung's (1997) findings that academic self-concept influences course selection, it seems that many students make decisions about courses that forever limit their future options.

More longitudinal research is needed to see if these patterns of sex differences hold across cultures and countries. Existing studies suggest that for most ethnic groups, males are more confident about their abilities in math and science. These differences between males and females are generally small, but consistent across studies (Kling, Hyde, Showers, & Buswell, 1999; Shapka & Keating, 2003).

Teachers' feedback, grading practices, evaluations, and communication of caring for students can make a difference in how students feel about their abilities in particular subjects. But the greatest increases in self-esteem come when students grow more competent in areas they value—including the social areas that become so important in adolescence. Thus, a teacher's greatest challenge is to help students achieve important understandings and skills.

# UNDERSTANDING OTHERS AND MORAL DEVELOPMENT

As we seek our own identity and form images of ourselves, we are also learning about right and wrong. One aspect of moral development is understanding the "significant others" around us. How do we learn to interpret what others are thinking and feeling?

## Theory of Mind and Intention

By age 2 or 3, children begin to develop a **theory of mind**, an understanding that other people are people, too, with their own minds, thoughts, feelings, beliefs, desires, and perceptions (Astington & Dack, 2008; Flavell, Miller, & Miller, 2002; Miller, 2009). Children need a theory of mind to make sense of other people's behaviour. Why is Sarah crying? Does she feel sad because no one will play with her? Children also need a theory of mind to understand that beliefs can differ from reality and that people can have different views. You will see in Chapter 4 that one explanation for autism is that children with this condition lack a theory of mind to help them understand their own and other people's emotions and behaviours.

Around the age of 2, children have a sense of intention, at least of their own intentions. They will announce, "I wanna peanut butter sandwich." As children develop a theory of mind, they also are able to understand that other people have intentions of their own. Older preschoolers who get along well with their peers are able to separate intentional from unintentional actions and to react accordingly. For example, they will not get angry when another child accidentally knocks over their block tower. But aggressive children have more trouble assessing intention. They are likely to attack anyone who topples their tower, even accidentally (Dodge & Pettit, 2003). As children mature, they are more able to assess and consider the intentions of others.

With a developing theory of mind, children are increasingly able to understand that other people have different feelings and experiences, and therefore may have a different viewpoint or perspective. This **perspective-taking ability** develops over time until it is quite sophisticated in adults. Being able to understand how others might think and feel is important in fostering cooperation and moral development, reducing prejudice, resolving conflicts, and encouraging positive social behaviours in general (Gehlbach, 2004). Some coaching in perspective-taking from the teacher might help if children mistreat peers and the mistreatment is not part of a deeper emotional or behavioural disorder (Woolfolk & Perry, 2012).

## Moral Development

Along with a more advanced theory of mind and an understanding of intention, children also develop a sense of right and wrong. In this section we focus on children's **moral reasoning**, their thinking about right and wrong and their *active construction* of moral judgments. Some of the earliest moral issues in classrooms involve dividing and sharing materials, or **distributive justice** (Damon, 1994). For young children (ages 5 to 6), fair

**Theory of mind** An understanding that other people are people, too, with their own minds, thoughts, feelings, beliefs, desires, and perceptions.

**Perspective-taking ability** Understanding that others have different feelings and experiences.

**Moral reasoning** The thinking process involved in judgments about questions of right and wrong.

**Distributive justice** Beliefs about how to divide materials or privileges fairly among members of a group; follows a sequence of development from equality to merit to benevolence.

distribution is based on equality; thus, teachers often hear, "Keshawn got more than I did—that's not fair!" In the next few years, children come to recognize that some people should get more based on merit—they worked harder or performed better. Finally, around age 8, children are able to take need into account and to reason based on benevolence; they can understand that some students may get more time or resources from the teacher because those students have special needs.

Another area that involves moral development is an understanding of rules. If you have spent time with young children, you know that there is a period when you can say, "Eating in the living room is not allowed!" and get away with it. For young children, rules simply exist. Piaget (1965) called this the state of **moral realism**. At this stage, the child of 5 or 6 believes that rules about conduct or rules about how to play a game are absolute and can't be changed. If a rule is broken, the child believes that the punishment should be determined by how much damage is done, not by the intention of the child or by other circumstances. So, accidentally breaking three cups is worse than intentionally breaking one, and in the child's eyes, the punishment for the three-cup offence should be greater.

As children interact with others and see that different people have different rules, there is a gradual shift to a **morality of cooperation**. Children come to understand that people make rules and people can change them. When rules are broken, both the damage done and the intention of the offender are taken into account.

**KOHLBERG'S THEORIES OF MORAL DEVELOPMENT.**   Lawrence Kohlberg's (1963, 1975, 1981) theory of moral development is based in part on Piaget's ideas, described earlier.

- - - - - - - - - - - - - - - - - - - - - - - - - - - - - - - - - - - - - -

**STOP & THINK** A man's wife is dying. There is one drug that could save her, but it is very expensive, and the druggist who invented it will not sell it at a price low enough for the man to buy it. Finally, the man becomes desperate and considers stealing the drug for his wife. What should he do, and why? •

- - - - - - - - - - - - - - - - - - - - - - - - - - - - - - - - - - - - - -

**Watch**
Kohlberg's Theories
of Moral Development

Kohlberg evaluated the moral reasoning of both children and adults by presenting them with **moral dilemmas**, or hypothetical situations in which people must make difficult decisions and justify them. Based on the individual's reasoning, Kohlberg proposed a detailed sequence of stages of moral reasoning, or judgments about right and wrong. He divided moral development into three levels: (1) *preconventional*, where judgment is based solely on a person's own needs and perceptions; (2) *conventional*, where the expectations of society and law are taken into account; and (3) *postconventional*, where judgments are based on abstract, more personal principles of justice that are not necessarily defined by society's laws. Each of these three levels is further divided into two stages.

### Preconventional Level

- Stage 1: *Obedience Orientation*—Obey rules to avoid punishments and bad consequences.
- Stage 2: *Rewards/Exchange Orientation*—Right and wrong are determined by personal needs and wants—"If I want it, it is right."

### Conventional Level

- Stage 3: *Being Nice/Relationships Orientation*—Being good means being nice and pleasing others.
- Stage 4: *Law and Order Orientation*—Laws and authorities must be obeyed; the social system must be maintained.

### Postconventional (Principled) Level

- Stage 5: *Social Contract Orientation*—The moral choice is determined by socially agreed upon standards—"the greatest good for the greatest number."
- Stage 6: *Universal Ethical Principles Orientation*—There are universal principles of human dignity and social justice that individuals should uphold, no matter what the law or other people say.

**Moral realism** Stage of development wherein children see rules as absolute.

**Morality of cooperation** Stage of development wherein children realize that people make rules and people can change them.

**Moral dilemmas** Situations in which no choice is clearly and indisputably right.

Moral reasoning is related to both cognitive and emotional development. As we have seen, abstract thinking becomes increasingly important in the higher stages of moral development, as children move from decisions based on absolute rules to decisions based on abstract principles such as justice and mercy. The ability to see another's perspective, to judge intentions, and to use formal operational thinking to imagine alternative bases for laws and rules also enters into judgments at the higher stages.

CRITICISMS OF KOHLBERG'S THEORY.     Even though there is evidence that the different levels of reasoning Kohlberg identified do form a hierarchy, with each stage representing an advancement in reasoning over the one before (Boom, Brugman, & van der Heijden, 2001), his stage theory has been criticized. First, in reality, the stages do not seem to be separate, sequenced, and consistent. People often give reasons for moral choices that reflect several different stages simultaneously. Or a person's choices in one instance may fit one stage, while his or her decisions in a different situation may reflect another stage. When asked to reason about helping someone else versus meeting their own needs, both children and adolescents reason at higher levels than when they are asked to reason about breaking the law or risking punishment (Arnold, 2000; Eisenberg, Shell, Pasernack, Lennon, Beller, & Mathy, 1987; Sobesky, 1983).

Second, in everyday life, making moral choices involves more than reasoning. Emotions, competing goals, relationships, and practical considerations all affect choices. People may be able to reason at higher levels but may make choices at lower levels based on these other factors (Carpendale, 2000). Kohlberg emphasized cognitive reasoning about morality, but he overlooked other aspects of moral maturity, such as character and virtue, that operate to solve moral problems in everyday life (Walker & Pitts, 1998).

GENDER DIFFERENCES: THE MORALITY OF CARING.     One of the most hotly debated criticisms of Kohlberg's theory is that the stages are biased in favour of Western male values that emphasize individualism. His stages do not represent the way moral reasoning develops in women or in other cultures, because the stage theory was based on a longitudinal study of American men only (Gilligan, 1982; Gilligan & Attanucci, 1988).

Carol Gilligan (1982) has proposed a different sequence of moral development, an "ethic of care." Gilligan suggests that individuals move from a focus on self-interests to moral reasoning based on commitment to specific individuals and relationships, and then to the highest level of morality based on the principles of responsibility and care for all people (which is a bit like Kohlberg's stage 3). If women never reach what Kohlberg considers the higher stages of justice, are they morally immature?

Some research supports this ethic of care and indicates that it is more typical of women's orientation to moral problem solving, especially when they reason about personal and real-life issues (Garmon, Basinger, Gregg, & Gibbs, 1996). However, a meta-analysis that combined the results of 113 studies found only small differences in moral orientation in line with Gilligan's theory (Jaffee & Hyde, 2000). The meta-analysis suggests both men and women use care to reason about interpersonal dilemmas and justice to reason about societal dilemmas. Moral reasoning was more strongly influenced by the context and content of the dilemma than by the gender of the reasoner. Even though men and women both seem to value caring and justice, there is some evidence that in everyday life, women feel more guilty about violating caring norms (being inconsiderate or untrustworthy) and men feel more guilty when they show violent behaviours (fighting or damaging property) (Williams & Bybee, 1994).

Caring for students and helping students learn to care has become a theme for many educators. For example, Nel Noddings (1995) urged that "themes of care" be used to organize the curriculum. Possible themes include "Caring for Self," "Caring for Family and Friends," and "Caring for Strangers and the World." Using the theme of "Caring for Strangers and the World," there could be units on crime, war, poverty, tolerance, ecology, or technology. Natural disasters (e.g., floods in Calgary, hurricanes in New Orleans and New Jersey, earthquakes in Haiti and Japan), homelessness, or the repercussions of recent wars (e.g., in Iraq and Afganistan) could be starting points for these units. Table 3.5 shows how a focus on crime and caring for strangers could be integrated into several high school classes.

TABLE 3.5 • **Using "Caring for Strangers and the World" as a Teaching Theme**

As part of a unit on "Caring for Strangers and the World," high school students examine the issue of crime in several classes. In every class, the study of aspects of crime would be continually tied to the theme of caring and to discussions of safety, responsibility, trust in each other and in the community, and commitment to a safer future.

| SUBJECT | ELEMENTS |
|---------|----------|
| Mathematics | Statistics: Gather data on the location and rates of crimes, ages of offenders, and costs of crime to society. Is there a correlation between severity of punishment and incidence of crime? What is the actual cost of a criminal trial? |
| English and social studies | Read *Oliver Twist*. Relate the characters to their social and historical context. What factors contributed to crime in nineteenth-century England?<br>Read popular mysteries. Are they literature? Are they accurate depictions of the criminal justice system? |
| Science | Genetics: Are criminal tendencies heritable? Are there sex differences in aggressive behaviour? Are women less competent than men in moral reasoning (and why did some social scientists think so)? How would you test this hypothesis? |
| Arts | Is graffiti art really art? |

*Source: Based on "Teaching Themes of Care," by Nel Noddings, Phi Delta Kappan, 76, pp. 675–679.*

## Moral Judgments, Social Conventions, and Personal Choices

**STOP & THINK**
1. If there were no law against it, would it be okay to blind someone?
2. If there were no rule against it, would it be okay to chew gum in class?
3. Who should decide your favourite vegetable or how to style your hair? •

We probably could agree that it is wrong to blind someone, wrong to break class rules, and wrong to dictate food preferences or hairstyles for other people—but it is a different kind of wrong in each case. The first question is about actions that are inherently immoral. The answer to the question is concerned with conceptions of justice, fairness, human rights, and human welfare. Even young children know that it is not okay to hurt other people or steal from them—law or no law. But some rules, like no gum chewing in question 2, are **social conventions**—agreed-upon rules and ways of doing things in a particular situation. Students (mostly) avoid chewing gum when the class rules (conventions) say so. It is not inherently immoral to chew gum—it is just against the rules. Some classes—in college or university, for example—work well using different rules. And it is not immoral to dislike lima beans (at least we hope not) or to wear your hair short if you are a female; these are *personal choices*—individual preferences and private issues.

Other criticisms of Kohlberg's stages are that they mix up moral judgments with decisions about social conventions and also overlook personal choice. Larry Nucci (2001) offers an explanation of moral development that covers all three domains or areas: *moral judgments, social conventions*, and *personal choice*. Children's thinking and reasoning develops across all domains, but the pace of development may not be the same in every area.

**MORAL VERSUS CONVENTIONAL DOMAINS.** For teachers, the most common "right and wrong" situations involve the moral and conventional domains. In the moral domain, beginning with a few basic ideas about right and wrong ("It is wrong to hurt others"), children move through the following stages: a sense that justice means equal treatment

**Social conventions** Agreed-upon rules and ways of doing things in a particular situation.

for all, an appreciation of equity and special needs, a more abstract integration of equity and equality along with a sense of caring in social relations, and, finally, a sense as adults that morality involves beneficence and fairness and that moral principles are independent of the norms of any particular group.

In the *conventional domain*, children begin by believing that the regularities they see are real and right—for example, men have short hair, women have longer hair, so that is the way it should be. As they mature, children see the exceptions (men with ponytails, women with very short cuts) and realize that conventions are arbitrary. Next, children understand that rules, even though they are arbitrary, are made to maintain order and that people in charge make the rules. As they move through adolescence, they swing from understanding conventions as the appropriate ways to operate in a social system to viewing them as nothing but society's standards that have become set because they are widely applied and seldom challenged. Finally, adults realize that conventions are useful in coordinating social life, but changeable, too. So, compared with young children, older adolescents and adults generally are more accepting of others who think differently about conventions and customs.

**IMPLICATIONS FOR TEACHERS.**   Nucci (2001) offers several suggestions for creating a moral atmosphere in your classroom. First, it is important to establish a community of mutual respect and warmth with a fair and consistent application of the rules. Without that kind of community, all your attempts to create a moral climate will be undermined. Second, teachers' responses to students should be appropriate to the domain of the behaviour—moral or conventional. For example, here are some responses to *moral issues* (Nucci, 2001, p. 146):

1. When an act is inherently hurtful or unjust, emphasize the harm done to others: "John, that really hurt Jamal."
2. Encourage perspective-taking: "Chris, how would you feel if someone stole from you?"

In contrast, here are two responses to rule or conventional issues:

3. Restate the rule: "Lisa, you are not allowed to be out of your seat during announcements."
4. Command: "Howie, stop swearing!"

In all four cases, the teacher's response fits the domain. To create an inappropriate response, just switch responses 1 or 2 with 3 or 4. For example, "Lisa, how would you feel if other people got out of their seat during announcements?" Lisa might feel just fine. And it is a weak response to a moral transgression to say, "John, it is against the rules to hit." It is more than against the rules—it hurts and it is wrong.

In the third domain of moral development—personal—children must sort out what decisions and actions are their personal choices and what decisions are outside personal choice. This process is the foundation for developing moral concepts related to individual rights, fairness, and democracy. Here, different cultures may have very different understandings about individual choice, privacy, and the role of individuality in the larger society.

## Diversity in Moral Reasoning

There are a number of broad cultural distinctions that might influence moral reasoning. Some cultures can be considered more traditional, with greater emphasis on customs and rituals that change slowly over time. In contrast, traditions and customs tend to change more rapidly in modern cultures. Nucci (2001) suggests that in more traditional cultures, customs may become "moralized." For example, not wearing head coverings in some cultures may seem to be in the conventional domain to outsiders, but is closer to the moral domain for members of the culture, especially when religious beliefs are involved.

One of Nucci's studies asked devout Hindus to rate 35 behaviours that violated community norms. An eldest son eating chicken a day after his father's death was considered the worst violation, and beating a disobedient wife was the least offensive. What seems like a convention (eating chicken) is a moral issue because the Hindus believed that the son's behaviour would prevent his father from receiving salvation—a terrible and eternal fate. So, to understand what is conventional and what is moral, we need to know about the beliefs of the culture.

In cultures that are more family-centred or group-oriented (often called *collectivist cultures*), the highest moral value might involve putting the opinions of the group before decisions based on individual conscience. Research has found that children's reasoning about moral, conventional, and personal domains is similar across cultures (Berk, 2005). Even in societies, such as China, that encourage deference to authority, children agree that adults have no right to dictate how children spend their free time. And people without authority, including children, should be obeyed when what they want you to do is fair and just, but disobeyed when what they dictate is immoral or unjust (Helwig, Arnold, Tan, & Boyd, 2003; Kim, 1998).

In the last years of his life, Kohlberg studied moral behaviour in schools. We turn to that topic now.

## Moral Behaviour

Three important influences on moral behaviour are modelling, internalization, and self-concept. First, children who have been consistently exposed to caring, generous adult models will tend to be more concerned for the rights and feelings of others (Eisenberg & Fabes, 1998; Woolfolk & Perry, 2015). Second, most theories of moral behaviour assume that young children's moral behaviour is first controlled by others through direct instruction, supervision, rewards and punishments, and correction. But in time, children **internalize** the moral rules and principles of the authority figures who have guided them; that is, children adopt the external standards as their own. If children are given reasons that they can understand when they are corrected—particularly reasons that highlight the effects of actions on others—then they are more likely to internalize moral principles. They learn to behave morally even when "no one is watching" (Hoffman, 2000).

Finally, we must integrate moral beliefs and values into our total sense of who we are, our self-concept.

> The tendency for a person to behave morally is largely dependent on the extent to which moral beliefs and values are integrated in the personality, and in one's sense of self. The influence our moral beliefs have on our lives, therefore, is contingent on the personal importance that we as individuals attach to them—we must identify and respect them as our own. (Arnold, 2000, p. 372)

AGGRESSION.   Aggression should not be confused with assertiveness, which means affirming or maintaining a legitimate right. Saying, "You are sitting in my chair!" is assertive. Pushing the invader out of the chair is aggressive. There are several forms of aggression. The most common form is **instrumental aggression**, which is intended to gain an object or privilege, such as shoving to get a chair or snatching a book from another student. The intent is to get what you want, not to hurt the other child, but the hurt may happen anyway. A second kind is **hostile aggression**—inflicting intentional harm. Hostile aggression can take the form of either **overt aggression**, such as threats or physical attacks (as in, "I'm gonna beat you up!"), or **relational aggression**, which involves threatening or damaging social relationships (as in, "I'm never going to speak to you again!"). Boys are more likely to use overt aggression, and girls, like Alison in the opening case, are more likely to use relational aggression, especially in middle school and beyond (Dodge, Coie, & Lynam, 2006; Ostrov & Godleski, 2010). A final kind of hostile aggression is a growing concern today, **cyber aggression**—using email, Twitter, Facebook, or other social media to spread rumours, make threats, or otherwise terrorize peers, as Stephanie's "friends" did in the case at the beginning of this chapter.

Aggressive students tend to believe that violence will be rewarded, and they use aggression to get what they want. They are more likely to believe that violent retaliation is acceptable: "It's OK to shove people when you're mad" (Egan, Monson, & Perry, 1998). Seeing violent acts go unpunished probably affirms and encourages these beliefs.

**Internalize** Process whereby children adopt external standards as their own.

**Instrumental aggression** Strong actions aimed at claiming an object, place, or privilege—not intended to harm, but may lead to harm.

**Hostile aggression** Bold, direct action that is intended to hurt someone else; unprovoked attack.

**Overt aggression** A form of hostile aggression that involves physical attack.

**Relational aggression** A form of hostile aggression that involves verbal attacks and other actions meant to harm social relationships.

**Cyber aggression** Using email, Twitter, Facebook, or other social media to spread rumours, make threats, or otherwise terrorize peers.

In addition, some children, particularly boys, have difficulty reading the intentions of others (Arsenio & Lemerise, 2004; Dodge, Coie, & Lynam, 2006; Dodge & Pettit, 2003). They assume another child "did it on purpose" when their block tower is toppled, they are pushed on the bus, or some other mistake is made. Retaliation follows and the cycle of aggression continues.

Children with more serious conduct problems often are identified during elementary school. But the problems are not new behaviours—usually they are behaviours the students have not outgrown from their early years (Petitclerc, Boivin, Dionne, Zoccolillo, & Tremblay, 2009). So waiting for children to "outgrow" aggressive behaviours does not work. For example, one study in Finland asked teachers to rate students' aggression by answering "never," "sometimes," or "often" to statements such as "hurts another child when angry." Teacher-rated aggression when students were age 8 predicted school adjustment problems in early adolescence and long-term unemployment in adulthood (Kokko & Pulkkinen, 2000). Similar results were found in a study conducted in Canada, New Zealand, and the United States. Boys (but not girls) who were often physically aggressive in elementary school were at risk for continuing violent and nonviolent forms of delinquency through adolescence (Broidy et al., 2003).

It is clear that helping children handle aggression can make a lasting difference in their lives. One of the best approaches for preventing problems with aggression later in life is to intervene early. For example, one study found that aggressive children whose teachers taught them conflict management strategies were diverted from a life path of aggression and violence (Aber, Brown, & Jones, 2003). Sandra Graham (1996) has successfully experimented with approaches that help aggressive grade 5 and 6 boys become better judges of others' intentions. Strategies include engaging in role-play, participating in group discussions of personal experiences, interpreting social cues from photographs, playing pantomime games, making videos, and writing endings to unfinished stories. The boys in the 12-session training group showed clear improvement in reading the intentions of others and responding with less aggression.

RELATIONAL AGGRESSION. Insults, gossip, exclusion, taunts—all are forms of relational aggression, sometimes called *social aggression* because the intent is to harm social connections. After grade 2 or 3, girls tend to engage in relational aggression more than boys, possibly because as girls become aware of gender stereotypes, they push their overt aggression underground into verbal, not physical, attacks. Relational aggression can be even more damaging than overt physical aggression—both to the victim and the aggressor. Victims, like Stephanie in the chapter opening, often are devastated. Teachers and other students may view relational aggressors as even more problematic than physical aggressors (Crick, Casas, & Mosher, 1997; Ostrov & Godleski, 2010). As early as preschool, children need to learn how to negotiate social relations without resorting to any kind of aggression. Interviews with adolescents reveal how much they count on their teachers and other adults in the school to protect them (Garbarino & deLara, 2002). We will examine more specific classroom strategies, especially strategies for handling bullying, in Chapter 13, *Creating Learning Environments*.

MEDIA, MODELLING, AND AGGRESSION. Modelling plays an important role in the expression of aggression (Bandura, Ross, & Ross, 1963). In a now seminal study, Albert Bandura and colleagues (Bandura, Ross, & Ross, 1963) arranged for a group of children to watch a film in which an adult interacted aggressively with an inflatable doll (e.g., punching the "Bobo" doll) while another group of children watched an adult playing appropriately with a set of Tinkertoys. After watching the film, researchers observed that children who had witnessed the aggressive interactions with the Bobo dolls played more aggressively than their peers who had observed the more appropriate play with Tinkertoys. Similarly, Canadian researchers (Cote, Vaillancourt, LeBlanc, Nagin, & Tremblay, 2006; Craig, Peters, & Konarski, 1998; Pepler, Craig, Jiang, & Connolly, 2008; Tremblay et al., 1996), working with data from the National Longitudinal Study of Children and Youth, have demonstrated strong associations between family membership and family functioning and aggressive behaviour. Children who grow up in homes

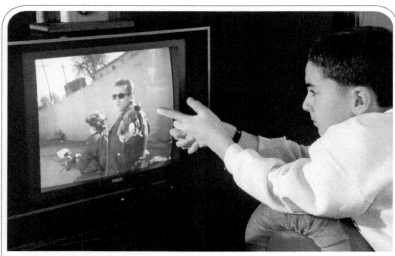

**MODELS OF AGGRESSION** One very real source of aggressive models is television programming with a high degree of violent content.

filled with harsh punishment and family violence are more likely to use aggression to solve their own problems.

One increasingly pervasive source of aggressive models is media entertainment. Almost every home in North America has a television and, by age 12, estimates are that most children will have witnessed over 8000 murders and over 100 000 other acts of violence on TV (Daly & Perez, 2009). But television isn't the only source of violent modelling. Students growing up in the inner cities see gang violence. The news (on TV, in print media, on the internet) is filled with stories of murders, rapes, and robberies. Many popular films are also filled with graphic depictions of violence, often performed by the "hero" who saves the day. Particularly disturbing is the fact that much of the violence children observe in the media goes unpunished. Again, children see that violent retaliation is acceptable—often it is rewarded. And what about those video games?

VIDEO GAMES AND AGGRESSIVE BEHAVIOUR.    Recently researchers reviewed 130 reports based on over 130 000 participants from Western countries such as the United States, Australia, Germany, Italy, the Netherlands, Portugal, and the United Kingdom, as well as from Japan (Anderson et al., 2010). They found that playing violent video games is a causal factor for increased aggressive thoughts, feelings, and actions, along with decreased feelings of empathy. Culture and gender had very little impact on how susceptible players were to the effects of these games. But playing positive video games can increase prosocial behaviours, so it is not that games themselves are bad. It appears that we learn what we play, but there are few prosocial games and many violent ones. So an important issue facing teachers, parents, and our whole society is determining what we should do to limit the risks to children. The *Guidelines* give some ideas for dealing with aggression and encouraging cooperation.

You can also reduce the negative effects of media violence by stressing three points with your students: (1) Most people do not behave in the aggressive ways shown in the media; (2) the violent acts observed in TV programs, films, and video games are not real, but are created by special effects and stunts; and (3) there are better ways to resolve conflicts, and these are the ways most real people solve their problems (Huesmann, Moise-Titus, Podolski, & Eron, 2003). Also, avoid using media as a reward or punishment because that makes them even more attractive to children (Slaby, Roedell, Arezzo, & Hendrix, 1995).

CHEATING.    About 80%–90% of high school and college and university students cheat at some point in school. In fact, the rates of academic cheating have been rising for the past 30 years, perhaps in response to increased pressures and high-stakes testing (Murdock & Anderman, 2006).

There are some individual differences in cheating. Most studies of adolescent and college- or university-age students find that males are more likely to cheat than females, and lower-achieving students are more likely to cheat than higher achievers. Students focusing on performance goals (making good grades, looking smart) as opposed to learning goals, and students with a low sense of academic self-efficacy (a belief that they probably can't do well in school), are more likely to cheat. Finally, students who are impulsive may be more likely to cheat (Anderman, Cupp, & Lane, 2009; Murdock & Anderman, 2006).

But cheating is not all about individual differences—the situation plays a role as well. In one study, the level of cheating decreased when students moved from math classes that emphasized competition and grades to classes that emphasized understanding and

Peter Byron/Photo Researchers, Inc.

## GUIDELINES

## Dealing With Aggression and Encouraging Cooperation

**Present yourself as a nonaggressive model.**
*Examples*
1. Do not use threats of aggression to win obedience.
2. When problems arise, model nonviolent conflict-resolution strategies (see Chapter 13).

**Ensure that your classroom has enough space and appropriate materials for every student.**
*Examples*
1. Prevent overcrowding.
2. Make sure prized toys or resources are plentiful.
3. Remove or confiscate materials that encourage personal aggression, such as toy guns.
4. Avoid highly competitive activities and evaluations.

**Make sure students do not profit from aggressive behaviours.**
*Examples*
1. Comfort the victim of aggression and make clear to the perpetrator that aggression is unacceptable in your view.
2. Use reasonable punishment, especially with older students.

**Teach directly about positive social behaviours.**
*Examples*
1. Incorporate lessons on social ethics/morality through reading selections and discussions.

2. Discuss the effects of antisocial actions such as stealing, bullying, and spreading rumours.
3. Provide models and encouragement—role-play appropriate conflict resolution.
4. Build self-esteem by building skills and knowledge.
5. Seek help for students who seem especially isolated and victimized.

**Provide opportunities for learning tolerance and cooperation.**
*Examples*
1. Emphasize the similarities among people rather than the differences.
2. Set up group projects that encourage cooperation.

*For more ideas, see the National Youth Violence Prevention Resource Center: http://www.safeyouth.gov/Resources/Prevention/Pages/PreventionHome.aspx.*

---

mastery (Anderman & Midgley, 2004). Students are less likely to cheat when they view their teacher as credible. If students trust the teacher as a credible source, they may be more likely to value the content being taught and therefore want to actually learn it (Anderman, Cupp, & Lane, 2009). Students also more prone to cheat when they are behind or "cramming for tests" or when they believe that their teachers do not care about them. For example, Erica had this perspective:

> I am a high school honors student, and I think there are different degrees of cheating. I'm a dedicated student, but when my history teacher bombards me with 50 questions due tomorrow or when a teacher gives me a fill-in-the-blanks worksheet on a night when I have swim practice, church, aerobics—and other homework—I'm going to copy from a friend! … Since I only do this when I need to, it isn't a habit. Every kid does this when they're in a pinch. (Jensen, Arnett, Feldman, & Cauffman, 2002, p. 210)

Tamera Murdock and Eric Anderman (2006) have proposed a model to integrate what we know about cheating with research to learn more about cheating. They suggest that in deciding to cheat, students ask three questions: What is my goal? Can I do it? What are the costs? See Table 3.6 for some example answers to these questions that might be associated with decisions to cheat or not to cheat, and some example strategies to support not cheating.

The implications for teachers are straightforward. To prevent cheating, try to avoid putting students in high-pressure situations. Make sure they are well prepared for tests, projects, and assignments so that they can do reasonably well without cheating. Be a credible and trustworthy source for information. Focus on learning and not on grades. Encourage collaboration on assignments and experiment with open-book, collaborative,

TABLE 3.6 • **When Do Students Cheat?**

Tamera Murdock and Eric Anderman have developed a model of academic cheating based on the answers to three questions.

| QUESTIONS | LESS LIKELY TO CHEAT: EXAMPLE ANSWERS | MORE LIKELY TO CHEAT: EXAMPLE ANSWERS | WHAT CAN THE TEACHER DO? EXAMPLE STRATEGIES |
|---|---|---|---|
| What is my goal? | The goal is to learn, get smarter, and be the best I can be.<br>It is my goal. | The goal is to look good, outperform others.<br>The goal is imposed on me. | Communicate that the point of the class is to learn—everyone can get better. |
| Can I do it? | I can do it with reasonable effort. | I doubt my ability to do it. | Build students' confidence by helping them take small but successful steps.<br>Point out students' past accomplishments. |
| What are the costs? | I will get caught and punished if I cheat.<br>I will feel morally wrong or dishonoured if I cheat. | I probably won't get caught and punished if I cheat.<br>Everyone does it, so it can't be wrong.<br>The pressure is too great—I can't fail. I have to cheat. | Make mistakes an opportunity to learn.<br>Take the pressure out of assignments with the chance to revise.<br>Monitor to prevent cheating and follow through with reasonable penalties. |

*Source: Adapted from Murdock, T. A., & Anderman, E. M. (2006). Motivational perspectives on student cheating: Toward an integrated model of academic dishonesty.* Educational Psychologist, 42, *129–145.*

or take-home tests. Consider telling students what concepts will be on the test and encourage them to discuss the concepts and their applications before the test. You might also make extra help available for those who need it. Be clear about your policies in regard to cheating, and enforce them consistently. Help students resist temptation by monitoring them carefully during testing.

# PERSONAL/SOCIAL DEVELOPMENT: LESSONS FOR TEACHERS

Certainly both Erikson and Bronfenbrenner stress that individuals are influenced by their social and cultural contexts. For example, here are a few big ideas we've discussed:

1. Students whose parents are divorcing can benefit from authoritative teachers who are both warm and clear about requirements.
2. For all students, self-concepts are increasingly differentiated over time—students may feel competent in one subject but not in others, or very capable as friends or family members but not as students.
3. For all students, it is a challenge to forge a meaningful identity that integrates their decisions about career, religion, ethnicity, gender roles, and connection to society. Teachers are in a position to support this quest.
4. Being rejected by peers is harmful for all students. Many students need guidance in developing social skills, in more accurately reading the intentions of others, in resolving conflicts, and in coping with aggression. Again, teachers can provide guidance.
5. When working under high pressure, with unreasonable workloads, and with little chance of being caught, many students will cheat. It is up to teachers and schools to do their best to avoid putting students in these unfavourable conditions.

# ▼ SUMMARY

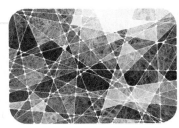

Color Symphony/Shutterstock

### Physical Development (pp. 64–70)

**Describe the changes in physical development of children in the preschool, elementary, and secondary grades.** During the preschool years, there is rapid development of children's gross and fine motor skills. Physical development continues throughout the elementary-school years, with girls often ahead of boys in size. With adolescence comes puberty and emotional struggles to cope with all the related changes.

**What are some of the consequences of early and late maturation for boys and girls?** Females mature about two years ahead of males. Early-maturing boys are more likely to enjoy high social status; they tend to be popular and to be leaders. But they also tend to engage in more delinquent behaviour, and this finding holds across many cultural groups. Early maturation is not generally beneficial for girls.

**What is the role of recess and physical activity in development?** Play supports brain development, language, and social development. Children release tensions, learn to solve problems, adapt to new situations, cooperate, and negotiate. The increase in childhood obesity is linked to inactivity and increased time spent watching TV and playing passive games, such as video and internet games.

**What are some of the signs of eating disorders?** Anorexic students may appear pale, have brittle fingernails, and have fine dark hairs developing all over their bodies. They are easily chilled because they have so little fat to insulate their bodies. They often are depressed, insecure, moody, and lonely. Girls may stop having their menstrual period.

### Bronfenbrenner: The Social Context for Development (pp. 70–81)

**Describe Bronfenbrenner's bioecological model of development.** This model takes into account both the biological aspects internal to the individual and the nested social and cultural contexts that shape development. Every person develops within a microsystem (immediate relationships and activities), inside a mesosystem (relationships among microsystems), embedded in an exosystem (larger social settings such as communities); all of these are part of the macrosystem (culture). In addition, all development occurs in and is influenced by the time period—the chronosystem.

**What are some aspects of the family that affect students in school?** Students probably have experienced different parenting styles and these styles can influence their social adjustment. At least in North American middle-class families, children of authoritative parents are more likely to be happy with themselves and relate well to others, whereas children of authoritarian parents have lower levels of self-control and may be less popular with peers. Children of permissive and rejecting/neglecting parents often have trouble in their relationships and are more likely to engage in risky and delinquent behaviour. But the research findings for parenting styles are not universal. Outcomes for children raised by authoritarian parents can differ across cultural, SES, and religious communities.

**How does divorce affect students?** During the divorce itself, conflict may increase as property and custody rights are being decided. After the divorce, the custodial parent may have to move to a less expensive home, go to work for the first time, or work longer hours. For the child, this can mean leaving behind important friendships just when support is needed the most, having only one parent who has less time than ever to be with them, or adjusting to new family structures when parents remarry.

**Why are peer relations important?** Peer relationships play a significant role in healthy personal and social development. There is strong evidence that adults who had close friends as children have higher self-esteem and are more capable of maintaining intimate relationships than adults who had lonely childhoods. Adults who were rejected as children tend to have more problems, such as dropping out of school or committing crimes.

**What are peer cultures?** Groups of students develop their own norms for appearance and social behaviour. Group loyalties can lead to rejection for some students, leaving them upset and unhappy.

**How can teachers' academic and personal caring affect students?** Students value caring in teachers. Caring can be expressed as support for academic learning and as concern for personal problems. For higher-achieving and higher SES students, academic caring may be more important, but for students who are alienated from school, personal caring may be more important.

**What are some signs of child abuse?** Signs of abuse or neglect include unexplained bruises, burns, bites, or other injuries, and fatigue, depression, frequent absences, poor hygiene, inappropriate clothing, problems with peers, and many others. Teachers must report suspected cases of child abuse and can be instrumental in helping students cope with other risks as well.

### Identity and Self-Concept (pp. 81–93)

**What are Erikson's stages of psychosocial development?** Erikson's emphasis on the relationship between society and the individual is a psychosocial theory of development—a theory that connects personal development (psycho) to the social environment (social). Erikson believed that people go through eight life stages, each of which involves a central crisis. Adequate resolution of each crisis leads to greater personal and social competence and a stronger foundation for solving future crises. In the first two stages, an infant must develop a sense of trust over mistrust and a sense of autonomy over shame and doubt. In early childhood, the focus of the third stage is on developing initiative and avoiding feelings of guilt. In the child's elementary school years, the fourth stage involves achieving a sense of industry and avoiding feelings of inferiority. In the fifth stage, identity versus role confusion, adolescents consciously attempt to solidify their identity. According to Marcia, these efforts may lead to identity diffusion, foreclosure, moratorium, or achievement. Erikson's three stages of adulthood involve struggles to achieve intimacy, generativity, and integrity.

**Describe the formation of ethnic and racial identities.** Ethnic and racial minority students are confronted with the challenge of forming an identity while living in two worlds—the values, beliefs, and behaviours of their group and of the larger culture. Most explanations for identity development describe stages moving from being unaware of differences between minority group and majority cultures, to different ways of negotiating the differences, and finally to an integration of cultures.

**How does self-concept change as children develop?** Self-concept (what we know about ourselves) becomes increasingly complex, differentiated, and abstract as we mature. Self-concept evolves through constant self-reflection, social interaction, and experiences in and out of school. Students develop a self-concept by comparing themselves to personal (internal) standards and social (external) standards. High self-esteem (how we feel about ourselves) is related to better overall school experience, both academically and socially. Gender and ethnic stereotypes are significant factors as well.

**Distinguish between self-concept and self-esteem.** Both self-concept and self-esteem are beliefs about the self. Self-concept is our attempt to build a scheme that organizes our impressions, feelings, and attitudes about ourselves. But this model is not stable. Self-perceptions vary from situation to situation and from one phase of our lives to another. Self-esteem is an evaluation of your self-worth. If people evaluate their worth positively, we say that they have high self-esteem. Self-concept and self-esteem are often used interchangeably, even though they have distinct meanings. Self-concept is a cognitive structure and self-esteem is an affective evaluation.

**Are there differences in self-concepts for girls and boys?** From grade 1 to grade 12, competence beliefs decline for both boys and girls in math, language arts, and sports. By high school, boys and girls express about the same competence in math, girls are higher in language arts, and boys are higher in sports. In terms of general self-esteem, both boys and girls report declines in the transition to middle school, but boys' self-esteem goes up in high school while girls' self-esteem stays the same.

## Understanding Others and Moral Development (pp. 93–102)

**What is a theory of mind and why is it important?** A theory of mind is an understanding that other people are people, too, with their own minds, thoughts, feelings, beliefs, desires, and perceptions. Children need a theory of mind to make sense of other people's behaviour. As children develop a theory of mind, they also are able to understand that other people have intentions of their own.

**How do perspective-taking skills change as students mature?** An understanding of intentions develops as children mature, but aggressive students often have trouble understanding the intentions of others. Social perspective-taking also changes as we mature. Young children believe that everyone has the same thoughts and feelings they do. Later, they learn that others have separate identities and therefore separate feelings and perspectives on events.

**What are the key differences among the preconventional, conventional, and postconventional levels of moral reasoning?** Kohlberg's theory of moral development includes three levels: (1) a preconventional level, where judgments are based on self-interest; (2) a conventional level, where judgments are based on traditional family values and social expectations; and (3) a postconventional level, where judgments are based on more abstract and personal ethical principles. Critics suggest that Kohlberg's view does not account for possible cultural differences in moral reasoning or differences between moral reasoning and moral behaviour.

**Describe Gilligan's levels of moral reasoning.** Carol Gilligan has suggested that because Kohlberg's stage theory was based on a longitudinal study of men only, it is very possible that the moral reasoning of women and the stages of women's development were not adequately represented. She has proposed an "ethic of care." Gilligan believes that individuals move from a focus on self-interests to moral reasoning based on commitment to specific individuals and relationships, and then to the highest level of morality based on the principles of responsibility and care for all people. Women are somewhat more likely to use a care orientation, but studies also show that both men and women *can* use both orientations.

**How does thinking in the moral and conventional domains change over time?** Beliefs about morality move from the young child's sense that justice means equal treatment for all to the adult's understanding that morality involves beneficence and fairness and that moral principles are independent of the norms of any particular group. In thinking about social conventions, children begin by believing that the regularities they see are real and right. After going through several stages, adults realize that conventions are useful in coordinating social life, but changeable, too.

**What influences moral behaviour?** Adults first control young children's moral behaviour through direct instruction, supervision, rewards and punishments, and correction. A second important influence on the development of moral behaviour is modelling. Children who have been consistently exposed to caring and generous adult models will tend to be more concerned for the rights and feelings of others.

**What are the different types of aggression?** Peer aggression can be instrumental (intended to gain an object or privilege), or hostile (intended to inflict harm). Hostile aggression can be either overt threats or physical attacks, or relational aggression, which involves threatening or damaging social relationships. Boys are more likely to use overt aggression and girls are more likely to use relational aggression. Today many social media applications and sites provide other avenues for relational aggression.

**How does ever-present media affect aggression and empathy?** The world and the media provide many negative models of behaviour. In time, children internalize the moral rules and principles of the authority figures who have guided them. If children are given reasons—particularly reasons that highlight the effects of actions on others—they can understand when they are corrected, and then they are more likely to internalize moral principles. Some schools have adopted programs to increase students' capacity to care for others.

**Why do students cheat?** In schools, cheating is a common behaviour problem that involves moral issues. The decision to cheat is based on three questions: What is my goal? Can I do this? What are the costs? Cheating is caused by both individual and situational factors, but if the pressure is great enough and the chance of getting caught is slim, many students will cheat.

# ▼ WHAT WOULD THEY DO?

## TEACHERS' CASEBOOK: Mean Girls

Here is how two practising teachers responded to the teaching situation described on the first page of this chapter.

### MEAGAN MANO

The Prince Charles School, Napanee, ON

To determine my actions in dealing with social issues in development, I would consider who was affected and how students could avoid problem situations and effectively deal with them in the future.

The actions of Alison and her clique are a form of harassment. I would make sure that my health program was geared toward educating the class, especially this group of girls, on harassment. Topics covered would include identifying ways of dealing with harassment and resources that can support someone experiencing it. As part of my program, I would arrange for a guest speaker to talk about relationships and about decision-making skills.

Harassment is not the only issue, as the girls seem to have found themselves in cliques. Again, to reach all students, I would analyze different case scenarios using an age-related film that involved several different cliques. In groups, I would have the students discuss the feelings of the characters in the film and brainstorm the characteristics of a true friend.

Since the email was forwarded to the entire school, it is important that the issues of harassment and bullying be addressed in every classroom. I would discuss the situation with the staff. One approach to ensure that all students were being exposed to these issues would be to set up a school-based program informing students about social skills.

I would speak one-on-one with Stephanie and Alison about friendship. They should both understand that although they were friends in the past, choosing different friends now is acceptable. It is common to hang out with people who share the same interests—and interests change. Alison should be made aware that there are ways of dealing with people that do not involve ridiculing them. I would have both of the girls brainstorm (on their own) different ways in which they could have dealt with the situation. Their ideas would help guide the discussion in my health program.

Finally, I would speak with Alison's and Stephanie's parents to inform them of the situation and of how I plan to address it at school. I would also suggest some topics they could raise at home to follow up my own conversations with the two girls.

### KATHLEEN BARTER

Seycove Secondary School, North Vancouver, BC

Cyberbullying is, unfortunately, all too commonplace in schools today. The biggest problem associated with cyberbullying is that often, as educators, we are unaware when it occurs. By the time we find out, the situation has often gone beyond the scope of the classroom teacher and may have gone "viral" in the school and on the internet. When a situation like this comes to light, teachers must respond in a timely manner. If the situation were not severe, the teacher would deal with the issue in a class discussion that focused on conflict resolution as a solution to bullying. Depending on the group and how many kids in the class know of the situation or were involved in it, the teacher could give a lesson on cyberbullying, ethics, and criminal activities. I might find a short story about bullying and have the students discuss responses and possible solutions, or find an historical or modern example of bullying to use as an analogy, having students discuss appropriate interventions and responses. However, given the severity of the situation with Stephanie and Alison, and the involvement of technology, this is a problem for the administrators in the school and the police liaison officer.

There are two key issues at play in this scenario: the bullying of Stephanie (which would be dealt with at the school), and the distribution of a pornographic image on the internet (which would be dealt with by police). The first step would be notification to the parents and a call to the police liaison officer. Once the police had completed their investigation and agreed on a resolution, the administration would become involved in resolving the bullying. Typically, administration and counsellors would work with the girls, both individually and in a group, using conflict resolution strategies. Following the individual conversations, they would bring all the girls in together and have each girl speak about why she participated in the bullying or how she felt as a victim or as a bully. The challenge is to make the girls understand the legal and moral impact of their actions and to understand how Stephanie felt as a result of being bullied. The girls need to understand that Stephanie might not be interested in the same things they are, but that doesn't mean they have to malign their past friendship.

Svkv/Shutterstock

# LEARNER DIFFERENCES AND LEARNING NEEDS

▶ **TEACHERS' CASEBOOK:** Including Every Student

It is a new school year, and you scan the list of students who will be registered in your classroom. Since your district follows the policy of inclusion, you always expect to have students whose academic abilities, social skills, and motivation for learning vary widely. This year you will have a student with a chronic health concern, asthma; a high-functioning student with Asperger's syndrome; a student with severe learning disabilities; and two students with ADHD. Add to this several students who are new to Canada and learning to speak English, and the class list has you feeling quite overwhelmed. In principle, you believe in the policy of inclusion, but meeting the needs of students in this class will be challenging.

## CRITICAL THINKING

- How will you design tasks and structure interactions with students to ensure they *all* make progress and learn to their full potential?

- What can you do to address the specific needs of students who are identified as having exceptional learning needs?

- How will you remain confident in your new situation?

## OVERVIEW AND OBJECTIVES

To answer the questions on the previous page, you need to understand that learners can differ in their learning strengths and needs. So far, we have talked little about students as individuals. We have discussed principles of development that apply to everyone—stages, processes, conflicts, and tasks. Our development as human beings is similar in many ways, but not in every way. Even among members of the same family, there are marked contrasts in appearance, interests, abilities, and temperament, and these differences have important implications for teaching. We will spend some time analyzing the concepts of intelligence and learning styles because these terms are so often misunderstood. Because it is highly likely you will have children with special needs in your class, whichever grade you teach, in this chapter we also explore both common and less frequently occurring learning problems that students may have. As we discuss each problem area, we will consider how a teacher might recognize problems, seek help, and plan instruction, using approaches such as response to intervention and universal designs for learning. By the time you have completed this chapter, you should be able to:

4.1   Discuss potential problems associated with categorizing and labelling students.

4.2   Describe current hierarchical theories and multiple theories of intelligence.

4.3   Explain how intelligence is measured, and discuss what these measurements tell teachers.

4.4   Discuss the values and limitations of considering students' learning styles.

4.5   Consider the implications of the *Canadian Charter of Rights and Freedoms* for your teaching.

4.6   Understand the special educational needs of students with learning challenges.

4.7   Recognize the special educational needs of students who are gifted and talented.

## LANGUAGE AND LABELLING

Every child has a distinctive collection of strengths and challenges that relate to learning and development. In that sense, all children can be regarded as "exceptional." However, some **exceptional students** have unusually high abilities in particular areas (e.g., music, art, math). Others have disabilities that impact learning and may require special education or other services. Although we will use a variety of terms, including developmental disabilities, communication disorders, and behavioural disorders, to describe particular groups of children's learning challenges throughout the chapter, a caution is in order: *Labelling students is a controversial issue.*

A label does not tell a teacher which methods to use with individual students. For example, few specific "treatments" automatically follow from a "diagnosis" of a behaviour disorder; many different teaching strategies and materials are appropriate. Furthermore, labels can become self-fulfilling prophecies. Everyone—teachers, parents, classmates, and even the students themselves—may see a label as a stigma that cannot be changed. Finally, labels are mistaken for explanations, as is evident in this line of thinking: "Chris gets into fights because he has a behaviour disorder." "How do you know he has a behaviour disorder?" "Because he gets into fights."

On the other hand, some educators argue that applying a label protects the child. For example, if classmates know that a student has a disability, they will be more willing to accept his or her behaviour. Labels still provide access to some special programs, useful information, special technology and equipment, or financial assistance. In truth, labels probably both stigmatize *and* help students.

**Exceptional students** Students who have unusually high abilities in particular areas or disabilities that impact learning and may require special education or other services.

**LABELS MAY PROMOTE FALSE STEREOTYPES** When labels take precedence over individual characteristics, the labels themselves constitute a handicap. Stereotypes about people who use wheelchairs might interfere with recognition of this young girl's other characteristics and her individuality.

Ted Foxx/Alamy

## Disabilities and Handicaps

A **disability** is just what the word implies—an inability to do something specific such as see or walk. A **handicap** is defined as a disadvantage in certain situations. Some disabilities lead to handicaps, but not in all contexts. For example, having a visual impairment is a handicap if you want to drive a car, but not when you are composing music or talking on the telephone. Stephen Hawking, the greatest living physicist, has Lou Gehrig's disease and no longer can walk or talk. He once said he is lucky that he became a theoretical physicist "because it is all in the mind. So my disability has not been a serious handicap." It is important that we do not create handicaps for people by the way we react to their disabilities. Some educators have suggested that we drop the word *handicap* altogether because the source of the word is demeaning. Handicap came from the phrase "cap-in-hand," used to describe people with disabilities who once were forced to beg just to survive (Hardman, Drew, & Egan, 2005).

We can think of all human characteristics as falling somewhere on a continuum. For instance, some people have very acute hearing while others are completely deaf. We all fall somewhere on that continuum, and our position on the continuum is likely to change over our lifetimes. As we age, for example, we are likely to experience changes in hearing, vision, and even some aspects of intellectual ability, as you will see later in this chapter.

When speaking about a person with a disability, it is important that we avoid the language of pity, as in "confined to a wheelchair" or "victim of AIDS." Wheelchairs are not confining. They allow people to get around. Using "victim of" or "suffering with" makes the person seem powerless. On their resources website, the United Spinal Association offers a free pdf booklet with many ideas about disability. Every teacher should read it. See Figure 4.1 for an example.

Another way of showing respect to individuals with disabilities is to use "person-first" language, discussed next.

**Disability** The inability to do something specific, such as walk or hear.

**Handicap** A disadvantage in a particular situation, sometimes caused by a disability.

## FIGURE 4.1

### DISABILITY ETIQUETTE

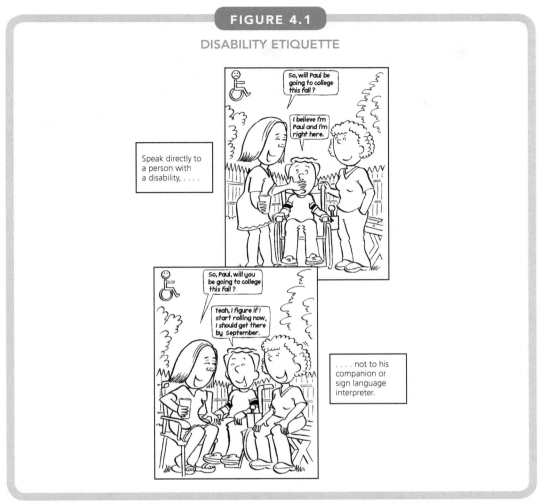

Source: Reprinted from "Disability Etiquette" © Permission granted by United Spinal Association. Go to www.unitedspinal.org for a free download of the full publication. Illustrations by Yvette Silver.

## People-First Language

Because everyone has a range of abilities, it makes sense to avoid using labels such as "emotionally disturbed student" or "at-risk student." Describing a complex person with one or two words implies that the condition labelled is the most important aspect of the person. Actually, the individual has many abilities, and to focus exclusively on the disability or high ability is to misrepresent the individual. An alternative is to use "people-first" language—to refer to "students with developmental disabilities" or "students placed at risk." Here the emphasis is on the students first.

| | | |
|---|---|---|
| Students with learning disabilities | NOT | Learning disabled students |
| Students receiving special education | NOT | Special education students |
| A person with epilepsy | NOT | An epileptic |
| A child with a physical disability | NOT | A crippled child |
| Children diagnosed with autism | NOT | Autistic children or autistics |

## Possible Biases in the Application of Labels

Even though there are many good tests and careful procedures for identifying students with disabilities and using labels properly, some racial and ethnic minority students are overrepresented in the disability categories and underrepresented in gifted programs.

What are likely causes of these over- and underrepresentations? Possible explanations include systematic biases in teachers' attitudes, curriculum, instruction, and the referral process itself; and teachers' lack of preparation for working effectively with ethnic minority students (Friend, 2011). To deal with the referral problem, educators have recommended gathering more information about a student before a formal referral is made. How long has the student been in the Canada? What about proficiency with English? Are there unusual stressors for the family? Does the curriculum build on the student's cultural knowledge (Chapter 5)? Is the classroom culturally compatible (Chapter 6) and engaging (Chapter 12)? Is the teacher knowledgeable about and respectful of the student's culture? Can the student's abilities be assessed using alternative approaches such as creativity tests and portfolios or performances (Chapter 15)? Considering a wide range of information about students and their circumstances should help teachers plan appropriately for their learning.

# INTELLIGENCE

Because the concept of intelligence is so important, so controversial, and so often misunderstood, we will spend quite a few pages discussing it. Let us begin with the basic question, "What does intelligence mean?"

## What Does Intelligence Mean?

STOP & THINK Who was the most intelligent person in your high school? Write down a name and the first four or five words that come to mind when you see that person in your mind's eye. What made you pick this individual? •

The idea that people vary in what we call **intelligence** has been with us for a long time. Plato discussed similar variations over 2000 years ago. Most early theories about the nature of intelligence involved one or more of the following three themes: (1) the capacity to learn; (2) the total knowledge a person has acquired; and (3) the ability to adapt successfully to new situations and to the environment in general. A recent definition captures these elements and stresses higher-order thinking: "the ability to reason deductively or inductively, think abstractly, use analogies, synthesize information, and apply it to new domains" (Kanazawa, 2010, p. 281).

INTELLIGENCE: ONE ABILITY OR MANY?   There are moderate to high correlations among scores on all mental tests. This "is arguably both the best established and the most striking phenomenon in the psychological study of intelligence" (van der Maas, Dolan, Grasman, Wicherts, Huizenga, & Raijmakers, 2006, p. 855). Because of these persistent intercorrelations, some psychologists believe intelligence is a basic ability that affects performance on all cognitively oriented tasks, from solving mathematical problems to analyzing poetry to taking history essay examinations. What could explain these results? Charles Spearman (1927) suggested that mental energy, which he called $g$ or general intelligence, is used to perform any mental test. Spearman added that each test also requires some specific abilities as well, so ability to do any mental task is based on $g$ + task-specific abilities. Today, psychologists generally agree that we can mathematically compute a common factor ($g$) across cognitive tests, but this computed factor is simply an indication or measure of **general intelligence**; it is not general intelligence itself (Kanazawa, 2010). Just having an overall mathematical indicator of intelligence isn't much help in understanding specific human abilities, so the notion of $g$ does not have much explanatory power (Blair, 2006).

Raymond Cattell and John Horn proposed a theory of fluid and crystallized intelligence that is more helpful in providing explanations of human abilities (Cattell, 1963, 1998; Horn, 1998). **Fluid intelligence** is the mental efficiency and reasoning ability included in Kanazawa's definition of intelligence, quoted above. The neurophysiological underpinnings of fluid intelligence may be related to changes in brain volume, myelinization (coating of neural fibres that makes processing faster), the density of dopamine receptors,

**Intelligence** Ability or abilities to acquire and use knowledge for solving problems and adapting to the world.

**General intelligence (g)** A general factor in cognitive ability that is related in varying degrees to performance on all mental tests.

**Fluid intelligence** Mental efficiency that is culture-free and nonverbal and is grounded in brain development.

or processing abilities in the prefrontal lobe of the brain, such as selective attention and working memory (Waterhouse, 2006), an aspect of brain functioning we will explore in Chapter 8. This aspect of intelligence increases until late adolescence (about age 22) because it is grounded in brain development, then declines gradually with age. Fluid intelligence is sensitive to injuries and diseases.

In contrast, **crystallized intelligence** is the ability to apply the problem-solving methods appropriate in your cultural context—the "application to new domains" part of Kanazawa's definition of intelligence. Crystallized intelligence can increase throughout the lifespan because it includes learned skills and knowledge such as reading, facts, and how to hail a cab, make a quilt, or design a unit on symbolism in poetry. By investing fluid intelligence in solving problems, we develop our crystallized intelligence, but many tasks in life, such as mathematical reasoning, draw on both fluid and crystallized intelligence (Ferrer & McArdle, 2004; Finkel, Reynolds, McArdle, Gatz, & Pederson, 2003; Hunt, 2000).

The most widely accepted view today is that intelligence, like self-concept, has many facets and is a hierarchy of abilities, with general ability positioned at the top and more specific abilities appearing at lower levels of the hierarchy (Carroll, 1997; Sternberg, 2000). John Carroll (1997) identifies one general ability, a few broad abilities (such as fluid and crystallized abilities, learning and memory, visual and auditory perception, and processing speed), and at least 70 specific abilities (such as language development, memory span, and simple reaction time). General ability may be related to the maturation and functioning of the frontal lobe of the brain, while specific abilities may be connected to other parts of the brain (Byrnes & Fox, 1998).

## Multiple Intelligences

While Howard Gardner was a developmental psychologist doing research with two very different groups—artistically gifted students at Harvard's Project Zero and patients with brain injuries at Boston's Veterans Administration Medical Center—he started thinking about a new theory of intelligence. Time and time again at the VA Medical Center, Gardner observed brain-injured patients who were lost spatially, but could do all kinds of verbal tasks, and other patients who had the opposite set of abilities and problems. He also worked with young children at Project Zero who could draw expertly but not craft a good sentence, and vice versa. Gardner concluded that there are several separate mental abilities, and developed his now-famous **theory of multiple intelligences**, which describes at least eight separate intelligences (1983, 2003, 2009).

WHAT ARE THESE INTELLIGENCES?    The eight intelligences in multiple intelligence (MI) theory are linguistic (verbal), musical, spatial, logical-mathematical, bodily-kinesthetic (movement), interpersonal (understanding others), intrapersonal (understanding self), and naturalist (observing and understanding natural and human-made patterns and systems). Gardner stresses that there may be more kinds of intelligence—eight is not a magic number. For example, he has speculated that there may be a spiritual intelligence and an existential intelligence, or the abilities to contemplate big questions about the meaning of life (Gardner, 2009). As Gardner witnessed first-hand in his early research with veterans and students, individuals may excel in one of these eight areas, but have no remarkable abilities, or may even have problems, in the other seven. Table 4.1 summarizes these eight intelligences.

Gardner believes that intelligence has a biological base. An intelligence is a "biopsychological potential to process information in certain ways in order to solve problems or create products that are valued in at least one culture or community" (Gardner, 2009, p. 5). Varying cultures and eras of history place different values on the eight intelligences. A naturalist intelligence is critical in farming cultures, whereas verbal and mathematical intelligences are important in technological cultures. In fact, Gardner suggests what industrialized cultures usually label as "intelligence" is just a combination of linguistic and logical mathematical skills, especially those taught in modern, secular schools (2009).

Crystallized intelligence Ability to apply culturally approved problem-solving methods.

Theory of multiple intelligences In Gardner's theory of intelligence, a person's eight separate abilities: linguistic, musical, spatial, logical-mathematical, bodily-kinesthetic, interpersonal, intrapersonal, and naturalist.

TABLE 4.1 • **Eight Intelligences**

Howard Gardner's theory of multiple intelligences suggests that there are eight kinds of human abilities. An individual might have strengths or weaknesses in one or several areas.

| INTELLIGENCE | END STATES | CORE COMPONENTS |
|---|---|---|
| Logical-mathematical | Scientist, Mathematician | Sensitivity to, and capacity to discern, logical or numerical patterns; ability to handle long chains of reasoning. |
| Linguistic | Poet, Journalist | Sensitivity to the sounds, rhythms, and meanings of words; sensitivity to the different functions of language. |
| Musical | Composer, Violinist | Abilities to produce and appreciate rhythm, pitch, and timbre; appreciation of the forms of musical expressiveness. |
| Spatial | Navigator, Sculptor | Capacities to perceive the visual-spatial world accurately and to perform transformations on one's initial perceptions. |
| Bodily-kinesthetic | Dancer, Athlete | Abilities to control one's body movements and to handle objects skillfully. |
| Interpersonal | Therapist, Salesman | Capacities to discern and respond appropriately to the moods, temperaments, motivations, and desires of other people. |
| Intrapersonal | Person with detailed, accurate self-knowledge | Access to one's own feelings and the ability to discriminate among them and draw on them to guide behaviour; knowledge of one's own strengths, weaknesses, desires, and intelligence. |
| Naturalist | Botanist, Farmer, Hunter | Abilities to recognize plants and animals, to make distinctions in the natural world, to understand systems and define categories (perhaps even categories of intelligence). |

*Source: From "Multiple Intelligences Go to School," by H. Gardner and T. Hatch, Educational Researcher, 18(8), p. 6. Copyright © 1989 by the American Educational Research Association. Reproduced by permission of the publisher. Also Educational Information and Transformation, edited by J. Kane. Published by Prentice Hall. Copyright © 2002 by Prentice Hall. Reprinted by permission of Pearson Education, Inc., Upper Saddle River, NJ.*

**EVALUATIONS OF MI THEORY.**  Gardner's MI theory has not received wide acceptance in the scientific community, even though many educators have embraced it. Lynn Waterhouse (2006) concluded that there have been no published studies that validate multiple intelligence theory. The eight intelligences are not independent; there are correlations among the abilities. In fact, logical-mathematical and spatial intelligences are highly correlated (Sattler, 2001). So, these "separate abilities" may not be so separate after all. Evidence linking musical and spatial abilities has prompted Gardner to consider that there may be connections among the intelligences (Gardner, 1998). In addition, some critics suggest that several intelligences are really talents (bodily-kinesthetic skill, musical ability) or personality traits (interpersonal ability). Other "intelligences" are not new at all. Many researchers have identified verbal and spatial abilities as elements of intelligence. Daniel Willingham (2004) has been even more blunt: "In the end, Gardner's theory is not that helpful. For scientists the theory is almost certainly incorrect. For educators, the daring applications forwarded by others in Gardner's name (and of which he disapproves) are unlikely to help students" (p. 24).

So there is not yet strong research evidence that adopting a multiple intelligences approach will enhance learning. In one of the few carefully designed evaluations, Callahan, Tomlinson, and Plucker (1997) found no significant gains in either achievement or self-concept for students who participated in START, a multiple intelligences approach to identifying and promoting talent in students who were at risk of failing.

**GARDNER RESPONDS.**   In response to these criticisms, defenders of MI theory say that the critics have a very narrow view of intelligence and research about intelligence. Gardner based his theory on a set of criteria that integrated a wide range of research in psychology:

- Potential isolation by brain damage
- The existence of prodigies and other exceptional individuals who are experts in some areas and average or below in others
- An identifiable core operation or set of operations
- A distinctive developmental trajectory, culminating in expert performances
- An evolutionary history and evolutionary plausibility
- Support from experimental psychological tasks
- Evidence from psychometric findings
- Susceptibility to encoding in a symbol system (Gardner, 2009, p. 5)

Supporters of the MI theory believe that newer research methods that look at dynamic models and study intelligence in cultural contexts will support it (Chen, 2004; Gardner & Moran, 2006). In addition, Gardner (2003, 2009) has responded to critics by identifying a number of myths and misconceptions about multiple intelligences theory and schooling. For example, he stresses that an intelligence is not the same as a sensory system—there is no "auditory intelligence" or "visual intelligence." Also, intelligences are not the same as learning styles. (Gardner doesn't believe that people actually have consistent learning styles.) Another misconception is that multiple intelligences theory disproves the idea of general intelligence. Gardner does not deny the existence of a general ability, but does question how useful general intelligence is as an explanation for human achievements. Stay tuned for more developments.

**MULTIPLE INTELLIGENCES GO TO SCHOOL.**   First let's consider a few misuses of MI theory in schools. Gardner particularly deplored an educational project in Australia that proclaimed different ethnic groups had certain specific intelligences but lacked others. Gardner went on television in Australia to call this program what it really was— "pseudoscience" and "veiled racism" (2009, p. 7). The project was cancelled. Some teachers embrace a simplistic version of Gardner's theory. They include every "intelligence" in every lesson, no matter how inappropriate.

A better way to use the theory is to focus on six entry points—narrative, logical-quantitative, aesthetic, experiential, interpersonal, and existential/foundational—in designing a curriculum (Gardner, 1991). For example, to teach about evolution, teachers might use the entry points as follows (Kornhaber, Fierros, & Veenema, 2004):

**Narrative:** Provide rich stories about Darwin's voyage to the Galapagos Islands or traditional folktales about the different plants and animals.
**Logical-quantitative:** Examine Darwin's attempts to map the distributions of the species or pose logical problems about what would happen to the ecosystem if one species disappeared.
**Aesthetic:** Examine Darwin's drawings of the species he studied on the Galapagos Islands.
**Experiential:** Do laboratory activities such as breeding fruit flies or completing virtual simulations of evolutionary processes.
**Interpersonal:** Form research teams or hold debates.
**Existential/foundational:** Consider questions about why species die out or the purpose for variation in species.

## Multiple Intelligences: Lessons for Teachers

After 20 years of work on his multiple intelligences theory, Gardner believes two lessons are most important for teachers (2009). First, teachers should take the individual differences among students seriously and differentiate their instruction to connect with each student. Much of this text will help you do just that. Second, any discipline, skill,

**Watch**
Multiple Intelligences:
Lessons for Teachers

Jim Cummins/Getty Images

**WHAT'S SMART?** There has been considerable controversy over the meaning of intelligence, whether there is more than one way to be "smart," and how we should measure intelligence.

or concept should be taught in several appropriate ways (but not eight ways every time). Anything worth knowing has different representations and multiple connections to various ways of thinking. And understandings can be expressed in words, images, movements, tables, charts, numbers, equations, poetry, and on and on. These two big ideas should *guide* educational interventions, but Gardner stresses that his theory is not itself an educational intervention. The MI theory expands our thinking about abilities and avenues for teaching, but learning is still hard work, even if there are multiple paths to knowledge.

## Intelligence as a Process

As you can see, the theories of Spearman, Cattell and Horn, Carroll, and Gardner tend to describe how individuals differ in the *content* of intelligence—the different abilities. Work in cognitive psychology has emphasized instead the *information processing* that is common to all people. How do humans gather and use information to solve problems and behave intelligently? New views of intelligence are growing out of this work. For example, the debates in the 2006 issue of *Behavioral and Brain Sciences* emphasized working memory capacity, the abilities to focus attention and inhibit impulses, and emotional self-regulation as aspects of fluid cognitive abilities.

Robert Sternberg's (1985, 2004; Stemler, Sternberg, Grigorenko, Jarvin, & Sharpes, 2009) **triarchic theory of intelligence** is a cognitive process approach to understanding intelligence. Sternberg uses the term *successful intelligence* to stress that intelligence is more than what is tested by mental abilities measures: Intelligence is about life success based on your own definition of success in your cultural context.

Sternberg believes the processes involved in intelligence are universal for humans. These processes are defined in terms of components—elementary information processes that are classified by the functions they serve and by how general they are. There are at least three different functions served. The first function—higher-order planning, strategy selection, and monitoring—is performed by *metacomponents* (sometimes called *executive processes*; see Chapter 8). A second function—implementing the strategies selected—is handled by *performance components*, such as taking notes to focus attention in class. The third function—gaining new knowledge—is performed by *knowledge-acquisition components*, such as separating relevant from irrelevant information as you try to understand a new concept. Some processes are specific; that is, they are necessary for only one kind of task, such as solving analogies. Other processes, such as monitoring progress and switching strategies, are very general and may be necessary in almost every cognitive task. This may help to explain the persistent correlations among all types of mental tests. People who are effective in selecting good problem-solving strategies, monitoring progress, and moving to a new approach when the first one fails are more likely to be successful on all types of tests.

Applying *metacomponents*, *performance components*, and *knowledge-acquisition components* allows individuals to solve problems in different situations and to develop three kinds of successful intelligence: analytic, creative, and practical. *Analytic intelligence* involves applying these components to situations with relatively familiar problems. *Creative intelligence* is necessary to cope successfully with new experiences in two ways: (1) using **insight**, or the ability to deal effectively with novel situations and find new solutions, and (2) using **automaticity**, the ability to become efficient and automatic in thinking and problem solving—the ability to quickly make the new solutions part of your cognitive toolkit, so to speak.

The third part of the triarchic theory, *practical intelligence*, highlights the importance of choosing an environment in which you can succeed, adapting to that environment, and

**Triarchic theory of intelligence** A three-part description of the mental abilities (thinking processes, coping with new experiences, and adapting to context) that lead to more or less intelligent behaviour.

**Insight** Sudden realization of a solution; the ability to deal effectively with novel situations.

**Automaticity** The result of learning to perform a behaviour or thinking process so thoroughly that the performance is automatic and does not require effort. Sometimes refers to excitement or stress.

reshaping it if necessary. People who are successful often seek situations in which their abilities will be valued, then work hard to capitalize on those abilities and compensate for any weaknesses. Thus, intelligence in this third sense involves practical matters such as career choice or social skills. In a field study in Voronezh, Russia, Elena Grigorenko and Robert Sternberg (2001) found that adults with higher practical and analytical intelligence coped better both mentally and physically with the stresses caused by rapid changes in that part of the world.

In recent years, Sternberg has added the concept of "wisdom" to his explanation of successful intelligence to create the *WICS theory* (Wisdom, Intelligence, Creativity Synthesized). According to WICS theory, the goal of education is to help citizens use "(a) creativity to generate new ideas and problems as well as possible solutions to the problems, (b) analytical intelligence to evaluate the quality of these solutions, (c) practical intelligence to implement decisions and persuade others of their value, and (d) wisdom to ensure that these decisions help achieve a common good over the long and short terms" (Grigorenko, Jarvin, Diffley, Goodyear, Shanahan, & Sternberg, 2009, p. 965).

Even though there are many theories of intelligence, teachers, students, and parents are most familiar with intelligence as a number or score on an IQ test.

## Measuring Intelligence

STOP & THINK How are a centimetre and a kilometre alike? What does *obstreperous* mean? Repeat these numbers backwards: 8 5 7 3 0 2 1 9 7. In what two ways is a lamp better than a candle? •

These items, adapted from Sattler (2001, p. 222), are similar to the verbal questions from a common individual intelligence test for children. Another part of the test asks the child to tell what is missing in a picture, put pictures in order to tell a story, copy a design using blocks, assemble part of a puzzle, complete mazes, and copy symbols. Even though psychologists do not agree on what intelligence is, they do agree that the intelligence measured in standard tests is related to learning in school. Why is this so? It has to do in part with the way intelligence tests were first developed.

BINET'S DILEMMA.   In 1904, Alfred Binet was confronted with the following problem by the minister of public instruction in Paris: How can students who will need special teaching and extra help be identified early in their school careers, before they fail in regular classes? Binet was also a political activist, very concerned with the rights of children. He believed that having an objective measure of learning ability could protect students from poor families who might be forced to leave school because they were the victims of discrimination and assumed to be slow learners.

Binet and his collaborator Theophile Simon wanted to measure not merely school achievement but the intellectual skills that students needed to do well in school. After trying many different tests and eliminating items that did not allow discrimination between successful and unsuccessful students, Binet and Simon finally identified 58 tests, several for each age group from 3 to 13. Binet's tests allowed the examiner to determine a **mental age** of a child. A child who succeeded on the items passed by most 6-year-olds, for example, was considered to have a mental age of 6, whether the child was actually 4, 6, or 8 years of age.

The concept of **intelligence quotient**, or **IQ**, was added after Binet's test was brought to North America and revised at Stanford University to give us the Stanford-Binet test. An IQ score was computed by comparing the mental-age score with the person's actual chronological age. The formula was as follows:

$$\text{Intelligence quotient} = \text{Mental age}/\text{Chronological age} \times 100$$

The first Stanford-Binet test, which was published in 1916, has been revised four times, most recently in 2003 (Roid, 2003). The practice of computing a mental age has been problematic because IQ scores calculated on the basis of mental age do not have the

**Mental age** In intelligence testing, a score based on average abilities for that age group.

**Intelligence quotient (IQ)** Score comparing mental and chronological ages.

same meaning as children get older. To cope with this problem, the concept of deviation IQ was introduced. The **deviation IQ** score is a number that tells exactly how much above or below the average a person scored on the test, compared with others in the same age group, as you will see in the next section.

WHAT DOES AN IQ SCORE MEAN?   Most intelligence tests are designed so that they have certain statistical characteristics. For example, the average score is 100; 50% of the people from the general population who take the tests will score 100 or above, and 50% will score below 100. About 68% of the general population will earn IQ scores between 85 and 115. Only about 16% will receive scores below 85, and only 16% will score above 115. Note, however, that these figures hold true for white, native-born Canadian children (assuming the use of Canadian versions of tests) whose first language is English. Whether IQ tests should even be used with ethnic and linguistic minority-group students is hotly debated.

GROUP VERSUS INDIVIDUAL IQ TESTS.   The Stanford-Binet test is an individual intelligence test. It has to be administered to one student at a time by a trained psychologist and takes about two hours to complete. Most of the questions are asked orally and do not require reading or writing. A student usually pays closer attention and is more motivated to do well when working directly with an adult. The *Guidelines* will help you to interpret students' IQ scores realistically.

Psychologists also have developed group tests that can be given to whole classes or schools. Compared with an individual test, a group test is much less likely to yield an accurate picture of any one person's abilities. When students take tests in a group, they may do poorly because they do not understand the instructions or have trouble reading,

**Deviation IQ**  Score based on statistical comparison of individuals' performance with the average performance of others in that age group.

## GUIDELINES

## Interpreting IQ Scores

**Check to see if the score is based on an individual or a group test. Be wary of group test scores.**
*Examples*

1.  Individual tests include the Wechsler Scales (WPPSI, WISC-III, WAIS-R), the Stanford-Binet, the McCarthy Scales of Children's Abilities, the Woodcock-Johnson Psycho-Educational Battery, and the Kaufman Assessment Battery for Children.

2.  Group tests include the Otis-Lennon School Abilities Tests, Slosson Intelligence Test, Raven Progressive Matrices, Naglieri Nonverbal Ability Test—Multiform, Differential Abilities Scales, and Wide Range Intelligence Test.

**Remember that IQ tests are only estimates of general aptitude for learning.**
*Examples*

1.  Ignore small differences in scores among students.

2.  Bear in mind that even an individual student's scores may change over time for many reasons, including measurement error.

3.  Be aware that a total score is usually an average of scores on several kinds of questions. A score in the middle or average range may mean that the student performed at the average on every kind of question or that the student did quite well in

some areas (for example, on verbal tasks) and rather poorly in other areas (for example, on quantitative tasks).

**Remember that IQ scores reflect a student's past experiences and learning.**
*Examples*

1.  Consider these scores as predictors of school abilities, not measures of innate intellectual abilities.

2.  If a student is doing well in your class, do not change your opinion or lower your expectations just because one score seems low.

3.  Be wary of IQ scores for ethnic-minority students and for students whose first language is not English. Even scores on "culture-free" tests are lower for students who are disadvantaged or "at risk" in some respect.

4.  Check to see if Canadian versions of the tests are used. Use caution when interpreting a student's scores acquired on American tests and normed for American students.

5.  Remember that both adaptive skills and scores on IQ tests are used to determine intellectual abilities and disabilities.

*For more information about interpreting IQ scores, see http://wilderdom. com/intelligence/IQUnderstandingInterpreting.html.*

because their pencils break or because other students distract them, or because they do not shine on paper-and-pencil tests (Sattler, 2001). As a teacher, you should be wary of IQ scores based on group tests.

THE FLYNN EFFECT: ARE WE GETTING SMARTER?   Ever since IQ tests were introduced in the early 1900s, scores in 20 different industrialized countries and in some more traditional cultures have been rising (Daley, Whaley, Sigman, Espinosa, & Neumann, 2003). In fact, in a generation, the average score goes up about 18 points on standardized IQ tests—maybe you really are smarter than your parents! This is called the **Flynn effect** after James Flynn, a political scientist who documented the phenomenon. Some explanations include better nutrition and medical care for children and parents, increasing complexity in the environment that stimulates thinking, the preponderance of smaller families who give more attention to their children, increased literacy of parents, more and better schooling, and better preparation for taking tests. One result of the Flynn effect is that the norms used to determine scores (you will read more about norms in Chapter 15) must be continually revised. In other words, to keep a score of 100 as the average, the test questions have to be made more difficult. This increasing difficulty has implications for any program that uses IQ scores as part of the entrance requirements. For example, some "average" students of the previous generation now might be identified as having intellectual disabilities because the test questions are harder (Kanaya, Scullin, & Ceci, 2003).

INTELLIGENCE AND ACHIEVEMENT.   Scoring higher on IQ tests is related to school achievement for children in all ethnic groups. But standard IQ tests measure only analytic IQ, not practical or creative IQs. Elena Grigorenko and her colleagues (2009) used the usual standardized test scores and GPA to predict middle-school students' achievement in high school, but also included tests of students' abilities to manage their own learning and motivation, along with measures of practical and creative intelligence. Using this broader picture of students' abilities, the researchers were able to make better predictions, not only of achievement in high school but also of the rate of growth. So IQ test scores can provide some prediction of achievement, but if measures of self-regulated learning skills, practical intelligence, and creativity are included, more accurate predictions are likely.

What about life after school? Do people who score high on IQ tests achieve more in life? Here the answer is less clear because life success and education are intertwined. On average, high school graduates earn more in their lifetime than nongraduates; college and university graduates and those with professional degrees earn even more (Cheeseman Day & Newurger, 2002). People with higher intelligence test scores tend to complete more years of school and to have higher-status jobs. However, when the number of years of education is held constant, the correlation decreases between IQ scores and income and success in later life. Just as Grigorenko and colleagues (2009) found, other factors such as motivation, social skills, and luck may make the difference (Goleman, 1995; Neisser et al., 1996; Sternberg & Wagner, 1993).

## Sex Differences in Intelligence

From infancy through the preschool years, most studies find few differences between boys and girls in overall mental and motor development or in specific abilities. During the school years and beyond, psychologists find no differences in general intelligence on the standard measures—these tests have been designed and standardized to minimize sex differences. However, scores on some tests of specific abilities show sex differences. The scores of males tend to be more variable in general, so there are more males than females with very high *and* very low scores on tests (Halpern, Benbow, Geary, Gur, Hyde, & Gernsbacher, 2007; Lindberg, Hyde, Peterson, & Linn, 2010). In addition, there are more boys diagnosed with learning disabilities, attention-deficit/hyperactivity disorder (ADHD), and autism. Diane Halpern and her colleagues (2007) summarize the research in the passage below:

> By the end of grade school and beyond, females perform better on assessments of verbal abilities when assessments are heavily weighted with writing and the language-usage items cover topics with which females are familiar; sex differences favoring females are much larger in these conditions than when assessments of verbal abilities do not

**Flynn effect** A steady rise in IQ test scores because of better health, smaller families, increased complexity in the environment, and more and better schooling.

including writing. In contrast, males excel on certain visuospatial-ability measures. Yet, of all the sex differences in cognitive abilities, differences in quantitative abilities have received the most attention because of the marked differences favoring males at the highest end of the ability distribution and because of their importance in so many occupations (p. 40).

There is a note of caution, however. In most studies of sex differences, race and socioeconomic status are not taken into account. For example, when ethnic groups are studied separately, there may be very small differences in mathematics performance favouring white males in high school and university, but slight differences favouring females among ethnic minority students. Also, there seem to be small differences in complex problem-solving skills favouring boys in high school, perhaps because problem solving is taught more in physics classes than in math, and boys are more likely than girls to take physics—another reason to encourage all students to get a good background in science (Lindberg, Hyde, Peterson, & Linn, 2010).

Several recent international *meta-analyses* (analyses that combine data from many different studies on the same topic) have found few differences in mathematics achievement for boys and girls. For example, Sara Lindberg and her colleagues analyzed data from 242 studies that included 1.3 million elementary through high school students. Overall, they found that, in the United States and some other nations, girls' and boys' performance in mathematics is comparable, but there are some differences across nations. Girls scored higher than boys in several countries such as Russia, Bahrain, and Mexico, and boys' scores were higher in other countries such as Switzerland, the Netherlands, and African nations (Else-Quest, Hyde, & Linn, 2010; Lindberg, Hyde, Peterson, & Linn, 2010). Also, the International Comparisons in Fourth-Grade Reading Literacy (Mullis, Martin, Gonzalez, & Kennedy, 2003) revealed that in 34 countries, grade 4 boys scored below girls in reading literacy. Finally, girls in general tend to get higher grades than boys in mathematics classes.

Males on average are better on tests that require mental rotation of a figure in space, prediction of the trajectories of moving objects, and navigating. Some researchers argue that evolution has favoured these skills in males (Buss, 1995; Geary, 1995, 1999), but others relate these skills to males' more active play styles, their greater experience with video games, and their participation in athletics (Else-Quest, Hyde, & Linn, 2010; Stumpf, 1995). Some educational psychologists believe that spatial skills are neglected in school curriculums and that even a small amount of instruction can make a big difference for students (Uttal, Hand, & Newcombe, 2009). The cross-cultural comparisons suggest that much of the difference in mathematics scores comes from learning, not biology. And studies showing that adults rated a math paper attributed to "John T. McKay" a full point higher on a five-point scale than the same paper attributed to "Joan T. McKay" suggests that discrimination and stereotyped expectations play a role as well (Angier & Chang, 2005).

Lindberg and her colleagues sum it up well: "Overall, it is clear that in the United States and some other nations, girls have reached parity with boys in mathematics performance. It is crucial that this information be made widely known to counteract stereotypes about female math inferiority held by gatekeepers such as parents and teachers and by students themselves" (2010, p. 1134). We agree that combating these stereotypes is critical. Melanie Steffens and her colleagues (2010) in Germany found that by age 9, girls already had developed implicit (out of awareness) math-gender stereotypes; the girls associated men with mathematics. These implicit beliefs grew stronger into adolescence, predicted girls' achievement in math, and affected their decisions to take elective math courses.

**HEREDITY OR ENVIRONMENT?**   Nowhere, perhaps, has the nature versus nurture debate raged so hard as in the area of intelligence. Should intelligence be seen as a potential, limited by our genetic makeup? Or does intelligence simply refer to an individual's current level of intellectual functioning, as influenced by experience and education?

Beware of either/or comparisons: It is impossible to separate intelligence "in the genes" from intelligence "due to experience." Today, most psychologists believe that differences in intelligence are due to both heredity and environment, probably in about equal proportions for children (Petrill & Wilkerson, 2000). And environmental influences include everything from the health of a child's mother during pregnancy to the amount of lead in the child's home to the quality of teaching a child receives. For example, Japanese and Chinese students know much more mathematics than North American students do, but their intelligence test scores are quite similar. This superiority in math is probably related to differences in the way mathematics is taught and studied in these countries and to the self-motivation skills of many Asian students (Baron, 1998; Stevenson & Stigler, 1992).

BEING SMART ABOUT IQ TESTS.    We saw that intelligence tests originally were developed, in part, to protect the rights of children from poorer families who might be denied an education on the false grounds that they weren't able to learn. We also saw that intelligence tests predict school success equally accurately for students of different races and income levels. Even so, these tests can never be free of cultural content, so they always will have some biases built in. Keep this in mind when you see your students' scores on any test. Finally, remember that the results of every assessment for every student should be used to support that student's learning and development and to identify effective practices, not to deny the student access to resources or appropriate teaching. For all adults caring for children—parents, teachers, administrators, counsellors, medical workers—it is especially important to realize that cognitive skills, like any other skills, are always improvable. *Intelligence is a current state of affairs, affected by past experiences and open to future changes.*

Now that you have a sense of what intelligence means, let's consider another kind of individual difference that often is misused and misunderstood in education—learning styles.

# LEARNING AND THINKING STYLES

For many years researchers have examined individual differences in "styles"—cognitive styles, learning styles, problem-solving styles, thinking styles, decision-making styles . . . the list goes on. Li-fang Zhang and Robert Sternberg (2005) organized the work on individual styles into three traditions. *Cognitive-centred* styles assess ways people process information, for example by being reflective or impulsive in responding (Kagan, 1976). *Personality-centred* styles assess more stable personality traits such as being extroverted versus introverted or relying on thinking versus feeling (Myers & McCaulley, 1988). *Activity-centred* styles assess a combination of cognition and personality that affects how people approach activities, so these styles may be of special interest to teachers.

One theme in activity-centred approaches is the differences between surface and deep approaches to processing information in learning situations (Snow, Corno, & Jackson, 1996). Students who take a surface-processing approach focus on memorizing the learning materials, not understanding them. These students tend to be motivated by rewards, grades, external standards, and the desire to be evaluated positively by others. Individuals who adopt the deep-processing approach see the learning activities as a means for understanding some underlying concepts or meanings. These students tend to learn for the sake of learning and are less concerned about how their performance is evaluated. Of course, the situation can encourage deep or surface processing, but there is evidence that individuals have tendencies to approach learning situations in characteristic ways (Biggs, 2001; Coffield, Moseley, Hall, & Ecclestone, 2004; Pintrich & Schrauben, 1992; Tait & Entwistle, 1998).

## Learning Styles and Preferences

You may have heard about **learning styles** or used the phrase yourself. Learning style usually is defined as the way a person approaches learning and studying. But beware—some conceptions of learning style have little research support; others are based on solid studies. First, the cautions.

CAUTIONS ABOUT LEARNING STYLES.    Since the late 1970s, a great deal has been written about differences in students' learning styles (Dunn & Dunn, 1978, 1987; Dunn & Griggs, 2003; Gregorc, 1982; Keefe, 1982). But we believe **learning preferences** is a more

**Learning styles** The way a person approaches learning and studying.

**Learning preferences** Preferred ways of studying and learning, such as using pictures instead of text, working with other people versus alone, learning in structured or in unstructured situations, and so on.

accurate label because most of this work describes preferences for particular learning environments. For example, where, when, with whom, or with what lighting, food, or music do you like to study? There are a number of instruments for assessing students' learning preferences—The Learning Style Inventory (Dunn, Dunn, & Price, 1989), Learning Styles Inventory (Revised) (Kolb and Kolb 2005), and the Learning Style Profile (Keefe & Monk, 1986).

Are these useful tools? Tests of learning style have been strongly criticized (Pashler, McDaniel, Rohrer, & Bjork, 2009). In fact, in an extensive examination of learning styles instruments, researchers at the Learning Skills Research Centre in England concluded, "with regard to work by Dunn and Dunn, Gregorc, and Riding, our examination of the reliability and validity of their learning style instruments strongly suggests that they should not be used in education or business" (Coffield, Moseley, Hall, & Ecclestone, 2004, p. 127). Most researchers are skeptical about the value of learning preferences. "The reason researchers roll their eyes at learning styles research is the utter failure to find that assessing children's learning styles and matching to instructional methods has any effect on their learning" (Stahl, 2002, p. 99). In fact, an experimental study had college students self-assess their learning style as auditory, visual, or kinesthetic and then taught the students in keeping with their professed style (Kratzig & Arbuthnott, 2006). Matching learning with teaching styles did not improve learning. When the researchers examined how people identified their own learning styles, they concluded that people's judgments represented preferences rather than superior skills in using auditory, visual, or kinesthetic modalities. If university students have trouble identifying their own learning style, think about grade 4 or 9 students!

In summary, the most recent review of learning styles research ends with these words: "The contrast between the enormous popularity of the learning-styles approach within education and the lack of credible evidence for its utility is, in our opinion, striking and disturbing. If classification of students' learning styles has practical utility, it remains to be demonstrated" (Pashler, McDaniel, Rohrer, & Bjork, 2009, p. 117).

So why are these ideas so popular? Part of the answer is that many thriving commercial companies are making large profits by providing advice to teachers, tutors, and managers about learning styles based on "inflated claims and sweeping conclusions which go beyond the current knowledge base" (Coffield, Moseley, Hall, & Ecclestone, 2004, p. 127). Money talks.

THE VALUE OF CONSIDERING LEARNING STYLES.    There is one learning styles distinction that has research support. Richard Mayer (e.g., Mayer & Massa, 2003) has been studying the distinction between visual and verbal learners, with a focus on learning from computer-based multimedia. Here, the assessment of learning styles is carefully done and more valid than assessments based on many of the commercial inventories. Mayer is finding that there is a visualizer–verbalizer dimension and that it has three facets: *cognitive spatial ability* (low or high), *cognitive style* (visualizer versus verbalizer), and *learning preference* (visual learner versus verbal learner), as shown in Table 4.2. So the picture is more complex than simply being a visual or a verbal learner. A student might have a preference for learning with pictures, but low spatial ability could make using pictures for learning less effective. To complicate matters even more, spatial abilities may be important for learning from static pictures, but less important for learning from animation—so the type of learning materials matters too (Hoeffler & Leutner, 2011). These differences can be reliably measured, but research has not identified the effects of teaching to these styles; certainly, presenting information in multiple modalities might be useful.

So before you try to accommodate all your students' learning styles, remember that students, especially younger ones, may not be the best judges of how they should learn. Preference for a particular style does not guarantee that using the style will be effective. Sometimes students, particularly poorer students, prefer what is easy and comfortable; real learning can be hard and uncomfortable. In some cases, students prefer to learn in a certain way because they have no alternatives; it is the only way they know how to approach the task. These students may benefit from developing new—and perhaps more effective—ways to learn. Learning styles probably are a minor factor in learning; factors such as teaching strategies and social connections in classrooms likely play much larger roles (Kratzig & Arbuthnott, 2006).

TABLE 4.2 • **Three Facets of the Visualizer-Verbalizer Dimension**

There are three dimensions to visual versus verbal learning: ability, style, and preference.
Individuals can be high or low on any or all of these dimensions.

| FACET | TYPES OF LEARNERS | DEFINITION |
|---|---|---|
| Cognitive ability | High spatial ability | Good abilities to create, remember, and manipulate images and spatial information |
| | Low spatial ability | Poor abilities to create, remember, and manipulate images and spatial information |
| Cognitive style | Visualizer | Thinks using images and visual information |
| | Verbalizer | Thinks using words and verbal information |
| Learning preference | Visual learner | Prefers instruction using pictures |
| | Verbal learner | Prefers instruction using words |

*Source: From R. E. Mayer & L. J. Massa (2003). "Three Facets of Visual and Verbal Learners: Cognitive Ability, Cognitive Style and Learning Preference."* Journal of Educational Psychology, 95(4), p. 838.

## Beyond Either/Or

Even though much of the work on matching learning styles and preferences to teaching is suspect, with unreliable measures and inflated claims, there is some value in thinking about learning styles. First, by helping students think about how they learn, you can develop thoughtful self-monitoring and self-awareness. In upcoming chapters, we will look at the value of such self-knowledge for learning and motivation. Second, looking at individual students' approaches to learning might help teachers appreciate, accept, and accommodate student differences and differentiate instruction (Coffield, Moseley, Hall, & Ecclestone, 2004; Rosenfeld & Rosenfeld, 2004).

Schools can make available learning options, such as having quiet, private corners as well as large tables for working; comfortable cushions as well as straight chairs; brightly lighted desks along with darker areas; headphones for listening to music as well as earplugs; structured as well as open-ended assignments; and information available from visuals, podcasts, and DVDs as well as books. Will making these alterations lead to greater learning? Here the answer is not clear. Very bright students appear to need less structure and to prefer quiet, solitary learning (Torrance, 1986) and the visual–verbal distinction seems to be valid. If nothing else, some accommodation of student preferences may make your classroom more inviting and student-friendly and communicate to your students that you care about them as individuals.

So far, we have focused on variability in students' abilities and learning preferences apart from specific exceptionalities. For the rest of the chapter, we will consider the needs of students whose high abilities and disabilities create particular challenges for teaching and learning.

## STUDENTS WHO ARE GIFTED AND TALENTED

Consider the following situation, a true story.

> Latoya was already an advanced reader when she entered 1st grade in a large urban school district. Her teacher noticed the challenging chapter books Latoya brought to school and read with little effort. After administering a reading assessment, the school's reading consultant confirmed that Latoya was reading at the 5th grade level. Latoya's parents reported with pride that she had started to read independently when she was 3 years old and "had read every book she could get her hands on" (Reis, Kaplan, Tomlinson, Westberg, Callahan, & Cooper, 2002).

In her struggling urban school, Latoya received no particular accommodations, and by grade 5, she was still reading at just above the grade 5 level. Her grade 5 teacher had no idea that Latoya had ever been an advanced reader.

Here is another true story:

> Alex Wade's field is linguistics. In his search for the perfect language—and "annoyed," he says, with Esperanto—he has created 10 languages and 30 or 40 alphabets, including one language without verbs, just for the challenge. He's taking courses at the University of Nevada, Reno, in Basque, linguistics, and microbiology (because he also has a talent for science).... Alex is 13 (Kronholz, 2011).

Latoya and Alex are not alone. They are members in a group of students with special needs that is often overlooked by the schools: students with gifts and talents. In the past, providing an enriched education for exceptionally bright or talented students was seen as undemocratic and elitist. Now there is a growing recognition that **gifted students** are being poorly served in most public schools. In 1996, Lupart and Pyryt at the University of Calgary estimated that, in a sample of 373 students they identified as having gifts and talents, 21% were underachieving in school. Because Lupart and Pyryt applied a very narrow definition of giftedness (referring to intellectual/academic talent), they claim that their estimate was fairly low. A more accurate estimate, according to these researchers, would be somewhere between 40 and 50%. Current research about this issue is hard to find, but experts believe the situation has not changed (M. Porath, personal communication, August 31, 2010).

## Who Are These Students?

There are many definitions of the term *gifted* because individuals can have many different gifts. Remember that Gardner (2003) identified eight separate kinds of "intelligences," and that Sternberg (1997) suggested a triarchic model. Renzulli and Reis (2003) also propose a three-part conception of giftedness: above-average general ability, a high level of creativity, and a high level of task commitment or motivation to achieve. In general, scholars emphasize that gifts and talents are often located in specific domains (i.e., individuals typically are not advanced in all areas). Reflecting this view, the *No Child Left Behind Act* in the United States characterizes students as gifted when they "give evidence of high achievement capability in areas such as intellectual, creative, artistic, or leadership capacity, or in specific academic fields, and who need services or activities not ordinarily provided by the school in order to fully develop those capabilities" (p. 544). Similarly, provincial ministries of education in Canada typically attend to definitions of high abilities or giftedness. However, some operational definitions of giftedness make additional distinctions based on measured IQ. For example, the Center for Gifted Education at the College of William and Mary makes the following distinctions: Gifted learners score above 130 on IQ tests, the highly gifted score above 145, the exceptionally gifted above 160, and the profoundly gifted above 175 (Kronholz, 2011).

Children who are truly gifted are not the students who simply learn quickly with little effort. The work of gifted students is original, extremely advanced for their age, and potentially of lasting importance. These children may read fluently with little instruction by the age of 3 or 4. They may play a musical instrument as would a skilful adult, turn a visit to the grocery store into a mathematical puzzle, and become fascinated with algebra when their friends are having trouble carrying in addition (Winner, 2000). Recent conceptions widen the view of giftedness to include attention to the children's culture, language, and other exceptionalities (Association for the Gifted, 2001). These newer conceptions of giftedness are more likely to identify children like Latoya and Alex.

What do we know about these remarkable individuals? A classic study of the characteristics of individuals with gifts was started decades ago by Lewis Terman and colleagues (1925, 1947, 1959; Holahan & Sears, 1995). This huge project has followed the lives of 1528 gifted males and females and continued until the year 2010. The subjects all have IQ scores in the top 1% of the population (140 or above on the Stanford-Binet individual test of intelligence). They were identified on the basis of these test scores and teacher recommendations.

**Gifted student** A very bright, creative, and talented student.

Terman and colleagues found that these children were larger, stronger, and healthier than the norm. Often, they began walking sooner and were more athletic. They were more emotionally stable than their peers and became better-adjusted adults than the average. They had lower rates of delinquency, emotional difficulty, divorce, drug problems, and so on. Of course, the teachers in Terman's study who made the nominations may have selected students who were better adjusted initially. And remember, Terman's study describes academically gifted students only. There are many other kinds of gifts.

**WHAT IS THE ORIGIN OF THESE GIFTS?** Studies of prodigies and geniuses in many fields document that deep and prolonged practice is necessary to achieve at the highest levels. For example, it took Newton 20 years to move from his first ideas to his ultimate contribution (Howe, Davidson, & Sloboda, 1998; Winner, 2000). We remember the early reports of Bloom's study of world-class concert pianists, sculptors, Olympic swimmers, research neurologists, mathematicians, and tennis champions (1982). To study talent in tennis, Bloom's research team had interviewed the top tennis players in the world, and their coaches, parents, siblings, and friends. One coach said that he would make a suggestion, and a few days later the young athlete would have mastered the move. Then the parents told how the child had practised that move for hours on end after getting the coach's tip. So, focused, intense practice plays a role. Also, the families of prodigies tend to be child-centred and to devote hours to supporting the development of their child's gifts. Bloom's research team described tremendous sacrifices made by families: rising before dawn to drive their child to a swimming coach or piano teacher in another city, working two jobs, or even moving the whole family to another part of the country to find the best teachers or coaches. The children responded to the family's sacrifices by working harder, and the families responded to the child's hard work by sacrificing more—an upward spiral of investment and achievement.

**ORIGINS OF GIFTEDNESS** For years, researchers have debated the nature versus nurture question about people with extraordinary abilities and talents. Studies of prodigies and geniuses in many fields document that deep and prolonged practice is necessary to achieve at the highest levels.

Toby Wales/Lebrecht Music & Arts

But hard work won't make each of us a world-class tennis player or a Newton. There is a role for nature as well. The children studied by Bloom showed early and clear talent in the areas they later developed. As children, great sculptors were constantly drawing and mathematicians were fascinated with dials, gears, and gauges. Parents' investments in their children came after the children showed early high-level achievement (Winner, 2000, 2003). Research suggests that gifted children, at least those with extraordinary abilities in mathematics, music, and visual arts, may have unusual brain organization—which can have both advantages and disadvantages. Giftedness in mathematics, music, and visual arts appears to be associated with superior visual-spatial abilities and enhanced development of the right side of the brain. Children with these gifts are also more likely not to have right-hand dominance—they may have left-hand dominance or mixed dominance. Also, this group is more likely to have language-related problems. These brain differences are evidence that "gifted children, child prodigies, and savants are not made from scratch but are born with unusual brains that enable rapid learning in a particular domain" (Winner, 2000, p. 160).

**WHAT PROBLEMS DO THE GIFTED FACE?** In spite of Bloom's and Terman's findings, it would be incorrect to say that every student with gifts and talents is superior in adjustment and emotional health. In fact, gifted adolescents, especially girls, are more likely to be depressed, and both girls and boys may be bored, frustrated, and isolated. Schoolmates may be consumed with baseball or worried about failing math, while the gifted child is fascinated with Mozart, focused on a social issue, or totally absorbed in computers, drama, or geology. Children who are gifted may also be impatient with friends, parents, and even teachers who do not share their interests or abilities (Woolfolk & Perry, 2015). Kronholz (2011) asked 13 000 gifted students to name one word for their experiences. The word they used most commonly was "waiting"—"Waiting for teachers to move ahead, waiting for classmates to catch up, waiting to learn something new—always waiting" (Kronholz, 2011, p. 3).

If their language is highly developed, students who are gifted may be seen as show-offs when they are simply expressing themselves. If they are highly sensitive to expectations and feelings of others, these students may be very vulnerable to criticisms and taunts. Because they are goal-directed and focused, these students may seem stubborn and uncooperative. Also, their keen sense of humour can be used as a weapon against teachers and other students. Adjustment problems seem to be greatest for children with the greatest gifts—those in the highest range of academic ability (i.e., above 180 IQ) (Hardman, Drew, & Egan, 2005; Robinson & Clinkenbeard, 1998). The chance of any teacher encountering a student in this highest IQ range is only about 1 in 80 over an entire 40-year career—but what if such a student walks into your class (Kronholz, 2011)?

## Identifying and Teaching Students Who Are Gifted

Identifying gifted children is not always easy, and teaching them well may be even more challenging. Many parents provide early educational experiences for their children. Children with these advantages can appear advanced relative to their peers when they enter elementary school, but this doesn't guarantee they will continue to be exceptional years later. In middle and high school, some very able students deliberately earn lower grades, making their abilities even harder to recognize. Girls are especially likely to hide their abilities (Lupart & Barva, 1998; Woolfolk & Perry, 2015).

RECOGNIZING STUDENTS' SPECIAL ABILITIES.   Marilyn Friend (2011) suggests asking the following questions to guide identification of children with gifts and talents:

- Who can easily manipulate abstract symbol systems such as mathematics?
- Who can concentrate for long periods of time on personal interests?
- Who remembers easily?
- Who developed language and reading early (as did Latoya, described at the beginning of this section)?
- Who is curious and has many interests?
- Whose work is original and creative?

Certainly Alex's interests and creativity in inventing languages, described earlier, fit these last two critieria. Students who are gifted may also prefer to work alone, have a keen sense of justice and fairness, be energetic and intense, form strong commitments to friends—often older students—and struggle with perfectionism.

Group achievement and intelligence tests tend to underestimate the IQs of very bright children. Group tests may be appropriate for screening, but they are not appropriate for making decisions about instruction. There is some evidence that using individual IQ tests such as the WISC-IV, which include evaluations of verbal comprehension and working memory, are the best predictors of achievement in reading and math for gifted students (Rowe, Kingsley, & Thompson, 2010). Many psychologists recommend a case study approach to identifying students with gifts and talents. This means gathering many kinds of information, including test scores, grades, examples of work, projects and portfolios, letters or ratings from teachers, self-ratings, and so on (Renzulli & Reis, 2003). Especially for recognizing artistic talent, experts in the field can be called in to judge the merits of a child's creations. Science projects, exhibitions, performances, auditions, and interviews are all possibilities. Creativity tests and assessments of self-regulation may identify some children not picked up by other measures, particularly students from minority groups who may be at a disadvantage on the other types of tests (Grigorenko, Jarvin, Diffley, Goodyear, Shanahan, & Sternberg, 2009). Remember, students with remarkable abilities in one area may have much less impressive abilities in others. In fact, some

TABLE 4.3 • **Recognizing and Supporting All Students with Gifts and Talents**

**Recognizing Gifted Students with Learning Disabilities.** Here are some ideas for supporting gifted students with learning disabilities (McCoach, Kehle, Bray, & Siegle, 2001):

- Identify these students by looking longitudinally at achievement.
- Remediate skill deficits, but also identify and develop talents and strengths.
- Provide emotional support; it is important for all students, but especially for this group.
- Help students learn to compensate directly for their learning problems, and assist them in "tuning in" to their own strengths and difficulties.

**Recognizing Gifts in Girls.** As young girls develop their identities in adolescence, they often reject being labelled as gifted—being accepted and popular and "fitting in" may become more important than achievement (Basow & Rubin, 1999; Stormont, Stebbins, & Holliday, 2001). How can teachers reach girls who are gifted?

- Notice when girls' test scores seem to decline in middle or high school.
- Encourage assertiveness, achievement, high goals, and demanding work from all students.
- Provide models of achievement through speakers, internships, or readings.
- Look for and support gifts in arenas other than academic achievement.

**Recognizing Gifted Students Who Live in Poverty.** Health problems, lack of resources, homelessness, fears about safety and survival, frequent moves, and responsibilities for the care of other family members all make achievement in school more difficult. To identify students with gifts:

- Use alternative assessment, teacher nomination, and creativity tests.
- Be sensitive to cultural differences in values about cooperative or solitary achievement (Ford, 2000).
- Use multicultural strategies to encourage both achievement and the development of racial identities.

students with gifts and talents also have learning disabilities. Their learning disabilities can mask their high abilities. Other groups who are underrepresented in gifted education programs include girls, children and youth who live in poverty, and children from some minority groups (Stormont, Stebbins, & Holliday, 2001). See Table 4.3 for ideas about identifying and supporting these students.

TEACHING GIFTED STUDENTS.    Some educators believe that students who are gifted should be *accelerated*—moved quickly through the grades or through particular subjects. Other educators prefer *enrichment*—giving the students additional, more sophisticated, and more thought-provoking work, but keeping them with their age group in school. Actually, both may be appropriate (Torrance, 1986). One way of doing this is through *curriculum compacting*. This strategy involves assessing students' knowledge of the material in an instructional unit, then teaching only for those goals not yet reached (Reis & Renzulli, 2004). Using curriculum compacting, teachers may be able to eliminate about half of the usual curriculum content for some gifted students without any loss of learning. The time saved can be used for learning goals that include enrichment, sophistication, and novelty (Werts, Culatta, & Tompkins, 2007).

**Acceleration.**  Many people object to acceleration, but most careful studies indicate that students who are truly gifted and who begin elementary school, junior high school, high school, college or university, or even graduate school early do as well as, and usually better than, other students who are progressing at the normal pace. Social and emotional adjustment does not appear to be impaired. Students who are gifted tend to prefer the company of older playmates and may be miserably bored if kept with children of their own age (Davis, Rimm, & Siegle, 2011).

An alternative to skipping grades is to accelerate students in one or two particular subjects but keep them with peers for most classes (Robinson & Clinkenbeard, 1998). However, for students who are extremely advanced intellectually (for example, those scoring 160 or higher on an individual intelligence test), the only practical solution may be to accelerate their education (Davis, Rimm, & Siegle, 2011; Kronholz, 2011).

**Methods and Strategies.** Teaching methods for students who are gifted should encourage abstract thinking (formal operational thought), creativity, and independence, not just the learning of greater quantities of facts. One approach that does *not* seem promising with gifted students is cooperative learning in mixed ability groups. Gifted students tend to learn more when they work in groups with other high-ability peers (Fuchs, Fuchs, Hamlett, & Karns, 1998; Robinson & Clinkenbeard, 1998). In fact, students in gifted programs appear to be less bored when they are ability grouped with others like themselves. An interesting tradeoff for gifted students is that their academic self-concepts tend to decrease when they are grouped with other high-ability students—an example of the "Little-Fish-in-a-Big-Pond" effect described in Chapter 3 (Preckel, Goetz, & Frenzel, 2010).

In working with students who are gifted and talented, teachers must be imaginative, flexible, and unthreatened by the capabilities of these students. The teacher must ask the following questions: What does this child need most? What is she ready to learn? Who can help me to challenge her? Challenge and support are critical for all students. But challenging students who know more than anyone else in the school about history or music or science or math can be a challenge! Answers might come from faculty members at nearby colleges and universities, retired professionals, books, museums, the internet, or older students. Strategies might be as simple as letting the child do math with the next grade. Other options include summer institutes; courses at nearby colleges and universities; classes with local artists, musicians, or dancers; independent research projects; selected classes in high school for younger students; honours classes; and special-interest clubs (Rosenberg, Westling, & McLeskey, 2011).

In the midst of providing challenge, don't forget the support. We have all seen the ugly sights of parents, coaches, or teachers forcing the joy out of talented children by demanding practice and perfection beyond the child's interest. Just as we should not force children to stop investing in their talent ("Oh, Michelangelo, quit fooling around with those sketches and go outside and play"), we should also avoid destroying intrinsic motivation with heavy doses of pressure and external rewards.

# Students With Learning Challenges

Most provinces and territories have adopted inclusive policies that place students with disabilities in neighbourhood schools within general education classrooms. As a result of these policies, you will have children from all of these categories in your classes.

Before we look at some of the specific learning challenges children face, let's review research that links brain functions to learning difficulties. With all of the new technology, the amount of research in this area has grown exponentially.

## Neuroscience and Learning Challenges

One of the early explanations for learning disabilities was minimal brain dysfunction. We now know that there are many other factors involved in the learning challenges children face, but certainly injuries or diseases of the brain can lead to disabilities in language, mathematics, attention, or behaviour.

Studies of the brains of students with learning disabilities and with attention deficit disorders show some differences in structure and activity compared to those of students without these problems. For example, people with attention disorders may have some areas of the brain that are smaller. The flow of blood appears to be less than is typical in the cerebellum and frontal lobes, and the levels of electrical activity are different in certain brain areas compared to people without attention deficits (Barkley, 2006). Elementary school students with specific language disabilities appear to have immature auditory systems—their brains process basic auditory information in a way similar to the brains of children 3 to 4 years younger (Goswami, 2004). The implications of these brain differences for instruction are still being worked out. It is difficult to determine exactly which came first, the learning problems or the brain differences (Friend, 2011).

Recently, a lot of attention has been given to the role of executive functions—referring to a set of supervisory, or self-regulatory, processes that support learners to engage in independent, goal-directed behaviour (Sesma, Mahone, Levine, Eason, & Cutting, 2009). At the most basic level, executive functions include attention, inhibition, cognitive flexibility, and working-memory. Higher-order functions include planning, monitoring, and problem-solving. Executive functions are linked to self-control and self-regulation, which are stronger predictors of children's success in school than are traditional measures of IQ (Diamond & Lee, 2011). These functions are needed when you are required to concentrate and then solve a problem, or when you control an impulse to act in a way that is inappropriate. Problems with executive functions are considered central to many learning challenges children and youth face, including learning disabilities, attention-deficit/hyperactivity disorder, and developmental disabilities (Meltzer, 2007).

Quite a bit of research on learning problems has focused on working memory (discussed in Chapter 8), partly because working memory capacity is a good predictor of a range of cognitive skills, including language understanding, reading and mathematics abilities, and fluid intelligence (Bayliss, Jarrold, Baddeley, Gunn, & Leigh, 2005). In addition, some studies indicate that children who have learning disabilities in reading and mathematics problem solving have considerable difficulties with working memory (Siegel, 2003; Swanson & Saez, 2003). Specifically, some research shows that children with learning disabilities have problems using the system of working memory that holds verbal and auditory information while you work with it. Because children with learning disabilities have trouble holding on to words and sounds, it is difficult for them to put the words together to comprehend the meaning of a sentence or to figure out what a math story problem is really asking about.

An even more serious problem may be difficulties retrieving needed information from long-term memory, so it is hard for these children to simultaneously hold on to information (such as the result from the first two figures multiplied in an algebra problem) while they have to transform new incoming information (such as the next numbers to add). Important bits of information keep getting lost. Finally, children with learning disabilities in mathematics and problem solving seem to have problems holding visual–spatial information, such as number lines or quantity comparisons, in working memory, so creating mental representations of "less than" and "greater than" problems is challenging (D'Amico & Guarnera, 2005).

More than half of all students receiving some kind of special education services in Canada are diagnosed as having learning disabilities. This is by far the largest category of students with disabilities.

## Students With Learning Disabilities

How do you explain what is wrong with a student who struggles to read, write, spell, or learn math, even though she is not developmentally delayed, emotionally disturbed, or educationally deprived and has normal vision, hearing, and language capabilities? The student likely has a **learning disability**. There is no fully agreed upon definition of *learning disability* (Fletcher, 2012), and there are slight differences in emphasis in the definitions used across Canada (Hutchinson, 2013). Many scholars believe that, in practice, too much emphasis is given to the discrepancy between students' IQ, as measured by an intelligence test, and their achievement in school. They would like to see equal, if not greater, emphasis placed on the psychological processing problems these students experience (e.g., phonological processing problems, memory problems, problems with number sense). Linda Siegel at the University of British Columbia has written extensively about this topic (1989, 1999). Most educational psychologists suggest that there are both physiological and environmental bases for learning disabilities, such as brain injury, exposure to toxins before birth by mothers who smoked or drank while pregnant, poor nutrition, lead-based paint in the home, or even poor instruction (Smith, 2004). Genetics plays a role as well. If parents have a learning disability, their children have a 30%–50% chance of having a learning disability, too (Friend, 2011).

The official definition of learning disabilities, adopted by the Learning Disabilities Association of Canada on January 30, 2002, emphasizes processing problems as the

**Learning disability** Problem with acquisition and use of language; may show up as difficulty with reading, writing, reasoning, or math.

primary characteristic of students with learning disabilities. See the excerpt below, taken from the association's website:

> "Learning Disabilities" refer to a number of disorders which may affect the acquisition, organization, retention, understanding or use of verbal or nonverbal information. These disorders affect learning in individuals who otherwise demonstrate at least average abilities essential for thinking and/or reasoning. As such, learning disabilities are distinct from global intellectual deficiency.

Learning disabilities result from impairments in one or more processes related to perceiving, thinking, remembering, or learning. These include, but are not limited to, language processing, phonological processing, visual–spatial processing, processing speed, memory and attention, and executive functions (e.g., planning, decision-making).

Learning disabilities range in severity and may interfere with the acquisition and use of one or more of the following:

- oral language (e.g., listening, speaking, understanding)
- reading (e.g., decoding, phonetic knowledge, word recognition, comprehension)
- written language (e.g., spelling, written expression)
- mathematics (e.g., computation, problem solving)

Learning disabilities may also involve difficulties with organizational skills, social perception, social interaction, and perspective taking.

Learning disabilities are lifelong. The way in which they are expressed may vary over an individual's lifetime, depending on the interaction between the demands of the environment and the individual's strengths and needs. Learning disabilities are suggested by unexpected academic underachievement or achievement, which is maintained only by unusually high levels of effort and support.

Learning disabilities are due to genetic and/or neurobiological factors or injury that alters brain functioning in a manner that affects one or more processes related to learning. These disorders are not due primarily to hearing and/or vision problems, socioeconomic factors, cultural or linguistic differences, lack of motivation, or ineffective teaching, although these factors may further complicate the challenges faced by individuals with learning disabilities. Learning disabilities may co-exist with various conditions, including attentional, behavioural, and emotional disorders, and sensory impairments or other medical conditions.

For success, individuals with learning disabilities require early identification and timely specialized assessments and interventions involving home, school, community and workplace settings. The interventions need to be appropriate for each individual's learning disability subtype and, at a minimum, include the provision of:

- specific skill instruction;
- accommodations;
- compensatory strategies; and
- self-advocacy skills.

STUDENT CHARACTERISTICS.   Students with learning disabilities are not all alike. The most common characteristics are specific difficulties in one or more academic areas; poor coordination; problems paying attention; hyperactivity and impulsivity; problems organizing and interpreting visual and auditory information; disorders of thinking, memory, speech, and hearing; and difficulties making and keeping friends (Hallahan, Kauffman, & Pullen, 2009; Rosenberg, Westling, & McLeskey, 2011). Many students with other disabilities (such as ADHD) and many students without disabilities may have some of the same characteristics, which makes identification complicated. To complicate the situation even more, not all students with learning disabilities will have these problems, and few will have all of these problems.

Most students with learning disabilities have difficulties reading. Table 4.4 lists some of the most common problems, although these problems are not always signs of learning disabilities. For English-speaking students, these difficulties appear to be caused by problems with relating sounds to letters that make up words, making spelling hard as well (Lyon, Shaywitz, & Shaywitz, 2003; Willcutt et al., 2001). For Chinese speakers, reading

TABLE 4.4 • **Reading Problems of Students With Learning Disabilities**

Do any of your students show these signs? They could be indications of reading disabilities.

---

**Anxiety around reading**

- Reluctant to read
- Cries or acts out to avoid reading
- Seems tense when reading

**Difficulty recognizing words or letters**

- Inserts an incorrect word, substitutes or skips words
- Reverses letters or numbers—48 for 24, for example
- Mispronounces words—"cape" for "cope"
- Mixes up order of words in sentences: "I can bikes ride" for "I can ride bikes."
- Reads very slowly and with little fluency—starts and stops often

**Poor vocabulary skills**

- Can't read new vocabulary words
- Has limited vocabulary

**Difficulty with understanding or remembering what was read**

- Can't recall basic facts from the reading
- Can't make inferences or identify the main idea

---

*Source: Based on information from Smith, D. D., & Tyler, N. C. (2010). Introduction to Special Education: Making a Difference (7th ed.). Columbus, OH: Merrill; Helpguide.org. www.helpguide.org/mental/learning_disabilities.htm.*

disabilities seem to be related to *morphological awareness*, or the ability to combine morphemes into words. Morphemes are the smallest units of meaning that makes sense alone. For example, "books" has two morphemes: "*book*" and "*s*"—the "*s*" has meaning because it makes *book* plural. Recognizing units of meaning in Chinese characters is helpful in learning the language (Shu, McBride-Chang, Wu, & Liu, 2006).

Math, both in terms of computation and problem solving, is the second most common problem for students with learning disabilities. Children with math learning disabilities tend to have significant difficulties with tasks that involve number sense. Nancy Perry and her colleagues at the University of British Columbia (MacKinnon McQuarrie, Siegel, Perry, & Weinberg, 2012) observed that children with math disabilities achieved lower scores on a test of quantitative concepts than their typically achieving peers—they had more difficulty with tasks involving counting, sequencing, and estimating. Also, these children had more difficulty doing some working memory tasks. This is consistent with a large body of research indicating that working memory problems interfere with retrieval and consolidation of basic math facts; execution of algorithms for addition, subtraction, multiplication, and division; math problem-solving tasks; and counting-based procedures (Geary, 2004; Passolunghi & Siegel, 2004). Importantly, MacKinnon McQuarrie and colleagues (2012) provided physiological evidence (through measures of cortisol levels in the children's saliva) that high reactivity (anxiety) may exacerbate some of the difficulties students with learning disabilities experience. It is important to support students with learning challenges emotionally as well as academically.

The writing of some students with learning disabilities is virtually unreadable (as you can see in Figure 4.2), and their spoken language can be halting and disorganized. As well, students with learning disabilities often lack effective ways of approaching academic tasks. They don't know how to focus on the relevant information, get organized, apply learning strategies and study skills, change strategies when one isn't working, or evaluate their learning. They tend to be passive learners, in part because they don't know *how* to learn—they have failed so often. Working independently is especially trying, so homework and seatwork are often left incomplete (Hallahan, Lloyd, Kauffman, Weiss, & Martinez, 2005).

**TEACHING STUDENTS WITH LEARNING DISABILITIES.** Nancy Perry (see Perry, McNamara, & Mercer, 2001) has argued that early diagnosis is important in order that

**FIGURE 4.2**

WRITING SAMPLE FROM A STUDENT WITH LEARNING DISABILITIES

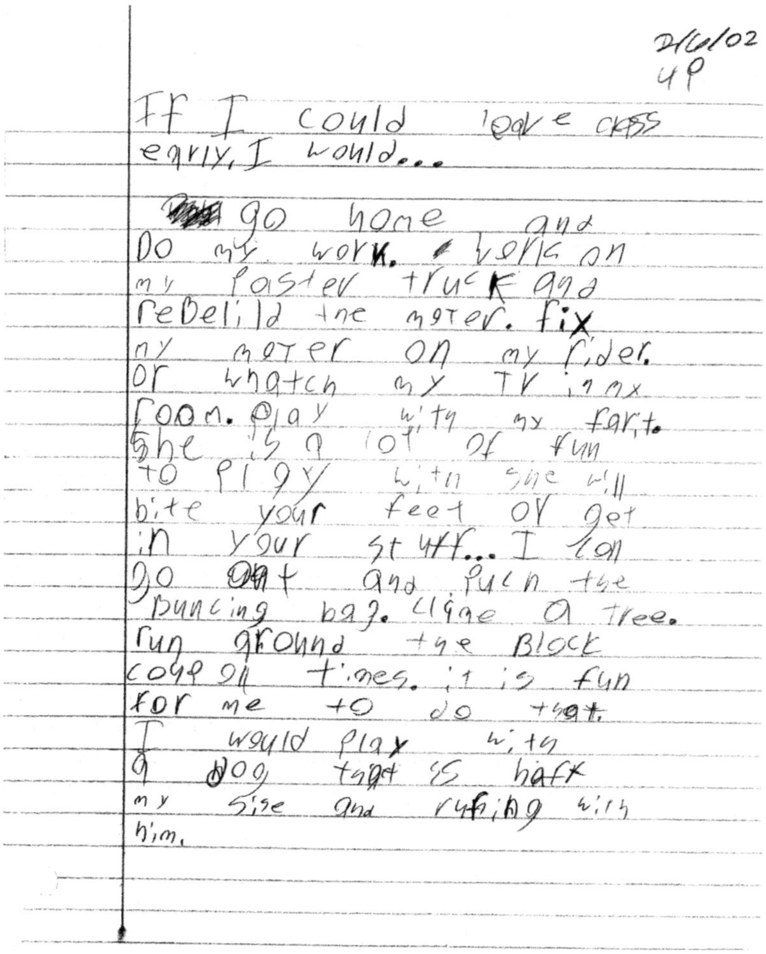

2/6/02
4P
If I could leave class
early, I would...
go home and
Do my work. work on
my faster truck and
rebelild the moter. fix
my moter on my rider.
or whatch my TV in my
room. play with my ferit.
She is a lot of fun
to play with she will
bite your feet or get
in your stuff... I can
go out and puch the
buncing bag. cline a tree.
run around the block
coupl of times. it is fun
for me to do that.
I would play with
a dog that is haft
my size and rufing with
him.

*Source: From Friend, M. (2008).* Special Education: Contemporary Perspectives for School Professionals, *2nd edition. Boston, MA: Allyn and Bacon, Boston. Adapted by permission of the publisher.*

students with learning disabilities get the remediation they need and do not become terribly frustrated and discouraged. It is also important to help students understand their disabilities. When students do not understand why they are having such trouble, they may become victims of **learned helplessness**. Students who experience learned helplessness believe that they cannot control or improve their own learning. This is a powerful belief. The students never exert the effort to discover that they can make a difference in their own learning, so they remain passive and helpless. This becomes a greater problem as students move through school and into life beyond. These students need to understand their disability and the accommodations they need in order to advocate for themselves.

Students with learning disabilities may try to compensate for their problems and develop bad learning habits in the process, or they may begin avoiding certain subjects out of fear of not being able to handle the work. Nancy Heath and her research team at McGill University study mental health in schools. Her early work (Heath, 1996; Heath & Ross, 2000) demonstrated that students with specific learning disabilities are at higher risk for social withdrawal and even depression than students in the general population. To support or prevent such mental health challenges, teachers must be sensitive to the emotional and motivational impact of students' academic difficulties. Refer students to the appropriate professionals in the school as soon as you recognize a reason for concern.

Learned helplessness The expectation, based on previous experiences involving lack of control, that all of one's efforts will lead to failure.

Two general approaches, preferably used together, have proved effective for students with learning disabilities (Friend, 2011). The first is *direct instruction*, described in Chapter 14. The basics of this approach are clear and involve explanations and demonstrations of new material, teaching in small steps with practice after each step, immediate feedback, and teacher guidance and support. The second general approach is *strategy instruction*, described in Chapter 9. Strategies are specific rules for focusing attention and accomplishing tasks, such as **TREE** for supporting elementary students' persuasive writing.

**T** opic sentence: Tell what you believe.
**R** easons: Tell three or more reasons why you believe this. Will your readers believe this?
**E** nding: Wrap it up!
**E** xamine: Check for all three parts.

These strategies have to be taught using good direct instruction—explanation, examples, and practice with feedback. See Chapters 9 and 14 for more details about these two approaches.

Some other general strategies for working with students with learning disabilities include keeping verbal instructions short and simple, having students repeat directions back to you to be sure they understand, giving multiple examples and repeating main points several times, and allowing more practice than usual, especially when the material is new. In addition, emphasizing study skills and methods for processing information in a given subject, such as reading or math, seems to be effective. Many of the principles of cognitive learning described in Chapters 8 and 9 can be applied to help students improve their attention, memory, and problem-solving abilities (Sawyer, Graham, & Harris, 1992). See, for example, Strategic Content Learning, developed by Deborah Butler at the University of British Columbia (Butler, 1998; Butler, Novak Lauscher, & Beckingham, 2005). Directly teach students self-monitoring strategies such as cueing students to ask, "Was I paying attention?" And teach students to use external memory strategies such as note-taking and devices such as assignment books, to-do lists, or electronic calendars (Hardman, Drew, & Egan, 2005). In every grade, connect new material to knowledge students already have.

You may be thinking that these are good ideas for many students who need more support and direct teaching of study skills. You are right.

## Students With Hyperactivity and Attention Disorders

**STOP & THINK** If a student is struggling with time management and organization issues, what kind of accommodations would you provide? •

You have probably heard and may even have used the term **hyperactivity**. The notion is a modern one; there were no hyperactive children 50 to 60 years ago. Today, if anything, the term is applied too often and too widely. Actually, hyperactivity is not one particular condition, but two kinds of problems that may or may not occur together—attention disorders and impulsive-hyperactivity problems.

**CHARACTERISTICS OF STUDENTS WITH HYPERACTIVITY AND ATTENTION DISORDERS.** Today, most psychologists agree that the main problem for children who are labelled hyperactive is directing and maintaining attention, not simply controlling their restlessness and physical activity. The American Psychiatric Association has established the diagnostic category of **attention-deficit/hyperactivity disorder (ADHD)** to identify children with this problem. APA defines ADHD as "a pervasive pattern of inattention, impulsivity and/or hyperactivity that is more frequent and severe than is typically observed in individuals at a comparable level of development" (American Psychiatric Association, *DSM-IV-TR*, 2000, p. 78). Some of the indicators listed in the *DSM-IV-TR* are

**Hyperactivity** Behaviour disorder marked by atypical, excessive restlessness and inattentiveness.

**Attention-deficit/hyperactivity disorder (ADHD)** Current term for disruptive behaviour disorders marked by overactivity, excessive difficulty sustaining attention, or impulsiveness.

**Watch**
ADHD

- **Inattention:** doesn't pay close attention to class activities, details of work, teacher directions, class discussions; can't organize work, notebooks, desk, assignments; easily distracted and forgetful
- **Hyperactivity:** fidgets and squirms; can't stay in assigned seat; can't move slowly, seems driven by a motor to go fast; talks excessively
- **Impulsivity:** Blurts out answers; has trouble waiting for a turn; interrupts

All children show some of these behaviours some of the time, but children with ADHD are likely to have some of these symptoms before age 7, the symptoms occur across many settings (not just school), and the symptoms lead to problems learning and getting along with others. ADHD usually is diagnosed in elementary school, but research suggests that problems with attention and hyperactivity may begin to show up as early as 3 years old (Friedman-Weieneth, Harvey, Youngswirth, & Goldstein, 2007). It is difficult to know how many children should be diagnosed with ADHD. The most common estimate is 3%–5% of the elementary school population in Canada (Hutchinson, 2013). More boys than girls are identified as hyperactive, but that gap appears to be narrowing. Girls have the same symptoms as boys, but tend to show the symptoms in less obvious ways, so they may not be identified as often and thus may miss getting appropriate support (Friend, 2011).

Just a few years ago, most psychologists thought that ADHD diminished as children entered adolescence, but now there is evidence that the problems can persist into adulthood for at least half of those with ADHD (Hirvikoski et al., 2011). Adolescence—with the increased stresses of puberty, transition to middle or high school, more demanding academic work, and more engrossing social relationships—can be an especially difficult time for students with ADHD (Taylor, 1998). When children diagnosed with ADHD become adults, about 30% have no more symptoms, 25% have persistent behavioural problems such as drug use or criminal behaviours, and around 25% develop major depression (Rosenberg, Westling, & McLeskey, 2011).

TREATMENT AND TEACHING STUDENTS WITH ADHD.   The most common intervention for students with ADHD is drug therapy. Ritalin and other prescribed drugs such as Adderall, Focalin, Dexedrine, and Cylert are stimulants, but in particular dosages, they tend to have paradoxical effects on many children with ADHD: Short-term effects include possible improvements in social behaviours such as cooperation, attention, and compliance. Research suggests that about 70%–80% of children with ADHD are more manageable when on medication. (Batschaw, 1997; Hutchinson, 2007). In general, students with ADHD who take stimulant medication engage in less stimulant-seeking behaviour and are more able to benefit from educational and social interventions (Hutchinson, 2007; Zentall, 1993).

The use of medication to treat ADHD is somewhat controversial. Mainly in the United States, and in the media, there are allegations that ADHD is over identified in the school-aged population and medications are being over prescribed. In their recent study of Canadian children and youth, Christine Brault and Eric Lacourse (2012) from the Université de Montréal concluded that the prevalence of prescribed medication and ADHD diagnosis in Canada is generally low. Of course, these drugs need to be carefully administered and their effects carefully monitored. Some children experience side effects such as loss of appetite or nausea, headaches, insomnia, and increased heart rate and blood pressure. For most children, these side effects are mild and can be controlled by adjusting the dosage. However, little is known about the long-term effects of drug therapy, so parents and teachers need to keep up with the research on treatments for ADHD. Table 4.5 lists some questions parents and teachers should ask about medication for children with ADHD.

ALTERNATIVES/ADDITIONS TO DRUG TREATMENTS.   While stimulant medications can improve the attention and behaviour of students with ADHD, in and of themselves they will not improve students' learning and achievement in school. For learning to occur, medication needs to be paired with other effective interventions. The methods that have proven most successful for helping students with ADHD are based on behavioural

TABLE 4.5 • **Questions for Teachers and Parents to Ask About Medication for Children With ADHD**

The most commonly prescribed medications for children and adolescents with ADHD are Ritalin (methylphenidate) and Dexedrine (dextroamphetamine). Parents and teachers should be well informed about these medications.

1. What is the medication? What information can I read about it?
2. Why is this medication prescribed for this adolescent? What changes should we expect to see at home? At school?
3. What behavioural program or behavioural therapy is being implemented in conjunction with this drug therapy?
4. How long will this medication be prescribed for this adolescent?
5. What are the side effects in the short term? In the long term?
6. What is the dosage? What is the schedule on which the medication will be taken?
7. How often will the adolescent be seen by the prescribing physician for re-evaluation?
8. Should the medication be stopped for a short period of time to see if it is still required? When?
9. Are there foods, beverages, or other substances that should not be consumed when one is taking this medication?
10. What kind of communication is necessary among home, school, and the adolescent to evaluate whether the medication is having the desired effect?
11. What procedures should be followed if the adolescent accidentally ingests an overdose?
12. Who explains all of this to the adolescent and what should the adolescent be told?

*Source: Hutchinson, N. L. (2004).* Teaching exceptional children and adolescents: A Canadian casebook. *Toronto: Prentice Hall. Reprinted by permission.*

principles of learning such as those described in Chapter 7. Gregory A. Fabiano and his colleagues (2009) identified 174 studies conducted between 1967 and 2006 that included almost 3000 participants in behavioural treatments for ADHD; all studies met rigorous standards of quality research. Behavioural treatments involve the application of methods derived from behavioural learning theories such as contingency management, time-out, shaping, self-regulation, and modelling. The researchers then compared treated with untreated groups or individuals before and after one or more different kinds of treatments. Their conclusion? Findings were clear and impressive. "Based on these results, there is strong and consistent evidence that behavioural treatments are effective for treating ADHD" (p. 129). In an interview, Gregory Fabiano said, "Our results suggest that efforts should be redirected from debating the effectiveness of behavioral interventions to dissemination, enhancing and improving the use of these programs in community, school and mental health settings." Researchers working with adults in Sweden also found that behavioural methods stressing a balance between accepting and changing ADHD symptoms and behaviours proved effective (Hirvikoski et al., 2011). Joe Lucyshyn (Cheremshynski, Lucyshyn, & Olson, 2013; Lucyshyn, Horner, Dunlap, Albin, & Ben, 2002) at the University of British Columbia is a proponent of positive behaviour support (PBS), which is linked to applied behaviour analysis. It helps families, educators, and psychologists identify and understand the full range of variables (e.g., personal, ecological) influencing problem behaviour. The goal of PBS is to foster more adaptive behaviour that supports learning.

The bottom line is that even if students in your class are on medication, it is critical that they also learn the academic and social skills they will need to succeed. The findings of one large study in Australia indicate what you might guess—we should attack the problem on all fronts:

> Multimodal approaches to intervention have been found to be most effective in terms of lasting change. For most, but not all children and adolescents, treatment with psycho-stimulants has beneficial effects, provided that it is accompanied by remedial tuition, counseling, and behavior management by parents/teachers, as required. Thus, advice from several different professions may be necessary. (van Kraayenoord, Rice, Carroll, Fritz, Dillon, & Hill, 2001, p. 7)

Even if students in your class are on medication, it is critical that they also learn the academic and social skills they will need to survive. Again, this will not happen by itself, even if behaviour improves with medication (Purdie, Hattie, & Carroll, 2002).

## Lessons for Teachers: Learning Disabilities and ADHD

Long assignments may overwhelm students with learning disabilities and attention deficits, so give them a few problems or paragraphs at a time with clear consequences for completion. Another promising approach combines instruction in learning and memory strategies with motivational training. The goal is to help students develop the "skill and will" to improve their achievement. They are also taught to monitor their own behaviour and encouraged to be persistent and to see themselves as "in control" (Pfiffner, Barkley, & DuPaul, 2006).

The notion of being in control is part of a therapy strategy for dealing with ADHD, one that stresses personal agency (Nylund, 2000). Rather than focusing on the child's problems, Nylund's idea is to enlist the child's strengths to conquer the child's problems—to put the child in control. New metaphors for the situation are developed. Rather than seeing the problems as inside the child, Nylund helps everyone see ADHD, trouble, boredom, and other enemies of learning as outside the child—demons to be conquered or unruly spirits to be enlisted in the service of what *the child* wants to accomplish. The focus is on solutions. The steps of Nylund's **SMART** approach are as follows (Nylund, 2000, p. xix):

**S** eparating the problem of ADHD from the child;
**M** apping the influence of ADHD on the child and family;
**A** ttending to the exceptions to the ADHD story;
**R** eclaiming special abilities of children diagnosed with ADHD; and
**T** elling and celebrating the new story.

As a teacher, you can look for times when the student is engaged—even short times. What is different about these times? Discover the student's strengths and allow yourself to be amazed by them. Make changes in your teaching that support the changes the student is trying to make. Nylund gives the following example. Nine-year-old Chris and his teacher, Ms. Baker, became partners in putting Chris in control of his concentration in school. Ms. Baker moved Chris's seat to the front of the room. The two designed a subtle signal to get Chris back on track, and Chris organized his messy desk. When Chris's concentration improved, Chris received an award at a party in his honour. Chris described how he was learning to listen in class: "You just have to have a strong mind and tell ADHD and Boredom not to bother you" (Nylund, 2000, p. 166). See Table 4.6 for suggestions that came from students working with Nylund, telling how their teachers can help them gain control.

TABLE 4.6 • **Students With ADHD Give Teachers Advice**

Students with ADHD make these recommendations for their teachers (Nylund, 2000).

- Use lots of pictures (visual clues) to help me learn.
- Recognize cultural and racial identity.
- Know when to bend the rules.
- Notice when I am doing well.
- Don't tell the other kids that I am taking Ritalin.
- Offer us choices.
- Don't just lecture—it's boring!
- Realize that I am intelligent.
- Let me walk around the classroom.
- Don't give tons of homework.
- More recess!
- Be patient.

## Students With Language and Communication Disorders

Language is a complex learned behaviour. Language disorders may arise from many sources, because so many different aspects of the individual are involved in learning language. A child with a hearing impairment may not learn to speak normally. Injuries can cause neurological problems that interfere with speech or language. Children who are not listened to, or whose perception of the world is distorted by emotional problems, will reflect these problems in their language development. Because speaking involves movements, any impairment of the motor functions involved with speech can cause language disorders. And because language development and thinking are so interwoven, any problems in cognitive functioning can affect ability to use language.

SPEECH IMPAIRMENTS.   Students who cannot produce sounds effectively for speaking are considered to have a **speech impairment**. About 5% of school-aged children have some form of speech impairment. Articulation problems and fluency disorders (stuttering) are the two most common problems.

**Articulation disorders** include distorting a sound like a lisp (*thumtimes* for *sometimes*), substituting one sound for another (*shairp* for *chair*), adding a sound (*chuch air* for *chair*), or omitting sounds (*chai* for *chair*) (Rosenberg, Westling, & McLeskey, 2011). Keep in mind, however, that most children are 6 to 8 years old before they can successfully pronounce all English sounds in normal conversation. The sounds of the consonants *l, r, y, s,* and *z* and the consonant blends *sh, ch, zh,* and *th* are the last to be mastered. Also, there are dialect differences based on geography that do not represent articulation problems. A student from Newfoundland might say *ideer* for *idea* but have no speech impairment.

**Stuttering** generally appears between the ages of 3 and 4. Causes of stuttering are unclear, but might include emotional or neurological problems or learned behaviour. If stuttering continues more than a year or so, the child should be referred to a speech therapist. Early intervention can make a big difference (Hardman, Drew, & Egan, 2005). When you are working with a student who stutters, speak to the child often, privately, and without hurrying, interrupting, or finishing the child's words and sentences. Pause often, especially after the child finishes speaking—communicate that it is okay to take time to think before you speak. Notice when the stuttering is more and less frequent. Avoid pressuring the child to speak quickly. In class discussions, call on her or him early in the discussion so tension won't build up, and ask a question that can be answered with few words. Speak frankly about the stuttering, but assure the student it is nothing to be ashamed of—many successful people, including kings, have shared the challenge and learned to improve (Friend, 2011; Rosenberg, Westling, & McLeskey, 2011).

**Voicing problems**, a third type of speech impairment, include speaking with an inappropriate pitch, quality, or loudness, or in a monotone. A student with any of these problems should be referred to a speech therapist. Recognizing the problem is the first step. Be alert for students whose pronunciation, loudness, voice quality, speech fluency, expressive range, or speaking rate is very different from that of their peers. Pay attention also to students who seldom speak. Are they simply shy, or do they have difficulties with language?

LANGUAGE DISORDERS.   Language differences are not necessarily language disorders. Students with language disorders are those who are markedly deficient in their ability to understand or express language, compared with other students of their own age and cultural group (Owens, 2012). Students who seldom speak, who use few words or very short sentences, or who rely only on gestures to communicate should be referred to a qualified school professional for observation or assessment. Table 4.7 gives ideas for how to promote language development in all students.

## Students With Emotional or Behavioural Disorders

Students with emotional and behavioural disorders can be among the most challenging to teach in general education classrooms, and are a source of concern for many prospective teachers (Avramidis, Bayliss, & Burden, 2000). About one-third of these students

**Speech impairment** Inability to produce sounds effectively for speaking.

**Articulation disorders** Any of a variety of pronunciation difficulties.

**Stuttering** Repetitions, prolongations, and hesitations that block flow of speech.

**Voicing problems** Speech impairments involving inappropriate pitch, quality, loudness, or intonation.

TABLE 4.7 • **Encouraging Language Development**

- Talk about things that interest children.
- Follow the children's lead. Reply to their initiations and comments. Share their excitement.
- Don't ask too many questions. If you must, use questions such as how *did/do...*, *why did/do...*, *and what happened...* that result in longer explanatory answers.
- Encourage children to ask questions. Respond openly and honestly. If you don't want to answer a question, say so and explain why. (*I don't think I want to answer that question; it's very personal.*)
- Use a pleasant tone of voice. You need not be a comedian, but you can be light and humorous. Children love it when adults are a little silly.
- Don't be judgmental or make fun of children's language. If you are overly critical of children's language or try to catch and correct all errors, they will stop talking to you.
- Allow enough time for children to respond.
- Treat children with courtesy by not interrupting when they are talking.
- Include children in family and classroom discussions. Encourage participation and listen to their ideas.
- Be accepting of children and of their language. Hugs and acceptance can go a long way.
- Provide opportunities for children to use language and to have that language work for them to accomplish their goals.

*Source: Adapted from information in Owens, R. E. Jr. (2010). Language Disorders: A Functional Approach to Assessment and Intervention, 5th edition. Published by Allyn and Bacon, Boston, MA. Copyright © 2010 by Pearson Education. Adapted by permission of the publisher.*

are arrested during their school years, and half are unemployed three to five years after leaving school (Rosenberg, Westling, & McLeskey, 2011), so early intervention is really important.

Professionals in education define **behaviour disorders** as behaviours that deviate so greatly from what is appropriate for the child's age group that it significantly interferes with the child's own growth and development and/or the lives of others. **Emotional disturbance** and behavioural disorders are actually umbrella terms that refer to a wide range of specific conditions, including anxiety and depressive disorders, conduct disorders, eating disorders, obsessive–compulsive disorders, and psychotic disorders (Center for Parent Information and Resources, 2014). Clearly, deviation implies a difference from some standard, and standards of behaviour differ from one situation, age group, culture, and historical period to another. Thus, what passes for team spirit in the football bleachers might be seen as disturbed behaviour in a bank or restaurant. In addition, a disorder is more than a temporary response to stressful events; the condition must be stable across time and in different situations. Table 4.8 describes a few of the specific disorders covered by the *Diagnostic and Statistical Manual of Mental Disorders* (4th edition, revised), also called the *DSM-IV-TR*, which is the guide professionals use to diagnose significant emotional and behavioural problems.

However they are defined, what you will observe as a teacher are students who are aggressive, anxious, withdrawn, or depressed and who often have difficulty following rules, paying attention, or interacting with others. One report estimates one in seven Canadian children/youth experience mental health disorders that significantly affect their lives at home, at school, and in the community at one time or another (Waddell, 2007). As with learning disabilities and ADHD, there are more boys than girls diagnosed with these disorders, and some ethnic and cultural groups are overrepresented in these categories (e.g., African American students in the United States, Aboriginal youth in Canada).

The range of possible emotional and behavioural disorders is wide. And students with other disabilities (e.g., learning disabilities, intellectual disabilities, ADHD) may also have emotional or behavioural problems. Often, these children are disliked by the other children, and even the adults, in their lives. They can be bullies, or they can be the ones being bullied. For children with behaviour problems, behaviour management approaches such as PBS (described earlier in this chapter) and those described in Chapter 7 often

**Emotional and behavioural disorders** Behaviours or emotions that deviate so much from the norm that they interfere with the child's own growth and development and/or the lives of others—inappropriate behaviours, unhappiness or depression, fears and anxieties, and trouble with relationships.

TABLE 4.8 ● **Examples of Emotional and Behavioural Disorders From the** *Diagnostic and Statistical Manual of Mental Disorders*

The medical community has identified many specific emotional and behavioural disorders, and these are included in the *Diagnostic and Statistical Manual of Mental Disorders* (fourth edition, text revision) (*DSM-IV-TR*). Instead of being called emotional and behaviour disorders, they are referred to as mental disorders. The following list, although not complete, includes examples of mental disorders listed in that publication that educators would consider emotional and behaviour disorders:

- **Anxiety disorders.** Anxiety disorders occur when students experience an overwhelming sense of fear or dread. One example is obsessive-compulsive disorder (OCD), in which students cannot stop themselves from worrying excessively about a specific concern—for example, germs. Other examples include phobias (fear of specific items, such as spiders, or fear of certain activities, such as going to school) and posttraumatic stress disorder (PTSD), in which students re-live in nightmares or flashbacks a traumatic event that they witnessed.

- **Disruptive behaviour disorders.** This category includes three types of disorders:
  - *Attention-deficit/hyperactivity disorder* is characterized by inattention, a high level of activity and impulsivity, or a combination of these. Note, though, that it often is not considered a disability.
  - *Oppositional defiant disorder* (ODD) is diagnosed when students are defiant with adults and vindictive or blaming with peers to an excessive degree over a long period of time.
  - *Conduct disorders* are diagnosed when students fight, bully, display cruelty to animals or people, or otherwise repeatedly break serious rules.

- **Eating disorders.** The most common eating disorder is anorexia nervosa, in which students believe they are overweight and refuse to eat, even when they are near starvation.

- **Mood disorders.** Also called *affective disorders*, this group includes depression and bipolar disorder, also called manic depression, in which students' moods swing from extreme highs (manic) to extreme lows (depression).

- **Tic disorders.** Tics are involuntary, rapid, stereotyped movements of specific muscle groups. Students with tics may blink their eyes or repeatedly sniff. The most well known tic disorder is Tourette syndrome, a disorder that ranges from mild to severe and includes both facial or other physical tics as well as vocal tics, often "barking" or profanity.

*Source: Adapted from Friend, M. (2008). Special Education: Contemporary Perspectives for School Professionals, 2nd edition. Published by Allyn and Bacon, Boston, MA. Copyright © 2008 by Pearson Education. Reprinted by permission of the publisher.*

are effective. Nancy Hutchinson (2013) at Queen's University recommends that students with emotional and behavioural disorders have the following supports in their classrooms to enhance their self-confidence, sense of responsibility and independence, and engagement in positive problem solving:

- structure, predictability, and consistency
- immediate, frequent, and specific feedback with consequences
- opportunities for academic success
- positive alternatives to current behaviours
- positive school-to-home support systems
- evidence that the student is making a change for the better

**Watch**
Students With Emotional or Behavioural Disorders

Early intervention and the classroom and school-wide initiatives described in Chapter 3 are also effective (Osher, Bear, Sprague, & Doyle, 2010; Sprague & Walker, 2000; Swearer, Espelage, Vaillancourt, & Hymel, 2010). Importantly, most students with behavioural problems need challenging and cognitively engaging work. According to Hutchinson (2013), we should not lower our expectations or excuse these students from learning. The future is not promising for those who never learn to control their behaviour and who also fail academically, so waiting for the students to "outgrow" their problems is seldom effective.

Children who are extremely anxious, withdrawn, shy, depressed, and hypersensitive, or who cry easily and have little confidence, may have an *anxiety disorder*. These children have few social skills and consequently very few friends. The most successful strategies for working with them appear to involve the direct teaching of social and emotional skills. **Social and emotional learning (SEL)** refers to the development of competencies for recognizing and managing emotions, developing care and concern for others, establishing positive relationships, making responsible decisions, and handling challenging situations effectively (Schonert-Reichl & Hymel, 2007). A number of evidence-based SEL programs are being implemented in school districts across Canada (e.g., search for Roots of Empathy or Mind Up on the internet). In Chapter 13, we will consider how to create a caring classroom community and help all students cope with social and emotional challenges that threaten both their own learning and the learning of others in the classroom.

Let's consider an area where teachers may be able to detect problems and make a difference—suicide.

SUICIDE.   Of course, not every student with emotional or behavioural problems will consider suicide, but depression often is associated with suicide. The Canadian Institutes of Health Research (CIHR, 2006) rates suicide as the second leading cause of death among youth aged 13–18, and for every youth who successfully dies by suicide there are another 200 who attempt to kill themselves. The rate of death by suicide is higher for boys than girls, but nonfatal, self-inflicted injuries are more common among girls. Some minority groups, including youth with disabilities and youth who are gay or lesbian (Galliher, Rostosky, & Hughes, 2004; Wilson, Armstrong, Furrie, & Walcot, 2009), are at higher risk for suicide than others. Suicide in Aboriginal youth populations is especially high compared with other groups. Health Canada (2014) estimates that the rates of suicide for First Nations youth are five to seven times that for non-Aboriginal youth, and rates of suicide for Inuit youth are among the highest in the world (11 times the national average).

There are several general risk factors, and they seem to apply to both boys and girls and across a number of ethnic groups: depression and substance abuse, history of suicide in the family, being under stress, tendency to be impulsive or perfectionistic, belief that a person goes to a better place after dying, and family rejection or conflict. Having more than one of these risk factors is especially dangerous (Friend, 2011; Steinberg, 2005).

Suicide is often regarded by youth as a response to life problems—problems that parents and teachers sometimes dismiss. There are many warning signs that trouble is brewing. Watch for changes in eating or sleeping habits, weight, grades, disposition, activity level, or interest in friends. Students at risk of suicide sometimes suddenly give away prized possessions such as cell phones, iPads, clothing, or pets. They may seem depressed or hyperactive and may say things like, "Nothing matters anymore," "You won't have to worry about me anymore," or "I wonder what dying is like." They may start missing school or quit doing work. The situation is especially dangerous if the student not only talks about suicide but also has a plan for carrying out a suicide attempt.

If you suspect that there is a problem, talk to the student directly. One feeling shared by many people who attempt suicide is that no one really takes them seriously. "A question about suicide does not provoke suicide. Indeed, teens (and adults) often experience relief when someone finally cares enough to ask" (Range, 1993, p. 145). Be realistic, not poetic, about suicide. Ask about specifics, and take the student seriously. Also, be aware that teenage suicides often occur in clusters. After one student acts or when stories about a suicide are reported in the media, other teens are more likely to copy the suicide (Lewinsohn, Rohde, & Seeley, 1994; Rice & Dolgin, 2002). Table 4.9 lists common myths and facts about suicide.

DRUG ABUSE.   Although drug abuse is not always associated with emotional or behavioural problems, and people without these challenges may abuse drugs, many adolescents with emotional problems also abuse drugs. Modern society makes growing up a very confusing process. Celebrities who are attractive and popular with youth drink alcohol, smoke cigarettes, and use drugs with seemingly little concern for their health. We have over-the-counter drugs for almost every common ailment. Coffee wakes us up, and a pill helps us sleep. And then we tell our youth to "say no" to drugs.

Social and emotional learning (SEL)  Refers to the development of competencies for recognizing and managing emotions, developing care and concern for others, establishing positive relationships, making responsible decisions, and handling challenging situations effectively.

TABLE 4.9 • **Myths and Facts About Suicide**

| Myth: | People who talk about suicide don't kill themselves; they are just trying to get attention. |
|---|---|
| Fact: | People who die by suicide usually talk about it first. They are in pain and oftentimes reach out for help because they do not know what to do and have lost hope. Always take talk about suicide seriously. Always. |
| Myth: | Only certain types of people commit suicide. |
| Fact: | All types of people commit suicide—male and female, young and old, rich and poor, country people and city people. It happens in every racial, ethnic, and religious group. |
| Myth: | You should never ask people who are suicidal if they are thinking about suicide or if they have thought about a method, because just talking about it will give them the idea. |
| Fact: | Asking people if they are thinking about suicide does not give them the idea for suicide. And it is important to talk about suicide with people who are suicidal because you will learn more about their mindset and intentions, and allow them to diffuse some of the tension that is causing their suicidal feelings. |
| Myth: | Most people who kill themselves really want to die. |
| Fact: | The vast majority of people who are suicidal do not want to die. They are in pain, and they want to stop the pain. Suicide is often intended as a cry for help. |
| Myth: | Young people never think about suicide; they have their entire life ahead of them. |
| Fact: | Suicide is the third leading cause of death for young people ages 15–24. Sometimes children under 10 die by suicide. |

*Source: Adapted from information by Kevin Caruso, Suicide Myths, Suicide.org. Available online at http://www.suicide.org/suicide-myths.html.*

The Youth Smoking Survey (YSS) (Health Canada, 2014) is administered to youth in grades 6 through 12 every other year. The YSS focuses mainly on students' tobacco use, but also collects information about their use of alcohol and drugs. The good news is that smoking, drinking, and drug use has been declining among youth since the YSS was first administered in 1994. This is expecially true for smoking. In the most recent administration of the YSS (2012–13), 13% of students in grades 6 through 9 reported *ever* having tried smoking tobacco—down from 45% in 1994. Even so, 4% of students in grades 6 through 12 (approximately 114 000 youth) reported that they are *current* smokers—2% reported daily smoking. Alcohol is the substance youth reported using most frequently, followed by marijuana. On average, youth consumed their first alcoholic beverage at age 13, and nearly 3 in 10 students reported drinking excessively (five or more drinks on one occasion) in the past 12 months. Students were asked how easy it would be for them to obtain drugs, including marijuana, other illicit drugs, and prescription and over-the-counter pain relievers. Nearly half of students surveyed indicated it would be "very" or "fairly" easy to get marijuana, and one-third of students indicated they had "very" or "fairly" easy access to pain relievers.

PREVENTION.   What can be done about preventing drug use among our students? First, we should distinguish between experimentation and abuse. Many students try a drug at a party but do not become regular users. Providing information or "scare" tactics such as the DARE drug prevention program seems to have little positive effect and may even encourage curiosity and experimentation (Dusenbury & Falco, 1995; Tobler & Stratton, 1997).

So what is more effective? Adam Fletcher and his colleagues analyzed research on school programs around the world. One overwhelmingly frequent finding was that after taking into account students' prior drug use and personal characteristics, "disengagement from school and poor teacher–student relations were associated with subsequent drug use and other risky health behaviors" (Fletcher, Bonell, & Hargreaves, 2008, p. 217). For example, the researchers describe one study that found, for young adolescents, being disconnected with school predicted their drug use two to four years later. One implication is that engaging adolescents in schools, forming positive relationships, and connecting the students to caring adults and peers is critical in creating a protective environment.

## Students With Developmental Disabilities

The term **developmental disabilities** refers to disabilities that affect all aspects of development and is used widely in Canada when referring to students who have significant limitations in cognitive abilities and adaptive behaviour. You may also have heard the terms *intellectual disabilities, cognitive impairment, cognitive disability,* or *mental retardation* (the term still used in the IDEA legislation in the United States). In general, these individuals learn at a far slower rate than other students, and they may reach a point at which their learning plateaus. Often, these individuals have difficulties maintaining skills without ongoing practice and generalizing skills learned in one context to another. Also, many of these students have difficulties carrying out tasks that involve combining or integrating multiple skills (e.g., doing laundry).

Intelligence tests are typically used to identify developmental delays, with a score below 70 being one of the indicators. An IQ score below 70 is one indicator of a developmental delay, but it is not enough evidence to diagnose a child as having a developmental disability. There must also be problems with adaptive behaviour, day-to-day independent living, and social functioning. This caution is especially important when interpreting the scores of students from different cultures. Defining developmental disabilities based on test scores alone can create what some critics call "six-hour retardates"—students who are seen as developmentally disabled only for that part of the day when they are in school.

Given the limitations of formal assessments, advocates for individuals with developmental disabilities are beginning to argue that it is better to focus efforts on identifying the amount and types of services these individuals require. In Canada, a distinction is often made between two levels of developmental disabilities, mild and severe (Hutchinson, 2013), primarily on the basis of the level of support required for adaptive functioning. Similarly, the American Association on Intellectual and Developmental Disabilities (AAIDD) now recommends a classification scheme based on the amount of support that a person requires to function at his or her highest level. Support varies from intermittent (e.g., as needed during stressful times), to limited (consistent support, but time-limited such as employment training), to extensive (daily care such as living in a group home), to pervasive (constant high-intensity care for all aspects of living) (Taylor, Richards, & Brady, 2005).

TEACHING STUDENTS WITH DEVELOPMENTAL DISABILITIES. As a general education teacher, you may not have contact with children needing extensive or pervasive support, but you will probably work with children with mild developmental disabilities. In the early grades, these students may simply learn more slowly than their peers. They need more time and more practice to learn and have difficulty transferring learning from one setting to another or putting small skills together to accomplish a more complex task. They often have difficulties with metacognitive skills and executive functioning required to plan, monitor, and redirect attention and learning strategies (Simon, 2010), so very structured and complete teaching and guidance makes sense. The *Guidelines* list more suggestions.

For many students with developmental disabilities between the ages of 9 and 13, learning goals include basic reading, writing, arithmetic, learning about the local environment, social behaviour, and personal interests. In middle school and high school, the emphasis is on vocational and domestic skills, literacy for living (using the telephone book; reading signs, labels, and newspaper ads; completing a job application), job-related behaviours such as courtesy and punctuality, health self-care, and citizenship skills. Today, there is a growing emphasis on **transition programming**—preparing the student to live and work in the community. Nancy Hutchinson and her colleagues at Queen's University, Kingston, are researching the benefits of cooperative education and on-the-job training

Developmental disabilities
Significantly below-average intellectual and adaptive social behaviour evident before the age of 18.

Transition programming Gradual preparation of exceptional students to move from high school into further education or training, employment, or community involvement.

## GUIDELINES

## Teaching Students With Intellectual Disabilities

1. Develop specific learning objectives based on an analysis of each student's learning strengths and weaknesses. No matter what a student knows, he or she is ready to learn the next step.
2. Work on practical skills and concepts based on the demands of adult life.
3. Analyze the task the student will be learning. Identify the specific steps involved in successful completion, and don't overlook any steps in your planning.
4. State and present objectives simply.
5. Present material in small, logical steps. Practise extensively before going on to the next step. Use resources such as computer drill and practice exercises in class, or have volunteers and family members continue guiding practice outside class.
6. Do not skip steps. Students with average intelligence can form conceptual bridges from one step to the next and make metacognitive judgments about how they are doing, but children with below-average intelligence need every step and bridge made explicit. Make connections for the student. Do not expect him or her to "see" the connections.
7. Be prepared to present the same idea in many different ways using different representations (verbal, visual, hands-on, etc.).
8. Go back to a simpler level if you see the student is not following.
9. Be especially careful to motivate the student and maintain attention. Allow and encourage different ways of expressing understanding—written, drawings, oral responses, gestures, etc.
10. Find materials that do not insult the student. A middle school boy may need the low vocabulary of "See Spot run," but will be insulted by the age of the characters and the content of the story.
11. Focus on a few target behaviours or skills so you and the student have a chance to experience success. Everyone needs positive reinforcement.
12. Be aware that students with below-average intelligence must overlearn, repeat, and practise more than children of average intelligence. They must be taught how to study, and they must frequently review and practice their newly acquired skills in different settings.
13. Pay close attention to social relations. Simply including students with below-average intelligence in a regular class will not guarantee that they will be accepted or that they will make and keep friends.
14. Establish peer tutoring programs and train all students in the class to serve as tutors and as tutees—see Chapter 10 for specifics.

For more information, visit www.aaidd.org.

for high school students with developmental disabilities. Their research shows that these students benefit from workplace experiences that gradually increase demands for independence and productivity (Hutchinson, Wintermute, Munby, Versnel, Chin, & Dalgamo, 2005; Hutchinson et al., 2011). As you will see later in the chapter, schools need to design an individualized educational program, or IEP, for every child with disabilities. An individualized transition plan, or ITP, may be part of the IEP for students with retardation (Hutchinson, 2013).

## Students With Physical Disabilities and Chronic Health Concerns

Some students must have special devices, such as braces, special shoes, crutches, or wheelchairs, to participate in school programs. If the school has the necessary architectural features, such as ramps, elevators, and accessible washrooms, and if teachers allow for the physical limitations of students, little needs to be done to alter the usual educational program. Later in this chapter, we discuss *universal* design as an approach to making schools and learning more accessible for students with disabilities. Other students have chronic health concerns that require moment-to-moment accommodations.

CEREBRAL PALSY.   **Cerebral palsy** (CP) is a disorder that affects muscle tone, movement, and motor skills—children with cerebral palsy have difficulty moving in a coordinated way (KidsHealth, 2009). Other vital functions that also involve motor skills and muscles may be involved and cause difficulty breathing, controlling bladder and bowel, and eating. The most common cause of cerebral palsy is lack of oxygen causing brain damage

Cerebral palsy Condition involving a range of motor or coordination difficulties due to brain damage.

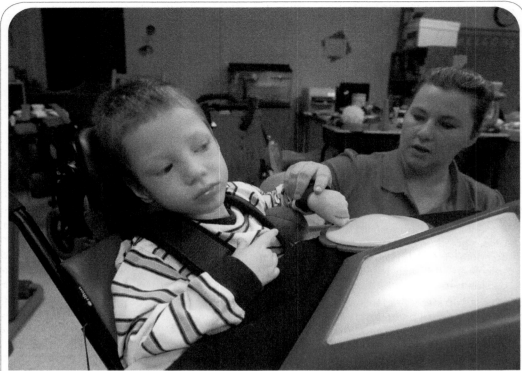

**INSTRUCTIONAL ACCOMMODATIONS** Physical and instructional accommodations can enable students with many kinds of disabilities to participate in general education classrooms. A specially designed desk enables this young girl with cerebral palsy to work independently in class.

at or before birth. However, cerebral palsy also can develop during the first three to five years of a child's life if, for example, a child contracts meningitis or viral encephalitis (American Academy of Family Physicians, 2009). Cerebral palsy can be mild or severe. For example, a child with mild CP may have awkward movements but require very little in the way of adaptations and accommodations. A child who has severe CP may not be able to walk or may have trouble speaking. Some children with CP will require lifelong care and assistance. Cerebral palsy is not degenerative; that is, it does not worsen over time (American Academy of Family Physicians, 2009). The most common form of cerebral palsy is characterized by **spasticity** (overly tight or tense muscles).

Many children with cerebral palsy have additional disabilities (KidsHealth, 2009). For example, many children with cerebral palsy also have hearing impairments, speech problems, or developmental disabilities. In classrooms and other settings, these secondary handicaps may create the greatest challenges. The strategies we describe for other children with language and learning disabilities and sensory impairments can work for these children, too. Assistive technologies, like those described near the end of this chapter, can help them do their work. Exercise and muscle training are critical, so physical and occupational therapy may be part of their individualized family or education plans. Importantly, professionals working as a multidisciplinary team with a coordinated plan can provide a wide range of resources to support development and learning in children with cerebral palsy and other physical disabilities.

**Spasticity** Overly tight or tense muscles, characteristic of some forms of cerebral palsy.

**Epilepsy** Disorder marked by seizures and caused by abnormal electrical discharges in the brain.

SEIZURE DISORDERS.   A seizure is a cluster of behaviour that occurs in response to abnormal neurochemical activities in the brain (Hardman, Drew, & Egan, 2005). The effects of the seizure depend on where the discharge of energy starts in the brain and how far it spreads. People with **epilepsy** have recurrent seizures, but not all seizures are the result of epilepsy; temporary conditions such as high fevers or infections can also trigger seizures. Seizures take many forms and differ with regard to the length, frequency, and movements involved.

Most **generalized seizures** (once called *grand mal*) are accompanied by uncontrolled jerking movements that ordinarily last from two to five minutes, possible loss of bowel or bladder control, and irregular breathing, followed by a deep sleep or coma. On regaining consciousness, the student may be very weary, confused, and in need of extra sleep. Most seizures can be controlled by medication. If a student has a seizure accompanied by convulsions in class, the teacher must take action so that the student will not be injured. The major danger to a student having a seizure is getting hurt by striking a hard surface during the violent jerking.

For this or any other medical emergency, it is important to stay calm and reassure the rest of the class. Do not try to restrain the child's movements; you can't stop the seizure once it starts. Lower the child gently to the floor, away from furniture or walls. Move hard objects away. Loosen scarves, ties, or anything that might make breathing difficult. Turn the child's head gently to the side and put a soft coat or blanket under the student's head. Never put anything in the student's mouth—it is *not* true that people having seizures can swallow their tongues. Don't attempt artificial respiration unless the student does not start breathing again after the seizure stops. Find out from the student's parents how the seizure is usually dealt with. If one seizure follows another and the student does not regain consciousness in between, if the student is pregnant, if the student has a medical ID that does not say "epilepsy, seizure disorder," if there are signs of injury, or if the seizure goes on for more than five minutes, get medical help right away (Friend, 2011). For more ideas and information, see www.epilepsy.ca.

Not all seizures are dramatic. Sometimes the student just loses contact briefly. The student may stare, fail to respond to questions, drop objects, and miss what has been happening for 1 to 30 seconds. These **absence seizures**, which were once called *petit mal,* can easily go undetected. If a child in your class appears to daydream frequently, does not seem to know what is going on at times, or cannot remember what has just happened when you ask, you should consult the school psychologist or nurse. The major problem for students with partial seizures is that they miss the continuity of the class interaction—these seizures can occur as often as 100 times a day. If their seizures are frequent, students will find the lessons confusing. Question these students to be sure they are understanding and following the lesson and be prepared to repeat yourself periodically.

OTHER SERIOUS HEALTH CONCERNS.    There are many other health problems that affect students' learning, in great part because they cause students to miss school, leading to lost instructional time and missed opportunities for friendships. Consider the following health concerns that you may have to deal with in your classroom:

- Asthma is a chronic lung condition that affects more than 11% of Canadian youth age 12 to 19 and over 15% of children aged 4 to 11 years (Asthma Society of Canada, 2014). It is the leading driver of children's health care costs, with more than $2 billion spent on asthma-related care each year. Since there is no cure for asthma, the goal is to control the symptoms. This can be done with medication and by helping children avoid what "triggers" their symptoms. Common triggers include pollens, pet dander, and especially second-hand smoke. Children can learn about asthma and how to take care of themselves at www.asthmakids.ca.

- Type 2 diabetes is a chronic condition that affects the way the body metabolizes sugar (glucose). This condition needs to be taken seriously because it can affect almost every major organ in the body, including the heart, blood vessels, nerves, eyes, and kidneys (Mayo Clinic, 2009). For most children, this disease can be managed, or prevented altogether, by eating healthy foods, being physically active, and maintaining a healthy body weight. When diet and exercise modifications are not enough, children will need medications, such as insulin, to manage their blood sugar (Rosenberg, Westling, & McLeskey, 2011; Werts, Culatta, & Tompkins, 2007).

- What once were terminal diseases in children are now illnesses they can survive or learn to live with. For example, the current survival rate from common childhood

**Generalized seizure** A seizure involving a large portion of the brain.

**Partial seizure or absence seizure** A seizure involving only a small part of the brain.

cancers (e.g., leukemia and brain and central nervous system tumours) exceeds 80% (Canadian Cancer Society, 2008; Daly, Kral, & Brown, 2008; National Cancer Institute, 2009). Unfortunately, the treatments (e.g., chemotherapy, radiation) often have negative long-term effects on development and learning.

In the case of each health condition, teachers need to talk to parents to know how the problems are handled, what the signs are that dangerous situations might be developing, and what resources are available for the student. Keep records of any incidents—they may be useful in the student's medical diagnosis and treatment, and consider appropriate accommodations on a case-by-case basis (e.g., some children may just need additional time on assignments, others will need emotional support and/or support for learning much like students with other disabilities).

## Students With Sensory Impairments

Sensory impairments refer to disabilities involving hearing and vision.

**STUDENTS WHO ARE VISUALLY IMPAIRED.**   Approximately one in 1000 students in Canada is visually impaired (Hutchinson, 2013). The majority of these students will be print users versus Braille users (American Printing House for the Blind, 2009). Students who have difficulty seeing often hold books either very close to or very far from their eyes. They may squint, rub their eyes frequently, or complain that their eyes burn or itch. Students with vision problems may misread material on the board, describe their vision as being blurred, be very sensitive to light, or hold their heads at an odd angle. They may become irritable when they have to work at a desk or lose interest if they have to follow an activity happening across the room (Hunt & Marshall, 2002). Any of these signs should be reported to a qualified school professional.

Mild vision problems can be overcome with corrective lenses. However, students with more significant visual impairments probably require special materials and equipment to function in general education classrooms. Most of these students have partial or **low vision**; that is, they have some useful vision between 20/70 and 20/200 (on the Snellen scale, where 20/20 is considered normal). For example, a person with 20/70 vision can only see at six metres what individuals with normal vision see at 21.3 metres. An individual with 20/200 vision is considered legally and **educationally blind**. Students who are educationally blind must use hearing and touch as their primary learning channels (Kirk, Gallagher, & Anastasiow, 1993).

Special materials and equipment that help these students function in regular classrooms include large-print typewriters; software that converts printed material to speech or to Braille; electronic organizers that have talking appointment books or address books; variable-speed tape recorders (which allow teachers to make time-compressed tape recordings that can be sped up in a way that changes the rate of speech without changing the voice pitch); special calculators; the abacus; three-dimensional maps, charts, and models; and special measuring devices. For students with visual problems, the quality of the print is often more important than the size, so watch out for hard-to-read handouts and blurry copies. Make yourself aware of local, provincial, and national resource centres (e.g., Special Education Technology, SET-BC, in British Columbia; the Canadian National Institute for the Blind, CNIB) that have resource materials and assistive technologies for students with sensory impairments.

The arrangement of your classroom is also an issue. Students with low vision or blindness need to know where things are, so consistency matters—a place for everything, and everything in its place. Leave plenty of space for moving around the room, and make sure to monitor possible obstacles and safety hazards such as garbage cans in aisles and open cabinet doors. If you rearrange the room, give students with visual problems a chance to learn the new layout. Make sure that each student has a buddy for fire drills or other emergencies (Friend, Bursuck, & Hutchinson, 1998).

**Low vision** Vision limited to close objects.

**Educationally blind** Needing Braille materials in order to learn.

**STUDENTS WHO ARE DEAF.**   You will hear the term *hearing impaired* used to describe students who have difficulties hearing. The deaf community and researchers prefer the

**SOME FACES OF ASPERGER SYNDROME** In his book *The Genesis of Artistic Creativity: Asperger Syndrome and the Arts,* Michael Fitzgerald (2005) speculates that the famous musicians Beethoven and Mozart and the artists van Gogh and Warhol displayed behaviours associated with Asperger syndrome.

terms *deaf* and *hard of hearing*. The number of deaf students has been declining over the past three decades, but when the problem does occur, the consequences for learning are serious (Hunt & Marshall, 2002). Signs of hearing problems are turning one ear toward the speaker, favouring one ear in conversation, or misunderstanding conversation when the speaker's face cannot be seen. Other indications include not following directions, seeming distracted or confused at times, frequently asking people to repeat what they have said, mispronouncing new words or names, and being reluctant to participate in class discussions. Take note particularly of students who have frequent earaches, sinus infections, or allergies.

In the past, educators have debated whether oral or manual approaches are better for children who are deaf or hard of hearing. Oral approaches involve **speech reading** (also called *lip reading*) and training students to use whatever limited hearing they may have. Manual approaches include **sign language** and **finger spelling**. Research indicates that children who learn some manual method of communicating perform better in academic subjects and are more socially mature than students who are exposed only to oral methods. Today, the trend is to combine both approaches (Hallahan, Kauffman, & Pullen, 2009).

Another perspective suggests that people who are deaf are part of a different culture with a different language, values, social institutions, and literature. Hunt and Marshall (2002) quote one deaf professional: "How would women like to be referred to as male-impaired, or whites like to be called black-impaired? I'm not impaired; I'm deaf!" (p. 348). From this perspective, a goal is to help deaf children become bilingual and bicultural, to be able to function effectively in both cultures. Technological innovations and the many avenues of communication possible through email and the internet have expanded communication possibilities for all people with hearing problems.

## Students With Autism Spectrum Disorders

You may be familiar with the term *autism*. According to the American Psychiatric Association (2000), **autism** is a developmental disability that significantly affects verbal and nonverbal communication, social interaction, and imaginative creativity, and is characterized by restrictive, repetitive, and stereotypic patterns of behaviour, interests, and activities. Generally, autism is evident before age 3. We use the term **autism spectrum disorders** to emphasize that autism includes a range of disorders, from mild to major. You might also hear the term *pervasive developmental disorder* (PDD), especially if you are talking with medical professionals.

**Speech reading** Using visual cues to understand language.

**Sign language** Communication system of hand movements that symbolize words and concepts.

**Finger spelling** Communication system that "spells out" each letter with a hand position.

**Autism and autism spectrum disorders** Developmental disability significantly affecting verbal and nonverbal communication, social interaction, and imaginative creativity, generally evident before age 3 and ranging from mild to major.

**Watch**
Students With Autism
Spectrum Disorders

From an early age, children with autism spectrum disorders may have difficulties in social relations. They do not form connections with others, avoid eye contact, or don't share feelings such as enjoyment or interest with others. Communication is impaired. About half of these students are nonverbal; they have very few or no language skills. Others make up their own language. They may obsessively insist on regularity and sameness in their environments—change is very disturbing. They may repeat behaviours and have restricted interests, watching the same DVD over and over, for example. They may be very sensitive to light, sound, touch, or other sensory information—sounds may be painful, for example. They may be able to memorize words or steps in problem solving, but not use them appropriately or be very confused when the situation changes or questions are asked in a different way (Franklin, 2007; Friend, 2011; Matson, Matson, & Rivet, 2007).

*Asperger syndrome* is one of the disabilities included in the autistic spectrum. These children have many of the characteristics described above, but their greatest trouble is with social relations. Language is less affected. Their speech may be fluent, but unusual, mixing up "I" and "you" pronouns, for example (Friend, 2011; Hutchinson, 2013). Many students with autism also have moderate to severe intellectual disabilities, but those with Asperger syndrome usually have average to above average intelligence (Friend, 2011).

THEORY OF MIND.    One current explanation for autism and Asperger syndrome is that children with these disorders lack a theory of mind (Miller, 2009)—an understanding that they and other people have minds, thoughts, and emotions. Students with autism have difficulty explaining their own behaviours, appreciating that other people might have different feelings, and predicting how behaviours might affect emotions. So, for example, a student may not understand why classmates are bored by his constant repetition of stories or obscure facts about topics he finds fascinating. Or the student may stand too close or too far away when interacting, not realizing that she is making other people uncomfortable (Friend, 2011; Harris, 2006; Hutchinson, 2013).

INTERVENTIONS.    Early and intense interventions that focus on communication and social relations are particularly important for children with autism spectrum disorders. Without interventions, behaviours such as poor eye contact and odd-seeming mannerisms tend to increase over time (Matson, Matson, & Rivet, 2007). As they move into elementary school, some of these students will be in inclusive settings, others in specialized classes, and many in some combination of these two. Collaboration among teachers and the family is particularly important. Strategies such as providing smaller classes, offering structured environments, finding a class "buddy" to give support, providing a safe "home base" for times of stress, ensuring consistency in instruction and transition routines, implementing assistive technologies, and using visual supports may be part of a collaborative plan (Friend, 2011; Harrower & Dunlap, 2001). Through adolescence and the transition to adulthood, instruction and guidance in life, work, and social skills are important educational goals.

# EXCEPTIONAL EDUCATION AND INCLUSION

We have been discussing in detail the many needs of exceptional learners because, no matter what grade or subject you teach, you will encounter these students in your classroom. The trend toward including exceptional students in general education classrooms began in the early 1970s and is currently the policy of ministries of education across Canada.

## Education Laws and Policies Pertaining to Exceptional Students

Canada does not have a national office of education, unlike Britain and the United States. Instead, each province has the authority to make its own laws concerning education, including exceptional education, and each province and territory has an **education or school act** that governs education in its elementary and secondary schools. As a teacher, you will need to become familiar with the laws and policies that govern education in your province or territory.

Education or school act Provincial or territorial legislation that governs education in elementary and secondary schools.

**Inclusion** is the current policy of the ministries of education in all of Canada's provinces and territories (Hutchinson, 2013). However, provinces differ in their definitions of inclusion. In British Columbia, for example, "Inclusion describes the principle that all students are entitled to equitable access to learning, achievement and the pursuit of excellence in all aspects of their educational programs" (British Columbia Special Education Branch, 2013, Section A, p. 2). However, the British Columbia Ministry of Education clarifies that **integration**—exceptional students' participation in activities with nonexceptional peers—is only one way to achieve inclusion, the preferred way. This definition of inclusion means that exceptional students may not spend 100% of every school day in general education activities or classrooms. The emphasis is on meeting the educational needs of all students, and this "does not preclude the appropriate use of resource rooms, self-contained classrooms, community-based training, or other specialized settings" (British Columbia Special Education Branch, 2013, Section A, p. 3). Consistent with British Columbia's policy in this regard, no jurisdiction uses the expression "full inclusion," and all provide alternatives to the general education classroom when that choice clearly does not meet the student's needs.

There is one national piece of legislation that has an impact on education across Canada—the **Canadian Charter of Rights and Freedoms**, which is part of the Constitution. Section 15.1 of the *Charter* outlines the equality provisions that apply to education:

> Every individual is equal before and under the law and has the right to equal protection and equal benefit of the law without discrimination and, in particular, without discrimination based on race, national or ethnic origin, colour, religion, sex, age, or mental or physical disability.

William MacKay (1986), a law professor at Dalhousie University in Nova Scotia, interpreted that there are three dimensions of "equality rights"—nondiscrimination, equal opportunity, and equal outcomes. For some students, having equal opportunities and achieving equal outcomes requires differential treatment—that is, a program that attends to and supports their exceptional learning needs.

Exceptional education in Canada has also been influenced by American legislation. In particular, Canadian practices in special education have embraced American practices of providing exceptional learners with a least restrictive placement and an individualized education program (IEP), and of protecting the rights of exceptional students and their families.

LEAST RESTRICTIVE PLACEMENT.  In the United States, federal law requires that students be educated in the least restrictive environment possible. Typically, this is interpreted to mean that exceptional students should be educated in general educational settings whenever possible or in settings that provide as close a match as possible to general educational settings. This practice is referred to as **least restrictive placement**. While there is no law requiring least restrictive placement in Canada, the principle is embodied in our practices. Some provinces (e.g., Prince Edward Island) refer to placement in the "most enabling environment" rather than the least restrictive environment (Hutchinson, 2013). Consistent with Canada's goal of becoming an inclusive society, it is generally accepted that the most enabling environment for most learners most of the time is the general education classroom. But as you can see in the *Point/Counterpoint*, inclusion challenges our education systems.

INDIVIDUALIZED EDUCATION PROGRAM.  Each student with exceptional learning needs must have an educational program tailored to his or her unique needs. The **individualized education program (IEP)** is written by a team that includes the student's teacher or teachers, a qualified school psychologist or special education supervisor, the parent(s) or guardian(s), and (when possible) the student. The program should be reviewed and updated each year and should address the following issues:

1. The student's present level of functioning.
2. Goals for the year and short-term measurable instructional objectives leading to those goals.

**Inclusion** The practice of integrating exceptional students into regular education classrooms; the emphasis is on participation rather than placement.

**Integration** The practice of having exceptional students participate in activities with their nonexceptional peers.

**Canadian Charter of Rights and Freedoms** Legislation that protects the rights of all Canadians and, in particular, Canadians who are members of minority groups, including Canadians with disabilities.

**Least restrictive placement** The practice of placing exceptional students in the most regular educational settings possible while ensuring that they are successful and receive support appropriate to their special needs.

**Individualized education program (IEP)** Annually revised program for an exceptional student detailing present achievement level, goals, and strategies, drawn up by teachers, family members, specialists, and (if possible) the student.

## POINT/COUNTERPOINT  Is Inclusion a Reasonable Approach to Teaching Exceptional Students?

Surveys indicate that the majority of Canadians and, in particular, teachers agree with the principle of inclusion (Human Resources and Social Development Canada, 2004). In general, teachers believe people with exceptionalities should be included in school; however, many teachers feel unprepared and unsupported in their efforts to meet the needs of these students in their classrooms (Hutchinson, 2013, p. 21). For this reason, inclusion continues to be a controversial issue in education in Canada.

### POINT

▶ **Inclusion makes sense.** Proponents of inclusion argue their case along two lines (Perry, Mirenda, & Siegel, 2007). Both in terms of human rights and effective instruction for all students, they argue it is the right thing to do. On the second point, they cite research indicating exceptional learners' academic performance is better in general versus special education settings (Katz & Mirenda, 2002; Stevens & Slavin, 1995). They argue that students receive higher quality instruction in general education classrooms compared with special education classrooms, where teachers' expectations tend to be lower and curriculum coverage less comprehensive. Furthermore, they argue that exceptional learners develop better communication and social skills and experience a greater sense of belonging in general education classrooms. Finally, they cite research showing that inclusion has no deleterious effects on the learning or behaviour of students without disabilities and, in fact, enhances their understandings about disabilities and commitment to inclusion.

### COUNTERPOINT

▶ **Inclusion is not working.** Although research points to the benefits of inclusion, there is plenty of anecdotal evidence concerning inclusion failures (Perry, Mirenda, & Siegel, 2007). Also, some research indicates that academic achievement and long-term life outcomes have not dramatically improved for individuals with disabilities, even after a quarter century of emphasis on inclusion in our public schools (Frattura & Capper, 2006). School dropout rates for special education students are still twice as high as for the general population and, when they leave school, they are significantly more likely to have difficulty finding and keeping employment and, therefore, living independently.

In defence of general education teachers, some skeptics ask: Is it reasonable to expect general education teachers who are already overburdened with responsibilities for low-achieving students, students coping with family crises, and students who speak little or no English to also handle the wide range of disabilities that could confront them? Currently, teacher preparation programs do little to prepare teacher candidates for the diversity of today's classrooms, and budgets for professional development have been cut for in-service teachers. The idea that extra support and consultation will be provided is good in theory, but it has been lacking in practice. Nancy Hutchinson (2007) agrees that effective inclusion has been an elusive goal in education. Perhaps it's prudent to ask what characterizes classroom and school contexts where inclusion is "working." According to Perry and colleagues (2007, p. 8), inclusion works when students receive excellent instruction from knowledgeable teachers in the context of coordinated and comprehensive approaches to programming. Ideally there is collaboration between general and special educators to produce plans for (a) remedial, tutorial, and skill-building instruction, and (b) adapting, modifying, and supplementing curricula, instruction, and classroom materials. In addition, inclusion works when children's learning challenges are identified early and support for inclusion is provided at all levels of the education system (i.e., school, district, province). Contexts like these do exist and, in them, *all* students learn and thrive and parents and teachers report positive perceptions of inclusion (Fisher, Roach, & Frey, 2002).

**Watch**
Individualized Education Program

3. A list of specific services to be provided to the student and details of when those services will be initiated.
4. A description of how fully the student will participate in the general education program.
5. A schedule telling how the student's progress toward the objectives will be evaluated and approximately how long the services described in the plan will be needed.
6. Beginning at the age of 16 (and as young as 14 for some students), a statement of needed transitional services to move the student toward further education or work in adult life.

The Ontario Ministry of Education posts sample IEPs on its website at www .ontariodirectors.ca/IEP-PEI/en.html.

## GUIDELINES — FAMILY AND COMMUNITY PARTNERSHIPS

### Productive Conferences

**Plan and prepare for a productive conference.**

*Examples*

1. Have a clear purpose and gather the needed information. If you want to discuss student progress, have work samples available.
2. Send home a list of questions, and ask families to bring the information to the conference. The following are sample questions from Friend and Bursuck (2002):
   - What is your child's favourite class activity?
   - Does your child have worries about any class activities? If so, what are they?
   - What are your priorities for your child's education this year?
   - What questions do you have about your child's education in my class this year?
   - How could we at school help make this the most successful year ever for your child?
   - Are there any topics you want to discuss at the conference that I might need to prepare for? If so, please let me know.
   - Would you like other individuals to participate in the conference? If so, please give me a list of their names.
   - Is there particular school information you would like me to have available? If so, please let me know.

**During the conference, create and maintain an atmosphere of collaboration and respect.**

*Examples*

1. Arrange the room for private conversation. Put a sign on your door to avoid interruptions. Meet around a conference table for better collaboration. Have tissues available.
2. Address families as "Mr." and "Ms.," not "Mom" and "Dad" or "Grandma." Use students' names.
3. Listen to families' concerns and build on their suggestions for their children.

**After the conference, keep good records and follow up on decisions.**

*Examples*

1. Make notes to yourself and keep them organized.
2. Summarize any actions or decisions in writing and send a copy to the family and any other teachers or professionals involved.
3. Communicate with families on other occasions, especially when there is good news to share.

For more information about parent conferences, see http://content.scholastic.com/browse/home.jsp and search using "parent teacher conference."

---

**THE RIGHTS OF STUDENTS AND PARENTS OR GUARDIANS.** As a teacher, you need to be aware of the expectations for the participation of parents and guardians in education in your province. Typically, parents and guardians are viewed as partners in the education of exceptional learners. They must approve any testing and special placements concerning their child, and they have the right to see all records kept by the school board that concern their child. They may obtain an independent evaluation, and they have the right to participate in planning their children's IEPs. Schools must maintain the confidentiality of students' records and ensure that testing practices do not discriminate against students from minority groups. Furthermore, schools should communicate with parents and guardians in their native languages (i.e., through interpreters and translators) and must have processes in place for them to appeal any decisions made by the school about their children. Finally, students are entitled to see all records that the school board keeps about them, and should, whenever possible, be involved in planning their educational programs. See the *Family and Community Partnerships Guidelines* for suggestions about how to conduct productive conferences with parents or guardians and students.

Response to intervention and universal designs for learning are two approaches that educators can use to support inclusion. We consider those next.

### Response to Intervention (RTI)

One of the problems for students with serious learning problems is that they have to struggle through the early grades, often falling further and further behind, until they are identified and assessed, meet criteria for a special education category, receive an IEP, and finally get appropriate help. A process called **response to intervention (RTI)** gives educators

**Response to intervention (RTI)** A process in which one of the main goals is to identify students who may have learning difficulties as early as possible so that they don't fall too far behind before their problems are recognized. A second goal is to document what works and what doesn't with each student for planning.

**RESPONSE TO INTERVENTION (RTI)** One of the main goals of the response to intervention (RTI) process is to identify students who may have learning difficulties as early as possible so that they don't fall too far behind before their problems are recognized. A second goal is to document what works and what doesn't with each student for planning.

a new option for assessing and educating students who might have serious learning problems early in their educational careers. The main goal of RTI is to make sure students get appropriate research-based instruction and support as soon as possible, in kindergarten if they need it, before they have fallen too far behind. A second goal is to make sure teachers are systematic in documenting what they have tried with these students and how well each intervention worked.

One common way of reaching these RTI goals is to use a three-tiered system (Fuchs & Fuchs, 2007). The *first tier* is to use a strong, well-researched way of teaching all the students (we will look at these kinds of approaches in Chapter 13). Students who do not do well with these methods are moved to the *second tier,* which typically involves getting extra support and additional small-group instruction. If some students still make limited progress, they move to the *third tier* for one-to-one intensive help and perhaps a special needs assessment. The approach has at least two advantages—students get extra help right away and the information gained based on their responses to the different interventions can inform further assessments and be used to guide future IEP planning, if the students reach the third stage of RTI.

If you decide that students in your class might benefit from special services, the first step is making a referral. How would you begin? Table 4.10 guides you through the referral process.

TABLE 4.10 • **Making a Referral**

1. Contact the student's parents. It is very important that you discuss the student's problems with the parents *before* you refer.
2. Before making a referral, check *all* the student's school records. Has the student ever
   - had a psychological evaluation?
   - qualified for special services?
   - been included in other special programs (e.g., for disadvantaged children; speech or language therapy)?
   - scored far below average on standardized tests?
   - been retained?

Do the records indicate
   - good progress in some areas but poor progress in others?
   - any physical or medical problem?
   - that the student is taking medication?

3. Talk to the student's other teachers and professional support personnel about your concern for the student. Have other teachers also had difficulty with the student? Have they found ways of dealing successfully with the student? Document the strategies you have used in your class to meet the student's educational needs. Your documentation will provide evidence that will be helpful to or required by the team of professionals who will evaluate the student. Demonstrate your concern by keeping written records. Your notes should include items such as

   - exactly what you are concerned about
   - why you are concerned about it
   - dates, places, and times you have observed the problem
   - precisely what you have done to try to resolve the problem
   - who, if anyone, helped you devise the plans or strategies you have used
   - evidence that the strategies have been successful or unsuccessful

*Remember that you should refer a student only if you can make a convincing case that the student may have a handicapping condition and probably cannot be served appropriately without special education. Referral for special education begins a time-consuming, costly, and stressful process that is potentially damaging to the student and has many legal ramifications.*

# UNIVERSAL DESIGNS FOR LEARNING

Architects have been thinking in terms of universal design for some time now; they are designing buildings, bridges, parks, and more to meet the needs of diverse users. Originally, their goal was to anticipate and eliminate barriers for individuals with disabilities. However, they soon recognized that buildings that incorporate the principles of universal design are more accessible and functional for everyone (Rose & Gravel, 2010; Moore, 2007). According to Rose and Gravel (2010), thinking in terms of universal design involves building options into initial designs and making better choices available to everyone. They point to television captioning as a good example of a tool that was originally designed for individuals who are deaf or hard of hearing. At one point it was an expensive "add-on" to a television purchase, but now captioning is built into every television and benefits not only individuals with hearing impairments, but also exercisers at health clubs, travellers in airports, and couples who go to sleep at different times (Rose & Gravel, 2010, p. 2).

In supporting students with exceptional learning needs, teachers can think in terms of **universal designs for learning (UDL)**—ensuring their classroom environment, the tasks they assign, and the resources they use (e.g., curricular, technological) are equally accessible and useable to a wide range of learners. The Center for Applied Special Technology (CAST, 2012) in the United States published a set of principles and guidelines for teachers wanting to use UDL in their teaching. These can be accessed on the website of the National Center on Universal Design for Learning (www.udlcenter.org/aboutudl/udl-guidelines_theorypractice). Jennifer Katz (2012) at the University of Manitoba published a helpful book on this topic titled *Teaching to Diversity: A Three Block Model of Universal Design for Learning*.

In Chapter 14, we discuss effective teaching and look at more ways to reach all of your students.

**Universal designs for learning** Considering the needs of all users in the design of new tools, learning programs, or websites.

## ▼ SUMMARY

### Language and Labelling (pp. 107–110)

**What are the advantages of and problems with labels?** Labels and diagnostic classifications of students with exceptionalities can easily become both stigmas and self-fulfilling prophecies, but they can also open doors to special programs and help teachers develop appropriate instructional strategies.

**What is people-first language?** People-first language ("students with developmental disabilities," "students with gifts and talents," etc.) is an alternative to labels that describe a complex person with one or two words, implying that the condition labelled is the most important aspect of the person. With person-first language, the emphasis is on the students first, not on the special challenges these students face.

**Distinguish between a disability and a handicap.** A disability is an inability to do something specific, such as see or walk. A handicap is a disadvantage in certain situations. Some disabilities lead to handicaps, but not in all contexts. Teachers must avoid imposing handicaps on learners who are disabled.

### Intelligence (pp. 110–119)

**What is *g*?** Spearman suggested that there is one mental attribute, which he called *g*, or general intelligence, that is used to perform any mental test, but that each test also requires some specific abilities in addition to *g*. A current version of the general-plus-specific-abilities theory is Carroll's work identifying

a few broad abilities (such as learning and memory, visual perception, verbal fluency) and at least 70 specific abilities. Fluid and crystallized intelligence are two of the broad abilities identified in most research.

Svkv/Shutterstock

**What is Gardner's view of intelligence and his position on *g*?** Gardner contends that an intelligence is a biological and psychological potential to solve problems and create products or outcomes that are valued by a culture. These intelligences are realized to a greater or lesser extent as a consequence of experiential, cultural, and motivational factors. Gardner argues for at least eight separate intelligences: linguistic, musical, spatial, logical-mathematical, bodily-kinesthetic, interpersonal, intrapersonal, naturalist, and perhaps existential. Gardner does not deny the existence of *g*, but he does question how useful *g* is as an explanation for human achievements.

**What are the elements of Sternberg's theory of intelligence?** Sternberg's triarchic theory of intelligence is a cognitive process approach to understanding intelligence. Analytic/componential intelligence involves the mental processes that are defined in terms of components: metacomponents, performance components, and knowledge-acquisition components. Creative/experiential intelligence involves coping with new experiences through insight or automaticity. Practical/contextual intelligence involves choosing to live and work in a context where success is likely, adapting to that context, and reshaping it if necessary. Practical intelligence is made up mostly of action-oriented tacit knowledge learned during everyday life.

**How is intelligence measured, and what does an IQ score mean?** Intelligence is measured through individual tests (Stanford-Binet, Wechsler, Woodcock-Johnson, etc.) and group tests (Otis-Lennon School Abilities Tests, Slosson Intelligence Test, etc.). Compared with an individual test, a group test is much less likely to yield an accurate picture of any one person's abilities. The average score is 100. About 68% of the general population will earn IQ scores between 85 and 115. Only about 16% of the population will receive scores below 85, and only 16% will score above 115. These figures hold true for white, native-born North Americans whose first language is Standard English. Intelligence test scores predict success in school, but they are less predictive of success in life when level of education is taken into account.

**What is the Flynn effect, and what are its implications?** Since the early 1900s, IQ scores have been rising. To keep 100 as the average for IQ test scores, questions have to be made more difficult. This increasing difficulty has implications for any program that uses IQ scores as part of the entrance requirements. For example, students who were not identified as having intellectual disabilities a generation ago might be identified as disabled now because the test questions are harder.

**Are there sex differences in cognitive abilities?** Girls seem to be better on verbal tests, especially when writing is involved. Males seem to be superior on tasks that require mental rotation of objects. The scores of males tend to be more variable in general, so there are more males than females with very high *and* very low scores on tests. Research on the causes of these differences has been inconclusive, except to indicate that academic socialization and teachers' treatment of male and female students in mathematics classes may play a role.

## Learning and Thinking Styles (pp. 119–121)

**Distinguish between learning styles and learning preferences.** Learning styles are the characteristic ways a person approaches learning and studying. Learning preferences are individual preferences for particular learning modes and environments. Even though learning styles and learning preferences are not related to intelligence or effort, they can affect school performance.

**Should teachers match instruction to individual learning styles?** Results of some research indicate that students learn more when they study in their preferred setting and manner, but most research does not show a benefit. Many students would benefit from developing new—and perhaps more effective— ways to learn.

**What learning style distinctions are the most well-supported by research?** One distinction that is repeatedly supported by the research is deep versus surface processing. Individuals who have a deep-processing approach see learning activities as a means for understanding some underlying concepts or meanings. Students who take a surface-processing approach focus on memorizing the learning materials, not understanding them. A second distinction is Mayer's visualizer–verbalizer dimension, which has three facets: cognitive spatial ability (low or high), cognitive style (a visualizer versus a verbalizer), and *learning preference* (a verbal learner versus a visual learner).

## Students Who Are Gifted and Talented (pp. 121–126)

**What are the characteristics of students who are gifted?** Students who are gifted learn easily and rapidly and retain what they have learned; use common sense and practical knowledge; know about many things that the other children don't; use a large number of words easily and accurately; recognize relations and comprehend meaning; are alert and keenly observant and respond quickly; are persistent and highly motivated on some tasks; and are creative or make interesting connections. Most students have gifts and talents in particular areas. Teachers should make special efforts to support students who are underrepresented in gifted programs— girls, students who also have learning disabilities, students from minority cultures, and students who are living in poverty.

**Is acceleration a useful approach with gifted students?** Many people object to acceleration, but most careful studies indicate that truly gifted students who are accelerated do as well as, and usually better than, other students who are progressing at the normal pace. Students who are gifted tend to prefer the company of older playmates and may be bored if kept with children their own age. Skipping grades may not be the best solution for a particular student, but for students who are extremely advanced intellectually (with a score of 160 or higher on an individual intelligence test), the only practical solution may be to accelerate their education.

## Students With Learning Challenges (pp. 126–146)

**What does research in neuroscience tell us about learning problems?** Studies of the brains of students with learning disabilities and with attention deficit disorders show some differences in structure and activity compared to those of students without problems. Problems with executive functions are central to many of the learning challenges children and youth face. Students with learning disabilities have problems in using the system of working memory that holds verbal and auditory information while you work with it. Because children with learning disabilities have trouble holding on to words and sounds, it is difficult for them to put the words together to comprehend the meaning of a sentence or to figure out what a math story problem is really asking about. There also may be difficulties retrieving needed information from long-term memory while transforming new incoming information, such as the next numbers to add. Important bits of information keep getting lost.

**What is a learning disability?** Specific learning disabilities involve significant difficulties in the acquisition and use of listening, speaking, reading, writing, reasoning, or mathematical abilities. These difficulties are intrinsic to the individual, presumed to be the result of central nervous system dysfunction, and may occur throughout the lifespan. Students with learning disabilities may become victims of learned helplessness when they come to believe that they cannot control or improve their own learning and therefore cannot succeed. A focus on learning strategies often helps students with learning disabilities.

**What is ADHD, and how is it handled in school?** *Attention-deficit/hyperactivity disorder (ADHD)* is the term used to describe individuals of any age with hyperactivity and attention difficulties. Use of medication to address ADHD is controversial, but generally effective. There can be negative side effects, such as headaches and nausea, but modifying the dosage can typically control these. Also, little is known about the long-term effects of drug therapy. The drugs alone will not lead to improvements in academic learning or peer relationships, two areas in which children with ADHD have great problems. Instructional methods that have proven most successful for helping students with ADHD are based on behavioural principles of learning such as those described in Chapter 7. One promising approach is positive behaviour support (PBS).

**What are the most common communication disorders?** Common communication disorders include speech impairments (articulation disorders, stuttering, and voicing problems) and oral language disorders. If these problems are addressed early, great progress is possible.

**What are the best approaches for students with emotional and behavioural disorders?** Behavioural approaches and direct teaching of social skills (as in social emotional learning) are two useful approaches. Students also may respond to structure and organization in the environment, schedules, activities, and rules.

**What are some warning signs of potential suicide?** Students at risk of suicide may show changes in eating or sleeping habits, weight, grades, disposition, activity level, or interest in friends. They sometimes suddenly give away prized possessions such as cell phones, iPads, clothing, or pets. They may seem depressed or hyperactive and may start missing school or quit doing work. Any thoughts or actions that could result in self-harm should be taken seriously and acted upon immediately.

**What defines intellectual disabilities?** Before age 18, students must score below about 70 on a standard measure of intelligence and must have problems with adaptive behaviour, day-to-day independent living, and social functioning. This caution is especially important when interpreting the scores of students from different cultures. The AAIDD now recommends a classification scheme based on the amount of support that a person requires to function at his or her highest level. Support varies from intermittent (e.g., as needed during stressful times), to limited (consistent support, but time limited such as employment training), to extensive (daily care such as living in a group home), to pervasive (constant high-intensity care for all aspects of living).

**How can schools accommodate the needs of physically disabled students?** If the school has the necessary architectural features, such as ramps, elevators, and accessible washrooms, and if teachers allow for the physical limitations of students, little needs to be done to alter the usual educational program. Identifying a peer to help with movements and transitions can be useful.

**How would you handle a seizure in class?** Do not restrain the child's movements. Lower the child gently to the floor, away from furniture or walls. Move hard objects away. Turn the child's head gently to the side, put a soft coat or blanket under the student's head, and loosen any tight clothing. Never put anything in the student's mouth. Find out from the student's parents how the seizure is usually dealt with. If one seizure follows another and the student does not regain consciousness in between, if the student is pregnant, or if the seizure goes on for more than five minutes, get medical help right away.

**What are some signs of vision and hearing impairment?** Holding books very close or far away, squinting, rubbing eyes, misreading the chalkboard, and holding the head at an odd angle are possible signs of visual problems. Signs of hearing problems are turning one ear toward the speaker, favouring one ear in conversation, or misunderstanding conversation when the speaker's face cannot be seen. Other indications include not following directions, seeming distracted or confused at times, frequently asking people to repeat what they have said, mispronouncing new words or names, and being reluctant to participate in class discussions.

**How does autism differ from Asperger syndrome?** Asperger syndrome is one of the autism spectrum disorders. Many students with autism also have moderate to severe intellectual disabilities, but those with Asperger syndrome usually have average to above average intelligence and better language abilities than other children with autism.

## Exceptional Education and Inclusion (pp. 146–151)

**What legislation affects special education across Canada?** Each province and territory has an education or school act that governs education in its elementary and secondary schools. Inclusion is the current policy of all the provinces and territories in Canada. Also, educating students in the least restrictive or most enabling environment, developing an individualized education plan (IEP) that meets the unique needs of each exceptional learner, and protecting the rights of students with exceptionalities and their families are principles shared by ministries of education across Canada. Only one piece of legislation has an impact on education across the country: the *Canadian Charter of Rights and Freedoms*, which is part of the Constitution.

**What is response to intervention (RTI)?** RTI is an approach to supporting students with learning problems as early as possible, not waiting for years to assess, identify, and plan a program. One RTI process is a three-tiered system. The first tier is to use a strong, well-researched way of teaching all the students. Students who do not do well with these methods are moved to the second tier by getting extra support and additional small-group instruction. If some students still make limited progress, they move to the third tier for one-to-one intensive help and perhaps a special needs assessment.

## ▼ WHAT WOULD THEY DO?

## TEACHERS' CASEBOOK: Including Every Student

Here is how two practising teachers responded to the teaching situation described on the first page of this chapter.

**BARB CADEL**
Poplar Bank Public School, Newmarket, ON

When setting up a classroom and planning programming, I find it beneficial to think about using universal design for learning. This way of thinking helps teachers design their classrooms to make the learning accessible for all students. Looking at learning as a continuum allows each student in the class, regardless of ability, to progress toward his or her learning goals in the most appropriate way, and to be assessed and evaluated fairly and accurately. Every student in every classroom is unique; recognizing this will help to ensure that every student will benefit. Assessing students' learning preferences will also help in planning a program that will help each to learn.

The physical set-up of the classroom will be important to ensure that the student with a hearing impairment and the English language learners will have the supports they require. I post a visual schedule of the day, which includes words and pictures to help all students understand what will happen during the course of the day. Labels throughout the classroom also assist with language development and allow students to "read the room."

The students identified as having a hearing impairment and a learning disability will have individualized education plans (IEPs), which will outline the specific program accommodations and modifications they require to be successful in the classroom. The IEPs will outline teaching, learning, and assessment strategies that will be beneficial to those students. It will also be important to have a sound understanding of any assistive technology the students may require (e.g., hearing aids, interpreter, computer technology).

When planning tasks and learning opportunities for the students, I would ensure that each student would be engaged each week working in a variety of groupings. Working in a small group will allow all students an opportunity to participate in meaningful discussion about their learning and to learn from and with each other. Tiered activities also provide all students with opportunities for success. With tiered instruction, the teacher plans a variety of activities around a central essential skill or concept that has varying degrees of complexity. All students will learn the basic skill or concept, but the students will achieve a variety of learning outcomes based on their learning strengths and needs.

It will also be important to consider the needs of all learners when planning assessments. Students should have the opportunity to be assessed in ways that allow them to best demonstrate their understanding; instead of traditional pen-and-paper tasks, many students will share their ideas orally; through art, drama, or music; using technology; or through an appropriate graphic organizer.

By looking first at a student's strengths and focusing on what the student can do, a teacher can plan appropriate programs to benefit all students and help them to learn in the most appropriate way.

### KAREN NOEL-BENTLEY
Choice School for Gifted Children, Vancouver, BC

In a diverse classroom, it is important that all students feel like they belong and that they can learn. Every student has something to offer in a community of learners. In the first weeks of school, I would design activities that foster a sense of community and cooperation. I would give all students the opportunity to demonstrate their areas of interest and strength, celebrating their diversity while finding areas of common interest and aspirations. This would provide me with insight into their learning preferences and would facilitate an atmosphere of acceptance and camaraderie.

To accommodate the unique learning needs of my students with exceptionalities, I would try to learn more about their needs and what support is available before the start of the year. How does my deaf student communicate? Sign language? Lip reading? Is there technology available to facilitate communication? Is there an audiologist or doctor with whom I can collaborate to support my deaf student? Does my school have a teacher with expertise in teaching English language learners? Is a pullout program offered for English language learners at my school? Are there other students in my class who speak the same language as the students who are learning to speak English? What are the needs of my student with a learning disability? Will he or she be in the classroom every day, and for how long? Will a Special Education Assistant be involved? I would hope to be able to work as a team with these experts, involving them in planning and consulting with them as needed.

The best way to manage planning for a diverse class is to design complex tasks that involve opportunities to differentiate content, process, and product. When designing a task for my diverse class, I would start with determining the big idea. What do all students need to learn? This is the main concept of the task, which all students would be expected to learn. What do most of the students need to learn? This would involve deeper learning that most students would be required to achieve, but would be optional for the students with exceptional learning needs. Finally, what do some students need to learn? This would include further enrichment for those students who are highly able and need advanced work to stay challenged. All students would be offered the choice to attempt a higher level of learning.

To differentiate the process of learning, I would consider what I know about how students in my class prefer to learn. For example, I would be sure to include a variety of visual and kinesthetic strategies that would be beneficial to my students with special needs, along with many other students who learn best visually or through direct manipulation. I would offer opportunities for cooperative learning, independent projects, and learning centres.

Learning materials would include books, videos, manipulatives, and discussions. All students would be exposed to a variety of learning tactics and strategies and would be offered choices for how they would acquire their information.

To provide all students with opportunities to demonstrate their learning, I would differentiate the products required from the learning tasks. For example, my student with a learning disability may not be able to write, but he may be able to dictate his thoughts to a scribe, type them on a computer, or draw a picture. Choices for some tasks could include drawing a map, creating a puppet show, or writing a diary. I would conduct regular and ongoing assessments with all students, using techniques such as interviews and observation. The students would maintain portfolios, indicating growth in their learning and giving them control over content. A variety of products and assessment strategies would ensure that all students can demonstrate their learning in ways that meet their unique needs.

The choices offered in all phases of learning and assessment give students control and understanding of their own learning. All students benefit when they understand their own strengths and areas of need. Students with exceptional needs become part of a continuum of learners within the classroom community. When teachers plan for this continuum, they can adjust the edges of the continuum to accommodate the specific needs of individual learners without feeling overwhelmed.

DG Design/Shutterstock

# CHAPTER
# 5

# LANGUAGE DEVELOPMENT, LANGUAGE DIVERSITY, AND IMMIGRANT EDUCATION

WHAT WOULD YOU DO?

▶ **TEACHERS' CASEBOOK:** Cultures Clash in the Classroom

Students from ethnic and language minority groups make up more than half of your high school classes this year. Mainly, these students are divided among three groups—Southeast Asians, Chinese Canadians, and Filipino Canadians. Students from each of the three groups seem to stick together, rarely making friends with students from "outside" their language and cultural groups. When you ask students to select partners for projects, the divisions are usually on ethnic lines. Occasionally, there are insults exchanged between the groups, and the atmosphere in class gets tense. When students communicate in their native language—one you don't understand— you sometimes get the sense that the joke is on you because of the looks and laughs directed your way. You realize that you are having trouble establishing positive relationships with many of the students whose language, culture, and background are very different from yours. You want to connect with all your students and create a classroom climate in which students interact and get along with one another, too.

**CRITICAL THINKING**

- What is the real problem here?
- How would you help the students (and yourself) to feel more comfortable with each other?
- What are your first goals in working on this problem?
- How will these issues affect the grade levels you will teach?

## OVERVIEW AND OBJECTIVES

Virtually all developed countries, and many developing ones, are becoming more diverse. Multiple languages fill many classrooms. For a range of reasons, including unrest across the globe, families are immigrating to find a better, safer life—and their children will likely be in your classrooms. In this chapter of our text we look at how the over 6000 natural languages in the world developed, what role culture plays, the stages in language development, and the emergence of literacy. Next we consider diversity in language development and dual language development. But language diversity is more than bilingualism. Because all of us speak at least one dialect, we examine what teachers need to know about dialects, and genderlects, along with the role of schools in second (or third) language learning. Finally we turn to the critical issue for you—how to become a capable and confident teacher of immigrant students and second language learners. What is the best approach to language instruction? Do the emotions and concerns of these students affect their learning? How can you identify English language learners with special talents or special needs? By the time you have completed this chapter, you should be able to:

5.1   Understand how language develops and know how to support emergent literacy.

5.2   Discuss what happens when children develop two languages.

5.3   Address whether dialect differences affect learning, and discuss what teachers can do.

5.4   Discuss whether English immersion or bilingual instruction is better for English language learners.

5.5   Describe the Generation 1.5 students, and explain their learning characteristics.

5.6   Define sheltered instruction, and explain how it works.

5.7   Discuss how teachers can recognize special learning needs and talents when they do not speak their students' first language.

# THE DEVELOPMENT OF LANGUAGE

All children in every culture master the complicated system of their native language unless severe deprivation or physical problems interfere. This knowledge is remarkable. To have a conversation, children must coordinate sounds, meanings, words and sequences of words, volume, voice tone, inflection, and turn-taking rules. Yet, by about age 4, most children have a vocabulary of thousands of words and knowledge of the grammar rules for basic conversations (Colledge et al., 2002).

## What Develops? Language and Cultural Differences

There are over 6000 natural languages in the world (Tomasello, 2006). In general, cultures develop words for the concepts that are important to them. For example, how many different shades of green can you name? Mint, olive, emerald, teal, sea foam, chrome, turquoise, chartreuse, lime, apple … An oil painting artist can add cobalt titanate green, cinnabar green, phthalo yellow green, viridian green, and many others. English-speaking countries have over 3000 words for colours. In contrast, the Himba people of Namibia and a tribe of hunter-gatherer people in Papua New Guinea who speak Berinmo have five words for colours, even though they can recognize many colour variations. But whether there are few or many colour terms, children gradually acquire the colour categories that are appropriate for their culture (Roberson, Davidoff, Davies, & Shapiro, 2004).

Languages change over time to reflect changing cultural needs and values. The Shoshoni Native Americans have one word that means "to make a crunching sound walking on the sand." This word was valuable in the past to communicate about hunting, but today new words describing technical tools have been added to the Shoshoni language, as the group's life moves away from nomadic hunting. To hear hundreds of new twenty-first-century tool words, listen to techies talk about computers (Price & Crapo, 2002).

**THE PUZZLE OF LANGUAGE.** It is likely that many factors—biological, cultural, and experiential—play a role in language development. To master a language, children must be able to (a) read the intentions of others so they can acquire the words, phrases, and concepts of their language and also (b) find patterns in the ways other people use these words and phrases to construct the grammar of their language (Tomasello, 2006). The important point is that children learn language as they develop other cognitive abilities by actively trying to make sense of what they hear and by looking for patterns and making up rules to put together the jigsaw puzzle of language.

**THE DEVELOPMENT OF LANGUAGE** The important point is that children learn language as they develop other cognitive abilities by actively trying to make sense of what they hear and by looking for patterns and making up rules to put together the jigsaw puzzle of language.

In this process, humans may have built-in biases, rules, and constraints about language that restrict the number of possibilities considered. For example, young children seem to have a constraint specifying that a new label refers to a whole object, not just a part. Another built-in bias leads children to assume that the label refers to a class of similar objects. So the child learning about the rabbit is equipped naturally to assume that "rabbit" refers to the whole animal (not just its ears) and that other similar-looking animals are also rabbits (Jaswal & Markman, 2001; Markman, 1992). Reward and correction play a role in helping children learn correct language use, but the child's thinking in putting together the parts of this complicated system is very important (Waxman & Lidz, 2006).

## When and How Does Language Develop?

Researchers who study language development, including Janet Werker at the University of British Columbia, have demonstrated how infants are born ready to learn any of the over 6000 languages spoken throughout the world (Kuhl, Stevens, Hayashi, Deguchi, Kiritani, & Iverson, 2006; Werker, 1989). In a now seminal article called "Becoming a Native Listener," Werker (1989) described how languages are formed from a set of speech sounds, called phones, and newborn infants can discriminate nearly every phonetic contrast on which they are tested, even those they haven't heard before. However, babies quickly begin to focus on and practice speech sounds they hear in their environment, and by 12 months are no longer able to distinguish sounds in all the world's languages. More recently, Werker and her colleagues (Byers-Heinlein, Burns, & Werker, 2010) demonstrated how, even in the womb, babies are sensitive to the rhythms and sounds of languages, and newborns prefer the sounds of languages that are rhythmically similar to the ones they heard in utero. This early selection, referred to as "perceptual narrowing," does not happen as quickly for bilingual babies as it does for babies in a monolingual environment. They remain more open, or "cognitively flexible," with regard to the sounds from different languages (Kuhl, cited in Klass, 2011).

Two processes known to support early language development are common in adult-child interactions: joint attention and child-directed speech. **Joint attention** occurs when a child and caregiver, or teacher, attend to the same object or event at the same time. Often the caregiver will describe it, label it, or ask questions about it. Such interactions promote sustained attention on the part of the infant/child, better comprehension, and faster vocabulary development (Flom & Pick, 2003; Silven, 2001). **Child-directed speech (CDS)** refers to a form of language characterized by short sentences with simple constructions

**Joint attention** Occurs when a child and caregiver, or teacher, attend to the same object or event at the same time.

**Child-directed speech (CDS)** Refers to a form of language characterized by short sentences with simple constructions and delivered in higher pitched, more prosodic, and exaggerated tones.

TABLE 5.1 • **Milestones in Early Childhood Language and Ways to Encourage Development**

| AGE RANGE | MILESTONE | STRATEGIES TO ENCOURAGE DEVELOPMENT |
|---|---|---|
| Between 2 and 3 | Identifies body parts; calls self "me" instead of name; combines nouns and verbs; has a 450-word vocabulary; uses short sentences; matches 3–4 colours; knows *big* and *little*; likes to hear same story repeated; forms some plurals; answers "where" questions | • Help the child listen and follow instructions by playing simple games.<br>• Repeat new words over and over.<br>• Describe what you are doing, planning, thinking.<br>• Have the child deliver simple messages for you.<br>• Show the child you understand what he or she says by answering, smiling, and nodding your head.<br>• Expand what the child says. Child: "more juice." You say, "Chris wants more juice." |
| Between 3 and 4 | Can tell a story; sentence length of 4–5 words; vocabulary about 1000 words; knows last name, name of street, several nursery rhymes | • Talk about how objects are the same or different.<br>• Help the child to tell stories using books and pictures.<br>• Encourage play with other children. Talk about places you've been or will be going. |
| Between 4 and 5 | Sentence length of 4–5 words; uses past tense; vocabulary of about 1500 words; identifies colours, shapes; asks many questions like "why?" and "who?" | • Help the child sort objects and things (e.g., things to eat, animals).<br>• Teach the child how to use the telephone.<br>• Let the child help you plan activities.<br>• Continue talking about the child's interests.<br>• Let the child tell and make up stories for you. |
| Between 5 and 6 At every age | Sentence length of 5–6 words; average 6-year-old has vocabulary of about 10 000 words; defines objects by their use; knows spatial relations (like "on top" and "far") and opposites; knows address; understands same and different; uses all types of sentences | • Praise children when they talk about feelings, thoughts, hopes, fears.<br>• Sing songs, rhymes.<br>• Talk with them as you would an adult.<br>• Listen and show your pleasure when the child talks to you.<br>• Carry on conversations with the child.<br>• Ask questions to get the child to think and talk.<br>• Read books to the child every day, increasing in length as the child develops. |

*Source: Adapted from LDOnLine.org with thanks to the Learning Disabilities Association of America.*

and delivered in higher pitched, more prosodic, and exaggerated tones (Snow, 1977). Also, CDS typically includes many interrogatives. Sometimes referred to as *motherese,* or colloquially as *baby talk,* this form of speech is observed when adults interact with infants across a variety of cultures. Even children use CDS to speak to infants and toddlers younger than themselves (Snow, 1977; Yont, Snow, & Vernon-Feagans, 2003). According to Snow, CDS reflects caregivers' belief that babies and young children are capable of reciprocal communication and their intention to invite babies into conversation. CDS promotes joint attention and turn-taking, and reflects adults' responsiveness to the language learning needs of children (Cameron-Faulkner, Lieven, & Tomasello, 2003).

Table 5.1 shows the milestones of language development, ages 2 to 6, in Western cultures, along with ideas for encouraging development.

SOUNDS AND PRONUNCIATION.　By about age 5, most children have mastered the sounds of their native language, but a few sounds may remain unconquered. You saw in the previous chapter that the sounds of the consonants *l, r, y, s, v,* and *z* and the consonant blends *sh, ch, ng, zh,* and *th* are the last to be mastered (Friend, 2011). Young children may understand and be able to use many words, but prefer to use the words they can pronounce easily. As children learn to hear differences in the sounds of language, they enjoy rhymes, songs, and general sound silliness. They like stories by Dr. Seuss partly because of the sounds, as is evidenced by the book titles—*All Aboard the Circus McGurkus* or *Wet Pet, Dry Pet, Your Pet, My Pet.* The young son of a friend of Anita's wanted to name his new baby sister Brontosaurus "just because it's fun to say."

**VOCABULARY AND MEANING.** As you can see in Table 5.1, children between ages 2 and 3 can use about 450 words (**expressive vocabulary**), even though they can understand many more (**receptive vocabulary**). By age 6, children's expressive vocabularies will grow to about 2600 words, and their receptive vocabularies will be an impressive 20 000 plus words (Otto, 2010). Some researchers estimate that students in the early elementary grades are learning up to 20 words a day (Bloom, 2002). In the early elementary years, some children may have trouble with abstract words, such as *justice* or *economy*. They also may not understand the subjunctive case ("If I were a butterfly") because they lack the cognitive ability to reason about things that are not true ("But you aren't a butterfly"). They may interpret all statements literally and thus misunderstand sarcasm or metaphor. For example, fables are understood concretely simply as stories instead of as moral lessons. Many children are in their preadolescent years before they are able to distinguish teasing from being taunting, or understand that a sarcastic remark should not be taken literally. By adolescence, students are able to use their developing cognitive abilities to learn abstract word meanings and to use poetic, figurative language (Owens, 2012).

"WHEN I SAY 'RUNNED', YOU KNOW I MEAN 'RAN'. LET'S NOT QUIBBLE."

Copyright © 2000 Sydney Harris. Reprinted with permission of Sydney Harris.

Young children begin to elaborate their simple language by adding plurals; endings for verbs such as *-ed* and *-ing*; small words like *and, but*, and *in*; articles (*a, the*); and possessives (*the girl's hair*). Jean Berko's (1958) classic study demonstrated that children could even apply these rules to make words that they had never encountered plural, possessive, or past tense. For example, when shown a picture of a single "wug," the preschool children in the study could answer correctly "wugs" when the researcher said, "Now there is another one. There are two of them. There are two _____." In the process of figuring out the rules governing these aspects of language, children make some very interesting mistakes.

**GRAMMAR AND SYNTAX.** For a brief time, children may use irregular forms of particular words properly, as if they are saying what they have heard. Then, as they begin to learn rules, they may **overregularize** words by applying the rules to everything. Children who once said, "Our car is broken" begin to insist, "Our car is broked." A child who once talked about her *feet* may discover the *-s* for plurals and refer to her *foots* or *feets*, then learn about *-es* for plurals (*horses, kisses*) and describe her *footses*, before she finally returns to talking about her *feet* (Flavell, Miller, & Miller, 2002). Parents often wonder why their child seems to be "regressing." Actually, these "mistakes" show how logical and rational children can be as they try to assimilate new words into existing schemes. Apparently these overregularizations happen in all languages, including American Sign Language. Because most languages have many irregular words, accommodation is necessary in mastering language. According to Joshua Hartshore and Michael Ullman (2006), girls tend to overregularize verb tenses more than boys, so they are more likely to say *holded* instead of *held*. The researchers speculate that because girls have better memory for words, they have better access to similar words (*folded, scolded*) and generalize to *holded*.

Early on, children master the basics of **syntax** (word order) in their native language, but overregularizing plays a role in mastering syntax, too. For example, because the usual order in English is subject–verb–object, preschoolers just mastering the rules of language have trouble with sentences in any other order. If 4-year-old Justin hears a statement in the passive voice, like "The truck was bumped by the car," he probably thinks the truck did the bumping to the car because "truck" came first in the sentence. Interestingly, however, in languages where the passive voice is more important, such as the South African language Sesotho, children use this construction much earlier, as young as 3 or 4 (Demuth, 1990). So in talking with young children, in English at least, it is generally better to use direct language. By early elementary school, many children can understand the meaning of passive sentences, but they do not use such constructions in their normal conversations, unless the passive construction is common in their culture.

**Expressive vocabulary** The words a person can speak.

**Receptive vocabulary** The words a person can understand in spoken or written words.

**Overregularize** To apply a rule of syntax or grammar in situations where the rule does not apply; e.g., "the bike was broked."

**Syntax** The order of words in phrases or sentences.

**PRAGMATICS: USING LANGUAGE IN SOCIAL SITUATIONS.**　**Pragmatics** involves the appropriate use of language to communicate in social situations—how to enter a conversation, tell a joke, interrupt, keep a conversation going, or adjust your language for the listener. Children show an understanding of pragmatics when they talk in simpler sentences to younger children or command their pets to "Come here!" in louder, deeper voices, or provide more detail when describing an event to a parent who was absent from the event (Flavell, Miller, & Miller, 2002; Rice, 1989). So even young children seem quite able to fit their language to the situation, at least with familiar people.

Rules for the appropriate use of language vary across cultures and communities. For example, Shirley Brice Heath (1983) spent many hours observing in two working-class communities in the United States. One was predominantly home to white families, the other to African American families. She found, across these groups, the adults asked different kinds of questions and encouraged different kinds of "talk." For example, in the white families, adults asked test-like questions with right answers, such as "How many cars are there?" or "Which car is bigger?" These questions seemed odd to African American children, whose families don't ask about what they already know. The African American child might wonder, "Why would my aunt ask me how many cars? She can see there are three." Instead, African American families encouraged rich storytelling and also teasing that hones their children's quick wit and assertive responses.

**METALINGUISTIC AWARENESS.**　Around the age of 5, children begin to develop **metalinguistic awareness**. This means their understanding about language and how it works becomes explicit—they are able to talk about language, and they have knowledge about language itself. They are ready to study and extend the rules that have been implicit—understood but not consciously expressed. This process continues throughout life, as we all become better able to use language. Learning to read and write, which begins with *emergent literacy*, encourages metalinguistic awareness.

## Emergent Literacy

Today, in most languages, reading is a cornerstone of learning, and the foundation for reading is built in early childhood. Because young children vary greatly in their knowledge and skills related to reading, research has expanded to study what supports these emerging literacy skills (often called **emergent literacy**). Figure 5.1 shows Kalla Terpenning's (from Galliano Island in British Columbia) emerging literacy skills just after she turned 6.

What are the most important skills that help literacy emerge? Here, the answers are not certain, but research has identified two broad categories of skills that are important for later reading: (1) skills related to understanding sounds and codes, such as knowing that letters have names, that sounds are associated with letters, and that words are made up of sounds; and (2) oral language skills such as expressive and receptive vocabulary, knowledge of syntax, and the ability to understand and tell stories, for example (Dickinson, McCabe, Anastopoulos, Peisner-Feinberg, & Poe, 2003; Storch & Whitehurst, 2002).

Some educators have emphasized decoding skills, others oral language, but a study by the National Institute of Child Health and Human Development (NICHD) Early Childhood Research Network (2005b) that followed over 1000 children from age 3 through grade 3 found that oral language skills at age 4 ½ predicted word decoding in grade 1 and reading comprehension in grade 3. The NICHD researchers concluded, "[m]ost recent investigations find that preschool oral language skills [for example, size of vocabulary, ability to use syntax, ability to understand and tell stories] play an important role alongside code skills in predicting reading in the transition to school" (p. 439). Because this was not an experimental design (see Chapter 1), we cannot be sure that early decoding and oral language skills cause later reading achievement. But the results of this study suggest that decoding and oral language skills are likely an important part of the puzzle; these skills often support each other. *Beware of either/or choices* between emphasizing decoding versus oral language—both are important.

**Pragmatics** The rules for when and how to use language to be an effective communicator in a particular culture.

**Metalinguistic awareness** Understanding about one's own use of language.

**Emergent literacy** The skills and knowledge, usually developed in the preschool years, that are the foundation for the development of reading and writing.

**FIGURE 5.1**

### A STORY AND A GROCERY LIST

Here are samples of Kalla Terpenning's emergent writing skills just after she turned 6. She knew quite a bit about reading and writing at that point in her development—letters make words that communicate meaning, writing goes from left to right, lists go down the page, and stories look different than shopping lists.

Me and Mommy went on the arplane. I saw the Librty BeL.

KALLA·S LiST UVe FRooTe
ToMmadoo Se.
AVooWCeAdooeS.
OriNiis.
APPLS.
PANYtS.

*Source: Woolfolk, A, Perry, N. E. (2012). Child and Adolescent Development, 1st Edition. Reprinted by permission of Pearson Education, Inc., Upper Saddle River, NJ.*

**BUILDING A FOUNDATION.**   What builds this foundation of emergent literacy skills? Two related activities are critical: (1) conversations with adults that develop knowledge about language; and (2) joint reading, using books as supports for talk about sounds, words, pictures, and concepts (NICHD Early Childhood Research Network, 2005a). Especially in the early years, children's home experiences are central in the development of language and literacy (Burgess, Hecht, & Lonigan, 2002; Sénéchal & LeFevre, 2002). In homes that promote literacy, parents and other adults value reading as a source of pleasure, and there are books and other printed materials everywhere. Parents read to their children, take them to bookstores and libraries, limit the amount of television everyone watches, and encourage literacy-related play such as setting up a pretend school or writing "letters" (Pressley, 1996; Snow, 1993; Whitehurst, Epstein, Angell, Payne, Crone, & Fischel, 1994). Child-care workers and teachers can help. In a study that followed almost 300 low-income children from kindergarten to grade 5, researchers found that the more families were involved with the school, the better their children's literacy development. School involvement was especially valuable when mothers had less education themselves (Dearing, Kreider, Simpkins, & Weiss, 2006).

**Watch**
Building a Foundation

## GUIDELINES

## Supporting Language and Promoting Literacy

### FOR FAMILIES

**Read with your children.**
*Examples*

1. Help children understand that books contain stories, that they can visit the stories as often as they like, that the pictures in the books go along with the story meaning, and that the words are always the same when they visit the story—that's reading! (Hulit & Howard, 2006)
2. Have a night-time reading ritual.

**Choose appropriate books and stories.**
*Examples*

1. Choose books with simple plots and clear illustrations.
2. Make sure illustrations precede the text related to the illustration. This helps children learn to predict what is coming next.
3. Ensure that language is repetitive, rhythmic, and natural.

### FOR TEACHERS

**Use stories as a springboard for conversations.**
*Examples*

1. Retell stories you have read with your students.
2. Talk about the words, activities, and objects in the books. Do the students have anything like these in their home or classroom?

**Identify and build on strengths the families already have (Delpit, 2003).**
*Examples*

1. What are the histories, stories, and skills of your students' family members? Children can draw or write about these.
2. Show respect for your students' language by celebrating poems or songs from the language.

**Provide home activities to be shared with family members.**
*Examples*

1. Encourage family members to work with children to read and follow simple recipes, play language games, keep diaries or journals for the family, and visit the library. Get feedback from families or your students about the activities.

2. Give families feedback sheets and ask them to help evaluate their children's schoolwork.
3. Provide lists of good children's literature available locally—work with libraries, clubs, and churches to identify sources.

### FOR SCHOOL COUNSELLORS AND ADMINISTRATORS

**Communicate with families about the goals and activities of your program.**
*Examples*

1. Have someone from the school district, the community, or even an older student translate into the languages of your students' families any material you plan to send home.
2. At the beginning of the school year, send home a description of the goals to be achieved in your class—make sure it is in a clear and readable format.
3. As you start each unit, send home a newsletter describing what students will be studying—give suggestions for home activities that support the learning.

**Involve families in decisions about curriculum.**
*Examples*

1. Have planning workshops at times family members can attend—provide child care for younger siblings, but let children and families work together on projects.
2. Invite parents to come to class to read to students, take dictation of stories, tell stories, record or bind books, and demonstrate skills.

**Make it easy for families to come to school.**
*Examples*

1. Provide babysitting for younger children while families meet with teachers.
2. Consider transportation needs of families—can they get to school?

*For more information on Family Literacy Partnerships, see www.famlit.org.*

*Source: Hulit, L. M., Howard, M. R. (2006). Born to Talk: An Introduction to Speech and Language Development, 4th edition. Reprinted by permission of Pearson Education, Inc., Upper Saddle River, NJ.*

## Emergent Literacy and Bilingual Children

Emergent literacy skills are critical for school readiness, regardless of the child's language or languages (Hammer, Farkas, & Maczuga, 2010). Most school programs in North America expect all children to learn to read and write in English. According to Carol Hammer and her colleagues, this emphasis on reading only in English may not be necessary. In fact, one key factor may facilitate literacy development—growth in receptive language. You probably remember that *receptive* language is made up of the words and language structures you understand, even if you do not use them in your *expressive* language, the words and structures you actually use when you talk.

Hammer followed 88 children for two years in a Head Start program (Hammer, Lawrence, & Miccio, 2007). The mothers of all the children spoke the Puerto Rican dialect of Spanish. There actually were two groups of students—those who had been expected to speak both English and Spanish from birth and those who were not expected to learn English until they started Head Start at age 3. The researchers found that it was not a particular score on any test, but *growth in receptive language* in general during the program that predicted early reading outcomes—and it did not matter if the students spoke English and Spanish from birth or if they just started speaking English in school. They concluded "that growth in children's English receptive language abilities during Head Start, as opposed to the level of English they had achieved by the end of Head Start, positively predicted the children's emergent reading abilities in English and the children's ability to identify letters and words in English. This was the case regardless of the level of the children's prior exposure to English" (p. 243). In addition, growth in Spanish language abilities predicted reading performance in Spanish.

One implication of Hammer and colleagues's (2007) research is that teachers and parents should focus on continuing language development and not worry about rushing children into speaking English exclusively. It seems that so long as children are progressing in their language development, in either their native language or English, positive early literacy outcomes will occur. These findings are consistent with the recommendations of the Society for Research in Child Development: "Investing in dual-language instead of English-only programs and encouraging pre-kindergarten attendance can improve learning opportunities for … children and increase their chances of success" (SRCD, 2009, p. 1). The *Guidelines* offer ideas about how to support children's early literacy development.

This brings us to a very important topic for teachers today—diversity in language development.

# DIVERSITY IN LANGUAGE DEVELOPMENT

Many children learn two or more languages simultaneously while they are growing up, and being bilingual or multilingual has many benefits, as we will see below.

## Dual Language Development

If you mastered your own first language, then added a second or third language, you are an example of *additive bilingualism* —you kept your first language and added another. But if you lost your first language when you added a second one, you experienced *subtractive bilingualism* (Norbert, 2005). If family members and the community value a child's first language, he or she is more likely to keep that language when a second one is learned. But if a child experiences discrimination against the first language, he or she may leave the first language behind as proficiency is gained in a new language (Hamers & Blanc, 2000; Montrul, 2010). Immigrants are more likely to experience discrimination and therefore "subtract" their first language.

If they are exposed to two languages from birth, **bilingual** children (children who speak two languages) reach the language milestones in both languages on the same schedule as **monolingual** children (children learning only one language). Initially, bilingual children may have a larger vocabulary in the language that they are learning from the person with whom they spend the most time or have the closest bond, so a child who stays home all day with a Chinese-speaking parent will likely use more Chinese words. But over time, these children can become fully and equally bilingual if the dual language exposure (a) begins early in life (before age 5), (b) occurs across a wide and rich range of contexts, and (c) is systematic, consistent, and sustained in the home and community (Petitto, 2009; Petitto & Kovelman, 2002). Another requirement is that the second language must provide more than 25% of the child's language input; with less exposure, the

**Bilingual** Speaking two languages and dealing appropriately with the two different cultures.

**Monolingual** Speaking only one language.

child is unlikely to learn the second language (Pearson, Fernandez, Lewedeg, & Oller, 1997). Bilingual children may mix vocabularies of the two languages when they speak, but this is not necessarily a sign that they are confused because their bilingual parents often intentionally mix vocabularies as well, selecting the word that best expresses their intent (Creese, 2009). So, with consistent and sustained engagement in two languages, children can be fully bilingual.

Recent research on the brain and bilingualism shows that people who learn two languages before about age 5 process both languages in the same way as those who learn only one language and use the same parts of their brains (mostly in the left hemisphere). In contrast, people who learn a second language later have to use both hemispheres of their brain as well as the frontal lobe and working memory. They have to apply more cognitive effort. As Laura-Ann Petitto (2009) notes, "*Later* bilingual exposure does *change* the typical pattern of the brain's neural organization for language processing, but early bilingual exposure does not" (p. 191).

SECOND LANGUAGE LEARNING.   What if you didn't learn two languages as you were growing up? When and how should you learn a second language? To answer that question, you have to remember the distinction between **critical periods** for learning (if learning doesn't happen then, it never will) and **sensitive periods**, times when we are especially responsive to learning. There is no critical period that limits the possibility of language learning by adults (Marinova-Todd, Marshall, & Snow, 2000). In fact, older children go through the stages of language learning faster than young children. Adults have more learning strategies and greater knowledge of language in general to bring to bear in mastering a second language (Diaz-Rico & Weed, 2002). But recent research on the brain and bilingualism suggests "*there is most definitely a 'sensitive period' for optimal bilingual language and reading exposure and mastery.* Age of first bilingual exposure predicts how strong a reader a bilingual child can and will become in each of their two languages" (Petitto, 2009, p. 192).

Even though there is no *critical* period for learning a language, there appears to be a critical period for learning accurate language pronunciation. The earlier people learn a second language, the more their pronunciation is near native. This is because from birth to about 4 months, infants can discriminate all the basic sound building blocks from any of the world's 6000 or so languages. Once they lose this capability and hone in on the sounds of the language, or languages, they are learning, near-native pronunciation of new languages is less likely (after 12-14 months). As we indicated above, however, the developmental window seems to stay open longer for children who are learning two or more languages at once, so these children can continue to differentiate sounds past their first year (Petitto, 2009).

After adolescence it is almost impossible to learn a new language without speaking with an accent (Anderson & Graham, 1994). Even if a child overhears a language, without actually learning it formally, this can improve later learning. After studying college students learning Spanish, Terry Au and colleagues concluded that "Although waiting until adulthood to learn a language almost guarantees a bad accent, having overheard the target language during childhood seems to lessen this predicament substantially" (Au, Knightly, Jun, & Oh, 2002, p. 242). So the best time to acquire two languages on your own through exposure (and to learn native pronunciation for both languages) is early childhood (Au, Oh, Knightly, Jun, & Romo, 2008).

BENEFITS OF BILINGUALISM.   There is no cognitive penalty for children who learn and speak two languages. In fact, there are benefits. Higher degrees of bilingualism are correlated with increased cognitive abilities in such areas as concept formation, creativity, theory of mind, cognitive flexibility, and understanding that printed words are symbols for language. In addition, these children have more advanced *metalinguistic* understanding of how language works; for example, they are more likely to notice grammar errors. Even more impressive, children from monolingual English-speaking families who attend

**Critical periods** If learning doesn't happen during these periods, it never will.

**Sensitive periods** Times when a person is especially ready for or responsive to certain experiences.

bilingual schools have been shown to have better phoneme awareness and reading comprehension than their peers who are educated in an English-only program. Looking at all this research, Petitto (2009) concluded that "early bilingualism offers no disadvantages; on the contrary, young bilinguals may be afforded a linguistic and a reading advantage... Moreover, learning to read in two languages may afford an advantage to children from monolingual homes in key phoneme awareness skills vital to reading success" (p. 193).

These conclusions hold as long as there is no stigma attached to being bilingual and as long as children are not expected to abandon their first language in order to learn the second (Bialystok, 2001; Bialystok, Majumder, & Martin, 2003; Galambos & Goldin-Meadow, 1990; Hamers & Blanc, 2000). Laura Petitto and Ioulia Kovelman (2003) suggest that perhaps humans evolved to speak multiple languages because this would have survival value, so maybe the "contemporary pockets of civilization where one language is spoken are the aberrant deviation; in other words, perhaps our brains were neurologically set to be multilingual" (p. 14). In addition, speaking two languages is an asset when graduates enter the business world (Mears, 1998).

**DIVERSITY IN LANGUAGE DEVELOPMENT** Higher degrees of bilingualism are correlated with increased cognitive abilities in such areas as concept formation, creativity, theory of mind, cognitive flexibility, and understanding that printed words are symbols for language.

Golden Pixels/Shutterstock

LANGUAGE LOSS.    Even though the advantages of bilingualism seem clear, many children and adults are losing their heritage language (Montrul, 2010). **Heritage language** is the language spoken in a student's home or by older relatives when the larger society outside the home speaks a different language (typically English or French in Canada). Often students who lose their heritage language were born in a new country after their parents or grandparents immigrated, so the students never lived in the country where everyone spoke their heritage language. In a large survey of grade 8 and 9 first- and second-generation children of immigrants in the United States, Portes and Hao (1998) found that only 16% had retained the ability to speak their heritage language well. And 72% said they preferred to speak English.

However, Indigenous languages are disappearing as well. According to the *National Household Survey* in 2011 (Statistics Canada, 2011), just 17.2% of Canadians who reported an Aboriginal identity indicated they could carry on a conversation in an Aboriginal language. This compares with 21% of respondents in the 2006 survey. These statistics vary across language groups and age groups and place of residence. For example, approximately 64% of Inuit individuals surveyed indicated they could speak an Aboriginal language, compared with 2.5% of individuals who identified as Métis. Older adults were also more likely to report speaking an Aboriginal language than youth, as were individuals living on versus off reserves.

Many First Nations peoples' intergenerational language transmission ceased as a result of the children being sent to residential schools during the first half of the twentieth century. Dr. Nicole Rosen at the University of Lethbridge is attempting to document one such language, called Michif, which is spoken by a few hundred Métis in Saskatchewan and Manitoba. As part of her efforts, she is involved in a language revitalization project with the Manitoba Métis Federation. The revitalization process follows a multipronged approach, with language learning targeted to both adults and children and taking place in both school and the home (Rosen, 2004).

Rather than losing one language to gain another, the goal should be **balanced bilingualism** —being equally fluent in both languages (Gonzalez, 1999). Students' home language connects them to extended family and important cultural traditions, but outside

Heritage language  The language spoken in the student's home or by members of the family.

Balanced bilingualism  Adding a second language capability without losing your heritage language.

TABLE 5.2 • **Some Schools That Support Heritage Languages in Canada and the United States**

| LANGUAGE | SCHOOL | DESCRIPTION |
|---|---|---|
| German | German Heritage Language School, Halifax Nova Scotia www.german-language-school.ca | Offers classes for adults and children. Lessons once a week for two hours on Thursday afternoons. German language skills (reading, writing, speaking, listening). |
| Chinese | Reidmount Saturday School, Markam, Ontario www.rhls.ca | A co-educational Saturday school that offers Chinese (Mandarin and Cantonese), Chinese history, English (grammar and writing), mathematics, science, communications, and drawing for students from junior kindergarten to grade 11. |
| Cree | Kihew Waciston Cree Immersion School Onion Lake First Nation, Saskatchewan www.onionlake.ca/education/kihew-waciston | The language of instruction for the children attending is Cree. The language—both spoken and written—permeates the building. |
| Many languages | The Alliance for the Advancement of Heritage Languages in America www.cal.org/heritage/index.html | The mission of the Alliance is to promote the maintenance and development of heritage languages for the benefit of individuals, communities, and society. |
| Spanish | Grupo Educa www.elgrupoeduca.org | Grupo Educa's mission is to enhance the Spanish language opportunities for children with a pre-existing knowledge of Spanish. Founded in June 2003 by a group of Southern California parents looking to expose their preschool-aged children to a dual-English/Spanish education. |
| Arabic and Hindi | Arabic and Hindi Heritage Language Classes, UCLA, Los Angeles http://www.hslanguages.ucla.edu/hslanguages | Intensive five-week courses for high school students who speak Hindi or Arabic at home and want to develop literacy and a deeper understanding of historical and contemporary South Asian culture. The project-based curriculum uses culturally relevant themes as a vehicle for listening, writing, speaking, and reading tasks. |

their homes, English connects them to academic, social, and economic opportunities (Borrero & Yeh, 2010).

Schools that focus on retaining heritage languages and cultures are being created in many countries with diverse language and cultural communities. Students attend these schools in the afternoons, on weekends, or during the summers in addition to attending their regular public school. In Great Britain, these institutions are called *supplementary* or *complementary* schools. In Australia they are called *community language* or *ethnic schools*. In Canada and the United States, the name often is *heritage language schools* (Creese, 2009). Look at Table 5.2 for a sampling of these schools and their missions.

Here are some ideas for learning about heritage schools in your area, suggested by Angela Creese (2009), a professor of educational linguistics at the University of Birmingham, United Kingdom:

- Find out which complementary/heritage schools are located in your area and make contact with them.
- When your students attend complementary/heritage schools, attend their awards ceremonies and presentations. Show your commitment to their bilingual and multicultural projects.
- Find out if teachers work in both the complementary/heritage and mainstream school sectors—ask them to undertake professional development workshops for other teachers in school.
- Ask a lead teacher of a complementary/heritage school to give an assembly.
- Encourage small-scale research and/or practical projects that would harness the potential links between complementary and mainstream schooling. (p. 272)

## Signed Languages

People who can communicate in both a spoken and a signed language or in two different signed languages are considered bilingual (Petitto, 2009). There are a number of other parallels between spoken languages and the many signed languages used around the world, such as American Sign Language (ASL), Signed English (USA, Ireland, New Zealand, Australia, Great Britain), Lingua de Signos Nicaraguense (Nicaraguan Sign Language), Warlpiri Sign Language (Australia Aboriginal), and Langue des Signes Quebecoise (LSQ) or Quebec Sign Language. Each of these languages is distinct and not simply a derived version of a spoken language. Moreover, people using Quebec Sign Language and French Sign Language may not understand each other. As is true for the spoken versions of these languages, there are differences in dialects across countries and even across regions within countries.

Both spoken and signed languages have large vocabularies and complex grammars. Laura Ann Petitto and Iugio Kovelman (2003) suggest that the same mechanisms for language acquisition are used for both spoken and signed languages. In addition, the milestones for signed language are the same as for spoken language. For example, children "say" their first words at about the same time, around 12 months, with both spoken and signed languages (Bloom, 2002). In fact, research with children learning a signed and a spoken language from infancy demonstrates that "being exposed to two languages from birth—and, in particular, being exposed to a signed and a spoken language from birth—does not cause a child to be language delayed or confused" (Petitto & Kovelman, 2003, p. 16). As with two spoken languages, children can become balanced bilinguals in a spoken and a signed language.

In the 1970s, language researchers were able to study the birth of a new socially shared signed language when Nicaragua established its first school for the deaf. The students came using their own unique invented sign languages. Over the years, a new language emerged that was based on the students' sign languages. As the children developed the new Lingua de Signos Nicaraguense (Nicaraguan Sign Language), it became more systematic. The vocabulary expanded and the grammar grew more complex. New students learned the developing Nicaraguan Sign Language as their native language (Hoff, 2006; Senghas & Coppola, 2001).

## What Is Involved in Being Bilingual?

In the 2011 Census of Population (Statistics Canada, 2014), more than 200 languages were reported as a home language or mother tongue across Canada. More than 14% of those surveyed reported speaking a language other than French or English, and 80% of individuals speaking an immigrant language live in the six largest metropolitan areas in Canada: Toronto, Montreal, Vancouver, Calgary, Edmonton, and Ottawa-Gatineau. With these numbers come many misconceptions about bilingualism, as you can see in Table 5.3.

What does it really mean to be bilingual? Some definitions of *bilingualism* focus exclusively on a language-based meaning: Bilingual people, or bilinguals, speak two languages. Other definitions are more rigorous and define bilinguals as "adults who had early, intensive, and maintained dual language exposure and who use their two languages in their adult daily life" (Petitto, 2009, p. 186). But being bilingual and bicultural also means mastering the knowledge necessary to communicate in two cultures as well as dealing with potential discrimination (Borrero & Yeh, 2010). Consider the experiences of two students who immigrated to Canada to study business at university (Lim, 2013):

> Student 1 immigrated to Canada from India: "I always heard about Canada to be open, friendly, smiling, caring, and safe. However, I found every day to be more mysterious than ever ... Some people are very open and gentle and some ... no smile and as rude as they can be."
>
> Student 2 came to Canada from Argentina: "Even though I decided to leave my home city for a better life, I found myself missing a lot all my good friends and family ... The change from Spanish to English and from a collectivist to individualist culture also had an impact on me."

TABLE 5.3 • **Myths and Misconceptions About Being Bilingual**

In the table below, L1 means the original language and L2 means the second language.

| MYTH | TRUTH |
|---|---|
| Learning a second language (L2) takes little time and effort. | Learning English as a second language takes two to three years for oral and five to seven years for academic language use. |
| All language skills (listening, speaking, reading, writing) transfer from L1 to L2. | Reading is the skill that transfers most readily. |
| Code-switching is an indication of a language disorder. | Code-switching indicates high-level language skills in both L1 and L2. |
| All bilinguals easily maintain both languages. | It takes great effort and attention to maintain high-level skills in both languages. |
| Children do not lose their first language. | Loss of L1 and underdevelopment of L2 are problems for second language learners (semilingual in L1 and L2). |
| Exposure to English is sufficient for L2 learning. | To learn L2, students need to have a reason to communicate, access to English speakers, interaction, support, feedback, and time. |
| To learn English, students' parents need to speak only English at home. | Children need to use both languages in many contexts. |
| Reading in L1 is detrimental to learning English. | Literacy-rich environments in either L1 or L2 support development of necessary prereading skills. |
| Language disorders must be identified by tests in English. | Children must be tested in both L1 and L2 to determine language disorders. |

*Source: Brice, A. E. (2002). The Hispanic Child: Speech, Language, Culture and Education, 1st Edition. Reprinted by permission of Pearson Education, Inc., Upper Saddle River, NJ.*

Being bilingual requires the ability to move back and forth between two cultures and two languages while still maintaining a sense of your own identity, so bilingualism requires biculturalism as well (Lee, Wong, & Alvarez, 2008). And being a successful bilingual student has one more requirement—learning *academic language*.

## Contextualized and Academic Language

Proficiency in a second language has two separate aspects: face-to-face communication (known as *basic* or *contextualized language skills*) and academic uses of language such as reading and doing grammar exercises (known as *academic language*) (Fillmore & Snow, 2000; Garcia, 2002). **Academic language** is the entire range of language used in elementary, secondary, and university level schools. Academic language includes the general words and concepts used in many subjects such as *analyze, evaluate,* or *summarize,* as well as words and strategies specific to disciplines such as *angle, factor the equation,* or *derivative* in math; a *factor* in statistics; or a *derivative* in finance (you see how complicated this gets when the same word has two very different meanings in different fields). Academic language is associated with abstract, higher-order, complex concepts (Vogt, Echevarria, & Short, 2010).

It takes about two to three years in a good-quality program for children who are learning a new language to be able to use basic or contextualized language

**Academic language** The entire range of language used in elementary, secondary, and university-level schools, including words, concepts, strategies, and processes from academic subjects.

TABLE 5.4 • **Common Errors and Accomplishments as Students Learn a Second Language**

| LANGUAGE STAGE | COMMON ERRORS AND LIMITATIONS | ACCOMPLISHMENTS |
|---|---|---|
| During the first year of learning the language | • No speech at all<br>• Only understands one word at a time<br>• Mispronounces words<br>• Leaves out words<br>• One or two word responses<br>• Relies heavily on context | • Uses pantomiming, gestures, pointing to communicate<br>• Can use "yes," "no," or single words |
| During the second year of learning the language | • Basic pronunciation and grammar mistakes<br>• Limited vocabulary | • Uses whole sentences<br>• Good comprehension (in context)<br>• Uses language to function well socially |
| During the third year and beyond of learning the language | • Some errors with complex grammar | • Can tell whole stories<br>• Good comprehension<br>• Beginning to understand and use academic language<br>• Larger vocabulary |

*Source: Based on information from Miranda, T. Z. (2008). Bilingual Education for All Students: Still Standing after All These Years. In L. S. Verplaetse & N. Migliacci (Eds.), Inclusive Pedagogy for English Language Learners: A Handbook of Research-Informed Practices (pp. 257–275). New York: Erlbaum.*

face to face in conversations. The stages for basic second language learning are shown in Table 5.4.

Mastering academic language skills such as reading texts in the new language takes much longer than three years—more like five to 10 years, depending on how much academic knowledge the student already had in his or her native language. So children who seem to "know" a second language in conversation may still have great difficulty with complex schoolwork in that language (Bialystok, 2001; Verplaetse & Migliacci, 2008).

The *Guidelines* give ideas for promoting language learning, but also keep cultural differences in mind as you teach. There are many ways that cultural differences might interfere with developing academic English and content understanding. For example, many Asian students come from a culture that believes asking the teacher questions is rude and inappropriate because questioning implies that the teacher has done a poor job of instruction. In Asian classrooms this might cause the teacher to lose face in front of the students—an entirely unacceptable situation. Thus teachers need to ask themselves why their English learners are not asking questions. For another example, class discussion may be considered a waste of time in cultures in which the teacher is viewed as the source of authoritative knowledge. How would students learn from other students who are not authorities? So beliefs about learning shaped by culture and previous experiences in different kinds of classrooms may explain why English learners seem quiet and reluctant to speak in class. English language learners also may think that their teachers are not very good because they do not explain everything. They also may strongly prefer memorization as a learning strategy if memorization was emphasized in their previous schools. (Thanks to Dr. Alan Hirvela at Ohio State University for pointing out these possible cultural differences in beliefs about schools and teachers.)

We turn to other language teaching issues next, as we consider dialects.

## GUIDELINES

### Promoting Language Learning

**Provide structures, frameworks, scaffolds, and strategies.**
*Examples*
1. "Think aloud" as you solve a problem by building on and clarifying the input of students.
2. Use visual organizers, story maps, or other aids to help students organize and relate information.

**Teach relevant background knowledge and key vocabulary concepts.**
*Examples*
1. Informally assess students' current background knowledge. Directly teach needed information, if missing.
2. Focus on key vocabulary words and use those words consistently.

**Give focused and useful feedback.**
*Examples*
1. Focus feedback on meaning, not grammar, syntax, or pronunciation.
2. Give frequent, brief, clear feedback—use words from the student's first language when you can.
3. Make sure to let students know when they are successful.
4. Break assignments and activities into smaller, "bite-sized pieces" with feedback after each "bite."

**Keeps students involved and engaged.**
*Examples*
1. Use small-group and pairs work.
2. Create situations where students talk at length.
3. Challenge students with clear higher-order questions—allow time to think and write out answers, maybe in pairs.

**Show authentic respect for students' culture and language.**
*Examples*
1. Learn about your students' personal and language background: What languages are spoken at home? When did the family arrive? How long have they lived in Canada? What schooling did they receive in other countries?
2. Learn about the students' religious background, food preferences and restrictions, and family customs; then incorporate students' experiences into writing and language arts activities.
3. Learn some key words in the students' languages.
4. View diversity as an asset; reject cultural deficit notions.

*Sources: Adapted from Peregoy, S. F., & Boyle, O. F. (2009). Reading, Writing, and Learning in ESL: A Resource Book for Teaching K–12 English Learners (5th ed.). Boston: Allyn & Bacon/Pearson; Echevarria, J., & Graves, A. (2011). Content Instruction: Teaching English Learners with Diverse Abilities (4th ed.). Columbus, OH: Pearson; Gersten, R. (1996b). Literacy Instruction for Language-Minority Students: The Transition Years. The Elementary School Journal, 96, 217–220.*

## DIALECT DIFFERENCES IN THE CLASSROOM

Communication is at the heart of teaching, but as we have seen in this chapter, culture affects communication. In this section, we will examine two kinds of language differences—dialect differences and genderlects.

### Dialects

**STOP & THINK** When you want a soft drink, what do you call it? Do you think people in other countries, or even in different regions of the same country, use the same term, even though we all speak English? •

Anita, one of your textbook authors, grew up in Texas. There, they always asked, "Do you want a *coke*?" If the answer was yes, the next question was, "What kind—Coca-Cola, root beer, 7-Up, orange?" Phil grew up just north of New York City. When he wanted a soft drink, he asked for *soda*. In Canada, we are more likely to refer to *pop*. Different countries and different regions within countries have different ways of speaking—both in their accents and word usage.

A **dialect** is any variety of a language spoken by a particular group. Eugene Garcia (2002) defines a dialect as "a regional variation of language characterized by distinct grammar, vocabulary, and pronunciation" (p. 218). The dialect is part of the group's

**Dialect** Any variety of a language spoken by a particular group.

collective identity. Actually, every person reading this text speaks at least one dialect, maybe more, because there is no one absolute standard English. The English language has several dialects—for example, Australian, Canadian, British, and American. Within each of these dialects are variations. A few examples of dialects of American English are Southern, Bostonian, Cajun, and African American Vernacular (Garcia, 2002). Similarly, Canadians in different regions of the country have different accents and dialects.

**Aboriginal or First Nations English dialects** are a group of dialects of English used by Aboriginal peoples of Canada. These dialects differ enough from mainstream Canadian speech that Aboriginal people are identifiable to non-Aboriginal people by the way they talk. As is the case with African American English, Aboriginal English is poorly understood and typically not well perceived by majority English speakers (Ball & Bernhardt, 2008). In fact, some practitioners and First Nations leaders have concerns about the dispropor-tionate numbers of Aboriginal children referred for speech language services, perhaps because features of their home English dialects are misinterpreted as speech language deficits or delays (Ball, Bernhardt, & Deby, 2006). Consequently, academics are calling for research to help speech language therapists and other educators distinguish between language impairments and dialectical differences, accept varieties of Aboriginal English as valid and part of the Aboriginal culture, and develop culturally relevant assessment and instructional practices (Ball & Bernhardt, 2008).

Dialects differ in their rules about pronunciation, grammar, and vocabulary, but it is important to remember that these differences are not errors. Each dialect is logical, com-plex, and rule-governed. An example of this is the use of the double negative. In many ver-sions of North American English, the double negative construction, such as "I don't have no more," is incorrect. But in many dialects, such as some varieties of African American vernacular English, and in other languages (for instance, Russian, French, Spanish, and Hungarian), the double negative is part of the grammatical rules. To say, "I don't want anything" in Spanish, you must literally say, "I don't want nothing," or *"No quiero nada."*

DIALECTS AND PRONUNCIATION.    Dialects also differ in pronunciation, which can lead to spelling problems. In some varieties of African American vernacular English and in Southern dialects, for instance, there is less attention paid to pronouncing the ends of words. A lack of attention to final consonants, such as *s*, can lead to failure to indicate possession, third-person singular verbs, and plurals in the standard way. So *John's book* might be *John book*, and the singular and plural will sound the same for words such as *thinks, wasps*, and *lists*. When endings are not pronounced, there are more *homonyms* (words that sound alike but have different meanings) in the student's speech than the unknowing teacher may expect; *spent* and *spend* might sound alike, for example. Even without the confusions caused by dialect differences, there are many homonyms in English. Usually, special atten-tion is given to words such as these when they come up in spelling lessons. If teachers are aware of the special homonyms in student dialects, they can teach these differences directly.

DIALECTS AND TEACHING.    How can teachers cope with linguistic diversity in the class-room? First, they can be sensitive to their own possible negative stereotypes about children who speak a different dialect. Second, teachers can ensure comprehension by repeating instructions using different words and by asking students to paraphrase instructions or give examples. The best teaching approach seems to be to focus on understanding the students and accepting their language as a valid and correct system, but to teach the alternative forms of English (or whatever the dominant language is in your country) that are used in more for-mal work settings and writing so that the students will have access to a range of opportuni-ties. For example, Lisa Delpit (1995) describes Martha Demientieff, a Native Alaskan teacher of Athabaskan children in a small village. The teacher's goal is for her students to become fluent in both their dialect, which she calls "Heritage English," and the "Formal English" of employers and others outside the village. She explains to her students that people outside the village will judge them by the way they talk and write. She goes on to explain:

> We have to feel sorry for them because they have only one way to talk. We're going to learn two ways to say things. One will be our Heritage way. The other will be Formal English. Then when we go to get jobs, we'll be able to talk like those people who only

**Watch**
Dialects and Teaching

**Aboriginal or First Nations English dialects** A group of dialects of English used by Aboriginal peoples of Canada.

**DIALECT DIFFERENCES IN THE CLASSROOM** Teachers should accept their linguistically diverse students' languages as valid and correct systems, but also teach the dominant language used in more formal work settings and writing so that the students will have access to a range of opportunities.

*Dennis Kitchen/PhotoEdit*

know and can only listen to one way. Maybe after we get the jobs we can help them to learn how it feels to have another language, like ours, that feels so good. We'll talk like them when we have to, but we'll always know our way is best. (p. 41)

Moving between two speech forms is called **code-switching**—something we all have learned to do. Sometimes, the code is formal speech for educational or professional communication. At other times, the code is informal for talk among friends and family. And occasionally, the codes are different dialects. Even young children recognize variations in codes. Delpit (1995) describes the reaction of one of her grade 1 students to her very first reading lesson. After she carefully recited the memorized introduction from the teacher's manual, a student raised his hand and asked, "Teacher, how come you talkin' like a white person? You talkin' just like my momma talk when she get on the phone."

Learning the alternative versions of a language is easy for most children, as long as they have good models, clear instruction, and opportunities for authentic practice.

## Genderlects

If you had to guess what **genderlects** are, based on what you know about dialects, you probably would figure out that genderlects are different ways of talking for males and females. There are some small differences between boys and girls—girls tend to be slightly more talkative and affiliative in their speech (*affiliative* speech is talk intended to establish and maintain relationships). But much of the research has been conducted with white, middle-class children, and the results do not necessarily hold for other groups and cultures. For example, some research reports that girls are more likely to cooperate and to talk about caring, whereas boys are more competitive and talk about rights and justice. But other studies have found that African American girls in one study were just as likely as boys to compete and talk about their rights in conversations (Leaper & Smith, 2004).

As with most aspects of language, there are cultural differences in genderlects. Interrupting is a good example. In studies with North American samples, boys have been found to interrupt more often than girls. However, studies in Africa, the Caribbean, South America, and Eastern Europe find females interrupt males much more often than they do in America. And in Thailand, Hawaii, Japan, and Antigua, the style of speaking for boys and girls is overlapping—this overlapping talk is not interruption but cooperative turn taking (Owens, 2005).

# TEACHING IMMIGRANT STUDENTS AND ENGLISH LANGUAGE LEARNERS

Akahdeep is in grade 5 and lives with his family in Surrey, British Columbia. He came with his family from Punjab, India, to Canada more than three years ago, so his father could take a job working on a farm owned by his uncle. The neighbourhood where Akahdeep and his family live has a large Punjabi population. Within the neighbourhood there are several temples, and many Punjabi restaurants and retail stores. Akahdeep's mother, who takes care of the home and children, speaks no English, but his father and his older brother, Dilpreet, both speak a little. Dilpreet was 15 when the family came to this country. He left school after one year in an English Language Learning (ELL) program, and went to work with his father on the farm. He is proud to be contributing to the family, but dreams of being a car mechanic; he spends all his free time fixing cars for neighbours

**Code-switching** Moving between two speech forms.

**Genderlects** Different ways of talking for males and females.

and earns a little extra money that way. Akahdeep's oldest sister is 15 now, and continues to receive ELL support in high school. Their parents have chosen a husband for her from "back home," and she plans to leave school as soon as she turns 16, although she would rather not marry the man her parents have chosen. Akahdeep's two younger sisters are 8 and 4; the youngest is in a special Head Start class to learn English, and the other is receiving special education support because she is having a hard time learning to read.

Akahdeep gets mostly Cs in school. He still struggles a bit with reading his textbooks, but he has many English-speaking friends in his class and has no trouble conversing in English with them; in fact, he translates for his parents when they come to school for parent conferences, which they do whenever his father can get off work. Math is his real talent; he consistently gets As on his tests. He attends a Challenge Program within his school district for math. The teacher at the Challenge Program tells him he could be an accountant or maybe an engineer when he grows up. Akahdeep likes this idea, but his father says that college would cost too much money and reminds him that the family plans to go back to India someday, once they have saved enough money to buy their own small farm, which is his father's dream.

There are many students like Akahdeep and his siblings in Canadian schools today. For the remainder of this chapter we explore ways of teaching these students so that their dreams of college and careers can come true wherever they finally live.

## Immigrants and Refugees

Figure 5.2 shows how ethnically diverse Canada has become. It is estimated that by the year 2016, 20% of Canada's population will be members of a visible minority group (Winzer, 2006). Many of these people will be immigrants. **Immigrants** are people who voluntarily leave their country to become permanent residents in a new place. **Refugees** are a special group of immigrants who also relocate voluntarily, but they are fleeing their home country because it is not safe. Canada determines refugee status on two grounds: Individuals are unable or unwilling to return to their home country because (a) they have a well-founded fear of persecution there, or (b) returning to their home country likely will result in torture, risk to life, or risk of cruel and unusual treatment or punishment (Citizenship and Immigration Canada, 2007). Since the Second World War, Canada has provided protection to more than 800 000 refugees, 147 000 in the years between 2002 and 2007.

**Immigrants** People who voluntarily leave their country to become permanent residents in a new place.

**Refugees** A special group of immigrants who also relocate voluntarily, but who are fleeing their home country because it is not safe.

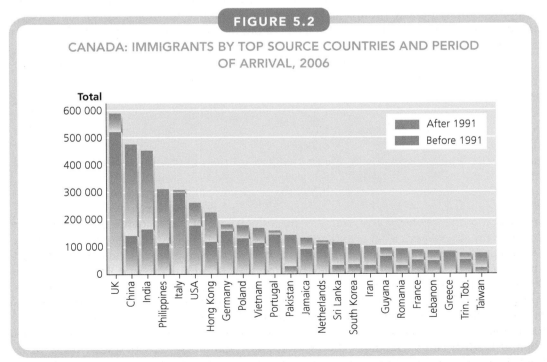

## FIGURE 5.2

### CANADA: IMMIGRANTS BY TOP SOURCE COUNTRIES AND PERIOD OF ARRIVAL, 2006

*Source: Canada Immigrant Job Issues. (n.d.). Retrieved September 13, 2010, from www.canadaimmigrants.com/statistics.asp.*

**TEACHING IMMIGRANT STUDENTS AND ENGLISH LANGUAGE LEARNERS** Most educational psychologists believe that no culture is deficient, but rather that there may be incompatibilities between the student's home culture and the expectations of the school.

Israel Images/Alamy

In the past, some educators suggested that immigrants, students from visible minority groups, and poor students had problems in school because they were "culturally disadvantaged" or "culturally handicapped." The assumption of this **cultural deficit model** was that the students' home culture was inferior because it had not prepared them to fit into the schools. Today, educational psychologists reject the idea of cultural deficits. They believe that no culture is deficient; rather, there may be incompatibilities between the student's home culture and the expectations of the school (Gallimore & Goldenberg, 2001). Multiculturalism is the goal. Multiculturalism rejects the idea of a **melting pot**, whereby ethnic minority groups are expected to assimilate into the mainstream society, and supports a society that values diversity—more like a salad bowl or mosaic with many contributions (Banks, 1997, 2006; Stinson, 2006).

## Classrooms Today

Immigration is now the main source of Canada's population growth, which has significant implications for our school systems, and for the preparation of teachers (Guo, 2012). As indicated earlier in this chapter, close to 20% of these families speak languages other than French or English at home. Consequently, many children who attend our schools have limited English proficiency. These changes are not limited to Canada. In the United States, nearly 21% of school-age children speak a language other than English at home, and there are projections that, by 2030, about 40% of the students in pre-kindergarten through grade 12 will have limited English skills. In fact, most developed countries have many immigrant students. For example, more than half of the students under age 12 in Amsterdam schools are from immigrant families (Crul & Holdaway, 2009).

Because immigrant families tend to live in particular neighbourhoods, the schools in these communities generally have the largest number of immigrants and English language learner (ELL) students. Some of these students also may not be able to read and write in their native language. Clearly, schools serving these students need extra resources to hire and train native-language–speaking teachers and aides, provide smaller classes, and purchase well-designed materials to teach complex academic subjects to students with limited English language skills (Crul & Holdaway, 2009). As you can guess, these extra resources are not always available.

**Cultural deficit model** A model that explains the school achievement problems of ethnic minority students by assuming that their culture is inadequate and does not prepare them to succeed in school.

**Melting pot** A metaphor for the absorption and assimilation of immigrants into the mainstream of society so that ethnic differences vanish.

FOUR STUDENT PROFILES.    Following are four general profiles of English learners in today's classrooms (Echevarria & Graves, 2011).

- *Balanced bilinguals.* These students speak, read, and write well both in their first language and in English. They have the academic knowledge needed to continue learning in both languages and the skills and attitudes to do so. These students may not present difficult teaching challenges, but they do need to maintain their skills in both languages and cultures.
- *Monolingual/literate students.* These students are literate in their native language (at or above grade level when working in their native language), but speak limited English. The teaching challenge here is to help the students develop English and continue to learn academic subjects.
- *Monolingual/preliterate students.* These students are not literate. They may not read or write in their native language, or they may have very limited literacy skills. Some have never have attended school. In addition, they speak limited English. These students require the greatest support in learning both academic subjects and language.
- *Limited bilingual.* These students can converse well in both languages, but for some reason they have trouble learning academically. There may be underlying challenges such as learning disabilities or emotional problems. Further assessment is often required to diagnose these problems.

These student profiles are related to the distinction we encountered earlier in the chapter between contextualized conversational language and academic language. You may remember that it takes two to three years to develop good conversational language, but five to 10 years to master academic language. *Conversational* skills include, for example, using appropriate vocabulary and sentences, asking and answering questions, starting and stopping conversations, listening, and understanding and using idioms.

*Academic language* includes reading and writing fluency; grammar and syntax; knowledge of specialized vocabulary; following written and oral directions; collaborating with other students on assignments; understanding different types of texts and forms of

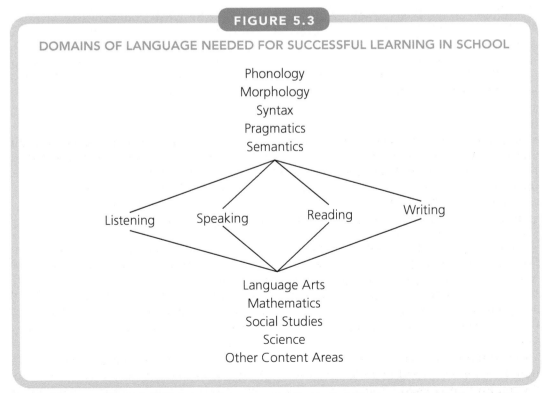

**FIGURE 5.3**

DOMAINS OF LANGUAGE NEEDED FOR SUCCESSFUL LEARNING IN SCHOOL

Phonology
Morphology
Syntax
Pragmatics
Semantics

Listening    Speaking    Reading    Writing

Language Arts
Mathematics
Social Studies
Science
Other Content Areas

*Source: Echevarria, J. J., Graves, A. (2011). Sheltered Content Instruction: Teaching English Language Learners with Diverse Abilities: Coursesmart ETextbook, 4th Edition. Reprinted by permission of Pearson Education, Inc., Upper Saddle River, NJ.*

writing such as fiction, poetry, math problems, science charts and graphs, and timelines in history; and study skills such as outlining, summarizing, and reading comprehension (Echevarria & Graves, 2011). So to be successful in learning content, English language learners must put together an understanding of language with knowledge of terms, concepts, and conventions specific to a particular subject such as mathematics or biology. Figure 5.3 shows all the different domains of language that must come together for learning.

If you teach at a school with many English language learners, there probably will be school personnel who do formal assessments to provide appropriate placements for these students.

# GENERATION 1.5: STUDENTS IN TWO WORLDS

**Generation 1.5** refers to children and youth, like Akahdeep, who were not born in Canada but immigrated here with their first-generation parents, typically before adolescence (Kim & Duff, 2012). They were not born in Canada, but they arrived early enough to spend most of their school years here. Often they perceive their national identity is divided between Canada and their country of birth. The language spoken in their homes may not be English, but they often speak fluent conversational English, even if their academic English is not as well developed.

These students may share several characteristics and challenges. They may not have strong literacy skills in the language used at home because they have not received much schooling in that language. They may have acquired much of their English through listening to and speaking with friends or older siblings, watching television, or listening to music. They have been called "ear learners" because they have built their knowledge of English on the language they have heard in their environment. But what they hear is often colloquial language or slang, so they may have trouble learning how to read and write accurately in English. Most native English speakers know if the grammar is correct in what we hear or read because we have heard (mostly) accurate grammar all our lives— our ears have taught us well. But for many Generation 1.5 students, their ear learning has given them an imperfect, even inaccurate conception of English grammar. Because they are "ear learners," they may use incorrect verb or noun forms, mispronounce plurals, or mix up words that sound very similar—for example, *confident* and *confidence*. They rely on context, gestures, facial cues, and intonations to make sense of language, so reading is more difficult and proofreading is hard because they cannot "hear" mistakes. Complex academic reading and writing assignments are very challenging (Harklau, Losey, & Siegal, 1999; Reid & Byrd 1998; Roberge, 2002). In contrast, many students who arrive in Canada to attend university can read and write quite well, but they have difficulty with oral interactions. These students learned English mostly as "eye learners" through reading, writing, and vocabulary and grammar exercises. Knowing what kind of students you have and how they first learned English should help you understand the mistakes they make and the challenges they face.

## Bilingual Education and English Learners

Two terms that you will see associated with bilingualism are **English language learners (ELL)**, describing *students* whose primary or heritage language is not English, and **English as a second language (ESL)** *classrooms*, where these students learn English. Limited proficiency in English often leads to lower academic achievement and poorer job prospects, so an important issue related to diversity in language development is how best to teach these students.

TWO APPROACHES TO ENGLISH LANGUAGE LEARNING. Virtually everyone agrees that all citizens should learn the official language, or languages, of their country. But when and how should instruction in that language begin? Is it better to teach English language learners to read first in their native language, or should they begin reading

---

**Structured English immersion (SEI)** An environment that teaches English rapidly by maximizing instruction in English and using English at a level appropriate to the abilities of the ELLs in the class.

**Semilingual** A lack of proficiency in any language; speaking one or more languages inadequately.

**Generation 1.5** Children and youth, like Akahdeep, who were not born in Canada but immigrated here with their first-generation parents, typically before adolescence.

**English language learners (ELLs)** Students who are learning English when their primary or heritage language is not English.

**English as a second language (ESL)** The classes devoted to teaching ELL students English.

## POINT/COUNTERPOINT  What Is the Best Way to Teach English Language Learners?

There are two basic positions on this question, which have given rise to two contrasting teaching approaches: one that focuses on *immersion* in English-only teaching and learning to make the transition to English as quickly as possible. The other approach attempts to *maintain or improve* the native language and use that language as the primary language for teaching and learning until English language skills are more fully developed.

**POINT**

▶ **Structured English immersion is the best approach for ELL students.** Proponents of the *immersion/fast transition* approach believe that English ought to be introduced as early and as intensively as possible; they argue that valuable learning time is lost if students are taught in their native language. Advocates cite the successes of the Canadian Immersion program as evidence that language immersion works (Baker, 1998). In an article for educational administrators, Kevin Clark claims, "These programs have the potential to accelerate ELLs' English language development and linguistic preparation for grade-level academic content" (2009, p. 42). Many schools today follow this line of thinking and offer **Structured English Immersion or SEI**. There are different perspectives on SEI, but usually it is defined as having two basic features: (1) Teachers use English as much as possible in instruction, but (2) the level of the students' abilities in the class determines how teachers use and teach English (i.e., English use and teaching must be appropriate for student abilities) (Ramirez, Yuen, & Ramey, 1991).

Immersion in a language is the best way to learn a new language and is the basis for many language-learning programs around the world (Clark, 2009). Moreover, in school systems like Montreal, Toronto, and Vancouver, where the student population speaks, literally, hundreds of languages, SEI seems the only reasonable approach.

**COUNTERPOINT**

▶ **Students' native language should be maintained.** Teaching *in* English and hoping students will figure it out is not the same as *teaching* English. Proponents of *native-language maintenance instruction* raise four important issues (Gersten, 1996b; Goldenberg, 1996; Hakuta & Garcia, 1989).

1. Deep learning in the first language supports second-language learning. For example, one study that followed a national sample of grade 8 students in the United States for 12 years found that Latino students' proficiency in their first language of Spanish predicted their reading ability in English, and their English reading ability predicted their achievement in school and in careers (Guglielmi, 2008). The metacognitive strategies and knowledge developed when students learn to read in their first language are transferred to reading in a second language as well (van Gelderen, Schoonen,

Stoel, de Glopper, & Hulstijn, 2007). So maintaining and increasing proficiency in the first language is important. The strategies and academic content (math, science, history, etc.) that students learn in their native language are not forgotten when they learn English.

2. Children who are forced to try to learn math or science in an unfamiliar language are bound to have trouble. What if you had been forced to learn fractions or biology in a second language that you had studied for only a semester? Some psychologists believe students taught by this approach may become **semilingual**; that is, they are not proficient in either language.

3. If the first language is neglected and the entire emphasis is on English, students may get the message that their home languages (and therefore, their families and cultures) are second class.

4. Years ago, Kenji Hakuta cited a "paradoxical attitude of admiration and pride for school-attained bilingualism on the one hand and scorn and shame for home-brewed immigrant bilingualism on the other" (1986, p. 229). Ironically, by the time students have mastered academic English and let their home language deteriorate, they reach secondary school and are encouraged to learn a "second" language. Sometimes native speakers of Spanish are encouraged to learn French or German, so they risk becoming semilingual in three languages (Miranda, 2008).

**Beyond Either/Or.** It is difficult to separate politics from practice in the debate about bilingual education. However, it is clear that high-quality bilingual education programs can have positive results. Students improve in their knowledge of subject matter taught in their native language, in their mastery of English, and in self-esteem as well (Crawford, 1997; Francis, Lesaux, & August, 2006). Fortunately attention today is shifting from debate about general approaches to a focus on effective teaching strategies. As you will see many times in this text, a combination of clarity of learning goals and direct instruction in needed skills—including learning strategies and tactics, teacher- or peer-guided practice leading to independent practice, authentic and engaging tasks, opportunities for interaction and conversation that are academically focused, and warm encouragement from the teacher—seems to be effective (Chamot & O'Malley, 1996; Gersten, 1996b; Goldenberg, 1996).

instruction in English? Do these children need some oral lessons in English before read-ing instruction can be effective? Should other subjects such as mathematics and social studies be taught in the primary (home) language until students are fluent in English? As you can see in the *Point/Counterpoint,* debates about this question have raged for quite a while.

RESEARCH ON BILINGUAL EDUCATION.   There are strong advantages for simultane-ous bilingual learning. Remember Petitto's (2009) finding that monolingual English speak-ers who participated in a bilingual program excelled in the skills needed for reading in both languages. When the National Literacy Panel on Language: Minority Children and Youth reviewed studies of English-only *immersion* versus native language *maintenance* programs in the United States, they found that the students in the native language mainte-nance programs performed better on many different measured outcomes (Francis, Lesaux, & August, 2006). In a study that directly compared immersion and maintenance programs in 128 classrooms in Texas and California, Lee Branum-Martin and his colleagues (2010) found that the amount of teaching conducted in English and Spanish could not be pre-dicted by type of program—there were many local variations. Some English immersion teachers used quite a bit of Spanish, and some Spanish language maintenance programs taught quite a bit in English. Another finding was that Spanish language maintenance programs had a positive impact on English performance.

A study funded by the U.S. Department of Education identified five major recom-mendations for ELLs (Gersten et al., 2007; Peregoy & Boyle, 2009), summarized here:

1. Begin instruction with a formative assessment (see Chapter 15) of reading to deter-mine exactly what the English learners know and what they are ready to learn, and to identify students who will need more help in reading.
2. Use small-group interventions to focus instruction on the areas of need identified in the assessments.
3. Target teaching essential vocabulary for the content in your curriculum as well as common words, phrases, and expressions used class.
4. Directly teach academic English—develop the students' abilities to read texts, write academic assignments, and use formal language and argument.
5. Make wide use of peer-assisted learning, particularly work in pairs, to complete aca-demic tasks.

BILINGUALISM FOR ALL: TWO-WAY IMMERSION.   Students need to master both con-versational and academic English to achieve at high levels, but they should not sacrifice their native language in the process. The goal of schools should be balanced bilingualism. One approach to reaching this goal is to create classes that mix students who are learn-ing a second language with students who are native speakers. The objective is for both groups to become fluent in both languages (Peregoy & Boyle, 2009; Sheets, 2005). Anita's daughter, whose first language is English, spent a summer in such a program in Quebec and was ahead in every French class she took after that.

For truly effective education for ELLs, we will need many bilingual teachers. If you have a competence in another language, you might want to develop it fully for your teaching. Because there is a shortage of qualified ESL teachers for ELLs (Hawkins, 2004), promoting language learning is a responsibility for most teachers, especially in communi-ties with large numbers of ELLs. Table 5.5 provides some ideas for supporting language and literacy development across the grade levels.

The challenge for most teachers working with immigrant and ELL students is to teach the subject matter and develop students' English language skills at the same time. Sheltered instruction is one approach that has proved successful in reaching both goals.

## Sheltered Instruction

**Sheltered instruction** teaches content to ELL students by putting the words and concepts of the content into context to make the content more understandable. Strategies include

**Sheltered instruction** Approach to teaching that improves English language skills while teaching content to ELL students by putting the words and concepts of the content into context to make the content more understandable.

TABLE 5.5 • **Ideas for Promoting Learning and Language Acquisition**

Effective teaching for students in bilingual and ESL classrooms combines many strategies—direct instruction, mediation, coaching, feedback, modelling, encouragement, challenge, and authentic activities.

1. Structures, frameworks, scaffolds, and strategies
   - Provide support to students by "thinking aloud," building on and clarifying input of students
   - Use visual organizers, story maps, or other aids to help students organize and relate information
2. Relevant background knowledge and key vocabulary concepts
   - Provide adequate background knowledge to students and informally assess whether students have background knowledge
   - Focus on key vocabulary words and use consistent language
   - Incorporate students' primary language meaningfully
3. Mediation/feedback
   - Give feedback that focuses on meaning, not grammar, syntax, or pronunciation
   - Give frequent and comprehensible feedback
   - Provide students with prompts or strategies
   - Ask questions that press students to clarify or expand on initial statements
   - Provide activities and tasks that students can complete
   - Indicate to students when they are successful
   - Assign activities that are reasonable, avoiding undue frustration
   - Allow use of native language responses (when context is appropriate)
   - Be sensitive to common problems in second-language acquisition
4. Involvement
   - Ensure active involvement of all students, including low-performing students
   - Foster extended discourse
5. Challenge
   - Provide implicit challenge (e.g., cognitive challenge, use of higher-order questions)
   - Provide explicit challenge (e.g., high but reasonable expectations)
6. Respect for—and responsiveness to—cultural and personal diversity
   - Show respect for students as individuals, respond to things students say, show respect for culture and family, and possess knowledge of cultural diversity
   - Incorporate students' experiences into writing and language arts activities
   - Link content to students' lives and experiences to enhance understanding
   - View diversity as an asset, reject cultural deficit notions

Source: *From Gersten, R. (1996). Literacy instruction for language minority students: The transition years. The Elementary School Journal, 96, 241–242. Copyright © 1996. Adapted by permission of the University of Chicago Press.*

simplifying and controlling language, giving attention to the relevant grammar and forms of English—helping students "crack the code," using visuals and gestures, and including real-life supports and examples. In addition, there is an emphasis on student talk and discussion instead of the teacher doing all the talking. In order to be clearer about what good sheltered instruction looks like, Jana Echevarría and her colleagues (2014) identified eight key elements: preparation, building background, comprehensibility, strategies, interaction, practice and application, lesson delivery, and review and assessment. Then the researchers developed an observational system to check that each element was included in teaching. The system is called the **Sheltered Instruction Observation Protocol or SIOP**. Figure 5.4 gives some examples of what each element of SIOP might include.

What might a SIOP lesson look like? There are many ways to design lessons that meet the standards in Figure 5.4. Table 5.6 describes seven different lesson structures and activities to help students understand content and develop language skills.

**Sheltered Instruction Observation Protocol or SIOP** An observational system to check that each element of sheltered instruction is present for a teacher.

**FIGURE 5.4**

## SOME EXAMPLES OF THE STRUCTURED INSTRUCTION OBSERVATION PROTOCOL

The SIOP has 30 characteristics or areas to assess during observation. Each characteristic is rated from 4 (Highly Evident) to 0 (Not Evident) or NA (Not Applicable). These ratings are converted into a score.

Observer: _____

Date: _____

Grade: _____

Class: _____

Teacher: _____

School: _____

ESL level: _____

Lesson: Multi-day Single-day (circle one)

*Directions:* Circle the number that best reflects what you observe in a sheltered lesson. You may give a score from 0–4. Cite under "Comments" specific examples of the behaviours observed. Total Score: _____ % Score _____ Tape #:_____

| | Highly Evident | | Somewhat Evident | | Not Evident | NA |
|---|---|---|---|---|---|---|
| **Preparation** | 4 | 3 | 2 | 1 | 0 | |
| 1. **Content objectives clearly defined,** displayed, and reviewed with students | ☐ | ☐ | ☐ | ☐ | ☐ | ☐ |
| 2. **Language objectives clearly defined,** displayed, and reviewed with students | ☐ | ☐ | ☐ | ☐ | ☐ | ☐ |
| 3. **Content concepts** appropriate for age and educational background level of students | ☐ | ☐ | ☐ | ☐ | ☐ | ☐ |
| 4. **Supplementary materials** used to a high degree, making the lesson clear and meaningful (e.g., computer programs, graphs, models, visuals) | ☐ | ☐ | ☐ | ☐ | ☐ | ☐ |
| 5. **Adaptation of content** (e.g., text, assignment) to all levels of student proficiency | ☐ | ☐ | ☐ | ☐ | ☐ | ☐ |
| 6. **Meaningful activities** that integrate lesson concepts (e.g., interviews, letter writing, simulations, models) with language practice opportunities for reading, writing, listening, and/or speaking | ☐ | ☐ | ☐ | ☐ | ☐ | ☐ |
| *Comments:* | | | | | | |
| **Building Background** | | | | | | |
| 7. **Concepts explicitly linked** to students' background experiences | ☐ | ☐ | ☐ | ☐ | ☐ | ☐ |
| 8. **Links explicitly made** between past learning and new concepts | ☐ | ☐ | ☐ | ☐ | ☐ | ☐ |
| 9. **Key vocabulary emphasized** (e.g., introduced, written, repeated, highlighted for students to see) | ☐ | ☐ | ☐ | ☐ | ☐ | ☐ |
| *Comments:* | | | | | | |
| **Comprehensible** | | | | | | |
| 10. **Speech** appropriate for students' proficiency level (e.g., slower rate, enunciation, and simple sentence structure for beginners) | ☐ | ☐ | ☐ | ☐ | ☐ | ☐ |
| 11. **Clear explanation** of academic tasks | ☐ | ☐ | ☐ | ☐ | ☐ | ☐ |
| 12. A variety of techniques used to make content **concepts clear** (e.g., modelling, visuals, hands-on activities, demonstration, gestures, body language) | ☐ | ☐ | ☐ | ☐ | ☐ | ☐ |
| *Comments:* | | | | | | |
| **Strategies** | | | | | | |
| 13. Ample opportunities for students to use **learning strategies** | ☐ | ☐ | ☐ | ☐ | ☐ | ☐ |
| 14. **Scaffolding techniques** consistently used assisting and supporting student understanding (e.g., think-alouds) | ☐ | ☐ | ☐ | ☐ | ☐ | ☐ |
| 15. A variety of questions or tasks that promote **higher-order thinking skills** (e.g., literal, analytical, interpretive questions) | ☐ | ☐ | ☐ | ☐ | ☐ | ☐ |
| *Comments:* | | | | | | |

|  | Highly Evident | | Somewhat Evident | | Not Evident | NA |
|---|---|---|---|---|---|---|
| **Interaction** | | | | | | |
| 16. Frequent opportunities for **interaction** and discussion between teacher/student and among students, which encourage elaborated responses about lesson concepts | ☐ | ☐ | ☐ | ☐ | ☐ | ☐ |
| 17. **Grouping configurations** support language and content objectives of the lesson | ☐ | ☐ | ☐ | ☐ | ☐ | ☐ |
| 18. Sufficient **wait time for student response** consistently provided | ☐ | ☐ | ☐ | ☐ | ☐ | ☐ |
| 19. Ample opportunities for students to **clarify key concepts in L1** as needed with aide, peer, or L1 text<br>*Comments:* | ☐ | ☐ | ☐ | ☐ | ☐ | ☐ |
| **Practice/Application** | | | | | | |
| 20. **Hands-on materials and/or manipulatives** provided for students to practice using new content knowledge | ☐ | ☐ | ☐ | ☐ | ☐ | ☐ |
| 21. Activities provided for students to **apply content and language knowledge** in the classroom | ☐ | ☐ | ☐ | ☐ | ☐ | ☐ |
| 22. Activities integrate all **language skills** (i.e., reading, listening, speaking)<br>*Comments:* | ☐ | ☐ | ☐ | ☐ | ☐ | ☐ |
| **Lesson Delivery** | | | | | | |
| 23. **Content objectives** clearly supported by lesson delivery | ☐ | ☐ | ☐ | ☐ | ☐ | ☐ |
| 24. **Language objectives** clearly supported by lesson delivery | ☐ | ☐ | ☐ | ☐ | ☐ | ☐ |
| 25. **Students engaged** approximately 90%–100% of the period | ☐ | ☐ | ☐ | ☐ | ☐ | ☐ |
| 26. **Pacing** of the lesson appropriate to the students' ability level<br>*Comments:* | ☐ | ☐ | ☐ | ☐ | ☐ | ☐ |
| **Review/Assessment** | | | | | | |
| 27. Comprehensive **review of key vocabulary** | ☐ | ☐ | ☐ | ☐ | ☐ | ☐ |
| 28. Comprehensive **review of key content concepts** | ☐ | ☐ | ☐ | ☐ | ☐ | ☐ |
| 29. Regular **feedback provided** to students on their output (e.g., language, content, work) | ☐ | ☐ | ☐ | ☐ | ☐ | ☐ |
| 30. **Assessment of student comprehension** and learning of all lesson objectives (e.g., spot checking, group response) throughout the lesson<br>*Comments:* | ☐ | ☐ | ☐ | ☐ | ☐ | ☐ |

*Source: Echevarria, J. J., Graves, A. (2011). Sheltered Content Instruction: Teaching English Language Learners with Diverse Abilities, Coursesmart ETextbook, 4th Edition. Reprinted by permission of Pearson Education, Inc., Upper Saddle River, NJ.*

## Affective and Emotional/Social Considerations

**STOP & THINK** You walk into one of your education classes. The instructor moves to the lectern and says:

> Mina-san, ohayō gozaimasu. Kyō wa, kyō iku shinrigaku no jū gyō ja arimasen. Kyō wa, nihon no bangō, ichi kara jū made benkyō -oshimasu. Soshite, kono kyōshitsu wa Amerika no kyōshitsu ja arimasen. Ima wa Nihon no kyō shitsu desu. Nihon no kyō shitsu dewa, shinakerebanaranai koto wa mittsu mo arimasu. Tatsu, rei, suwaru. Mina-san, tatte kudasai. Doshite tatteimasen ka? Wakarimasen ka?

The class continues in the same way until you are handed the "test" and told to "Do your best—this is 20% of your grade." You can't believe it! What would you do? •

Does this seem impossible? Actually, a doctoral student (Yough, 2010) designed this lesson (without the test) so his educational psychology class would experience how it feels to have important content taught in a language you don't speak (assuming your

TABLE 5.6 • **Ideas for Lesson Structures in SIOP That Encourage Understanding of Content and Build Language Skills**

| STRUCTURE | EXAMPLE/WHAT DOES IT LOOK LIKE? | RATIONALE/WHY DOES IT WORK? |
|---|---|---|
| Think-Pair-Share (see Chapter 10) | Instead of asking questions to the whole class and calling on two or three students to respond, the teacher asks everyone to think of an answer or respond to a prompt, and tell it to a partner. Then, the teacher calls on some students to share their responses with the whole class. | All students have a chance to think and speak about the topic. Allows teachers to monitor student understanding of the content and language objectives during a lesson. |
| Chunk and Chew | The teacher pauses after every 10 minutes and directs students to talk with a partner or in a small group about what they have just learned. In SIOP lessons, the teacher carefully structures student talk with specific prompts and/or sentence starters, such as "If I could interview any author we read this year, it would be … because … " | Makes new information easier to learn by "chunking" it into learnable, bite-size pieces (see Chapter 8 for why this is important). Gives students a chance to talk using concepts and content from the lesson. |
| Roam and Review | The teacher poses a reflection question (e.g., "What was the most important thing you learned today?" or "What surprised you in our studies today?") and students think silently, then stand and roam the classroom, discussing their ideas with classmates. | Students synthesize what they have learned and communicate it in a conversational manner. They practice communicating. |
| Podcasts | Students prepare a two- to three-minute oral summary on a topic they have selected or the teacher has assigned. They rehearse and then record it on a podcast or an audio file for use on the class computer. | Provides practice in speaking and the chance to hear and improve language. Having an audience increases motivation and encourages careful preparation. |
| TV Talk Show | Small groups plan a talk show on a topic with multiple parameters that they have studied. One student is the host and interviewer; others are the guests. For example, after studying extreme weather phenomena, one guest might be an expert on hurricanes, another on blizzards, a third on earthquakes, and a fourth on tornadoes. | Video recording of the show allows the teacher or the students to assess how well the students spoke, used key vocabulary, responded to host questions, and so forth. Having an audience increases motivation and encourages careful preparation. |
| Writing Headlines | Students capture the essence of a day's lesson, section of a text read, video watched, or information presented orally by writing a headline, and then sharing their headline. | Encourages students to use descriptive language and focus on word choice to create compelling headlines. |
| E-Journals and Wiki Entries | Students write in an e-journal daily or once a week to reflect on what they have been learning. At the end of a unit, the teacher might ask students to write an online entry for a class wiki that presents key information on a topic being studied. | Encourages synthesizing information and writing longer pieces. |

*Source: Based on Echevarria, J., Vogt, M., & Short, D. J. (2014b). Making content comprehensible for secondary English learners: The SIOP® Model (2nd edition.), pp. 198–199. Boston: Pearson.*

Japanese is a bit rusty!). Research on ELL students shows that they may experience severe challenges and stress in school. They may feel that they don't belong, and that others are making fun of them or just ignoring them. Everyone else seems to know the rules and the right words. It takes courage and persistence to keep trying to communicate; it is easier to say as little as possible. The practice in communicating that these students desperately need just doesn't happen.

What can teachers do to support students' courage and persistence in communicating? The first step is to create a classroom community that is caring and respectful. We explore strategies for creating classroom community in Chapter 13. Echevarria and Graves (2011) suggest additional steps to provide emotional support and increase self-esteem for ELL students, as you can see in the *Guidelines*.

Another problem is related to cultural differences. As we saw earlier, students who immigrate to Canada in their middle or high school years may have experienced very different educational systems and educational values "back home." They may have been very successful in those systems, perhaps by excelling in the memorizing required by the curriculum. When they encounter a different approach to education, suddenly they may

## GUIDELINES

### Providing Emotional Support and Increasing Self-Esteem for English Language Learners

**Create learning activities that promote success in reading and writing.**
*Examples*
1. Have weekly individual conferences with younger students and record their retelling of a story. Let students edit and revise the dictation and read it to a partner.
2. Do interactive journals with older students—collect each week and write back.

**Make sure students have plenty of time to practise and get careful, targeted corrections.**
*Examples*
1. Point out privately what is correct, almost correct, and wrong in written work.
2. Be sensitive about public oral corrections and build on what is correct, but do not accept clearly incorrect answers.

**Connect teaching to relevant knowledge from students' lives.**
*Examples*
1. Ask students to survey family members about favourite films—use film characters to discuss elements of literature—plot, point of view, etc.
2. Have students create construction firms and plan projects to learn math concepts.

**Actively involve learners.**
*Examples*
1. Use timelines in history compared to personal timelines based on family history.
2. Do projects in science based on animals or farming for rural students.

**Use different grouping strategies.**
*Examples*
1. Try pairs for writing stories and practising oral presentations.
2. Create small teams to research recent immigrant groups' culture and language.

**Provide native language support.**
*Examples*
1. Learn and use as much of the students' language as possible—if they can learn, so can you.
2. Find internet translation sources and local native speaking volunteers.
3. Bring native language magazines and books into the classroom.

**Involve family and community members.**
*Examples*
1. Bring in storytellers, local business owners, artists, craftspeople.
2. Create a Welcome Centre for your class.

**Hold high expectations for all students, and communicate these expectations clearly.**
*Examples*
1. Keep scrapbooks of previous students who have gone on to careers or college.
2. Don't accept mediocre work.
3. Be a model of respect for diversity and an enemy of bigotry.

*Source: Echevarria, J. J., Graves, A. (2011). Sheltered Content Instruction: Teaching English Language Learners with Diverse Abilities, Coursesmart ETextbook, 4th Edition. Reprinted by permission of Pearson Education, Inc., Upper Saddle River, NJ.*

struggle and feel as if they know little or nothing. As a teacher, you need to learn the strengths of these students and acknowledge their abilities—and build on their knowledge. We turn to that topic next.

## Working With Families: Using the Tools of the Culture

Luis Moll and his colleagues wanted a better way to teach the children of working-class Mexican American families in the barrio schools of Tucson, Arizona (Moll, Amanti, Neff, & Gonzalez, 1992). Rather than adopt a model of remediating the students' deficits, Moll decided to identify and build on the tools and cultural **funds of knowledge** of their families. By interviewing the families, the researchers identified their extensive knowledge about agriculture, economics, medicine, household management, mechanics, science, and religion. When teachers based their assignments on these funds of knowledge, students were more engaged and teachers were educated about their students' lives. For example, by participating in a funds of knowledge project, one teacher realized that she always had thought about her students in terms of deficits and problems—poor achievement, alienation, family troubles, and poverty. But then she got to know the families by focusing

Funds of knowledge
Knowledge that families and community members have acquired in many areas of work, home, and religious life that can become the basis for teaching.

on their resources, not their limitations. She also learned that her students' actions often were misinterpreted:

> Strong family values and responsibility are characteristics of the families I visited. . . . My students were expected to participate in household chores such as cleaning house, car maintenance, food preparation, washing dishes, and caring for younger siblings. I learned what this insight meant when one of my students was unable to attend school drama and chorus rehearsals one day. In my journal entry detailing this project, I noted the following incident:
>
> -Wednesday (11/25/92) The music teacher commented (to me), "You know, Leticia has missed two chorus rehearsals." Before I could answer, the school drama teacher stepped in to add, "Oh, she's very irresponsible." She had signed up to be in the Drama Club and had only been to two meetings. I said "Wait a minute. . . ." I then told her how Leticia's younger brother was being hospitalized for a series of operations, and when the mother had to leave, she left Leticia in charge of caring for her two younger siblings. In fact, her missing after-school rehearsals was an act of responsibility, obedience and loyalty to her family. (Gonzales et al., 1993)

By engaging with students' families, this teacher learned about the valuable cognitive resources in the community, and her respect for her students and their families increased. Moll's work also was the basis for the Welcome Center project in a prekindergarten through grade 5 elementary school in the Southwestern United States. Within four years the school had gone from 12% to 43% Latino/a, with most of these students recently arrived immigrants. The Welcome Center was a "social and instructional space where recent immigrant families in the school would come to trade a variety of expertise, meet each other, gather information about their children's education, and share general information on practical matters" (DaSilva Iddings, 2009, p. 207). The Center was a bright, comfortable, informal space with a small kitchen, picnic tables, computer and printer, books and magazines in Spanish and English, math manipulatives, showcases for children's work, and other welcoming features. Grade 5 students offered homework assistance after school at the centre. Spanish-speaking families taught classes in Spanish, cooking, and dancing for community members. English literacy activities were provided for adults and children learning together. The centre produced many success stories—teachers who connected with students' families and came to appreciate the value of their students' language and culture, immigrant families who moved toward citizenship, and others who opened businesses and restaurants. Connections with families may be especially important for the success of immigrant students. The Family and Community Partnerships *Guidelines* have more ideas.

## GUIDELINES — FAMILY AND COMMUNITY PARTNERSHIPS

### Welcoming All Families

**Make sure communication with families is understandable.**
*Examples*
1. Use the families' home languages wherever possible.
2. Use oral forms of communication—phone calls or home visits—whenever possible.

**Balance positive and negative messages.**
*Examples*
1. Send home notes or descriptions about their child's accomplishments or acts of kindness.
2. Explain disciplinary actions as ways of helping children succeed.

**Establish systems for welcoming new families.**
*Examples*
1. Assign more experienced "buddy" parents to communicate with new families.
2. Connect with multilingual media in your community to make announcements about school.

**Make sure messages get through.**
*Examples*
1. Establish telephone trees or texting networks.
2. Set the expectation that there will be a weekly note sent home so parents can ask their children about it.
3. Establish a class newsletter or website and incorporate multiple languages.

# SPECIAL CHALLENGES: ENGLISH LANGUAGE LEARNERS WITH DISABILITIES AND SPECIAL GIFTS

If you remember the four profiles of ELLs described earlier, you know that one type of student may have learning disabilities, but it is very difficult to tell because the student's language is limited. English language learners with disabilities are difficult to diagnose—expert assessment is necessary (Garcia & Tyler, 2010). Sometimes students are inappropriately placed in special education just because they have problems with English, but other times, students who would benefit from special services are denied placement because their problems are assumed to be simply language learning issues (USDE, 2004). In addition, students with special talents and gifts may be difficult to recognize.

## English Language Learners With Disabilities

As a teacher, one of your decisions will be whether to refer a struggling ELL student for testing. Of course, the first step is to use the best teaching approaches, incorporating sheltered instruction to develop both subject matter learning and English language development. But if progress seems much slower than usual, you might ask the following questions, suggested by George De George (2008): What is the student's educational background, and what is the background of his or her family? When did the student come to Canada? Being born in Canada but speaking another language at home or immigrating when very young actually can make learning in the early grades more difficult. Students who immigrate after successfully learning in their home country schools have literacy skills to build on. They know some academic content, and they know they can learn in school. In contrast, the children who speak another language at home and have never been to school have no oral English to use as they learn the letters and sounds of written English. Bilingual instruction is the best strategy here.

Other questions to ask when considering a referral are: Were there any problems or complications during the mother's pregnancy? Has the child experienced any serious injuries or illnesses? Has the child moved around a great deal? Has the child had adequate opportunities to learn in a good bilingual or ELL program? Have the teachers who worked with the child been trained in teaching English language learning? Is the student making progress, even if he or she is behind others the same age? Does the student have any talents or special skills to build on? These questions will help you determine if the student's difficulties are due to lack of learning opportunities, inadequate teaching, or a disability. No matter what the diagnosis—attention and appropriate teaching are needed. Students who have difficulties with English are much more likely to drop out of school (USDE, 2004).

## Reaching Every Student: Recognizing Giftedness in Bilingual Students

Because they may be struggling with academic English, even though they are very knowledgeable, bilingual students may be overlooked for gifted and talented programs. A grade 10 boy from Mexico, in the United States for two years, told an interviewer in Spanish:

> High school is hard for me because my English is so limited. . . . There are times when I feel a lot of pressure because I want to say something, but I don't know how to say it. There are many times when the teacher is asking questions, I know the answer, but I am afraid that people might laugh at me. (Walqui, 2008, p. 104)

This student might well be gifted. To identify gifted bilingual students, you can use a case study or portfolio approach in order to collect a variety of evidence, including interviews with parents and peers, formal and informal assessments, samples of student work and performances, and student self-assessments. The checklist in Table 5.7, from Castellano and Diaz (2002), is a useful guide.

TABLE 5.7 • **Identifying Bilingual Students With Gifts and Talents**

Here are some ideas for identifying bilingual students with gifts and talents. Watch for students who:

_____ Learn English quickly

_____ Take risks in trying to communicate in English

_____ Practice English skills by themselves

_____ Initiate conversations with native English speakers

_____ Do not frustrate easily

_____ Are curious about new words or phrases and practise them

_____ Question word meanings; for example, "How can a bat be an animal and also something you use to hit a ball?"

_____ Look for similarities between words in their native language and English

_____ Are able to modify their language for less capable English speakers

_____ Use English to demonstrate leadership skills; for example, use English to resolve disagreements and to facilitate cooperative learning groups

_____ Prefer to work independently or with students whose level of English proficiency is higher than theirs

_____ Are able to express abstract verbal concepts with a limited English vocabulary

_____ Are able to use English in a creative way; for example, can make puns, poems, jokes, or original stories in English

_____ Become easily bored with routine tasks or drill work

_____ Have a great deal of curiosity

_____ Are persistent; stick to a task

_____ Are independent and self-sufficient

_____ Have a long attention span

_____ Become absorbed with self-selected problems, topics, and issues

_____ Retain, easily recall, and use new information

_____ Demonstrate social maturity, especially in the home or community

*Source: Castellano, J. A., Diaz, E. (2002). Reaching New Horizons: Gifted and Talented Education for Culturally and Linguistically Diverse Students, 1st Edition. Reprinted by permission of Pearson Education, Inc., Upper Saddle River, NJ.*

## ▼ SUMMARY

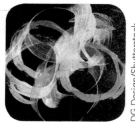

DG Design/Shutterstock

### The Development of Language (pp. 156–163)

**How are humans predisposed to develop language? What roles do culture and learning play?** Cultures create words for the concepts that are important to them. Children develop language as they build on other cognitive abilities by actively trying to make sense of what they hear, looking for patterns, and making up rules. In this process, built-in biases and rules may limit the search and guide the pattern recognition. Reward and correction play a role in helping children learn correct language use, but the child's thought processes are very important.

**What are the elements of language?** By age 5, most children have mastered almost all the sounds of their native language. In terms of vocabulary, we understand more words than we use. By age 6, children understand up to 20 000 words and use about 2600 words. Understanding of words that express abstract ideas and hypothetical situations comes later as cognitive abilities develop. As children develop an understanding of grammar, they may apply new rules too widely, saying "broked" for "broken," for example. Understanding the passive voice in syntax develops after understanding active voice.

**What are pragmatics and metalinguistic awareness?** Pragmatics is knowledge about how to use language—when, where, how, and to whom to speak. Metalinguistic awareness, knowledge about your own use of language and how language works, begins around age 5 or 6 and grows throughout life.

**What are the most important skills that help literacy emerge?** Research has identified two broad categories of skills that are important for later reading: (1) understanding sounds and codes such as knowing that letters have names, that sounds are associated with letters, and that words are made up of sounds; and (2) oral language skills, such as expressive and receptive vocabulary, knowledge of syntax, and the ability to understand and tell stories. For bilingual students, growth in receptive language in L1 or L2 predicts early reading outcomes. Parents and teachers can support emerging literacy by reading with children, retelling stories and talking about them, and limiting time spent watching television.

## Diversity in Language Development (pp. 163–170)

**What is involved in learning two languages?** Children can learn two languages at once if they have adequate opportunities in both languages. There are cognitive advantages to learning more than one language, so it is valuable to retain your heritage language even as you learn another. The best time to learn accurate pronunciation is early childhood, but people of any age can learn a new language. Having overheard a language as a child can improve one's ability to learn that language as an adult. Even though the advantages of bilingualism seem clear, many children and adults are losing their heritage language. Rather than losing one language to gain another, the goal should be balanced bilingualism—being equally fluent in both languages. People who can communicate in both a spoken and a signed language or in two different signed languages are considered bilingual.

**What does it mean to be truly bilingual?** Some definitions of bilingualism focus exclusively on a language-based meaning: Bilingual people, or bilinguals, speak two languages. Other definitions are more rigorous and define bilinguals as adults who use their two languages effectively in their adult daily life, which includes being bicultural as well—moving back and forth between two cultures and two languages while still maintaining a sense of identity. Proficiency in a second language has two separate aspects: face-to-face communication (*contextualized language skills*) that take about two to three years in a good program to develop, and academic uses of language such as reading and doing grammar exercises (known as *academic English*) that take about five to 10 years to develop. Bilingual students also often struggle with social adjustment problems relating to biculturalism.

**How do cultural differences affect bilingual students?** Cultural differences might interfere with developing academic English and content understanding. For example, many Asian students come from a culture that believes asking the teacher questions is rude and inappropriate because questioning implies that the teacher has done a poor job of instruction. Thus teachers need to ask themselves why their English language learners are not asking questions. Beliefs about learning shaped by culture and previous experiences in different kinds of classrooms may explain why ELLs seem quiet and reluctant to speak in class. These students may also think that their teachers are not very good because the teachers do not explain everything. They also may strongly prefer memorization as a learning strategy if memorization was emphasized in their previous schools.

## Dialect Differences in the Classroom (pp. 170–172)

**What is a dialect?** A dialect is any variety of a language spoken by a particular group. The dialect is part of the group's collective identity. Every person reading this text speaks at least one dialect, maybe more, because there is no one absolute standard form of English. Dialects differ in their rules about pronunciation, grammar, and vocabulary, but it is important to remember that these differences are not errors. Each dialect is logical, complex, and rule-governed. There are even some differences in how men and women talk, called genderlects.

**How should teachers take dialects into account?** Teachers can be sensitive to their own possible negative stereotypes about children who speak a different dialect. Teachers also can ensure comprehension by repeating instructions using different words and by asking students to paraphrase instructions or give examples. The best teaching approach seems to be to focus on understanding the students and to accept their language as a valid and correct system, but to teach the alternative forms of English (or whatever the dominant language is in your country) that are used in more formal work settings and writing so that the students will have access to a range of opportunities.

## Teaching Immigrant Students and English Language Learners (pp. 172–175)

**Distinguish between the terms *immigrant* and *refugee*.** Immigrants are people who voluntarily leave their country to become permanent residents in a new place. Refugees are a special group of immigrants who also relocate voluntarily, but they are fleeing their home country because it is not safe.

**Distinguish between the "melting pot" and multiculturalism.** Statistics point to increasing cultural diversity in North American society. Multiculturalism is the goal. Multiculturalism rejects the idea of a melting pot, whereby ethnic minority groups are expected to assimilate into the mainstream society, and supports a society that values diversity—more like a salad bowl or mosaic with many contributions.

**What are four general profiles of English language learners?** *Balanced bilinguals* speak, read, and write well both in their first language and in English. *Monolingual/literate students* are literate in their native language (at or above grade level when working in their native language), but speak limited English. *Monolingual/preliterate students* are not literate. They may not read or write in their native language, or they may have very limited literacy skills. *Limited bilingual* students can converse well in both languages, but for some reason they have trouble learning academically. There may be underlying challenges such as learning disabilities or emotional problems.

## Generation 1.5: Students in Two Worlds (pp. 176–184)

**What is Generation 1.5?** Generation 1.5 are students who were not born in Canada, but came with their families when they were young (typically before adolescence) and have received most of their schooling here. The language spoken in their homes may not be English, but they often speak fluent conversational English, even if their academic English is not as well developed. They may tend to be "ear learners" who have mastered language by listening to and interacting with the language models around them. They may perceive their national identify as divided between Canada and their country of birth.

**What terms are related to English learners?** Two terms that you will see associated with bilingualism are English language learners (ELL), describing *students* whose primary or heritage language is not English, and English as a second language (ESL) *classrooms*, where these students learn English. Limited proficiency in English often leads to lower academic achievement and poorer job prospects so an important issue related to diversity in language development is how best to teach these students.

**What is bilingual education?** Although there is much debate about the best way to help ELLs master English, studies show it is best if they are not forced to abandon their first language. The more proficient students are in their first language, the faster they will master the second.

**What is sheltered instruction?** Sheltered instruction is one approach that has proved successful in teaching English and academic content. Sheltered instruction teaches content to ELLs by putting the words and concepts of the content into context to make the content more understandable. Strategies include simplifying and controlling language, giving attention to the relevant grammar and forms of English—helping students "crack the code," using visuals and gestures, and including real-life supports and examples. In addition, there is an emphasis on student talk and discussion instead of the teacher doing all the talking. There are affective and emotional considerations for English language learners. They may experience severe challenges and stress in school. They may feel that they don't belong, that others are making fun of them, or just ignoring them. Building on students' funds of cultural knowledge is one way to make classrooms more supportive and teaching more effective.

### Special Challenges: English Language Learners with Disabilities and Special Gifts (pp. 185–186)

**How do teachers deal with the special needs of English language learners?** As a teacher, one of your decisions will be whether to refer a struggling ELL student for testing. Of course, the first step is to use the best teaching approaches, incorporating sheltered instruction to develop both subject matter learning and English language development. But if progress seems much slower than usual, you might refer the student for observation or testing. No matter what the diagnosis, attention and appropriate teaching are needed. Students who have difficulties with English are much more likely to drop out of school. And because language differences can mask giftedness, teachers should make special efforts to identify bilingual students and English language learners who have gifts and talents.

## ▼ WHAT WOULD THEY DO?

## TEACHERS' CASEBOOK: Cultures Clash in the Classroom

Here is how several expert teachers responded to the teaching situation described on the first page of this chapter.

### MAUREEN SHAW

John Fraser Secondary School, Mississauga, ON

This problem provides teachers and students with an opportunity to increase their emotional intelligence (EQ), cross-cultural understanding, and language skills.

The teacher addressing these issues should first engage in self-reflection: Are the students really talking about the teacher, or is the teacher insecure? In a multilingual environment, students and teachers need to develop tolerance for hearing foreign languages. Language learners will need to communicate in their first language (L1) during the early stages of language acquisition and be encouraged to speak it less often as they reach "conversational competence."

**Diagnosing the problem(s):** Use the following questions to diagnose the problem.

- Are the students capable of expressing their ideas and feelings in English?
- Do their cultural backgrounds and past experiences make it stressful to make language mistakes in front of their peers?
- Do they believe they can succeed in our educational system?
- Have these students ever been taught explicitly the behaviours expected during group work?

**Addressing the problem(s):** The students are likely talking about themselves, not the teacher, and they may feel uncomfortable speaking English. Use the following strategies to break down barriers.

- Ask students to write individually about a time when they felt left out.
- Discuss how this can happen during group work.
- Ask students whether they participated in group work in their former countries.
- Explain what teachers want students to accomplish in group work.
- Describe the benefits of group work and the challenges associated with it.
- Encourage students to set goals. For example, ask students to rate on a scale of 1 to 10 how much they want to improve their English language skills. If the results are high, encourage them to make a promise to use English in every class.

- Create mixed-language groups, in which the rule is: Don't talk with people outside your group. Ask students to create a Venn diagram that shows the beliefs and experiences they have in common.
- Ask each group to list suitable and unsuitable occasions for L1 conversation.

Keep in mind that in multilingual schools, these issues affect all grade levels. If these issues aren't addressed, students will have difficulty succeeding in almost all their classes. Group work is a common requirement.

### ALLISON JORDAN

Castlebrooke Secondary School, Brampton, ON

On the first day of school, I organize a series of ice-breaker activities with my students to encourage them to get to know their classmates and their teacher. I also ask them to fill out a "Get to Know You" sheet, so I can learn about their interests, cultures, and backgrounds. I incorporate the information from these "Get to Know You" sheets into lessons throughout the course to provide students with learning experiences that are authentic, relevant, and meaningful.

To make the classroom a welcoming and supportive learning environment, I always model respectful behaviour, and actively encourage students to demonstrate respect for themselves, their peers, and their teacher. My students and I co-construct a list of "respectful behaviours," that I post in a prominent place in the classroom and refer to throughout the semester if students need reminding.

When planning classroom activities, I make a conscious effort to place students into mixed ability and mixed language groups; I then change the members in the groups for each new activity. I want to encourage the students to work with all of their classmates—not just those students who speak their first language. To encourage a welcoming environment in the classroom, I explain to students how speaking in their native language during group work can cause other students to feel excluded and upset. I also have the students participate in role-play exercises throughout the course to help them develop positive social interactions while speaking in English with their peers.

# CULTURE AND DIVERSITY

WHAT WOULD YOU DO?

▶ **TEACHERS' CASEBOOK:** White Girls Club

You teach in a fairly homogeneous primary school. In fact, most of your kindergarten–grade 1 students are middle- or upper middle-class and white. In January, a new student came to your school. Her family is Muslim and from Iran, and children notice that her mom dresses differently than their moms, wearing loose-fitting clothing and a scarf, or hijab, that is the tradition in their religious community. After a few weeks, you notice that the new student is not being included in many activities. She sits alone in the library and plays alone at recess. No one sits with her at lunch, and at recess she is the last to be chosen for any team. This is troubling enough, but then one day you overhear two of your higher-achieving girls talking about their "White Girls Club."

**CRITICAL THINKING**

- Would you investigate to learn more about this "club"? How?
- If you found that your students had created a club that excluded nonwhite students, what would you do?
- If you teach older students, what can you do about student groups that define themselves by who *cannot* be members?

## OVERVIEW AND OBJECTIVES

The face of Canadian classrooms is changing. The same can be said for many countries today. In a talk to the American Educational Research Association, Frank Pajares said, "The critical questions in education involve matters that cannot be settled by universal prescription. They demand attention to the cultural forces that shape our lives" (Pajares, 2000, p. 5). We believe he is right. In this chapter, we examine the many cultures that form the fabric of our society. We begin by considering the meaning of culture and the diverse student population in schools—you will meet four students whose stories reflect this diversity. Within this broad conception of culture, we examine three important dimensions of every student's identity: social class, race/ethnicity, and gender. We consider multicultural education, a general process of school reform that incorporates and embraces diversity, and we look at approaches to creating culturally compatible and resilient classrooms. The last section presents three general principles for teaching every student. By the time you have completed this chapter, you should be able to:

6.1 Describe how social class, ethnicity, and race influence teaching and learning in a diverse society.

6.2 Explain the meaning of *stereotype threat*, and examine its possible effects on student achievement.

6.3 Describe the development of gender identity and the role of gender in teaching.

6.4 Define multicultural education.

6.5 Apply research on diversity to the creation of culturally compatible classrooms.

**Listen**
Today's Diverse
Classrooms

# TODAY'S DIVERSE CLASSROOMS

In this text, we take a broad interpretation of cultural diversity, so we will examine social class, race, ethnicity, and gender as aspects of diversity. We begin with a look at the meaning of culture. Many people associate this concept with the "cultural events" section of the newspaper—art galleries, museums, Shakespearean festivals, classical music, and so on. Culture has a much broader meaning; it embraces the whole way of life of a group of people.

## Culture and Group Membership

There are many definitions of **culture**. Most include some or all of the following: the knowledge, skills, rules, norms, practices, traditions, self-definitions, institutions (educational, legal, communal, religious, political, etc.), language, and values that shape and guide beliefs and behaviour in a particular group of people as well as the art, literature, folklore, and artifacts produced and passed down to the next generation (Cohen, 2009, 2010; Pai & Alder, 2001). The group creates a culture—a program for living—and communicates the culture to members. Groups can be defined along regional, ethnic, religious, racial, gender, social class, or other lines. Each of us is a member of many groups, so we all are influenced by many different cultures. Sometimes the influences are incompatible or even contradictory. For example, if you are a feminist but also a Roman Catholic, you may have trouble reconciling the two different cultures' beliefs about the ordination of women as priests. Your personal belief will be based, in part, on how strongly you identify with each group.

There are many different cultures, of course, in every modern country. In Canada, students living in the suburbs of Toronto certainly differ in a number of ways from students growing up on a farm in Quebec. In the United States, students growing

**Culture** The knowledge, rules, traditions, attitudes, and values that guide the behaviour of a group of people and allow them to solve the problems of living in their environment.

## FIGURE 6.1

### CULTURE AS AN ICEBERG

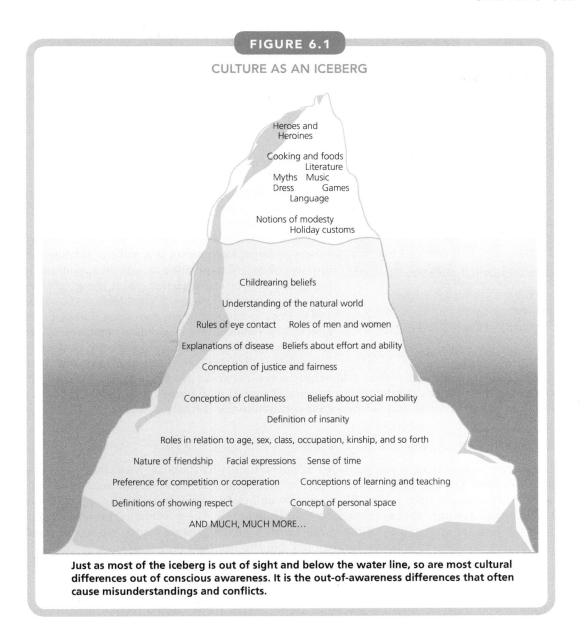

Heroes and Heroines

Cooking and foods
Literature
Myths    Music
Dress        Games
Language

Notions of modesty
Holiday customs

Childrearing beliefs

Understanding of the natural world

Rules of eye contact    Roles of men and women

Explanations of disease    Beliefs about effort and ability

Conception of justice and fairness

Conception of cleanliness    Beliefs about social mobility

Definition of insanity

Roles in relation to age, sex, class, occupation, kinship, and so forth

Nature of friendship    Facial expressions    Sense of time

Preference for competition or cooperation    Conceptions of learning and teaching

Definitions of showing respect    Concept of personal space

AND MUCH, MUCH MORE...

**Just as most of the iceberg is out of sight and below the water line, so are most cultural differences out of conscious awareness. It is the out-of-awareness differences that often cause misunderstandings and conflicts.**

up in a small rural town in the Great Plains are part of a cultural group that is very different from that of students in a large Northeastern urban centre or students in a Florida suburb. Within those small towns in the Great Plains or Quebec, the son or daughter of a convenience store clerk grows up in a different culture from the child of the town doctor or dentist. Individuals of African, Asian, Aboriginal, or European descent have distinctive histories and traditions. The experiences of males and females are different in most ethnic and economic groups. Everyone living within a particular country shares many common experiences and values, especially because of the influence of the mass media, but other aspects of their lives are shaped by differing cultural backgrounds.

Ricardo Garcia (1991) compares culture to an iceberg. One-third of the iceberg is visible; the rest is hidden and unknown. The visible signs of culture, such as costumes and marriage traditions, reflect only a small portion of the differences among cultures, as you can see in Figure 6.1.

Many of the differences are "below the surface." They are implicit, unstated, even unconscious biases and beliefs (Sheets, 2005). Cultures differ in rules for conducting

**JUST ONE CULTURE?** Definitions of *culture* apply to regional, ethnic, religious, racial, gender, social class, and other areas of difference. Each of us is a member of many groups, so we all are influenced by many different cultures.

Ryan McVey/Getty Images

interpersonal relationships, for example. In some groups, listeners give a slight affirmative nod of the head and perhaps an occasional "uh huh" to indicate they are listening carefully. But members of other cultures listen without giving acknowledgment, or with eyes downcast, as a sign of respect. In some cultures, high-status individuals initiate conversations and ask the questions, and low-status individuals only respond. In other cultures, the pattern is reversed.

Cultural influences are widespread and pervasive. Some psychologists even suggest that culture defines intelligence. For example, physical grace is essential in Balinese social life, so the ability to master physical movements is a mark of intelligence in that culture. Manipulating words and numbers is important in Western societies, so in these cultures such skills are indicators of intelligence (Gardner, 1983). Even symptoms of psychological disorders are affected by culture. In industrialized cultures where cleanliness is emphasized, people with obsessive-compulsive disorders often become obsessed with cleaning their hands, whereas in Bali, where social networks are emphasized, people with obsessive-compulsive disorders often become obsessed with knowing all the details about the lives of their friends and family—their social network (Lemelson, 2003).

## Meet Four Students

In Chapter 1 you read some statistics about students in Canada. Look back at those statistics now. As you can see, classrooms are becoming more diverse. But teachers do not work with statistics; they work with students—unique individuals. Nancy Knapp from the University of Georgia invites us to meet four individuals. These students are not specific people; they are composites of the characteristics of real people Nancy has known and taught. The names and schools are fictional, but the lives are very real.

**Ternice Mattox** is a grade 7 student who lives with her mother and three younger siblings in a large city. Her mother works the 7:00–3:00 shift at a dry-cleaning plant and then cleans offices some nights and weekends to make ends meet, so Ternice gets her brothers and sister up and ready for school every day, feeds them dinner when they get home, and makes sure they do their homework at night; she has been doing this since she was 10.

School hasn't ever been very hard for Ternice; in elementary school she usually got Bs, even though a lot of the teachers said she talked too much. But she never really liked school until last year. Her grade 6 English teacher seemed to want students to talk. She had them reading stories about real people, like you could meet any day downtown. In class, she got people talking about what the characters should do and why the authors wrote the stories the way they did. Best of all, she let you write about whatever you wanted, even your own life, and she didn't count off for every mistake right away, but let you work with her and with the other kids until you had a final copy you could be really proud of. In that class, Ternice found out that she really liked to write, and her teacher said she was good at it. One of her stories even got published in the school newspaper. Ternice talked and wrote so much in that class that Anthony Bailey got on her about why she was "actin' so white." She got mad and told him that acting foolish was worse than acting white, but it still bothered her. She and Anthony kind of go together, and she likes him a lot; she has "Ternice and "Tone" written all over her notebooks.

Her English class this year is not nearly as good. Her teacher from last year wants her to take some tests to see if she can get into the gifted program, but Ternice is not so sure about that. Even if she got in, she's afraid she wouldn't know anyone. Almost all the kids in "gifted" are white, and the few African American kids are from another part of town. Besides, her friends might not like it, especially Anthony. At her school, "brains" don't go around with "regulars," and vice versa. Her mom wants her to try and says there's no telling where she can go from there, but Ternice doesn't want to go anywhere that's away from all her friends. Still, she wishes she could have more classes like her English class last year.

**Benjamin Whittaker** lives in a suburban community. His father is the vice president at a local bank and member of the board of a local hospital. His mother and father are divorced. Ben lives with his father, but still sees his mom every two weeks for the weekend. His older sister is in her second year of university taking a pre-veterinary course. Ben started high school this year; he's taking algebra, world history, French, English, and first-year chemistry. His course schedule was his father's idea, especially the chemistry. Ben feels completely out of his league in that class, but his father insisted that if he was going to get into pre-med in college, he had to get a jump-start on science. Ben's mother says medicine is where the money is, and she knows Ben can do it if he just gets focused.

Ben's not so sure. He has never been a star student like his sister, and he really struggled at the beginning of middle school. He just couldn't get the hang of taking notes; either he couldn't figure out what was most important so he'd try to write down everything the teachers said, or he'd get distracted by something and miss whole sections of the lecture. He also had a hard time keeping track of his assignments, and when he did remember to do them, his notebooks and backpack were such a mess that sometimes he'd lose them before he got them turned in. At the end of the first semester, his homeroom teacher suggested he be evaluated for ADHD, and his family doctor put him on a trial dose of Ritalin, which seemed to help. With some additional coaching on organizational skills, Ben gradually improved and finished grade 8 with a solid B average. He still takes Ritalin on school days, but not on the weekends, which is when he does most of his artwork.

Art is what Ben really loves. Since he was a little boy he has been drawing people and animals and whole scenes out of his imagination. Sometimes when he's working on a drawing, he loses all track of time. His mom calls it being "zoned in," and teases him that he'd forget to eat if she didn't come up and get him. Lately, he's been experimenting with the graphics program on his computer, and he's even drawn a few panels of his own web comic. He's only shown it to some friends, but they thought it was pretty funny. It's weird, he never has trouble focusing on his art, but even with the Ritalin, he's having more and more trouble focusing on his schoolwork this year. He's worried his grades won't be very good; he may even flunk chemistry. Ben knows he could do better if he took a lighter load, especially if he could move out of the advanced track and take some art courses. His parents say art is nice for a hobby, but it's no way to make a living.

**Davy Walker** is in grade 2 and worries that he is not doing well, but he's afraid to ask his teacher about it. He doesn't really like asking questions, anyway, because everyone looks at you, and sometimes they laugh if you ask a dumb one. The problem is, he just can't seem to catch on to reading the way most of the other kids do. He can read some of the words if he has enough time, especially if no one is listening to him, but he hates it when the teacher has them take turns reading aloud. Everyone else seems to read so much better and faster that he just freezes up and makes stupid mistakes.

His teacher had a conference with his mom and dad last fall and told them he needed to read more at home. His parents own a family restaurant in a small town where they live, and his mom and dad both work pretty long hours there; even his older sister helps out some on weekends. His mom tried for a while to get him to read to her when she put him to bed at night, but it didn't work out very well. He got sick of the baby books that were all he could read, and when she got him to try something harder, it went so slowly that she got impatient and quit. Davy was just as glad. When he grows up, he's going to run the restaurant for his dad. He can already clear tables and stack the dishes in the big dishwasher, and sometimes his dad lets him help run the cash register and make change. When he's older, he'll learn to take orders and work the grill. Davy doesn't see what reading has to do with running a good restaurant.

**Jessie Kinkaid** is in grade 12. She lives with her mother, who works as a doctor's receptionist, in a small house in town. Her father owns a car dealership and lives just outside of town with his second wife and Jessie's 3-year-old half-brother, so she sees him pretty often.

Jessie is in the vocational track at school and mostly makes Cs, with a few Ds. Once in a while, she fails a course, but she'll have enough credits to graduate by the end of next year, which is all she really cares about. Her home economics teacher says she has a real flair for cooking, and wants Jessie to bring up her grades so she can apply to chef's school. Jessie likes to cook and knows she's good at it, but doesn't see any point in going to more school. She's only graduating to please her parents; she knows what she's going to do with her life. After graduation she's going to get a job in town somewhere for a couple years to save up some money and then she'll marry Walter Aiken. They have been going together since she began high school. Walt graduated last year and started a program in animal science at a small local university this year. They plan to wait until he is finished before they get married. Then they'll move into the small house on the Aiken's farm until Walt's dad is ready to retire, probably in another three or four years. Then Walt will take over the farm, and they'll move into the big house. Jessie hopes they'll have at least one child by then.

So Jessie doesn't see any point in worrying about her grades, as long as she graduates. Her father agrees it would be foolish to waste time and money on extra schooling she'll never use. Jessie's mother, who left school at 17 to marry, is the one urging Jessie to think about going on. She says she just wants Jessie to "keep all her options open."

Ternice, Ben, Davy, and Jessie are just four students—there are millions more, all with unique collections of abilities and experiences. They speak different languages, have different ethnic and racial backgrounds, and live in different kinds of communities. Some come from families in poverty, others from families with power and privilege, but all face challenges in their education. For the remainder of the chapter we will look at the dimensions of cultural differences in schools today.

## Cautions About Interpreting Cultural Differences

Before we examine the bases for cultural differences, two cautions are necessary. First, we will consider social class, ethnicity, and gender separately, because much of the available research focuses on only one of these variables. Of course, real children are not just Asian, or middle-class, or female; they are complex beings and members of many groups, just like the four students we have just described.

The second caution is that group membership is not destiny. Just knowing a student is a member of a particular cultural group does not tell you what that student is like. People are individuals. For example, if a student in your class consistently arrives late, you should not assume that the student's behaviour reflects a cultural difference in beliefs about punctuality. It may be that the student has a job before school or must walk a long distance or that he or she dreads school.

CULTURAL CONFLICTS AND COMPATIBILITIES.    The differences between cultures may be very obvious, tip-of-the iceberg characteristics such as holiday customs and dress, or they may be very subtle, below-the-surface differences such as how to get your turn in conversations. When subtle cultural differences meet, misunderstandings and conflicts are common. These conflicts can happen when the values and competencies of the dominant, mainstream culture are used to determine what is considered "normal" or appropriate behaviour in schools. In these cases, children who have been socialized in a different culture may be perceived as acting inappropriately, not following the rules, or being rude and disrespectful.

Rosa Hernandez Sheets (2005) describes a 5-year-old Mexican American girl who tried to bring a bread roll, part of her school cafeteria lunch, home to give to her little brother every day. Her parents were proud of her for sharing, but the school officials made her throw the roll away, because it was against school rules to take food from the cafeteria. The girl was conflicted about following school rules versus honouring her family's cultural values. The teacher in this case solved the problem by talking to the cafeteria cook, getting the roll in a baggie, and putting the baggie in the girl's backpack to be taken home after school.

Not all cultural differences lead to clashes in school, however. Jim Anderson (1995), a professor at the University of British Columbia, asked Chinese Canadian, Indo-Canadian, and European Canadian parents to describe five things they were doing to promote the reading and writing development of their children in kindergarten through grade 2. Parents in all three groups indicated that they read to their children, engaged in some form of direct teaching (e.g., teaching children how to spell or how to decode difficult words), and tried to teach their children about the value and uses of literacy (e.g., implicitly through modelling or through direct teaching). What was evident across all responses was that children in all three groups experienced a wide array of literacy activities. What differed among groups was the relative emphasis placed on directly teaching literacy skills versus involving children in naturally occurring literacy events. Anderson suggests that some differences across cultures may not really matter if teachers understand these differences and are willing to accommodate them.

**DANGERS IN STEREOTYPING.**   Even positive stereotypes can have an negative impact. For example, there are dangers in characterizing all Asian students in the North American context as model students—quiet, hardworking, and passive. Acting on these stereotypes can reinforce conformity and stifle assertiveness. Moreover, Stacey Lee (2006) describes how Asian Americans are seen as perpetual foreigners. No matter how many decades their families have lived in America, even fourth- or fifth-generation Asian American students are not seen as "real" Americans. In fact, Lee's research shows that teachers tend to refer to these students as "Asian," not "Asian American" or "American." That would be like calling Nancy an Irish student because her father came to Canada from Ireland. She was born in Oshawa, Ontario, and has only been to Ireland once, when she was 8 years old. Too often, students take these stereotypes to heart and feel "foreign" even in the country of their birth—Canada or America. One high school student told Lee (2004), "Watching MTV affected the way I acted very much. I wanted to be more Americanized. I changed my hair color. I got colored contact lenses" (p. 44). Later in this chapter, we will explore ways to make classrooms compatible with the home cultures of students. First, however, we need to examine some of the effects of cultural conflicts and discrimination on student achievement.

**Watch**
Dangers in Stereotyping

# ECONOMIC AND SOCIAL CLASS DIFFERENCES

Even though most researchers would agree that social class is one of the most meaningful cultural dimensions in people's lives, those same researchers have great difficulty defining social class (Liu, Ali, Soleck, Hopps, Dunston, & Pickett, 2004). Different terms are used—social class, socioeconomic status (SES), economic background, wealth, poverty, or privilege. Some people consider only economic differences; others add considerations of power, influence, mobility, control over resources, and prestige.

## Social Class and SES

In modern societies, levels of wealth, power, and prestige are not always consistent. Some people—for instance, university professors—are members of professions that are reasonably high in terms of social status, but provide little wealth or power. Other people have political power even though they are not wealthy, or they may be members of the "social register" in a town, even though their family money is long gone. Most people are generally aware of their social class—that is, they perceive that some groups are above them in social class and some are below them. They may even show a kind of "*classism*" (like racism or sexism), believing that they are "better" than members of lower social classes and avoiding association with them. For example, in an ethnographic study (see Chapter 1 if you don't remember what ethnographic means), Marissa, a member of the most popular and privileged clique in her high school, described the "grits"—the least popular group:

> Grits are poor. I think they mostly live in the country. We—[quickly correcting herself] some of my friends call them hicks or rednecks. I guess most live on the Hill—that's over on the west side of town. It's the slums. Grits smoke, do drugs, dress grungy. They have those hick accents. They usually get bad grades. They don't like school so I think they drop out a lot. They don't really fit in. They are troublemakers. I don't see them much; they aren't in any of my classes. (Brantlinger, 2004, pp. 109–110)

In addition to social class, there is another way of thinking about differences that is commonly used in research. Sociologists and psychologists combine variations in wealth, power, control over resources, and prestige into an index called **socioeconomic status, or SES**. In contrast to social class, most people are not conscious of their SES designation. SES is usually ascribed to people by researchers; different formulas for determining SES might lead to different assignments (Liu, Ali, Soleck, Hopps, Dunston, & Pickett, 2004; Sirin, 2005). No single variable, not even income, is an effective measure of SES. When collecting data about children and youth, Statistics Canada (2008) considers family income, parents' occupations, and parents' education to arrive at an overall indicator of SES.

## Poverty and School Achievement

You saw in Chapter 1 that about one in seven children in Canada live in poverty (Canada 2000, 2013). For particular groups of children the rate is far higher (e.g., between 33%–40% for immigrant refugee and Indigenous children, respectively). Children in lone-parent families and children who have parents with low levels of education also have a particularly high risk of poverty (29% and 39% respectively, UNICEF, 2012). Canada is ranked twenty-fourth of 35 "rich" industrialized nations in the UNICEF report—we are at the top of the bottom third. There is ample evidence showing how children suffer—developmentally, medically, socially, and academically—as a result of poverty. That the rate of child poverty in Canada is higher than the rate for the general population and higher than the rate for elderly Canadians suggests our tax and social policies are not making them a priority, which makes little sense from an economic and social welfare perspective.

What about SES and school achievement? The average correlation between SES and school achievement is moderate, about .30 to .40 (Sackett, Kuncel, Arneson, Cooper, & Waters, 2009; Sirin, 2005). In general, high-SES students of all ethnic groups show higher average levels of achievement and stay in school longer than low-SES students (Berliner, 2005; Gutman, Sameroff, & Cole, 2003). Poor children are at least twice as likely as non-poor children to be kept back in school. And the longer the child is in poverty, the stronger the impact is on achievement. For example, even when we take into account parents' education, the chance that children will be retained in grades or placed in special education classes increases by 2%–3% for every year the children live in poverty (Ackerman, Brown, & Izard, 2004; Bronfenbrenner, McClelland, Wethington, Moen, & Ceci, 1996).

What are the effects of low socioeconomic status that might explain the lower school achievement of these students? No one cause is to blame (Evans, 2004). Poor health care for mother and child, dangerous or unhealthy environments, limited resources, family stress, interruptions in schooling, exposure to violence, overcrowding, homelessness, discrimination, and other factors lead to school failures and low-paying jobs—and another generation born in poverty. Evans (2004), Jensen (2009), and McLoyd (1998) describe other possible explanations. Let's take a closer look at each of them.

**Socioeconomic status (SES)** Relative standing in the society based on income, power, background, and prestige.

HEALTH, ENVIRONMENT, AND STRESS.    The negative effects of poverty begin even before a child is born. Families in poverty have less access to good prenatal and infant health care and nutrition. Over half of all adolescent mothers receive no prenatal care at all. Poor mothers and adolescent mothers are more likely to have premature babies, and prematurity is associated with many cognitive and learning problems. Children in poverty are more likely to be exposed to both legal drugs (nicotine, alcohol) and illegal drugs (cocaine, heroin) before birth. Children whose mothers take drugs during pregnancy can have problems with organization, attention, and language skills.

In the early years, children in poverty experience higher levels of stress hormones than children in middle-class and wealthy families. High levels of these hormones can interfere with the flow of blood in the brain, and the development of synaptic connections (Shonkoff, 2006). In addition, stress hormones can deplete tryptophan (Richell, Deakin, & Anderson, 2005), an amino acid that calms impulsive and violent behaviours (Hudley & Novak, 2007). Poor children are four times as likely to experience stress due to evictions, lack of food, overcrowding, or utility disconnections. Increased stress is related to increased school absences, decreased attention and concentration, problems with memory and thinking, reduced motivation and effort, increased depression, and reduced neurogenesis (growth of new brain cells) (Jensen, 2009). As they grow, poor children breathe more polluted air and drink more contaminated water (Evans, 2004). Poor children are at least twice as likely as non-poor children to suffer lead poisoning, which is associated with lower school achievement and long-term neurological impairment (McLoyd, 1998).

LOW EXPECTATIONS—LOW SELF-ESTEEM.    Because low-SES students may wear old clothes, or be less familiar with books and school activities, teachers and other students may assume that these students are not bright. The teacher may avoid calling on them, assuming they don't know the answer, may set lower standards, and may accept poor work. Thus, low expectations become institutionalized, and the educational resources provided are inadequate (Borman & Overman, 2004). Low expectations, along with a lower-quality educational experience, can lead to a sense of learned helplessness, described in Chapter 4. Low-SES children, particularly those who also encounter racial discrimination, may decide that school is a dead end. Without a high school diploma, these students find few rewards awaiting them in the work world. Many available jobs barely pay a living wage.

PEER INFLUENCES AND RESISTANCE CULTURES.    Some researchers have suggested that low-SES students may become part of a **resistance culture**. To members of this culture, making it in school means selling out and trying to act "middle class." In order to maintain their identity and their status within the group, low-SES students must reject the behaviour that would make them successful in school—studying, cooperating with teachers, even coming to class (Bennett, 2011; Ogbu, 1987, 1997). John Ogbu linked identification in a resistance culture to poor Hispanic American, Native American, and African American groups, but similar reactions have been noted for poor white students, both in the United States and in England, and high school students in Papua New Guinea (Woolfolk Hoy, Demerath, & Pape, 2002).

This is not to say that all low-SES students resist achievement. Data from the *Canadian National Longitudinal Study of Children and Youth (NLSCY)* have demonstrated that some students, despite the enormous challenges they face, do well in school and in life. These students are said to be *resilient*. And we should not forget that some aspects of schooling—competitive grading, public reprimands, stressful testing and assignments, and repetitive work that is too hard or too easy—can encourage resistance in all students (Okagaki, 2001). To focus solely on students' resistance is a way of blaming students for their lower achievement; instead, educators should focus on making school an inclusive place that does not invite resistance (Stinson, 2006). Judy Lupart and Vianne Timmons (2003) summarized a national study of how students "at risk" for learning difficulties are identified across Canada and what provinces and schools are doing for these

Resistance culture Group values and beliefs about refusing to adopt the behaviours and attitudes of the majority culture.

Michael J. Doolittle/The Image Works

**SUMMER SETBACKS.** Children in poverty lose ground academically during the summers while middle- and upper-class families provide many educational experiences over the summer for their children. One study suggests that the four summer vacations between grade 2 and grade 6 account for 80% of the achievement differences between poor and advantaged students.

students. They concluded that students' at-risk status is not simply a characteristic of individuals; rather, it is the result of interactions among a "confluence of factors within social, economic, cultural, and community contexts" (p. 219). According to Lupart and Timmons, successful programs are personalized and seek to eliminate the environmental conditions that contribute to students' problems.

HOME ENVIRONMENT AND RESOURCES. Families in poverty seldom have access to high-quality preschool care for their young children, the kind of care that enhances cognitive and social development (Duncan & Brooks-Gunn, 2000; Vandell, 2004). Poor children read less and spend more time watching television; they have less access to books, computers, libraries, trips, and museums (Evans, 2004; Kim & Guryan, 2010). Again, not all low-income families lack resources. Many of these families provide rich learning environments for their children. When parents of any SES level support and encourage their children—by reading to them, providing books and educational toys, taking the children to the library, making time and space for learning—the outcomes for their children are better. Home and neighbourhood resources seem to have the greatest impact on children's achievement when school is not in session—during the summer or before students enter school.

SUMMER SETBACKS.    Over the past decade, evidence has been mounting that students in poverty begin school about six months behind in reading compared to students from wealthier homes, but the difference between the groups grows to almost three years by grade 6. One explanation for this growing gap is that the children from poorer homes lose ground over the summer. Even though both groups make comparable achievement gains during the school year, every summer vacation creates about a three-month reading achievement gap between poor and advantaged children (Kim & Guryan, 2010). One study suggested that the four summer vacations between grade 2 and grade 6 accounted for 80% of the achievement differences between poor and advantaged students (Allington & McGill-Frazen, 2003, 2008). This truly is a case of the rich getting richer. Wealthier children have greater access to books all the time, but especially over the summer. They read more, and the more children read, the better readers they become—volume of reading matters.

TRACKING: POOR TEACHING.    Another explanation for the lower achievement of many low-SES students is that these students experience **tracking**—placement in classes or strands based on judgments of ability—and, therefore, have a different academic socialization. They are actually taught differently (Oakes, 1990b). If they are tracked into "low-ability" or "general" classes, they may be taught to memorize and be passive. Middle-class students are more likely to be encouraged to think and create in their classes. Is tracking a problem? Read the arguments in the Point/ *Counterpoint* box.

Even if they are not tracked, low-income students are more likely to attend schools with inadequate resources and less-effective teachers (Evans, 2004). When low-SES students receive an inferior education, their academic skills are inferior and their life chances are limited, beginning with not being prepared for higher education (Anyon, 1980; Knapp & Woolverton, 2003). See the *Guidelines* for a few ideas about quality teaching for students who live in poverty.

**Tracking** Assignment to different classes and academic experiences based on achievement.

## POINT/COUNTERPOINT  Is Tracking an Effective Strategy?

Streaming or tracking students into different classes or strands (college/university prep, vocational, remedial, gifted, etc.) has been practised in Canada and other developed countries for decades (Krahn & Taylor, 2008), but does it work? Critics say tracking is harmful, while supporters claim it is useful, even though it presents challenges.

▶ **Tracking is harmful and should be eliminated.**
Tom Loveless, writing in the April 1999 issue of *Educational Leadership*, argued, "Prominent researchers and prestigious national reports have argued that tracking stands in the way of equal educational opportunity" (Loveless, 1999, p. 28). More recently, Scott Davies and Neil Guppy (2006) reported findings from Canadian research that support this argument; it is more common for students from wealthier and more advantaged family backgrounds to take courses that keep post-secondary options open, while students from poorer and relatively less advantaged backgrounds are disproportionately represented in vocational programs.

What is the evidence against tracking? A few well-done and carefully designed studies found that tracking increases the gap between high and low achievers by depressing the achievement of low-track students and boosting the achievement of high-track students (Gamoran, 1987; Kerckhoff, 1986). Gamoran found that the achievement gap between low- and high-track students is greater than the gap between students who drop out of school and students who graduate. And, because low-income students are overrepresented in the lower tracks, they suffer the greatest harm from tracking (Krahn & Taylor, 2008; Oakes, 1990b; Oakes & Wells, 2002). In an interview with Marge Scherer (1993), Jonathan Kozol described the cruel predictive side of tracking:

> [T]racking is so utterly predictive. The little girl who gets shoved into the low reading group in 2nd grade is very likely to be the child who is urged to take cosmetology instead of algebra in the 8th grade, and most likely to be in vocational courses, not college courses, in the 10th grade, if she hasn't dropped out by then. (p. 8)

Therefore, students from disadvantaged backgrounds should benefit most from the elimination of tracking. Is this likely?

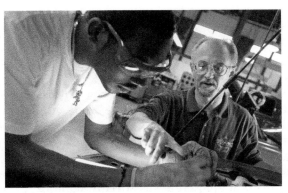

Patrick White/Pearson Allyn and Bacon/ Merrill Education

▶ **Eliminating tracking will hurt many students.**
Researchers who have looked closely at tracking believe that tracking may be harmful for some students some of the time, but not for all students and not all of the time. First, as most people agree, tracking seems to have positive effects for the high-track students. Gifted programs, honours classes, and advanced placement classes seem to work (Fuchs, Fuchs, Hamlett, & Karns, 1998; Robinson & Clinkenbeard, 1998). No one, especially parents, wants to eliminate the positive effects of these programs. And data from the *Youth in Transition Study* in Canada indicate that students traditionally thought to be disadvantaged by tracking (immigrant students, students from visible minority groups, female students) are, in fact, remaining in the academic stream and keeping their options open for post-secondary education (Krahn & Taylor, 2008).

What would happen if schools eliminated tracking? Loveless (1999) identified some possible hidden costs. First, results of a large national study suggest that when low-track grade 10 students are assigned to heterogeneous classes rather than low tracks, they gain about 5 percentage points in achievement. So far, so good. But average students lose 2 percentage points when put into heterogeneous classes and high-ability students lose about 5 points. Another consequence of eliminating tracking is *bright flight*—the withdrawal of the brightest students from the schools. Proponents of tracking argue that students with different abilities and aptitudes should have opportunities to take different sequences of courses during high school (Krahn & Taylor, 2008). They contend students can learn better and enjoy learning more when grouped homogeneously. Finally, they argue that teachers can attend to and accommodate student differences more easily when students within classes are less diverse.

**Beware of Either/Or.** In some classes, using a mixed-ability structure seems to hinder the achievement of all students. For example, students in heterogeneous algebra classes don't learn as much as students in tracked classes—whatever the ability level of the students (Epstein & MacIver, 1992). And a meta-analysis of student self-esteem found that students in low-track classes did *not* have lower self-esteem than students in heterogeneous classes (Kulik & Kulik, 1997).

So what is the answer? As usual, it is more complicated than simply eliminating or implementing tracking. Avoiding overrepresentation or unwarranted representation of certain groups in the so-called "lower tracks" is important, but so is providing alternatives for students who prefer to pursue educational goals that don't lead to college and university programs. Careful attention to every student's interests and achievement may mean different answers for different students at different times.

## GUIDELINES

## Teaching Students Who Live in Poverty

**Educate yourself about the effects of poverty on student learning.**
*Examples*

1. Read articles from good journals.
2. Seek reliable sources such as Eric Jensen's (2009) *Teaching with Poverty in Mind: What Being Poor Does to Kids' Brains and What Schools Can Do about It.*

**Set and maintain high expectations.**
*Examples*

1. Guard against feeling sorry for students, excusing poor work, and expecting less. Replace pity with empathy based on solid knowledge of your students.
2. Communicate to students that they can succeed with good effort.
3. Provide constructive criticism because you believe your students can do quality work.
4. Add challenging subjects and AP classes.

**Develop caring relationships with your students.**
*Examples*

1. Use inclusive language—"our class," "our projects," "our school," "our efforts."
2. Talk to students outside class. Make a point to identify their interests and abilities.
3. Attend sports or other events where your students participate.
4. Create a class welcome centre for families (see Chapter 5).

**Build learning and self-regulation skills as part of the curriculum.**
*Examples*

1. Teach students how to organize work, focus attention, or seek appropriate help.
2. Include conflict management and social problem-solving skills in lessons.

**Notice health problems.**
*Examples*

1. Notice who seems to be absent or tardy often.
2. Check to see whether some students struggle to hear the class discussions. Can they see from the back of the room?
3. Model healthy eating and physical activity.

**Assess student knowledge; start where they are, but don't stay there (Milner, 2010).**
*Examples*

1. Use short ungraded assessments that target the learning objectives for each unit.
2. Differentiate instruction (see Chapter 14) based on results.

*Many examples adapted from Jensen, E. (2009). Teaching with Poverty in Mind: What Being Poor Does to Kids' Brains and What Schools Can do About It. Alexandria, VA: Association for Supervision and Curriculum Development.*

# ETHNICITY AND RACE DIFFERENCES IN TEACHING AND LEARNING

Canada truly is a diverse society. According to the *National Household Survey* (Statistics Canada, 2013), 6.8 million of Canada's residents are foreign born, and one in five people living in Canada are members of visible minority groups. Before we look at the research on ethnicity and race, let's clarify some terms.

## Terms: Ethnicity and Race

**Ethnicity** usually refers to a group's shared common cultural characteristics such as history, homeland, language, traditions, or religion. We all have some ethnic heritage, whether our background is Canadian, Italian, Ukrainian, Hmong, Chinese, Japanese, Navajo, Hawaiian, Puerto Rican, Cuban, Hungarian, German, African, or Irish—to name only a few.

**Race**, on the other hand, is defined as "a category composed of men and women who share biologically transmitted traits that are defined as socially significant," such as skin colour or hair texture (Macionis, 2003, p. 354). In effect, race is a label that people apply to themselves and to others based on appearances. There are no biologically pure races. In fact, for any two humans chosen at random, an average of only .012% (about

**Ethnicity** A cultural heritage shared by a group of people.

**Race** A group of people who share common biological traits that are seen as self-defining by the people of the group.

one-hundredth of 1%) of the alphabetic sequence of their genetic codes is different due to race (Myers, 2005). Today many psychologists emphasize that ethnicity and race are socially constructed ideas. Still, race is a powerful construct. At the individual level, race is part of our identity—how we understand ourselves and interact with others. At the group level, race is involved with economic and political structures (Omi & Winant, 1994).

Sociologists sometimes use the term **minority group** to label a group of people that receives unequal or discriminatory treatment. Strictly speaking, however, the term refers to a numerical minority compared with the total population. Referring to particular racial or ethnic groups as "minorities" is technically incorrect in some situations, because in certain places the "minority" group is actually the majority—for example, students from Pacific Rim countries in some of the inner-city schools in Vancouver. This practice of referring to people as "minorities" because of their racial or ethnic heritage has been criticized because it is misleading and has negative historical connotations.

## Ethnic and Racial Differences in School Achievement

A major concern in schools is that some ethnic groups consistently achieve below the average for all students (Matthews, Kizzie, Rowley, & Cortina, 2010; Uline & Johnson, 2005). This pattern of results tends to hold for standardized achievement tests, but (at least in the United States) the gaps have been narrowing over the past four to five decades (Raudenbush, 2009). For example, on the National Assessment of Educational Progress in mathematics, the gap between scores of white and African American grade 4 students narrowed from 34 points in 1996 to 26 points in 2009. The gap between white and Hispanic grade 4 students narrowed from 25 in 1996 to 21 in 2009 (NCES, 2009).

Proponents of this notion of an "achievement gap" have been criticized for taking a narrow view, assuming that the scores of white, middle-class students are the norm that all other students must be compared to and measured by. Multicultural scholar H. Richard Milner (2010) reminds teachers that "people of color may experience a different type of 'normal' life and that excellence can and does emerge in multiple and varied forms: people of color from all walks of life are successful" (p. 9). He suggests that we think about other kinds of "gaps," such as teacher education and quality gaps, affordable housing gaps, challenging curriculum gaps, health care and nutrition gaps, school funding gaps, and quality child-care gaps—all culminating in *opportunity gaps* for many students of colour.

Opportunity gaps lead to education completion gaps. Across all the United States in 2007, about 80% of white students graduated from high school, compared to 60% of African American students, 62% of Latino/a students, 91% of Asian/Pacific Islanders, and 61% of Native Americans. Similarly, in Canada the dropout rate for students from some minority ethnic groups is higher than it is for white students and, although the dropout rate for Aboriginal youth is higher than for any other group, particularly for Aboriginal youth living on reserve (Richards, 2011).

Although there are consistent differences among ethnic groups on tests of cognitive abilities, most researchers agree that these differences are mainly the legacy of discrimination, the product of cultural mismatches, or a result of growing up in poverty. Because many students from minority groups are also economically disadvantaged, it is important to separate the effects of these two sets of influences on school achievement (Roberts, Mohammed, & Vaughn, 2010). For example, a recent study found that learning and self-regulation skills (such as attentiveness, persistence, organization, learning independence) explained the literacy development of African American boys from kindergarten to grade 5, even after taking into account the effects of the boys' SES, home environment, and problem behaviours (Matthews, Kizzie, Rowley, & Cortina, 2010). So early development of these learning skills can help to close the opportunity gap, at least for African American boys, and probably for others.

Rather than focusing on achievement gaps, many educators have called for more research on the successes of minority students. Berry (2005) conducted an in-depth study of two middle-school-aged African American boys who were successful in mathematics. In the lives of those students, Berry found support and high expectations from family

**Minority group** A group of people who have been socially disadvantaged—not always a minority in actual numbers.

and teachers; positive math experiences in preschool and elementary school; connections to church and athletic extracurricular activities; and positive identities as math students. Berry encouraged educators and researchers to focus on the success stories of minority students and to identify the strengths, skills, and other significant factors that lead to success.

One final theme characterized the successful African American boys above—their families had prepared them to understand and deal with discrimination, our next topic.

## The Legacy of Discrimination

When we considered explanations for why low-SES students have trouble in school, we listed the low expectations and biases of teachers and fellow students. Many ethnic-minority students have similar experiences. Imagine that the children described below are your own. What would you do?

> Almost forty years ago, in the city of Topeka, Kansas, a minister walked hand in hand with his seven-year-old daughter to an elementary school four blocks from their home. Linda Brown wanted to enroll in the 2nd grade, but the school refused to admit her. Instead, public school officials required her to attend another school two miles away. This meant that she had to walk six blocks to a bus stop, where she sometimes waited half an hour for the bus. In bad weather, Linda Brown would be soaking wet by the time the bus came; one day she became so cold at the bus stop that she walked back home. Why, she asked her parents, could she not attend the school only four blocks away? (Macionis, 2003, p. 353)

In Canada, residential schools were built for First Nations children, who were then educated off the reserve.

> [The schools] were funded by the federal government who inspected the curriculum, and operated by the Christian churches who provided administrators, teachers, and additional funds. . . . The residential schools were not successful academically, vocationally, or socially, but they persisted into the 1960s. . . . In 1961, scholars at the University of British Columbia reported to the government . . . that the schools represented a severe discontinuity in experience for the native youth. Nearly all dropped out before grade 12, few went to university, and many suffered social and emotional difficulties. (Crealock & Bachor, 1995, p. 518)

**LINDA BROWN** Nine-year-old Linda Brown, the plaintiff in *Brown* v. *Board of Education of Topeka.*

Carl Iwasaki/Time & Life Pictures/Getty Images

Linda Brown's parents filed a suit against the Board of Education of Topeka and challenged the school segregation policy. The outcome of that landmark case, *Brown v. Board of Education of Topeka,* is the basis for the principle of free and appropriate education for *all* students, a principle adopted in Canada as well as the United States. However, some Aboriginal communities have increasingly moved to create and control schools for their children and to inject more and more Aboriginal content into their curricula. Many Aboriginal bands want to take full responsibility for the care and education of children in their communities (Ball, 2008; Crealock & Bachor, 1995).

Years of research on the effects of desegregation have mostly shown that legally mandated integration is not a quick solution to the detrimental effects of centuries of racial inequality. Too often, minority-group students are re-segregated in low-ability tracks even in integrated schools. Simply putting people in the same building does not mean that they will come to respect each other or even that they will experience the same quality of education (Ladson-Billings, 2004; Pettigrew, 1998).

The University of British Columbia (UBC) and several other institutions across Canada have developed teacher education programs especially for preservice teachers of First Nations ancestry. The hope is that once students in the Native Indian Teacher Education Program (NITEP) at UBC complete their degrees, they will return to their band schools or teach in public schools and provide high-quality, culturally sensitive instruction to First Nations students.

Gwen Point is an Aboriginal educator whose history was profiled in *Connected,* a publication of the British Columbia College of Teachers (2004). She learned *her* language from her grandmother, along with the stories and songs of her people. However, when she went to school, she learned about discrimination and shame: "I became ashamed of being Indian." At school, Point did not have the opportunity to speak Halq'eméylem. None of her teachers were Aboriginal, and there was no First Nations content in the curriculum. Point's grandmother told her to go to university and "come home and help your people," which is exactly what she did.

Point has had a distinguished career as an educator and advocate for Aboriginal culture. Especially, she has been instrumental in restoring the Halq'eméylem language, which was on the verge of extinction, to the Sto:lo community. In cooperation with Simon Fraser University and the British Columbia College of Teachers, Point developed a certificate program that allows adults to learn the language and prepare to teach it to students in public and First Nations schools. One graduate of the program says, "We give our children opportunities to learn the language. And by sharing the language with others, we help to build awareness and self-esteem."

Point believes that this is a remarkable shift "from not being allowed to speak our language. It's a validation of our people and our elders. . . . As a parent, grandparent, and educator, I can see it's helping our students."

What is the legacy of unequal treatment and discrimination?

**GWEN POINT** A distinguished educator and advocate for Aboriginal culture, Gwen Point developed a program that prepares adults from First Nations communities to teach their language to students in public and First Nations schools.

Courtesy of Gwen Point

**WHAT IS PREJUDICE?**   The word *prejudice* is closely related to the word *pre-judge*. **Prejudice** is a rigid and irrational generalization—a prejudgment—about an entire category of people. Prejudice is made up of beliefs, emotions, and tendencies toward particular actions. For example, you are prejudiced against people who are overweight if you believe they are lazy (belief), feel disgusted (emotion), and refuse to date them (action) (Myers, 2010). Prejudice can be positive or negative; that is, you can have positive as well as negative irrational beliefs about a group, but the word usually refers to negative attitudes. Targets of prejudice can be based on race, ethnicity, religion, politics, geographic location, language, sexual orientation, gender, or appearance.

**THE DEVELOPMENT OF PREJUDICE.**   Racial prejudice is pervasive, and it starts early. By about age 6, close to 85% of students in a Canadian sample had significant pro-white, anti–African American biases (Doyle & Aboud, 1995). Two popular beliefs are that young children are innocently colour-blind and that they will not develop biases unless their parents teach them to be prejudiced. Although these beliefs are appealing, they are not supported by research. Even without direct coaching from their parents, many young children develop racial prejudice. Current explanations of the development of prejudice combine personal and social factors (Katz, 2003; McKown, 2005).

One source of prejudice is the human tendency to divide the social world into two categories—*us* and *them,* or the *in-group* and the *out-group.* These divisions may be made on the basis of race, religion, sex, age, ethnicity, or even athletic team membership. We tend to see members of the out-group as inferior and different from us, but similar to each other—"They all look alike" (Aboud, 2003; Lambert, 1995). Also, those who have more (more money, more social status, more prestige) may justify their privilege by assuming that they deserve to "have" because they are superior to the "have-nots." This can lead to blaming the victims:

**prejudice** Prejudgment, or irrational generalization about an entire category of people.

**Doonesbury**                                                                 BY GARRY TRUDEAU

People who live in poverty or women who are raped are seen as causing their problems by their behaviour—"They got what they deserved." Emotions play a part as well. When things go wrong, we look for someone or some whole group to blame. For example, in the United States, after the tragic events of 9/11, some people vented their anger by attacking innocent Arab Americans (Myers, 2010).

But prejudice is more than a tendency to form in-groups, a self-justification, or an emotional reaction—it is also a set of cultural values. Children learn about valued traits and characteristics from their families, friends, teachers, and the world around them. And for years, most of the models presented in books, films, television, and advertising were middle- and upper-class European Americans. People of different ethnic and racial backgrounds were seldom the "heroes" (Ward, 2004). This is changing. In 2002, the Academy Awards for best actress and best actor went to African Americans, although Denzel Washington won for his portrayal of a villain. However, in 2005, Jamie Foxx won for his remarkable portrayal of Ray Charles—a hero. And since then, the United States has elected a African American president, Barack Obama.

---

**STOP & THINK** List three traits most characteristic of:
- First-year college or university students
- Politicians
- Athletes
- Buddhists
- Members of the Dominion of Canada Rifle Association •

---

Prejudice is difficult to combat because it can be part of our thinking processes. You saw in Chapter 2 that children develop schemes, or schemas, as they are referred to in Chapter 7—organized bodies of knowledge—about objects, events, and actions. We have schemas that organize our knowledge about drinking from a straw, people we know, the meaning of words, and so on. We can also form schemas about groups of people. When asked to list the traits most characteristic of college or university students, politicians, athletes, Buddhists, or members of the Canada Rifle Association, you probably could generate a list. That list would show that you have a **stereotype**—a schema—that organizes what you know about the group.

As with any schema, we use our stereotype to make sense of the world. You will see in Chapter 8 that having a schema allows you to process information more quickly and efficiently, but it also allows you to distort information to make it better fit your schema (Macrae, Milne, & Bodenhausen, 1994). This is the danger in racial and ethnic stereotypes. We notice information that confirms or agrees with our stereotype—our schema—and miss or dismiss information that does not fit. For example, if a juror has a negative stereotype of Asian Canadians and is listening to evidence in the trial of an Asian Canadian, the juror may interpret the evidence more negatively. The juror may actually forget testimony in favour of the defendant but remember more damaging testimony. Information that fits the stereotype is even processed more quickly (Anderson, Klatzky, & Murray, 1990; Baron, 1998).

CONTINUING DISCRIMINATION. Prejudice consists of beliefs and feelings (usually negative) about an entire category of people. The third element of prejudice is a tendency to act, called discrimination. **Discrimination** is unequal treatment of particular categories of people. Members of minority groups face prejudice and discrimination in subtle or blatant ways every day. For example, in the United States, people of Latino, African American, and Native American descent make up about 25% of the U.S. population, but only 17% of the House of Representatives and 6% of the Senate (Koppleman, 2011). In the 2007–2008 school year, less than 4% of the doctorates awarded went to Latino students, 6% to African Americans, and .4% to Native Americans. In contrast, 27% of the doctorates were awarded to non-residents of the United States (NCES, 2010). Less than 9% of the scientists, engineers, and mathematicians in the United States are either African American or Hispanic American.

**Stereotype** Schema that organizes knowledge or perceptions of a category.

**Discrimination** Treating particular categories of people unfairly.

Even though their attitudes toward science and math are more favourable than the attitudes of white students, African American and Hispanic students begin to lose out in science and math as early as elementary school. They are chosen less often for gifted classes and acceleration or enrichment programs. They are more likely to be tracked into "basic skills" classes. As they progress through middle school, high school, and university or college, their paths take them farther and farther out of the pipeline that produces scientists. If they do persist and become scientists or engineers, as a group they—along with women—will still be paid proportionately less than white men for the same work (Mendoza & Johnson, 2000; National Science Foundation, 2011). Comparable figures for Canadian minorities are more difficult to find. However, what is available paints a similar picture for ethnic groups in Canada, particularly those from Aboriginal groups (Ezeife, 2011, 2013). Minorities in Canada are underrepresented in math, science, and engineering programs in tertiary education and, therefore, in careers in those disciplines.

The families of racial and ethnic minority students often have to be vigilant about discrimination to protect their children. They may teach their children to notice and resist possible discrimination. Teachers may unintentionally offend these families if they are not sensitive to possible messages of discrimination. Carol Orange (2005) described a teacher who sent home a holiday worksheet that featured an alphabetical list of all the students in the class. Three students' names were not in the typed list, but were handwritten, out of order, and on the side of the sheet. Two of these students were members of visible minority groups. The mother of one student was very upset that her son was truly "marginalized" (written in the margins) on the list. These three students were added to the class (and hence, the list) late in the school year, after the list was set up, but the teacher could have avoided this insult (unintended on her part) by redoing the list to give every student a place—a small but important symbol that she valued each one of them.

There is another problem caused by stereotypes and prejudice that can undermine academic achievement—stereotype threat.

## Stereotype Threat

**Stereotype threat** is an "apprehensiveness about confirming a stereotype" (Aronson, 2002, p. 282). The basic idea is that when stereotyped individuals are in situations where the stereotype applies, they bear an extra emotional and cognitive burden. The burden is the possibility of confirming the stereotype, either in the eyes of others or in their own eyes. Thus when girls are asked to solve complicated mathematics problems, for example, they are at risk of confirming widely held stereotypes that girls are inferior to boys in mathematics. It is not necessary that the individual even believe the stereotype. All that matters is that the person is *aware* of the stereotype and *cares about performing* well enough to disprove its unflattering implications (Aronson, Lustina, Good, Keough, Steele, & Brown, 1999; Huguet & Régner, 2007). What are the results of stereotype threat? Recent research provides answers that should interest all teachers.

SHORT-TERM EFFECTS: TEST PERFORMANCE.   One review of the research on women, math, and stereotype threat concluded that very subtle clues that might activate anxiety, such as asking test takers to indicate their gender on an answer sheet before taking a math test, tend to lower math scores for women, especially when tests are difficult, the women are moderately identified with the math field, and being female is an important part of their identity. The differences are small on average—something like a female with average math ability scoring 450 instead of the expected average of 500 on an SAT- or GRE-type test. One study estimated that removing stereotype threat might mean an additional 6% of women getting a passing score on a high-stakes calculus test (Nguyen & Ryan, 2008; Wout, Dasco, Jackson, & Spencer, 2008). In other studies, girls in high school and college have scored below boys on a math test when stereotype threats are present, but the same as boys when these threats are not present (Smith & Hung, 2008). Just telling the girls that the math test they are about to take does not reveal gender differences is enough to eliminate any differences in scores.

**Stereotype threat** The extra emotional and cognitive burden that one's performance in an academic situation might confirm a stereotype that others hold.

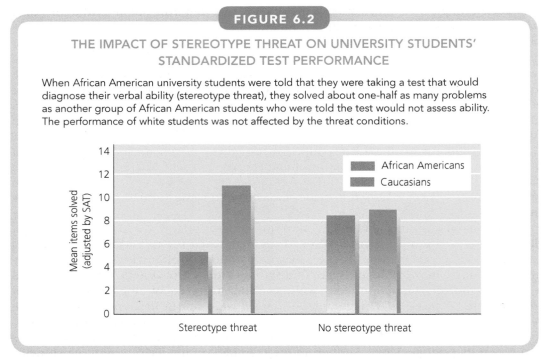

**FIGURE 6.2**

THE IMPACT OF STEREOTYPE THREAT ON UNIVERSITY STUDENTS'
STANDARDIZED TEST PERFORMANCE

When African American university students were told that they were taking a test that would diagnose their verbal ability (stereotype threat), they solved about one-half as many problems as another group of African American students who were told the test would not assess ability. The performance of white students was not affected by the threat conditions.

*Source: Adapted from Aronson, J., Steele, C. M., Salinas, M. F., & Lustina, M., J. (2007). The Effect of Stereotype Threat on the Standardized Test Performance of College Students. Readings About the Social Animal, 10th ed. Worth Publishers. Reprinted by permission of Joshua Aronson, Ph.D.*

In a series of experiments, Joshua Aronson, Claude Steele, and their colleagues demonstrated that when minority-group university students are put in situations that induce stereotype threat, their performance suffers (Aronson, 2002; Aronson & Steele, 2005; Okagaki, 2006). For example, African American and white undergraduate subjects in an experiment at Stanford University were told that the test they were about to take would precisely measure their verbal ability. A similar group of subjects was told that the purpose of the test was to understand the psychology of verbal problem solving and not to assess individual ability. As shown in Figure 6.2, when the test was presented as diagnostic of verbal ability, the African American students solved about half as many problems as the white students. In the non-threat situation, the two groups solved about the same number of problems.

All groups, not just minority-group students, can be susceptible to stereotype threat. In another study, the subjects were white male university students who were very strong in mathematics. One group was told that the test they were taking would help experimenters determine why Asian students performed so much better than white students on that particular test. Another group just took the test. The group that faced the stereotype threat of confirming that "Asians are better in math" scored significantly lower on the test (Aronson, Lustina, Good, Keough, Steele, & Brown, 1999). The individuals most vulnerable to stereotype threat are those who care the most and who are most deeply invested in high performance (Ryan & Ryan, 2005).

Why does stereotype threat affect test performance? Anxiety is part of a model developed by Katherine and Allison Ryan (2005) to explain the links between stereotype threat and lower math performance for women and African Americans. When these students are in situations that evoke stereotype threats, such as high-pressure tests, they tend to adopt performance-avoidance goals. We will examine this kind of goal more deeply in Chapter 12, but the short version is that setting performance-avoidance goals means the students want to avoid looking dumb. Students who set these kinds of self-protective goals don't persist or use effective strategies. They tend to adopt self-handicapping strategies such as not trying or procrastinating—they just want to survive without looking stupid. But because they put off studying or didn't try, they are anxious and unprepared during the test. Ryan and Ryan sum up their model:

> Concerns about fulfilling a negative stereotype (females and Blacks do not do well in math) bring about a performance-avoid goal orientation towards the test-taking situation for students who are invested in doing well on the test. A performance-avoid goal will lead to an increase in the worry component of test anxiety, make self-efficacy vulnerable, and [lead] to cognitive disorganization or diminishment. (2005, p. 60)

Two other related explanations are that stereotype threat reduces working memory capacity, so students can't hold as much in their minds (Okagaki, 2006), and that it also decreases interest and engagement in the task—why get absorbed in a task that will make you look incompetent (Smith, Sansone, & White, 2007)?

LONG-TERM EFFECTS: DISIDENTIFICATION.   If students continue to adopt performance-avoidance goals and develop self-defeating strategies to avoid looking stupid, they may withdraw, claim to not care, exert little effort, or even drop out of school—they psychologically disengage from success in the domain and claim "math is for nerds" or "school is for losers." Once students define academics as "uncool," it is unlikely they will exert the effort needed for real learning. There is some evidence that African American male students are more likely than African American female students and white students to *disidentify* with academics—that is, to separate their sense of self-esteem from their academic achievement (Cokley, 2002; Major & Schmader, 1998; Steele, 1992). Other studies have questioned this connection, however. Historically, education has been valued among African American communities (Walker, 1996). One study found that African American adolescents who had strong Afrocentric beliefs also had higher achievement goals and self-esteem than adolescents who identified with the larger white culture (Spencer, Noll, Stoltzfus, & Harpalani, 2001).

A challenge for teachers is to help all students see academic achievement as part of their ethnic, racial, and gender identity.

COMBATTING STEREOTYPE THREAT.   Aronson, Fried, and Good (2002) demonstrated the powerful effects of changing beliefs about intelligence. In their study, African American and white undergraduates at Stanford University were asked to write letters to at-risk middle school students to encourage them to persist in school. Some of the undergraduates were given evidence that intelligence is *improvable* and encouraged to communicate this information to their pen pals. Others were given information about multiple intelligences, but were not told that these multiple abilities can be improved. The middle school students were not real, but the process of writing persuasive letters about improving intelligence proved powerful. The African American college students—and the white students to a lesser extent—who were encouraged to believe that intelligence can be improved had higher grade point averages and reported greater enjoyment of and engagement in school when contacted at the end of the next school quarter. Changing their beliefs about the improvability of intelligence also led to higher year-end math achievement scores for middle school girls (Good, Aronson, & Inzlicht, 2003). So, believing that intelligence can be improved might inoculate students against stereotype threat. In another study, reframing a threatening test as a "challenge" that "sharpens the mind" decreased the impact of stereotype threat for grade 4 to grade 6 African American students and for Princeton University students from high schools that rarely send students to Ivy League schools (Alter, Aronson, Darley, Rodriguez, & Ruble, 2010).

In Chapter 12, we will discuss test anxiety and how to overcome the negative effects of anxiety. Many of these strategies are also appropriate for helping students resist stereotype threat.

# GENDER IN TEACHING AND LEARNING

In this section, we examine the development of two related identities—sexual identity and gender-role identity. We particularly focus on how men and women are socialized and the role of teachers in providing an equitable education for both sexes.

## Sex and Gender

The word *gender* usually refers to traits and behaviours that a particular culture judges to be appropriate for men and for women. In contrast, *sex* refers to biological differences (Brannon, 2002; Deaux, 1993). An individual's identity in terms of gender and sex has three components: gender identity, sexual orientation, and gender-role behaviours (Patterson, 1995; Ruble, Martin, & Berenbaum, 2006). **Gender identity** is a person's self-identification as male or female. *Gender-role behaviours* are those behaviours and characteristics that the culture associates with each gender, and *sexual orientation* involves the person's choice of a sexual partner.

Relations among these three elements are complex. For example, a woman may identify herself as a female (gender identity), but behave in ways that are not consistent with the gender role (play football or wrestle), and may be heterosexual, bisexual, or homosexual in her sexual orientation. So **sexual identity** is a complicated construction of beliefs, attitudes, and behaviours. Erikson and many other earlier psychologists thought that identifying your gender identity was straightforward; you simply realized that you were male or female and acted accordingly. But today, we know that some people experience conflicts about their gender. For example, transsexuals often report feeling trapped in the wrong body; they experience themselves as female, but their biological sex is male, or vice versa (Ruble, Martin, & Berenbaum, 2006; Yarhouse, 2001).

SEXUAL ORIENTATION.   During adolescence, about 8% of boys and 6% of girls report engaging in some same-sex activity or feeling strong attractions to individuals of their own sex. Males are more likely than females to experiment with same-sex partners as adolescents, but females are more likely to experiment later, often in college. Fewer adolescents actually have a homosexual or bisexual orientation—about 4% of adolescents identify themselves as gay (males who choose male partners), lesbian (females who choose female partners), or bisexual (people who have partners of both sexes). This number increases to 5%–13% for adults (Savin-Williams, 2006).

Scientists debate the origins of homosexuality. Most of the research has been with men, so less is known about women. Evidence so far suggests that both biological and social factors are involved. For example, sexual orientation is more similar for identical twins than for fraternal twins, but not all identical twins have the same sexual orientation (Ruble, Martin, & Berenbaum, 2006).

There are quite a few models describing the development of sexual orientation as part of identity. Generally, the models include the following or similar stages (Yarhouse, 2001):

- *Feeling different*—Beginning around age 6, the child may be less interested in the activities of other children who are the same sex. Some children may find this difference troubling and fear being "found out." Others do not experience these anxieties.
- *Feeling confused*—In adolescence, as they feel attractions for peers of the same sex, students may be confused, upset, lonely, and unsure of what to do. They may lack role models and may try to change themselves by becoming involved in activities and dating patterns that fit heterosexual stereotypes.
- *Acceptance*—As young adults, many individuals sort through sexual orientation issues and identify themselves as gay, lesbian, or bisexual. They may or may not make their sexual orientation public, but might share the information with a few friends.

The problem with phase models of identity development is that the identity achieved is assumed to be final. Actually, newer models emphasize that sexual orientation can be flexible, complex, and multifaceted; it can change over the lifetime. For example, people may have dated or married opposite-sex partners at one point in their lives, but have same-sex attractions or partners later in their lives, or vice versa (Garnets, 2002).

Parents and teachers are seldom the first people to hear about the adolescent's sexual identity concerns. But if a student does seek your counsel, Table 6.1 provides some ideas for reaching out.

**Gender identity** The sense of self as male or female as well as the beliefs one has about gender roles and attributes.

**Sexual identity** A complex combination of beliefs about gender roles and sexual orientation.

TABLE 6.1 • **Reaching Out to Help Students Struggling With Sexual Identity**

These ideas come from the *Attic Speakers Bureau*, a program of The Attic Youth Center, where trained peer educators reach out to youth and youth-service providers in schools, organizations, and health-care facilities.

---

**REACHING OUT**

If a lesbian, gay, bisexual, or transgender youth or a youth questioning his or her own sexual orientation should come to you directly for assistance, remember the following simple, 5-point plan:

LISTEN It seems obvious, but the best thing that you can do in the beginning is allow that individual to vent and express what is going on in his or her life.

AFFIRM Tell them, "You are not alone." This is crucial. A lot of LGBTQ youth feel isolated and lack peers with whom they can discuss issues around sexual orientation. Letting them know that there are others dealing with the same issues is invaluable. This statement is also important because it does not involve a judgment call on your part.

REFER You do not have to be the expert. A referral to someone who is trained to deal with these issues is a gift you are giving to that student, not a dismissal of responsibility.

ADDRESS Deal with harassers—do not overlook issues of verbal or physical harassment around sexual orientation. It is important to create and maintain an environment where all youth feel comfortable and welcome.

FOLLOW-UP Be sure to check in with the individual to see if the situation has improved and if there is anything further you may be able to do.

There are also some things that you as an individual can do to better serve LGBTQ youth and youth dealing with issues around sexual orientation:

- Work on your own sense of comfort around issues of sexual orientation and sexuality.
- Get training on how to present information on sexual orientation effectively.
- Dispel myths around sexual orientation by knowing facts and sharing that information.
- Work on setting aside your own personal biases to better serve students dealing with issues around sexual orientation and sexuality.

---

*Source: From Figure 3. Copyright © The Attic Speakers Bureau and Carrie E. Jacobs, Ph.D. Reprinted with permission.*

## Gender Roles

*Gender roles* are expectations about how males and females should behave—about what is masculine and what is feminine. Gender roles vary by culture, time, and place. What was expected of women in Canada in the 1700s definitely has changed, even though women generally still are the primary caregivers and in charge of the home.

When and how do children develop gender roles? As early as age 2, children are aware of gender differences—they know whether they are girls or boys and that mommies are girls and daddies are boys. By age 3 or so, they realize that their sex cannot be changed; they will always be male or female. Biology plays a part in gender role development. Very early, hormones affect activity level and aggression, with boys tending to prefer active, rough, noisy play. Play styles lead young children to prefer same-sex play partners with similar styles, so by age 4, children spend three times as much play time with same-sex playmates as with opposite-sex playmates; by age 6, the ratio is 11 to 1 (Benenson, 1993; Hines, 2004; Maccoby, 1998).

But biology is not the whole story; boys and girls may be treated differently, too. Researchers have found that boys are given more freedom to roam the neighbourhood and are allowed to tackle potentially dangerous activities earlier, such as crossing the street alone. Thus, independence and initiative seem to be encouraged more in boys than in girls. In fact, parents, peers, and teachers may reward behaviours that seem gender appropriate—gentle kindness in girls and strong assertiveness in boys (Brannon, 2002).

And then there are the toys! Walk through any store's toy section and see what is offered to girls and boys. Dolls and kitchen sets for girls and toy weapons for boys have been with us for decades. But we cannot blame the toy makers alone. Adults buying for children favour gender-typed toys; fathers also tend to discourage young sons from playing with "girl's" toys (Brannon, 2002).

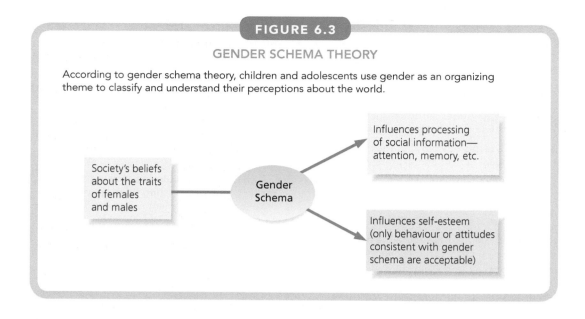

**FIGURE 6.3**

GENDER SCHEMA THEORY

According to gender schema theory, children and adolescents use gender as an organizing theme to classify and understand their perceptions about the world.

Society's beliefs about the traits of females and males → Gender Schema →

Influences processing of social information—attention, memory, etc.

Influences self-esteem (only behaviour or attitudes consistent with gender schema are acceptable)

Through their interactions with family, peers, teachers, toys, and the environment in general, children begin to form **gender schemas,** or organized networks of knowledge about what it means to be male or female. Gender schemas help children make sense of the world and guide their behaviour (see Figure 6.3). So a young girl whose schema for "girls" includes "girls play with dolls and not with trucks" or "girls can't be scientists" will pay attention to, remember, and interact more with dolls than trucks, and she may avoid science activities (Golombok, Rust, Zervoulis, Croudace, Golding, & Hines, 2008; Leaper, 2002; Liben & Signorella, 1993). Of course, these are averages, and individuals do not always fit the average. An individual girl might decide, for example, that the gender schema "trucks are for boys" doesn't matter to her. She plays with the truck if it interests her (Liben & Bigler, 2002).

By age 4, children have an initial sense of gender roles, and by 5 or so, they have developed a gender schema that describes what clothes, games, toys, behaviours, and careers are "right" for boys and girls—and these ideas can be quite rigid (Brannon, 2002). Even in this era of great progress toward equal opportunity, a preschool girl is more likely to tell you she wants to become a nurse than to say she wants to be an engineer. After she had given a lecture on the dangers of sex stereotyping in schools, a colleague of Anita Woolfolk brought her young daughter to her university class. The students asked the little girl, "What do you want to be when you grow up?" The child immediately replied, "A doctor," and her professor/mother beamed with pride. Then the girl whispered to the students in the front row, "I really want to be a nurse, but my mommy won't let me." Actually, this is a common reaction for young children. Preschoolers tend to have more stereotyped notions of sex roles than older children, and all ages seem to have more rigid and traditional ideas about male occupations than about what occupations females should pursue (Woolfolk & Perry, 2012). Later, as adolescents go through puberty, they may become even more focused on behaving in "masculine" or "feminine" ways, as defined by their peer culture. So many factors, from biology to cultural norms, play a role in gender role development. Beware of either/or explanations.

Anita was proofreading this very page for a previous edition while travelling on a train. The conductor stopped beside her seat. He said, "I'm sorry, dear, for interrupting your homework, but do you have a ticket?" She had to smile at his (likely unintended) sexism. She doubts he made the same comment to the man across the aisle writing on his legal pad. Like racial discrimination, messages of sexism can be subtle, and they can appear in classrooms.

Gender schemas Organized cognitive structures that include gender-related information that influences how children think and behave.

## Gender Bias in Curriculum

Unfortunately, schools often foster **gender biases** in a number of ways. Publishers have established guidelines to prevent gender bias in teaching materials, but it still makes sense to check for stereotypes. For example, even though children's books now have an equal number of males and females as central characters, there still are more males in the titles and the illustrations, and the characters (especially the boys) continue to behave in stereotypical ways. Boys are more aggressive and argumentative, and girls are more expressive and affectionate. Girl characters sometimes cross gender roles to be more active, but boy characters seldom show "feminine" expressive traits (Brannon, 2002; Evans & Davies, 2000). Also, video learning packages, virtual worlds, social media sites, and sources such as YouTube have not been carefully screened like most texts for gender, racial, ethnic, economic, religious, or age stereotypes and biases, and they can be sources of stereotyped messages (Henry, 2011). DVDs, computer programs, and testing materials often feature boys more than girls and include other biases. One look at the body builds of males and females in video combat games shows what unreal and unhealthy body images they promote.

Another "text" that students read long before they arrive in your classroom is television. A content analysis of television commercials found that white male characters were more prominent than any other group. Even when only the actor's voice could be heard, men were 10 times more likely to narrate commercials. And the same pattern of men as the "voice of authority" on television occurred in the United Kingdom, Europe, Australia, and Asia. Women were more likely than men to be shown as dependent on men and often were depicted at home (Brannon, 2002). So, before and after going to school, students are likely to encounter texts that over-represent males.

## Gender Bias in Teaching

There has been quite a bit of research on teachers' treatment of male and female students. You should know, however, that most of these studies have focused on white students, so the results reported in this section hold mostly for white male and female students.

Many studies document what seem like biases favouring boys. One of the best-documented findings of the past 25 years is that teachers have more overall interactions and more negative interactions, but not more positive interactions, with boys than with girls (Jones & Dindia, 2004). This is true from preschool to college or university. Teachers ask more questions of males, give males more feedback (praise, criticism, correction), and give more specific and valuable comments to boys. The effect of these differences is that from preschool through college/university, girls, on the average, receive 1800 fewer hours of attention and instruction than boys (Sadker, Sadker, & Klein, 1991). Of course, these differences are not evenly distributed. Some boys, generally high-achieving white students, receive more than their share, whereas high-achieving girls receive the least teacher attention.

Not all biases in school favour boys. In the past 10 years in North America, Western Europe, Australia, and some Asian countries there have been questions about whether schools serve boys well. This concern is fuelled by data from many countries that seem to show underachievement in boys. For example, data from a U.S. government survey show the average grade 11 boy writes at the level of an average grade 8 girl (Younger & Warrington, 2006). More dramatic accusations include that schools are trying to destroy "boys' culture" and force "feminine, frilly content" on boys.

> Discrimination against girls has ended, the argument runs. Indeed, thanks to feminism, girls have special treatment and special programs. Now, what about the boys? It is boys who are slower to learn to read, more likely to drop out of school, more likely to be disciplined, more likely to be in programs for children with special needs. In school it is girls who are doing better, boys who are in trouble—and special programs for boys that are needed. (Connell, 1996, p. 207)

One explanation for why boys struggle in school is that the expectations of schooling do not fit the way boys learn (Gurian & Henley, 2001). Another suggestion is that boys sabotage their own learning by resisting school expectations and rules to "display their

**Gender biases** Different views of males and females, often favouring one gender over the other.

masculinity and get respect" (Kleinfield, 2005, p. B6). Critics of the schools suggest that boys need changes such as smaller classes, more discussions, better discipline, mentoring programs, and men in their schools—by far the majority of elementary school teachers are female (Svoboda, 2001).

A current suggestion for making schools more effective for both boys and girls is to establish single-sex classrooms. A story in the *New York Times Magazine* (Weil, 2008) indicates research from around the world shows that teaching boys and girls in separate classes can have positive effects on student learning, motivation, and engagement, but only if certain demanding conditions are met. Teachers must realize that there are no boy- or girl-specific teaching strategies—good teaching is good teaching. Regrouping students by sex does not make teaching easier; in fact, it can make class management more difficult. To succeed, the teachers and students must understand that the goal of the single-sex classrooms is better learning for everyone in a classroom atmosphere that supports more open discussions with less concern about making impressions with peers (Younger & Warrington, 2006). The *Guidelines* box provides additional ideas about how to avoid gender bias in your classroom.

We have dealt with a wide range of differences in this chapter. How can teachers provide an appropriate education for all of their students? One answer is multicultural education with culturally compatible classrooms.

## GUIDELINES

### Avoiding Gender Bias in Teaching

**Check to see if textbooks and other materials you are using present an honest view of the options open to both males and females.**
*Examples*

1. Identify whether both males and females are portrayed in traditional and nontraditional roles at work, at leisure, and at home.
2. Discuss your analyses with students, and ask them to help you find sex-role biases in other materials—magazine advertising, TV programs, news reporting, for example.

**Watch for any unintended biases in your own classroom practices.**
*Examples*

1. Monitor whether you group students by sex for certain activities. Is the grouping appropriate?
2. Monitor whether you call on one sex or the other for certain answers—boys for math and girls for poetry, for example.
3. Monitor your metaphors. Don't ask students to "tackle the problem."

**Look for ways in which your school may be limiting the options open to male or female students.**
*Examples*

1. Find out what advice guidance counsellors give to students in course and career decisions.
2. Look into whether there is a good sports program for both girls and boys.
3. See if girls are encouraged to take advanced placement courses in science and mathematics and if boys are encouraged in English and foreign language classes.

**Use gender-free language as much as possible.**
*Examples*

1. Make sure you speak of "law-enforcement officer" and "mail carrier" instead of "policeman" and "mailman."
2. Be sure you name a committee "head" instead of a "chairman."

**Provide role models.**
*Examples*

1. Assign articles in professional journals written by female research scientists or mathematicians.
2. Have recent female graduates who are majoring in science, math, engineering, or other technical fields come to class to talk about college.
3. Create electronic mentoring programs for both male and female students to connect them with adults working in areas of interest to the students.

**Make sure all students have a chance to do complex, technical work.**
*Examples*

1. Experiment with same-sex lab groups so girls do not always end up as the secretaries, boys as the technicians.
2. Rotate jobs in groups or randomly assign responsibilities.

---

*What if you witness gender bias as a student teacher? See this site for ideas: www.ehow.com/info_8637186_ways-stop-gender-bias-classroom.html.*

# MULTICULTURAL EDUCATION: CREATING CULTURALLY COMPATIBLE CLASSROOMS

**Multicultural education** can be defined as follows:

> [a] process of comprehensive school reform and basic education for all students. It challenges and rejects racism and other forms of discrimination in schools and society and accepts and affirms the pluralism (ethnic, racial, linguistic, religious, economic, and gender, among others) that students, their communities, and their teachers reflect. (Nieto & Bode, 2008, p. 44)

James Banks (2006) suggests that multicultural education has five dimensions, as shown in Figure 6.4. Many people are familiar only with the dimension of *content integration,* using examples and content from a variety of cultures when teaching a subject. Because they believe that multicultural education is simply a change in curriculum, some teachers assume that it is irrelevant for subjects such as science and mathematics. But if you consider the other four dimensions—helping students understand how knowledge is influenced by beliefs, reducing prejudice, creating social structures in schools that support learning and development for all students, and using teaching methods that reach all students—then you will see that this view of multicultural education is relevant to all subjects and all students.

An examination of the alternative approaches to multicultural education is beyond the scope of an educational psychology text, but be aware that there is no general agreement about the "best" approach. Many educators have suggested that culturally relevant pedagogy should be an element in multicultural education reform.

## Culturally Relevant Pedagogy

Several researchers have focused on teachers who are especially successful with students from visible minority groups and students in poverty (Delpit, 1995; Ladson-Billings, 1994, 1995; Moll, Amanti, Neff, & Gonzalez, 1992; Siddle Walker, 2001). The work of Gloria

**Multicultural education**
Education that promotes equity in the schooling of all students.

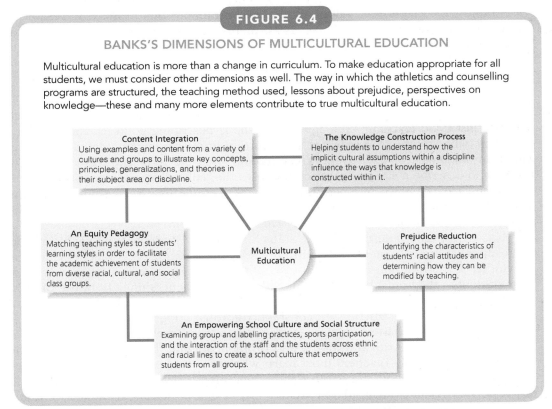

**FIGURE 6.4**

**BANKS'S DIMENSIONS OF MULTICULTURAL EDUCATION**

Multicultural education is more than a change in curriculum. To make education appropriate for all students, we must consider other dimensions as well. The way in which the athletics and counselling programs are structured, the teaching method used, lessons about prejudice, perspectives on knowledge—these and many more elements contribute to true multicultural education.

**Content Integration**
Using examples and content from a variety of cultures and groups to illustrate key concepts, principles, generalizations, and theories in their subject area or discipline.

**The Knowledge Construction Process**
Helping students to understand how the implicit cultural assumptions within a discipline influence the ways that knowledge is constructed within it.

**An Equity Pedagogy**
Matching teaching styles to students' learning styles in order to facilitate the academic achievement of students from diverse racial, cultural, and social class groups.

**Multicultural Education**

**Prejudice Reduction**
Identifying the characteristics of students' racial attitudes and determining how they can be modified by teaching.

**An Empowering School Culture and Social Structure**
Examining group and labelling practices, sports participation, and the interaction of the staff and the students across ethnic and racial lines to create a school culture that empowers students from all groups.

*Source: Reprinted with the permission of James A. Banks from James A. Banks, An Introduction to Multicultural Education (4th edition). Boston: Allyn and Bacon, page 32.*

Ladson-Billings (1990, 1992, 1995) is a good example. For three years, she studied excellent teachers in a California school district that served an African American community. In order to select the teachers, she asked parents and principals for nominations. Parents nominated teachers who respected them, created enthusiasm for learning in their children, and understood their children's need to operate successfully in two different worlds—the home community and the white world beyond. Principals nominated teachers who had few discipline referrals, high attendance rates, and high standardized test scores. Ladson-Billings was able to examine in depth eight of the nine teachers who were nominated by *both parents and principals.*

Based on her research, Ladson-Billings developed a conception of teaching excellence that encompasses but goes beyond considerations of sociolinguistics and social organizations. She uses the term **culturally relevant pedagogy** to describe teaching that rests on three propositions.

1. *Students must experience academic success.* "Despite the current social inequities and hostile classroom environments, students must develop their academic skills. The ways those skills are developed may vary, but all students need literacy, numeracy, technological, social, and political skills in order to be active participants in a democracy" (Ladson-Billings, 1995, p. 160).

2. *Students must develop/maintain their cultural competence.* As they become more academically skilled, students must still retain their cultural competence. "Culturally relevant teachers utilize students' culture as a vehicle for learning" (Ladson-Billings, 1995, p. 161). For example, one teacher used rap music to teach about literal and figurative meaning, rhyme, alliteration, and onomatopoeia in poetry. In some Canadian contexts, teachers might bring in a community expert to explain the history of a local First Nations band. Follow-up lessons could include student-designed projects about the art, food, language, and political structures of the band.

3. *Students must develop a critical consciousness to challenge the status quo.* In addition to developing academic skills while retaining cultural competence, excellent teachers help students "develop a broader sociopolitical consciousness that allows them to critique the social norms, values, mores, and institutions that produce and maintain social inequities" (Ladson-Billings, 1995, p. 162). For example, in one school, students were upset that their textbooks were out of date. They mobilized to investigate the funding formulas that allowed middle-class students to have newer books, wrote letters to the newspaper editor to challenge these inequities, and updated their texts with current information from other sources.

Ladson-Billings (1995) noted that many people have said that her three principles "are just good teaching." She agrees that she is describing good teaching, but she questions "why so little of it seems to be occurring in classrooms populated by African American students" (p. 159). Geneva Gay (2000) uses the term *culturally responsive teaching* to describe a similar approach that uses the "cultural knowledge, prior experiences, frames of reference, and performance styles of ethnically diverse students to make learning encounters more relevant to and effective for them. It *teaches to and through* the strengths of these students. It is culturally *validating and affirming*" (p. 29).

Lisa Delpit (2003) describes three steps for teaching students from visible minority groups that are consistent with culturally relevant pedagogy: (1) Teachers must be convinced of the inherent intellectual capability, humanity, and spiritual character of their students—they must believe in the children. (2) Teachers must fight the foolishness that high test scores or scripted lessons are evidence of good learning and good teaching. Successful instruction is "constant, rigorous, integrated across disciplines, connected to students' lived cultures, connected to their intellectual legacies, engaging, and designed for critical thinking and problem solving that is useful beyond the classroom" (p. 18). (3) Teachers must learn who their students are and the legacies they bring. Then, students can explore their own intellectual legacies and understand the important reasons for academic, social, physical, and moral excellence—not just to "get a job" but also "for our community, for your ancestors, for your descendents" (p. 19).

**Culturally relevant pedagogy** Excellent teaching for students from visible minorities that includes academic success and developing/maintaining cultural competence and critical consciousness to challenge the status quo.

TABLE 6.2 • **Research-Based Characteristics of Schools and Teachers That Successfully Serve Diverse Groups of Students**

| CHARACTERISTICS OF SCHOOLS | CHARACTERISTICS OF EFFECTIVE TEACHING | OTHER CHARACTERISTICS |
|---|---|---|
| Strong administrative leadership | Dedicated teachers who are accountable to produce results | Much total academic time: A very long functional school day/week, including before-school-hours to after-school-hours interactions and tutoring, good use of almost every minute of every class hour, and summer school for students who need it |
| Frequent evaluation of student progress | Much teacher scaffolding, encouraging student self-regulation | Students who help one another with academics |
| Emphasis on academics | Curriculum and instruction emphasizing understanding | Strong family–school connections |
| Safe and orderly environment | Mentoring, especially with regard to college admissions | Donors and visibly supportive, successful alumni |
| High expectations for student achievement including selective recruitment/retention of students, with the school weeding out students who are not using the opportunity well in favour of students who will (i.e., weeding out misbehaving students, students not meeting academic standards) | Intentional, massive, and frequent attempts to motivate students, including use of the following mechanisms:<br><br>• Positive expectations<br>• Visible care by teachers and administrators<br>• Praise of specific accomplishments<br>• Generally positive atmosphere, encouragement of effort attributions<br>• Cooperative learning experiences<br>• Tangible rewards for achievements | Motivational mechanisms not often encountered in schools:<br><br>• Extreme community celebrations of academic achievements<br>• Encouragement of a possible self as college graduate and successful professional<br>• Discouragement of negative possible selves<br>• Development of informed pride in cultural heritage and life |
| Excellent classroom management in most classrooms, resulting in/including a high proportion of academic time on task | Teachers who provide strong instructional supports for academic achievement (e.g., study guides, test expectations made apparent, informative feedback on homework and before exams) | Many extracurricular and curricular-enrichment activities—almost all academically oriented or intended to increase commitment to academic pursuits<br>An attractive school building loaded with resources to support academic pursuits |

*Source: Adapted from Pressley, M., Rahael, L., Gallagher, J. D., & DiBella, J. (2004). Providence St. Mel School: How a school that works for African American students works. Journal of Educational Psychology, 96(2), 234–235.*

Michael Pressley and his colleagues (2004) did a case study of a very successful K–12 school that served an ethnically diverse community. They associated the characteristics shown in Table 6.2 with the school's success.

In the past, discussions of teaching low-income students from racial, ethnic, or language minority groups have focused on remediating problems or overcoming perceived deficits. Today, teaching to the strengths and recognizing the resilience of these students are emphasized.

## Fostering Resilience

In any given week, the 12%–15% of school-age children who have urgent needs for social and emotional support are not getting help. Community and mental health services often don't reach the students who are at the highest risk. But many children at risk for academic failure not only survive—they thrive. They are resilient students. What can we learn from these students? What can teachers and schools do to encourage **resilience**?

Resilience The ability to adapt successfully in spite of difficult circumstances and threats to development.

**PROMOTING RESILIENCE** Stresses can build up for even the most resilient students. How can you create a classroom community that supports resilience? One important factor is having connected relationships.

Bill Aron/PhotoEdit

**RESILIENT STUDENTS.**   Students who are able to thrive in spite of serious challenges are actively engaged in school. They have good interpersonal skills, confidence in their own ability to learn, positive attitudes toward school, pride in their ethnicity, and high expectations (Borman & Overman, 2004; Lee, 2005). Also, students who have high intelligence or valued talents are more protected from risks. Being easy-going and optimistic is associated with resilience as well. Factors outside the student—interpersonal relationships and social support—matter, too. It helps to have a warm relationship with a parent who has high expectations and supports learning by organizing space and time at home for study. But even without such a parent, a strong bond with someone competent—a grandparent, aunt, uncle, teacher, mentor, or other caring adult—can serve the same supportive function. Involvement in school, community, or religious activities can provide more connections to concerned adults and also teach lessons in social skills and leadership (Berk, 2005).

**RESILIENT CLASSROOMS.**   You can't choose personalities or parents for your students. Even if you could, stresses can build up for even the most resilient students. Beth Doll and her colleagues (2005) suggest that we have to change classrooms instead of kids because "alternative strategies will be more enduring and most successful when they are integrated into naturally occurring systems of support [like schools] that surround children" (p. 3). So how can you create a classroom that supports resilience?

In their book on resilient classrooms, Doll and her colleagues (2005) draw on research in education and psychology on best practices for children in poverty and children with disabilities to describe the characteristics of resilient classrooms. There are two strands of elements that bind students to their classroom community: self-agency and connected relationships.

**SELF-AGENCY STRAND.**   The self-agency strand emphasizes students' capacity to set and pursue goals and includes academic self-efficacy, self-control, and self-determination.

- *Academic self-efficacy* is a belief in your own ability to learn, and is one of the most consistent predictors of academic achievement. As you will see in Chapter 11, self-efficacy emerges when students tackle challenging, meaningful tasks with the support needed to be successful and observe other students doing the same thing. Accurate and encouraging feedback from teachers also helps.
- *Behavioural self-control*, a form of self-regulation, is essential for a safe and orderly learning environment. Chapters 7, 11, and 13 will give you ideas for helping students develop self-regulation of knowledge and skills.
- *Academic self-determination*, which also involves self-regulation, making choices, setting goals, and following through, is the third element in the self-agency strand. As you will see in Chapter 12, students who are self-determined are more motivated and committed to learning.

**RELATIONSHIP STRAND.**   The relationship strand emphasizes caring and connected relationships in the classroom and the school with teachers, peers, and families.

- *Caring teacher–student relationships* are consistently associated with better school performance, especially for students who face serious challenges. We saw the power of caring teachers in Chapters 1 and 3 and will continue to see the value of these relationships throughout this text.
- *Effective peer relations*, as we saw in Chapter 3, also are critical in connecting students to school.

- *Effective home–school relationships* are the final element in building a caring, connected network for students. In the School Development Program, James Comer has found that when parents stay involved, their children's grades and test scores improve (Comer, Haynes, & Joyner, 1996). The *Family and Community Partnerships Guidelines* box gives some ideas for how to connect with families and communities.

## Diversity in Learning

Over two decades ago, Roland Tharp (1989) outlined several dimensions of classrooms that reflect the diversity of the students and can be tailored to better fit their backgrounds.

SOCIAL ORGANIZATION.  "A central task of educational design is to make the organization of teaching, learning, and performance compatible with the social structures in which students are most productive, engaged, and likely to learn" (Tharp, 1989, p. 350). Social structure or social organization in this context means the ways people interact to accomplish a particular goal. For example, the social organization of Hawaiian society

---

## GUIDELINES — FAMILY AND COMMUNITY PARTNERSHIPS

### Building Learning Communities

Joyce Epstein (1995) describes six types of family–school–community partnerships. The following guidelines are based on her six categories.

**Parenting partnerships: Help all families establish home environments to support children as students.**
*Examples*
1. Offer workshops, videos, courses, family literacy fairs, and other informational programs to help parents cope with parenting situations that they identify as important.
2. Establish family support programs to assist with nutrition, health, and social services.
3. Find ways to help families share information with the school about the child's cultural background, talents, and needs. Learn from the families.

**Communication: Design effective forms for school-to-home and home-to-school communication.**
*Examples*
1. Make sure that communications fit the needs of families. Provide translations, visual support—whatever is needed to make communication effective.
2. Visit families in their territory after gaining their permission. Don't expect family members to come to school until a trusting relationship is established.
3. Balance messages about problems with communications of accomplishments and positive information.

**Volunteering: Recruit and organize parent help and support.**
*Examples*
1. Do an annual postcard survey to identify family talents, interests, times available, and suggestions for improvements.
2. Establish a structure (telephone tree, group email, classroom website or Facebook page, etc.) to keep all families informed. Make sure that families without telephones are included.

3. If possible, set aside a room for volunteer meetings and projects.

**Learning at home: Provide information and ideas for families about how to help children with school work and learning activities.**
*Examples*
1. Provide assignment schedules, homework policies, and tips on how to help with school work without doing the work.
2. Get family input into curriculum planning—have idea and activity exchanges.
3. Send home learning packets and enjoyable learning activities, especially over holidays and summers.

**Decision-making partnerships: Include families in school decisions, developing family and community leaders and representatives.**
*Examples*
1. Create family advisory committees for the school with parent representatives.
2. Make sure that all families are in a network with their representative.

**Community partnerships: Identify and integrate resources and services from the community to strengthen school programs, family practices, and student learning and development.**
*Examples*
1. Have students and parents research existing resources; build a database based on this research.
2. Identify service projects for students; explore service learning.
3. Identify community members who are school alumni and get them involved in school programs.

*Source: From Epstein, J. L. (1995). School/family/community partnerships: Caring for the children we share. Phi Delta Kappan, 76, 704–705. Reprinted by permission of Phi Delta Kappan and the author.*

depends heavily on collaboration and cooperation. Children play together in groups of friends and siblings, with older children often caring for the younger ones. When cooperative work groups of four or five boys and girls were established in Hawaiian classrooms, student learning and participation improved (Okagaki, 2001, 2006). But when Okagaki tried the same structure in a Navajo classroom, students would not work together. These students are socialized to be more solitary and not to play with the opposite sex. However, by setting up same-sex working groups of only two or three Navajo students, teachers encouraged them to help each other. If you have students from several cultures, you may need to provide choices and variety in grouping structures.

CULTURAL VALUES AND LEARNING PREFERENCES.    Results of research conducted by Jim Anderson and Lee Gunderson (1997) at the University of British Columbia showed cultural differences in beliefs about learning to read and write. They interviewed more than 60 parents and 100 students from Chinese, Iranian, and Indo-Canadian communities and compared their beliefs and preferences concerning the teaching and learning of literate behaviour. Many North American teachers support an emergent model of reading, believing that learning to read and write are imprecise processes, that approximation and invention are part of the learning process, and that adult standards for correctness and conventions will not be met in the early stages of reading and writing. This was not the view of many of the parents Anderson and Gunderson interviewed. These parents believed that accuracy and precision were important from the beginning. They criticized practices such as invented spelling and recognizing children's early attempts at reading—"It's not real reading," they said. Parents from these communities also believed that teachers should engage in more direct instruction and that students should talk less, receive more homework, and be asked to memorize more facts.

These cultural values also were evident in students' behaviour. Consider Alice's preferences for reading and writing activities:

> Alice was an extraordinary third grader. She was an immigrant who in two years had become fluent in English; her intelligence had qualified her as an intellectually gifted student. Alice was most content at school when she was filling out pages in a workbook. She and her family believed that answering questions and filling in bubbles in multiple-choice workbook items were essential learning activities that represented the basic goal of literacy learning: to master a set of discrete skills. (Anderson & Gunderson, 1997, p. 514)

Anderson and Gunderson urged teachers to recognize that there are many ways to learn reading and writing and to encourage parents to support their children's literacy learning in ways that are familiar to them. At the same time, teachers can help parents understand other approaches to the teaching through regular communication and involvement in the classroom. Also, teachers can engage students in a wide range of activities in the classroom, including some that build on what students experience at home.

For Aboriginal Canadians, oral communication has historically been the primary method of teaching among Aboriginal groups, resulting in less attention to written forms of communication (Crealock & Bachor, 1995). In fact, some Aboriginal languages are only now being coded in a manner that will standardize their written forms and make them available to Aboriginal and non-Aboriginal Canadians. Traditionally, Aboriginals have not written books for children, and storybook reading has not been valued as a preschool activity to the extent it is in most European Canadian families. This may put First Nations students at a disadvantage when they enter school. Furthermore, Aboriginal cultures train and reward visual-motor and spatial skills, while the dominant culture trains and rewards verbal skills (Crealock & Bachor, 1995). As a result, many Aboriginal students have above-average spatial skills and high mechanical aptitude but never have these strengths reinforced in school. Ensuring that these students have opportunities to engage in activities such as map-making, or making patterns or clothes, is one way to recognize these strengths.

Finally, some educators suggest that Asian children tend to value teacher approval and to work well in structured, quiet learning environments where there are clear goals and social support (Manning & Baruth, 1996). Anderson and Gunderson's research (above) seems to corroborate this view. However, other research suggests that there are clear and deep differences in Asian and Western styles of learning. Students from Asian cultures tend be more interdependent and to value learning with others, while Western cultures emphasize independence and individual learning (Chang, Mak, Li, Wu, Chen, & Lu, 2011). But, as you saw earlier, there are dangers in stereotyping any group, especially in terms of cultural learning styles.

CAUTIONS (AGAIN) ABOUT LEARNING STYLES RESEARCH.   In considering this research on learning styles, you should keep two points in mind. First, the validity of some of the learning styles research has been strongly questioned, as we saw in Chapter 3. Second, there is a heated debate today about whether identifying ethnic group differences in learning styles and preferences is a dangerous, racist, sexist exercise. We can move too quickly to stereotypes. We have included the information about differences in learning styles or preferences because we believe that, used sensibly, this information can help you better understand your students. But it is dangerous and incorrect to assume that every individual in a group shares the same learning style (Sheets, 2005). The best advice for teachers is to be sensitive to individual differences in all your students and to make available alternative paths to learning. Never prejudge how a student will learn best based on assumptions about the student's ethnicity or race. Get to know the individual.

SOCIOLINGUISTICS.   **Sociolinguistics** is the study of "the courtesies and conventions of conversation across cultures" (Tharp, 1989, p. 351). Knowledge of sociolinguistics will help you understand why communication sometimes breaks down in classrooms. The classroom is a special setting for communicating; it has its own set of rules for when, how, to whom, about what subject, and in what manner to use language. Sometimes, the sociolinguistic skills of students do not fit the expectations of teachers or counsellors, as we saw earlier.

In order to be successful, students must know the communication rules; that is, they must understand the **pragmatics** of the classroom—when, where, and how to communicate. This is no easy task. As class activities change, rules change. Sometimes you have to raise your hand (during the teacher's presentation), but sometimes you don't (during story time on the rug). Sometimes it is good to ask a question (during discussion), but other times it isn't so good (when the teacher is reprimanding you). These differing activity rules are called **participation structures**, and they define appropriate participation for each class activity. Most classrooms have many different participation structures. To be competent communicators in the classroom, students sometimes have to read very subtle, nonverbal cues telling them which participation structures are currently in effect. For example, when the teacher moves to the white board, students should look up and be ready for instructions.

SOURCES OF MISUNDERSTANDINGS.   Some children are simply better than others at reading the classroom situation because the participation structures of the school match the structures they have learned at home. The communication rules for most school situations are similar to those in middle-class homes, so children from these homes often appear to be more competent communicators. They know the unwritten rules. Students who are not white and middle class may not know the rules. For example, researchers found that Pueblo Indian students participated twice as much in classes where teachers waited longer to react. Waiting longer also helps girls to participate more freely in math and science classes (Grossman & Grossman, 1994). Students from different cultural backgrounds may have learned participation structures that conflict with the behaviours expected in school. For example, one study found that the home conversation style of Hawaiian children is to chime in with contributions to a story. In school, however, this overlapping style is viewed as "interrupting." When the teachers in one school learned about these differences and made their reading groups more like their students' home conversation groups, the young Hawaiian children in their classes improved in reading (Au, 1980; Tharp, 1989).

It seems that even students who speak the same language as their teachers may still have trouble communicating, and thus learning school subjects. What can teachers do? Especially in the early grades, you should make communication rules for activities clear and explicit. Do not assume students know what to do. Use cues to signal students when changes occur. Explain and demonstrate appropriate behaviour. We have seen teachers show young children how to use their "inside voice," "six-inch voice," or "whisper voice."

**Sociolinguistics** The study of the formal and informal rules for how, when, about what, to whom, and how long to speak in conversations within cultural groups.

**Pragmatics** The rules for when and how to use language to be an effective communicator in a particular culture.

**Participation structures** The formal and informal rules for how to take part in a given activity.

One teacher said and then demonstrated, "If you have to interrupt me while I'm working with other children, stand quietly beside me until I can help you." Be consistent in responding to students. If students are supposed to raise their hands, don't call on those who break the rules. In these ways you teach students how to communicate and learn in school.

## Lessons for Teachers: Teaching Every Student

The goal of this chapter is to give you a sense of the diversity in today's and tomorrow's schools and to help you meet the challenges of teaching in a multicultural classroom. How will you understand and build on all the cultures of your students? How will you deal with many different languages? Here are three general teaching principles to guide you in finding answers to these questions.

KNOW YOUR STUDENTS.   We must learn who our students are and the legacies they bring (Delpit, 2003). Nothing you read in a chapter on cultural differences will teach you enough to understand the lives of all your students. If you can take other courses or read about other cultures, we encourage you to do it. But reading and studying are not enough. You should get to know your students' families and communities. Elba Reyes, a successful bilingual teacher for children with special needs, describes her approach as follows:

> Usually I find that if you really want to know a parent, you get to know them on their own turf. This is key to developing trust and understanding the parents' perspective. First, get to know the community. Learn where the local grocery store is and what the children do after school. Then schedule a home visit at a time that is convenient for the parents. The home environment is not usually as ladened with failure. I sometimes observed the child being successful in the home, for example, riding a bicycle or helping with dinner. (Bos & Reyes, 1996, p. 349)

Try to spend time with students and parents on projects outside school. Ask parents to help in class or to speak to your students about their jobs, hobbies, history, and heritage. In the elementary grades, don't wait until a student is in trouble to have the first meeting with a family member. Watch and listen to the ways your students interact in large and small groups. Have students write to you, and write back to them. Eat lunch with one or two students. Spend some non-teaching time with them.

**Watch**
Respect Your Students

RESPECT YOUR STUDENTS.   From knowledge ought to come respect for your students' learning strengths—for the struggles they face and the obstacles they overcome. We must believe in our students (Delpit, 2003). For a child, genuine acceptance is a necessary condition for developing self-esteem. Sometimes the self-image and occupational aspirations of minority-group children actually decline in their early years in public school, probably because of the emphasis on majority culture values, accomplishments, and history. By presenting the accomplishments of particular members of an ethnic group or by bringing that group's culture into the classroom (in the form of literature, art, music, or any cultural knowledge), teachers can help students maintain a sense of pride in their cultural group. This integration of culture must be more than the "tokenism" of sampling ethnic foods or wearing costumes. Students should learn about the socially and intellectually important contributions of the various groups. There are many excellent references that provide background information, history, and teaching strategies for different groups of students (e.g., Banks, 2002; Gay, 2000; Irvine & Armento, 2001; Ladson-Billings, 1995).

TEACH YOUR STUDENTS.   The most important thing you can do for your students is to teach them to read, write, speak, compute, think, and create—through constant, rigorous, culturally connected instruction (Delpit, 2003). Too often, goals for low-SES or minority-group students have focused exclusively on basic skills. Students are taught words and sounds, but the meaning of the story is supposed to come later. Knapp, Turnbull, and Shields (1990) make these suggestions:

- Focus on meaning and understanding from beginning to end—for example, by orienting instruction toward comprehending reading passages, communicating important ideas in written text, or understanding the concepts underlying number facts.

- Balance routine skill learning with novel and complex tasks from the earliest stages of learning.
- Provide context for skill learning that establishes clear reasons for needing to learn the skills.
- Influence attitudes and beliefs about the academic content areas as well as skills and knowledge.
- Eliminate unnecessary redundancy in the curriculum (e.g., repeating instruction in the same mathematics skills year after year). (p. 5)

And finally, teach students directly about how to be students. In the early grades, this could mean directly teaching the courtesies and conventions of the classroom: how to get a turn to speak, how and when to interrupt the teacher, how to whisper, how to get help in a small group, how to give an explanation that is helpful. In the later grades, it may mean teaching the study skills that fit your subject. You can ask students to learn "how we do it in school" without violating the second principle above—respect your students. Ways of asking questions around the kitchen table at home may be different from ways of asking questions in school, but students can learn both ways, without deciding that either way is superior. Also you can expand ways of doing it in school to include more possibilities. The *Guidelines* box gives more ideas.

## GUIDELINES

### Culturally Relevant Teaching

**Experiment with different grouping arrangements to encourage social harmony and cooperation.**
*Examples*
1. Try "study buddies" and pairing students together.
2. Organize heterogeneous groups of four or five.
3. Establish larger teams for older students.

**Provide a range of ways to learn material to accommodate students' cultural and learning preferences.**
*Examples*
1. Give students verbal materials at different reading levels.
2. Offer visual materials—charts, diagrams, models.
3. Provide tapes for listening and viewing.
4. Set up activities and projects.

**Teach classroom procedures directly, even ways of doing things that you think everyone already knows.**
*Examples*
1. Tell students how to get the teacher's attention.
2. Explain when and how to interrupt the teacher if students need help.
3. Show which materials students can take and which require permission.
4. Demonstrate acceptable ways to disagree with or challenge another student.

**Learn the meaning of different behaviour for your students.**
*Examples*
1. Ask students how they feel when you correct or praise them. What gives them this message?

2. Talk to family and community members and other teachers to discover the meaning of expressions, gestures, or other responses that are unfamiliar to you.

**Emphasize meaning in teaching.**
*Examples*
1. Make sure that students understand what they read.
2. Try storytelling and other modes that don't require written materials.
3. Use examples that relate abstract concepts to everyday experiences; for instance, relate negative numbers to being overdrawn in your chequebook.

**Get to know the customs, traditions, and values of your students.**
*Examples*
1. Use holidays as a chance to discuss the origins and meaning of traditions.
2. Analyze different traditions for common themes.
3. Attend community fairs and festivals.

**Help students detect racist and sexist messages.**
*Examples*
1. Analyze curriculum materials for biases.
2. Make students "bias detectives," reporting comments from the media.
3. Discuss the ways in which students communicate biased messages about each other and what should be done when this happens.
4. Discuss expressions of prejudice such as anti-Semitism.

# ▼ SUMMARY

### Today's Diverse Classrooms (pp. 190–195)

**What is culture?** There are many conceptions of culture, but most include the knowledge, skills, rules, traditions, beliefs, and values that guide behaviour in a particular group of people: Culture is a program for living. Everyone is a member of many cultural groups, defined in terms of geographic region, nationality, ethnicity, race, gender, social class, and religion. Membership in a particular group does not determine behaviour or values, but makes certain values and kinds of behaviour more likely. Wide variations exist within each group. You met four individuals, Ternice, Benjamin, Davy, and Jessie, who embody that diversity.

### Economic and Social Class Differences (pp. 195–200)

**What is SES, and how does it differ from social class?** Social class reflects a group's prestige and power in a society. Most people are aware of the social class that they share with similar peers. Socioeconomic status (SES) is a term used by sociologists for variations in wealth, power, control over resources, and prestige. Socioeconomic status is determined by several factors—not just income—and often overpowers other cultural differences. No single variable is an effective measure of SES.

**What is the relationship between SES and school achievement?** Socioeconomic status and academic achievement are moderately correlated. High-SES students of all ethnic groups show higher average levels of achievement on test scores and stay in school longer than low-SES students. The longer the child is in poverty, the stronger the impact is on achievement. Why is there a correlation between SES and school achievement? Low-SES students may suffer from inadequate health care, teachers' lowered expectations of them, low self-esteem, learned helplessness, participation in resistance cultures, school tracking, understimulating home environments, and summer setbacks. This last striking finding is that low-SES children lose academic ground outside school over the summer, while higher-SES children continue to advance.

### Ethnicity and Race Differences in Teaching and Learning (pp. 200–207)

**Distinguish between ethnicity and race.** Ethnicity (culturally transmitted behaviour) and race (biologically transmitted physical traits) are socially significant categories people use to describe themselves and others. Minority groups (either numerically or historically unempowered) are rapidly increasing in population.

**How can differences in ethnicity of teachers and students affect school performance?** Conflicts can arise from differences between teachers and students in culture-based beliefs, values, and expectations. Cultural conflicts are usually about below-the-surface differences, because when subtle cultural differences meet, misunderstandings are common. Students in some cultures learn attitudes and behaviours that are more consistent with school expectations. Differences among ethnic groups in cognitive and academic abilities are largely the legacy of racial segregation and continuing prejudice and discrimination.

Uttam Gurjar/Shutterstock

**Distinguish among prejudice, discrimination, and stereotype threat.** Prejudice is a rigid and irrational generalization—a prejudgment or attitude—about an entire category of people. Prejudice may target people in particular racial, ethnic, religious, political, geographic, or language groups, or it may be directed toward the gender or sexual orientation of the individual. Discrimination is unequal treatment of or actions toward particular categories of people. Stereotype threat is the extra emotional and cognitive burden that your performance in an academic situation might confirm a stereotype that others hold about you. It is not necessary that the individual even believe the stereotype. All that matters is that the person is *aware* of the stereotype and *cares about performing* well enough to disprove its unflattering implications. In the short run, the fear that you might confirm a negative stereotype can induce test anxiety and undermine performance. Over time, experiencing stereotype threat may lead to disidentification with schooling and academic achievement.

### Gender in Teaching and Learning (pp. 207–212)

**What are the stages of achieving a sexual orientation for gay and lesbian youth?** Stages of achieving a sexual orientation for gay and lesbian students can follow a pattern from discomfort to confusion to acceptance. Some researchers contend that sexual identity is not always permanent and can change over the years.

**What are gender roles and how do they develop?** Gender role is the image each individual has of himself or herself as masculine or feminine in characteristics—a part of self-concept. Biology (hormones) plays a role, as does the differential behaviour of parents and teachers toward male and female children. Through their interactions with family, peers, teachers, and the environment in general, children begin to form gender schemas, or organized networks of knowledge about what it means to be male or female.

**How are gender biases communicated?** In children's books, there are more males in the titles and the illustrations, and the characters (especially the boys) continue to behave in stereotypic ways. Girl characters sometimes cross gender roles to be more active, but boy characters seldom show "feminine" expressive traits. Some overrepresentation of gender exists in television commercials, too. Teachers interact more with boys in both positive and negative ways. Lately some educators have claimed that schools are not supportive for boys, and same-sex classrooms have been suggested as an answer. The research on the value of these classrooms is mixed.

### Multicultural Education: Creating Culturally Compatible Classrooms (pp. 213–221)

**What is multicultural education?** Multicultural education is a field of study designed to increase educational equity for all students. According to the multicultural ideal, Canada should be transformed into a society that values diversity. James Banks suggests that multicultural education has five dimensions: integrating content, helping students understand how knowledge is influenced by beliefs, reducing prejudice, creating social structures in schools that support learning and development for all students, and using teaching methods that reach all students.

**What is culturally relevant pedagogy?** "Culturally relevant pedagogy is an approach to teaching that uses the cultural knowledge, prior experiences, frames of references, and learning styles of ethnically diverse students to make learning encounters more relevant and effective for them. It teaches *to and through* the strengths of these students" (Gay, 2000). Gloria Ladson-Billings describes culturally relevant teaching that rests on three propositions: Students must experience academic success, develop/maintain their cultural competence, and develop a critical consciousness to challenge the status quo.

**What are the elements of a resilient classroom?** There are two strands of elements that bind students to their classroom community. One strand emphasizes the self-agency of students—their capacity to set and pursue goals. This includes academic self-efficacy, self-control, and self-determination. The second strand emphasizes caring and connected relationships with the teacher, peers, and the home.

## ▼ WHAT WOULD YOU DO?
## TEACHERS' CASEBOOK: White Girls Club

Here is how two practising teachers responded to the teaching situation described on the first page of this chapter.

**SARA VINCENT** • Special Education
Langley High School

Discrimination and racism often occur because of ignorance. The best solution to minimize discrimination is educating individuals about diverse cultures. The teacher can invite the new student's family into the classroom to talk about their backgrounds and experiences, or she can have the entire class complete a project on family history. Once the other students in the classroom learn more about the new student's culture, they will be more likely to accept her differences and understand that she is not much different from them. In addition, the teacher can have the new student be team leader at recess or in the classroom so that she will not be picked last. This will help her gain confidence in befriending her peers. While the teacher attempts to focus on positive aspects of educating her students, she should make the administration aware of the "White Girls Club" situation. Administrators should intervene and bring attention to the situation if the troubling behaviors of the other girls continue.

**PAULA COLEMERE** • Special Education Teacher—English, History
McClintock High School

In one of my favorite lessons for the beginning of the year I give each student five mixed beans and have students choose which is the "best" one. We then discuss why they chose the bean as the best and discuss the differences in beans before connecting to people. After the discussion, we role play different scenarios that deal with diversity; this is a good lesson because it addresses self-esteem in addition to diversity. While all students can use a boost to self-esteem, it would hopefully help the new girl to feel better about the situation. This lesson can be tailored to younger or older students. Since these students are young, I would hope this would be a gentle way for the girls in the "club" to see that what they have been doing is wrong. My next step would be to conference with the girls and mediate if necessary.

# CHAPTER

## 7

Irina_QQQ/Shutterstock

# BEHAVIOURAL VIEWS OF LEARNING

## WHAT WOULD YOU DO?

## ▶ TEACHERS' CASEBOOK: Out of Control

You were hired in January to take over the classes of a teacher who moved away. This is a great district and a terrific school. If you do well, you might be in line for a full-time opening next fall. As you are introduced around the school, you get a number of sympathetic looks and many—too many—offers of help: "Let me know if I can do anything for you."

After the first hour, you begin to understand why so many teachers volunteered their help. Evidently the previous teacher had no management system—no order. Several students walk around the room while you are talking to the class, interrupt you when you are working with a group, torment each other, and open their lunches (or those of other students) for a self-determined snack. There is one very charismatic leader who causes regular disruptions, resists your authority, and destroys your efforts to develop a community of learners. Simply taking attendance and introducing the first activity lasts 10 minutes. You end the first day exhausted and discouraged, having lost both your voice and your patience. You wonder how you can possibly establish a workable management system and still teach students what they will need to know in order to complete the province-wide spring reading, writing, and mathematics proficiency tests.

### CRITICAL THINKING

- How would you approach the situation?
- Which problem behaviours would you tackle first?
- Would giving rewards or administering punishments be useful in this situation?
- Why or why not?

## OVERVIEW AND OBJECTIVES

We begin this chapter with a general definition of learning that takes into account the opposing views of different theoretical groups. We will highlight one group, the behavioural theorists, in this chapter and another major group, the cognitive theorists, in Chapters 8 and 9; then, we will look at constructivism in Chapter 10 and social cognitive views in Chapter 11. As you will see, there are many ways to look at learning, and each has something to offer educators.

Our discussion in this chapter will focus on four behavioural learning processes: contiguity, classical conditioning, operant conditioning, and observational learning, with the greatest emphasis placed on the last two processes. After examining the implications of applied behaviour analysis for teaching, we look at a recent direction in behavioural approaches to learning—self-management. Finally, we investigate Bandura's challenge to behavioural views of learning as well as other criticisms, cautions, and ethical considerations for educators.

By the time you have completed this chapter, you should be able to:

**7.1**   Define learning, and distinguish among the processes involved in learning through contiguity, classical conditioning, and operant conditioning.

**7.2**   Distinguish between positive and negative reinforcement, and presentation and removal punishment.

**7.3**   Apply behavioural approaches to modifying behaviour in and out of the classroom.

**7.4**   Describe newer approaches to applied behavioural analysis, including functional behavioural assessment and self-management.

**7.5**   Discuss contemporary challenges to behavioural theories of learning, and address concerns about their application.

# UNDERSTANDING LEARNING

When we hear the word *learning,* most of us think of studying and school. We think about subjects or skills we intend to master, such as algebra, Mandarin, chemistry, or karate. But learning is not limited to school. We learn every day of our lives. Babies learn to kick their legs to make the mobile above their cribs move, young girls learn the lyrics to all their favourite Carly Rae Jepson songs, middle-aged people like Anita, Phil, and Nancy learn to change their diet and exercise patterns, and every few years we all learn to find a new style of dress attractive when the old styles (the ones we once loved) go out of fashion. This last example shows that learning is not always intentional. We don't try to like new styles and dislike old ones; it just seems to happen that way. We don't intend to become nervous when we hear a teacher call our name or when we step onto a stage, yet many of us do. So what is this powerful phenomenon called *learning?*

In the broadest sense, **learning** occurs when experience (including practice) causes a relatively permanent change in an individual's knowledge or behaviour. The change may be deliberate or unintentional, for better or for worse, correct or incorrect, and conscious or unconscious (Mayer, 2011; Schunk, 2012). To qualify as learning, this change must be brought about by experience—by the interaction of a person with his or her environment. Changes simply caused by maturation, such as growing taller or turning grey, do not qualify as learning. Temporary changes resulting from illness, fatigue, drugs, or hunger are also excluded from a general definition of learning. A person who has gone without food for two days does not learn to be hungry, and a person who is ill does not learn to move more slowly. Of course, learning plays a part in how we respond to hunger or illness.

**Learning** Process through which experience causes permanent change in knowledge or behaviour.

Our definition specifies that the changes resulting from learning take place in the individual's knowledge or behaviour. Most psychologists would agree with this statement, but some tend to emphasize the change in knowledge, whereas others focus on the change in behaviour. Cognitive psychologists, who focus on changes in knowledge, believe learning is an internal mental activity that cannot be observed directly. As you will see in the next chapter, cognitive psychologists studying learning are interested in unobservable mental activities such as thinking, remembering, and solving problems (Schwartz, Wasserman, & Robbins, 2002).

The psychologists discussed in this chapter, on the other hand, favour **behavioural learning theories**. The behavioural view generally assumes that the outcome of learning is a change in behaviour, and it emphasizes the effects of external events on the individual. Some early behaviourists such as J. B. Watson took the radical position that because thinking, intentions, and other internal mental events could not be seen or studied rigorously and scientifically, these "mentalisms," as he called them, should not even be included in an explanation of learning.

**WHAT IS LEARNING?** Behavioural views of learning generally assume that the outcome of learning is a change in behaviour. The focus is on what can be observed.

Ryan McVay/Thinkstock/Getty Images

## Neuroscience of Behavioural Learning

You saw in Chapter 2 that we are learning more and more about the brain. Researchers conducting animal and human studies have discovered quite a bit about the areas of the brain that are involved with learning new behaviours. For example, parts of the cerebellum are involved in simple reflex learning, like learning to blink following a particular tone, and that other parts of the brain are involved in learning how to avoid painful stimulation such as shock (Schwartz, Wasserman, & Robbins, 2002). Other lines of research ask why animals and people will behave in certain ways to gain stimulation or reinforcers. Stimulation to certain parts of the brain will cause hungry rats to ignore food and keep doing whatever it takes to keep the stimulation coming. These same brain systems are associated with the pleasures people experience from many things, including food and music. It is likely that many parts of the brain and complex patterns of activity allow us to enjoy some experiences, "learn to want them, and learn how to get them" (Bernstein & Nash, 2008, p. 187).

Before we look in depth at behavioural explanations of learning, let's step into an actual classroom and note the possible results of learning.

## Learning Is Not Always What It Seems

After weeks of working with her cooperating teacher in a grade 8 social studies class, Elizabeth Chan was ready to begin her first day of solo teaching. As she rose from her desk and started toward the front of the room, she glimpsed another adult in the classroom door. It was her supervisor from the university, B. J. Ross. Elizabeth's neck and facial muscles suddenly became very tense and her hands trembled.

> "I've stopped by to observe your teaching," Dr. Ross said. "This will be my first of six visits. I tried to reach you last night to tell you."
>
> Elizabeth tried to hide her reaction, but her hands trembled as she gathered the notes for the lesson.
>
> "Let's start today with a kind of game. I will say some words, then I want you to tell me the first words you can think of. Don't bother to raise your hands. Just say the words out loud, and I will write them on the board. Don't all speak at once, though. Wait until someone else has finished to say your word. Okay, here is the first word: Métis."

**Behavioural learning theories** Explanations of learning that focus on external events as the cause of changes in observable behaviours.

"Red River." "Louis Riel." "Rebellion." The answers came very quickly, and Elizabeth was relieved to see that the students understood the game.

"All right, very good," she said. "Now try another one: Batoche."

"Duck Lake." "Fish Creek." "John A. Macdonald." "Big Mac." "Sir Ronald McDonald!" With this last answer, a ripple of laughter moved across the room.

"Ronald McDonald?" Elizabeth sighed wearily. "Get serious." Then she laughed too. Soon, all the students were laughing. "Okay, settle down," Elizabeth said. "These ideas are getting a little off base!"

"Off base? Baseball," shouted the boy who had first mentioned Ronald McDonald. He stood up and started throwing balls of paper to a friend in the back of the room, simulating the style of Trystan Magnuson.

"Red Sox." "No, the Blue Jays." "The Rogers Centre." "Hot dogs." "Popcorn." "Hamburgers." "Ronald McDonald." The responses now came too fast for Elizabeth to stop them. For some reason, the Ronald McDonald line got an even bigger laugh the second time around, and Elizabeth suddenly realized she had lost the class.

"Okay, since you know so much about the Rebellion, close your books and take out a pen," Elizabeth said, obviously angry. She passed out the worksheet that she had planned as a cooperative, open-book project. "You have 20 minutes to finish this test!"

"You didn't tell us we were having a test!" "This isn't fair!" "We haven't even covered this stuff yet!" "I didn't do anything wrong!" There were moans and disgusted looks, even from the most mellow students. "I'm reporting you to the principal; it's a violation of students' rights!"

This last comment hit hard. The class had just finished discussing human rights as preparation for this unit on the Northwest Rebellion. As she listened to the protests, Elizabeth felt terrible. How was she going to grade these "tests"? The first section of the worksheet involved facts about events leading up to the Northwest Rebellion, and the second section asked students to create a news-style program interviewing ordinary people touched by the war.

"All right, all right, it won't be a test. But you do have to complete this worksheet for a grade. I was going to let you work together, but your behaviour this morning tells me that you are not ready for group work. If you can complete the first section of the sheet working quietly and seriously, you may work together on the second section." Elizabeth knew that her students would like to work together on writing the script for the news interview program.

It appears, on the surface at least, that very little learning of any sort was taking place in Elizabeth's classroom. In fact, Elizabeth had some good ideas; but she also made some mistakes in her application of learning principles. We will return to this episode later in the chapter to analyze various aspects of what took place. To get us started, three events can be singled out, each possibly related to a different learning process.

First, Elizabeth's hands trembled when her university supervisor entered the room. Second, the students were able to associate the phrases *Red River* and *Louis Riel* with the word *Métis*. Third, one student continued to disrupt the class with inappropriate responses. The three learning processes represented are classical conditioning, contiguity, and operant conditioning. In the following pages, we will examine these three kinds of learning, starting with contiguity.

## EARLY EXPLANATIONS OF LEARNING: CONTIGUITY AND CLASSICAL CONDITIONING

**Contiguity** Association of two events because of repeated pairing.

**Stimulus** Event that activates behaviour.

**Response** Observable reaction to a stimulus.

One of the earliest explanations of learning came from Aristotle (384–322 B.C.E.). He said that we remember things together (1) when they are similar, (2) when they contrast, and (3) when they are contiguous. This last principle is the most important, because it is included in all explanations of learning by association. The principle of **contiguity** states that whenever two or more sensations occur together often enough, they will become associated. Later, when only one of these sensations (a **stimulus**) occurs, the other will be remembered too (a **response**) (Rachlin, 1991; Schwartz et al., 2002). Contiguity also plays a major role in another learning process best known as *classical conditioning*.

**STOP & THINK** Close your eyes and focus on a vivid image of the following: The smell of French fries cooking. A time you were really embarrassed in school. The taste of chocolate fudge. The sound of a dentist's drill. What did you notice as you formed these images? •

If you are like Nancy, imagining the sound of the dentist's drill tightens your neck muscles. Phil actually salivates when he imagines salty fries or smooth rich chocolate (especially because it is 7:00 p.m. and he hasn't had dinner yet). **Classical conditioning** focuses on the learning of involuntary emotional or physiological responses such as fear, increased muscle tension, salivation, or sweating. These sometimes are called **respondents** because they are automatic responses to stimuli. Through the process of classical conditioning, humans and animals can be trained to react involuntarily to a stimulus that previously had no effect—or a very different effect—on them. The stimulus comes to elicit, or bring forth, the response automatically.

Classical conditioning was discovered in the 1920s by Ivan Pavlov, a Russian physiologist who was trying to determine how long it took a dog to secrete digestive juices after it had been fed. But the intervals of time kept changing. At first, the dogs salivated as expected while they were being fed. Then the dogs began to salivate as soon as they saw the food, and finally they salivated as soon as they heard the scientists walking toward the lab. Pavlov decided to make a detour from his original experiments and examine these unexpected interferences, or "psychic reflexes" as he called them at first.

In one of his first experiments, Pavlov began by sounding a tuning fork and recording a dog's response. As expected, there was no salivation. At this point, the sound of the tuning fork was a **neutral stimulus** because it brought forth no salivation. Then Pavlov fed the dog. The response was salivation. The food was an **unconditioned stimulus (US)** because no prior training or "conditioning" was needed to establish the natural connection between food and salivation. The salivation was an **unconditioned response (UR)**, again because it was elicited automatically—no conditioning required.

Using these three elements—the food, the salivation, and the tuning fork—Pavlov demonstrated that a dog could be *conditioned* to salivate after hearing the tuning fork. He did this by contiguous pairing of the sound with food. He sounded the fork and then quickly fed the dog. After Pavlov repeated this several times, the dog began to salivate after hearing the sound, but before receiving the food. Now the sound had become a **conditioned stimulus (CS)** that could bring forth salivation by itself. The response of salivating after the tone was now a **conditioned response (CR)**.

If you think that Pavlovian conditioning is of historical interest only, consider this news story describing an advertising campaign for products aimed at "Gen Y," those people born between 1977 and 1994:

> Mountain Dew executives have their own term for this [advertising strategy]: the Pavlovian connection. By handing out samples of the brand at surfing, skateboard and snowboard tournaments, "There's a Pavlovian connection between the brand and the exhilarating experience," says Dave Burwich, a top marketing executive at Pepsi, which makes Mountain Dew. (Horovitz, April 22, 2002, p. B2)

Maybe they could hand out math homework, too! The *Guidelines* give some other ideas.

It is possible that many of our emotional reactions to various situations are learned in part through classical conditioning. Physicians have a term, "white coat syndrome," that describes people whose blood pressure (an involuntary response) goes up when it is tested in the doctor's office, usually by someone in a white coat. Another example, Elizabeth's trembling hands when she saw her university supervisor, might be traced to previous unpleasant experiences during past evaluations of her performance. Now just the thought of being observed elicits a pounding heart and sweaty palms. Classical conditioning has implications for teachers as well as marketing managers. Remember that emotions and attitudes as well as facts and ideas are learned in classrooms. This emotional learning can sometimes interfere with academic learning. Procedures based on classical conditioning also can be used to help people learn more adaptive emotional responses, as the *Guidelines* suggest.

**Classical conditioning** Association of automatic responses with new stimuli.

**Respondents** Responses (generally automatic or involuntary) elicited by specific stimuli.

**Neutral stimulus** Stimulus not connected to a response.

**Unconditioned stimulus (US)** Stimulus that automatically produces an emotional or physiological response.

**Unconditioned response (UR)** Naturally occurring emotional or physiological response.

**Conditioned stimulus (CS)** Stimulus that evokes an emotional or physiological response after conditioning.

**Conditioned response (CR)** Learned response to a previously neutral stimulus.

## GUIDELINES

### Applying Classical Conditioning

**Associate positive, pleasant events with learning tasks.**
*Examples*
1. Emphasize group competition and cooperation over individual competition. Many students have negative emotional responses to individual competition that may generalize to other learning.
2. Make division drills fun by having students decide how to divide refreshments equally, then letting them eat the results.
3. Make voluntary reading appealing by creating a comfortable reading corner with pillows, colourful displays of books, and reading props such as puppets (see Morrow & Weinstein, 1986, for more ideas).

**Help students to risk anxiety-producing situations voluntarily and successfully.**
*Examples*
1. Assign a shy student the responsibility of teaching two other students how to distribute materials for map study.
2. Devise small steps toward a larger goal. For example, give ungraded practice tests daily, and then weekly, to students who tend to "freeze" in test situations.

3. If a student is afraid of speaking in front of the class, let the student read a report to a small group while seated, then read it while standing, then give the report from notes instead of reading it verbatim. Next, move in stages toward having the student give a report to the whole class.

**Help students recognize differences and similarities among situations so they can discriminate and generalize appropriately.**
*Examples*
1. Explain that it is appropriate to avoid strangers who offer gifts or rides, but safe to accept favours from adults when parents are present.
2. Assure students who are anxious about taking university entrance exams that this test is like all the other achievement tests they have taken.

_____

*If you would like to learn more about classical conditioning, see www.class.uidaho.edu/psyc390/lessons/lesson02/lesson2.htm.*

## OPERANT CONDITIONING: TRYING NEW RESPONSES

So far, we have concentrated on the automatic conditioning of reflex-like responses such as salivation and fear. Clearly, not all human learning is so unintentional, and not all behaviours are so automatic. People actively "operate" on their environment. These deliberate actions are called **operants**. The learning process involved in operant behaviour is called **operant conditioning** because we learn to behave in certain ways as we operate on the environment.

The person generally thought to be responsible for developing the concept of operant conditioning is B. F. Skinner (1953). Skinner began with the belief that the principles of classical conditioning account for only a small portion of learned behaviours. Many human behaviours are operants, not respondents. Classical conditioning describes only how existing responses might be paired with new stimuli; it does not explain how new operant behaviours are acquired.

Behaviour, like response or action, is simply a word for what a person does in a particular situation. Conceptually, we may think of a behaviour as sandwiched between two sets of environmental influences: those that precede it (its **antecedents**) and those that follow it (its **consequences**) (Skinner, 1950). This relationship can be shown very simply as antecedent–behaviour–consequence, or A–B–C (Kazdin, 2008). As behaviour is ongoing, a given consequence becomes an antecedent for the next ABC sequence. Research in operant conditioning shows that operant behaviour can be altered by changes in the antecedents, the consequences, or both. Early work focused on consequences, often using rats or pigeons as subjects.

**Operants** Voluntary (and generally goal-directed) behaviours emitted by a person or an animal.

**Operant conditioning** Learning in which voluntary behaviour is strengthened or weakened by consequences or antecedents.

**Antecedents** Events that precede an action.

**Consequences** Events that follow an action.

## Types of Consequences

According to the behavioural view, consequences determine to a great extent whether a person will repeat the behaviour that led to the consequences. The type and timing of consequences can strengthen or weaken behaviours. We will look first at consequences that strengthen behaviour.

**REINFORCEMENT.**   Although **reinforcement** is commonly understood to mean "reward," this term has a particular meaning in psychology. A **reinforcer** is any consequence that strengthens the behaviour it follows. So, by definition, reinforced behaviours increase in frequency or duration. Whenever you see a behaviour persisting or increasing over time, you can assume the consequences of that behaviour are reinforcers for the individual involved (Alberto & Troutman, 2009; Landrum & Kauffman, 2006). The reinforcement process can be diagrammed as follows:

**Listen**
Reinforcement

CONSEQUENCE            EFFECT
Behaviour ⟶ Reinforcer ⟶ Strengthened or repeated behaviour

We can be fairly certain that food will be a reinforcer for a hungry animal, but what about people? It is not clear why an event acts as a reinforcer for an individual, but there are many theories about why reinforcement works. For example, some psychologists suggest that reinforcers are preferred activities or that they satisfy needs, whereas other psychologists believe that reinforcers reduce tension or stimulate a part of the brain (Rachlin, 1991; Schwartz et al., 2002). Whether the consequences of any action are reinforcing probably depends on the individual's perception of the event and the meaning it holds for her or him. For example, students who repeatedly get sent to the principal's office for misbehaving may be indicating that something about this consequence is reinforcing for them, even if it doesn't seem desirable to you. By the way, Skinner did not speculate about why reinforcers increase behaviour. He believed that it was useless to talk about "imaginary constructs" such as meaning, expectations, needs, or tensions. Skinner simply described the tendency for a given operant behaviour to increase after certain consequences (Skinner, 1953, 1989).

There are two types of reinforcement. The first, called **positive reinforcement,** occurs when the behaviour produces a new stimulus. Examples include a pigeon's pecking on the red key, producing food; your wearing a new outfit, producing many compliments; or a student falling out of his chair, producing cheers and laughter from classmates.

Notice that positive reinforcement can occur even when the behaviour being reinforced (falling out of a chair) is not "positive" from the teacher's point of view. In fact, positive reinforcement of inappropriate behaviours occurs unintentionally in many classrooms. Teachers help maintain problem behaviours by inadvertently reinforcing them. For example, Elizabeth may have unintentionally reinforced problem behaviour in her class by laughing the first time the boy answered, "Ronald McDonald." The problem behaviour may have persisted for other reasons, but the consequence of Elizabeth's laughter could have played a role.

**Reinforcement** Use of consequences to strengthen behaviour.

**Reinforcer** Any event that follows a behaviour and increases the chances that the behaviour will occur again.

**Positive reinforcement** Strengthening behaviour by presenting a desired stimulus after the behaviour.

When the consequence that strengthens a behaviour is the *appearance* (addition) of a new stimulus, the situation is defined as *positive reinforcement*. In contrast, when the consequence that strengthens a behaviour is the *disappearance* (subtraction) of a stimulus, the process is called **negative reinforcement**. If a particular action leads to avoiding or escaping an irritating or unpleasant—an **aversive**—situation, the action is likely to be repeated in a similar situation. A common example is the car seat-belt buzzer. As soon as you put on your seat belt, the irritating buzzer stops. You are likely to *repeat* this "buckling up" action in the future (so the process is *reinforcement*) because the behaviour made an aversive buzzing stimulus *disappear* (so the kind of reinforcement is *negative*).

It is important to remember that the "negative" in negative reinforcement does not imply that the behaviour being reinforced is necessarily negative or bad. The meaning is closer to that of using a negative sign in arithmetic—*something is subtracted*. Try to associate positive and negative reinforcement with the *consequence* of adding or subtracting something following a behaviour that has the *effect* of strengthening (reinforcing) the behaviour.

PUNISHMENT.   Negative reinforcement is often confused with punishment. To avoid this mistake, remember that the process of reinforcement (positive or negative) always involves strengthening behaviour. **Punishment**, on the other hand, involves *decreasing* or *suppressing* behaviour. A behaviour followed by a punisher is less likely to be repeated in similar situations in the future. Again, it is the effect that defines a consequence as punishment, and different people have different perceptions of what is punishing. One student may find suspension from school punishing, whereas another student wouldn't mind the break at all. The process of punishment is diagrammed as follows:

|CONSEQUENCE|EFFECT|
|---|---|

Behaviour → Punisher → Weakened or decreased behaviour

Like reinforcement, punishment may take one of two forms. The first type has been called Type I punishment, but this name isn't very informative, so we use the term **presentation punishment**. It occurs when presenting or adding a stimulus following the behaviour suppresses or decreases the behaviour. When teachers reprimand students, assign extra work, or make students run extra laps, and so on, they are using presentation punishment. We call the other type of punishment (Type II punishment) **removal punishment** because it involves removing a stimulus. When teachers or parents take away privileges after a young person has behaved inappropriately, they are applying removal punishment. With both types, the effect is to decrease the behaviour that led to the punishment. Figure 7.1 summarizes the processes of reinforcement and punishment.

## Reinforcement Schedules

When individuals are learning a new behaviour, they will learn it faster if they are reinforced for every correct response. This is a **continuous reinforcement schedule**. Then, when the new behaviour has been mastered, they will maintain it best if they are reinforced intermittently rather than every time. An **intermittent reinforcement schedule** helps students to maintain skills without expecting constant reinforcement.

There are two basic types of intermittent reinforcement schedules. One—called an **interval schedule**—is based on the amount of time that passes between reinforcers. The other—a **ratio schedule**—is based on the number of responses learners give between reinforcers. Interval and ratio schedules may be either fixed (predictable) or variable (unpredictable). Table 7.1 summarizes the five possible reinforcement schedules (the continuous schedule and the four kinds of intermittent schedules).

What are the effects of different schedules? Speed of performance depends on control. If reinforcement is based on the number of responses you give, then you have more control over the reinforcement: The faster you accumulate the correct number of responses, the faster the reinforcement will come. A teacher who says, "As soon as you complete these 10 problems correctly, you may listen to your iPod," can expect higher rates of performance than a teacher who says, "Work on these 10 problems for the next 20 minutes. Then I will check your papers and those with 10 correct may listen to their iPods."

**Negative reinforcement** Strengthening behaviour by removing an aversive stimulus when the behaviour occurs.

**Aversive** Irritating or unpleasant.

**Punishment** Process that weakens or suppresses behaviour.

**Presentation punishment** Decreasing the chances that a behaviour will occur again by presenting an aversive stimulus following the behaviour; also called *Type I punishment*.

**Removal punishment** Decreasing the chances that a behaviour will occur again by removing a pleasant stimulus following the behaviour; also called *Type II punishment*.

**Continuous reinforcement schedule** Presenting a reinforcer after every appropriate response.

**Intermittent reinforcement schedule** Presenting a reinforcer after some but not all responses.

**Interval schedule** Length of time between reinforcers.

**Ratio schedule** Reinforcement based on the number of responses between reinforcers.

## FIGURE 7.1

### KINDS OF REINFORCEMENT AND PUNISHMENT

Negative reinforcement and punishment are often confused. It may help you to remember that reinforcement is always associated with increases in behaviours, and punishment always involves decreasing or suppressing behaviour.

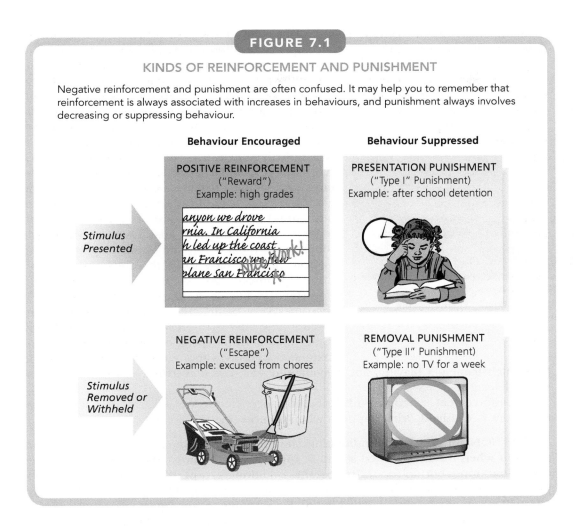

TABLE 7.1 • **Five Reinforcement Schedules**

| SCHEDULE | DEFINITION | EXAMPLE | RESPONSE PATTERN | REACTION WHEN REINFORCEMENT STOPS |
|---|---|---|---|---|
| Continuous | Reinforcement after every response | Turning on the television | Rapid learning of response | Very little persistence; rapid disappearance of response |
| Fixed-interval | Reinforcement after a set period of time | Weekly quiz | Response rate increases as time for reinforcement approaches, then drops after reinforcement | Little persistence; rapid drop in response rate when time for reinforcement passes and no reinforcer appears |
| Variable-interval | Reinforcement after varying lengths of time | Pop quizzes | Slow, steady rate of responding; very little pause after reinforcement | Greater persistence; slow decline in response rate |
| Fixed-ratio | Reinforcement after a set number of responses | Piece work Bake sale | Rapid response rate; pause after reinforcement | Little persistence; rapid drop in response rate when expected number of responses are given and no reinforcer appears |
| Variable-ratio | Reinforcement after a varying number of responses | Slot machines | Vary high response rate; little pause after reinforcement | Greatest persistence; response rate stays high and gradually drops off |

*Source: From Sulzer-Azaroff, B., & Mayer, G. R. (1994). Achieving Educational Excellence: Behavior Analysis for School Personnel (Figure, p. 89). San Marcos, CA: Western Image. Reprinted by permission of the authors.*

Visions of America, LLC/Alamy

**INTERMITTENT REINFORCEMENT** Casino slot machines are a good example of the effectiveness of intermittent reinforcement: People "learn" to persist in losing their money, because they might be rewarded with a jackpot, albeit infrequently and unpredictably.

Persistence in performance depends on unpredictability. Continuous reinforcement and both kinds of fixed reinforcement (ratio and interval) are quite predictable. We come to expect reinforcement at certain points and are generally quick to give up when the reinforcement does not meet our expectations. To encourage persistence of response, variable schedules are most appropriate. A great example of student persistence on a variable schedule was presented in an article about Valorie Lewis, an award-winning teacher. Describing Lewis's grade 3 class, one of her colleagues said that the students are "afraid to be absent because they don't want to take the chance they will miss anything. Mrs. Lewis doesn't tell them when she is planning something special, so they have to be there every day just in case" (Johnson, 2008, p. 7D). In fact, if the reinforcement schedule is gradually changed until it becomes very "lean"—meaning that reinforcement occurs only after many responses or a after a long time interval—then people can learn to work for extended periods without any reinforcement at all. Just watch gamblers playing slot machines to see how powerful a lean reinforcement schedule can be.

Reinforcement schedules influence how persistently we will respond when reinforcement is withheld. What happens when reinforcement is completely withdrawn?

**EXTINCTION.**   In classical conditioning, the conditioned response is extinguished (disappears) when the conditioned stimulus appears, but the unconditioned stimulus does not follow (tone, but no food). In operant conditioning, a person or an animal will not persist in a certain behaviour if the usual reinforcer is withheld long enough. The behaviour will eventually be extinguished (stop). For example, if you repeatedly email a professor but never get a reply, you may give up. Removal of reinforcement altogether leads to **extinction**. The process may take a while, however, as you know if you have tried to extinguish a child's tantrums by withholding your attention. Often the child wins—because you give up ignoring her—and instead of extinction, intermittent reinforcement occurs. This, of course, may encourage even more persistent tantrums in the future.

## Antecedents and Behaviour Change

In operant conditioning, antecedents—the events preceding behaviours—provide information about which behaviours will lead to positive consequences and which will lead to unpleasant ones. Skinner's pigeons learned to peck for food when a light was on, but not to bother when the light was off, because no food followed pecking when the light was off. In other words, they learned to use the antecedent light as a cue to discriminate the likely consequence of pecking. The pigeons' pecking was under **stimulus control**—that is, controlled by the discriminative stimulus of the light. This happens in humans, too. For example, Anita found herself (more than once) about to turn into her old office parking lot, even after her department had been relocated to a new building across town. As she drove, the old landmark cues kept her heading automatically to the old office. Another example is the supposedly true story of a getaway car driver in a bank robbery who sped through town, only to be caught by the police when she dutifully stopped at a red light. The stimulus of the red light had come to have automatic control.

We all learn to discriminate—to read situations. When should you ask to borrow your roommate's car—after a major disagreement or after you both have had a great time at a party? The antecedent cue of a school principal standing in the hall helps students discriminate the probable consequences of running or attempting to break into a locker. We often respond to such antecedent cues without fully realizing that they are influencing our behaviour. But teachers can use cues deliberately in the classroom.

**Extinction** The disappearance of a learned response.

**Stimulus control** Capacity for the presence or absence of antecedents to cause behaviours.

**EFFECTIVE INSTRUCTION DELIVERY.**   One important antecedent to increase positive student responses is the type of instructions you give. Research on **effective instruction delivery (EID)** has found instructions that are concise, clear, and specific, and that communicate an expected result, are more effective than vague directions. Statements work better than questions. You should be within a few metres of the students; directions shouted from across the room are less likely to work. Ideally, you should make eye contact with the students first, and then give the directions (Roberts, Tingstrom, Olmi, & Bellipanni, 2008).

**CUEING.**   By definition, **cueing** is the act of providing an antecedent stimulus just before a specific behaviour is supposed to take place. Cueing is particularly useful in setting the stage for behaviours that must occur at a given time, but are easily forgotten. In working with young people, teachers often find themselves correcting behaviours after the fact, asking students, "When are you going to start remembering to . . . ?" These reminders often lead to irritation. The mistake is already made, and the young person is left with only two choices: to promise to try harder or to think, "Why don't you leave me alone?" Neither response is very satisfying. Presenting a nonjudgmental cue can help prevent such negative confrontations. When a student performs the appropriate behaviour after a cue, the teacher can reinforce the student's accomplishment instead of punishing failure.

**PROMPTING.**   Sometimes students need help learning to respond to a cue in an appropriate way so the cue becomes a discriminative stimulus. One approach is to provide an additional cue, called a **prompt**, following the first cue. There are two principles for using a cue and a prompt to teach a new behaviour. First, make sure the environmental stimulus that you want to become a cue occurs immediately before the prompt you are using, so students will learn to respond to the cue and not rely only on the prompt. Second, fade (gradually reduce or delay) the prompt as soon as possible so students do not become dependent on it (Alberto & Troutman, 2009).

One way to incorporate cueing and prompting is by providing students with a checklist or reminder sheet. Figure 7.2 is a checklist for the steps in peer tutoring. Working in pairs is the cue; the checklist is the prompt. As students learn the procedures, the teacher

> **Effective instruction delivery (EID)** Instructions that are concise, clear, and specific, and that communicate an expected result. Statements work better than questions.
>
> **Cueing** Providing a stimulus that "sets up" a desired behaviour.
>
> **Prompt** A reminder that follows a cue to make sure the person reacts to the cue.

---

## FIGURE 7.2

### WRITTEN PROMPTS: A PEER TUTORING CHECKLIST

By using this checklist, students are reminded how to be effective tutors. As they become more proficient, the checklist may be less necessary.

 Remember to…

 _____ 1. Have the lesson ready.

 _____ 2. Talk clearly.

 _____ 3. Be friendly.

 _____ 4. Tell the student when the answer is right.

 _____ 5. STOP! Correct mistakes.

 _____ 6. Praise good work!

 _____ 7. Make the lesson fun.

 _____ 8. Do not give TOO MUCH help.

 _____ 9. Fill out the daily sheet.

_____ 10. Can you add a suggestion?

*Source: From Suzler-Azaroof, B., & Mayer, G. R. (1994). Achieving Educational Excellence: Behavior Analysis for School Personnel (Figure, p. 89). San Marcos, CA: Western Image. Reprinted by permission of the authors.*

may stop using the checklist, but may remind the students of the steps. When no written or oral prompts are necessary, the students have learned to respond appropriately to the environmental cue of working in pairs—they have learned how to behave in peer tutoring situations. However, the teacher should continue to monitor the process, recognize good work, and correct mistakes. Before a peer tutoring session, the teacher might ask students to close their eyes and "see" the checklist, focusing on each step. As students work, the teacher could listen to their interactions and continue to provide coaching as they improve their peer tutoring skills.

What would these principles look like in action? We turn to that next.

# APPLIED BEHAVIOUR ANALYSIS

**Applied behaviour analysis** is the application of behavioural learning principles to change behaviour. The method is sometimes called **behaviour modification**, but this term has negative connotations for many people and is often misunderstood (Alberto & Troutman, 2009; Kazdin, 2001, 2008).

Ideally, applied behaviour analysis requires clear specification of the behaviour to be changed; careful measurement of the behaviour; analysis of the antecedents and reinforcers that might be maintaining inappropriate or undesirable behaviour; interventions based on behavioural principles to change the behaviour; and careful measurement of changes. In research on applied behaviour analysis, an ABAB design (described in Chapter 1) is common. That is, researchers take a baseline measurement of the behaviour (A), then apply the intervention (B), then stop the intervention to see if the behaviour goes back to the baseline level (A), and then reintroduce the intervention (B).

In classrooms, teachers usually cannot follow all the ABAB steps, but they can do the following:

1. Clearly specify the behaviour to be changed and note the current level. For example, if a student is "careless," does this mean two, three, four, or more computation errors for every 10 problems?
2. Plan a specific intervention using antecedents, consequences, or both. For example, offer the student one extra minute of computer time for every problem completed with no errors.
3. Keep track of the results, and modify the plan if necessary.

Let's consider some specific methods for accomplishing step 2—the intervention.

## Methods for Encouraging Behaviours

As we discussed earlier, to encourage behaviour is to reinforce it. There are several specific ways to encourage existing behaviours or teach new ones. These include teacher attention and praise, the Premack principle, shaping, and positive practice.

REINFORCING WITH TEACHER ATTENTION.  Many psychologists advise teachers to "accentuate the positive"—praise students for good behaviour, while ignoring misbehaviour. In fact, some researchers believe that "the systematic application of praise and attention may be the most powerful motivational and classroom management tool available to teachers" (Alber & Heward, 1997, p. 277; Alber & Heward, 2000). A related strategy is *differential reinforcement*, or ignoring inappropriate behaviours, while being sure to reinforce appropriate behaviours as soon as they occur. For example, if a student is prone to making irrelevant comments ("When is the game this Friday?"), you should ignore the off-task comment, but recognize a task-related contribution as soon as it occurs (Landrum & Kauffman, 2006).

This praise-and-ignore approach can be helpful, but don't expect it to solve all classroom management problems. Several studies have shown that disruptive behaviours persist when teachers use positive consequences (mostly praise) as their only classroom management strategy (McGoey & DuPaul, 2000; Pfiffner & O'Leary, 1987; Sullivan & O'Leary, 1990). Also, if attention from other students is reinforcing the problem behaviours, the teacher's ignoring them won't help much.

Applied behaviour analysis The application of behavioural learning principles to understand and change behaviour.

Behaviour modification Systematic application of antecedents and consequences to change behaviour.

There is a second consideration in using praise. The positive results found in research occur when teachers carefully and systematically praise their students (Landrum & Kauffman, 2006). Merely "handing out compliments" will not improve behaviour. To be effective, praise must (1) be contingent on the behaviour to be reinforced, (2) specify clearly the behaviour being reinforced, and (3) be believable (O'Leary & O'Leary, 1977). In other words, the praise should be sincere recognition of a well-defined behaviour so students understand what they did to warrant the recognition. Teachers who have not received special training often violate these conditions (Brophy, 1981). Ideas for using praise effectively, based on Brophy's extensive review of the subject and Alan Kazdin's (2008) work with parents and teachers, are presented in the *Guidelines*.

Some psychologists have suggested that teachers' use of praise tends to focus students on learning to win approval rather than on learning for its own sake. Perhaps the best advice is to be aware of the potential dangers of the overuse or misuse of praise and to navigate accordingly.

SELECTING REINFORCERS: THE PREMACK PRINCIPLE.   In most classrooms, there are many readily available reinforcers other than teacher attention, such as the chance to talk to other students, work at computers, or feed the class animals. However, teachers tend

## GUIDELINES

## Using Praise Appropriately

**Be clear and systematic in giving praise.**
*Examples*
1. Make sure praise is tied directly to appropriate behaviour.
2. Make sure the student understands the specific action or accomplishment that is being praised. Say, "I am impressed that you made sure everyone in your group got a chance to speak," not, "Good job leading the group."

**Make praise "appreciative" not "evaluative" (Ginott, 1972).**
*Examples*
1. Praise and appreciate the student's efforts, accomplishments, and actions—especially when the actions help others.
2. Don't evaluate the student's character or personality—praise the action, not the person.

**Set standards for praise based on individual abilities and limitations.**
*Examples*
1. Praise progress or accomplishment in relation to the individual student's past efforts.
2. Focus the student's attention on his or her own progress, not on comparisons with others.

**Attribute the student's success to effort and ability so the student will gain confidence that success is possible again.**
*Examples*
1. Don't imply that the success may be based on luck, extra help, or easy material.
2. Ask students to describe the problems they encountered and how they solved them.

**Make praise really reinforcing.**
*Examples*
1. Don't attempt to influence the rest of the class by singling out some students for praise. This tactic frequently backfires, because students know what's really going on. In addition, you risk embarrassing the student you have chosen to praise.
2. Don't give undeserved praise to students simply to balance failures. It is seldom consoling and calls attention to the student's inability to earn genuine recognition.
3. Don't use "caboosing"—tacking a criticism on at the end, as in "Good job on completing your homework this week. Why can't you do that every week?" (Kazdin, 2008).

**Recognize genuine accomplishments.**
*Examples*
1. Reward the attainment of specified goals, not just participation.
2. Do not reward uninvolved students just for being quiet and not disrupting the class.
3. Tie praise to students' improving competence or to the value of their accomplishment. Say, "I noticed that you double-checked all your problems. Your score reflects your careful work."

*For more information on teacher praise, see www.apa.org/education/k12/using-praise.aspx?item=1.*

**GRANDMA'S RULE** "First, do what I want you to do, and then you may do what you want to do." According to the Premack principle, by making preferred activities contingent on learning and positive behaviour, teachers can greatly increase both.

Richard Hutchins/PhotoEdit

to offer these opportunities in a rather haphazard way. Just as with praise, by making privileges and rewards directly contingent on learning and positive behaviour, the teacher can greatly increase both learning and desired behaviour.

A helpful guide for choosing the most effective reinforcers is the **Premack principle**, named for David Premack (1965). According to the Premack principle, a high-frequency behaviour (a preferred activity) can be an effective reinforcer for a low-frequency behaviour (a less-preferred activity). This is sometimes referred to as "Grandma's rule": First, do what I want you to do, and then you may do what you want to do. Elizabeth used this principle in her class when she told them they could work together on their worksheets after they quietly completed the first section of the worksheet on their own.

If students didn't have to study, what would they do? The answers to this question may suggest many possible reinforcers. For most students, talking, moving around the room, sitting near a friend, being exempt from assignments or tests, reading magazines, using the computer, or playing games are preferred activities. The best way to determine appropriate reinforcers for your students may be to watch what they do in their free time.

For the Premack principle to be effective, the low-frequency (less preferred) behaviour must happen first. In the following dialogue, observe how the teacher loses a perfect opportunity to use the Premack principle:

> **Students:** Oh, no! Do we have to work on grammar again today? The other classes got to discuss the play we saw in the auditorium this morning.
>
> **Teacher:** But the other classes finished the lesson on sentences yesterday. We're almost finished, too. If we don't finish the lesson, I'm afraid you'll forget the rules we reviewed yesterday.
>
> **Students:** Why don't we finish the sentences at the end of the period and talk about the play now?
>
> **Teacher:** Okay, if you promise to complete the sentences later.

Discussing the play could have served as a reinforcer for completing the lesson. As it is, the class may well spend the entire period discussing the play. Just as the discussion becomes fascinating, the teacher will have to end it and insist that the class return to the grammar lesson.

SHAPING.   What happens when students continually fail to gain reinforcement because they simply cannot perform a skill in the first place? Consider these examples:

- A grade 4 student looks at the results of the latest mathematics test. "No credit on almost half of the problems again because I made one dumb mistake in each problem. I hate math!"
- A grade 10 student finds some excuse each day for avoiding the softball game in gym class. The student cannot catch a ball and now refuses to try.

In both situations, the students are receiving no reinforcement for their work because the end product of their efforts is not good enough. A safe prediction is that the students will soon learn to dislike the class, the subject, and perhaps the teacher and school in general. One way to prevent this problem is the strategy of **shaping**, also called **successive approximations**. Shaping and successive approximation involves reinforcing progress for small steps toward a larger, complex behaviour instead of waiting for perfection.

In order to use shaping, the teacher must take the final complex behaviour the student is expected to master and break it down into a number of small, manageable steps. One approach that identifies the small steps is **task analysis**, originally developed by R. B. Miller (1962) to help the armed services train personnel. Miller's system begins with

**Premack principle** Principle stating that a more-preferred activity can serve as a reinforcer for a less-preferred activity.

**Shaping** Reinforcing each small step of progress toward a desired goal or behaviour.

**Successive approximations** Small components that make up a complex behaviour.

**Task analysis** System for breaking down a task hierarchically into basic skills and subskills.

a definition of the final performance requirement—what the trainee (or student) must be able to do at the end of the program or unit. Then, the steps that will lead to the final goal are specified. The procedure simply breaks skills and processes down into subskills and subprocesses—small steps to success.

Consider an example of task analysis in which students must write a position paper based on research. If the teacher assigned the position paper without analyzing the task, what could happen? Some of the students might not know how to do systematic computer research. They might read one or two entries in Wikipedia, and then write about their position based only on this brief reading. Another group of students might know how to use computers and search engines to do research online and how to find information from indexes in books, but have difficulty integrating information to reach conclusions. They might hand in lengthy papers listing summaries of different ideas without any synthesis or conclusions. Another group of students might be able to draw conclusions, but their written presentations might be so confusing and grammatically incorrect that the teacher could not understand what they were trying to say. Each of the groups would have failed to fulfill the assignment, but for different reasons.

A task analysis gives a picture of the logical sequence of steps leading toward the final goal. An awareness of this sequence can help teachers make sure that students have the necessary skills before they move to the next step. In addition, when students have difficulty, the teacher can pinpoint problem areas. Many behaviours can be improved through shaping, especially the acquisition of skills that involve persistence, endurance, increased accuracy, greater speed, or extensive practice to master. Because shaping is a time-consuming process, however, it should not be used if success can be attained through simpler methods such as cueing.

POSITIVE PRACTICE.    In **positive practice**, students replace one behaviour with another. This approach is especially appropriate for dealing with academic errors. When students make a mistake, they must correct it as soon as possible and practise the correct response. The same principle can be applied when students break classroom rules. Instead of being punished, the student might be required to practise the correct alternative action; for example, entering the room and immediately putting backpacks in assigned places. This process sometimes is called *positive practice overcorrection* because the correct behaviour is practised until it becomes almost automatic (Cole, Montgomery, Wilson, & Milan, 2000; Marvin, Rapp, Stenske, Rojas, Swanson, & Bartlett, 2010).

The *Guidelines* summarize approaches encouraging positive behaviour.

## Handling Undesirable Behaviour

No matter how successful you are at accentuating the positive, there are times when you must cope with undesirable behaviour, either because other methods fail or because the behaviour itself is dangerous and calls for direct action. For this purpose, negative reinforcement, reprimands, response cost, and social isolation all offer possible solutions.

NEGATIVE REINFORCEMENT.    Recall the basic principle of negative reinforcement: If an action stops or avoids something unpleasant, then that action is likely to occur again in similar situations. Negative reinforcement was operating in Elizabeth's classroom. When they moaned and complained, her students escaped the test, so negative reinforcement probably increased the frequency of complaining in the future.

Negative reinforcement can also be used to enhance learning. To do this, you place students in mildly unpleasant situations so they can "escape" when their behaviour improves. Consider these examples:

Teacher to a grade 3 class: "When the supplies are put back in the cabinet and each of you is sitting quietly, we will go outside. Until then, we will miss our recess."

High-school teacher to a student who seldom finishes in-class assignments: "As soon as you complete the assignment, you may join the class in the auditorium. But until you finish, you must work in the study hall."

Antonio Banderas in the film *Take the Lead:* Working with a group of totally uncooperative students, Banderas blasts the students with music they hate, only turning it off when the entire class is lined up and ready to practise their ballroom dance moves.

Positive practice Practising correct responses immediately after errors.

## GUIDELINES

### Encouraging Positive Behaviours

**Make sure you recognize positive behaviour in ways that students value.**
*Examples*

1. When presenting class rules, set up positive consequences for following rules as well as negative consequences for breaking rules.
2. Recognize honest admissions of mistakes by giving a second chance: "Because you admitted that you copied your paper from a book, I'm giving you a chance to rewrite it."
3. Offer desired rewards for academic efforts, such as extra recess time, exemptions from homework or tests, or extra credit on major projects.

**When students are tackling new material or trying new skills, give plenty of reinforcement.**
*Examples*

1. Find and comment on something right in every student's first life drawing.
2. Reinforce students for encouraging each other. "French pronunciation is difficult and awkward at first. Let's help each other by eliminating all giggles when someone is brave enough to attempt a new word."

**After new behaviours are established, give reinforcement on an unpredictable schedule to encourage persistence.**
*Examples*

1. Offer surprise rewards for good participation in class.
2. Start classes with a short, written extra-credit question. Students don't have to answer, but a good answer will add points to their total for the semester.
3. Make sure the good students get compliments for their work from time to time. Don't take them for granted.

**Use the Premack principle to identify effective reinforcers.**
*Examples*

1. Watch what students do with their free time.
2. Notice which students like to work together. The chance to work with friends is often a good reinforcer.

**Use cueing to help establish new behaviours.**
*Examples*

1. Put up humorous signs in the classroom to remind students of rules.
2. At the beginning of the year, as students enter class, call their attention to a chart posted on the board listing all of the materials they should have with them when they come to class.

**Make sure all students, even those who often cause problems, receive some praise, privileges, or other rewards when they do something well.**
*Examples*

1. Review your class list occasionally to make sure all students are receiving some reinforcement.
2. Set standards for reinforcement so that all students will have a chance to be rewarded.
3. Check your biases. Are boys getting more opportunities for reinforcement than girls, or vice versa? How about students of different races?

**Establish a variety of reinforcers.**
*Examples*

1. Let students suggest their own reinforcers or choose from a "menu" of reinforcers with "weekly specials."
2. Talk to other teachers or parents about ideas for reinforcers.

Actually, a true behaviourist might object to identifying these situations as examples of negative reinforcement because too much student thinking and understanding is required to make the negative reinforcers work. Teachers cannot treat students like lab animals, subjecting them to loud noises or cold environments until they give a right answer. But teachers can make sure that unpleasant situations improve when student behaviour improves.

You may wonder why the negative reinforcement examples above are not considered punishment. Surely staying in during recess, not accompanying the class to a special program, or being subjected to music you hate is punishing. But the focus in each case is on strengthening specific behaviours (putting away supplies, finishing in-class assignments, lining up and cooperating with the teacher). The teacher strengthens (reinforces) the behaviours by removing something aversive as soon as the desired behaviours occur. Because the consequence involves removing or "subtracting" a stimulus, the reinforcement is negative.

Negative reinforcement also gives students a chance to exercise control. Missing recess or hearing music you hate are unpleasant situations, but in each case, the students retain control. As soon as they perform the appropriate behaviour, the unpleasant situation ends. In contrast, punishment occurs after the fact, and a student cannot so easily control or terminate it.

There are several rules for negative reinforcement: Describe the desired change in a positive way. Don't bluff. Make sure you can enforce your unpleasant situation. Follow through despite complaints. Insist on action, not promises. If the unpleasant situation terminates when students promise to be better next time, you have reinforced making promises, not making changes (Alberto & Troutman, 2009; O'Leary, 1995).

REPRIMANDS.  In the *Junction Journal,* Anita's daughter's elementary school newspaper, the following lines appeared in a story called "Why I Like School," written by a grade 4 student: "I also like my teacher. She helps me understand and learn. She is nice to everyone. I like it when she gets mad at somebody, but she doesn't yell at them in front of the class, but speaks to them privately."

Soft, calm, private **reprimands** are more effective than loud, public reprimands in decreasing disruptive behaviour (Landrum & Kauffman, 2006). Research has shown that when reprimands are loud enough for the entire class to hear, disruptions increase or continue at a constant level. Some students enjoy public recognition for misbehaviour, or they don't want classmates to see them "lose" to the teacher. If they are not used too often, and if the classroom is generally a positive, warm environment, then students usually respond quickly to private reprimands (Kaplan, 1991).

**DELIVERING REPRIMANDS** Research has shown that scolding a student in front of the entire class may actually reinforce his or her disruptive behaviour by drawing more attention to it. Calm, private reprimands may be more effective.

Bill Aron/PhotoEdit

RESPONSE COST.  The concept of **response cost** is familiar to anyone who has ever paid a fine. For certain infractions of the rules, people must lose some reinforcer—money, time, privileges (Walker, Shea, & Bauer, 2004). In a class, the concept of response cost can be applied in a number of ways. The first time a student breaks a class rule, the teacher gives a warning. The second time, the teacher makes a mark beside the student's name in the grade book. The student loses two minutes of recess for each mark accumulated. For older students, a certain number of marks might mean losing the privilege of working in a group or using the computers.

SOCIAL ISOLATION.   One of the most controversial behavioural methods for decreasing undesirable behaviour is the strategy of **social isolation**, often called **time out**, from reinforcement. The process involves removing a highly disruptive student from the classroom for five to 10 minutes. The student is placed in an empty, uninteresting room alone—the punishment is brief isolation from other people. A trip to the principal's office or confinement to a chair in the corner of the regular classroom does not have the same effect as sitting alone in an empty room. But beware. If a brief time out does not help improve the situation, don't try a longer time out. Alan Kazdin (2008), who has been helping teachers and parents work positively with children for decades, says, "If you are giving longer and longer time-outs, it means your strategy is failing. The answer is not to escalate—just the opposite in fact. If you are giving more and longer time-outs, this should tell you that you need to do more to positively reinforce good behaviours to replace the unwanted behaviours" (p. 10)—good advice for any form of punishment.

SOME CAUTIONS ABOUT PUNISHMENT.   Unfortunately, punishment seems to be a very common part of parenting and schooling. We say *unfortunately* because study after study shows that punishment by itself, as usually practised in homes and schools, just doesn't work. It tells children what to stop doing (often, they knew that already), but it does not teach them what to do instead (Kazdin, 2008). Whenever you consider the use

**Reprimands** Criticisms for misbehaviour; rebukes.

**Response cost** Punishment by loss of reinforcers.

**Social isolation** Removal of a disruptive student for five to 10 minutes.

**Time out** Technically, the removal of all reinforcement. In practice, isolation of a student from the rest of the class for a brief time.

of punishment, you should make it part of a two-pronged attack. The first goal is to carry out the punishment and suppress the undesirable behaviour. The second goal is to make clear what the student should be doing instead and to provide reinforcement for those desirable actions. Thus, while the problem behaviours are being suppressed, positive alternative responses are being strengthened. As you will see in the next section, recent approaches really emphasize supporting positive behaviours. The *Guidelines* give ideas for using punishment for positive purposes.

We repeat. Punishment in and of itself does not lead to any positive behaviour. Harsh punishment communicates to students that "might makes right" and may encourage retaliation. In addition, punishment works best when the potential punisher—the teacher—is around. Students learn to "be good" when the teacher is in the room, but when the teacher leaves or there is a substitute teacher, the system might fall apart. Punishment tends to

## GUIDELINES

## Using Punishment

**Try to structure the situation so you can use negative reinforcement rather than punishment.**
*Examples*

1. Allow students to escape unpleasant situations (completing additional workbook assignments, weekly tests of math facts) when they reach a level of competence.
2. Insist on actions, not promises. Don't let students convince you to change the terms of the agreement.

**If you do use punishment, keep it mild and brief—then pair it with doing the right thing.**
*Examples*

1. Time out for young children—no more than two to five minutes; loss of points—no more than one sticker if the student can earn five in a day (Kazdin, 2008).
2. Pair the brief, mild punishment with reinforcement for doing the right thing or restitution. If a student writes graffiti in the washroom, use brief punishment plus cleaning off the graffiti.

**Be consistent in your application of punishment.**
*Examples*

1. Avoid inadvertently reinforcing the behaviour you are trying to punish. Keep confrontations private, so that students don't become heroes for standing up to the teacher in a public showdown.
2. Let students know in advance the consequences of breaking the rules by posting major class rules for younger students or outlining rules and consequences in a course syllabus for older students.
3. Tell students they will receive only one warning before punishment is given. Give the warning in a calm way, and then follow through.
4. Make punishment as unavoidable and immediate as is reasonably possible.
5. Don't punish when you are angry—you may be too harsh, then need to take it back later—which shows a lack of consistency.

**Focus on the students' actions, not on the students' personal qualities.**
*Examples*

1. Reprimand in a calm but firm voice.
2. Avoid vindictive or sarcastic words or tones of voice. You might hear your own angry words later when students imitate your sarcasm.
3. Stress the need to end the problem behaviour instead of expressing any dislike you might feel for the student.
4. Be aware that visible minority students are disproportionately punished, sent to detention, and expelled from school. Are your policies fair?

**Adapt the punishment to the infraction.**
*Examples*

1. Ignore minor misbehaviours that do not disrupt the class, or stop these misbehaviours with a disapproving glance or a move toward the student.
2. Make sure the punishment isn't worse than the crime—don't take away all the free time a student has earned for one infraction of the rules, for example (Landrum & Kauffman, 2006). Less punishment is more effective, as long as it is paired with reinforcement for doing the right thing.
3. Don't use homework as a punishment for misbehaviours such as talking in class.
4. When a student misbehaves to gain peer acceptance, removal from the group of friends can be effective, because this is really time out from a reinforcing situation.
5. If the problem behaviours continue, analyze the situation and try a new approach. Your punishment may not be very punishing, or you may be inadvertently reinforcing the misbehaviour.

_____

*For more information on punishment, see https://pubs.ext.vt.edu/350/350-111/350-111_pdf.pdf.*

focus students on the consequences of their actions for themselves instead of challenging them to think about the impact of their behaviour on others; as a result punishment does not instill compassion or empathy for others. Finally, punishment can interfere with developing a caring relationship with your students (Alberto & Troutman, 2009; Hardin, 2008; Kohn, 1996a, 1996b, 2005; Walker, Shea, & Bauer, 2004).

# PUTTING IT ALL TOGETHER: BEHAVIOURAL APPROACHES TO TEACHING AND MANAGEMENT

The behavioural approach to learning has inspired several important contributions to instruction, including systems for specifying learning objectives and direct instruction (we will look at these topics in Chapter 14 when we discuss teaching) and class management systems such as group consequences, contingency contracts, and token economies (Landrum & Kauffman, 2006). These approaches are useful when the goal is to learn explicit information or change behaviours and when the material is sequential and factual.

Remember, there is one element that is part of every behavioural learning program—specific practice of correct behaviours. Contrary to popular wisdom, practice does not make perfect. Instead, practice makes permanent the behaviours practised, so practising accurate behaviours is important. As other examples of a behavioural approach, consider group consequences, contingency contracts, and token reinforcement.

## Group Consequences

A teacher can base reinforcement for the class on the behaviour of selected target students (for example, "If Noah, Evan, and Mei stay on their mats until the end of nap time, then we will have a special snack"). Also, the class can earn rewards based on the collective behaviour of everyone in the class, usually by adding each student's points to a class or a team total. The **good behaviour game** is an example of this approach. Teachers and students discuss what would make the classroom a better place. Then, they identify behaviours that get in the way of learning. Based on this discussion, class rules are developed, and the class is divided into two or three teams. Each time a student breaks one of the rules, that student's team is given a mark. The team with the fewest marks at the end of the period receives a special reward or privilege (longer recess, first to lunch, the team "spaceship" is moved closer to the "moon," and so on). If all teams earn fewer than a preestablished number of marks, all receive the reward. Sometimes a class needs a "no tattling" rule so the teams don't spend all their time pointing out each other's mistakes. Most studies indicate that even though the game generates only small improvements in academic achievement, it can produce definite improvements in the behaviours listed in the good behaviour rules, and it can prevent many behaviour problems (Embry, 2002; Tingstrom, Sterling-Turner, & Wilczynski, 2006).

What happens if we add interventions that target academic achievement to the proven power of the good behaviour game? Catherine Bradshaw and her colleagues did just that (Bradshaw, Zmuda, Kellam, & Ialongo, 2009). They followed 678 mostly African American students from urban grade 1 classes through their high school years. In grade 1 these students participated in either a control group or one of two specific programs: (a) a classroom-centred intervention that combined the good behaviour game with an enhanced academic curriculum (read-alouds, journal writing, Reader's Theatre, critical thinking skills, Mimosa math, small group activities, etc.), or (b) a family-centred intervention that promoted parent involvement in home reading and math activities and helped parents develop better child management strategies. Students who participated in the classroom intervention that combined the good behaviour game with an enhanced academic curriculum in grade 1 had higher scores on standardized achievement tests in grade 12, reduced referrals for special education services, higher rates of high school graduation, and higher rates of college attendance 12 years later! The parent involvement program had positive but not significant effects on all these measures and a small significant effect on reading test scores. So early investment in helping students learn positive behaviours and academic skills can make a difference for years to come.

**Good behaviour game** Arrangement where a class is divided into teams and each team receives demerit points for breaking agreed-upon rules of good behaviour.

You can also use **group consequences** without dividing the class into teams; that is, you can base reinforcement on the behaviour of the whole class. However, caution is needed using group approaches—the whole group should not suffer for the misbehaviour or mistakes of one individual if the group has no real influence over that person. Anita once saw an entire class break into cheers when the teacher announced that one boy was transferring to another school. The chant "No more points! No more points!" filled the room. The "points" referred to the teacher's system of giving one point to the whole class each time anyone broke a rule. Every point meant five minutes of recess lost. The boy who was transferring had been responsible for the loss of many recess periods. He was not very popular to begin with, and the point system, though quite effective in maintaining order, had made the boy an outcast in his own class.

Peer pressure in the form of support and encouragement, however, can be a positive influence. Group consequences are recommended when students care about the approval of their peers (Theodore, Bray, Kehle, & Jenson, 2001). If the misbehaviour of several students seems to be encouraged by the attention and laughter of other students, then group consequences could be helpful. Teachers might show students how to give support and constructive feedback to classmates. If a few students seem to enjoy sabotaging the system, those students may need separate arrangements such as putting all the saboteurs together in their own group.

## Contingency Contracts and Token Reinforcement

In a **contingency contract** program, the teacher draws up an individual contract with each student, describing exactly what the student must do to earn a particular privilege or reward. In some programs, students suggest behaviours to be reinforced and the rewards that can be gained. The negotiating process itself can be an educational experience, as students learn to set reasonable goals and abide by the terms of a contract. And, if students participate in setting the goals, they often are more committed to reaching them (Locke & Latham, 2002; Schunk, 2012; Schunk, Pintrich, & Meece, 2008).

An example of a contract for completing assignments that is appropriate for intermediate and upper-grade students is presented in Figure 7.3. This chart serves as a contract, assignment sheet, and progress record. Information about progress can support student motivation. Something like this might even help you keep track of assignments and due dates in your university classes.

---

**STOP & THINK** Have you ever participated in a program where you earned points or credits that you could exchange for a reward? Are you a member of a frequent flyer club, or do you get points on your credit card? Do you get one free coffee for every 10 coffee purchases or a free smoothie when you fill a punch card? Does being a part of such a program affect your buying habits? How? Phil knows he pays for everything he can with his credit card to get the points and always tries to fly on one airline for the same reason. •

---

Group consequences Rewards or punishments given to a class as a whole for adhering to or violating rules of conduct.

Contingency contract A contract between the teacher and a student specifying what the student must do to earn a particular reward or privilege.

Token reinforcement system System in which tokens earned for academic work and positive classroom behaviour can be exchanged for some desired reward.

Often, it is difficult to provide positive consequences for all the students who deserve them. A **token reinforcement system** can help solve this problem by allowing all students to earn tokens for both academic work and positive classroom behaviour. The tokens may be points, checks, holes punched in a card, chips, play money, or anything else that is easily identified as the student's property. Periodically, the students exchange the tokens they have earned for some desired reward (Alberto & Troutman, 2009; Kazdin, 2001).

Depending on the age of the student, the rewards could be small toys, school supplies, free time, special class jobs, positive notes sent home, time to listen to music, or other privileges. When a "token economy," as this kind of system is called, is first established, the tokens should be given out on a fairly continuous schedule, with chances to exchange the tokens for rewards available early and often. Once the system is working well, however, tokens should be distributed on an intermittent schedule and saved for longer periods of time before they are exchanged for rewards.

Another variation is to allow students to earn tokens in the classroom and then exchange them for rewards at home. These plans are very successful when parents are

## FIGURE 7.3

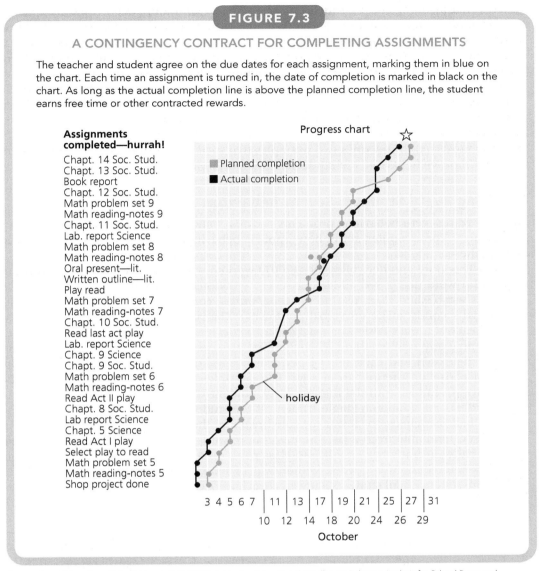

### A CONTINGENCY CONTRACT FOR COMPLETING ASSIGNMENTS

The teacher and student agree on the due dates for each assignment, marking them in blue on the chart. Each time an assignment is turned in, the date of completion is marked in black on the chart. As long as the actual completion line is above the planned completion line, the student earns free time or other contracted rewards.

**Assignments completed—hurrah!**

Chapt. 14 Soc. Stud.
Chapt. 13 Soc. Stud.
Book report
Chapt. 12 Soc. Stud.
Math problem set 9
Math reading-notes 9
Chapt. 11 Soc. Stud.
Lab. report Science
Math problem set 8
Math reading-notes 8
Oral present—lit.
Written outline—lit.
Play read
Math problem set 7
Math reading-notes 7
Chapt. 10 Soc. Stud.
Read last act play
Lab. report Science
Chapt. 9 Science
Chapt. 9 Soc. Stud.
Math problem set 6
Math reading-notes 6
Read Act II play
Chapt. 8 Soc. Stud.
Lab report Science
Chapt. 5 Science
Read Act I play
Select play to read
Math problem set 5
Math reading-notes 5
Shop project done

Progress chart

■ Planned completion
■ Actual completion

holiday

3 4 5 6 7 | 11 | 13 | 17 | 19 | 21 | 25 | 27 | 31
        10  12   14   18  20   24  26   29

October

Source: From Sulzer-Azaroff, B., & Mayer, G. R. (1994). Achieving Educational Excellence: Behavior Analysis for School Personnel (Figure, p. 89). San Marcos, CA: Western Image. Reprinted by permission of the authors.

willing to cooperate. Usually a note or report form is sent home daily or twice a week. The note indicates the number of points earned in the preceding time period. The points may be exchanged for minutes of television viewing, access to special toys, or private time with parents. Points can also be saved up for larger rewards such as trips. Do not use this procedure, however, if you suspect the child might be pressured for perfection or punished for poor reports (Jurbergs, Palcic, & Kelly, 2007).

Token reinforcement systems are complicated and time-consuming. Generally, they should be used in only three situations: (1) to motivate students who are completely uninterested in their work and have not responded to other approaches; (2) to encourage students who have consistently failed to make academic progress; and (3) to deal with a class that is out of control. Some groups of students seem to benefit from token economies more than others. Students with intellectual disabilities, children who have failed often, students with few academic skills, and students with behaviour problems all seem to respond to the concrete, direct nature of token reinforcement.

Before you try a token system, you should be sure that your teaching methods and materials are right for the students. Sometimes, class disruptions or lack of motivation

**Watch**
Contingency Contracts and Token Reinforcement

indicate that teaching practices need to be changed. Maybe the class rules are unclear or are enforced inconsistently. Perhaps your instructions are vague. Maybe the text is too easy or too hard or the pace is wrong. If these problems exist, a token system may improve the situation temporarily, but the students will still have trouble learning the academic material. Improve your teaching first. The few pages devoted here to token reinforcement and contingency contracts can offer only an introduction to these programs. If you want to set up a large-scale reward program in your classroom, you should probably seek professional advice. Often, the school psychologist, counsellor, or principal can help.

The next section describes two examples that successfully applied behavioural principles to improve behaviours of students with special needs.

## Reaching Every Student: Severe Behaviour Problems

Students with severe behaviour problems provide some of the most difficult challenges for teachers. Three studies show how applied behavioural principles can be useful in helping these students.

Lea Theodore and her colleagues (2001) worked with the teacher of five adolescent males who were diagnosed as having severe emotional disorders. A short list of clear rules was established (e.g., use no obscene words, comply with the teacher's requests within five seconds, make no verbal putdowns). The rules were written on index cards taped to each student's desk. The teacher had a checklist on his desk with each student's name to note any rule breaking. This checklist was easily observable, so students could monitor their own and each other's performance. At the end of the 45-minute period, a student chose a "criterion" from a jar. The possible criteria were: performance of the whole group, student with the highest score, student with the lowest score, the average of all students, or a random single student. If the student or students selected to be the criterion had five checks or fewer for rule-breaking, then the whole class got a reward, also chosen randomly from a jar. The possible rewards were things like a power drink, a bag of chips, a candy bar, or a late-to-class pass. An ABAB design was used—baseline, two-week intervention, two-week withdrawal of intervention, and two-week return to group consequences. All students showed clear improvement in following the rules when the reward system was in place. Students liked the approach and the teacher found it easy to implement.

In the second study, Kara McGoey and George DuPaul (2000) worked with teachers in three preschool classrooms to address problem behaviours of four students diagnosed as having attention-deficit hyperactive disorder. The teachers tried both a token reinforcement program (students earned small and large buttons on a chart for following class rules), and a response cost system (students began with five small buttons and one large button per activity each day and lost buttons for not following rules). Both procedures were effective in lowering rule breaking, but the teachers found the response cost system easier to implement.

Behavioural interventions are often used with children with autism (see Bartlett, Rapp, Krueger, & Henrickson, 2011; Hall, Grundon, Pope, & Romero, 2010; Soares, Vannest, & Harrison, 2009). For example, Sara Bartlett and her colleagues tested a *response cost* strategy to treat the problem of spitting by Evan, an 8-year-old boy with autism who had very limited verbal abilities. The researchers let the boy listen to a radio, identified as a favourite toy by his teachers, as he worked at a table in a therapy room in his school. When the boy spit, the radio was removed for 10 seconds, and then replaced. Evan's spitting went to near zero rates during these training sessions. Then the researchers stopped the response cost strategy and the radio was not removed when Evan spit. The rates of spitting went back up. Next the researchers reinstituted the response cost, removing the radio for 10 seconds, and Evan's spitting went back down again to near zero. (Notice this also is an example of an ABAB research design—baseline, treatment, return to baseline, reinstate treatment.) The researchers moved Evan back into the classroom and conducted his training sessions there. Finally they taught Evan's teachers to use the strategy, and Evan's spitting stayed at near zero in his regular classroom through the entire four-month follow-up period.

## Functional Behavioural Assessment and Positive Behaviour Supports

Teachers in both regular and special education classes have had success with a new approach that begins by asking, "What are students getting out of their problem behaviours—what functions do these behaviours serve?" The focus is on the *why* of the behaviour, not on the *what* (Lane, Falk, & Wehby, 2006; Stage et al., 2008; Warren et al., 2006). The reasons for problem behaviours generally fall into four categories (Barnhill, 2005; Maag & Kemp, 2003). Students act out to:

1. Receive attention from others—teachers, parents, or peers
2. Escape from some unpleasant situation—an academic or social demand
3. Get a desired item or activity
4. Meet sensory needs, such as stimulation from rocking or flapping arms for some children with autism

**FUNCTIONAL BEHAVIOURAL ASSESSMENT** These approaches focus on the "why" of student behaviour or misbehaviour. Teachers observe student behaviours in context and may interview the student, peers, and parents.

David Mager/Pearson Learning Photo Studio

If the reason for the behaviour is known, then the teacher can devise ways of supporting positive behaviours that will serve the same "why" function. For example, Anita once worked with a middle-school principal who was concerned about a boy who had lost his father a few years earlier and was having trouble in a number of subjects, especially math. The student disrupted math class at least twice a week and ended up in the principal's office. There, the boy enjoyed the principal's undivided attention. After a scolding, they talked about sports because the principal liked the student and was concerned that he had no male role models. It is easy to spot the function of the classroom disruptions—they always led to (1) escape from math class (negative reinforcement) and (2) one-on-one time with the principal (positive reinforcement after a little bit of reprimanding). The principal, teacher, and Anita developed a way to support the student's positive behaviours in math by getting him some extra tutoring and by giving him time with the principal when he completed math problems instead of when he acted up in class. The new positive behaviours served many of the same functions as the old problem behaviours.

DISCOVERING THE "WHY": FUNCTIONAL BEHAVIOURAL ASSESSMENTS. The process of understanding the "why" of a problem behaviour is known as **functional behavioural assessment (FBA)**. Using a wide range of procedures to map the A-B-Cs of the situation—the antecedents, behaviours, and consequences—teachers try to identify the reason for the behaviour (Barnhill, 2005). Many different procedures might help you determine the functions of a behaviour. You can begin by interviewing students about their behaviours. In one study, students were asked to describe what they did that got them in trouble in school, what happened just before they acted out, and what happened right after. Even though the students were not always sure why they acted out, they seemed to benefit from talking to a concerned adult who was trying to understand their situation, not just reprimand them (Murdock, O'Neill, & Cunningham, 2005). But you will need to do more than just talk to students. You might also talk to parents or other teachers. You could conduct an A-B-C observation with these questions in mind: When and where does the problem behaviour occur? What people or activities are involved? What happens right before—what do others do or say, and what did the target student do or say? What happens right after the behaviour—what did you, other students, or the target student do or say? What does the target student gain or escape from by engaging in the behaviour—what changes after the student acts out? A more structured approach is shown in Figure 7.4—an observation guide for functional behavioural assessment based on a simple ABC analysis. Using this information, the teacher found out that the student acted out whenever the class was transitioning to another activity. The sources of reinforcement for the student are clear, too.

Functional behavioural assessment (FBA) Procedures used to obtain information about antecedents, behaviours, and consequences to determine the reason or function of the behaviour.

## FIGURE 7.4

### A SIMPLE STRUCTURED OBSERVATION GUIDE FOR FUNCTIONAL BEHAVIOURAL ANALYSIS USING THE ABC FRAME

Student Name: Denton R.
Location: Math—Mrs. B
Start time: 1:02

Date: 2/25/2012
Observer: Mr. B.
Stop time: 1:15

| A: ANTECEDENTS | B: BEHAVIOURS | C: CONSEQUENCES |
| --- | --- | --- |
| 1:03 Students get out books and open to begin class. | D. pulls out his cap and puts it on. | Students around D. start laughing and saying "Hey." |
| 1:05 Teacher notices D. and tells him to remove his cap. | D. stands, slowly removes his cap, and bows. | Students applaud. |
| 1:14 Teacher asks D. a question. | D. says, "Man, I don't know." | Another student says, "Yeah, you're stupid." Others laugh. |

Source: Friend, M., & Bursuck, W. D. (2012). Including Students with Special Needs: A Practical Guide for Classroom Teachers, 6th Edition. Reprinted by permission of Pearson Education, Inc., Upper Saddle River, NJ.

The same behaviours may serve different functions for different students. For example, a functional behavioural assessment of three preschool students found that two of the students were aggressive and uncooperative in order to gain the teacher's attention, but the third child actually was trying to escape or avoid teacher attention (Dufrene, Doggett, Henington, & Watson, 2007). With information from a functional behavioural assessment, teachers developed an intervention package, including positive behaviour supports for each child. Two students met specific standards to get the teacher attention they wanted, but the third child got to be "left alone" as long as he met certain standards.

**Watch**
Positive Behaviour Supports

Positive behaviour supports (PBS) Interventions designed to replace problem behaviours with new actions that serve the same purpose for the student.

Precorrection A tool for positive behaviour support that involves identifying the context for a student's misbehaviour, clearly specifying the alternative expected behaviour, modifying the situation to make the problem behaviour less likely, then rehearsing the expected positive behaviours in the new context and providing powerful reinforcers.

POSITIVE BEHAVIOUR SUPPORTS. **Positive behaviour supports (PBS)** are the actual interventions designed to replace problem behaviours with new actions that serve the same purpose for the student. These supports can help students with disabilities succeed in inclusion classrooms. For example, the disruptive behaviour of a 5-year-old boy with an intellectual disability was nearly eliminated in a relatively short time through a PBS intervention that was based on a functional assessment conducted by the regular teaching staff and the special education teacher. The intervention included making sure the tasks assigned were at the right difficulty level, providing assistance with these tasks, teaching the student how to request assistance, and teaching the student how to request a break from assigned work (Soodak & McCarthy, 2006; Umbreit, 1995).

But these approaches are not only for students with special needs. Research shows that disciplinary referrals decrease when the whole school uses these approaches for all students (Lewis, Sugai, & Colvin, 1998). Because about 5% of students account for about 50% of the discipline referrals, it makes sense to develop interventions for those students. Positive behaviour interventions based on functional assessments can reduce these behaviour problems by 80% (Crone & Horner, 2003). At the classroom level, teachers are encouraged to use such preventive strategies as **precorrection**, which involves identifying the context for a student's misbehaviour, clearly specifying the alternative expected behaviour, modifying the situation to make the problem behaviour less likely—for example, providing a cue or moving the student away from tempting distractions—then rehearsing the expected positive behaviours in the new context and providing powerful reinforcers when the positive behaviours occur. There is an emphasis on keeping students engaged, providing a positive focus, consistently enforcing school/class rules, correcting disruptive behaviour proactively, and planning for smooth transitions (Freiberg, 2006).

Positive behaviour supports also can be part of a school-wide program. At the school level, the teachers and administrators can:

- Agree on a common approach for supporting positive behaviours and correcting problems
- Develop a few positively stated, specific behavioural expectations and procedures for teaching these expectations to all students
- Identify a continuum of ways (from small and simple, to more complex and stronger) to acknowledge appropriate behaviours and correct behavioural errors
- Integrate the positive behaviour support procedures with the school's discipline policy

Research on school-wide positive behaviour supports is limited, but results so far have been good. A study comparing middle-school students in a behaviour support program with students outside the program showed that program students reported more positive reinforcement for appropriate behaviour. Disciplinary referrals as well as verbal and physical aggression significantly decreased. In addition, students' perceptions of school safety improved (Metzler, Biglan, Rusby, & Sprague, 2001). Studies of school-wide PBS efforts also indicate decreases in disciplinary referrals (Lewis, Sugai, & Colvin, 1998, 1997; Soodak & McCarthy, 2006).

Even with new approaches such as PBS, in recent years, most behavioural psychologists have found that operant conditioning offers too limited an explanation of learning. As behavioural approaches to learning developed, some researchers added a new element—thinking about behaviour.

## Self-Management

STOP & THINK What area of your life needs some self-management? Write down one behaviour you would like to increase and one behaviour you would like to eliminate. •

As you will see throughout this text, the role of students in managing their own learning is a major concern of psychologists and educators today. This concern is not restricted to any one group or theory. Different areas of research and theory all converge on one important idea: that the responsibility and the ability to learn rest within the student. Students must be active—no one can learn for someone else (Mace, Belfiore, & Hutchinson, 2001; Manning & Payne, 1996; Winne, 1995; Zimmerman & Schunk, 2004). From a behavioural perspective, students may be involved in any or all of the steps in a basic behaviour change program. They may help set goals, observe their own work, keep records of it, and evaluate their own performance. Finally, they can select and deliver reinforcement.

GOAL SETTING. It appears that the goal-setting phase is very important in **self-management** (Reeve, 1996; Schunk, Pintrich, & Meece, 2008). In fact, some research suggests that setting specific goals and making them public may be the critical elements of self-management programs. For example, S. C. Hayes and his colleagues identified university students who had serious problems with studying and taught them how to set specific study goals. Students who set goals and announced them to the experimenters performed significantly better on tests covering the material they were studying than students who set goals privately and never revealed them to anyone (Hayes, Rosenfarb, Wulfert, Munt, Korn, & Zettle, 1985). A review of 20 years of research on self-management found that adults most often set the goals for students (Briesch & Chafouleas, 2009).

Higher standards tend to lead to higher performance (Locke & Latham, 2002). Unfortunately, student-set goals have a tendency to reflect increasingly lower expectations. Teachers can help students maintain high standards by monitoring the goals set and reinforcing high standards.

MONITORING AND EVALUATING PROGRESS. Students may also participate in the monitoring and evaluation phases of a behaviour change program. In fact, these are the elements of self-management that most often are handled by the students themselves (Briesch & Chafouleas, 2009; Mace, Belfiore, & Hutchinson, 2001). Some examples of behaviours

**Self-management** Management of your own behaviour and acceptance of responsibility for your own actions; use of behavioural learning principles to change your own behaviour.

that are appropriate for self-monitoring are the number of assignments completed, time spent practising a skill, number of books read, number of problems correct, and time taken to run a mile. Tasks that must be accomplished without teacher supervision such as homework or private study are also good candidates for self-monitoring. Students keep a chart, diary, or checklist that records the frequency or duration of the behaviours in question. A progress record card can help older students break down assignments into small steps, determine the best sequence for completing the steps, and keep track of daily progress by setting goals for each day. The record card itself serves as a prompt that can be faded out.

Self-evaluation is somewhat more difficult than simple self-recording because it involves making a judgment about quality. Students can evaluate their behaviour with reasonable accuracy, especially if they learn standards for judging a good performance or product. One key to accurate self-evaluation seems to be for the teacher to periodically check students' assessments and give reinforcement for accurate judgments. Older students may learn accurate self-evaluation more readily than younger students. Again, bonus points can be awarded when the teachers' and students' evaluations match (Kaplan, 1991). Self-correction can accompany self-evaluation. Students first evaluate, then alter and improve their work, and finally, compare the improvements to the standards again (Mace, Belfiore, & Hutchinson, 2001).

**SELF-REINFORCEMENT.**   The last step in self-management is **self-reinforcement**. There is some disagreement, however, as to whether this step is actually necessary. Some psychologists believe that setting goals and monitoring progress alone are sufficient and that self-reinforcement adds nothing to the effects (Hayes et al., 1985). Others believe that rewarding yourself for a job well done can lead to higher levels of performance than simply setting goals and keeping track of progress (Bandura, 1986). If you are willing to be tough and really deny yourself something you want until your goals are reached, then perhaps the promise of the reward can provide extra incentive for work. With that in

**Self-reinforcement** Controlling your own reinforcers.

---

## GUIDELINES — FAMILY AND COMMUNITY PARTNERSHIPS

### Student Self-Management

**Introduce the system to parents and students in a positive way.**
*Examples*

1. Invite family participation and stress possible benefits to all family members.
2. Consider starting the program just with volunteers.
3. Describe how you use self-management programs yourself.

**Help families and students establish reachable goals.**
*Examples*

1. Have examples of possible self-management goals for students such as starting homework early in the evening or keeping track of books read.
2. Show families how to post goals and keep track of progress. Encourage everyone in the family to work on a goal.

**Give families ways to record and evaluate their child's progress (or their own).**
*Examples*

1. Divide the work into easily measured steps.
2. Provide models of good work where judgments are more difficult, such as in creative writing.

3. Give families a record form or checklist to keep track of progress.

**Encourage families to check the accuracy of student records from time to time, and help their children to develop forms of self-reinforcement.**
*Examples*

1. Have many checkups when students are first learning, and fewer later.
2. Have siblings check one another's records.
3. Where appropriate, test the skills that students are supposed to be developing at home, and reward students whose self-evaluations match their test performances.
4. Have students brainstorm ideas with their families for rewarding themselves for jobs well done.

---

*For more about self-management, see www.selfmanagementforkids.org.*

mind, you may want to think of some way to reinforce yourself when you finish reading this chapter. A similar approach helped us write chapters in the first place.

Sometimes, teaching students self-management can solve a problem for teachers and provide fringe benefits as well. For example, the coaches of a competitive swim team with members ages 9 to 16 were having difficulty persuading swimmers to maintain high work rates. Then the coaches drew up four charts indicating the training program to be followed by each member and posted the charts near the pool. The swimmers were given the responsibility of recording both their numbers of laps and their completion of each training unit. Because the recording was public, swimmers could see their own and their teammates' progress and keep accurate track of the work units completed. Work output increased by 27%. The coaches also liked the system because swimmers could begin to work immediately without waiting for instructions (McKenzie & Rushall, 1974).

At times, families can be enlisted to help their children develop self-management abilities. Working together, teachers and parents can focus on a few goals and, at the same time, support the growing independence of the students. The *Family and Community Partnerships Guidelines* give some ideas.

# CHALLENGES, CAUTIONS, AND CRITICISMS

In this section we look at some of the challenges to earlier behavioural approaches to learning as well as some important criticisms and cautions.

## Beyond Behaviourism: Bandura's Challenge

Over 35 years ago, Alberta-born psychologist Albert Bandura (1977) noted that the traditional behavioural view of learning had many limitations. Sometimes Bandura has been characterized as a neo-behaviourist, but he has corrected that label:

> At the time of my graduate training, the entire field of psychology was behaviorally oriented with an almost exclusive focus on the phenomenon of learning. But I never really fit the behavioral orthodoxy. At the time virtually all of the theorizing and research centered on learning through the effects of reinforcing outcomes. In my first major program of research, I argued against the primacy of conditioning in favor of observational learning, in which people neither emit responses nor receive reinforcements during the process of learning. (quoted in Pajares, 2008, p. 1)

In his early work on **social learning theory**, which emphasizes learning by observing others, Bandura pointed out two key distinctions between enactive and observational learning and between learning and performance.

ENACTIVE AND OBSERVATIONAL LEARNING. Bandura distinguished between enactive and vicarious or observational learning. **Enactive learning** is learning by doing and experiencing the consequences of your actions. This may sound like operant conditioning all over again, but it is not, and the difference has to do with the role of consequences. Proponents of operant conditioning believe that consequences strengthen or weaken behaviour. In enactive learning, however, consequences are seen as providing information. Bandura emphasized reinforcement does not "stamp in" responses, but instead instills expectations about outcomes—what will happen if I do that behaviour? He explained this position in his early book, *Social Learning Theory* (1977). In other words, our interpretations of the consequences create expectations, influence motivation, and shape beliefs (Schunk, 2012).

Vicarious learning is learning by observing others, so it often is called **observational learning**. People and animals can learn merely by observing another person or animal learn, and this fact challenges the behaviourist idea that cognitive factors are unnecessary in an explanation of learning. If people can learn by watching, they must be focusing their attention, constructing images, remembering, analyzing, and making decisions that affect learning. Thus, much is going on mentally before performance and reinforcement can even take place. Cognitive apprenticeships, discussed in Chapter 10, are examples of vicarious learning—learning by observing others.

**Social learning theory** Theory that emphasizes learning through observation of others.

**Enactive learning** Learning by doing and experiencing the consequences of your actions.

**Observational learning** Learning by observation and imitation of others—vicarious learning.

**OBSERVATIONAL LEARNING** Observational theories of learning consider the importance of learning by doing and learning by observing others.

**LEARNING AND PERFORMANCE.** To explain some limitations of the behavioural model, Bandura also distinguished between the acquisition of knowledge (learning) and the observable performance based on that knowledge (behaviour). In other words, Bandura suggested that we all may know more than we show. An example is found in one of Bandura's early studies (1965). Preschool children saw a film of a model kicking and punching an inflatable "Bobo" doll. One group saw the model rewarded for the aggression, another group saw the model punished, and a third group observed no consequences. When they were moved to a room with the Bobo doll, the children who had seen the punching and kicking reinforced on the film were the most aggressive toward the doll. Those who had seen the attacks punished were the least aggressive. But when the children were promised rewards for imitating the model's aggression, all of them demonstrated that they had learned the behaviour.

Thus, incentives can affect performance. Even though learning may have occurred, it may not be demonstrated until the situation is appropriate or there are incentives to perform. This might explain why some students don't perform "bad behaviours" such as swearing or smoking that they all see modelled by adults, peers, and the media. Personal consequences may discourage them from performing the behaviours. In other examples, children may have learned how to write the alphabet, but perform badly because their fine motor coordination is limited, or they may have learned how to simplify fractions, but perform badly on a test because they are anxious. In these cases, their performance is not an indication of their learning.

Bandura provided an alternative to the behavioural theories of the time. His work continued as he developed *social cognitive theory*—one of the most influential theories of learning and motivation in educational psychology today. We will devote Chapter 11 to a closer look at social cognitive theory.

## Criticisms of Behavioural Methods

This chapter gave you an overview of several strategies for changing classroom behaviour. However, you should be aware that these strategies are tools that can be used either responsibly or irresponsibly. What, then, are some issues you should keep in mind?

**STOP & THINK** During your job interview, the principal asks, "A teacher last year got in trouble for bribing his students with homework exemptions to get them to behave in class. What do you think about using rewards and punishments in teaching?" What will you say? •

While you think about your answer to this question, look at the *Point/Counterpoint* on "Should Students Be Rewarded for Learning?" to see two different perspectives. Properly used, the strategies in this chapter can be effective tools to help students learn academically and grow in self-sufficiency. Effective tools, however, do not automatically produce excellent work, and behavioural strategies are often implemented haphazardly, inconsistently, incorrectly, or superficially (Landrum & Kauffman, 2006). The indiscriminate use of even the best tools can lead to difficulties.

Some psychologists fear that rewarding students for all learning will cause them to lose interest in learning for its own sake (Deci, 1975; Deci & Ryan, 1985; Kohn, 1993, 1996b; Lepper & Greene, 1978; Lepper, Keavney, & Drake, 1996; Ryan & Deci, 1996). Studies have suggested that using reward programs with students who are already interested in the subject matter may, in fact, cause students to be less interested in the subject

## POINT/COUNTERPOINT  Should Students Be Rewarded for Learning?

For years, educators and psychologists have debated whether students should be rewarded for schoolwork and academic accomplishments. In the early 1990s, Paul Chance and Alfie Kohn exchanged opinions in several issues of *Phi Delta Kappan* (March 1991; November 1992; June 1993). Then, Judy Cameron and W. David Pierce (1996) of the University of Alberta published an article on reinforcement in the *Review of Educational Research* that precipitated extensive criticisms and rebuttals in the same journal from Mark Lepper, Mark Keavney, Michael Drake, Alfie Kohn, Richard Ryan, and Edward Deci (Kohn, 1996; Lepper, Keavney, & Drake, 1996; Ryan & Deci, 1996). Many of the same people exchanged opinions in the November 1999 issue of *Psychological Bulletin* (Deci, Koestner, & Ryan, 1999; Eisenberg, Pierce, & Cameron, J., 1999). What are the arguments?

### POINT

▶ **Students are punished by rewards.** Alfie Kohn (1993) argues, "Applied behaviorism, which amounts to saying, 'do this and you'll get that,' is essentially a technique for controlling people. In the classroom it is a way of doing things to children rather than working *with* them" (p. 784). He contends that rewards are ineffective because when the praise and prizes stop, the behaviours stop, too. After analyzing 128 studies of extrinsic rewards, Edward Deci, Richard Koestner, and Richard Ryan (1999) concluded that "tangible rewards tend to have a substantial effect on intrinsic motivation, with the limiting conditions we have specified. Even when tangible rewards are offered as indicators of good performance, they typically decrease intrinsic motivation for interesting activities" (pp. 658–659).

The problem with rewards does not stop here. According to Kohn, rewarding students for learning actually makes them less interested in the material:

*All of this means that getting children to think about learning as a way to receive a sticker, a gold star, or a grade—or even worse, to get money or a toy for a grade, which amounts to an extrinsic motivator for an extrinsic motivator—is likely to turn learning from an end into a means. Learning becomes something that must be gotten through in order to receive the reward. Take the depressingly pervasive program by which children receive certificates for pizzas when they have read a certain number of books. John Nicholls of the University of Illinois comments, only half in jest, that the likely consequence of this program is "a lot of fat kids who don't like to read." (p. 785)*

*Source: From Chance, P., (1993). Sticking Up for Rewards. Phi Delta Kappan, pp. 787–790. Reprinted with permission of Phi Delta Kappan and the author. From Kohn, A. (1993). Rewards versus Learning: A Response to Paul Chance, Phi Delta Kappan, pp. 783, 785. Reprinted from Phi Delta Kappan with the author's permission.*

### COUNTERPOINT

▶ **Learning should be rewarding.** According to Paul Chance (1993):

*Behavioral psychologists in particular emphasize that we learn by acting on our environment. As B. F. Skinner put it: "[People] act on the world, and change it, and are changed in turn by the consequences of their actions." Skinner, unlike Kohn, understood that people learn best in a responsive environment. Teachers who praise or otherwise reward student performance provide such an environment . . . . If it is immoral to let students know they have answered questions correctly, to pat students on the back for a good effort, to show joy at a student's understanding of a concept, or to recognize the achievement of a goal by providing a gold star or a certificate—if this is immoral, then count me a sinner. (p. 788)*

Do rewards undermine interest? In their review of research, Cameron and Pierce (1994) concluded, "When tangible rewards (e.g., gold star, money) are offered contingent on performance on a task [not just on participation] or are delivered unexpectedly, intrinsic motivation is maintained" (p. 49). In a later review of research, Eisenberg, Pierce, and Cameron (1999) added, "Reward procedures requiring specific high task performance convey a task's personal or social significance, increasing intrinsic motivation" (p. 677). Even psychologists such as Edward Deci and Mark Lepper who suggest that rewards might undermine intrinsic motivation agree that rewards can also be used positively. When rewards provide students with information about their growing mastery of a subject or when the rewards show appreciation for a job well done, then the rewards bolster confidence and make the task more interesting to the students, especially students who lacked ability or interest in the task initially. Nothing succeeds like success. As Chance points out, if students master reading or mathematics with the support of rewards, they will not forget what they have learned when the praise stops. Would they have learned without the rewards? Some would, but some might not. Would you continue working for a company that didn't pay you, even though you liked the work? Will freelance writer Alfie Kohn, for that matter, lose interest in writing because he gets paid fees and royalties?

when the reward program ends, as you saw in the *Point/Counterpoint*. In addition, there is some evidence that praising students for being intelligent when they succeed can undermine their motivation if they do not perform as well the next time. After they fail, students who had been praised for being smart may be less persistent and enjoy the task less compared to students who had been praised earlier for working hard (Mueller & Dweck, 1998).

*"Hey wait a minute! You're cleaning erasers as a punishment? I'm cleaning them as a reward!"*

© 1991 Tony Saltzmann. Reprinted by permission.

Just as you must take into account the effects of a reward system on the individual, you must also consider its impact on other students. Using a reward program or giving one student increased attention may have a detrimental effect on the other students in the classroom. Is it possible that other students will learn to be "bad" in order to be included in the reward program? Most of the evidence on this question suggests that using individual adaptations such as reward programs does not have any adverse effects on students who are not participating if the teacher believes in the program and explains the reasons for using it to the nonparticipating students. After interviewing 98 students in grades 1 through 6, Cindy Fulk and Paula Smith (1995) concluded, "Teachers may be more concerned about equal treatment of students than students are" (p. 416). If the conduct of some students does seem to deteriorate when their peers are involved in special programs, many of the same procedures discussed in this chapter should help them return to previous levels of appropriate behaviour (Chance, 1992, 1993).

## Ethical Issues

The ethical questions related to the use of the strategies described in this chapter are similar to those raised by any process that seeks to influence people. What are the goals? How do these goals fit with those of the school as a whole? What effect will a strategy have on the individuals involved? Is too much control being given to the teacher, or to a majority?

GOALS.   The strategies described in this chapter could be applied exclusively to teaching students to sit still, raise their hands before speaking, and remain silent at all other times (Winett & Winkler, 1972). This certainly would be an unethical use of the techniques. It is true that a teacher may need to establish some organization and order, but stopping with improvements in conduct will not ensure academic learning. On the other hand, in some situations, reinforcing academic skills may lead to improvements in conduct. Whenever possible, emphasis should be placed on academic learning. Academic improvements generalize to other situations more successfully than do changes in classroom conduct.

STRATEGIES.   Punishment can have negative side effects: It can serve as a model for aggressive responses, and it can encourage negative emotional reactions. Punishment is unnecessary and even unethical when positive approaches, which have fewer potential dangers, might work as well. When simpler, less-restrictive procedures fail, then more complicated procedures should be tried.

A second consideration in the selection of a strategy is the impact of the strategy on the individual student. For example, some teachers arrange for students to be rewarded at home with a gift or special activities based on good work in school. But if a student has a history of being severely punished at home for bad reports from school, a home-based reinforcement program might be very harmful to that student. Reports of unsatisfactory progress at school could lead to increased abuse at home.

## Behavioural Approaches: Lessons for Teachers

There is great diversity in the learning histories of students. Every person in your class will come to you with different fears and anxieties. Some students may be terrified of speaking in public or of failing at competitive sports. Others will be anxious around various animals. Different activities or objects will serve as reinforcers for some students, but not others. Some students will work for the promise of good grades—others couldn't care less. All of your students will have learned different behaviours in their homes, neighbourhoods, churches, or communities.

The research and theories presented in this chapter should help you understand how the learning histories of your students might have taught them to respond automatically to tests with sweaty palms and racing hearts—possible classical conditioning at work. Their learning histories might have included being reinforced for persistence, or for whining—operant conditioning at work. The chance to work in a group may be a reinforcer for some students and a punisher for others. Remember, what works for one student may not be right for another. And students can get "too much of a good thing"; reinforcers can lose their potency if they are overused.

Even though your students will have many different learning histories, there are some convergences—principles that apply to all people:

1. No one eagerly repeats behaviours that have been punished or ignored. Without some sense of progress, it is difficult to persist.
2. When actions lead to consequences that are positive for the person involved, those actions are likely to be repeated.
3. Teachers often fail to use reinforcement to recognize appropriate behaviour; they respond instead to inappropriate behaviours, sometimes providing reinforcing attention in the process.
4. To be effective, praise must be a sincere recognition of a real accomplishment.
5. Whatever their current level of functioning, students can learn to be more self-managing.

## ▼ SUMMARY

Irina_QQQ/Shutterstock

### Understanding Learning (pp. 226–228)

**What is learning?** Although theorists disagree about the definition of learning, most would agree that learning occurs when experience causes a change in a person's knowledge or behaviour. Changes simply caused by maturation, illness, fatigue, or hunger are excluded from a general definition of learning. Behavioural theorists emphasize the role of environmental stimuli in learning and focus on behaviour—observable responses. Behavioural learning processes include contiguity learning, classical conditioning, operant conditioning, and observational learning.

### Early Explanations of Learning: Contiguity and Classical Conditioning (pp. 228–230)

**How does a neutral stimulus become a conditioned stimulus?** In classical conditioning, which was discovered by Pavlov, a previously neutral stimulus is repeatedly paired with a stimulus that evokes an emotional or physiological response. Later, the previously neutral stimulus alone evokes the response—that is, the neutral stimulus is conditioned to bring forth a conditioned response. The neutral stimulus has become a conditioned stimulus.

**What are some everyday examples of classical conditioning?** Here are a few; add your own: salivating when you smell your favourite foods, tension when you hear a dentist's drill, nervousness when you step on stage.

### Operant Conditioning: Trying New Responses (pp. 230–236)

**What defines a consequence as a reinforcer? As a punisher?** According to Skinner's concept of operant conditioning, people learn through the effects of their deliberate responses. For an individual, the effects of consequences following an action may serve as either reinforcers or punishers. A consequence is defined as a reinforcer if it strengthens or maintains the response that brought it about, but as a punishment if it decreases or suppresses the response that brought it about.

**Negative reinforcement is often confused with punishment. How are they different?** The process of reinforcement (positive or negative) always involves strengthening behaviour. The teacher strengthens (reinforces) desired behaviours by removing something aversive as soon as the desired behaviours occur. Because the consequence involves removing or "subtracting" a stimulus, the reinforcement is negative. Punishment, on the other hand, involves decreasing or suppressing behaviour. A behaviour followed by a "punisher" is less likely to be repeated in similar situations in the future.

**How can you encourage persistence in a behaviour?** Ratio schedules (based on the number of responses) encourage higher rates of response, and variable schedules (based on varying numbers of responses or varying time intervals) encourage persistence of responses.

**What is the difference between a cue and a prompt?** A cue is an antecedent stimulus just before a particular behaviour is to take place. A prompt is an additional cue following the first cue. Make sure the environmental stimulus that you want to become a cue occurs immediately before the prompt you are using, so students will learn to respond to the cue and not rely only on the prompt. Then, fade the prompt as soon as possible so students do not become dependent on it.

### Applied Behaviour Analysis (pp. 236–243)

**What are the steps in applied behaviour analysis?** The steps are: (1) Clearly specify the behaviour to be changed and note the current level; (2) plan a specific intervention using antecedents, consequences, or both; and (3) keep track of the results, and modify the plan if necessary.

**How can the Premack principle help you identify reinforcers?** The Premack principle states that a high-frequency behaviour (a preferred activity) can be an effective reinforcer for a low-frequency behaviour (a less-preferred activity). The best way to determine appropriate reinforcers for your students may be to watch what they do in their free time. For most students, talking, moving around the room, sitting near a friend, being exempt from assignments or tests, computer time, or playing games are preferred activities.

**When is shaping an appropriate approach?** Shaping helps students develop new responses a little at a time, so it is useful for building complex skills, working toward difficult goals, and increasing persistence, endurance, accuracy, or speed. Because shaping is a time-consuming process, however, it should not be used if success can be attained through simpler methods such as cueing.

**What are some cautions in using punishment?** Punishment in and of itself does not lead to any positive behaviour or compassion for others, and it may interfere with developing caring relationships with students. Thus, whenever you consider the use of punishment, you should make it part of a two-pronged attack. First, carry out the punishment and suppress the undesirable behaviour. Second, make clear what the student should be doing instead and provide reinforcement for those desirable actions. Thus, while the problem behaviours are being suppressed, positive alternative responses are being strengthened.

### Putting It All Together: Behavioural Approaches to Teaching and Management (pp. 243–251)

**Describe the managerial strategies of group consequences, contingency contracts, and token programs.** Using group consequences involves basing reinforcement for the whole class on the behaviour of the whole class. In a contingency contract program, the teacher draws up an individual contract with each student, describing exactly what the student must do to earn a particular privilege or reward. In token programs, students earn tokens (points, checks, holes punched in a card, chips, etc.) for both academic work and positive classroom behaviour. Periodically, the students exchange the tokens they have earned for some desired reward. A teacher must use these programs with caution, emphasizing learning and not just "good" behaviour.

**How can functional behavioural assessment and positive behaviour supports be used to improve student behaviours?** In doing a functional behavioural assessment, a teacher studies the antecedents and consequences of problem behaviours to determine the reason or function of the behaviour. Then, positive behaviour supports are designed to replace problem behaviours with new

actions that serve the same purpose for the student, but do not have the same problems.

**What are the steps in self-management?** Students can apply behaviour analysis on their own to manage their own behaviour. Teachers can encourage the development of self-management skills by allowing students to participate in setting goals, keeping track of progress, evaluating accomplishments, and selecting and giving their own reinforcers.

### Challenges, Cautions, and Criticisms (pp. 251–255)

**What was Bandura's challenge to behavioural learning?** Bandura believed that the traditional behavioural view of learning had many limitations. Even though he was educated during a time when behavioural learning was dominant, he never really fit the behavioural orthodoxy. He argued in favour of observational learning, in which people neither emit responses nor receive reinforcements during the process of learning.

**Distinguish between enactive and vicarious (observational) learning.** Enactive learning is learning by doing and experiencing the consequences of your actions. Vicarious (observational) learning is learning by observing, which challenges the behaviourist idea that cognitive factors are unnecessary in an explanation of learning. Much is going on mentally before performance and reinforcement can even take place. In behavioural views, reinforcement and punishment directly affect behaviour. In social learning theory, seeing another person, a model, reinforced or punished can have similar effects on the observer's behaviour. Social cognitive theory expanded social learning theory to include cognitive factors such as beliefs, expectations, and perceptions of self.

**Distinguish between learning and performance.** Social learning theory recognized the differences between learning and performance—in other words, we all may know more than we show. You can learn something, but not perform it until the situation and incentives are right. Even though learning may have occurred, it may not be demonstrated until the situation is appropriate or there are incentives to perform.

**What are the main criticisms of behavioural approaches?** The misuse or abuse of behavioural learning methods is unethical. Critics of behavioural methods also point out the danger that reinforcement could decrease interest in learning by overemphasizing rewards and could have a negative impact on other students. Teachers can use behavioural learning principles appropriately and ethically.

## ▼ WHAT WOULD THEY DO?

## TEACHERS' CASEBOOK: Out of Control

Here is how some expert teachers responded to the situation described at the beginning of the chapter about the disruptive student.

**ALICIA CUZNER**
Astolot Educational Centre, Ottawa, ON

**BEING CONSISTENT**
To working toward resolving this issue, I would first make a list of my expectations for the classroom. In doing so, I would know my own specific goals for the class. I would then share these expectations

with the students, and class rules would be posted somewhere in the classroom. These rules would be written in positive language and would describe desired behaviours. For example, rather than saying, "No talking," the rule might say, "Listen to others when they are speaking." This strategy will help students understand what I am striving for.

I would also establish duties and responsibilities for every student. Students who misbehave may benefit from specific classroom responsibilities because it may give them a sense of belonging. This could include vacuuming after class, wiping the tables, cleaning the whiteboard, or taking attendance. By taking on the tasks that help to make a class function, students will feel as though they are part of a community and that their presence matters.

I would be consistent with my rules and consequences, while also using positive reinforcement to encourage desired behaviours. I would give praise when students help one another, use words to describe how they're feeling, or follow the rules. I would also be consistent about applying the consequences to students who do not follow the rules. I would place a chair outside my room door, away from distractions or influences, where students can sit when they disrupt the class. This strategy has worked for me in the past because the student is situated close enough to the classroom that, after the student spends a few minutes sitting on the chair, I can speak to him or her about the undesirable behaviour and how to earn his or her way back into the classroom. Often, students need to be removed from the classroom only briefly to calm down, and then they can rejoin the class after they have regained control of their emotions. Thanks in part to repetition, students begin to understand which actions are desirable and which are not tolerated. When it comes to a misbehaving student, it is essential to remove him or her from the room immediately so that the undesired behaviour can be defused quickly.

### NICOLE THERRIEN
Huronia Centennial Elementary School, Elmvale, ON

With the range of behaviours and diversity of students within any class, class management is complex and requires a multifaceted approach. Students are sensitive to energy and excitement, so conveying a love for learning with students gets me great mileage. I would begin by demonstrating my genuine enthusiasm for working with this group of students and state that *the main goal for all of us is to learn together*. All actions within the class need to contribute to that goal. Using this as the trunk of the tree, the branches (self-regulation, collaboration, initiative, independent work, responsibility, organization) then become natural extensions in which I involve the students to determine what success looks like. I remind them repeatedly to reflect on the question, "How is what I am doing right now contributing to our learning together?"

With the main purpose for our time together established, next comes the task of setting up the students for success. In the case of attendance and instructions taking too much time, consider turning these areas into opportunities for whole-class competition. Establish an attendance game and involve the students in setting a realistic time this should take. For every minute they shave off toward that time, offer a reward. I'm in favour of allowing the students to choose their reward from options that don't involve food and usually involve exercise, outdoor time, social time, or self-directed time.

Next begins the journey of allowing students a way to demonstrate their strengths. Any inventory of skills, intelligences, and learning preferences can be used. However, what you do with the information is most important. I make a point of displaying the results and conference briefly with the students. I relate this to everyday classroom scenarios as often as possible (e.g., using math manipulatives is ideal for the visual and kinaesthetic learner). I let them know that over the course of any block of learning time, they will have the opportunity to shine because a variety of learning scenarios will be available. Also, I explain that I understand that some activities and times of the day will be a challenge for them. From then on, it becomes standard that I set the bar high any chance I can for students who struggle the most with the success criteria established. For example, for kinaesthetic and interpersonal learners, I point out that the four-corners activity is tailored for them and that I can't wait to hear their contributions. Amazingly, when students believe that many opportunities during the school day are tailored to them, they shine.

Martin Capek/Shutterstock

# COGNITIVE VIEWS OF LEARNING

▶ **TEACHERS' CASEBOOK:** Remembering the Basics

The students in your senior history classes seem to equate understanding with memorizing. They prepare for each unit test by memorizing the exact words of the textbook. Even the best students seem to think that the use of flash cards is the only learning strategy possible. In fact, when you try to encourage students to think about history by reading some original sources, debating issues in class, or examining art and music from the time period you are studying, they rebel. "Will this be on the test?" "Why are we looking at these pictures—will we have to know who painted them and when?" "What's this got to do with history?" Even the students who participate in the debates seem to use words and phrases straight from the textbook without knowing what they are saying.

**CRITICAL THINKING**

- What are these students' beliefs and expectations, and how do these affect their learning?

- Why do you think they insist on using the rote memory approach?

- How would you use what the students already know to help them learn in better, more meaningful ways?

- How will these issues affect the grade levels you will teach?

## OVERVIEW AND OBJECTIVES

We turn from behavioural theories of learning to the cognitive perspective in this chapter. This means a shift from "viewing the learners and their behaviours as products of incoming environmental stimuli" to seeing the learners as "sources of plans, intentions, goals, ideas, memories, and emotions actively used to attend to, select, and construct meaning from stimuli and knowledge from experience" (Wittrock, 1982, pp. 1–2). We will begin with a discussion of the general cognitive approach to learning and memory and the importance of knowledge in learning. To understand memory, we will consider early information processing models of memory, along with the recent improvements on those models suggested by findings in the interdisciplinary fields of cognitive science. These new models point to key processes of working memory, cognitive load, and knowledge. Then, we turn to ideas about how teachers can help their students become more knowledgeable. By the time you have completed this chapter, you should be able to:

8.1 Differentiate between behavioural and cognitive views of learning.

8.2 Explain early information processing models of memory and recent cognitive science models, including working memory and cognitive load theory.

8.3 Discuss the role of different kinds of knowledge in learning and remembering.

8.4 Describe the processes involved in storing and retrieving different types of information from long-term memory.

8.5 Identify some developmental and individual differences in memory.

8.6 Describe processes and strategies involved in becoming knowledgeable.

## ELEMENTS OF THE COGNITIVE PERSPECTIVE

The cognitive perspective is both the oldest and one of the youngest members of the psychological community. It is old because discussions of the nature of knowledge, the value of reason, and the contents of the mind date back at least to the ancient Greek philosophers (Gluck, Mercado, & Myers, 2008). From the late 1800s until several decades ago, however, cognitive studies fell from favour and behaviourism thrived. Today, there is renewed interest in learning, thinking, and problem solving. The focus is the scientific study of memory and cognition—broadly defined as "the mental events and knowledge we use when we recognize an object, remember a name, have an idea, understand a sentence, or solve a problem" (Ashcraft & Radvansky, 2010, p. 2). The emphasis is on everyday thinking, even though the study of abnormal thinking (as in schizophrenia) can help us understand cognition better at times. The **cognitive view of learning** is a generally agreed-upon philosophical orientation that views learning as an active mental process of acquiring, remembering and using knowledge. Most importantly, cognitive psychologists assume that mental processes exist, that they can be studied scientifically, and that humans are active information processors.

In the past few years, the study of memory and cognition has become interdisciplinary and often is called **cognitive science**—the study of thinking, language, and, increasingly, the brain. Cognitive science views cognition as the operation of a very complex but coordinated system of multiple memory components interacting rapidly and simultaneously (Ashcraft & Radvansky, 2010). In Chapter 10 we will look more closely at cognitive science, or as it is sometimes called even more broadly, *the learning sciences*.

### Comparing Cognitive and Behavioural Views

The cognitive and behavioural views differ in their assumptions about what is learned. According to the cognitive view, knowledge and strategies are learned, then changes in

**Cognitive view of learning** A general approach that views learning as an active mental process of acquiring, remembering, and using knowledge.

**Cognitive science** The interdisciplinary study of thinking, language, intelligence, knowledge creation, and the brain.

 **Listen**
Comparing Cognitive and Behavioural Views

259

Juice Images/Alamy

**COGNITIVE VIEWS** These students are literally building their understanding as they try to construct models and solve problems.

knowledge and strategies make changes in behaviour possible. According to the behavioural view, the new behaviours themselves are learned. Both behavioural and cognitive theorists believe reinforcement is important in learning, but for different reasons. The strict behaviourist maintains that reinforcement strengthens responses; cognitive theorists perceive reinforcement as a source of information about what is likely to happen if behaviours are repeated or changed.

**VIEWS OF LEARNING.** In the cognitive view, learning is extending and transforming the understanding we already have, not simply writing associations on the blank slates of our brains (Greeno, Collins, & Resnick, 1996). Instead of being passively influenced by environmental events, people actively choose, practise, pay attention, ignore, reflect, and make many other decisions as they pursue goals. Older cognitive views emphasized the acquisition of knowledge, but newer approaches stress its construction (Anderson, Reder, & Simon, 1996; Mayer, 2011).

**GOALS.** The goal of behavioural researchers is to identify a few general laws of learning that apply to all higher organisms—including humans, regardless of age, intelligence, or other individual differences. Cognitive psychologists, on the other hand, study a wide range of learning situations. Because of their focus on individual and developmental differences in cognition, they have not been as concerned with general laws of learning. This is one of the reasons that there is no single cognitive model or theory of learning that represents the entire field.

## The Brain and Cognitive Learning

The brain continues to change throughout life, and learning affects those changes. One study found that part of the brain hippocampus is larger in taxi drivers than in other car drivers, and this increased size is related to the length of time the person has been driving a taxi. The explanation is that part of the brain grew larger because it was used more in navigating around the city (Maguire et al., 2000). In another study, when people learned to read musical notations, they developed an automatic response to just looking at a sheet of music—they read it without being told to, and their motor cortex prepared to play the notes (Stewart, Henson, Kampe, Walsh, Turner, & Frith, 2003). Observing and visualizing also support learning because the brain automatically responds. For example, when observing someone perform an action, the area of the observer's brain that would be involved in that action is activated just by watching—the brain rehearses the action it sees another person perform. These areas of the brain that fire both during perception of an action and when performing the action have been called *mirror neurons* in monkeys (where they were first discovered) and **mirror systems** in humans because the activated areas in humans contain millions of neurons (Ehrenfeld, 2011; Rizzolatti, Fadiga, Gallese, & Fogassi, 1996). When you actually look at an object, a certain area of the brain is activated. Just mentally visualizing the object activates at least two-thirds of the same area of the brain (Ganis, Thompson, & Kosslyn, 2004).

Clearly the brain is involved whenever learning takes place. As Blakemore and Frith (2005) note in their book on lessons for education from research in neuroscience: "We start with the idea that the brain has evolved to educate and be educated, often instinctively and effortlessly" (p. 459). The brain shapes and is shaped by cognitive processing activities. Even at the neural level, new synapses are formed a few minutes after a child is unsuccessful at processing information. So unsuccessful processing triggers development, too (Siegler, 2004).

Because of the continuing development of the brain, particularly as the prefrontal cortex matures, children become more able to integrate past and present experiences. An infant or a toddler reacts impulsively, but the 8-year-old can remember and reflect. Analysis, control, abstraction, memory space, speed of processing, and interconnection of information make self-regulation and continuing cognitive development possible. Many

**Mirror systems** Areas of the brain that fire both during perception of an action by someone else and when performing the action.

of these developmental and brain changes involve knowledge—a key element in the cognitive perspective.

## The Importance of Knowledge in Cognition

STOP & THINK Quickly, list 10 terms that pertain to educational psychology. Now list 10 terms that relate to ceramic engineering •

Unless you are studying ceramic engineering, it probably took you longer to list 10 terms from that field than from educational psychology. Or, maybe you're still asking, "What is ceramic engineering anyway?" Your answers depend on your knowledge. (Hint: Think fibre optics, ceramic teeth and bones, ceramic semi-conductors for computers, heat-shielding tiles for space shuttles.)

Knowledge and knowing are the outcomes of learning. When we learn the history of cognitive psychology, the products of ceramic engineering, or the rules of tennis, we know something new. However, knowing is more than the end product of previous learning; it also guides new learning. (The cognitive approach suggests that one of the most important elements in the learning process is what the individual brings to new learning situations.) What we already know is the foundation and frame for constructing all future learning. Knowledge determines to a great extent what we will pay attention to, perceive, learn, remember, and forget (Bransford, Brown, & Cocking, 2000; Sawyer, 2006b). For example, compared to grade 4 students with little knowledge of soccer, grade 4 students who were soccer experts learned and remembered far more new soccer terms, even though the abilities of the two groups to learn and remember nonsoccer terms were the same. The difference was the soccer experts used their soccer knowledge to organize and cluster the soccer terms, which helped them remember (Schneider & Bjorklund, 1992).

GENERAL AND SPECIFIC KNOWLEDGE.   Knowledge in the cognitive perspective includes both subject-specific understandings (math, history, soccer, etc.) and general cognitive skills such as planning, solving problems, and comprehending language (Greeno, Collins, & Resnick, 1996). So, there are different kinds of knowledge. Some is **domain-specific knowledge** that pertains to a particular task or subject. For example, knowing that the shortstop plays between second and third base is specific to the domain of baseball. Some knowledge, on the other hand, is general—it applies to many different situations. For example, **general knowledge** about how to read or use a computer or focus attention is useful both in and out of school.

Of course, there is no absolute line between general and domain-specific knowledge. When you were first learning to read, you may have studied specific facts about the sounds of letters. At that time, knowledge about letter sounds was specific to the domain of reading. But now you can use both knowledge about letter sounds and the ability to read in more general ways (Bruning, Schraw, & Norby, 2011; Schunk, 2008). And learning in school generally requires both domain-specific and domain-general knowledge and skills. For example, Steven Hecht and Kevin Vagi (2010) followed students from grades 4 through 5 as the students were learning about fractions. Difficulty mastering fractions was associated both with lack of specific knowledge about fractions and lack of general knowledge about how to behave and pay attention in class.

To have knowledge of something is to remember it over time and to be able to find it when you need it. Cognitive psychologists have studied memory extensively and have learned more about knowledge in the process. Let's see what they have learned.

## COGNITIVE VIEWS OF MEMORY

There are a number of theories of memory, but the most common are the information processing explanations (Ashcraft & Radvansky, 2010; Bruning, Schraw, Norby, 2011; Sternberg & Sternberg, 2012). We will use this well-researched framework for examining learning and memory.

**Domain-specific knowledge** Information that is useful in a particular situation or that applies mainly to one specific topic.

**General knowledge** Information that is useful in many different kinds of tasks; information that applies to many situations.

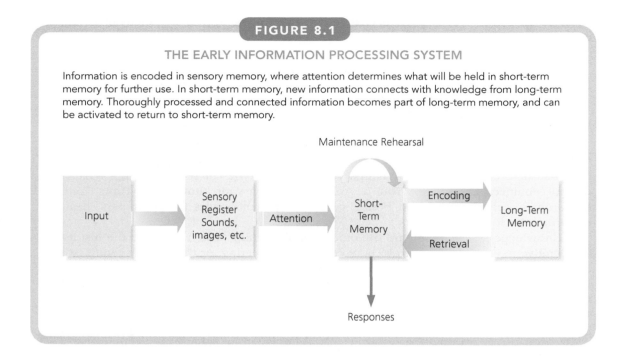

**FIGURE 8.1**

THE EARLY INFORMATION PROCESSING SYSTEM

Information is encoded in sensory memory, where attention determines what will be held in short-term memory for further use. In short-term memory, new information connects with knowledge from long-term memory. Thoroughly processed and connected information becomes part of long-term memory, and can be activated to return to short-term memory.

Early **information processing** views of memory used the computer as a model. Like the computer, the human mind takes in information, performs operations on it to change its form and content, stores the information, retrieves it when needed, and generates responses to it. But for most cognitive psychologists, the computer model is only a metaphor for human mental activity. Figure 8.1 is a schematic representation of an early information processing model of memory (Atkinson & Shiffrin, 1968).

According to this model, stimuli from the environment (input) flow into the sensory registers, one for each sensing modality (seeing, hearing, tasting, etc.). From there, some information is encoded and moves to short-term memory. Short-term memory holds information very briefly, combines it with information from long-term memory, and, with enough effort, moves some information into long-term memory storage. Short-term memory is also responsible for generating responses or output.

This model proved helpful, but also incomplete. For example, in the model, information moved through the system mostly in one way, from sensory registers to long-term memory, but research indicated many more interactions and connections among the processes. The model could not explain how out-of-awareness memories or knowledge could influence learning or how several cognitive processes could happen simultaneously—like many small computers operating in parallel. A more recent cognitive science information processing model retains some of the features of the old approach, but emphasizes the role of working memory, attention, and the interactions among the elements of the system, as shown in Figure 8.2, which is based on several sources (Ashcraft & Radvansky, 2010; Bruning, Schraw, & Norby, 2011; Sternberg & Sternberg, 2012).

In order to understand this model, let's examine each element more carefully.

**Information processing** The human mind's activity of taking in, storing, and using information.

**Sensory memory** System that holds sensory information very briefly.

## Sensory Memory

Stimuli from the environment (sights, sounds, smells, etc.) constantly bombard our body's mechanisms for seeing, hearing, tasting, smelling, and feeling.(**Sensory memory** is the initial processing that transforms these incoming stimuli into information so we can make sense of them. Other names for the sensory memory are *sensory buffer, iconic memory* (for images), and *echoic memory* (for sounds).)

## A RECENT VERSION OF THE INFORMATION PROCESSING SYSTEM

Information is encoded in sensory memory, where perception and attention determine what will be held in working memory for further use. In working memory, executive processes manage the flow of information and integrate new information with knowledge from long-term memory. Thoroughly processed and connected information becomes part of long-term memory, and when activated again, becomes part of working memory. Implicit memories are formed without conscious effort. All three elements of the system interact with each other to guide perception; represent, organize, and interpret information; apply and modify propositions, concepts, images, schemas, and strategies; construct knowledge; and solve problems. Attention has a role in all three memory processes and in the interactions among them.

**CAPACITY, DURATION, AND CONTENTS OF SENSORY MEMORY.** The capacity of sensory memory is very large, and it can take in more information than we can possibly handle at once. But this vast amount of sensory information is fragile in duration. It lasts less than three seconds.

---

**STOP & THINK** Wave a pencil (or your finger) back and forth before your eyes while you stare straight ahead. What exactly do you see? Pinch your arm and let go. What do you feel just after you let go? •

---

You just experienced this brief holding of sensory information in your own sensory memory. You could see a trace of the pencil after the actual stimulus had been removed and feel the pinch after you let go. The sensory memory held information about the stimuli very briefly after the actual stimulus had left (Lindsay & Norman, 1977).

The information content of sensory memory resembles the sensations from the original stimulus. Visual sensations are coded briefly as images, almost like photographs.

Auditory sensations are coded as sound patterns, similar to echoes. It may be that the other senses also have their own codes. Thus, for a second or so, a wealth of data from sensory experience remains intact. In these moments, we have a chance to select and organize information for further processing. Perception and attention are critical at this stage.

PERCEPTION.    The process of detecting a stimulus and assigning meaning to it is called **perception**. This meaning is constructed based on both physical representations from the world and our existing knowledge. For example, consider these marks: **I3**. If asked what the letter is, you would say "B." If asked what the number is, you would say "13." The actual marks remain the same; their meaning changes in keeping with your expectation to recognize a letter or a number and your knowledge of what Arabic numbers and the Latin alphabet look like. To a child without appropriate knowledge, the marks would probably be meaningless. Context matters, too. In the series **A I3 C**, I3 is a *letter*, but in the series **12 I3 14,** it is a *number* (Bruning, Schraw, Norby, 2011).

The process from sensory input to recognized objects probably goes through several stages. In the first phase, features are extracted or analyzed to give a rough sketch. This feature analysis has been called *data-driven* or **bottom-up processing** because the stimulus must be analyzed into features or components and assembled into a meaningful pattern "from the bottom up." For example, a capital letter A consists of two relatively straight lines joined at a 45-degree angle and a horizontal line through the middle. Whenever we see these features, or anything close enough, including A, *A*, **A**, A, 𝒜, and 𝓐, we are on the road to recognizing an A (Anderson, 2010). This explains how we are able to read words written in other people's handwriting, and why humans, but not computer bots, can fill in those annoying security codes such as axq𝓔𝓮. .

As perception continues, the features are organized into patterns. These processes were studied in Germany early in this century (and later in North America) by psychologists called *Gestalt theorists*. **Gestalt**, which means "pattern" or "configuration" in German, refers to people's tendency to organize sensory information into patterns or relationships. Figure 8.3 presents a few Gestalt principles.

If all perception relied only on feature analysis and Gestalt principles, learning would be very slow. At the last stage of perception, the features and patterns detected are combined in relation to the context of the situation and our existing knowledge—called **top-down** or conceptually driven processing. So to recognize patterns rapidly, in addition to noting features, we use context and what we already know about the situation—our knowledge about words or pictures or the way the world generally operates. For example, you would not have seen the earlier marks as the letter A if you had no knowledge of the Latin alphabet. So, what you know also affects what you are able to perceive. In Figure 8.2, the role of knowledge in perception is represented by the double arrow between long-term memory (stored knowledge), working memory, and sensory memory.

**Perception** Interpretation of sensory information.

**Bottom-up processing** Perceiving based on noticing separate defining features and assembling them into a recognizable pattern.

**Gestalt** German for *pattern* or *whole*. Gestalt theorists hold that people organize their perceptions into coherent wholes.

**Top-down** Making sense of information by using context and what we already know about the situation; sometimes called *conceptually drivien perception*.

---

### FIGURE 8.3

#### EXAMPLES OF GESTALT PRINCIPLES

Gestalt principles of perception explain how we "see" patterns in the world around us.

**a. Figure-ground**
What do you see? Faces or a vase? Make one figure—the other ground.

**b. Proximity**
You see these lines as 3 groups because of the proximity of the lines.

**c. Similarity**
You see these lines as an alternating pattern because of the similarity in height of lines.

**d. Closure**
You perceive a circle instead of a series of curved lines.

---

*Source: Schunk, D. H. (1996). Learning Theories: An Educational Perspective, 2nd Edition. Reprinted by permission of Pearson Education, Inc., Upper Saddle River, NJ.*

**THE ROLE OF ATTENTION.** If every variation in colour, movement, sound, smell, temperature, and other features ended up in working memory, life would be impossible. But attention is selective. By paying **attention** to selected stimuli and ignoring others, we limit the possibilities of what we will perceive and process. What we pay attention to is guided to a certain extent by what we already know and what we need to know, so attention is involved in and influenced by all three memory processes shown in Figure 8.2. Attention is also affected by what else is happening at the time, by the type and complexity of the task, by the resources you bring to the situation, and by your ability to control or focus your attention. Some students with attention-deficit disorder have great difficulty focusing attention or ignoring competing stimuli.

But attention takes effort and is a limited resource. We imagine you have to work a bit to pay attention to these words about attention! People can pay attention to only one cognitively demanding task at a time (Sternberg & Sternberg, 2012). For example, when Nancy was learning to drive, she couldn't listen to the radio and drive at the same time. After some practice, she could listen, but she had to turn the radio off when traffic was heavy. After years of practice, she can plan a class, listen to the radio, and carry on a conversation as she drives. This is possible because many processes that initially require attention and concentration become automatic with practice. Actually, **automaticity**, or the ability to carry out complex behaviour with little mental effort, probably is a matter of degree; we are not completely automatic, but rather more or less automatic in our performances depending on how much practice we have had, the situation, and whether we are intentionally focusing our attention and directing our own cognitive processing. For example, even experienced drivers might become very attentive and focused during a blinding blizzard—and no one should text or talk on a cell phone while driving. Researchers at Dalhousie University found that using a cell phone while driving increases your risk of a car crash by 70% (Asbridge, Brubacher, & Chan, 2013)

**EYES (AND ATTENTION) ON THE ROAD** The girl in the picture has it right. You can talk to passengers, but a text or phone conversation while driving is dangerous for everyone because the demands on attention are too great.

Martin Novak / Shutterstock

**ATTENTION AND MULTITASKING.** Drivers who text or chat say they are multitasking, and often they think all is fine. You may be multitasking right now. Adolescents are multitasking more than ever, perhaps because they have access to so much technology. In one survey of 8- to 18-year-olds, about one-third of them reported multitasking with multimedia while they do their homework (Azzam, 2006). These students reported using media about six to seven hours each day on average, but with the multitasking, they actually were exposed to more than eight to nine hours of media.

Is multitasking a good idea? Research by David Meyer and his colleagues at the Brain, Cognition, and Actions Laboratory says it depends (Hamilton, 2009). Actually, there are two types of multitasking—*sequential multitasking*, in which you switch back and forth from one task to another, but focus on only one at a time, and *simultaneous multitasking*, in which there is overlapping focus on several tasks at time. Also, the content of the tasks makes a difference. Some tasks, such as walking and chewing gum, call on different cognitive and physical resources—and both walking and chewing are pretty automatic. But other complex tasks, such as driving and talking on the phone, require some of the same cognitive resources—paying attention to traffic and paying attention to what the caller is saying. The problem with multitasking comes with *simultaneous, complex* tasks.

For tasks that are at all complicated, no matter how good you have become at multitasking, your performance of the task will suffer (David Meyer interviewed by Hamilton, 2009, p. 1). In fact, it can take up to 400% longer to do a homework assignment if you are multitasking (Paulos, 2007). In complicated situations, the brain prioritizes and focuses on one thing. You may be able to listen to quiet instrumental music in the background

**Attention** Focus on a stimulus.

**Automaticity** The result of learning to perform a behaviour or thinking process so thoroughly that the performance is automatic and does not require effort. Sometimes refers to excitement or stress.

## Gaining and Maintaining Attention

**Use signals.**
*Examples*

1. Develop a signal that tells students to stop what they are doing and focus on you. Some teachers move to a particular spot in the room, flick the lights, tap the table, or play a chord on the class piano. Mix visual and auditory signals.
2. Avoid distracting behaviours, such as tapping a pencil while talking, that interfere with both signals and attention to learning.
3. Give short, clear directions before, not during, transitions.
4. Be playful with younger children: Use a dramatic voice, sensational hat, or clapping game (Miller, 2005).

**Reach out rather than call out (Miller, 2005).**
*Examples*

1. Walk to the child, look into his or her eyes.
2. Speak in a firm but nonthreatening voice.
3. Use the child's name.

**Make sure the purpose of the lesson or assignment is clear to students.**
*Examples*

1. Write the goals or objectives on the board and discuss them with students before starting. Ask students to summarize or restate the goals.
2. Explain the reasons for learning, and ask students for examples of how they will apply their understanding of the material.

3. Tie the new material to previous lessons—show an outline or map of how the new topic fits with previous and upcoming material.

**Incorporate variety, curiosity, and surprise.**
*Examples*

1. Arouse curiosity with questions such as "What would happen if?"
2. Create shock by staging an unexpected event such as a loud argument just before a lesson on communication.
3. Alter the physical environment by changing the arrangement of the room or moving to a different setting.
4. Shift sensory channels by giving a lesson that requires students to touch, smell, or taste.
5. Use movements, gestures, and voice inflection—walk around the room, point, and speak softly and then more emphatically.

**Ask questions and provide frames for answering.**
*Examples*

1. Ask students why the material is important, how they intend to study, and what strategies they will use.
2. Give students self-checking or self-editing guides that focus on common mistakes or have them work in pairs to improve each other's work—sometimes it is difficult to pay attention to your own errors.

*For more ideas about gaining student attention, see www.atozteacherstuff.com/Tips/Attention_Getters.*

---

while you study, but favourite songs with words will steal your attention away and it will take time to get back to what you were doing.

ATTENTION AND TEACHING.   The first step in learning is paying attention. Students cannot process information that they do not recognize or perceive (Lachter, Forster, & Ruthruff, 2004). But how successfully information is processed depends on several things, not just attention. Some tasks are *resource-limited*. Performance on those tasks will improve if we allocate more resources—for example, turn off the iPod and give the complicated lecture your full attention. Other tasks are *data-limited*, which means that successful processing depends on the amount and quality of the data available. If the quality of the information available is inadequate, then no matter how hard we focus attention, we will not be successful. For example, if you just can't hear the lecture or you know very few of the terms being used, more focused attention will not help you understand. We have already discussed a third kind of task—*automated*—that happens without much attention because we have practised it so thoroughly—for example, the way an expert musician moves her fingers on the strings of a guitar (Bruning, Schraw, Norby, 2011).

Many factors in the classroom influence student attention. Bright colours, underlining or highlighting of written or spoken words, calling students by name, surprise events, intriguing questions, variety in tasks and teaching methods, and changes in voice level, lighting, or pacing can all be used to *gain* attention. But then students have to *maintain* attention—they have to stay focused on the important features of the learning situation. The *Guidelines* offer ideas for capturing and maintaining students' attention.

## Working Memory

**Working memory** is the "workbench" of the memory system, the interface where new information is held temporarily and combined with knowledge from long-term memory to solve problems or comprehend a lecture, for example. Working memory "contains" what you are thinking about at the moment. For this reason, some psychologists consider the working memory to be synonymous with "consciousness" (Sweller, van Merriënboer, & Paas, 1998). Unlike sensory memory or long-term memory, working memory capacity is very limited—something many of your professors seem to forget as they race through a lecture while you work to hold on to and make sense of their words and PowerPoints.

In Figure 8.1 you saw **short-term memory**. Short-term memory is not exactly the same as working memory. Working memory includes both temporary storage and active processing—the workbench of memory—where active mental effort is applied to both new and old information. But short-term memory usually means just storage, the immediate memory for new information that can be held about 15 to 20 seconds (Baddeley, 2001). Early experiments suggested that the capacity of short-term memory was only about five to nine (the "magic 7," + or − 2) separate new bits of information at once (Miller, 1956). Later, we will see that this limitation can be overcome using strategies such as chunking or grouping, but the five to nine limit generally holds true in everyday life. It is quite common to remember a new phone number after finding it on the internet, as you make the call. But what if you have two phone calls to make in succession? Two new phone numbers (14 digits) probably cannot be stored simultaneously.

Alan Baddeley and his colleagues are responsible for the model of working memory that is central to our current understanding of human cognition. In this model, working memory is composed of at least four elements: *the central executive* that controls attention and other mental resources (the "worker" of working memory), the *phonological loop* that holds verbal and acoustical (sound) information, the *visuospatial sketchpad* for visual and spatial information, and the *episodic buffer* where information from the phonological loop, visuospatial sketchpad, and long-term memory is integrated together to create representations based on verbal, spatial, and visual information. The phonological loop and visuospatial sketchpad are short-term memory storage for sounds and images, so they are like what was considered short-term memory in earlier information processing models. The phonological loop, visuospatial sketchpad, and episodic buffer do some lower-level work for the central executive—holding on to and combining information. Baddeley also said there may be other lower-level worker/storage systems for different information, but phonological loop, visuospatial sketchpad, and episodic buffer are the ones we know about (Baddeley, 2007; Baddeley, Hitch, & Allen, 2009; Jarrold, Tam, Baddeley, & Harvey, 2011). Figure 8.4 shows the working memory system—let's experience that system in action.

---

**STOP & THINK** Solve this problem from Ashcraft and Radvansky (2010, p. 161) and pay attention to how you go about the process:

$$\frac{(4 + 5) \times 2}{3 + (12/4)} \bullet$$

---

**THE CENTRAL EXECUTIVE.**   As you solved the arithmetic problem in the Stop & Think, the central executive of your working memory focused your attention on the facts that you needed (what is 4 + 5? what is 12/4?), retrieved rules for which operations to do first, and recalled how to divide. The **central executive** supervises attention, makes plans, and decides what information to retrieve and how to allocate resources, as you can see in Figure 8.4.

**THE PHONOLOGICAL LOOP.**   The **phonological loop** is a speech- and sound-related system for holding and rehearsing (refreshing) words and sounds in short-term memory. It briefly holds verbal information and keeps it active by keeping it "in the loop"—rehearsing and paying attention to the information. The short-term storage of the phonological loop

**Working memory**   The information that you are focusing on at a given moment.

**Short-term memory**   Component of memory system that holds information for about 20 seconds.

**Central executive**   The part of working memory that is responsible for monitoring and directing attention and other mental resources.

**Phonological loop**   Part of working memory. A speech- and sound-related system for holding and rehearsing (refreshing) words and sounds in short-term memory for about 1.5 to 2 seconds.

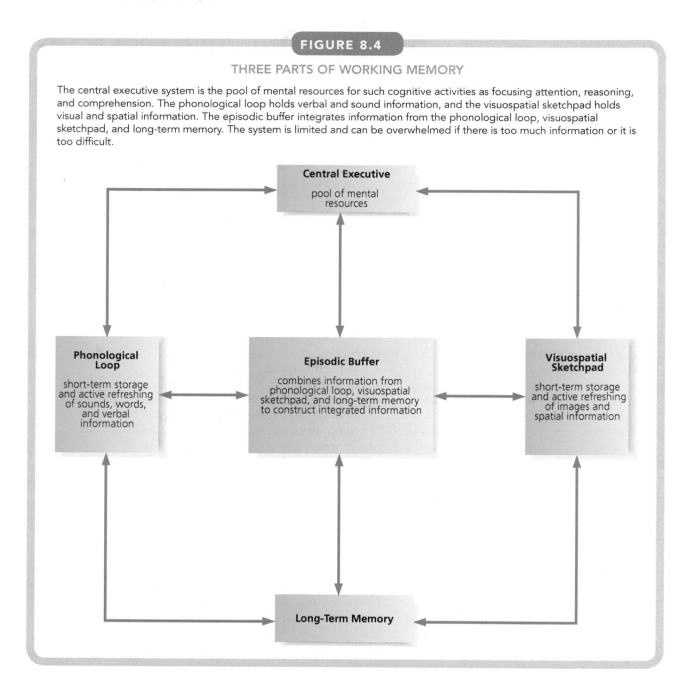

**FIGURE 8.4**

THREE PARTS OF WORKING MEMORY

The central executive system is the pool of mental resources for such cognitive activities as focusing attention, reasoning, and comprehension. The phonological loop holds verbal and sound information, and the visuospatial sketchpad holds visual and spatial information. The episodic buffer integrates information from the phonological loop, visuospatial sketchpad, and long-term memory. The system is limited and can be overwhelmed if there is too much information or it is too difficult.

**Central Executive**

pool of mental resources

**Phonological Loop**

short-term storage and active refreshing of sounds, words, and verbal information

**Episodic Buffer**

combines information from phonological loop, visuospatial sketchpad, and long-term memory to construct integrated information

**Visuospatial Sketchpad**

short-term storage and active refreshing of images and spatial information

**Long-Term Memory**

is where you put the "18" ($4 + 5 = 9$; $9 \times 2 = 18$) from the top line of the problem while you calculated the $3 + (12/4)$ on the bottom of the problem. Baddeley (2001, 2007) suggests that we can hold as much in the phonological loop as we can rehearse (say to ourselves) in 1.5 to 2 seconds. The seven-digit telephone number fits this limitation. But what if you tried to hold these seven words in mind: *disentangle appropriation gossamer anti-intellectual preventative foreclosure documentation* (Gray, 2011)? Besides being a mouthful, these words take longer than two seconds to rehearse and are more difficult to hold in working memory than seven single digits or seven short words. In addition, some of the words may be unfamiliar to you, so they are harder to rehearse.

Remember—put in your working memory—that we are discussing temporarily holding new information. In daily life we certainly can hold more than five to nine bits or 1.5 seconds of information at once. While you are keying in that seven-digit phone number you just looked up, you are bound to have other things "on your mind"—in your memory—such as how to use a telephone, whom you are calling, and why. You don't have to pay attention to these things; they are not new knowledge. Some of the processes, such as using the keypad on the phone, are *automated* tasks. However, because of the working memory's limitations, if you were in a foreign country and were attempting to use an unfamiliar telephone system, you might very well have trouble remembering the phone number because your central executive was searching for strategies to use the phone system at the same time. Even a few bits of new information can be too much to remember if the new information is very complex or unfamiliar or if you have to integrate several elements to make sense of a situation (Sweller, van Merriënboer, & Paas, 1998).

THE VISUOSPATIAL SKETCHPAD.    Now try this problem.

- - - - - - - - - - - - - - - - - - - - - - - - - - - - - - - - - - - - - - - - - - - - - - - - - - - - -

STOP & THINK If you rotate a *d* 180 degrees clockwise, do you get a *b* or a *p*? •

- - - - - - - - - - - - - - - - - - - - - - - - - - - - - - - - - - - - - - - - - - - - - - - - - - - - -

Most people answer this question by creating a visual image of a "d" and rotating it. The **visuospatial sketchpad** is the place in your mind where you manipulated the image (after your central executive retrieved the meaning of "180 degrees," and "clockwise" of course). Working in the visuospatial sketchpad has some of the same aspects as actually looking at a picture or object. If you have to solve the "d" problem and also pay attention to an image on a screen, you will be slowed down just like you would be if you had to look back and forth between two different objects. But if you had to solve the "d" problem while repeating digits, there is little slow down. You can use your phonological loop and your visuospatial sketchpad at the same time, but each is quickly filled and easily overburdened. In fact, each kind of task—verbal and visual—appears to happen in different areas of the brain and there are some individual differences in the capacities of these systems, too (Ashcraft & Radvansky, 2010; Gray, 2011).

THE EPISODIC BUFFER.    If working memory is the workbench of memory, the episodic buffer is the workbench of working memory. The **episodic buffer** is the process that brings together and integrates information from the phonological loop, visuospatial sketchpad, and long-term memory under the supervision of the central executive, to create complex memories, such as storing the appearance, voice, words, and actions of an actor in a film to create a complete character.

THE DURATION AND CONTENTS OF WORKING MEMORY.    It is clear that the duration of information in the working memory system is short, about 5 to 20 seconds, unless you keep rehearsing the information or process it in some other way. It may seem to you that a memory system with a 20-second time limit is not very useful, but, without this system, you would have already forgotten what you read in the first part of this sentence before you came to these last few words. This would clearly make understanding sentences difficult.

The contents of information in working memory may be in the form of sounds and images that resemble the representations in sensory memory, or the information may be structured more abstractly, based on meaning.

## Cognitive Load and Retaining Information

Let's get back to that professor who raced through a lecture, taxing your working memory. Some tasks make more demands than others on working memory. **Cognitive load** is a term that refers to the amount of mental resources, mostly working memory, required to perform a particular task. The concept is only about 25 years old, but in 2010 there was an entire special issue of *Educational Psychology Review* dedicated to cognitive load theory (van Gog, Paas, & Sweller, 2010).

THREE KINDS OF COGNITIVE LOAD.    The cognitive load of a task is not an absolute "weight." The extent of cognitive load in a given situation depends on many things, including what the person already knows about the task and what resources are available. There

**Visuospatial sketchpad**  Part of working memory. A holding system for visual and spatial information.

**Episodic buffer**  The process that brings together and integrates information from the phonological loop, visuospatial sketchpad, and long-term memory under the supervision of the central executive.

**Cognitive load**  The volume of resources necessary to complete a task.

are three kinds of cognitive load. One is unavoidable, one gets in the way, and one is valuable.

**Intrinsic cognitive load** is unavoidable—it is the amount of cognitive processing required to figure out the material. That amount depends on how many elements you have to take into account, how complicated the interactions among the elements are, and your level of expertise in problem area (Antonenko, Paas, Grabner, & van Gog, 2010). Even though working memory can hold five to nine new bits of information, it can process only about two to four at a time. So, if you have to understand how many separate elements interact in a complex system, such as grasping the structure and function of DNA, you will be in trouble unless you already understand some of the parts—vocabulary, concepts, procedures, and so on (van Merriënboer & Sweller, 2005). Intrinsic cognitive load is essential to the task—it cannot be eliminated. But good instruction can help manage intrinsic load.

**Extraneous cognitive load** is the cognitive capacity you use to deal with problems not related to the learning task, like trying to get your roommate (spouse, children, partner) to quit interrupting you or struggling with a disorganized lecture or a poorly written textbook (not this one, we hope!). Instruction can help manage extraneous load by providing supports, focusing attention on the main ideas, and generally supplying scaffolding (see Chapter 2).

The valuable cognitive load is called *germane* because it is directly related to (germane to) high quality learning. **Germane cognitive load** comes from extensive processing of relevant information—organizing and integrating the material with what you already know and forming new understandings. Instruction can support this process by asking students to explain the material to each other or to themselves, to draw or chart their understandings, to take useful notes, and to use other strategies we will discuss in upcoming chapters (Berthold & Renkl, 2009; Mayer, 2011, van Gog, Pass, & Sweller, 2010). The three kinds of cognitive load are summarized in Table 8.1. Just a note: Some psychologists

**Intrinsic cognitive load** The resources required by the task itself, regardless of other stimuli.

**Extraneous cognitive load** The resources required to process stimuli irrelevant to the task.

**Germane cognitive load** Deep processing of information related to the task, including the application of prior knowledge to a new task or problem.

TABLE 8.1 • **Three Kinds of Cognitive Load**

There are three types of cognitive load that make demands during learning, with different causes and effects.

| TYPE OF COGNITIVE LOAD | WHAT IS IT? | WHAT CAUSES IT? | WHAT'S AN EXAMPLE? | WHAT HAPPENS? |
|---|---|---|---|---|
| Intrinsic | *Unavoidable:* the essential processing needed to attend to and represent the material | Caused by the inherent complexity of the task: the more complex, the more basic processing needed | More intrinsic processing needed to recognize and organize a complicated task such as quadratic equations | Processing focuses attention and begins to organize learning, rote learning possible |
| Extraneous | *Avoidable or manageable:* unhelpful processing needed to deal with problems that are not related to the learning task itself | Caused by poor learning strategies, divided attention and distractibility, poor instruction, inadequate background knowledge | Students scan back and forth between the text and a graph, but don't know how to read the graph or integrate the visual and verbal information | Inappropriate processing, no learning, possible discouragement |
| Germane | *Desirable:* the deep processing (organizing, integrating, connecting to prior knowledge) required to generate understandings | Learner motivation to understand, make strong effort, try new strategies when first attempts fall short | Learner diagrams relationships in a problem, connects to key ideas in the text | Appropriate organizing, elaborating, and visualizing lead to deep learning |

Source: *Adapted from Bruning, R. H., Schraw, G. J., & Norby, M. M. (2011). Cognitive Psychology and Instruction (5th ed.). Boston: Pearson, pp. 220–224; Mayer, R. E. (2011). Applying the Science of Learning. Boston: Pearson, pp. 62–71.*

suggest that there is no practical distinction between intrinsic and germane load—a student must deal with both to learn (Kalyuga, 2011).

RETAINING INFORMATION IN WORKING MEMORY.  Information in working memory must be kept activated in order for it to be retained. Activation is high as long as you are focusing on information, but activation decays or fades quickly when attention shifts away. Holding information in working memory is like a circus performer keeping a series of plates spinning on top of several poles. The performer gets one plate spinning, moves to the next plate, and the next, but has to return to the first plate before it slows down too much and falls off its pole. If we don't keep the information "spinning" in working memory—keep it activated—it will "fall off" (Anderson, 1995, 2010). When activation fades, forgetting follows.

To keep information activated, most people continue rehearsing the information mentally. There are two types of rehearsal. **Maintenance rehearsal** involves repeating the information in your phonological loop or refreshing information in your visuospatial sketchpad. As long as you revisit the information, it can be maintained in working memory indefinitely. Maintenance rehearsal is useful for retaining something you plan to use and then forget, such as a phone number or a location on a map.

**Elaborative rehearsal** involves connecting the information you are trying to remember with something you already know—with knowledge from long-term memory. For example, if you meet someone at a party whose name is the same as your brother's, you don't have to repeat the name to keep it in memory; you just have to make the connection. This kind of rehearsal not only retains information in working memory but also helps create long-term memories. Rehearsal is a process the central executive controls to manage the flow of information through the information processing system (Ashcraft & Radvansky, 2010).

The limited capacity of working memory can also be somewhat circumvented by the process of **chunking**. Because the number of bits of information, not the size of each bit, is a limitation for working memory, you can retain more information if you can group individual bits of information. You can experience this effect of chunking by trying to hold these letters in memory:

BMOLOLPMODNACTV

Now try these:

BMO LOL PMO DNA CTV

You just used chunking to group the string of letters into memorable (and meaningful) chunks, so you could hold more in memory. Also, you brought your knowledge of the world to bear on the memory task. Chunking helps you remember a password or social security number.

FORGETTING.  Information may be lost from working memory through *interference* or *decay*. **Interference** is fairly straightforward: Processing new information interferes or gets confused with old information. As new thoughts accumulate, old information is lost from working memory. Information is also lost by time **decay**. If you don't continue to pay attention to information, the activation level decays (weakens) and finally drops so low that the information cannot be reactivated—it disappears altogether. Some cognitive psychologists argue that interference is the main factor in forgetting in working memory—your mind starts processing other information and the previous information is "written over" (Sternberg & Sternberg, 2012).

Actually, forgetting is very useful. Without forgetting, people would quickly overload their working memories and learning would cease. Also, it would be a problem if you remembered permanently every sentence you ever read, every sound you ever heard, every picture you ever saw . . . you get the idea. Finding a particular bit of information in all that sea of knowledge would be impossible. It is helpful to have a system that provides temporary storage and that "weeds out" some information from everything you experience.

**Maintenance rehearsal**  Keeping information in working memory by repeating it to yourself.

**Elaborative rehearsal**  Keeping information in working memory by associating it with something else you already know.

**Chunking**  Grouping individual bits of data into meaningful larger units.

**Interference**  Processing new information interferes or gets confused with old information.

**Decay**  The weakening and fading of memories with the passage of time.

## Individual Differences and Working Memory

As you might expect, there are both developmental and individual differences in working memory. Let's examine a few.

DEVELOPMENTAL DIFFERENCES.   There are three basic aspects of memory: memory span or the amount of information that can be held in short-term/working memory, memory processing efficiency, and speed of processing. As they get older, children can process many different kinds of information—verbal, visual, mathematical, etc.—faster, so increased speed of processing seems to be a general factor. In addition, the increase in speed with age is the same for North American and Korean children, so increasing processing speed with age may be universal (Kail, 2000; Kail & Park, 1994).

These three basic capacities act together and influence each other; more efficient processing allows greater amounts to be held in memory, for example (Demetriou, Christou, Spanoudis, & Platsidou, 2002). You experienced this effect of efficient processing when you remembered BMOLOLPMODNACTV by chunking the letters into BMO LOL PMO DNA CTV. Your more efficient and faster processing expanded your memory span. Young children have fewer strategies and less knowledge, so they have more trouble with memorizing a longer series. But as they grow older, children develop more effective strategies for remembering information. Most children spontaneously discover rehearsal around age 5 or 6 and continue to use it. Also around age 6, most children discover the value of using organizational strategies, and by 9 or 10, they use these strategies spontaneously. So, given the following words to learn:

> couch, orange, rat, lamp, pear, sheep, banana, rug, pineapple, horse, table, dog

an older child or an adult might organize the words into three short lists of furniture, fruit, and animals. Also remember that expertise in an area helps you use categories to organize and remember, as we saw with the expert soccer players earlier. Younger children can be taught to use rehearsal or organization to improve memory, but they probably won't apply the strategies unless they are reminded. Children also become more able to use elaboration as they mature, but this strategy develops late in childhood. Creating images or stories to assist in remembering ideas is more likely for older elementary school students and adolescents (Siegler, 1998).

In terms of strategies, for young children, using a new strategy or operation—such as reaching for a toy, counting, or finding a word—takes up a large portion of their working memory. But once an operation is mastered and becomes more automatic, there is more working memory available for short-term storage of new information (Johnson, 2003). So, through changes in the brain, faster processing of information, the development and automating of strategies, and added knowledge, working memory increases in capacity from age 4 through adolescence (Alloway, Gathercole, & Pickering, 2006; Gathercole, Pickering, Ambridge, & Wearing, 2004). Children are 10 to 11 years old before they have adult-like memories (Bauer, 2006).

INDIVIDUAL DIFFERENCES.   Besides developmental differences, there are other individual variations in working memory, and these differences have implications for learning. Try this:

- - - - - - - - - - - - - - - - - - - - - - - - - - - - - - - - - - - - - - - -

STOP & THINK Read the following sentences and words in caps out loud once:
*For many years my family and friends have been working on the farm.* SPOT
*Because the room was stuffy, Bob went outside for some fresh air.* TRAIL
*We were fifty miles out to sea before we lost sight of the land.* BAND
Now cover the sentences and answer these questions (be honest):
Name the words that were in all caps. Who was in the stuffy room? Who worked on the farm? •

- - - - - - - - - - - - - - - - - - - - - - - - - - - - - - - - - - - - - - - -

You have just taken a few items from a test of working memory span (Engle, 2001). The test required you to both process and store—process the meaning of the sentences and store the words. How did you do?

The more educational psychologists study working memory, the more we realize how important it is in learning and development at every age (Alloway, Banner, & Smith, 2010; Welsh, Nix, Blair, Bierman, & Nelson, 2010). For adolescents and adults, the correlation between scores on a test of working memory span (like the one you just took in the *Stop & Think* exercise above) and the verbal portion of standardized tests of achievement that American students take to compete for university admission is about .59. But there is no correlation between those tests and simple short-term memory span (repeating digits). For elementary school students, growth in working memory (but not simple short-term memory) is related to reading abilities and reading comprehension; problems with working memory are associated with reading disabilities. Working memory is related to academic achievement, math computation, and solving complex word problems in math in elementary school. For young children, growth in working memory and attention control during the preschool years predicts emergent literacy and number skills.

Working-memory span is also related to scores on intelligence tests. If a task requires controlled attention or higher-level thinking, then working memory probably is a factor in performing that task (Ackerman, Beier, & Boyle, 2005; Hambrick, Kane, & Engle, 2005; Unsworth & Engle, 2005). Some people seem to have more efficient working memories than others (Cariglia-Bull & Pressley, 1990; Di Vesta & Di Cintio, 1997; Jurden, 1995), and differences in working memory may be associated with giftedness in math and verbal areas.

We turn next to long-term memory. Because this is such an important topic for teachers, we will spend quite a bit of time on it.

## LONG-TERM MEMORY

Working memory holds the information that is currently activated, such as the name of the person you just met. **Long-term memory** holds the information that is well learned, such as the names of all the people you know.

### Capacity, Duration, and Contents of Long-Term Memory

There are a number of differences between working and long-term memory. Information enters working memory very quickly, but it takes time and effort to store memories for the long term. Whereas the capacity of working memory is limited, the capacity of long-term memory appears to be, for all practical purposes, unlimited. In addition, once information is securely stored in long-term memory, it can remain there permanently. Our access to information in working memory is immediate because we are thinking about the information at that very moment. But gaining access to information in long-term memory requires time and effort.

Recently, some psychologists have suggested that there are not two separate memory stores (working and long-term). Rather, working memory is the part of long-term memory that works on (processes) currently activated information. The difference between working memory and long-term memory just may be in how activated or inactive a particular memory is (Anderson, 2010; Wilson, 2001). This model sees memory as a set of nested systems with very short-term storage (phonological loop, visuospatial sketchpad, other brief holding areas) nested in working memory, which is just the active part of long-term memory that does the integrating of old and new information (Sternberg & Sternberg, 2012).

#### CONTENTS OF LONG-TERM-MEMORY: DECLARATIVE, PROCEDURAL, AND SELF-REGULATORY KNOWLEDGE.
Earlier, we talked about general and specific knowledge. Another way to categorize knowledge is as *declarative*, *procedural*, or *self-regulatory* (Schraw, 2006).

**Declarative knowledge** is knowledge that can be declared, through words and symbol systems of all kinds—Braille, sign language, dance or musical notation, mathematical symbols, and so on. Declarative knowledge is "knowing that" something is the case. The range of declarative knowledge is tremendous. You can know very specific facts (the atomic weight of gold is 196.967), or generalities (leaves of some trees change colour in autumn), or personal preferences (I don't like lima beans), or rules (to divide fractions,

**Long-term memory** Permanent store of knowledge.

**Declarative knowledge** Verbal information; facts; "knowing that" something is the case.

TABLE 8.2 • **Kinds of Knowledge**

| | GENERAL KNOWLEDGE | DOMAIN-SPECIFIC KNOWLEDGE |
|---|---|---|
| Declarative | Hours the library is open<br>Rules of grammar | The definition of "hypotenuse"<br>The lines of the poem "The Raven" |
| Procedural | How to use your cell phone<br>How to drive | How to solve an oxidation-reduction equation<br>How to throw a pot on a potter's wheel |
| Conditional | When to give up and try another approach<br>When to skim and when to read carefully | When to use the formula for calculating volume<br>When to rush the net in tennis |

invert the divisor and multiply). Small units of declarative knowledge can be organized into larger units; for example, principles of reinforcement and punishment can be organized in your thinking into a theory of behavioural learning.

**Procedural knowledge** is "knowing how" to do something such as divide fractions or design a website—it is knowledge in action. Procedural knowledge must be demonstrated. Notice that repeating the rule "to divide fractions, invert the divisor, and multiply" shows declarative knowledge—the student can state the rule. But to show procedural knowledge, the student must act. When faced with a fraction to divide, the student must divide correctly. Students demonstrate procedural knowledge when they translate a passage into French, correctly categorize a geometric shape, or craft a coherent paragraph.

**Self-regulatory knowledge** is knowing how to manage your learning—knowing how and when to use your declarative and procedural knowledge (Schraw, 2006; Winne, 2011). It takes self-regulatory knowledge to know when to read every word in a text and when to skim or when to apply a strategy for overcoming procrastination. Self-regulatory knowledge has also been called *conditional knowledge* (Paris & Cunningham, 1996). For many students, this kind of knowledge is a stumbling block. They have the facts and can do the procedures, but they don't seem to understand how to apply what they know at the appropriate time. Self-regulatory knowledge can be specific to a subject area (when to use the formula for calculating area, not perimeter, in geometry) or more general (how to summarize key points or use diagrams to organize information). In fact, all three kinds of knowledge—declarative, procedural, and self-regulatory—can be either general or domain-specific, as you can see in Table 8.2 (Schraw, 2006).

Most cognitive psychologists distinguish between two categories of long-term memory, explicit and implicit, with subdivisions under each category, as shown in Figure 8.5. **Explicit memory** is knowledge from long-term memory that can be recalled and consciously considered. We are aware of these memories—we know we have remembered them. **Implicit memory**, on the other hand, is knowledge that we are not conscious of recalling, but that influences behaviour or thought without our awareness. These different kinds of memory are associated with different parts of the brain (Ashcraft & Radvansky, 2010; Gray, 2011).

This view has been challenged recently. Lynne Reder and her colleagues claim that implicit and explicit are not different memory systems, but just different kinds of tasks that are accomplished with one memory system (Reder, Park, & Kieffaber, 2009). Stay tuned as new theories develop. For now, we will stick with the idea of explicit and implicit systems, and look at explicit memories first.

## Explicit Memories: Semantic and Episodic

In Figure 8.5, you will see that explicit memories can be either semantic (based on meaning) or episodic (based the sequence of events).

**Semantic memory**, very important in schools, is memory for meaning, including words, facts, theories, and concepts—*declarative* knowledge, so sometimes the name

---

**Procedural knowledge** Knowledge that is demonstrated when we perform a task; "knowing how."

**Self-regulatory knowledge** Knowing how to manage your learning, or knowing how and when to use your declarative and procedural knowledge.

**Explicit memory** Long-term memories that involve deliberate or conscious recall.

**Implicit memory** Knowledge that we are not conscious of recalling, but that influences our behaviour or thought without our awareness.

**Semantic memory** Memory for meaning.

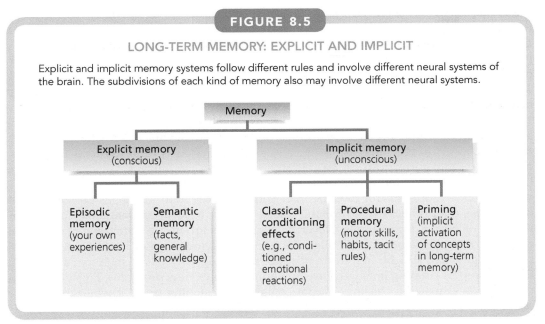

**FIGURE 8.5**

**LONG-TERM MEMORY: EXPLICIT AND IMPLICIT**

Explicit and implicit memory systems follow different rules and involve different neural systems of the brain. The subdivisions of each kind of memory also may involve different neural systems.

*Source: From Gray, P. (2011). Psychology. Published by Worth Publishers. Copyright © 1991, 1994, 1999, 2002, 2011 by Worth Publishers. Adapted with permission of the publisher.*

*declarative memory* is used. These memories are not tied to particular experiences and are represented and stored as propositions, images, concepts, and schemas (Anderson, 2010; Schraw, 2006; Winne, 2011).

PROPOSITIONS AND PROPOSITIONAL NETWORKS.    How do we represent the meaning of sentences and pictures in our memories? One answer is with propositions connected in networks. A proposition is the smallest unit of knowledge that can be judged true or false (Anderson, 2010). Here is an example of a statement with three propositions: "The prime minister, who is head of Canada's government and lives at 24 Sussex Drive, is appointed by the governor general." The three basic propositions are:

1. The prime minister is head of Canada's government.
2. The prime minister lives at 24 Sussex Drive.
3. The prime minister is appointed by the governor general.

Propositions that share information are linked in what cognitive psychologists call **propositional networks**. It is the meaning, not the exact words or word order, that is stored in the network. The same propositional network would apply to the sentence: "Appointed as Canada's head of government by the governor general, the prime minister lives at 24 Sussex Drive." The meaning is the same, and it is this meaning that is stored in memory as a set of relationships among propositions.

It is possible that most information is stored and represented in propositional networks. When we want to recall a bit of information, we can translate its meaning (as represented in the propositional network) into familiar phrases and sentences, or mental pictures. Also, because propositions are networked, recall of one bit of information can trigger or activate recall of another. We are not aware of these networks, for they are not part of our conscious memory (Anderson, 2010). In much the same way, we are not aware of underlying grammatical structure when we form a sentence in our own language; we don't have to diagram a sentence in order to say it.

**Propositional network** Set of interconnected concepts and relationships in which long-term knowledge is held.

IMAGES.    **Images** are representations based on the structure or appearance of the information (Anderson, 2010). As we form images (like you did in the rotating "d" problem), we try to remember or recreate the physical attributes and spatial structure of information.

**Images** Representations based on the physical attributes—the appearance—of information.

For example, when asked what store is beside the Tim Hortons at a particular intersection in town, many people would look "in their mind's eye" to view the intersection and then "look" beside the Tim Hortons. However, researchers don't agree on exactly how images are stored in memory. Some psychologists believe that images are stored as pictures; others believe we store propositions in long-term memory (The Source is beside Tim Hortons) and convert to pictures in working memory when necessary. The debate continues (Sternberg & Sternberg, 2012).

There probably are features of each process involved—some memory for images and some verbal or propositional descriptions of the image. Seeing images "in your mind's eye" is not exactly the same as seeing the actual image. It is more difficult to perform complicated transformations on mental images than on real images. For example, if you had a plastic "d" magnet on your refrigerator, you could very quickly rotate it. Rotating mentally takes more time for most people. And it is easier to form images for some words or concepts than others—it is probably easier for you to form an image of Tim Hortons than one of *justice*, for example. Nevertheless, images are useful in making many practical decisions such as how a sofa might look in your living room or how to line up a golf shot. Images may also be helpful in abstract reasoning. Physicists, such as Faraday and Einstein, report creating images to reason about complex new problems. Einstein claimed that he was visualizing chasing a beam of light and catching up to it when the concept of relativity came to him (Kosslyn & Koenig, 1992).

**TWO ARE BETTER THAN ONE: WORDS AND IMAGES.** Allan Paivio (1986, 2006; Clark & Paivio, 1991), previously of the University of Western Ontario, proposed the **dual coding theory**. It suggests that information is stored in long-term memory as either visual images or verbal units, or both. Psychologists who agree with this point of view believe that information coded both visually and verbally is easiest to learn (Butcher, 2006). This may be one reason why explaining an idea with words and then representing it visually in a figure, as we do in textbooks, has proved helpful to students.

**STOP & THINK** What makes a cup a cup? List the characteristics of *cupness*. What is a fruit? Is a banana a fruit? Is a tomato a fruit? How about a squash? A watermelon? A sweet potato? An olive? A coconut? How did you learn what makes a fruit a fruit? •

**CONCEPTS.** Most of what we know about cups and fruits and the world involves concepts and relations among concepts (Ashcraft & Radvansky, 2010). But what exactly is a concept? A **concept** is a category used to group similar events, ideas, objects, or people. When we talk about a particular concept such as *student*, we refer to a category of people who are similar to one another—they all study a subject. The people may be old or young, in school or not; they may be studying basketball or Bach, but they all can be categorized as students. Concepts are abstractions. They do not exist in the real world. Only individual examples of concepts exist. Concepts help us organize vast amounts of information into manageable units. For instance, there are about 7.5 million distinguishable differences in colours. By categorizing these colours into some dozen or so groups, we manage to deal with this diversity quite well (Bruner, 1973).

In early research, psychologists assumed that people create concepts based on rules about **defining attributes**, or distinctive features. For example, books all contain pages that are bound together in some way. (But what about "ebooks"?) Your concept of a cat might include defining attributes such as a round head on a small body, triangle-shaped ears, whiskers, four legs, and fur. This concept enables you to identify cats whether they are calico or Siamese without relearning "cat" each time you encounter a new cat. The defining attributes theory of concepts suggests that we recognize specific examples by noting key required features.

Since about 1970, however, these views about the nature of concepts have been challenged (Ashcraft & Radvansky, 2010). Although some concepts, such as equilateral triangle, have clear-cut defining attributes, most concepts do not. Take the concept of *party*. What are the defining attributes? You might have difficulty listing these attributes, but

**Dual coding theory** Suggests that information is stored in long-term memory as either visual images or verbal units, or both.

**Concept** A category used to group similar events, ideas, objects, or people.

**Defining attribute** Qualities that connect members of a group to a specific concept.

you probably recognize a party when you see or hear one (unless, of course we are talking about political parties, or the other party in a lawsuit, where the sound might not help you recognize the "party"). What about the concept of *bird*? Your first thought might be that birds are animals that fly. But is an ostrich a bird? What about a penguin? A bat?

PROTOTYPES, EXEMPLARS, AND THEORY-BASED CATEGORIES. One current view of concept learning suggests that we have in our minds a prototype of a party or a bird or the letter A—an image that captures the essence of each concept. A **prototype** is the best representative of its category. For instance, the best representative of the "birds" category for many North Americans might be a robin (Rosch, 1973). Other members of the category may be very similar to the prototype (sparrow) or similar in some ways but different in others (chicken, ostrich). At the boundaries of a category, it may be difficult to determine if a particular instance really belongs. For example, is a television "furniture"? Is an elevator a "vehicle"? Is an olive a "fruit"? Whether something fits into a category is a matter of degree or graded membership. Thus, categories have fuzzy boundaries. Some events, objects, or ideas are simply better examples of a concept than others (Ashcraft & Radvansky, 2010).

**CHANGING CONCEPTS** Concepts have many attributes and may not remain constant. Recent technological applications such as text messaging have changed the concept of conversation.

Stockbyte/Getty Images

Another explanation of concept learning suggests that we identify members of a category by referring to exemplars. **Exemplars** are our actual memories of specific birds, parties, furniture, and so on that we use to compare with an item in question to see if that item belongs in the same category as our exemplar. Prototypes probably are built from experiences with many exemplars. This happens naturally because memories of particular events (episodic memories) tend to blur together over time, creating an average or typical sofa prototype from all the sofa exemplars you have experienced (Smith & Kosslyn, 2007).

There are some drawbacks to prototype and exemplar theories. For example, how do you know what "bird experiences" to blur or average together to create a bird concept if you don't already have a bird concept? One answer is that our classifications are essentially **theory-based** ideas about the world that we create to make sense of things. So a *brick,* a *rock,* and a *shoe* are in the same category if the category is "things to pound a nail with if you don't have a hammer." Our theory of what might work creates the "things to pound with" category. Some of the knowledge used to create concepts based on theories may be implicit and out of awareness, for example, what makes for "good music"—you just know it when you hear it (Ashcraft & Radvansky, 2010; Sternberg & Sternberg, 2012).

Jacob Feldman (2003) suggests a final aspect of concept formation—the simplicity principle. Feldman theorizes that when humans are confronted with examples, they induce the simplest category or rule that would cover all the examples. Sometimes it is easy to come up with a simple rule (triangles) and sometimes it is more difficult (fruit), but humans seek a simple hypothesis for collecting all the examples under one concept. Feldman suggests that this simplicity principle is one of the oldest ideas in cognitive psychology: "organisms seek to understand their environment by reducing incoming information to a simpler, more coherent, and more useful form" (p. 231). Does this remind you of the Gestalt principles of perception?

SCHEMAS. Propositions, concepts, and single images are fine for representing single ideas and simple relationships, but often our knowledge about a topic combines many concepts, images, and propositions. To explain this kind of complex knowledge, psychologists developed the idea of a schema. **Schemas** (sometimes called schemata) are abstract knowledge structures that organize vast amounts of information. A schema (the singular

**Prototype** A best example or best representative of a category.

**Exemplar** An actual memory of a specific object.

**Theory-based** An explanation for concept formation that suggests our classifications are based on ideas about the world that we create to make sense of things.

**Schemas (singular, schema)** Basic structures for organizing information; concepts.

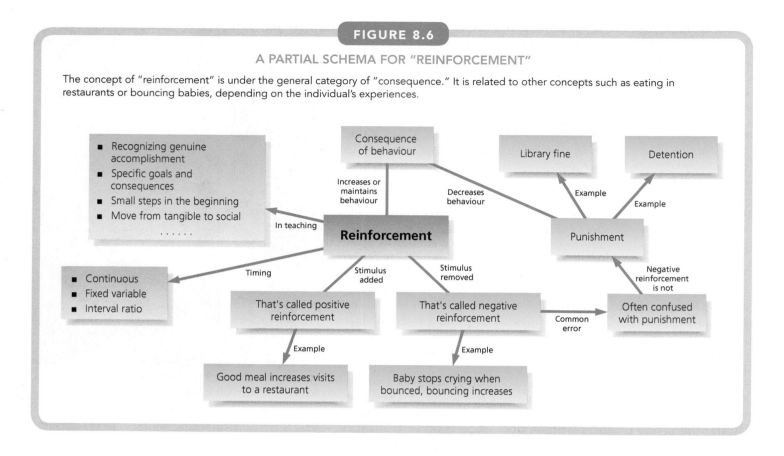

**FIGURE 8.6**

### A PARTIAL SCHEMA FOR "REINFORCEMENT"

The concept of "reinforcement" is under the general category of "consequence." It is related to other concepts such as eating in restaurants or bouncing babies, depending on the individual's experiences.

form) is a mental framework that guides our perception and helps us make sense of our experience based on what we already know and what we expect to happen (Sternberg & Sternberg, 2012). Figure 8.6 is a partial representation of a schema for knowledge about reinforcement.

The schema tells you what features are typical of a category, what to expect about an object or situation. The pattern has "slots" that are filled with specific information as we apply the schema in a particular situation. And schemas are personal. For example, my schema of reinforcement is less richly developed than Skinner's schema must have been. You encountered a very similar concept of *scheme* in the discussion of Piaget's theory of cognitive development in Chapter 2.

When you hear the sentence, "The prime minister, who is head of Canada's government and lives at 24 Sussex Drive, is appointed by the governor general," you know even more about it than the three propositions. You probably can infer that being head of government requires quite a lot of negotiating with the other political parties. Your schema for "political parties" gives you some sense of topics they debate and negotiate. None of this information was explicitly stated in the sentence.

Schematic knowledge helps us to form and understand concepts. How do we know that counterfeit money is not "real" money, even though it perfectly fits our "money" prototype and exemplars and looks like real money? We know because of its history. The "wrong" people printed the money. So our understanding of the concept of money is connected with concepts of crime, forgery, the federal treasury, and many others in a larger schema for "money."

Another type of schema, a **story grammar** (sometimes called a *schema for text* or *story structure*) helps students to understand and remember stories. A general story grammar is: setting, initiating events, reactions, goals, actions, outcomes, and endings (van den Broek, Lorch, & Thurlow, 1996). A more specific story grammar could be something like this: murder discovered, search for clues, murderer's fatal mistake identified, trap set to

**Story grammar**   Typical structure or organization for a category of stories.

trick suspect into confessing, murderer takes bait . . . mystery solved! To comprehend a story, we select a schema that seems appropriate. Then, we use this framework to decide which details are important, what information to seek, and what to remember. It is as though the schema is a theory about what should occur in the story. The schema guides us in "interrogating" the text, pointing to the specific information we expect to find so that the story makes sense. If we activate our "murder mystery schema," we may be alert for either clues or a murderer's fatal mistake. Without an appropriate schema, trying to understand a story, textbook, or classroom lesson is a very slow, difficult process, something like finding your way through a new town without a map or GPS.

To review, propositions, images, concepts, and schemas are all explicit *semantic* memories. The second kind of explicit memory is *episodic.*

EPISODIC MEMORY.   Memory for information tied to a particular place and time, especially information about the events or episodes of your own life, is called **episodic memory**. Episodic memory is about events we have experienced, so we often can explain when the event happened. In contrast, we usually can't describe when we acquired a semantic memory. For example, you may have a difficult time remembering when you developed semantic memories for the meaning of the word *injustice*, but you can easily remember a time that you felt unjustly treated. Episodic memory also keeps track of the order of things, so it is a good place to store jokes, gossip, or plots from films.

Memories for dramatic or emotional moments in your life are called **flashbulb memories**. These memories are vivid and complete, as if your brain demanded that you "record this moment." Under stress, more glucose energy goes to fuel brain activity, while stress-induced hormones signal the brain that something important is happening (Myers, 2005; Sternberg & Sternberg, 2012). So when we have intense emotional reactions, memories are stronger and more lasting. Many people have vivid memories of very positive or very negative events in school such as winning a prize or being humiliated. You probably know just where you were and what you were doing on 9/11 or when Canada's national hockey team defeated the United States to win the Olympic gold medal in 2010.

**PROCEDURAL MEMORY** Procedural memory applies to skills, habits, and "how to do things." It may take a while to learn a procedure, such as serving a tennis ball, but once learned, the procedure tends to be remembered for a long time.

Guy Drayton/Dorling Kindersley, Ltd.

## Implicit Memories

Look back at Figure 8.5. You will see that there are three kinds of implicit or out-of-awareness memories: *classical conditioning*, *procedural memory*, and *priming effects*. In classical conditioning, as we saw in Chapter 7, some out-of-awareness memories may cause you to feel anxious as you take a test or make your heart rate increase when you hear a dentist's drill or a siren.

The second type of implicit memory is **procedural memory** for skills, habits, and how to perform tasks—in other words, memory for procedural knowledge. It may take a while to learn a procedure—such as how to ski, factor an equation, or design a teaching portfolio, but once learned, this knowledge tends to be remembered for a long time. Procedural knowledge is represented as scripts and condition-action rules, sometimes called *productions.*

**Scripts** are action sequences or plans for actions stored in memory (Schraw, 2006). We all have scripts for events like ordering food in restaurants, and these scripts differ depending on whether the restaurant is a four-star bistro or a fast-food drive-through. Even young children have scripts for how to behave during snack time at preschool or at a friend's birthday party, as you can see in Figure 8.7. In fact, for very young children, scripts seem to help them organize and remember the predictable aspects of their world.

**Episodic memory**   Long-term memory for information tied to a particular time and place, especially memory of the events in a person's life.

**Flashbulb memories**   Clear, vivid memories of emotionally important events in your life.

**Procedural memory**   Long-term memory for how to do things.

**Script**   Schema or expected plan for the sequence of steps in a common event such as buying groceries or ordering pizza.

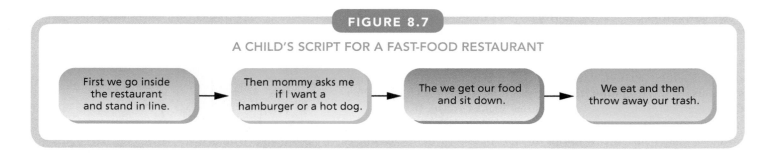

**FIGURE 8.7**

A CHILD'S SCRIPT FOR A FAST-FOOD RESTAURANT

| | | | |
|---|---|---|---|
| First we go inside the restaurant and stand in line. | Then mommy asks me if I want a hamburger or a hot dog. | The we get our food and sit down. | We eat and then throw away our trash. |

This frees up some working memory to learn new things and recognize when something is out of place in the situation. In terms of human survival, it probably is useful to remember what is likely to keep happening and to notice when something is out of place (Nelson & Fivush, 2004).

**Productions** specify what to do under certain conditions: If A occurs, then do B. A production might be something like, "If you want to snow ski faster, lean back slightly," or "If your goal is to increase student attention and a student has been paying attention a bit longer than usual, then praise the student." People can't necessarily state all their scripts and condition-action rules, and they don't even realize that they are following these rules, but they act on them nevertheless. The more practised the procedure, the more automatic the action and the more implicit the memory (Anderson, 2010; Schraw, 2006).

**STOP & THINK** Fill in these blanks: MEM _ _ _ •

The final type of implicit memory involves **priming**, or activating information that already is in long-term memory through some out-of-awareness process. You might have seen an example of priming in the fill-in-the-blank question above. If you wrote MEMORY instead of MEMOIR or MEMBER, or other MEM words, then priming may have played a role because the word *memory* has occurred many times in this chapter. Priming may be the fundamental process for retrieval as associations are activated and spread through the memory system (Ashcraft & Radvansky, 2010).

## Storing and Retrieving Information in Long-Term Memory

Just what is done to "save" information permanently—to create explicit and implicit memories? How can we make the most effective use of our practically unlimited capacity to learn and remember? The way you learn information in the first place—the way you process it in working memory at the outset—strongly affects its recall later. One important requirement is that you integrate new information with existing knowledge as you construct an understanding. Here, *elaboration, organization, imagery*, and *context* play a role.

**Elaboration** is adding meaning to new information by connecting with already existing knowledge. In other words, we apply our schemas and draw on already existing knowledge to construct an understanding. Frequently, we change our existing knowledge in the process. We often elaborate automatically. For example, a paragraph about an historic figure in ancient Rome tends to activate our existing knowledge about that period; we use the old knowledge to understand the new.

Material that is elaborated when first learned will be easier to recall later. First, as we saw earlier, elaboration is a form of rehearsal. It keeps the information activated in working memory long enough to have a chance for the new information to be integrated with knowledge in long-term memory. Second, elaboration builds extra links to existing knowledge. The more one bit of information or knowledge is associated with other bits, the more routes there are to follow to get to the original bit. To put it another way, you have several "handles" or priming/retrieval cues to "pick up" or recognize the information you might be seeking (Bruning, Schraw, & Norby, 2011).

**Productions** The contents of procedural memory; rules about what actions to take, given certain conditions.

**Priming** Activating a concept in memory or the spread of activation from one concept to another.

**Elaboration** Adding and extending meaning by connecting new information to existing knowledge.

## GUIDELINES — FAMILY AND COMMUNITY PARTNERSHIPS

### Organizing Learning

**Give families specific strategies to help their children practise and remember.**

*Examples*

1. Develop "super learner" homework assignments that include material to be learned and a "parent coaching card" with a description of a simple memory strategy—appropriate for the material—that parents can teach their child.
2. Provide a few comprehension check questions so a family member can review reading assignments and check the child's understanding.
3. Describe the value of distributed practice and give family members ideas for how and when to work skills practice into home conversations and projects.

**Ask family members to share their strategies for organizing and remembering.**

*Examples*

1. Create a family calendar.

2. Encourage planning discussions in which family members help students break large tasks into smaller jobs, identify goals, and find resources.

**Discuss the importance of attention in learning.**

*Examples*

1. Encourage families to create study spaces that are away from distractions.
2. Make sure parents know the purpose of homework assignments.

_____

*For a website dedicated to high-school study skills that might help parents, see www.mtsu.edu/~studskl/hsindex.html.*

---

The more students elaborate new ideas, the more they "make them their own," the deeper their understanding and the better their memory for the knowledge will be. We help students to elaborate when we ask them to:

- translate information into their own words
- create examples
- explain to a peer
- create a metaphor
- draw a diagram of the situation
- act out the relations
- apply the information to new problems

Of course, if students elaborate new information by developing misguided explanations, these misconceptions will be remembered, too.

**Organization** is a second element of processing that improves learning. Material that is well organized is easier to learn and to remember than bits and pieces of information, especially if the material is complex or extensive. Chunking is one kind of organization—putting small bits of information into larger, more meaningful chunks. Placing a concept in a structure also will help you learn and remember both general definitions and specific examples. The structure serves as a guide back to the information when you need it. For example, Table 8.2 organizes information about types of knowledge, and Figure 8.6 organizes our knowledge about reinforcement. The *Family and Community Partnerships Guidelines* give ideas for working with families to give all your students more support and practice in organizing learning.

IMAGERY.   You may remember that the dual coding theory of memory suggests that information coded both visually and verbally is easiest to learn (Butcher, 2006; Paivio, 2006). Imagery can support memory if the information to be learned lends itself to images—it is easier to form an image for *car* than for *internal combustion*, for example, at least for us. Also the ability to form and use mental images appears to vary among individuals—some people are simply better at this task than others (Bruning, Schraw, &

**Organization** Ordered and logical network of relations.

Norby, 2011). That said, is a picture worth 1000 words in teaching? Richard Mayer (2001, 2005) has studied this question for several years and has found that the right combination of pictures and words can make a significant difference in students' learning, at least for older students. Mayer's cognitive theory of multimedia learning includes three ideas that should be familiar to you now:

**Dual Coding**: Visual and verbal materials are processed in different systems (Clark & Paivio, 1991).

**Limited Capacity**: Working memory for verbal and visual material is severely limited. Cognitive load has to be managed (Baddeley, 2001; van Merriënboer & Sweller, 2005).

**Generative Learning**: Meaningful learning happens when students focus on relevant information and generate or build connections (Mayer, 2008, 2011).

*The problem:* How to build complex understandings that integrate information from visual (pictures, diagrams, graphs, animations, films) and verbal (text, lecture) sources, given the limitations of working memory. *The solution:* Make sure the information is available at the same time or in focused small bites. Mayer and Gallini (1990) provide an example. They used three kinds of texts to explain how a bicycle pump works. One text used only words, the second had pictures that just showed the parts of the pump system and the steps, and the third (this one improved student learning and recall) showed both the "on" and the "off" states of the pumps with labels right on the illustration for each step in the pumping process, as you can see in Figure 8.8.

There are several cautions about using multiple representations to teach, however. First, Vernon Hall and his colleagues (Hall, Bailey, & Tillman, 1997) found that students who drew their own illustrations of how a pump works did as well as students who were

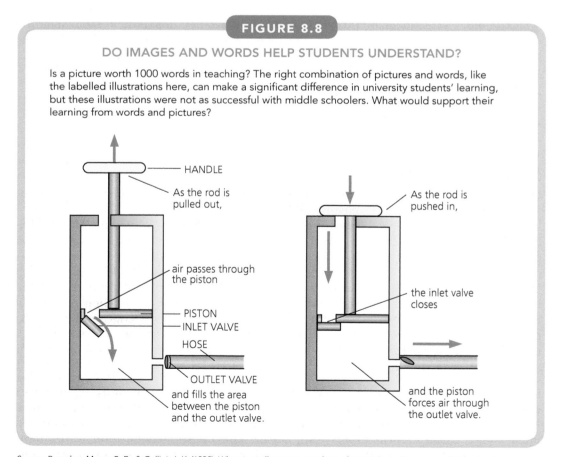

**FIGURE 8.8**

### DO IMAGES AND WORDS HELP STUDENTS UNDERSTAND?

Is a picture worth 1000 words in teaching? The right combination of pictures and words, like the labelled illustrations here, can make a significant difference in university students' learning, but these illustrations were not as successful with middle schoolers. What would support their learning from words and pictures?

HANDLE

As the rod is pulled out,

air passes through the piston

PISTON
INLET VALVE

HOSE

OUTLET VALVE

and fills the area between the piston and the outlet valve.

As the rod is pushed in,

the inlet valve closes

and the piston forces air through the outlet valve.

*Source: Based on Mayer, R. E., & Gallini, J. K. (1990). When is an illustration worth ten thousand words?* Journal of Educational Psychology, 82, 715–726.

provided Mayer's illustrations. Second, the students in both Mayer's and Hall's studies were in college. When Erin McTigue (2009) tried to replicate these kinds of results with middle school students in life and physical sciences, the labelled pictures led to small improvements in students' understanding for life science texts, but not for physical science texts.

So research has shown that just using multiple representations (words, pictures, diagrams, charts, animations, etc.) does not necessarily lead to better learning. Students, especially younger ones, need supports such as colour coding to draw attention to relevant relations in pictures and diagrams, or frequent checks for understanding with corrections if they are forming misconceptions (Berthold & Renkl, 2009). The moral of the story? Give students multiple ways to understand—pictures and explanations. But don't overload working memory—"package" the visual and verbal information together in bite-size (or memory-size) pieces and teach students directly how to learn from illustrations or how to draw their own.

**Context** is a fourth element of processing that influences learning. Aspects of physical and emotional context—places, rooms, moods, who is with us—are learned along with other information. Later, if you try to remember the information, it will be easier if the current context is similar to the original one (Ashcraft & Radvansky, 2010). Context is a kind of priming that activates the information. For example, in a classic study, scuba divers who learned a list of words underwater and then were tested underwater remembered more than scuba divers who learned underwater but were tested on dry land (Godden & Baddeley, 1975). In another study, students who learned material in one type of room performed better on tests taken in a similar room than they did on comparable tests taken in a very different-looking room (Smith, Glenberg, & Bjork, 1978). So, studying for a test under "test-like" conditions (not at Tim Hortons, for example) may result in improved performance. Of course, you can't always go back to the same place or a similar one in order to recall something. But if you can picture the setting, the time of day, and your companions, you may eventually reach the information you seek.

**LEVELS OF PROCESSING THEORY.** Craik and Lockhart (1972), psychologists at the University of Toronto, first proposed their **levels of processing theory** as an alternative to short-/long-term memory models, but levels of processing theory is particularly related to the notion of elaboration described earlier. Craik and Lockhart suggested that what determines how long information is remembered is how extensively the information is analyzed and connected with other information. The more completely information is processed, the better are our chances of remembering it. For example, according to the levels of processing theory, if we ask you to sort pictures of dogs based on the colour of their coats, you might not remember many of the pictures later. But if we ask you to rate each dog on how likely it is to chase you as you jog, you probably would remember more of the pictures. To rate the dogs, you must pay attention to details in the pictures, relate features of the dogs to characteristics associated with danger, and so on. This rating procedure requires deeper processing and more focus on the *meaning*, not surface features, of the photos.

**RETRIEVING INFORMATION FROM LONG-TERM MEMORY.** When we need to use information from long-term memory, we search for it. Sometimes, the search is conscious, as when you see a friend approaching and search for her name. At other times, locating and using information from long-term memory is automatic, as when you enter a computer password or the word *memory* pops to mind when you see MEM _ _ _. Think of long-term memory as a huge cabinet full of tools (skills, procedures) and supplies (knowledge, concepts, schemas) ready to be brought to the workbench of working memory to accomplish a task. The cabinet (long-term memory) stores an incredible amount, but it may be hard to find what you are looking for quickly. The workbench (working memory) is small, but anything on it is immediately available. Because it is small, however, supplies (bits of information) sometimes are lost when the workbench is overloaded or when one bit of information covers (interferes with) another (E. Gagné, 1985). Of course you have to walk into the room through the door of attention in order to get to the workbench and the cabinet (Silverman, 2008).

**Context** The total setting or situation that surrounds and interacts with a person or event. It includes internal and external circumstances and situations that interact with the individual's thoughts, feelings, and actions to shape development and learning.

**Levels of processing theory** Theory that recall of information is based on how deeply it is processed.

SPREADING ACTIVATION.   The size of the network in long-term memory is huge, but only small parts from it are activated at any one time—in fact, as you saw earlier, some psychologists say the smaller activated part of long-term memory *is* working memory. Information is retrieved in this network through **spreading activation**. When a particular proposition or image is active—when we are thinking about it—other closely associated knowledge can be primed or triggered as well, and activation can spread through the network (Anderson, 2010). Thus, as Phil focuses on the propositions, "I'd like to go for a drive to see the fall leaves," related ideas such as, "I should rake leaves," and "The car needs an oil change," come to his mind. As activation spreads from the "car trip" to the "oil change," the original thought, or active memory, disappears from working memory because of the limited space. Thus, **retrieval** from long-term memory occurs partly through the spreading of activation from one bit of knowledge to related ideas in the network.

RECONSTRUCTION.   In long-term memory, the information is still available, even when it is not activated, even when you are not thinking about it at the moment. If spreading activation does not "find" the information we seek, then we might still come up with an answer through **reconstruction**, a cognitive tool or problem-solving process that makes use of logic, cues, and other knowledge to construct a reasonable answer by filling in any missing parts (Koriat, Goldsmith, & Pansky, 2000). Sometimes reconstructed recollections are incorrect. For example, in 1932, F. C. Bartlett conducted a series of famous studies on remembering stories. He read a complex, unfamiliar First Nations tale to students at England's Cambridge University and, after various lengths of time, asked the students to recall the story. Stories the students recalled were generally shorter than the original and were translated into the concepts and language of the Cambridge student culture. The story told of a seal hunt, for instance, but many students remembered (reconstructed) a "fishing trip," an activity closer to their experiences and more consistent with their schemas.

FORGETTING AND LONG-TERM MEMORY.   Over 100 years ago, Hermann Ebbinghaus (1885/1964), a pioneer in studying memory for verbal information, said simply, "All sorts of ideas, if left to themselves, are gradually forgotten. This fact is generally known" (p. 62). Information appears to be lost from long-term memory through time decay and interference. For example, memory for Spanish–English vocabulary decreases for about three years after a person's last course in Spanish, then stays level for about 25 years, then drops again for the next 25 years. One explanation for this decline is that neural connections, like muscles, grow weak without use. After 25 years, it may be that the memories are still somewhere in the brain, but they are too weak to be reactivated. Also, the physiological deterioration that comes with age could account for the later declines because some neurons simply die (Anderson, 2010). Finally, newer memories may interfere with or obscure older memories, and older memories may interfere with memory for new material.

Even with decay and interference, long-term memory is remarkable. Information in working memory can be lost and forgotten, but information stored in long-term memory may be available for a long time, given the right cues (Erdelyi, 2010). Teaching strategies that encourage student engagement, deeper processing of information, and higher levels of initial learning are associated with longer retention. Examples of such strategies are frequent reviews and tests, elaborated feedback, high standards, mastery learning, and active involvement in learning projects.

## Individual Differences and Long-Term Memory

The major individual difference that affects long-term memory is knowledge. As we saw with the young soccer experts, when people have more domain-specific declarative and procedural knowledge, they are better at learning and remembering material in that domain (Alexander, 1997). Think about what it is like to read a very technical textbook in an area you know little about. Every line is difficult. You have to stop and look up words or turn back to earlier sections to read about concepts you don't understand. It is hard to remember what you are reading because you are trying to understand and remember at the same time. But with a good basis of knowledge, learning and remembering become

**Spreading activation**  Retrieval of pieces of information based on their relatedness to one another. Remembering one bit of information activates (stimulates) recall of associated information.

**Retrieval**  Process of searching for and finding information in long-term memory.

**Reconstruction**  Recreating information by using memories, expectations, logic, and existing knowledge.

easier; the more you know, the easier it is to know more. This may be why classes in your major seem easier than the required classes outside your major. Another factor could be interest. To develop expert understanding and recall in a domain requires the "continuous interplay of skill (i.e., knowledge) and thrill (i.e., interest)" (Alexander, Kulikowich, & Schulze, 1994, p. 334).

Now let's turn to the really important question: How can teachers support the development of long-lasting knowledge?

# BECOMING KNOWLEDGEABLE: SOME BASIC PRINCIPLES

We will discuss the development of *declarative* and *procedural* knowledge separately, but keep in mind that real learning is a combination and integration of these elements. We look at developing the third type, *self-regulatory* knowledge, in the next chapter when we discuss metacognition.

## Reaching Every Student: Development of Declarative Knowledge

As you have seen, people learn best when they have a good base of knowledge in the area they are studying. With many well-elaborated schemas and scripts to guide them, new material makes more sense, and there are many possible spots in the long-term memory network for connecting new information with old. What are some possible strategies? Perhaps the best single method for helping students learn is to make each lesson as meaningful as possible.

MAKING IT MEANINGFUL.   Meaningful lessons are presented in vocabulary that makes sense to the students. New terms are clarified through ties with more familiar words and ideas. Meaningful lessons are well organized, with clear connections between the different elements of the lesson. Finally, meaningful lessons make natural use of old information to help students understand new information through examples or analogies.

The importance of meaningful lessons is emphasized below in an example presented years ago by Smith (1975).

-------------------------------------------------------------

STOP & THINK Look at the three lines below. Begin by covering all but the first line. Look at it for a second, close the book, and write down all the letters you remember. Then repeat this procedure with the second and third lines.
1.   KBVODUWGPJMSQTXNOGMCTRSO
2.   READ JUMP WHEAT POOR BUT SEEK
3.   KNIGHTS RODE HORSES INTO WAR •

-------------------------------------------------------------

Each line has the same number of letters, but the chances are great that you remembered all the letters in the third line, a good number of letters in the second line, and very few in the first line. The first line makes no sense. There is no way to organize it in a brief glance. Working memory is simply not able to hold and process all those bits of information quickly. The second line is more meaningful. You do not have to see each letter because your long-term memory brings prior knowledge of spelling rules and vocabulary to the task. The third line is the most meaningful. Just a glance and you can probably remember all of it because you bring to this task prior knowledge not only of spelling and vocabulary but also of rules about syntax and probably some historical information about knights (they didn't ride in tanks). This sentence is meaningful because you have existing schemas for assimilating it (Sweller, van Merriënboer, & Paas, 1998).

The challenge for teachers is to make lessons less like learning the first line and more like learning the third line. Although this may seem obvious, think about the times when you have read a sentence in a text or heard an explanation from a professor that might just as well have been KBVODUWGPJMSQTXNOGMCTRSO. But beware, attempts to change the ways that students are used to learning—moving from memorizing to meaningful—are not always greeted with student enthusiasm. Students may be concerned about their grades; at least when memorization gains an A, they know what is expected. Meaningful learning can be riskier and more challenging. In Chapter 9, 10, and 11 we will examine a variety of ways in which teachers can support meaningful learning and understanding.

What can you do when students don't have a good base of knowledge? Mnemonics is a memory strategy for getting started.

**MNEMONICS.**   **Mnemonics** are systematic procedures for improving memory (Atkinson et al., 1999; Levin, 1994; Rummel, Levin, & Woodward, 2003). When information has little inherent meaning, mnemonic strategies build in meaning by connecting what is to be learned with established words or images.

The **loci method** derives its name from the plural of the Latin word *locus,* meaning "place." To use loci, you must first imagine a very familiar place, such as your own house or apartment, and pick out particular locations to serve as "pegs" to "hang" memories. For instance, let's say you want to remember to buy milk, bread, butter, and cereal at the store. Imagine a giant jug of milk blocking the entry hall, a lazy loaf of bread sleeping on the living room couch, a stick of butter melting all over the dining room table, and cereal covering the kitchen floor. When you want to remember the items, all you have to do is take an imaginary walk through your house.

If you need to remember information for long periods of time, an acronym may be the answer. An **acronym** is a form of abbreviation—a word formed from the first letter of each word in a phrase, for example, HOMES to remember the Great Lakes (Huron, Ontario, Michigan, Erie, Superior). Another method forms phrases or sentences out of the first letter of each word or item in a list, for example, Every Good Boy Does Fine to remember the lines on the G clef—E, G, B, D, F. Because the words must make sense as a sentence, this approach also has some characteristics of **chain mnemonics**, methods that connect the first item to be memorized with the second, the second item with the third, and so on. In one type of chain method, each item on a list is linked to the next through some visual association or story. Another chain-method approach is to incorporate all the items to be memorized into a jingle such as "i before e except after c."

The mnemonic system that has been most extensively researched in teaching is the **keyword method**. Joel Levin and his colleagues use a mnemonic (the 3 Rs) to teach the keyword mnemonic method:

- **R**ecode the to-be-learned vocabulary item as a more familiar, concrete keyword—this is the keyword.
- **R**elate the keyword clue to the vocabulary item's definition through a sentence.
- **R**etrieve the desired definition.

The keyword method has been used extensively in foreign language learning. For example, the French word *carte* (meaning "map") sounds like the English word *cart. Cart* becomes the keyword: You imagine a shopping cart filled with a huge collection of maps, or you make up a sentence such as "The cart full of maps tipped over" (Pressley, Levin, & Delaney, 1982). A similar approach has been used to help students connect artists with particular aspects of their paintings. For example, students are told to imagine that the heavy dark lines of paintings by Rouault are made with a *ruler* (Rouault) dipped in black paint (Carney & Levin, 2000, 2002).

Vocabulary learned with keywords can be easily forgotten if students are given keywords and images instead of being asked to supply words and images that are relevant to them. When the teacher provides the memory links, these associations may not fit the students' existing knowledge and may be forgotten or confused later; as a result, remembering suffers (Wang & Thomas, 1995; Wang, Thomas, & Ouellette, 1992). Younger students have some difficulty forming their own images. For them, memory aids that rely on auditory cues—rhymes such as "Thirty days hath September" seem to work better (Willoughby, Porter, Belsito, & Yearsley, 1999). Not all educators agree, however, as you will see in the *Point/Counterpoint*.

**Watch**
Mnemonics

**Mnemonics**  Techniques for remembering; the art of memory.

**Loci method**  Technique of associating items with specific places.

**Acronym**  Technique for remembering by using the first letter of each word in a phrase to form a new, memorable word.

**Chain mnemonics**  Memory strategies that associate one element in a series with the next element.

**Keyword method**  System of associating new words or concepts with similar-sounding cue words and images.

Until we have some knowledge to guide learning, it may help to use some mnemonic approaches to build vocabulary and facts.

ROTE MEMORIZATION. Very few things need to be learned by rote. The greatest challenge teachers face is to help students think and understand, not just memorize. Unfortunately, many students view **rote memorizing** and learning as the same thing (Iran-Nejad, 1990).

On rare occasions we do have to memorize something word for word, such as lines in a song, poem, or play. How would you do it? If you have tried to memorize a list of items that are all similar to one another, you may have found that you tended to remember items at the beginning and at the end of the list, but forgot those in the middle. This is called the **serial-position effect**. **Part learning**, breaking the list into smaller segments, can

> **Rote memorization**
> Remembering information by repetition without necessarily understanding the meaning of the information.
>
> **Serial-position effect** The tendency to remember the beginning and the end, but not the middle of a list.
>
> **Part learning** Breaking a list of items into shorter lists.

## POINT/COUNTERPOINT  What's Wrong With Memorizing?

For years, students have relied on memorization to learn vocabulary, procedures, steps, names, and facts. Is this a bad idea?

▶ **POINT Rote memorization creates inert knowledge.** Years ago William James (1912) described the limitations of rote learning by telling a story about what can happen when students memorize but do not understand:

*A friend of mine, visiting a school, was asked to examine a young class in geography. Glancing at the book, she said: "Suppose you should dig a hole in the ground, hundreds of feet deep, how should you find it at the bottom—warmer or colder than on top?" None of the class replying, the teacher said: "I'm sure they know, but I think you don't ask the question quite rightly. Let me try." So, taking the book, she asked: "In what condition is the interior of the globe?" And received the immediate answer from half the class at once. "The interior of the globe is in a condition of igneous fusion." (p. 150)*

The students had memorized the answer, but they had no idea what it meant. Perhaps they didn't understand the meaning of "interior," "globe," or "igneous fusion." At any rate, the knowledge was useful to them only when they were answering test questions, and only then when the questions were phrased exactly as they had been memorized. Students often resort to memorizing the exact words of definitions when they have no hope for actually understanding the terms or when teachers count off for definitions that are not exact.

Howard Gardner has been a vocal critic of rote memorization and a champion of "teaching for understanding." In an interview in *Phi Delta Kappan* (Siegel & Shaughnessy, 1994), Gardner says:

*. . . even our better students in our better schools are just going through the motions of education. In* The Unschooled Mind, *I review ample evidence that suggests an absence of understanding—the inability of students to take knowledge, skills, and other apparent attainments and apply them successfully in new situations. In the absence of such flexibility and adaptability, the education that the students receive is worth little. (pp. 563–564)*

▶ **COUNTERPOINT Rote memorization can be effective.** Memorization may not be such a bad way to learn new information that has little inherent meaning, such as foreign language vocabulary. Alvin Wang, Margaret Thomas, and Judith Ouellette (1992) compared learning Tagalog (the national language of the Philippines) using either rote memorization or the keyword approach for associating new words with existing words and images. In their study, even though the keyword method led to faster and better learning initially, long-term forgetting was *greater* for students who had used the keyword method than for students who had learned by rote memorization.

A study of preservice teachers found that they believed memorization is valuable for young children to build basic skills (Beghetto, 2008). There are times when students must memorize and we do them a disservice if we don't teach them how. For example, "memorization in simple mathematics or word reading activities in the early grades may be desirable and promote future academic success; constructivist, problem-based learning by itself may not be as successful as a combination of both constructivist problem solving and memorization together" (Chang et al., 2011, p. 25).

**Beware of Either/Or.** Every discipline has its own terms, names, facts, and rules. As adults, we want to work with physicians who have memorized the correct names for the bones and organs of the body or the drugs needed to combat particular infections. Of course, they can look up some information or research certain conditions, but they have to know where to start. We want to work with accountants who give us accurate information about the new tax codes, information they probably had to memorize because it changes from year to year in ways that are not necessarily rational or meaningful. We want to deal with computer salespeople who have memorized their stock and know exactly which printers will work with our computer. Just because something was learned through memorization does not mean it is inert knowledge. The real question, as Gardner points out, is whether you can *use* the information flexibly and effectively to solve new problems.

help prevent this effect, because breaking a list into several shorter lists means there will be fewer middle items to forget.

Another strategy for memorizing a long selection or list is the use of **distributed practice**. A student who studies Hamlet's soliloquy intermittently throughout the weekend will probably do much better than a student who tries to memorize the entire speech on Sunday night. Studying for an extended period is called *massed practice*. **Massed practice** leads to cognitive overload, fatigue, and lagging motivation. Distributed practice gives time for deeper processing and strengthens the connections in the neural network of the brain (Mumford, Costanza, Baughman, Threlfall, & Fleishman, 1994; Paul, 2011). What is forgotten after one session can be relearned in the next with distributed practice. Still, there is debate in education about how much memorization should be encouraged, as you can see in the *Point/Counterpoint*.

## Development of Procedural Knowledge

One characteristic that distinguishes experts from novices in every arena, from reading to medical diagnosis, is that the experts' declarative knowledge has become "proceduralized"—that is, incorporated into routines they can apply automatically without making many demands on working memory. Explicit memories have become implicit and the expert is no longer aware of them. Skills that are applied without conscious thought are called **automated basic skills**. An example is shifting gears in a standard transmission car. At first, you have to think about every step, but as you become more expert (if you do), the procedure becomes automatic. But not all procedures can be automatic, even for experts in a particular domain. For example, no matter how expert you are in driving, you still have to consciously watch the traffic around you. This kind of conscious procedure is called a *domain-specific strategy*. Automated basic skills and domain-specific strategies are learned in different ways (Gagné, Yekovich, & Yekovich, 1993).

AUTOMATED BASIC SKILLS.   Most psychologists identify three stages in the development of an automated skill: *cognitive, associative*, and *autonomous* (Anderson, 2010; Fitts & Posner, 1967). At the cognitive stage, when we are first learning, we rely on declarative knowledge and general problem-solving strategies to accomplish our goal. For example, to learn how to assemble a bookshelf, we might try to follow steps in the instruction manual, putting a check beside each step as we complete it to keep track of progress. At this stage, we have to "think about" every step and perhaps refer back to the pictures of parts to see what a "10 cm metal bolt with lock nut" looks like. The cognitive load on working memory is heavy. There can be quite a bit of trial-and-error learning at this stage when, for example, the bolt we chose doesn't fit.

At the *associative stage*, individual steps of a procedure are combined or "chunked" into larger units. We reach for the right bolt and put it into the right hole. One step smoothly cues the next. With practice, the associative stage moves to the *autonomous stage*, where the whole procedure can be accomplished without much attention. So if you assemble enough bookshelves, you can have a lively conversation as you do, paying little attention to the assembly task. This movement from the cognitive to the associative to the autonomous stage holds for the development of basic cognitive skills in any area, but science, medicine, chess, and mathematics have been most heavily researched. One thing is clear—it takes many hours of successful practice to make skills automatic.

What can teachers do to help their students pass through these three stages and become more expert learners? In general, it appears that two factors are critical: *prerequisite knowledge* and *practice with feedback*. First, if students don't have the essential prior knowledge (concepts, schemas, skills, etc.), the cognitive load on working memory will be too great. Second, practice with feedback allows you to form associations, recognize cues automatically, and combine small steps into larger condition-action rules or **productions**. Even from the earliest stage, some of this practice should include a simplified version of the whole process in a real context. Practice in real contexts helps students learn not only *how* to do a skill but also *why and when* (Collins, Brown, & Newman, 1989; Gagné, Yekovich, & Yekovich, 1993). Of course, as every athletic coach knows, if a

**Distributed practice**   Practice in brief periods with rest intervals.

**Massed practice**   Practice for a single extended period.

**Automated basic skills**   Skills that are applied without conscious thought.

**Productions**   The contents of procedural memory; rules about what actions to take, given certain conditions.

particular step, component, or process is causing trouble, that element might be practised alone until it is more automatic, and then put back into the whole sequence, to lower the cognitive load on working memory (Anderson, Reder, & Simon, 1996; Ericsson, 2011).

**DOMAIN-SPECIFIC STRATEGIES.** As we saw earlier, some procedural knowledge, such as monitoring the traffic while you drive, is not automatic because conditions are constantly changing. Once you decide to change lanes, the manoeuvre may be fairly automatic, but the decision to change lanes was conscious, based on the traffic conditions around you. **Domain-specific strategies** are consciously applied skills that organize thoughts and actions to reach a goal. To support this kind of learning, teachers need to provide opportunities for practice in many different situations—for example, practice reading with package labels, magazines, books, letters, operating manuals, web pages and so on. In the next chapter's discussion of problem-solving and study strategies, we will examine other ways to help students develop domain-specific strategies. For now, let's summarize these ideas for developing declarative and procedural knowledge in a set of *Guidelines*. We will spend quite a bit of time in the next chapter on developing self-regulatory knowledge.

> **Domain-specific strategies**
> Consciously applied skills to reach goals in a particular subject or problem.

## GUIDELINES

### Helping Students Understand and Remember

**Make sure you have the students' attention.**
*Examples*
1. Develop a signal that tells students to stop what they are doing and focus on you. Make sure students respond to the signal—don't let them ignore it. Practise using the signal.
2. Move around the room, use gestures, and avoid speaking in a monotone.
3. Begin a lesson by asking a question that stimulates interest in the topic.
4. Regain the attention of individual students by walking closer to them, using their names, or asking them a question.

**Help students separate essential from nonessential details and focus on the most important information.**
*Examples*
1. Summarize instructional objectives to indicate what students should be learning. Relate the material you are presenting to the objectives as you teach: "Now I'm going to explain exactly how you can find the information you need to meet Objective One on the board—determining the tone of the story."
2. When you make an important point, pause, repeat, ask a student to paraphrase, note the information on the board in coloured chalk, or tell students to highlight the point in their notes or readings.

**Help students make connections between new information and what they already know.**
*Examples*
1. Review prerequisites to help students bring to mind the information they will need to understand new material: "Who can tell us the definition of a quadrilateral? Now, what is a rhombus? Is a square a quadrilateral? Is a square a rhombus? What did we say yesterday about how you can tell? Today we are going to look at some other quadrilaterals."
2. Use an outline or diagram to show how new information fits with the framework you have been developing. For example, "Now that you know the duties of the Canadian Space Agency, where would you expect to find it in this diagram of the branches of the Canadian government?"
3. Give an assignment that specifically calls for the use of new information along with information already learned.

**Provide for repetition and review of information.**
*Examples*
1. Begin the class with a quick review of the homework assignment.
2. Give frequent, short tests.
3. Build practice and repetition into games, or have students work with partners to quiz each other.

**Present material in a clear, organized way.**
*Examples*
1. Make the purpose of the lesson very clear.
2. Give students a brief outline to follow. Put the same outline on an overhead transparency so you can keep yourself on track. When students ask questions or make comments, relate these to the appropriate section of the outline.
3. Use summaries in the middle and at the end of the lesson.

**Focus on meaning, not memorization.**
*Examples*
1. In teaching new words, help students associate the new word to a related word they already understand: "*Enmity* is from the same base as *enemy*."
2. In teaching about remainders, have students group 12 objects into sets of 2, 3, 4, 5, 6, and ask them to count the "leftovers" in each case.

---

*For more information on information processing, see www.edpsycinteractive.org/topics/cognition/infoproc.html.*

# ▼ SUMMARY

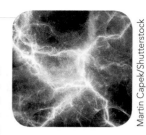

Martin Capek/Shutterstock

## Elements of the Cognitive Perspective (pp. 259–261)

**Contrast cognitive and behavioural views of learning in terms of what is learned and the role of reinforcement.** According to the cognitive view, knowledge is learned, and changes in knowledge make changes in behaviour possible. According to the behavioural view, the new behaviours themselves are learned. Both behavioural and cognitive theorists believe reinforcement is important in learning, but for different reasons. The strict behaviourist maintains that reinforcement strengthens responses; cognitive theorists see reinforcement as a source of feedback about what is likely to happen if behaviours are repeated or changed—as a source of information.

**How does knowledge affect learning?** The cognitive approach suggests that one of the most important elements in the learning process is knowledge the individual brings to the learning situation. What we already know determines to a great extent what we will pay attention to, perceive, learn, remember, and forget.

**What is the brain's role in cognition?** The human brain seems to both impact and be impacted by learning. For example, individuals who regularly complete tasks such as taxi driving develop certain regions of the brain more than others who do not engage in such activities. Research also suggests that learning changes communication among neurons. These changes enable children to engage in complex tasks such as integrating past and present experiences by approximately age 7.

## Cognitive Views of Memory (pp. 261–273)

**Describe the path from sensory input to recognizing objects.** The first phase in the process is feature analysis, or bottom-up processing, because the stimulus must be analyzed into features or components and assembled into a meaningful pattern. The Gestalt principles are one explanation for how features are organized into patterns. In addition to noting features and using these Gestalt principles, to recognize patterns rapidly we use what we already know about the situation, information from the context, and our knowledge of prototypes or best examples.

**What is working memory?** Working memory is both short-term storage in the phonological loop and visuospatial sketchpad and processing in the episodic buffer, guided by the central executive—it is the workbench of conscious thought. To keep information activated in working memory for longer than 20 seconds, people use maintenance rehearsal (mentally repeating) and elaborative rehearsal (making connections with knowledge from long-term memory). Elaborative rehearsal also helps move new information to long-term memory. The limited capacity of working memory can also be somewhat circumvented by the control process of chunking. There are individual differences in working memory, and working memory span is related to performance on tasks that require higher-level thinking and controlled attention such as IQ tests and the Law School Admissions Test.

**What is cognitive load and how does it impact information processing?** Cognitive load refers to the volume of cognitive resources, including perception, attention and memory, necessary to perform a task. These resources must be devoted not only to organizing and understanding the task, but also to analyzing the solution and ignoring irrelevant stimuli. If cognitive load is high, it can decrease or even inhibit one's ability to perform a task.

## Long-Term Memory (pp. 273–285)

**Compare declarative, procedural, and self-regulatory knowledge.** Declarative knowledge is knowledge that can be declared, usually in words or other symbols. Declarative knowledge is "knowing that" something is the case. Procedural knowledge is "knowing how" to do something; it must be demonstrated. Self-regulatory knowledge is "knowing when and why" to apply your declarative and procedural knowledge.

**How is information represented in long-term memory, and what role do schemas play?** Memories may be explicit (semantic or episodic) or implicit (procedural, classical conditioning, or priming). In long-term memory, bits of information may be stored and interrelated in terms of propositional networks, images, concepts, and schemas. A concept is a category used to group similar events, ideas, objects, or people such as books, students, or cats. Concepts provide a manner of organizing diversity among members of a group. Concepts are often represented by prototypes (an ideal example) and exemplars (a representative memory). Long-term memories include concepts that enable people to identify and recognize members of a group. To organize propositions, images, and concepts, we have schemas, which are data structures that allow us to represent large amounts of complex information, make inferences, and understand new information. Today some psychologists suggest that working memory is just the part of long-term memory that is currently activated—that you are thinking about at any given time.

**What learning processes improve long-term memory?** The way you learn information in the first place affects its recall later. One important requirement is to integrate new material with knowledge already stored in long-term memory using elaboration, organization, imagery, and context. The dual coding theory suggests that information coded both verbally and visually is easier to remember. Pictures and words help students learn as long as they are well organized and do not overload working memory. Another view of memory is the levels of processing theory, in which recall of information is determined by how completely it is processed.

**Why do we forget?** Information lost from working memory truly disappears, but information in long-term memory may be available, given the right cues. Information appears to be lost from long-term memory through time decay (neural connections, like muscles, grow weak without use) and interference (newer memories may obscure older memories, and older memories may interfere with memory for new material).

## Becoming Knowledgeable: Some Basic Principles (pp. 285–289)

**Describe three ways to develop declarative knowledge.** Declarative knowledge develops as we integrate new information with our existing understanding. The most useful and effective way to learn and remember is to understand and use new information. Making the information to be remembered meaningful is important and often is the greatest challenge for teachers. Mnemonics are memorization aids: They include approaches such as the loci method, acronyms, chain mnemonics, and the keyword method.

A powerful but limiting way to accomplish this is rote memorization, which can best be supported by part learning and distributed practice.

**Describe some methods for developing procedural knowledge.** Automated basic skills and domain-specific strategies—two types of procedural knowledge—are learned in different ways. There are three stages in the development of an automated skill: cognitive (following steps or directions guided by declarative knowledge),

associative (combining individual steps into larger units), and autonomous (where the whole procedure can be accomplished without much attention). Prerequisite knowledge and practice with feedback help students move through these stages. Domain-specific strategies are consciously applied skills of organizing thoughts and actions to reach a goal. To support this kind of learning, teachers need to provide opportunities for practice and application in many different situations.

# ▼ WHAT WOULD THEY DO?

## TEACHERS' CASEBOOK: Remembering the Basics

Here is how some expert teachers responded to the situation described at the beginning of the chapter.

### GARTH NICHOLS
Bayview Glen School, Toronto, ON

At its heart, history is the study of humanity, the application of critical thinking, and the constant recreation of past events. People, places, and events can rarely be understood with full clarity due to bias in the construction of history. If I were faced with this situation in my own classroom, I would stop and take a long, reflective look at the way history is being taught in the younger grades, as well as at the language, resources, and assessments that I use in my own classes.

Using an inquiry-based approach, I would problematize the topic under study by presenting varying perspectives of one event, as well as different interpretations of that event during different time periods. As the zeitgeist of a culture changes, so, too, does the popular interpretation of events, and one culture may view an event from subtle or widely varying points of view. My assessments would contain content but would begin to reflect this movement away from facts and more toward the application of ideas to make sense of the topic.

To accomplish this, I would embed within my units and lessons a critical thinking continuum. At the foundation would be the descriptive analysis, where students would learn or research the who, what, where, when, why, and how of the topic. Once this has been established to a reasonable degree, students would then apply a critical thinking lens analyzing one, or more, of the acronym PERMS: What is Politically, Economically, Religiously, Socially, Militarily, and Socially significant or important within this topic? I would get my students learning, understanding, and applying the six historical thinking concepts: use of primary documents, establishing historical significance, exploring causes and consequences, taking historical perspectives, identifying continuity and change, and understanding the ethical dimensions of historical interpretations.

With this continuum in place, and with a systemic review of the history courses being taught, it is hoped that the students' view of historical events would shift over time to appreciate that facts are not without interpretation, and that history is a subject that can inform us of the past but also help us understand our present and future.

### CLAIRE FRANKEL-SALAMA
Formerly from Bishop's College High School St. John's, NL

Most students are motivated to obtain good marks and, for many, these have been achieved through rote learning. True learning through the association of ideas has not been part of their school

experience. Why is this the case? Why is the rote memory approach still the favoured method of "learning"?

In many schools, teachers have to deal with the unpleasant logistical realities of extremely large classes, multiple preparations, heavy course loads, and extracurricular activities. In the interest of expedience, there is a strong emphasis on multiple-choice and factually strict questioning techniques that afford little room for independent thinking and development of good writing skills. In fact, the increased use of standardized testing has served only to exacerbate this problem by precluding more pedagogically sound qualitative forms of evaluation and feedback. Teachers feel increasingly pressured to prepare students for the exam rather than to develop keen, critical minds.

How can we, as educators, deal with these realities and still work toward a more synthetic approach to learning?

Certainly it is valuable to consider an interdisciplinary approach to teaching, especially at the high school level, where courses tend to be taught as separate units. Meetings between departments should take place, and multidisciplinary projects should be encouraged. For example, it may be possible to accommodate a history presentation or essay in a literature, or even a science, assignment. This should not be considered cheating; indeed, such an effort should have the cooperation of all departments involved. In this way, the student begins to realize the impact of science on literature, of music on history, of mathematics on art, and so on. A co-directed paper on socialism in literature will surely have more intellectual impact than a simple research paper in one restricted area.

Another effective way to encourage analysis and synthesis involves the use of authentic documents and oral histories. A reading of Rabelais's recommendation of a good Renaissance education helps us question our own. The study of caricatures from different sources regarding the same historical event deepens understanding of different political viewpoints. A survivor's account of the Triangle Shirtwaist Factory fire helps us "feel" the need for labour reform. A study of socialist art and its relationship to an economic system will explain what the ideology is really about. The comprehension of contextualities will certainly deepen understanding.

Teachers should neither despair nor think that these efforts will bear no fruit. After all, wisdom comes with age and experience. It is not unusual to receive visits or letters from former students thanking a teacher for introducing a particular author, some interesting paintings, a meaningful destination, or previously unheard music. Germination requires a confluence of several seemingly unrelated conditions. Eventually, some seeds will bloom, perhaps even beyond expectations.

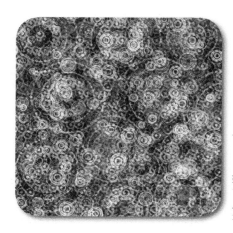

Liubomir/Shutterstock

# CHAPTER 9

# COMPLEX COGNITIVE PROCESSES

► **TEACHERS' CASEBOOK:** Uncritical Thinking

This year's class is worse than any you've ever had. You assigned a research paper and you find more and more students are using the web for their information. In itself, using the web is okay, but the students appear to be completely uncritical about what they find. "If it is on the web, it must be right" seems to be their attitude. Their first drafts are filled with quotes that seem very biased to you, and there are no sources cited or listed. It is not just that students don't know how to reference their work. You are more concerned that they cannot critically evaluate what they are reading. And all they are reading is information on the web!

**CRITICAL THINKING**

- How would you help your students evaluate the information they are finding on the web?

- Beyond this immediate issue, how will you help students think more critically about the subjects you are teaching?

- How will you take into account the cultural beliefs and values of your students as you support their critical thinking?

## OVERVIEW AND OBJECTIVES

In the previous chapter we focused on how knowledge develops—how people make sense of and remember information and ideas. In this chapter, we consider complex cognitive processes that lead to understanding. Understanding is more than memorizing. It is more than retelling in your own words. Understanding involves appropriately transforming and using knowledge, skills, and ideas. These understandings are considered "higher-level cognitive objectives" in a commonly used system of educational objectives (Anderson & Krathwohl, 2001; Bloom, Engelhart, Frost, Hill, & Krathwohl, 1956). We will focus on implications of cognitive theories for the day-to-day practice of teaching.

Because the cognitive perspective is a philosophical orientation and not a unified theoretical model, teaching methods derived from it are varied. In this chapter, we will first examine the complex cognitive process of metacognition—using knowledge and skills about learning, motivation, and yourself to plan and regulate your own learning. Next we explore four important areas in which cognitive theorists have made suggestions for learning and teaching: learning strategies, problem solving, creativity, and critical thinking, including argumentation. Finally, we will consider the question of how to encourage the transfer of learning from one situation to another to make learning more useful.

When you have completed this chapter, you should be able to:

9.1   Discuss roles of metacognition in learning and remembering.
9.2   Describe several learning and study strategies that help students develop their metacognitive abilities.
9.3   Explain processes involved in problem solving and factors that can interfere with successful problem solving.
9.4   Explain how creativity is defined, assessed, and encouraged in the classroom.
9.5   Identify factors that influence students' abilities to think critically and to form and support arguments.
9.6   Discuss how, why, and when knowledge learned in one situation might be applied to new situations and problems.

# METACOGNITION

In Chapter 8 we examined **executive control processes**, including attention, rehearsal, organization, imagery, and elaboration. These executive control processes are sometimes called *metacognitive* skills, because they can be intentionally used to regulate cognitive activities like encoding, and storing and retrieving information from memory.

## Metacognitive Knowledge and Regulation

Donald Meichenbaum, professor emeritus at the University of Waterloo, and his colleagues described **metacognition** as people's "awareness of their own cognitive machinery and how the machinery works" (Meichenbaum, Burland, Gruson, & Cameron, 1985, p. 5). Metacognition literally means cognition about cognition—or thinking about thinking—something William James wrote about over 100 years ago (although he did not give it that name). The term was introduced into discussions of child development by John Flavell and his colleagues in the early 1970s. Metacognition is higher-order knowledge about your own thinking as well as your ability to use this knowledge to manage your own cognitive processes such as comprehending and problem solving (Bruning, Schraw, & Norby, 2011). People differ in how well and how quickly they learn partly because they differ in their metacognitive knowledge and skills.

 **Watch**
Metacognitive Knowledge and Regulation

**Executive control processes** Processes such as selective attention, rehearsal, elaboration, and organization that influence encoding, storage, and retrieval of information in memory.

**Metacognition** Knowledge about our own thinking processes.

**METACOGNITION** Metacognition sets the stage for choosing the best way to approach a learning task. Students with well-developed metacognitive skills set goals, organize their activities, select among various approaches to learning, and change strategies if needed.

Anthony Magnacca/Merrill

Metacognition involves all three kinds of knowledge we discussed earlier: (1) *declarative knowledge* about yourself as a learner, factors that influence your learning and memory, and skills, strategies, and resources you need to perform a task—*knowing what* to do; (2) *procedural knowledge* or *knowing how* to use the strategies; and (3) *self-regulatory knowledge* to ensure the completion of the task—*knowing the conditions*, when and why, to apply the procedures and strategies (Bruning, Schraw, & Norby, 2011). Metacognition is strategically applying this declarative, procedural, and self-regulatory knowledge to accomplish goals and solve problems (Schunk, 2012). Metacognition also includes knowledge about the value of applying cognitive strategies in learning (Pressley & Harris, 2006).

Metacognition regulates thinking and learning (Brown, 1987; Nelson, 1996). There are three essential skills: *planning, monitoring,* and *evaluating. Planning* involves deciding how much time to give to a task, which strategies to use, how to start, which resources to gather, what order to follow, what to skim and what to give intense attention to, and so on. *Monitoring* is the real-time awareness of "How I'm doing." Monitoring is asking questions like, "Is this making sense? Am I trying to work too fast? Have I studied enough?" *Evaluating* involves making judgments about the processes and outcomes of thinking and learning. "Should I change strategies? Get help? Give up for now? Is this paper (painting, model, poem, plan . . .) finished?" The notion of *reflection* in teaching—thinking back on what happened in class and why, and thinking forward to what you might do next time—is really metacognition about teaching (Sawyer, 2006a).

Of course, we don't have to be metacognitive all the time. Some actions become routine or automatic. Metacognition is most useful when tasks are challenging, but not too difficult. And even when we are planning, monitoring, and evaluating, these processes are not necessarily conscious, especially in adults. We may use them without being aware of our efforts (Perner, 2000). Experts in a particular field plan, monitor, and evaluate as second nature; they have difficulty describing their metacognitive knowledge and skills (Pressley & Harris, 2006; Reder, 1996).

## Individual Differences in Metacognition

Some differences in metacognitive abilities are the result of development. Younger children, for example, may not be aware of the purpose of a lesson—they may think the point is simply to finish. They also may not be good at gauging the difficulty of a task—they may think reading for fun and reading a science book are the same (Gredler, 2009). As children grow older, they are more able to exercise executive control over strategies. For example, they are more able to determine if they have understood instructions or if they have studied enough to remember a set of items. Metacognitive abilities begin to develop around ages 5 to 7 and improve throughout school (Flavell, Green, & Flavell, 1995; Woolfolk & Perry, 2012).

Not all differences in metacognitive abilities have to do with age or maturation. Some individual differences in metacognitive abilities are probably caused by differences in biology or learning experiences. In fact, many students diagnosed as having learning disabilities have problems monitoring their attention (Hallahan & Kauffman, 2006), particularly in long tasks. Working to improve metacognitive skills can be especially important for students who often have trouble in school (Schunk, 2012; Swanson, 1990).

## Lessons for Teachers: Developing Metacognition

Like any knowledge or skill, metacognitive knowledge and skills can be learned and improved.

**METACOGNITIVE DEVELOPMENT FOR YOUNGER STUDENTS.** In his grade 2 classroom, Daric Desautel (2009) worked with mostly Latino/a and Asian students. As part of teaching literacy, Desautel decided to focus on student metacognitive knowledge and skills such as setting goals, planning, evaluating achievements, and self-reflection. He wanted to help students develop the habit of "looking in" at their own thinking. He also included self-reflections to help students evaluate their writing and gain insight into themselves as readers and writers. For example, one self-reflection activity included a checklist asking:

- Did you pick a topic that you know all about?
- Did you write a special beginning that makes the reader want more?
- Did you organize your thoughts and make a table of contents?
- Did you pick the right kind of paper and illustrate your book clearly?
- Did you re-read your work to check for *sound*, *sense*, *order*, and *goofs*?

Desautel was successful in helping all his students, not just the most verbal and advanced, develop metacognitive knowledge. One student noted in his reflection, "I worked hard and did my best to make this book. I like nonfiction books better than stories. Next time, I would write about a different sport."

In her work with grade 1 and 2 students, Nancy found that asking students two questions helped them become more metacognitive. The questions were "What did you learn about yourself as a reader/writer today?" and "What did you learn that you can do again and again and again?" When teachers regularly asked these questions during class, even young students demonstrated fairly sophisticated levels of metacognitive understanding and action (Perry, VandeKamp, Mercer, & Nordby, 2000).

Many of the cooperating teachers we work with use a strategy called **KWL** to guide reading and inquiry in general. It can be used with most grade levels. The steps are:

**K** What do I already *know* about this subject?
**W** What do I *want* to know?
**L** At the end of the reading or inquiry, what have I *learned*?

The KWL strategy encourages students to "look within" and identify what they bring to each learning situation, where they want to go, and what they actually achieved. It's a very metacognitive approach to learning. Marilyn Friend and William Bursuck (2002, pp. 362–363) describe how one teacher used modelling and discussion to teach the KWL strategy. After reviewing the steps, the teacher models an example and a nonexample of using KWL to learn about "crayons."

> **Teacher:** What do we do now that we have a passage assigned to read? First, I brainstorm, which means I try to think of anything I already know about the topic and write it down.

The teacher writes on the board or overhead known qualities of crayons, such as "made of wax," "come in many colours," "can be sharpened," "several different brands."

> **Teacher:** I then take this information I already know and put it into categories, like "what crayons are made of" and "crayon colours." Next, I write down any questions I would like to have answered during my reading, such as "Who invented crayons? When were they invented? How are crayons made? Where are they made?" At this point, I'm ready to read, so I read the passage on crayons. Now I must write down what I learned from this passage. I must include any information that answers the questions I wrote down before I read and any additional information. For example, I learned that coloured crayons were first made in the United States in 1903 by Edwin Binney and E. Harold Smith. I also learned that the Crayola Company owns the company that made the original magic markers. Last, I must organize this information into a map so I can see the different main points and any supporting points.

**KWL** One cooperative learning strategy used by many teachers to guide reading and inquiry is called KWL: What do I know? What do I want to know? What have I learned?

Anthony Magnacca/Merrill

**KWL** A strategy to guide reading and inquiry: Before—What do I already *know*? What do I *want* to know? After—What have I *learned*?

At this point, the teacher draws a map on the chalkboard or overhead.

> **Teacher:** Let's talk about the steps I used and what I did before and after I read the passage.

A class discussion follows.

> **Teacher:** Now I'm going to read the passage again, and I want you to evaluate my textbook reading skills based on the KWL Plus strategy we've learned.

The teacher then proceeds to demonstrate the strategy *incorrectly*.

> **Teacher:** The passage is about crayons. Well, how much can there really be to know about crayons besides there are hundreds of colours and they always seem to break in the middle? Crayons are for little kids, and I'm in junior high so I don't need to know that much about them. I'll just skim the passage and go ahead and answer the question. Okay, how well did I use the strategy steps?

The class discusses the teacher's inappropriate use of the strategy. Notice how the teacher provides both an *example* and a *nonexample*—good teaching.

**METACOGNITIVE DEVELOPMENT FOR SECONDARY AND UNIVERSITY STUDENTS (LIKE YOU).** For older students, teachers can include metacognitive questions into their lessons, lectures, and assignments. For example, David Jonassen (2011) suggests that instructional designers incorporate these questions into hypermedia learning environments to help students be more self-reflective:

What are my intellectual strengths and weaknesses?

How can I motivate myself to learn when I need to?

How good am I at judging how well I understand something?

How can I focus on the meaning and significance of new information?

How can I set specific goals before I begin a task?

What questions should I ask about the material before I begin?

How well have I accomplished my goals once I'm finished?

Have I learned as much as I could have once I finish a task?

Have I considered all options after I solve a problem?

Metacognition includes knowledge about using many strategies in learning—our next topic.

# LEARNING STRATEGIES

Most teachers will tell you that they want their students to "learn how to learn." Years of research indicate that using effective learning strategies helps students learn and that these strategies can be taught (Hamman, Berthelot, Saia, & Crowley, 2000; Pressley & Harris, 2006). But were you taught "how to learn"? Powerful and sophisticated learning strategies and study skills are seldom taught directly until high school or even university, so most students have little practice with them (Winne, 2013). In contrast, early on, students usually discover repetition and rote learning on their own, so they have extensive practice with these strategies. Unfortunately, some teachers think memorizing is learning (Beghetto, 2008; Woolfolk Hoy & Murphy, 2001). This may explain why many students cling to flash cards and memorizing—they don't know what else to do (Willoughby, Porter, Belsito, & Yearsley, 1999).

As we saw in Chapter 9, the way something is learned in the first place greatly influences how readily we remember the information and how appropriately we can apply the knowledge later. First, students must be *cognitively engaged* to learn—they have to *focus attention* on relevant or important aspects of the material. Second, to think and *process deeply,* they have to *invest effort*, make connections, elaborate, translate, invent, organize, and reorganize—the greater the practice and processing, the stronger the learning. Finally, students must *regulate and monitor* their learning—keep track of what is making sense and noticing when a new approach is needed, That is, they must be *metacognitive*. The emphasis today is on helping students develop effective learning strategies that focus attention and effort, process information deeply, and monitor understanding.

## Being Strategic About Learning

**Learning strategies** are flexible kinds of procedural knowledge—*knowing how* to do something. There are thousands of strategies. Some are general and taught in school, such as summarizing or outlining. Others are specific to a subject, such as using a mnemonic to remember the order of the planets: "My Very Educated Mother Just Served Us Nachos" for Mercury, Venus, Earth, Mars, Jupiter, Saturn, Uranus, and Neptune. Other strategies may be unique, invented by an individual to learn Chinese characters, for example. Learning strategies can be cognitive (summarizing, identifying the main idea), metacognitive (monitoring comprehension—Do I understand?), or behavioural (using an internet dictionary, setting a timer to work till time's up) (Cantrell, Almasi, Carter, Rintamaa, & Madden, 2010). All are ways of accomplishing a learning task that are intentionally applied when usual methods have not worked and strategic effort is needed (Harris, Alexander, & Graham, 2008). Over time, as you become more expert at using strategies, less intentional effort is needed. Ultimately you may become more automatic in applying the strategies; in other words, the strategies will become your usual way of accomplishing that kind of task, until they don't work and new strategies are needed.

Skilled learners have a wide range of learning strategies they can apply fairly automatically. Using learning strategies and study skills is related to modestly higher GPAs in high school and persistence in university (Robbins et al., 2004; Winne, 2013). Researchers have identified several important principles:

1. Students should be exposed to a number of different strategies, not only general learning strategies but also very specific strategies for particular subjects, such as the graphic strategies described later in this section.
2. Students should be taught conditional knowledge about when, where, and why to use various strategies. Although this may seem obvious, teachers often neglect this step. A strategy is more likely to be maintained and employed if students know when, where, and why to use it.
3. Students may know when and how to use a strategy, but unless they also develop the desire to employ these skills, general learning ability will not improve. Several learning strategy programs include a motivational training component.
4. Students need to believe that they can learn new strategies, that the effort will pay off, and that they can "get smarter" by applying these strategies.
5. Students need some background knowledge and useful schemas in the area being studied to make sense of learning materials. It will be difficult to find the main idea in a paragraph about ichthyology, for example, if you don't know much about fish. So students may need direct instruction in schematic (content) knowledge along with strategy training. Table 9.1 summarizes several learning strategies.

DECIDING WHAT IS IMPORTANT.   You can see from the first entry in Table 9.1 that learning begins with focusing attention—deciding what is important. But distinguishing the main idea from less important information is not always easy. Often students focus on the "seductive details" or the concrete examples, perhaps because these are more interesting (Gardner, Brown, Sanders, & Menke, 1992). You may have had the experience of remembering a joke or an intriguing example from a lecture, but not being clear about the larger point the professor was presenting. Finding the central idea is especially difficult if you lack knowledge in an area and the amount of new information provided is extensive. Teachers can give students practice in identifying and using signals in texts such as headings, bold words, outlines, or other indicators to identify key concepts and main ideas (Lorch, Lorch, Ritchey, McGovern, & Coleman, 2001).

SUMMARIES.   Creating summaries can help students learn, but students have to be taught how to summarize (Byrnes, 1996; Palincsar & Brown, 1984). Jeanne Ormrod

**Learning strategies** A special kind of procedural knowledge—*knowing how* to approach learning tasks.

TABLE 9.1 • **Examples of Learning Strategies**

|  | EXAMPLES |
| --- | --- |
| **Planning and Focusing Attention** | Setting goals and timetables |
|  | Underlining and highlighting |
|  | Skimming, looking for headings and topic sentences |
| **Organizing and Remembering** | Making organizational charts |
|  | Creating flowcharts, Venn diagrams |
|  | Using mnemonics, imagery |
| **Comprehension** | Concept mapping, webs |
|  | Summarizing, outlining and note-taking |
|  | Creating examples |
|  | Explaining to a peer |
| **Cognitive Monitoring** | Making predictions |
|  | Self-questioning and self-testing |
|  | Identifying what doesn't make sense |
| **Practice** | Using part practice |
|  | Using whole practice |

(2004) summarizes these suggestions for helping students create summaries. Ask students to:

- Find or write a topic sentence for each paragraph or section.
- Identify big ideas that cover several specific points.
- Find some supporting information for each big idea.
- Delete any redundant information or unnecessary details.

Begin by doing summaries of short, easy, well-organized readings. Introduce longer, less organized, and more difficult passages gradually. Ask students to compare their summaries and discuss what ideas they thought were important and why—what's their evidence?

Two other study strategies that are based on identifying key ideas are underlining texts and taking notes.

**STOP & THINK** How do you make notes as you read? Look back over the past several pages of this chapter. Are any words highlighted yellow or pink? Are there marks or drawings in the margins and if so, do the notes pertain to the chapter content or are they grocery lists and doodles? •

**UNDERLINING AND HIGHLIGHTING.**   Do you underline or highlight key phrases in textbooks? Underlining and note-taking are probably two of the most frequent but ineffectively used strategies among post-secondary students. One common problem is that students underline or highlight too much. It is better to be selective. In studies that limit how much students can underline—for example, only one sentence per paragraph—learning has improved (Snowman, 1984). In addition to being selective, you also should actively transform the information into your own words as you underline or take notes. Don't rely on the words of the book. Note connections between what you are reading and other things you already know. Draw diagrams to illustrate relationships. Finally, look for organizational patterns in the material and use them to guide your underlining or note-taking.

TAKING NOTES.  Taking good lecture notes is not easy. You have to hold the lecture information in working memory; select, organize, and transform the important ideas and themes before the information "falls off" your working memory workbench; and write down the ideas and themes—all while you are still following the lecture (Peverly et al., 2007). As you fill your notebook with words and try to keep up with a lecturer, you may wonder if taking notes makes a difference. It does, if the strategy is used well.

- Taking notes focuses attention during class. Of course, if taking notes interferes with actually listening to and making sense of the lecture, then note-taking may not be effective (Kiewra, 1989, 2002; Van Meter, Yokoi, & Pressley, 1994).
- Taking notes makes you construct meaning from what you are hearing, seeing, or reading, so you elaborate, translate into your own words, and remember (Armbruster, 2000). Even if students don't review notes before a test, taking them in the first place appears to aid learning, especially for those who lack prior knowledge in an area.
- Notes provide extended external storage that allows you to return and review. Students who use their notes to study tend to perform better on tests, especially if they take many high-quality notes—more is better as long as you are capturing key ideas, concepts, and relationships, not just intriguing details (Kiewra, 1985, 1989; Peverly, Brobst, Graham, & Shaw, 2003).
- Expert students match notes to their anticipated use and modify strategies after tests or assignments; use personal codes to flag material that is unfamiliar or difficult; fill in holes by consulting relevant sources (including other students in the class); and record information verbatim only when a verbatim response will be required. In other words, they are *strategic* about taking and using notes (Van Meter, Yokoi, & Pressley, 1994).

Even though taking notes is valuable from middle school through graduate school, students with learning disabilities often have trouble (Boyle, 2010a, 2010b). Middle school and high school students with learning disabilities who used a strategic note-taking form recalled and understood significantly more key ideas from science lectures than students in control groups who used conventional note-taking methods (Boyle, 2010b; Boyle & Weishaar, 2001). For an example of this kind of form see www.ldonline.org/article/6210. Figure 9.1 is a general form that can be used in many note-taking situations. Dividing up the page is an idea from Cornell notes, described in Pauk's classic guide, *How to Study in College*. It is still available (Pauk & Owens, 2010). This form could be useful for any student who needs extra guidance in note-taking,

## Visual Tools for Organizing

To use underlining and note-taking effectively, you must identify main ideas. In addition, you must understand the organization of the text or lecture—the connections and relationships among ideas. Some visual strategies have been developed to help students with this key organizational element (Van Meter, 2001). A **concept map** is a drawing that charts the relations among ideas, as shown in Figure 9.2, which is a concept map describing a website for creating concept maps! You may have referred to these interconnected ideas as *webs*.

In a review of 55 studies with students from grade 4 to graduate school and subjects ranging from science to statistics to nursing, John Nesbit and Olusola Adesope (2006) of Simon Fraser University concluded that, "in comparison with activities such as reading text passages, attending lectures, and participating in class discussions, concept mapping activities are more effective for attaining knowledge retention and transfer" (p. 434). "Mapping" relationships by noting causal connections, comparison/contrast connections, and examples improves recall. Anita's students use **Cmaps**, the free downloadable tools from the website shown in Figure 9.2, that are used for creating concept maps. One student even planned his dissertation and organized all the reading for his doctoral examinations with tools from the website. Computer Cmaps can be linked to the internet, and

**Concept map** A drawing that charts the relationships among ideas.

**Cmaps** Tools for concept mapping developed by the Institute for Human and Machine Cognition that are connected to many knowledge maps and other resources on the internet.

## FIGURE 9.1

### A FORM FOR TAKING NOTES STRATEGICALLY

| Topic: | What do I already know about this topic? |
|---|---|
| Key Points/ Key Terms | Notes |
| | |

Summaries: Write 3 to 5 sentences that capture the main ideas.

1.

2.

3.

4.

5.

Questions: What is still confusing or unclear?

*Source: Based on ideas from Pauk, W., Owens, R. J. Q. (2010) [1962]. How to Study in College (10th ed.). Florence, KY: Cengage Learning; http://academic.cuesta.edu/acasupp/as/618.htm; and www.ldonline.org/article/6210.*

students in different classrooms and schools all over the world can collaborate on them. Students should compare their filled-in "maps" and discuss the differences in their thinking with each other.

There are other ways to visualize organization, such as Venn diagrams, which show how ideas or concepts overlap, and tree diagrams, which show how ideas branch off each other. Time lines organize information in sequence and are useful in classes such as history or geology.

## FIGURE 9.2

### THE WEBSITE FOR THE INSTITUTE FOR HUMAN AND MACHINE COGNITION CMAP TOOLS AT HTTP://CMAP.IHMC.US

At this site, you can download concept mapping tools to construct, share, and criticize knowledge on any subject.

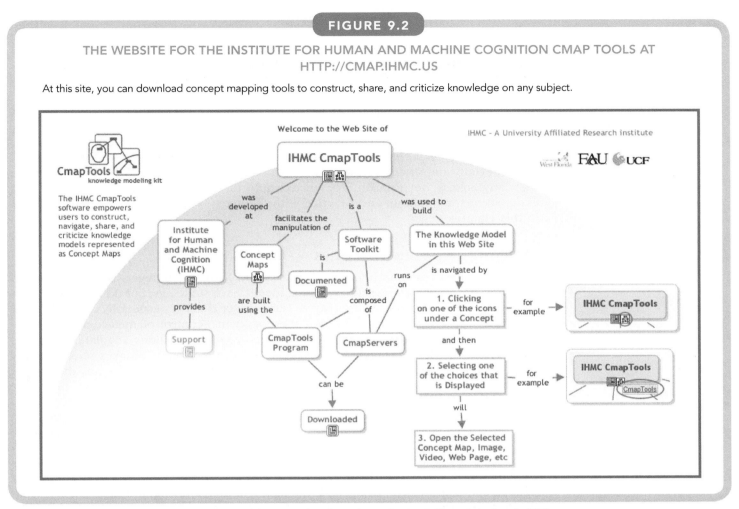

Source: Institute for Human and Machine Cognition Cmap Tools home page. http://cmap.ihmc.us. Reprinted with permission from the IHMC.

## Reading Strategies

As we saw earlier, effective learning strategies should help students *focus attention*, invest effort (connect, elaborate, translate, organize, summarize) so they *process information deeply*, and *monitor* their understanding. There are a number of strategies that support these processes in reading. Many use mnemonics to help students remember the steps involved. For example, one strategy that can be used for any grade above later elementary is the five-step **READS**:

**R** Review headings and subheadings.
**E** Examine boldface words.
**A** Ask, "What do I expect to learn?"
**D** Do it—Read!
**S** Summarize in your own words. (Friend & Bursuck, 2012)

A strategy that can be used in reading literature is **CAPS**:

**C** Who are the characters?
**A** What is the aim of the story?
**P** What problem happens?
**S** How is the problem solved?

There are several reasons why strategies like the ones we've described are effective. First, following the steps makes students more aware of the organization of a given chapter. How often have you skipped reading headings entirely and thus missed major clues about the way the information was organized? Next, these steps require students to study the chapter in sections instead of trying to learn all the information at once. This makes use of *distributed practice*. Answering questions about the material forces students to process the information more deeply and with greater elaboration.

No matter what strategies you use, students have to be taught how to use them. *Direct teaching, explanation, modelling*, and *practice with feedback* are necessary and are especially important for students with learning challenges and students whose first language is not English. For an example of direct teaching of strategies with explanations, modelling, and practice with feedback, see the KWL discussion earlier in this chapter.

## Applying Learning Strategies

One of the most common findings in research on learning strategies is a phenomenon known as **production deficiencies**, where students learn strategies, but do not apply them when they could or should (Pressley & Harris, 2006). This is especially a problem for students with learning disabilities. For these students, control of metacognitive strategies such as planning, organizing, monitoring progress, and making adaptations often is underdeveloped (Kirk, Gallagher, Anastasiow, & Colemen, 2006). It makes sense to teach these strategies directly. To ensure that students actually use the strategies they learn, several conditions must be met.

APPROPRIATE TASKS.   First, of course, the learning task must be *appropriate*. Why would students use more complex learning strategies when the task the teacher set is to "learn and return" the exact words of the text or lecture? With these tasks, memorizing will be rewarded and the best strategies involve distributed practice and perhaps mnemonics (described in Chapter 9). But we hope that there are few of these kinds of tasks in contemporary teaching, so if the task is *understanding*, not memorizing, what else is necessary?

VALUING LEARNING.   The second condition for using sophisticated strategies is that students must *care* about learning and understanding. They must have goals that can be reached using effective strategies (Zimmerman & Schunk, 2001). Anita was reminded of this in her educational psychology class one semester when she enthusiastically shared a magazine article about study skills. The gist of the article was that students should continually revise and rewrite their notes from a course, so that by the end, all their understanding could be captured in one or two pages. Of course, the majority of the knowledge at that point would be reorganized and connected well with other knowledge. "See," she told the class, "these ideas are real—not just trapped in texts. They can help you study smarter." After a heated discussion, one of the best students said in exasperation, "I'm carrying 18 hours—I don't have time to *learn* this stuff!" She did not believe that her goal—to survive the overloaded semester—could be reached by using time-consuming study strategies.

EFFORT AND EFFICACY.   This student also was concerned about effort. The third condition for applying learning strategies is that students must believe the effort and investment required to apply the strategies are reasonable, given the likely return (Winne, 2001). And students must believe they are capable of using the strategies; that is, they must have self-efficacy for using the strategies to learn the material in question (Schunk, 2012). This is related to another condition: Students must have a base of knowledge and/or experience in the area. No learning strategies can help students accomplish tasks that are completely beyond their current understandings.

The *Guidelines* provide a summary of ideas for you and your students.

**Production deficiencies** Failing to activate a learning strategy—a production—when it is appropriate and useful to use the strategy.

## GUIDELINES

### Becoming an Expert Student

**Make sure you have the necessary declarative knowledge (facts, concepts, ideas) to understand new information.**
*Examples*

1. Keep definitions of key vocabulary available as you study.
2. Review required facts and concepts before attempting new material.

**Find out what type of test the teacher will give (essay, short answer), and study the material with that in mind.**
*Examples*

1. For a test with detailed questions, practise writing answers to possible questions.
2. For a multiple-choice test, use mnemonics to remember definitions of key terms.

**Make sure you are familiar with the organization of the materials to be learned.**
*Examples*

1. Preview the headings, introductions, topic sentences, and summaries of the text.
2. Be alert for words and phrases that signal relationships, such as *on the other hand, because, first, second, however, since*.

**Know your own cognitive skills and use them deliberately.**
*Examples*

1. Use examples and analogies to relate new material to something you care about and understand well, such as sports, hobbies, or films.
2. If one study technique is not working, try another—the goal is to stay involved, not to use any particular strategy.

**Study the right information in a productive way.**
*Examples*

1. Be sure you know exactly what topics and readings the test will cover.
2. Spend your time on the important, difficult, and unfamiliar material that will be required for the test or assignment.
3. Keep a list of the parts of the text that give you trouble, and spend more time on those pages.
4. Process the important information thoroughly by using mnemonics, forming images, creating examples, answering questions, making notes in your own words, and elaborating on the text. Do not try to memorize the author's words—use your own.

**Monitor your own comprehension.**
*Examples*

1. Use questioning to check your understanding.
2. When reading speed slows down, decide if the information in the passage is important. If it is, note the problem so you can reread or get help to understand. If it is not important, ignore it.
3. Check your understanding by working with a friend and quizzing one another.

*For more resources on studying, see http://www.ucc.vt.edu/stdysk/stdyhlp.html or http://www.d.umn.edu/student/loon/acad/strat.*

*Source: From Armbruster, B. B., & Anderson, T. H. (1993). Research Synthesis on Study Skills. Educational Leadership, 39. Reprinted with permission from ASCD. All rights reserved. The Association for Supervision and Curriculum Development is a worldwide community of educators advocating sound policies and sharing best practices to achieve the success of each learner. To learn more, visit ASCD at www.ascd.org.*

### Reaching Every Student: Learning Strategies for Struggling Students

Reading is key in all learning. Strategy instruction can help many struggling readers. As you have seen, some approaches make use of mnemonics to help students remember the steps. For example, Susan Cantrell (2010) and her colleagues identified 862 students in grades 6 to 9 who were at least two years behind in reading. The students were from 23 different schools. Students were randomly assigned to either a Learning Strategies Curriculum (Deshler & Schumaker, 2005) or the traditional curriculum. The Learning Strategies Curriculum focused on six strategies: word identification, visual imagery, self-questioning, LINCS vocabulary strategy, sentence writing, and paraphrasing. The **LINCS Vocabulary Strategy** uses stories and imagery to help students learn how to identify, organize, define, and remember words, which increases their ownership of their learning. The LINCS steps are:

**L** "List the parts." Identify the vocabulary word and key information.
**I** "Identify a reminding word." Pick a known word that reminds them of the vocabulary word.

**LINCS Vocabulary Strategy** A strategy that uses stories and imagery to help students learn how to identify, organize, define, and remember words and their meanings.

TABLE 9.2 • **Teaching Strategies for Improving Students' Metacognitive Knowledge and Skills**

- These eight guidelines taken from Pressley and Woloshyn (1995) should help you in teaching any metacognitive strategy.
- Teach a few strategies at a time, intensively and extensively as part of the ongoing curriculum.
- Model and explain new strategies.
- If parts of the strategy were not understood, model again and re-explain strategies in ways that are sensitive to those confusing or misunderstood aspects of strategy use.
- Explain to students where and when to use the strategy.
- Provide plenty of practice, using strategies for as many appropriate tasks as possible.
- Encourage students to monitor how they are doing when they are using strategies.
- Increase students' motivation to use strategies by heightening their awareness that they are acquiring valuable skills—skills that are at the heart of competent functioning.
- Emphasize reflective processing rather than speedy processing; do everything possible to eliminate high anxiety in students; encourage students to shield themselves from distractions so they can attend to academic tasks.

*For a list of strategies and links to resources about them, see http://pedagogy.merlot.org/TeachingStrategies.html.*
*Source: Adapted from Pressley, M., & Woloshyn, V. (1995). Cognitive Strategy Instruction That Really Improves Children's Academic Performance. Cambridge, MA: Brookline Books, p. 18.*

**N** "Note a LINCing story." Create a story that bridges the vocabulary word with the known word.

**C** "Create a LINCing picture." Draw a picture that represents the story.

**S** "Self-test." Check their learning of the vocabulary word by reciting all the parts of their LINCS.

After a year, the grade 6 students who had participated in the Learning Strategies Curriculum performed significantly better on reading comprehension and strategy use, but there were no differences for grade 9 students. It is possible that reading strategy instruction is most effective in elementary and early middle school when students are learning how to learn through reading (Cantrell, Almasi, Carter, Rintamaa, & Madden, 2010).

Of course, you have to do more than just tell students about the strategy—you have to teach it. Michael Pressley, formerly of the University of Western Ontario, and his colleague Vera Woloshyn at Brock University (1995) developed the Cognitive Strategies Model as a guide for teaching students to improve their metacognitive strategies. Table 9.2 describes the steps in teaching these strategies.

# PROBLEM SOLVING

**STOP & THINK** You're interviewing with the district superintendent for a position as a school psychologist. The superintendent is known for his unorthodox interview questions. He hands you a pad of paper and a ruler and says, "Tell me, what is the exact thickness of a single sheet of paper?" •

This is a true story—Anita was asked the paper thickness question in an interview years ago. The answer was to measure the thickness of the entire pad and divide by the number of pages in the pad. She got the answer and the job, but what a tense moment that was. It seems the superintendent was interested in her ability to solve problems—under pressure!

A **problem** has an initial state (the current situation), a goal (the desired outcome), and a path for reaching the goal (operations or activities that move you toward the goal). Problem solvers often have to set and reach subgoals as they move toward the final solution. For example, if your goal is to drive to the beach, but at the first stop sign you skid through the intersection, you may have to reach a subgoal of fixing your brakes before you can continue toward the original goal (Schunk, 2012). Also, problems

**Problem** Any situation in which you are trying to reach some goal and must find a means to do so.

can range from *well structured* to *ill structured*, depending on how clear-cut the goals are and how much structure is provided for solving them. Most arithmetic problems are well structured, but finding the right university major is ill structured. Ill-structured problems have many different solutions and paths to solutions. Life presents many ill-structured problems.

**Problem solving** is usually defined as formulating new answers, going beyond the simple application of previously learned rules to achieve a goal. Problem solving is what happens when no solution is obvious—when, for example, you can't afford new brakes for the car that skidded on the way to the beach (Mayer & Wittrock, 2006). Some psychologists suggest that most human learning involves problem solving (Anderson, 1993).

There is debate about problem solving. Some psychologists believe that effective problem-solving strategies are specific to the problem area. That is, the problem-solving strategies in mathematics are unique to math; the strategies in art are unique to art; and so on. The other side of the debate claims that there are some general problem-solving strategies that can be useful in many areas.(General problem-solving strategies usually include the steps of *identifying* the problem, *setting goals*, *exploring* possible solutions and consequences, *acting*, and finally *evaluating* the outcome.)

Actually, there is evidence for the value of both general and specific strategies. In their research with grades 4 and 5 students, Steven Hecht and Kevin Vagi (2010) found that both domain-specific and general factors affected performance on problems involving fractions. The influences were specific conceptual knowledge about fractions and the general information processing skill of attentive classroom behaviour. Another study with children in grade 3 found that both specific arithmetic knowledge and general attention-focusing skills were related to arithmetic problem solving (Fuchs et al., 2006). Finally, Robert Kail and Lynda Hall (1999) found that both domain-specific arithmetic knowledge and general information processing skills, including reading and information processing time, were related to success in solving word problems.

It appears that people move between general and specific approaches, depending on the situation and their level of expertise. Early on, when we know little about a problem area or domain, we can rely on general learning and problem-solving strategies to make sense of the situation. As we gain more domain-specific knowledge (particularly procedural knowledge about how to do things in the domain), we consciously apply the general strategies less and less; our problem solving becomes more automatic. But if we encounter a problem outside our current knowledge, we may return to relying on general strategies to attack the problem (Alexander, 1992, 1996).

A key first step in any problem solving—general or specific—is identifying that a problem exists (and perhaps treating the problem as an opportunity).

## Identifying: Problem Finding

**Watch**
Identifying: Problem Finding

Problem identification is not always straightforward. We are reminded of a story about tenants who were angry because the elevators in their building were slow. Consultants hired to "fix the problem" reported that the elevators were no worse than average and improvements would be very expensive. One day, as the building supervisor watched people waiting impatiently for an elevator, he realized that the problem was not slow elevators, but the fact that people were bored; they had nothing to do while they waited. When the boredom problem was identified and seen as an opportunity to improve the "waiting experience," the simple solution of installing a mirror by the elevator on each floor eliminated complaints.

Even though problem identification is a critical first step, research indicates that people often "leap" to naming the first problem that comes to mind ("the elevators are too slow!"). Experts in a field are more likely to spend time carefully considering the nature of the problem (Bruning, Schraw, & Norby, 2011). Finding a solvable problem and turning it into an opportunity is the process behind many successful inventions, such as the ballpoint pen, garbage disposal, appliance timer, alarm clock, self-cleaning oven, and thousands of others.

Once a solvable problem is identified, what next?

**Problem solving** Creating new solutions for problems.

## Defining Goals and Representing the Problem

Let's take a real problem: The machines designed to pick tomatoes are damaging the tomatoes. What should we do? If we represent the problem as a faulty machine design, then the goal is to improve the machine. But if we represent the problem as a faulty design of the tomatoes, then the goal is to develop a tougher tomato. The problem-solving process follows two entirely different paths, depending on which representation and goal are chosen (Bransford & Stein, 1993). To represent the problem and set a goal, you have to *focus attention* on relevant information, *understand the words* of the problem, and *activate the right schema* to understand the whole problem.

**STOP & THINK** If you have black socks and white socks in your drawer, mixed in the ratio of four to five, how many socks will you have to take out to make sure you have a pair the same colour (adapted from Sternberg & Davidson, 1982)? •

**FOCUSING ATTENTION ON WHAT IS RELEVANT.**   Representing the problem often requires finding the relevant information and ignoring the irrelevant details. For example, what information was relevant in solving the above sock problem? Did you realize that the information about the four-to-five ratio of black socks to white socks is irrelevant? As long as you have only two different colours of socks in the drawer, you will have to remove only three socks before two of them match.

**UNDERSTANDING THE WORDS.**   The second task in representing a problem is understanding the meaning of the words, sentences, and factual information in the problem. So problem solving requires comprehending the language and relations in the problem. In math word problems, it also involves assigning mathematical operators (addition, division, etc.) to relations among numbers (Jitendra et al., 2009; Lee, Ng, & Ng, 2009). All this makes a demand on working memory. For example, a major stumbling block in representing many word problems is the students' understanding of part-whole relations (Cummins, 1991). Students have trouble figuring out what is part of what, as is evident in this dialogue between a teacher and a grade 1 student:

> **Teacher:** Pete has three apples. Ann also has some apples. Pete and Ann have nine apples altogether. How many apples does Ann have?
>
> **Student:** Nine.
>
> **Teacher:** Why?
>
> **Student:** Because you just said so.
>
> **Teacher:** Can you retell the story?
>
> **Student:** Pete had three apples. Ann also had some apples. Ann had nine apples. Pete also has nine apples. (Adapted from De Corte & Verschaffel, 1985, p. 19)

The student interprets "altogether" (the whole) as "each" (the parts).

A common difficulty for older students is understanding that ratio and proportion problems are based on multiplicative relations, not additive relations (Jitendra et al., 2009). So to solve

$$2 : 14 = ? : 35$$

many students subtract to find the difference between 2 and 14 ($14 - 2 = 12$) and then subtract 12 from 35 to get 23, giving them the (wrong) answer

$$2 : 14 = 23 : 35$$

The real question is about the *proportional* relationship between 2 and 14. How many times larger than 2 is 14? The answer: 7 times larger. Then the real question is "35 is 7 times larger than what number?" The answer is 5 ($7 \times 5 = 35$). So

$$2 : 14 = 5 : 35$$

Sometimes, students are taught to search for key words (*more, less, greater,* etc.), pick a strategy or formula based on the key words (*more* means "add"), and apply the formula. Actually, this gets in the way of forming a conceptual understanding of the whole problem—the next challenge (Van de Walle, Karp, & Bay-Williams, 2010).

UNDERSTANDING THE WHOLE PROBLEM.   The third task in representing a problem is to assemble all the relevant information and sentences into an accurate understanding or translation of the total problem. This means that students need to form a conceptual model of the problem—they have to understand what the problem is *really asking* (Jonassen, 2003). Consider this example.

STOP & THINK Two train stations are 50 miles apart. At 2 p.m. one Saturday afternoon, two trains start toward each other, one from each station. Just as the trains pull out of the stations, a bird springs into the air in front of the first train and flies ahead to the front of the second train. When the bird reaches the second train, it turns back and flies toward the first train. The bird continues to do this until the trains meet. If both trains travel at the rate of 25 miles per hour and the bird flies at 100 miles per hour, how many miles will the bird have flown before the trains meet? (Posner, 1973) •

Your interpretation of the problem is called a *translation* because you translate the problem into a schema that you understand. If you translate this as a *distance* problem (activate a distance schema) and set a goal ("I have to figure out how far the bird travels before it meets the oncoming train and turns around, then how far it travels before it has to turn again, and finally add up all the trips back and forth"), then you have a very difficult task on your hands. But there is a better way to structure the problem. You can represent it as a question of *time* and focus on the time the bird is in the air. The solution could be stated like this:

> The trains are going the same speed so they will meet in the middle, 25 miles from each station. This will take one hour because they are traveling 25 mph. In an hour, the bird will cover 100 miles because it is flying at 100 miles per hour. Easy!

Research shows that students can be too quick to decide what a problem is asking. Once a problem is categorized—"Aha, it's a distance problem!"—a particular schema is activated. The schema directs attention to particular information and sets up expectations for what the right answer should look like. For example, if you use a distance schema in the above problem, the right answer looks like adding up many small distance calculations (Kalyuga, Chandler, Tuovinen, & Sweller, 2001; Reimann & Chi, 1989).

When students lack the necessary schemas to represent problems, they often rely on surface features of the situation and represent the problem incorrectly, like the student who wrote "15 + 24 = 39" as the answer to, "Joan has 15 bonus points and Louise has 24. How many more does Louise have?" This student saw two numbers and the word *more,* so he applied the *add to get more* procedure. When students use the wrong schema, they overlook critical information, use irrelevant information, and may even misread or misremember critical information to "make" it fit the schema. But when students use the proper schema to represent a problem, they are less likely to be confused by irrelevant information or tricky wording, such as the presence of the word *more* in a problem that really requires *subtraction* (Fenton, 2007; Resnick, 1981). Figure 9.3 gives examples of different ways students might represent a simple mathematics problem. Exposure to different ways of representing and solving problems helps develop mathematical understanding (Star & Rittle-Johnson, 2009).

How can students who lack a good base of knowledge improve their translation and schema selection? To answer this question, we usually have to move to area-specific problem-solving strategies because schemas are specific to content areas.

TRANSLATION AND SCHEMA TRAINING: DIRECT INSTRUCTION IN SCHEMAS.   For students with little knowledge in an area, teachers can begin by directly teaching the

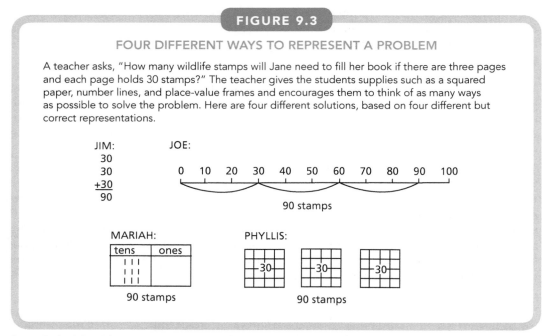

**FIGURE 9.3**

**FOUR DIFFERENT WAYS TO REPRESENT A PROBLEM**

A teacher asks, "How many wildlife stamps will Jane need to fill her book if there are three pages and each page holds 30 stamps?" The teacher gives the students supplies such as a squared paper, number lines, and place-value frames and encourages them to think of as many ways as possible to solve the problem. Here are four different solutions, based on four different but correct representations.

*Source: Riedesel, C. A, Schwartz, J. E. (1999).* Essentials of Elementary Mathematics, *2nd Edition. Reprinted by permission of Pearson Education, Inc., Upper Saddle River, NJ.*

necessary schema using demonstration, modelling, and "think-alouds." As we just saw, ratio/proportion problems like the following are a big challenge for many students.

> Ernesto and Dawn worked separately on their social studies projects this weekend. The ratio of the number of hours Ernesto spent on the project to the number of hours Dawn spent on the project was 2:3. If Ernesto spent 16 hours on the project, how many hours did Dawn spend on the project? (Jitendra et al., 2009, p. 257)

The teacher used a "think-aloud" to focus students on the key schema for solving this problem, so she said, "**First,** I figure this is a ratio problem, because it compared the number of hours that Ernesto worked **to** the number of hours Dawn worked. This is a **part-part ratio** that tells about a **multiplicative relationship** (2:3) between the hours Ernesto and Dawn worked." The teacher went on to think aloud, "**Next,** I represented the information. . . . **Finally,** I used the equivalent fractions strategy and . . . ." The think-aloud demonstration can be followed by providing students with many *worked examples*. In mathematics and physics it appears that in the *early stages* of learning, students benefit from seeing many different kinds of example problems worked out correctly for them (Moreno, Ozogul, & Reisslein, 2011). But before we explore worked examples in the next section, a caution is in order. Students with advanced knowledge improve when they solve new problems, not when they focus on already worked-out examples. Worked examples can actually interfere with the learning of more expert students. This has been called the *expert reversal effect* because what works for experts is the *reverse* of what works for beginners (Kalyuga & Renkl, 2010).

**TRANSLATION AND SCHEMA TRAINING: WORKED EXAMPLES.**   Worked examples reflect all the stages of problem solving—identifying the problem, setting goals, exploring solutions, solving the problem, and finally evaluating the outcome (Schworm & Renkl, 2007; van Gog, Paas, & Sweller, 2010). Worked examples are useful in many subject areas. Adrienne Lee and Laura Hutchinson (1998) found that undergraduate students learned more when they were provided with examples of chemistry problem solutions that were annotated to show an expert problem solver's thinking at critical steps. In Australia, Slava Kalyuga and colleagues (2001) found that worked-out examples helped apprentices to learn about electrical circuits when the apprentices had less experience in the area. Silke Schworm and Alexander Renkl (2007) used video examples to help student teachers learn how to make convincing arguments for or against a position.

Why are examples effective? Part of the answer is in *cognitive load theory*, discussed in the previous chapter. When students lack specific knowledge in domains—for example, fractions or proportions—they try to solve the problems using general strategies such as looking for key words or applying rote procedures. But these approaches put great strain on working memory—too much to "keep in mind" at once overloads memory. In contrast, worked examples chunk some of the steps, provide cues and feedback, focus attention on relevant information, and make fewer demands on memory, so the students can use cognitive resources to understand instead of searching randomly for solutions (Wittwer & Renkl, 2010).

To get the most benefit from worked examples, however, students have to actively engage—just "looking over" the examples is not enough. This is not too surprising when you think about what supports learning and memory. You need to pay attention, process deeply, and connect with what you already know. Students should explain the examples to themselves. This *self-explanation* component is a critical part of making learning from worked examples active, not passive. Examples of self-explanation strategies include trying to predict the next step in a solution, then checking to see if you are right or trying to identify an underlying principle that explains how to solve the problem. In their study with student teachers, Schworm and Renkl (2007) embedded prompts that required the student teachers to think about and explain elements of the arguments they saw on the tape, such as, "Which argumentative elements does this sequence contain? How is it related to Kirsten's statement?" (p. 289). Students have to be mentally engaged in making sense of the examples—and self-explanation is one key to engagement (Atkinson & Renkl, 2007; Wittwer & Renkl, 2010).

Another way to use worked examples is to have students compare examples that reach a right answer, but are worked out in different ways. What is the same about each solution? What is different? Why? (Rittle-Johnson & Star, 2007) Also, worked-out examples should deal with one source of information at a time rather than having students move between text passages, graphs, tables, and so on. The cognitive load will be too heavy for beginners if they have to integrate many sources of information to make sense of the worked examples (Marcus, Cooper, & Sweller, 1996).

Worked examples can serve as analogies or models for solving new problems. But beware. Without explanations and coaching, novices may remember the surface features of a worked example or case instead of the deeper meaning or the structure. It is the meaning or structure, not the surface similarities, that helps in solving new, analogous problems (Gentner, Lowenstein, & Thompson, 2003). We have heard students complain that the test preparation problems in their math classes were about boats and river currents, but the test asked about airplanes and wind speed. They protested, "There were no problems about boats on the test!" In fact, the problems on the test about wind were solved in exactly the same way as the "boat" problems, but the students were focusing only on the surface features. One way to overcome this tendency is to have students compare examples or cases so they can develop a problem-solving schema that captures the common structure, not the surface features, of the cases (Gentner, Loewenstein, & Thompson, 2003).

How else might students develop the schemas they will need to represent problems in a particular subject area? Mayer (1983b) has recommended giving students practice in the following: (1) recognizing and categorizing a variety of problem types;

**WORKED OUT EXAMPLES** Students benefit from seeing many different kinds of example problems worked out correctly for them, especially when they show an expert problem solver's thinking at critical steps.

Spencer Grant/PhotoEdit

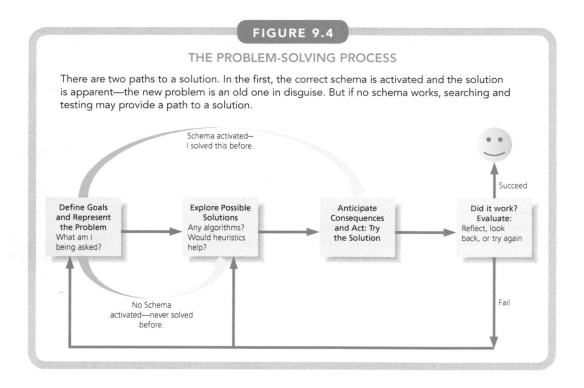

**FIGURE 9.4**

THE PROBLEM-SOLVING PROCESS

There are two paths to a solution. In the first, the correct schema is activated and the solution is apparent—the new problem is an old one in disguise. But if no schema works, searching and testing may provide a path to a solution.

(2) representing problems—either concretely in pictures, symbols, or graphs, or in words; and (3) selecting relevant and irrelevant information in problems.

THE RESULTS OF PROBLEM REPRESENTATION.   There are two main outcomes of the problem representation stage of problem solving, as shown in Figure 9.4. If your representation of the problem suggests an immediate solution, your task is done. In one sense, you haven't really solved a new problem; you have simply recognized the new problem as a "disguised" version of an old problem that you already knew how to solve. Seeing through a disguised problem to recognize it as one that can be solved using an "old" schema is called **schema-driven problem solving**. In terms of Figure 9.4, you can use the schema-activated route and proceed directly to a solution.

But what if you have no existing way of solving the problem or your activated schema fails? Time to search for a solution!

## Exploring Possible Solution Strategies

In conducting your search for a solution, you have available two general kinds of procedures: algorithmic and heuristic. Both of these are forms of procedural knowledge (Schraw, 2006).

ALGORITHMS.   An **algorithm** is a step-by-step procedure for achieving a goal. It usually is domain specific, meaning it is tied to a particular subject area. In solving a problem, if you choose an appropriate algorithm (e.g., to find the arithmetic mean, you add all the scores, then divide by the number of scores) and implement it properly, a right answer is guaranteed. Unfortunately, students often apply algorithms unsystematically, trying out one first, and then another. They may even happen on the right answer, but not understand how they got there, or they may forget the steps they used to find the answer. For some students, applying algorithms haphazardly could be an indication that formal operational thinking and the ability to work through a set of possibilities systematically (as described by Piaget) is not yet developed. But many problems cannot be solved by algorithms. What then?

**Schema-driven problem solving** Recognizing a problem as a "disguised" version of an old problem for which one already has a solution.

**Algorithm** Step-by-step procedure for solving a problem; prescription for solutions.

HEURISTICS.    A **heuristic** is a general strategy that might lead to the right answer (Schoenfeld, 2011). Because many of life's problems (careers, relationships, etc.) are not straightforward and have ill-defined problem statements and no apparent algorithms, the discovery or development of effective heuristics is important (Korf, 1999). Let's examine a few.

In **means-ends analysis**, the problem is divided into a number of intermediate goals or subgoals, and then a means of solving each intermediate subgoal is figured out. For example, writing a 20-page term paper can loom as an insurmountable problem for some students. They would be better off breaking this task into several intermediate goals, such as selecting a topic, locating sources of information, reading and organizing the information, making an outline, and so on. As they attack a particular intermediate goal, they may find that other goals arise. For example, locating information may require that they find someone to refresh their memory about using the library computer search system. Keep in mind that psychologists have yet to discover an effective heuristic for students who are just starting their term paper the night before it is due.

Some problems lend themselves to a **working-backward strategy**. Using this heuristic, you begin at the goal and work back to the unsolved initial problem. Working backward is sometimes an effective heuristic for solving geometry proofs. It can also be a good way to set intermediate deadlines ("Let's see, if I have to submit this chapter in four weeks, I should have a first draft finished by the eleventh, and that means I better stop searching for new references and start writing by . . .").

Another useful heuristic is **analogical thinking** (Copi, 1961; Gentner, Loewenstein, & Thompson, 2003). This heuristic limits your search for solutions to situations that have something in common with the one you currently face. When submarines were first designed, for example, engineers had to figure out how battleships could determine the presence and location of vessels hidden in the depths of the sea. Studying how bats solve an analogous problem of navigating in the dark led to the invention of sonar. Take note, however—to use analogies effectively, you must focus on meaning and not surface similarities. So focusing on bats' appearance would not have helped to solve the submarine problem.

The possible analogies students bring to the classroom are bound to vary based on their experience and culture. For example, Zhe Chen and his colleagues (Chen, 2004) wondered if postsecondary students might use familiar folk tales—one kind of cultural knowledge—as analogies to solve problems. That is just what happened. Chinese students were better at solving a problem of weighing a statue because the problem was similar to their folk tale about how to weigh an elephant (by water displacement). North American students were better at solving a problem of finding the way out of a cave (leaving a trail), by using an analogy to Hansel and Gretel, a common folk tale.

Putting your problem-solving plan into words and giving reasons for selecting it can lead to successful problem solving (Lee & Hutchinson, 1998). You may have discovered the effectiveness of this **verbalization** process accidentally, when a solution popped into your head as you were explaining a problem to someone else.

## Anticipating, Acting, and Looking Back

After representing the problem and exploring possible solutions, the next step is to select a solution and anticipate the consequences. For example, if you decide to solve the damaged tomato problem by developing a genetically modified tougher tomato, how will consumers react? If you take time to learn a new graphics program to enhance your term paper (and your grade), will you still have enough time to finish the paper?

After you choose a solution strategy and implement it, evaluate results by checking for evidence that confirms or contradicts your solution. Many people tend to stop working before they reach the best solution and simply accept an answer that works in some cases. In mathematical problems, evaluating the answer might mean applying a checking routine, such as adding to check the result of a subtraction problem or, in a long addition problem, adding the column from bottom to top instead of top to bottom. Another possibility is estimating the answer. For example, if the computation was $11 \times 21$, the answer should be around 200, because $10 \times 20$ is 200. A student who reaches an answer of 2311

**Heuristic** General strategy used in attempting to solve problems.

**Means-ends analysis** Heuristic in which a goal is divided into subgoals.

**Working-backward strategy** Heuristic in which one starts with the goal and moves backward to solve the problem.

**Analogical thinking** Heuristic in which one limits the search for solutions to situations that are similar to the one at hand.

**Verbalization** Putting your problem-solving plan and its logic into words.

or 32 or 562 should quickly realize these answers cannot be correct. Estimating an answer is particularly important when students rely on calculators or computers, because they cannot go back and spot an error in the figures.

## Factors That Hinder Problem Solving

Sometimes problem solving requires looking at things in new ways. People may miss out on a good solution because they fixate on conventional uses for materials. This difficulty is called **functional fixedness** (Duncker, 1945). In your everyday life, you may often exhibit functional fixedness. Suppose a screw on a dresser-drawer handle is loose. Will you spend 10 minutes searching for a screwdriver, or will you fix it with a ruler edge or a dime?

Another kind of fixation that blocks effective problem solving is **response set**, getting stuck on one way of representing a problem. Try this:

In each of the four matchstick arrangements below, move only one stick to change the equation so that it represents a true equality such as V = V.

$$V = VII \qquad VI = XI \qquad XII = VII \qquad VI = II$$

You probably figured out how to solve the first example quite quickly. You simply move one matchstick from the right side over to the left to make VI = VI. Examples two and three can also be solved without too much difficulty by moving one stick to change the V to an X or vice versa. But the fourth example (taken from Raudsepp & Haugh, 1977) probably has you stumped. To solve this problem, you must change your response set or switch schemas, because what has worked for the first three problems will not work this time. The answer here lies in changing from Roman numerals to Arabic numbers and using the concept of square root. By overcoming response set, you can move one matchstick from the right to the left to form the symbol for square root; the solution reads $\sqrt{1} = 1$, which is simply the symbolic way of saying that the square root of 1 equals 1. Recently, a creative reader of this text emailed some other solutions. Jamaal Allan, then a master's student, pointed out that you could use any of the matchsticks to change the = sign to ≠. Then, the last example would be V ≠ II, or 5 does not equal 2, an accurate statement. He suggested that you also might move one matchstick to change = to < or >, and the statements would still be true (but not equalities as specified in the problem above). Bill Wetta offered another solution that used both Arabic and Roman numerals. You can move one matchstick to make the first V an X. Then VI = II becomes XI = II, or eleven (in Roman numerals) equals 11 (in Arabic numerals). Just this morning, another creative approach was submitted by Ray Partlow, an educational psychology student. He noted, "Simply remove a matchstick from the V from the left-hand side, and place it directly on top of the I, getting II = II." Covering one matchstick with another opens up a whole new set of possibilities! Can you come up with any other solutions? Be creative!

SOME PROBLEMS WITH HEURISTICS.   We often apply heuristics automatically to make quick judgments; that saves us time in everyday problem solving. The mind can react automatically and instantaneously, but the price we often pay for this efficiency may be bad problem solving, which can be costly. Making judgments by invoking stereotypes leads even smart people to make dumb decisions. For example, we might use a **representativeness heuristic** to make judgments about possibilities based on our prototypes—what we think is representative of a category. Consider this:

If I ask you whether a slim, short stranger who enjoys poetry is more likely to be a truck driver or an Ivy League classics professor, what would you say?

You might be tempted to answer based on your prototypes of truck drivers or professors. But consider the odds. Depending how you count, there are about 200 universities and colleges in Canada with perhaps an average of two or so classics professors per school. So, we have 400 professors. Say about 20% are both short and slim—that's 80; and half of those like poetry—we are left with 40. Suppose there are 200 000 truck drivers in Canada. If only one in every 1000 of those truck drivers were short, slim, poetry lovers, we have 200 truck drivers who fit the description. With 40 professors versus 200 truck drivers, it's five times more likely that our stranger is a truck driver (Myers, 2005).

**Functional fixedness** Inability to use objects or tools in a new way.

**Response set** Rigidity; the tendency to respond in the most familiar way.

 **Representativeness heuristic** Judging the likelihood of an event based on how well the events match your prototypes—what you think is representative of the category.

Teachers and students are busy people, and they often base their decisions on what they have in their minds at the time. When judgments are based on the availability of information in our memories, we are using the **availability heuristic**. If instances of events come to mind easily, we think they are common occurrences, but that is not necessarily the case; in fact, it is often wrong. For example, you may have been surprised to read in Chapter 4 that accelerating gifted students' pace through the grades does not undermine their social development. Data may not support a judgment, but **belief perseverance**, or the tendency to hold on to our beliefs even in the face of contradictory evidence, may make us resist change.

The **confirmation bias** is the tendency to search for information that confirms our ideas and beliefs: This arises from our eagerness to get a good solution. You have often heard the saying "Don't confuse me with the facts." This aphorism captures the essence of the confirmation bias. Most people seek evidence that supports their ideas more readily than they search for facts that might refute them. For example, once you decide to buy a certain car, you are likely to notice reports about the good features of the car you chose, not the good news about the cars you rejected. Our automatic use of heuristics to make judgments, our eagerness to confirm what we like to believe, and our tendency to explain away failure combine to generate *overconfidence*. Students usually are overconfident about how fast they can get their papers written; it typically takes twice as long as they estimate (Buehler, Griffin, & Ross, 1994). In spite of their underestimation of their completion time, they remain overly confident of their next prediction.

The *Guidelines* give some ideas for helping students become good problem solvers.

## Expert Knowledge and Problem Solving

Most psychologists agree that effective problem solving is based on having an ample store of knowledge about the problem area (Schoenfeld, 2011). In order to solve the matchstick problem, for example, you had to understand Roman and Arabic numbers as well as the concept of square root. You also had to know that the square root of 1 is 1. Let's take a moment to examine this expert knowledge.

**Availability heuristic** Judging the likelihood of an event based on what is available in your memory, assuming those easily remembered events are common.

**Belief perseverance** The tendency to hold on to beliefs, even in the face of contradictory evidence.

**Confirmation bias** Seeking information that confirms our choices and beliefs, while disconfirming evidence.

## GUIDELINES

### Problem Solving

**Ask students if they are sure they understand the problem.**
*Examples*
1. Can they separate relevant from irrelevant information?
2. Are they aware of the assumptions they are making?
3. Encourage them to visualize the problem by diagramming or drawing it.
4. Ask them to explain the problem to someone else. What would a good solution look like?

**Encourage attempts to see the problem from different angles.**
*Examples*
1. Suggest several different possibilities yourself, and then ask students to offer some.
2. Give students practice in taking and defending different points of view on an issue.

**Let students do the thinking; don't just hand them solutions.**
*Examples*
1. Offer individual problems as well as group problems, so that each student has the chance to practise.

2. Give partial credit if students have good reasons for "wrong" solutions to problems.
3. If students are stuck, resist the temptation to give too many clues. Let them think about the problem overnight.

**Help students develop systematic ways of considering alternatives.**
*Examples*
1. Think out loud as you solve problems.
2. Ask, "What would happen if?"
3. Keep a list of suggestions.

**Teach heuristics.**
*Examples*
1. Use analogies to solve the problem of limited parking in the downtown area. How are other "storage" problems solved?
2. Use the working backward strategy to plan a party.

*For more resources on problem solving, see www.hawaii.edu/suremath/home.html.*

KNOWING WHAT IS IMPORTANT.   Experts know where to focus their attention. For example, knowledgeable baseball fans pay attention to the moves of the shortstop to learn if the pitcher will throw a fastball, curveball, or slider. But those with little knowledge about baseball may never see the movements of the shortstop, unless the ball is hit toward that part of the field (Bruning, Schraw, & Norby, 2011). In general, experts know what to pay attention to when judging a performance or product such as an Olympic high dive or a prize-winning chocolate cake. To nonexperts, most good dives or cakes look about the same, unless of course they "flop"!

MEMORY FOR PATTERNS AND ORGANIZATION.   The modern study of expertise began with investigations of chess masters (Simon & Chase, 1973). Results indicated that masters can quickly recognize about 50 000 different arrangements of chess pieces. They can look at one of these patterns for a few seconds and remember where every piece on the board was placed. It is as though they have a "vocabulary" of 50 000 patterns. Michelene Chi (1978) demonstrated that grade 3 through 8 chess experts had a similar ability to remember chess piece arrangements. For all the masters, patterns of pieces are like words. If you were shown any word from your vocabulary store for just a few seconds, you would be able to remember every letter in the word in the right order (assuming you could spell the word). But a series of letters arranged randomly is hard to remember, as you saw in Chapter 9. An analogous situation holds for chess masters. When chess pieces are placed on a board randomly, masters are no better than average players at remembering the positions of the pieces. The master's memory is for patterns that make sense or could occur in a game.

A similar phenomenon occurs in other fields. There may be an intuition about how to solve a problem based on recognizing patterns and knowing the "right moves" for those patterns. Experts in physics, for example, organize their knowledge around central principles (e.g., Boyle's or Newton's laws), whereas beginners organize their smaller amounts of physics knowledge around the specific details stated in the problems (e.g., levers or pulleys) (Ericsson, 1999; Fenton, 2007).

PROCEDURAL KNOWLEDGE.   In addition to representing a problem very quickly, experts know what to do next and are able do it. They have a large store of *productions* or IF-THEN schemas about what action to take in various situations. Thus, the steps of understanding the problem and choosing a solution happen simultaneously and fairly automatically (Ericsson & Charness, 1999). Of course, this means that they must have many, many schemas available. A large part of becoming an expert is simply acquiring a great store of *domain knowledge,* or knowledge that is particular to a field (Alexander, 1992). To do this, you must encounter many different kinds of problems in that field, observe others solving problems, and practise solving many yourself. Some estimates are that it takes 10 years or 10 000 hours of deliberate, focused, sustained practice to become an expert in most fields (Ericsson, 2011; Ericsson & Charness, 1994; Simon, 1995). Experts' rich store of knowledge is elaborated and well practised, so that it is easy to retrieve from long-term memory when needed (Anderson, 1993).

PLANNING AND MONITORING.   Experts spend more time analyzing problems, drawing diagrams, breaking large problems down into subproblems, and making plans. Whereas a novice might begin immediately—writing equations for a physics problem or drafting the first paragraph of a paper, experts plan out the whole solution and often make the task simpler in the process. As they work, experts monitor progress, so time is not lost pursuing dead ends or weak ideas (Schunk, 2012).

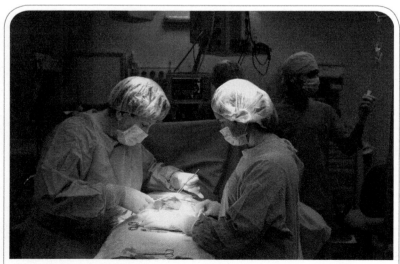

**EXPERT KNOWLEDGE** A large part of becoming an expert is simply acquiring a great store of *domain knowledge,* or knowledge that is particular to a field. This surgeon has likely invested years of deliberate, focused, sustained practice to become an expert.

Levent Konuk/Shutterstock

So what can we conclude? Experts (1) know where to focus their attention, (2) perceive large, meaningful patterns in given information and are not confused by surface features and details, (3) hold more information in working and long-term memories, in part because they have organized the information into meaningful chunks and procedures, (4) take a great deal of time to analyze a given problem, (5) have automatic procedures for accomplishing pieces of the problem, and (6) are better at monitoring their performance. When the area of problem solving is well defined, such as chess or physics, then these skills of expert problem solvers hold fairly consistently. But when the problem-solving area is less well defined and has fewer clear underlying principles, such as problem solving in economics or psychology, then the differences between experts and novices are not as clear-cut (Alexander, 1992).

# CREATIVITY AND CREATIVE PROBLEM SOLVING

**STOP & THINK** Consider this student. He had severe dyslexia—a learning disability that made reading and writing exceedingly difficult. He described himself as an "underdog." In school, he knew that if the reading assignment would take others an hour, he had to allow two or three hours. He knew that he had to keep a list of all of his most frequently misspelled words in order to be able to write at all. He spent hours alone in his room. Would you expect his writing to be creative? Why or why not? •

The person described in the box above is John Irving, celebrated author of what one critic called "wildly inventive" novels such as *The World According to Garp*, *The Cider House Rules*, and *A Prayer for Owen Meany* (Amabile, 2001). How do we explain his amazing creativity? What is creativity?

## Defining Creativity

**Creativity** is the ability to produce work that is original, but still appropriate and useful (Plucker, Beghetto, & Dow, 2004). Most psychologists agree that there is no such thing as "all-purpose creativity"; people are creative in a particular area, as John Irving was in writing fiction. But to be creative, the "invention" must be intended. An accidental spilling of paint that produces a novel design is not creative unless the artist recognizes the potential of the "accident," or she uses the spilling technique intentionally to create new works (Weisberg, 1993). Although we frequently associate the arts with creativity, any subject can be approached in a creative manner.

## Assessing Creativity

**STOP & THINK** How many uses can you list for a brick? Take a moment and brainstorm—write down as many as you can. •

Like the author John Irving, Paul Torrance had a learning disability. He became interested in educational psychology when he was a high school English teacher (Neumeister & Cramond, 2004). Torrance was known as the "Father of Creativity." He developed two types of creativity tests: verbal and graphic (Torrance, 1972; Torrance & Hall, 1980). In the verbal test, you might be instructed to think up as many uses as possible for a brick (as you did above) or asked how a particular toy might be changed to make it more fun. On the graphic test, you might be given 30 circles and asked to create 30 different drawings, with each drawing including at least one circle. Figure 9.5 shows the creativity of an 8-year-old girl in completing this task.

These tests require **divergent thinking**, an important component of many conceptions of creativity. Divergent thinking is the ability to propose many different ideas or answers. **Convergent thinking** is the more common ability to identify only one answer. Responses to all these creativity tasks are scored for originality, fluency, and flexibility—three aspects of divergent thinking. *Originality* is usually determined statistically. To be original, a response must be given by fewer than five or 10 people out of every 100 who take the test. *Fluency*

**Creativity** Imaginative, original thinking or problem solving.

**Divergent thinking** Coming up with many possible solutions.

**Convergent thinking** Narrowing possibilities to a single answer.

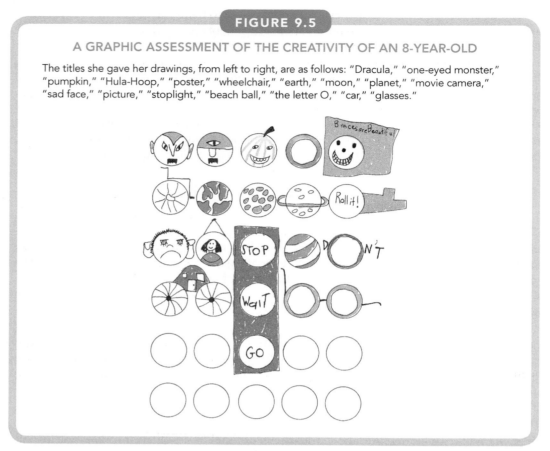

**FIGURE 9.5**

A GRAPHIC ASSESSMENT OF THE CREATIVITY OF AN 8-YEAR-OLD

The titles she gave her drawings, from left to right, are as follows: "Dracula," "one-eyed monster," "pumpkin," "Hula-Hoop," "poster," "wheelchair," "earth," "moon," "planet," "movie camera," "sad face," "picture," "stoplight," "beach ball," "the letter O," "car," "glasses."

Source: Torrance, E. P. (1986, 2000). A Graphic Assessment of the Creativity of an Eight-Year-Old. The Torrance Test of Creative Thinking. Reprinted with permission of Scholastic Testing Service, Inc., Bensonville, IL.

is the number of different responses. *Flexibility* is generally measured by the number of different categories of responses. For instance, if you listed 20 uses of a brick, but each was to build something, your fluency score might be high, but your flexibility score would be low. Of the three measures, fluency—the number of responses—is the best predictor of divergent thinking, but there is more to real-life creativity than divergent thinking (Plucker, Beghetto, & Dow, 2004).

A few possible indicators of creativity in your students are curiosity, concentration, adaptability, high energy, humour (sometimes bizarre), independence, playfulness, nonconformity, risk taking, attraction to the complex and mysterious, willingness to fantasize and daydream, intolerance for boredom, and inventiveness (Sattler & Hoge, 2006).

## What Are the Sources of Creativity?

Researchers have studied cognitive processes, personality factors, motivational patterns, and background experiences to explain creativity (Simonton, 2000). Teresa Amabile (1996) proposes a three-component model of creativity. Individuals or groups must have:

1. *Domain-relevant skills*, including talents and competencies that are valuable for working in the domain, such as Michelangelo's skills in shaping stone, developed when he lived with a stonecutter's family as a child.
2. *Creativity-relevant processes*, including work habits and personality traits such as John Irving's habit of working 10-hour days to write and rewrite and rewrite until he perfected his stories.
3. *Intrinsic task motivation* or a deep curiosity and fascination with the task. This aspect of creativity can be greatly influenced by teachers and parents who support autonomy, stimulate curiosity, encourage fantasy, and provide challenge.

**CREATIVITY AND COGNITION.** Having a rich store of knowledge in an area is the basis for creativity, but something more is needed. For many problems, that "something more" is the ability to see things in a new way—**restructuring** the problem, which leads to a sudden **insight**, a realization of a solution. Often this happens when a person has struggled with a problem or project, and then sets it aside for a while. Some psychologists believe that time away allows for *incubation*, a kind of unconscious working through the problem. Actually, it is more complex than that. Incubation seems to help more on divergent thinking tasks than on verbal or visual tasks. Also, incubation is more helpful when a longer preparation period precedes the individual's setting the problem aside (Sio & Ormerod, 2009). Leaving the problem for a time probably interrupts rigid ways of thinking so you can restructure your view of the situation and think more divergently (Gleitman, Fridlund, & Reisberg, 1999). Creativity requires extensive knowledge, flexibility, and the continual reorganizing of ideas. And we saw that motivation, persistence, and social support play important roles as well.

**CREATIVITY AND DIVERSITY.** As Dean Simonton said, even with years of research on creativity, "Psychologists still have a long way to go before they come anywhere close to understanding creativity in women and minorities" (2000, p. 156). Thus far, white males have been the focus of creativity research and writing over the years. However, patterns of creativity in other groups are complex—sometimes matching and sometimes diverging from patterns found in traditional research.

In another connection between creativity and culture, research suggests that being on the outside of mainstream society, being bilingual, or being exposed to other cultures might encourage creativity (Simonton, 2000). In fact, true innovators often break rules. "Creators have a desire to shake things up" (Winner, 2000, p. 167). In addition, even for those who are not outside the mainstream, it appears that participation in multicultural experiences fosters creativity. Angela Ka-Yee Leung and her colleagues (Leung & Chiu, 2008; Maddux, Leung, Chiu, & Galinsky, 2009) reviewed theory and research, including experimental studies that exposed participants to information and images about other cultures. The researchers concluded that multicultural experiences support both creative processes, such as retrieving novel or unconventional ideas from memory, and creative performance, such as generating insightful solutions to problems. These effects are especially strong when people open themselves up to divergent ideas, and when the situation does not emphasize finding quick, firm answers. Multicultural individuals are particularly willing to consider and build on unfamiliar ideas, entertain conflicting alternatives, and make unlikely connections between ideas (Leung & Chiu, 2010; Maddux & Galinsky, 2009). So even though your students may not be able to travel to Tibet or Turkey, they still could become more creative problem solvers if they learned about different cultures.

**SOCIAL ACCEPTANCE OF CREATIVITY** History is filled with examples of creative breakthroughs rejected in their time (for example, Galileo's theory of the sun as the centre of the solar system). Is today's society ready to welcome creative contributions in the field of alternative energies?

Paul Whitfield/Dorling Kindersley, Ltd.

## Creativity in the Classroom

Today's and tomorrow's complex problems require creative solutions. And creativity is important for an individual's psychological, physical, social, and career success (Plucker, Beghetto, & Dow, 2004). How can teachers promote creative thinking? All too often, in the crush of day-to-day classroom life, teachers stifle creative ideas without realizing what they are doing. Teachers are in an excellent position to encourage or discourage creativity through their acceptance or rejection of the unusual and imaginative. The *Guidelines*, adapted from Fleith (2000) and Sattler and Hoge (2006), describe other possibilities for encouraging creativity.

Restructuring Conceiving of a problem in a new or different way.

Insight Sudden realization of a solution; the ability to deal effectively with novel situations.

## Encouraging Creativity

**Accept and encourage divergent thinking.**
*Examples*

1. During class discussion, ask, "Can anyone suggest a different way of looking at this question?"
2. Reinforce attempts at unusual solutions to problems, even if the final product is not perfect.
3. Offer choices in topics for projects or modes of presentation (written, oral, visual or graphic, using technology).

**Tolerate dissent.**
*Examples*

1. Ask students to support dissenting opinions.
2. Make sure nonconforming students receive an equal share of classroom privileges and rewards.

**Encourage students to trust their own judgment.**
*Examples*

1. When students ask questions you think they can answer, rephrase or clarify the questions and direct them back to the students.
2. Give ungraded assignments from time to time.

**Emphasize that everyone is capable of creativity in some form.**
*Examples*

1. Avoid describing the feats of great artists or inventors as if they were superhuman accomplishments.

2. Recognize creative efforts in each student's work. Have a separate grade for originality on some assignments.

**Provide time, space, and materials to support creative projects.**
*Examples*

1. Collect "found" materials for collages and creations— buttons, stones, shells, paper, fabric, beads, seeds, drawing tools, clay—try flea markets and friends for donations. Have mirrors and pictures for drawing faces.
2. Make a well-lighted space available where children can work on projects, leave them, and come back to finish them.
3. Follow up on memorable occasions (field trips, news events, holidays) with opportunities to draw, write, or make music.

**Be a stimulus for creative thinking.**
*Examples*

1. Use class brainstorming sessions whenever possible.
2. Model creative problem solving by suggesting unusual solutions for class problems.
3. Encourage students to delay judging a particular suggestion for solving a problem until all the possibilities have been considered.

*For more ideas, see*
*http://eric.ed.gov/?id=ED389474.*

---

In addition to encouraging creativity through everyday interactions with students, teachers can try brainstorming. The basic tenet of **brainstorming** is to generate ideas without evaluating them, because evaluation often inhibits generation (Osborn, 1963). Evaluation, discussion, and criticism are postponed until all possible suggestions have been made. In this way, one idea inspires others; people do not withhold potentially creative solutions out of fear of criticism. John Baer (1997, p. 43) gives these rules for brainstorming:

1. Defer judgment.
2. Avoid ownership of ideas. When people feel that an idea is "theirs," egos sometimes get in the way of creative thinking. They are likely to be more defensive later when ideas are critiqued, and they are less willing to allow their ideas to be modified.
3. Feel free to "hitchhike" on other ideas. This means that it's okay to borrow elements from ideas already on the table, or to make slight modifications of ideas already suggested.
4. Encourage wild ideas. Impossible, totally unworkable ideas may lead someone to think of other, more possible, more workable ideas. It's easier to take a wildly imaginative bad idea and tone it down to fit the constraints of reality than it is to take a boring bad idea and make it interesting enough to be worth thinking about.

**Brainstorming** Generating ideas without stopping to evaluate them.

Individuals as well as groups may benefit from brainstorming. In writing this text, for example, we have sometimes found it helpful to list all the different topics that could be covered in a chapter, then leave the list and return to it later to evaluate the ideas.

## The Big C: Revolutionary Innovation

Ellen Winner (2000) describes the "big-C creativity," or innovation that establishes a new field or revolutionizes an old one. Even child prodigies do not necessarily become adult innovators. Prodigies have mastered well-established domains very early, but innovators change the entire domain. "Individuals who ultimately make creative breakthroughs tend from their earliest days to be explorers, innovators, and tinkerers. Often this adventurousness is interpreted as insubordination, though more fortunate tinkerers receive from teachers or peers some form of encouragement for their experimentation" (Gardner, 1993, pp. 32–33). What can parents and teachers do to encourage these potential creators? Winner (2000) lists four dangers to avoid:

1. Avoid pushing so hard that the child's intrinsic passion to master a field becomes a craving for extrinsic rewards.
2. Avoid pushing so hard that the child later looks back on a missed childhood.
3. Avoid freezing the child into a safe, technically perfect way of performing that has led to lavish rewards.
4. Be aware of the psychological wounds that can follow when the child who can perform perfectly becomes the forgotten adult who can do nothing more than continue to perform perfectly—without ever creating something new.

Finally, teachers and parents can encourage students with outstanding abilities and creative talents to give back to the society—service learning, discussed in Chapter 11, is one opportunity.

We may not all be revolutionary in our creativity, but we all can be experts in one area—critical thinking.

# CRITICAL THINKING AND ARGUMENTATION

Many educational psychologists believe that good thinking can and should be developed in school. One way to develop students' thinking is to create a *culture of thinking* in your classrooms (Perkins, Jay, & Tishman, 1993). This means that there is a spirit of inquisitiveness and critical thinking, a respect for reasoning and creativity, and an expectation that students will learn to make and counter arguments based on evidence.

## Developing Critical Thinking

**Critical thinking** skills involve evaluating conclusions by logically and systematically examining the problem, the evidence, and the solution. They are useful in almost every life situation—even in evaluating the media ads that constantly bombard us. When you see a group of gorgeous people extolling the virtues of a particular brand of orange juice as they frolic in skimpy bathing suits, you must decide if sex appeal is a relevant factor in choosing a fruit drink (remember Pavlovian advertising from Chapter 7).

No matter what approach you use to develop critical thinking, it is important to follow up with additional practice. One lesson is not enough. For example, if your class examined a particular historical document to determine if it reflected bias or propaganda, you should follow up by analyzing other written historical documents, contemporary advertisements, or news stories. Unless thinking skills become overlearned and relatively automatic, they are not likely to be transferred to new situations (Mayer & Wittrock, 2006). Instead, students will use these skills only to complete the lesson in social studies, not to evaluate the claims made by friends, politicians, car manufacturers, or diet plans. Table 9.3 describes the characteristics of a critical thinker.

## Critical Thinking in Specific Subjects

The characteristics of critical thinkers in Table 9.3 would be useful in any subject. But some critical thinking skills are specific to a particular subject. For example, to teach history, Jeffrey Nokes and his colleagues investigated (1) using traditional texts versus multiple readings, and (2) direct teaching of critical thinking skills versus no direct teaching of critical thinking skills (Nokes, Dole, & Hacker, 2007). The multiple texts included historical

**Critical thinking** Evaluating conclusions by logically and systematically examining the problem, the evidence, and the solution.

TABLE 9.3 • **What Is a Critical Thinker?**

Assuming that critical thinking is reasonable reflective thinking focused on deciding what to believe or do, a critical thinker:

1. Is open minded and mindful of alternatives.
2. Tries to be well informed.
3. Judges well the credibility of sources.
4. Identifies conclusions, reasons, and assumptions.
5. Judges well the quality of an argument, including the acceptability of its reasons, assumptions, and evidence.
6. Can well develop and defend a reasonable position.
7. Asks appropriate clarifying questions.
8. Formulates plausible hypotheses; plans experiments well.
9. Defines terms in a way appropriate for the context.
10. Draws conclusions when warranted, but with caution.
11. Integrates all items in this list when deciding what to believe or do.

*Source: Adapted from Robert H. Ennis. Retrieved May 26, 2011, from http://faculty.ed.uiuc.edu/rhennis/index.html.*

fiction, excerpts from speeches, government documents, photographs, charts and historical data, and short sections from texts. The history critical thinking skills taught were:

- **Sourcing:** Looking at the source of the document before reading and using that information to help interpret and make inferences about the reading. Is the source biased? Can I trust it?
- **Corroboration:** Making connections between the information in different texts and noting similarities and contradictions.
- **Contextualization:** Imaging the time, place, people, and culture that is the context for the event, with all the political and social forces that might be operating.

Students who learned with multiple texts instead of traditional textbooks actually learned more history content. Also, students were able to learn and apply two of the three critical thinking skills, *sourcing* and *corroboration*, when they were *directly taught* how to use the skills. Contextualization proved more difficult, perhaps because the students lacked the background knowledge to fill in contextual information. So critical thinking for specific subjects can be taught along with the subject. But as you can see in the *Point/Counterpoint*, educators don't agree about the best way to foster critical thinking in schools.

## Argumentation

The ability to construct and support a position—to argue—is essential in science, politics, persuasive writing, and critical thinking, to name just a few areas. The heart of **argumentation** (the process of debating a claim with someone else) is supporting your position with evidence and understanding, and then refuting your opponent's claims and evidence. Children are not good at argumentation, adolescents are a bit better, and adults are better still, but not perfect. Children don't pay very much attention to the claims and evidence of the other person in the debate. Adolescents understand that their opponent in a debate has a different position, but they tend to spend much more time presenting their own position than they do trying to understand and critique their opponent's claims. It is as if the adolescents believe "winning an argument" means making a better presentation, but they don't appreciate the need to understand and weaken the opponent's claims (Kuhn & Dean, 2004).

Children and adolescents focus more on their own positions because it is too demanding to remember and process both their own and their opponent's claims and evidence at the same time—the *cognitive load* is just too much. In addition, argumentation skills are not natural. They take both time and instruction to learn (Kuhn, Goh, Iordanou, & Shaenfield, 2008; Udell, 2007).

But what has to be learned? In order to make a case while understanding and refuting the opponent's case, you must be aware of what you are saying, what your opponent is saying, and how to refute your opponent's claims. This takes planning, evaluating how the plan is going, reflecting on what the opponent has said, and changing strategies as

**Argumentation** The process of debating a claim with someone else.

## POINT/COUNTERPOINT   Should Schools Teach Critical Thinking and Problem Solving?

The question of whether schools should focus on process or content, problem-solving skills or core knowledge, higher-order thinking skills or academic information has been debated for years. Some educators suggest that students must be taught how to think and solve problems, while other educators assert that students cannot learn to "think" in the abstract. They must be thinking about something—some content. Should teachers focus on knowledge or thinking?

**POINT**

▶ **Problem solving and higher-order thinking can and should be taught.** An article in the April 28, 1995, issue of the *Chronicle of Higher Education* makes this claim:

*Critical thinking is at the heart of effective reading, writing, speaking, and listening. It enables us to link together mastery of content with such diverse goals as self-esteem, self-discipline, multicultural education, effective cooperative learning, and problem solving. It enables all instructors and administrators to raise the level of their own teaching and thinking. (p. A-71)*

Closer to home for you, Peter Facione (2011) claims that critical thinking is related to GPA in university and to reading comprehension. How can students learn to think critically? Some educators recommend teaching thinking skills directly with widely used techniques such as the Productive Thinking Program or CoRT (Cognitive Research Trust). Other researchers argue that learning computer programming languages will improve students' minds and teach them how to think logically. Finally, because expert readers automatically apply certain metacognitive strategies, many educators and psychologists recommend directly teaching novice or poor readers how to apply these strategies. Michael Pressley's Good Strategy User model (Pressley & Harris, 2006) and Palincsar and Brown's (1984) reciprocal teaching approach are successful examples of direct teaching of metacognitive skills. Research on these approaches generally shows improvements in achievement and comprehension for students of all ages who participate (Pressley & Harris, 2006; Rosenshine & Meister, 1994).

Jess Yu/Shutterstock

**COUNTERPOINT**

▶ **Thinking and problem-solving skills do not transfer.** According to E. D. Hirsch (1996), a vocal critic of critical thinking programs:

*But whether such direct instruction of critical thinking or self-monitoring does in fact improve performance is a subject of debate in the research community. For instance, the research regarding critical thinking is not reassuring. Instruction in critical thinking has been going on in several countries for over a hundred years. Yet researchers found that students from nations as varied as Israel, Germany, Australia, the Philippines, and the United States, including those who have been taught critical thinking continue to fall into logical fallacies. (p. 136)*

The CoRT program has been used in over 5000 class-rooms in 10 nations. But Polson and Jeffries (1985) report that "after 10 years of widespread use we have no adequate evidence concerning the effectiveness of the program" (p. 445). In addition, Mayer and Wittrock (1996) note that field studies of problem solving in real situations show that people often fail to apply the mathematical problem-solving approaches they learn in school to actual problems encountered in the grocery store or home.

Even though educators have been more successful in teaching metacognitive skills, critics still caution that there are times when such teaching hinders rather than helps learning. Robert Siegler (1993) suggests that teaching self-monitoring strategies to low-achieving students can interfere with the students' development of adaptive strategies. Forcing students to use the strategies of experts may put too much burden on working memory as the students struggle to use an unfamiliar strategy and miss the meaning or content of the lesson. For example, rather than teach students strategies for figuring out words from context, it may be helpful for students to focus on learning more vocabulary words.

**Beware of Either/Or.** One clear message from current research on learning is that both subject-specific knowledge and learing strategies are important. Students today need to be critical consumers of all kinds of knowledge, but critical thinking alone is not enough. Students need the knowledge, vocabulary, and concepts to understand what they are reading, seeing, and hearing. The best teachers can teach math content and how to learn math at the same time, or history and how to critically assess history sources.

needed—in other words, *metacognitive knowledge and skills for argumentation*. Deanna Kuhn and her colleagues (2008) designed a process for developing metacognitive argumentation skills. They presented a class of grade 6 students with the following dilemma.

The Costa family has moved to the edge of town from far away Greece with their 11-year-old son Nick. Nick was a good student and soccer player back home in Greece. Nick's parents have decided that in this new place, they want to keep Nick at home with them, and not have him be at the school with the other children. The family speaks only Greek, and they think Nick will do better if he sticks to his family's language and doesn't try to learn English. They say they can teach him everything he needs at home. What should happen? Is it okay for the Costa family to live in the town but keep Nick at home, or should they be required to send their son to the town school like all the other families do? (p. 1313)

Based on their initial position on the dilemma, the 28 students in the class were divided into two groups—"Nick should go to school" or "Nick should be taught at home." These two groups were divided again into same-gender pairs, and all the "Nick should go to school" pairs moved to a room next door to their class. For about 25 minutes, each pair from one side "debated" a pair in the other room using instant messaging (IM). Later in the week the process was repeated, but with different pairs debating. In all, there were seven IM debates, so every "go to school" pair debated every "stay home" pair over several weeks. After four of the seven sessions, the pairs were given a transcript of the dialogue from their last debate, along with worksheets that scaffolded their *reflection* on their own arguments or the arguments of their opponents. The students evaluated their arguments and tried to improve them, with some adults coaching. These reflective sessions were repeated three times.

Next, there was a "showdown" debate—the entire "go to school" team debated the entire "stay home" team via one computer per team and a smart board. For this debate, half of each team prepared as experts on their position and half as experts *on the opponent's arguments*. After winter break and again after spring break, the whole process was repeated with new dilemmas.

You can see that there were three techniques employed in the study, supported by technology, to help students become more metacognitive about argumentation. First, they had to work in pairs to collaborate and agree on each communication with the opposing pair. Second, the researchers provided the pairs with transcripts of parts of their dialogue with the opponents so the partners could reflect on the discussions. Third, the dialogues were conducted via instant messaging, so the pairs had a permanent record of the discussion.

So what happened? The pairs, IM, and reflection strategies were successful for most students in helping them take into account the opponent's position and create strategies for rebutting the opponent's arguments. Working in pairs seemed to be especially helpful. When adolescents and even adults work alone, they often are not successful at creating effective counterarguments and rebuttals (Kuhn & Franklin, 2006).

# TEACHING FOR TRANSFER

**STOP & THINK** Think back for a moment to a class in one of your high school subjects that you have not studied in university. Imagine the teacher, the room, the textbook. Now remember what you actually learned in class. If it was a science class, what were some of the formulas you learned? Oxidation reduction? Boyle's law? •

If you are like most of us, you may remember *that* you learned these things, but you will not be quite sure exactly *what* you learned. Were those hours wasted? This question relates to the important topic of learning transfer. Let's begin with a definition of *transfer*.

Whenever something previously learned influences—for good or bad—current learning, or when solving an earlier problem affects how you solve a new problem, **transfer** has occurred. Erik De Corte (2003) calls transfer "the productive use of cognitive tools and motivations" (p. 142). This meaning of *transfer* emphasizes doing something new (productive), not just reproducing a previous application of the tools. If students learn a mathematical principle in one class and use it to solve a physics problem days or weeks later in another class, then transfer has taken place. However, the effect of past learning on present learning is not always positive. Functional fixedness and response set (described earlier in this chapter) are examples of negative transfer because they are attempts to apply familiar but *inappropriate* strategies to a new situation.

Actually, there are several dimensions of transfer (Barnett & Ceci, 2002). You can transfer learning across subjects (math skills used in science problems), across physical contexts (learned in school, used on the job), across social contexts (learned alone, used

**Transfer** Influence of previously learned material on new material; the productive (not reproductive) uses of cognitive tools and motivations.

with your family or team), across time periods (learned in university, used months or years later), across functions (learned for academics, used for hobbies and recreation), and across modalities (learned from watching the Home and Garden cable channel, used to discuss ideas for a patio with a landscape architect). So transfer can refer to many different examples of applying knowledge and skills beyond where, when, and how you learned them.

## The Many Views of Transfer

Transfer has been a focus of research in educational psychology for over 100 years. After all, the productive use of knowledge, skills, and motivations across a lifetime is a fundamental goal of education (Pugh & Bergin, 2006; Shaffer, 2010). Early work focused on specific transfer of skills and the general transfer of *mental discipline* gained from studying rigorous subjects such as Greek or mathematics. But in 1924, E. L. Thorndike demonstrated that there was no mental discipline benefit from learning Greek. Learning Greek just helped you learn more Greek. So, thanks to Thorndike, you were not required to take Greek in high school.

More recently, researchers have distinguished between the automatic, direct use of skills such as reading or writing in everyday applications and the thoughtful transfer of knowledge and strategies to arrive at creative solutions to problems (Bereiter, 1995; Bransford & Schwartz, 1999; Salomon & Perkins, 1989). The key to thoughtful transfer is *mindful abstraction*, or the deliberate identification of a principle, main idea, strategy, or procedure that is not tied to one specific problem or situation, but could apply to many. Such an abstraction becomes part of your metacognitive knowledge, available to guide future learning and problem solving. Bransford and Schwartz (1999) added another key—a resource-rich environment that supports productive, appropriate transfer. Table 9.4 summarizes the types of transfer.

## Teaching for Positive Transfer

Years of research and experience show that students will master new knowledge, problem-solving procedures, and learning strategies, but usually they will not use them unless prompted or guided. For example, studies of real-world mathematics show that people do not always apply math procedures learned in school to solve practical problems in their homes or at grocery stores (Lave, 1988; Lave & Wenger, 1991). This happens because learning is *situated*—tied to specific situations. Because knowledge is learned as a tool to solve particular problems, we may not realize that the knowledge is relevant when we encounter a problem that seems different, at least on the surface (Driscoll, 2005; Singley & Anderson, 1989). How can you make sure your students will use what they learn, even when situations change?

TABLE 9.4 • **Kinds of Transfer**

| | DIRECT-APPLICATION | PREPARATION FOR FUTURE LEARNING |
|---|---|---|
| **Definition** | Automatic transfer of highly practiced skill | Conscious application of abstract knowledge to a new situation<br><br>Productive use of cognitive tools and motivations |
| **Key Conditions** | Extensive practice<br><br>Variety of settings and conditions<br><br>Overlearning to automaticity | Mindful focus on abstracting a principle, main idea, or procedure that can be used in many situations<br><br>Learning in powerful teaching-learning environments |
| **Examples** | Driving many different cars<br><br>Finding your gate in an airport | Applying KWL or READS strategies<br><br>Applying procedures from math in designing a page layout for the school newspaper |

**HIGHER-LEVEL TRANSFER** Students will be more likely to transfer knowledge to new situations if they have been actively involved in the learning process. They should be encouraged to form abstractions that they will apply later, so the students know transfer is an important goal.

**WHAT IS WORTH LEARNING?** First, you must answer the question "What is worth learning?" The learning of basic skills such as reading, writing, computing, cooperating, and speaking will definitely transfer to other situations, because these skills are necessary for later work both in and out of school—writing job applications, reading novels, paying bills, working on a team, locating and evaluating health care services, among others. All later learning depends on positive transfer of these basic skills to new situations.

Teachers must also be aware of what the future is likely to hold for their students, both as a group and as individuals. What will society require of them as adults? As children, none of us studied anything about computers; yet now we spend most of every day using them, and Phil even designs software for researching how students learn. He also learned to use a slide rule. Now, calculators and computers have made this skill obsolete. We were encouraged to take advanced math and physics instead of typing in high school. Those were great classes, but we still struggle with keyboarding—who knew? Undoubtedly, changes as extreme and unpredictable as these await the students you will teach. For this reason, the general transfer of principles, attitudes, learning strategies, self-motivation, time management skills, and problem solving will be just as important for your students as the specific transfer of basic skills.

**HOW CAN TEACHERS HELP?** For basic skills, greater transfer can also be ensured by **overlearning**, practising a skill past the point of mastery. Many of the basic facts students learn in elementary school, such as the multiplication tables, are traditionally overlearned. Overlearning helps students develop automated basic skills as we saw in Chapter 9.

For higher-level transfer, students must first learn and understand. Students will be more likely to transfer knowledge to new situations if they have been actively involved in the learning process. Students should be encouraged to form abstractions that they will apply later, so they know transfer is an important goal. It also helps if students form deep connections between the new knowledge and their existing structures of knowledge as well as connections to their everyday experiences (Pugh & Bergin, 2007). Erik De Corte (2003) believes that teachers support transfer, the productive use of cognitive tools and motivations, when they create powerful teaching-learning environments using these design principles:

- The environments should support constructive learning processes in all students.
- The environments should encourage the development of student self-regulation, so that teachers gradually give over more and more responsibilities to the students.
- Learning should involve interaction and collaboration.
- Learners should deal with problems that have personal meaning for them, that are similar to those they will face in the future.
- The classroom culture should encourage students to become aware of and develop their cognitive and motivational processes. In order to be productive users of these tools, students must know about and value them.

The next three chapters delve in depth about how to support constructive learning, motivation, self-regulation, collaboration, and self-awareness in all students. For now, the *Family and Community Partnerships Guidelines* give ideas for enlisting support from families to encourage transfer.

There is one last kind of transfer that is especially important for students—the transfer of the *learning strategies* we encountered earlier. Learning strategies are meant to be applied across a wide range of situations.

**Overlearning** Practising a skill past the point of mastery.

**STAGES OF TRANSFER FOR STRATEGIES.**   Gary Phye (1992, 2001; Phye & Sanders, 1994) describes three stages in developing strategic transfer. In the *acquisition phase*, students should not only receive instruction about a strategy and how to use it, but also rehearse the strategy and practise being aware of when and how they are using it. In the *retention phase*, more practice with feedback helps students hone their strategy use. In the *transfer phase*, students should be given new problems that can be solved with the same strategy, even though the problems appear different on the surface. To enhance motivation, teachers should point out to students how using the strategy will help them solve many problems and accomplish different tasks. These steps help build both procedural and self-regulatory knowledge—*how* to use the strategy as well as *when* and *why*.

For all students, there is a positive relationship between using learning strategies and academic gains such as high school GPA and retention in university (Robbins, Le, & Lauver, 2005). Some students will learn productive strategies on their own, but all students can benefit from direct teaching, modelling, and practice of learning strategies and study skills. This is one important way to prepare all of your students for the future. Newly mastered concepts, principles, and strategies must be applied in a wide variety of situations and with many types of problems (Chen & Mo, 2004). Positive transfer is encouraged when skills are practised under authentic conditions, similar to those that will exist when the skills are needed later. Students can learn to write by corresponding with email pen pals in other countries. They can learn historical research methods by studying their own family history. Some of these applications should involve complex, ill-defined, unstructured problems, because many of the problems to be faced in later life, both in school and out, will not come to students complete with instructions.

## GUIDELINES — FAMILY AND COMMUNITY PARTNERSHIPS

### Promoting Transfer

**Keep families informed about their child's curriculum so they can support learning.**
*Examples*
1. At the beginning of units or major projects, send a letter summarizing the key goals, a few of the major assignments, and some common problems students have in learning the material for that unit.
2. Ask parents for suggestions about how their child's interests could be connected to the curriculum topics.
3. Invite parents to school for an evening of "strategy learning." Have the students teach their family members one of the strategies they have learned in school.

**Give families ideas for how they might encourage their children to practise, extend, or apply learning from school.**
*Examples*
1. To extend writing, ask parents to encourage their children to write letters or emails to companies or civic organizations asking for information or free products. Provide a shell letter form for structure and ideas, and include addresses of companies that provide free samples or information.
2. Ask family members to include their children in some projects that require measurement, halving or doubling recipes, or estimating costs.

3. Suggest that students work with grandparents to do a family memory book. Combine historical research and writing.

**Show connections between learning in school and life outside school.**
*Examples*
1. Ask families to talk about and show how they use the skills their children are learning in their jobs, hobbies, or community involvement projects.
2. Ask family members to come to class to demonstrate how they use reading, writing, science, math, or other knowledge in their work.

**Make families partners in practising learning strategies.**
*Examples*
1. Focus on one learning strategy at a time—ask families to simply remind their children to use a particular strategy with homework that week.
2. Develop a lending library of books and videos to teach families about learning strategies.
3. Give parents a copy of the Becoming an Expert Student Guidelines on page 303, rewritten for your grade level.

*For more information on promoting transfer, see http://education.purduecal.edu/Vockell/EdPsyBook.*

# ▼ SUMMARY

Liubomir/Shutterstock

## Metacognition (pp. 293–296)

**What are the three metacognitive skills?** The three metacognitive skills used to regulate thinking and learning are planning, monitoring, and evaluating. Planning involves deciding how much time to give to a task, which strategies to use, how to start, and so on. Monitoring is the real-time awareness of "how I'm doing." Evaluating involves making judgments about the processes and outcomes of thinking and learning and acting on those judgments.

**What are some sources of individual differences in metacognition?** Individual differences in metacognition may result from different paces of development (maturation) or biological differences among learners. For example, young students may not be able to understand a lesson's purpose as well as older students.

**How can teachers help students develop metacognitive knowledge and skills?** With younger students, teachers can help students "look inside" to identify what they do to read, write, or learn better. Systems such as KWL can help if teachers demonstrate, explain, and model the strategy. For older students, teachers can build self-reflective questions into assignments and learning materials.

## Learning Strategies (pp. 296–304)

**What are learning strategies?** Learning strategies are a special kind of procedural knowledge—*knowing how* to do something. A strategy for learning might include mnemonics to remember key terms, skimming to identify the organization, and then writing answers to possible essay questions. Use of strategies and tactics reflects metacognitive knowledge.

**What key functions do learning strategies play?** Learning strategies help students become cognitively engaged—focus attention on the relevant or important aspects of the material. Second, they encourage students to invest effort, make connections, elaborate, translate, organize, and reorganize in order to think and process deeply—the greater the practice and processing, the stronger the learning. Finally, strategies help students regulate and monitor their own learning—keep track of what is making sense and notice when a new approach is needed.

**Describe some procedures for developing learning strategies.** Expose students to a number of different strategies, not only general learning strategies but also very specific tactics, such as the graphic strategies. Teach conditional knowledge about when, where, and why to use various strategies. Develop motivation to use the strategies and tactics by showing students how their learning and performance can be improved. Provide direct instruction in content knowledge needed to use the strategies.

**When will students apply learning strategies?** If they have appropriate strategies, students will apply them if they are faced with a task that requires good strategies, value doing well on that task, think the effort to apply the strategies will be worthwhile, and believe that they can succeed using the strategies. Also, to apply deep processing strategies, students must assume that knowledge is complex and takes time to learn and that learning requires their own active efforts.

## Problem Solving (pp. 304–315)

**What is problem solving?** Problem solving is both general and domain specific. Also, problems can range from *well structured* to *ill structured*, depending on how clear cut the goal is and how much structure is provided for solving the problem.

General problem-solving strategies usually include the steps of *identifying* the problem, *setting goals*, *exploring* possible solutions and consequences, *acting*, and finally *evaluating* the outcome. Both general and specific problem solving are valuable and necessary.

**Why is the representation stage of problem solving so important?** To represent the problem accurately, you must understand both the whole problem and its discrete elements. Schema training may improve this ability. The problem-solving process follows entirely different paths, depending on what representation and goal are chosen. If your representation of the problem suggests an immediate solution, the task is done; the new problem is recognized as a "disguised" version of an old problem with a clear solution. But if there is no existing way of solving the problem or if the activated schema fails, then students must search for a solution. The application of algorithms and heuristics—such as means-ends analysis, working backward, analogical thinking, and verbalization—may help students solve problems.

**Describe factors that can interfere with problem solving.** Factors that hinder problem solving include functional fixedness or rigidity (response set). These disallow the flexibility needed to represent problems accurately and to have insight into solutions. Also, as we make decisions and judgments, we may overlook important information because we base judgments on what seems representative of a category (representativeness heuristic) or what is available in memory (availability heuristic), then pay attention only to information that confirms our choices (confirmation bias) so that we hold on to beliefs, even in the face of contradictory evidence (belief perseverance).

**What are the differences between expert and novice knowledge in a given area?** Expert problem solvers have a rich store of declarative, procedural, and conditional knowledge. They organize this knowledge around general principles or patterns that apply to large classes of problems. They work faster, remember relevant information, and monitor their progress better than novices.

## Creativity and Creative Problem Solving (pp. 315–319)

**What is creativity and how is it assessed?** Creativity is a process that involves independently restructuring problems to see things in new, imaginative ways. Creativity is difficult to measure, but tests of divergent thinking can assess originality, fluency, and flexibility. Originality is usually determined statistically. To be original, a response must be given by fewer than five or 10 people out of every 100 who take the test. Fluency is the number of different responses. The number of different categories of responses measures flexibility.

**What can teachers do to support creativity in the classroom?** Multicultural experiences appear to help students think flexibly and creatively. Teachers can encourage creativity in their interactions with students by accepting unusual, imaginative answers, modelling divergent thinking, using brainstorming, and tolerating dissent.

## Critical Thinking and Argumentation (pp. 319–322)

**What is critical thinking?** Critical thinking skills include defining and clarifying the problem, making judgments about the consistency and adequacy of the information related to a problem, and drawing conclusions. No matter what approach you use to develop critical thinking, it is important to follow up activities with additional practice. One lesson is not enough—overlearning will help students use critical thinking in their own lives.

**What is argumentation?** The heart of argumentation (the process of debating a claim with someone else) is supporting your position with evidence and understanding, and then refuting your opponent's claims and evidence. Argumentation skills are not natural. They take both time and instruction to learn. It is especially difficult for children and adolescents to pay attention to, understand, and refute the opponent's position with evidence.

### Teaching for Transfer (pp. 322–325)

**What is transfer?** Transfer occurs when a rule, fact, or skill learned in one situation is applied in another situation; for example, applying rules of punctuation to write a job application letter. Transfer also involves applying to new problems the principles learned in other, often dissimilar situations.

**What are some dimensions of transfer?** Information can be transferred across a variety of contexts. Some examples include transfer from one subject to another, one physical location to another, or one function to another. These types of transfer make it possible to use skills developed in one area for many other tasks.

**Distinguish between automatic and mindful, intentional transfer.** Spontaneous application of well-learned knowledge and skills is automatic transfer. Mindful, intentional transfer involves reflection and deliberate application of abstract knowledge to new situations. Learning environments should support active constructive learning, self-regulation, collaboration, and awareness of cognitive tools and motivational processes. In addition, students should deal with problems that have meaning in their lives. In addition, teachers can help students transfer learning strategies by teaching strategies directly, providing practice with feedback, and then expanding the application of the strategies to new and unfamiliar situations.

## ▼ WHAT WOULD THEY DO?

## TEACHERS' CASEBOOK: Uncritical Thinking

Here is how some practising teachers would help students learn to critically evaluate the information they find on the internet.

### JOHN BALDASSARRE
Formerly from Archbishop Oscar Romero High School, Edmonton, AB

When assigning a "research" paper, I find it extremely valuable to start the process early in the year by presenting students with a website that features a fake news story that appears to be real. I ask students to begin to discuss and evaluate the story that is presented and to discuss any similar events that are taking place in the world at the time. After a lengthy discussion, I reveal to the students the fact that the website and the news story are fake and begin to show them how to establish the validity of a website or author. I ask students to consider the following basic questions:

- Who is the author of the news story or website, and what is his or her background? Is there anything on the site that could bias the information?
- What is the purpose of the website? Is it affiliated with any other sites (political parties, social action groups, etc.)? Is it associated with a specific domain, or is it a personal site?
- How active and recent is the website?
- Is the content based on opinions or on studies and/or articles? Can those studies or articles be accessed?
- Can you find the same information stated on other websites or within more traditional, print-based research materials?

I then ask students to apply the above criteria to each research paper that I assign. Students come to realize that they need to research more than one source of information and that they must develop the ability to discern information and to filter bias and opinions from the objective facts. In teaching and advocating this type of methodology and critical thinking process, I also try to function as a role model and demonstrate to students how to filter through a plethora of information to find the sources that are best suited to the task.

### ALANNA KING
Orangeville District Secondary School, Orangeville, ON

One technique I use to help students critically evaluate research obtained through internet sources is to show four examples of websites and then walk the students through how to rank the sites from worst to best. For this activity, I break the class into small groups and ask students to develop their own criteria and to sort the examples. As a class, we then list all of the criteria together. Rather than give the students the criteria in advance, they are expected to actively engage with these exemplars for comparison and to express their own ideas about the websites. Together, we develop a common class lexicon for discussing the authority and reliability of websites for research. Students now have a clear understanding of the expectations associated with choosing internet research sources. Another advantage of this activity is that the students become dissatisfied with websites that are inadequate after interacting with good ones.

This activity also involves asking the students to engage with a "citation tool" from the beginning of their research, which reinforces the value of finding quality internet sources. Most digital citation tools now produce excellent quality reference pages based on user input. Poor websites have very little information to plug into the citation tool, and sometimes students find that they can't even locate an author or copyright date. Using the citation tool during the research process, rather than at the end of an assignment, helps students to manage their own research process.

Many students don't know how to use research material as evidence for an argument, so finding deeper web-based sources is critical to success. I think students undervalue their own voices and don't know how to recognize and appreciate their own ideas during research. I model how to analyze a paragraph on my digital projector, and think aloud in front of the students, so they can see how I'm developing ideas and connecting them to my research question. Next, I give students a reading from a website and invite them to listen to their own thoughts as they read silently. I suggest that these thoughts might help to

- predict what is next
- connect to their own experiences
- connect to other texts they've experienced
- connect to current events

During this close reading, students recognize once again the importance of choosing quality internet research. Engaging with the text on multiple levels helps students learn how to critically evaluate web sources.

Kelia Neokow/Shutterstock

# THE LEARNING SCIENCES
## AND CONSTRUCTIVISM

▶ **TEACHERS' CASEBOOK:** Dilemma on Day 1

You have finally landed a job teaching English and writing in a high school. The first day of class, you discover that a number of students appear to be just beginning to learn English. You make a mental note to meet with them to determine how much and what kind of reading they can handle. To get a sense of the class's interest, you ask them to write a review of the last book they read, as if they were on TV doing a "book talk" program. There is a bit of grumbling, but the students seem to be writing, so you take a few minutes to try to talk with a student who seems to have trouble with English.

That night you look over the book reviews. Either the students are giving you a hard time, or no one has read anything lately. Several students mention a text from another class, but their reviews are one-sentence evaluations—usually containing the words *lame* or *useless* (often misspelled). In stark contrast are the papers of three students— they are a pleasure to read, worthy of publication in the school literary magazine (if there were one), and reflect a fairly sophisticated understanding of some good literature.

**CRITICAL THINKING**

- How would you adapt your lesson plans for this group?
- What will you do tomorrow?
- What teaching approaches do you think will work with this class?
- How will you work with the three students who are more advanced and with the students who are just learning English?

## OVERVIEW AND OBJECTIVES

In the past three chapters, we have analyzed different aspects of learning. We considered behavioural, information processing, and cognitive science explanations of what and how people learn. We examined complex cognitive processes such as metacognitive skills and problem solving. These views of learning focus on the individual and what is happening in his or her "head." In this chapter, we expand our investigation of learning to include insights from a relatively recent interdisciplinary approach called the *learning sciences*. This approach brings together work in many fields that study learning, including educational psychology, computer science, neuroscience, and anthropology. One of the foundations of the learning sciences is constructivism, a broad perspective that calls attention to two critical aspects of learning: social and cultural factors. In this chapter, we examine the role of other people and the cultural context in learning. Sociocultural constructivist theories have roots in cognitive perspectives, but have moved well beyond these early explanations. We will explore a number of teaching strategies and approaches that are consistent with cognitive perspectives—inquiry, problem-based learning, cooperative learning, cognitive apprenticeships, and service learning. Finally, we will examine learning in this digital age, including the considerations about learning in technology-rich environments.

By the time you have completed this chapter, you should be able to:

**10.1** Describe the collaborative approach that led to the interdisciplinary field of learning sciences.

**10.2** Explain different perspectives on constructivism as a theory of learning and teaching.

**10.3** Identify the common elements in most contemporary constructivist theories.

**10.4** Apply constructivist principles to classroom practice.

**10.5** Evaluate the use of community-based activities/service learning.

**10.6** Describe positive and negative influences of technology on the learning and development of children and adolescents.

# THE LEARNING SCIENCES

In the previous three chapters, psychologists were responsible for most of the theory and research we discussed. But many other people have also studied learning: Today, there are multiple perspectives included in the learning sciences.

## What Are the Learning Sciences?

The interdisciplinary field of the **learning sciences** brings together research in psychology, education, computer science, philosophy, sociology, anthropology, neuroscience, and other fields that study learning. You already have explored some of the foundations of the learning sciences in Chapters 8 and 9, including the make-up of working memory and the role of cognitive load in learning; how information is represented in complex structures such as schemas; what experts know and how their knowledge is different from that of novices; metacognition; problem solving; thinking and reasoning; and how knowledge transfers (or doesn't transfer) from the classroom to the world beyond.

No matter what their focus, knowledge workers in the learning sciences are interested in how deep knowledge in subjects like science, mathematics, and literacy is acquired and applied in the real world of scientists and mathematicians and writers. In the *Cambridge Handbook of Learning Sciences*, R. Keith Sawyer (2006) contrasts what it takes for deep learning to occur with traditional classroom practices that have dominated schooling in many countries for decades. Look at Table 10.1 to see the differences.

**Learning sciences** An interdisciplinary science of learning based on research in psychology, education, computer science, philosophy, sociology, anthropology, neuroscience, and other fields that study learning.

TABLE 10.1 • **How Deep Learning Contrasts With Learning in Traditional Classrooms**

| LEARNING IN TRADITIONAL CLASSROOMS | BUT FINDINGS FROM COGNITIVE SCIENCE SHOW THAT DEEP LEARNING REQUIRES THAT: |
|---|---|
| Class material is not related to what students already know. Example: Teacher says, "Igneous rocks are . . . " | Learners relate new understandings to what they already know and believe. Example: Teacher says, "Have any of you seen granite counter tops on TV home shows? Or maybe you have one in your house. What do they look like . . .?" |
| Class material presented and learned as disconnected bits of knowledge. "The definition of metamorphic rocks is. . . ." | Learners integrate and interconnect their knowledge in expanding conceptual systems. "We already have learned about two kinds of rocks. We also learned last week about how the earth has changed over the centuries, with some ocean floors becoming land areas. Today we will learn about how marble and diamonds. . . . " |
| Lessons involve memorizing facts and doing procedures without understanding how or why. "To divide fractions, invert and multiply . . ." | Learners search for patterns and recognize or invent underlying principles. "Remind me what it means to divide. . . . Okay, so ¾ divided by ½ means how many sets of what are in. . . .?" |
| Learners have trouble understanding ideas that are not straight from the textbook or explained in the same way. "What does your textbook say about . . ." | Learners evaluate new ideas, even if not in the text, and integrate them into their thinking. "On TV yesterday there was a story about a new drug that is effective in curing one out of eight cases of . . . . What is the probability of a cure?" |
| Authorities and experts are the source of unchanging and accurate facts and procedures. "Scientists agree. . . ." | Learners understand that knowledge is socially constructed by people, so ideas require critical examination. "Here is an excerpt from the political debates last week. Let's think about how you would determine what statements are more supported by evidence . . ." |
| Learners simply memorize everything instead of thinking about the purpose of learning and the best strategies for that purpose. "This will be on the test." | Learners think about why they are learning, monitor their understanding, and reflect on their own learning processes. "How could you use this concept in your own life? How can you tell if you are understanding it?" |

Source: Based on Sawyer, K. (2006). The new science of learning. In R. K. Sawyer (Ed.). The Cambridge handbook of the learning sciences (p. 4). New York: The Cambridge University Press. New York: Oxford University Press.

## Basic Assumptions of the Learning Sciences

Even though the different fields in the learning sciences approach their study from varying perspectives, there is growing agreement about some basic assumptions (Sawyer, 2006b):

- **Experts have deep conceptual knowledge.** Experts know many facts and procedures, but just learning facts and procedures will not make you an expert. Experts have deep conceptual understanding that allows them to put their knowledge into action; they are able to apply and modify their knowledge to fit each situation. Experts' deep conceptual knowledge generates problem finding and problem solving.
- **Learning comes from the learner.** Better instruction alone will not transfer deep understandings from teachers to students. Learning is more than receiving and processing information transmitted by teachers or texts. Rather, students must actively participate in their own personal construction of knowledge. We are knowledge inventors, not copy machines (de Kock, Sleegers, & Voeten, 2004).

- **Schools must create effective learning environments.** It is the job of the school to create environments where students are active in constructing their own deep understandings so they can reason about real-world problems and transfer their learning from school to their lives beyond the school walls.
- **Prior knowledge is key.** Students come into our classrooms filled with knowledge and beliefs about how the world works. Some of these preconceptions are right, some are part right, and some are wrong. If teaching does not begin with what the students "know," then the students will learn what it takes to pass the test, but their knowledge and beliefs about the world will not change.
- **Reflection is necessary to develop deep conceptual knowledge.** Students need to express and perform the knowledge they are developing through writing, conversations, drawings, projects, skits, portfolios, reports, and so on. But the performance is not enough. To develop deep conceptual knowledge, students need to reflect—thoughtfully analyze their own work and progress.

### Embodied Cognition

Recently a new theme has emerged in the cognitive and learning sciences that "the way we think about and represent information reflects the fact that we need to interact with the world" (Ashcraft & Radvansky, 2010, p. 32). This view, called **embodied cognition**, acknowledges that these interactions occur through our senses and bodies, and the way our bodies interact with the world to achieve our goals affects our thinking. In other words, our cognitive processes have deep roots in the interactions of our bodies with the real world—what develops cognitively depends on our sensorimotor engagement with the world. Consequently, the body, not the mind, is primary, but the body needs the mind to successfully interact in the world. In some ways, this perspective is similar to Piaget's idea that thinking emerges early on from the infant's sensorimotor interaction in the world. Instead of being just simple conduits for outside world sounds and images, our senses and motor responses are central to how we think. So we have to understand how our physical body interacts with the world in order to understand our mind (Wilson, 2002).

Actually, it appears that humans are capable of both real-time, situation-by-situation, adaptive, ever-changing interactions (where the *mind is serving the body* to succeed—for example, driving in traffic or doing a jigsaw puzzle) and abstract thinking using symbols and representations developed in earlier times to solve current problems (where *the body-brain control system is serving the mind*—for example, in using images or analogies to learn a new language). Humans' abilities to mentally represent and manipulate symbols that are not present in real time is critical. In fact, Margret Wilson (2002) suggests:

> This takeover by the mind, and the concomitant ability to mentally represent what is distant in time or space, may have been one of the driving forces behind the runaway train of human intelligence that separated us from other hominids. (p. 635)

In educational psychology, these fundamental assumptions of the learning sciences and embodied cognition all lead to the conclusion that thinking is constructive. In the next section we look at both cognitive and social constructivism—topics you will hear about repeatedly in your preparation for teaching.

## COGNITIVE AND SOCIAL CONSTRUCTIVISM

Consider this situation:

> A young child who has never been to the hospital is in her bed in the pediatric wing. The nurse at the station down the hall calls over the intercom above the bed, "Hi, Chelsea, how are you doing? Do you need anything?" The girl looks puzzled and does not answer. The nurse repeats the question with the same result. Finally, the nurse says emphatically, "Chelsea, are you there? Say something!" The little girl responds tentatively, "Hello wall—I'm here."

**Embodied cognition** Theory stating that cognitive processes develop from real-time, goal-directed interactions between humans and their environment.

Chelsea encountered a new situation—a talking wall. The wall is persistent. It sounds like a grown-up wall. She shouldn't talk to strangers, but she is not sure about walls. She uses what she knows and what the situation provides to construct meaning and to act.

Here is another example of constructing meaning. This time, Kate and her 9-year-old son Ethan co-construct understandings as they buy groceries:

**Ethan:** (running to get a shopping cart) Do we need the big one?

**Kate:** We might—better too big than not big enough. Here is our list—where do we go first?

**Ethan:** We need ice cream for the party! (Ethan heads toward frozen foods.)

**Kate:** Whoa! What happened to the ice cream carton you left out on the kitchen counter?

**Ethan:** It melted, and it wasn't out that long. I promise!

**Kate:** Right, and we may be in this store awhile, so let's start with things that won't melt while we are shopping—I usually buy produce first.

**Ethan:** What's "produce"?

**Kate:** Things that grow—fruits and vegetables "produced" by farmers.

**Ethan:** Okay, the list says cucumbers. Here they are. Wait there are two kinds. Which do you want? The little ones say "local." What's local?

**Kate:** Local means from around here—close to us, close to our "location." Hmmm— the big ones are 75 cents *each*, and these smaller ones are $1.15 *a pound*. How would you decide which is a better deal?

**Ethan:** I guess bigger is better, right? Or is local better?

**Kate:** Well, I wonder if they cost the same for the amount you get—per pound. How could you figure that out?

**Ethan:** I don't know—the price for a pound isn't on the big ones, just the price each.

**Kate:** When the doctor wants to know how many pounds you weigh, she puts you on a scale. What if you weighed a big cucumber over there on that food scale?

**Ethan:** Okay—it weighs half a pound.

**Kate:** So half a pound costs 75 cents—what would a whole pound cost—that's two halves make a whole?

**Ethan:** 75 cents plus 75 cents—$1.50. Gee, the bigger ones are more expensive. So the smaller ones are better and they are "local"—that's good, too, right?

**Kate:** Maybe. I like to support our local farmers. Where are the small cucumbers from? Look at the tiny print on the label.

**Ethan:** Delta. Is that close to us?

**Kate:** Pretty close—it is just about an hour's drive from the market here at Univercity . . .

Look at the knowledge being co-constructed about planning ahead, vocabulary, math, problem solving, and even geography. Constructivist theories of learning focus on how people make meaning, both on their own like Chelsea and in interaction with others like Ethan.

## Constructivist Views of Learning

**Constructivism** is a broad term used by philosophers, curriculum designers, psychologists, educators, and others that emphasizes the active role of the learner in building understanding and making sense of information. Ernst von Glasersfeld calls it "a vast and woolly area in contemporary psychology, epistemology, and education" (1997, p. 204). Constructivist perspectives are grounded in the research of Piaget; Vygotsky; the Gestalt psychologists; Bartlett, Bruner, and Rogoff; as well as the philosophy of John Dewey and the work in anthropology of Jean Lave, to mention just a few intellectual roots.

There is no one constructivist theory of learning, but most constructivist theories agree on two central ideas:

**Central Idea 1:** Learners are active in constructing their own knowledge.

**Central Idea 2:** Social interactions are important in this knowledge construction process (Bruning, Schraw, & Norby, 2011).

Constructivist approaches in science and mathematics education, in educational psychology and anthropology, and in computer-based education all embrace these two ideas. But even though many psychologists and educators use the term *constructivism*,

Constructivism   View that emphasizes the active role of the learner in building understanding and making sense of information.

they often mean very different things (Martin, 2006; McCaslin & Hickey, 2001; Phillips, 1997).

One way to organize constructivist views is to talk about two forms of constructivism: psychological and social construction (Palincsar, 1998; Phillips, 1997). We could oversimplify a bit and say that psychological constructivists focus on how individuals use information, resources, and help from others to build and improve their mental models and problem-solving strategies—see Central Idea 1. In contrast, social constructivists view learning as increasing our abilities to participate with others in activities that are meaningful in the culture—see Central Idea 2 (Windschitl, 2002). Let's look a bit closer at each type of constructivism.

**CONSTRUCTIVIST VIEWS** Constructivist theories are based on the ideas that learners actively develop their knowledge, rather than passively receive it, in package form, from teachers or outside sources.

### PSYCHOLOGICAL/INDIVIDUAL/COGNITIVE CONSTRUCTIVISM.

Many psychological theories include some kind of constructivism because these theories embrace the idea that individuals construct their own cognitive structures as they interpret their experiences in particular situations (Palincsar, 1998). These psychological constructivists "are concerned with how individuals build up certain elements of their cognitive or emotional apparatus" (Phillips, 1997, p. 153). Because they study individual knowledge, beliefs, self-concept, or identity, they are sometimes called *individual constructivists* or *cognitive constructivists;* they all focus on the inner psychological life of people. When Chelsea talked to the wall in the previous section, she was making meaning using her own individual knowledge and beliefs about how to respond when someone (or something) talks to you. She was using what she knew to impose intellectual structure on her world (Piaget, 1971; Windschitl, 2002). When children observe that most plants need soil to grow and then conclude that plants "eat dirt," they are using what they know about how eating supports life to make sense of plant growth (Linn & Eylon, 2006).

Using these standards, most recent information processing theories are constructivist because they are concerned with how individuals construct internal representations (propositions, images, concepts, schemas) that can be remembered and retrieved (Mayer, 1996). The outside world is viewed as a source of input, but once the sensations are perceived and enter working memory, the important work is assumed to be happening "inside the head" of the individual (Schunk, 2012; Vera & Simon, 1993). Some psychologists, however, believe that information processing is "trivial" or "weak" constructivism because the individual's only constructive contribution is to build accurate internal representations of the outside world (Derry, 1992; Garrison, 1995; Marshall, 1996; Windschitl, 2002).

In contrast, Piaget's psychological (cognitive) constructivist perspective is less concerned with "correct" representations and more interested in meaning as an individual constructs it. As we saw in Chapter 2, Piaget proposed that as children develop, their thinking becomes more organized and adaptive and less tied to concrete events. Piaget's special concern was with logic and the construction of universal knowledge that cannot be learned directly from the environment—knowledge such as conservation or reversibility (Miller, 2011). Such knowledge comes from reflecting on and coordinating our own cognitions or thoughts, not from mapping external reality. Piaget saw the social environment as an important factor in development, but did not believe that social interaction was the main mechanism for changing thinking (Moshman, 1997). Some educational and developmental psychologists have referred to Piaget's kind of constructivism as **first wave constructivism** or "solo" constructivism, with its emphasis on Central Idea 1, individual meaning making (De Corte, Greer, and Verschaffel, 1996; Paris, Byrnes, & Paris, 2001).

**First wave constructivism** A focus on the individual and psychological sources of knowing, as in Piaget's theory.

Gabbro/Alamy

At the extreme end of individual constructivism is the notion of **radical constructivism**. This perspective holds that there is no reality or truth "in the world," only the individual's perceptions and beliefs. Each of us constructs meaning from our own experiences, but we have no way of understanding or "knowing" the reality of others (Woods & Murphy, 2002). A difficulty with this position is that, when pushed to the extreme of relativism, all knowledge and all beliefs are equal because they are all valid individual perceptions. There are problems with this thinking for educators. First, teachers have a professional responsibility to emphasize some values, such as honesty or justice, over others, such as bigotry and deception. All perceptions and beliefs are not equal. As teachers, we ask students to work hard to learn. If learning cannot advance understanding because all understandings are equally good, then, as David Moshman (1997) notes, "we might just as well let students continue to believe whatever they believe" (p. 230). Also, it appears that some knowledge, such as counting and one-to-one correspondence, is not constructed, but universal. Knowing one-to-one correspondence is part of being human (Geary, 1995; Schunk, 2012).

VYGOTSKY'S SOCIAL CONSTRUCTIVISM.   As you also saw in Chapter 2, Vygotsky emphasized Central Idea 2 above—social interaction, cultural tools, and activity shape individual development and learning. Ethan's interactions and activities in the grocery store with his mother shaped his learning about anticipating possible consequences (running out of space in the shopping cart and melted ice cream), the meaning of "produce" and "local," how to calculate price per pound, and geography (Martin, 2006). By participating in a broad range of activities with others, learners *appropriate* the outcomes produced by working together; these outcomes could include both new strategies and knowledge. **Appropriating** means being able to reason, act, and participate using cultural tools—for example, using conceptual tools such as "force" and "acceleration" to reason in physics (Mason, 2007). In psychological (cognitive) constructivism, learning means individually possessing knowledge. But in social constructivism, learning means belonging to a group and participating in the social construction of knowledge (Mason, 2007). Putting learning in social and cultural contexts, as Vygotsky did, is known as **second wave constructivism** (Paris, Byrnes, & Paris, 2001).

Because his theory relies heavily on social interactions and the cultural context to explain learning, most psychologists classify Vygotsky as a social constructivist (Palincsar, 1998; Prawat, 1996). However, some theorists categorize him as a psychological constructivist because he was primarily interested in development within the individual (Moshman, 1997; Phillips, 1997). In a sense, Vygotsky was both. One advantage of Vygotsky's theory of learning is that it gives us a way to consider both the psychological and the social: He bridges both camps. For example, Vygotsky's concept of the *zone of proximal development*—the area in which a child can solve a problem with the help (scaffolding) of an adult or more able peer—has been called a place where culture and cognition create each other (Cole, 1985). Culture creates cognition when the adult uses tools and practices from the culture (language, maps, computers, looms, music) to steer the child toward goals the culture values (reading, writing, weaving, dance). Cognition creates culture as the adult and child together generate new practices and problem solutions to add to the cultural group's repertoire (Serpell, 1993). So people are both products and producers of their societies and cultures (Bandura, 2001). One way of integrating individual and social constructivism is to think of knowledge as both *individually constructed* and *socially mediated* (Windschitl, 2002).

The term **constructionism** is sometimes used to describe how public knowledge in math, science, history, and other subjects is created. Although this is not our main concern in educational psychology, it is worth a quick look.

CONSTRUCTIONISM.   Social constructionists do not focus on individual learning. Their concern is how public knowledge is constructed in the disciplines such as economics and even educational psychology. Beyond this kind of academic knowledge, constructionists also are interested in how common-sense ideas, everyday beliefs, and commonly held understandings about people and the world are communicated to new members of a

Radical constructivism Knowledge is assumed to be the individual's construction; it cannot be judged right or wrong.

Appropriating   Being able to internalize or take for yourself knowledge and skills developed in interaction with others or with cultural tools.

Second wave constructivism   A focus on the social and cultural sources of knowing, as in Vygotsky's theory.

Constructionism   How public knowledge in disciplines such as science, math, economics, or history is constructed.

sociocultural group (Gergen, 1997; Phillips, 1997). Questions raised might include who determines what constitutes history, what is the proper way to behave in public, or how to get elected class president. Social constructionists believe all knowledge is socially constructed, and, more important, some people have more power than others to define what constitutes such knowledge. Relationships between and among teachers, students, families, and the community are the important issues. Collaboration to understand diverse viewpoints is encouraged, and traditional bodies of knowledge often are challenged (Gergen, 1997). The philosophies of Jacques Dierrida and Michel Foucault are important sources for constructionists. Vygotsky's theory, with its attention to the way cognition creates culture, has some elements in common with constructionism.

These different perspectives on constructivism raise some general questions, and they disagree on the answers. These questions can never be fully resolved, but different theories tend to favour different positions. Let's consider the questions.

## How Is Knowledge Constructed?

One tension among different approaches to constructivism is based on how knowledge is constructed. Moshman (1982) describes three explanations.

1. *The realities and truths of the external world direct knowledge construction.* Individuals reconstruct outside reality by building accurate mental representations such as propositional networks, concepts, cause-and-effect patterns, and condition-action production rules that reflect "the way things really are." The more the person learns, the deeper and broader his or her experience is, the closer that person's knowledge is to objective reality. Information processing holds this view of knowledge (Cobb & Bowers, 1999).

2. *Internal processes such as Piaget's organization, assimilation, and accommodation direct knowledge construction.* New knowledge is abstracted from old knowledge. Knowledge is not a mirror of reality, but rather an abstraction that grows and develops with cognitive activity. Knowledge is not true or false; it just grows more internally consistent and organized with development.

3. *Both external and internal factors direct knowledge construction.* Knowledge grows through the interactions of internal (cognitive) and external (environmental and social) factors. Vygotsky's description of cognitive development through the appropriation and use of cultural tools such as language is consistent with this view (Bruning, Schraw, & Norby, 2011). Another example is Bandura's theory of reciprocal interactions among people, behaviours, and environments described in Chapter 11 (Schunk, 2012). Table 10.2 summarizes the three general explanations about how knowledge is constructed.

## Knowledge: Situated or General?

A second question that cuts across many constructivist perspectives is whether knowledge is internal, general, and transferable, or bound to the time and place in which it is constructed—situated. Psychologists who emphasize the social construction of knowledge and situated learning affirm Vygotsky's notion that learning is inherently social and embedded in a particular cultural setting (Cobb & Bowers, 1999). What is true in one time and place—such as the "fact" before Columbus's time that the earth was flat—becomes false in another time and place. Particular ideas may be useful within a specific **community of practice**—a social situation or context in which ideas are judged useful or true—such as fifteenth-century navigation, but useless outside that community. What counts as new knowledge is determined in part by how well the new idea fits with current accepted practice. Over time, the current practice may be questioned and even overthrown, but until such major shifts occur, current practice will shape what is considered valuable.

**Situated learning** emphasizes that learning in the real world is not like studying in school. It is more like an apprenticeship where novices, with the support of an expert guide and model, take on more and more responsibility until they are able to function independently. Proponents of this view believe situated learning explains learning in

**Community of practice** Social situation or context in which ideas are judged useful or true.

**Situated learning** The idea that skills and knowledge are tied to the situation in which they were learned and that they are difficult to apply in new settings.

TABLE 10.2 • **How Knowledge Is Constructed**

| TYPE | ASSUMPTIONS ABOUT LEARNING AND KNOWLEDGE | EXAMPLE THEORIES |
|---|---|---|
| External Direction | Knowledge is acquired by constructing a representation of the outside world. Direct teaching, feedback, and explanation affect learning. Knowledge is accurate to the extent that it reflects the "way things really are" in the outside world. | Information processing |
| Internal Direction | Knowledge is constructed by transforming, organizing, and reorganizing previous knowledge. Knowledge is not a mirror of the external world, even though experience influences thinking and thinking influences knowledge. Exploration and discovery are more important than teaching. | Piaget |
| Both External and Internal Direction | Knowledge is constructed based on social interactions and experience. Knowledge reflects the outside world as filtered through and influenced by culture, language, beliefs, interactions with others, direct teaching, and modelling. Guided discovery, teaching, models, and coaching as well as the individual's prior knowledge, beliefs, and thinking affect learning. | Vygotsky |

factories, around the dinner table, in high school halls, in street gangs, in the business office, and on the playground. The ideas, skills, and knowledge a person learns are tied to the situation in which they were learned and may be difficult to apply in new settings.

Situated learning is sometimes described as "enculturation," or adopting the norms, behaviours, skills, beliefs, language, and attitudes of a particular community. The community might be mathematicians or gang members or writers or students in your grade 8 class or soccer players—any group that has particular ways of thinking and doing. Knowledge is viewed not as an individual's cognitive structures, but rather as a creation of the community over time. The practices of the community—the ways of interacting and getting things done, as well as the tools the community has created—constitute the knowledge of that community. Learning means becoming more able to participate in those practices and use the tools (Greeno, Collins, & Resnick, 1996; Mason, 2007; Rogoff, 1998).

At the most basic level, "situated learning emphasizes the idea that much of what is learned is specific to the situation in which it is learned" (Anderson, Reder, & Simon, 1996, p. 5). Thus, some would argue, learning to do calculations in school may help students do more school calculations, but it may not help them balance a chequebook, because the skills can be applied only in the context in which they were learned—namely school (Lave, 1997; Lave & Wenger, 1991). But it also appears that knowledge and skills can be applied across contexts that were not part of the initial learning situation, as when you use your ability to read and calculate to do your income taxes, even though income tax forms were not part of your high school curriculum (Anderson, Reder, & Simon, 1996).

Learning that is situated in school does not have to be doomed or irrelevant (Bereiter, 1997). As you saw in Chapter 9, a major question in educational psychology—and education in general—concerns the transfer of knowledge from one situation to another. How can you encourage this transfer from one situation to another? Help is on the way in the next section.

## Common Elements of Constructivist Student-Centred Teaching

**STOP & THINK** What makes a lesson student-centred? List the characteristics and features that put the student in the centre of learning. •

We have looked at some areas of disagreement among the constructivist perspectives, but what about areas of agreement? All constructivist theories assume that knowing develops as learners, like Chelsea and Ethan, try to make sense of their experiences. "Learners, therefore, are not empty vessels waiting to be filled, but rather active organisms seeking meaning" (Driscoll, 2005, p. 487). Humans construct mental models or schemas and continue to revise them to make better sense of their experiences. Again, we are knowledge inventors, not filing cabinets. Our constructions do not necessarily resemble external reality; rather, they are our unique interpretations, like Chelsea's friendly, persistent wall. This doesn't mean that all constructions are equally useful or viable. Learners test their understandings against experience and the understandings of other people—they negotiate and co-construct meanings like Ethan did with his mother.

Constructivists share similar goals for learning. They emphasize knowledge *in use* rather than *storing* inert facts, concepts, and skills. Learning goals include developing abilities to find and solve ill-structured problems, critical thinking, inquiry, self-determination, and openness to multiple perspectives (Driscoll, 2005). Even though there is no single constructivist theory, many constructivist approaches recommend five conditions for learning:

1. Embed learning in complex, realistic, and relevant learning environments.
2. Provide for social negotiation and shared responsibility as a part of learning.
3. Support multiple perspectives and use multiple representations of content.
4. Nurture self-awareness and an understanding that knowledge is constructed.
5. Encourage ownership in learning. (Driscoll, 2005; Marshall, 1992)

Before we discuss particular teaching approaches, let's look more closely at these dimensions of constructivist teaching.

COMPLEX LEARNING ENVIRONMENTS AND AUTHENTIC TASKS. Constructivists believe that students should not be given stripped-down, simplified problems and basic skills drills. Instead, students should encounter **complex learning environments** that present "fuzzy," ill-structured problems. The world beyond school presents few simple problems or step-by-step directions, so schools should be sure that every student has experience solving complex problems. Complex problems are not just difficult ones; rather, they have many parts. There are multiple, interacting elements in complex problems and multiple possible solutions. There is no one right way to reach a conclusion, and each solution may bring a new set of problems.

These complex problems should be embedded in authentic tasks and activities, the kinds of situations that students would face as they apply what they are learning in the real world (Needles & Knapp, 1994). Students may need support (*scaffolding*) as they work on these complex problems, with teachers helping them find resources, keeping track of their progress, breaking larger problems down into smaller ones, and so on. This aspect of constructivist approaches is consistent with situated learning in emphasizing learning in situations where the knowledge will be applied.

SOCIAL NEGOTIATION. Many constructivists share Vygotsky's belief that higher mental processes develop through **social negotiation**—an aspect of the learning process that relies on collaboration with others and respect for different perspectives—and interaction. So, collaboration in learning is valued. A major goal of teaching is to develop students' abilities to establish and defend their own positions while respecting the positions of others and working together to negotiate or co-construct meaning. To accomplish this exchange, students must talk and listen to each other. It is a challenge for children in cultures that are individualistic and competitive to adopt what has been called an **intersubjective attitude**—a commitment to build shared meaning by finding common ground and exchanging interpretations.

MULTIPLE PERSPECTIVES AND REPRESENTATIONS OF CONTENT. When students encounter only one model, one analogy, one way of understanding complex content, they often oversimplify as they try to apply that one approach to every situation. Anita saw this

**Complex learning environments** Problems and learning situations that mimic the ill-structured nature of real life.

**Social negotiation** Aspect of learning process that relies on collaboration with others and respect for different perspectives.

**Intersubjective attitude** A commitment to build shared meaning with others by finding common ground and exchanging interpretations.

AUTHENTIC TASKS AND SOCIAL INTERACTIONS Constructivist approaches recommend that educators emphasize complex, realistic, and relevant learning environments, as well as the importance of social interactions in the learning process. For example, the students here are collaborating to create a household budget.

Ian Shaw/Alamy

happen in her educational psychology class when six students were presenting an example of guided discovery learning. The students' presentation was a near copy of a guided discovery demonstration earlier in the semester, but with some major misconceptions. Anita's students knew only one way to represent discovery learning. Resources for the class should have provided **multiple representations of content** using different analogies, examples, and metaphors. This idea is consistent with Jerome Bruner's (1966) **spiral curriculum**, a structure for teaching that introduces the fundamental structure of all subjects—the "big ideas"—at a basic level early in the school years, then successively revisits those ideas in more and more complex forms over time.

**UNDERSTANDING THE KNOWLEDGE CONSTRUCTION PROCESS.** Constructivist approaches emphasize making students aware of their role in constructing knowledge. The assumptions we make, our beliefs, and our experiences shape what each of us comes to "know" about the world. Different assumptions and different experiences lead to different knowledge, as we saw in Chapter 6 when we explored the role of cultural differences in shaping knowledge. If students are aware of the influences that shape their thinking, they will be more able to choose, develop, and defend positions in a self-critical way while respecting the positions of others.

**STUDENT OWNERSHIP OF LEARNING.** "While there are several interpretations of what [constructivist] theory means, most agree that it involves a dramatic change in the focus of teaching, putting the students' own efforts to understand at the center of the educational enterprise" (Prawat, 1992, p. 357). Student ownership does not mean that the teacher abandons responsibility for instruction. Because the design of teaching is a central issue in our text, we will spend the rest of this chapter discussing examples of *ownership of learning* and *student-centred instruction*.

## APPLYING CONSTRUCTIVIST PERSPECTIVES

Even though there are many applications of constructivist views of learning, we can recognize constructivist approaches by the activities of the teacher and the students. Mark Windschitl (2002) suggests that the following activities encourage meaningful learning:

- Teachers elicit students' ideas and experiences in relation to key topics, then fashion learning situations that help students elaborate on or restructure their current knowledge.
- Students are given frequent opportunities to engage in complex, meaningful, problem-based activities.
- Teachers provide students with a variety of information resources as well as the tools (technological and conceptual) necessary to mediate learning.
- Students work collaboratively and are given support to engage in task-oriented dialogue with one another.
- Teachers make their own thinking processes explicit to learners and encourage students to do the same through dialogue, writing, drawings, or other representations.
- Students are routinely asked to apply knowledge in diverse and authentic contexts, explain ideas, interpret texts, predict phenomena, and construct arguments based on evidence, rather than focus exclusively on the acquisition of predetermined "right answers."

**Multiple representations of content** Considering problems using various analogies, examples, and metaphors.

**Spiral curriculum** Bruner's design for teaching that introduces the fundamental structure of all subjects early in the school years, then revisits the subjects in more and more complex forms over time.

- Teachers encourage students' reflective and autonomous thinking in conjunction with the conditions in this list.
- Teachers employ a variety of assessment strategies to understand how students' ideas are evolving and to give feedback on the processes as well as the products of their thinking. (p. 137)

In addition, constructivist approaches include **scaffolding**, providing supports students need to develop expertise and, as they succeed, gradually withdrawing those supports. One implication of Vygotsky's theory of cognitive development is that deep understanding requires that students grapple with problems in their zone of proximal development; they need scaffolding to work productively in that zone that stretches just beyond their current level of competence. Here is a good description of scaffolding that emphasizes the dynamic interactive nature of scaffolding as well as the knowledge that both teacher and student bring—both are experts on something: "Scaffolding is a powerful conception of teaching and learning in which teachers and students create meaningful connections between teachers' cultural knowledge and the everyday experience and knowledge of the student" (McCaslin & Hickey, 2001, p. 137). Look back at the grocery store conversation between Ethan and his mother at the beginning of the previous section. Notice how the mother used the melted ice cream on the kitchen counter and the scale in the doctor's office—connections to Ethan's experience and knowledge—to scaffold Ethan's understanding.

Even though there are different views of scaffolding, most educational psychologists agree on three characteristics (van de Pol, Volman, & Beishuizen, 2010):

1. **Contingency Support**: The teacher is constantly adjusting, differentiating, and tailoring responses to the student.
2. **Fading**: The teacher gradually withdraws support as the student's understanding and skills deepen.
3. **Transferring Responsibility**: Students assume more and more responsibility for their own learning.

In the next sections, we will examine three specific teaching approaches that put the student at the centre and provide scaffolding: inquiry and problem-based learning, cognitive apprenticeships, and cooperative learning.

## Inquiry and Problem-Based Learning

John Dewey described the basic **inquiry learning** format in 1910 as an approach in which the teacher presents a puzzling situation and students solve the problem by gathering data and testing their conclusions. There have been many adaptations of this strategy, but the form usually includes the following student activities (Echevarria, 2003; Lashley, Matczynski, & Rowley, 2002) after the teacher presents a puzzling event, question, or problem:

- Formulate hypotheses to explain the event or solve the problem;
- collect data to test the hypotheses;
- draw conclusions; and
- reflect on the original problem and the thinking processes needed to solve it.

**EXAMPLES OF INQUIRY.** Shirley Magnusson and Annemarie Palincsar have developed a teachers' guide for planning, implementing, and assessing different phases of inquiry science units, called *Guided Inquiry Supporting Multiple Literacies or GisML* (Hapgood, Magnusson, & Palincsar, 2004; Palincsar, Magnusson, Collins, & Cutter, 2001; Palincsar, Magnusson, Marano, Ford, & Brown, 1998). The teacher first identifies a curriculum area and some general guiding questions, puzzles, or problems. For example, the teacher chooses *communication* as the area and asks this general question: "How and why do humans and animals communicate?" Next, several specific focus questions are posed. "How do whales communicate?" "How do gorillas communicate?" The focus questions have to be carefully chosen to guide students toward important understandings. One

**Scaffolding** Support for learning and problem solving; the support could be clues, reminders, encouragement, breaking the problem down into steps, providing an example, or anything else that allows the student to grow in independence as a learner.

**Inquiry learning** Approach in which the teacher presents a puzzling situation and students solve the problem by gathering data and testing their conclusions.

**Watch**
Examples of Inquiry

key idea in understanding animal communication is the relationship among the animal's structures, survival functions, and habitat. Animals have specific *structures* such as large ears or echo-locators, which function to find food, attract mates, or identify predators, and these structures and functions are related to the animals' *habitats*—large ears for navigating in the dark, for example. Thus, focus questions must ask about animals with different structures for communication, different functional needs for survival, and different habitats. Questions about animals with the same kinds of structures or the same habitats would not be good focus points for inquiry (Magnusson & Palincsar, 1995).

The next phase is to engage students in the inquiry, perhaps by playing an audio recording of different animal sounds, having students make guesses and claims about communication, and asking the students questions about their guesses and claims. Then, the students conduct both first-hand and second-hand investigations. First-hand investigations are direct experiences and experiments—for example, measuring the size of bats' eyes and ears in relation to their bodies (using pictures or videos—not real bats!). In second-hand investigations, students consult books, the internet, interviews with experts, and other resources to find specific information or get new ideas. As part of their investigating, the students begin to identify patterns. The curved line in Figure 10.1 shows that cycles can be repeated. In fact, students might go through several cycles of investigating, identifying patterns, and reporting results before moving on to constructing explanations and making final reports. Another possible cycle is to evaluate explanations before reporting by making and then checking predictions, applying the explanation to new situations.

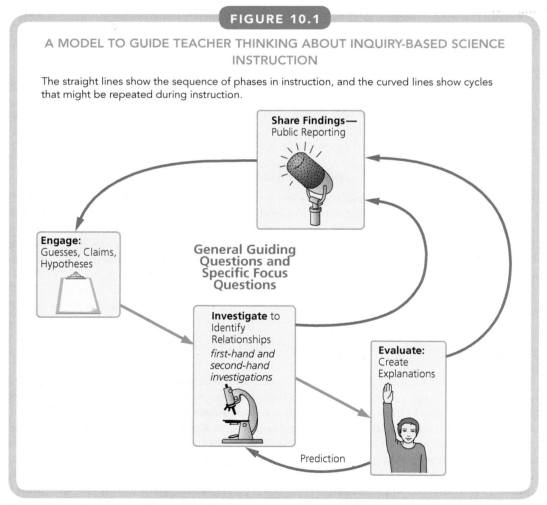

### FIGURE 10.1

### A MODEL TO GUIDE TEACHER THINKING ABOUT INQUIRY-BASED SCIENCE INSTRUCTION

The straight lines show the sequence of phases in instruction, and the curved lines show cycles that might be repeated during instruction.

**Share Findings—** Public Reporting

**Engage:** Guesses, Claims, Hypotheses

General Guiding Questions and Specific Focus Questions

**Investigate** to Identify Relationships *first-hand and second-hand investigations*

**Evaluate:** Create Explanations

Prediction

*Source: Based on Palinscar, A. S., Magnusson, S. J., Marano, D., Ford, D., & Brown, N. (1988). Designing a Community of Practice: Principles and Practices of the GisML Community. Teaching and Teacher Education, 14, p. 12.*

Inquiry teaching allows students to learn content and process at the same time. In the examples just discussed, students learned about how animals communicate and how structures are related to habitats. In addition, they learned the inquiry process itself—how to solve problems, evaluate solutions, and think critically.

PROBLEM-BASED LEARNING.    Whereas inquiry learning grew out of practices in science, problem-based learning grew out of research on expert knowledge in medicine (Schmidt, van der Molen, te Winkel, & Wijnen, 2009). The goals of **problem-based learning** are to help students develop knowledge that is useful and flexible, not inert, by providing realistic problems that don't necessarily have "right" answers. *Inert knowledge* is information that is memorized but seldom applied (Cognition and Technology Group at Vanderbilt [CTGV], 1996; Whitehead, 1929). Other goals of problem-based learning are to enhance intrinsic motivation and skills in problem solving, collaboration, evidence-based decision making, and self-directed lifelong learning.

In problem-based learning, students are confronted with a problem that launches their inquiry as they collaborate to find solutions. The students identify and analyze the problem based on the facts from the scenario; and then they begin to generate hypotheses about solutions. As they suggest hypotheses, they identify missing information—what do they need to know to test their solutions? This launches a phase of research. Then, students apply their new knowledge, evaluate their problem solutions, recycle to research again if necessary, and finally reflect on the knowledge and skills they have gained. Throughout the entire process, students are not alone or unguided. Their thinking and problem solving is scaffolded by the teacher, computer software supports, models, coaching, expert hints, guides and organizational aids, or other students in the collaborative groups—so working memory is not overloaded. For example, as students work, they may have to fill in a diagram that helps them distinguish between "claims" and "reasons" in a scientific argument (Derry, Hmelo-Silver, Nagarajan, Chernobilsky, & Beitzel, 2006; Hmelo-Silver, Ravit, & Chinn, 2007).

In true problem-based learning, the problem is real and the students' actions matter. For example, during the 2010 Deepwater oil spill in the Gulf of Mexico, many teachers used the problem as a springboard for learning. Their students researched how this spill compared to others in size, location, costliness, causes, and attempted solutions. What could be done? How do currents and tides play a role? What locations, businesses, and wildlife are in the greatest danger? What will the short-term and long-term financial and environmental impacts be? What actions can students take to play a positive role? A number of teachers blogged about using the oil spill in problem-based learning and collected resources for other teachers (see www.edutopia.org/blog/oil-spill-project-based-learning-resources).

Some problems are not authentic because they do not directly affect the students' lives, but they are engaging. For example, in a computer simulation called the *River of Life Challenge* (Sherwood, 2002), students meet Billy and his lab partner, Suzie, who are analyzing the quality of water from a local river. Suzie is concerned that Billy's conclusions are careless and incomplete. Billy is challenged to research the issue in more depth by the Legacy League, a multi-ethnic group of characters who raise questions and direct Billy and Suzie to helpful resources so they can research the answers. The format for the challenge in the STAR Legacy Cycle includes six phases: Encounter the challenge, generate ideas, consider multiple perspectives, research and revise your ideas, test your mettle (check your understanding), and go public about your conclusions. Undergraduate science education students who used this simulation improved their graph-reading skills as well as their conceptual understanding of several topics such as the composition of air and classes of organisms in a river ecosystem (Kumar & Sherwood, 2007).

Let's look at these phases more closely as they might take place in an upper-level science class (Klein & Harris, 2007).

1. The cycle begins with an *intriguing challenge* to the whole class. For example, in biomechanics it might be "Assume you are a living cell in a bioreactor. What things will influence how long you live?" or "Your grandmother is recovering from a broken hip. In which hand should she hold the cane to help her balance?" The question

**Problem-based learning** Methods that provide students with realistic problems that don't necessarily have "right" answers.

## POINT/COUNTERPOINT Are Inquiry and Problem-Based Learning Effective Teaching Approaches?

Inquiry, discovery learning, and problem-based learning are very appealing, but are they effective? Specifically, does problem-based learning lead to deep understanding for most students?

**POINT**

▶ **Problem-based learning is overrated.** Paul Kirschner and his colleagues were clear and critical in their article in the *Educational Psychologist*. Even the title of the article was blunt: "Why minimal guidance during instruction does not work: An analysis of the failure of constructivist, discovery, problem-based, experiential, and inquiry-based teaching." They argued:

*Although unguided or minimally guided instructional approaches are very popular and intuitively appealing, the point is made that these approaches ignore both the structures that constitute human cognitive architecture and evidence from empirical studies over the past half-century that consistently indicate that minimally guided instruction is less effective and less efficient than instructional approaches that place a strong emphasis on guidance of the student learning process. (Kirschner, Sweller, & Clark, 2006, p. 75)*

These respected researchers (and others more recently) cited decades of research demonstrating that unguided discovery/inquiry and problem-based learning are ineffective, especially for students with limited prior knowledge (Kalyuga, 2011; Klahr & Nigam, 2004; Tobias, 2010). Louis Alfieri and his colleagues (2011) examined the results from 108 studies going back over 50 years and found that explicit teaching was more beneficial than unassisted discovery, especially for studies published in the most well-rated journals. Their conclusion: "unassisted discovery generally does not benefit learning" (p. 12).

But what about problem-based learning in particular? Much of the research on problem-based learning has taken place in medical schools, and results have been mixed. In one study, students learning through problem-based instruction were better at clinical skills such as problem formation and reasoning, but they were worse in their basic knowledge of science and felt less prepared in science (Albanese & Mitchell, 1993). A review of problem-based learning curricula in medical schools concluded that this approach was not effective in promoting higher levels of student knowledge (Colliver, 2000).

**COUNTERPOINT**

▶ **Problem-based learning is a powerful teaching approach.** Problem-based learning has some advantages. In one study, medical students who learned with problem-based approaches created more accurate and coherent solutions to medical problems (Hmelo, 1998). In an extensive study of a problem-based medical program in the Netherlands, Schmidt and his colleagues (2009) concluded that, compared to graduates of conventional programs, graduates of the problem-based learning program performed better in practical medical and interpersonal skills, took less time to graduate, and had small positive differences in their medical knowledge and diagnostic reasoning. MBA students who learned a concept using problem-based methods were better at explaining the concept than students who had learned the concept from lecture and discussion (Capon & Kuhn, 2004). Students who are better at self-regulation may benefit more from problem-based

is framed in a way that makes students bring to bear their current knowledge and preconceptions.

2. Next, students *generate ideas* to compile what they currently know and believe using individual, small-group, or whole-group brainstorming or other activities.

3. *Multiple perspectives* are added to the process in the form of outside experts (live, on video, or from texts), websites, magazine or journal articles, or a CD on the subject. In the river challenge, the Legacy League guided Billy and Suzie to explore multiple perspectives.

4. Students go deeper to *research and revise.* They consult more sources or hear class lectures, all the while revising ideas and perhaps journaling about their thinking.

5. Students *test their mettle* by getting feedback from other students or the teacher about their tentative conclusions. Some formative (ungraded) tests might check their understanding at this point.

6. Students *go public* with their final conclusions and solutions in the form of an oral presentation, poster/project, or final exam.

Project-based science is a multimedia learning environment similar to problem-based learning that focuses on grades K-12 (Krajcik & Czerniak, 2007). MyProject is a web-based science learning environment used in college (Papanikolaou & Boubouka, 2011). The teacher's role in problem-based learning is to identify engaging problems and methods (Evensen, Salisbury-Glennon, & Glenn, 2001), but using problem-based methods over time can help all students to develop self-directed learning skills.

Cindy Hmelo-Silver (2004; Hmelo-Sliver, Ravit, & Chinn, 2007) reviewed the research and found good evidence that problem-based learning supports the construction of flexible knowledge and the development of problem-solving and self-directed learning skills. But there is less evidence that participating in problem-based learning is intrinsically motivating or that it teaches students to collaborate. In studies of high school economics and mathematics, recent research favours problem-based approaches for learning more complex concepts and solving multistep word problems.

Laurence Gough/Shutterstock

**Beware of Either/Or.** You don't have to choose between inquiry and content-focused methods. The best approach in elementary and secondary schools may be a balance of content-focused and inquiry or problem-based methods. For example, Eva Toth, David Klahr, and Zhe Chen (2000) tested a balanced approach for teaching grade 4 students how to use the controlled variable strategy in science to design good experiments. The method had three phases: (1) In small groups, students conducted exploratory experiments to identify variables that made a ball roll farther down a ramp; (2) the teacher led a discussion, explained the controlled variable strategy, and modelled good thinking about experiment design; and (3) the students designed and conducted application experiments to isolate which variables caused the ball to roll farther. The combination of inquiry, discussion, explanation, and modelling was successful in helping the students understand the concepts. Clearly scaffolding supports are key factors in successful inquiry and problem-based learning.

The difference seems to come down to completely unguided discovery versus guided, supported, and well-scaffolded inquiry. Alfieri and his colleagues (2011) concluded:

> Overall, the effects of unassisted-discovery tasks seem limited, whereas enhanced-discovery tasks requiring learners to be actively engaged and constructive seem optimal. On the basis of the current analyses, optimal approaches should include at least one of the following: (a) guided tasks that have scaffolding in place to assist learners, (b) tasks requiring learners to explain their own ideas and ensuring that these ideas are accurate by providing timely feedback, or (c) tasks that provide worked examples of how to succeed in the task. (p. 13)

appropriate resources; orient students to the problem by describing objectives and rationales; organize the students by helping them set goals and define tasks; support, coach, and mentor students as they gather information, craft solutions, and prepare artifacts (models, reports, videos, PowerPoints, portfolios, etc.); and support student reflection on their own learning outcomes and processes (Arends & Kilcher, 2010).

RESEARCH ON INQUIRY AND PROBLEM-BASED LEARNING.   Does using inquiry or problem-based learning activities lead to greater achievement? The debate has waged for years. Some research results say, "Yes." For example, using an open-ended and software-supported inquiry science approach called GenScope that explores genetics, students in high school science classrooms learned significantly more compared to students in traditional classrooms (Hickey, Kindfield, Horwitz, & Christie, 1999, Hickey, Wolfe, & Kindfield, 2000). In a study of almost 20 000 middle-school students in a large urban district who used inquiry-based materials, those who participated in inquiry learning had significantly higher passing rates on standardized tests. African American males especially benefited from these methods (Geier et al., 2008). Several other studies point to increases in student engagement and motivation with inquiry learning (Hmelo-Silver, Ravit, & Chinn, 2007), as long as the learning is supported and students have adequate background knowledge. But not every educational psychologist agrees that problem-based learning is valuable, at least for all students, as you can see in the *Point/Counterpoint*.

Another constructivist approach that relies heavily on scaffolding is cognitive apprenticeships.

## Cognitive Apprenticeships and Reciprocal Teaching

Over the centuries, apprenticeships have proved to be an effective form of education. By working alongside a master and perhaps other apprentices, young people have learned many skills, trades, and crafts. Knowledgeable guides provide models, demonstrations, and corrections, as well as a personal bond that is motivating. The performances required of the learner are real and important and grow more complex as the learner becomes more competent (Collins, 2006; Linn & Eylon, 2006; Hung, 1999). With *guided participation* in real tasks comes *participatory appropriation*—students appropriate the knowledge, skills, and values involved in doing the tasks (Rogoff, 1995, 1998). In addition, both the newcomers to learning and the old-timers contribute to the community of practice by mastering and remastering skills—and sometimes improving these skills in the process (Lave & Wenger, 1991).

Allan Collins (2006) suggests that knowledge and skills learned in school have become too separated from their use in the world beyond school. To correct this imbalance, some educators recommend that schools adopt many of the features of apprenticeships. But rather than learning to sculpt or dance or build a cabinet, apprenticeships in school would focus on cognitive objectives such as reading comprehension, writing, or mathematical problem solving. There are many cognitive apprenticeship models in which a less experienced learner acquires knowledge and skills under the guidance of an expert, but most share six features:

- Students observe an expert (usually the teacher) *model* the performance.
- Students get external support through *coaching* or tutoring (including hints, tailored feedback, models, and reminders).
- Students receive conceptual *scaffolding*, which is then gradually faded as the student becomes more competent and proficient.
- Students continually *articulate* their knowledge—putting into words their understanding of the processes and content being learned.
- Students *reflect* on their progress, comparing their problem solving to an expert's performance and to their own earlier performances.
- Students are required to *explore* new ways to apply what they are learning—ways that they have not practised at the master's side.

As students learn, they are challenged to master more complex concepts and skills and to perform them in many different settings.

How can teaching provide cognitive apprenticeships? Mentoring in teaching is one example. Another is cross-age grouping. In some schools, students of different ages work side by side for part of every day on a "pod" designed to have many of the qualities of an apprenticeship. The pods might focus on a craft or a discipline. Examples include gardening, architecture, and "making money." Many levels of expertise are evident in the students of different ages, so students can move at a comfortable pace, but still have the model of a master available. Community volunteers, including many parents, visit to demonstrate a skill that is related to the pod topic.

Alan Schoenfeld's (1989, 1994) teaching of mathematical problem solving is another example of the cognitive apprenticeship instructional model.

**Cognitive apprenticeship** A relationship in which a less experienced learner acquires knowledge and skills under the guidance of an expert.

**Reciprocal teaching** Designed to help students understand and think deeply about what they read.

COGNITIVE APPRENTICESHIPS IN READING: RECIPROCAL TEACHING. The goal of **reciprocal teaching** is to help students understand and think deeply about what they read (Palincsar, 1986; Palincsar & Brown, 1984, 1989). To accomplish this goal, students in small reading groups learn four strategies: *summarizing* the content of a passage, *asking a question* about the central point, *clarifying* the difficult parts of the material, and *predicting* what will come next. These are strategies skilled readers apply almost automatically, but poor readers seldom do—or they don't know how. To use the strategies effectively, poorer readers need direct instruction, modelling, and practice in actual reading situations.

First, the teacher introduces these strategies, perhaps focusing on one strategy each day. As the expert, the teacher explains and models each strategy and encourages student apprentices to practise. Next, the teacher and the students read a short passage silently. Then, the teacher again provides a model by summarizing, questioning, clarifying, or predicting based on the reading. Everyone reads another passage, and the students gradually begin to assume the teacher's role. The teacher becomes a member of the group, and may finally leave, as the students take over the teaching. Often, the students' first attempts are halting and incorrect. But the teacher gives clues, guidance, encouragement, support doing parts of the task (such as providing question stems), modelling, and other forms of scaffolding to help the students master these strategies. The goal is for students to learn to apply these strategies independently as they read so they can make sense of text.

APPLYING RECIPROCAL TEACHING.   Although reciprocal teaching seems to work with almost any age student, most of the research has been done with younger adolescents who can read aloud fairly accurately, but who are far below average in reading comprehension. After 20 hours of practice with this approach, many students who were in the bottom quarter of their class moved up to the average level or above on tests of reading comprehension. Palincsar has identified three guidelines for effective reciprocal teaching ("When Student Becomes Teacher," 1986):

1. *Shift gradually.* The shift from teacher to student responsibility must be gradual.
2. *Match demands to abilities.* The difficulty of the task and the responsibility must match the abilities of each student and grow as these abilities develop.
3. *Diagnose thinking.* Teachers should carefully observe the "teaching" of each student for clues about how the student is thinking and what kind of instruction he or she needs.

In contrast to some approaches that try to teach 40 or more strategies, an advantage of reciprocal teaching is that it focuses attention on four powerful strategies. But these strategies must be taught—not all students develop them on their own. One study of reciprocal teaching spanning over three years found that questioning was the strategy used most often, but that students had to be taught how to ask higher-level questions because most student questions were literal or superficial (Hacker & Tenent, 2002). Another advantage of reciprocal teaching is that it emphasizes practising these four strategies in the context of actual reading—reading literature and reading texts. Finally, the idea of scaffolding and gradually moving the student toward independent and fluid reading comprehension is a critical component in reciprocal teaching and cognitive apprenticeships in general (Rosenshine & Meister, 1994).

## Collaboration and Cooperation

Even with all the concern today about academic standards, performance on proficiency tests, and international comparisons of student achievement, schooling has always been about more than academic learning. Of course, academics are the prime directive, but an education also prepares students to live and work cooperatively with all kinds of people:

> Most corporations are looking for employees who are not only good at the mastery of a particular set of academic skills but who also have the ability to work harmoniously with a wide variety of coworkers as a cooperative team, to demonstrate initiative and responsibility, and to communicate effectively. (Aronson, 2000, p. 91)

**NURTURING INDEPENDENT READERS** The concept of scaffolding and gradually moving the student toward independent and fluid reading comprehension is a critical component in reciprocal teaching and cognitive apprenticeships.

Patrick White/Merrill

For the past four decades, researchers have examined collaboration and cooperation in schools. Although there are some inconsistencies, the majority of the studies indicate that truly cooperative groups have positive effects—from preschool to college—on students' empathy, tolerance for differences, feelings of acceptance, friendships, self-confidence, awareness of the perspectives of others, higher-level reasoning, problem solving, and even school attendance (Galton, Hargreaves, & Pell, 2009; Gillies & Boyle, 2011; Solomon, Watson, & Battistich, 2001). It is even argued that cooperative learning experiences are crucial in preventing many of the social problems that plague children and adolescents (Gillies, 2003, 2004).

**((• Listen**
Collaboration and Cooperation

**COLLABORATION, GROUP WORK, AND COOPERATIVE LEARNING.**    The terms *collaboration, group work*, and *cooperative learning* often are used as if they mean the same thing. Certainly there is some overlap, but there are differences as well. The distinctions between collaboration and cooperation are not always clear. Ted Panitz (1996) suggests **collaboration** is a philosophy about how to relate to others—how to learn and work. Collaboration is a way of dealing with people that respects differences, shares authority, and builds on the knowledge that is distributed among other people. **Cooperation**, on the other hand, is a way of working with others to attain a shared goal (Gillies, 2003). Collaborative learning has roots in the work of British teachers who wanted their students to respond to literature in more active ways as they learned. Cooperative learning has North American roots in the work of psychologists John Dewey and Kurt Lewin. You could say that *cooperative* learning is one way to *collaborate* in schools.

Group work, on the other hand, is simply several students working together—they may or may not be cooperating. Many activities can be completed in groups. For example, students can work together to conduct a local survey. How do people feel about the plan to build a new mall that will bring more shopping and more traffic? Would the community support or oppose the building of a nuclear power plant? If students must learn 10 new definitions in a biology class, why not let them divide up the terms and definitions and teach one another? Be sure, however, that everyone in the group can handle the task. Sometimes, one or two students end up doing the work of the entire group.

Group work can be useful, but true cooperative learning requires much more than simply putting students in groups and dividing up the work. Angela O'Donnell and Jim O'Kelly describe a teacher who claimed to be using "cooperative learning" by asking students to work in pairs on a paper, each writing one part. Unfortunately, the teacher allowed no time to work together and provided no guidance or preparation in cooperative social skills. Students got a grade for their individual part and a group grade for the whole project. One student received an A for his part, but a C for the group project because his partner earned an F—he never turned in any work. So one student was punished with a C for a situation he could not control while the other was rewarded with a C for doing no work at all. This was not cooperative learning—it wasn't even group work (O'Donnell & O'Kelly, 1994).

**Collaboration**  A philosophy about how to relate to others—how to learn and work.

**Cooperation**  Way of working with others to attain a shared goal.

**Cooperative learning** Situations in which elaboration, interpretation, explanation, and argumentation are integral to the activity of the group and where learning is supported by other individuals.

**BEYOND GROUPS TO COOPERATION.**    David and Roger Johnson (2009a), two of the founders of cooperative learning in North America, define formal **cooperative learning** as "students working together, for one class period to several weeks, to achieve shared learning goals and complete jointly specific tasks and assignments" (p. 373). Cooperative learning has a long history in education, moving in and out of favour over the years. Today, evolving constructivist perspectives have fuelled a growing commitment to learning situations that rely on elaboration, interpretation, explanation, and argumentation—that is, cooperative learning (Webb & Palincsar, 1996, p. 844). David and Roger Johnson (2009a) note:

> From being discounted and ignored, cooperative learning has steadily progressed to being one of the dominant instructional practices throughout the world. Cooperative learning is now utilized in schools and universities throughout most of the world in every subject area and from preschool through graduate school and adult training programs. (p. 365)

Different learning theory approaches favour cooperative learning for different reasons (O'Donnell, 2002, 2006). Information processing theorists point to the value of group discussion in helping participants rehearse, elaborate, and expand their knowledge. As group members question and explain, they have to organize their knowledge, make connections, and review—all processes that support information processing and memory. Advocates of a Piagetian perspective suggest the interactions in groups can create the cognitive conflict and disequilibrium that lead an individual to question his or her understanding and try out new ideas—or, as Piaget (1985) said, "to go beyond his current state and strike out in new directions" (p. 10). Those who favour Vygotsky's theory suggest that social interaction is important for learning because higher mental functions such as reasoning, comprehension, and critical thinking originate in social interactions and are then appropriated and internalized by individuals. Students can accomplish mental tasks with social support before they can do them alone. Thus, cooperative learning provides the social support and scaffolding students need to move learning forward. To benefit from these dimensions of cooperative learning, groups must be cooperative—all members must participate. But, as any teacher or parent knows, cooperation is not automatic when students are put into groups.

**COOPERATION: A WORTHY GOAL** While academics are the key goal, education also prepares students to live and work cooperatively with all kinds of people. Studies of cooperative learning indicate its positive influence on students' empathy, tolerance, friendships, self-confidence, and even school attendance.

Patrick White/Merrill

WHAT CAN GO WRONG: MISUSES OF GROUP LEARNING.   Without careful planning and monitoring by the teacher, group interactions can hinder learning and reduce rather than improve social relations in classes (Gillies & Boyle, 2011). For example, if there is pressure in a group for conformity—perhaps because rewards are being misused or one student dominates the others—interactions can be unproductive and unreflective. Misconceptions might be reinforced, or the worst, not the best, ideas may be combined to construct a superficial or even incorrect understanding (Battistich, Solomon, & Delucci, 1993). Students who work in groups but arrive at wrong answers may be more confident that they are right—a case of "two heads are worse than one" (Puncochar & Fox, 2004). Also, the ideas of low-status students may be ignored or even ridiculed while the contributions of high-status students are accepted and reinforced, regardless of the merit of either set of ideas (Anderson, Holland, & Palincsar, 1997; Cohen, 1986). Mary McCaslin and Tom Good (1996) list several other disadvantages of group learning:

- Students often value the process or procedures over the learning. Speed and finishing early take precedence over thoughtfulness and learning.
- Rather than challenging and correcting misconceptions, students support and reinforce misunderstandings.
- Socializing and interpersonal relationships may take precedence over learning.
- Students may simply shift dependency from the teacher to the "expert" in the group—learning is still passive and what is learned can be wrong.
- Status differences may be increased rather than decreased. Some students learn to "loaf" because the group progresses with or without their contributions. Others become even more convinced that they are unable to understand without the support of the group.

The next sections examine how teachers can avoid these problems and encourage true cooperation.

## Tasks for Cooperative Learning

Like other decisions in teaching, plans for using cooperative groups begin with a goal. What are students supposed to accomplish? Successful teachers interviewed in one study emphasized that group activities must be well planned, students need to be prepared to work in groups, and teachers' expectations for the task have to be explicitly stated (Gillies & Boyle, 2011). What is the task? Is it a true group task—one that builds on the knowledge and skills of several students—or is the task more appropriate for individuals (Cohen, 1994; O'Donnell, 2006)?

Tasks for cooperative groups may be more or less structured. Highly structured tasks include work that has specific answers—drill and practice, applying routines or procedures, answering questions from readings, computations in mathematics, and so on. Ill-structured complex tasks have multiple answers and unclear procedures, requiring problem finding and higher-order thinking. These ill-structured problems are true group tasks; that is, they are likely to require the resources (knowledge, skills, problem-solving strategies, creativity) of all the group members to accomplish, whereas individuals often can accomplish highly structured tasks just as effectively as groups. These distinctions are important because ill-structured, complex, true group tasks appear to require more and higher-quality interactions than routine tasks if learning and problem solving are to occur (Cohen, 1994; Gillies, 2004; Gillies & Boyle, 2011).

**Watch**
Highly Structured, Review, and Skill-Building Tasks

**HIGHLY STRUCTURED, REVIEW, AND SKILL-BUILDING TASKS.** A relatively structured task such as reviewing previously learned material for an exam might be well served by a structured technique such as STAD (Student Teams Achievement Divisions), in which teams of four students compete to determine which team's members can amass the greatest improvement over previous achievement levels (Slavin, 1995). Praise, recognition, or extrinsic rewards can enhance motivation, effort, and persistence under these conditions, and thus increase learning. Focusing the dialogue by assigning narrow roles also may help students stay engaged when the tasks involve practice or review.

**ILL-STRUCTURED, CONCEPTUAL, AND PROBLEM-SOLVING TASKS.** If the task is ill structured and more cognitive in nature, then an open exchange and elaborated discussion will be more helpful (Cohen, 1994; Ross & Raphael, 1990). Thus, strategies that encourage extended and productive interactions are appropriate when the goal is to develop higher-order thinking and problem solving. In these situations, a tightly structured process, competition among groups for rewards, and rigid assignment of roles are likely to inhibit the richness of the students' interactions and to interfere with progress toward the goal. Open-ended techniques such as reciprocal questioning (King, 1994), reciprocal teaching (Palincsar & Brown, 1984; Rosenshine & Meister, 1994), pair-share (Kagan, 1994), or Jigsaw (Aronson, 2000) should be more productive because, when used appropriately, they encourage more extensive interaction and elaborative thought in situations where students are being exposed to complex materials. In these instances, the use of rewards may well divert the group away from the goal of in-depth cognitive processing. When rewards are offered, the goal often becomes achieving the reward as efficiently as possible, which could mean having the highest-achieving students do all the work (Webb & Palincsar, 1996).

**SOCIAL SKILLS AND COMMUNICATION TASKS.** When the goal of peer learning is enhanced social skills or increased intergroup understanding and appreciation of diversity, the assignment of specific roles and functions within the group might support communication (Cohen, 1994; Kagan, 1994). In these situations, it can be helpful to rotate leadership roles so that minority group students and females have the opportunity to demonstrate and develop leadership skills; in addition, all group members can experience the leadership capabilities of each individual (Miller & Harrington, 1993). Rewards probably are not necessary, and they may actually get in the way because the goal is to build community, a sense of respect, and responsibility for all team members.

## Preparing Students for Cooperative Learning

David and Roger Johnson (2009a) explain five elements that define true cooperative learning groups:

- Positive interdependence
- Promotive interaction
- Individual accountability
- Collaborative and social skills
- Group processing

Group members experience *positive interdependence*. The members believe they can attain their goals only if the others in the group attain their goals as well, so they need each other for support, explanations, and guidance. *Promotive interaction* means that group members encourage and facilitate each other's efforts. They usually interact face to face and close together, not across the room, but they also could interact via digital media around the world. Even though they feel a responsibility to the group to work together and help each other, students must ultimately demonstrate learning on their own; they are held *individually accountable* for learning, often through individual tests or other assessments. *Collaborative and social skills* are necessary for effective group functioning. Often, these skills, such as giving constructive feedback, reaching consensus, and involving every member, must be taught and practised before the groups tackle a learning task. Finally, members monitor *group processes* and relationships to make sure the group is working effectively and to learn about the dynamics of groups. They take time to ask, "How are we doing as a group? Is everyone working together? What should we do more or less of next time?"

Research in grades 8 through 12 in Australia found that students in cooperative groups that were structured to require positive interdependence and mutual helping learned more in math, science, and English than students in unstructured learning groups (Gillies, 2003). In addition, compared to students in the unstructured groups, students in the structured groups also said learning was more fun.

SETTING UP COOPERATIVE GROUPS. How large should a cooperative group be? Again, the answer depends on your learning goals. If the purpose is for the group members to review, rehearse information, or practise, four to six students is about the right size. But if the goal is to encourage each student to participate in discussions, problem solving, or computer learning, then groups of two to four members work best. Also, when setting up cooperative groups, it often makes sense to balance the number of boys and girls. Some research indicates that when there are just a few girls in a group, they tend to be left out of the discussions unless they are the most able or assertive members. By contrast, when there are only one or two boys in the group, they tend to dominate and be "interviewed" by the girls unless these boys are less able than the girls or are very shy. In some studies, but not all, of mixed-gender groups, girls avoided conflict and boys dominated discussion (O'Donnell & O'Kelly, 1994; Webb & Palincsar, 1996). Whatever the case, teachers must monitor groups to make sure everyone is contributing and learning.

If a group includes some students who are perceived as different or who are often rejected, then it makes sense to be sure that there are group members who are tolerant and kind. One successful teacher interviewed by Gillies and Boyle (2011) put it this way:

> I also try to make sure that there are one or two people in the group who have the ability to be tolerant. At least the kid in question will know that, while the other group members may not be his best friends, they won't give him a hard time. I try to put the least reactive kids in the group with the child in question. This year I've had a couple of girls who have been very good with difficult kids. They don't put up with nonsense but they don't over-react and are prepared to demonstrate some good social skills. (p. 72)

GIVING AND RECEIVING EXPLANATIONS. In practice, the effects of learning in a group vary, depending on what actually happens in the group and who is in it. If only a few people take responsibility for the work, these people will learn, but the nonparticipating members probably will not. Students who ask questions, get answers, and attempt explanations are more likely to learn than students whose questions go unasked or unanswered. In fact, there is evidence that the more a student provides elaborated, thoughtful explanations to other students in a group, the more the *explainer* learns. Giving good explanations appears to be even more important for learning than receiving explanations (O'Donnell, 2006; Webb, Farivar, & Mastergeorge, 2002). In order to explain, you have to organize the information, put it into your own words, think of examples and analogies (which connect the information to things you already know), and test your understanding by answering questions. These are excellent learning strategies (King, 1990, 2002; O'Donnell & O'Kelly, 1994).

Good explanations are relevant, timely, correct, and elaborated enough to help the listener correct misunderstandings; the best explanations tell why (Webb, Farivar, & Mastergeorge, 2002; Webb & Mastergeorge, 2003). For example, in a middle-school mathematics class, students worked in groups on the following problem:

> Find the cost of a 30-minute telephone call to the prefix 604 where the first minute costs $0.22 and each additional minute costs $0.13.

The level of explanation and help students received was significantly related to learning; the higher the level of explanation, the more learning took place. Table 10.3 shows the different levels of help. Of course, the students must pay attention to and use the help in order to learn. And the help-receiver also has responsibilities if learning is to go well. For example, if a helper says, "13 times 29," then the receiver should say, "Why is it 29?" Asking good questions and giving clear explanations are critical, and usually these skills must be taught.

ASSIGNING ROLES.    Some teachers assign roles to students to encourage cooperation and full participation. Several roles are described in Table 10.4. If you use roles, be sure that they support learning. In groups that focus on social skills, roles should support listening, encouragement, and respect for differences. In groups that focus on practice, review, or mastery of basic skills, roles should support persistence, encouragement, and participation. In groups that focus on higher-order problem solving or complex learning, roles should encourage thoughtful discussion, sharing of explanations and insights, probing, brainstorming, and creativity. Make sure that you don't communicate to students that the major purpose of the groups is simply to do the procedures—the roles. Roles are supports for learning, not ends in themselves (Woolfolk Hoy & Tschannen-Moran, 1999).

TABLE 10.3 • **Levels of Help in Cooperative Groups**

Students are more likely to learn if they give and get higher-level help.

| LEVEL | DESCRIPTION AND EXAMPLE |
|---|---|
| Highest | |
| 6 | Verbally labelled explanation of how to solve part or all of the problem ("Multiply 13 cents by 29, because 29 minutes are left after the first minute.") |
| 5 | Numerical rule with no verbal labels for the numbers ("This is 30, so you minus 1.") |
| 4 | Numerical expression or equation ("13 times 29.") |
| 3 | Numbers to write or copy ("Put 13 on top, 29 on the bottom. Then you times it.") |
| 2 | Answer to part or all of the problem ("I got $3.77.") |
| 1 | Non-content or non-informational response ("Just do it the way she said.") |
| 0 | No response |
| Lowest | |

*Source: Adapted from Webb, N. M., Troper, J. D., & Fall, R. (1995). Constructive activity and learning in collaborative small groups.* Journal of Educational Psychology, 87, *p. 411.*

TABLE 10.4 • **Possible Student Roles in Cooperative Learning Groups**

Depending on the purpose of the group and the age of the participants, having these assigned roles might help students cooperate and learn. Of course, students may have to be taught how to enact each role effectively, and roles should be rotated so students can participate in different aspects of group learning.

| ROLE | DESCRIPTION |
| --- | --- |
| Encourager | Encourages reluctant or shy students to participate |
| Praiser/Cheerleader | Shows appreciation of others' contributions and recognizes accomplishments |
| Gate Keeper | Equalizes participation and makes sure no one dominates |
| Coach | Helps with the academic content, explains concepts |
| Question Commander | Makes sure all students' questions are asked and answered |
| Checker | Checks the group's understanding |
| Taskmaster | Keeps the group on task |
| Recorder | Writes down ideas, decisions, and plans |
| Reflector | Keeps group aware of progress (or lack of progress) |
| Quiet Captain | Monitors noise level |
| Materials Monitor | Picks up and returns materials |

*Source: Based Kagan, S. (1994). Cooperative Learning. San Clemente: Kagan Publishing.*

Often, cooperative learning strategies include group reports to the entire class. If you have been on the receiving end of these class reports, you know that they can be deadly dull. To make the process more useful for the audience as well as the reporters, Annemarie Palincsar and Leslie Herrenkohl (2002) taught the class members to use *intellectual roles* as they listened to reports. These roles were based on the scientific strategies of predicting and theorizing, summarizing results, and relating predictions and theories to results. Some audience members were assigned the role of checking the reports for clear relationships between predictions and theories. Other students in the audience listened for clarity in the findings. And the rest of the students were responsible for evaluating how well the group reports linked prediction, theories, and findings. Research shows that using these roles promotes class dialogue, thinking and problem solving, and conceptual understanding (Palincsar & Herrenkohl, 2002).

## Designs for Cooperation

Developing deep understandings in cooperative groups requires that all the group members *participate* in *high-quality discussions*. Discussions that support learning include talk that interprets, connects, explains, and uses evidence to support arguments. We now turn to different strategies that build in structures to support both participation and high-quality discussions.

RECIPROCAL QUESTIONING. **Reciprocal questioning** is where students work on realistic problems that don't necessarily have "right" answers. It requires no special materials or testing procedures and can be used with a wide range of ages. After a lesson or presentation by the teacher, students work in pairs or triads to ask and answer questions about the material (King, 1990, 1994, 2002). The teacher provides question stems (see Table 10.5), and then students are taught how to develop specific questions on the lesson material using the generic question stems. The students create questions, and then take turns asking and answering. This process has proved more effective than traditional discussion groups because it seems to encourage deeper thinking about the material.

**Reciprocal questioning**
Students work in pairs or triads to ask and answer questions about lesson material.

TABLE 10.5 • **Question Stems to Encourage Dialogue in Reciprocal Questioning**

After participating in a lesson or studying an assignment on their own, students use these stems to develop questions, create and compare answers, and collaborate to create the best response.

What is an everyday application of . . . ?
How would you define . . . in your own words?
What are the advantages and disadvantages of . . . ?
What do you already know about . . . ?
Explain why . . . applies to . . . ?
How does . . . influence . . . ?
What is the value of . . . ?
What are the reasons for . . . ?
What are some arguments for and against . . . ?
What is the your first choice about . . . ? Your second choice? Why?
What is the best . . . and why?
Compare . . . and . . . based only on . . .
How would . . . be different if . . . ?
Do you agree or disagree with this claim? What is your evidence?

Questions such as those in Table 10.5, which encourage students to make connections between the lesson and previous knowledge or experience, seem to be the most helpful.

For example, using question stems like those in Table 10.5, a small group in Mr. Garcia's grade 9 world cultures class had the following discussion about the concept of culture:

> **Sally**: In your own words, what does culture mean?
>
> **Jim**: Well, Mr. Singh said in the lesson that a culture is the knowledge and understandings shared by the members of a society. I guess it's all the things and beliefs and activities that people in a society have in common. It includes things like religion, laws, music, medical practices, stuff like that.
>
> **Sally**: And dance, art, family roles.
>
> **Barry**: Knowledge includes language. So, I guess cultures include language, too.
>
> **Jim**: I guess so. Actually, I have a question about that: How does a culture influence the language of a society?
>
> **Barry**: Well, for one thing, the language is made up of words that are important to the people of that culture. Like, the words name things that the people care about, or need, or use. And so, different cultures would have different vocabularies. Some cultures may not even have a word for *telephone,* because they don't have any. But, phones are important in our culture, so we have lots of different words for phones, like *cell phone, digital phone, desk phone, cordless phone, phone machine,* and . . .
>
> **Jim** (laughing): I'll bet desert cultures don't have any words for *snow* or *skiing.*
>
> **Sally** (turning to Barry): What's your question?
>
> **Barry**: I've got a great question! You'll never be able to answer it. What would happen if there were a group somewhere without any spoken language? Maybe they were all born not being able to speak, or something like that. How would that affect their culture, or could there even be a culture?
>
> **Sally**: Well, it would mean they couldn't communicate with each other.
>
> **Jim**: And they wouldn't have any music! Because they wouldn't be able to sing.
>
> **Barry**: But wait! Why couldn't they communicate? Maybe they would develop a nonverbal language system, you know, the way people use hand signals, or the way deaf people use sign language. (King, 2002, pp. 34–35)

**Jigsaw Classroom** A learning process in which each student is part of a group and each group member is given part of the material to be learned by the whole group. Students become "expert" on their piece and then teach it to the others in their group.

JIGSAW.    Elliot Aronson and his graduate students invented the **Jigsaw Classroom** when Aronson was a professor of social psychology (and Anita was a student) at the University of Texas at Austin. Some of her friends worked on his research team. Aronson developed the approach "as a matter of absolute necessity to help defuse a highly explosive situation" (Aronson, 2000, p. 137). The Austin schools had just been desegregated by court order. White, African American, and Hispanic students were together in classrooms for the first time. Hostility and turmoil ensued, with fistfights in corridors and classrooms. Aronson's answer was the Jigsaw Classroom, a learning process in which each student is part of a group and each group member is given part of the material to be learned by the whole group. Students become "expert" on their piece and then teach it to the others in their group.

Because students have to learn and be tested on every piece of the larger "puzzle," everyone's contribution is important—the students truly are interdependent. A more recent version, Jigsaw II, adds expert groups in which the students who are responsible for the same material from each learning group confer to make sure they understand their assigned part and then plan ways to teach the information to their learning group members. Next, students return to their learning groups, bringing their expertise to the sessions. In the end, students take an individual test covering all the material and earn points for their learning team score. Teams can work for rewards or simply for recognition (Slavin, 1995).

STRUCTURED CONTROVERSIES.   Constructive conflict resolution is essential in classrooms because conflicts are inevitable and even necessary for learning. Piaget's theory tells us that developing knowledge requires cognitive conflict. David and Roger Johnson (2009b) make a powerful case for constructive intellectual conflict:

> Conflict is to student learning what the internal combustion engine is to the automobile. The internal combustion engine ignites the fuel and the air with a spark to create the energy for movement and acceleration. Just as the fuel and the air are inert without the spark, so, ideas in the classroom are inert without the spark of intellectual conflict. (p. 37)

One study of grade 10 students found that students who were wrong, but for different reasons, were sometimes able to correct their misunderstandings if they argued together about their conflicting wrong answers (Schwarz, Neuman, & Biezuner, 2000). Individuals trying to exist in groups will have interpersonal conflicts, too, which also can lead to learning. In fact, research over the past 40 years demonstrates that constructive controversy in classrooms can lead to greater learning, open-mindedness, seeing the perspectives of others, creativity, motivation, engagement, and self-esteem (Johnson & Johnson, 2009b). Table 10.6 shows how academic and interpersonal conflicts can be positive forces in a learning community.

As you can see in Table 10.6, the structured part of **structured controversies** is that students work in pairs within their four-person cooperative groups to research a particular

**Structured controversy** Students work in pairs within their four-person cooperative groups to research a particular controversy.

TABLE 10.6 • **Structured Controversies: Learning From Academic and Interpersonal Conflicts**

Conflict, if handled well, can support learning. Academic conflicts can lead to critical thinking and conceptual change. Conflicts of interest are unavoidable, but can be handled so no one is the loser.

| ACADEMIC CONTROVERSY | CONFLICTS OF INTEREST |
|---|---|
| One person's ideas, information, theories, conclusions, and opinions are incompatible with those of another, and the two seek to reach an agreement. | The actions of one person attempting to maximize benefits prevents, blocks, or interferes with another person maximizing her or his benefits. |
| *Controversy Procedure* | *Integrative (Problem-Solving) Negotiations* |
| Research and prepare positions | Describe wants |
| Present and advocate positions | Describe feelings |
| Refute opposing position and refute attacks on own position | Describe reasons for wants and feelings |
| Reverse perspectives | Take other's perspective |
| Synthesize and integrate best evidence and reasoning from all sides | Invent three optional agreements that maximize joint outcomes. Choose one and formalize agreement |

*Source: From Johnson, D., & Johnson, R. (1999). The Three Cs of School and Classroom Management. In H. J. Freiberg (Ed.), Beyond Behaviourism: Changing the Classroom Management Paradigm. Boston: Allyn and Bacon. Adapted with permission.*

## GUIDELINES

## Using Cooperative Learning

**Fit group size and composition to your learning goals.**
*Examples*

1. For social skills and team-building goals, use groups of two to five, common interest groups, mixed groups, or random groups.
2. For structured fact and skill-based practice and review tasks, use groups of four to six, mixed ability such as high-middle and middle-low or high-low and middle-middle group compositions.
3. For higher-level conceptual and thinking tasks, use groups of two to four; select members to encourage interaction.

**Assign appropriate roles.**
*Examples*

1. For social skills and team-building goals, assign roles to monitor participation and conflict; rotate leadership of the group.
2. For structured fact and skill-based practice and review tasks, assign roles to monitor engagement and insure low-status students have resources to offer, as in Jigsaw.
3. For higher-level conceptual and thinking tasks, assign roles only to encourage interaction, divergent thinking, and extended, connected discourse, as in debate teams or group facilitator. Don't let roles get in the way of learning.

**Make sure you assume a supporting role as the teacher.**
*Examples*

1. For social skills and team-building goals, be a model and encourager.
2. For structured fact and skill-based practice and review tasks, be a model, director, or coach.

3. For higher-level conceptual and thinking tasks, be a model and facilitator.

**Move around the room and monitor the groups.**
*Examples*

1. For social skills and team-building goals, watch for listening, turn-taking, encouraging, and managing conflict.
2. For structured fact and skill-based practice and review tasks, watch for questioning, giving multiple elaborated explanations, attention, and practice.
3. For higher-level conceptual and thinking tasks, watch for questioning, explaining, elaborating, probing, divergent thinking, providing rationales, synthesizing, using and connecting knowledge sources.

**Start small and simple until you and the students know how to use cooperative methods.**
*Examples*

1. For social skills and team-building goals, try one or two skills, such as listening and paraphrasing.
2. For structured fact and skill-based practice and review tasks, try pairs of students quizzing each other.
3. For higher-level conceptual and thinking tasks, try reciprocal questioning using pairs and just a few question stems.

*For more information on cooperative learning, see www.co-operation.org.*

*Source: Based on Woolfolk Hoy, A., & Tschannen-Moran, M. (1999). Implications of Cognitive Approaches to Peer Learning for Teacher Education. In A. O'Donnell and A. King (Eds.),* Cognitive Perspectives on Peer Learning *(pp. 257–284). Mahwah, NJ: Lawrence Erlbaum.*

controversy, such as whether lumber companies should be allowed to cut down trees in national forests. Each pair of students researches the issue, develops a pro or con position, presents their position and evidence to the other pair, discusses the issue, and then reverses positions and argues for the other perspective. Then, the group develops a final report that summarizes the best arguments for each position and reaches a consensus (Johnson & Johnson, 2009b; O'Donnell, 2006).

In addition to these approaches, Spencer Kagan (1994) has developed many cooperative learning structures designed to accomplish different kinds of academic and social tasks. The *Guidelines* give you ideas for incorporating cooperative learning in to your classes.

### Reaching Every Student: Using Cooperative Learning Wisely

Cooperative learning always benefits from careful planning, but sometimes including students with special needs requires extra attention to planning and preparation. For example, cooperative structures such as scripted questioning and peer tutoring depend on a balanced interaction between the person taking the role of questioner or explainer and the student who is answering or being taught. In these interactions, you want to see and hear explaining and teaching, not just telling or giving right answers. But many students with learning disabilities have difficulties understanding new concepts, so both the explainer and the student can get frustrated, and social rejection for the student with learning disabilities might follow. Because students with learning disabilities often have problems with social relations, it is not a good idea to put them in situations where more rejection is likely. So, when you are teaching new or difficult-to-grasp concepts, cooperative learning might not be the best choice for students with learning disabilities (Kirk, Gallagher, Anastasiow, & Coleman, 2006). In fact, research has found that cooperative learning in general is not always effective for students with learning disabilities (Smith, 2006).

Gifted students also may not benefit from cooperative learning when groups are mixed in ability. The pace often is too slow, the tasks too simple, and there is just too much repetition. In addition, gifted students often fall into the role of teacher or end up just doing the work quickly for the whole group. If you use mixed-ability groups and include gifted students, the challenges are to use complex tasks that allow work at different levels and keep gifted students engaged without losing the rest of the class (Smith, 2006).

Cooperative learning may be an excellent choice for learners developing skills in English as an additional language (EALs), however. The Jigsaw cooperative structure is especially helpful because all students in the group, including the EAL students, have information that the group needs, so they also must talk, explain, and interact. In fact, the Jigsaw approach was developed in response to the need to create high interdependence in diverse groups. In many classrooms today, there are four, five, six, or more languages represented. Teachers can't be expected to master every heritage language spoken by all of their students every year. In these classrooms, cooperative groups can help as students work together on academic tasks. Students who speak two languages can help translate and explain lessons to others in the group. Speaking in a smaller group may be less anxiety provoking for students who are learning another language; thus, EAL students may get more language practice with feedback in these groups (Smith, 2006).

Cooperative learning is only as good as its design and implementation. Cooperative methods probably are both misused and underused in schools, in part because using cooperative learning well requires time and investment in teaching students how to learn in groups (Blatchford, Baines, Rubie-Davis, Bassett, & Chowne, 2006).

## Dilemmas of Constructivist Practice

Years ago, Larry Cremin (1961) observed that progressive, innovative pedagogies require exceptionally skilled teachers. Today, the same could be said about constructivist teaching. We have already seen that there are many varieties of constructivism and many practices that flow from these different conceptions. We also know that all teaching today happens in a context of high-stakes testing and accountability. In these situations, constructivist teachers face many challenges. Mark Windschitl (2002) identified four teacher dilemmas of constructivism in practice, summarized in Table 10.7. The first is conceptual: How do I make sense of cognitive versus social conceptions of constructivism and reconcile these different perspectives with my practice? The second dilemma is pedagogical: How do I teach in truly constructivist ways that both honour my students' attempts to think for themselves, but still insure that they learn the academic material? Third are cultural dilemmas: What activities, cultural knowledge, and ways of talking will build a community in a diverse classroom? Finally, there are political dilemmas: How can I teach for deep understanding and critical thinking, but still satisfy the accountability demands of parents?

TABLE 10.7 • **Teachers' Dilemmas of Constructivism in Practice**

Teachers face conceptual, pedagogical, cultural, and political dilemmas as they implement constructivist practices. Here are explanations of these dilemmas and some representative questions that teachers face as they confront them.

| TEACHERS' DILEMMA CATEGORY | REPRESENTATIVE QUESTIONS OF CONCERN |
|---|---|
| I. *Conceptual dilemmas:* Grasping the underpinnings of cognitive and social constructivism; reconciling current beliefs about pedagogy with the beliefs necessary to support a constructivist learning environment. | Which version of constructivism is suitable as a basis for my teaching? Is my classroom supposed to be a collection of individuals working toward conceptual change or a community of learners whose development is measured by participation in authentic disciplinary practices? If certain ideas are considered correct by experts, should students internalize those ideas instead of constructing their own? |
| II. *Pedagogical dilemmas:* Honouring students' attempts to think for themselves while remaining faithful to accepted disciplinary ideas; developing deeper knowledge of subject matter; mastering the art of facilitation; managing new kinds of discourse and collaborative work in the classroom. | Do I base my teaching on students' existing ideas rather than on learning objectives? What skills and strategies are necessary for me to become a facilitator? How do I manage a classroom where students are talking to one another rather than to me? Should I place limits on students' construction of their own ideas? What types of assessments will capture the learning I want to foster? |
| III. *Cultural dilemmas:* Becoming conscious of the culture of your classroom; questioning assumptions about what kinds of activities should be valued; taking advantage of experiences, discourse patterns, and local knowledge of students with varied cultural backgrounds. | How can we contradict traditional, efficient classroom routines and generate new agreements with students about what is valued and rewarded? How do my own past images of what is proper and possible in a classroom prevent me from seeing the potential for a different kind of learning environment? How can I accommodate the worldviews of students from diverse backgrounds while at the same time transforming my own classroom culture? Can I trust students to accept responsibility for their own learning? |
| IV. *Political dilemmas:* Confronting issues of accountability with various stakeholders in the school community; negotiating with key others the authority and support to teach for understanding. | How can I gain the support of administrators and parents for teaching in such a radically different and unfamiliar way? Should I make use of approved curriculums that are not sensitive enough to my students' needs, or should I create my own? How can diverse problem-based experiences help students meet specific state and local standards? Will constructivist approaches adequately prepare my students for high-stakes testing for college admissions? |

*Source: Adapted from Windschitl, M. (2002). Framing constructivism in practice as the negotiation of dilemmas: An analysis of the conceptual, pedagogical, cultural, and political challenges facing teachers. Review of Educational Research, 72, p. 133. Reproduced with permission of the publisher.*

# SERVICE LEARNING

Service learning combines academic learning with personal and social development for secondary and college students (Woolfolk Hoy, Demerath, & Pape, 2002). A more formal definition of **service learning** is "a teaching and learning strategy that integrates meaningful community service with instruction and reflection to enrich the learning experience, teach civic responsibility, and strengthen communities" (National Service Learning Clearing House, n.d.). Common characteristics of service learning strategies in Canada include:

- are organized and meet actual community needs
- are integrated into the student's curriculum
- provide time to reflect and write about the service experience
- provide opportunities to apply newly learned academic skills and knowledge
- enhance both academic learning and a sense of caring for others

Service learning activities may involve direct service (tutoring, serving meals at homeless shelters), indirect service (collecting food for shelters, raising money), or advocacy (designing and distributing posters about a food drive, writing newspaper articles) (Johnson & Notah, 1999). Service learning also could be a form of problem-based learning.

**Service learning** Combines academic learning with personal and social development for secondary and college students.

Participation in service learning can promote political and moral development for adolescents. Through service learning projects, adolescents experience their own competence and agency by working with others in need. Students see themselves as political and moral agents, rather than as merely good citizens (Youniss & Yates, 1997). In addition, service learning can help adolescents think in new ways about their relationships with people who are unlike them, and thus can lead them to become more tolerant of differences (Tierney, 1993). Finally, service learning experiences foster an "ethic of care" that can result in a growing commitment to confront difficult social problems (Rhodes, 1997). In this sense, student involvement in service learning can motivate and empower adolescents to critically reflect on their role in society (Woolfolk Hoy, Demerath, & Pape, 2002). A number of schools now have participation in service learning as a graduation requirement, but some educators question if "required" service is fair or appropriate. At least three of the school requirements have been challenged in court, but, so far, the requirements have been upheld (Johnson & Notah, 1999).

**SERVICE LEARNING** Community service projects can promote adolescents' moral development, feelings of competence and agency, and tolerance of differences, and encourage them to reflect critically on their roles in society.

Jeff Greenberg/PhotoEdit

Studies of service learning have produced mixed results. Some studies have found modest gains on measures of social responsibility, tolerance for others, empathy, attitude toward adults, and self-esteem (Solomon, Watson, & Battistich, 2001). A case study at an urban parochial high school describes a successful service learning experience program that was required for juniors and was part of a year-long course on social justice (Youniss & Yates, 1999). In the class, students examined the moral implications of current social issues such as homelessness, poverty, exploitation of immigrant labourers, and urban violence. Students also were required to serve four times (approximately 20 hours) at an inner-city soup kitchen. The researchers concluded that students emerged from the course with "a deeper awareness of social injustice, a greater sense of commitment to confront these injustices, and heightened confidence in their abilities overall" (Yates & Youniss, 1999, p. 64).

Your students may be involved in service learning both inside and outside the school. You might share the *Family and Community Partnership Guidelines* with families and use them yourself. Many are taken from Richard Sagor (2003) and Elias and Schwab (2006).

# LEARNING IN A DIGITAL WORLD

It seems that computers, smartphones, iPods, iPads, iTouches, tablets, digital readers, and interactive video games, along with iCloud, Facebook, Twitter, Google, Yahoo!, and other digital tools and media have changed life for everyone. Homes and schools are filled with media. For students, doing homework often involves exchanging messages with friends via email, texting, or cell phones; searching the web; and downloading resources—all the time listening to music via an iPod or watching television (Roberts, Foehr, & Rideout, 2005). A recent Ipsos-Reid poll found that, in early 2010, Canadians were spending slightly more than 18 hours per week online, while they watched television for just under 17 hours per week (Ipsos, 2010).

**Watch**
Learning in a Digital World

## Learning Environments and Technology

With all the technology available today, there is growing interest in *technology-rich learning environments*, or TREs. These environments include virtual worlds, computer

## GUIDELINES · FAMILY AND COMMUNITY PARTNERSHIPS

### Service Learning

**The service should be ongoing, not just a brief project.**
*Examples*

1. Instead of having a two-week food drive with a party for the class that collected the most, encourage a longer commitment to cook or serve food at shelters for homeless families.
2. Contact local agencies to identify real needs that your students could address or search online by postal code: www.volunteermatch.org.

**Consider virtual volunteering. See www.serviceleader.org/virtual.**
*Examples*

1. Translate a document into another language.
2. Provide multimedia expertise, such as preparing a PowerPoint, QuickTime, or other computer-based presentation.
3. Design an agency's newsletter or brochure, or copy edit an agency's publication or proposal.
4. Proofread drafts of papers and online publications.
5. Research and write articles for brochures, newsletters, websites.
6. Design a logo for an agency or program, or fill other illustration needs.

**Be aware of service learning projects in school. Make sure learning is at the centre.**
*Examples*

1. Have clear learning objectives for the projects.
2. Examine grade-level standards in science, history, health, literature, and other areas to see how some might be met through service projects—for example, how might

concepts in biology be learned through designing a nutrition education project for senior citizens or preschool students?
3. Do students reflect over time about their experiences, keep journals, write or draw what they have learned, and include these reflections in class discussions?

**Make sure the service draws on your child's talents and skills so that it is actually valuable to the recipients and he or she gains a sense of accomplishment and usefulness from applying skills to help others.**
*Examples*

1. Youth who have artistic talents might help redecorate a game room at a senior citizens' centre.
2. Individuals who are good storytellers could work with children at a day care centre or in a children's clinic.
3. Students who are bilingual might help teachers translate school newsletters into the languages of fellow students' families or serve as translators at local clinics.

**Design service learning opportunities so they are inclusive (Dymond, Renzaglia, & Chun, 2007).**
*Examples*

1. Consider transportation needs for children with disabilities.
2. Link service learning projects to life skills such as social skills on the job, safety, and punctuality.
3. Encourage teachers to monitor interactions in groups for all students; be aware of how students with special needs are included.

*For more ideas, see*
*www.communityservicelearning.ca/en/resources.htm.*

---

simulations that support problem-based learning such as the *River of Life Challenge* described earlier, intelligent tutoring systems, educational games, audio recordings, hand-held wireless devices, and multimedia environments—to name just a few.

There are three kinds of uses for technology in schools. First, teachers can design technology-based activities for their classrooms, for virtual learning environments, or for blended models using both in-class and virtual environments. Second, students can interact with technologies in a variety of ways, such as by using a computer or tablet to complete assignments, or by collaborating in a virtual environment with other students or teachers using interactive **cloud computing** applications. Cloud computing allows computer users online access to applications such as a Google documents or Microsoft Web Mail along with computing assets such as network-accessible data storage and processing. Finally, administrators use technology to track teacher, class, and student information in school, district, or provincial systems. You could be involved with any or all three uses of technology in your teaching.

The primary goal for integrating technology into a classroom is to support student learning. The process may seem difficult and troublesome at first, especially for teachers with few technological skills. Starting points include researching your school or district technology policies and procedures, identifying internal resources such as technology

**Cloud computing** Allows computer users to access applications such as a Google document or Microsoft Web Mail, as well as computing assets such as network-accessible data storage and processing to use online applications.

integration teams, seeking out training resources, and working with teachers who already use technology in their classes. Becoming familiar with available technological resources will help you to identify and include new technologies that will enhance your teaching. A golden rule for technology integration in any classroom is that you do not need to reinvent the wheel. Focus on identifying centres of expertise where existing resources are available to adapt and build on.

## Virtual Learning Environments

**Virtual Learning Environment (VLE)** is a broad term that describes many ways of learning in virtual systems. The most traditional VLE is referred to as a **Learning Management System (LMS)**. LMSs deliver e-learning using applications such as Moodle, BlackBoard, RCampus, and Desire2Learn. Learning management systems are large, complex, and costly—Phil's university uses a system called Canvas to support every course on all three of the university's campuses. Canvas sites have readings, discussion groups, a calendar, and many other resources. Professors taught classes without these assets for decades, but the learning management system has expanded their teaching and learning options. To deal with costs, some institutions use free *open-source software* to construct virtual learning environments. Tools that support open-source software include Moodle, Google Apps, Microsoft SharePoint, and PBWorks.

There are different kinds of virtual learning environments. A **Personal Learning Environment (PLE)** framework provides tools that support individualized learning in a variety of contexts and situations; the learners assume control of how and when their learning occurs. Students working in personal learning environments can download an assignment at Panera, read the material on the bus, and then post an analysis on the discussion board at 4:00 a.m. from their room—learning is asynchronous, it takes place anytime and anywhere. Complex personal learning environments include tools that assess learners' knowledge and then adapt the next content to fit their needs. Tools that support PLEs include computer-based training modules, ebooks, cognitive tutors, quizzes, and self-assessment tools.

A **Personal Learning Network (PLN)** is a framework in which knowledge is constructed through online peer interactions. PLNs consist of both synchronous (real time) and asynchronous technologies using interactive web conferencing, hybrid classes, or online discussions. A PLN can be used for K–12 instructional purposes and also as a resource for professional development. Social networking tools such as Facebook, Twitter, Edutopia, and EdWeb allow the instruction to move outside the school, city, and even country to include learners with similar interests around the globe. Tools that support personal learning networks include web conferencing tools such as Adobe Connect and Elluminate, instant messaging, interactive video and audio messaging, social networking, discussion boards, and blogs.

The most complex VLE is an **Immersive Virtual Learning Environment (IVLE)**. The IVLE is a simulation of a real-world environment that immerses students in tasks like those required in a professional practicum. The purpose is to learn through enculturation, for example by being eco explorers in the rainforest or reporters covering a story about an outbreak of food poisoning in a local school (Gee, 2003; Gibson, Aldrich, & Prensky, 2006; Shaffer et al., 2009). Immersive Virtual Learning Environments are designed to be domain specific using realistic scenarios (Bagley & Shaffer, 2009; Shaffer et al., 2009). IVLE experiences mimic tasks required in a professional practicum, such as interviewing sources for a news story about food poisoning, following leads to identify the source of a problem, and crafting an accurate engaging article, thus blending real-world engagement in a virtual scenario. These immersive environments often include *cognitive tutors*—the technology is programmed to interact as a tutor by providing prompts after analyzing the student's response.

**Massive Multi-player Online Games (MMOGs)** are interactive gaming environments constructed in virtual worlds in which the learner assumes a character role of avatar. Virtual world simulations incorporating MMOGs have been used for experiential and didactic learning in the medical field for several years and quickly are gaining attention

**Virtual Learning Environment (VLE)** A broad term that describes many ways of learning in virtual or online systems.

**Learning Management System (LMS)** System that delivers e-learning, provides tools and learning materials, keeps records, administers assessments, and manages learning.

**Personal Learning Environment (PLE)** Provides tools that support individualized learning in a variety of contexts and situations.

**Personal Learning Network (PLN)** Framework in which knowledge is constructed through online peer interactions.

**Immersive Virtual Learning Environment (IVLE)** A simulation of a real-world environment that immerses students in tasks like those required in a professional practicum.

**Massive Multi-player Online Games (MMOGs)** Interactive gaming environments constructed in virtual worlds where the learner assumes a character role of avatar.

in PK–12 classrooms. The pedagogic value in good gaming design is the ability to create complex scenarios by developing lessons using modelling and problem-based learning scenarios as alternative methods of instruction (Gee, 2008). For example, Project Evoke is a game developed by the World Bank (www.urgentevoke.com). As they play the game, adolescents from around the world work collectively to solve major world problems such as hunger. Stay tuned for more exciting learning worlds.

## Developmentally Appropriate Computer Activities for Young Children

Digital media are appealing, but are they appropriate for preschool children? This is hotly debated. Computers should not be used to do solitary drill-and-practice activities. Developmentally appropriate ways to use computers with 3- and 4-year-olds are different from the ways we use computers in kindergarten and the primary grades (www. kidsource.com/education/computers.children.html). With developmentally appropriate computer activities, young children can benefit cognitively without sustaining losses in creativity (Haugland & Wright, 1997). Software for children should include simple spoken directions; the activities should be open-ended and encourage discovery, exploration, problem solving, and understanding of cause and effect. Children should be able to remain in control of the activities through a variety of responses. Finally, the content should be appropriate for and respectful of diverse cultures, ages, and abilities (Fischer & Gillespie, 2003; Frost, Wortham, & Reifel, 2005). Linda Tsantis and her colleagues suggest that you ask this question about any program you are considering: "Does this software program help create learning opportunities that did not exist without it?" (Tsantis, Berwick, & Thouvebelle, 2003).

There is another important consideration—does the program's multimedia features (e.g., embedded videos, zoom-ins, music, added sounds, images) add to learning or take away from it? One danger is that programs will include attractive visuals or sound effects that actually interrupt and interfere with the development of important concepts. For example, do the sounds of a buzz saw and the thud of a falling tree in a Peter Rabbit storytelling program foster distractibility and interfere with understanding the story, plot, and characters? Maybe (Tsantis, Bewick, & Thouvenelle, 2003).

Dealing with all of this stimulation might make children better at multitasking, but also worse at deeper thought processes such as developing perspective-taking skills and understanding the plot, theme, and sequence of the story. So children learn to do several things at once, but have a superficial understanding of what they are doing (Carpenter, 2000).

Research in the Netherlands, however, demonstrated that multimedia storybooks can provide support for understanding stories and remembering linguistic information for kindergarten students from families with low educational levels who are behind in language and literacy skills (Verhallen, Bus, & de Jong, 2006). The difference in this study seemed to be that the multimedia features of the story supported understanding and memory by providing multiple pathways to meaning, giving visual and verbal representations of key story elements, focusing attention on important information, and reinforcing key ideas. This extra scaffolding may be especially important for students with limited language and literacy skills. So the bottom line is that multimedia elements should focus on meaning and not just provide attractive "bells and whistles."

## Computers and Older Students

There is evidence that using computers—especially games that require multiple activities, visual attention, imagery, and fast action—supports the development of visual skills, as long as the tasks fit the student's level of ability (Subrahmanyam, Greenfield, Kraut, & Gross, 2001). But does computer use support academic learning? The answer is complex and even surprising. After reviewing hundreds of studies, including five other research reviews, Roschelle, Pea, Hoadley, Gordon, and Means (2000) concluded that there were no strong conclusions. Using computer tutorial programs appeared to improve achievement

## GUIDELINES

## Using Computers

### IF YOU HAVE ONLY ONE COMPUTER IN YOUR CLASSROOM

**Provide convenient access.**
*Examples*
1. Find a central location if the computer is used to display material for the class.
2. Find a spot on the side of the room that allows seating and view of the screen, but does not crowd or disturb other students if the computer is used as a workstation for individuals or small groups.

**Be prepared.**
*Examples*
1. Check to be sure software needed for a lesson or assignment is installed and working.
2. Make sure instructions for using the software or doing the assignment are in an obvious place and clear.
3. Provide a checklist for completing assignments.

**Create "trained experts" to help with computers.**
*Examples*
1. Train student experts, and rotate experts.
2. Use adult volunteers—parents, grandparents, aunts and uncles, older siblings—anyone who cares about the students.

**Develop systems for using the computer.**
*Examples*
1. Make up a schedule to insure that all students have access to the computer and no students monopolize the time.
2. Create standard ways of saving student work.

### IF YOU HAVE MORE THAN ONE COMPUTER IN YOUR CLASSROOM

**Plan the arrangement of the computers to fit your instructional goals.**
*Examples*
1. For cooperative groups, arrange so students can cluster around their group's computer.
2. For different projects at different computer stations, allow for easy rotation from station to station.

**Experiment with other models for using computers.**
*Examples*
1. Navigator Model—four students per computer: One student is the (mouse and keyboard) driver, another is the "navigator." "Back-seat driver 1" manages the group's progress and "back-seat driver 2" serves as the timekeeper. The navigator attends a 10-minute to 20-minute training session in which the facilitator provides an overview of the basics of particular software. Navigators cannot touch the mouse. Driver roles are rotated.
2. Facilitator Model—six students per computer: the facilitator has more experience, expertise, or training—serves as the guide or teacher.
3. Collaborative Group Model—seven students per computer: Each small group is responsible for creating some component of the whole group's final product. For example, one part of the group writes a report, another creates a map, and a third uses the computer to gather and graph census data.

### NO MATTER HOW MANY COMPUTERS YOU HAVE IN YOUR CLASSROOM

**Select developmentally appropriate programs that encourage learning, creativity, and social interaction.**
*Examples*
1. Encourage two children to work together rather than having children work alone.
2. Check the implicit messages in programs. For example, some drawing programs allow children to "blow up" their projects if they don't like them, so instead of solving a problem they just destroy it. Tsantis and colleagues (2003) recommend a recycle metaphor instead of a "blow it up" option.
3. Look for programs that encourage discovery, exploration, problem solving, and multiple responses.

**Monitor children as they work at computers.**
*Examples*
1. Make sure computers are in areas where adults can observe them.
2. Discuss with children why some programs or websites are off limits.
3. Balance computer time with active play such as hands-on projects, blocks, sand, water, and art.

**Keep children safe as they work at computers.**
*Examples*
1. Teach children to shield their identity on the internet and monitor any "friends" they may be communicating with.
2. Install filtering software to protect children from inappropriate content.

*Sources: Suggestions are taken from Frost, J. L., Wortham, S. C., & Reifel, S. (2005). Play and child development (2nd ed.). Upper Saddle River, NJ: Prentice-Hall, pp. 76–80; Tsantis, L. A., Bewick, C. J., & Thouvenelle, S. (2003, November). Examining some common myths about computer use in the early years. Beyond the Journal: Young Children on the Web (pp. 1–9).*

Anthony Magnacca/Merrill

**DIGITALLY DISADVANTAGED?** Many students have limited access to technology at home or in their communities. This split in access to technology has been called the digital divide.

test scores for K–12 students, but simulations and enrichment programs had few effects—perhaps another example that when you teach and test specific skills, children learn the skills. More recent research reports similar results. Computers may be more useful in improving mathematics and science skills than other subjects and not very successful in improving reading (Slavin, Lake, Chambers, Cheung, & Davis, 2009). Like any teaching tool, computers can be effective if used well, but just being on a computer will not automatically increase academic achievement, especially achievement as measured by standardized tests (Richtel, 2011). Roschelle and colleagues (Roschelle, Pea, Hoadley, Gordon, & Means, 2000) concluded that computers are more likely to increase achievement if they support the basic processes that lead to learning: active engagement, frequent interaction with feedback, authenticity and real-world connection, and productive group work (Jackson et al., 2006). See the *Guidelines* for more ideas.

## Media/Digital Literacy

With the advent of digital media comes a new concern with literacy—media or digital literacy. Today, to be literate—that is to be able to read, write, and communicate—children have to read and write in many media, not just printed words. Films, videos, DVDs, computers, photographs, artwork, magazines, music, television, billboards, and more communicate through images and sounds. How do children read these messages? This is a new area of research and application in educational and developmental psychology (Hobbs, 2004).

As an example of practice, consider Project Look Sharp, directed by Cynthia Scheibe, a developmental psychologist (www.ithaca.edu/looksharp). The goal of the project is to provide materials, training, and support as teachers integrate media literacy and critical thinking about media into their class lessons. Teachers participating in the project help their students become critical readers of media. One group of elementary school students studied ants in science, and then viewed the animated film *Antz*. In the discussion after the movie, students were challenged to describe what was accurate and inaccurate in the film's portrayal of ants. What were the messages of the film? How was product placement (e.g., an ant drinking a bottle of Pepsi) used? Tests immediately and six months later indicated that the children performed best on the questions related to the discussion about the accuracy of the film (Scheibe, 2004). Project Look Sharp suggests these questions to guide discussion of media:

1. Who made—and who sponsored—this message, and what is their purpose?
2. Who is the target audience, and how is the message specifically tailored to that audience?
3. What are the different techniques used to inform, persuade, entertain, and attract attention?
4. What messages are communicated (and/or implied) about certain people, places, events, behaviours, lifestyles, and so forth?
5. How current, accurate, and credible is the information in this message?
6. What is left out of the message that might be good to know? (p. 63)

The *Guidelines* give more ideas from Scheibe and Rogow (2004) for supporting the development of media literacy in your students.

## GUIDELINES

## Supporting the Development of Media Literacy

**Use media to practise general observation, critical thinking, analysis, perspective-taking, and production skills.**
*Examples*

1. Ask students to think critically about the information presented in advertising, "news" programs, and textbooks—would different people interpret the messages in differing ways?
2. Foster creativity by having students produce their own media on a topic you are studying.
3. Ask students to compare ways information might be presented in a documentary, TV news report, advertisement, public service announcement, etc.
4. Give examples of how word selection, background music, camera angles, colour, etc. can be used to set a mood or bias a message.

**Use media to stimulate interest in a new topic.**
*Examples*

1. Analyze a magazine article about the topic.
2. Read sections from a novel or view film clips on the topic.

**Help students identify what they already know or believe about a topic based on popular media content. Help them identify erroneous beliefs.**
*Examples*

1. What do students "know" about space travel?
2. What have they learned about biology from advertisements?

**Use media as a standard pedagogical tool.**
*Examples*

1. Provide information about a topic through many different media sources—internet, books, DVDs, audio recordings, online newspapers, etc.
2. Assign homework that makes use of different media.
3. Have students express opinions or attempt to persuade using different media—photographs, collages, videos, poems, songs, animated films, etc.

**Analyze the effects that media had on historical events.**
*Examples*

1. How were First Nations Canadians portrayed in art and in films?
2. What sources of information were available 50 years ago? 100 years ago?

*For more ideas, see*
*www.ithaca.edu/looksharp.*

## ▼ SUMMARY

### The Learning Sciences (pp. 329–331)

**What are some basic assumptions of the learning sciences?** Key assumptions in the learning sciences are that experts develop deep conceptual knowledge, learning comes from the learner, creating learning environments is the responsibility of the school, students' prior knowledge is key, and reflection is a critical component of learning. These common assumptions enable researchers from various disciplines to address the same issues of learning from a variety of perspectives.

### Cognitive and Social Constructivism (pp. 331–338)

**Describe two kinds of constructivism, and distinguish these from constructionism.** *Psychological* constructivists such as Piaget are concerned with how individuals make sense of their world, based on individual knowledge, beliefs, self-concept, or identity— also called *first wave constructivism*. *Social* constructivists such as Vygotsky believe that social interaction, cultural tools, and activity shape individual development and learning—also called *second wave constructivism*. By participating in a broad range of activities with others, learners appropriate the outcomes produced by working together; they acquire new strategies and knowledge of their world. Finally, constructionists are interested in how public knowledge in academic disciplines is constructed as well as how everyday beliefs about the world are communicated to new members of a sociocultural group.

**In what ways do constructivist views differ about knowledge sources, accuracy, and generality?** Constructivists debate whether knowledge is constructed by mapping external reality, by adapting and changing internal understandings, or by an interaction of external forces and internal understandings. Most psychologists believe there is a role for both internal and external factors, but differ in how much they emphasize one or the other. Also, there is discussion about whether knowledge can be constructed in one situation and applied to another or whether knowledge is situated—that is, specific and tied to the context in which it was learned.

Kelia Neokow/Shutterstock

**What is meant by thinking as enculturation?** Enculturation is a broad and complex process of acquiring knowledge and understanding consistent with Vygotsky's theory of mediated learning. Just as our home culture taught us lessons about the use of language, the culture of a classroom can teach lessons about thinking by giving us models of good thinking; providing direct instruction in thinking processes; and encouraging practice of those thinking processes through interactions with others.

**What are some common elements in most constructivist views of learning?** Even though there is no single constructivist theory, many constructivist approaches recommend complex, challenging learning environments and authentic tasks; social negotiation and co-construction; multiple representations of content; understanding that knowledge is constructed; and student ownership of learning.

## Applying Constructivist Perspectives (pp. 338–356)

**Distinguish between inquiry methods and problem-based learning.** The inquiry strategy begins when the teacher presents a puzzling event, question, or problem. The students ask questions (only yes/no questions in some kinds of inquiry) and then formulate hypotheses to explain the event or solve the problem; collect data to test the hypotheses about casual relationships; form conclusions and generalizations; and reflect on the original problem and the thinking processes needed to solve it. Problem-based learning may follow a similar path, but the learning begins with an authentic problem—one that matters to the students. The goal is to learn math or science or history or some other important subject while seeking a real solution to a real problem.

**Describe six features that most cognitive apprenticeship approaches share.** Students observe an expert (usually the teacher) model the performance; get external support through coaching or tutoring; and receive conceptual scaffolding, which is then gradually faded as the student becomes more competent and proficient. Students continually articulate their knowledge—putting into words their understanding of the processes and content being learned. They reflect on their progress, comparing their problem solving to an expert's performance and to their own earlier performances. Finally, students explore new ways to apply what they are learning—ways that they have not practised at the master's side.

**Describe the use of dialogue in reciprocal teaching.** The goal of reciprocal teaching is to help students understand and think deeply about what they read. To accomplish this goal, students in small reading groups learn four strategies: summarizing the content of a passage, asking a question about the central point, clarifying the difficult parts of the material, and predicting what will come next. These strategies are practised in a classroom dialogue about the readings. Teachers first take a central role, but as the discussion progresses, the students take more and more control.

**What are the differences between collaboration and cooperation?** One view is that collaboration is a philosophy about how to relate to others—how to learn and work. Collaboration is a way of dealing with people that respects differences, shares authority, and builds on the knowledge that is distributed among other people. Cooperation, on the other hand, is a way of working together with others to attain a shared goal.

**What are the learning theory underpinnings of cooperative learning?** Learning can be enhanced in cooperative groups through rehearsal and elaboration (information processing theories), creation and resolution of disequilibrium (Piaget's theory), or scaffolding of higher mental processes (Vygotsky's theory).

**Describe five elements that define true cooperative learning.** Students interact face to face and close together, not across the room. Group members experience positive interdependence—they need each other for support, explanations, and guidance. Even though they work together and help each other, members of the group must ultimately demonstrate learning on their own—they are held individually accountable for learning, often through individual tests or other assessments. If necessary, the collaborative skills important for effective group functioning, such as giving constructive feedback, reaching consensus, and involving every member, are taught and practised before the groups tackle a learning task. Finally, members monitor group processes and relationships to make sure the group is working effectively and to learn about the dynamics of groups.

**How should tasks match design in cooperative learning?** A relatively structured task works well with a structured technique; extrinsic rewards can enhance motivation, effort, and persistence under these conditions; roles, especially those that focus attention on the work to be accomplished, also may be productive. On the other hand, strategies that encourage extended and productive interactions are appropriate when the goal is to develop higher-order thinking and problem solving. The use of rewards may well divert the group away from the goal of in-depth cognitive processing. When the goal of peer learning is enhanced social skills or increased intergroup understanding and appreciation of diversity, the assignment of specific roles and functions within the group might support communication. Rewards probably are not necessary and may actually get in the way because the goal is to build community, a sense of respect, and responsibility for team members.

**What are some possible strategies for cooperative learning?** Strategies include reciprocal questioning, Jigsaw, structured controversy, and many cooperative structures described by Spencer Kagan.

## Service Learning (pp. 356–357)

**What are some key characteristics of service learning?** Service learning activities should be organized around and designed to meet actual community needs, and integrated into the student's curriculum. Teachers should provide time for students to reflect on and write about their service experience, offer opportunities to apply newly learned academic skills and knowledge, and strive to enhance both academic learning and a sense of caring for others. Service learning activities ought not be supplementary to students' regular activities, but instead should be an integral part of their learning.

## Learning in a Digital World (pp. 357–363)

**What are some possible uses of technology in education?** Technology such as computers, iPods, smartphones, digital readers, and interactive gaming systems are extremely popular among young people. In fact, the many ways of communicating and interacting with others through technology may even shape the way students think about what it means to socialize. These technologies can be useful teaching tools, but they do have limitations. First, technology cannot necessarily replace the teacher when it comes to direct instruction (and not all programs are able to bring about learning). Classrooms of the future may take greater advantage of learning environments that immerse students in virtual worlds where they work alone or with others to solve problems, create projects, simulate the skills of experts, visit historical sites, tour world-class museums, or play games that teach and apply academic skills. The results of research on technology-enhanced learning emphasize that technology by itself will not guarantee improvement in academic achievement—like any tool, technology must be used well by confident, competent teachers.

# ▼ WHAT WOULD YOU DO?

## TEACHERS' CASEBOOK: Dilemma on Day 1

Here is how some practising teachers responded to the situation described at the beginning of the chapter.

### ELAINE TAN COMEAU
Lakeview Elementary School, Burnaby, BC

As a new teacher myself, I understand the initial excitement this teacher was feeling. Rather than feel helpless at this point, remember that these book reviews reflect only one type of assessment—the written form. Today's multi-ability-level classrooms require a variety of assessment methods to address diverse backgrounds and learning styles and to give students more opportunities to demonstrate progress. The key here is to focus less on what needs to be covered and more on how it will be covered—process over content!

The first assignment might have caused some students to feel incapable because they lacked English grammar and writing skills and used an underdeveloped vocabulary. The key for English language learners is to provide lower-language and higher-interest visuals; for example, to use key words that connect ideas, sentence frames, or line maps. All students will benefit from vocabulary building. Select key vocabulary in each lesson and ask students to discuss, use, and apply those words.

The teacher should also adapt various instructional methods. For example, supplement long novels with videos or short stories written at appropriate levels to access students' different learning styles and means of understanding; integrate fine art to appeal to another type of learning style. Try the same activity again by grouping students in twos and threes, providing each with an interesting article she or he can relate to and write about. Prepare in advance a set of sentence frames to be completed for the students' articles.

Make use of the capable students, since all students benefit from shared learning experiences. Ask these three students to function as peer tutors in small groups. Cooperative learning groups assist with the inherent behavioural management challenge and help to reduce the isolation, boredom, and fear of sharing some students feel. Small groups also give the English language learner access to a fluent English speaker while simultaneously building the confidence and self-esteem of the peer tutor.

Where possible, assign world literature selections based on students' countries of origin to heighten interest and attention span. English language learners may want to write responses in their first languages. Ask peer tutors to assist these students in translating their ideas into English. This provides major language and interpersonal benefits for both groups of students, along with challenges for the advanced students.

### LESLEY PETERSON
Formerly from Sister High School, Winnipeg, MB

The first thing to determine is whether this writing task was a reasonably reliable diagnostic tool. Did you check that the students were familiar with the conventions of the review form and/or ensure that your expectations were clearly articulated to students? It might be worth assigning another writing task before deciding that the students whose papers were lacking in coherence were, in fact, unable to write coherent papers. However, in my experience, weak students tend to interpret every writing task as an invitation to retell the story. If these students have failed to do even that coherently, the problem is probably a real one.

Determining how to proceed with the very weak students, then, assuming that their weaknesses are validated, requires reference to the program policy and course outline. Also, if the course is required for university entrance or is a prerequisite for such a course, you cannot solely grade on effort and improvement. There must be standards. You should be prepared to differentiate your teaching in terms of the material that students read, the assignments they may choose, and the criteria by which they are evaluated. Differentiating instruction is still a good strategy for the standards-driven curriculum while retaining the same evaluation criteria for all students.

Central to the design of courses like this is a strong emphasis on the writing process. You should plan to teach writing, reading, and revision strategies that will be helpful to all or most students. If this is your goal, however, I strongly suggest changing this first assignment. Instead, ask the students to write reviews of the "best" book they have ever read. Knowing what they consider to be the "best" books is invaluable for planning a wide range of readings that engage students' interest. If you're well and widely read in world literature, you'll be able to find novels, short stories, and poems that intersect with what engages students. It's that basic old principle of teaching that needs to be put into action here: Find out where they are, then meet them, and take them forward from there.

If this is a university-entrance course, you should gather more data about the students who appear weak. Check their final marks in the prerequisite course and talk to previous English teachers. If you still feel a student does not have the reading, writing, and thinking skills necessary for success in this course, consider requesting conferences with the student's parents. Advise parents that this course will be a struggle for their child. An early recommendation to see a guidance counsellor or to change a timetable can turn into a real favour to the student. Better that the student enroll in an appropriate course now than sit in the wrong one, have her or his self-esteem battered for months, and then drop the course.

As for the really advanced writers, they need to be recognized, supported, and challenged. Nurture and challenge their love of literature and writing. Assigning advanced students assignments that are too easy can hurt students' self-esteem and lead to underachievement (not to mention boredom). Encourage these students to get involved in whatever writing communities are available. If a school magazine doesn't exist, encourage them to start one. Many cities have organizations similar to the Manitoba Writers' Guild, which sponsors readings and open-microphone sessions, organizes workshops, and so on that can be very helpful to advanced writers.

Teaching a separate, gifted program to three students is more work than most English teachers have time for. But there are community resources you can access. Does your town library, university, or college have a "writer in residence?" If your school has a work experience coordinator, can he or she hook up these students with a professional journalist? Our local theatre gave one of my students a volunteer position reading and making recommendations on scripts. It changed her life.

Find out what kind of writing these students are most interested in and introduce them to other people who care about it as much as they do. You definitely shouldn't "punish" these students for their ability by giving them extra work. It might be possible for them to earn a separate credit for their extra involvement—talk to a guidance counsellor, work experience coordinator, or administrator to find out what's available. And have the grace to admit that these students might learn more if you let them spend part of your class time in the library. They'll respect you more for it, not less.

# CHAPTER 1

Echo3005/Shutterstock

# SOCIAL COGNITIVE VIEWS OF LEARNING AND MOTIVATION

## WHAT WOULD YOU DO?

**TEACHERS' CASEBOOK:** Failure to Self-Regulate

You know your students need to be organized and self-regulating to do well in both their current and their future classes. But many of the students just don't seem to know how take charge of their own learning. They have trouble completing larger projects—many wait until the last minute. They can't organize their work or decide what is most important. Some can't even keep up with assignments. Their book bags are disaster areas—filled with long overdue assignment sheets and class handouts from last semester crumbled in with school newsletters and permission slips for field trips. You are concerned because they will need to be much more organized and on top of their work as they progress through their education. You have so much material to cover to meet district guidelines, but many of your students are drowning in the amount of work they already have.

### CRITICAL THINKING

- What organizational skills do students need to be successful in your subject or class?
- What could you do to teach these skills, while still covering the material?
- How would you help students develop an authentic sense of efficacy for guiding their own learning?

## OVERVIEW AND OBJECTIVES

For the past four chapters, we have analyzed different aspects of learning. We considered behavioural and information processing explanations of what and how people learn. We have examined cognitive science and complex cognitive processes such as concept learning and problem solving. These explanations of learning focus on the individual and what is happening in his or her "head." Recent perspectives have called attention to two other aspects of learning that are critical: social and cultural factors. In the previous chapter, we examined social constructivism and the interdisciplinary learning sciences. In this chapter, we look at social cognitive theory—a current view of learning and motivation that discusses dynamic interactions among many of the behavioural, personal, and cultural factors involved in learning and motivation.

Social cognitive theory has its roots in Bandura's early criticisms of behavioural views of learning, as you read in Chapter 7. Social cognitive theory moved beyond behaviourism to focus on humans as self-directed agents who make choices and marshal resources to reach goals. Concepts such as self-efficacy and self-regulated learning are key in social cognitive theories. These concepts are important in understanding motivation as well, so this chapter provides a good path from learning to the discussion of motivation in the next chapter. We end the chapter with a look back at our tour through different models of instruction. Rather than debating the merits of each approach, we will consider the contributions of these different models of instruction, grounded in different theories of learning. Don't feel that you must choose the "best" approach—there is no such thing. Even though theorists argue about which model is best, excellent teachers don't debate. They apply all the approaches, using each one when appropriate.

By the time you have completed this chapter, you should be able to:

11.1   Define the basic principles of social cognitive theories of learning and motivation, including triarchic reciprocal causality, modelling/observational learning, self-efficacy, and agency.

11.2   Discuss the roles of observation and self-efficacy in learning.

11.3   Describe important components of self-regulated learning.

11.4   Apply self-regulated learning principles to teaching.

# SOCIAL COGNITIVE THEORY

As we saw in Chapter 7, in the early 1960s, Albert Bandura demonstrated that people can learn by observing both the actions of others and the consequences of those actions. Most of what is known today as *social cognitive theory* is based on the work begun by Bandura in the 1950s at Stanford University. Before we talk about the theory, let's meet the man.

## A Self-Directed Life: Albert Bandura

Albert Bandura's life story should be a movie. His parents were immigrants from Eastern Europe; they chose the rugged land of northern Alberta for their family farm. Bandura's parents never went to school, but they valued education. His father taught himself to read in three languages, giving young Albert a great model of self-regulated learning— a concept that figures prominently in social cognitive theory today. On the way to finishing high school, Bandura worked many jobs, including a stint as a carpenter at a furniture factory and one as a road worker on the Alaska Highway in the Yukon. He finished his undergraduate degree at the University of British Columbia in three years, even though he had to cram all his classes into the morning to have time for his afternoon jobs. Because he needed a morning class to fill one time slot, he enrolled in introductory psychology and found his future profession (Bandura, 2007, p. 46). His next stop was graduate school at the epicentre of psychological research in 1950—the University of Iowa. After earning his PhD (in three years again), Bandura joined the faculty at Stanford in 1953—he was 28 years old. He is still at Stanford nearly 60 years later, and now teaches some of the children of his former students. During his PhD studies, Phil was lucky enough to be able to enroll in a seminar he taught.

Pajares' short biography of Bandura (see http://stanford.edu/dept/psychology/bandura/pajares/bandurabio.html) reveals how much his theories reflected his life as a self-directed, self-regulating learner growing up in a challenging environment. Describing his experiences in his two-teacher high school, Bandura (2007) said,

**ALBERT BANDURA** You may remember Albert Bandura from Chapter 7. Pictures from his famous Bobo doll experiment on observational learning are in the background. Most of what we know today as social cognitive theory is based on the work he began in the 1950s at Stanford University.

Jon Brenneis/Time & Life Pictures/Getty Images

> We had to take charge of our own learning. Self-directed learning was an essential means of academic self-development, not a theoretical abstraction. The paucity of educational resources turned out to be an enabling factor that has served me well rather than an insurmountable handicapping one. The content of courses is perishable, but self-regulatory skills have lasting functional value whatever the pursuit might be. (p. 45)

In the next section we will look at the key features of Bandura's work and social cognitive theory by considering four topics: moving beyond behaviourism, the concept of triarchic reciprocal causality, the power of observational learning, and the key beliefs of agency and self-efficacy.

## Beyond Behaviourism

Bandura's early **social learning theory** was concerned with observing and modelling others who were reinforced or punished for their particular behaviours. But as you know from Chapter 7, he found basic behaviourism to be too limited. In his autobiography, Bandura (2007) describes the shortcomings of behaviourism and the need to put people in social context:

> I found this behavioristic theorizing discordant with the obvious social reality that much of what we learn is through the power of social modeling. I could not imagine a culture in which its language; mores; familial customs and practices; occupational competencies; and educational, religious, and political practices were gradually shaped in each new member by rewarding and punishing consequences of their trial-and-error performances. (p. 55)

Over time, Bandura's explanations of learning included more attention to cognitive factors such as *expectations* and *beliefs* in addition to the social influences of models (Bandura, 1986, 1997, 2001). His current perspective, **social cognitive theory**, retains an emphasis on the role of other people serving as models and teachers (the *social* part of social cognitive theory), but includes thinking, believing, expecting, anticipating, self-regulating, and making comparisons and judgments (the *cognitive* part). Social cognitive theory is a *dynamic system* that explains human adaptation, learning, and motivation. The theory addresses how people develop social, emotional, cognitive, and behavioural capabilities; how people regulate their own lives; and what motivates them (Bandura, 2007; Bandura & Locke, 2003). In fact, many of the concepts from this chapter will help you understand motivation in the upcoming chapter.

**Social learning theory** Theory that emphasizes learning through observation of others.

**Social cognitive theory** Theory that adds concern with cognitive factors such as beliefs, self-perceptions, and expectations to social learning theory.

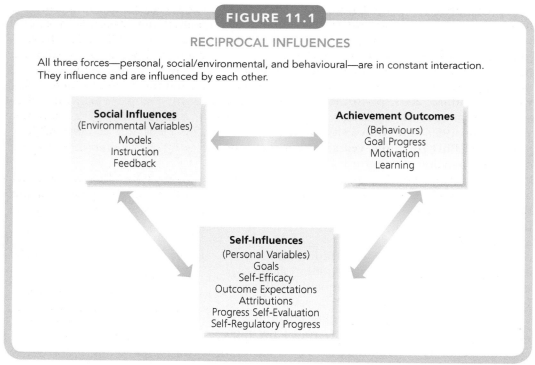

Sources: From Schunk, D. H. (1999). Social-Self Interaction and Achievement Behavior. Educational Psychologist, 34, p. 221. Adapted with permission of Lawrence Erlbaum Associates, Inc. and the author.

## Triarchic Reciprocal Causality

We claimed that social cognitive theory describes a system. This system, called **triarchic reciprocal causality**, is the dynamic interplay among three kinds of influences: personal, environmental, and behavioural, as shown in Figure 11.1. Personal factors (beliefs, expectations, attitudes, knowledge), the physical and social environment (resources, consequences of actions, other people, models and teachers, physical settings), and behaviour (individual actions, choices, verbal statements) all influence and are influenced by each other—they reciprocate to shape behaviour.

Figure 11.1 shows the interaction of person, environment, and behaviour in learning settings (Schunk, Pintrich, & Meece, 2008). External factors such as models, instructional strategies, or teacher feedback (elements of the environment for students) can affect student personal factors such as goals, sense of efficacy for the task (described in the next section), attributions (beliefs about causes for success and failure), and processes of self-regulation such as planning, monitoring, and controlling distractions. For example, teacher feedback can lead students to feel either more confident or more discouraged, and then the students adjust their goals accordingly. Environmental and personal factors encourage behaviours such as effort and persistence that lead to learning. But these behaviours also reciprocally impact personal factors. For example, as students achieve through increased effort (behaviour), their confidence and interest increase (personal). And behaviours also affect the social environment. For example, if students do not persist or if they seem to misunderstand, teachers may change instructional strategies or learning group assignments, thus changing the learning environment for the students.

Think for a minute about the power of reciprocal causality in classrooms. If personal factors, behaviours, and the environment are in constant interaction, then cycles of events are progressive and self-perpetuating. Suppose a student who is new to the school walks into class late because he got lost in the unfamiliar building. The student has a tattoo and several visible pierced body parts. He is anxious about his first day and hopes to

**Triarchic reciprocal causality** An explanation of behaviour that emphasizes the mutual effects of the individual and the environment on each other.

do better at this new school, but the teacher's initial reaction to his late entry and dramatic appearance is a bit hostile. The student feels insulted and responds in kind, so the teacher begins to form expectations about him and acts more vigilant, less trusting. The student senses the distrust. He decides that this school will be just as worthless as his previous one—and wonders why he should bother to try. The teacher sees the student's disengagement, invests less effort in teaching him, and the cycle continues. These reciprocal effects are more than hypothetical. When Trevor and Kitty Williams (2010) examined data on high school students' confidence in mathematics and achievement in mathematics in 30 different countries, they found evidence that math confidence and math achievement reciprocally influenced each other in 26 of the countries, just as Bandura would predict.

Two key elements of social cognitive theory are observational learning and self-efficacy. We will examine each of these more closely, with special emphasis on their implications for teaching.

## MODELLING: LEARNING BY OBSERVING OTHERS

Learning by observing others is a key element of social cognitive theory. What causes an individual to learn and perform behaviours and skills modelled by others? Several factors play a role. The developmental level of the observer makes a difference in learning. As children grow older, they are able to focus attention for longer periods of time, use memory strategies to retain information, and motivate themselves to practise, as you can see in Table 11.1. A second influence is the status of the model. Children are more likely to imitate the actions of others who seem competent, powerful, prestigious, and enthusiastic, so parents, teachers, older siblings, athletes, action heroes, rock stars, or film personalities may serve as models, depending on the age and interests of the child. Third, by watching others, we learn about what behaviours are appropriate for people like ourselves, so models who are seen as similar are more readily imitated

**Watch**
Modelling: Learning by Observing Others

TABLE 11.1 • **Factors That Affect Observational Learning**

| CHARACTERISTIC | EFFECTS ON MODELLING PROCESS |
|---|---|
| Developmental Status | Improvements with development include longer attention and increased capacity to process information, use of strategies, comparing of performances with memorial representations, and adopting intrinsic motivators. |
| Model Prestige and Competence | Observers pay greater attention to competent, high-status models. Consequences of modelled behaviours convey information about functional value. Observers attempt to learn actions they believe they will need to perform. |
| Vicarious Consequences | Consequences to models convey information about behavioural appropriateness and likely outcomes of actions. Valued consequences motivate observers. Similarity in attributes or competence signals appropriateness and heightens motivation. |
| Outcome Expectations | Observers are more likely to perform modelled actions they believe are appropriate and will result in rewarding outcomes. |
| Goal Setting | Observers are likely to attend to models who demonstrate behaviours that help observers attain goals. |
| Self-efficacy | Observers attend to models when they believe they are capable of learning or performing the modelled behaviour. Observation of similar models affects self-efficacy ("If they can do it, I can, too"). |

*Source: Adapted from Schunk, D. H. (2002). Learning Theories: An Education Perspective (4th ed.). © 2004 by Prentice Hall. Reprinted by permission of Pearson Education, Inc., Upper Saddle River, NJ.*

(Schunk, Pintrich, & Meece, 2008). All students need to see successful, capable models who look and sound like them, no matter what their ethnicity, socioeconomic status, or gender.

Looking at Table 11.1, we see the last three influences involve goals and expectations. If observers expect that certain actions of models will lead to particular outcomes for the models (such as specific practice regimens leading to improved athletic performance) and the observers value those outcomes or goals, then the observers will pay attention to the models and try to reproduce the models' behaviours. Finally, observers are more likely to learn from models if the observers have a high level of self-efficacy—that is, if they believe they are capable of doing the actions needed to reach the goals, or at least of learning how to do so (Bandura, 1997; Schunk, Pintrich, & Meece, 2008).

## Elements of Observational Learning

STOP & THINK Your interview for a position in the middle school is going well. The next question is: "Who are your models as teachers? Do you hear yourself saying or see yourself doing things that other teachers have done? Are there teachers from films or books that you would like to emulate?" •

Through observational learning, we learn not only *how* to perform a behaviour but also what will happen to us in specific situations if we perform it. Observation can be a very efficient learning process. The first time children hold hairbrushes, cups, or tennis rackets, they usually brush, drink, or swing as well as they can, given their current muscle development and coordination. Let's take a closer look at how observational learning occurs. Bandura (1986) notes that observational learning includes four elements: paying attention, retaining information or impressions, producing behaviours, and being motivated to repeat the behaviours.

ATTENTION.   In order to learn through observation, we have to pay attention. In teaching, you will have to ensure students' attention to the critical features of the lesson by making clear presentations and highlighting important points. In demonstrating a skill (for example, threading a sewing machine or operating a lathe), you may need to have students look over your shoulder as you work. Seeing your hands from the same perspective as they see their own directs their attention to the right features of the situation and makes observational learning easier.

RETENTION.   To imitate the behaviour of a model, you have to remember it. This involves mentally representing the model's actions in some way, probably as verbal steps ("Hwa-Rang, the eighth form in Tae Kwan Do karate, is a palm-heel block, then a middle riding stance punch, then . . ."), or as visual images, or both. Retention can be improved by mental rehearsal (imagining imitating the behaviour) or by actual practice. In the retention phase of observational learning, practice helps us remember the elements of the desired behaviour, such as the sequence of steps.

PRODUCTION.   Once we "know" how a behaviour should look and remember the elements or steps, we still may not perform it smoothly. Sometimes, we need a great deal of practice, feedback, and coaching about subtle points before we can reproduce the behaviour of the model. In the production phase, practice makes the behaviour smoother and more expert.

MOTIVATION AND REINFORCEMENT.   As you saw in Chapter 7, social learning theory distinguishes between acquisition and performance. We may acquire a new skill or behaviour through observation, but we may not perform that behaviour until there is some motivation or incentive to do so. Reinforcement can play several roles in observational learning. If we anticipate being reinforced for imitating the actions of a model, we may be more motivated to pay attention, remember, and reproduce the behaviours. In addition, reinforcement is important in maintaining learning. A person who tries a new behaviour is unlikely to persist without reinforcement (Schunk, 2008). For example, if an unpopular student adopted the dress of the "in" group, but was ignored or ridiculed, it is unlikely that the imitation would continue.

Bandura identifies three forms of reinforcement that can encourage observational learning. First, of course, the observer may reproduce the behaviours of the model and receive direct reinforcement, as when a gymnast successfully executes a front flip/round-off combination and the coach/model says, "Excellent!"

But the reinforcement need not be direct—it may be **vicarious reinforcement**, where an observer may simply see others reinforced for a particular behaviour and then increase his or her production of that behaviour. For example, if you compliment two students on the excellent illustrations in their lab reports, several other students who observe your compliments may turn in illustrated lab reports next time. Most TV ads hope for this kind of effect. People in TV commercials become deliriously happy when they drive a particular car or drink a specific energy drink, and the viewer is supposed to do the same; the viewer's behaviour is reinforced vicariously by the actors' obvious pleasure. Punishment can also be vicarious: You may slow down on a stretch of highway after seeing several people get speeding tickets there.

The final form of reinforcement is **self-reinforcement**, or controlling your own reinforcers. This sort of reinforcement is important for both students and teachers. In fact, if one goal of education is to produce people who are capable of educating themselves, then students must learn to manage their own lives, set their own goals, and provide their own reinforcement. In adult life, rewards are sometimes vague and goals often take a long time to reach. Think about how many small steps are required to complete an education and find your first job. As a teacher, sometimes self-reinforcement is all that keeps you going. Life is filled with tasks that call for this sort of self-regulation—a topic we will address later in this chapter (Rachlin, 2004).

Social cognitive theory has some powerful implications for teaching. In this section, we will look more closely at using observational learning in teaching.

## Observational Learning in Teaching

STOP & THINK How would you incorporate observational learning into your teaching? What are the skills, attitudes, and strategies that can be modelled in teaching your subject? •

There are five possible outcomes of observational learning: directing attention, encouraging existing behaviours, changing inhibitions, teaching new behaviours and attitudes, and arousing emotions. Let's look at each of these as they occur in classrooms.

DIRECTING ATTENTION.   By observing others, we not only learn about actions but also notice the objects and circumstances involved in the actions. For example, in a preschool class, when one child plays enthusiastically with a toy that has been ignored for days, many other children may want to have the toy, even if they play with it in different ways or simply carry it around. This happens, in part, because the children's attention has been drawn to that particular toy.

FINE-TUNING ALREADY-LEARNED BEHAVIOURS.   All of us have had the experience of looking for cues from other people when we find ourselves in unfamiliar situations. Observing the behaviour of others tells us which of our already-learned behaviours to use: the proper fork for eating the salad, when to leave a gathering, what kind of language is appropriate, and so on. Adopting the dress and grooming styles of TV or music idols is another example of this kind of effect.

STRENGTHENING OR WEAKENING INHIBITIONS.   If class members witness one student breaking a class rule and getting away with it, they may learn that undesirable consequences do not always follow rule breaking. If the rule breaker is a well-liked, high-status

**Vicarious reinforcement** Increasing the chances that we will repeat a behaviour by observing another person being reinforced for that behaviour.

**Self-reinforcement** Controlling (selecting and administering) your own reinforcers.

DO AS I DO . . . Modelling has long been used to teach dance, sports, and crafts, and skills such cooking, chemistry, and welding. Modelling can also be applied deliberately in the classroom to teach mental skills and to broaden horizons—to teach new ways of thinking.

Imagebroker/Alamy

class leader, the effect of the modelling may be even more pronounced. This "contagious" spreading of behaviours through imitation is a **ripple effect** (Kounin, 1970) that can work for the teacher's benefit. When the teacher deals effectively with a rule breaker, especially a class leader, the idea of breaking this rule may be inhibited for the other students viewing the interaction. This does not mean that teachers must reprimand each student who breaks a rule, but once a teacher has called for a particular action, following through is an important part of capitalizing on the ripple effect.

TEACHING NEW BEHAVIOURS.   Modelling has long been used, of course, to teach dance, sports, and crafts, as well as skills in subjects such as food science, chemistry, and welding. Modelling can also be applied deliberately in the classroom to teach mental skills and to broaden horizons—to teach new ways of thinking. Teachers serve as models for a vast range of behaviours, from pronouncing vocabulary words, to reacting to the seizure of a student with epilepsy, to being enthusiastic about learning. For example, a teacher might model critical thinking skills by thinking "out loud" about a student's question. Or a high school teacher concerned about girls who seem to have stereotyped ideas about careers might invite women with nontraditional jobs to speak to the class. Studies indicate that modelling can be most effective when the teacher makes use of all the elements of observational learning—attention, retention, production, and especially reinforcement and practice.

Models who are the same age as the students may be particularly effective. For example, Schunk and Hanson (1985) compared two methods for teaching subtraction to grade 2 students who had difficulties learning this skill. One group of students observed other students learning the procedures, while another group watched a teacher's demonstration. Then, both groups participated in the same instructional program. The students who observed peer models learning not only scored higher on tests of subtraction after instruction but also gained more confidence in their own ability to learn. For students who doubt their own abilities, a good model is a low-achieving peer who keeps trying and finally masters the material (Schunk, 2004).

AROUSING EMOTION.   Finally, through observational learning, people may develop emotional reactions to situations they have never experienced personally, such as flying or driving. A child who watches a friend fall from a swing and break an arm may become fearful of swings. After the terrible events of September 11, 2001, children may be anxious when they see airplanes flying close to the ground. News reports of shark attacks have many of us anxious about swimming in the ocean. Note that hearing and reading about a situation are also forms of observation. Some terrible examples of modelling occur with "copy-cat killings" or suicide clusters in schools. When frightening things happen to people who are similar in age or circumstances to your students, they may need to be given an opportunity to talk about their emotions.

The *Guidelines* will give you some ideas about using observational learning in the classroom.

Self-efficacy is a key element of social cognitive theory that is especially important in learning and teaching.

**Ripple effect** "Contagious" spreading of behaviours through imitation.

## GUIDELINES

## Using Observational Learning

**Model behaviours and attitudes you want your students to learn.**
*Examples*

1. Show enthusiasm for the subject you teach.
2. Be willing to demonstrate both the mental and the physical tasks you expect the students to perform. Anita once saw a teacher sit down in the sandbox while her 4-year-old students watched her demonstrate the difference between "playing with sand" and "throwing sand."
3. When reading to students, model good problem solving. Stop and say, "Now let me see if I remember what happened so far," or "That was a hard sentence. I'm going to read it again."
4. Model good problem solving—think out loud as you work through a difficult problem.

**Use peers, especially class leaders, as models.**
*Examples*

1. In group work, pair students who do well with those who are having difficulties.
2. Ask students to demonstrate the difference between "whispering" and "silence—no talking."

**Make sure students see that positive behaviours lead to reinforcement for others.**
*Examples*

1. Point out the connections between positive behaviour and positive consequences in stories.
2. Be fair in giving reinforcement. The same rules for rewards should apply to both the students with problems and the students who do not cause trouble.

**Enlist the help of class leaders in modelling behaviours for the entire class.**
*Examples*

1. Ask a well-liked student to be friendly to an isolated, fearful student.
2. Let high-status students lead an activity when you need class cooperation or when students are likely to be reluctant at first. Popular students can model dialogues in foreign-language classes or be the first to tackle dissection procedures in biology.

*For more information on observational learning, see: www.readwritethink.org/lessons/lesson_view.asp?id=275.*

## SELF-EFFICACY AND AGENCY

Bandura (1986, 1994, 1997) suggests that predictions about possible outcomes of behaviour are critical for learning because they affect goals, effort, persistence, strategies, and resilience. "Will I succeed or fail? Will I be liked or laughed at? Will I be more accepted by teachers in this new school?" These predictions are affected by **self-efficacy**—our beliefs about our personal competence or effectiveness in a given area. Bandura (1994) defines self-efficacy as "people's beliefs about their capabilities to produce designated levels of performance that exercise influence over events that affect their lives" (p. 71).

Bandura's more recent efforts (2006) and the work of many other researchers have focused on the role of self-efficacy in **human agency**—the *exercising influence over life events* part of the definition above. Agency involves the ability to make intentional choices and action plans, design appropriate courses of action, and then motivate and regulate the execution of these plans and actions to reach goals. When we discuss self-regulation later in the chapter, you will see how students and teachers can become more *agentic*—more self-directing and in charge of their own learning and motivation.

### Self-Efficacy, Self-Concept, and Self-Esteem

Most people assume self-efficacy is the same as self-concept or self-esteem, but it isn't. *Self-efficacy* is future-oriented, "a context-specific assessment of competence to perform a specific task" (Pajares, 1997, p. 15). *Self-concept* is a more global construct that contains many perceptions about the self, including self-efficacy. Self-concept is developed as a

**Self-efficacy** A person's sense of being able to deal effectively with a particular task.

**Human agency** The capacity to coordinate learning skills, motivation, and emotions to reach your goals.

**CAN I DO IT?** Self-efficacy refers to the knowledge of one's own ability to successfully accomplish a particular task with no need for comparisons with others' ability—the question is "Can I do it?" not "Are others better than I am?"

Mason Trullinger/Alamy

result of external and internal comparisons, using other people or other aspects of the self as frames of reference. But self-efficacy focuses on your ability to successfully accomplish a particular task with no need for comparisons—the question is whether *you* can do it, not whether others would be successful. Also, self-efficacy beliefs are strong predictors of behaviour, but self-concept has weaker predictive power (Anderman & Anderman, 2009; Bandura, 1997).

Self-efficacy is "context specific," which means it varies depending on the subject or task. For example, Phil's sense of efficacy for singing is really low, but he feels confident in his ability to read a map and navigate (except in certain cities that are hopeless). Even young students have different efficacy beliefs for different tasks. One study found that by grade 1, students already differentiated among their sense of efficacy for reading, for writing, and for spelling (Wilson & Trainin, 2007).

Self-efficacy is concerned with judgments of personal competence; self-esteem is concerned with judgments of self-worth. There is no direct relationship between self-esteem and self-efficacy. It is possible to feel highly efficacious in one area and still not have a high level of self-esteem, or vice versa (Valentine, DuBois, & Cooper, 2004). For example, as Phil confessed earlier, he has very low self-efficacy for singing, but his self-esteem is not affected, probably because his life does not require singing. But if his self-efficacy for teaching a particular class started dropping after several bad experiences, he's sure his self-esteem would suffer because he values teaching.

## Sources of Self-Efficacy

Bandura identified four sources of self-efficacy expectations: mastery experiences, physiological and emotional arousal, vicarious experiences, and social persuasion. **Mastery experiences** are our own direct experiences—usually the most powerful source of efficacy information. Successes raise efficacy beliefs, while failures lower efficacy. Level of **arousal** affects self-efficacy, depending on how the arousal is interpreted.

**Mastery experiences** Our own direct experiences—the most powerful source of efficacy information.

**Arousal** Physical and psychological reactions causing a person to feel alert, excited, or tense.

TABLE 11.2 • **Sources of Self-Efficacy**

| SOURCE | EXAMPLE |
|---|---|
| Mastery Experiences | Past successes and failures in similar situations, as perceived by the individual. To increase efficacy, the success must be attributed to the ability, effort, choices, and strategies of the individual—not to luck or extensive help from others. |
| Vicarious Experiences | Seeing other people like you succeed on a task or reach a goal that is similar to the one you face. |
| Social Persuasion | Encouragement, informational feedback, useful guidance from a trusted source. |
| Physiological Arousal | Positive or negative arousal—excitement and a feeling of being "psyched" and ready (increases efficacy) or a sense of anxiety and foreboding (decreases efficacy). |

As you face the task, are you anxious and worried (lowers efficacy) or excited and "psyched" (raises efficacy) (Bandura, 1997; Schunk, Pintrich, & Meece, 2008; Usher & Pajares, 2009)?

In **vicarious experiences**, someone else models accomplishments. The more closely the observer identifies with the model, the greater the impact on self-efficacy will be. When the model performs well, the student's efficacy is enhanced, but when the model performs poorly, efficacy expectations decrease. Although mastery experiences generally are acknowledged as the most influential source of efficacy beliefs in adults, Keyser and Barling (1981) found that children (grade 6 students in their study) rely more on **modelling** as a source of self-efficacy information.

**Social persuasion** can be a "pep talk" or specific performance feedback. Social persuasion alone can't create enduring increases in self-efficacy, but a persuasive boost in self-efficacy can lead a student to make an effort, attempt new strategies, or try hard enough to succeed (Bandura, 1982). Social persuasion can counter occasional setbacks that might have instilled self-doubt and interrupted persistence. The potency of persuasion depends on the credibility, trustworthiness, and expertise of the persuader (Bandura, 1997). Table 11.2 summarizes the sources of self-efficacy.

## Self-Efficacy in Learning and Teaching

**Listen**
Self-Efficacy in Learning and Teaching

**STOP & THINK** On a scale from one to 100, how confident are you that you will finish reading this chapter today? •

Let's assume your sense of efficacy is around 90 for completing this chapter. Greater efficacy leads to greater effort and persistence in the face of setbacks, so even if you are interrupted in your reading, you are likely to return to the task. Nancy believes she can finish writing this section today, so she resumed work on it after her computer crashed and she had to start over on several pages.

Self-efficacy also influences motivation through goal setting. If we have a high sense of efficacy in a given area, we will set higher goals, be less afraid of failure, and find new strategies when old ones fail. If your sense of efficacy for reading this chapter is high, you are likely to set high goals for completing the chapter—maybe you will take some notes, too. If your sense of efficacy is low, however, you may avoid the reading altogether or give up easily when problems arise or you are interrupted with a better offer (Bandura, 1993, 1997; Pajares & Schunk, 2001). See the *Guidelines* for ideas about encouraging self-efficacy.

**Vicarious experiences** Accomplishments that are modelled by someone else.

**Modelling** Changes in behaviour, thinking, or emotions that happen through observing another person—a model.

**Social persuasion** A "pep talk" or specific performance feedback—one source of self-efficacy.

## GUIDELINES

### Encouraging Self-Efficacy

**Emphasize students' progress in a particular area.**
*Examples*

1. Return to earlier material in reviews and show how "easy" it is now.
2. Encourage students to improve projects when they have learned more.
3. Keep examples of particularly good work in portfolios.

**Set learning goals for your students, and model a mastery orientation for them.**
*Examples*

1. Recognize progress and improvement.
2. Share examples of how you have developed your abilities in a given area, and provide other models of achievement who are similar to your students—no supermen or superwomen whose accomplishments seem unattainable.
3. Read stories about students who overcame physical, mental, or economic challenges.
4. Don't excuse failure because a student has problems outside school. Help the student succeed inside school.

**Make specific suggestions for improvement, and revise grades when improvements are made.**
*Examples*

1. Return work with comments noting what the students did right, what they did wrong, and why they might have made the mistakes.
2. Experiment with peer editing.
3. Show students how their revised, higher grade reflects greater competence and raises their class average.

**Stress connections between past efforts and past accomplishments.**
*Examples*

1. Have individual goal-setting and goal-review conferences with students, in which you ask students to reflect on how they solved difficult problems.
2. Confront self-defeating, failure-avoiding strategies directly.

*For more information on self-efficacy,*
*see www.uky.edu/~eushe2/Pajares/self-efficacy.html.*

**Listen**
Guidelines: Encouraging
Self-Efficacy

What is the most motivating level of efficacy? Should students be accurate, optimistic, or pessimistic in their predictions? There is evidence that a higher sense of self-efficacy supports motivation, even when the efficacy is an overestimation. Children and adults who are optimistic about the future are more mentally and physically healthy, less depressed, and more motivated to achieve (Flammer, 1995; Seligman, 2006).

As you might expect, there are dangers in underestimating abilities because then students are more likely to put out a weak effort and give up easily. But there are dangers in continually overestimating performance as well. Students who think that they are better readers than they actually are may not be motivated to go back and repair misunderstandings as they read. They don't discover that they did not really understand the material until it is too late (Pintrich & Zusho, 2002).

In schools, we are particularly interested in self-efficacy for learning mathematics, writing, history, science, sports, and other subjects, as well as self-efficacy for using learning strategies and for the many other challenges that classrooms present. For example, in research with students, self-efficacy is related to writing and math performance for students from grade 3 through high school (Fast et al., 2010; Kenney-Benson, Pomerantz, Ryan, & Patrick, 2006; Pajares, 2002), life satisfaction for adolescents (Vecchio, Gerbino, Pastorelli, Del Bove, & Caprara, 2007), reported use of deep processing learning strategies for college students (Prat-Sala & Redford, 2010), choice of college major (Pajares, 2002), and performance in college for older students (Elias & MacDonald, 2007). The value of self-efficacy seems to be cross-cultural. For example, self-efficacy is related to math/science goals and interests for Mexican American youth (Navarro, Flores, & Worthington, 2007), academic achievement in math for both male and female middle-school students (Kenney-Benson, Pomerantz, Ryan, & Patrick, 2006), and mathematics achievement for both Anglo and South Asian Canadian middle-school students (Klassen, 2004).

**TEACHER SELF-EFFICACY** Research shows that teachers' sense of efficacy grows from real success with students. Experience or training that helps teachers succeed in the day-to-day tasks of teaching will contribute to their sense of efficacy.

Juice Images/Alamy

So, maybe you are thinking, sure higher self-efficacy is related to higher achievement because students who have more ability have higher self-efficacy. But these relationships between self-efficacy and achievement hold even when we take ability into account. For example, when students with the same ability in math are compared, the ones with higher self-efficacy for math perform better in math (Wigfield & Wentzel, 2007).

Research indicates that performance in school is improved and self-efficacy is increased when students (a) adopt short-term goals so it is easier to judge progress; (b) are taught to use specific learning strategies such as outlining or summarizing that help them focus attention; and (c) receive rewards based on achievement, not just engagement, because achievement rewards signal increasing competence (Graham & Weiner, 1996).

## Teachers' Sense of Efficacy

You saw in Chapter 1 that much of Anita's research has focused on **teachers' sense of efficacy**, defined as a teacher's belief that he or she can reach even difficult students to help them learn. This confident belief appears to be one of the few personal characteristics of teachers that predict student achievement (Tschannen-Moran & Woolfolk Hoy, 2001; Tschannen-Moran, Woolfolk Hoy, & Hoy, 1998; Woolfolk Hoy & Burke-Spero, 2005; Woolfolk Hoy, Hoy, & Davis, 2009). As with any kind of efficacy, there may be both benefits and dangers in overestimating abilities. Optimistic teachers probably set higher goals, work harder, reteach when necessary, and persist in the face of problems. But some benefits might follow from having doubts about your efficacy. The *Point/Counterpoint* looks at both sides of teachers' efficacy judgments.

It takes self-efficacy to be self-regulated. We turn to this issue next to explore how you can help your students lead a self-directed life.

**Teachers' sense of efficacy** A teacher's belief that he or she can reach even the most difficult students and help them learn.

## POINT/COUNTERPOINT   Are High Levels of Teacher Efficacy Beneficial?

Based on Bandura's research on self-efficacy, we probably would assume that high sense of efficacy for teachers is a good thing. But not everyone agrees. Here is the debate.

▶ **POINT   Higher efficacy is better than lower.** The research on teachers' sense of efficacy points to many positive outcomes related to higher efficacy. Anita, her husband, and a colleague summarized this research (Woolfolk Hoy, Hoy, & Davis, 2009). Here are a few of the findings. Teachers with a strong sense of efficacy tend be more enthusiastic and spend more time teaching in subject areas where their sense of efficacy is higher, and they tend to avoid subjects when efficacy is lower. Teachers with higher efficacy judgments tend to be more open to new ideas; more willing to experiment with new methods to better meet the needs of their students; more likely to use powerful but potentially difficult-to-manage methods such as inquiry and small-group work; and less likely to use easy-to-adopt but weaker methods such as lectures. Higher efficacy teachers are less likely to criticize students and more persistent in following up on incorrect student answers. Teachers with a higher sense of efficacy tend to select strategies that support student learning rather than those that simply cover the curriculum. Compared to low-efficacy teachers, those who report a higher sense of efficacy tend to be more active in monitoring seatwork and maintaining academic focus, and they respond quickly to student misbehaviour by redirecting attention without showing anger or becoming threatened. What about the students? In addition to being related to student achievement, teachers' sense of efficacy has been associated with other student outcomes such as motivation and students' own sense of efficacy.

▶ **COUNTERPOINT   There are problems with high efficacy.** In spite of the large body of literature describing positive outcomes associated with higher self-efficacy, several researchers have questioned whether higher is always better. For example, Karl Wheatley (2002, 2005) suggested that several forms of teacher self-efficacy might be problematic. One is the excessive optimism of beginning teachers that interferes with their ability to accurately judge their own effectiveness. In an analysis of students who were about to begin their student teaching, Carol Weinstein (1988) found a strong sense of "unrealistic optimism"—the tendency to believe that problems experienced by others would not happen to them. Interestingly, the unrealistic optimism was greatest for activities having to do with controlling students (e.g., maintaining discipline, establishing and enforcing class rules). These findings are consistent with Emmer and Hickman's (1991) observations that student teachers who had trouble managing their classes still reported high levels of classroom management efficacy. Another problematic consequence of higher efficacy is resistance to acquiring new knowledge and skills and a tendency to "stick with what works"—with the ways of teaching that have provided the sense of mastery in the past. Overconfident efficacy may quickly be followed by giving up if the task proves more difficult than first thought. Wheatley (2002) believes "lower efficacy beliefs are essential for teacher learning; doubt motivates change" (p. 18).

**Beyond Either/Or.** It is true that persistent high efficacy perceptions in the face of poor performance (unrealistic optimism) can produce avoidance rather than action and interfere with teacher learning, but we believe that a sense of *efficacy for learning to teach* would be necessary to respond in these positive ways to the doubts described above. The challenge is to develop an authentic sense of self-efficacy—one that is accurate or just a bit optimistic.

## SELF-REGULATED LEARNING

As you may remember from the beginning of this chapter, Albert Bandura said his early education in a tiny school in Canada had given him self-regulation skills that lasted a lifetime. He also noted,

> A major goal of formal education is to equip students with the intellectual tools, self-beliefs, and self-regulatory capabilities to educate themselves throughout their lifetime. The rapid pace of technological change and accelerated growth of knowledge are placing a premium on capability for self-directed learning. (Bandura, 2007, p. 10)

Today, people change jobs an average of seven times before they retire. Many of these career changes require new learning that must be self-initiated and self-directed (Martinez-Pons, 2002). Thus, one goal of teaching, as Bandura noted, should be to free students from the need for teachers, so the students can continue to learn independently throughout their lives. To continue learning independently throughout life, you must be self-regulated—what we refer to in conversations as a *self-starter*.

**STOP & THINK** Think about the class you are taking where you are using this text. On a seven-point scale—from 1= *not at all true of me*, to 7= *very true of me*—answer the following questions:

1. When I study for a test, I try to put together the information from class and from the text.
2. When I do homework, I try to remember what the teacher said in class so I can answer the questions correctly.
3. I know I will be able to learn the material for this class.
4. I expect to do well in this class.
5. I ask myself questions to make sure I know the material I have been studying.
6. Even when study materials are dull and uninteresting, I keep working until I finish. •

You have just answered six items from the Motivated Strategies for Learning Questionnaire (MSLQ) (Midgley et al., 1998; Pintrich & De Groot, 1990). This questionnaire has been used in hundreds of studies to assess students' perceptions of their self-regulated learning and motivation. How did you describe yourself? The first two questions reflect how you perceive you use *cognitive strategies*, like those we discussed in Chapter 9. The second two questions assess your *sense of efficacy* for this class. But the last two questions (five and six) specifically assess **self-regulation**, defined by Barry Zimmerman and Dale Schunk (2011) as the process we use to activate and sustain our thoughts, behaviours, and emotions in order to reach our goals. Bandura (2007) summarizes self-regulation as setting goals and mobilizing the efforts and resources needed to reach those goals. When the goals involve learning, we talk about *self-regulated learning* (Dinsmore, Alexander, & Loughlin, 2008). Self-regulated learners are "metacognitive, motived to learn, and strategic" (Perry & Rahim, 2011, p. 122).

Self-regulated learners have a combination of academic learning skills and self-control that makes learning more productive, so they are more motivated; in other words, they have the skill and the will to learn (Murphy & Alexander, 2000; Schunk, 2005). Self-regulated learners transform their mental abilities, whatever they are, into academic skills and strategies (Zimmerman & Schunk, 2011). Many studies link strategy use to different measures of academic achievement, especially for middle-school and high school students (Fredricks, Blumenfeld, & Paris, 2004). For younger students, self-regulation of attention and emotion are critical for learning and achieving in school (Valiente, Lemery-Chalfant, & Swanson, 2010).

## What Influences Self-Regulation?

The concept of self-regulated learning integrates much of what is known about effective learning and motivation. As you can see from the processes described above, three factors influence skill and will: knowledge, motivation, and self-discipline or volition. In addition, there are developmental differences among students.

**KNOWLEDGE.** To be productive self-regulated learners, students need knowledge about themselves, the subject, the task, strategies for learning, and the contexts in which they will apply their learning. "Expert" students know about themselves and how they learn best. For example, they know their preferred learning approaches; what is easy and what is hard for them; how to cope with the difficult parts; what their interests and talents are; and how to use their strengths. These experts also know quite a bit about the subject being studied—and the more they know, the easier it is to learn more (Alexander, Schallert, & Reynolds, 2009). They probably understand that different learning tasks require different approaches on their part. A simple memory task, for example, might require a mnemonic strategy (see Chapter 8), whereas a complex comprehension task might be approached by means of concept maps of the key ideas (see Chapter 9). Also, these self-regulated learners know that learning is often difficult and knowledge

**Self-regulation** Process of activating and sustaining thoughts, behaviours, and emotions in order to reach goals.

is seldom absolute; there usually are different ways of looking at problems as well as different solutions (Greene, Muis, & Pieschl, 2010; Winne, 1995).

These expert students not only know what each task requires but also can apply the strategy that's needed. They can skim or read carefully. They can use memory strategies or reorganize the material. As they become more knowledgeable in a field, they apply many of these strategies automatically. In short, they have mastered a large, flexible repertoire of learning strategies (see Chapter 9). Finally, self-regulated learners think about the contexts in which they will apply their knowledge—when and where they will use their learning—so they can set motivating goals and connect present work to future accomplishments (Weinstein, 1994; Winne, 1995).

MOTIVATION.   Self-regulated learners are motivated to learn (see Chapter 12). They find many tasks in school interesting because they value learning, not just performing well in the eyes of others. They believe their own intelligence and abilities are improvable. Even if they are not intrinsically motivated by a particular task, they are serious about getting the intended benefit from it. They focus their attention and other cognitive and emotional resources on the task at hand. They know why they are studying, so their actions and choices are self-determined and not controlled by others (Zimmerman, 2011). However, knowledge and motivation are not always enough. Self-regulated learners need volition or self-discipline. "Where motivation denotes commitment, volition denotes follow-through" (Corno, 1992, p. 72).

**Volition** Willpower; self-discipline; work styles that protect opportunities to reach goals by applying self-regulated learning.

**Co-regulation** A transitional phase during which students gradually appropriate self-regulated learning and skills through modelling, direct teaching, feedback, and coaching from teachers, parents, or peers.

**Shared regulation** Students working together to regulate each other through reminders, prompts, and other guidance.

VOLITION.   It is a bright winter day. Phil and Nancy's dog, Abby, is looking like she'd like to track deer on a walk in the forest, but Phil wants to keep writing because the deadline for this chapter is very near. He has knowledge and motivation, but to keep going he needs a good dose of volition. **Volition** is an old-fashioned word for willpower. The more technical definition for volition is *planning for and protecting opportunities to reach goals*. Self-regulated learners know how to protect themselves from distractions—where to study, for example, so they are not interrupted. They know how to cope when they feel anxious, drowsy, or lazy (Corno, 2011; Snow, Corno, & Jackson, 1996). And they know what to do when they are tempted to stop working.

Volition is deliberate and effortful, but with practice it can become more automatic—a habit or a "work ethic" (Corno, 2011). William James knew this over 100 years ago. One of Anita's favourite James quotes is about making volition a habit. He said, "do every day or two something for no other reason than that you would rather not do it, so that when the hour of dire need draws nigh, it may find you not unnerved and untrained to stand the test" (James, 1890, IV, p. 126).

DEVELOPMENT OF SELF-REGULATION.   There are developmental differences in self-regulation. Self-regulation generally improves over time. In the early grades, girls may be better than boys in self-regulation (Greene, Muis, & Pieschl, 2010; Matthews, Ponitz, & Morrison, 2009).

How do students develop knowledge, motivation, and volition? Two social processes support the development of self-regulation: co-regulation and shared regulation. **Co-regulation** is a transitional phase during which students gradually appropriate self-regulated learning and skills through modelling, direct teaching, feedback, and coaching from teachers, parents, or peers. **Shared regulation** happens when students work together to regulate each other through reminders, prompts, and other guidance (Hadwin, Jäevelä & Miller, 2011).

**THE SKILL AND THE WILL** Self-regulated learners have a combination of academic learning skills and self-control that makes learning easier; they have the *skill* and the *will* to learn.

What does self-regulation look like when it has developed? Let's examine some models.

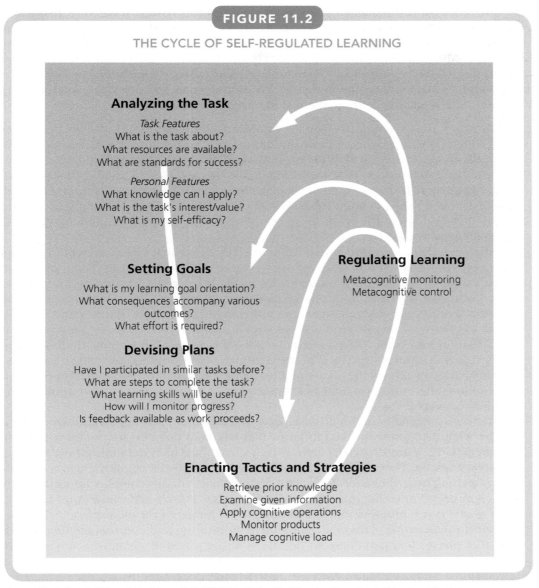

**FIGURE 11.2**

THE CYCLE OF SELF-REGULATED LEARNING

**Analyzing the Task**

*Task Features*
What is the task about?
What resources are available?
What are standards for success?

*Personal Features*
What knowledge can I apply?
What is the task's interest/value?
What is my self-efficacy?

**Setting Goals**

What is my learning goal orientation?
What consequences accompany various outcomes?
What effort is required?

**Devising Plans**

Have I participated in similar tasks before?
What are steps to complete the task?
What learning skills will be useful?
How will I monitor progress?
Is feedback available as work proceeds?

**Regulating Learning**

Metacognitive monitoring
Metacognitive control

**Enacting Tactics and Strategies**

Retrieve prior knowledge
Examine given information
Apply cognitive operations
Monitor products
Manage cognitive load

Source: Woolfolk, A. E., Winne, P. H., & Perry, N. E. (2006). The Cycle of Self-Regulated Learning. In Educational Psychology (3rd Canadian ed.), p. 307, Fig 8.9. Adapted with permission of Pearson Education Canada and Philip Winne.

## Models of Self-Regulated Learning and Agency

Albert Bandura may have gone from high-school graduate to professor in six years using his self-regulated learning knowledge and skills, but not all of your students will be Banduras with established *habits of volition*. In fact, some psychologists suggest that you think of this capacity as one of many characteristics that distinguish individuals (Snow, Corno, & Jackson, 1996). Some students are much better at it than others. How can you help more students become self-regulated learners in school? What is involved in being self-regulated?

Theoretical models of **self-regulated learning** describe how learners—like you!—set goals and mobilize the efforts and resources needed to reach those goals, making adaptation as needed to succeed. There are several models of self-regulated learning, but all agree that the cognitive processes needed for self-regulated learning require effort (Greene, Muis, & Pieschl, 2010; Puustinen & Pulkkinen, 2001; Winne, 2011). Let's look at one Phil developed with his University of Victoria colleague Allyson Hadwin (1998). It's shown in Figure 11.2. This depiction of self-regulated learning has many facets, as it should when the topic at hand is how you manage your academic life.

**Self-regulated learning** A view of learning as skills and will applied to analyzing learning tasks, setting goals and planning how to do the task, applying skills, and especially making adjustments about how learning is carried out.

The model of self-regulated learning in Figure 11.2 is based on the view that learners are *agents*. As we saw earlier, agency is the capacity to coordinate learning skills, motivation, and emotions to reach your goals. Agents are not puppets on strings held by teachers, textbook authors, or webpage designers. Instead, agents control many factors that influence how they learn. Self-regulating learners exercise agency as they engage in a cycle with four main stages: analyzing the task, setting goals and devising plans, enacting strategies, and regulating learning by making needed adjustments.

1. *Analyzing the learning task.* You are familiar with this stage of self-regulated learning. What do you do when a professor announces there will be a test? You ask about conditions you believe will influence how you'll study. Is it essay or multiple-choice? Is your best friend up to date on the material to be tested and available to study with you? In general, learners examine whatever information they think is relevant in order to construct a sense of what the task is about, what resources to bring to bear, and how they feel about the work to be done—are they interested? confident? anxious? knowledgeable? clueless?

2. *Setting goals and devising plans.* Knowing conditions that influence work on tasks provides information that learners use to create goals for learning. Then, plans can be developed about how to reach those goals. What goals for studying might you set for a quiz covering only one chapter that counts just 3% toward your course grade? Would your goals change if the test covered the last six chapters and counted 30% toward your course grade? What targets are identified in these goals—repeating definitions, being able to discuss how a teacher could apply findings from key research studies described in the textbook, or critiquing theoretical positions? Choosing goals affects the shape of a learner's plans for how to study. Is practising definitions the best approach? Is a better plan to create examples and applications of key concepts?

3. *Enacting strategies to accomplish the task.* In this phase, self-regulated learners consider what they know or need to know that will help them be successful with these strategies. They are especially alert as they enact their plan to monitor how well the plan is working. They ask themselves these questions: Is the cognitive load too great? Am I getting overwhelmed? What can I do to manage all this complex information? Is the approach I'm taking too effortful for the results I'm are achieving? Am I reaching my goals? Is my progress rate fast enough to be prepared for the test?

4. *Regulating learning.* This is metacognitive monitoring and control (see Chapter 9). In this phase, learners come to decisions about whether changes are needed in any of the three preceding phases. For example, if learning is slow, they ask these questions: Should I study with my best friend? Do I need to review some prior material that provides the foundation for the content I am now studying? Do I need to start over—identifying what the task really is and then setting new (higher, lower, different) goals?

## An Individual Example of Self-Regulated Learning

Students today are faced with constant distractions. Barry Zimmerman (2002, p. 64) describes Tracy, a high-school student who is devoted to Facebook and Twitter:

> An important mid-term math exam is two weeks away, and she had begun to study while listening to popular music "to relax her." Tracy has not set any study goals for herself—instead she simply tells herself to do as well as she can on the test. She uses no specific learning strategies for condensing and memorizing important material and does not plan out her study time, so she ends up cramming for a few hours before the test. She has only vague self-evaluative standards and cannot gauge her academic preparation accurately. Tracy attributes her learning difficulties to an inherent lack of mathematical ability and is very defensive about her poor study methods. However, she does not ask for help from others because she is afraid of "looking stupid," or seek out supplementary materials from the library because she "already has too much to learn." She finds studying to be anxiety-provoking, has little self-confidence in achieving success, and sees little intrinsic value in acquiring mathematical skill.

Clearly, Tracy is unlikely to do well on the test. What would help? For an answer, let's consider Zimmerman's cycle of self-regulated learning. His cycle has three phases—*forethought, performance, reflection*—and is consistent with the Winne and Hadwin model described above. In Zimmerman's phase 1, the *forethought phase* (like Winne and Hadwin's steps 1 and 2 of analyzing the task and setting goals), Tracy needs to set clear, reasonable goals and plan a few strategies for accomplishing those goals. And Tracy's beliefs about motivation make a difference at this point, too. If Tracy had a sense of self-efficacy for applying the strategies that she planned, if she believed that using those strategies would lead to math learning and success on the test, if she saw some connections between her own interests and the math learning, and if she were trying to master the material—not just look good or avoid looking bad—then she would be on the road to self-regulated learning.

Moving from forethought to Zimmerman's *performance phase* (similar to Phil's and Hadwin's step 3 of enacting the strategies) brings new challenges. Now Tracy must have a repertoire of self-control (volitional) and learning strategies, including using imagery, mnemonics, attention focusing, and other techniques such as those described in Chapters 8 and 9 (Kiewra, 2002). She also will need to self-observe—that is, monitor how things are going so she can change strategies if needed. Actual recording of time spent, problems solved, or pages written may provide clues about when or how to make the best use of study time. Turning off the music would help, too.

Finally, Tracy needs to move to Zimmerman's phase 3 of *reflection* (similar to Winne and Hadwin's step 4 of regulating learning) by looking back on her performance and reflecting on what happened. It will help her develop a sense of efficacy if she attributes successes to effort and good strategy use and avoids self-defeating actions and beliefs such as making weak efforts, pretending not to care, or assuming she is "no good at math."

Both Zimmerman's model and the model proposed by Phil and Allyson Hadwin emphasize the cyclical nature of self-regulated learning: Each phase flows into the next, and the cycle continues as students encounter new learning challenges. Both models begin with being informed about the task so you can set good goals. Having a repertoire of learning strategies and tactics also is necessary in both models. And self-monitoring of progress followed by modifying plans if needed are critical to both. Notice also that the way students think about the task and their ability to do it—their *sense of efficacy for self-regulation*—is key as well (Zimmerman, 2011).

## Two Classrooms

Students differ in their self-regulation knowledge and skills. But teachers must work with an entire classroom, and still "reach every student." Here are two examples of real situations where teachers did just that. The first involves writing, the second math problem solving—both complex tasks.

WRITING.    Carol is a grade 2 student described by Nancy and her colleague Lynn Drummond (2002). Lynn was Carol's teacher; she characterizes Carol as "a very weak writer." Carol has difficulty finding facts and then transforming those facts into meaningful prose for a research report. Also, she has difficulty with the mechanics of writing, which, according to Lynn, "holds her back."

Over the course of the year, Lynn involved her grade 2 and 3 students in three projects about animals. Through this writing, she wanted students to learn how to (a) do research, (b) write expository text, (c) edit and revise their writing, and (d) use the computer as a tool for researching and writing. For the first report, the class worked on one topic together (chipmunks). They did the fact-finding and writing together, because Lynn needed to show them how to do research and write a report. Also, the class developed frameworks for working collaboratively as a community of learners. When they wrote the second report (on penguins), Lynn offered students many more choices and encouraged them to depend more on themselves and one another. Finally, for the third report, students chose an animal, conducted a self-regulated research project, and wrote a report. Now that they knew how to do research and write a report, they could work alone or together and be successful at this complex task.

Carol worked with a student in grade 3 who was doing research on a related topic. He showed Carol how to use a table of contents and offered advice about how to phrase ideas in her report. Also, Carol underlined words she thought were misspelled so she could check them later when she met with Lynn to edit her report. Unlike many low-achieving students who have not learned strategies for self-regulating learning, Carol was not afraid to attempt challenging tasks, and she was confident about her ability to develop as a writer. Reflecting on her progress across the school year, Carol said, "I learned a lot from when I was in grade 1 because I had a lot of trouble then."

MATH PROBLEM SOLVING.   Lynn Fuchs and her colleagues (2003) assessed the value of incorporating self-regulated learning strategies into math problem-solving lessons in real classrooms. The researchers worked with 24 teachers. All of the teachers taught the same content in their grade 3 classes. Some of these teachers (randomly chosen) taught in their usual way. Another randomly chosen group incorporated strategies to encourage problem-solving transfer—using skills and knowledge learned in the lessons to solve problems in other situations and classes. The third group of teachers added transfer and self-regulated learning strategies to their units on math problem solving. Here are a few of the transfer and self-regulated learning strategies that were taught:

- Using a key, students scored their homework and gave it to a homework collector (a peer).
- Students graphed their completion of homework on a class report.
- Students used individual thermometer graphs that were kept in folders to chart their daily scores on individual problems.
- At the beginning of each session, students inspected their previous charts and set goals to beat their previous scores.
- Students discussed with partners how they might apply problem-solving strategies outside class.
- Before some lessons, students reported to the group about how they had applied problem-solving skills outside class.

Both transfer and self-regulated learning strategies helped students learn mathematical problem solving and apply this knowledge to new problems. The addition of self-regulated learning strategies was especially effective when students were asked to solve problems that were very different from those they encountered in the lessons. Students at every achievement level as well as students with learning disabilities benefited from learning the strategies.

## Technology and Self-Regulation

In the previous chapter, we saw some examples of using technology-rich environments to explore complex concepts. But to learn in these rich environments, students need meta-cognitive and self-regulatory skills so they won't get lost in a sea of information. If the concepts they are learning are challenging and complicated, then some scaffolding is needed to support the students' developing understandings (Azevedo, 2005; Azevedo, Johnson, Chauncey, & Graesser, 2011). For example, Roger Azevedo and his colleagues (Azevedo, Cromley, & Seibert, 2004) studied undergraduate students who were learning about the circulatory system using a hypermedia encyclopedia. The materials available to them included texts, diagrams, photographs, video clips, and animated examples of how the circulatory system works. There were three different learning conditions. One group of students was told just to learn all they could about the circulatory system. A second group got the same instructions, but, in addition, they had a list of 10 subgoals to guide their learning. The third group had the list of subgoals plus a self-regulation "coach," who helped them plan their learning, monitor their developing understanding, try different strategies, and handle problems when they arose. Students in all three conditions were asked to "think out loud" as they used the hypermedia materials—describing what they were thinking as they went through the materials. Students who had the support of a self-regulation coach who focused on task analysis, goal setting, using strategies, and monitoring progress developed more complete and complex mental models of the circulatory system.

How could you provide this kind of self-regulation teaching and coaching for your students? Maybe peer coaches would be one way, or enlisting the help of families.

## GUIDELINES — FAMILY AND COMMUNITY PARTNERSHIPS

### Supporting Self-Regulation at Home and in School

**Emphasize the value of encouragement.**
*Examples*
1. Teach students to encourage each other.
2. Tell families about the areas that are most challenging for their child—those that will be the most in need of encouragement.

**Model self-regulation.**
*Examples*
1. Target small steps for improving an academic skill. Tailor goals to the students' current achievement level.
2. Discuss with your students how you set goals and monitor progress.
3. Ask parents and caregivers to show their children how they set goals for the day or week, write to-do lists, or keep appointment books.

**Make families a source of good strategy ideas.**
*Examples*
1. Have short, simple materials describing a "strategy of the month" that students can practise at home.

2. Create a lending library of books about goal setting, motivation, learning, and time-management strategies for students.
3. Encourage families to help their children focus on problem-solving processes and not turn immediately to the answers at the back of the book when doing homework.

**Provide self-evaluation guidelines.**
*Examples*
1. Develop rubrics for self-evaluation with students (see). Model how to use them.
2. Provide record-keeping sheets for assignments early in the year; then gradually have students develop their own.
3. Encourage parents and caregivers to model self-evaluation as they focus on areas they want to improve.
4. For family conferences, have examples of materials other families have successfully used to keep track of progress.

*For more ideas to share with parents and caregivers, see www.pbs.org/wholechild/parents/building.html.*

## Reaching Every Student: Families and Self-Regulation

Children begin to learn self-regulation in their homes. Families can teach and support self-regulated learning through modelling, encouragement, facilitation, rewarding of goal setting, good strategy use, and other processes described in the next section (Martinez-Pons, 2002). The *Family and Community Partnerships Guidelines* give some ideas for helping students become more self-regulating.

## Another Approach to Self-Regulation: Cognitive Behaviour Modification

When some psychologists were studying a behaviour modification approach called *self-management*—using reinforcement and punishment to manage your own behaviour—Donald Meichenbaum, now retired from the University of Waterloo, was having success teaching impulsive students to "talk themselves through" tasks (Meichenbaum, 1977). He called his method *cognitive behaviour modification* (Manning & Payne, 1996). **Cognitive behaviour modification** focuses on self-talk and self-instruction as tools for to regulating your behaviour.

You may remember from Chapter 2 that there is a stage in cognitive development when young children seem to guide themselves through a task using private speech. Using **self-instruction**, they talk to themselves, often repeating the words of a parent or teacher. In cognitive behaviour modification, students are taught directly how to use self-instruction. Meichenbaum (1977) outlined the steps:

1. An adult model performs a task while talking to him- or herself out loud (cognitive modelling).
2. The child performs the same task under the direction of the model's instructions (overt, external guidance).
3. The child performs the task while instructing him- or herself aloud (overt, self-guidance).

**Cognitive behaviour modification** Procedures based on both behavioural and cognitive learning principles for changing your own behaviour by using self-talk and self-instruction.

**Self-instruction** Talking oneself through the steps of a task.

**SELF-REGULATION BEGINS AT HOME** Parents can teach and support self-regulated learning through modelling, encouragement, facilitation, and rewarding of goal setting in order to help children become more self-regulating.

Corbis Premium RF/Alamy

4. The child whispers the instructions to him- or herself as he/she goes through the task (faded, overt self-guidance).
5. The child performs the task while guiding his/her performance via private speech (covert self-instruction). (p. 32)

Brenda Manning and Beverly Payne (1996) list four skills that can increase student learning: listening, planning, working, and checking. How might cognitive self-instruction help students develop these skills? One possibility is to use personal booklets or class posters that prompt students to "talk to themselves" about these skills. For example, one grade 5 class designed a set of prompts for each of the four skills and posted the prompts around the classroom. The prompts for listening included "Does this make sense?" "Am I getting this?" "I need to ask a question now before I forget." "Pay attention!" "Can I do what he's saying to do?" Planning prompts were "Do I have everything together?" "Do I have my friends tuned out for right now?" "Let me get organized first." "What order will I do this in?" "I know this stuff!" Posters for these and the other two skills, working and checking, are shown in Figure 11.3. Part of the power of this process is in getting students involved in thinking about and creating their own guides and prompts. Having the discussion and posting the ideas makes students more self-aware and in control of their own learning.

Actually, cognitive behaviour modification as it is advocated by Meichenbaum and others has many more components than just teaching students to use self-instruction. Meichenbaum's methods also include dialogue and interaction between teacher and student, modelling, guided discovery, motivational strategies, feedback, careful matching of the task with the student's developmental level, and other principles of good teaching. The student is even involved in designing the program (Harris, 1990; Harris & Pressley, 1991). Given all this, it is no surprise that students seem to be able to generalize the skills developed with cognitive behaviour modification to new learning situations (Harris, Graham, & Pressley, 1992).

Today, there are entire school intervention programs based on cognitive behaviour modification. For example, the *Coping Power Program* includes training for both parents and their children, beginning in the last half of one academic year and continuing through the entire next school year. The training for students often focuses on anger and aggression.

**FIGURE 11.3**

POSTERS TO REMIND STUDENTS TO "TALK THEMSELVES THROUGH" LISTENING, PLANNING, WORKING, AND CHECKING IN SCHOOL

These four posters were designed by a grade 5 class to help them remember to use self-instruction. Some of the reminders reflect the special world of these preadolescents.

### Poster 1
**While Listening:**
1. Does this make sense?
2. Am I getting this?
3. I need to ask a question now before I forget.
4. Pay attention.
5. Can I do what he's saying to do?

### Poster 3
**While Working:**
1. Am I working fast enough?
2. Stop staring at my girlfriend and get back to work.
3. How much time is left?
4. Do I need to stop and start over?
5. This is hard for me, but I can manage.

### Poster 2
**While Planning:**
1. Do I have everything together?
2. Do I have my friends tuned out for right now?
3. Let me get organized first.
4. What order will I do this in?
5. I know this stuff!

### Poster 4
**While Checking:**
1. Did I finish everything?
2. What do I need to recheck?
3. Am I proud of this work?
4. Did I write all the words? Count them.
5. I think I finished. I organized myself. Did I daydream too much?

*Source: Manning M. L., Payne, B. D. (1994). Self-Talk for Teachers and Students: Metacognitive Strategies for Personal and Classroom Use, 1st edition. Reprinted by permission of Pearson Education, Inc., Upper Saddle River, NJ.*

Different training sessions emphasize personal goal-setting, awareness of feelings (especially anger), learning to relax and change the focus away from the angry feelings, making coping self-statements, developing organizational and study skills, seeing the perspectives of others, developing social problem-solving skills, and dealing with peer pressure by practising how to say no (Lochman & Wells, 2003). Another similar approach is *Tools for Getting Along* (Daunic, Smith, Brank, & Penfield, 2006). Both programs have been effective in helping aggressive middle-school students to "get along" with their classmates and teachers. In addition, in psychotherapy, tools based on cognitive behaviour modification have proved to be some of the most effective ways of dealing with psychological problems such as depression.

Both the *Coping Power Program* and *Tools for Getting Along* include emotional self-regulation skills. We turn to this area of self-regulation next.

## Emotional Self-Regulation

Social and emotional competences and self-regulation are critical for both academic and personal development. The Collaborative for Academic, Social, and Emotional Learning (CASEL) lists five core social and emotional skills and competencies:

- **Self-awareness**—accurately assessing your feelings, interests, values, and strengths; maintaining a well-grounded sense of self-confidence
- **Self-management**—regulating your emotions to handle stress, control impulses, and persevere in overcoming obstacles; setting and monitoring progress toward personal and academic goals; expressing emotions appropriately

- **Social awareness**—taking the perspective of and empathizing with others; recognizing and appreciating individual and group similarities and differences; recognizing and using family, school, and community resources
- **Relationship skills**—establishing and maintaining healthy and rewarding relationships based on cooperation; resisting inappropriate social pressure; preventing, managing, and resolving interpersonal conflict; seeking help when needed
- **Responsible decision-making**—making decisions based on consideration of ethical standards, safety concerns, appropriate social norms, respect for others, and likely consequences of various actions; applying decision-making skills to academic and social situations; contributing to the well-being of one's school and community (http://casel.org/why-it-matters/what-is-sel/skills-competencies)

A number of studies that followed students over several years in the United States and in Italy have found that prosocial behaviours and social competence in the early grades are related to academic achievement and popularity with peers as many as five years later (Elias & Schwab, 2006). Developing emotional self-regulation is especially important in the early years when students are learning how to learn in schools. For example, Carlos Valiente and his colleagues (Valiente, Lemery-Chalfant, & Swanson, 2010) followed almost 300 students through kindergarten to assess the relations between effortful self-control, emotionality, and academic achievement. They found that students' anger, sadness, and shyness were negatively related to achievement and that self-control was positively related to achievement, particularly for students who showed lower levels of negative emotions. So helping students develop emotional self-regulation can set them on a good path for learning in school, and probably can help them in social relations with their peers as well. How can teachers help students develop these skills? The *Guidelines* give some ideas.

## GUIDELINES

### Encouraging Emotional Self-Regulation

**Create a climate of trust in your classroom.**
*Examples*

1. Avoid listening to "tattle tale" stories about students.
2. Follow through with fair consequences.
3. Avoid unnecessary comparisons and give students opportunities to improve their work.

**Help students recognize and express their feelings.**
*Examples*

1. Provide a vocabulary of emotions and note descriptions of emotions in characters or stories.
2. Be clear and descriptive about your own emotions.
3. Encourage students to write in journals about their own feelings. Protect the privacy of these writings (see trust above).

**Help students recognize emotions in others.**
*Examples*

1. For young children, "Look at Chandra's face. How do you think she feels when you say those things?"

2. For older students, use readings, analysis of characters in literature or films, or role reversals to help them identify the emotions of others.

**Provide strategies for coping with emotions.**
*Examples*

1. Discuss or practise alternatives such as stopping to think how the other person feels, seeking help, and using anger management strategies such as self-talk or leaving the scene.
2. Model strategies for students. Talk about how you handle anger, disappointment, or anxiety.

**Help students recognize cultural differences in emotional expression.**
*Examples*

1. Have students write about or discuss how they show emotions in their family.
2. Teach students to "check it out"—ask the other people how they are feeling.

_____

*For ideas about promoting emotional competence, see http://casel.org.*

# TEACHING TOWARD SELF-EFFICACY AND SELF-REGULATED LEARNING

**STOP & THINK** How are you studying right now? What goals have you set for your reading today? What is your plan for learning, and what strategies are you using right now to learn? How did you learn those strategies? •

Most teachers agree that students need to develop skills and attitudes for independent, lifelong learning (*self-regulated learning* and a *sense of efficacy for learning*). Fortunately, there is a growing body of research that offers guidance about how to design tasks and structure classroom interactions to support students' development of and engagement in self-regulated learning (Neuman & Roskos, 1997; Perry, 1998; Sinatra & Taasoobshirazi, 2011; Stoeger & Ziegler, 2011; Wharton-McDonald, Pressley, Rankin, Mistretta, Yokoi, & Ettenberger, 1997; Zimmerman & Schunk, 2011). This research indicates that students develop academically effective forms of self-regulated learning (SRL) and a sense of efficacy for learning when teachers involve them in *complex meaningful tasks* that extend over *long periods of time*, much like the constructivist activities described in Chapter 10. Also, to develop self-regulated learning and self-efficacy for learning, students need to have some *control over their learning processes and products*—they need to make choices about what to work on, where, and with whom. They also need to have *control over the difficulty* of the task—how much to read or write, at what pace, and with what level of support. And because self-monitoring and self-evaluation are key to effective SRL and a sense of efficacy, teachers can help students develop SRL by involving them in *setting criteria* for evaluating their learning processes and products, and then giving them opportunities to *reflect* on and make judgments about their progress using those standards. It helps to work in *collaboration* with peers and seek feedback from them. As you saw earlier, this has been called *shared regulation*. Throughout the entire process, teachers must *co-regulate* the task by "providing just enough and just in time information and support to facilitate students' acquisition and application of SRL" (Perry & Rahim, 2011, p. 130). Let's examine each of these more closely.

## Complex Tasks

Teachers don't want to assign students tasks that are too difficult and that lead to frustration. This is especially true when students have learning difficulties or disabilities. In fact, research indicates that the most motivating and academically beneficial tasks for students are those that challenge, but don't overwhelm them (Rohrkemper & Corno, 1988; Turner, 1997); complex tasks need not be overly difficult for students.

The term *complex* refers to the design of tasks, not their level of difficulty. From a design point of view, tasks are complex when they address multiple goals and involve large chunks of meaning—for example, projects and thematic units. Furthermore, complex tasks extend over long periods of time, engage students in a variety of cognitive and metacognitive processes, and allow for the production of a wide range of products (Perry, VandeKamp, Mercer, & Nordby, 2002; Wharton-McDonald, Pressley, Rankin, Mistretta, Yokoi, & Ettenberger, 1997). For example, a study of Egyptian pyramids might result in the production of written reports, maps, diagrams, skits, and models.

Even more important, complex tasks provide students with information about their learning progress. These tasks require them to engage in deep, elaborative thinking and problem solving. In the process, students develop and refine their cognitive and metacognitive strategies. Furthermore, succeeding at such tasks increases students' self-efficacy and intrinsic motivation (McCaslin & Good, 1996; Turner, 1997). Rohrkemper and Corno (1988) advised teachers to design complex tasks that provide opportunities for students to modify the learning conditions in order to cope with challenging problems. Learning to cope with stressful situations and make adaptations is an important educational goal. Remember from Chapter 4 that according to Sternberg, one aspect of intelligence is choosing or adapting environments so that you can succeed.

**DEVELOPING STUDENT CONTROL** In order to develop self-regulated learning and self-efficacy for learning, students need to have some control over their learning processes and products; teachers can help by involving students in evaluating their learning processes, products, and progress.

Spencer Grant/Alamy

## Control

Teachers can share control with students by giving them choices. When students have choices (e.g., about what to produce, how to produce it, where to work, whom to work with), they are more likely to anticipate a successful outcome (increased self-efficacy) and consequently increase effort and persist when difficulty arises (Turner & Paris, 1995). Also, by involving students in making decisions, teachers invite them to take responsibility for learning by planning, setting goals, monitoring progress, and evaluating outcomes (Turner, 1997). These are qualities of highly effective, self-regulating learners.

Giving students choices creates opportunities for them to adjust the level of challenge that particular tasks present (e.g., they can choose easy or more challenging reading materials, determine the nature and amount of writing in a report, supplement writing with other expressions of learning). But what if students make poor academic choices? Highly effective, high-SRL teachers carefully consider the choices they give to students. They make sure students have the knowledge and skills they need to operate independently and make good decisions (Perry & Rahim, 2011). For example, when students are learning new skills or routines, teachers can offer choices with constraints (e.g., students must write a minimum of four sentences/paragraphs/pages, but they can choose to write more; they must demonstrate their understanding of an animal's habitat, food, and babies, but they can write, draw, or speak their knowledge).

Highly effective teachers also teach and model good decision making. For example, when students are choosing partners, teachers can ask them to consider what they need from their partner (e.g., shared interest and commitment, perhaps knowledge or skills that they need to develop). When students are making choices about how best to use their time, these teachers ask, "What can you do when you're finished? What can you do if you are waiting for my help?" Often, lists are generated and posted, so students can refer to them while they work. Finally, highly effective teachers give students feedback about the choices they make and tailor the choices they give to suit the unique characteristics of particular learners. For example, they might encourage some students to select research topics for which resources are readily available and written at a level that is accessible to the learner. Alternatively, they might encourage some students to work collaboratively versus independently to ensure they have the support and shared regulation they need to be successful.

**Watch**
Self-Evaluation

## Self-Evaluation

Evaluation practices that support SRL are nonthreatening. They are embedded in ongoing activities, emphasize process as well as products, focus on personal progress, and help students to interpret errors as opportunities for learning to occur. In these contexts, students enjoy and actually seek challenging tasks because the cost of participation is low (Paris & Ayres, 1994). Involving students in generating evaluation criteria and evaluating their own work also reduces the anxiety that often accompanies assessment by giving students a sense of control over the outcome. Students can judge their work in relation to a set of qualities both they and their teachers identify as "good" work. They can consider the effectiveness of their approaches to learning and alter their behaviours in ways that enhance it (Winne, 2011; Winne & Perry, 2000).

In high-SRL classrooms, there are both formal and informal opportunities for students to evaluate their learning. For example, one student teacher asked grades

4 and 5 students to submit reflections journals describing the games they designed with a partner or small group of collaborators for a probability and statistics unit (Perry, Phillips, & Dowler, 2004). Their journals explained their contribution to the group's process and product, and described what they learned from participating. The student teacher took these reflections into account when she evaluated the games. More informally, teachers ask students, "What have you learned about yourself as a writer today?" "What do good researchers and writers do?" "What can we do that we couldn't do before?" Questions like these, posed to individuals or embedded in class discussions, prompt students' metacognition, motivation, and strategic action—the components of SRL.

## Collaboration

The Committee on Increasing High School Students' Motivation to Learn (2004) concluded that when students can put their heads together, they are more receptive to challenging assignments—the very kind of complex task that develops self-regulation. The Committee noted:

> Collaborative work also can help students develop skills in cooperation. Furthermore, it helps create a community of learners who have responsibility for each other's learning, rather than a competitive environment, which is alienating to many students, particularly those who do not perform as well as their classmates. (p. 51)

The most effective uses of cooperative/collaborative relationships to support SRL are those that reflect a climate of community and shared problem solving (Perry & Drummond, 2002; Perry, VandeKamp, Mercer, & Nordby, 2002). In these contexts, teachers and students actually co-regulate one another's learning (McCaslin & Good, 1996), offering support, whether working alone, in pairs, or small groups. This support is instrumental to individuals' development and use of metacognition, intrinsic motivation, and strategic action (e.g., sharing ideas, comparing strategies for solving problems, identifying everyone's area of expertise). Teachers who promote SRL spend time at the start of each school year teaching routines and establishing norms of participation (e.g., how to give constructive feedback and how to interpret and respond to peers' suggestions). As you will see in Chapter 13, developing useful management and learning procedures and routines takes time at the beginning of the year, but it is time well spent. Once routines and patterns of interaction are established, students can focus on learning and teachers can attend to teaching academic skills and the curriculum.

# BRINGING IT ALL TOGETHER: THEORIES OF LEARNING

How can we make sense of the diversity in perspectives on learning we have explored for the last four chapters? We have considered behavioural, cognitive, constructivist (individual and social), and social cognitive explanations of what people learn and how they learn it. Table 11.3 presents a summary of several of these perspectives on learning.

Rather than debating the merits of each approach, consider their contributions to understanding learning and improving teaching. Don't feel that you must choose the "best" approach—there is no such thing. Chemists, biologists, and nutritionists rely on different theories to explain and improve health. Different views of learning can be used together to create productive learning environments for the diverse students you will teach. Behavioural theory helps us understand the role of cues in setting the stage for behaviours and the role of consequences and practice in encouraging or discouraging particular behaviours. But much of humans' lives and learning is more than behaviours. Language and higher-order thinking require complex information processing and memory—something the cognitive models help us understand. And what about the person as a creator and constructor of knowledge, not just a processor

TABLE 11.3 • **Four Views of Learning**

There are variations within each of these views of learning and overlaps as well, especially in constructivist views.

| | **BEHAVIOURAL** | **COGNITIVE** | **CONSTRUCTIVIST** | | **SOCIAL COGNITIVE** |
|---|---|---|---|---|---|
| | Applied Behavioural Analysis *B. F. Skinner* | Information Processing *J. Anderson* | Individual *Jean Piaget* | Social/Situated *Lev Vygotsky* | Social Cognitive Theory *Albert Bandura* |
| Knowledge | Fixed body of knowledge to acquire Stimulated from outside | Fixed body of knowledge to acquire Stimulated from outside Prior knowledge influences how information is processed | Changing body of knowledge, individually constructed in social world Built on what learner brings | Socially constructed knowledge Built on what participants contribute, construct together | Changing body of knowledge, constructed in interaction with others and the environment |
| Learning | Acquisition of facts, skills, concepts Occurs through drill, guided practice | Acquisition of facts, skills, concepts, and strategies Occurs through the effective application of strategies | Active construction, restructuring prior knowledge Occurs through multiple opportunities and diverse processes to connect to what is already known | Collaborative construction of socially defined knowledge and values Occurs through socially constructed opportunities | Active construction of knowledge based on observation, interacting in the physical and social world, and developing agency—becoming more self-regulating |
| Teaching | Transmission presentation (telling) | Transmission Guide students toward more "accurate" and complete knowledge | Challenge, guide thinking toward more complete understanding | Co-construct knowledge with students | Presenting models, demonstrating, supporting self-efficacy and self-regulation |
| Role of Teacher | Manager, supervisor Correct wrong answers | Teach and model effective strategies Correct misconceptions | Facilitator, guide Listen for student's current conceptions, ideas, thinking | Facilitator, guide Co-participant Co-construct different interpretation of knowledge; listen to socially constructed conceptions | Model, facilitator, motivator Model of self-regulated learning |
| Role of Peers | Not usually considered | Not necessary but can influence information processing | Not necessary but can stimulate thinking, raise questions | Ordinary and necessary part of process of knowledge construction | Serve as models Ordinary and necessary part of process of knowledge construction |
| Role of Student | Passive recipient of information Active listener, direction-follower | Active processor of information, strategy user Organizer and reorganizer of information Rememberer | Active construction (within mind) Active thinker, explainer, interpreter, questioner | Active co-construction with others and self Active thinker, explainer, interpreter, questioner Active social participator | Active co-construction with others and self Active thinker, explainer, interpreter, questioner Active social participator |

of information? Here, constructivist perspectives have much to offer. Finally, social cognitive theory highlights the important role of agency and self-direction. Life requires self-regulated learning.

We like to think of the four main learning theories in Table 11.3 as four pillars for teaching. Students must first understand and make sense of the material (constructivist); then, they must remember what they have understood (cognitive—information processing); then, they must practise and apply (behavioural) their new skills and understanding to make them more fluid and automatic—a permanent part of their repertoire. Finally, they must take charge of their own learning (social cognitive). Failure to attend to any part of the process results in lower-quality learning.

## ▼ SUMMARY

### Social Cognitive Theory (pp. 368–371)

**Distinguish between social learning and social cognitive theories.** Social learning theory expanded behavioural views of reinforcement and punishment. In behavioural views, reinforcement and punishment directly affect behaviour. In social learning theory, observing another person, a model, being reinforced or punished can have similar effects on the observer's behaviour. Social cognitive theory expands social learning theory to include cognitive factors such as beliefs, expectations, and perceptions of self. Current social cognitive theory is a dynamic system that explains human adaptation, learning, and motivation. The theory addresses how people develop social, emotional, cognitive, and behavioural capabilities; how people regulate their own lives; and what motivates them.

**What is triarchic reciprocal causality?** Triarchic reciprocal causality is the dynamic interplay between three kinds of influences: personal, environmental, and behavioural. Personal factors (beliefs, expectations, attitudes, and knowledge), the physical and social environment (resources, consequences of actions, other people, models and teachers, and physical settings), and behaviour (individual actions, choices, and verbal statements) all influence and are influenced by each other.

### Modelling: Learning by Observing Others (pp. 371–375)

**What is modelling?** Learning by observing others is a key element of social cognitive theory. Modelling is influenced by the developmental characteristics of the observer, the status and prestige of the model, the consequences of the model's actions as seen by the observer, the observer's expectations about performing the observed behaviours (will I be rewarded?), the links that the observers perceive between their goals and the models' behaviours (will doing what the model does get me what I want?), and the observer's self-efficacy (can I do it?).

**What kinds of outcomes can observational learning encourage?** Observational learning can lead to five possible outcomes, including directing attention, encouraging existing behaviours, changing inhibitions, teaching new behaviours and attitudes, and arousing emotions. By directing attention, we gain insight into how others do things and what objects are involved in their actions. Encouraging or fine-tuning existing behaviours can lead to the development of good habits or make

Echo3005/Shutterstock

work more efficient. Observing others also has the capacity to cue us in to others' attention, which can cause us to become more or less "self-conscious" about our behaviour; when others are doing something, it's easier for us to do the same. Young children in particular learn by watching and emulating others, but everyone can gain insight into how something is done well (or poorly) by observing someone else do it. Finally, observing can lead to the association of emotions with certain activities. If others are observed enjoying an activity, the observer may learn to enjoy the activity as well.

### Self-Efficacy and Agency (pp. 375–380)

**What is self-efficacy, and how is it different from other self-schemas?** Self-efficacy is distinct from other self-schemas in that it involves judgments of capabilities specific to a particular task. Self-concept is a more global construct that contains many perceptions about the self, including self-efficacy. Compared to self-esteem, self-efficacy is concerned with judgments of personal capabilities; self-esteem is concerned with judgments of self-worth.

**What are the sources of self-efficacy?** Four sources are mastery experiences (direct experiences), level of arousal as you face the task, vicarious experiences (accomplishments are modelled by someone else), and social persuasion (a "pep talk" or specific performance feedback).

**How does self-efficacy affect motivation?** Greater efficacy leads to greater effort, persistence in the face of setbacks, higher goals, and finding new strategies when old ones fail. If sense of efficacy is low, however, people may avoid a task altogether or give up easily when problems arise.

**What is teachers' sense of efficacy?** One of the few personal characteristics of teachers related to student achievement is a teacher's efficacy belief that he or she can reach even difficult students to help them learn. Teachers with a high sense of efficacy work harder, persist longer, and are less likely to experience burnout. Teachers' sense of efficacy is higher in schools where the other teachers and administrators have high expectations for students and where teachers receive help from their principals in solving instructional and management problems. Efficacy grows from real success with students, so any experience or training that helps you succeed in the day-to-day tasks of teaching will give you a foundation for developing a sense of efficacy in your career. There may be some benefits to lower efficacy, if this encourages teachers to pursue professional development and improvement.

### Self-Regulated Learning (pp. 380–390)

**What factors are involved in self-regulated learning?** One important goal of teaching is to prepare students for lifelong learning. To reach this goal, students must be self-regulated learners; that is, they must have a combination of the knowledge, motivation to learn, and volition that provides the skill and will to learn independently and effectively. Knowledge includes an understanding of self, subject, task, learning strategy, and contexts for application. Motivation to learn provides the commitment, and volition is the follow-through that combats distraction and protects persistence.

**What is the self-regulated learning cycle?** There are several models of self-regulated learning. Winne and Hadwin describe a four-phase model: analyzing the task, setting goals and designing plans, enacting strategies to accomplish the task, and regulating learning. Zimmerman notes three similar phases: forethought (which includes setting goals, making plans, self-efficacy, and motivation); performance (which involves self-control and self-monitoring); and reflection (which includes self-evaluation and adaptations, leading to the forethought/planning phase again).

**What are some examples of teaching students to be more self-regulating?** Self-regulating learners engage in four types of activities: analyzing the task, setting goals and designing plans, engaging in learning, and adjusting their approach to learning. Teaching students to be more self-regulating might take the form of providing opportunities to identify and analyze the task at hand. Students should ask themselves: What is the task? What is an ideal outcome of the task? Students may also benefit from goal-setting practice; they may ask: What are my short-term goals? What are my long-term goals? Learning strategies such as identifying important details and developing a big picture of material is the next step in the process. Finally, students need to reflect on whether they were successful and devise strategies for overcoming shortcomings in their self-regulation process. They may ask themselves: Where was I successful? Where do I need to improve in order to meet my goals in the future?

**What is cognitive behaviour modification?** Cognitive behaviour modification is a process in which self-talk is used to regulate behaviour. Cognitive behaviour modification may take many forms, including helping to keep students engaged in their learning or helping them deal effectively with anger and aggression. Some research has identified four skills that are particularly helpful self-talk strategies: listening, planning, working, and checking. Cognitive behaviour modification can be used with students of all ages, but helping students engage in self-talk may require more adult assistance and guidance for younger children, or those who have not had opportunities to practise good self-regulation strategies.

**What are the skills involved in emotional self-regulation?** Emotionally self-regulating individuals are aware of their own emotions and the feelings of others—realizing that inner emotions can differ from outward expressions. They can talk about and express emotions in ways that are appropriate for their cultural group. They can feel empathy for others in distress and also cope with their own distressing emotions—they can handle stress. These individuals know that relationships are defined in part by how emotions are communicated within the relationship. All these skills come together to produce a capacity for emotional self-regulation.

### Teaching Toward Self-Efficacy and Self-Regulated Learning (pp. 391–393)

**How can teachers support the development of self-efficacy and self-regulated learning?** Teachers should involve students in complex meaningful tasks that extend over long periods of time; provide them control over their learning processes and products—they need to make choices. They should involve students in setting criteria for evaluating their learning processes and products, and then give them opportunities to make judgments about their progress using those standards. Finally, teachers should encourage students to work collaboratively with and seek feedback from peers.

### Bringing It All Together: Theories of Learning (pp. 393–395)

**What is the value of the four different perspectives on learning?** The behavioural, cognitive, constructivist, and social cognitive learning theories are four pillars for teaching. Students must first understand and make sense of the material (constructivist); then, they must remember what they have understood (cognitive—information processing); then, they must practise and apply (behavioural) their new skills and understanding to make them more fluid and automatic—a permanent part of their repertoire. Finally, they must take charge of their own learning (social cognitive). Failure to attend to any part of the process results in lower-quality learning.

---

## ▼ WHAT WOULD THEY DO?

## TEACHERS' CASEBOOK: Failure to Self-Regulate

Here is how several expert teachers responded to the situation at the beginning of the chapter of the teacher with a class of disorganized students.

### JAMES HATHAWAY
Stephen Lewis Secondary School, Thornhill, ON

In order to help students learn to become more organized in general, I build organizational skills into daily lessons. For example, I post a classroom agenda, drawn up on chart paper, on one wall so that the students can refer to it on a daily basis. It includes the date, a page number for their binder, and the topic of the day. Students can update their own binders at the same time as the wall agenda is updated, and this takes only a few moments from every day. Besides keeping the class on the same "page," encouraging students to use their own binders also becomes habit forming, something that they can use in other courses.

When it comes to helping students stay on top of large projects, I break the project into smaller and more manageable parts that they complete throughout the course or over several weeks. This way the students won't be overwhelmed by the amount of work to be done; it also provides me with checkpoints to monitor student progress. In addition, if students fall behind on a smaller task, it isn't too hard for them to catch up, and they are less likely to just give up and not complete the work.

### SARAH MACNEIL, HIGH SCHOOL SOCIAL STUDIES
Park View Education Centre, Bridgewater, NS

At the high school level, students spend a lot of time travelling from classroom to classroom, which means the possibility of them losing important papers and materials is quite high. The need to stay organized is paramount. I ask students to bring a three-ring binder when they attend my class and to use dividers to indicate when we move from unit to unit. In the first few days of class, I spend a lot of time introducing students to my classroom. There are various plastic bins (labelled by class) around the room, which are used for handouts and for handing in homework. Teacher course materials are also readily visible in my classroom so students can observe how materials can be organized. They see me use the materials on a daily basis and can recognize how easy it is for me to locate certain items because they are organized. Binders are labelled by subject and topic area. Other resource materials (i.e., books) are organized by topic. I also make an effort to discuss timelines for assignment completion with my students. Together we assess what a fair timeline is and, in some cases (depending on the size of the assignment), we set up various due dates for different stages of the assignment. I also discuss my own timelines for having assignments marked and returned to students. I find this is an effective way to let students know that timelines are important for both students and teachers. Being consistent with routines for organization helps students to become more self-reliant.

Thrashem/Shutterstock

# MOTIVATION IN LEARNING AND TEACHING

▶ **TEACHERS' CASEBOOK:** Motivating Students When Resources Are Thin

It is July, and you have finally been offered a teaching position. The district wasn't your first choice, but job openings were really scarce, so you're pleased to have a job in your field. You are discovering that the teaching resources in your school are slim to none; the only materials available are some aging texts and the workbooks that go with them. Every idea you have suggested for software, simulation games, DVDs, field trips, or other more active teaching materials has been met with the same response: "There's no money in the budget for that." As you look over the texts and workbooks, you wonder how the students could be anything but bored by them. To make matters worse, the texts look pretty high level for your students. But the objectives in the workbooks are important. Besides, the provincial curriculum requires these units.

## CRITICAL THINKING

- How would you arouse student curiosity and interest about the topics and tasks in the workbooks?

- How would you establish the value of learning this material?

- How would you handle the difficulty level of the texts?

- What do you need to know about motivation to solve these problems?

- What do you need to know about your students in order to motivate them?

## OVERVIEW AND OBJECTIVES

Most educators agree that motivating students is one of the critical tasks of teaching. To learn, students must be cognitively, emotionally, and behaviourally engaged in productive class activities. We begin with the question "What is motivation?" and examine many of the answers that have been proposed, including a discussion of intrinsic and extrinsic motivation and five general theories of motivation: behavioural, humanistic, cognitive, social cognitive, and sociocultural. Next, we consider more closely several personal factors that frequently appear in discussions of motivation: needs, goal orientations, beliefs and self-perceptions, interests and curiosity, emotions, and anxiety.

How do we put all this information together in teaching? How do we create environments, situations, and relationships that encourage motivation and engagement in learning? First, we consider how the personal influences on motivation come together to support motivation to learn. Then, we examine how motivation is influenced by the academic work of the class, the value of the work, and the setting in which the work must be done. Finally, we discuss a number of strategies for developing motivation as a constant state in your classroom and as a permanent trait in your students.

By the time you have completed this chapter, you should be able to:

12.1   Define motivation, and differentiate among five theoretical explanations for learner motivation.

12.2   Explain how learners' needs influence their motivation to learn.

12.3   Describe the different kinds of goal orientations and their influences on motivation.

12.4   Discuss how students' beliefs and attributions can influence motivation.

12.5   Describe the roles of interests, curiosity, emotions, and anxiety in motivation.

12.6   Explain how teachers can influence and encourage students' motivation to learn.

---

We began examining motivation in the previous chapter when we explored students' beliefs about their capabilities—their self-efficacy. We will spend another chapter on motivation because students' motivation has a direct and powerful impact on their social interactions and academic achievement in your classroom. Students with the same abilities and prior knowledge may perform quite differently, based on their motivation (Wigfield & Wentzel, 2007). So how does that work? Let's start with a basic question.

# WHAT IS MOTIVATION?

**Motivation** is usually defined as an internal state that arouses, directs, and maintains behaviour. Psychologists studying motivation have focused on five basic questions:

1. What choices do people make about their behaviour? Why do some students, for example, focus on their homework and others watch television?
2. How long does it take to get started? Why do some students start their homework right away, while others procrastinate?
3. What is the intensity or level of involvement in the chosen activity? Once the backpack is opened, is the student engrossed and focused, or is he just going through the motions?
4. What causes someone to persist or to give up? Will a student read the entire Shakespeare assignment or just a few pages?
5. What is the person thinking and feeling while engaged in the activity? Is the student enjoying Shakespeare, feeling competent, or worrying about an upcoming test (Graham & Weiner, 1996; Pintrich, Marx, & Boyle, 1993)?

**Motivation** An internal state that arouses, directs, and maintains behaviour.

## Meeting Some Students

Many factors influence motivation and engaged learning. To get a sense of the complexity of motivation, let's step into a high-school science classroom just after the teacher has given directions for a lab activity. The student profiles are adapted from Stipek (2002).

**Hopeless Hunter** won't even start the assignment—as usual. He just keeps saying, "I don't understand," or "This is too hard." When he answers your questions correctly, he "guessed" and he "doesn't really know." Hunter spends most of his time staring into space; he is falling further and further behind.

**Safe Sienna** checks with you about every step—she wants to be perfect. You once gave her bonus points for doing an excellent colour drawing of the apparatus, and now she produces a work of art for lab every time. But Sienna won't risk getting a B. If it isn't required or on the test, Sienna isn't interested in doing the work.

**Satisfied Seth**, on the other hand, is interested in this project. In fact, he knows more than you do about it. Evidently he spends hours reading about chemistry and performing experiments. But his overall grade in your class is between B– and C because he never turns in homework. Seth is satisfied with the C he can get on tests without even trying.

**Defensive Danica** doesn't have her lab manual—again, so she has to share with another student. Then she pretends to be working, but spends most of her time making fun of the assignment or trying to get answers from other students when your back is turned. She is afraid to try because if she makes an effort and fails, she fears that everyone will know she is "dumb."

**Anxious Alexandra** is a good student in most subjects, but she freezes on science tests and "forgets" everything she knows when she has to answer questions in class. Her parents are scientists and expect her to become one, too, but her prospects for this future look dim.

---

**STOP & THINK** Each of these students has problems with at least one of the five areas of motivation: (1) choices, (2) getting started, (3) intensity, (4) persistence, or (5) thoughts and feelings. Can you diagnose the problems? The answers are on page 402. •

---

Each student presents a different motivational challenge, yet you have to figure out how to motivate and teach the entire class. In the next few pages, we will look more closely at the meaning of motivation so we can better understand these students.

## Intrinsic and Extrinsic Motivation

We all know how it feels to be motivated, to move energetically toward a goal or to work hard, even if we are bored by the task. What energizes and directs our behaviour? The explanation could be drives, basic desires, needs, incentives, fears, goals, social pressure, self-confidence, interests, curiosity, beliefs, values, expectations, and more. Some psychologists have explained motivation in terms of personal *traits* or individual characteristics. Certain people, so the theory goes, have a strong need to achieve, a fear of tests, a curiosity about mechanical objects, or an enduring interest in art, so they work hard to achieve, avoid tests, tinker endlessly in their garages, or spend hours in art galleries. Other psychologists see motivation more as a *state*, a temporary situation. If, for example, you are reading this paragraph because you have a test tomorrow, you are motivated (at least for now) by the situation. Of course, the motivation we experience at any given time usually is a combination of trait and state. You may be studying because you value learning *and* because you are preparing for a test.

A classic distinction is made between intrinsic and extrinsic motivation. **Intrinsic motivation** is the natural human tendency to seek out and conquer challenges because the activity itself is satisfying and rewarding—we do not need incentives or punishments (Anderman & Anderman, 2010; Deci & Ryan, 2002; Reiss, 2004). Satisfied Seth studies chemistry outside school simply because he loves learning about chemistry; no one makes him do it. Intrinsic motivation is associated with many positive outcomes in school such as academic achievement, creativity, reading comprehension and enjoyment, and using deep learning strategies (Corpus, McClintic-Gilbert, & Hayenga, 2009).

Intrinsic motivation Motivation associated with activities that are their own reward.

In contrast, when we do something to earn a grade, avoid punishment, please the teacher, or for some other reason that has very little to do with the task itself, we experience **extrinsic motivation**. We are not really interested in the activity for its own sake; we care only about what it will gain us. Safe Sienna works for the grade; she has little interest in the subject itself. Extrinsic motivation has been associated with negative emotions, poor academic achievement, and maladaptive learning strategies (Corpus, McClintic-Gilbert, & Hayenga, 2009).

According to psychologists who adopt the intrinsic/extrinsic concept of motivation, it is impossible to tell just by looking if a behaviour is intrinsically or extrinsically motivated. The essential difference between the two types of motivation is the student's *reason* for acting, that is, whether the **locus of causality** for the action (the location of the cause) is internal or external—inside or outside the person. Students who read or practise their backstroke or paint may be reading, swimming, or painting because they freely chose the activity based on personal interests (*internal locus of causality/intrinsic motivation*), or because someone or something else outside is influencing them (*external locus of causality/extrinsic motivation*) (Reeve, 2002; Reeve & Jang, 2006a, 2006b).

**FOR THE MEDAL ONLY?** Is this athlete motivated just by a piece of metal hanging from a ribbon, or is he also likely intrinsically motivated to achieve what he has in his sport?

As you think about your motivation, you probably realize that the dichotomy between intrinsic and extrinsic motivation is too either/or—too all-or-nothing. There are two explanations that avoid either/or thinking. One is that our activities fall along a continuum from fully self-determined (intrinsic motivation) to fully determined by outside factors (extrinsic motivation). For example, students may freely choose to work hard on activities they don't find particularly enjoyable because they know the activities are important in reaching a valued goal—such as spending hours studying educational psychology in order to become a good teacher. Is this intrinsic or extrinsic motivation? Actually, it is in between—the person is freely choosing to accept outside causes such as licensure requirements and then is trying to get the most benefit from the requirements. The person has *internalized an external cause* (Vansteenkiste, Lens, & Deci, 2006).

A second explanation is that intrinsic and extrinsic motivations are not two ends of a continuum. Instead, intrinsic and extrinsic tendencies are two independent possibilities, and, at any given time, we can be motivated by some aspects of each (Covington & Mueller, 2001). Teaching can create intrinsic motivation by connecting to students' interests and helping them develop competence. But you know this won't work all the time. Did you find fractions inherently interesting? Was your curiosity piqued by irregular verbs? If teachers count on intrinsic motivation to energize all their students all of the time, they will be disappointed. There are situations where incentives and external supports are necessary. Teachers must encourage and nurture intrinsic motivation, while making sure that extrinsic motivation supports learning (Anderman & Anderman, 2010; Brophy, 2003). To do this, they need to know about the factors that influence motivation.

## Five General Approaches to Motivation

**STOP & THINK** Why are you reading this chapter? Are you curious about motivation and interested in the topic? Or is there a test in your near future? Do you need this course to meet provincial standards for credentialing? Maybe you believe that you will do well in this class, and that belief keeps you working. Perhaps it is some combination of these reasons. What motivates you to study motivation? •

**Extrinsic motivation** Motivation created by external factors such as rewards and punishments.

**Locus of causality** The location—internal or external—of the cause of behaviour.

Motivation is a vast and complicated subject encompassing many theories. Some theories were developed by studying animals in laboratories. Others are based on research with humans in situations that used games or puzzles. Research in clinical or industrial psychology inspired additional theories as well. Our examination of the field must be selective; otherwise we would have to leave out the rest of what's in this book.

BEHAVIOURAL APPROACHES TO MOTIVATION.    According to the behavioural view, understanding student motivation begins with a careful analysis of the incentives and rewards present in the classroom. A **reward** is an attractive object or event supplied as a consequence of a particular behaviour. For example, Safe Sienna was *rewarded* with bonus points when she drew an excellent diagram. An **incentive** is an object or event that encourages or discourages behaviour. The promise of an A+ was an *incentive* to Sienna. Actually receiving the grade was a *reward*. Providing grades, stars, stickers, and other compensations for learning—or demerits for misbehaviour—is an attempt to motivate students by extrinsic means of incentives, rewards, and punishments.

HUMANISTIC APPROACHES TO MOTIVATION.    In the 1940s, proponents of humanistic psychology such as Carl Rogers argued that neither of the dominant schools of psychology, behavioural or Freudian, adequately explained why people act as they do. **Humanistic interpretations** of motivation emphasize such intrinsic sources of motivation as a person's needs for "self-actualization" (Maslow, 1968, 1970), the inborn "actualizing tendency" (Rogers & Freiberg, 1994), or the need for "self-determination" (Deci, Vallerand, Pelletier, & Ryan, 1991). So, from the humanistic perspective, to motivate means to encourage people's inner resources—their sense of competence, self-esteem, autonomy, or self-actualization. Maslow's theory and Deci and Ryan's self-determination theory, discussed later, are influential humanistic explanations of motivation.

COGNITIVE APPROACHES TO MOTIVATION.    In cognitive theories, people are viewed as naturally active and curious, searching for information to solve personally relevant problems. Thus, cognitive theorists emphasize intrinsic motivation. In many ways, cognitive theories of motivation also developed as a reaction to the behavioural views. Cognitive theorists believe that behaviour is determined by our thinking, not simply by whether we have been rewarded or punished for the behaviour in the past (Stipek, 2002). Behaviour is initiated and regulated by plans (Miller, Galanter, & Pribram, 1960), goals (Locke & Latham, 2002), schemas (Ortony, Clore, & Collins, 1988), expectations (Vroom, 1964), and attributions (Weiner, 2010). We will look at goals, expectations, and attributions later in this chapter.

SOCIAL COGNITIVE THEORIES.    Many influential social cognitive explanations of motivation can be characterized as **expectancy × value theories**. This means that motivation is seen as the result of multiplying two main forces: the individual's *expectation* of reaching a goal and the *value* of that goal to him or her. In other words, the important questions are, "If I try hard, can I succeed?" and "If I succeed, will the outcome be valuable or rewarding to me?" Motivation is a product of these two factors because, if either

**Reward** An attractive object or event supplied as a consequence of a behaviour.

**Incentive** An object or event that encourages or discourages behaviour.

**Humanistic interpretation** Approach to motivation that emphasizes personal freedom, choice, self-determination, and striving for personal growth.

**Expectancy × value theories** Explanations of motivation that emphasize individuals' expectations for success combined with their valuing of the goal.

**STOP & THINK ANSWERS** Hopeless Hunter has trouble with getting started (2) and with a sense of despair (5); during the activity he feels defeated and helpless. Safe Sienna makes good choices (1), gets started right away (2), and persists (4). But she is not really engaged and takes little pleasure in the work (4 and 5). As long as he is following his own choices (1), Satisfied Seth is prompt in getting started (2), engaged (3), persistent (4), and enjoys the task (5). Defensive Danica makes poor choices (1), procrastinates (2), avoids engagement (3), and gives up easily (4) because she is so concerned about how others will judge her (5). Anxious Alexandra's problems have to do with what she thinks and how she feels as she works (5). Her worry and anxiety may lead her to make poor choices (1) and procrastinate (2), which only makes her more anxious at test time. •

factor is zero, then there is no motivation to work toward the goal. For example, if I believe I have a good chance of making the basketball team (high expectation), and if making the team is very important to me (high value), then my motivation should be strong. But if either factor is zero (I believe I haven't a prayer of making the team, or I couldn't care less about playing basketball), then my motivation will be zero, too (Tollefson, 2000).

Jacqueline Eccles and Allan Wigfield add the element of *cost* to the expectancy × value equation. Values have to be considered in relation to the cost of pursuing them. How much energy will be required? What could I be doing instead? What are the risks if I fail? Will I look stupid (Eccles, 2009; Eccles & Wigfield, 2002)?

SOCIOCULTURAL CONCEPTIONS OF MOTIVATION.    Finish this sentence: "I am a/an _____." What is your identity? With which groups do you identify most strongly? **Sociocultural views of motivation** emphasize participation in communities of practice where people engage in activities to establish their identities and their interpersonal relations within the community. Thus, students are motivated to learn if they are members of a classroom or school community that values learning. Just as we learn through socialization to speak or dress or order food in restaurants—by watching and learning from more capable members of the culture—we also learn to be students by watching and learning from members of our school community. In other words, we learn by the company we keep (Eccles, 2009; Hickey, 2003; Rogoff, Turkanis, & Bartlett, 2001). When we see ourselves as soccer players, or sculptors, or engineers, or teachers, or psychologists, we are claiming an identity within a group. In building an identity in the group, we move from legitimate peripheral participation to central participation. **Legitimate peripheral participation** means that beginners are genuinely involved in the work of the group, even if their abilities are undeveloped and their contributions are small. The novice weaver learns to dye wool before spinning and weaving, and the novice teacher learns to tutor one child before working with the whole group. Each task is a piece of the real work of the expert. The identities of both the novice and the expert are bound up in their participation in the community. Each is motivated to learn the values and practices of the community to keep their identity as community members (Lave & Wenger, 1991; Wenger, 1998).

The behavioural, humanistic, cognitive, social cognitive, and sociocultural approaches to motivation are summarized in Table 12.1. These theories differ in their answers to the question, "What is motivation?" but each contributes in its own way toward a comprehensive understanding.

To organize the many ideas about motivation in a way that is useful for teaching, let's examine four broad areas. Most contemporary explanations of motivation include a discussion of needs, goals, beliefs, and, finally, the emotional "hot" side of motivation—interests, curiosity, emotions, and anxiety (Murphy & Alexander, 2000).

**Sociocultural views of motivation** Perspectives that emphasize participation, identities, and interpersonal relations within communities of practice.

**Legitimate peripheral participation** Genuine involvement in the work of the group, even if your abilities are undeveloped and contributions are small.

TABLE 12.1 • **Five Views of Motivation**

|  | BEHAVIOURAL | HUMANISTIC | COGNITIVE | SOCIAL COGNITIVE | SOCIOCULTURAL |
|---|---|---|---|---|---|
| Source of Motivation | Extrinsic | Intrinsic | Intrinsic | Intrinsic and Extrinsic | Intrinsic |
| Important Influences | Reinforcers, rewards, incentives, and punishers | Need for self-esteem, self-fulfillment, and self-determination | Beliefs, attributions for success and failure, expectations | Goals, expectations, intentions, self-efficacy | Engaged participation in learning communities; maintaining identity through participation in activities of group |
| Key Theorists | Skinner | Maslow Deci | Weiner Graham | Locke & Latham Bandura | Lave Wenger |

# NEEDS

Early research in psychology conceived of motivation in terms of trait-like needs or consistent personal characteristics. Three of the main needs studied extensively in this earlier work were the needs for *achievement, power*, and *affiliation* (Pintrich, 2003). Abraham Maslow's influential theory emphasized a hierarchy that included all these needs and more.

**Watch**
Maslow's Hierarchy
of Needs

## Maslow's Hierarchy of Needs

Maslow (1970) suggested that humans have a **hierarchy of needs** ranging from lower-level needs for survival and safety that we focus on first to higher-level needs for intellectual achievement and finally self-actualization that we address once lower-level needs are satisfied. **Self-actualization** is Maslow's term for self-fulfillment, the realization of personal potential. Each of the lower needs must be met before the next higher need can be addressed.

Maslow (1968) considered the four lower-level needs—for survival, then safety, followed by belonging, and then self-esteem—**deficiency needs**. When these needs are satisfied, the motivation for fulfilling them decreases. He described the three higher-level needs—intellectual achievement, then aesthetic appreciation, and finally self-actualization—**being needs**. When they are met, a person's motivation does not cease; instead, it increases to seek further fulfillment. Unlike the deficiency needs, these being needs can never be completely filled. For example, the more successful you are in your efforts to develop as a teacher, the harder you are likely to strive for even greater improvement.

Maslow's theory has been criticized for the very obvious reason that people do not always appear to behave as the theory would predict. Most of us move back and forth among different types of needs and may even be motivated by many needs at the same time. Some people deny themselves safety or friendship to achieve knowledge, understanding, or greater self-esteem.

Criticisms aside, Maslow's theory does give us a way of looking at the whole student, whose physical, emotional, and intellectual needs are all interrelated. A child whose feelings of safety and sense of belonging are threatened by his parents' divorce may have little interest in learning how to divide fractions. If school is a fearful, unpredictable place where neither teachers nor students know where they stand, both are likely to be more concerned with security and less with teaching and learning, respectively. Belonging to a social group and maintaining self-esteem within that group, for example, are important to students. If doing what the teacher says conflicts with group rules, students may choose to ignore the teacher's wishes or even defy the teacher.

Self-determination theory is a more recent approach to motivation that focuses on human needs (Deci & Ryan, 2002; Reeve, 2009).

## Self-Determination: Need for Competence, Autonomy, and Relatedness

Self-determination theory suggests that we all need to feel competent and capable, to have some choices and a sense of control over our lives, and to be connected to others—to belong to a social group. Notice that these are similar to earlier conceptions of basic needs: *competence* (achievement), *autonomy and control* (power), and *relatedness* (affiliation). Because different cultures have divergent conceptions of self, some psychologists have asked whether the needs for competence, autonomy, and relatedness are universal. In a series of studies, Hyungshim Jang and her colleagues (Jang, Reeve, Ryan, Kim, 2009) found that experiences of competence, autonomy, and relatedness were associated with satisfying learning experiences for Korean high school students, so even in a collectivistic culture, these needs may be important.

**Need for autonomy** is central to self-determination because it is the desire to have our wishes, rather than external rewards or pressures, determine our actions (Deci & Ryan, 2002; Reeve, 2009; Reeve, Deci, & Ryan, 2004). People strive to have authority in their lives, to be in charge of their behaviour. They constantly struggle against pressure

**Hierarchy of needs** Maslow's model of seven levels of human needs, from basic physiological requirements to the need for self-actualization.

**Self-actualization** Fulfilling one's potential.

**Deficiency needs** Maslow's four lower-level needs, which must be satisfied first.

**Being needs** Maslow's three higher-level needs, sometimes called *growth needs*.

**Need for autonomy** The desire to have our own wishes, rather than external rewards or pressures, determine our actions.

from external controls such as the rules, schedules, deadlines, orders, and limits imposed by others. Sometimes, even help is rejected so the individual can remain in command (deCharms, 1983).

SELF-DETERMINATION IN THE CLASSROOM. Classroom environments that support student self-determination and autonomy are associated with greater student interest and curiosity (even interest in homework assignments!), sense of competence, creativity, conceptual learning, grades, school attendance and satisfaction, engagement, use of self-regulated learning strategies, psychological well-being, and preference for challenge. These relationships appear to hold from grade 1 through graduate school (Jang, Reeve, & Deci, 2010; Moller, Deci, & Ryan, 2006; Reeve, 2009; Shih, 2008). When students have the authority to make choices, they are more likely to believe schoolwork is important, even if it is not "fun." Thus, they tend to internalize educational goals and take them as their own.

**SELF-DETERMINED STUDENTS** Classroom environments that support student self-determination and autonomy are associated with greater student interest and curiosity, sense of competence, creativity, conceptual learning, and preference for challenge.

In contrast to autonomy-supporting classrooms, controlling environments tend to improve performance only on simple, low-level tasks. When students are pressured to perform, they often seek the quickest, easiest solution. But even though controlling styles of teaching are less effective, teachers are under pressure from administrators, accountability requirements, and cultural expectations to be "in charge," along with parents' expectations for class "discipline." In addition, students often are passive and unengaged or even defiant. Finally, some teachers equate control with useful structure or feel more comfortable with a controlling style (Reeve, 2009). Assuming you are willing to resist those pressures, how can you support student autonomy? One answer is to focus on information, not control, in your interactions with students.

INFORMATION AND CONTROL. **Cognitive evaluation theory** (Deci & Ryan, 2002) explains how students' experiences such as being praised or criticized, reminded of deadlines, assigned grades, given choices, or lectured about rules can influence their intrinsic motivation by affecting their sense of self-determination and competence. According to this theory, all events have two aspects: *controlling* and *informational*. If an event is highly controlling—that is, if it pressures students to act or feel a certain way—then students will experience less control and their intrinsic motivation will be diminished. If, on the other hand, the event provides information that increases the students' sense of competence, then intrinsic motivation will increase. Of course, if the information provided makes students feel less competent, it is likely that motivation will decrease (Pintrich, 2003). Here is an example of a more *controlling* communication:

> Your paper is due on Monday. Today, we are going to the school library. In the library, you will find information from books and internet sites to use for your paper. Don't waste your time; don't goof off; make sure to get your work done. In the library, you may work by yourself or with a partner. (Reeve, 2009, p. 169)

This teacher may believe he is supporting autonomy because he offered a *choice*. Contrast his message with the following statement that gives *information* about why the library visit is valuable:

> Your paper is due on Monday. As a way of helping you write a well-researched paper, we are going to where the information is—the school library. The reason we are going to the library is to find the information you need from books and internet sites. While there, you may be tempted to goof off, but students in the past have found that a trip to the library was a crucial part of writing an excellent paper. To help you write your best possible paper, you may work in the way you wish—by yourself or with a partner. (Reeve, 2009, p. 169)

**Cognitive evaluation theory** Suggests that events affect motivation through the individual's perception of the events as controlling behaviour or providing information.

Michelle D. Bridwell/PhotoEdit

## GUIDELINES

### Supporting Self-Determination and Autonomy

**Allow and encourage students to make choices.**
*Examples*

1. Design several different ways to meet a learning objective (e.g., a paper, a collection of interviews, a test, a news broadcast), and let students choose one. Encourage them to explain the reasons for their choice.
2. Appoint student committees to make suggestions about streamlining procedures such as caring for class pets or distributing equipment.
3. Provide time for independent and extended projects.
4. Allow students to choose work partners as long as they focus on the task.

**Help students plan actions to accomplish self-selected goals.**
*Examples*

1. Experiment with using goal cards. Students list their short- and long-term goals and then record three or four specific actions that will move them toward those goals. Goal cards are personal—like credit cards.
2. Encourage middle and high school students to set goals in each subject area, record them in a goal book or on a computer thumb drive, and check progress toward the goals on a regular basis.

**Hold students accountable for the consequences of their choices.**
*Examples*

1. If students choose to work with friends and do not finish a project because too much time was spent socializing, grade the project as it deserves and help the students see the connection between lost time and poor performance.

2. When students choose a topic that captures their imagination, discuss connections between their investment in the work and the quality of the products that follow.

**Provide rationales for limits, rules, and constraints.**
*Examples*

1. Explain reasons for rules.
2. Respect rules and constraints in your own behaviour.

**Acknowledge that negative emotions are valid reactions to teacher control.**
*Examples*

1. Explain that it is okay (and normal) to feel bored waiting for a turn, for example.
2. Communicate that sometimes important learning involves frustration, confusion, and weariness.
3. Acknowledge students' perspective: "Yes, this problem is difficult," or "I can understand why you might feel that way."

**Use noncontrolling, positive feedback.**
*Examples*

1. See poor performance or behaviour as a problem to be solved, not a target of criticism.
2. Avoid controlling language, such as "should," "must," "have to."

_____

*For more information on self-determination theory see www.psych.rochester.edu/SDT.*

*Source: From Raffini, J. P. (1996). 150 Ways to Increase Intrinsic Motivation in the Classroom. Allyn and Bacon: Boston, MA. © Pearson Education; Reeve, J. (1996). Motivating Others: Nurturing Inner Motivational Resources. Allyn and Bacon: Boston, MA. © 1996 Pearson Education. Adapted by permission of the publisher.*

As a teacher, what can you do to support student needs for autonomy and competence? An obvious first step is to limit your controlling messages to students because controlling language (*must, ought, have* to, *should* ...) can undermine student motivation (Vansteenkiste, Simons, Lens, Sheldon, & Deci, 2004). Make sure the information you provide highlights students' growing competence. The *Guidelines* provide some suggestions for ways you can support autonomy and self-determination in your classroom.

THE NEED FOR RELATEDNESS.   The need for relatedness is the desire to establish close emotional bonds and attachments with others. When teachers and parents are responsive and demonstrate that they care about the children's interests and well-being, the children show high intrinsic motivation. Students who feel a sense of relatedness to teachers, parents, and peers are more emotionally engaged in school (Furrer & Skinner, 2003).

All students need caring teachers, but students at risk for failure have an even greater need for this good care. Positive relationships with teachers increase the likelihood that students will succeed in high school and go on to pursue post-secondary education (Stipek, 2006; Thompson, 2008; Woolfolk Hoy & Weinstein, 2006). In addition, emotional and physical problems—ranging from eating disorders to suicide—are more common among individuals who lack social relationships (Baumeister & Leary, 1995). Relatedness is similar to a sense of belonging, discussed in Chapter 3 (Osterman, 2000).

## Needs: Lessons for Teachers

From infancy to old age, people want to be competent, connected, and in control. Students are more likely to participate in activities that help them grow more competent. They are less likely to engage in activities that hold the possibility of failure. This means your students need appropriately challenging tasks—not too easy, but not impossible either. They also benefit from watching their competence grow, perhaps through self-monitoring systems or portfolios. To be connected, students need to feel that people in school care about them and can be trusted to help them learn.

What else matters in motivation? Many theories include goals as key elements.

# GOAL ORIENTATIONS

A **goal** is an outcome or attainment an individual is striving to accomplish (Locke & Latham, 2002). When students strive to read a chapter or make the top GPA, they are involved in goal-directed behaviour. In pursuing goals, students are generally aware of some current condition (I haven't even opened my textbook), some ideal condition (I have understood every page), and the discrepancy between the two. Goals motivate people to reduce the discrepancy between "where they are" and "where they want to be." Goal setting is usually effective for Phil. In addition to the routine tasks, such as eating lunch, which will happen without much attention, he often sets goals for each day. For example, today he intends to finish this section, reserve a bike for spin class, edit his notes for tomorrow's class, and wash a load of clothes (we know—not too exciting). Having decided to do these things, he will feel uncomfortable if he doesn't complete the list.

According to Gary Locke at the University of Toronto and his colleague Edwin Latham (Locke & Latham, 2002), there are four main reasons why goal setting improves performance. Goals:

1. Direct attention to the task at hand and away from distractions. Every time Phil's mind wanders from this chapter, his goal of finishing the section helps direct attention back to the writing.
2. Energize effort. The more challenging the goal, to a point, the greater the effort.
3. Increase persistence. When we have a clear goal, we are less likely to give up until we reach the goal: Hard goals demand effort and tight (but reasonable) deadlines lead to faster work.
4. Promote the development of new knowledge and strategies when old strategies fall short. For example, if your goal is making an A and you don't reach that goal on your first quiz, you might try a new study approach for the next quiz, such as explaining the key points to a friend.

## Types of Goals and Goal Orientations

The types of goals we set influence the amount of motivation we have to reach them. Goals that are *specific, elaborated, moderately difficult*, and *likely to be reached* in the near future tend to enhance motivation and persistence (Schunk, Pintrich, & Meece, 2008; Stipek, 2002).

*Specific, elaborated* goals provide clear standards for judging performance. If performance falls short, we keep going. For example, Ralph Ferretti and his colleagues (Ferretti, Lewis, Andrews-Weckerly, 2009) gave grades 4 and 6 students either a general goal for writing a persuasive essay ("write a letter to a teacher about whether or not students should be given more out-of-class assignments . . . ") or the general goal elaborated with specific subgoals such as:

- You need to say very clearly what your opinion or viewpoint is.
- You need to think of two or more reasons to back up your opinion.
- You need to explain why those reasons are good reasons for your opinion. (p. 580)

**Goal** What an individual strives to accomplish.

David Mager/Pearson Learning Photo Studio

**"MEASURING UP" ISN'T THE POINT** When students set mastery goals, the quality of their engagement in the task is higher—they are more invested. They are less worried about how their performance compares to that of others in the class.

Both students with and without learning disabilities wrote more persuasive essays when they were given specific subgoals.

*Moderate difficulty* provides a challenge, but not an unreasonable one. Finally, goals that can be reached *fairly soon* are not likely to be pushed aside by more immediate concerns. Groups such as Alcoholics Anonymous show they are aware of the motivating value of short-term goals when they encourage their members to stop drinking "one day at a time."

**STOP & THINK** On a scale from 1 (Strongly Agree) to 5 (Strongly Disagree), how would you answer these questions:

I feel really pleased in school when

___ I solve problems by working hard.
___ I know more than the others.
___ I don't have to work hard.
___ I keep busy.
___ I finish first.
___ All the work is easy.
___ I learn something new.
___ I am the only one who gets an A.
___ I am with my friends. •

**FOUR ACHIEVEMENT GOAL ORIENTATIONS IN SCHOOL.** Goals are specific targets. **Goal orientations** describe the reasons we pursue goals and the standards we use to evaluate progress toward those goals. For example, your target might be to make an A in this course. Are you doing so in order to *master* educational psychology—to learn all about it, or to *perform*—to look good in the eyes of your friends and family? There are four main goal orientations— mastery (learning), performance (looking good), work-avoidance, and social (Schunk, Pintrich, & Meece, 2008). In the *Stop & Think* exercise you just completed, can you tell which goal orientations are reflected in the different answers? Most of the questions were adapted from a study on students' theories about learning mathematics (Nicholls, Cobb, Wood, Yackel, & Patashnick, 1990).

The most common distinction in research on students' goals is between mastery goals (also called *task goals* or *learning goals*) and performance goals (also called *ability goals* or *ego goals*). The standard of a **mastery goal** is to improve, to learn, no matter how awkward you appear. When students set mastery goals, their engagement in the task is higher—they are more invested. Students with mastery goals tend to seek challenges, persist when they encounter difficulties, and feel better about their work (Midgley, 2001). They focus on the task at hand and are not worried about how their performance "measures up" compared to others in the class. We often say that these students "get lost in their work." In addition, they are more likely to seek appropriate help, use more elaborate cognitive processing strategies, and generally approach academic tasks with confidence (Anderman & Patrick, 2012; Kaplan & Maehr, 2007).

The second kind of goal is a performance goal. Standards for students with **performance goals** are about demonstrating their ability to others. These students may be focused on getting good test scores and grades, or they may be more concerned with winning and outperforming other students. Students whose goal is outperforming others may do things to look smart, such as reading easy books in order to "read the most books." Evaluations of their performance by others, not what they learn, is what matters. Students with performance goals may act in ways that actually interfere with learning. For example, they may cheat or use short-cuts to get finished, work hard only on graded assignments, be upset and hide papers with low grades, choose tasks that are

**Goal orientations** Patterns of beliefs about goals related to achievement in school.

**Mastery goal** A personal intention to improve abilities and learn, no matter how performance suffers.

**Performance goal** A personal intention to seem competent or perform well in the eyes of others.

easy, and be very uncomfortable with assignments that have unclear evaluation criteria (Anderman & Anderman, 2010; Stipek, 2002).

WAIT—ARE PERFORMANCE GOALS ALWAYS BAD? Performance goals sound pretty dysfunctional, don't they? Earlier research indicated that performance goals generally were detrimental to learning, but like extrinsic motivation, a performance goal orientation may not be all bad, all of the time. In fact, some research indicates that both mastery and performance goals are associated with using active learning strategies and high self-efficacy (Midgley, Kaplan, & Middleton, 2001; Stipek, 2002). For college students, pursuing performance goals has been related to higher achievement. And, as is the case with intrinsic and extrinsic motivation, students can, and often do, pursue mastery and performance goals at the same time (Anderman & Patrick, 2012).

To account for these recent findings, educational psychologists have added the distinction of approach/avoidance to the mastery/performance distinction. In other words, students may be motivated to either approach mastery or avoid misunderstanding. They may approach performance or avoid looking incompetent. Table 12.2 shows examples and the effects of each kind of goal orientation. Where do you see the most problems? Do you agree that the real problems are with avoidance? Students who fear they may misunderstand (mastery avoid) may be perfectionist—focused on getting it exactly right. Students who avoid looking dumb (performance avoid) may adopt defensive, failure-avoiding strategies like Defensive Danica described earlier—they pretend not to care, make a show of "not really trying," or cheat (Harackiewiz, Barron, Pintrich, Elliot, & Thrash, 2002; Harackiewiz & Linnenbrink, 2005).

One final caution—performance approach goals can turn into performance avoidance goals if students are not successful in looking smart or winning. The path might lead from performance approach (trying to win), to performance avoidance (saving face and trying not to look dumb), to learned helplessness (I give up!). So wise teachers avoid trying to motivate using competition and social comparisons (Brophy, 2005).

BEYOND MASTERY AND PERFORMANCE. Some students don't want to learn, look smart, or avoid looking dumb; they just want to finish fast or avoid work altogether. These students try to complete assignments and activities as quickly as possible without exerting much effort (Schunk, Pintrich, & Meece, 2008). John Nicholls called these students **work-avoidant learners**—they feel successful when they don't have to try hard, when the work is easy, or when they can "goof off" (Nicholls & Miller, 1984).

**Work-avoidant learners** Students who don't want to learn or to look smart, but just want to avoid work.

TABLE 12.2 • **Goal Orientations**

Students may have either an approach or an avoidance focus for mastery and performance goal orientations.

| GOAL ORIENTATION | APPROACH FOCUS | AVOIDANCE FOCUS |
| --- | --- | --- |
| Mastery | *Focus:* Mastering the task, learning, understanding<br><br>*Standards Used:* Self-improvement, progress, deep understanding (task-involved) | *Focus:* Avoiding misunderstanding or not mastering the task<br><br>*Standards Used:* Just don't be wrong; perfectionists don't make mistakes |
| Performance | *Focus:* Being superior, winning, being the best<br><br>*Standards Used:* Normative—getting the highest grade, winning the competition (ego-involved goal) | *Focus:* Avoiding looking stupid, avoiding losing<br><br>*Standards Used:* Normative—don't be the worst, get the lowest grade, or be the slowest (ego-involved goal) |

*Source: From Pintrich, P. R., & Schunk, D. H. (2002). Motivation in Education: Theory, Research and Applications, 2nd edition. Allyn and Bacon: Boston, MA. © 2002 Pearson Education. Adapted by permission of the publisher.*

A final category of goals becomes more important as students get older—**social goals**. Social goals include a wide variety of needs and motives that have different relationships to learning. As students move into adolescence, their social networks change to include more peers. Nonacademic activities such as athletics, dating, and "hanging out" compete with schoolwork. Some social goals help, but others hinder learning. For example, adolescents' goal of maintaining friendships can get in the way of learning when cooperative learning group members don't challenge wrong answers or misconceptions because they are afraid to hurt each other's feelings (Anderson, Holland, & Palincsar, 1997). Certainly, pursuing social goals such as having fun with friends or avoiding being labelled a "nerd" can get in the way of learning. But the goal of bringing honour to your family or team by working hard or being part of a peer group that values academics certainly can support learning (Pintrich, 2003; A. Ryan, 2001; Urdan & Maehr, 1995).

We talk about goals in separate categories, but students can and do pursue several goals at once (Bong, 2009; Darnon, Dompnier, Gillieron, & Butera, 2010). They have to coordinate their goals so they can make decisions about what to do and how to act. What if social and academic goals are incompatible? For example, if students do not see a connection between achievement in school and success in life, particularly because discrimination prevents them from succeeding, then they are not likely to set academic achievement as a goal. Such anti-academic peer groups probably exist in every high school (Committee on Increasing High School Students' Engagement and Motivation to Learn, 2004; Wentzel, 1999). Sometimes, succeeding in the peer group means not achieving in school—and succeeding in the peer group is important. The need for social relationships is basic and strong for most people.

GOALS IN SOCIAL CONTEXT.    You have seen in other chapters that current thinking in educational psychology puts people in context. Goal orientation theory is no exception. The people in the situation socially construct the meaning of an activity, such as an assignment in a biology class. Goals set for the activity will reflect the participants' understanding of "what they are doing." So, in a highly competitive classroom climate, students might be more likely to adopt performance goals. In contrast, in a supportive, learner-centred classroom, even a student with a lower sense of self-efficacy might be encouraged to aim for higher mastery goals. Goals are constructed as part of the triadic reciprocal interaction of person, environment, and behaviour described by social cognitive theory—"interlocking perceptions of 'meaning,' 'purpose,' and 'self' in guiding and framing action, thought and emotion" (Kaplan & Maehr, 2007).

The way students perceive their class defines the *classroom goal structure*—the goals that students think are emphasized in the class (Murayama & Elliot, 2009). Lisa Fast and her colleagues (Fast, Lewis, Bryant, Bocian, Cardullo, Rettig, & Hammond, 2010) found that grades 4 through 6 students had significantly higher levels of self-efficacy and mathematics achievement when they perceived their math classes as caring, challenging, and mastery oriented. So challenge, support, and focusing on learning more than emphasizing not looking good seem to create a positive classroom environment.

## Feedback, Goal Framing, and Goal Acceptance

Besides having specific goals and creating supportive social relationships, three additional factors make goal setting in the classroom effective. The first is *feedback*. To be motivated by a discrepancy between "where you are" and "where you want to be," you must have an accurate sense of both your current status and how far you have to go. There is evidence that feedback emphasizing progress is the most effective. In one study, feedback to adults emphasized either that they had accomplished 75% of the standards set or that they had fallen short of the standards by 25%. When the feedback highlighted accomplishment, the subjects' self-confidence, analytic thinking, and performance were all enhanced (Bandura, 1997).

The second factor affecting motivation to pursue a goal is *goal framing*. Activities or assignments can be explained or framed as contributing to students' intrinsic goals, such as growing competence, self-determination, positive relationships with friends or

**Social goals** A wide variety of needs and motives to be connected to others or part of a group.

teachers, or well-being. The alternative is portraying activities as helping students reach extrinsic goals such as working for a grade, meeting requirements, getting ready for classes next year, and so on. When activities are linked to students' intrinsic goals of becoming more competent, self-directed, and connected with others, then the students process information more deeply and persist longer to gain a conceptual (not superficial) understanding. Linking activities to the extrinsic goals of meeting someone else's standards promotes rote learning, but not deep understanding or persistence (Vansteenkiste, Lens, & Deci, 2006).

The third factor is *goal acceptance*. Commitment matters: The relationship between higher goals and better performance is strongest when people are committed to the goals (Locke & Latham, 2002). If students reject goals set by others or refuse to set their own goals, then their motivation will suffer. Generally, students are more willing to commit to the goals of others if the goals seem realistic, reasonably difficult, and meaningful—and if the goals are validated by connecting activities to students' intrinsic interests (Grolnick, Gurland, Jacob, & Decourcey, 2002).

## Goals: Lessons for Teachers

Students are more likely to work toward goals that are clear, specific, reasonable, moderately challenging, and attainable within a relatively short period of time. If teachers focus on student performance, high grades, and competition, they may encourage students to set performance goals. This could undermine the students' ability to learn and become task-involved and set them on a path toward alienation from learning in school and learned helplessness (Anderman & Maehr, 1994; Brophy, 2005). Students may not yet be expert at setting their own goals or keeping these goals in mind, so encouragement and accurate feedback are necessary. If you use any reward or incentive systems, be sure the goal you set is to learn and improve in some area, not just to perform well or look smart. And be sure the goal is not too difficult. Students, like adults, are unlikely to stick with tasks or respond well to teachers who make them feel insecure or incompetent. This leads to our next topic—the power of beliefs in motivation.

# BELIEFS AND SELF-PERCEPTIONS

Thus far, we have talked about needs and goals, but yet another factor must be considered in explaining motivation. What do students believe about learning and about themselves—their competence and the causes for success or failure? Let's start with a basic question—What do they believe about knowing?

## Beliefs About Knowing: Epistemological Beliefs

What students believe about knowledge and learning makes up their **epistemological beliefs**. Epistemological beliefs influence students' motivation and the kinds of strategies they use.

---

**STOP & THINK** How would you answer these questions taken from Chan and Sachs (2001)?
1. Which of the following is the most important thing in learning math? (a) Remember what the teacher has taught you, (b) practise lots of problems, (c) understand the problems you work on.
2. Which of the following is the important thing to do in learning science? (a) Faithfully do the work the teacher tells you, (b) try to see how the explanation makes sense, (c) try to remember everything you are supposed to know.
3. If you wanted to know everything there is about something, say animals, how long would you have to study it? (a) Less than a year if you study hard, (b) about one or two years, (c) forever.
4. What happens when you learn more and more about something? (a) The questions get more and more complex, (b) the questions get easier and easier, (c) all the questions all get answered. •

---

**Epistemological beliefs** Beliefs about the structure, stability, and certainty of knowledge, and how knowledge is best learned.

Using questions like those in *Stop and Think,* researchers have identified several dimensions of epistemological beliefs (Chan & Sachs, 2001; Schommer, 1997; Schommer-Aikins, 2002; Schraw & Olafson, 2002). For example:

- **Structure of Knowledge:** Is knowledge in a field a simple set of facts or a complex structure of concepts and relationships?
- **Stability/Certainty of Knowledge:** Is knowledge fixed or does it evolve over time?
- **Ability to Learn:** Is the ability to learn fixed (based on innate ability) or changeable?
- **Speed of Learning:** Can we gain knowledge quickly or does it take time to develop knowledge?
- **Nature of Learning:** Does learning mean memorizing facts passed down from authorities and keeping the facts isolated, or does it mean developing your own integrated understandings?

Students' beliefs about knowing and learning affect the goals they set and the learning strategies they apply. For example, if you believe knowledge should be gained quickly, you are likely to try one or two quick strategies (read the text once, spend two minutes trying to solve the word problem) and then stop. If you believe that learning means developing integrated understandings, you will process the material more deeply, connect to existing knowledge, create your own examples, or draw diagrams, and generally elaborate on the information to make it your own (Kardash & Howell, 2000; Muis & Franco, 2009). In one study, elementary school students (grades 4 and 6) who believed that learning is understanding processed science texts more deeply than others who believed that learning is reproducing facts (Chan & Sachs, 2001). The *Stop & Think* questions you just answered were used in that study to assess the students' beliefs. The answers associated with a belief in complex, evolving knowledge that takes time to understand and grows from active learning are 1c, 2b, 3c, and 4a.

Beliefs about one dimension discussed above—ability to learn—are particularly powerful. Read on.

## Beliefs About Ability

**STOP & THINK** Rate these statements taken from Dweck (2000) on a scale from 1 (Strongly Agree) to 6 (Strongly Disagree).

\_\_\_\_ You have a certain amount of intelligence and you really can't do much to change it.
\_\_\_\_ You can learn new things, but you can't really change your basic intelligence.
\_\_\_\_ No matter who you are, you can change your intelligence a lot.
\_\_\_\_ No matter how much intelligence you have, you can always change it quite a bit. •

Some of the most powerful beliefs affecting motivation in school are about ability. Adults use two basic concepts of ability (Dweck, 2002, 2006). An **entity view of ability** assumes that ability is a stable, uncontrollable trait—a characteristic of the individual that cannot be changed. According to this view, some people have more ability than others, but the amount each person has is set. An **incremental view of ability**, on the other hand, portrays ability as unstable and controllable—"an ever-expanding repertoire of skills and knowledge" (Dweck & Bempechat, 1983, p. 144). By hard work, study, or practice, knowledge can be increased and thus ability can be improved. What is your view of ability? Look back at your answers to the *Stop & Think* questions.

Young children tend to hold an exclusively incremental view of ability. Through the early elementary grades, most students believe that effort is the same as intelligence. Smart people try hard, and trying hard makes you smart. If you fail, you aren't smart and you didn't try hard (Dweck, 2000; Stipek, 2002). At around age 11 or 12, children can differentiate among effort, ability, and performance. At about this time, they come to believe that someone who succeeds without working at all must be really smart. This is when beliefs about ability begin to influence motivation (Anderman & Anderman, 2010).

Students who hold an *entity* (unchangeable) view of intelligence tend to set performance avoid goals to avoid looking bad in the eyes of others. They seek situations where

**Entity view of ability** Belief that ability is a fixed characteristic that cannot be changed.

**Incremental view of ability** Belief that ability is a set of skills that can be changed.

they can look smart and protect their self-esteem. Like Safe Sienna, they keep doing those things they can do well without expending too much effort or risking failure, because either one—working hard or failing—indicates (to them) low ability. To work hard but still fail would be devastating. Students with learning disabilities are more likely to hold an entity view.

In contrast, holding an *incremental* view of ability is associated with greater motivation and learning. Believing that you can improve your ability helps you focus on the *processes* of problem solving and applying good strategies, instead of on the *products* of test scores and grades (Chen & Pajares, 2010).

Teachers who hold *entity* views are quicker to form judgments about students and slower to modify their opinions when confronted with contradictory evidence (Stipek, 2002). Teachers who hold *incremental* views, in contrast, tend to set mastery goals and seek situations in which students can improve their skills because improvement means getting smarter. Failure is not devastating; it simply indicates more work is needed. Ability is not threatened. Incremental theorists tend to set moderately difficult goals, the kind we have seen are the most motivating.

Beliefs about ability are related to other beliefs about what you can and cannot control in learning.

## Beliefs About Causes and Control: Attribution Theory

One well-known explanation of motivation begins with the assumption that we try to make sense of our behaviour and the behaviour of others by searching for explanations and causes. To understand our own successes and failures, particularly unexpected ones, we all ask, "Why?" Students ask themselves, "Why did I flunk my midterm?" or "Why did I do so well this grading period?" They may attribute their successes and failures to ability, effort, mood, knowledge, luck, help, interest, clarity of instructions, the interference of others, unfair policies, and so on. To understand others' successes and failures, we also make attributions—the others are smart or lucky or work hard, for example. **Attribution theories** of motivation describe how the individual's explanations, justifications, and excuses influence motivation (Anderman & Anderman, 2010).

Bernard Weiner is one of the main educational psychologists responsible for relating attribution theory to school learning (Weiner, 2000, 2010). According to Weiner, most of the attributed causes for successes or failures can be characterized in terms of three dimensions:

1. **Locus** (location of the cause—internal or external to the person). For example, attributing a great piano performance to your musical talent or hard work are internal attributions. Explaining the performance as due to coaching from a great teacher is an external attribution.
2. **Stability** (whether the cause of the event is the same across time and in different situations). For example, talent is stable, but effort can change.
3. **Controllability** (whether the person can control the cause). For example, effort and finding a great teacher are controllable, but innate musical talent is not.

Every cause for success or failure can be categorized simultaneously on these three dimensions. For instance, luck is external (locus), unstable (stability), and uncontrollable (controllability). In attribution theory, ability is usually considered stable and uncontrollable, but incremental theorists (described earlier) would argue that ability is unstable and controllable. Weiner's locus and controllability dimensions are closely related to Deci's concept of locus of causality.

Weiner believes these three dimensions have important implications for motivation because they affect expectancy and value. The *stability* dimension, for example, seems to be closely related to expectations about the future. If students attribute their failure to stable factors such as the difficulty of the subject or an unfair teacher, they will expect to keep failing in that subject or with that teacher. But if they attribute the outcome to unstable factors such as mood or luck, they can hope for better outcomes next time. The *internal/external locus* seems to be closely related to feelings of self-esteem. If

**Attribution theories** Descriptions of how individuals' explanations, justifications, and excuses influence their motivation and behaviour.

**UNMOTIVATED?** The greatest motivational problems arise when students attribute failures to uncontrollable causes and focus on their own inadequacy. Apathy is a logical reaction if students believe the causes of failure are beyond their control.

Lon C. Diehl/PhotoEdit

success or failure is attributed to internal factors, success will lead to pride and increased motivation, whereas failure will diminish self-esteem. The *controllability* dimension is related to emotions such as anger, pity, gratitude, or shame. If we feel responsible for our failures, we may feel guilt; if we feel responsible for successes, we may feel proud. Failing at a task we cannot control can lead to shame or anger (Weiner, 2010).

Feeling in control of your own learning is related to choosing more difficult academic tasks, putting out more effort, using better strategies, and persisting longer in school work (Schunk, 2000; Weiner, 1994a, 1994b). Factors such as continuing discrimination against women, people of colour, and individuals with special needs can affect these individuals' perceptions of their ability to control their lives (van Laar, 2000).

ATTRIBUTIONS IN THE CLASSROOM. People with a strong sense of **self-efficacy** (see Chapter 11) for a given task ("I'm good at math") tend to attribute their failures to lack of effort ("I should have double-checked my work"), misunderstanding directions, or just not studying enough. These are internal, controllable attributions. As a consequence, students with a strong sense of efficacy usually focus on strategies for succeeding next time. This response often leads to achievement, pride, and a greater feeling of control. But students with a low sense of self-efficacy ("I'm terrible at math") tend to attribute their failures to lack of ability ("I'm just dumb"). If this is the case, why bother?

The greatest motivational problems arise when students attribute failures to stable, uncontrollable causes. Such students may seem resigned to failure, depressed, helpless—what we generally call "unmotivated" (Weiner, 2000, 2010). These students respond to failure by focusing even more on their own inadequacy; their attitudes toward schoolwork may deteriorate even further. Apathy is a logical reaction to failure if students believe the causes are stable, unlikely to change, and beyond their control anyway. In addition, students who view their failures in this light are less likely to seek help; they believe nothing and no one can help, so they conceal their needs for help. This creates a downward spiral of failure and concealment—"the motivationally 'poor' children, by concealing their difficulties, become 'poorer'" (Marchland & Skinner, 2007). You can see that if a student held an entity view (ability cannot be changed) and a low sense of self-efficacy, motivation would be destroyed when failures were attributed to lack of ability ("I just can't do this and I'll never be able to learn") (Bandura, 1997; Schunk, Pintrich, & Meece, 2008; Stipek, 2002).

TEACHER ACTIONS AND STUDENT ATTRIBUTIONS. We also make attributions about the causes of other people's successes and failures. When a teacher assumes that student failure is attributable to forces beyond the student's control, the teacher tends to respond with sympathy and avoid giving punishments. If, however, the failures are attributed to a controllable factor such as lack of effort, the teacher's response is more likely to be irritation or anger, and reprimands may follow. These tendencies seem to be consistent across time and cultures (Weiner, 1986, 2000).

What do students make of these reactions from their teachers? Sandra Graham (1991, 1996) gives some surprising answers. There is evidence that when teachers respond to students' mistakes with pity, praise for a "good try," or unsolicited help, the students are more likely to attribute their failure to an uncontrollable cause—usually lack of ability. Does this mean that teachers should be critical and withhold help? Of course not! But it is a reminder that over-solicitous help can give unintended messages.

**Self-efficacy** A person's sense of being able to deal effectively with a particular task.

Graham (1991) suggests that many minority group students could be the victims of well-meaning pity from teachers. Seeing the very real problems that the students face, teachers may "ease up" on requirements so the students will "experience success." But a subtle communication may accompany the pity, praise, and extra help: "You don't have the ability to do this, so I will overlook your failure." Graham warns that a student's history of academic failure can increase the odds that student will be a target of sympathetic feedback, so these students experience lots of low-ability cues (Graham, 1991). This kind of "benevolent" feedback, even if well intended, can be a subtle form of racial or ethnic discrimination.

## Beliefs About Self-Worth

Whatever the label, most theorists agree that a sense of efficacy, control, or self-determination is critical if people are to feel intrinsically motivated.

LEARNED HELPLESSNESS.   When people come to believe the events and outcomes in their lives are mostly uncontrollable, so failure is inevitable, they have developed **learned helplessness** (Seligman, 1975). To understand the power of learned helplessness, consider this classic experiment (Hiroto & Seligman, 1975): People received either solvable or unsolvable puzzles. In the next phase of the experiment, they were given a series of solvable puzzles. Those who struggled with unsolvable puzzles in the first phase of the experiment usually solved significantly fewer puzzles in the second phase. They had learned that they could not control the outcome, so why even try?

Learned helplessness appears to cause three types of deficits: *motivational, cognitive*, and *affective*. Students who feel hopeless, like Hopeless Hunter described earlier, expect to fail, so why should they even try—thus *motivation* suffers. Because they are pessimistic about learning, these students miss opportunities to practise and improve skills and abilities, so they develop *cognitive* deficits. Finally, because they are performing poorly, they often suffer from *affective* problems such as depression, anxiety, and listlessness (Alloy & Seligman, 1979). Once established, it is very difficult to reverse the effects of learned helplessness.

SELF-WORTH.   What are the connections between attributions and beliefs about ability, self-efficacy, and self-worth? Covington and his colleagues suggest these factors come together in three kinds of motivational sets: *mastery oriented, failure avoiding*, and *failure accepting*, as shown in Table 12.3 (Covington, 1992; Covington & Mueller, 2001).

**Learned helplessness** The expectation, based on previous experiences with a lack of control, that all one's efforts will lead to failure.

TABLE 12.3 • **Mastery-Oriented, Failure-Avoiding, and Failure-Accepting Students**

|  | ATTITUDE TOWARD FAILURE | GOALS SET | ATTRIBUTIONS | VIEW OF ABILITY | STRATEGIES |
|---|---|---|---|---|---|
| Mastery-Oriented | Low fear of failure | Learning goals: moderately difficult and challenging | Effort, use of effective strategies, sufficient knowledge is cause of success | Incremental; improvable | Adaptive strategies; e.g., try another way, seek help, practise/ study more |
| Failure-Avoiding | High fear of failure | Performance goals; very hard or very easy | Lack of ability is cause of failure | Entity; set | Self-defeating strategies; e.g., make a feeble effort, pretend not to care |
| Failure-Accepting | Expectation of failure; depression | Performance goals or no goals | Lack of ability is cause of failure | Entity; set | Learned helplessness; likely to give up |

**Mastery-oriented students** tend to value achievement and see ability as improvable (an incremental view), so they set mastery goals to increase their skills and abilities. They are not fearful of failure, because failing does not threaten their sense of competence and self-worth. This allows them to set moderately difficult goals, take risks, and cope with failure constructively. They generally attribute success to their own effort, and thus they assume responsibility for learning and have a strong sense of self-efficacy. They learn faster, have more self-confidence and energy, are more aroused, welcome concrete feedback (it does not threaten them), and are eager to learn "the rules of the game" so that they can succeed. All of these factors make for persistent, successful learning (Covington & Mueller, 2001; McClelland, 1985).

**Failure-avoiding students** tend to hold an entity (fixed) view of ability, so they set performance goals. They lack a strong sense of their own competence and self-worth separate from their performance. In other words, they feel only as smart as their last test grade, so they never develop a solid sense of self-efficacy. In order to feel competent, they must protect themselves (and their self-worth) from failure. If they have been generally successful, they may seek to avoid failure like Safe Sienna, simply by taking few risks and "sticking with what they know." If, on the other hand, they have experienced a good bit of failure, then they, like Defensive Danica, may adopt self-defeating strategies such as feeble efforts, setting very low or ridiculously high goals, or claiming not to care. Just before a test, a student might say, "I didn't study at all!" or "All I want to do is pass." Then, any grade above passing is a success. Procrastination is another example. Low grades do not imply low ability if the student can claim, "I did okay considering I didn't start the term paper until last night." All these are **self-handicapping** strategies because the students are imposing handicaps that block their success in order to avoid testing their true ability. Very little learning is going on.

Unfortunately, failure-avoiding strategies generally lead to the very failure the students were trying to avoid. If failures continue and excuses wear thin, the students may finally decide that they are incompetent. Their sense of self-worth and self-efficacy deteriorates. They give up and thus become **failure-accepting students**. They are convinced that their problems are due to low ability. As we saw earlier, those students who attribute failure to low ability and believe ability is fixed are likely to become depressed, apathetic, and helpless. Like Hopeless Hunter, they have little hope for change.

Teachers may be able to prevent some failure-avoiding students from becoming failure accepting by using varied measures of outcomes and setting a number of goals. In this way all students have a realistic chance of succeeding on some outcome measures and reaching at least a few goals (Chen, Wu, Kee, Lin, & Shui, 2009). Also, many students may need support in aspiring to higher levels in the face of sexual or ethnic stereotypes about what they "should" want or what they "should not" be able to do well. This kind of support could make all the difference. Instead of pitying or excusing these students, teachers can teach them how to learn and then hold them accountable for their learning. This will help the students develop a sense of self-efficacy for learning and avoid learned helplessness. The *Guidelines* discuss how to encourage self-worth.

## Beliefs and Attributions: Lessons for Teachers

If students believe they lack the ability to understand higher mathematics, they will probably act on this belief even if their actual abilities are well above average. These students are likely to have little motivation to tackle trigonometry or calculus because they expect to do poorly in these areas. If students believe that failing means they are stupid, they are likely to adopt many self-handicapping, self-defeating strategies. And teachers who stress performance, grades, and competition can encourage self-handicapping without realizing they are doing so (Anderman & Anderman, 2010). Just telling students to "try harder" is not particularly effective. Students need real evidence that effort will pay off, that setting a higher goal will not lead to failure, that they can improve, and that abilities can be changed. They need authentic mastery experiences.

What else do we know about motivation? Feelings matter.

**Mastery-oriented students** Students who focus on learning goals because they value achievement and see ability as improvable.

**Failure-avoiding students** Students who avoid failure by sticking to what they know, by not taking risks, or by claiming not to care about their performance.

**Self-handicapping** Students may engage in behaviour that blocks their own success in order to avoid testing their true ability.

**Failure-accepting students** Students who believe their failures are due to low ability and there is little they can do about it.

## GUIDELINES

### Encouraging Self-Worth

**Emphasize that abilities are not set, but are always improvable.**
*Examples*
1. Share examples of how you have improved your knowledge and skills, for example in writing, at a sport, or doing a craft.
2. Tell about your own failures that became successes when you tried new strategies or got the right help.
3. Save first drafts and finished products from students in previous classes to show how much the students improved with effort and support.

**Teach directly about the difference between learning goals and performance goals.**
*Examples*
1. Encourage students to set a small-step goal for one subject.
2. Recognize improvements often with private authentic praise.
3. Use personal best goals, not between-student competition.

**Make the classroom a place where failure is just diagnostic—failure tells what needs to be improved.**
*Examples*
1. If a student gives a wrong answer in class, say, "I bet others would give that answer, too. Let's examine why that is not the best answer. This gives us a chance to dig deeper—excellent!"
2. Encourage revising, improving, polishing, and redoing with an emphasis on improvement.
3. Show students connections between their revised work and a higher grade, but emphasize their growing competence.

**Encourage help seeking and help giving.**
*Examples*
1. Teach students how to ask explicit questions about what they do not understand.
2. Recognize students who are helpful.
3. Train class experts for some ongoing needs such as technology guides or progress checkers.

# INTERESTS, CURIOSITY, EMOTIONS, AND ANXIETY

Do you remember starting school? Were you curious about what might be in store, excited about your new world, interested and challenged? Many children are. But a common concern of parents and teachers is that this curiosity and excitement about learning is replaced by a sense of drudgery and disinterest. School becomes a job you have to do—a workplace where the work is not that interesting (Wigfield & Wentzel, 2007). In fact, interest in school decreases over time from elementary to high school, with boys showing greater declines than girls. The transition to middle school is particularly linked to a decline in interest. These declines are troubling because results of research on learning in school show that interest is related to students' attention, goals, grades, and depth of learning (Dotterer, McHale, & Crouter, 2009; Hidi & Renninger, 2006).

## Tapping Interests

**STOP & THINK** As part of your interview for a job in a large high school, the principal asks, "How would you interest students in learning? Could you tap their interests in your teaching?" •

There are two kinds of interests—*personal* (individual) and *situational*—the trait and state distinction again. Personal or individual interests are more long-lasting aspects of the person, such as an enduring tendency to be attracted to or to enjoy subjects such as languages, history, or mathematics, or activities such as sports, music, or films. Students with individual interests in learning in general seek new information and have more positive attitudes toward schooling. Situational interests are more short-lived aspects of the activity, text, or materials that catch and keep the student's attention. Both personal and situational interests are related to learning from texts—greater interest leads to more positive emotional responses to the material, then to greater persistence in learning, deeper

**INTEREST AND EXCITEMENT** Students' interest in and excitement about what they're learning are two of the most important factors in education.

UpperCut Images/Alamy

processing, better remembering of the material, and higher achievement (Ainley, Hidi, & Berndorf, 2002; Hofer, 2010; Pintrich, 2003). And interests increase when students feel competent, so even if students are not initially attracted to a subject or activity, they may develop interests as they experience success (Stipek, 2002).

Ann Renninger (2009) describes a four-phase model of interest development:

situational interest triggered ⟶ situational interest maintained ⟶ emerging individual interest ⟶ well-developed individual interest

For example, consider Julia, a graduating senior in college described by Hidi and Renninger (2006). As she waits nervously in the dentist's office, flipping through a magazine, her attention is drawn (*situational interest trigger*) to an article about a man who left his engineering job to become a facilitator in legal conflict resolution. When she is called to the dentist's chair, she is still reading the article, so she marks her place and returns to finish reading after her appointment (*situational interest maintained*). She takes notes, and, over the next weeks, searches the internet, visits the library, and meets with her advisor to get more information about this career option (*emerging individual interest*). Four years later, Julia is enjoying her job as a facilitator as she handles more and more arbitration cases for a law firm (*well-developed, enduring individual interest*).

In the early stages of this four-phase model, emotions play a big role—feelings of excitement, pleasure, fun, and curiosity. Situational interest may be triggered by positive feelings, as when Julia started reading. Curiosity followed and helped Julia stay engaged as she learned more about becoming a facilitator. As Julia added knowledge to her curiosity and positive feelings, her personal interest emerged, and the *cycle of positive feelings, curiosity, and knowledge* continued to build enduring interest.

**Watch**
Catching and Holding
Interests

**CATCHING AND HOLDING INTERESTS.**    Whenever possible, it helps to connect academic content to students' enduring individual interests. But given that the content you will teach is probably largely set by the province, it will be difficult to tailor lessons to each student's interests. You will have to rely more on triggering and maintaining situational interest. Here, the challenge is to not only *catch* but also *hold* students' interest (Pintrich,

2003). For example, Mathew Mitchell (1993) found that using computers, groups, and puzzles caught students' interest in secondary mathematics classes, but the interests did not hold. Lessons that held the students' interest over time included math activities that were related to real-life problems and active participation in laboratory activities and projects. Another source of interest is fantasy. Cordova and Lepper (1996) found students learned more math facts during a computer exercise in which they were challenged, as captains of star ships, to navigate through space by solving math problems. The students got to name their ships, stock the (imaginary) galley with their favourite snacks, and name all the crew members after their friends. In a study of math learning with older adolescents, Durik and Harackiewicz (2007) concluded that catching interest by using colourful learning materials with pictures was helpful for students with low initial interest in mathematics, but not for students who were already interested. For the interested students, holding interest by showing how math could be personally useful was more effective.

There are other cautions in responding to students' interests, as you can see in the *Point/Counterpoint.*

## POINT/COUNTERPOINT    Does Making Learning Fun Make for Good Learning?

When many beginning teachers are asked about how to motivate students, they often mention making learning fun. But is it necessary for learning to be fun?

▶ **Teachers should make learning fun.** A search for "making learning fun" on Google.com yields "about 240 000" resources and references. Clearly, there is interest in making learning fun. Research shows that passages in texts that are more interesting are remembered better (Schunk, Pintrich, & Meece, 2008). For example, students who read books that interested them spent more time reading, read more words in the books, and felt more positively about reading (Guthrie & Alao, 1997).

Games and simulations can make learning more fun, too. For example, when Anita's daughter was in grade 8, all the students in her grade spent three days playing a game her teachers had designed called ULTRA. Students were divided into groups and formed their own "countries." Each country had to choose a name, symbol, national flower, and bird. They wrote and sang a national anthem and elected government officials. The teachers allocated different resources to the countries. To get all the materials needed for the completion of assigned projects, the countries had to establish trade with one another. There was a monetary system and a stock market. Students had to work with their fellow citizens to complete cooperative learning assignments. Some countries "cheated" in their trades with other nations, and this allowed debate about international relations, trust, and war. Liz says she had fun—but she also learned how to work in a group without the teacher's supervision and gained a deeper understanding of world economics and international conflicts.

A highly motivating grade 3 teacher in another study had her class set up a post office for the whole school. Each classroom in the school had an address and postal code. Students had jobs in the post office, and everyone in the school used the post office to deliver letters to students and teachers. Students designed their own stamps and set postal rates. The teacher said that the system "improves their creative writing without them knowing it" (Dolezal, Welsh, Pressley, & Vincent, 2003, p. 254).

▶ **Fun can get in the way of learning.** As far back as the early 1900s, educators warned about the dangers of focusing on fun in learning. None other than John Dewey, who wrote extensively about the role of interest in learning, cautioned that you can't make boring lessons interesting by mixing in fun like you can make bad chili good by adding some spicy hot sauce. Dewey wrote, "When things have to be made interesting, it is because interest itself is wanting. Moreover, the phrase itself is a misnomer. The thing, the object, is no more interesting than it was before" (Dewey, 1913, pp. 11–12).

There is a good deal of research now indicating that adding interest by incorporating fascinating but irrelevant details actually gets in the way of learning the important information. These "seductive details," as they have been called, divert the readers' attention from the less interesting main ideas (Harp & Mayer, 1998). For example, students who read biographies of historical figures remembered more very interesting—but unimportant—information compared to interesting main ideas (Wade, Schraw, Buxton, & Hayes, 1993).

Shannon Harp and Richard Mayer (1998) found similar results with high school science texts. These texts added emotional interest and seductive details about swimmers and golfers who are injured by lightning to a lesson on the process of lightning. They concluded that, "in the case of emotional interest versus cognitive interest, the verdict is clear. Adjuncts aimed at increasing emotional interest failed to improve understanding of scientific explanations" (p. 100). The seductive details may have disrupted students' attempts to follow the logic of the explanations and thus interfered with their comprehending the text. Harp and Mayer conclude that "the best way to help students enjoy a passage is to help them understand it" (p. 100).

## Curiosity: Novelty and Complexity

Nearly 50 years ago, psychologists suggested that individuals are naturally motivated to seek novelty, surprise, and complexity (Berlyne, 1966). Exploration probably is innate; infants must explore the world to learn about it (Bowlby, 1969). More recently, Reiss (2004) listed curiosity as one of the 16 basic human motivations, and Flum and Kaplan (2006) made the case that schools should target developing an exploratory orientation in students as a major goal.

Interest and curiosity are related. Curiosity is a tendency to be interested in a wide range of areas (Pintrich, 2003). According to Renninger's (2009) four-phase model of interest described in the previous section, our individual interests begin to emerge as we raise and answer "curiosity questions" that help us organize our knowledge about a topic. In order for situational interests to develop into long-term individual interests, curiosity and the desire for exploration are necessary.

George Lowenstein (1994) suggests that curiosity arises when attention is focused on a gap in knowledge. These information gaps cause a sense of deprivation—a need to know that we call "curiosity." This idea is similar to Piaget's concept of disequilibrium, discussed in Chapter 2, and has a number of implications for teaching. First, students need some base of knowledge before they can experience gaps in that knowledge leading to curiosity. Second, students must be aware of the gaps in order for curiosity to result. In other words, they need a metacognitive awareness of what they know and don't know (Hidi, Renninger, & Krapp, 2004). Asking students to make guesses and then providing feedback can be helpful. Also, proper handling of mistakes can stimulate curiosity by pointing to missing knowledge. Finally, the more we learn about a topic, the more curious we may become about that subject. As Maslow (1970) predicted, fulfilling the need to know increases, not decreases, the need to know more. See the *Guidelines* for more about building interest and curiosity in the classroom.

## Emotions and Anxiety

How do you feel about learning? Excited, bored, curious, fearful? Today, researchers emphasize that learning is not just about the *cold cognition* of reasoning and problem solving. Learning and information processing also are influenced by emotion, so *hot cognition* plays a role in learning as well (Pintrich, 2003). Research on emotions, learning, and motivation is expanding, in part because we know more about the brain and emotion.

NEUROSCIENCE AND EMOTION.   In mammals, including humans, stimulation to a small area of the brain called the *amygdala* seems to trigger emotional reactions such as the "fight or flight" response. The responses in nonhuman animals can be strong. But human emotions are the outcome of physiological responses triggered by the brain, combined with interpretations of the situation and other information. So, hearing startling sounds during an action movie might cause a brief emotional reaction, but hearing the same sounds in the middle of the night as you are walking through a dark alley could lead to stronger and more lasting emotional reactions. Even though the amygdala plays a key role in emotions, many other brain regions are also involved. Emotions are a "constant interplay between cognitive assessments, conscious feelings, and bodily responses, with each able to influence the other" (Gluck, Mercado, & Myers, 2007, p. 418). Humans are more likely to pay attention to, learn about, and remember events, images, and readings that provoke emotional responses (Murphy & Alexander, 2000; Cowley & Underwood, 1998; Reisberg & Heuer, 1992). Emotions can affect learning by changing brain dopamine levels that influence long-term memory and by directing attention toward one aspect of the situation (Pekrun, Elliot, & Maier, 2006). Sometimes, emotions interfere with learning by taking up attention or working memory space that could be used for learning (Pekrun, Goetz, Titz, & Perry, 2002).

In teaching, we are concerned about particular emotions—those related to achievement in school. Experiences of success or failure can provoke achievement emotions such as pride, hope, boredom, anger, or shame (Pekrun, Elliot, & Maier, 2006). How can we use these findings to support learning in school?

## GUIDELINES

## Building on Students' Interests and Curiosity

**Relate content objectives to student experiences.**
*Examples*

1. With a teacher in another school, establish pen pals across the classes. Through writing letters, students exchange personal experiences, photos, drawings, written work, and ask and answer questions ("Have you learned cursive writing yet?" "What are you doing in math now?" "What are you reading?"). Letters can be mailed in one large mailer to save stamps or sent via email.

2. Identify classroom experts for different assignments or tasks. Who knows how to use the computer for graphics? How to search the internet? How to cook? How to use an index?

3. Have a "Switch Day" when students exchange roles with a school staff or support person. Students must research the role by interviewing their staff member, prepare for the job, dress the part for the day they take over, and then evaluate their success after the switch.

**Identify student interests, hobbies, and extracurricular activities that can be incorporated into class lessons and discussions.**
*Examples*

1. Have students design and conduct interviews and surveys to learn about each other's interests.

2. Keep the class library stocked with books that connect to students' interests and hobbies.

3. Allow choices (stories in language arts or projects in science) based on students' interests.

**Support instruction with humour, personal experiences, and anecdotes that show the human side of the content.**
*Examples*

1. Share your own hobbies, interests, and favourites.

2. Tell students there will be a surprise visitor; then dress up as the author of a story and tell about "yourself" and your writing.

**Use original source material with interesting content or details.**
*Examples*

1. Letters and diaries in history.

2. Darwin's notes in biology.

**Create surprise and curiosity.**
*Examples*

1. Have students predict what will happen in an experiment, then show them whether they were right or wrong.

2. Provide quotes from history and ask students to guess who said it.

---

*For more information on students' interests and motivation, see http://mathforum.org/~sarah/Discussion.Sessions/biblio.motivation.html.*

*Source: From Raffini, J. (1996). 150 Ways to Increase Intrinsic Motivation in the Classroom. Allyn and Bacon: Boston, MA. © Pearson Education. Adapted by permission of the publisher; Pintrich, P, & Schunk, D. (2002). Motivation in Education (2nd ed.). Merrill/Prentice-Hall, pp. 298–299.*

---

**ACHIEVEMENT EMOTIONS.** In the past, with the exception of anxiety, emotions generally were overlooked in research on learning and motivation (Linnenbrink-Garcia & Pekrun, 2011). But as you saw above, research in the neurosciences has shown that emotions are both causes and consequences of learning processes. Reinhard Pekrun and his colleagues (Pekrun, Elliot, & Maier, 2006, 2009) have tested a model that relates different goal orientations to boredom and other emotions in older adolescents from the United States and Germany. The goal orientations are those we discussed earlier: mastery, performance approach, and performance avoidance.

With a *mastery goal*, students focused on an activity. They valued the activity as a way to get smarter, and they felt in control. They were not afraid of failing, so they could focus on the task at hand. The researchers found that having mastery goals predicted enjoyment in learning, hope, and pride. Students with mastery goals were less likely to feel angry or bored about learning. Boredom is a big problem in classrooms because it is associated with difficulties in paying attention, lack of intrinsic motivation, weak effort, shallow processing of information, and poor self-regulated learning (Pekrun, Goetz, Daniels, Stupinsky, & Perry, 2010)

With a *performance-approach goal*, students wanted to look good or be the best, and they focused their attention on positive outcomes. Performance-approach goals were related mostly to pride. Students with *performance-avoidance goals* focused on the fear of failing and the possibility of looking stupid. Performance-avoidance goals predicted feelings of anxiety, hopelessness, and shame. These findings are summarized in Table 12.4.

TABLE 12.4 • **How Different Achievement Goals Influence Achievement Emotions**

Different goals are associated with different emotions that can impact motivation.

| GOAL ORIENTATION | STUDENT EMOTIONS |
|---|---|
| *Mastery*<br>Focus on activity, controllability, positive value of activity | Increases: enjoyment of activity, pride, hope<br>Decreases: boredom, anger |
| *Performance-approach*<br>Focus on outcome, controllability, positive outcome value | Increases: pride |
| *Performance-avoidance*<br>Focus on outcome, lack of controllability, negative outcome value | Increases: anxiety, hopelessness, shame |

*Source: Adapted from Pekrun, R., Elliot, A. J., & Maier, M. A. (2006). Achievement goals and discrete achievement emotions: A theoretical model and prospective test. Journal of Educational Psychology, 98, 583–597.*

How can you increase positive achievement emotions and decrease boredom in the subject you teach? Students are more likely to feel bored if they believe they have little control over the learning activities and they don't value the activities. Matching challenge to the students' skill levels and giving choices can increase the students' sense of control. In addition, efforts to build student interest and show the value of the activities also help to fight boredom. And remember, achievement emotions are domain specific. The fact that students enjoy and feel proud of their work in math does not mean they will enjoy English or history (Goetz, Frenzel, Hall, & Pekrun, 2008; Pekrun, Goetz, Daniels, Stupinsky, & Perry, 2010). In addition, teachers who enjoy their subjects tend to be more enthusiastic and encourage student enjoyment, so make sure, as much as possible, that you are teaching from your own interests and passions (Brophy, 2008; Frenzel, Goetz, Lüdtke, Pekrun, & Sutton, 2009).

AROUSAL AND ANXIETY. Just as we all know how it feels to be motivated, we all know what it is like to be aroused. **Arousal** involves both psychological and physical reactions—changes in brain wave patterns, blood pressure, heart rate, and breathing rate that cause you to feel alert, wide awake, even excited.

To understand the effects of arousal on motivation, think of two extremes. The first is late at night. You are trying for the third time to understand a required reading, but you are so sleepy. Your attention drifts as your eyelids droop. You decide to go to bed and get up early to study (a plan that you know seldom works). At the other extreme, imagine that you have a critical test tomorrow—one that determines whether you will get a scholarship. You feel tremendous pressure from everyone to do well. You know that you need a good night's sleep, but you are wide awake. In the first case, arousal is too low, and in the second, too high. Psychologists have known for years that there is an optimum level of arousal for most activities (Yerkes & Dodson, 1908). Generally speaking, higher levels of arousal are helpful on simple tasks such as sorting laundry, but lower levels of arousal are better for complex learning tasks.

ANXIETY IN THE CLASSROOM. At one time or another, everyone has experienced **anxiety**, or a general uneasiness, feeling of self-doubt, and sense of tension. The effects of anxiety on school achievement are clear. Anxiety can be both a cause and an effect of school failure—students do poorly because they are anxious, and their poor performance increases their anxiety. Anxiety probably is both a *trait* and a *state*. Some students tend to be anxious in many situations (trait anxiety), but some situations are especially anxiety provoking (state anxiety) (Covington, 1992; Zeidner, 1998).

Anxiety seems to have both cognitive and affective components. The cognitive side includes worry and negative thoughts—thinking about how bad it would be to fail and worrying that you will, for example. The affective side involves physiological and emotional reactions such as sweaty palms, upset stomach, racing heartbeat, or fear (Jain

**Arousal** Physical and psychological reactions causing a person to feel alert, excited, or tense.

**Anxiety** General uneasiness, a feeling of tension.

& Dowson, 2009; Schunk, Pintrich, & Meece, 2008). Whenever there are pressures to perform, severe consequences for failure, and competitive comparisons among students, anxiety may be encouraged (Wigfield & Eccles, 1989). Research with school-age children shows a relationship between the quality of sleep (how quickly and how well you sleep) and anxiety. Better-quality sleep is associated with positive arousal or an "eagerness" to learn. Poor-quality sleep, on the other hand, is related to debilitating anxiety and decreased school performance. You may have discovered these relationships for yourself in your own school career (Meijer & van den Wittenboer, 2004).

**HOW DOES ANXIETY INTERFERE WITH ACHIEVEMENT?**    Anxiety interferes with learning and test performance at three points: focusing attention, learning, and testing. When students are learning new material, they must pay attention to it. Highly anxious students evidently divide their attention between the new material and their preoccupation with how worried and nervous they are feeling. Instead of concentrating, they keep noticing the tight feelings in their chest, thinking, "I'm so tense, I'll never understand this stuff!" From the beginning, anxious students may miss much of the information they are supposed to learn because their thoughts are focused on their own worries (Cassady & Johnson, 2002).

But the problems do not end here. Even if they are paying attention, many anxious students have trouble learning material that is somewhat disorganized and difficult—material that requires them to rely on their memory. Unfortunately, much material in school could be described this way. In addition, many highly anxious students have poor study habits. Simply learning to be more relaxed will not automatically improve these students' performance; their learning strategies and study skills must be improved as well (Jain & Dowson, 2009; Naveh-Benjamin, 1991).

Finally, anxious students often know more than they can demonstrate on a test. They may lack critical test-taking skills, or they may have learned the material, but "freeze and forget" on tests (Naveh-Benjamin, McKeachie, & Lin, 1987).

## Reaching Every Student: Coping With Anxiety

Some students, particularly those with learning disabilities or emotional disorders, may be especially anxious in school. When students face stressful situations such as tests, they can use three kinds of coping strategies: problem-focused self-regulating learning strategies, emotional management, and avoidance. *Problem-focused self-regulating strategies* might include planning a study schedule, borrowing good notes, or finding a protected place to study. *Emotion-focused strategies* are attempts to reduce the anxious feelings, for example, by using relaxation exercises or describing the feelings to a friend. Of course, the latter might become an *avoidance strategy*, along with going out for pizza or suddenly launching an all-out desk-cleaning attack. (Can't study until you get organized!) Different strategies are helpful at different points—for example, self-regulated learning before and emotion management during an exam. Different strategies fit different people and situations (Zeidner, 1995, 1998).

Teachers should help highly anxious students to set realistic goals, because these individuals often have difficulty making wise choices. They tend to select either extremely difficult or extremely easy tasks. In the first case, they are likely to fail, which will increase their sense of hopelessness and anxiety about school. In the second case, they will probably succeed on the easy tasks, but they will miss the sense of satisfaction that could encourage greater effort and ease their fears about schoolwork. Goal cards, progress charts, or goal-planning journals may help here. In addition, directly teaching students self-regulated learning strategies and supporting their self-efficacy can help them be more in control of their learning and their anxiety (Jain & Dowson, 2009).

## Curiosity, Interests, and Emotions: Lessons for Teachers

Make efforts to keep the level of arousal right for the task at hand. If students are going to sleep, energize them by introducing variety, piquing their curiosity, surprising them, or giving them a brief chance to be physically active. Learn about their interests and incorporate these interests into lessons and assignments. If arousal is too great, follow the *Guidelines* for dealing with anxiety.

## GUIDELINES

### Coping With Anxiety

**Use competition carefully.**
*Examples*

1. Monitor activities to make sure no students are being put under undue pressure.
2. During competitive games, make sure all students involved have a reasonable chance of succeeding.
3. Experiment with cooperative learning activities.

**Avoid situations in which highly anxious students will have to perform in front of large groups.**
*Examples*

1. Ask anxious students questions that can be answered with a simple yes or no, or some other brief reply.
2. Give anxious students practice in speaking before smaller groups.

**Make sure all instructions are clear. Uncertainty can lead to anxiety.**
*Examples*

1. Write test instructions on the board or on the test itself instead of giving them orally.
2. Check with students to make sure they understand. Ask several students how they would do the first question, exercise, or sample question on a test. Correct any misconceptions.
3. If you are using a new format or starting a new type of task, give students examples or models to show how it is done.

**Avoid unnecessary time pressures.**
*Examples*

1. Give occasional take-home tests.
2. Make sure all students can complete classroom tests within the period given.

**Remove some of the pressures from major tests and exams.**
*Examples*

1. Teach test-taking skills; give practice tests; provide study guides.
2. Avoid basing most of a report-card grade on one test.
3. Make extra-credit work available to add points to course grades.
4. Use different types of items in testing because some students have difficulty with particular formats.

**Develop alternatives to written tests.**
*Examples*

1. Try oral, open-book, or group tests.
2. Have students do projects, organize portfolios of their work, make oral presentations, or create a finished product.

**Teach students self-regulation strategies (Schutz & Davis, 2000).**
*Examples*

1. Before the test: Encourage students to see the test as an important and challenging task that they have the capabilities to prepare for. Help students stay focused on the task of getting as much information as possible about the test.
2. During the test: Remind students that the test is important (but not overly important). Encourage task focus—pick out the main idea in the question, slow down, stay relaxed.
3. After the test: Think back on what went well and what could be improved. Focus on controllable attributions—study strategies, effort, careful reading of questions, relaxation strategies.

*For more information about test anxiety, see www.counselingcenter.uiuc.edu/?page_id=193.*

---

How can we put together all this information about motivation? How can teachers create environments, situations, and relationships that encourage motivation? We address these questions next.

## MOTIVATION TO LEARN IN SCHOOL: ON TARGET

Teachers are concerned about developing a particular kind of motivation in their students—the **motivation to learn**, defined as "a student tendency to find academic activities meaningful and worthwhile and to try to derive the intended academic benefits from them" (Brophy, 1988, pp. 205–206). Motivation to learn involves more than wanting or intending to learn. It includes the quality of the student's mental efforts. For example, reading the text 11 times may indicate persistence, but motivation to learn implies more thoughtful, active study strategies, such as summarizing, elaborating the basic ideas, outlining in your own words, drawing graphs of the key relationships, and so on (Brophy, 1988).

It would be wonderful if all our students came to us filled with the motivation to learn, but they don't. As teachers, we have three major goals. The first is to involve students productively with the work of the class; in other words, to *catch* their interest and

**Motivation to learn** The tendency to find academic activities meaningful and worthwhile and to try to benefit from them.

TABLE 12.5 • **Building a Concept of Motivation to Learn**

Motivation to learn is encouraged when the following five elements come together.

| SOURCE OF MOTIVATION | OPTIMUM CHARACTERISTICS OF MOTIVATION TO LEARN | CHARACTERISTICS THAT DIMINISH MOTIVATION TO LEARN |
|---|---|---|
| Type of Goal Set | INTRINSIC: Personal factors such as needs, interests, curiosity, enjoyment | EXTRINSIC: Environmental factors such as rewards, social pressure, punishment |
| Type of Involvement | LEARNING GOAL: Personal satisfaction in meeting challenges and improving; tendency to choose moderately difficult and challenging goals<br><br>TASK-INVOLVED: Concerned with mastering the task | PERFORMANCE GOAL: Desire for approval for performance in others' eyes; tendency to choose very easy or very difficult goals<br><br>EGO-INVOLVED: Concerned with self in others' eyes |
| Achievement Motivation | Motivation to ACHIEVE: Mastery orientation | Motivation to AVOID FAILURE: Prone to anxiety |
| Likely Attributions | Successes and failures attributed to CONTROLLABLE effort and ability | Successes and failures attributed to UNCONTROLLABLE causes |
| Beliefs About Ability | INCREMENTAL VIEW: Belief that ability can be improved through hard work and added knowledge and skills | ENTITY VIEW: Belief that ability is a stable, uncontrollable trait |

create a *state* of motivation to learn. The second and longer-term goal is to develop in our students enduring individual interests and the *trait* of being motivated to learn so they will be able to educate themselves for the rest of their lives. And finally, we want our students to be *cognitively engaged*—to think deeply about what they study. In other words, we want them to be thoughtful (Blumenfeld, Puro, & Mergendoller, 1992).

Earlier in this chapter we examined the roles of intrinsic and extrinsic motivation, attributions, goals, beliefs, self-perceptions, interests, curiosity, and emotions in motivation. Table 12.5 shows how each of these factors contributes to motivation to learn.

The central question for the remainder of the chapter is: How can teachers use their knowledge about attributions, goals, beliefs, self-perceptions, interests, and emotions to increase motivation to learn? To organize our discussion, we will use the TARGET model (Ames, 1992; Epstein, 1989), identifying six areas where teachers make decisions that can influence student motivation to learn.

**T:** task that students are asked to do
**A:** autonomy or authority students are allowed in working
**R:** recognition for accomplishments
**G:** grouping practices
**E:** evaluation procedures
**T:** time in the classroom

## Tasks for Learning

An **academic task** includes work the student must accomplish, including the content covered and the mental operations required. To understand how academic tasks can affect students' motivation, we need to analyze the task. Tasks have different values for students.

**TASK VALUE.** As you probably recall, many theories suggest that the strength of our motivation in a particular situation is determined by both our *expectation* that we can succeed and the *value* of that success to us. Perceptions of task value predict the choices

**Academic tasks** The work the student must accomplish, including the content covered and the mental operations required.

students make, such as whether to enroll in advanced science classes or join the track team. Efficacy expectations predict achievement in actually doing the task—how well the students will perform in the science class or on the track team (Wigfield & Eccles, 2002b).

We can think of task value as having four components: importance, interest, utility, and cost (Eccles & Wigfield, 2002; Hulleman, Godes, Hendricks, & Harackiewicz, 2010). **Importance or attainment value** is the significance of doing well on the task—how success on the task meets personal needs (the need to be well liked, athletic, etc.). For instance, if someone has a strong need to appear smart and believes that a high grade on a test proves you are smart, then the test has high attainment value for that person. A second component is **interest or intrinsic value**. This is simply the enjoyment one gets from the activity itself. Some people like the experience of learning. Others enjoy the feeling of hard physical effort or the challenge of solving puzzles. Tasks also can have **utility value**, the contribution the task makes toward achieving a short-term or long-term goal such as earning a degree. Finally, tasks have costs—negative consequences that might follow from doing the task such as not having time to do other things or looking awkward as you perform the task.

You can see from our discussion of task value that personal and environmental influences on motivation interact constantly. The task we ask students to accomplish is an aspect of the environment; it is external to the student. But the value of accomplishing the task is bound up with the internal needs, beliefs, and goals of the individual. Because task value has to do with choices, positive values toward academic tasks can be life-changing because choices about courses in high school and education after high school affect career and life opportunities (Durik, Vida, & Eccles, 2006).

BEYOND TASK VALUE TO GENUINE APPRECIATION.    Jere Brophy (2008, p. 140) reminds teachers that there is more to value than interest or utility—there is the power of knowing: "Powerful ideas expand and enrich the quality of students' subjective lives." These ideas give us lenses for viewing the world, tools for making decisions, and frames for appreciating the beauty in words and images. An entire issue of *Theory Into Practice*, the journal Anita edits, is devoted to Jere's ideas about engaging students in the value and appreciation of learning (Turner, Patrick, & Meyer, 2011). One way to build appreciation is with authentic tasks.

AUTHENTIC TASKS.    Recently, there has been a great deal written about the use of authentic tasks in teaching. An **authentic task** has some connection to the real-life problems and situations that students will face outside the classroom, both now and in the future. If you ask students to memorize definitions they will never use, to learn the material only because it is on the test, or to repeat work they already understand, then there can be little motivation to learn. But if the tasks are authentic, students are more likely to see the genuine utility value of the work and are also more likely to find the tasks meaningful and interesting (Pugh & Phillips, 2011). **Problem-based learning**, where students tackle realistic problems that don't necessarily have right answers, and service learning (Chapter 10) are two examples of the use of authentic tasks in teaching. For example, a physics teacher might use skateboarding as a basis for problems and examples, knowing that skateboarding is an authentic task for many of her students (Anderman & Anderman, 2010). For younger students, compare these two teachers described by Anderman and Anderman (2010):

> Mrs. Byrnes gives her class an initial lesson on halves and quarters, divides students into groups of three, and gives each group two Twinkies and a plastic knife. She asks the students to cut one Twinkie into two equally-sized pieces, and the other Twinkie into four equally-sized pieces. Next comes the challenge—use the Twinkie pieces to determine which fraction is bigger, one-half (1/2) or three-fourths (3/4). Mrs. Byrnes then visits each group; the members must explain their work to her. When they are correct, they get to eat the Twinkies.
>
> Mr. Fletcher gives the same initial lesson on halves and quarters. He then provides each student with a worksheet with a few simple questions that are designed to help the students to learn about fractions. For these questions, the students are supposed to imagine that they have several pieces of paper, and that they cut the paper with scissors into various quantities (e.g., they cut one paper into four equal-size pieces, they cut another paper into two equal-size pieces). The students are then asked to demonstrate whether one-half (1/2) or three-fourths (3/4) is the bigger fraction. They then have to write down their answer, along with a brief explanation.

**Importance or attainment value** The importance of doing well on a task; how success on the task meets personal needs.

**Interest or intrinsic value** The enjoyment a person gets from a task.

**Utility value** The contribution of a task to meeting one's goals.

**Authentic task** Tasks that have some connection to real-life problems the students will face outside the classroom.

**Problem-based learning** Methods that provide students with realistic problems that don't necessarily have "right" answers.

The students in Mrs. Byrnes's class were involved in a more authentic (and tasty) task involving cutting and dividing food, cooperating with others, and enjoying the fruits (or Twinkies) of their labour. They also had to figure out how to share two halves and four quarters equally among three people—advanced cooperation.

## Supporting Autonomy and Recognizing Accomplishment

The second area in the TARGET model involves how much choice and autonomy students are allowed. Choice and control in schools are not the norm. Children and adolescents spend literally thousands of hours in schools where other people decide what will happen. Yet we know that self-determination and a sense of internal locus of causality are critical to maintaining intrinsic motivation and student engagement (Jang, Reeve, & Deci, 2010; Reeve, Nix, & Hamm, 2003). What can teachers do to support choice without creating chaos?

SUPPORTING CHOICES.    Choices should provide a range of selections that allow students to follow their interests and pick an option that is important and relevant to them (Katz & Assor, 2007). But beware of giving too many choices. Like totally unguided discovery or aimless discussions, unstructured or unguided choices can be counterproductive for learning (Garner, 1998). Graduate students in our classes can find it disconcerting if they are asked to design a final project that will determine their grade.

The alternative is *bounded choice*—giving students a range of options that set valuable tasks for them, but also allow them to follow personal interests. The balance must be just right: "too much autonomy is bewildering and too little is boring" (Guthrie et al., 1998, p. 185). Students can have input about work partners, seating arrangements, how to display work, or suggestions for class rules. But the most important kind of autonomy support teachers can provide probably is cognitive autonomy support—giving students opportunities to discuss different cognitive strategies for learning, approaches to solving problems, or positions on an issue (Stefanou, Perencevich, DiCintio, & Turner, 2004). Students also can exercise autonomy about how they receive feedback from the teacher or from classmates. Figure 12.1 describes a strategy called "Check It Out," in which students specify the skills

### FIGURE 12.1

#### STUDENT AUTONOMY: CHECK IT OUT

Using this technique to support student autonomy, the teacher decides on a set of skills that will be developed over a unit, but the student decides which skill(s) will be evaluated on any given assignment. Over the course of the unit, all the skills have to be "checked out." This student has indicated that she wants the teacher to "check out" her creativity and verb tense.

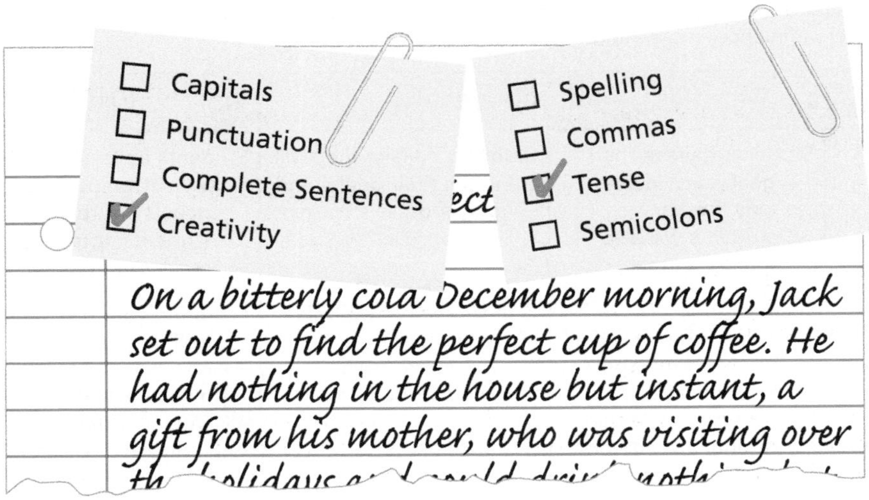

□ Capitals
□ Punctuation
□ Complete Sentences
☑ Creativity

□ Spelling
□ Commas
☑ Tense
□ Semicolons

*On a bitterly cold December morning, Jack set out to find the perfect cup of coffee. He had nothing in the house but instant, a gift from his mother, who was visiting over th* ...

*Source: From Raffini, J. P. (1996). 150 Ways to Increase Intrinsic Motivation to the Classroom. Allyn and Bacon: Boston, MA. © Pearson Education. Reprinted/Adapted by permission of the publisher.*

that they want to have evaluated in a particular assignment. Over the course of a unit, all the skills have to be "checked out," but students choose when each one is evaluated.

**RECOGNIZING ACCOMPLISHMENT.** The third TARGET area is recognition for accomplishments. Students should be recognized for improving on their own personal best, for tackling difficult tasks, for persisting, and for creativity—not just for performing better than others. In Chapter 7 we noted that giving students rewards for activities that they already enjoy can undermine intrinsic motivation. What sort of recognition leads to engagement? One answer comes from a study by Ruth Butler (1987). Students in grades 5 and 6 were given interesting divergent thinking tasks that were followed up by one of the following teacher responses: individual personalized comments, standardized praise ("very good"), grades, or no feedback. Interest, performance, attributions to effort, and task involvement were higher after personalized comments. Ego-involved motivation (the desire to look good or do better than others) was greater after grades and standard praise.

## Grouping, Evaluation, and Time

You may remember a teacher who motivated you to work hard—someone who made a subject come alive. Or you may remember how many hours you spent practising as a member of a team, orchestra, choir, or theatre troupe. If you do, then you know the motivational power of relationships with other people.

**GROUPING AND GOAL STRUCTURES.** Motivation can be greatly influenced by the ways we relate to the other people who are also involved in accomplishing a particular goal. Johnson and Johnson (2009a) have labelled this interpersonal "climate" of how students work together in striving for a goal the **goal structure** of the task. There are three goal structures: cooperative, competitive, and individualistic, as shown in Table 12.6.

When a task involves complex learning and problem-solving skills, cooperation leads to higher achievement than competition, especially for students with lower abilities. Students learn to set attainable goals and negotiate. They become more altruistic. The interaction with peers that students enjoy so much becomes a part of the learning process. The result? The need for belonging described by Maslow is more likely to be met and motivation is increased (Stipek, 2002; Webb & Palincsar, 1996). There are many approaches to peer learning or group learning, as you saw in Chapter 11. For example, to encourage motivation with a cooperative goal structure, form reading groups based on student interests instead of abilities, and change the groups every month (Anderman & Anderman, 2010).

**Goal structure** The way students relate to others who are also working toward a particular goal.

TABLE 12.6 • **Different Goal Structures**

Each goal structure is associated with a different relationship between the individual and the group. This relationship influences motivation to reach the goal.

| | **COOPERATIVE** | **COMPETITIVE** | **INDIVIDUALISTIC** |
|---|---|---|---|
| Definition | Students believe their goal is attainable only if other students will also reach the goal. | Students believe they will reach their goal if and only if other students do not reach the goal. | Students believe that their own attempt to reach a goal is not related to other students' attempts to reach the goal. |
| Examples | Team victories—each player wins only if all the team members win: a relay race, a quilting bee, a barn raising, a symphony, a play. | Golf tournament, singles tennis match, a 100-metre dash, valedictorian. | Lowering your handicap in golf, jogging, learning a new language, enjoying a museum, losing or gaining weight, stopping smoking. |

*Source: Based on Johnson, D., & Johnson, R. (1999). Learning Together and Alone: Cooperation, Competition, and Individualization (5th ed.). Allyn and Bacon: Boston, MA. © Pearson Education.*

EVALUATION. The greater the emphasis on competitive evaluation and grading, the more students will focus on performance goals rather than mastery. And low-achieving students who have little hope of either performing well or mastering the task may simply want to get it over with (Brophy, 2005). How can teachers prevent students from simply focusing on the grade or doing the work "just to get finished"? The most obvious answer is to de-emphasize grades and to emphasize learning in the class. Students need to understand the value of the work. Instead of saying, "You will need to know this for the test," tell students how the information will be useful in solving problems they want to solve. Suggest that the lesson will answer some interesting questions. Communicate that understanding is more important than finishing. Unfortunately, many teachers do not follow this advice.

TIME. Most experienced teachers know that there is too much work and not enough time in the school day. Even if students become engrossed in a project, they must stop and turn their attention to another class when the bell rings or when the teacher's schedule indicates it's time to move on to a new subject. Furthermore, students must progress as a group. If particular individuals can move faster or if they need more time, they may still have to follow the pace of the whole group. So scheduling often interferes with motivation by making students move faster or slower than would be appropriate or by interrupting their involvement. It is difficult to develop persistence and a sense of self-efficacy when students are not allowed to stick with a challenging activity. As a teacher, will you be able to make time for engaged and persistent learning? Some elementary classrooms have *DEAR* time—Drop Everything And Read—to give extended periods when everyone, even the teacher, reads. Some middle and high schools have *block scheduling* in which teachers work in teams to plan larger blocks of class time.

PUTTING IT ALL TOGETHER. How do these motivational elements come together in real classrooms? Sara Dolezal and her colleagues observed and interviewed grade 3 teachers in eight Catholic schools and determined if their students were low, moderate, or high in their level of motivation (Dolezal, Welsh, Pressley, & Vincent, 2003). Table 12.7 summarizes the dramatic differences in these classrooms between the use of strategies that support motivation and those that undermine it. Students in the *low-engagement* classes were restless and chatty as they faced their easy, undemanding seatwork. The classrooms were bare, unattractive, and filled with management problems. Instruction was disorganized. The class atmosphere was generally negative. The *moderately engaged* classrooms were organized to be "student friendly," with reading areas, group work areas, posters, and student artwork. The teachers were warm and caring, and they connected lessons to students' background knowledge. Management routines were smooth and organized, and the class atmosphere was positive. The teachers were good at catching student attention, but they had trouble *holding* attention, probably because the tasks were too easy. *Highly engaging* teachers had all the positive qualities of student-friendly classrooms—but they added more challenging tasks along with the support the students needed to succeed. These excellent motivators did not rely on one or two approaches to motivate their students; they applied a large repertoire of strategies from Table 12.7.

## Diversity in Motivation

Because students differ in terms of language, culture, economic privilege, personality, knowledge, and experience, they will also differ in their needs, goals, interests, emotions, and beliefs. Teachers encourage motivation to learn by taking this diversity into account using TARGET—designing tasks, supporting autonomy, recognizing accomplishments, grouping, making evaluations, and managing time. Take interest, for example. Embedding student writing tasks in cultural contexts is one way to catch and hold situational interest (Alderman, 2004; Bergin, 1999). When ethnic immigrant students in middle-school classes moved from writing using worksheets and standard assignments to writing about such topics as immigration, bilingualism, and gang life—issues that were important to them and to their families—their papers got longer and the writing quality was better (Rueda & Moll, 1994).

TABLE 12.7 • **Strategies That Support and Undermine Motivation in the Classroom**

| A FEW STRATEGIES THAT SUPPORT MOTIVATION | |
|---|---|
| STRATEGY | EXAMPLE |
| Messages of accountability and high expectations | The teacher asks students to have parents review and sign some assignments. |
| Teacher communicates importance of work | "We need to check it for at least one minute, which means looking over it carefully." |
| Clear goals/directions | The teacher explains exactly how the students are to separate into groups and complete their nominations for their favourite book. |
| Connections across the curriculum | The teacher relates the concept of ratios in math to compare/contrast skills in reading. |
| Opportunities to learn about and practise dramatic arts | After studying about historical figures, students write and produce their own plays. |
| Attributions to effort | During a word game, the teacher says to a student, "Did you study last night?" The student nods. "See how it helps?" |
| Encouraging risk-taking | "I need a new shining face. Someone I haven't called on yet. I need a risk-taker." |
| Uses games and play to reinforce concept or review material | During a math lesson using balance, students spend five minutes weighing the favourite toy they were asked to bring in that day. |
| Home–school connections | As part of math science unit, a recycling activity asks families to keep a chart of everything they recycle in a week. |
| Multiple representations of a task | The teacher uses four ways to teach multiplication: "magic multipliers," sing-along multiplication facts, whole-class flash card review, "Around-the-World" game. |
| Positive classroom management, praise, private reprimands | "Thumbs up when you are ready to work. Table 7 has thumbs up. I like the way table 7 is waiting patiently." |
| Stimulating creative thought | "We are going to use our imaginations today. We are going to take a trip to an imaginary theatre in our heads." |
| Opportunities for choice | Students can choose to use prompts for their journal writing or pick their own topic. |
| Teacher communicates to students that they can handle challenging tasks | "This is hard stuff and you are doing great. I know adults who have trouble with this." |
| Value students—communicate caring | The teacher allows a new student to sit with a buddy for the day. |
| A FEW STRATEGIES THAT DO NOT SUPPORT MOTIVATION TO LEARN | |
| Attributions to intellect rather than effort | When students remark during a lesson, "I'm stupid" or "I'm a dork," the teacher says nothing, then replies, "Let's have someone who is smart." |
| Teacher emphasizes competition rather than working together | The teacher conducts a poetry contest where students read poems to the class and the class members hold up cards with scores rating how well each student performed. |
| No scaffolding for learning a new skill | The teacher is loud and critical when students have trouble: "Just look back in the glossary and don't miss it because you are too lazy to look it up." |
| Ineffective/negative feedback | "Does everyone understand?" A few students say yes and the teacher moves on. |
| Lack of connections | The day before Thanksgiving holiday, the teacher leads a brief discussion about that tradition, then the remainder of the activities are about Confederation. |
| Easy tasks | The teacher provides easy work and "fun" activities that teach little. |
| Negative class atmosphere | "Excuse me, I said page number. If you follow and listen, you would know." |
| Punitive classroom management | The teacher threatens bad grades if students do not look up words in the glossary. |
| Work that is much too difficult | The teacher assigns independent math work that only one or two students can do. |
| Slow pacing | The pace is set for the slowest students—others finish and have nothing to do. |
| Emphasis on finishing, not learning | The teacher communicates the purpose is to finish, not learn or use the vocabulary. |
| Sparse, unattractive classroom | There are no decorated bulletin boards, maps, charts, or displays of student work. |
| Poor planning | Missing handouts force the teacher to have large instead of smaller work groups. |
| Public punishment | All students stand, and the teacher reads a list of those who finished the assignment and they sit down. The teacher gives public lecture on responsibility to those left standing. |

*Source: Adapted from Dolezal, S. E., Welsh, L. M., Pressley, M., & Vincent, M. (2003). How do nine third-grade teachers motivate their students? Elementary School Journal, 103, pp. 247–248.*

Language is a central factor in students' connections with the school. When bilingual students are encouraged to draw on both English and their heritage language, motivation and participation can increase. Robert Jimenez (2000) found in his study of bilingual Latino/a students that successful readers viewed reading as a process of making sense; they used both of their languages to understand the material. For instance, they might look for Spanish word parts in English words to help them translate. Less-successful students had a different goal. They believed that reading just meant saying the words correctly in English. It is likely their interest and sense of efficacy for reading in English would be less, too.

## Lessons for Teachers: Strategies to Encourage Motivation

Until four basic conditions are met for every student and in every classroom, no motivational strategies will succeed. First, the classroom must be relatively organized and free from constant interruptions and disruptions. (Chapter 13 will give you the information you need to make sure this requirement is met.) Second, the teacher must be a patient, supportive person who never embarrasses the students because they made mistakes. Everyone in the class should view mistakes as opportunities for learning (Clifford, 1990, 1991). Third, the work must be challenging, but reasonable. If work is too easy or too difficult, students will have little motivation to learn. They will focus on finishing, not on learning. Finally, the learning tasks must be authentic. And as we have seen, what makes a task authentic is influenced by the students' culture (Bergin, 1999; Brophy & Kher, 1986; Stipek, 1993).

Once these four basic conditions are met, the influences on students' motivation to learn in a particular situation can be summarized in four questions: Can I succeed at this task? Do I want to succeed? What do I need to do to succeed? Do I belong? (Committee on Increasing High School Students' Engagement and Motivation to Learn, 2004; Eccles & Wigfield, 1985). We want students to have confidence in their ability so they will approach learning with energy and enthusiasm. We want them to see the value of the tasks involved and work to learn, not just try to get the grade or get finished. We want students to believe that success will come when they apply good learning strategies instead of believing that their only option is to use self-defeating, failure-avoiding, face-saving strategies. When things get difficult, we want students to stay focused on the task, and not get so worried about failure that they "freeze." And we want students to feel as though they belong in school—that their teachers and classmates care about them and can be trusted.

CAN I DO IT? BUILDING CONFIDENCE AND POSITIVE EXPECTATIONS.    No amount of encouragement or "cheerleading" will substitute for real accomplishment. To ensure genuine progress:

1. *Begin work at the students' level and move in small steps.* One possibility is to have very easy and very difficult questions on every test and assignment, so all students are both successful and challenged. When grades are required, make sure all the students in class have a chance to make at least a C if they work hard.
2. *Make sure learning goals are clear, specific, and possible to reach in the near future.* Break long-term projects into subgoals. If possible, give students a range of goals at different levels of difficulty, and let them choose.
3. *Stress self-comparison, not comparison with others.* Give specific feedback and corrections. Tell students what they are doing right as well as what is wrong and why it is wrong. Periodically, give students a question or problem that was once hard for them but now seems easy. Point out how much they have improved.
4. *Communicate to students that academic ability is improvable* and specific to the task at hand. In other words, the fact that a student has trouble in algebra doesn't necessarily mean that geometry will be difficult. Don't undermine your efforts to stress improvement by displaying only the 100% papers on the bulletin board.
5. *Model good problem solving,* especially when you have to try several approaches. Students need to see that learning is not smooth and error-free, even for the teacher.

DO I WANT TO DO IT? SEEING THE VALUE OF LEARNING.   Teachers can use intrinsic and extrinsic motivation strategies to help students see the value of the learning task.

**Attainment and Intrinsic Value.**   To establish attainment value, we must connect the learning task with the needs of the students. It must be possible for students to meet their needs for safety, belonging, and achievement in our classes. Many students are quietly wounded by their teachers' words or school practices that embarrass, label, or demean (Olson, 2008). We must make it clear that both women and men can be high achievers in all subjects: no subjects are the territory of only one sex. It is not "unfeminine" to be strong in mathematics, car mechanics, or sports. It is not "unmasculine" to be good in literature, art, or French.

There are many strategies for encouraging intrinsic (interest) motivation. Several of the following are taken from Brophy (1988).

1. *Tie class activities to student interests* in sports, music, current events, pets, common problems or conflicts with family and friends, fads, television, and movie personalities, or other significant features of their lives (Schiefele, 1991).
2. *Arouse curiosity*. Point out puzzling discrepancies between students' beliefs and the facts. For example, Stipek (1993) describes a teacher who asked her grade 5 class if there were "people" on some of the other planets. When the students said yes, the teacher asked if people needed oxygen to breathe. Because the students had just learned this fact, they responded yes. Then the teacher told them that there is no oxygen in the atmosphere of the other planets. This surprising discrepancy between what the children knew about oxygen and what they believed about life on other planets led to a rousing discussion of the atmospheres of other planets.
3. *Make the learning task fun*. Many lessons can be taught through simulations or games (see the *Point/Counterpoint*). Used appropriately so that the activity connects with learning, these experiences can be very worthwhile and fun, too.
4. *Make use of novelty and familiarity*. Don't overuse a few teaching approaches or motivational strategies. We all need some variety. Varying the goal structures of tasks (cooperative, competitive, individualistic) can help. When the material being covered in class is abstract or unfamiliar to students, try to connect it to something they know and understand. For example, talk about the size of a large area, such as the Acropolis in Athens, in terms of football fields.

**Instrumental Value.**   Sometimes it is difficult to encourage intrinsic motivation, and so teachers must rely on the utility or "instrumental" value of tasks. It is important to learn many skills because they will be needed in more advanced classes or for life outside school.

1. When these connections are not obvious, you should *explain the connections* to your students or ask them to explain how the material will be important in their lives (Hulleman, Godes, Hendricks, & Harackiewicz, 2010).
2. In some situations, teachers can *provide incentives and rewards* for learning (see Chapter 7). Remember, though, that giving rewards when students are already interested in the activity may undermine intrinsic motivation.
3. *Use ill-structured problems and authentic tasks* in teaching. Connect problems in school to real problems outside, such as buying your first car, making decisions about mobile phone plans, or writing a persuasive letter to a potential employer.

WHAT DO I NEED TO DO TO SUCCEED? STAYING FOCUSED ON THE TASK.   When students encounter difficulties, as they must if they are working at a challenging level, they need to keep their attention on the task. If the focus shifts to worries about performance, fear of failure, or concern with looking smart, then motivation to learn is lost.

1. *Give students frequent opportunities to respond* through questions and answers, short assignments, or demonstrations of skills and correct problems quickly. You don't want students to practise errors too long.
2. When possible, *have students create a finished product*. They will be more persistent and focused on the task when the end is in sight. For example, Phil often begins a

house-painting project thinking he will work for just an hour and then finds himself still painting hours later because he wants to see the finished product.

3. *Avoid heavy emphasis on grades and competition.* An emphasis on grades forces students to focus on performance, not learning. Anxious students are especially hard hit by highly competitive evaluation.

4. *Reduce the task risk without oversimplifying it.* When tasks are risky (failure is likely and the consequences of failing are grave), student motivation suffers. For difficult, complex, or ambiguous tasks, provide students with plenty of time, support, resources, help, and the chance to revise or improve work.

5. *Model motivation to learn* for your students. Talk about your interest in the subject and how you deal with difficult learning tasks.

6. *Teach the particular learning strategies* that students will need to master the material being studied. Show students how to learn and remember so they won't be forced to fall back on self-defeating strategies or rote memory.

**DO I BELONG IN THIS CLASSROOM?** This last question will take more than a page or two to address, so I have devoted a large part of Chapter 13 to the notion of creating learning communities. The support of families can be helpful as you design strategies for your students. The *Family and Community Partnerships Guidelines* give ideas for working with families.

---

### GUIDELINES — FAMILY AND COMMUNITY PARTNERSHIPS

## Motivation to Learn

**Understand family goals for children.**
*Examples*

1. In an informal setting, around coffee or snacks, meet with families individually or in small groups to listen to what their goals are for their children.
2. Mail out questionnaires or send response cards home with students, asking what skills the families believe their children most need to work on. Pick one goal for each child, and develop a plan for working toward the goal both inside and outside school. Share the plan with the families and ask for feedback.

**Identify student and family interests that can be related to goals.**
*Examples*

1. Ask a member of the student's family to share a skill or hobby.
2. Identify "family favourites"—favourite foods, music, vacations, sports, activities, hymns, movies, games, snacks, recipes, memories. Tie class lessons to interests.

**Give families a way to track progress toward goals.**
*Examples*

1. Provide simple "progress charts" or goal cards that can be posted on the refrigerator.
2. Ask for parents' or caregivers' feedback (and mean it) about your effectiveness in helping their children.

**Work with families to build confidence and positive expectations.**
*Examples*

1. Avoid comparing one child in a family to another during conferences and discussions with family members.

2. Ask family members to highlight strong points of homework assignments. They might attach a note to assignments describing the three best aspects of the work and one element that could be improved.

**Make families partners in showing the value of learning.**
*Examples*

1. Invite family members to the class to demonstrate how they use mathematics or writing in their work.
2. Involve parents or caregivers in identifying skills and knowledge that could be applied at home and prove helpful to the family right now—for example, keeping records on service agencies, writing letters of complaint to department stores or landlords, or researching vacation destinations.

**Provide resources that build skill and will for families.**
*Examples*

1. Give family members simple strategies for helping their children improve study skills.
2. Involve older students in a "homework hotline" telephone network for helping younger students.

**Have frequent celebrations of learning.**
*Examples*

1. Invite families to a "museum" at the end of a unit on dinosaurs. Students create the museum in the auditorium, library, or cafeteria. After visiting the museum, families go to the classroom to examine their child's portfolio for the unit.
2. Place mini-exhibits of student work at local grocery stores, libraries, or community centres.

# ▼ SUMMARY

### What Is Motivation? (pp. 399–403)

**Define motivation.** Motivation is an internal state that arouses, directs, and maintains behaviour. The study of motivation focuses on how and why people initiate actions directed toward specific goals, how long it takes them to get started in the activity, how intensively they are involved in the activity, how persistent they are in their attempts to reach these goals, and what they are thinking and feeling along the way.

**What is the difference between intrinsic and extrinsic motivation?** Intrinsic motivation is the natural tendency to seek out and conquer challenges as we pursue personal interests and exercise capabilities—it is motivation to do something when we don't have to. Extrinsic motivation is based on factors not related to the activity itself. We are not really interested in the activity for its own sake; we care only about what it will gain us.

**How does locus of causality apply to motivation?** The essential difference between intrinsic and extrinsic motivation is the person's reason for acting—that is, whether the locus of causality for the action is inside or outside the person. If the locus is internal, the motivation is intrinsic; if the locus is external, the motivation is extrinsic. Most motivation has elements of both. In fact, intrinsic and extrinsic motivation may be two separate tendencies—both can operate at the same time in a given situation.

**What are the key factors in motivation according to a behavioural viewpoint? A humanistic viewpoint? A cognitive viewpoint? A social cognitive viewpoint? A sociocultural viewpoint?** Behaviourists tend to emphasize extrinsic motivation caused by incentives, rewards, and punishment. Humanistic views stress the intrinsic motivation created by the need for personal growth, fulfillment, and self-determination. Cognitive views stress a person's active search for meaning, understanding, and competence, and the power of the individual's attributions and interpretations. Social cognitive theories take into account both the behaviourists' concern with the consequences of behaviour and the cognitivists' interest in the impact of individual beliefs and expectations. Many influential social cognitive explanations of motivation can be characterized as expectancy × value theories. Sociocultural views emphasize legitimate engaged participation and identity within a community.

**What are expectancy × value theories?** Expectancy × value theories suggest that motivation to reach a goal is the product of our expectations for success and the value of the goal to us. If either is zero, our motivation is zero also.

**What is legitimate peripheral participation?** Legitimate peripheral participation means that beginners are genuinely involved in the work of the group, even if their abilities are undeveloped and their contributions are small. The identities of the novice and the expert are bound up in their participation in the community. They are motivated to learn the values and practices of the community to keep their identity as community members.

### Needs (pp. 404–407)

**Distinguish between deficiency needs and being needs in Maslow's theory.** Maslow called four lower-level needs—survival, safety, belonging, and self-esteem—deficiency needs. When these needs are satisfied, the motivation for fulfilling them decreases. He labelled the three higher-level needs—intellectual achievement,

aesthetic appreciation, and self-actualization—being needs. When they are met, a person's motivation increases to seek further fulfillment.

**What are the basic needs that affect motivation, and how does self-determination affect motivation?** Self-determination theory suggests that motivation is affected by the need for competence, autonomy and control, and relatedness. When students experience self-determination, they are intrinsically motivated—they are more interested in their work, have a greater sense of self-esteem, and learn more. Whether students experience self-determination depends in part on if the teacher's communications with students provide information or seek to control them. In addition, teachers must acknowledge the students' perspective, offer choices, provide rationales for limits, and treat poor performance as a problem to be solved rather than a target for criticism.

### Goal Orientations (pp. 407–411)

**What kinds of goals are the most motivating?** Goals increase motivation if they are specific, moderately difficult, and able to be reached in the near future.

**Describe mastery, performance, work-avoidant, and social goals.** A mastery goal is the intention to gain knowledge and master skills, leading students to seek challenges and persist when they encounter difficulties. A performance goal is the intention to get good grades or to appear smarter or more capable than others, leading students to be preoccupied with themselves and how they appear (ego-involved learners). Students can approach or avoid these two kinds of goals—the problems are greatest with avoidance. Another kind of avoidance is evident with work-avoidant learners, who simply want to find the easiest way to handle the situation. Students with social goals can be supported or hindered in their learning, depending on the specific goal (i.e., have fun with friends or bring honour to the family).

**What makes goal setting effective in the classroom?** In order for goal setting to be effective in the classroom, students need accurate feedback about their progress toward goals, and they must accept the goals set. Generally, students are more willing to adopt goals that seem realistic, reasonably difficult, meaningful, and validated by activities connecting them to their intrinsic interests.

### Beliefs and Self-Perceptions (pp. 411–417)

**What are epistemological beliefs and how do they affect motivation?** Epistemological beliefs are ways of understanding how you think and learn. Individuals' epistemological beliefs can impact their approach to learning, their expectations of themselves and the work they do, and the extent to which they engage in academic tasks. Specifically, epistemological beliefs include your understanding of the structure, stability, and certainty of knowledge. A belief that knowledge can be organized into a grand scheme in which all things are related, for example, may lead students to try to connect all new knowledge with previous knowledge in a meaningful way. If the task proves excessively challenging, these students may believe the new information is not relevant to them or worth understanding.

**How do beliefs about ability affect motivation?** When people hold an entity theory of ability—that is, they believe that ability is fixed—they tend to set performance goals and strive to protect themselves from failure. When they believe ability is improvable (an incremental theory), however, they tend to set mastery goals and handle failure constructively.

**What are the three dimensions of attributions in Weiner's theory?** According to Weiner, most of the attributed causes for successes or failures can be characterized in terms of three dimensions: locus (location of the cause internal or external to the person), stability (whether the cause stays the same or can change), and responsibility (whether the person can control the cause). The greatest motivational problems arise when students attribute failures to stable, uncontrollable causes. These students may seem resigned to failure, depressed, helpless—what we generally call "unmotivated."

**What is learned helplessness and what deficits does it cause?** When people come to believe that the events and outcomes in their lives are mostly uncontrollable, they have developed learned helplessness, which is associated with three types of deficits: motivational, cognitive, and affective. Students who feel hopeless will be unmotivated and reluctant to attempt work. They miss opportunities to practise and improve skills and abilities, so they develop cognitive deficits and they often suffer from affective problems such as depression, anxiety, and listlessness.

**How does self-worth influence motivation?** Mastery-oriented students tend to value achievement and see ability as improvable, so they focus on mastery goals, take risks, and cope with failure constructively. A low sense of self-worth seems to be linked with the failure-avoiding and failure-accepting strategies intended to protect the individual from the consequences of failure. These strategies may seem to help in the short term, but are damaging to motivation and self-esteem in the long run.

### Interests, Curiosity, Emotions, and Anxiety (pp. 417–424)

**How do interests and emotions affect learning?** Learning and information processing are influenced by emotion. Students are more likely to pay attention to, learn, and remember events, images, and readings that provoke emotional responses or that are related to their personal interests. However, there are cautions in responding to students' interests. "Seductive details," interesting bits of information that are not central to the learning, can hinder learning.

**How does curiosity affect learning, and what can teachers do to stimulate curiosity in their subject area?** Curiosity is the tendency toward interest in a variety of things. Students' curiosity is guided by their interests, and thus provides them with a self-driven motivation to explore new ideas and concepts. As a result, curiosity can be a powerful motivational tool that captures and maintains students' attention in school. Teachers can foster curiosity by tapping into students' interests, illustrating connections between course material and applications that may be interesting to students, and allowing students to find these connections for themselves. An example might include asking students to identify which simple machines are at work in a skateboard or rollercoaster.

**What is the role of arousal in learning?** There appears to be an optimum level of arousal for most activities. Generally speaking, a higher level of arousal is helpful on simple tasks, but lower levels of arousal are better for complex tasks. When arousal is too low, teachers can stimulate curiosity by pointing out gaps in knowledge or using variety in activities. Severe anxiety is an example of arousal that is too high for optimal learning.

**How does anxiety interfere with learning?** Anxiety can be the cause or the result of poor performance; it can interfere with attention to, learning of, and retrieval of information. Many anxious students need help in developing effective test-taking and study skills.

### Motivation to Learn in School: On TARGET (pp. 424–433)

**Define motivation to learn.** Teachers are interested in a particular kind of motivation—student motivation to learn. Student motivation to learn is both a trait and a state. It involves taking academic work seriously, trying to get the most from it, and applying appropriate learning strategies in the process.

**What does TARGET stand for?** TARGET is an acronym for the six areas in which teachers make decisions that can influence student motivation to learn: the nature of the *task* that students are asked to do, the *autonomy* students are allowed in working, how students are *recognized* for their accomplishments, *grouping* practices, *evaluation* procedures, and the scheduling of *time* in the classroom.

**How do tasks affect motivation?** The tasks that teachers set affect motivation. When students encounter tasks that are related to their interests, stimulate their curiosity, or are connected to real-life situations, they are more likely to be motivated to learn. Tasks can have attainment, intrinsic, or utility value for students. Attainment value is the importance to the student of succeeding. Intrinsic value is the enjoyment the student gets from the task. Utility value is determined by how much the task contributes to reaching short-term or long-term goals.

**Distinguish between bounded and unbounded choices.** Like totally unguided discovery or aimless discussions, unstructured or unbounded choices can be counterproductive for learning. The alternative is bounded choice—giving students a range of options that set out valuable tasks for them, but also allow them to follow personal interests. The balance must be just right so that students are not bewildered by too much choice or bored by too little room to explore.

**How can recognition undermine motivation and a sense of self-efficacy?** Recognition and reward in the classroom will support motivation to learn if the recognition is for personal progress rather than competitive victories. Praise and rewards should focus on students' growing competence. At times, praise can have paradoxical effects when students use the teacher's praise or criticism as cues about capabilities.

**List three goal structures and distinguish among them.** How students relate to their peers in the classroom is influenced by the goal structure of the activities. Goal structures can be competitive, individualistic, or cooperative. Cooperative goal structures can encourage motivation and increase learning, especially for low-achieving students.

**How does the evaluative climate affect goal setting?** The more competitive the grading, the more students set performance goals and focus on "looking competent," that is, they are more ego-involved. When the focus is on performing rather than learning, students often see the goal of classroom tasks as simply finishing, especially if the work is difficult.

**What are some effects of time on motivation?** In order to foster motivation to learn, teachers should be flexible in their use of time in the classroom. Students who are forced to move faster or slower than they should or who are interrupted as they become involved in a project are not likely to develop persistence for learning.

# ▼ WHAT WOULD THEY DO?

## TEACHERS' CASEBOOK: Motivating Students When Resources Are Thin

Here is how some practising teachers responded to motivate students when resources are slim.

### LINDY HENDERSON
Beaver Brae School, Kenora, ON

In the teaching world, lack of resources is a reality as well as a perfect opportunity to design authentic learning experiences for students. Educators are required to be well-versed in curriculum expectations and mandatory content for their subject area or grade. From there, the choice is yours as to how you centre the content in an authentic learning experience.

So, where to begin? Start with the big ideas that need to be covered. Using the overall expectations regarding content as your guide, ask big, open-ended questions. This will frame the thinking around the topic, and the learning will always be content-driven and student-centred. Then, make connections. Does other curriculum exist that relates? What are your students' interests? What do your students talk about most often, or do, in their spare time? What learning opportunities have they enjoyed in the past? Making connections to that which is intrinsically of interest to your learners will not only motivate them, but also let them know that they are active participants in their learning. Using the framework of the big ideas (content), link existing print materials. Then encourage students to ask and answer their own questions. Let's face it: No one looks back on that awesome worksheet they completed a few years back, but we all recall an authentic learning experience!

Humans are naturally inquisitive. It is our nature to ask questions and seek answers. Educators who model their own wonderment foster the same in others. By providing students with time, space, context, and connections, student motivation will fall into place. Connecting with other students or experts, collaboratively problem-solving, showcasing learning in a variety of ways—these are a few ways students will be motivated and active during their learning journey. While print resources may be limited or questionably useful at times, the world is connected through the internet. Making connections of your own—with colleagues in your building and beyond—provides exponentially more opportunities to be creative and versatile in your teaching practice.

### KATE WHITTON
Meadowview Public School, Addison, ON

Part of the reality of teaching today is that there never seems to be enough funds for the adoption of stimulating new material.

As a result, teachers have had to become even more creative and versatile with the resources that are available. As well, many excellent free resources can be found outside the school. I would begin by searching within the local community for guest speakers and for free programs and materials offered by government and private agencies and by public libraries. Sometimes local industry can offer products, such as paper, that would otherwise be discarded. Other wonderful sources are the internet, the Board Learning Resources centres, and inter-school swaps.

By experiencing concrete results students will begin to comprehend the concept of the value of learning, so these results have to be meaningful for them. Creating assignments that integrate the various learning styles in the classroom will initiate and maintain student interest. One possible approach is to find a common theme that incorporates the objectives in the workbooks and then develop problem-solving projects or assignments based on this theme. The Stability strand in science, for example, could be combined with the social studies Pioneers strand by having students create a 3-D model of pioneer life that includes components of language (skit, written report, brochure) and math (geometry, measurement, number sense).

Breaking down material into smaller chunks helps students understand it without feeling overwhelmed. Going on to apply it in a more concrete, hands-on way will extend and solidify students' knowledge. The project approach gives students a goal to work toward and acts as an incentive to work through some of the more "boring" workbook material. Furthermore, everyone can be successful on some level with a multi-faceted project. Kids love to problem solve; however, they do require parameters within which to work, and as they become accustomed to this style of learning these parameters can become less stringent. Another advantage of this approach is that teachers can continue making more connections with other curriculum requirements. The key is to remain flexible and open-minded when it comes to altering your own "gems," even at the last minute!

Motivation is highly individualistic. Setting realistic goals and hooking students on some level will enable them to work through most difficult areas, especially when they can bring their own visions and experiences to a project or assignment. Kids usually enjoy working in groups or pairs as they apply concepts in a more active and creative manner. In short, rather than dictating to students, teachers should be more facilitative.

Irina_QQQ/Shutterstock

# CREATING LEARNING ENVIRONMENTS

## TEACHERS' CASEBOOK: Bullies and Victims

Two boys are terrorizing one of your students. They are larger, stronger, and older than the boy being victimized, who is small and shy. Unfortunately, the bullies are fairly popular, in part because they are successful athletes. There are incidents on the bus before and after school, in the gym, and at lunch, including intimidation, extortion of lunch money, tripping, shoving, and verbal taunts—"homo" is a favourite chant. You do not have the two bullies in any of your classes. Your student has started to miss school routinely, and when he is in class, the quality of his work is declining. The other students in your class see what is going on and know you are aware of the problem, too.

### CRITICAL THINKING

- How do you handle this situation?
- Who should be involved?
- What would you do about the verbal homophobic insults?
- What if the bullies were members of your classroom?
- What would you do if the bullies and victim were girls?

## OVERVIEW AND OBJECTIVES

This chapter looks at the ways that teachers create social and physical environments for learning by examining classroom management—one of the main concerns of teachers, particularly beginning teachers. The very nature of classes, teaching, and students makes good management a critical ingredient of success; we will investigate why this is true. Successful managers create more time for learning, involve more students, and help students to become self-managing.

A positive learning environment must be established and maintained throughout the year. One of the best ways to do this is to try to prevent problems from occurring at all. But when problems arise—as they inevitably do—an appropriate response is important. What will you do when students challenge you openly in class, when one student asks for your advice on a difficult personal problem, or when another withdraws from all participation? We will examine the ways in which teachers can communicate effectively with their students in these and many other situations.

By the time you have completed this chapter, you should be able to:

13.1 Relate academic learning time and student cooperation to creating and maintaining a classroom climate conducive to academic achievement and socio-emotional well-being.

13.2 Summarize the research on the roles of rules, procedures, and consequences in classroom management.

13.3 Explain how the physical environment can support or interfere with learning, and plan an appropriate arrangement for your classroom.

13.4 Identify strategies for preventing and addressing student misbehaviours, including bullying.

13.5 Characterize successful teacher–student communication.

## THE NEED FOR ORGANIZATION

In study after study of the factors related to student achievement, classroom management stands out as the variable with the largest impact (Marzano & Marzano, 2003). Knowledge and expertise in classroom management are marks of expertise in teaching; stress and exhaustion from managerial difficulties are precursors of burnout in teaching (Emmer & Stough, 2001). Why is classroom management so critical?

Classes are particular kinds of environments. They have distinctive features that influence their inhabitants no matter how the students or the desks are organized or what the teacher believes about education (Doyle, 1986, 2006). Classrooms are *multidimensional*. They are crowded with people, tasks, and time pressures. Many individuals, all with differing goals, preferences, and abilities, must share resources, accomplish various tasks, use and reuse materials without losing them, move in and out of the room, and so on. In addition, actions can have multiple effects. Calling on students of low ability may encourage their participation and thinking but may slow the discussion and lead to management problems if the students cannot answer. And events occur *simultaneously*—everything happens at once, and the pace is fast. Teachers have literally hundreds of exchanges with students during a single day.

In this rapid-fire existence, events are *unpredictable*. Even when plans are carefully made, a lesson can still be interrupted by technology glitch or a loud, angry discussion right outside the classroom. Because classrooms are *public*, the way the teacher handles these unexpected intrusions is seen and judged by all. Students are always noticing if the teacher is being "fair." Is there favouritism? What happens when a rule is broken? Finally,

**COOPERATION IS KEY** Gaining student cooperation is the first task of classroom management. There are lessons, materials, time, space, and people to coordinate to keep learning on track.

AGStockUSA/Alamy

classrooms have *histories*. The meaning of a particular teacher's or student's actions depends in part on what has happened before. The fifteenth time a student arrives late requires a different response from the teacher than the first late arrival. In addition, the history of the first few weeks of school affects life in the class all year.

## The Basic Task: Gain Their Cooperation

The basic management task for teachers is to achieve order and harmony by gaining and maintaining student cooperation in class activities (Doyle, 2006). Given the multi-dimensional, simultaneous, immediate, unpredictable, public, and historical nature of classrooms, this is quite a challenge. Gaining student cooperation means planning activities, having materials ready, making appropriate behavioural and academic demands on students, giving clear signals, accomplishing transitions smoothly, foreseeing problems and stopping them before they start, selecting and sequencing activities so that flow and interest are maintained—and much more. Also, different activities require different managerial skills. For example, a new or complicated activity may be a greater threat to classroom management than a familiar or simple activity.

Obviously, gaining the cooperation of kindergartners is not the same task as gaining the cooperation of students in grade 12. During kindergarten and the first few years of elementary school, direct teaching of classroom rules and procedures is important because these students are still learning how to behave in school. For children in the middle elementary years, many school and classroom routines have become relatively automatic, but new rules and procedures for a particular activity may need to be taught directly, and the entire system still needs monitoring and maintenance. Toward the end of elementary school and middle school and the beginning of high school, some students begin to test and defy authority. The management challenges at this stage are to deal productively with these disruptions and to motivate students who are becoming less concerned with teachers' opinions and more interested in their social lives. By the end of high school, the challenges are to manage the curriculum, fit academic material to students' interests and abilities, and help students become more self-managing (Emmer & Evertson, 2013; Evertson & Emmer, 2013).

## The Goals of Classroom Management

**Listen**
The Goals of Classroom Management

**STOP & THINK** You are interviewing for a job in a great school district—it is known for innovation. The vice principal looks at you for a moment and then asks, "What is classroom management?" How would you answer? •

The aim of **classroom management** is to maintain a positive, productive learning environment. But order for its own sake is an empty goal. As we discussed in Chapter 6, it is unethical to use class management techniques just to keep students docile and quiet. What, then, is the point of working so hard to manage classrooms? There are at least three reasons why management is important.

ACCESS TO LEARNING.   Each classroom activity has its own rules for participation. Sometimes these rules are clearly stated by the teacher, but often they are implicit and unstated. Teacher and students may not even be aware that they are following different rules for different activities (Berliner, 1983). For example, in a reading group students may have to raise their hands to make a comment, but in a show-and-tell circle in the same class they may simply have to catch the teacher's eye.

As we saw in Chapter 6, the rules defining who can talk; what they can talk about; and when, to whom, and how long they can talk are often called **participation structures**. In order to participate successfully in a given activity, students must understand the participation structure. Some students, however, seem to come to school less able to participate than others. The participation structures they learn at home in interactions with siblings, parents, and other adults do not match the participation structures of school activities (Cazden, 2001). What can we conclude? To reach the first goal of classroom management—giving all students access to learning—you must make sure that everyone knows *how to participate* in class activities. The key is awareness. What are your rules and expectations? Are they understandable, given your students' cultural backgrounds and home experiences? What unspoken rules or values may be operating? Are you clearly signalling appropriate ways to participate? For some students, particularly those with behavioural and emotional challenges, direct teaching and practice of the important behaviours may be required (Emmer & Stough, 2001).

MORE TIME FOR LEARNING.   If you were to use a stopwatch to time the commercials during a TV game show, you'd likely find that almost half of the program was devoted to commercials. Then, if you timed all the "small talk," you'd find that very little time is spent actually playing the game. If you used a similar approach in classrooms, timing all the different activities throughout the day, you might be surprised by how little actual teaching takes place. Many minutes are lost each day through interruptions, disruptions, late starts, and rough transitions. Obviously, students will learn only what they encounter. Almost every study examining time and learning has found a significant relationship between time spent on content and student learning (Weinstein, Romano, & Mignano, 2011). Thus, one important goal of classroom management is to expand the sheer number of minutes available for learning. This time is sometimes called **allocated time**.

**Classroom management**
Techniques used to maintain a healthy learning environment, relatively free of behavioural problems.

**Participation structures** The formal and informal rules for how to take part in a given activity.

**Allocated time** Time set aside for learning.

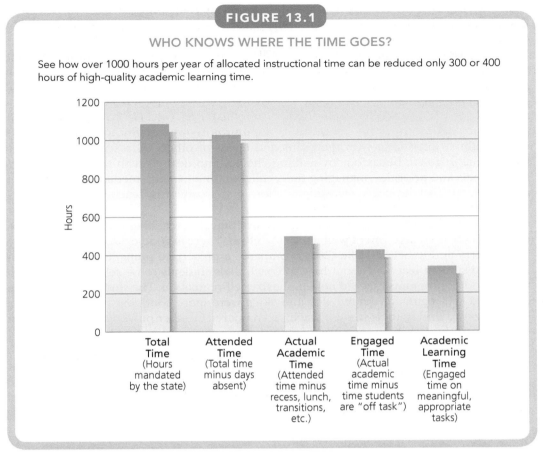

**FIGURE 13.1**

WHO KNOWS WHERE THE TIME GOES?

See how over 1000 hours per year of allocated instructional time can be reduced only 300 or 400 hours of high-quality academic learning time.

Source: From Weinstein, C. S., & Mignano, A. J. (2007). Elementary Classroom Management (4th ed.). New York: McGraw-Hill. © The McGraw-Hill Companies. Adapted with permission of the McGraw-Hill Companies, Inc.

Simply making more time available for learning will not automatically lead to achievement. To be valuable, time must be used effectively. As you saw in the chapters on cognitive learning, how students process information is a central factor in what they learn and remember. Basically, students will learn what they practise and think about. The time spent actively involved in specific learning tasks is often called **engaged time**, or sometimes **time on task**.

Again, however, engaged time doesn't guarantee learning. Students may be struggling with material that is too difficult or using the wrong learning strategies. When students are working with a high rate of success—really learning and understanding—we call the time spent **academic learning time**. So the second goal of class management is to increase academic learning time by keeping students *actively engaged in worthwhile, appropriate learning activities*. Figure 13.1 shows how the 1000+ hours of time mandated for school can become only about 333 hours of high-quality academic learning time for a typical student.

Getting students engaged in learning early in their school careers can make a big difference. Several studies have shown that teachers' rating of students' on-task, persistent engagement in grade 1 predicts achievement test score gains and grades through grade 4, as well as the decision to drop out of high school (Fredricks, Blumenfeld, & Paris, 2004).

**MANAGEMENT FOR SELF-MANAGEMENT.** The third goal of any management system is to help students become better able to manage themselves. If teachers focus on student compliance, they will spend much of the teaching/learning time monitoring and correcting. Students come to see the purpose of school as just following rules, not constructing deep understanding of academic knowledge. And complex learning structures

**Engaged time/time on task** Time spent actively engaged in the learning task at hand.

**Academic learning time** Time when students are actually succeeding at the learning task.

such as cooperative or problem-based learning require student *self-management*. Compliance with rules is not enough to make these learning structures work (Evertson & Weinstein, 2006).

The movement from demanding obedience to teaching self-regulation and self-control is a fundamental shift in discussions of classroom management today (Weinstein, 1999). Tom Savage (1999) says simply, "the most fundamental purpose of discipline is the development of self-control. Academic knowledge and technological skill will be of little consequence if those who possess them lack self-control" (p. 11). Through self-control and self-regulation, students demonstrate *responsibility*—the ability to fulfill their own needs without interfering with the rights and needs of others (Glasser, 1990). Students learn to self-regulate behaviour by making choices and dealing with the consequences, setting goals and priorities, managing time, collaborating to learn, mediating disputes and making peace, and developing trusting relations with trustworthy teachers and classmates (Bear, 2005; Rogers & Frieberg, 1994).

Encouraging **self-management** requires extra time, but teaching students how to take responsibility is an investment well worth the effort. There is good evidence for this claim. Nancy Perry and Rebecca Collie (2011) compared a preservice preparation program that instructed student teachers about how to coach their students to be self-regulated learners with other programs that did not emphasize self-regulation. The student teachers who developed self-regulation knowledge and skills were more confident, less stressed, and more engaged during their student teaching compared to other prospective teachers who did not learn how to help their students to become self-regulated. This makes sense—if you teach your students to manage their own behaviour and learning, you should have fewer management problems, less stress, and more time to teach, which would support your growing sense of teacher efficacy. When elementary and secondary teachers have effective class management systems but neglect to set student self-management as a goal, their students often have trouble working independently after graduating from these "well-managed" classes.

## CREATING A POSITIVE LEARNING ENVIRONMENT

When making plans for your class, much of what you have already learned in this text should prove helpful. You know, for example, that problems are prevented when student differences, such as those discussed in Chapters 2 through 6, are taken into account in instructional planning. Sometimes students become disruptive because the work assigned is too difficult. And students who are bored by lessons well below their ability levels may be interested in finding more exciting activities to fill their time.

In one sense, teachers prevent discipline problems whenever they make an effort to motivate students. A student involved in learning is usually not involved in a clash with the teacher or other students at the same time. All plans for motivating students are steps toward preventing problems.

### Some Research Results

What else can teachers do to create a positive learning environment? For several years, educational psychologists at the University of Texas at Austin studied classroom management quite thoroughly (Emmer & Stough, 2001; Emmer, Evertson, & Anderson, 1980; Emmer & Gerwels, 2006). Their general approach was to study a large number of classrooms, making frequent observations during the first weeks of school and less frequent visits later in the year. After several months, there were dramatic differences among the classes. Some had very few management problems, while others had many. The most and least effective teachers were identified on the basis of the quality of classroom management and student achievement later in the year.

Next, the researchers looked at their observation records of the first weeks of class to see how the effective teachers got started. Other comparisons were made between the teachers who ultimately had harmonious, high-achieving classes and those whose classes

**Self-management** Management of your own behaviour and acceptance of responsibility for your own actions; use of behavioural learning principles to change your own behaviour.

were fraught with problems. On the basis of these comparisons, management principles were developed. The researchers then taught these principles to a new group of teachers; the results were quite positive. Teachers who applied the principles had fewer problems, their students spent more time learning and less time disrupting, and achievement was higher. The findings of these studies formed the basis for two books on classroom management (Emmer & Evertson, 2009, 2013). Many of the ideas on the following pages are from these books.

## Routines and Rules Required

---

STOP & THINK What are the three or four most important rules you will have for your classroom? •

---

At the elementary school level, teachers must lead 20 to 30 students of varying abilities through many different activities each day. Without efficient rules and procedures, a great deal of time is wasted answering the same question over and over. "My pencil broke. How can I do my math?" "I'm finished with my story. What should I do now?" "Steven hit me!" "I left my homework in my locker."

At the secondary school level, teachers must deal daily with more than 100 students who use dozens of materials and often change rooms for each class. Secondary school students are also more likely to challenge teachers' authority. The effective teachers studied by Emmer, Evertson, and their colleagues had planned procedures and rules for coping with these situations.

ROUTINES AND PROCEDURES. How will materials and assignments be distributed and collected? Under what conditions can students leave the room? How will grades be determined? What are the special routines for handling equipment and supplies in science, art, or vocational classes? **Procedures** and **routines** describe how activities are accomplished in classrooms, but they are seldom written down; they are simply the ways of getting things done in class. Carol Weinstein and colleagues (Weinstein & Novodvorsky, 2011; Weinstein, Romano, & Mignano, 2011) recommend that teachers establish procedures to cover the following areas:

1. *Administrative routines*, such as taking attendance
2. *Student movement*, such as entering and leaving or going to the bathroom
3. *Housekeeping*, such as watering plants or storing personal items
4. *Routines for accomplishing lessons*, such as how to collect assignments or return homework
5. *Interactions between teacher and student*, such as how to get the teacher's attention when help is needed
6. *Talk among students*, such as giving help or socializing

You might use these six areas as a framework for planning your class procedures and routines. The *Guidelines* should help you as you plan.

RULES. Unlike routines, rules are often written down and posted because **rules** specify expected and forbidden actions in the class. They are the dos and don'ts of classroom life. In establishing rules, Jack Martin and Jeff Sugarman (1993) at Simon Fraser University in British Columbia recommend considering what kind of atmosphere you want to create. What student behaviour will help you teach effectively? What limits do the students need to guide their behaviour? The rules you set should be consistent with school rules and also in keeping with principles of learning. For example, we know from the research on small-group learning that students benefit when they explain work to peers. They learn as they teach. A rule that forbids students to help each other may be inconsistent with good learning principles. Or a rule that says "No erasures when writing" may make students focus more on preventing mistakes than on communicating clearly in their writing (Burden, 1995; Emmer & Stough, 2001; Weinstein, Romano, & Mignano, 2011).

**Procedures/routines** Prescribed steps for an activity.

**Rules** Statements specifying expected and forbidden behaviour; dos and don'ts.

## GUIDELINES

### Establishing Class Routines

**Determine procedures for student upkeep of desks, classroom equipment, and other facilities.**
*Examples*

1. Set aside a cleanup time each day or once a week in self-contained classes.
2. Demonstrate and have students practise how to push chairs under the desk, take and return materials stored on shelves, sharpen pencils, use the sink or water fountain, assemble lab equipment, and so on.
3. Put a rotating monitor in charge of equipment or materials.

**Decide how students will be expected to enter and leave the room.**
*Examples*

1. Have a procedure for students to follow as soon as they enter the room. Some teachers have a standard assignment ("Have your homework out and be checking it over").
2. Inform students under what conditions they can leave the room, and make sure they understand when they need to ask for permission to do so.
3. Tell students how they should gain admission to the room if they are late.
4. Set up a policy about class dismissal. Many teachers require students to be in their seats and quiet before they can leave at the end of class. The teacher, not the bell, dismisses class.

**Establish signals for getting students' attention, and teach them to your students.**
*Examples*

1. In the classroom, flick the lights on and off, sound a chord on a piano or recorder, sound a bell like the "ring bell for service" at a sales counter, move to the podium and stare silently at the class, use a phrase like "Eyes, please," take out your grade book, or move to the front of the class.
2. In the halls, raise a hand, clap once, or use some other signal to indicate "Stop."
3. On the playground, whistle or raise a hand to indicate "line up."

**Set routines for student participation in class.**
*Examples*

1. Decide whether you will have students raise their hands for permission to speak or simply require that they wait until the speaker has finished.
2. Determine a signal to indicate that you want everyone to respond at once. Some teachers raise a cupped hand to their ear. Others preface the question with "Everyone."
3. Make sure you are clear about differences in procedures for different activities: reading group, learning centre, discussion, teacher presentation, seatwork, video watching, peer learning group, library, and so forth.
4. Establish how many students at a time can be at the pencil sharpener, teacher's desk, learning centre, sink, bookshelves, reading corner, or bathroom.

**Determine how you will communicate, collect, and return assignments.**
*Examples*

1. Establish a place for listing assignments. Some teachers reserve a particular corner of the board for listing assignments. Others write assignments in coloured chalk. For younger students, it may be better to prepare assignment sheets or folders, colour-coding them for math workbook, reading packet, and science kit.
2. Be clear about how and where assignments should be collected. Some teachers collect assignments in a box or bin; others have a student collect work while they introduce the next activity.

*For ideas about involving students in developing rules and procedures, see http://publications.sreb.org/2004/04V03_Ten_Strategies.pdf and www.nassp.org/tabid/3788/default.aspx?topic=Expectations_Do_You_Have_Them_Do_Students_Get_Them.*

Rules should be positive and observable (raise your hand to be recognized). Having a few general rules that cover many specifics is better than listing all the dos and don'ts. But if specific actions, such as chewing gum in class or smoking cigarettes in the bathrooms, are forbidden, a rule should make this clear (Emmer & Gerwels, 2006).

RULES FOR ELEMENTARY SCHOOL.   Evertson and Emmer (2009) give four examples of general rules for elementary school classes:

1. *Respect and be polite to all people.* Give clear explanations of what you mean by "polite," including not hitting, fighting, or teasing. Examples of polite behaviour include waiting your turn, saying "please" and "thank you," and not calling names. This applies to behaviour toward adults (including substitute teachers) and children.
2. *Be prompt and prepared.* This rule highlights the importance of the academic work in the class. Being prompt includes the beginning of the day and transitions between activities.

3. *Listen quietly while others are speaking.* This applies to the teacher and other students, in both large-class lessons and small-group discussions.

4. *Obey all school rules.* This reminds students that all school rules apply in your classroom. Then students cannot claim, for example, that they thought it was okay to chew gum or listen to music from their iPod in your class, even though these are against school rules, "because you never made a rule against it for us."

Whatever the rule, students need to be taught the behaviour that the rule includes and excludes. Examples, practice, and discussion will be needed before learning is complete.

As you've seen, different activities often require different rules. This can be confusing for elementary students until they have thoroughly learned all the rules. To prevent confusion, you might consider making signs that list the rules for each activity. This provides clear and consistent cues about participation structures so all students, not just the "well-behaved," know what is expected. Of course, these rules must be explained and discussed before the signs can have their full effect.

RULES FOR SECONDARY SCHOOL.    Emmer and Evertson (2009) suggest six examples of rules for secondary school students:

1. *Bring all needed materials to class.* The teacher must specify the type of pen, pencil, paper, notebook, texts, and so on.

2. *Be in your seat and ready to work when the bell rings.* Many teachers combine this rule with a standard beginning procedure for the class, such as a warm-up exercise on the board or a requirement that students have paper with a proper heading ready when the bell rings.

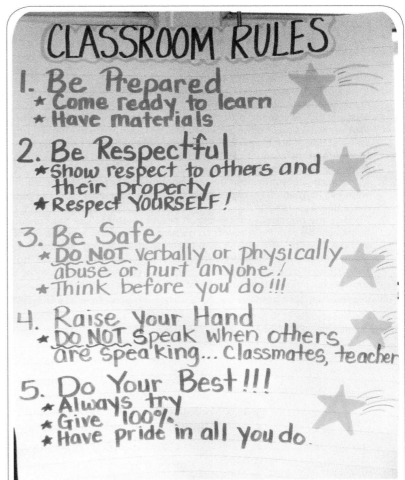

Richard mittleman/Alamy

**RULES PROMOTE RESPECT** Classroom rules that are understood clearly by all students can help maintain a classroom environment that is respectful and more conducive to effective learning.

3. *Respect and be polite to all people.* This rule covers fighting, verbal abuse, and general troublemaking. *All people* includes the teacher.

4. *Listen and stay seated while someone else is speaking.* This applies when the teacher or other students are talking.

5. *Respect other people's property.* This means property belonging to the school, the teacher, or other students.

6. *Obey all school rules.* As with the elementary class rules, this covers a variety of behaviour and situations, so you do not have to repeat every school rule for your class. It also reminds the students that you will be monitoring them inside and outside your class. Make sure that you know all the school rules. Some secondary students are adept at convincing teachers that their misbehaviour "really isn't against the rules."

These rules are more than ways to maintain order. In their study of 34 middle school classrooms, Lindsay Matsumura and her colleagues (2008) found that having explicit rules in the classroom about respecting others predicted the number of students who participated in class discussion, so respect is a gateway to student engagement with the academic material and class dialogue that supports learning.

CONSEQUENCES.    As soon as you decide on your rules and procedures, you must consider what you will do when a student breaks a rule or does not follow a procedure. It is too late to make this decision after the rule has been broken. For many infractions, the

TABLE 13.1 • **Seven Categories of Consequences for Students**

1. *Expressions of disappointment.* If students like and respect their teacher, then a serious, sorrowful expression of disappointment may cause students to stop and think about their behaviour.
2. *Loss of privileges.* Students can lose free time. If they have not completed homework, for example, they can be required to do it during a free period or recess.
3. *Exclusion from the group.* Students who distract their peers or fail to cooperate can be separated from the group until they are ready to cooperate. Some teachers give a student a pass for 10 to 15 minutes. During this time, the student goes to another class or study hall, where the other students and teachers ignore him or her. Some students may perceive this consequence as a reward.
4. *Written reflections on the problem.* Students can write in journals, write essays about what they did and how it affected others, or write letters of apology—if this is appropriate. Another possibility is to ask students to describe objectively what they did; then the teacher and the student can discuss and sign and date this statement. These records are available if parents or administrators need evidence of the students' behaviour.
5. *Detentions.* Detentions can be very brief meetings after school, during a free period, or at lunch. The main purpose is to talk about what has happened. (In high school, detentions are often used as punishments; suspensions and expulsions are available as more extreme measures.)
6. *Visits to the principal's office.* Expert teachers tend to use this consequence rarely, but they do use it when the situation warrants. Some schools require students to be sent to the office for certain offences, such as fighting. If you tell a student to go to the office and the student refuses, you might call the office saying that the student has been sent. Then the student has the choice of either going to the office or facing the principal's penalty for "disappearing" on the way.
7. *Contact with parents.* If problems become a repeated pattern, most teachers contact the student's family. This is done to seek support for helping the student, not to blame the parents or punish the student.

*Source: From Weinstein, C. S., & Mignano, A. J. (2007). Elementary Classroom Management (4th ed.). New York: McGraw-Hill. © The McGraw-Hill Companies. Adapted with permission of the McGraw-Hill Companies, Inc.*

logical consequence is having to go back and "do it right." Students who run in the hall may have to return to where they started and walk properly. Incomplete papers can be redone. Materials left out should be put back. You can use **natural or logical consequences** to support social and emotional development by doing the following (Elias & Schwab, 2006):

- Separate the deed from the doer—the problem is the behaviour, not the student.
- Emphasize to students that they have the power to choose their actions and thus avoid losing control.
- Encourage student reflection, self-evaluation, and problem solving—avoid teacher lecturing.
- Help students identify and give a rationale for what they could do differently next time in a similar situation.

The main point here is that decisions about penalties (and rewards) must be made early on, so that students know before they break a rule or use the wrong procedure what this will mean for them. Anita encourages her student teachers to get a copy of the school rules and their cooperating teacher's rules, and then plan their own. Sometimes, consequences are more complicated. In their case studies of four expert elementary school teachers, Weinstein and Mignano (2007) found that the teachers' negative consequences fell into seven categories, as shown in Table 13.1.

 **Watch**
Who Sets the Rules and Consequences?

WHO SETS THE RULES AND CONSEQUENCES?   If you are going to involve students in setting rules or creating a constitution, you may need to wait until you have established a sense of community in your classroom. Before students can contribute meaningfully to the class rules, they need to trust the teacher and the situation (Elias & Schwab, 2006). In Chapter 1, we described Ken, an expert teacher who worked with his students to establish a students' and teacher's "Bill of Rights" instead of defining rules. These "rights" cover most situations that might require a "rule" and help the students move toward the goal of becoming self-managing. In another class, the Bill of Rights included the rights to whisper when the teacher is not talking, be treated politely, have a two-minute break between working periods, make choices about the day's schedule, have privacy and not have people take your things, and chew gum without blowing bubbles, among several others.

Developing rights and responsibilities rather than rules makes a very important point to students. "Teaching children that something is wrong because there is a rule against it is

**Natural/logical consequences** Instead of punishing, having students redo, repair, or in some way face the consequences that naturally flow from their actions.

TABLE 13.2 • **Laws to Protect Our Rights**

---

1. Follow directions the first time.
2. Speak nicely, be courteous, and respect other people, their feelings and their things. Follow the Bill of Rights.
3. Laugh at the right time for the right time.
4. Respect others' right to learn. Do not distract others. Don't be nosy. Don't yell. Remember to get quiet at countdown.
5. Talk at the right times with the right tone of voice and volume.
6. Transitions and movements are calm, quiet, careful, and elegant.
7. Follow all classroom and school procedures, like: bathroom; pencil; lunch and recess; morning; dismissal; and . . .

---

*Source: From Weinstein., C. S., & Mignano, A. J. (2007). Elementary Classroom Management (4th ed.). New York: McGraw-Hill. © The McGraw-Hill Companies. Adapted with permission of the McGraw-Hill Companies, Inc.*

not the same as teaching them that there is a rule against it because it is wrong, and helping them to understand why this is so" (Weinstein, 1999, p. 154). Students should understand that the rules are developed so that everyone can work and learn together. It should be noted that when Ken has had some very difficult classes, he and his students have had to establish some "laws" that protect students' rights, as you can see in Table 13.2.

Another kind of planning that affects the learning environment is designing the physical arrangement of the class furniture, materials, and learning tools.

## Planning Spaces for Learning

**STOP & THINK** Think back over all the classrooms in all the schools you have attended. Which ones stand out as inviting or exciting? Which ones were cold and empty? Did any teachers have designs that let different students do different things at once? How did they accomplish this? •

Spaces for learning should invite and support the activities you plan in your classroom, and they should respect the inhabitants of the space. This respect begins at the classroom door for young children by helping them identify their class. One school that won awards for its architecture painted each classroom door a different bright colour so that young children could find their "home" (Herbert, 1998). Once inside, spaces can be created that invite quiet reading, group collaboration, or independent research. If students are to use materials, they should be able to reach them. In an interview with Marge Scherer (1999), Herb Kohl describes how he creates a positive environment in his classes:

> What I do is put up the most beautiful things I know—posters, games, puzzles, challenges—and let the children know these are provocations. These are ways of provoking them into using their minds. You have to create an environment that makes kids walk in and say, "I really want to see what's here. I would really like to look at this." (p. 9)

In terms of classroom arrangements, there are two basic ways of organizing space: one focusing on personal territories and one focusing on interest areas.

**PERSONAL TERRITORIES.** Can the physical setting influence teaching and learning in classrooms organized by territories? Front-seat location does seem to increase participation for students who are predisposed to speak in class, whereas a seat in the back will make it more difficult to participate and easier to sit back and daydream (Woolfolk & Brooks, 1983). But the **action zone**, where participation is greatest, may be in other areas, such as on one side or near a particular learning centre (Good, 1983a; Lambert, 1994). To "spread the action around," Weinstein, Romano, and Mignano (2011) suggest that teachers move around the room when possible, establish eye contact with and direct questions to students seated far away, and vary the seating so that the same students are not always consigned to the back.

*Horizontal rows* share many of the advantages of the traditional row and column arrangements. Both are useful for independent seatwork and teacher, student, or media

**Action zone** Area of a classroom where the greatest amount of interaction takes place.

presentations; they encourage students to focus on the presenter and simplify housekeeping. Horizontal rows also permit students to work more easily in pairs. However, this is a poor arrangement for large-group discussion.

*Clusters of four or circle* arrangements are best for student interaction. Circles are especially useful for discussions but still allow for independent seatwork. Clusters permit students to talk, help one another, share materials, and work on group tasks. Both arrangements, however, are poor for whole-group presentations and may make class management more difficult.

The *fishbowl or stack* special formation, where students sit close together near the focus of attention (the back row may even be standing), should be used only for short periods of time, because it is not comfortable and can lead to discipline problems. On the other hand, the fishbowl can create a feeling of group cohesion and is helpful when the teacher wants students to watch a demonstration, brainstorm on a class problem, or see a small visual aid.

INTEREST AREAS.    The design of interest areas can influence the way the areas are used by students. For example, working with a classroom teacher, Carol Weinstein (1977) was able to make changes in interest areas that helped the teacher meet her objectives of having more girls involved in the science centre and having all students experiment more with a variety of manipulative materials. In a second study, changes in a library corner led to more involvement in literature activities throughout the class (Morrow & Weinstein, 1986). If you design areas of interest for your class, keep the suggestions in the *Guidelines* in mind.

Personal territories and interest areas are not mutually exclusive; many teachers use a design that combines these types of organizations. Individual students' desks—their territories—are placed in the centre, with interest areas in the back or around the periphery of the room. This allows the flexibility needed for both large- and small-group activities. Figure 13.2 shows an elementary classroom that combines interest area and personal territory arrangements.

## FIGURE 13.2

### AN ELEMENTARY CLASSROOM ARRANGEMENT

This grade 4 teacher has designed a space that allows teacher presentations and demonstrations, small-group work, computer interactions, math manipulatives activities, informal reading, art, and other projects without requiring constant rearrangements.

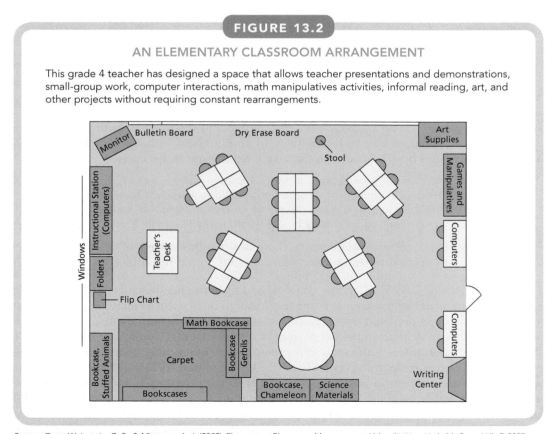

*Source: From Weinstein, C. S., & Mignano, A. J. (2007). Elementary Classroom Management (4th ed.). New York: McGraw-Hill. © 2007 The McGraw-Hill Companies. Adapted with permission of the McGraw-Hill Companies, Inc.*

## GUIDELINES

### Designing Learning Spaces

**Note the fixed features and plan accordingly.**
*Examples*
1. Remember that the audiovisual centre and computers need an electrical outlet.
2. Keep art supplies near the sink, and small-group work by a blackboard.

**Create easy access to materials and a well-organized place to store them.**
*Examples*
1. Make sure materials are easy to reach and visible to students.
2. Have enough shelves so that materials need not be stacked.

**Provide students with clean, convenient surfaces for studying.**
*Examples*
1. Put bookshelves next to the reading area, and games by the game table.
2. Prevent fights by avoiding crowded work spaces.

**Avoid dead spaces and "racetracks."**
*Examples*
1. Don't have all the interest areas around the outside of the room, leaving a large dead space in the middle.
2. Avoid placing a few items of furniture right in the middle of this large space, which creates a "racetrack" around the furniture.

**Arrange things so you can see your students and they can see all instructional presentations.**
*Examples*
1. Make sure you can see over partitions.
2. Design seating so that students can see instruction without moving their chairs or desks.

**Make sure work areas are private and quiet.**
*Examples*
1. Make sure there are no tables or work areas in the middle of traffic lanes; a person should not have to pass through one area to get to another.
2. Keep noisy activities as far as possible from quiet ones. Increase the feeling of privacy by placing partitions, such as bookcases or pegboards, between areas or within large areas.

**Provide choices and flexibility.**
*Examples*
1. Establish private cubicles for individual work, open tables for group work, and cushions on the floor for whole-class meetings.
2. Give students a place to keep their personal belongings. This is especially important if students don't have personal desks.

**Try new arrangements, then evaluate and improve.**
*Examples*
1. Have a "two-week arrangement," then evaluate.
2. Enlist the aid of your students. They have to live in the room, too, and designing a classroom can be a very challenging educational experience.

---

*For more ideas on classroom design, see www.edutopia.org/blog/8-tips-and-tricks-redesign-your-classroom.*

## Getting Started: The First Weeks of Class

Determining a room design, rules, and procedures are first steps toward having a well-managed class, but how do effective teachers gain students' cooperation in those first critical days and weeks? One study carefully analyzed the first weeks' activities of effective and ineffective elementary teachers and found striking differences (Emmer, Evertson, & Anderson, 1980). By the second or third week of school, students in the ineffective teachers' classrooms were more and more disruptive, and less and less on task.

EFFECTIVE MANAGERS FOR ELEMENTARY STUDENTS.   In the effective teachers' classrooms, the very first day was well organized. Name tags were ready. There was something interesting for each child to do right away. Materials were set up. The teachers had planned carefully to avoid any last-minute tasks that might take them away from their students. These teachers dealt with the children's pressing concerns first. "Where do I put my things?" "How do I pronounce my teacher's name?" "Can I whisper to my neighbour?" "Where is the washroom?" The effective teachers had a workable, easily understood set of rules and taught the students the most important rules right away.

They taught the rules as they would any other subject, with a lot of explanation, examples, and practice.

Throughout the first weeks, the effective teachers continued to spend quite a bit of time teaching rules and procedures. Some used guided practice to teach procedures; others used rewards to shape behaviour. Most taught students to respond to a bell or some other signal to gain their attention. These teachers worked with the class as a whole on enjoyable academic activities. They did not rush to get students into small groups or to get them started in readers. This whole-class work gave the teachers a better opportunity to continue monitoring all students' learning of the rules and procedures. Misbehaviour was stopped quickly and firmly, but not harshly.

In the poorly managed classrooms, the first weeks were quite different. Rules were not workable; they were either too vague or very complicated. For example, one teacher made a rule that students should "be in the right place at the right time." Students were not told what this meant, so their behaviour could not be guided by the rule. Neither positive nor negative behaviour had clear, consistent consequences. After students broke a rule, ineffective teachers might give a vague criticism, such as "Some of my children are too noisy," or issue a warning, but not follow through with the threatened consequence.

In the poorly managed classes, procedures for accomplishing routine tasks varied from day to day and were never taught or practised. Instead of dealing with these obvious needs, ineffective teachers spent time on procedures that could have waited. For example, one teacher had the class practise for a fire drill the first day, but left unexplained other procedures that would be needed every day. Students wandered aimlessly and had to ask each other what they should be doing. Often, the students talked to one another because they had nothing productive to do. Ineffective teachers frequently left the room. Many became absorbed in paperwork or in helping just one student. They had not made plans for how to deal with late-arriving students or other interruptions. One ineffective teacher tried to teach students to respond to a bell as a signal for attention but later let the students ignore it. All in all, the first weeks in these classrooms were disorganized and filled with surprises for teachers and students alike.

EFFECTIVE MANAGERS FOR SECONDARY STUDENTS.   What about getting started in a secondary school class? It appears that many of the differences between effective and ineffective elementary school teachers hold at the secondary level as well. Again, effective teachers focus on establishing rules, procedures, and expectations on the first day of class. These standards for academic work and class behaviour are clearly communicated to students and consistently enforced during the first weeks of class. Student behaviour is closely monitored, and infractions of the rules are dealt with quickly. In classes with students of lower ability, work cycles are shorter; students are not required to spend long, unbroken periods on one type of activity. Instead, during each period, they are moved smoothly through several different tasks. In general, effective teachers carefully follow each student's progress so that students cannot avoid work without facing consequences (Emmer & Evertson, 1982).

With all this close monitoring and consistent enforcement of the rules, you may wonder if effective secondary teachers have to be grim and humourless. Not necessarily. The effective teachers in one study also smiled and joked more with their students (Moskowitz & Hayman, 1976). As any experienced teacher can tell you, there is much more to smile about when the class is cooperative.

# CREATING A LEARNING COMMUNITY

Nel Noddings (1992, 1995) has written about the need to create caring educational environments where students take more responsibility for governing their school and classroom. As we saw in Chapter 11 when we discussed the need for relatedness, students are more intrinsically motivated when they feel that their teachers care about them (Grolnick, Ryan, & Deci, 1991). When Blakeburn Elementary School in Port Coquitlam, British Columbia, opened in 2000, one of its school-wide goals was to develop supportive, caring relationships among colleagues, with parents, and among students (Blakeburn Elementary &

Laidlaw, 2001; Laidlaw, 2004). The school focused on helping students become socially responsible. This required consistency and modelling at all levels, and the students learned the language of solving problems, respecting diversity, and contributing to the classroom and the school. In interviews, students talked about feeling safe, included, and happy to be at school. Parents said, "There is a different atmosphere at this school. . . . There is a sense of mutual trust. The expectation is that the kids will manage and get along, and they do" (Blakeburn Elementary & Laidlaw, 2001, p. 1). Historically, however, North American schools have emphasized regulating students' behaviour through rules, not through relationships.

GETTING STARTED ON COMMUNITY.   Whether you are working as an individual or as part of a school-wide team, creating the kind of community that is visible in the day-to-day routines at Blakeburn Elementary School does not happen automatically (Blakeburn Elementary & Laidlaw, 2001, p. 4). It involves input from many different levels to develop a philosophy and participation structures that will foster self-control and social responsibility on the part of students. At Blakeburn, the "leadership team" met first and talked about how to create a caring and socially responsible learning community. Team members used the provincial ministry's Performance Standards for Social Responsibility as a framework for developing a common language and set of expectations. Then they involved the children and their families. The first week of school was devoted to the articulation of what it means (for all members) to be part of a socially responsible community. Students participated in multi-aged "family" groups on relevant activities. Throughout this process, the staff recognized that this work must be multifaceted and integrated in all the curricula and interactions in their classrooms and at the school. They realized that creating positive classroom and school climates requires more than the implementation of prepackaged programs at a scheduled time in the day. It involves "living the principles of inclusion and responsibility ... all day, every day" (Blakeburn Elementary & Laidlaw, 2001, p. 4).

# Maintaining a Good Environment for Learning

A good start is just that—a beginning. Effective teachers build on this beginning. They maintain their management system by preventing problems and keeping students motivated and engaged in productive learning activities. We have discussed several ways to keep students motivated and engaged. In the previous chapter on motivation, for example, we considered stimulating curiosity, relating lessons to student interests, encouraging cooperative learning, establishing learning goals instead of performance goals, and having positive expectations. What else can teachers do?

## Encouraging Engagement

**Watch**
Encouraging Engagement

STOP & THINK What activities keep you completely engaged—the time just seems to disappear? What about those activities keeps you focused? •

In general, as teacher supervision increases, students' engaged time also increases (Emmer & Evertson, 1981). One study found that elementary students working directly with a teacher were on task 97% of the time, while students working on their own were on task only 57% of the time (Frick, 1990). This does not mean that teachers should eliminate independent work for students. It simply means that this type of activity usually requires careful monitoring.

When the task provides continuous cues for the student about what to do next, involvement will be greater. Activities with clear steps are likely to be more absorbing, because one step leads naturally to the next. When students have all the materials they need to complete a task, they tend to stay involved. If their curiosity is piqued, students will be motivated to continue seeking an answer. And, as you now know, students will be

## GUIDELINES

## Keeping Students Engaged

### Make basic work requirements clear.
*Examples*

1. Specify and post the routine work requirements for headings, paper size, pen or pencil use, and neatness.
2. Establish and explain rules about late or incomplete work and absences. If a pattern of incomplete work begins to develop, deal with it early; speak with parents if necessary.
3. Make due dates reasonable and stick to them unless the student has a very good excuse for lateness.

### Communicate the specifics of assignments.
*Examples*

1. With younger students, have a routine procedure for giving assignments, such as writing them on the board in the same place each day. With older students, assignments may be dictated, posted, or given in a syllabus.
2. Remind students of coming assignments.
3. With complicated assignments, give students a sheet describing what to do, what resources are available, due dates, and so on. Explain your grading criteria to older students.
4. Demonstrate how to do the assignment, do the first few questions together, or provide a sample worksheet.

### Monitor work in progress.
*Examples*

1. When you give an in-class assignment, make sure that each student gets started correctly. If you check only students who raise their hands for help, you will miss those who think they know what to do but don't really understand, those who are too shy to ask for help, and those who don't plan to do the work at all.
2. Check progress periodically. In discussions, make sure that everyone has a chance to respond.

### Give frequent academic feedback.
*Examples*

1. Elementary students should get papers back the day after they are handed in.
2. Good work can be displayed in class and graded papers sent home to parents each week.
3. Students of all ages can keep records of grades, projects completed, and extra credits earned.
4. For older students, break up long-term assignments into several phases, giving feedback at each point.

*For more ideas, see www.edutopia.org/classroom-student-participation-tips and http://archive.brookespublishing.com/articles/ed-article-0212.htm.*

---

more engaged if they are involved in authentic tasks—activities that have connections to real life. Also, activities are more engaging when the level of challenge is higher and when students' interests are incorporated into the tasks (Emmer & Gerwels, 2006).

Of course, teachers can't supervise every student all the time, or rely on curiosity to keep students motivated. Something else must keep students working on their own. In their study of elementary and secondary teachers, Evertson, Emmer, and their colleagues found that effective class managers at both levels had well-planned systems for encouraging students to manage their own work (Emmer & Evertson, 2009, 2013). The suggestions in the *Guidelines* are based on their findings.

## Prevention Is the Best Medicine

The ideal way to manage problems, of course, is to prevent them in the first place. Martin and Sugarman (1993) note that "many difficulties in classroom management can be prevented by effective teaching" (p. 51) that interests students, avoids confusion, and keeps activities moving. In a classic study, Jacob Kounin (1970) examined classroom management by comparing effective teachers, whose classes were relatively free of problems, with ineffective teachers, whose classes were continually plagued by chaos and disruption. Observing both groups in action, Kounin found that the teachers were not very different in the way they handled discipline once problems arose. The difference was that the successful teachers were much better at preventing problems. Kounin concluded that effective classroom teachers were especially skilled in four areas: "*withitness*," *overlapping activities*, *group focusing*, and *movement management* (Doyle, 1977). More recent research confirms the importance of these factors (Emmer & Stough, 2001).

## Withitness

**Withitness** means communicating to students that you are aware of everything that is happening in the classroom, that you aren't missing anything. "With-it" teachers seem to have eyes in the backs of their heads. They avoid becoming absorbed or interacting with only a few students, since such behaviour encourages the rest of the class to wander. These teachers are always scanning the room, making eye contact with individual students, so that the students know they are being monitored (Charles, 2011; Weinstein, Romano, & Mignano, 2011).

These teachers prevent minor disruptions from becoming major. They also know who instigated the problem, and they make sure that the right people are dealt with. In other words, they do not make what Kounin called *timing errors* (waiting too long before intervening) or *target errors* (blaming the wrong student and letting the real perpetrators escape responsibility for their behaviour).

If two problems occur at the same time, effective teachers deal with the more serious one first. For example, a teacher who tells two students to stop whispering but ignores even a brief shoving match at the pencil sharpener communicates to students a lack of awareness. Students begin to believe that they can get away with almost anything if they are clever.

OVERLAPPING AND GROUP FOCUS.   **Overlapping** means keeping track of and supervising several activities at the same time. For example, a teacher may have to check the work of an individual and at the same time keep a small group working by saying, "Right, go on," and stop an incident in another group with a quick "look" or reminder (Burden, 1995; Charles, 2011).

Maintaining a **group focus** means keeping as many students as possible involved in appropriate class activities and avoiding narrowing in on just one or two students. All students should have something to do during a lesson. For example, the teacher might ask everyone to write the answer to a question, then call on individuals to respond while the other students compare their answers. Choral responses might be required while the teacher moves around the room to make sure everyone is participating (Charles, 2002b). For example, during a grammar lesson the teacher might say, "Everyone who thinks the answer is *have run*, hold up the red side of your card. If you think the answer is *has run*, hold up the green side" (Hunter, 1982). This is one way teachers can ensure that all students are involved and that everyone understands the material.

MOVEMENT MANAGEMENT.   **Movement management** means keeping lessons and the group moving at an appropriate (and flexible) pace, with smooth transitions and variety. The effective teacher avoids abrupt transitions, such as announcing a new activity before gaining the students' attention or starting a new activity in the middle of something else. In these situations, one-third of the class will be doing the new activity, many will be working on the old lesson, several will be asking other students what to do, some will be taking the opportunity to have a little fun, and most will be confused. Another transition problem Kounin noted is the *slowdown*, or taking too much time to start a new activity. Sometimes teachers give too many directions. Problems also arise when teachers have students work one at a time while the rest of the class waits and watches.

STUDENT SOCIAL SKILLS AS PREVENTION.   But what about the students? What can they do? When students lack social and emotional skills such as being able to share materials, read the intentions of others, or handle frustration, classroom management problems often follow. So all efforts to teach social and emotional self-regulation are steps for preventing management problems. Over the short term, educators can teach and model these skills, then give students feedback and practice using them in a variety of settings. Over the long term, teachers can help to change attitudes that value aggression over cooperation and compromise (Elias & Schwab, 2006).

Debra Stipek and her colleagues (1999) describe many ways teachers embed social skills lessons into school subjects and informal discussions. For example, class rules emphasize respect ("there are no stupid questions"), students learn to give "put ups" not

**Withitness** According to Kounin, awareness of everything happening in a classroom.

**Overlapping** Supervising several activities at once.

**Group focus** The ability to keep as many students as possible involved in activities.

**Movement management** Keeping lessons and the group moving at an appropriate (and flexible) pace, with smooth transitions and variety.

"put downs," the lives of historical figures provide opportunities to discuss choices and how to deal with stresses, and student conflicts become life lessons in relationships. In addition, students are given a "Toolbox of Coping Skills" that contains concrete objects to be used to address problems. The Toolbox includes Post-it notes to record student concerns and troubling situations so the incidents can be dealt with at an appropriate time. Exit and U-turn signs remind students that the best strategy may be to "exit" the situation. "Exiting to a safe place, without explanation, is taught as one appropriate face-saving, and possibly life-saving, response" (Stipek, de la Sota, & Weishaupt, 1999, p. 443). Indicators are that students do learn to use these skills.

## Caring Relationships: Connections With School

All efforts at building positive relationships with students and classroom community are steps toward preventing management problems. Students respect teachers who maintain their authority without being rigid or harsh, who are fair and honest with them, who make sure they understand the materials, who ask if something is wrong when they seem upset, and who use creative instructional practices to "make learning fun." Students also value teachers who show academic and personal caring by acting like real people (not just as teachers), sharing responsibility, minimizing the use of external controls, including everyone, searching for students' strengths, communicating effectively, and showing an interest in their students' lives and pursuits (Elias & Schwab, 2006; Wentzel, 2002; Woolfolk Hoy & Weinstein, 2006).

SCHOOL CONNECTIONS.   Students who feel connected with school are happier, more self-disciplined, and less likely to engage in dangerous behaviours such as substance abuse, violence, and early sexual activity (Freiberg, 2006; McNeely, Nonnemaker, & Blum, 2002; Ponitz, Rimm-Kaufman, Grimm, & Curby, 2009). In fact, in a synthesis of 119 studies conducted from 1948 to 2004, Jeffrey Cornelius-White (2007) concluded that positive, warm, encouraging relationships with teachers are related to many student outcomes including participation in class, critical thinking, dropout prevention, self-esteem, motivation, less disruptive behaviour, and attendance. When Barbara Bartholomew (2008) asked a veteran special education teacher what keeps students engaged and motivated, the teacher replied without hesitation, "Students need to know that no matter what, you will never give up on them" (p. 58).

An example of respect for students and their lives comes from Esme Codell. "Madame Esme" (the name she preferred) had a morning ritual as follows:

In the morning, three things happen religiously. I say good morning, real chipper, to every single child and make sure they say good morning back. Then I collect "troubles" in a "Trouble Basket," a big green basket into which the children pantomime unburdening their home worries so they can concentrate on school. Sometimes a kid has no troubles. Sometimes a kid piles it in, and I in turn pantomime bearing the burden. This way, too, I can see what disposition the child is in when he or she enters. Finally, before they can come in, they must give me a word, which I print on a piece of tag board and keep in an envelope. It can be any word, but preferably one that they heard and don't really know or one that is personally meaningful. We go over the words when we do our private reading conferences. (Codell, 2001, p. 30)

"DON'T GIVE UP ON ME" Students who feel connected with school are happier, more self-disciplined, and less likely to engage in negative behaviours. Believing that they matter and that their teachers are "on their side" helps keep students engaged and motivated.

Liz Moore/Merrill

When students perceive their schools are competitive places where they are treated differently based on race, gender, or ethnicity, then they are more likely to act out or withdraw altogether. But when they feel that they have choices, that the emphasis is on personal improvement and not comparisons, and when they feel respected and supported by teachers, students are more likely to bond with schools (Osterman, 2000). One way of expressing respect and caring is by connecting with students' families and home lives. For example, students in China describe their teachers as high on caring. This may be because Chinese teachers spend quite a bit of time in students' homes, learning about their home life, and offering help outside school. These teachers show respect for the families and cultures of their students by their willingness to visit and to help (Jia, Ling, Yoshikawa, Chen, & Hughes, 2009; Suldo, Friedrich, White, Farmer, Minch, & Michalowski, 2009).

**CREATING COMMUNITIES OF CARE FOR ADOLESCENTS.** The transition to high school is a particularly important time to maintain caring teacher–student relationships. Students have more teachers and fewer close relationships, just at a time when emotional, social, and academic stresses are increasing. One diverse urban school with over 2000 students confronted this problem by creating small communities of care. These were interdisciplinary teams of students and teachers who shared common interests and participated in a "Freshman Focus" class during the first nine weeks of school. The class helped students adjust to high school, get oriented to the building, and develop school skills like taking notes, social skills, and even skills for getting along with parents. The programs led to the development of positive teacher beliefs about students, supportive teacher–student relationships, and the promotion of academic and life skills (Ellerbrock & Kiefer, 2010).

# DEALING WITH DISCIPLINE PROBLEMS

Being an effective manager does not mean publicly correcting every minor infraction of the rules. This kind of public attention may actually reinforce the misbehaviour, as we saw in Chapter 7. The key is being aware of what is happening and knowing what is important so that you can prevent problems.

## Stopping Problems Quickly

Most students comply quickly when the teacher gives a desist order (a "stop doing that") or redirects behaviour. But some students are the targets of more than their share of desists. One study found that these disruptive students seldom complied with the first teacher request to stop. Often, the disruptive students responded negatively, leading to an average of four to five cycles of teacher desists and student responses before the student complied (Nelson & Roberts, 2000). Emmer and Evertson (2009) and Levin and Nolan (2000) suggest seven simple ways to stop misbehaviour quickly, moving from least to most intrusive:

- *Make eye contact* with, or move closer to, the offender. Other nonverbal signals, such as pointing to the work students are supposed to be doing, might be helpful. Make sure the student actually stops the inappropriate behaviour and gets back to work. If you do not, students will learn to ignore your signals.
- *Try verbal hints* such as "name-dropping" (simply insert the student's name into the lecture), asking the student a question, or making a humorous (not sarcastic) comment such as, "I must be hallucinating. I swear I heard someone shout out an answer, but that can't be because I haven't called on anyone yet!"
- Ask students *if they are aware* of the negative effects of their actions, or send an "I" message, described later in the chapter.
- If they are not performing a class procedure correctly, *remind the students* of the procedure and have them follow it correctly. You may need to quietly collect a toy, comb, magazine, or note that is competing with the learning activities, while privately informing the students that their possessions will be returned after class.
- In a calm, unhostile way, *ask the student to state the correct rule or procedure* and then to follow it. Glasser (1969) proposes three questions: "What are you doing? Is it against the rules? What should you be doing?"

- Tell the student in a clear, assertive, and unhostile way to *stop the misbehaviour*. (Later in the chapter we will discuss assertive messages to students in more detail.) If students "talk back," simply repeat your statement.
- *Offer a choice*. For example, when one student continued to call out answers no matter what the teacher tried, the teacher said, "John, you have a choice. Stop calling out answers immediately and begin raising your hand to answer or move your seat to the back of the room and you and I will have a private discussion later. You decide." (Levin & Nolan, 2000, p. 177).

Many teachers prefer the use of *logical consequences*, described earlier, as opposed to penalties. For example, if one student has harmed another, you can require the offending student to make an "Apology of Action," which includes a verbal apology plus somehow repairing the damage done. This restorative approach provides opportunities for victims, offenders, and community members to come together to discuss the harm and, hopefully, leads to reconciliation (Canadian Resource Centre for Victims of Crime, 2011). Offenders can develop empathy and social perspective-taking as they think about what would be an appropriate "repair" (Elias & Schwab, 2006). Restorative justice, with its emphasis on forgiveness, making things right, and restoring balance and harmony, has roots in faith communities (Canadian Resource Centre for Victims of Crime, 2011), but also it is consistent with Aboriginal "peacemaking circles." In 1996, the Criminal Code was amended to include restorative approaches to sentencing, and schools in Canada and throughout North America are using principles of restorative justice to solve problems and structure discipline.

If you must impose penalties, the *Guidelines*, taken from Weinstein and Novodvorsky (2011) and Weinstein, Romano, and Mignano (2011), give ideas about how to do it. The examples are taken from the actual words of the expert teachers described in their book.

## GUIDELINES

### Imposing Penalties

**Delay the discussion of the situation until you and the students involved are calmer and more objective.**
*Examples*

1. Say calmly to a student, "Sit there and think about what happened. I'll talk to you in a few minutes," or, "I don't like what I just saw. Talk to me during your free period today."
2. Say, "I'm really angry about what just happened. Everybody take out journals; we are going to write about this." After a few minutes of writing, the class can discuss the incident.

**Impose penalties privately.**
*Examples*

1. Make arrangements with students privately. Stand firm in enforcing arrangements.
2. Resist the temptation to "remind" students in public that they are not keeping their side of the bargain.
3. Move close to a student who must be disciplined and speak so that only the student can hear.

**After imposing a penalty, re-establish a positive relationship with the student immediately.**
*Examples*

1. Send the student on an errand or ask him or her for help.
2. Compliment the student's work or give a symbolic "pat on the back" when the student's behaviour warrants. Look hard for such an opportunity.

**Set up a graded list of penalties that will fit many occasions.**
*Examples*

1. Establish a list of penalties for not turning in homework: (1) receive reminder; (2) receive warning; (3) hand homework in before close of school day; (4) stay after school to finish work; (5) participate in a teacher–student–parent conference to develop an action plan.

**Always teach problem-solving strategies along with penalties to help students learn what to do next time (Elias & Schwab, 2006).**
*Examples*

1. Use Problem Diaries, where students record what they were feeling, identify the problem and their goal, then think of other possible ways to solve the problem and achieve the goal.
2. Try *Keep Calm 5-2-5*: At the first physical signs of anger, students say to themselves: "Stop. Keep Calm," then take several slow breaths, counting to five breathing in, two holding breath, and five breathing out.

*For more ideas, see www.teachercertification.org/a/maintaining-a-positive-classroom-environment.html or www.cfchildren.org.*

TABLE 13.3 • **What Does Bullying Look Like?**

| TYPE OF BULLYING | DESCRIPTION | BEHAVIOURS THAT COUNT AS BULLYING |
|---|---|---|
| Physical | Any unwanted physical contact in which one participant exerts power or force over another | Hitting, pinching, punching, kicking, shoving Withholding, stealing, destroying property |
| Verbal | Any comment considered offensive or threatening to the victim | Hurtful teasing, name-calling, criticizing, humiliating, threatening, making derogatory comments about others' religion, race, sex, abilities or disabilities |
| Social/Relational | Intentional manipulation of people's social lives, friendships, or reputation | Leaving people out on purpose, spreading rumours, convincing others not to be friends with someone, damaging friendships or reputations, setting someone up to look foolish |
| Cyberbullying | Using an electronic platform to bully (e.g., Facebook, cell phones, the internet) | Spreading rumours through Facebook, texting embarrassing/compromising pictures |

*Source: Adapted from Woolfolk, A. & Perry, N.E. (2015). Child and Adolescent Development, 2nd ed. Pearson. Table 10.4 on p. 422.*

There is a caution about penalties, however. Never use lower achievement status (moving to a lower reading group, giving a lower grade, giving excess homework) as a punishment for breaking class rules. These actions should be done only if the benefit of the action outweighs the possible risk of harm. As Carolyn Orange (2000) notes, "Effective, caring teachers would not use low achievement status, grades, or the like as a means of discipline. This strategy is unfair and ineffective. It only serves to alienate the student" (p. 76).

## Bullying and Cyberbullying

**Watch**
Bullying and Cyberbullying

*Bullying* is a type of aggression characterized by systematic and repeated abuse of power intended to harm the victim (Merrell, Isava, Gueldner, & Ross, 2008). Table 13.3 describes different types of bullying along with examples of behaviours that count as bullying. The three most common types of bullying are physical, verbal, and social/relational, but cyberbullying is becoming more common, especially for adolescents, who often have greater access to the internet and social media than young children do (Woolfolk & Perry, 2015). The line between good-natured exchanges and hostile teasing may seem thin, but a rule of thumb is that teasing someone who is less powerful or less popular or using any racial, ethnic, or religious slur should *not* be tolerated. Between 10%–30% of children and youth report being involved in bullying, and this seems to be the case around the world (Cook, Williams, Guerra, Kim, & Sadek, 2010; Guerra, Williams, & Sadek, 2011). Both bullies and victims are at risk for long-term academic, psychological, and behavioural problems (Swearer, Espelage, Vaillancourt, & Hymel, 2010).

VICTIMS. Studies from both Europe and the United States indicate that about 10% of children are chronic victims—the constant targets of physical or verbal attacks. One kind of victim tends to have low self-esteem and to feel anxious, lonely, insecure, and unhappy. These students often are prone to crying and withdrawal; in general, when attacked, they won't defend themselves. These victims may believe that they are rejected because they have flaws that they cannot change or control—no wonder they are depressed and helpless! There is a second kind of victim—highly emotional and hot-tempered students who seem to provoke aggressive reactions from their peers. Members of this group have few friends (Pellegrini, Bartini, & Brooks, 1999).

TABLE 13.4 • **Dos and Don'ts About Teasing**

Teasing has led to some tragic situations. Discuss what to do about it in your class.

| DO | DON'T |
|---|---|
| 1. Be careful of others' feelings. | 1. Tease someone you don't know well. |
| 2. Use humour gently and carefully. | 2. [If you are a boy] tease girls about sex. |
| 3. Ask whether teasing about a certain topic hurts someone's feelings. | 3. Tease about a person's body. |
| 4. Accept teasing from others if you tease. | 4. Tease about a person's family members. |
| 5. Tell others if teasing about a certain topic hurts your feelings. | 5. Tease about a topic when a student has asked you not to. |
| 6. Know the difference between friendly gentle teasing and hurtful ridicule or harassment. | 6. Tease someone who seems agitated or whom you know is having a bad day. |
| 7. Try to read others' "body language" to see if their feelings are hurt—even when they don't tell you. | 7. Be thin-skinned about teasing that is meant in a friendly way. |
| 8. Help a weaker student when he or she is being ridiculed. | 8. Swallow your feelings about teasing—tell someone in a direct and clear way what is bothering you. |

*Source: From Weinstein, C. S. (2007). Middle and Secondary Classroom Management: Lessons from Research and Practice (4th ed.), © 2007 McGraw-Hill. Adapted with permission from The McGraw-Hill Companies, Inc.*

Garbarino and deLara (2002) estimate that 160 000 children avoid school every day and thousands more drop out of school altogether because they are always afraid. Children who have been chronic victims through elementary and middle school are more depressed and more likely to attempt suicide as young adults (Graham, 1998; Hodges & Perry, 1999). Consider the case of Rehtaeh Parsons, a teenager in Dartmouth, Nova Scotia, who ended her life in April 2014 after she was gang raped (17 months prior) by a group of four teenage boys. The incident was recorded and then distributed online through social media. Rehtaeh's mother attributes her daughter's death to the rape but also to the humiliation and isolation Rehtaeh experienced as a result of the "constant bullying and messaging and harassment" she experienced online (Wikipedia, 2014). And students who kill or injure others in schools are more often victims than bullies (Reinke & Herman, 2002a, 2002b). In the past years, we have seen tragic consequences when bullied students turned guns on their tormentors in schools.

BULLYING AND TEASING.    A longitudinal study that followed a representative sample of students in grades 1 through 6 for two years found that aggressive children whose teachers taught them conflict management strategies were moved away from a life path of aggression and violence (Aber, Brown, & Jones, 2003). But when teachers are silent about aggression and teasing, students may "hear" agreement with the insult (Weinstein & Novodvorsky, 2011). Table 13.4 presents a list of dos and don'ts about teasing in schools.

Besides following these guidelines, research has shown that having a strong sense of community in your classroom is associated with more student empathy for the victims of bullying and less "blaming the victim" for being attacked (Gini, 2008). So anything you do to develop class community will be a step toward dealing with bullying. In particular, students standing up for one another can really make a difference. Anti-Bullying or Pink Shirt Day originated in 2007 when two boys, David Shepherd and Travis Price of Berwick, Nova Scotia, decided to show solidarity with a grade 9 student who was bullied for wearing a pink shirt on the first day of school. They went to a discount store and bought and distributed 50 pink shirts to their classmates. Other students in the school got on board and also wore pink clothes to school the next day. When the bullied student arrived for school that day, he was met with a "sea of pink." Shepherd and Price describe how he looked "like there had been a weight lifted off his shoulder . . . and there's been nary a peep from bullies since" (CBC, 2007). The boys' activism captured widespread media attention around the world. Since then, various countries have identified an anti-bullying day and, in 2012, the United Nations declared May 4 Anti-Bullying Day (Wikipedia, 2014).

In a study of over 2500 students in 59 schools, Nancy Guerra and her colleagues (2011) found that providing opportunities for success, promoting achievement and self-esteem, and improving teacher–student relationships also help to prevent bullying. Some schools and school systems are being proactive and implementing bullying prevention programs. An important consideration, though, is whether the programs have been proven effective. Unfortunately, the results are mixed on the effectiveness of many school-wide bullying prevention programs. It's important to look for scientific evidence that the programs work—according to Swearer and colleagues (Swearer, Espelage, Vaillancourt, & Hymel, 2010), many don't.

CHANGING ATTRIBUTIONS.    Cynthia Hudley and her colleagues (2007) at UCLA have developed a program to reduce physical aggression in elementary school. The program, called *BrainPower*, is grounded in attribution theory, discussed in Chapter 12. The central goal of *BrainPower* is to teach aggressive students to presume negative social encounters (e.g., a peer knocks over your milk or bumps into you as you are getting ready to go out at recess) are due to accidental causes rather than intentional hostility.* The program also teaches accurate reading of social cues, so that students recognize when aggression against them is intentional. After students become more skilful at judging social cues, they learn and practise appropriate responses such as asking questions, being assertive—not aggressive, or seeking adult help. Two decades of research on this program shows it has been successful in changing many students' attributions and behaviours (Hudley, Graham, & Taylor, 2007).

CYBERBULLYING.    With all the positive possibilities associated with technology come problems, too. Now bullies can use technology—YouTube, social media, web blogs—to torment their victims, as was the case for Rehtaeh Parsons. Amanda Todd is another devastating example of how harmful cyberstalking and bullying can be. She committed suicide at the age of 15 in her home in Port Coquitlam, BC, after experiencing relentless online stalking and bullying. When she was in grade 7, she met a stranger online who convinced her to bare her breasts, took a photo of them, and, when she refused to repeat the action, proceeded to seek out and share the photo with Todd's friends online. As a result, Todd was ostracized and bullied by her peers. In October 2012, after enduring several years of this torment, Todd posted a nine-minute video on YouTube telling her story through a series of flashcards, before ending her life (Wikipedia, 2014). This kind of bullying is difficult to combat because the perpetrators can hide, but the damage can be long term. Table 13.5 has some ideas for dealing with cyberbullying.

## Special Problems With Secondary Students

Many secondary students never complete their work. Besides encouraging student responsibility, what else can teachers do to deal with this frustrating problem? Because students at this age have many assignments and teachers have many students, both teachers and students may lose track of what has and has not been completed. It often helps to teach students how to use a daily planner. In addition, the teacher must keep accurate records. The most important thing is to enforce the established consequences for incomplete work. Do not pass a student because you know that he or she is "bright enough" to pass. Make it clear to these students that the choice is theirs: they can do the work and pass, or they can refuse to do the work and face the consequences. You might also ask, in a private moment, if there is anything interfering with the student's ability to get to the work.

There is also the problem of students who continually break the same rules—always forgetting materials, for example, or getting into fights. What should you do? Seat these students away from others who might be influenced by them. Try to catch them before they break the rules, but if rules are broken, be consistent in applying established

---

*Source: Based on Legacy Program Summary, Brain Power, NREPP, SAMHSA, http://www.nrepp.samhsa.gov/ViewLegacy .aspx?id=3

TABLE 13.5  •  **Dealing With Cyberbullying**

- Develop an explicit policy for acceptable in-school use of the internet, and include it in the school handbook (or your class rules).
- The policy should spell out what constitutes cyberbullying and list consequences.
- Make sure that children and young people are aware that bullying will be dealt with seriously.
- Ensure that parents/guardians who express cyberbullying concerns are taken seriously.
- Explain to students that they
  - should never share or give out personal information, PIN numbers, phone numbers, etc.
  - should not delete messages; they do not have to read them, but they should show them to an adult they trust. Messages can be used to take action against cyberbullies.
  - should not open a message from someone they don't know.
  - should never reply to the message.
  - can block the sender's message if they are being bullied through email or instant messaging.
  - can forward the messages to their internet service provider.
  - should tell an adult.
  - should show the message to the police if it contains physical threats.
  - should speak out against cyberbullying.
  - should never send messages when they are angry.
  - should never send messages they wouldn't want others to see.
- Make parents aware of the fact that all of the major internet service providers offer some form of parental controls. For example, AOL has developed "AOL Guardian,"* which reports with whom youngsters exchange messages and what websites they visit, and monitors chat rooms for children 13 and under.
- Encourage parents to keep computers in a public room in the house.
- Invite members of the local police department to come to school to speak with parents and students about proper internet use.
- Make sure ethics is included in any computer instruction given at your school.

\* AOL Canada provides a similar service in Canada.

Source: From Weinstein C. S. (2007). Middle and Secondary Classroom Management: Lessons from Research and Practice (4th ed.). © 2007 McGraw-Hill. Adapted with permission from The McGraw-Hill Companies, Inc.

consequences. Do not accept promises to do better next time (Levin & Nolan, 2000). Teach the students how to monitor their own behaviour; some of the self-regulation techniques described in Chapter 11 should be helpful. Finally, remain friendly with the students. Try to catch them in a good moment so that you can talk to them about something other than their rule breaking.

A defiant, hostile student can pose serious problems. If there is an outburst, try to get out of the situation as soon as possible; everyone loses in a public power struggle. One possibility is to give the student a chance to save face and cool down by saying, "It's your choice to cooperate or not. You can take a minute to think about it." If the student complies, the two of you can talk later about controlling the outbursts. If the student refuses to cooperate, you can tell him or her to wait in the hall until you get the class started on work, then step outside for a private talk. If the student refuses to leave, send another class member for the assistant principal. Again, follow through. If the student complies before help arrives, do not let him or her off the hook. If outbursts occur frequently, you might have a conference with the counsellor, parents, or other teachers. If the problem is an irreconcilable clash of personalities, the student should be transferred to another teacher. There is quite a bit of discussion today about zero tolerance for rule breaking in schools. Is this a good idea? The *Point/Counterpoint* box looks at both sides of the issue.

It is sometimes useful to keep records of the incidents by logging the student's name, words and actions, date, time, place, and teacher's response. These records may help identify patterns and can prove useful in meetings with administrators, parents, or special services personnel (Burden, 1995). Some teachers have students sign each entry to verify the incidents.

## POINT/COUNTERPOINT    Is Zero Tolerance a Good Idea?

With the very visible violence in schools today, some districts have instituted "zero-tolerance" policies for rule breaking. One result? An elementary school in Langley, British Columbia, banned kindergarten children from touching one another on the playground (CTV, 2013). The ban was a response to injuries resulting from games and other forms of "hands-on" play. Parents were asked to speak with their children about the ban and coach them to play games that don't involve touching. Do zero-tolerance policies make sense?

▶ **POINT** **Zero tolerance means zero common sense.** An internet search using keywords "zero-tolerance" and schools will locate a wealth of information about the policy—much of it against. For example, Oren Dorrell reported this incident in the November 2, 2009, edition of *USA Today* :

*The most recent high-profile case [of zero tolerance] involved Zachary Christie, a 6-year-old who was suspended for five days on Sept. 29 after he brought a camping utensil that was part knife, fork and spoon to Downes Elementary in Newark, Del. School officials considered it a dangerous instrument and suspended the boy, adding that he couldn't return to Downes until he completed at least 45 days at an alternative school. (Dorrell, 2009)*

What does the research say? In 2006, the American Psychological Association set up a Zero Tolerance Task force to answer that question (American Psychological Association Zero Tolerance Task Force, 2008). Analyzing a decade of research, they reached the following conclusions:

- Schools are not any safer or more effective in disciplining students now than before they instituted zero tolerance.
- The higher rates of suspension caused by zero tolerance have not led to less racial bias in disciplining students.
- Zero tolerance policies can actually lead to increases in bad behaviour that then lead to higher dropout rates.

In addition, zero tolerance policies can discourage students from informing teachers when the students learn that a classmate is "planning to do something dangerous." The zero tolerance rules get in the way of trusting relationships between teachers and students (Syvertsen, Flanagan, & Stout, 2009). Adolescents need both structure and support, but zero tolerance policies can create a highly structured, rigid environment that ignores the need for support. Finally, many of the popular zero-tolerance interventions such as increased security guards, hallway monitors, and the introduction of metal detectors have no apparent effect on the incidence of school bullying (Hyman, Kay, Tabori, Weber, Mahon, & Cohen, 2006; NCES, 2003).

▶ **COUNTERPOINT** **Zero tolerance is necessary for now.** The arguments for zero tolerance focus on school safety and the responsibilities of schools and teachers to protect the students and themselves. Of course, many of the incidents reported in the news seem to be overreactions to childhood pranks, or worse, overzealous applications of zero tolerance to innocent mistakes or lapses of memory. But how do school officials separate the innocent from the dangerous? For example, it has been widely reported that Andy Williams, a boy who killed two classmates in Santee, California, assured his friends before the shootings that he was only joking about "pulling a Columbine."

Gregg Toppo (2003), writing for *USA Today*, described how a grade 2 student used his shoe to attack his teacher; a kindergartner hit a pregnant teacher in the stomach; and an 8-year-old threatened to use gasoline to burn down his suburban elementary school. Toppo noted, "Elementary school principals and safety experts say they're seeing more violence and aggression than ever among their youngest students, pointing to what they see as an alarming rise in assaults and threats to classmates and teachers" (p. A2).

Incidents such as these have pressed schools to take a hard line on aggressive behaviour, and their response has often been to adopt the so-called zero-tolerance policy.

**Beyond Either/Or.** Surely we can ask adults to use good judgment in applying rules in dangerous situations, but not feel trapped by the rules when student actions are not intended to harm and are not dangerous.

Violence or destruction of property is a difficult and potentially dangerous problem, so it needs to be taken seriously. The first step is to send for help and get the names of participants and witnesses. Then get rid of any crowd that may have gathered; an audience will only make things worse. Do not try to break up a fight without help. Make sure that the school office is aware of the incident and follow the school policy in dealing with the situation. What else can you do? Consult the *Guidelines* for handling potentially explosive situations. The suggestions are taken from Weinstein and Novodvorsky (2011).

## GUIDELINES

## Handling Potentially Explosive Situations

**Move slowly and deliberately toward the problem situation.**
*Examples*
1. Walk slowly, then be as still as possible.
2. Establish eye-level position.

**Be respectful.**
*Examples*
1. Keep a reasonable distance.
2. Do not crowd the student. Do not get "in the student's face."
3. Speak respectfully. Use the student's name.
4. Avoid pointing or gesturing.

**Be brief.**
*Examples*
1. Avoid long-winded statements or nagging.
2. Stay with the agenda. Stay focused on the problem at hand. Do not get sidetracked.
3. Deal with less severe problems later.

**Avoid power struggles.**
*Examples*
1. Speak privately if possible.
2. Do not get drawn into "I won't, you will" arguments.
3. Don't make threats or raise your voice.

**Inform the student of the expected behaviour and the negative consequence as a choice or decision for the student to make. Then withdraw from the student and allow some time for the student to decide.**
*Examples*
1. Say, "Michael, you need to return to your desk, or I will have to send for the principal. You have a few seconds to decide." Then move away, perhaps attending to other students.
2. If Michael does not choose the appropriate behaviour, deliver the negative consequences ("You are choosing to have me call the principal"). Follow through with the consequence.

---

*For more ideas, see www.njcap.org/templated/Programs.html.*

*Source: Adapted from Weinstein, C. S. (2007). Middle and Secondary Classroom Management: Lessons from Research and Practice, 4th ed. © McGraw-Hill. Adapted with permission from The McGraw-Hill Companies, Inc.*

# THE NEED FOR COMMUNICATION

**STOP & THINK** A student says to you, "That book you assigned is really stupid—I'm not reading it!" What do you say? •

Communication between teachers and students is essential when problems arise. Communication is more than "teachers talk—students listen." It is more than the words exchanged between individuals. We communicate in many ways. Our actions, movements, voice tone, facial expressions, and other nonverbal behaviour send messages to our students. Many times, the messages we intend to send are not the messages our students receive.

## Message Sent—Message Received

**Teacher:** Carl, where is your homework?

**Carl:** I left it in my dad's car this morning.

**Teacher:** Again? You'll have to bring me a note tomorrow from your father saying that you actually did the homework. No grade without the note.

**Message Carl receives:** I can't trust you. I need proof that you did the work.

**Teacher:** Sit at every other desk. Put all your things under your desk. Jane and Laurel, you're sitting too close together. One of you move!

**Message Jane and Laurel receive:** I expect you two to cheat on this test.

> A new student comes to Ms. Tung's kindergarten. The child is messy and unwashed. Ms. Tung puts her hand lightly on the girl's shoulder and says, "I'm glad you're here." Her muscles tense, and she leans away from the child.

**Message student receives:** I don't like you. I think you are bad.

In all interactions, a message is sent and a message is received. Sometimes teachers believe that they are sending one message, but their voices, body positions, choices of words, and gestures may communicate a different message.

Students may hear the hidden message and respond to it. For example, a student may respond with hostility if she or he feels insulted by the teacher (or by another student), but may not be able to say exactly where the feeling of being insulted came from. Perhaps it was in the teacher's tone of voice, not the words actually spoken. In such cases, the teacher may feel attacked for no reason. The first principle of communication is that people respond to what they think was said or meant, not necessarily to the speaker's intended message or actual words.

There are many exercises for practising sending and receiving messages accurately. One such exercise uses the **paraphrase rule**. Before any participant, including the teacher, is allowed to respond to any other participant in a class discussion, he or she must summarize what the previous speaker said. If the summary is wrong, indicating that the speaker was misunderstood, the speaker must explain again. The respondent then tries again to paraphrase. The process continues until the speaker agrees that the listener has heard the intended message.

Paraphrasing is more than a classroom exercise. It can be the first step in communicating with students. Before teachers can deal appropriately with any student problem, they must know what the real problem is. A student who says, "This book is really dumb! Why did we have to read it?" may really be saying, "The book was too difficult for me. I couldn't read it, and I feel dumb."

## Diagnosis: Whose Problem Is It?

As a teacher, you may find some student behaviour unacceptable, unpleasant, or troubling. It is often difficult to stand back from these problems, take an objective look, and decide on an appropriate response. According to Thomas Gordon (1981), the key to good teacher–student relationships is determining why you are troubled by a particular behaviour and whose problem it is. The teacher must begin by asking who "owns" the problem. The answer to this question is critical. If it is really the student's problem, the teacher must become a counsellor and supporter, helping the student find his or her own solution. But if the teacher "owns" the problem, it is the teacher's responsibility to find a solution through problem solving with the student.

Diagnosing who owns the problem is not always straightforward. Let's look at three troubling situations to get some practice in this skill:

1. A student writes obscene words and draws sexually explicit illustrations in a school encyclopedia.
2. A student tells you that his parents had a bad fight and he hates his father.
3. A student quietly reads a newspaper in the back of the room.

Why is this behaviour troubling? If you cannot accept the student's behaviour because it has a serious effect on you as a teacher—if you are blocked from reaching your goals by the student's action—then you own the problem. It is your responsibility to confront the student and seek a solution. A teacher-owned problem appears to be present in the first situation described above—the young pornographer—because teaching materials are damaged.

If you feel annoyed by the behaviour because it is getting in the student's own way or because you are embarrassed for the child, but the behaviour does not directly interfere with your teaching, it is probably the student's problem. The test question is: Does this

Paraphrase rule Policy whereby listeners must accurately summarize what a speaker has said before being allowed to respond.

student's action tangibly affect you or prevent you from fulfilling your role as a teacher? The student who hates his father would not prevent you from teaching, even though you might wish the student felt differently. The problem is really the student's, and he must find his own solution.

The third situation is more difficult to diagnose. One argument is that the teacher is not interfered with in any way, so it is the student's problem. Another argument is that teachers might find reading the paper distracting during a lecture, so it is their problem, and they must find a solution. In a grey area such as this, the answer probably depends on how the teacher actually experiences the student's behaviour. After deciding who owns the problem, it is time to act.

## Counselling: The Student's Problem

Let's pick up the situation in which the student found the reading assignment "dumb." How might a teacher handle this positively?

**Student:** This book is really dumb! Why did we have to read it?

**Teacher:** You're pretty upset. This seemed like a worthless assignment to you. [Teacher paraphrases the student's statement, trying to hear the emotions as well as the words.]

**Student:** Yeah! Well, I guess it was worthless. I mean, I don't know if it was. I couldn't exactly read it.

**Teacher:** It was just too hard to read, and that bothers you.

**Student:** Sure, I felt really dumb. I know I can write a good report, but not with a book this tough.

**Teacher:** I think I can give you some hints that will make the book easier to understand. Can you see me after school today?

**Student:** Okay.

Here the teacher used **empathetic listening** to allow the student to find a solution. (As you can see, this approach relies heavily on paraphrasing.) By trying to hear the student and by avoiding the tendency to jump in too quickly with advice, solutions, criticisms, reprimands, or interrogations, the teacher keeps the communication lines open. Here are a few *unhelpful* responses the teacher might have made:

- I chose the book because it is the best example of this author's style in our library. You will need to have read it before your IB (International Baccalaureate) English class next year. (The teacher justifies the choice; this prevents the student from admitting that this "important" assignment is too difficult.)
- Did you really read it? I bet you didn't do the work, and now you want out of the assignment. (The teacher accuses; the student hears, "The teacher doesn't trust me!" and must defend herself or himself or accept the teacher's view.)
- Your job is to read the book, not ask me why. I know what's best. (The teacher pulls rank, and the student hears, "You can't possibly decide what is good for you!" The student can rebel or passively accept the teacher's judgment.)

Empathetic, active listening is more than a parroting of the student's words; it should capture the emotions, intent, and meaning behind them. Sokolove, Garrett, Sadker, and Sadker (1986, p. 241) have summarized the components of active listening: (1) blocking out external stimuli; (2) attending carefully to both the verbal and nonverbal messages; (3) differentiating between the intellectual and the emotional content of the message; and (4) making inferences regarding the speaker's feelings.

When students realize that they really have been heard and not evaluated negatively for what they have said or felt, they feel freer to trust the teacher and to talk more openly. Sometimes the true problem surfaces later in the conversation.

## Confrontation and Assertive Discipline

Now let's assume that a student is doing something that actively interferes with teaching. The teacher decides that the student must stop. The problem is the teacher's. Confrontation, not counselling, is required.

**Empathetic listening** Hearing the intent and emotions behind what another says and reflecting them back by paraphrasing.

**"I" MESSAGES.** Gordon (1981) recommends sending an "I" message in order to intervene and change a student's behaviour. Basically, this means telling a student in a straightforward, assertive, and nonjudgmental way what she or he is doing, how it affects you as a teacher, and how you feel about it. The student is then free to change voluntarily, and often does so. Here are two "I" messages:

- If you leave your book bags in the aisles, I might trip and hurt myself.
- When you all call out, I can't concentrate on each answer, and I'm frustrated.

**ASSERTIVE DISCIPLINE.**   Lee and Marlene Canter (1992; Canter, 1996) suggest other approaches for dealing with a teacher-owned problem. They call their method **assertive discipline**. Many teachers are ineffective with students because they are either wishy-washy and passive or hostile and aggressive (Charles, 2011).

**EMPATHETIC LISTENING** When students realize they really have been heard and not evaluated negatively for what they have said or felt, they begin to trust the teacher and to talk more openly. Sometimes the true problem surfaces later in the conversation.

Spencer Grant/Alamy

Instead of telling the student directly what to do, *passive* teachers tell, or often ask, the student to try or to think about the appropriate action. The passive teacher might comment on the problem behaviour without actually telling the child what to do differently: "Why are you doing that? Don't you know the rules?" or "Sam, are you disturbing the class?" Or the teacher might clearly state what should happen, but never follow through with the established consequences, giving the students "one more chance" every time. Finally, passive teachers might ignore behaviour that should receive a response or may wait too long before responding.

A *hostile response style* involves different mistakes. Teachers may make "you" statements that condemn the student without stating clearly what the student should be doing: "You should be ashamed of the way you're behaving!" or "You never listen!" or "You're acting like a baby!" Teachers may also threaten students angrily but follow through too seldom, perhaps because the threats are too vague—"You'll be very sorry you did that when I get through with you!"—or too severe. For example, a teacher tells a student in a physical education class that he will have to "sit on the bench for three weeks." A few days later the team is short one member and the teacher allows the student to play, never returning him to the bench to complete the three-week sentence. Often, a teacher who has been passive becomes hostile and explodes when students persist in misbehaving.

In contrast to both the passive and the hostile styles, an *assertive response* communicates to the students that you care too much about them and the process of learning to allow inappropriate behaviour to persist. Assertive teachers clearly state what they expect. To be most effective, the teachers often look into a student's eyes when speaking and address the student by name. Assertive teachers' voices are calm, firm, and confident. They are not sidetracked by accusations such as "You just don't understand!" or "You don't like me!" Assertive teachers do not get into a debate about the fairness of the rules. They expect changes, not promises or apologies.

Not all educators believe that assertive discipline is useful. Earlier critics questioned the penalty-focused approach and emphasized that assertive discipline undermined student self-management (Render, Padilla, & Krank, 1989). John Covaleskie (1992) observed, "What helps children become moral is not knowledge of the rules, or even obedience to the rules, but discussions about the reasons for acting in certain ways" (p. 56). These critics have had an impact. More recent versions of assertive discipline focus on teaching students how to behave responsibly and working to establish mutual respect and trust (Charles, 2011).

**"I" message** Clear, nonaccusatory statement of how something is affecting you.

**Assertive discipline** Clear, firm, unhostile response style.

CONFRONTATIONS AND NEGOTIATIONS. If "I" messages or assertive responses fail and a student persists in misbehaving, the teacher and student are in a conflict. Several pitfalls now loom. The two individuals become less able to perceive each other's behaviour accurately. Research has shown that the angrier you get with another person, the more you see the other as the villain and yourself as an innocent victim. Because you feel that the other person is in the wrong, and he or she feels just as strongly that the conflict is all your fault, very little mutual trust is possible. A cooperative solution to the problem is almost impossible. In fact, by the time the discussion has gone on a few minutes, the original problem is lost in a sea of charges, countercharges, and self-defence (Baron & Byrne, 2003).

There are three methods of resolving a conflict between teacher and student. One is for the teacher to impose a solution. This may be necessary during an emergency, as when a defiant student refuses to go to the hall to discuss a public outbreak, but it is not a good solution for most conflicts. The second method is for the teacher to give in to the student's demands. You might be convinced by a particularly compelling student argument, but again, this method should be used sparingly. It is generally a bad idea to be talked out of a position, unless the position was wrong in the first place. Problems arise when either the teacher or the student gives in completely.

Gordon (1981) recommends a third approach, which he calls the "no-lose method." Here the needs of both the teacher and the students are taken into account in the solution. No one person is expected to give in completely; all participants retain respect for themselves and each other. The no-lose method is a six-step problem-solving strategy:

1. *Define the problem*. What exactly is the behaviour involved? What does each person want? (Use active listening to help students pinpoint the real problem.)
2. *Generate many possible solutions*. Brainstorm, but remember to not allow any evaluations of ideas yet.
3. *Evaluate each solution*. Any participant may veto any idea. If no solutions are found to be acceptable, brainstorm again.
4. *Make a decision*. Choose one solution through consensus, not voting. In the end, everyone must be satisfied with the solution.
5. *Determine how to implement the solution*. What will be needed? Who will be responsible for each task? What is the timetable?
6. *Evaluate the success of the solution*. After trying the solution for a while, ask, "Are we satisfied with our decision? How well is it working? Should we make some changes?"

Many of the conflicts in classrooms can be important learning experiences for all concerned.

## Reaching Every Student: Peer Mediation and Negotiation

Handling conflict is difficult for most of us—and for young people it can be even harder. Nearly 40 years ago, a large study of more than 8000 middle and high school students and 500 faculty from three major cities concluded that 90% of the conflicts among students are resolved in destructive ways or are never resolved at all (DeCecco & Richards, 1974). The few studies conducted since that time have reached similar conclusions. Avoidance, force, and threats seem to be the major strategies for dealing with conflict (Johnson, Johnson, Dudley, Ward, & Magnuson, 1995). But there are better ways—like peer mediation and negotiation strategies that teach lifelong lessons.

David Johnson and his colleagues (1995) provided conflict resolution training to 227 students in grades 2 through 5. Students learned a five-step negotiating strategy:

1. *Jointly define the conflict*. Separate the person from the problem and the actions involved, avoid win–lose thinking, and get both parties' goals clear.
2. *Exchange positions and interests*. Present a tentative proposal and make a case for it; listen to the other person's proposal and feelings; and stay flexible and cooperative.

3. *Reverse perspectives.* See the situation from the other person's point of view and reverse roles and argue for that perspective.
4. *Invent at least three agreements that allow mutual gain.* Brainstorm, focus on goals, think creatively, and make sure everyone has power to invent solutions.
5. *Reach an integrative agreement.* Make sure both sets of goals are met. If all else fails, flip a coin, take turns, or call in a third party—a mediator.

In addition to learning conflict resolution, all students in Johnson and Johnson's study were trained in mediation strategies. The role of the mediator was rotated—every day the teacher chose two students to be the class mediators and to wear the mediators' T-shirts. Johnson and his colleagues found that students learned the conflict resolution and mediation strategies and used them successfully to handle conflicts in a more productive way, both in school and at home.

Peer mediation has also been successful with older students and those with serious problems (Sanchez & Anderson, 1990). In one program, selected gang members were given mediation training, and then all members were invited to participate voluntarily in the mediation process, supervised by school counsellors. Strict rules governed the process leading to written agreements signed by gang representatives. Sanchez and Anderson (1990) found that gang violence in the school was reduced to a bare minimum—"The magic of the mediation process was communication" (p. 56).

Even if you do not have formal peer mediation training in your school, you can help your students handle conflict more productively. For example, Esme Codell, the excellent first-year teacher you met earlier in this chapter, taught her grade 5 students a simple four-step process and posted the steps on a bulletin board: "1. Tell person what you didn't like. 2. Tell person how it made you feel. 3. Tell person what you want in the future. 4. Person responds with what they can do. Congratulations! You are a Confident Conflict Conqueror!" (Codell, 2001, p. 23).

We have looked at quite a few perspectives on classroom management. Clearly, there is not a one-size-fits-all strategy for creating social and physical spaces for learning. What does the research tell us? Are some better than others?

## Research on Management Approaches

Emmer and Aussiker (1990) conducted a meta-analysis of three general perspectives on management: *influencing* students through listening and problem solving, as described by Gordon (1981); *group management* through class meetings and student discussion, as advocated by Glasser (1969, 1990); and *control* through rewards and punishments, as exemplified by Canter and Canter (1992). No clear conclusions could be drawn about the impact of these approaches on student behaviours. However, some evaluations have found positive effects for Freiberg's (1999) Consistency Management program and for programs that use rewards and punishments (Lewis, 2001).

INTEGRATING IDEAS. In a study conducted in Australia, Ramon Lewis (2001) found that recognizing and rewarding appropriate student behaviours, talking with students about how their behaviour affects others, involving students in class discipline decisions, and providing nondirective hints and descriptions about unacceptable behaviours were associated with students taking greater responsibility for their own learning. It is interesting that these interventions represent all three of the general approaches reviewed by Emmer and Aussiker—influence, group management, and control. In a study of over 3000 grade 9 students in Singapore, Youyan Nie and Shun Lau (2009) found that both caring and control were positively related to student engagement, so blending control, influence, caring, and group management strategies may be necessary in order to create positive learning environments. This is not always easy. Lewis also concluded that teachers sometimes find using these interventions difficult when students are aggressive—and most in need of the approaches. When teachers feel threatened, it can be difficult for them to do what students need, but that may be the most important time to act positively and combine caring with control.

FAMILY AND COMMUNITY PARTNERSHIPS

## Classroom Management

**Make sure that families know the expectations and rules of your class and school.**
*Examples*

1. At a Family Fun Night, have your students do skits showing the rules—how to follow them and what breaking them "looks like" and "sounds like."

2. Make a poster for the refrigerator at home that describes, in a light way, the most important rules and expectations.

3. For older students, give families a list of due dates for the major assignments, along with tips about how to encourage high-quality work by pacing the effort—avoiding last-minute panic.

4. Communicate in appropriate ways; for example, use the family's first language when possible. Tailor messages to the reading level of the home.

**Make families partners in recognizing good citizenship.**
*Examples*

1. Send positive notes home when students, especially students who have had trouble with classroom management, work well in the classroom.

2. Give ideas for ways in which any family, even one with few economic resources, can celebrate accomplishment—a favourite food; the chance to choose a movie to rent; a comment to a special person such as an aunt, grandparent, or minister; the chance to read to a younger sibling.

**Identify talents in the community to help build a learning environment in your class.**
*Examples*

1. Have students write letters to carpet and furniture stores asking for donations of remnants to carpet a reading corner.

2. Find family members who can build shelves or room dividers, paint, sew, laminate manipulatives, write stories, repot plants, or network computers.

3. Contact businesses for donations of computers, printers, or other equipment.

**Seek cooperation from families when behaviour problems arise.**
*Examples*

1. Talk to families over the phone or in their home. Have good records about the problem behaviour.

2. Listen to family members and solve problems with them.

*For more ideas see www.educationworld.com.*

**COMMUNICATING WITH FAMILIES ABOUT CLASSROOM MANAGEMENT.** As we have seen throughout this text, families are important partners in education. This statement applies to classroom management as well. When parents and teachers share the same expectations and support each other, they can create a more positive classroom environment and more time for learning. The *Family and Community Partnerships Guidelines* provide ideas for how to work with families and the community.

## DIVERSITY: CULTURALLY RESPONSIVE MANAGEMENT

Research on discipline shows that students from minority groups may be disciplined for behaviours they never meant to be disruptive or disrespectful because of a communication breakdown. For example, studies involving African Americans, especially males, indicate that these students are punished more often and more harshly than other students. These students lose time from learning as they spend more hours in detention or suspension (Ferguson, 2000; Monroe & Obidah, 2002; Skiba, Michael, Nardo, & Peterson, 2000). Why?

The notion that African American and Latin American students are punished more because they commit more serious offences is *not* supported by the data. Instead, these students are punished more severely for minor offences such as rudeness or defiance—words and actions that are interpreted by teachers as meriting severe punishment. One explanation is a lack of cultural synchronization between teachers and students. "The language, style of walking, glances, and dress of black children, particularly males, have engendered fear, apprehension, and overreaction among many teachers and school administrators" (Irvine, 1990, p. 27). African American students may be disciplined for behaviours that were never intended to be disruptive or disrespectful. According to Joyce Barakett of Concordia University, teachers in Canada also "call upon cultural differences" to explain students' behaviour (Barakett, 1986, p. 98). In interviews, teachers reported that children from Yugoslavia "posed problems of control," and Greek children were more motivated (Barakett, 1986, p. 99). Teachers do their students and themselves a service if they work at helping them to become bicultural—helping their students to learn how to function in both mainstream and home cultures, but also learning the meaning of their students' words and actions—so they do not misinterpret and then punish their students' unintended insults (Gay, 2006).

**Culturally responsive management** is simply a part of the larger concept of culturally relevant teaching. Geneva Gay (2006) sums it up:

> If the classroom is a comfortable, caring, embracing, affirming, engaging, and facilitative place for students then discipline is not likely to be much of an issue. It follows then that both classroom management and school achievement can be improved for students from different ethnic, racial, social, and linguistic backgrounds by ensuring that curriculum and instruction are culturally relevant and personally meaningful for them.

Anita once asked a gifted educator in an urban New Jersey high school which teachers were most effective with the really tough students. He said there are two kinds: teachers who can't be intimidated or fooled and expect their students to learn, and teachers who really care about the students. When I asked, "Which kind are you?" he answered "Both!" He is an example of a "**warm demander**," a teacher who seems to be most effective with students placed at risk for experiencing any of a wide variety of negative outcomes (Irvine & Armento, 2001; Irvine and Fraser, 1998). Sometimes these warm demanders appear harsh to outside observers (Burke-Spero, 1999; Burke-Spero & Woolfolk Hoy, 2002).

Carla Monroe and Jennifer Obidah (2002) studied Ms. Simpson, a grade 8 science teacher. She described herself as having high expectations for academics and behaviour in her classes—so much so that she believed that her students perceived her as "mean." Yet, she often used humour and dialect to communicate her expectations, as in the following exchange:

> **Ms. Simpson [addressing the class]:** If you know you're going to act the fool just come to me and say, "I'm going to act the fool at the pep rally," so I can go ahead and send you to wherever you need to go. [Class laughs.]
>
> **Ms. Simpson:** I'm real serious. If you know you're having a bad day, you don't want anybody touching you, you don't want nobody saying nothing to you, somebody bump into you you're going to snap—you need to come up to me and say, "I'm going to snap and I can't go to the pep rally." [The students start to call out various comments.]
>
> **Ms. Simpson:** Now, I just want to say I expect you to have the best behaviour because you're the most mature students in the building … don't make me stop the pep rally and ask the grade students to leave.
>
> **Edward:** We'll have silent lunch won't we? [Class laughs.]
>
> **Ms. Simpson:** You don't want to dream about what you're going to have. [Class laughs.] Okay, 15 minutes for warm-ups. [The students begin their warm-up assignment.]

Some students may be more accustomed to a directive kind of management and discipline outside of school. Their families might say, "Put down that candy" or "Go to bed," whereas other parents might ask, "Can we eat candy before dinner?" or "Isn't it time for bed?" As H. Richard Milner (2006) says, "The question should not be which approach is right or wrong but which approach works with and connects with the students' prior knowledge and ways of knowing."

**Culturally responsive management** Taking cultural meanings and styles into accour when developing management plans and responding to stude

**Warm demanders** Effective teachers who show both high expectations and great carin their students.

# ▼ SUMMARY

### The Need for Organization (pp. 438–442)

**What are the challenges of classroom management?** Classrooms are by nature multidimensional, full of simultaneous activities, fast-paced and immediate, unpredictable, public, and affected by the history of students' and teachers' actions. A teacher must juggle all these elements every day. Productive classroom activity requires students' cooperation. Maintaining cooperation is different for each age group. Young students are learning how to "go to school" and need to learn the general procedures of school. Older students need to learn the specifics required for working in different subjects. Working with adolescents requires teachers to understand the power of the adolescent peer group.

**What are the goals of good classroom management?** The goals of effective classroom management are to make ample time for learning; improve the quality of time use by keeping students actively engaged; make sure participation structures are clear, straightforward, and consistently signalled; and encourage student self-management, self-control, and responsibility.

### Creating a Positive Learning Environment (pp. 442–447)

**Distinguish between rules and procedures.** Rules are the specific dos and don'ts of classroom life. They usually are written down or posted. Procedures cover administrative tasks, student movement, housekeeping, and routines for accomplishing lessons, interactions between students and teachers, and interactions among students. Rules can be written in terms of rights and students may benefit from participating in establishing these rules. Consequences should be established for following and breaking the rules and procedures so that the teacher and the students know what will happen.

**Distinguish between personal territories and interest-area spatial arrangements.** There are two basic kinds of spatial organization, territorial (the traditional classroom arrangement) and functional (dividing space into interest or work areas). Flexibility is often the key. Access to materials, convenience, privacy when needed, ease of supervision, and a willingness to re-evaluate plans are important considerations in the teacher's choice of physical arrangements.

**[C]ontrast the first school week of effective and ineffective [cla]ssroom managers.** Effective classroom managers spent the [first] days of class teaching a workable, easily understood set of [rules] and procedures by using a lot of explanation, examples, and [practi]ce. In these classes, students were occupied with organized, [worka]ble activities and learned to function cooperatively in the [room]. Quick, firm, clear, and consistent responses to infractions [of] rules characterized effective teachers. The teachers had [planned] carefully to avoid any last-minute tasks that might have [taken] them away from their students. These teachers dealt with [chil]dren's pressing concerns first. In contrast, for ineffec[tive man]agers, procedures for accomplishing routine tasks varied [day] to day and were never taught or practised. Students [related to] one another because they had nothing productive to [do. Ineff]ective teachers frequently left the room. Many became [absorbed] in paperwork or in helping just one student. They had [no] plans for how to deal with typical problems such as late [s]tudents or interruptions.

Irina_QQQ/Shutterstock

### Creating a Learning Community (pp. 450–451)

**How can teachers foster a learning community in their classroom and school?** Whether you are working as an individual teacher or as part of a school-wide team, creating a learning community involves input from many different levels to develop a philosophy and participation structures that will foster self-control and social responsibility on the part of students. Recall how the staff at Blakeburn met first and talked about how to create a caring and socially responsible learning community. Then they involved the children and their families. The first week of school was devoted to the articulation of what it means (for all members) to be part of a socially responsible community. Throughout this process, the staff recognized that this work must be multifaceted and integrated in all the curricula and interactions in their classrooms and at the school.

### Maintaining a Good Environment for Learning (pp. 451–455)

**How can teachers encourage engagement?** In general, as teacher supervision increases, students' engaged time also increases. When the task provides continuous cues for the student about what to do next, involvement will be greater. Activities with clear steps are likely to be more absorbing, because one step leads naturally to the next. Making work requirements clear and specific, providing needed materials, and monitoring activities all add to engagement.

**Explain the factors identified by Kounin that prevent management problems in the classroom.** To create a positive environment and prevent problems, teachers must take individual differences into account, maintain student motivation, and reinforce positive behaviour. Successful problem preventers are skilled in four areas described by Kounin: "withitness," overlapping, group focusing, and movement management. When penalties have to be imposed, teachers should impose them calmly and privately. In addition to applying Kounin's ideas, teachers can prevent problems by establishing a caring classroom community and teaching students to use social skills and emotional self-regulation skills.

**How do teachers help students form connections with schools?** To get started on building connections, teachers should make expectations for both academic work and student behaviours clear. Respect for students' needs and rights should be at the centre of class procedures. Students know that their teachers care about them when teachers try to make classes interesting, are fair and honest with them, make sure they understand the materials, and have ways to cope with students' concerns and troubles.

### Dealing With Discipline Problems (pp. 455–461)

**Describe seven levels of intervention in misbehaviour.** Teachers can first make eye contact with the student or use other nonverbal signals, then try verbal hints such as simply inserting the student's name into the lecture. Next the teacher asks if the offender is aware of the negative effects of the actions, then reminds the student of the procedure and has her or him follow it correctly. If this does not work, the teacher can ask the student to state the correct rule or procedure and then to follow it, and then move to telling the student in a clear, assertive, and unhostile way to stop the misbehaviour. If this fails, too, the teacher can offer a choice—stop the behaviour or meet privately to work out the consequences.

**What can teachers do about bullying, teasing, and cyberbullying?** Teachers often underestimate the amount of peer conflict and bullying that happens in schools. Bullying involves both an imbalance of power between students and repeated attempts at harm and may take place in a variety of settings—including those in which students are not face-to-face with one another at school. Teachers can think of bullying as a form of violence and approach strategies for overcoming bullying as they would strategies to overcoming other violent acts. For example, prevention of bullying can take the form of developing a respectful classroom community and discussing conflict.

**What are some challenges in secondary classrooms?** Teachers working in secondary schools should be prepared to handle students who don't complete school work, repeatedly break the same rule, or openly defy teachers. These students may also be experiencing new and powerful stressors. As a result, secondary students may benefit if teachers provide opportunities or point out resources for these students to seek out help and support. Teachers might also find consultation with guidance counsellors and parents helpful.

### The Need for Communication (pp. 462–468)

**What is meant by "empathetic listening"?** Communication between teacher and student is essential when problems arise. All interactions between people, even silence or neglect, communicate some meaning. Empathetic, active listening can be a helpful response when students bring problems to teachers. Teachers must reflect back to the students what they hear them saying. This reflection is more than a parroting of words; it should capture the emotions, intent, and meaning behind them.

**Distinguish among passive, hostile, and assertive response styles.** The passive style can take several forms. Instead of telling the student directly what to do, the teacher simply comments on the behaviour, asks the student to think about the appropriate action, or threatens but never follows through. In a hostile response style, teachers may make "you" statements that condemn the student without stating clearly what the student should be doing. An assertive response communicates to the students that the teacher cares too much about them and the process of learning to allow inappropriate behaviour to persist. Assertive teachers clearly state what they expect.

**What is peer mediation?** Peer mediation is one good possibility for preventing violence in schools. The steps for peer mediation are: (1) Jointly define the conflict. (2) Exchange positions and interests. (3) Reverse perspectives. (4) Invent at least three agreements that allow mutual gain. (5) Reach an integrative agreement.

### Diversity: Culturally Responsive Management (pp. 468–469)

**What is culturally responsive management, and why is it needed?** African Americans and Latino/a Americans, especially males, are punished more often and more harshly than other students, but they do not commit more serious offences. Instead, these students are punished more severely for minor offences such as rudeness or defiance—words and actions that are interpreted by teachers as meriting severe punishment. One explanation is a lack of cultural synchronization between teachers and students. Culturally responsive management combines high expectaions for students' appropriate behaviour with warmth and caring for the students as individuals.

## ▼ WHAT WOULD THEY DO?

## TEACHERS' CASEBOOK: Bullies and Victims

Here is how a practising teacher responded to the teaching situation described on the first page of this chapter.

### SANDRA BORZELLINO
Mackenzie Glen Public School, Maple, ON

Bullying is never a one-size-fits-all approach. Not all strategies or techniques will work for all children, and in responding to negative behaviour, several factors need to be considered. For instance, what are the ages of the students involved? Is this a first-time occurrence? When is the best time to deal with this issue? Differences need to be honoured when dealing with bullying. However, before dealing with bullying, a lot of work should be invested in prevention. Anti-bullying campaigns and zero tolerance school-board policies don't always include step-by-step programs that can be incorporated for students at different ages and stages in life. Teacher training programs are often vague, brief, and disconnected from actual situations that are prevalent in specific schools and classrooms.

Bullying is a problem that is often linked to issues of poor self-esteem, anger, and inadequate self-regulation skills. These concerns need to be pushed to the forefront when building a learning community, particularly in the classroom.

As educators, we need increased mindfulness around building self-confidence. Promoting self-esteem begins at an early age. Often, by the time children begin grade school, they already have a strong sense of who they are and their strengths and weaknesses. Developing self-confidence takes time and requires teachers to evaluate their daily practice. Recognizing that how we speak, and the material we present to our children, may alter students' perception of the way they see themselves is a transformative practice that requires deep examination.

Identifying students' triggers is essential. How can we help students deal with their emotions? We are taught not to hit another person, yet we are often not given alternatives to what we *should* do instead. Children require assistance in recognizing their own personal "sparks" that could lead to them losing control. This requires explicit teaching, role playing, and ongoing communication.

Teaching children to self-regulate their emotions or impulses is a critical piece to the puzzle. Ironically, many school boards have recently identified self-regulation as a key learning skill. Teaching this skill requires practice, and through appropriate activities, teachers can model self-regulation as it pertains to schoolwork and behaviour. The goal is for kids to learn to apply suitable responses independently as a life skill.

Consequences of bullying can vary, since there are conflicting styles and approaches. Ensuring that all students feel safe is vital. The outcome of a bullying situation sends a clear message to other students who may have witnessed the incident or heard about it indirectly. In the case of a homophobic remark, it may be an issue of communicating and breaking down what words mean and how their use can be hurtful. Inappropriate and unrealistic consequences can also influence the likelihood of reoccurrence. Modelling respect and empathy for all parties shows that we can all make mistakes and that mistakes can be forgiven. Communicating with parents, staff, and administrators sends a transparent message to children, and instituting realistic consequences at home can help to maintain stability for a child.

Even if bullying occurs at school, that does not render it as isolated to that location. The problem lies deeper. Building self-esteem, addressing feelings and emotions, and teaching self-regulation strategies are just some of the strategies to prevent bullying. Addressing these real-life skills are as important as learning to read and write, and are critical to developing a student population that is better equipped to face the realities of everyday social interactions.

### SHELLY VOHRA
*Educator and Instructional Coach, Peel District School Board, Toronto, ON*

Bullying is a serious problem that affects millions of children. It can interfere with their social, emotional, and academic development. As a teacher, you need to take all bullying incidents seriously.

In this case, it is essential that at the start of the school year you get to know your students and build relationships with them. It shows that you value a safe environment where students feel comfortable sharing their opinions, values, and thoughts. Trust will go a long way in ensuring that students will report any incidents of bullying to you. There are several ways to build a warm and welcoming class community: (a) Have students complete an interest inventory; (b) complete icebreaker activities; (c) participate in team building games; (d) host weekly community circles; and (e) complete outdoor activities that involve team work. During the first month of school, I would discuss bullying with my students, providing examples, role-playing some common scenarios, and making it clear that it is never okay to bully.

During this time, be sure to discuss classroom rules and consequences, including the issue of bullying. In my classroom, my students generate these rules and consequences. This gives them ownership over their own behaviour in addition to the consequences of their actions. We write the rules and consequences on Bristol board and sign it, signifying our agreement. A copy is sent home to parents; this is a great way for parents to initiate a conversation with their child about bullying and expected behaviour in and out of the classroom.

In this case, I would hope that this student would approach me with his side of the story. If not, I would conduct a weekly community circle to review and discuss bullying and why people are bullied in hopes of providing the student with the opportunity to discuss the incidents. Let your students know that if they are victims of bullying, you will deal with it. If he did not approach me on his own, I would ask him if everything was okay, and if there was anything he wanted to tell me. If the response is no, don't push, or you risk alienating the student. Reassure him that you have an open-door policy and that you will protect his privacy. Offer him the chance to write down what is bothering him if he is not comfortable talking about it. Be sure to keep a close eye on this student and watch not only what he says but also his body language. Students who are shy, less confident, and have trouble finding classmates to work with are highly susceptible to bullying.

Speak to other teachers to see if they have noticed unusual behaviours or if the student has said anything that might arouse concern. Also speak to the guidance counsellor; often the guidance counsellor is better equipped to deal with these issues. Guidance counsellors are privy to students' histories, so speaking with with them can be an important step in solving the issue. Consider briefing the principal, who should be prepared in case a parent calls him or her directly. Finally, document everything. Your notes and observations will come in handy should the need arise. As well, be prepared for a phone call from parents or guardians, if they suspect that something is not right with their child.

The best approach is to implement a school-wide anti-bullying program to ensure that school is a place where all students feel safe to learn. The first step is to identify the "hot spots" where bullying usually occurs (e.g., bathrooms, hallways, the lunchroom, and the playground during recess).

Bullying is a complex issue. We must not forget about the bullies; they need support and guidance, too. These students are usually struggling with their own issues, and it sometimes comes out in the form of bullying. All students need to believe that their teachers care about them and will do what is required to help and protect them.

Mxz/Shutterstock

# TEACHING EVERY STUDENT

WHAT WOULD YOU DO?

▶ **TEACHERS' CASEBOOK:** Reaching and Teaching
Every Student

You have started a new job in a high school in your home town. When you were in school, the students were fairly similar—white, working to middle class, and English speaking. There was a special education class for students who had serious learning or developmental problems. But in the classes you will be teaching, you find a wide range of reading levels, family incomes, and learning challenges. Two of your students are virtually ready for post-secondary education, while several struggle to read the texts, and their writing is impossible to decipher. Reading English texts is a challenge for some of your students, though they seem to speak English with little trouble.

**CRITICAL THINKING**

- How would you differentiate instruction for this diverse group of students?
- Do different philosophies of teaching provide different answers to this question?
- How will you grade work if you have successfully differentiated instruction?

## OVERVIEW AND OBJECTIVES

Much of this text has been about learning and learners. In this chapter, we focus on teaching and teachers. Are there particular characteristics that distinguish effective from ineffective teachers? Research on whole-class teaching points to the importance of several factors that we will explore.

What else do we know about teaching? We look at how teachers plan, including how to use taxonomies of learning objectives or themes as a basis for planning.

With this foundation of knowing how to set goals and make plans, as well as an understanding of the characteristics of effective teachers, we move to a consideration of some general teacher-centred strategies: lecturing, seatwork, homework, questioning, recitation, and group discussion.

In the final section of this chapter, we will focus on how to match teaching to the needs and abilities of students through differentiated instruction, flexible grouping, and adaptive teaching. Finally we explore how teachers' beliefs about their students' abilities—teacher expectations—might influence student learning and teacher–student relationships.

By the time you have completed this chapter, you should be able to:

**14.1**  Identify the characteristics of effective teachers and effective classroom climates.

**14.2**  Develop learning objectives using Bloom's taxonomy.

**14.3**  Describe the processes involved in planning a lesson, and distinguish among basic formats for putting plans into action.

**14.4**  Discuss the appropriate uses of direct instruction, homework, questioning, and group discussion.

**14.5**  Define differentiated instruction and adaptive teaching, and apply the approach to teaching a diverse group of students.

**14.6**  Explain the possible effects of teacher expectations, and know how to avoid the negative implications.

# RESEARCH ON TEACHING

This chapter is about teaching, so we start with findings from several decades of research.

How would you go about identifying the keys to successful teaching? You might ask students, principals, college or university professors of education, or experienced teachers to list the characteristics of good teachers. Or you could do intensive case studies of a few classrooms over a long period. You might observe classrooms, rate different teachers on certain characteristics, and then see which characteristics were associated with teachers whose students either achieved the most or were the most motivated to learn. (To do this, of course, you would have to decide how to assess achievement and motivation.) You could identify teachers whose students, year after year, learned more than students working with other teachers; then you could watch the more successful teachers, and note what they do. You might also train teachers to apply several different strategies to teach the same lesson and then determine which strategy led to the greatest student learning. You could videotape teachers, and then ask them to view the recordings and report what they were thinking about as they taught and what influenced their decisions while teaching, called *stimulated recall*. You might study transcripts of classroom dialogue to learn what helped students understand the material. You might use the relationships identified between teaching and learning as the basis for developing teaching approaches and testing these approaches in *design experiments*.

All these approaches and more have been used to investigate teaching (Floden, 2001; Greeno, Collins, & Resnick, 1996; Gröschner, Seidel, & Shavelson, 2012). Let's examine some of the specific knowledge about teaching gained from these projects.

## Characteristics of Effective Teachers

**STOP & THINK** Think about the most effective teacher you ever had—the one you learned the most from. What were the characteristics of that person? What made that teacher so effective? •

Some of the earliest research on effective teaching focused on the personal qualities of the teachers themselves. Results revealed some lessons about three teacher characteristics: clarity, warmth, and knowledge. Recent research has focused on knowledge, so we will spend some extra time on that characteristic.

CLARITY AND ORGANIZATION.   When Barak Rosenshine and Norma Furst (1973) reviewed about 50 studies of teaching, they concluded *clarity* was the most promising teacher behaviour for future research on effective teaching. Teachers who provide clear presentations and explanations tend to have students who learn more and who rate their teachers more positively (Comadena, Hunt, & Simonds, 2007; Hines, Cruickshank, & Kennedy, 1985). Teachers with more knowledge of the subject tend to be less vague in their explanations to the class. The less vague the teacher, the more the students learn (Evertson & Emmer, 2009, 2013).

WARMTH AND ENTHUSIASM.   As you are well aware, some teachers are much more enthusiastic than others. Some studies have found that ratings of teachers' enthusiasm for their subject are correlated with student achievement gains (Keller, Neumann, & Fischer, 2012), whereas warmth, friendliness, and understanding seem to be the teacher traits most strongly related to students liking the teacher and the class in general (Madsen, 2003; Hamann, Baker, McAllister, & Bauer, 2000; Soar & Soar, 1979). But note that these are correlational studies. The results do not tell us that teacher enthusiasm causes student learning or that warmth causes positive attitudes, only that the two variables tend to occur together. Two possible connections are that when teachers are enthusiastic, they capture and hold student attention, and that enthusiastic teachers model engagement and interest in learning. Student attention, interest, and engagement lead to learning. Of course, it is easier to be an enthusiastic teacher when your students are learning (Keller et al., 2012).

What about another important teacher characteristic—knowledge?

## Teachers' Knowledge

As you saw in Chapters 8 and 9, knowledge is the defining characteristic of expertise. **Expert teachers** have elaborate systems of knowledge for understanding problems in teaching. For example, when a beginning teacher is faced with students' wrong answers on math or history tests, all of these answers may seem about the same—wrong. But for an expert teacher, wrong answers are part of a rich system of knowledge that could include how to recognize several types of wrong answers, the misunderstanding or lack of information behind each kind of mistake, the best way to reteach and correct the misunderstanding, materials and activities that have worked in the past, and several ways to test whether the reteaching was successful. This unique kind of teacher knowledge that combines mastery of *academic content* with knowing *how to teach* the content and how to match instruction to *student differences* is called **pedagogical content knowledge** (Gess-Newsome, 2012). In addition, expert teachers have clear goals and take individual differences into account when planning for their students. These teachers are **reflective** practitioners, constantly trying to understand and improve their work with students (Hogan, Rabinowitz, & Craven, 2003).

What do expert teachers know that allows them to be so successful? Lee Shulman (1987) has studied this question, and he has identified seven areas of professional knowledge. Expert teachers know:

1. the academic subjects they teach—their content knowledge is deep and interconnected;
2. general teaching strategies that apply in all subjects (such as the principles of classroom management, effective teaching, and evaluation that you will discover in this text);

**Expert teachers** Experienced, effective teachers who have developed solutions for classroom problems. Their knowledge of teaching process and content is extensive and well organized.

**Pedagogical content knowledge** Teacher knowledge that combines mastery of *academic content* with knowing *how to teach* the content and how to match instruction to *student differences*.

**Reflective** Thoughtful and inventive. Reflective teachers think back over situations to analyze what they did and why and to consider how they might improve learning for their students.

**EFFECTIVE TEACHERS** Effective teachers know how to transform their knowledge into examples, explanations, illustrations, and activities.

Monkey Business Images/Shutterstock

3. the curriculum materials and programs appropriate for their subject and grade level;
4. subject-specific knowledge for teaching: special ways of teaching certain students and particular concepts, such as the best ways to explain negative numbers to lower-ability students;
5. the characteristics and cultural backgrounds of learners;
6. the settings in which students learn—pairs, small groups, teams, classes, schools, and the community;
7. the goals and purposes of teaching.

This is quite a list. Obviously, one course cannot give you all the information you need to teach. In fact, a whole program of courses won't make you an expert. That takes time and experience. But studying educational psychology has added to your professional knowledge because at the heart of educational psychology is a concern with learning wherever it occurs.

Do teachers who know more about their subject have a more positive impact on their students? It depends on the subject. When Hill, Rowan, and Ball (2005) tested grade 1 and grade 3 teachers' specific knowledge of the math concepts that they actually teach and their understanding of how to teach those concepts, they found that teachers with greater *content* and *pedagogical content knowledge* had students who learned more mathematics. Similarly, high school students appear to learn more mathematics from teachers with degrees or significant coursework in mathematics (Wayne & Youngs, 2003). And studies in German high schools have found that math teachers with more pedagogical content knowledge have students who are more cognitively engaged and more supported in learning, and this higher quality instruction predicts higher student math achievement (Baumert et al., 2010).

When we look at teachers' knowledge of facts and concepts in other subjects, as measured by test scores and university grades, the relationship to student learning is unclear and may be indirect (Aloe & Becker, 2009). We know from Darling-Hammond and Youngs's (2002) work that the quality of teachers—as measured by whether the teachers were fully certified and have a major in their teaching field—is related to student performance. When we look at scores on teacher certification tests, there is a modest positive relationship between teachers' scores and students' achievement—the strongest evidence for this relationship is again in mathematics (Boyd, Goldhaber, Lankford, & Wyckoff, 2008).

The indirect effects are that teachers who know more may make clearer presentations and recognize student difficulties more easily. They are ready for any student questions and do not have to be evasive or vague in their answers. Thus, knowledge is necessary for effective teaching because being more knowledgeable helps teachers be *clearer*, more *organized*, and more *responsive* to student questions.

## Recent Research on Teaching

In a program of large-scale, longitudinal research, Robert Pianta and his colleagues (Pianta, 2005, 2008; Crosnoe et al., 2010; Jerome, Harme, & Pianta, 2009; Luckner & Pianta, 2011) have identified three aspects of classroom climate that are related to the development and learning of preschool and elementary school students. These three dimensions are consistent with the characteristics of effective teachers identified in earlier research on teaching, and they cover affective, behavioural, and cognitive dimensions, as you can see in Table 14.1. The *affective* dimension in Pianta's model is teacher *emotional support*, similar

TABLE 14.1 • **Dimensions of Classroom Climate**

| AREA OF TEACHING | CLASSROOM CLIMATE DIMENSION | COMPONENTS | DEFINITIONS AND EXAMPLES |
|---|---|---|---|
| Affective | Emotional Support | *Positive Climate* | Warmth, mutual respect, positive emotional connections between teacher and students |
| | | *Negative Climate (negative predictor of learning)* | Disrespect, anger, hostility |
| | | *Teacher Sensitivity* | Consistency and effectiveness in responding to students' academic and emotional needs |
| | | *Regard for Students' Perspectives* | Activities encourage student autonomy and emphasize students' interests, motivations, and points of view |
| Cognitive | Instructional Support | *Concept Development* | Activities and discussion promote higher-order thinking skills and cognition |
| | | *Quality of Feedback* | Consistency in providing specific, process-oriented feedback and back-and-forth exchanges to extend students' learning |
| Behavioural | Classroom Organization | *Behaviour Management* | Teachers' effectiveness in monitoring, preventing, and redirecting misbehaviour |
| | | *Productivity* | How consistently learning is maximized with clear activities and routines, teacher preparation, efficient transitions, and minimal disruptions |
| | | *Instructional Learning Formats* | How well materials, modalities, and activities are used to engage students in learning |

*Source: Based on Brown, J. L., Jones, S. M., LaRusso, M. D., & Aber, J. L. (2010). Improving classroom quality: Teacher influences and experimental impacts of the 4Rs Program. Journal of Educational Psychology, 102, 153–167.*

to teacher warmth and enthusiasm identified in early research. The *cognitive* dimension is instructional support, which includes concept development (activities and discussions that promote student higher-order thinking) and quality feedback that is specific and focused on the learning process. Concept development and quality feedback may be easier for teachers with greater knowledge for teaching. Pianta's third dimension is classroom organization, which includes *behavioural* concerns such as classroom and lesson management, with clear activities and routines that make more time for student learning and are really engaging—similar to the teacher characteristics of clarity and organization.

Now let's get to the specifics of teaching—the first step is planning.

## THE FIRST STEP: PLANNING

**STOP & THINK** Greta Morine-Dershimer (2006) asks which of the following are true about teacher planning:

Time is of the essence.

Plans are made to be broken.

Don't look back.

A little planning goes a long way.

You can do it yourself.

One size fits all. •

**Watch**
Research on Planning

### Research on Planning

When you thought about the "What Would You Do?" challenge at the beginning of this chapter, you were planning. In the past few years, educational researchers have become very interested in teachers' planning. They have interviewed teachers about how they plan, asked teachers to "think out loud" while planning or to keep journals describing their plans, and even studied teachers intensively for months at a time. What have they found?

First, planning influences what students will learn, since planning transforms the available time and curriculum materials into activities, assignments, and tasks for students—*time is of the essence planning*. When a teacher decides to devote seven hours to language arts and 15 minutes to science in a given week, the students in that class will learn more language than science. Planning done at the beginning of the year is particularly important because many routines and patterns, such as time allocations, are established early. So *a little planning does go a long way* in terms of what will be taught and what will be learned.

Second, teachers engage in several levels of planning—by the year, term, unit, week, and day. All the levels must be coordinated. Accomplishing the year's plan requires breaking the work into terms, the terms into units, and the units into weeks and days. For experienced teachers, unit planning seems to be the most important level, followed by weekly and then daily planning. As you gain experience in teaching, it will become easier to coordinate these levels of planning (Morine-Dershimer, 2006).

Third, plans reduce—but do not eliminate—uncertainty in teaching. Planning must allow flexibility. There is some evidence that when teachers "overplan"— fill every minute and stick to the plan no matter what—their students do not learn as much as students whose teachers are flexible (Shavelson, 1987). So *plans are not made to be broken—but sometimes they need to be bent a bit*.

In order to plan creatively and flexibly, teachers need to have wide-ranging knowledge about students, their interests, and their abilities; the subjects being taught; alternative ways to teach and assess understanding; working with groups; the expectations and limitations of the school and community; how to apply and adapt materials and texts; and how to pull all this knowledge together into meaningful activities. The plans of beginning teachers sometimes don't work because the teachers lack knowledge about the students or the subject—they can't estimate how long it will take students to complete an activity, for example, or they stumble when asked for an explanation or a different example (Calderhead, 1996).

In planning, *you can do it yourself*—but *collaboration* is better. Working with other teachers and sharing ideas is one of the best experiences in teaching. Some educators think that a collaborative approach to planning used in Japan called *kenshu* or "mastery through study" is one reason why Japanese students do so well on international tests. A basic part of the *kenshu* process involves a small group of teachers developing a lesson, then videotaping one of the group members teaching the lesson. Next, all members review the recording, analyze student responses, and improve the lesson further. Other teachers try the revised lesson and more improvements follow. At the end of the school year, all the study groups may publish the results of

**EXPERT PLANNING** In planning, you can go it alone, but collaboration is better. Sharing ideas with colleagues can be one of the best experiences in teaching.

Krista Greco/Merrill

their work. To learn about this approach, search the internet using the keywords "lesson study." While you are out there in cyberspace, explore some of the lesson plans available using the keywords "lesson plans," or search by subject or grade—for example, "math lesson plans" or "grade 4 lesson plans."

But even great lesson plans taken from a terrific website on science have to be adapted to your situation. Some of the adaptation comes before you teach and some comes after. In fact, much of what experienced teachers know about planning comes from looking back—reflecting—on what worked and what didn't, so *do look back* on your plans and grow professionally in the process. Collaborative reflection and revising lessons are major components of the **lesson study** approach to planning.

Finally, there is no one model for effective planning. *One size does* not *fit all* in planning. For experienced teachers, planning is a creative problem-solving process. They know how to accomplish many lessons and segments of lessons. They know what to expect and how to proceed, so they don't necessarily continue to follow the detailed lesson-planning models they learned during their teacher-preparation programs. Planning is more informal—"in their heads." However, many experienced teachers think it was helpful to learn this detailed system as a foundation (Clark & Peterson, 1986).

*"And then, of course, there's the possibility of being just the slightest bit too organized."*

Glen Dines/Phi Delta Kappan

No matter how you plan, you must have a learning goal in mind. In the next section, we consider the range of goals you might have for your students.

## Objectives for Learning

We hear quite a bit today about visions, goals, outcomes, and standards. At a very general, abstract level are the grand goals society may have for graduates of public schools (e.g., that all graduates have effective communication and problem-solving skills). However, very general goals are meaningless as potential guidelines for instruction. Therefore, many provinces (e.g., British Columbia, Manitoba, Ontario) have developed standards that provide more specific descriptions of how students will demonstrate progress toward the attainment of grand goals (e.g., students will develop the concept of fractions, mixed numbers, and decimals and use models to relate fractions to decimals and

**Lesson study** As a group, teachers develop, test, improve, and retest lessons until they are satisfied with the final version.

to find equivalent fractions). At this level, the indicators are close to being instructional objectives (Airasian, 2005).

AN EXAMPLE OF STANDARDS: TECHNOLOGY.  Here is an example of standards that relate to you—the teacher—and what you should know about technology. Two widely adopted technology standards are from the International Society for Technology in Education (ISTE) and the Partnership for 21st Century Skills. The ISTE produced the ISTE Standards for Teachers shown below (ISTE•T; www.iste.org/standards/nets-for-teachers/nets-for-teachers-2008.aspx):

1. **Facilitate and Inspire Student Learning and Creativity***
   Teachers use their knowledge of subject matter, teaching and learning, and technology to facilitate experiences that advance student learning, creativity, and innovation in both face-to-face and virtual environments.
2. **Design and Develop Digital-Age Learning Experiences and Assessments**
   Teachers design, develop, and evaluate authentic learning experiences and assessment incorporating contemporary tools and resources to maximize content learning in context and to develop the knowledge, skills, and attitudes identified in the ISTE•T.
3. **Model Digital-Age Work and Learning**
   Teachers exhibit knowledge, skills, and work processes representative of an innovative professional in a global and digital society.
4. **Promote and Model Digital Citizenship and Responsibility**
   Teachers understand local and global societal issues and responsibilities in an evolving digital culture and exhibit legal and ethical behaviour in their professional practices.
5. **Engage in Professional Growth and Leadership**
   Teachers continuously improve their professional practice, model lifelong learning, and exhibit leadership in their school and professional community by promoting and demonstrating the effective use of digital tools and resources.

But what about your teaching? Let's move into the classroom.

CLASSROOMS: INSTRUCTIONAL OBJECTIVES.  Norman Gronlund and Susan Brookhart (2009) define **instructional objectives** as intended learning outcomes, or the types of performance students will demonstrate after instruction to show what they have learned. People with behavioural views write objectives that focus on observable and measurable changes in the learner. Behavioural objectives use terms such as *list, define, add,* or *calculate.* Cognitive objectives, on the other hand, emphasize thinking and comprehension, so they are more likely to include words such as *understand, recognize, create,* or *apply.* Let us look more closely at two different methods of writing instructional objectives: one that reflects behaviourist views of learning and another based on cognitive views of learning.

MAGER: START WITH THE SPECIFIC.  Robert Mager developed a very influential system for writing instructional objectives (Mager, 1975). His idea is that objectives ought to describe what students will be doing when demonstrating their achievement and how you will know they are doing it, so these are generally regarded as **behavioural objectives**. According to Mager, a good objective has three parts. First, it describes the intended *student behaviour.* What must the student do? Second, it lists the *conditions* under which the behaviour will occur. How will this behaviour be recognized or tested? Third, it gives the *criteria* for acceptable performance on the test. For example, an objective in social studies might be: "Given a recent article from the local newspaper [conditions], the student will mark each statement with an F for fact or an O for opinion [observable student behaviour], with 75 percent of the statement correctly marked [criteria]." With this emphasis on final behaviour, Mager's system requires a very explicit statement. Mager contends that often students can teach themselves if they are given well-stated objectives.

**Instructional objectives** Clear statements of what students are intended to learn through instruction.

**Behavioural objectives** Instructional objectives stated in terms of observable behaviour.

---

*Reprinted with permission from *National Educational Technology Standards For Teachers.*Copyright © 2007, 2008 by ISTE (International Society for Technology in Education). All rights reserved.

TABLE 14.2 • **A Combined Method for Creating Objectives**

| GENERAL OBJECTIVE |
|---|
| Comprehends scientific concepts. |
| **SPECIFIC EXAMPLES** |
| 1. Describes the concept in his or her own words.<br>2. Gives an example of the concept [that is new].<br>3. States hypotheses based on the concept.<br>4. Describes how the process functions in a given situation.<br>5. Describes an experiment that illustrates the process. |

*Source: Based on Gronlund, N. E., & Brookhart, S. M. (2009). Gronlund's writing instructional objectives (8th ed.). Upper Saddle River, NJ: Pearson Education, Inc.*

**GRONLUND: START WITH THE GENERAL.** Gronlund and Brookhart (2009) offer a different approach, often used for writing **cognitive objectives**. They believe that an objective should be stated first in general terms (*understand, solve, appreciate,* etc.). Then the teacher should clarify by listing examples of behaviour that would provide evidence that the student has attained the objective. Look at the example in Table 14.2. The goal here is *comprehending* a scientific concept. A teacher could never list all the behaviours that might be involved in "presenting and defending," but stating an initial, general objective along with specific examples makes the purpose clear.

The most recent research on instructional objectives tends to favour approaches similar to Gronlund's. James Popham (2005a), a former proponent of very specific objectives, makes this recommendation:

> Strive to come up with a half dozen or so truly salient, broad, yet measurable instructional objectives for your own classroom. Too many small-scope, hyperspecific objectives will be of scant value to you because, if you're at all normal, you'll soon disregard [them]. On the other hand, a small number of intellectually manageable, broad, yet measurable objectives will not only prove helpful to you instructionally but will also help you answer the what-to-assess question (pp. 104–105).

## Flexible and Creative Plans—Using Taxonomies

---

**STOP & THINK** Think about your assignments for one of your classes. What kind of thinking is involved in doing the assignments?
  Remembering facts and terms?
  Understanding key ideas?
  Applying information to solve problems?
  Analyzing a situation, task, or problem?
  Making evaluations or giving opinions?
  Creating or designing something new? •

---

Almost 60 years ago, a group of experts in educational evaluation led by Benjamin Bloom set out to improve college and university examinations. The impact of their work has touched education at all levels around the world (Anderson & Sosniak, 1994). Bloom and his colleagues developed a **taxonomy**, or classification system, of educational objectives. Objectives were divided into three domains: cognitive, affective, and psychomotor. A handbook describing the objectives in each area was eventually published. In real life, of course, behaviour from these three domains occurs simultaneously. While students are writing (psychomotor), they are also remembering or reasoning (cognitive), and they are likely to have some emotional response to the task as well (affective).

**THE COGNITIVE DOMAIN.** Bloom's taxonomy of the thinking or **cognitive domain** is considered one of the most significant educational writings of the twentieth century

**Cognitive objectives** Instructional objectives stated in terms of higher-level thinking operations.

**Taxonomy** Classification system.

**Cognitive domain** In Bloom's taxonomy, memory and reasoning objectives.

TABLE 14.3 • **A Revised Taxonomy in the Cognitive Domain**

The revised taxonomy includes cognitive processes operating on different kinds of knowledge. The verbs in the chart are examples of what might be used to create objectives.

| | THE COGNITIVE PROCESS DIMENSION | | | | | |
|---|---|---|---|---|---|---|
| **THE KNOWLEDGE DIMENSION** | 1. REMEMBER | 2. UNDERSTAND | 3. APPLY | 4. ANALYZE | 5. EVALUATE | 6. CREATE |
| **A. Factual Knowledge** | list | summarize | classify | order | rank | combine |
| **B. Conceptual Knowledge** | describe | interpret | experiment | explain | assess | plan |
| **C. Procedural Knowledge** | tabulate | predict | calculate | differentiate | conclude | compose |
| **D. Metacognitive Knowledge** | appropriate use | execute | select strategy | change strategy | reflect | invent |

*Source: From Anderson, L. W., Krathwohl, D. R. (2001).* A Taxonomy for Learning, Teaching, and Assessing. *Allyn and Bacon: Boston, MA. © Pearson Education. Reprinted by permission of the publisher.*

(Anderson & Sosniak, 1994). The six basic objectives in Bloom's taxonomy are *knowledge, comprehension, application, analysis, synthesis,* and *evaluation* (Bloom, Engelhart, Frost, Hill, & Krathwohl, 1956).

It is common in education to consider these objectives as a hierarchy, each skill building on those below, but such a view is not entirely accurate. Some subjects, such as mathematics, do not fit this structure very well (Kreitzer & Madaus, 1994). Still, you will hear many references to *lower-level* and *higher-level objectives*, with knowledge, comprehension, and application considered lower level and the other categories considered higher level. As a rough way of thinking about objectives, this classification can be helpful (Gronlund & Brookhart, 2009). The taxonomy of objectives can also be helpful in planning assessments because different procedures are appropriate for objectives at the various levels, as you will see in Chapter 15.

In 2001, a group of educational researchers published the first major revision of the cognitive taxonomy, and this is the one we use today (Anderson & Krathwohl, 2001).

1. *Remembering*: Remembering or recognizing something without necessarily understanding, using, or changing it
2. *Understanding*: Understanding the material being communicated without necessarily relating it to anything else
3. *Applying*: Using a general concept to solve a particular problem
4. *Analyzing*: Breaking something down into its parts
5. *Evaluating*: Judging the value of materials or methods as they might be applied in a particular situation
6. *Creating*: Creating something new by combining different ideas

The 2001 revision of Bloom's taxonomy added a new dimension—to recognize that cognitive processes must process *something* —you have to remember or understand or apply some form of knowledge. If you look at Table 14.3, you will see the result. We now have the six processes of *remembering, understanding, applying, analyzing, evaluating,* and *creating* acting on four kinds of knowledge—*factual, conceptual, procedural,* and *metacognitive.*

Consider how this revised taxonomy might suggest objectives for a social studies/language arts class. An objective that targets analyzing conceptual knowledge is:

After reading an historical account of the framing of Canada's constitution, students will be able to explain the author's point of view or bias.

An objective for evaluating metacognitive knowledge might be:

> Students will reflect on and describe their strategies for identifying the biases of the author.

See http://projects.coe.uga.edu/epltt/index.php?title=Bloom%27s_Taxonomy for more explanations and examples.

THE AFFECTIVE DOMAIN. The objectives in the taxonomy of the **affective domain**, or domain of emotional response, have not yet been revised from the original version. They range from least committed to most committed (Krathwohl, Bloom, & Masia, 1964). At the lowest level, students simply pay attention to a certain idea. At the highest level, students adopt an idea or a value and act consistently with that idea. There are five basic objectives in the affective domain:

1. *Receiving:* Being aware of or attending to something in the environment. This is the "I'll-listen-to-the-concert-but-I-won't-promise-to-like-it" level.
2. *Responding:* Showing some new behaviour as a result of experience. At this level, a person might applaud after the concert or hum some of the music the next day.
3. *Valuing:* Showing some definite involvement or commitment. At this point, a person might choose to go to a concert instead of a film.
4. *Organization:* Integrating a new value into one's general set of values, giving it some ranking among one's general priorities. This is the level at which a person would begin to make long-range commitments to concert attendance.
5. *Characterization by value:* Acting consistently with the new value. At this highest level, a person would be firmly committed to a love of music and demonstrate it openly and consistently.

Like the basic objectives in the cognitive domain, these five objectives are very general. To write specific learning objectives, you must state what students will actually be doing when they are receiving, responding, valuing, and so on. For example, an objective for a nutrition class at the valuing level (showing involvement or commitment) might be stated: After completing the unit on food contents and labelling, at least 50% of the class will commit to a junk-food boycott project by giving up candy for a month.

THE PSYCHOMOTOR DOMAIN. Until recently, the **psychomotor domain**, or the realm of physical ability objectives, has been mostly overlooked by teachers not directly involved with physical education. There are several taxonomies in this domain (e.g., Harrow, 1972; Simpson, 1972) that generally move from basic perceptions and reflex actions to skilled, creative movements. James Cangelosi (1990) provides a useful way to think about objectives in the psychomotor domain as either (1) voluntary muscle capabilities that require endurance, strength, flexibility, agility, and speed, or (2) the ability to perform a specific skill.

Objectives in the psychomotor domain should be of interest to a wide range of educators, including those in fine arts, vocational-technical education, and special education. Many other subjects, such as chemistry, physics, and biology, also require specialized movements and well-developed hand and eye coordination. Using lab equipment, the mouse on a computer, or art materials means learning new physical skills. Here are two examples of psychomotor objectives:

> Four minutes after completing a 1.6-kilometre run in eight minutes or under, your heart rate will be below 120.
> Use a computer mouse effectively to "drag and drop" files.

Whatever your instructional objectives for your students, Terry TenBrink (2006, p. 57) suggests the following four criteria. Objectives should be:

1. Student-oriented (emphasis on what the student is expected to do).
2. Descriptive of an appropriate learning *outcome* (both developmentally appropriate and appropriately sequenced, with more complex objectives following prerequisite objectives).
3. Clear and understandable (not too general or too specific).
4. Observable (avoid outcomes you can't see such as "appreciating" or "realizing").

**Affective domain** Objectives focusing on attitudes and feelings.

**Psychomotor domain** Realm of physical ability and coordination objectives.

The *Guidelines* should help you whether you use objectives for every lesson or for just a few assignments.

## GUIDELINES

### Using Instructional Objectives

**Avoid "word magic"—phrases that sound noble and important but say very little, such as, "Students will become deep thinkers."**
*Examples*

1. Keep the focus on specific changes that will take place in the students' knowledge of skills.
2. Ask students to explain the meaning of the objectives. If they can't give specific examples of what you mean, the objectives are not communicating your intentions to your students.

**Suit the activities to the objectives.**
*Examples*

1. If the goal is the memorization of vocabulary, give the students memory aids and practice exercises.
2. If the goal is the ability to develop well-thought-out positions, consider position papers, debates, projects, or mock trials.

3. If you want students to become better writers, give many opportunities for writing and rewriting.

**Make sure that your tests are related to your objectives.**
*Examples*

1. Write objectives and rough drafts for tests at the same time. Revise these drafts of tests as the units unfold and objectives change.
2. Weight the tests according to the importance of the various objectives and the time spent on each.

*For additional ideas, see www.personal.psu.edu/staff/b/x/bxb11/ Objectives or http://edtech.tennessee.edu/~bobannon/objectives.html.*

## Planning From a Constructivist Perspective

**STOP & THINK** Think about the same course assignments you analyzed in the previous *Stop & Think* activity. What are the big ideas that run through all those assignments? What other ways could you learn about those ideas besides completing the assignments? •

Traditionally, it has been the teacher's responsibility to do most of the planning for instruction, but new ways of planning are emerging. In **constructivist approaches**, planning is shared and negotiated. The teacher and students together make decisions about content, activities, and approaches. Rather than having specific student behaviour and skills as objectives, the teacher has overarching goals—"big ideas"—that guide planning (Borich, 2011). These goals are understandings or abilities that the teacher returns to again and again. Today, teaching with themes and integrated content are major elements in planning and designing lessons and units, from kindergarten (Roskos & Neuman, 1998) through high school (Clarke & Agne, 1997). For example, Elaine Homestead and Karen McGinnis (middle school teachers) and Elizabeth Pate (a college professor) designed a unit on "Human Interactions" that included studying racism, world hunger, pollution, and air and water quality. Students researched issues by reading textbooks and outside sources, learning to use databases, interviewing local officials, and inviting guest speakers into class. Students had to develop knowledge in science, mathematics, and social studies. They learned to write and speak persuasively, and in the process, raised money for hunger relief in Africa (Pate, McGinnis, & Homestead, 1995).

Elementary-age students can benefit from integrated planning, too. There is no reason to work on spelling skills, then listening skills, then writing skills, and then social studies or science. All these abilities can be developed together if students work to solve authentic problems. Some topics for integrating themes with younger children are people,

**Constructivist approach** View that emphasizes the active role of the learner in building understanding and making sense of information.

TABLE 14.4 • **Some Themes for Integrated Planning for Middle and High School Students**

| Courage | Time and space |
|---|---|
| Mystery | Groups and institutions |
| Survival | Work |
| Human interaction | Motion |
| Communities of the future | Cause and effect |
| Communication/language | Probability and prediction |
| Human rights and responsibilities | Change and conservation |
| Identity/coming of age | Diversity and variation |
| Interdependence | Autobiography |

*Sources: Based on Clarke, J. H., & Agne, R. M. (1997). Curriculum Development; Interdisciplinary High School Teaching. Boston: Allyn & Bacon; Thompson, G. (1991). Teaching through Themes. New York: Scholastic. See Thompson for resources and strategies to develop some of these themes in elementary school and Clarke and Agne for ideas at the high school level.*

friendship, gardens as habitats, communities, and patterns. Possibilities for older children are given in Table 14.4.

Let's assume you have an idea of what you want students to understand, but *how* do you teach to encourage understanding? You still need to decide what's happening on Monday. You need to design teaching that is appropriate for the objectives.

# TEACHING APPROACHES

In this section we will provide some basic formats for putting plans into action. The first challenge is to match your teaching methods to your objectives. We begin with strategies for teaching explicit facts and concepts.

## Direct Instruction

For many people, the image of teaching is an instructor explaining material to students— lecture is a classic form. There was an explosion of research in the 1970s and 1980s that focused on these more traditional forms of teaching. The results of all this work identified a model of teaching that was related to improved student learning. Barak Rosenshine and Robert Stevens (1986) call this approach **direct instruction** or **explicit teaching**. Tom Good (1983a) uses the term **active teaching** to describe a similar approach.

The direct instruction model fits a specific set of circumstances because it was derived from a particular approach to research. Researchers identified the elements of direct instruction by comparing teachers whose students learned more than expected (based on entering knowledge) with teachers whose students performed at an expected or average level. The researchers focused on existing practices in American classrooms. Because the focus was on traditional forms of teaching, the research could not identify successful innovations. Effectiveness was usually defined as average improvement in standardized test scores for a whole class or school. So the results hold for large groups, but not necessarily for every student in the group. Even when the average achievement of a group improves, the achievement of some individuals may decline (Good, 1996; Shuell, 1996).

Given these conditions, direct instruction applies best to the teaching of **basic skills**— clearly structured knowledge and essential skills, such as science facts, mathematics computations, reading vocabulary, and grammar rules (Rosenshine & Stevens, 1986). These

**Direct instruction or explicit teaching** Systematic instruction for mastery of basic skills, facts, and information.

**Active teaching** Teaching characterized by high levels of teacher explanation, demonstration, and interaction with students.

**Basic skills** Clearly structured knowledge that is needed for later learning and that can be taught step by step.

skills involve tasks that are relatively unambiguous; they can be taught step by step and tested objectively. Franz Weinert and Andreas Helmke (1995) describe effective direct instruction as having the following features:

> (a) the teacher's classroom management is especially effective and the rate of student interruptive behaviors is very low; (b) the teacher maintains a strong academic focus and uses available instructional time intensively to initiate and facilitate students' learning activities; (c) the teacher insures that as many students as possible achieve good learning progress by carefully choosing appropriate tasks, clearly presenting subject-matter information and solution strategies, continuously diagnosing each student's learning progress and learning difficulties, and providing effective help through remedial instruction. (p. 138)

To this list, Xin Ma (2012) adds moving at a brisk pace and having a warm and accepting classroom climate.

How would a teacher turn these themes into actions?

ROSENSHINE'S SIX TEACHING FUNCTIONS. Rosenshine and his colleagues (Rosenshine, 1988; Rosenshine & Stevens, 1986) have identified the following six teaching functions based on the research on effective instruction. These can serve as a checklist or framework for teaching basic skills.

1. *Review and check the previous day's work.* Reteach if students misunderstood or made errors.
2. *Present new material.* Make the purpose clear, teach in small steps, and provide many examples and non-examples.
3. *Provide guided practice.* Question students, give practice problems, and listen for misconceptions and misunderstandings. Reteach if necessary. Continue guided practice until students answer about 80% of the questions correctly.
4. *Give feedback and correctives* based on student answers. Reteach if necessary.
5. *Provide independent practice.* Let students apply the new learning on their own, in seatwork, cooperative groups, or homework. The success rate during independent practice should be about 95%. This means that students must be well prepared for the work by the presentation and guided practice, and that assignments must not be too difficult. The point is for the students to practise until the skills become overlearned and automatic—until the students are confident. Hold students accountable for the work they do—check it.
6. *Review weekly and monthly* to consolidate learning. Include some review items as homework. Test often, and reteach material missed on the tests.

These six functions are not steps to be followed in a particular order, but all of them are elements of effective instruction. For example, feedback, review, or reteaching should occur whenever necessary and should match the abilities of the students. Also, keep in mind the age and prior knowledge of your students. The younger or the less prepared your students, the briefer your explanations should be. Use more and shorter cycles of presentation, guided practice, feedback, and correctives.

ADVANCE ORGANIZERS. Teachers using direct instruction often begin with an **advance organizer**. This is an introductory statement broad enough to encompass all the information that will follow. The organizers can serve three purposes: They direct your attention to what is important in the coming material, they highlight relationships among ideas that will be presented, and they remind you of relevant information you already have.

Advance organizers fall into one of two categories, comparative and expository (Mayer, 1984). *Comparative organizers* activate (bring into working memory) already existing schemas. They remind you of what you already know, but may not realize is relevant. A comparative advance organizer for a history lesson on revolutions might be a statement that contrasts military uprisings with the physical and social changes involved in the Industrial Revolution; you could also compare the common aspects of the French, English, Mexican, Russian, Iranian, Egyptian, and American revolutions (Salomon & Perkins, 1989).

**Advance organizer** Statement of inclusive concepts to introduce and sum up material that follows.

In contrast, *expository organizers* provide new knowledge that students will need in order to understand the upcoming information. In an English class, you might begin a large thematic unit on rites of passage in literature with a very broad statement of the theme and why it has been so central in literature—something like, "A central character coming of age must learn to know himself or herself, often makes some kind of journey of self-discovery, and must decide what in the society is to be accepted and what should be rejected." Such an organizer might precede reading novels such as *The Adventures of Huckleberry Finn*.

The general conclusion of research on advance organizers is that they do help students learn, especially when the material to be learned is quite unfamiliar, complex, or difficult—as long as two conditions are met (Langan-Fox, Waycott, & Albert, 2000; Morin & Miller, 1998). First, to be effective, the organizer must be understood by the students. This was demonstrated dramatically in a classic study by Dinnel and Glover (1985). They found that instructing students to paraphrase an advance organizer—which, of course, requires them to understand its meaning—increased the effectiveness of the organizer. Second, the organizer must really be an organizer: It must indicate relations among the basic concepts and terms that will be used. Concrete models, diagrams, or analogies seem to be especially good organizers (Robinson, 1998; Robinson & Kiewra, 1995).

**ADVANCE ORGANIZERS** Advance organizers remind students of information they already know that will help them understand the new material or present key concepts they will need. This teacher is helping students bring to mind what they already know about bones in the human body before launching into the lesson.

Fuse/Getty Images

**WHY DOES DIRECT INSTRUCTION WORK?** Well-organized presentations with advance organizers, clear explanations, the use of explanatory links, and reviews can all help students perceive connections among ideas. If done well, therefore, a direct instruction lesson may be a resource that students use to construct understanding. For example, reviews activate prior knowledge, so that students are ready to understand. Brief, clear presentations and guided practice avoid overloading the students' information processing systems and taxing their working memories. Numerous examples and explanations give many pathways and associations for building networks of concepts. Guided practice can also give the teacher a snapshot of the students' thinking as well as their misconceptions, allowing the teacher to address them directly as misconceptions rather than simply as "wrong answers."

Every subject, even university-level English or chemistry, can require some direct instruction. Noddings (1990) reminds teachers that students may need some direct instruction in how to use various manipulative materials to get the possible benefits from them. Students working in cooperative groups may need guidance, modelling, and practice in how to ask questions and give explanations. And to solve difficult problems, students may need some direct instruction in possible problem-solving strategies.

Some studies have found that teachers' presentations take up one-sixth to one-fourth of all classroom time. Teacher explanation is appropriate for communicating a large amount of material to many students in a short period of time, introducing a new topic, giving background information, or motivating students to learn more on their own. Teacher presentations are therefore most appropriate for cognitive and affective objectives at the lower levels of the taxonomies described earlier: for remembering, understanding, applying, receiving, responding, and valuing (Arends, 2001; Kindsvatter, Wilen, & Ishler, 1992).

**EVALUATING DIRECT INSTRUCTION.** Direct instruction, particularly when it involves extended teacher presentations or lectures, has some disadvantages. You may find that some students have trouble listening for more than a few minutes at a time and that they

TABLE 14.5 • **Active Learning and Teacher Presentations**

Here are some ideas we use for keeping students cognitively engaged in lessons. They can be adapted for many ages.

| | |
|---|---|
| **Write an Answer:** Pose a question, ask everyone to write a brief answer, then call on students to share what they wrote. | **Voting:** Pose two alternative explanations; ask how many agree with each (may be a good idea to ask the student to close their eyes and vote so they won't be swayed by the votes of others). |
| **I used to think_____, but now I know_____:** After a lesson, ask students to fill in the blanks, then share their results with the person beside them | **Choral Response:** Have the whole class restate in unison important facts and ideas, such as "In a right triangle, $a^2 + b^2 = c^2$." |
| **Think-Pair-Share:** Pose a question, students think of an answer on their own, then consult with a neighbour to improve the answer, then volunteers share their ideas. | **One-Minute Write:** After a section of the lesson, students write for one minute to summarize the key points or raise a question about what is not clear to them. |

simply tune you out. Teacher presentations can put the students in a passive position by doing much of the cognitive work for them and may prevent students from asking or even thinking of questions (Freiberg & Driscoll, 2005). **Scripted cooperation** is one way to incorporate active learning into lectures. Several times during the presentation, the teacher asks students to work in pairs. One person is the summarizer and the other critiques the summary. This activity gives students a chance to check their understanding, organize their thinking, and translate ideas into their own words. Other possibilities are described in Table 14.5.

Critics also claim that direct instruction is based on a wrong theory of learning. Teachers break material into small segments, present each segment clearly, and reinforce or correct, thus transmitting accurate understandings from teacher to student. The student is viewed as an "empty vessel" waiting to be filled with knowledge, rather than an active constructor of knowledge (Berg & Clough, 1991; Driscoll, 2005). These criticisms of direct instruction echo the criticisms of behavioural learning theories.

There is ample evidence, however, that direct instruction and explanation can help students learn actively, not passively (Leinhardt, 2001). For younger and less prepared learners, student-controlled learning without teacher direction and instruction can lead to systematic deficits in the students' knowledge. Without guidance, the understandings that students construct may be incomplete and misleading (Sweller, Kirschner, & Clark, 2007). For example, Harris and Graham (1996) describe the experiences of their daughter Leah in a whole-language/progressive education school, where the teachers successfully developed their daughter's creativity, thinking, and understanding.

> Skills, on the other hand, have been a problem for our daughter and for other children. At the end of kindergarten, when she had not made much progress in reading, her teacher said she believed Leah had a perceptual problem or a learning disability. Leah began asking what was wrong with her, because other kids were reading and she wasn't. Finally, an assessment was done. (p. 26)

The testing indicated no learning disability, strong comprehension abilities, and poor word attack skills. Luckily, Leah's parents knew how to teach word attack skills. Direct teaching of these skills helped Leah become an avid and able reader in about six weeks. Deep understanding and fluent performance—whether in dance or mathematical problem solving or reading—require models of expert performance and extensive practice with feedback (Anderson, Reder, & Simon, 1995). Guided and independent practice and feedback are at the heart of the direct instruction model. See the *Guidelines* for more ideas about teaching effectively.

**Scripted cooperation** Learning strategy in which two students take turns summarizing material and criticizing the summaries.

## GUIDELINES

## Teaching Effectively

**Use advance organizers.**
*Examples*

1. English: Shakespeare used the social ideas of his time as a framework for his plays—*Julius Caesar*, *Hamlet*, and *Macbeth* deal with concepts of natural order, a nation as the human body, etc.
2. Social studies: Geography dictates economy in preindustrialized regions or nations.
3. History: Important concepts during the Renaissance were symmetry, admiration of the classical world, the centrality of the human mind.

**Use a number of examples.**
*Examples*

1. In mathematics class, ask students to point out all the examples of right angles that they can find in the room.
2. In teaching about islands and peninsulas, use maps, slides, models, postcards.

**Organize your lessons carefully.**
*Examples*

1. Provide objectives that help students focus on the purpose of the lesson.
2. Begin lessons by writing a brief outline on the board, or work on an outline with the class as part of the lesson.
3. If possible, break the presentation into clear steps or stages.
4. Review periodically.

**Anticipate and plan for difficult parts in the lesson.**
*Examples*

1. Plan a clear introduction to the lesson that tells students what they are going to learn and how they are going to learn it.
2. Do the exercises and anticipate student problems—consult the teachers' manual for ideas.
3. Have definitions ready for new terms, and prepare several relevant examples for concepts.
4. Think of analogies that will make ideas easier to understand.
5. Organize the lesson in a logical sequence; include checkpoints that incorporate oral or written questions or problems to make sure the students are following the explanations.

**Strive for clear explanations.**
*Examples*

1. Avoid vague words and ambiguous phrases. Steer clear of "the somes"—*something, someone, sometime, somehow;*

"the not verys"—*not very much, not very well, not very hard, not very often;* and other unspecific fillers, such as *most, not all, sort of, and so on, of course, as you know, I guess, in fact,* or *whatever,* and *more or less.*
2. Use specific (and, if possible, colourful) names instead of *it, them,* and *thing.*
3. Refrain from using pet phrases such as *you know, like,* and *okay?* Another idea is to record a lesson on tape to check yourself for clarity.
4. Give explanations at several levels so that all students, not just the brightest, will understand.
5. Focus on one idea at a time and avoid digressions.

**Make clear connections by using explanatory links such as because, if—then, or therefore.**
*Examples*

1. Use statements, such as, "Explorers found it difficult to get to the west coast of Canada because it was so hard to cross the Rockies."
2. Use helpful explanatory links in labelling visual material such as graphs, concept maps, or illustrations.

**Signal transitions from one major topic to another with phrases.**
*Examples*

1. Use transitional phrases such as, "The next area …," "Now we will turn to …," or "The second step is… ."
2. Outline topics by listing key points, drawing concept maps on the board, or using an overhead projector.

**Communicate an enthusiasm for your subject and the day's lesson.**
*Examples*

1. Tell students why the lesson is important. Have a better reason than "This will be on the test" or "You will need to know it next year." Emphasize the value of the learning itself.
2. Be sure to make eye contact with the students.
3. Vary your pace and volume in speaking. Use silence for emphasis.

*For more ideas about effective teaching, see www.effectiveteachingsolutions.com.*

## Seatwork and Homework

**SEATWORK.** The conclusions of the limited research on **seatwork** (independent classroom-desk work) are clear; this technique is often overused. For example, a summary of research from 1975 to 2000 found a similar problem in reading instruction for students

**Seatwork** Independent classroom work.

**Watch**
Seatwork

with disabilities. These students, who often have trouble learning without teacher guidance, spent about 40% of their time on individual seatwork (Vaughn, Levy, Coleman, & Bos, 2002).

Seatwork should follow up a lesson and give students supervised practice. It should not be the main mode of instruction. Unfortunately, many workbook pages do little to support the learning of important objectives. Before you assign work, ask yourself, "Does doing this work help students learn anything that matters?" Students should see the connection between the seatwork or homework and the lesson. Tell them why they are doing the work. The objectives should be clear, all the materials that might be needed should be provided, and the work should be easy enough that students can succeed on their own. Success rates should be high—near 100%. When seatwork is too difficult, students often resort to guessing or copying just to finish.

There are several alternatives to completing workbook assignments, such as reading silently and reading aloud to a partner; writing for a "real" audience; writing letters or journals; transcribing conversations and punctuating them properly; making up problems; working on long-term projects and reports; solving brain teasers and puzzles; and engaging in computer activities (Weinstein, Romano, & Mignano, 2011). One of our favourites is creating a group story. Two students begin a story on the computer. Then two more add a paragraph. The story grows with each new pair's addition. The students are reading and writing, editing, and improving. With so many different authors, each writer may spark the creative thinking of other contributors.

Any independent work requires careful monitoring. Being available to students doing seatwork is more effective than offering students help before they ask for it. Short, frequent contacts are best (Brophy & Good, 1986). Sometimes you may be working with a small group while other students do seatwork. In these situations, it is especially important for students to know what to do if they need help. Nancy has observed in classrooms where students follow the rule "Ask three, then me." Students have to consult three classmates before seeking help from the teacher. Teachers in these classrooms spend time early in the year showing students *how* to help each other—how to ask questions and how to explain.

**STOP & THINK**  Think back to your elementary and high school days. Do you remember any homework assignments? What sticks in your mind about those assignments? •

**HOMEWORK.**  In contrast to the limited research on seatwork, educators have been studying the effects of homework for over 75 years (Cooper, 2004; Cooper, Robinson, & Patall, 2006; Corno, 2000; Trautwein, 2007).

To benefit from homework, students must understand the assignment. It may help to do the first few questions as a class, to clear up any misconceptions. This is especially important for students who may have no one at home to consult if they have problems with the assignment. A second way to keep students involved is to hold them accountable for completing the work correctly, not just for filling in the page. This means the work should be checked, the students given a chance to correct the errors or revise work, and the results counted toward the class grade (Brophy & Good, 1986). Expert teachers often have ways of correcting homework quickly during the first minutes of class by having students check each other's or their own work. There are other concerns about making homework effective, as you can see in the *Point/Counterpoint.*

If students get stuck on homework, they need help at home from someone who can scaffold their work without just "giving the answer" (Pressley, 1995). But many family members don't know how to help (Hoover-Dempsey et al., 2001; Hoover-Dempsey, Bassler, & Burow, 1995). The *Family and Community Partnerships Guidelines* include ideas for helping families deal with homework.

## Questioning and Discussion

Teachers pose questions, students answer. This form of teaching, sometimes called *recitation,* has been with us for many years (Weinstein, Romano, & Mignano, 2011). The

## POINT/COUNTERPOINT    Is Homework a Valuable Use of Time?

Like so many methods in education, homework has moved in and out of favour. In the early 1900s, homework was seen as an important path to mental discipline, but by the 1940s, homework was criticized as too much drill and low-level learning. Then in the 1950s, homework was rediscovered as a way to catch up with the Soviet Union in science and mathematics, only to be seen as too much pressure on students during the more laid-back 1960s. By the 1980s, homework was in again as a way to improve the standing of North American children compared to students around the world (Cooper & Valentine, 2001). Today, homework is increasing in early elementary schools (Hofferth & Sandberg, 2000). Everyone has done homework—were those hours well spent?

▶ **POINT** **Homework does not help students learn.** No matter how interesting an activity is, students will eventually get bored with it—so why give them work both in and out of school? They will simply grow weary of learning. And important opportunities are lost for community involvement or leisure activities that would create well-rounded citizens. When parents help with homework, they can do more harm than good—sometimes confusing their children or teaching them incorrectly. And students from poorer families often must work, so they miss doing the homework; then the learning discrepancy between the rich and poor grows even greater. Besides, the research is inconsistent about the effects of homework. For example, one study found that in-class work was better than homework in helping elementary students learn (Cooper & Valentine, 2001). In his book *The Homework Myth: Why Our Kids Get Too Much of a Bad Thing*, Alfie Kohn (2006) suggests the schools adopt no homework as the default policy. "Changing the default to no homework would likely have two practical consequences: The number of assignments would decline and the quality of those assignments would rise. Both of these, I believe, represent significant improvements in our children's education" (p. 168).

Harris Cooper and his colleagues reviewed many studies of homework and concluded that there is little relationship between homework and learning for young students, but the relationship between homework and achievement grows progressively stronger for older students. Most of the studies involved math and reading or English homework, however, not social studies, science, or other subjects.

▶ **COUNTERPOINT** **Well-planned homework can work for many students.** There is recent evidence that students in high school who do more homework (and watch less television after school) have higher grades, even when other factors such as gender, grade level, ethnicity, socioeconomic status (SES), and amount of adult supervision are taken into consideration (Cooper, Robinson, & Patall, 2006; Cooper & Valentine, 2001; Cooper, Valentine, Nye, & Kindsay, 1999). The Canadian Council on Learning (CCL, 2009) agrees that homework can be beneficial, but only if it is assigned judiciously and engages students. Specifically, their review of studies on homework conducted between 2003 and 2007 indicates the following:

- Homework that asks students to consider alternative strategies for solving problems is more likely to be effective than rote learning.
- Homework does not benefit children in the primary grades.
- Lower-achieving students benefit the most from homework.
- Homework each day should not exceed a student's grade $\times$ 10 (Cooper's rule of thumb)—that is, a student in grade 5 should not do more that 50 minutes of homework each day.

Most research examines the relationship between amount of time spent on homework (as reported by students or parents) and achievement in terms of grades or achievement tests. Another approach is to focus on effort instead of time. Students' self-reported effort on homework is consistently and positively related to student achievement (Trautwein, Schnyder, Niggli, Neumann, & Lüdtke, 2009). "High homework effort means that a student does his or her best to solve the tasks assigned. There need not be a close relationship between effort and time on homework: A student putting as much effort as possible into a homework assignment might finish in 5 minutes or still be working after an hour" (Trautwein & Lüdtke, 2007, p. 432). Students are more likely to put in effort if they see the homework as interesting, valuable, reasonably challenging, and not anxiety provoking—this could require some differentiated homework assignments (Dettmers, Trautwein, Ludtke, Kunter, & Baumert, 2010). So the challenge is to get students to put their best efforts into appropriate homework and to get teachers to assign only high-quality homework.

teacher's questions develop a framework for the subject matter involved. The students' answers are often followed by reactions from the teacher such as praise, correction, or requests for further information. The pattern from the teacher's point of view consists of *initiation* (teacher asks questions), *response* (student answers), and *evaluation* (praising,

## GUIDELINES — FAMILY AND COMMUNITY PARTNERSHIPS

### Homework

**Make sure that families know what students are expected to learn.**
*Examples*

1. At the beginning of a unit, send home a list of the main objectives, examples of major assignments, key due dates, homework "calendar," and a list of resources available for free at libraries or on the internet.
2. Provide a clear, concise description of your homework policy—how homework is counted toward class grades; consequences for late, forgotten, or missing homework; and so on.

**Help families find a comfortable and helpful role in their child's homework.**
*Examples*

1. Remind families that "helping with homework" means encouraging, listening, monitoring, praising, discussing, brainstorming—not necessarily teaching and never doing the work for their child.
2. Encourage families to set aside a quiet time and place for everyone in the family to study. Make this time a regular part of the daily routine.
3. Have some homework assignments that are fun and involve the whole family—puzzles, family albums, watching a television program together and doing a "review."
4. In conferences, ask families what they need to play a helpful role in their child's homework.

**Solicit and use suggestions from families about homework.**
*Examples*

1. Find out what responsibilities the child has at home—how much time is available for homework.

2. Periodically, have a "homework hotline" for call-in questions and suggestions.

**If no one is at home to help with homework, set up other support systems.**
*Examples*

1. Assign study buddies who can be available over the phone.
2. If students have computers, provide lists of internet helplines.
3. Locate free help in public libraries and make these resources known.

**Take advantage of family and community "funds of knowledge" to connect homework with life in the community, and life in the community with lessons in school (Moll, Amanti, Neff, & Gonzales, 1992).**
*Examples*

1. Create a lesson about how family members use math and reading in sewing and in housing construction (Epstein & Van Voorhis, 2001).
2. Design interactive homework projects that families do together to evaluate needed products for their home; for example, deciding on the best buy on shampoo or paper towels.

_____

*For more ideas, see*
*www.ncpie.org/DevelopingPartnerships.*

*For help for parents and an article from teachers' points of view, see*
*www.edu.gov.on.ca/abc123/eng/tips/homework.html and*
*http://kidshealth.org/parent/positive/learning/homework.html.*

correcting, probing, or expanding), or "IRE" (Burbules & Bruce, 2001). These steps are repeated over and over.

Let us consider the heart of recitation—the initiation, or questioning, phase. Effective questioning techniques may be among the most powerful tools teachers employ during lessons. An essential element of innovations such as cognitive apprenticeships, peer learning techniques, authentic learning activities, and nearly all other contemporary learning techniques is keeping students cognitively engaged—and that is where skilful questioning strategies are especially effective. Questions play several roles in cognition. They can help students rehearse information for effective recall. They can work to identify gaps in their knowledge base and provoke curiosity and long-term interest. They can initiate cognitive conflict and promote the disequilibrium that results in a changed knowledge structure. They can serve as cues, tips, or reminders. And students as well as teachers should learn to question effectively. We tell our students that the first step in doing a good research project is asking a good question.

For now, we will focus on teachers' questions and how to make them as helpful as possible for students. Many beginning teachers are surprised to discover how valuable good questions can be and how difficult they are to create.

STOP & THINK Think back to your most recent class. What kinds of questions does your professor ask? What sort of thinking is required to answer the questions? Remembering, understanding, applying, analyzing, evaluating, or creating? How long does the professor wait for an answer? •

KINDS OF QUESTIONS. Some educators have estimated that the typical teacher asks between 30 and 120 questions an hour, or about 1 500 000 questions over a teaching career (Sadker & Sadker, 2006). What sorts of questions do teachers ask? Many can be categorized in terms of Bloom's taxonomy of objectives in the cognitive domain. Table 14.6 offers examples of questions at the different taxonomic levels.

Another way to categorize questioning is in terms of **convergent questions** (those with one correct answer only) or **divergent questions** (those with many possible answers). Questions about concrete facts are convergent: "Who ruled England in 1540?" "Who wrote

TABLE 14.6 • **Classroom Questions for Objectives in the Cognitive Domain**

Questions can be posed that encourage thinking at every level of Bloom's taxonomy in the cognitive domain. Of course, the thinking required depends on what has gone before in the discussion.

| CATEGORY | TYPE OF THINKING EXPECTED | EXAMPLES |
|---|---|---|
| Knowledge (Remembering) | Recalling or recognizing information as learned | Define . . . . <br> What is the capital of . . . ? <br> What did the text say about . . . ? |
| Comprehension (Understanding) | Demonstrating understanding of the materials; transforming, reorganizing, or interpreting | Explain in your own words.... . <br> Compare . . . <br> What is the main idea of ... ? <br> Describe what you saw.... . |
| Application (Applying) | Using information to solve a problem with a single correct answer | Which principle is demonstrated in . . . ? <br> Calculate the area of . . . . <br> Apply the rule of . . . to solve . . . . |
| Analysis (Analyzing) | Critical thinking; identifying reasons and motives; making inferences based on specific data; analyzing conclusions to see if supported by evidence | What influenced the writings of . . . ? <br> Why was Ottawa chosen . . . ? <br> Which of the following are facts and which are opinions . . . ? <br> Based on your experiment, what is the chemical . . . ? |
| Synthesis (Creating) | Divergent, original thinking; original plan, proposal, design, or story | What's a good name for . . . ? <br> How could we raise money for . . . ? <br> What would the Canada be like if the Bloc Québécois were the official opposition? |
| Evaluation (Evaluating) | Judging the merits of ideas, offering opinions, applying standards | Which Canadian premier is the most effective? Why? <br> Which painting do you believe to be better? Why? <br> Why would you favour . . . ? |

*Source: Based on Sadker, M., & Sadker, D. (1986). Questioning Skills. In J. Cooper (Ed.), Classroom Teaching Skills: A Handbook (3rd ed.) (pp. 143–160). Boston, D. C. Heath.*

Convergent questions Questions that have a single correct answer.

Divergent questions Questions that have no single correct answer.

the original *Peter Pan*?" Questions dealing with opinions or hypotheses are divergent: "In this story, which character is most like you and why?" "In 100 years, which of the past five prime ministers will be most admired?"

**FITTING THE QUESTIONS TO THE STUDENTS.** All kinds of questions can be effective (Barden, 1995). Different patterns seem to be better for different students, however. The best pattern for younger students and for lower-ability students of all ages is to use simple questions that allow a high percentage of correct answers, ample encouragement, help when the student does not have the correct answer, and praise. For high-ability students, the successful pattern includes the use of harder questions at both higher and lower levels and more critical feedback (Berliner, 1987; Good, 1988).

Whatever their age or ability, all students should have some exposure to thought-provoking questions and, if necessary, help in learning how to answer them. As we saw in Chapter 9, to master critical thinking and problem-solving skills, students must have a chance to practise the skills. They also need time to think about their answers. But research shows that teachers wait an average of only one second for students to answer (Rowe, 1974). When teachers learn to pose a question, then wait at least three to five seconds before calling on a student to answer, students tend to give longer answers; more students are likely to participate, ask questions, and volunteer appropriate answers; student comments involving analysis, synthesis, inference, and speculation tend to increase; and the students generally appear more confident in their answers (Berliner, 1987; Rowe, 1974; Sadker & Sadker, 2006).

This seems to be a simple method of improving in teaching, but five seconds of silence is not that easy to handle. It takes practice. You might try asking students to jot down ideas or even to discuss the question with another student and formulate an answer together. This makes the wait more comfortable and gives students a chance to think. Of course, if it is clear that students are lost or don't understand the question, waiting longer will not help. When your question is met with blank stares, rephrase the question or ask if anyone can explain the confusion. Also, there is some evidence that extending wait times does not affect learning in university classes (Duell, 1994), so with advanced high school students, you may want to conduct your own evaluation of wait time.

A word about selecting students to answer questions. If you call only on volunteers when selecting students to answer questions, you may get the wrong idea about how well students understand the material. Also, the same people volunteer over and over again. Many expert teachers have some systematic way of making sure that they call on everyone; they may pull names from a jar or check names off a list as each student speaks (Weinstein & Novodvorsky, 2011; Weinstein, Romano, & Mignano, 2011). Another possibility is to put each student's name on an index card, then shuffle the cards and go through the deck as you call on people. You can use the cards to make notes about students' answers or extra help they seem to need.

**RESPONDING TO STUDENT ANSWERS.** What do you do after the student answers? The most common response, occurring about 50% of the time in most classrooms, is simple acceptance—"Okay" or "Uh-huh" (Sadker & Sadker, 2006). But there are better reactions, depending on whether the student's answer is correct, partly correct, or wrong. If the answer is quick, firm, and correct, simply accept the answer or ask another question. If the answer is correct but hesitant, give the student feedback about why the answer is correct: "That's right, Chris, the Governor General is the Queen's representative in Canada." This allows you to explain the material again. If this student is unsure, others may be confused as well. If the answer is partially or completely wrong but the student has made an honest attempt, you should probe for more information, give clues, simplify the question, review the previous steps, or reteach the material. If the student's wrong answer is silly or careless, however, it is better simply to correct the answer and go on (Good, 1988; Rosenshine & Stevens, 1986).

John Hattie and Helen Timperley (2007), researchers at the University of Auckland in New Zealand, reviewed several decades of research on feedback and constructed a model to guide teachers. The model proposes three feedback questions: "Where am I going?"

"How am I going?" and "Where to next?" The first question is about goals and goal clarity. The second is about progress—movement toward goals. The third question is about moving forward to improve understandings when goals are not met yet or to build on attained goals. The Hattie and Timperley model also considers the focus of the feedback on four levels: task, process, self-regulation, and self-feedback. Here are some examples (p. 90):

*Task Feedback*: "You need to include more about the Treaty of Versailles."

*Process Feedback*: "This page may make more sense if you use the strategies we talked about earlier."

*Self-Regulation Feedback*: "You already know the key features of the opening of an argument. Check to see whether you have incorporated them in your first paragraph."

**GROUP DISCUSSIONS** Small-group discussions allow greater student participation and exchange of ideas, but students may need help to stay focused.

*Will Hart/PhotoEdit*

*Self-Feedback*: "You are a great student." "That's an intelligent response, well done."

Hattie and Timperley argue that feedback about *process* and *self-regulation* is the most powerful because it helps students move toward deep understanding, mastery, and self-direction in learning. Feedback about self (usually praise) is common in classes, but is not effective unless the praise provides information about how effort, persistence, or self-regulation moved the student forward, as in "You are terrific—you stuck with this, revised again, and now this essay makes a powerful argument."

**GROUP DISCUSSION.** **Group discussion** is in some ways similar to the recitation strategy. A teacher may pose questions, listen to student answers, react, and probe for more information, but in a true group discussion, the teacher does not have a dominant role. Students ask questions, answer each other's questions, and respond to each other's answers (Beck, McKeown, Worthy, Sandora, & Kucan, 1996; Burbules & Bruce, 2001; Parker & Hess, 2001).

There are many advantages to group discussions. The students are directly involved and have the chance to participate. Group discussion helps students learn to express themselves clearly, to justify opinions, and to tolerate different views. Group discussion also gives students a chance to ask for clarification, examine their own thinking, follow personal interests, and assume responsibility by taking leadership roles in the group. Thus, group discussions help students evaluate ideas and synthesize personal viewpoints. Discussions are also useful when students are trying to understand difficult concepts that go against common sense. By thinking together, challenging each other, and suggesting and evaluating possible explanations, students are more likely to reach a genuine understanding.

Of course, there are disadvantages. Class discussions are quite unpredictable and may easily digress into exchanges of ignorance. You may have to do a good deal of preparation to ensure that participants have a background of knowledge on which to base the discussion. Some members of the group may have great difficulty participating and may become anxious if forced to speak. And large groups are often unwieldy. In many cases, a few students will dominate the discussion while the others daydream (Arends, 2004; Freiberg & Driscoll, 2005).

Are discussions effective learning tools? In a major review of research conducted from 1964 to 2003 on the value of discussing texts for improving student comprehension, Karen Murphy and her colleagues (2009) reached some surprising conclusions.

**Group discussion** Conversation in which the teacher does not have the dominant role; students pose and answer their own questions.

## GUIDELINES

### Productive Group Discussions

**Invite shy children to participate.**
*Examples*

1. "What's your opinion, Joel?" or "Does anyone have another opinion?"
2. Don't wait until there is a deadly silence to ask shy students to reply. Most people, even those who are confident, hate to break a silence.

**Direct student comments and questions back to another student.**
*Examples*

1. "That's an unusual idea, Steve. Kim, what do you think of Steve's idea?"
2. "That's an important question, John. Maura, do you have any thoughts about how you'd answer that?"
3. Encourage students to look at and talk to one another rather than wait for your opinion.

**Make sure that you understand what a student has said. If you are unsure, other students may be unsure as well.**
*Examples*

1. Ask a second student to summarize what the first student said; then, the first student can try again to explain if the summary is incorrect.
2. "Karen, I think you're saying … Is that right, or have I misunderstood?"

**Probe for more information.**
*Examples*

1. "That's a strong statement. Do you have any evidence to back it up?"

2. "Did you consider any other alternatives?"
3. "Tell us how you reached that conclusion. What steps did you go through?"

**Bring the discussion back to the subject.**
*Examples*

1. "Let's see, we were discussing … and Sarah made one suggestion. Does anyone have a different idea?"
2. "Before we continue, let me try to summarize what has happened thus far."

**Give time for thought before asking for responses.**
*Examples*

1. "How would your life be different if television had never been invented? Jot down your ideas on paper, and we will share reactions in a minute." After a minute: "Hiromi, will you tell us what you wrote?"

**When a student finishes speaking, look around the room to judge reactions.**
*Examples*

1. If other students look puzzled, ask them to describe why they are confused.
2. If students are nodding assent, ask them to give an example of what was just said.

---

*For more ideas, see*
*www.edutopia.org/blog/productive-group-work-andrew-miller or*
*www.extension.umn.edu/distribution/citizenship/components/00018e.html.*

---

They examined a wide range of discussion formats, including Instructional Conversations, Junior Great Books Shared Inquiry, Questioning the Author, Literature Circles, Book Club, and Grand Conversation—to name just a few. They found many of these approaches were very successful in increasing student talk, limiting teacher talk, and promoting students' literal interpretations of the texts they discussed. But getting students to talk more did not necessarily promote their critical thinking, reasoning, or argumentation skills. Also, discussion was more effective for students whose comprehension abilities are below average, perhaps because average and higher-ability students already have the skills to comprehend texts. A few discussion structures, such as Junior Great Books Shared Inquiry, used over a longer period of time seemed to support both comprehension of text and critical thinking. The researchers concluded, "Simply putting students into groups and encouraging them to talk is not enough to enhance comprehension and learning; it is but a step in the process" (p. 760). The *Guidelines* give some ideas for facilitating a productive group discussion.

### Fitting Teaching to Your Goals

In the midst of all our discussions about methods, we have to keep in mind that the first questions should be: What should students learn? and What is worth knowing today? Then, we can match methods to goals. Deanna Kuhn (2007) said it well:

As for direct instruction, of course it has a place. Each young student does not need to reinvent knowledge from the ground up. The challenge is to formulate what we want direct instruction to be. In doing so, it is well to keep in mind that it is students who construct meaning from such instruction and decide what it is that they will learn. (p. 112)

There is no one best way to teach. Different goals and student needs require different teaching methods. Direct instruction often leads to better performance on achievement tests, whereas the open, informal methods such as discovery learning or inquiry approaches are associated with better performance on tests of creativity, abstract thinking, and problem solving. In addition, the open methods are better for improving attitudes toward school and for stimulating curiosity, cooperation among students, and lower absence rates (Borich, 2011; Walberg, 1990). According to these conclusions, when the goals of teaching involve problem solving, creativity, understanding, and mastering processes, many approaches besides direct instruction should be effective. These guidelines are in keeping with Tom Good's conclusion that teaching should become less direct as students mature and when the goals involve affective development and problem solving or critical thinking (Good, 1983a). Every student may require direct, explicit teaching for some learning goals some of the time, but all students also need to experience more open, constructivist, student-centred teaching as well. So far, we have talked about approaches to teaching—general strategies. But in today's diverse classrooms, one size does not fit all. Within the general approach, teachers have to fit their instruction to the needs and abilities of their students—they have to differentiate instruction.

# DIFFERENTIATED INSTRUCTION

We introduced **differentiated instruction** in Chapter 1. Actually, the idea of adapting teaching to the abilities and needs of the learner is an ancient one. To prove it, Lyn Corno (2008, p. 161) quotes these words of Quintilian from the fifth century B.C.E.:

> Some students are slack and need to be encouraged; others work better when given a freer rein. Some respond best when there is some threat or fear; others are paralyzed by it. Some apply themselves to the task over time, and learn best; others learn best by concentration and focus in a single burst of energy. (Quintilian, trans. 1921)

Obviously Quintilian appreciated the need for fitting instruction to the student. One way to do this when teachers have many students is to use appropriate groupings.

## Within-Class and Flexible Grouping

It is not unusual to have three- to five-year differences in any given classroom (Castle, Deniz, & Tortora, 2005). But even if you decided to simply forge ahead and teach the same material in the same way to your entire class, you would not be alone. Differences in student prior knowledge are a major challenge for teachers, especially in subjects that build on previous knowledge and skills such as math and science (Loveless, 1998). One answer has been to use the strategy known as ability grouping, but that has problems, too.

THE PROBLEMS WITH ABILITY GROUPING. Students in many classes and schools are grouped by ability, even though there is no clear evidence that this **within-class ability grouping** is superior to other approaches. In a random sample of primary-grade teachers in the United States, 63% reported using within-class ability groups for reading. Students in lower-ability groups were less likely to be asked critical comprehension questions and given fewer opportunities to make choices about what to read (Chorzempa & Graham, 2006). For schools with lower-SES students, grouping often means that these students are segregated into lower-ability tracks. According to Paul George (2005):

> In my 3 decades of experience with this issue, when homogenous grouping is the primary strategy for organizing students in schools with significant racial and ethnic diversity in the population, the result is almost always deep, and often starkly obvious, division of students on the basis of race, ethnicity, and social class. (p. 187)

**Differentiated instruction** Teaching that takes into account students' abilities, prior knowledge, and challenges so that instruction matches not only the subject being taught but also students' needs.

**Within-class ability grouping** System of grouping in which students in a class are divided into two or three groups based on ability in an attempt to accommodate student differences.

## GUIDELINES

## Using Flexible Grouping

**Form and re-form groups based on accurate assessments of students' *current performance* in the subject being taught.**
*Examples*

1. Use scores on the most recent reading assessments to establish reading groups, and rely on current math performance to form math groups.
2. Assess continuously. Change group placement frequently when students' achievements change.

**Make sure different groups get appropriately different instruction, not just the same material. Make sure teaching methods and pace are adjusted to fit the needs of the group.**
*Examples*

1. Vary more than pace; fit teaching to students' interests and knowledge.
2. If all groups are doing research reports, request that some be written, while others are oral or PowerPoint presentations.
3. Organize and teach groups so that low-achieving students get appropriate extra instruction—not just the same material again. Make lower-achieving groups smaller so students get extra attention.
4. Make sure all work is meaningful and respectful—no worksheets for lower-ability groups while the higher-ability groups do experiments and projects.
5. Try alternatives. For example, DeWayne Mason and Tom Good (1993) found that supplementing whole-class instruction in math with remediation and enrichment for students when they needed it worked better than dividing the class into two ability groups and teaching these groups separately.

**Discourage comparisons between groups and encourage students to develop a whole-class spirit.**
*Examples*

1. Don't seat groups together outside the context of their reading or math group.
2. Avoid naming ability groups—save the names for mixed-ability or whole-class teams.

**Group by ability for one or, at the most, two subjects.**
*Examples*

1. Make sure there are many lessons and projects that mix members from the groups.
2. Experiment with learning strategies in which cooperation is stressed (described in Chapter 10).
3. Keep the number of groups small (two or three at most) so that you can provide as much direct teaching as possible—leaving students alone for too long leads to less learning.

_____

*For more information about classroom grouping, see these two sites: www.eduplace.com/science/profdev/articles/valentino.html and www.nwrel.org/scpd/sirs/1/cu2.html.*

Thoughtfully constructed and well-taught ability groups in math and reading can be effective, but the point of any grouping strategy should be to provide appropriate challenge and support—that is, to reach children within their "zone of proximal development" (Vygotsky, 1997). Flexible grouping is one possible answer.

FLEXIBLE GROUPING. In **flexible grouping**, students are grouped and regrouped based on their learning needs. Assessment is continuous so that students are always working within their zone of proximal development. Arrangements might include small groups, partners, individuals, and even the whole class—depending on which grouping best supports each student's learning of the particular academic content. Flexible grouping approaches include high-level instruction and high expectations for all students, no matter what their group placement (Corno, 2008). One five-year longitudinal study of flexible grouping in a high-needs urban elementary school found 10%–57% increases in students who reached mastery level, depending on the subject area and grade level. Teachers received training and support in the assessment, grouping, and teaching strategies needed, and by the end of the study, 95% of the teachers were using flexible grouping. The teachers in the study believed that some of the gains came because students were more focused on learning and more confident (Castle, Deniz, & Tortora, 2005).

Another way to use flexible grouping is the nongraded elementary school. Students of several ages (for example, 6, 7, and 8) are together in one class, but they are flexibly grouped within the class for instruction based on achievement, motivation, or interest in different subjects. This cross-grade grouping seems to be effective for students of all

**Flexible grouping** Grouping and regrouping students based on learning needs.

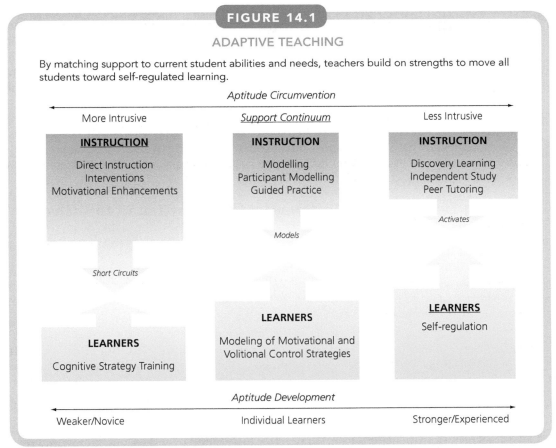

**FIGURE 14.1**

ADAPTIVE TEACHING

By matching support to current student abilities and needs, teachers build on strengths to move all students toward self-regulated learning.

*Aptitude Circumvention*

More Intrusive          *Support Continuum*          Less Intrusive

| **INSTRUCTION** | **INSTRUCTION** | **INSTRUCTION** |
| Direct Instruction | Modelling | Discovery Learning |
| Interventions | Participant Modelling | Independent Study |
| Motivational Enhancements | Guided Practice | Peer Tutoring |

*Activates*

*Models*

*Short Circuits*

**LEARNERS**
Self-regulation

**LEARNERS**
Modeling of Motivational and
Volitional Control Strategies

**LEARNERS**
Cognitive Strategy Training

*Aptitude Development*

Weaker/Novice          Individual Learners          Stronger/Experienced

*Source: Based on Corno, L. (2008). On teaching adaptively. Educational Psychologist, 43 (3), 161–173; and Randi, J., & Corno, L., Teaching and learner variation, in Pedagogy—Learning from Teaching, British Journal of Educational Psychology, Monograph Series II (3), pp. 47–69.*

abilities as long as the grouping allows teachers to give more direct instruction to the groups. But be sensible about cross-age grouping. Mixing students in grades 3, 4, and 5 for math or reading class based on what they are ready to learn makes sense. However, sending a large boy in grade 4 to grade 2, where he is the only older student and stands out like a sore thumb, isn't likely to work well. Also, when cross-age classes are created just because there are too few students for one grade—and not in order to better meet the students' learning needs—the results are not positive (Veenman, 1997). As we have seen repeatedly throughout this text, working at a challenging level, but one you can master with effort and support, is more likely to encourage learning and motivation.

If you ever decide to use flexible grouping in your class, the *Guidelines* should help you make the approach more effective (Arends, 2007; Good & Brophy, 2008).

## Adaptive Teaching

Lyn Corno (2008) has developed a model of **adaptive teaching** that also addresses learner differences. In this approach, teachers see "learner variation as an opportunity for learning from teaching rather than as obstacles to be overcome" (p. 171). Adaptive teaching provides all students with challenging instruction and uses supports when needed, but removes those supports as students become able to handle more on their own. Figure 14.1 shows the continuum of support and type of instruction that matches students' needs. As shown on the far left of the figure, when students are novices in an area or have little prior knowledge and skills, the teaching is more direct and includes well-designed motivational strategies to keep them engaged. At the same time, students are taught how to apply appropriate cognitive strategies, to give them the "skills" to learn. There are short cycles

**Adaptive teaching** Provides all students with challenging instruction and uses supports when needed, but removes these supports as students become able to handle more on their own.

of teaching, checking for understanding, and reteaching. As students develop aptitudes in the subject, teaching moves to modelling, guided practice, and coaching. By this time, students should have improved their cognitive "skills" strategies, so teaching can also focus on motivational and volitional strategies—the "will" to learn. Finally as students gain more knowledge and skills, teaching can move to guided discovery, independent study, and peer tutoring, with an emphasis on self-regulated learning—the kind of learning the students will need for the rest of their lives.

Adaptive teaching makes sure that everyone is challenged. For example, one teacher at a magnet school described how he "iced" his curriculum with some content "just beyond the reach" of even his most advanced students. He wanted to be sure all his students found some assignments difficult. He believed "everyone needs to stretch in my class" (Corno, 2008, p. 165).

## Reaching Every Student: Differentiated Instruction in Inclusive Classrooms

**STOP & THINK** When you think about teaching in an inclusive classroom, what are your concerns? Do you have enough training? Will you get the support you need from school administrators or specialists? Will working with the students with disabilities take time away from your other responsibilities? •

These questions are common, and sometimes concerns are justified. But effective teaching for exceptional students does not require a unique set of skills. It is a combination of good teaching practices and sensitivity to all your students. Students with disabilities need to *learn the academic material,* and they need to be *full participants in the day-to-day life of the classroom.*

To accomplish the first goal of academic learning, students with learning disabilities appear to benefit from using extended practice distributed over days and weeks and from *advance organizers* such as focusing students on what they already know or stating clear objectives (Swanson, 2001).

To accomplish the second goal of integrating students with disabilities into the day-to-day life of the classroom, Marilyn Friend and William Bursuck (2002) recommend the INCLUDE strategy:

**I**dentify the environmental, curricular, and instructional demands of your classroom.
**N**ote students' learning strengths and needs.
**C**heck for potential areas of student success.
**L**ook for potential problem areas.
**U**se information gathered to brainstorm instructional adaptations.
**D**ecide which adaptations to try.
**E**valuate student progress.

Table 14.7 shows how the INCLUDE strategy might be applied to students with learning and behavioural disabilities.

When students have special needs, they may be referred to child study teams, school psychologists, or teachers of students with special needs for evaluation (see Table 4.10 on page 150 for guidelines about referring students for evaluation). The outcome of this process sometimes includes the preparation of an individualized education program, or IEP, as described in Chapter 4. Chapter 4 also describes some ways technology can support student differences in the classroom. Finally, review the section on teaching toward self-regulated learning in Chapter 11. There are some good tips in there about how to differentiate instruction and learning to address the needs of all students.

## Mentoring Students as a Way of Differentiating Teaching

One way to make all instruction more appropriate and effective is to know your students and develop trusting relationships with them. The knowledge you gain about the students

TABLE 14.7 • **Making Adaptations for Students with Learning and Behavioural Disabilities Using Steps in the INCLUDE Strategy**

| IDENTIFY CLASSROOM DEMANDS | NOTE STUDENT STRENGTHS AND NEEDS | CHECK FOR POTENTIAL SUCCESSES; LOOK FOR POTENTIAL PROBLEMS | DECIDE ON ADAPTATIONS |
|---|---|---|---|
| Student desks in clusters of four | *Strengths* Good vocabulary skills  *Needs* Difficulty attending to task | *Success* Student understands instruction if on task  *Problem* Student off task—does not face instructor as she teaches | Change seating so student faces instructor |
| Small-group work with peers | *Strengths* Good handwriting  *Needs* Oral expressive language—problem with word finding | *Success* Student acts as secretary for cooperative group  *Problem* Student has difficulty expressing self in peer learning groups | Assign as secretary of group; place into compatible small group; develop social skills instruction for all students |
| Expect students to attend class and be on time | *Strengths* Good drawing skills  *Needs* Poor time management | *Success* Student uses artistic talent in class  *Problem* Student is late for class and frequently does not attend at all | Use individualized student contract for attendance and punctuality—if goals met, give student artistic responsibility in class |
| Textbook difficult to read | *Strengths* Good oral communication skills  *Needs* Poor reading accuracy; lacks systematic strategy for reading text | *Success* Student participates well in class; good candidate for class dramatizations  *Problem* Student is unable to read text for information | Provide taped textbooks; highlight student text |
| Lecture on women's suffrage movement to whole class | *Strengths* Very motivated and interested in class  *Needs* Lack of background knowledge | *Success* Student earns points for class attendance and effort  *Problem* Student lacks background knowledge to understand important information in lecture | Give student video to view before lecture; build points for attendance and working hard into grading system |
| Whole class instruction on telling time to the quarter hour | *Strengths* Good colouring skills  *Needs* Cannot identify numbers 7–12; cannot count by fives | *Success* Student is able to colour clock faces used in instruction  *Problem* Student is unable to acquire telling time skills | Provide extra instruction on number identification and counting by fives |

*Source: From Friend, M., & Bursuck, W. D. (2002). Including Students with Special Needs: A Practical Guide for Classroom Teachers, 3rd edition. Allyn and Bacon: Boston, MA. © Pearson Education. Adapted by permission of the publisher.*

should help in adapting your teaching, and the positive relationship you establish will help students stay engaged in learning. See the *Guidelines* for ideas.

No matter how you differentiate instruction, there is one part of your teaching that should be the same for all your students—*appropriate high expectations.*

## GUIDELINES

### Teachers as Mentors

**Beware of stereotypes in your thinking and teaching.**
*Examples*

1. See every student as an individual, and communicate that clearly to the student.
2. Analyze curriculum materials for biases, and teach students to become bias detectors.

**Take advantage of technology.**
*Examples*

1. Use a web program like Eyes to the Future, which link middle school girls with high school girls in their districts who have stayed interested in math and science as well as women who use science, math, and technology in their careers. The purpose is to help middle school girls see how their work at school relates to "real life." (http://etf.terc.edu)
2. Establish "email pals" for students, with retired adults or successful former students as their mentors.
3. Download resources from NWREL's National Mentoring Center, especially their school-based mentoring and tutoring materials (www.nwrel.org/mentoring/topic_pubs.php#5).

**Let students know you believe in them.**
*Examples*

1. Set standards high and give critical feedback, but also provide support and encouragement.
2. Showcase accomplishments of former students.

**Take the time to establish and maintain relationships.**
*Examples*

1. Don't expect trust right away; you may have to earn it.
2. Stay in touch with students, and keep the door open to provide guidance in the future.
3. Spend some time with students outside academics—before or after school, as part of clubs or extracurricular activities. Have some fun together. Find common interests.

**If you set up a more formal mentoring system, be sure participants are trained and monitored.**
*Examples*

1. Use materials from national mentor groups for training, for example, Elements of Effective Practice from MENTOR/ National Mentoring Partnership (www.mentoring.org/start_a_ program/planning_and_design).
2. Have regular times to provide ongoing training and to deal with problems that may arise.

## TEACHER EXPECTATIONS

Nearly 40 years ago, a study by Robert Rosenthal and Lenore Jacobson (1968) captured the attention of the media in a way that few studies by psychologists have since then. The study also caused great controversy within the professional community. Debate about the meaning of the results continues (De Boer, Bosker, & van der Werf, 2010; Jussim, 2012; Jussim, Robustelli, & Cain, 2009; Rosenthal, 1995; Snow, 1995).

What did Rosenthal and Jacobson say that caused such a stir? They chose several students at random in a number of elementary school classrooms, and then told the teachers that these students probably would make significant intellectual gains during the year. The students did indeed make larger gains than normal that year. The researchers presented data suggesting the existence of a **Pygmalion effect** or self-fulfilling prophecy in the classroom. A **self-fulfilling prophecy** is a groundless expectation that leads to behaviours that then make the original expectation come true (Merton, 1948). An example is a false belief that a bank is failing, leading to a rush to withdraw money that then causes the bank to fail as expected.

**Pygmalion effect** Exceptional progress by a student as a result of high teacher expectations for that student; named for the mythological king Pygmalion, who made a statue, then caused it to be brought to life.

**Self-fulfilling prophecy** A groundless expectation that is confirmed because it has been expected.

**STOP & THINK** When you thought about the most effective teacher you ever had, was one of the characteristics that the teacher believed in you or demanded the best from you? How did the teacher communicate that belief? •

## Two Kinds of Expectation Effects

Actually, two kinds of expectation effects can occur in classrooms. In the self-fulfilling prophecy described above, the teacher's beliefs about the students' abilities have no basis in fact, but student behaviour comes to match the initially inaccurate expectation. The second kind of expectation effect occurs when teachers are fairly accurate in their initial reading of students' abilities and respond to students appropriately. The problems arise when students show some improvement, but teachers do not alter their expectations to take account of the improvement. This is called a **sustaining expectation effect**, because the teacher's unchanging expectation sustains the student's achievement at the expected level. The chance to raise expectations, provide more appropriate teaching, and thus encourage greater student achievement is lost. In practice, self-fulfilling prophecy effects seem to be stronger in the early grades, and sustaining effects are more likely in the later grades (Kuklinski & Weinstein, 2001).

## Sources of Expectations

**Listen**
Sources of Expectations

There are many possible sources of teachers' expectations, including intelligence test scores (especially when not interpreted appropriately), gender (more behaviour problems for boys and higher academic achievement for girls), notes from previous teachers, the medical or psychological reports in students' permanent files, knowledge of older brothers and sisters, appearance (higher expectations for attractive students), previous achievement, socioeconomic status, race and ethnicity, and the actual behaviours of the student (Van Matre, Valentine, & Cooper, 2000). Even the student's after-school activities can be a source of expectations. Teachers tend to hold higher expectations for students who participate in extracurricular activities than for students who do not. And recent research shows that some teachers may even hold expectations at the class level—that is, they have higher or lower expectations for all the students in a particular class (Rubie-Davies, 2010).

Some students are more likely than others to be the recipients of sustaining expectations. For example, withdrawn children provide little information about themselves, so teachers may sustain their expectations about these children for lack of new input (Jones & Gerig, 1994). Also, self-fulfilling prophecy effects tend to be stronger for students from lower-SES families and for some minority groups (de Boer, Bosker, & van der Werf, 2010). In a synthesis of over 50 studies in the United States, Harriet Tenenbaum and Martin Ruck (2007) found that teachers held higher expectation for and directed more positive questions and encouragement toward European American compared to African American and Latino/a students. The highest expectations were reserved for Asian American students. It appears that early childhood teachers may hold higher expectations for students who are more socially competent (Hinnant, O'Brien, & Ghazarian, 2009). For example, in another study of 110 students whose development was followed from age 4 to age 18, Jennifer Alvidrez and Rhona Weinstein (1999) found that teachers tended to overestimate the abilities of preschool children they rated as independent and interesting and to underestimate the abilities of children perceived as immature and anxious.

Expectations and beliefs focus attention and organize memory, so teachers may pay attention to and remember the information that fits the initial expectations (Fiske, 1993; Hewstone, 1989). Even when student performance does not fit expectations, the teacher may rationalize and attribute the performance to external causes beyond the student's control. For example, a teacher may assume that the low-ability student who did well on a test must have cheated and that the high-ability student who failed must have been upset that day. In both cases, behaviour that seems out of character is dismissed. It may take many instances of supposedly uncharacteristic behaviour to change the teacher's beliefs about a particular student's abilities. Thus, expectations often remain in the face of contradictory evidence (Brophy, 1998).

## Do Teachers' Expectations Really Affect Students' Achievement?

The answer to this question is more complicated than it might seem. There are two ways to investigate the issue. One is to give teachers unfounded expectations about their students and note if these baseless expectations have any effects. The other approach is to

**Sustaining expectation effect** Student performance maintained at a certain level because teachers don't recognize improvements.

identify the naturally occurring expectations of teachers and study the effects of these expectations. The answer to the question of whether teacher expectations affect student learning depends in part on which approach is taken to study the question.

The original Rosenthal and Jacobson experiment used the first approach—giving teachers groundless expectations and noting the effects. A careful analysis of the results revealed that even though students in grades 1 through 6 participated in the study, the self-fulfilling prophecy effects could be traced to dramatic changes in just five students in grades 1 and 2. After reviewing the research on teacher expectations, Raudenbush (1984) concluded that these expectations have only a small effect on student IQ scores (the outcome measure used by Rosenthal and Jacobson) and only in the early years of a new school setting—in the first years of elementary school and then again in the first years of middle or junior high school.

But what about the second approach—naturally occurring expectations? Research shows that teachers do indeed form beliefs about students' capabilities. Many of these beliefs are accurate assessments based on the best available data and are corrected as new information is collected (Jussim & Haber, 2005). But inaccuracies can make a difference. Alvidrez and Weinstein (1999) found teachers' judgments of student ability at age 4 predicted student grade-point average at age 18. The strongest predictions were for students whose abilities were *underestimated*. If teachers decide that some students are less able, and if the teachers lack effective strategies for working with lower-achieving students, then students may experience a double threat—low expectations and inadequate teaching (Good & Brophy, 2008).

Even though it is clear that teacher expectations can affect student achievement, the effects are modest on average and tend to dissipate somewhat over the years (Jussim, 2012). The power of the expectation effect depends on the age of the students (generally speaking, younger students are more susceptible) and on how differently a teacher treats high versus low-expectation students, an issue we turn to next (Kuklinski & Weinstein, 2001). Teachers may use different instructional strategies and also have different relationships with students based on expectations.

INSTRUCTIONAL STRATEGIES. Different grouping processes may well have a marked effect on students because different groups get different instruction (de Boer, Bosker, & van der Werf, 2010). And some teachers leave little to the imagination; they make their expectations all too clear. For example, Alloway (1984) recorded comments such as these directed to low-achieving groups:

> "I'll be over to help you slow ones in a minute." "The blue group will find this hard."

In these remarks the teacher not only tells the students that they lack ability, but also communicates that finishing the work, not understanding, is the goal.

Once teachers assign students to ability groups, they usually assign different learning activities. To the extent that teachers choose activities that challenge students and increase achievement, these differences are probably necessary. Activities become inappropriate, however, when students who are ready for more challenging work are not given the opportunity to try it because teachers believe they cannot handle it. This is an example of a *sustaining expectation effect*.

TEACHER–STUDENT INTERACTIONS. However the class is grouped and whatever the assignments, the quantity and the quality of teacher–student interactions are likely to affect the students. Students who are expected to achieve tend to be asked more and harder questions, to be given more chances and a longer time to respond, and to be interrupted less often than students who are expected to do poorly. Teachers also give these high-expectation students cues and prompts, communicating their belief that the students can answer the question (Good & Brophy, 2008; Rosenthal, 1995). They tend to smile at these students more often and to show greater warmth through such nonverbal responses as leaning toward the students and nodding their heads as the students speak (Woolfolk & Brooks, 1983, 1985).

In contrast, with low-expectation students, teachers ask easier questions, allow less time for answering, and are less likely to give prompts. They are more likely to respond

## GUIDELINES

### Avoiding the Negative Effects of Teacher Expectations

**Use information about students from tests, cumulative folders, and other teachers very carefully.**
*Examples*
1. Avoid reading cumulative folders at the beginning of the year.
2. Be critical and objective about the reports you hear from other teachers.
3. Be flexible in your expectations—a student's label or your judgment might be wrong.

**Be flexible in your use of grouping strategies.**
*Examples*
1. Review work of students often and experiment with new groupings.
2. Use different groups for different subjects.
3. Use mixed-ability groups in cooperative exercises.

**Provide both challenge and support.**
*Examples*
1. Don't say, "This is easy; I know you can do it."
2. Offer a wide range of problems and encourage all students to try a few of the harder ones for extra credit. Find something positive about these attempts.
3. Make sure your high expectations come with academic and emotional support for students' struggles. "Holding high standards without providing a warm environment is merely harsh. A warm environment without high standards lacks backbone" (Jussim, 2012).

**Be especially careful about how you respond to low-achieving students during class discussions.**
*Examples*
1. Give them prompts, cues, and time to answer.
2. Give ample praise for good answers.
3. Call on low achievers as often as high achievers.

**Use materials that show a wide range of ethnic groups.**
*Examples*
1. Check readers and library books. Is there ethnic diversity?
2. If few materials are available, ask students to research and create their own, based on community or family sources.

**Make sure that your teaching does not reflect racial, ethnic, or sexual stereotypes or prejudice.**
*Examples*
1. Use a checking system to be sure you call on and include all students.
2. Monitor the content of the tasks you assign. Do boys get the "hard" math problems to work at the board? Do you avoid having students with limited English give oral presentations?

**Be fair in evaluation and disciplinary procedures.**
*Examples*
1. Make sure that equal offences receive equal punishment. Find out from students in an anonymous questionnaire whether you seem to be favouring certain individuals.
2. Try to grade student work without knowing the identity of the student. Ask another teacher to give you a second opinion from time to time.

**Communicate to all students that you believe they can learn—and mean it.**
*Examples*
1. Return papers that do not meet standards with specific suggestions for improvements.
2. If students do not have the answers immediately, wait, probe, and then help them think through an answer.

**Involve all students in learning tasks and in privileges.**
*Examples*
1. Use some system to make sure that you give each student practice in reading, speaking, and answering questions.
2. Keep track of who gets to do what job. Are some students always on the list while others seldom make it?

**Monitor your nonverbal behaviour.**
*Examples*
1. Do you lean away or stand farther away from some students? Do some students get smiles when they approach your desk while others get only frowns?
2. Does your tone of voice vary with different students?

*For more information see*
*http://chiron.valdosta.edu/whuitt/files/teacherexpect.html.*

with sympathetic acceptance or even praise for inadequate answers from low-achieving students, but to criticize these same students for wrong answers. Even more disturbing, low-achieving students receive less praise than high-achieving students for similar correct answers. This inconsistent feedback can be very confusing for low-ability students. Imagine how hard it would be to learn if your wrong answers were sometimes praised, sometimes ignored, and sometimes criticized, and your right answers received little recognition (Good, 1983a, 1983b; Hattie & Timperley, 2007). Even though the effects of these communications may be small each day, there can be huge effects as the expectation differences build year after year with many teachers (Trouilloud, Sarrazin, Bressoux, & Bois, 2006).

Of course, not all teachers form inappropriate expectations or act on their expectations in unconstructive ways (Babad, Inbar, & Rosenthal, 1982). The *Guidelines* may help you avoid some of these problems. But avoiding the problem may be more difficult than it seems. In general, low-expectation students also tend to be the most disruptive students. (Of course, low expectations can reinforce their desire to disrupt or misbehave.) Teachers may call on these students less, wait a shorter time for their answers, and give them less praise for right answers, partly to avoid the wrong, careless, or silly answers that can cause disruptions, delays, and digressions. The challenge is to deal with these very real threats to classroom management without communicating low expectations to some students or fostering their own low expectations of themselves. And sometimes, low expectations become part of the culture of the school—beliefs shared by teachers and administrators alike (Weinstein, Madison, & Kuklinski, 1995).

## ▼ SUMMARY

### Research on Teaching (pp. 474–478)

**What methods have been used to study teaching?** For years, researchers have tried to unravel the mystery of effective teaching using classroom observation, case studies, interviews, experimentation with different methods, stimulated recall (teachers view videos and explain their teaching), analysis of lesson transcripts, and other approaches to study teaching in real classrooms.

**What are the general characteristics of good teaching?** A variety of teacher qualities are related to good teaching. Research suggests teachers who receive proper training and certification have more successful students. Although it is important, teacher knowledge of a subject is not sufficient for effective teaching. Thorough knowledge does lead to greater clarity and better organization, which are both tied to good teaching. Teachers who provide clear presentations and explanations tend to have students who learn more and who rate their teachers more positively. Teacher warmth, friendliness, and understanding seem to be the traits most strongly related to positive student attitudes about the teacher and the course in general.

**What do expert teachers know?** It takes time and experience to become an expert teacher. These teachers have a rich store of well-organized knowledge about the many specific situations of teaching. This includes knowledge about the subjects they teach, their students, general teaching strategies, subject-specific ways of teaching, settings for learning, curriculum materials, and the goals of education. Expert teachers also know how to be reflective practitioners—how to use their experience as a way to grow and improve in their teaching.

**What does the new latest research on teaching show?** A program of large-scale, longitudinal research has identified three aspects of classroom climate that are related to the development and learning of preschool and elementary school students. These three dimensions are consistent with the characteristics of teachers identified in earlier research on teaching and cover affective, behavioural, and cognitive dimensions. The *affective* dimension is teacher *emotional support*, similar to teacher warmth and enthusiasm identified in early research. The *cognitive*

dimension is instructional support, which includes concept development (activities and discussions that promote student higher-order thinking) and quality feedback that is specific and focused on the learning process. The third dimension is classroom organization, which includes *behavioural* concerns such as classroom and lesson management with clear activities and routines that make more time for learning and really engage students—similar to the teacher characteristics of clarity and organization.

### The First Step: Planning (pp. 478–485)

**What are the levels of planning, and how do they affect teaching?** Teachers engage in several levels of planning—by the year, term, unit, week, and day. All the levels must be coordinated. The plan determines how time and materials will be turned into activities for students. There is no single model of planning, but all plans should allow for flexibility. Planning is a creative problem-solving process for experienced teachers. It is more informal—"in their heads."

**What is an instructional objective?** An instructional objective is a clear and unambiguous description of your educational intentions for your students. Mager's influential system for writing behavioural objectives states that a good objective has three parts—the intended student behaviour, the conditions under which the behaviour will occur, and the criteria for acceptable performance. Gronlund's alternative approach suggests that an objective should be stated first in general terms, and then the teacher should clarify by listing sample behaviours that would provide evidence that the student has attained the objective. The most recent research on instructional objectives tends to favour approaches similar to Gronlund's.

**Describe the three taxonomies of educational objectives.** Bloom and others have developed taxonomies categorizing basic objectives in the cognitive, affective, and psychomotor domains. In real life, of course, behaviours from these three domains occur simultaneously. A taxonomy encourages systematic thinking about relevant objectives and ways to evaluate them. Six basic objectives are listed in the cognitive domain: knowing, understanding, applying, analyzing, evaluating, and creating. A recent revision of this taxonomy adds that these processes can act on four kinds of knowledge: factual, conceptual, procedural, and metacognitive. Objectives in the affective domain run from least committed to most committed. Objectives in the psychomotor domain generally move from basic perceptions and reflex actions to skilled, creative movements.

**Describe constructivist planning.** In teacher-centred approaches, teachers select learning objectives and plan how to get students to meet those objectives. Teachers control the "what" and "how" of learning. In contrast, planning is shared and negotiated in student-centred, or constructivist, approaches. Rather than having specific student behaviours as objectives, the teacher has overarching goals or "big ideas" that guide planning. Integrated content and teaching with themes are often part of the planning. Assessment of learning is ongoing and mutually shared by teacher and students.

## Teaching Approaches (pp. 485–497)

**What is direct instruction?** Direct instruction is appropriate for teaching basic skills and explicit knowledge. It includes the teaching functions of review/overview, presentation, guided practice, feedback and correctives (with reteaching if necessary), independent practice, and periodic reviews. The younger or less able the students, the shorter the presentation should be with more cycles of practice and feedback.

**Distinguish between convergent and divergent and high-level versus low-level questions.** Convergent questions have only one right answer. Divergent questions have many possible answers. Higher-level questions require analysis, synthesis, and evaluation—students have to think for themselves. The best pattern for younger students and for lower-ability students of all ages is simple questions that allow a high percentage of correct answers, ample encouragement, help when the student does not have the correct answer, and praise. For high-ability students, the successful pattern includes harder questions at both higher and lower levels and more critical feedback. Whatever their age or ability, all students should have some experience with thought-provoking questions and, if necessary, help in learning how to answer them.

**How can wait time affect student learning?** When teachers learn to pose a question, then wait at least three to five seconds before calling on a student to answer, students tend to give longer answers; more students are likely to participate, ask questions, and volunteer appropriate answers; student comments involving analysis, synthesis, inference, and speculation tend to increase; and the students generally appear more confident in their answers.

**What are the advantages and disadvantages of group discussion?** Group discussion helps students participate directly, express themselves clearly, justify opinions, and tolerate different views. Group discussion also gives students a chance to ask for clarification, examine their own thinking, follow personal interests, and assume responsibility by taking leadership roles in the group. Thus, group discussions help students evaluate ideas and synthesize personal viewpoints. However, discussions are quite unpredictable and may easily digress into exchanges of ignorance.

**How can you match teaching to your goals?** Different goals and student needs require different teaching methods. Direct instruction often leads to better performance on achievement tests, whereas the open, informal methods such as discovery learning or inquiry approaches are associated with better performance on tests of creativity, abstract thinking, and problem solving. In addition, the open methods are better for improving attitudes toward school and for stimulating curiosity, cooperation among students, and lower absence rates.

## Differentiated Instruction (pp. 497–502)

**What are the problems with ability grouping?** Academic ability groupings can have both disadvantages and advantages for students and teachers. Students in higher-ability groups may benefit, but students in lower-ability groups are less likely to be asked critical comprehension questions and are given fewer opportunities to make choices about readings and assignments. For schools with lower-SES students, grouping often means that these students are segregated even in their own classes, so ability grouping can create segregation within diverse schools.

**What are the alternatives available for grouping in classes, including flexible grouping?** Cross-age grouping by subject can be an effective way to deal with ability differences in a school. Within-class ability grouping, if handled sensitively and flexibly, can have positive effects, but alternatives such as cooperative learning may be better.

**What is adaptive teaching?** Adaptive teaching provides all students with challenging instruction and uses supports when needed, but removes those supports as students are able to handle more on their own.

**What characterizes effective teaching for exceptional students?** Effective teaching for exceptional students does not require a unique set of skills. It is a combination of good teaching practices and sensitivity to all students. Students with disabilities need to learn the academic material, and they need to be full participants in the day-to-day life of the classroom.

**What resources do teachers have to work effectively with exceptional children?** When students have special needs, they may be referred to specialists such as child study teams, school psychologists, or teachers of students with special needs for evaluation. The outcome of this process sometimes includes the preparation of an individualized educational program, or IEP, as described in Chapter 4, which will have teaching ideas and guidelines. In addition, differentiated instruction can improve learning for all students, and developing mentoring relationships with students can help teachers connect with student abilities and needs.

## Teacher Expectations (pp. 502–506)

**What are some sources of teacher expectations?** Sources include intelligence test scores, gender, notes from previous teachers and the medical or psychological reports found in cumulative folders, ethnic background, knowledge of older brothers and sisters, physical characteristics, previous achievement, socioeconomic status, and the actual behaviours of the student.

**What are the two kinds of expectation effects and how do they happen?** The first is the self-fulfilling prophecy: the teacher's beliefs about the students' abilities have no basis in fact, but student behaviour comes to match the initially inaccurate expectation. The second is a sustaining expectation effect: teachers are fairly accurate in their initial reading of students' abilities and respond to students appropriately but teachers do not alter their expectations to take account of the improvement. When this happens, the teacher's unchanging expectation can sustain the student's achievement at the expected level. In practice, sustaining effects are more common than self-fulfilling prophecy effects.

**What are the different avenues for communicating teacher expectations?** Some teachers tend to treat students differently, depending on their own views of how well the students are likely to do. Differences in treatment toward low-expectation students may include setting less challenging tasks, focusing on lower-level learning, giving fewer choices, providing inconsistent feedback, and communicating less respect and trust. Students may behave accordingly, fulfilling teachers' predictions or staying at an expected level of achievement.

## ▼ WHAT WOULD THEY DO?

## TEACHERS' CASEBOOK: Reaching and Teaching Every Student

Here is how two practising teachers responded to the teaching situation described on the first page of this chapter.

**LENORE KLASSEN** • Formerly Special Needs Coordinator, Edmonton, AB

This scenario certainly describes many of our classes in a busy urban Alberta school. The teachers in my junior high school face this problem daily, as junior high in our district is the last truly inclusive level, with all students being in the same classroom—in high school our students are streamed according to ability into levelled courses. Thus in most of our classes (grades 7–9) you will find a wide spectrum of students with differing language backgrounds, cultural backgrounds, skill levels, SES, and (dis)abilities.

In order to differentiate teaching, we focus on providing *adaptations* to both the instructional and assessment components of the curriculum. Only in extreme circumstances do we change the learning outcomes (*modifications*) for students. In my school, the four core academic departments (math, language arts, social studies, and science) have determined core learning outcomes for each unit, and have also created a list of the 10 essential learning outcomes for each subject (what the student must learn in order to be successful at the next level). By reducing the curriculum to these 10 essential outcomes, we can focus on teaching the core material to all students, and then supplement the essential material with extra material according to student capabilities.

Adaptations to instruction are crucial for student success. In our school, the core material is taught explicitly. First, key vocabulary is reviewed, and for ESL students, an opportunity to translate into first language is given. Second, background knowledge is given and discussed as a class so that weaker students can learn from stronger students. Our teachers often illustrate key components using a mixed media/smartboard/video format to increase interest and student attention, and teachers provide plenty of classroom time to practise. Assignments can be adapted for length for weaker students, if needed, but the key skills needed for the course are not compromised—instead students practise until mastery is reached. Much of the work done in class is marked as "For Learning" (teacher feedback) and only assignments done in class, under the teacher's direct supervision are used for "Of Learning" (marks for the report card). The analogy is that learning academics is like learning a sport—much practice must occur under a coach's direction before an athlete participates in a real match/event.

Our grading practice has been to assign letter grades according to the level of proficiency and level of adaptations needed for success. A letter grade of C is given if a student demonstrates mastery/knowledge of the basic material. A letter grade of B is given if a student shows mastery of the more complex material. A letter grade of A is given if a student not only shows mastery of the material taught, but also is able to go beyond what is taught and apply it to untaught material. Assessments are written as a department and are designed to follow this grading practice. For example, the first part of a unit final exam will demonstrate basic knowledge items (C-level questions), the second part of the test will ask more difficult questions (B-level questions), and the third part will include a few challenging, never-seen-before questions (A-level questions). Giving a student a grade on an assessment becomes more transparent when you have tests designed on this principle.

If students receive minor adaptations in a course (such as extra time, a quiet space, oral questions), then they are graded using standard grading practices. If they receive major adaptations (open book, A-level questions removed, translator used), then they can receive only a grade of C for that course. The idea is that students need to be "weaned" off major adaptations.

Teaching is becoming more complex as our classrooms become more diverse. Good teaching is always about being willing to make learning work for all students.

**LEYTON SCHNELLERT** • Prog Coord, Master of Ed in Educ Practic prog (and former teacher of elementary, middle, and secondary schl students), Simon Fraser University, Burnaby, BC

I have been a teacher for 18 years now. I think the first thing that I would do in this scenario is take a deep breath! One of the most important things I can do is tell myself that this might take a little while to figure out and that's okay. Complex situations take time to sort out. Another thing I would do is find out more about the students from their perspective. If I want to develop pathways for information to flow to and from them, then I need to find out what they are interested in, what has worked for them in the past, and what their expectations are of me. I can adjust my teaching without asking these questions, but I have headed in the wrong direction many times before when I just could have asked!

I usually look for trends in what students tell me. I recently had three different Humanities 9 classes with three different profiles: the first was filled with quiet students who were afraid to fail and wanted a lot of structure and visuals; the second was a group of very chatty kids, who knew a lot about popular culture and liked asking questions and having discussions—they wanted to know details; finally, the third class needed movement breaks—lots of kids were into sports, electronics, and art. Across all three classes there were some similarities— students were worried that I would not like them or their work, students liked to read (if not at "grade" level), and none, not even the chatty folks, wanted to give oral presentations. So I took this into account, and while I planned similar lessons for each class, I adjusted my plans with the class "personality" in mind.

Knowing that the students liked to read, I worked with colleagues and the librarian to create "text sets." These are groups of texts on the same theme. I introduced each text with a sales pitch (i.e., a book talk) and then students chose which text to read. Some texts had a lot of visuals or larger print; others were news articles or more factual texts. Many were easier to read. This way, the students had a choice, and I appealed to their need for visuals and different levels of text. What is important is that the students knew what to do with the text. I typically had them process the text in a small group, with support to activate their prior knowledge, and then I had them extract key information and combine what they thought before they read the text with what they learned from reading the text.

One of the most powerful ways I have found to engage diverse classes of students is to offer them more than one way to show what they know. If I am clear with them about the "learning intention" (i.e., outcome) or ask an inquiry question that we develop our knowledge around, they can collect information and show what they know in a variety of ways. I do teach each method (e.g., webbing vs. two-column notes vs. flow chart vs. paragraph synthesis), but ultimately it is so students can choose multiple paths to the same outcome.

One of the benefits of having a diverse class is that the class's diversity becomes a strength. If I differentiate instruction with a few kids in mind (e.g., Sarah will need an option to draw), all kids can benefit from seeing and using other ways to synthesize information. In fact, one of the best ways to demonstrate understanding is to show what you know in more than one modality. I have learned to make my classes a place where students can help determine the criteria for an assignment and the options available for demonstrating their learning. While I have the curriculum to refer to, I have found that even my more disengaged learners participate when they have a voice in creating the assignments. When a student asks for an alternative way to show what he or she knows, the route often benefits others—it also reduces the pressure on me. Rather than guessing what students need and want, I co-construct it with them.

Recently, a group of students asked me if they could create a slide show about the Napoleonic Era. I had to refer them back to our shared criteria several times, as they did not have much explanation behind their points. That's been key—being clear that a PowerPoint presentation or painting still needs to be explained, just like any other form of communication. As long as this is in the criteria, I can justify the mark I give. Yet there is differentiation here, too. In this unit, I had students create an artifact for a museum show based on a significant moment in Napoleon's "reign" that showed him to be a hero. Knowing that they had to explain their piece, some students stood beside their artifact and explained it as others came by, others wrote up supporting documents to be placed beside their artifacts, and two students recorded their commentary so that passersby could listen on headphones. All of these were viable options.

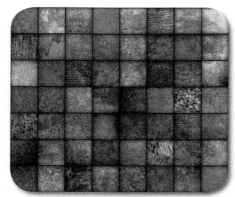

# CLASSROOM ASSESSMENT, GRADING, AND TESTING

▶ **TEACHERS' CASEBOOK:** Giving Meaningful Grades

Your school requires that you give letter grades to your class. You can use any method you want, as long as an A, B, C, D, or F appears for each of the subject areas on every student's report card, every grading period. Some teachers are using worksheets, quizzes, homework, and tests. Others are assigning group work and portfolios. A few teachers are individualizing standards by grading on progress and effort more than final achievement. Some are trying contract approaches and experimenting with longer-term projects, while others are relying almost completely on daily class work to assign grades. Two teachers who use group work are considering giving credit toward grades for being a "good group member" or competitive bonus points for the top-scoring group. Others are planning to use improvement points for class rewards, but not for grades. Your only experience with grading was using written comments and a mastery approach that rated the students as making satisfactory or unsatisfactory progress toward particular objectives. You want to use a system that is reliable, fair, and manageable, but also encourages learning based on feedback, not just working purely for grades.

## CRITICAL THINKING

- What would you choose as your major graded assignments and projects?
- Would you include credit for behaviours such as group participation or effort?
- How would you put all the elements together to determine a grade for every student for every marking period?
- How would you justify your system to the principal and to the students' families, especially when the teachers in your school are using so many different criteria?
- What do you think of the wide range of criteria being used by different teachers—is this fair to students?
- How will these issues affect the grade levels you will teach?

## OVERVIEW AND OBJECTIVES

As you read this chapter, you will examine assessment, testing, and grading, focusing not only on the effects they are likely to have on students, but also on practical ways to develop better methods for testing and grading.

We begin by considering basic concepts in assessment, including validity and reliability. Next we examine the many types of tests teachers prepare each year and approaches to assessment that don't rely on traditional testing. Then, we explore effects grades are likely to have on students, as well as the very important topic of communicating with students and families. How will you justify the grades you give? Finally, because standardized tests are in use today, we spend some time looking at them, the meaning of test scores, and alternatives to traditional testing.

By the time you have completed this chapter, you should be able to:

**15.1** Distinguish among evaluation, measurement, and assessment, and describe the functions of each.

**15.2** Distinguish between norm-referenced and criterion-referenced assessments.

**15.3** Describe how reliability, validity, and absence of bias are used to understand and judge assessments.

**15.4** Describe two kinds of traditional classroom testing, and how authentic assessment can be used as an alternative to traditional assessments.

**15.5** Describe the effects of grading on students and the types of strategies teachers can use to communicate to parents about grades.

**15.6** Explain how to interpret common standardized test scores (percentile rank, z scores).

**15.7** Identify some of the current issues in standardized testing.

## BASICS OF ASSESSMENT

Assessments are critical because teaching involves making many kinds of judgments—decisions based on values: "Is this software appropriate for my students?" "Will Jacob do better if he repeats grade 2?" "Should Emily get a B– or a C+ on the project?" This chapter is about judgments that are informed by measurement, testing, and grading, and all forms of assessment.

A **standardized test** is any test that is administered, scored, and interpreted in a standard manner—the same directions, time limits, and scoring for all (Popham, 2011). Standard methods of developing items, administering the test, scoring it, and reporting the scores are all implied by the term *standardized test*. The schools where you teach probably will use standardized tests, especially to screen students with exceptionalities and, in some provinces, to document achievement of students and schools and to participate in international studies of students' achievement.

**Classroom assessments**, on the other hand, are created by teachers. These assessments can take many different forms—unit tests, essays, portfolios, projects, performances, oral presentations—the list is long. We emphasize classroom assessment because teachers are responsible for them. Let's begin by examining some key issues beginning with the difference between measurement and assessment.

### Measurement and Assessment

**Measurement** is quantitative—numbers describe a particular feature of an event or a characteristic of a student. Measurement tells how much, how often, or how well by providing scores, ranks, or ratings. Instead of saying, "Sarah doesn't seem to understand addition," a teacher might say, "Sarah answered only two of the 15 problems correctly in her addition

**Standardized tests** Tests given, usually nationwide, under uniform conditions and scored according to uniform procedures.

**Classroom assessments** Classroom assessments are selected and created by teachers and can take many different forms—unit tests, essays, portfolios, projects, performances, oral presentations, etc.

**Measurement** An evaluation expressed in quantitative (number) terms.

**SUMMATIVE ASSESSMENT** The final exam is a classic example of a summative assessment. This type of assessment occurs at the end of instruction and provides a summary of accomplishment.

homework." Measurement, when done well, also allows a teacher to compare one student's performance on a particular task with either a specific standard or to the performances of other students on the same task.

Not all decisions teachers make involve measurement. Some decisions are based on information that is difficult or inappropriate to express numerically: student preferences, discussions with families, previous experience, even intuition. But measurement does play a large role in many classroom decisions, and, when properly done, it can provide accurate, unbiased data for decision making.

Increasingly, the term *assessment* is reserved for describing the process of gathering information about students' learning. **Assessment** is broader than measurement because it includes all kinds of ways to sample and observe students' skills, knowledge, and abilities (Linn & Miller, 2005). Assessments can be formal, such as unit tests, or informal, such as observing who emerges as a leader in group work. Assessments can be designed by classroom teachers or by local, provincial, or international agencies. And today, assessments can go well beyond paper-and-pencil exercises to judgments based on students' performances, portfolios, projects, or products (Popham, 2011).

FORMATIVE AND SUMMATIVE ASSESSMENT.   There are two general uses or functions for assessment: formative and summative. **Formative assessment** occurs before or during instruction. The purposes of formative assessment are to guide the teacher in planning and improving instruction and to help students improve learning. In other words, formative assessment helps *form* instruction by providing feedback that is "nonevaluative, supportive, timely, and specific" (Shute, 2008, p. 153). Often students are given a formative test prior to instruction, a **pretest** that helps the teacher and students determine what they already know. Sometimes a test is given during instruction to see what areas of weakness remain so teaching can be directed toward problem areas. These formative tests are not graded, so students who tend to be very anxious about "real" tests may find this low-pressure practice in test taking especially helpful.

**Summative assessment** occurs at the end of instruction. Its purpose is to inform the teacher and the students about the level of accomplishment attained. Summative assessment, therefore, provides a summary of accomplishment. The final exam is a classic example.

The distinction between formative and summative assessment is based on how the results are used. And any method of assessment—traditional, performance, project, oral, portfolio, and so on—can be used for either formative or summative purposes. If the purpose of the assessment is to improve your teaching and help students guide their learning, the evaluation is *formative*. But if the purpose is to evaluate final achievement (and help determine a course grade), the assessment is *summative* (Nitko & Brookhart, 2011). In fact, the same assessment could be used as a formative evaluation at the beginning of the unit and as a summative evaluation at the end. Table 15.1 gives some examples of different uses of assessment.

The formative uses of assessment are really the most important in teaching. In fact, Popham believes "any teacher who uses tests dominantly to determine whether students get high or low grades should receive a solid F in classroom assessment" (Popham, 2008, p. 256). Tests and all assessments should be used to help teachers make better instructional decisions.

The answers given on any type of test have no meaning by themselves; we must make some kind of comparison to interpret test results. There are two basic types of

**Assessment** Procedures used to obtain information about student performance.

**Formative assessment** Ungraded testing used before or during instruction to aid in planning and diagnosis.

**Pretest** Formative test for assessing students' knowledge, readiness, and abilities.

**Summative assessment** Testing that follows instruction and assesses achievement.

TABLE 15.1 • **Using Tests to Make Instructional Decisions**

The best use of assessment is to plan, guide, and target instruction. Here are some decisions that can benefit from assessment results.

| DECISION CATEGORY | TYPICAL ASSESSMENT STRATEGY | DECISION OPTIONS |
|---|---|---|
| What to teach in the first place? | Preassessment before instruction | Whether to provide instruction for specific objectives? |
| How long to keep teaching toward a particular instructional objective? | En route assessments of students' progress | Whether to continue or cease instruction for an objective either for an individual or for the whole class? |
| How effective was an instructional sequence? | Comparing students' posttest to pretest performances | Whether to retain, discard, or modify a given instructional sequence the next time it's used? |

*Source: From Popham, W. J. (2005). Classroom Assessment: What Teachers Need to Know, 4/e. Allyn and Bacon: Boston, MA. © Pearson Education. Adapted by permission of the publisher.*

comparisons: In *norm-referenced comparison*, a particular student's test score is compared to scores obtained by other people who have taken the same test. The second type is *criterion-referenced*. Here, the student's score is compared to a fixed benchmark or minimum passing score. Actually, the same test can be interpreted either in a norm-referenced or criterion-referenced way.

NORM-REFERENCED TEST INTERPRETATIONS.  In **norm-referenced testing** and grading, scores for the people who have taken the test provide information or norms for interpreting the meaning of a given individual's score. A *norm* is typical performance for a particular group. By comparing the individual's raw score (the actual number correct) to the norm, we can determine if the person's score is above, below, or around the average for the group that person belongs to. There are at least three types of **norm groups** (comparison groups) in education—the class or school itself, the school district, and national samples. Students in national norm groups used to interpret large-scale international assessments. Just like it's important to know whether the temperature is Celsius or Farenheit, validly interpreting a student's score in a norm-referenced way requires careful consideration about whether the student really belongs to the norm group.

Norm-referenced tests typically cover a wide range of general objectives. They are especially appropriate when only the top few candidates can be admitted to a program, such as for law school or a scholarship. However, norm-referenced measurement, like any kind of measurement, has its limitations. The results of a norm-referenced test do not tell you whether students are ready to move on to more advanced material. For instance, knowing that a student is in the top 3% of the class on a test of algebraic concepts will not tell you if he or she is ready to move on to advanced math; everyone else in the class may have a limited understanding of the algebraic concepts.

Nor are norm-referenced tests particularly appropriate for measuring affective and psychomotor objectives. To measure individuals' psychomotor learning, you need a clear description of standards. (Even the best gymnast in school performs certain exercises better than others and needs specific guidance about how to improve.) In the affective area, attitudes and values are personal; comparisons among individuals are not really appropriate. For example, how could we measure an "average" level of political values or opinions? Finally, norm-referenced tests tend to encourage competition and comparison of scores. Some students compete to be the best. Others, realizing that being the best is impossible, may compete to be the worst. Both goals have their casualties.

It's important to note that norm-referenced tests aren't necessarily large-scale standardized tests. Any class in which a teacher's tests graded "on the curve" is norm-referenced.

**Norm-referenced testing** Testing in which scores are compared with the average performance of others.

**Norm group** Large sample of students serving as a comparison group for scoring tests.

**VALIDITY AND RELIABILITY** The validity and reliability decisions based on tests may be affected by the extent to which the tests measure intelligence, knowledge, motivation, or differences in life experiences.

**CRITERION-REFERENCED TEST INTERPRETATIONS.** When test scores are compared, not to the scores of others, but to a given standard of performance, this is **criterion-referenced testing** or grading. To decide who should be allowed to drive a car, it is important to determine just what standard of performance is necessary for selecting safe drivers. It does not matter how your test results compare to others'. If your performance on the test was in the top 10%, but you consistently ran through red lights, you would not be a good candidate for a driver's licence, even though your score was high.

Criterion-referenced tests measure mastery of very specific objectives. The results of a criterion-referenced test should tell the teacher exactly what a student can and cannot do, at least under certain conditions. For example, a criterion-referenced test would be useful in measuring students' skill in adding three-digit numbers. A test could be designed with 20 different problems, and the standard for mastery could be set at 17 correct out of 20. Now you see an issue with criterion-referenced interpretations. The standard is often somewhat arbitrary. If two students receive scores of 7 and 14, it does not matter that one student did much better than the other because neither met the standard of 17. Both need more help with addition.

In teaching basic skills, there are many instances where comparison to a preset standard is more important than comparison to other's performance. It is not very comforting to know, as a parent, that your child is better in reading than most of the students in her class if none of the students is reading adequately. Sometimes standards for meeting the criterion should be set at 100% correct. You would not like to have your appendix removed by a surgeon who left surgical instruments inside the body *only* 10% of the time.

Criterion-referenced tests are not appropriate for every situation, however. Some subjects cannot be analyzed into a set of specific objectives. Moreover, although standards are important in criterion-referenced testing, they can often be arbitrary, as we noted. When deciding whether a student has mastered adding three-digit numbers comes down to the difference between 16 or 17 correct answers, it seems difficult to justify one particular standard over another. Finally, at times, it is valuable to know how the students in your class compare to other students at their grade level both locally and provincially. Each type of test is well suited for certain situations, but each also has its limitations.

## Assessing the Assessments: Reliability and Validity

One of the most common problems with the use of assessments, especially tests, is misinterpretation of results. This often happens when people believe tests are precise measurements of a student's knowledge or skill. No test provides a perfect picture of a person's abilities; a test is only one small sample. Three factors are important in developing good tests and interpreting results: *reliability, validity,* and *absence of bias.*

RELIABILITY OF TEST SCORES.   Scores are reliable if a test gives a consistent and stable "reading" of a person's ability from one occasion to the next, assuming the person's ability remains the same. A reliable thermometer works in a similar manner, giving you a reading of 100°C each time you measure the temperature of boiling water. Measuring **reliability** this way, by giving the test on two different occasions, indicates *stability* or *test-retest reliability*. If a group of people take two equivalent versions of a test and the scores on both tests are comparable, this indicates *alternate-form reliability*. Reliability can also

**Criterion-referenced testing** Testing in which scores are compared to a set performance standard.

**Reliability** Consistency of test results.

Corbis

refer to the *internal consistency* or the precision of a test. One approach to calculating this type of reliability, known as *split-half reliability,* is by comparing performance on odd-numbered test questions with performance on even-number items. If, for example, someone did quite well on all the odd-numbered items and poorly on the even-numbered items, it would not be wise to assume the full set of items was consistent or precise in measuring what was intended.

There are several ways to compute reliability. All of them give numbers between 0.0 and 1.0, like a correlation coefficient. Above .90 is considered very reliable; .80 to .90 is good, and below .80 is not very good reliability. Generally speaking, longer tests are more reliable than shorter ones.

ERROR IN SCORES.    All tests are imperfect estimators of the qualities or skills we are trying to measure. There are errors in scores generated in every testing situation. Some sources of error relate to the student such as mood, motivation, test-taking skills, or even cheating. Sometimes errors are in your favour and you score higher than your ability might warrant; sometimes the errors go against you. There are also sources of error related to the test itself—the directions may be unclear, the reading level is too high, the items are ambiguous, or the time limits are inappropriate.

Every test score always includes some amount of error. How can error be reduced? As you might guess, this returns us to the issue of reliability. The more reliable the test scores are, the less error there is in the score we observe. On standardized tests, like intelligence tests, developers take this into consideration and make estimations of how much students' scores would probably vary just due to errors. This estimation is called the **standard error of measurement**. Thus, a reliable test can also be defined as one with a small standard error of measurement.

CONFIDENCE INTERVAL.    Never base an evaluation of a student's ability or achievement on the raw score the student obtains. Instead, consider a **confidence interval**, or "standard error band," that encloses the student's score. A confidence interval based on the standard error of measurement allows you to consider a range of scores that might include a student's **true score**—the score the student would get if it were possible to obtain a measurement that was completely accurate and error-free.

Let us assume, for example, you are a teacher in British Columbia. Two students in your class take the provincial examination in Social Studies 11. Suppose the standard error of measurement for this test is 5. One student receives a score of 79, and the other, a score of 85. At first glance, these scores seem quite different. But that changes when you consider the standard error bands around the scores because the bands overlap. About two-thirds of the time, the first student's true score might be estimated to be anywhere between 74 and 84 (that is, the student's actual score of 79 plus and minus the standard error of 5). The second student's true score might be anywhere between 80 and 90. Both students could have the same true score of 80, 81, 82, 83, or 84 because the score bands overlap at those numbers. It is crucial to keep in mind the idea of standard error bands when selecting students for special programs. No child should be selected or rejected simply because the score obtained missed the cutoff by one or two points. The student's true score might well be above the cutoff point.

VALIDITY.    If test scores are sufficiently reliable, the next question is whether judgments and decisions based on the test scores are valid. To have **validity**, the decisions and inferences based on the test must be supported by evidence or acceptable reasons. It follows that that the validity of a decision or inference is judged in relation to a particular use or purpose—that is, in relation to the actual decision being made and the evidence for it. A particular test might be valid for one purpose but not for another (Frisbie, 2005; Oosterhof, 2009; Popham, 2011).

There are different kinds of evidence to support a particular judgment. If the purpose of a test is to measure skills covered in a course or unit, then we would hope to see test questions on all the important topics and not on extraneous information. If this condition is met, we would have *content-related evidence of validity*. Have you ever taken a

**Standard error of measurement** Hypothetical estimate of variation in scores if testing were repeated.

**Confidence interval** Range of scores within which an individual's particular score is likely to fall.

**True score** The score the student would get if the measurement were completely accurate and error-free.

**Validity** Degree to which a test measures what it is intended to measure.

test that dealt only with a few ideas from one lecture or just a few pages of the textbook? In these cases, decisions based on just that test (like your grade) almost certainly lacked content-related evidence for validity.

Some tests are designed to predict outcomes. The Law School Admissions Test (LSAT), for example, is intended to predict performance in law school. If LSAT scores correlate with academic performance in law school, then we have *criterion-related evidence of validity* for the use of the LSAT in admissions decisions.

Most commercial standardized tests are designed to measure a psychological characteristic or "construct" such as reasoning ability, reading comprehension, achievement motivation, intelligence, creativity, and so on. It is a bit more difficult to gather *construct-related evidence of validity*, yet this is a very important requirement—probably the most important. Construct-related evidence of validity is gathered over many years. It is indicated by a pattern of scores. For example, older children can answer more questions on intelligence tests than younger children. This fits with our *construct* of intelligence. If the average 5-year-old answered as many questions correctly on a test as the average 13-year-old, we would doubt that the test really measured intelligence. Construct-related evidence for validity can also be demonstrated when the results of a test correlate with the results of other well-established, reliable measures of the same construct.

Today, many psychologists suggest that construct-related evidence of validity is the broadest category and that gathering content- and criterion-related evidence is another way of determining if the test actually measures the construct it was designed to measure. Nearly 40 years ago, Sam Messick (1975) raised two important questions to consider in making any decisions about using a test: *Is the test a good measure of the characteristic it is assumed to assess? Should the test be used for the proposed purpose?* The first question is about construct-related evidence of validity; the second is about ethics and values.

A test must be reliable in order for decisions and inferences based on it to be valid. For example, if an intelligence test yields different results each time it is given to the same child over the course of a few months, then, by definition, it is not reliable. Certainly, it couldn't support valid inferences about a student's intelligence because intelligence is assumed to be fairly stable, at least over a short period of time. However, reliability will not guarantee validity. If that intelligence test gave the same score every time for a particular child, but didn't predict school achievement, speed of learning, or other characteristics associated with intelligence, then performance on the test would not be a useful indicator of intelligence. The test would be reliable—but inferences based on it would be invalid. Reliability and validity are issues with all assessments, not just standardized tests. Classroom tests should yield scores that are *reliable*, that are as free from error as possible, and that are *valid*—accurately measuring what they are supposed to.

ABSENCE OF BIAS.   The third important criterion for judging assessments is absence of bias. **Assessment bias** "refers to qualities of an assessment instrument that offend or unfairly penalize a group of students because of the students' gender, ethnicity, socio-economic status, religion, or other such group-defining characteristic" (Popham, 2011, p. 111). Biases are aspects of the test such as content, language, or examples that might distort the performance of a group—either for better or for worse. For example, if a provincial exam requires understanding passages that describe boxing or football scenarios, we might expect males on average to do better than females.

Two forms of assessment bias are *unfair penalization* and *offensiveness*. The reading assessment with heavy sports content is an example of unfair penalization—girls may be penalized for their lack of knowledge about boxing or football. Offensiveness occurs when a particular group might be insulted by the content of the assessment. Offended, angry students may not perform at their best.

What about biases based on ethnicity or social class? Research on test bias shows that most commercial standardized tests predict school achievement equally well across all groups of students (Sattler, 2001). But even so, many people believe that the tests still can be unfair to some groups. Tests may not have *procedural fairness*; that is, some

**Assessment bias** Qualities of an assessment instrument that offend or unfairly penalize a group of students because of the students' gender, SES, race, ethnicity, etc.

groups may not have an equal opportunity to show what they know on the test. Here are a few examples:

1. The language of the test and the tester is often different from the languages of the students.
2. Answers that support middle-class values are often rewarded with more points.
3. On individually administered intelligence tests, being very verbal and talking a lot is rewarded. This favours students who feel comfortable in that particular situation.

Also, tests may not be fair because different groups have had different opportunities to learn the material tested. The questions asked tend to centre on experiences and facts more familiar to the dominant culture than to minority-group students. Consider this test item for grade 4 students described by Popham (2011, p. 371):

My uncle's field is computer programming.

Look at the sentences below. In which sentence does the word *field* mean the same as it does in the boxed sentence above?

    A. The softball pitcher knew how to field her position.
    B. They prepared the field by spraying and plowing it.
    C. I know the field I plan to enter when I finish college.
    D. The doctor used a wall chart to examine my field of vision.

Items like this are included on most standardized and many textbook tests. But not all families describe their work as a field of employment. If your parents work in professional jobs such as computers, medicine, law, or education, the item would make sense. But what if your parents work at a grocery store or a car repair shop? Are these fields? Life outside class has prepared some students, but not others, for this item.

Concern about cultural bias in testing has led some psychologists to try to develop **culture-fair** or **culture-free tests**. These efforts have not been very successful. On many of the so-called culture-fair tests, the performance of students from lower-SES backgrounds and ethnic groups has been the same as or worse than their performance on the standard Wechsler and Binet Intelligence scales (Sattler, 2001). And when you think about it, how can you separate culture from cognition? Every student's learning is embedded in his or her culture, and every test question emerges from some kind of cultural knowledge.

Today, most commercial and provincial standardized tests are checked carefully for assessment bias, but teacher-made tests may have biased content as well. It makes sense to have colleagues check your tests for bias, especially when you are getting started in teaching (Popham, 2011).

With this background in the basic concepts of formative and summative assessments; norm-referenced and criterion-referenced interpretations; and attention to reliability, validity, and absence of bias, we are ready to enter the classroom, where *learning is supported by frequent assessments using cumulative questions that ask students to apply and integrate knowledge.*

## CLASSROOM ASSESSMENT: TESTING

**STOP & THINK** Think back to your most recent test. What was the format? Did you feel that the test results were an accurate reflection of your knowledge or skills? Have you ever had to design a test? What makes a good, fair test? •

When most people think of assessments in a classroom, they usually think of testing. As you will see shortly, teachers today have many other options, but testing is still a significant activity in most classrooms. In this section, we will examine how to evaluate the tests that accompany standard curriculum materials and show you how to write your own test questions.

**Listen**
Classroom Assessment: Testing

**Culture-fair or culture-free test**
A test without cultural bias.

## Using the Tests From Textbooks

Most elementary and secondary school texts today come complete with supplemental materials such as teaching manuals and ready-made tests. Using these tests can save time, but is this good teaching practice? The answer depends on your objectives for your students, the way you teach the material, and the quality of the tests provided. If the textbook test is of high quality, matches your testing plan, and fits the instruction you actually provided for your students, then it may be the right test to use. Check the reading level of the items provided and be prepared to revise/improve them (Airasian, 2005; McMillan, 2004). Table 15.2 gives key points to consider in evaluating textbook tests.

What if there are no tests available for the material you cover, or the tests provided in your teachers' manuals are not appropriate for your students? Then it's time for you to create your own tests. We will consider the two major kinds of traditional tests—objective and essay.

## Objective Testing

Multiple-choice questions, matching exercises, true/false statements, and short-answer or fill-in responses are all types of **objective test** items. The word *objective* in relation to testing means "not open to many interpretations," or "not subjective." Scoring objective items is relatively straightforward compared to scoring essay questions because the answers are more clear-cut.

How should you decide which item format is best for a particular test? Use the one that provides the most direct measure of the learning outcome you intended for your students (Gronlund & Waugh, 2009). In other words, if you want to see how well students can write a letter, have them write a letter, don't ask multiple-choice questions about letters. But if many different item formats will work equally well, then use multiple-choice questions because they are easier to score fairly and can cover many topics. Switch to other formats if writing good multiple-choice items for the material is not possible or appropriate. For example, if related concepts such as terms and definitions need to be linked, then a matching item is a better format than multiple-choice. If it is difficult to come up with several wrong answers for a multiple-choice item, try a true/false question instead. Alternatively, ask the student to supply a short answer that completes a statement (fill in the blank). Variety in objective testing can lower students' anxiety because the entire grade does not depend on one type of question that a particular student may find difficult. We will look closely at the multiple-choice format because it is the most versatile—and the most difficult to use well.

TABLE 15.2 ● **Key Points to Consider in Judging Textbook Tests**

1. The decision to use a textbook test or pre-made standard achievement test must come *after* a teacher identifies the objective that he or she has taught and now wants to assess.
2. Textbook and standard tests are designed for the typical classroom, but since few classrooms are typical, most teachers deviate somewhat from the text in order to accommodate their pupils' needs.
3. The more classroom instruction deviates from the textbook, the less valid the textbook tests are likely to be.
4. The main consideration in judging the adequacy of a textbook or standard achievement test is the match between its test questions and what pupils were taught in their classes:

   a. Are questions similar to the teacher's objectives and instructional emphases?
   b. Do questions require pupils to perform the behaviours they were taught?
   c. Do questions cover all or most of the important objectives taught?
   d. Is the language level and terminology appropriate for pupils?
   e. Does the number of items for each objective provide a sufficient sample of pupil performance?

*Source: From Airasian, P. W. (2005). Classroom Assessment: Concepts and Applications (5th ed.). New York: McGraw-Hill, p. 161. With permission from The McGraw-Hill Companies.*

**Objective testing** Multiple-choice, matching, true/false, short-answer, and fill-in tests; scoring answers does not require interpretation.

USING MULTIPLE-CHOICE TESTS.   Even though about three-fourths of education professors reject the use of multiple-choice tests in determining students' grades, about half of public school teachers endorse them (Banks, 2005). You should know how to use these tests well. Of course, multiple-choice items can test facts, but these items can assess more than recall and recognition if they require the student to deal with new material by applying or analyzing a concept or principle being tested (Gronlund & Waugh, 2009; McMillan, 2004). For example, the following multiple-choice item is designed to assess students' ability to recognize unstated assumptions, one of the skills involved in analyzing an idea:

> An educational psychology professor states, "A *z* score of +1 on a test is equivalent to a percentile rank of approximately 84." Which of the following assumptions is the professor making?
>
> 1. The scores on the test range from 0 to 100.
> 2. The standard deviation of the test scores is equal to 3.4.
> 3. The distribution of scores on the test is normal. (Correct answer)
> 4. The test is valid and reliable.

If you did not know the correct answer above, don't worry. We will get to *z* scores later in this chapter and it will all make sense.

WRITING MULTIPLE-CHOICE QUESTIONS.   All test items require skillful construction, but good multiple-choice items are a particular challenge. Some students jokingly refer to multiple-choice tests as "multiple-guess" tests—a sign that these tests are often poorly designed. Your goal in writing test items is to design them so they measure students' achievement, not test-taking skills or guessing.

The **stem** of a multiple-choice item is the part that asks the question or poses the problem. The choices that follow are called *alternatives*. The wrong answers among the alternatives are called **distractors** because their purpose is to distract students who have only a partial understanding of the material. If there were no good distractors, students with only a vague understanding would have no difficulty in finding the right answer. The *Guidelines* should help you write good stems and alternatives.

## Essay Testing

The best way to measure some learning objectives is to ask students to create answers on their own. Essay questions are one way to accomplish this. The most difficult part of essay testing is judging the quality of the answers, but writing good, clear questions is not particularly easy, either. We will look at writing, administering, and grading essay tests.

We will also consider factors that can bias the scoring of essay questions and ways you can overcome these problems.

CONSTRUCTING ESSAY TESTS.   Because answering takes time, true essay tests cover less material than objective tests. Thus, for efficiency, essay tests should be limited to assessing important, complex learning outcomes. A good essay question gives students a clear and precise task and indicates the elements to be covered in the answer. The students should know how extensive their answer needs to be and about how much time they should spend on each question. Evaluate these two essay questions from Popham (2011, pp. 183–184):

1. (High school level) You have just viewed a video containing three widely seen television commercials. What is the one classic propaganda technique present in all three commercials?
2. (Middle school level) Thinking back over the mathematics lesson and homework assignments you had during the past 12 weeks, what conclusions can you draw? Take no more than one page for your response.

Question 1 is pretty clear (do you agree?), but some indication of desired length would be helpful. Question 2 gives a page limit, but would you know what is being asked? What is the specific question here?

**Stem** The question part of a multiple-choice item.

**Distractors** Wrong answers offered as choices in a multiple-choice item.

## GUIDELINES

### Writing Objective Test Items

**Make the stem clear and simple, and present only a single problem. Unessential details should be left out.**
*Example*

| *Poor* | *Better* |
| --- | --- |
| There are several different kinds of standard or derived scores. An IQ score is especially useful because _____. | An advantage of an IQ score is _____. |

**State the problem in the stem in positive terms. Negative language is confusing. If you must use words such as *not*, *no*, or *except*, underline them or type them in all capitals.**
*Example*

| *Poor* | *Better* |
| --- | --- |
| Which of the following is not a standard score? | Which of the following is *not* a standard score? |

**Do not expect students to make extremely fine discriminations among answer choices.**
*Example*
The percentage of area in a normal curve falling between +1 and −1 standard deviations is about:

| *Poor* | | *Better* | |
| --- | --- | --- | --- |
| a. 66% | b. 67% | a. 14% | b. 34% |
| c. 68% | d. 69% | c. 68% | d. 95% |

**Make sure each alternative answer fits the grammatical form of the stem, so that no answers are obviously wrong.**
*Example*

| *Poor* | *Better* |
| --- | --- |
| The Stanford-Binet test yields an | The Stanford-Binet is a test of |
| a. IQ score. | a. intelligence. |
| b. reading level. | b. reading level. |
| c. vocational preference. | c. vocational preference. |
| d. mechanical aptitude. | d. mechanical aptitude. |

**Avoid including two distractors that have the same meaning.**
If only one answer can be right and if two answers are the same, then these two must both be wrong. This narrows down the choices considerably.

**Avoid using categorical words such as *always*, *all*, *only*, or *never* unless they can appear consistently in all the alternatives.**
Most smart test takers know that categorical answers are usually wrong.

**Avoid using the exact wording found in the textbook.**
Poor students may recognize the answers without knowing what they mean.

**Avoid overuse of *all of the above* and *none of the above*.**
Such choices may be helpful to students who are simply guessing. In addition, using *all of the above* may trick a quick student who sees that the first alternative is correct and does not read on to discover that the others are correct, too.

**Avoid obvious patterns on a test—they aid students who are guessing.**
The position of the correct answer should be varied, as should its length.

Students need ample time for answering. If more than one essay is assigned in the same class period, you may want to suggest time limits for each question. Remember, however, time pressure increases anxiety and may interfere with accurate assessment of some students. Whatever your approach, do not try to make up for the limited amount of material an essay test can cover by including a large number of questions. It would be better to plan on more frequent testing than to include more than two or three essay questions in a single class period. Combining an essay question with a number of objective items is one way to avoid the problem of limited sampling of course material (Gronlund & Waugh, 2009).

**EVALUATING ESSAYS.** Gronlund and Waugh (2009) offer several strategies for grading essays. When possible, a good first step is to construct a set of scoring criteria or a rubric (more on rubrics later) and share it with students. Then, decide what type of information should be in every answer. Here is an example from TenBrink (2003, p. 326).

*Question:* Defend or refute the following statement: Civil wars are necessary to the growth of a developing country. Cite reasons for your argument, and use examples from history to help substantiate your claim.
*Scoring Rubric:* All answers, regardless of the position taken, should include (1) a clear statement of the position, (2) at least five logical reasons, (3) at least four examples from history that clearly substantiate the reasons given.

Once you have set your expectations for answers, you can assign points to the various parts of the essay. You might also give points for the organization of the answer and the coherence of the essay. You can then assign grades such as 1 to 5 or A, B, C, D, and F, and sort the papers into piles by grade. As a final step, skim the papers in each pile to see if they are comparable in quality, then re-classify papers if necessary. These techniques will help ensure fairness and accuracy in grading.

When grading essay tests that contain several questions, it's best to grade all responses to one question before moving on to the next. This helps prevent the quality of a student's answer to one question from influencing your reaction to the student's other answers. After you finish reading and scoring the first question, shuffle the papers so no students end up having all their questions graded first (when you may be taking more time to give feedback or are applying stricter standards, for example) or last (when you may be tired of writing feedback or more lax in your standards). You may realize greater objectivity if you ask students to put their names on the back of the paper, so that grading is anonymous. A final check on your fairness as a grader is to have another teacher who is equally familiar with your goals and subject matter look over a few of your tests without knowing what grades you have assigned. This can give you valuable insights into areas of bias in your grading practices.

THE VALUE OF TRADITIONAL TESTING.   Right answers are important. Even though schooling is about learning to think and solve problems, it is also about knowledge. Students must have something to think with—facts, ideas, concepts, principles, theories, explanations, arguments, images, and opinions. Well-designed traditional tests can evaluate students' knowledge effectively and efficiently (Airasian, 2005). Some educators believe that traditional testing should play an even greater role than it currently does. Some analysts suggest that students may lack essential knowledge if schools emphasize processes such as critical thinking and problem solving more than content. To teach more about content, teachers will need to determine how well their students are learning that content. Traditional testing provides useful information about content learning. Tests are also valuable in motivating and guiding students' learning. There is research evidence that frequent testing encourages learning and retention. In fact, taking more frequent tests improves learning, even if there is no feedback from the test—bad teaching, but a powerful result (Roediger & Karpicke, 2006)

CRITICISMS OF TRADITIONAL TESTS.   Traditional testing has been under fire since at least the 1990s. As Grant Wiggins (1991) noted then:

We do not judge Xerox . . . or Dom Perignon vineyards on the basis of indirect, easy to test, and common indicators. Nor would the workers in those places likely produce quality if some generic, secure test served as the only measure of their success in meeting a standard. Demanding and getting quality, whether from students or adult workers, means framing standards in terms of the work that we undertake and value. (p. 22)

**NONTRADITIONAL ASSESSMENTS** Alternatives to traditional testing have emerged that address what are seen as its limits, including that it emphasizes recall of facts instead of thinking and problem solving. Alternative approaches include authentic assessment, student exhibitions, and student portfolios.

Wiggins continues to argue for assessment that makes sense, that tests knowledge as it is applied in real-world situations. Understanding cannot be measured by tests that ask students to use skills and knowledge out of context.

Your stand on traditional testing is part of your philosophy of teaching. Let's look at a few alternative approaches to classroom assessment.

# AUTHENTIC CLASSROOM ASSESSMENTS

**Authentic assessments** ask students to apply skills and abilities as they would in real life. For example, they might use fractions to enlarge or reduce recipes. Grant Wiggins (1989) made this argument over 20 years ago:

> If tests determine what teachers actually teach and what students will study for—and they do—then the road to reform is a straight but steep one: test those capabilities and habits we think are essential, and test them in context. Make [tests] replicate, within reason, the challenges at the heart of each academic discipline. Let them be—authentic. (p. 41)

Wiggins goes on to say that if our instructional goals for students include the abilities to write, speak, listen, create, think critically, do research, solve problems, or apply knowledge, then our tests should ask students to write, speak, listen, create, think, research, solve, and apply. How can this happen?

Many educators suggest we look to the arts and sports for analogies to solve this problem. If we think of the "test" as being the recital, exhibition, game, mock court trial, or other performance, then teaching to the test is just fine. All coaches, artists, and musicians gladly "teach" to these "tests" because performing well on these tests is the whole point of instruction. Authentic assessment asks students to perform. The performances may be thinking performances, physical performances, creative performances, or other forms. So **performance assessment** is any form of assessment that requires students to carry out an activity or produce a product to demonstrate learning (Airasian, 2005).

It may seem odd to talk about thinking as a performance, but there are many parallels. Serious thinking is risky, because real-life problems are not well defined. Often, the outcomes of our thinking are public—others evaluate our ideas. Like a dancer auditioning for the Winnipeg Ballet, we must cope with the consequences of being evaluated. Like a potter looking at a lump of clay, a student facing a difficult problem must experiment, observe, redo, imagine, and test solutions, apply both basic skills and inventive techniques, make interpretations, decide how to communicate results to the intended audience, and often accept criticism and improve the initial solution (Eisner, 1999; Herman, 1997).

## Portfolios and Exhibitions

The concern with authentic assessment has led to developing several approaches based on the goal of performance in context. Instead of circling answers to "factual" questions about nonexistent situations, students are required to solve real problems. Facts are used in a context where they apply—for example, instead of asking students, "If you bought a pencil for $1.69 and paid a toonie, how much change would you get back?" have students work in pairs with real money to role play making different purchases, or set up a mock class store and have students make purchases and give change (Gronlund & Waugh, 2009). Here's a sample for a grade 10 science project.

**Description**  Students gather data about the effects on temperature of water in two test tubes, each half filled with water. One test tube is wrapped in a dry paper towel and the other is wrapped in a wet paper towel with water at room temperature. After taking 10 measurements of water temperature n each test tube, they plot their data. They then consider how these results lead to predicting why we sweat and why dogs, who can not sweat, pant with their tongues hanging out on very warm days.

**Overall Task Content Area**  Life Science

**Specific Knowledge Areas**  Homeostatic mechanisms

**Authentic assessments**
Assessment procedures that test skills and abilities as they would be applied in real-life situations.

**Performance assessments**  Any form of assessment that requires students to carry out an activity or produce a product in order to demonstrate learning.

**Performance Expectations**

- taking measurements
- organizing data
- plotting information
- drawing inferences from data
- applying scientific principles to explain

Students completing this "test" will use scientific knowledge to understand a real-life phenomenon—perspiration. In the process, they will have to think critically and write persuasively.

Portfolios and exhibitions are two approaches to assessment that require performance in context. With these approaches, it is difficult to tell where instruction stops and assessment starts because the two processes are interwoven (Oosterhof, 2009; Popham, 2011).

PORTFOLIOS.    For years, photographers, artists, models, and architects have had portfolios to display their skills and talents, and show to prospective employers. A **portfolio** is a systematic collection of work, often including work in progress, revisions, student self-analyses, and reflections on what the student has learned. Written work or artistic pieces are common in portfolios, but student portfolios might also include letters to the portfolio readers describing each entry and its importance. Portfolios also might include graphs, diagrams, pictures or digital slideshows, PowerPoint presentations, recordings of the students reading their work, unedited and final drafts of persuasive essays or poems, lists of books read, annotated website addresses, peer comments, videos, laboratory reports, and computer programs—anything that demonstrates learning in the area being taught and assessed (Popham, 2011). Similar to the difference between formative and summative evaluation, there is a distinction between process portfolios and final or "best work" portfolios. Process portfolios document learning and show progress. Best work portfolios showcase final accomplishments (Johnson & Johnson, 2002). Table 15.3 shows some examples for both individuals and groups.

EXHIBITIONS.    An **exhibition** is a performance test that has two additional features. First, it is public, so students preparing exhibitions must take the audience into account; communication and understanding are essential. Second, an exhibition often requires many hours of preparation, because it is the culminating experience of a whole program of study. Thomas Guskey and Jane Bailey (2001) suggest that exhibits help students understand qualities of good work and recognize those qualities in their own productions and performances. Students also benefit when they select examples of their work to exhibit and articulate their reasons for making the selections. Being able to judge quality can encourage student motivation by setting clear goals. The *Guidelines* give some ideas for using portfolios in your teaching.

 **Watch**
Exhibitions

## Evaluating Portfolios and Performances

Checklists, rating scales, and scoring rubrics are helpful when you assess performances, because assessments of performances, portfolios, and exhibitions are criterion-referenced, not norm-referenced. In other words, the students' products and performances are compared to established public standards, not ranked in relation to other students' work (Wiggins, 1991).

SCORING RUBRICS.    A checklist or rating scale gives specific feedback about elements of a performance. **Scoring rubrics** are rules that for determining the quality of a student performance, often on a four-point scale from "excellent" (4) to "inadequate" (1), or on a scale that assigns points to each category—10 points for excellent, 6 for good, and so on (Mabry, 1999). For example, a rubric describing excellent *delegation of responsibility* in a group research project might be:

> Each student in the group can clearly explain what information is needed by the group, what information s/he is responsible for locating, and when the information is needed.

**Portfolio** A collection of the student's work in an area, showing growth, self-reflection, and achievement.

**Exhibition** A performance test or demonstration of learning that is public and usually takes an extended time to prepare.

**Scoring rubrics** Rules that are used to determine the quality of a student's performance.

TABLE 15.3 • **Process and Best Works Portfolios for Individuals and Groups**

Here are a few examples of how to use portfolios in different subjects.

| THE PROCESS PORTFOLIO | | |
|---|---|---|
| **Subject Area** | **Individual Student** | **Cooperative Group** |
| Science | Documentation (running records or logs) of using the scientific method to solve a series of laboratory problems | Documentation (observation checklists) of using the scientific method to solve a series of laboratory problems |
| Mathematics | Documentation of mathematical reasoning through double-column mathematical problem solving (computations on the left side and running commentary explaining thought processes on the right side) | Documentation of complex problem solving and use of higher-level strategies |
| Language Arts | Evolution of compositions from early notes through outlines, research notes, response to others' editing, and final draft | Rubrics and procedures developed to ensure high-quality peer editing |
| THE BEST WORKS PORTFOLIO | | |
| **Subject Area** | **Individual Student** | **Cooperative Group** |
| Language Arts | The best compositions in a variety of styles—expository, humour/satire, creative (poetry, drama, short story), journalistic (reporting, editorial columnist, reviewer), and advertising copy | The best dramatic production, video project, TV broadcast, newspaper, advertising display |
| Social Studies | The best historical research paper, opinion essay on historical issue, commentary on current event, original historical theory, review of a historical biography, account of academic controversy participated in | The best community survey, paper resulting from academic controversy, oral history compilation, multidimensional analysis of historical event, press corps interview with historical figure |
| Fine Arts | The best creative products such as drawings, paintings, sculptures, pottery, poems, thespian performance | The best creative products such as murals, plays written and performed, inventions thought of and built |

*Source: From Johnson, D. W., & Johnson, R. T. (2002).* Meaningful Assessment: A Meaningful and Cooperative Process. *Allyn and Bacon: Boston, MA.*

This rubric was generated using Rubistar (http://rubistar.4teachers.org), an online service for educators that allows you to select a subject area and category, then create a rubric. To get the rubric, we chose the subject of writing—"group planning and research project"—and the category of "delegation of responsibility." The *Guidelines* give more ideas; some are taken from Goodrich (1997), Johnson and Johnson (2002), and Popham (2011).

Performance assessment requires careful judgment on the part of teachers and clear communication to students about what is good and what needs improving. In some ways, the approach is similar to the clinical method first introduced by Binet to assess intelligence: It is based on observing the student perform a variety of tasks and comparing his

## GUIDELINES

## Creating Portfolios

**Involve students in selecting the pieces that will make up their portfolios.**
*Examples*

1. During the unit or semester, ask each student to select work that fits certain criteria, such as "my most difficult problem," "my best work," "my most improved work," or "three approaches to."
2. For their final submissions, ask students to select pieces that best show how much they have learned.

**Make sure the portfolios include information that shows student self-reflection and self-criticism.**
*Examples*

1. Ask students to include a rationale for their selections.
2. Have each student write a "guide" to his or her portfolio, explaining how strengths and weaknesses are reflected in the work included.
3. Include self- and peer critiques, indicating specifically what is good and what might be improved.
4. Model self-criticism of your own productions.

**Make sure the portfolios reflect the students' activities in learning.**
*Examples*

1. Include a representative selection of projects, writings, drawings, and so forth.
2. Ask students to relate the goals of learning to the contents of their portfolios.

**Be aware that portfolios can serve different functions at different times of the year.**
*Examples*

1. Early in the year, it might hold unfinished work or "problem pieces."
2. At the end of the year, it should contain only what the student is willing to make public.

**Be certain portfolios demonstrate students' growth.**
*Examples*

1. Ask students to make a "history" of their progress along certain dimensions and to illustrate points in their growth with specific works.
2. Ask students to include descriptions of activities outside class that reflect the growth illustrated in the portfolio.

**Teach students how to create and use portfolios.**
*Examples*

1. Keep models of very well done portfolios as examples, but stress that each portfolio is an individual statement.
2. Examine your students' portfolios frequently, especially early in the year when they are just getting used to the idea. Give constructive feedback.

*For more ideas about using portfolios, see* www.teachervision.fen.com/assessment/teaching-methods/20153.html.

## GUIDELINES

## Developing a Rubric

1. **Look at models:** Show students examples of good and not-so-good work based on composites of work not linked to individual students. Identify the characteristics that make the good ones good and the bad ones bad.
2. **List criteria:** Use the discussion of models to begin a list of what counts in quality work.
3. **Articulate gradations of quality:** Describe the best and worst levels of quality; then fill in the middle levels based on your knowledge of common problems and the discussion of not-so-good work.
4. **Practise on models:** Have students use the rubrics to evaluate the models you gave them in Step 1.
5. **Use self- and peer assessment:** Give students their task. As they work, stop them occasionally for self- and peer assessment.
6. **Revise:** Always give students time to revise their work based on the feedback they get in Step 5.

7. **Use teacher assessment:** In your grading, be sure to use the same rubric students used to assess their work.

Note: *Step 1 may be necessary only when you are asking students to engage in a task with which they are unfamiliar. Steps 3 and 4 are useful but time consuming; you can do these on your own, especially when you've been using rubrics for a while. A class experienced in rubric-based assessment can streamline the process so that it begins with listing criteria, after which the teacher writes out the gradations of quality, checks them with the students, makes revisions, then uses the rubric for self-, peer, and teacher assessment.*

*For a great explanation of using rubrics, see* http://pareonline.net/getvn.asp?v=7&n=25.

*The article includes several links such as* www.teach-nology.com/web_tools/rubrics *and* http://rubistar.4teachers.org *that allow you to create and customize rubrics for your class.*

or her performance to a standard. Just as Binet never wanted to assign a single number to represent the child's intelligence, teachers who use authentic assessments do not try to assign one score to the student's performance. Even if rankings, ratings, and grades have to be given, these judgments are not the ultimate goals—improvement of learning is.

It is often helpful to have students join in to develop rating scales and scoring rubrics. When students participate, they are challenged to decide what quality work looks or sounds like in a particular area. They know in advance what is expected. As students gain practice in designing and applying scoring rubrics, their work and their learning often improve. Figure 15.1 gives three alternatives—numerical, graphic, and descriptive—for rating an oral presentation.

**RELIABILITY, VALIDITY, GENERALIZABILITY.**   Because the teacher's personal judgment plays such a central role in evaluating performances, issues of reliability, validity, and generalizability are critical considerations. One teacher's "excellent" could be another

---

**FIGURE 15.1**

**THREE WAYS OF RATING AN ORAL PRESENTATION**

**Numerical Rating Scale**

**Directions:**

Indicate how often the pupil performs each of these behaviours while giving an oral presentation. For each behaviour circle **1** if the pupil **always** performs the behaviour, **2** if the pupil **usually** performs the behaviour, **3** if the pupil **seldom** performs the behaviour, and **4** if the pupil **never** performs the behaviour.

*Physical Expression*

A. Stands straight and faces audience.

   **1  2  3  4**

B. Changes facial expression with change in the tone of the presentation.

   **1  2  3  4**

**Graphic Rating Scale**

**Directions:**

Place an **X** on the line that shows how often the pupil did each of the behaviours listed while giving an oral presentation.

*Physical Expression*

A. Stands straight and faces audience.

  **always    usually    seldom    never**

B. Changes facial expression with change in the tone of the presentation.

  **always    usually    seldom    never**

**Descriptive Rating Scale**

**Directions:**

Place an **X** on the line at the place that best describes the pupil's performance of each behaviour.

*Physical Expression*

A. Stands straight and faces audience.

| **stands straight, always looks at audience** | **weaves, fidgets, eyes roam from audience to ceiling** | **constant, distracting movements, no eye contact with audience** |
|---|---|---|

B. Changes facial expression with change in the tone of the presentation.

| **matches facial expressions to content and emphasis** | **facial expressions usually appropriate, occasional lack of expression** | **no match between tone and facial expression; expression distracts** |
|---|---|---|

*Source: From Airasian, P. W. (2005). Classroom Assessment: Concepts and Applications (5th ed.). New York: McGraw-Hill, p. 251. With permission of The McGraw-Hill Companies.*

teacher's "adequate." Research shows that when raters are experienced and scoring rubrics are well developed and refined, reliability may improve (Herman & Winters, 1994; LeMahieu, Gitomer, & Eresh, 1993). Some of this improvement in reliability occurs because a rubric focuses the raters' attention on a few dimensions of the work and limits scoring levels that can be used. If scorers can give only a rating of 1, 2, 3, or 4, they are more likely to agree than if they could score based on a 100-point scale. So the rubrics may achieve reliability not because they capture underlying agreement among raters, but because the rubrics limit options and thus limit variability in scoring (Mabry, 1999).

In terms of validity, there is some evidence that students who are classified as "master" writers on the basis of portfolio assessment are judged less capable using standard writing assessments. Which form of assessment is the best reflection of enduring qualities? It is hard to say. In addition, when rubrics are developed to assess specific tasks, the results of applying them may not predict performance on anything except very similar tasks, so we do not know whether a student's performance on a specific task will generalize to the larger area of study (Haertel, 1999; Herman & Winters, 1994; McMillan, 2004).

DIVERSITY AND BIAS IN PERFORMANCE ASSESSMENT.    Equity is an issue in all assessment and no less so with performances and portfolios. With a public performance, there could be bias effects based on a student's appearance and speech or the student's access to expensive audio, video, or graphic tools. Performance assessments have the same potential as other tests to discriminate unfairly against students who are not wealthy or who are culturally different (McDonald, 1993). And the extensive group work, peer editing, and out-of-class time devoted to portfolios means that some students may have access to greater networks of support and outright help. Many students in your classes will come from families that have sophisticated computer graphics and desktop publishing capabilities. Others may have few opportunities like that. These differences can be sources of bias and inequity, especially in portfolios and exhibitions.

## Informal Assessments

**Informal assessments** are ungraded (formative) assessments that gather information from multiple sources to help teachers make decisions (Banks, 2005). Early on in the unit, assessments should be formative (provide feedback, but not count toward a grade), saving the actual graded assessments for later in the unit when all students have had the chance to learn the material (Tomlinson, 2005a). Some examples of informal assessment are journals, student observations and checklists, questioning, and student self-assessment.

JOURNALS.    Journals are very flexible and widely used informal assessments. Students usually have personal or group journals and write in them on a regular basis. In their study, Michael Pressley and his colleagues (Pressley, Mohan, Raphael, Fingeret, 2007) found that excellent grade 1 literacy teachers used journaling for three purposes:

- as communication tools that allowed students to express their own thoughts and ideas
- as an opportunity to apply what they have learned
- as an outlet to encourage fluency and creative expression in language usage

Teachers may use journals to learn about their students in order to better connect their teaching to the students' concerns and interests. But often journals focus on academic learning, usually through responses to prompts. Banks (2005) describes one high school physics teacher who asked his students to respond to these three questions in their journals:

1. How can you determine the coefficient of friction if you know only the angle of the inclined plane?
2. Compare and contrast magnetic, electronic, and gravitational fields.
3. If you were to describe the physical concept of sound to your best friend, what music would you use to demonstrate this concept?

Informal assessments Ungraded (formative) assessments that gather information from multiple sources to help teachers make decisions.

TABLE 15.4 • **Aligning Different Assessment Tools With Their Targets**

Different learning outcomes require different assessment methods.

| ASSESSMENT METHOD | | | | |
|---|---|---|---|---|
| **Target to Be Assessed** | **Selected Response** | **Essay** | **Performance Assessment** | **Personal Communication** |
| **Knowledge Mastery** | Multiple-choice, true/false, matching, and fill-in can sample mastery of elements of knowledge | Essay exercises can tap understanding of relationships among elements of knowledge | Not a good choice for this target—three other options preferred | Can ask questions, evaluate answers, and infer mastery—but a time-consuming option |
| **Reasoning Proficiency** | Can assess understanding of basic patterns of reasoning | Written descriptions of complex problem solutions can provide a window into reasoning proficiency | Can watch students solve some problems and infer about reasoning proficiency | Can ask student to "think aloud" or can ask follow-up questions to probe reasoning |
| **Skills** | Can assess mastery of the prerequisites of skilful performance—but cannot tap the skill itself | Can assess mastery of the prerequisites of skilful performance—but cannot tap the skill itself | Can observe and evaluate skills as they are being performed | Strong match when skill is oral communication proficiency; also can assess mastery of knowledge prerequisite to skilful performance |
| **Ability to Create Products** | Can assess mastery of knowledge prerequisite to the ability to create quality products—but cannot assess the quality of products themselves | Can assess mastery of knowledge prerequisite to the ability to create quality products—but cannot assess the quality of products themselves | A strong match can assess: (a) proficiency in carrying out steps in product development and (b) attributes of the product itself | Can probe procedural knowledge and knowledge of attributes of quality products—but not product quality |

*Source: Based on Stiggins, R. J. (2002). Where Is Our Assessment Future and How Can We Get There? In R. W. Lissitz, W. D. Schafer (Eds.),* Meaningful Assessment: A Meaningful and Cooperative Process. *Allyn and Bacon: Boston, MA. © Pearson Education.*

When reading the students' journals, the teacher realized that many of the students' basic assumptions about friction, acceleration, and velocity came from personal experiences and not from scientific reasoning. His approach to teaching had to change to reach the students. The teacher never would have known to make the changes in his instruction without reading the journals (Banks, 2005).

There are many other kinds of informal assessments—keeping notes and observations about students' performance, rating scales, and checklists. Every time teachers ask questions or watch students perform skills, the teachers are conducting informal assessments. Look at Table 15.4, which summarizes the possibilities and limitations of aligning different assessment tools with their targets. One major message in this chapter is the importance of correctly matching the type of assessment tools used to the target—to what is being assessed.

 **Watch**
Involving Students in Assessments

**INVOLVING STUDENTS IN ASSESSMENTS.** One way to connect teaching and assessment while developing students' sense of efficacy for learning is to involve the students in the assessment process. Students can keep track of their own progress and assess their improvement. Here are other ideas, some taken from Stiggins and Chappuis (2005). Students might:

- Learn about the criteria for judging work by examining and discussing with a peer examples of good, average, and poor products or performances. Then pick a poor example and revise to improve it.
- Describe to the teacher or a peer (orally or in writing) the way they approached an assignment, the problems they encountered, the options they considered, and the final result.
- Analyze their strengths and weaknesses before starting a project, then discuss with the teacher or peers how they will use their strengths and overcome their weaknesses as they work on the project.
- In pairs, make up questions that might be on the test, explain why those are good questions, and then answer them together.
- Look back at earlier work and analyze how they have grown by describing "I used to think . . . but now I know. . . ." After doing a few of these analyses, summarize using a frame such as: What did I know before I started? What did I learn? What do I want to learn next?
- Before a major test, do a free write on these prompts "What exactly will be on the test?" "What kinds of questions will be asked (multiple-choice, essay, etc.)?" "How well will I do?" "What do I need to study to make sure I am ready?"

One last idea—the teacher arranges items on a test according to specific learning targets, and prepares a "test analysis" chart for students, with three boxes: "My strengths," "Quick review," and "Further study." After handing back the corrected test, students identify learning targets they have mastered and write them in the "My strengths" box. Next, students categorize their wrong answers as either "simple mistake" or "further study." Then, students list the simple mistakes in the "Quick review" box. Last, students write the rest of the learning targets represented by wrong answers in the "Further study" box.

No matter how you assess students, ultimately you will assign grades. We turn to that job next.

# GRADING

STOP & THINK Think back on your report cards and grades over the years. Did you ever receive a grade that was lower than you expected? How did you feel about yourself, the teacher, the subject, and school in general as a result of the lower grade? What could the teacher have done to help you understand and profit from the experience? •

In determining a final grade, the teacher must make a major decision. Should a student's grade reflect the student's status in comparison with the rest of the class, or should the grade reflect the amount of material learned and how well it has been learned? In other words, should grading be *norm-referenced* or *criterion-referenced*?

## Norm-Referenced Versus Criterion-Referenced Grading

In **norm-referenced grading**, the student's standing is based on a comparison with others who also took the course. If a student studies very successfully and almost everyone else does, too, the student may receive a disappointing grade, perhaps a C or D. One common type of norm-referenced grading is called **grading on the curve**. This system distributes grades in proportions based on the normal or bell-shaped curve so that only a few students receive very high or very low grades and most students receive grades between C+ and B−. How you feel about this approach probably depends on where your grades generally fall along that "curve." There is good evidence that this type of grading damages relationships among students and between teachers and students, and also diminishes motivation for most students (Krumboltz & Yeh, 1996). When you think about it, if the

**Norm-referenced grading** Assessment of students' achievement in relation to one another.

**Grading on the curve** Norm-referenced grading that compares students' performance to an average level.

## FIGURE 15.2

### A CRITERION-REFERENCED REPORT CARD

This is one example of a criterion-referenced report card. Other forms are possible, but all criterion-referenced reports indicate student progress toward specific goals.

**LINCOLN ELEMENTARY SCHOOL**
**GRADE 5**

Student _____  Teacher _____  Principal _Muriel Simms_  Quarter  2  3  4

E = Excellent  S = Satisfactory  P = Making Progress  N = Needs improvement

**READING PROGRAM**

Materials Used: _____
_____

____ Reads with understanding
____ Is able to write about what is read
____ Completes reading group work accurately and on time
____ Shows interest in reading

**Reading Skills**
____ Decodes new words
____ Understands new words

**Independent Reading Level**
Below/At Grade Level/Above

**LANGUAGE ARTS**
____ Uses oral language effectively
____ Listens carefully
____ Masters weekly spelling

**Writing skills**
____ Understands writing as process
____ Creates a rough draft
____ Makes meaningful revisions
____ Creates edited, legible final draft

**Editing skills**
____ Capitalizes
____ Punctuates
____ Uses complete sentences
____ Uses paragraphs
____ Demonstrates dictionary skills

**Writing skill level:**
Below/At Grade Level/Above

**MATHEMATICS**

**Problem Solving**
____ Solves teacher-generated problems
____ Solves self-/student-generated problems
____ Can create story problems

**Interpreting Problems**
____ Uses appropriate strategies
____ Can use more than one strategy
____ Can explain strategies in written form
____ Can explain strategies orally

**Math Concepts**
  **Understands Base Ten**
Beginning/Developing/Sophisticated
  **Multiplication, Basic facts**
Beginning/Developing/Sophisticated
  **2-Digit Multiplications**
Beginning/Developing/Sophisticated
  **Division**
Beginning/Developing/Sophisticated
  **Geometry**
Beginning/Developing/Sophisticated

**Overall Math Skill Level:**
Beginning/Developing/Sophisticated

**Attitude/Work Skills**
____ Welcomes a challenge
____ Persistent
____ Takes advantage of learning from others
____ Listens to others
____ Participates in discussion

**It Figures**
Is working on: _____

**Goals:** _____
Is working on achieving goal:
_____

**SOCIAL STUDIES**
____ Understands subject matter
____ Shows curiosity and enthusiasm
____ Contributes to class discussions
____ Uses map skills
____ Demonstrates control of reading skills by interpreting text
Topics covered: individual cultures, Columbus–first English colonies

**SCIENCE**
____ Shows curiosity about scientific subject matter
____ Asks good scientific questions
____ Shows knowledge of scientific method
____ Uses knowledge of scientific method to help set up and run experiment(s)
____ Makes good scientific observations
____ Has researched scientific topic(s)
  Topic(s) _____

**I Wonder**
Is currently working on_____
_____

**WORKING SKILLS**
____ Listens carefully
____ Follows directions
____ Works neatly and carefully
____ Checks work
____ Completes work on time
____ Uses time wisely
____ Works well independently
____ Works well in a group
____ Takes risks in learning
____ Welcomes a challenge

**HOMEWORK**
____ Self-selects homework
____ Completes work accurately
____ Completes work on time

**PRESENTATIONS/PROJECTS**
_____
_____

**HUMAN RELATIONS**
____ Shows courtesy
____ Respects rights of others
____ Shows self-control
____ Interacts well with peers
____ Shows a cooperative and positive attitude in class
____ Shows a cooperative attitude when asked to work with other students
____ Is willing to help other students
____ Works well with other adults (subs, student teacher, parents, etc.)

| Attendance | | | | |
|---|---|---|---|---|
| | 1st | 2nd | 3rd | 4th |
| Present | | | | |
| Absent | | | | |
| Tardy | | | | |

Placement for next year:

curve arbitrarily limits the number of good grades that can be given, then, in the game of grading, most students will be losers (Guskey & Bailey, 2001; Haladyna, 2002; Kohn, 1996b). Over 30 years ago, Benjamin Bloom (of Bloom's taxonomy) and his colleagues (1981) pointed out the fallacy of grading on the curve:

> There is nothing sacred about the normal curve. It is the distribution most appropriate to chance and random activity. Education is a purposeful activity, and we seek to have students learn what we have to teach. If we are effective in our instruction, the distribution

of achievement should be very different from the normal curve. In fact, we may even insist that our educational efforts have been unsuccessful to the extent that the distribution of achievement approximates the normal distribution. (pp. 52–53)

In **criterion-referenced grading**, the grade represents accomplishments. If clear objectives have been set for the course, the grade may represent a certain number of objectives met satisfactorily. When a criterion-referenced system is used, criteria for each grade generally are spelled out in advance. It is then up to the student to earn the grade she or he wants to receive. Theoretically, in this system, every student can achieve an A if every one reaches the criteria. Criterion-referenced grading has the advantage of relating judgments about a student to the achievement of clearly defined instructional goals. Some school districts have developed reporting systems where report cards list objectives along with judgments about the student's attainment of each. Reporting is done at the end of each unit of instruction. The elementary school report card shown in Figure 15.2 demonstrates the relationship between assessment and the goals of the unit.

Most schools have a specified grading system, so we won't spend time here on the many possible systems. Let's consider a different question—one with research behind it. What is the effect of grades on students?

## Effects of Grading on Students

When we think of grades, we often think of competition. Highly competitive classes may be particularly hard on anxious students, students who lack self-confidence, and students who are less prepared. So, although high standards and competition do tend to be generally related to increased academic learning, it is clear that a balance must be struck between high standards and a reasonable chance to succeed. Rick Stiggins and Jan Chappuis (2005) observe:

> From their very earliest school experiences, our students draw life-shaping conclusions about themselves as learners on the basis of the information we provide to them as a result of their teachers' classroom assessments. As the evidence accumulates over time, they decide if they are capable of succeeding or not. They decide whether the learning is worth the commitment it will take to attain it. They decide . . . whether to risk investing in the schooling experience. These decisions are crucial to their academic well-being. (p. 11)

It may sound as though low grades and failure should be avoided in school. But the situation is not that simple.

THE VALUE OF FAILING?   After reviewing many years of research on the effects of failure from several perspectives, Margaret Clifford (1990, 1991) concluded:

> It is time for educators to replace easy success with challenge. We must encourage students to reach beyond their intellectual grasp and allow them the privilege of learning from mistakes. There must be a tolerance for error-making in every classroom, and gradual success rather than continual success must become the yardstick by which learning is judged. (1990, p. 23)

Some level of failure may be helpful for most students, especially if teachers help their students see connections between hard work and improvement. Efforts to protect students from failure and to guarantee success may be counterproductive. Carol Tomlinson, an expert on differentiated instruction, puts it this way: "Students whose learning histories have caused them to believe that excellence can be achieved with minimal effort do not learn to expend effort, and yet perceive that high grades are an entitlement for them" (2005b, p. 266). So maybe not failure, but accurate and critical feedback can be especially important for students who are used to easy As (Shute, 2008).

RETENTION IN GRADE.   So far, we have been talking about the effects of failing a test or perhaps a course. But what about the effect of failing an entire grade—that is, of being "held back"? Is retention a good policy? See the *Point/Counterpoint* to examine the issue.

Criterion-referenced grading Assessment of each student's mastery of course objectives.

## POINT/COUNTERPOINT    Should Children Be Held Back?

For the past 100 years, parents and educators have debated about the value of retention versus *social promotion* (passing students on to the next grade with their peers). What does the evidence say? What are the arguments?

**POINT**

▶ **Yes, it just makes sense.** Retention in kindergarten for children considered "not ready" for grade 1 is a common practice. Compared to students who are relatively younger (born September to November), students who are relatively older (January to August birthdays) have higher achievement in school on average (Cobley, McKenna, Baker, & Wattie, 2009). In fact, some parents hold their son or daughter back to give the child an edge over peers in each grade thereafter or because the child was born late in the year—a practice sometimes called "academic red-shirting." The results on academic "red-shirting" are mixed. Some studies have found benefits for students who have been held back by their parents, but other studies have found no benefits.

With the increased emphasis on high standards and accountability, the idea of social promotion has come under fire and retention is seen as the better way. Guanglei Hong and Stephen Raudenbush (2005) summarize this and other arguments that have been made in favour of retention:

*A widely endorsed argument is that, when low-achieving students are retained in a grade, the academic status of children in a classroom will become more homogeneous, easing the teacher's task of managing instructional activities (Byrnes, 1989; also see Shepard & Smith, 1988, for a review). In particular, retaining some children in kindergarten may allow the first-grade teacher to teach at a higher level, benefiting those who would be promoted under the policy. Meanwhile, children who view grade retention as a punishment may study harder to avoid being retained in the future. Some have argued that, in comparison with the social promotion policy, repeating a grade is perhaps developmentally more appropriate and may make learning more meaningful for children who are struggling (Plummer & Graziano, 1987; Smith & Shepard, 1988). If these arguments are correct, adopting a policy of grade retention will benefit those promoted and those retained, thus boosting achievement overall. (p. 206)*

**COUNTERPOINT**

▶ **No, retention is not effective.** After summarizing the arguments in favour of kindergarten retention, Hong and Raudenbush (2005) reviewed the findings of almost a century of research. They noted that even though there are a small number of studies that support the value of retention, the weight of the evidence indicates that it is not helpful and may even be harmful. Most research finds that grade retention is associated with poor long-term outcomes such as dropping out of school, higher arrest rates, fewer job opportunities, lower self-esteem (Jimerson, 1999; Jimerson, Anderson, & Whipple, 2002; Jimerson & Ferguson, 2007; Shepard & Smith, 1989). In a study of children in Manitoba, even after taking into account students' socioeconomic status, the frequency they had changed schools, and other factors, being retained in a grade strongly predicted withdrawal from school: "Retention does not solve the problems of children struggling in school, it exacerbates these problems" (Guèvremont, Roos, & Brownell, 2007).

The study by Hong and Raudenbush (2005) examined data on 11 843 kindergarten students in the United States who participated in a longitudinal study that followed them to the end of grade 1. The researchers were able to compare retained and promoted students from schools that practice retention as well as promoted students from schools that practice social promotion. They found no evidence that retention improved either reading or mathematics achievement. In addition, retention did not seem to improve instruction in grade 1 by making the class more similar in academic ability. After one year, the retained students were an average of one year behind, and evidence indicated that these children would have done better if promoted. The researchers concluded that retention "seemed to have constrained the learning potential for all but the highest-risk children" (p. 220). Another U.S. study that followed retained and promoted students for four years found some short-term advantages for retained students in social and behavioural skills, followed by long-term problems and vulnerabilities. The authors suggested that the "struggle-succeed-struggle" pattern may undermine academic motivation for retained students and interfere with peer relations (Wu, West, & Hughes, 2010).

**Beware of Either/Or: Using Research for Children.** No matter what, children who are having trouble should get help, whether they are promoted or retained. However, just covering the same material again in the same way won't solve the children's academic or social problems. According to Jeannie Oakes (1999), social promotion as it is sometimes thought of—just promoting children into the next grade—is not something any sensible person would advocate. The best approach may be to promote the children along with their peers, but to give them special programming during the summer or over the next year (Mantzicopoulos & Morrison, 1992). In addition, because the inability to focus attention and self-regulate is an important aspect of readiness to learn (Blair, 2002), help should also focus on improving these skills as well. An even better approach would be to prevent the problems before they occur by providing extra resources in the early years (McCoy & Reynolds, 1999).

Matthew Benoit/Shutterstock

## Grades and Motivation

If you are relying on grades to motivate students, you had better think again (Smith, Smith, & De Lisi, 2001). The assessments you give should support students' motivation to learn—not their motivation to work for a good grade. But is there really a difference between working for a grade and working to learn? The answer depends in part on how a grade is determined. If you test only at a simple but detailed level of knowledge, you may force students to choose between complex learning and a good grade. But when a grade reflects meaningful learning, working for a grade and working to learn become the same thing. As a teacher, you can use grades to motivate the kind of learning you intend students to achieve in your course. Finally, low grades generally do not encourage greater efforts. Students receiving low grades are more likely to withdraw, blame others, decide that the work is "dumb," or feel responsible for the low grade but helpless to make improvements. They give up on themselves or on school (Tomlinson, 2005b). Rather than assigning a failing grade, you might consider the work incomplete and give students support in revising or improving. Maintain high standards and give students a chance to reach them (Guskey, 2011; Guskey & Bailey, 2001).

Another effect on motivation that occurs in high schools is the race for valedictorian. Sometimes, students and families find clever ways to move ahead of the competition—but the strategies have little to do with learning. As Tom Guskey and Jane Bailey (2001) note, when a valedictorian wins by a 1/1000 of decimal point, how meaningful is the learning behind the difference? Some high schools now name multiple valedictorians—as many as meet the highest standards of the school—because they believe that the educators' job is "not to select talent, but, rather, to develop talent" (Guskey & Bailey, 2001, p. 39).

The *Guidelines* give ideas for using any grading system in a fair and reasonable way.

## Beyond Grading: Communicating With Families

No number or letter grade conveys the totality of a student's experience in a class or course. Students, families, and teachers sometimes are too focused on the end point—the grade. But communicating with families should involve more than just sending home grades. There are a number of ways to communicate with and report to families. Many teachers have a beginning-of-the-year newsletter or student handbook that communicates homework, behaviour, and grading policies to families. Other options described by Guskey and Bailey (2001) are:

- notes attached to report cards
- phone calls, especially "good news" calls
- school open houses
- student-led conferences
- portfolios or exhibits of student work
- homework hotlines
- school or class webpages
- home visits

Conferences with parents or caregivers are often expected of teachers in elementary school and can be equally important in middle and high school. Clearly, the more skilled teachers are at communicating, the more effective they will be at conducting these conferences. Listening and problem-solving skills such as those discussed in Chapter 13 can be particularly important. When you are dealing with families or students who are angry or upset, make sure you really hear their concerns, not just their words. The atmosphere should be friendly and unrushed. Any observations about the student should be as factual as possible, based on observation or information from assignments. Information gained from a student or a parent/caregiver should be kept confidential.

One kind of information that will interest parents is their child's standardized test scores. We look at these tests in the next section.

## GUIDELINES

### Using Any Grading System

**Explain your grading policies to students early in the course and remind them of the policies regularly.**
*Examples*

1. Give older students a handout describing the assignments, tests, grading criteria, and schedule.
2. Explain to younger students in a low-pressure manner how their work will be evaluated.

**Base grades on clearly specified, reasonable standards.**
*Examples*

1. Specify standards by developing a rubric with students—have anonymous examples of poor, good, and excellent work from previous classes.
2. Discuss workload and grading standards with more experienced teachers.
3. Give a few formative tests to get a sense of your students' knowledge and skills before you give a graded test.
4. Take tests yourself first to gauge the difficulty of the test and to estimate the time your students will need.

**Base your grades on as much objective evidence as possible.**
*Examples*

1. Plan in advance how and when you will test.
2. Keep a portfolio of student work. This may be useful in student or parent conferences.

**Be sure students understand test directions.**
*Examples*

1. Outline the directions on the board.
2. Ask several students to explain the directions.
3. Go over a sample question first.

**Correct, return, and discuss test questions as soon as possible.**
*Examples*

1. Have students who wrote good answers read their responses for the class; make sure they are not the same students each time.
2. Discuss why wrong answers, especially popular wrong choices, are incorrect.
3. As soon as students finish a test, give them the answers to questions and the page numbers where answers are discussed in the text.

**As a rule, do not change a grade.**
*Examples*

1. Make sure you can defend the grade in the first place.
2. *Do* change clerical or calculation errors.

**Guard against bias in grading.**
*Examples*

1. Ask students to put their names on the backs of their papers.
2. Use an objective point system or model papers when grading essays.

**Keep pupils informed of their standing in the class.**
*Examples*

1. Write the distribution of scores on the board after tests.
2. Schedule periodic conferences to go over work from previous weeks.

## STANDARDIZED TESTING

For as long as we can remember, educators and policy-makers have been concerned about students' performance on tests, particularly standardized tests. These tests are common in several provinces, particularly in reading, mathematics, and science. Understanding what standardized test scores really mean and how they can be used and misused is critical. Let's look first at the results you will see from these tests—the scores. First, we examine scores used when commercially developed tests are employed, such as an intelligence test or a diagnostic test. Then we consider reports from provincial tests, which are usually presented in terms of "meeting expectations."

### Types of Scores for Commercially Developed Tests

**STOP & THINK** At your first parent conference, a mother and father are concerned about their child's IQ score of 86. They say that they expect their child to "get close to 100%." Do they understand the meaning of these scores? •

**Give students the benefit of the doubt. All measurement techniques involve error.**
*Examples*
1. Unless there is a very good reason not to, give the higher grade in borderline cases.
2. If a large number of students miss the same question in the same way, revise the question for the future and consider throwing it out for that test.

**Avoid reserving high grades and high praise for answers that conform to your ideas or to those in the textbook.**
*Examples*
1. Give extra points for correct and creative answers.
2. Withhold your opinions until all sides of an issue have been explored.
3. Reinforce students for disagreeing in a rational, productive manner.
4. Give partial credit for partially correct answers.

**Make sure each student has a reasonable chance to be successful, especially at the beginning of a new task.**
*Examples*
1. Pretest students to make sure they have prerequisite abilities.
2. When appropriate, provide opportunities for students to retest to raise their grades, but make sure the retest is as difficult as the original.
3. Consider failing efforts as "incomplete," and encourage students to revise and improve.
4. Base grades more on work at the end of the unit; give ungraded work in the beginning of the unit.

**Balance written and oral feedback.**
*Examples*
1. Consider giving short, lively written comments with younger students and more extensive written comments with older students.
2. When the grade on a paper is lower than the student might have expected, be sure the reason for the lower grade is clear.
3. Tailor comments to the individual student's performance; avoid writing the same phrases over and over.
4. Note specific errors, possible reasons for errors, ideas for improvement, and work done well.

**Make grades as meaningful as possible.**
*Examples*
1. Tie grades to the mastery of important objectives.
2. Give ungraded assignments to encourage exploration.
3. Experiment with performances and portfolios.

**Base grades on more than just one criterion.**
*Examples*
1. Use essay questions as well as multiple-choice items on a test.
2. Grade oral reports and class participation.

---

*For more thoughts about grading, see*
http://www.bced.gov.bc.ca/classroom_assessment/09_report_student_prog.pdf.

*Source:* Based on Drayer, A. M. (1979). General conferencing guidelines adapted from *Problems in Middle and High School Teaching: A Handbook for Student Teachers and Beginning Teachers* (pp. 182–187). Boston: Allyn and Bacon. © Allyn and Bacon.

---

To understand the scores from some standardized tests, you need to know some basics about different types of scores and what they tell you. But first you should be familiar with some easy statistics.

MEASUREMENTS OF CENTRAL TENDENCY AND STANDARD DEVIATION. You have probably had a great deal of experience with means. A **mean** is simply the arithmetical average of a group of scores. You know how calculate the mean: Add the scores and divide the sum by the number of scores. The mean is one way to describe **central tendency**, a score that is typical or representative of the whole set or distribution of scores. Very high or very low scores—outliers—affect the mean. Two other measures of central tendency are the median and the mode. The **median** is the middle score in a ranked list of scores. It's the point at which half the scores are larger and half are smaller. When there are a few very high or low scores, the median may be a better representative of the central tendency of a group than the mean. The **mode** is the score that occurs most often.

A score at the mean, median, or mode is representative of the set of scores, but it does not tell you anything about how the scores spread out around that point. Two sets of scores may both have a mean of 50, but be alike in no other way. Consider these two

**Mean** Arithmetical average.

**Central tendency** Typical score for a group of scores.

**Median** Middle score in a group of scores.

**Mode** Most frequently occurring score.

sets of scores: 45, 45, 50, 50, 50, 55, and 55; and scores of 0, 10, 50, 50, 50, 90, and 100. In both cases, the mean, median, and mode are all 50, but how the scores are distributed across the scale from 0 to 100 is quite different.

The **standard deviation** is a measure of how widely the scores vary around the mean. The larger the standard deviation, the more spread out the scores are. The smaller the standard deviation, the more the scores are clustered near the mean. For example, in the set of scores 45, 45, 50, 50, 50, 55, and 55, the standard deviation is much smaller than in the distribution 1, 10, 50, 50, 50, 90, and 100. Another way of saying this is that distributions with very small standard deviations have less **variability** in the scores.

Knowing the mean and the standard deviation of a set of scores gives you a clearer picture of the meaning of an individual score relative to others. For example, suppose you received a score of 78 on a test. You would be very pleased with the score if the mean of the test were 70 and the standard deviation were 4. In this case, your score would be 2 standard deviations above the mean, a score very much above average.

Consider the difference if the mean of the test had remained at 70, but the standard deviation had been 20. In this second case, your score of 78 would be less than 1 standard deviation from the mean. You would be much closer to the middle of the group, with a score above average, but not high. Knowing the standard deviation tells you much more than simply knowing the **range** of scores, the difference between the highest and the lowest scores. That's because one or two really extreme scores make the range large but can't be taken as evidence that other scores are widely variable.

THE NORMAL DISTRIBUTION.   Standard deviations are especially helpful if the results of the tests form a **normal distribution**. You know about the normal distribution. It is the bell-shaped curve that describes many naturally occurring physical and social phenomena. In a normal distribution, many scores fall in the middle, giving the curve its bell appearance. You find fewer and fewer scores as you look out toward the far right and far left, or *tails*, of the distribution. The normal distribution has been thoroughly analyzed by statisticians. The mean of a normal distribution is also its midpoint. Half the scores are above the mean, and half are below it. In a normal distribution, the mean, median, and mode are all the same point.

Another very helpful property of the normal distribution is that it is easy to determine what percentage of scores fall between two scores. In Figure 15.3, you can see that a student scoring within plus or minus 1 standard deviation of the mean has lots of company. Many scores pile up here. In fact, 68% of all scores are located in the curve from 1 standard deviation below to 1 standard deviation above the mean. Only about 16% of the scores are higher than 1 standard deviation above the mean. And within this higher group, only 2% are higher than 2 standard deviations above the mean. Because the curve has the same properties on the side to the left of the mean, only about 16% of the scores are less than 1 standard deviation below the mean, and in that group only about 2% are lower than 2 standard deviations below the mean. At 2 standard deviations from the mean in either direction, the scorer has left the pack.

Many commercially developed tests used in Canadian schools are engineered so their scores have a normal distribution. For example, the Stanford-Binet Intelligence Scales combines scores from 10 subscales to create a full-scale score. Full-scale scores are normed to have a mean of 100 points and a standard deviation of 15 points. A student scoring 115 points would be 1 standard deviation above the mean. About 84% of students have scores lower than this, and 16% have higher scores.

Now we are ready to look at different kinds of test scores.

PERCENTILE RANK SCORES.   Ranking is the basis for one very useful kind of score reported on some standardized tests, a **percentile rank** score. In percentile ranking, each student's *raw score* (actual number correct) is compared with the raw scores of the students in the *norm group* (comparison group). The percentage of students in the norm group who scored at or below a particular raw score is the percentile rank. If Phil's score were the same as or higher than three-quarters of students in the norm group, Phil would score at the *75th percentile*, and he would have a percentile rank of 75. It's important

---

Standard deviation Measure of how widely scores vary from the mean.

Variability Degree of difference or deviation from mean.

Range Distance between the highest and the lowest scores in a group.

Normal distribution The most commonly occurring distribution, in which scores are distributed evenly around the mean.

Percentile rank Percentage of those in the norming sample who scored at or below an individual's score.

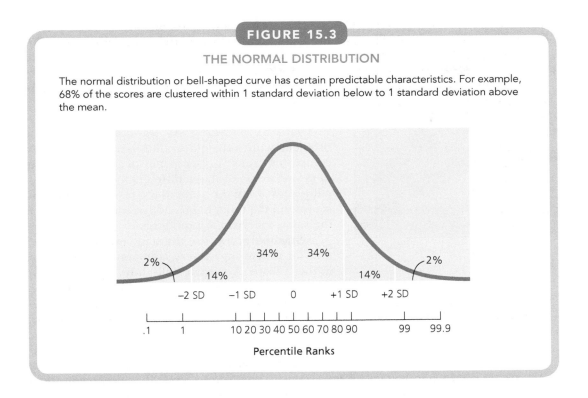

**FIGURE 15.3**

**THE NORMAL DISTRIBUTION**

The normal distribution or bell-shaped curve has certain predictable characteristics. For example, 68% of the scores are clustered within 1 standard deviation below to 1 standard deviation above the mean.

to realize that Phil's percentile score does not mean he had a raw score of 75 correct answers or that he answered 75% of the questions correctly. The 75 refers to the percentage of people in the norm group whose scores on the test were equal to or below his. A percentile rank of 50 means that a student has scored as well as or better than 50% of the norm group and has achieved an average score.

Be cautious when interpreting percentile scores. Differences between percentile ranks do not match differences in raw score points. For example, the difference between the 50th and 60th percentile near the middle of a set of scores might be just 2 raw points, whereas the difference on the same test between the 90th and 99th percentile, far on the high side of scores, could be about 10 points. Just one or two answers right or wrong can make a bigger difference in percentile scores if you are near the middle.

GRADE-EQUIVALENT SCORES.  **Grade-equivalent scores** are generally obtained from separate norm groups for each grade level. The average of the scores of all the grade 10 students in the norm group defines the grade 10 equivalent score. Suppose the raw-score average of the grade 10 norm group is 38. Any student who attains a raw score of 38 on that test will be assigned a grade-equivalent score of grade 10. Grade-equivalent scores are generally listed in numbers such as 8.3, 4.5, 7.6, 11.5, and so on. The whole number gives the grade. The decimals stand for tenths of a year, but they are usually interpreted as months.

Suppose a student with the grade-equivalent score of 10 is in grade 7. Should this student be promoted immediately? No. Different forms of tests are used at different grade levels. So the grade 7 student may not have had to answer items that would be given to students in higher grades. This student's high score represents superior mastery of material at the grade 7 level rather than a capacity for doing advanced work. Even though an average grade 10 student could do as well as our grade 7 student on this particular test, the grade 10 student would certainly know much more than was covered in this test for grade 7 students. Also, grade-equivalent score units do not mean the same thing at every grade level. For example, a grade 2 student reading at the grade 1 level would have more trouble in school than a grade 11 student who reads at the grade 10 level.

**Grade-equivalent score** Measure of grade level based on comparison with norming samples from each grade.

**STANDARDIZED TESTS** You can tell these students are concentrating. What will their scores tell us? What do they mean?

Mary Ann Chastain/AP Images

Because grade-equivalent scores are misleading and often misinterpreted, especially by parents, most educators and psychologists strongly believe *they should not be used at all*. We agree. There are other forms of reporting available that are more appropriate.

**STANDARD SCORES.**   As we noted earlier, one problem with percentile ranks is the difficulty in comparing ranks. A discrepancy of a certain number of raw-score points has a different meaning at different places along the scale of the test. With standard scores, on the other hand, a difference of 5 points is the same everywhere on the scale.

**Standard scores** use the standard deviation as a unit for measuring. A very common standard score is the **z score**. A *z* score tells how many standard deviations a raw score is above or below the mean. In the example described earlier, in which you scored 78 on a test where the mean was 70 and the standard deviation was 4, your *z* score would be +2, exactly 2 standard deviations above the mean. If your friend scored 64 on this test, that score is 1.5 standard deviation units below the mean, and the *z* score would be −1.5. A *z* score of 0 would be no standard deviations above the mean—in other words, right on the mean. Measurements similar to *z* scores are used when you take a bone density test. Your score will compare your bone density to that of a healthy 30-year-old. If your score is below −1, you are moving toward osteoporosis. Below −2, you are there.

To calculate the *z* score for a given raw score, subtract the mean from the raw score and divide the difference by the standard deviation. The formula is:

$$z = \frac{\text{Raw Score} - \text{Mean}}{\text{Standard Deviation}}$$

Because it is often inconvenient to use negative numbers, other standard scores have been devised. The **T score** has a mean of 50 and uses a standard deviation of 10. Thus, a *T* score of 50 indicates average performance. If you multiply the *z* score by 10 (which eliminates the decimal) and add 50 (which gets rid of the negative number), you get the equivalent *T* score as the answer. The person whose *z* score was −1.5 would have a *T* score of 35.

First multiply the *z* score by 10:   $-1.5 \times 10 = -15$
Then add 50:   $-15 + 50 = 35$

**DISCUSSING TEST RESULTS WITH FAMILIES.**   Teachers often have formal conferences and informal talks with parents or caregivers. Often the topic is testing results. At times, you will be expected to explain or describe test results to your students' families. The *Family and Community Partnerships Guidelines* give some ideas.

## Accountability and High-Stakes Testing

**Standard scores** Scores based on the standard deviation.

**z score** Standard score indicating the number of standard deviations above or below the mean.

**T score** Standard score with a mean of 50 and a standard deviation of 10.

**STOP & THINK** How has standardized testing affected your life so far? What opportunities have been opened or closed to you based on test scores? Was the process fair? •

Every day, there are many decisions made about individuals that are based on the results of tests. Should Russell be issued a driver's licence? How many and which students from grade 8 would benefit from an accelerated program in science? Who needs extra tutoring? Who will be admitted to university or professional school? Test scores may affect

**GUIDELINES** — FAMILY AND COMMUNITY PARTNERSHIPS —

## Conferences and Explaining Test Results

### GENERAL CONFERENCING GUIDELINES

**Decide on a few clear goals for the conference.**
*Examples*

- gathering information about the student to help in your instruction
- explaining grades or test results
- letting parents know what is coming during the next unit or marking period
- soliciting help from parents
- making suggestions for use at home

**Begin and end with a positive statement.**
*Examples*

"Jacob is a natural leader."

"Eve really enjoys the science centre."

"Yesim is really supportive when other students are upset."

"Ashanti's sense of humour keeps the class positive."

**Listen actively.**
*Examples*

Accept the emotions of parents or caregivers. Don't try to talk them out of what they feel.

"You seem to feel frustrated when Lee doesn't do his homework."

**Respect family members' time and their concern about their child—establish a partnership.**
*Examples*

Speak plainly, briefly, and avoid jargon.

Be tactful, but don't avoid talking about tough issues.

Ask families to follow through on class goals at home: "Ask Ashley for her homework checklist and help her keep it up to date. I will do the same at school."

**Learn from the family members.**
*Examples*

What are the students' strengths as revealed in hobbies or extracurricular activities?

What are the students' interests?

**Follow-up and follow through.**
*Examples*

Send a brief note thanking the family members for attending.

Share student successes through notes or email messages.

Keep families informed before problems develop.

### EXPLAINING AND USING TEST RESULTS

**Explain, in nontechnical terms, what each type of score on the test report means and why tests are not "perfect."**
*Examples*

1. If the test is norm-referenced, know what the comparison group was (national, provincial, district). Explain that the child's score shows how he or she performed in relation to the other students in the comparison group.
2. If the test is criterion-referenced, explain that the scores show how well their child performs specific tasks such as word problems or reading comprehension.
3. Encourage parents to think of the score not as a single point, but as a range or band that includes the score.
4. Ignore small differences between scores.

**For norm-referenced tests, use percentile scores. They are the easiest to understand.**
*Examples*

1. Percentile scores tell what percentage of students in the comparison group made the same score or lower—higher percentiles are better, and 99 is as high as you can get: 50 is average.
2. Percentile scores do not tell the "percent correct," so scores that would be bad on a classroom test (say 65% to 75% or so) often are above average—even good—as percentile scores.

**Avoid using grade-equivalent scores.**
*Examples*

1. If parents want to focus on the "grade level" of their child, tell them that high grade-equivalent scores reflect a thorough understanding of the current grade level and *not* the capacity to do higher grade-level work.
2. Tell parents that the same grade-equivalent score has different meanings in different subjects—reading versus mathematics, for example.

*Source:* Based on ideas from Fromberg, D. P., & Driscoll, M. (2011). *The Successful Classroom: Management Strategies for Regular and Special Education Teachers.* Teachers College, Columbia University: Scholastic; Planning for parent conferences, www2.scholastic.com/browse/article.jsp?id=4194

*For more help explaining tests to parents, see* http://pareonline.net/getvn.asp?v=1&n=1.

progressions thorugh the grades, high school graduation, access to special programs, placement in special education classes, and opportunities for scholarships and school funding.

MAKING DECISIONS.   In making these decisions, it is important to distinguish between the *quality* of the test itself and the way the test is *used*. Even the best assessments can be, and have been, misused. Years ago, for example, using otherwise valid and reliable individual intelligence tests, many students were inappropriately identified as having mental retardation, the term used at that time (Snapp & Woolfolk, 1973). The problem was not with the tests, but with the fact that the test score was the only information used to classify students. Much more information is always needed to make this type of placement decision.

Behind all the statistics and terminology are issues related to values and ethics. Who will be tested? What are the consequences of choosing one test over another for a particular purpose with a given group? What is the effect of the testing on the students? How will the test scores of minority-group students be interpreted? What do we really mean by *intelligence, competence,* and *scholastic aptitude*? Do our views agree with those implied by the tests we use to measure these constructs? How will test results be integrated with other information about the individual to make judgments? Answering these questions requires choices based on values, as well as accurate information about what tests can and cannot tell us. Keep these values issues in mind as we examine testing uses and decisions.

Because the decisions affected by test scores are so critical, many educators call this process **high-stakes testing**. One of the high-stakes uses for test results is to hold teachers, schools, and administrators **accountable** for student performance. For example, the Fraser Institute uses provincially administered tests in Alberta, British Columbia, Ontario, and Quebec as some of the data for ranking schools. We've already noted issues with interpreting ranks. As you might predict, there is quite a bit of controversy surrounding such practices.

Teachers are often frustrated that test results can come too late in the year to help them plan instruction or remediation for their current students. They also are troubled by the amount of time that testing takes—to prepare for the tests and to give them. They complain that the tests cover material that their curriculum does not include. Are they right?

DOCUMENTED PROBLEMS WITH HIGH-STAKES TESTING.   When so much can ride on the results of a test, you would assume that the test actually measured what had been taught. In the past, this match has been a problem. Recently, the overlap between what is taught and what is tested has been improving, but it still makes sense to be aware of possible mismatches.

What about time? In Canada, we lack research about how much time teachers devote to preparing for provincial examinations. Another unintended consequence of the early-warning testing in elementary school may be to nudge students who believe they are not going to do well to leave school. No matter how good the test, some uses of high-stakes tests are not appropriate. Table 15.5 describes some of them.

USING HIGH-STAKES TESTING WELL.   To be valuable, testing programs must have a number of characteristics. Of course, the tests used must be reliable, valid for the purposes used, and free of bias. In addition, the testing program must:

1. Match the content standards of the district—this is a vital part of reaching valid interpretations of test scores.
2. Be part of the larger assessment plan. No individual test provides all the necessary information about student achievement. It is critical that schools avoid making pass/fail decisions based on a single test.
3. Test complex thinking, not just basic skills and factual knowledge.
4. Provide alternate assessment strategies for students with identifiable disabilities.
5. Provide opportunities for retesting when the stakes are high.

High-stakes testing Standardized tests whose results have powerful influences when used by school administrators, other officials, or employers to make decisions.

Accountable Making teachers and schools responsible for student learning, usually by monitoring learning with high-stakes tests.

TABLE 15.5 • **Inappropriate Uses for High-Stakes Test Results**

Beware of some uses for standardized test results. Tests were not designed for these purposes.

| | |
|---|---|
| **Province-to-Province Comparisons** | You cannot really compare provinces using standardized test scores. Provinces do not have the same curriculum, tests, resources, or challenges. If comparisons are made, they usually tell us what we already know—some provinces have more funding for schools and families with higher incomes or education levels. |
| **Evaluation of Teachers or Schools** | Many influences on test scores—family and community resources—are outside the control of teachers and schools. Often students move from school to school, so many students taking a test in spring may have been in the school only for a few weeks. |
| **Identifying Where to Buy a House** | Generally speaking, the schools with the highest test scores are in the neighbourhoods where families have the highest levels of education and income. They may not be the "best schools" in terms of teaching, programs, or leadership, but they are the schools lucky enough to have the "right" students. |

*Source: Adapted from Haladyna, T. H. (2002). Essentials of Standardized Achievement Testing: Validity and Accountability. Allyn and Bacon: Boston, MA. © Pearson Education. Adapted by permission of the publisher.*

6. Include all students in the testing, but also provide informative reports of the results that make the students' situations clear if they have special challenges or circumstances such as disabilities.
7. Provide appropriate remediation when students fail.
8. Make sure all students taking the test have adequate opportunities to learn the material being tested.
9. Take into account the student's language. Students who have difficulty reading or writing in English will not perform well on tests that require English proficiency.
10. Use test results for children, not against them (Haladyna, 2002).

This is important, so we will repeat it: High-stakes standardized **achievement tests** must be chosen so that the items on the test actually measure knowledge gained in the classes. Also, students must have the necessary skills to take the test. If students score low on a science test not because they lack knowledge about science, but because they have difficulty reading the questions, don't speak English fluently, or have too little time to finish, then the test is not a good basis for validly interpreting science achievement for those students.

## Reaching Every Student: Helping Students With Disabilities Prepare for High-Stakes Tests

Erik Carter and his colleagues (2005) tested a procedure for preparing students with learning disabilities, mild intellectual disabilities, and language impairments for a high-stakes test. The students were ages 15 to 19; over half were males from a minority and all had IEPs (Individual Educational Programs—see Chapter 4) to guide their education. All were struggling in school. Over six class periods, an instructor taught the students strategies such as how to fill in bubbles on answer sheets completely, sorting problems by difficulty and doing the easy ones first, using rounding to estimate answers in math, identifying exactly what the question is asking by underlining key words and phrases, and eliminating alternatives that have redundant information or extreme qualifiers.

**Achievement tests** Standardized tests measuring how much students have learned in a given content area.

## GUIDELINES

### Preparing Yourself and Your Students for Testing

#### ADVICE FOR TEACHERS

**Make sure the test actually covers the content of the unit of study.**
*Examples*

1. Compare test questions to course objectives. Make sure that there is good overlap.
2. Check to see if the test is long enough to cover all important topics.
3. Find out if there are any difficulties your students experience with the test, such as not enough time, too difficult a level of reading, and so on. If there are, discuss these problems with appropriate school personnel.

**Make sure students know how to use all the test materials.**
*Examples*

1. Several days before the testing, do a few practice questions with a similar format.
2. Demonstrate the use of the answer sheets, especially computer-scored answer sheets.
3. Check with new students, shy students, slower students, and students who have difficulty reading to make sure they understand the questions.
4. Make sure students know if and when guessing is appropriate.

**Follow instructions for administering the test exactly.**
*Examples*

1. Practise giving the test before you actually use it.
2. Follow the time limits exactly.

**Make students as comfortable as possible during testing.**
*Examples*

1. Do not create anxiety by making the test seem like the most important event of the year.

2. Help the class relax before beginning the test, perhaps by telling a joke or having everyone take a few deep breaths. Don't be tense yourself!
3. Make sure the room is quiet.
4. Discourage cheating by monitoring the room. Don't become absorbed in your own paperwork.

#### ADVICE FOR STUDENTS

**Use the night before the test effectively.**
*Examples*

1. Study the night before the exam, ending with a final look at a summary of the key points, concepts, and relationships.
2. Get a good night's sleep. If you know you generally have trouble sleeping the night before an exam, try getting extra sleep on several previous nights.

**Set the situation so you can concentrate on the test.**
*Examples*

1. Give yourself plenty of time to eat and get to the exam room.
2. Don't sit near a friend. It may make concentration difficult. If your friend leaves early, you may be tempted to do so, too.

**Make sure you know what the test is asking.**
*Examples*

1. Read the directions carefully. If you are unsure, ask the instructor or proctor for clarification.
2. Read each question carefully to spot tricky words, such as *not, except, all of the following but one.*
3. On an essay test, read every question first, so you know the size of the job ahead of you and can make informed decisions about how much time to spend on each question.
4. On a multiple-choice test, read every alternative, even if an early one seems right.

The good news is that after completing the preparation program, students improved their scores on the tests. But the bad news is that the increases were not large enough to bring most of the students to the passing level. The authors recommend that preparation for testing should occur much earlier for students with disabilities. At an average age of 16, the students in this study already were discouraged. The strategies taught should be closely aligned with the specific types of problems that the students will encounter on the test and should be embedded in good content instruction. Finally, these students often are anxious about the negative consequences of failing—not receiving a regular diploma, or no access to college or trade school. The best way to deal with this anxiety is to better equip the students with the academic skills they will need to succeed (Carter et al., 2005). The *Guidelines* should help you and all your students prepare for high-stakes testing.

**Use time effectively.**
*Examples*

1. Begin working right away and move as rapidly as possible while your energy is high.
2. Do the easy questions first.
3. Don't get stuck on one question. If you are stumped, mark the question so you can return to it easily later, and go on to questions you can answer more quickly.
4. On a multiple-choice test, if you know you will not have time to finish, fill in all the remaining questions with the same letter if there is no penalty for guessing.
5. If you are running out of time on an essay test, do not leave any questions blank. Briefly outline a few key points to show the instructor you knew the answer but needed more time.

**Know when to guess on multiple-choice or true-false tests.**
*Examples*

1. Always guess when only right answers are scored.
2. Always guess when you can eliminate some of the alternatives.
3. Don't guess if there is a penalty for guessing, unless you can confidently eliminate at least one alternative.
4. Are correct answers always longer? Shorter? In the middle? More likely to be one letter? More often true than false?
5. Does the grammar give the right answer away or eliminate any alternatives?

**Check your work.**
*Examples*

1. Even if you can't stand to look at the test another minute, reread each question to make sure you answered the way you intended.

2. If you are using a machine-scored answer sheet, check occasionally to be sure the number of the question you are answering corresponds to the number of the answer on the sheet.

**On essay tests, answer as directly as possible.**
*Examples*

1. Avoid flowery introductions. Answer the question in the first sentence and then elaborate.
2. Don't save your best ideas till last. Give them early in the answer.
3. Unless the instructor requires complete sentences, consider listing points, arguments, and so on by number in your answer. It will help you organize your thoughts and concentrate on the important aspects of the answer.

**Learn from the testing experience.**
*Examples*

1. Pay attention when the teacher reviews the answers. You can learn from your mistakes, and the same question may reappear in a later test.
2. Notice if you are having trouble with a particular kind of item; adjust your study approach next time to handle this type of item better.

---

*For more test-taking strategies see* www.testtakingtips.com.

## Lessons for Teachers: Quality Assessment

Quality teaching and quality assessment share the same basic principles, and these principles hold for all students. Carol Tomlinson (2005b, pp. 265–266) suggests that good instruction and good grading both depend on a teacher who:

- is aware of and responds to student differences
- specifies clear learning outcomes
- uses pretests and formative assessments to monitor student progress toward learning goals
- adapts instruction in a variety of ways to ensure, as much as possible, that each student continues to progress
- makes sure students know the criteria for success on summative assessments that are tightly aligned to the stated learning goals
- provides varied forms of assessment to ensure that students have an unobstructed opportunity to express what they have learned

# ▼ SUMMARY

Angela Waye/Shutterstock

## Basics of Assessment (pp. 511–517)

**Distinguish between measurement and assessment.** Measurement is the description of an event or characteristic using numbers. Assessment includes measurement, but is broader because it includes all kinds of ways to sample and observe students' skills, knowledge, and abilities.

**Distinguish between formative and summative assessment.** In the classroom, assessment may be formative (ungraded, diagnostic) or summative (graded). Formative assessment helps form instruction, and summative assessment summarizes students' accomplishments.

**Distinguish between norm-referenced and criterion-referenced tests.** In norm-referenced tests, a student's performance is compared to the average performance of others. In criterion-referenced tests, scores are compared to a pre-established standard. Norm-referenced tests cover a wide range of general objectives. However, results of norm-referenced tests do not tell whether students are ready for advanced material, and they are not appropriate for affective and psychomotor objectives. Criterion-referenced tests measure the mastery of very specific objectives.

**What is test reliability?** Some tests are more reliable than others; that is, they yield more stable and consistent estimates. Care must be taken in the interpretation of test results. Each test is only a sample of a student's performance on a given day. The score is only an estimate of a student's hypothetical true score. The standard error of measurement takes into account the possibility for error and is one index of test reliability.

**What is test validity?** The most important consideration about a test is the validity of the decisions and judgments that are based on the test results. Evidence of validity can be related to content, criterion, or construct. Construct-related evidence for validity is the broadest category and encompasses the other two categories of content and criterion. Tests must be reliable to be valid, but reliability does not guarantee validity.

**What is absence of bias?** Tests must be free of assessment bias. Bias occurs when tests include material that offends or unfairly penalizes a group of students because of the students' gender, SES, race, or ethnicity. Culture-fair tests have not proved to solve the problem of assessment bias.

## Classroom Assessment: Testing (pp. 517–522)

**How can testing support learning?** Learning is supported by frequent testing using cumulative questions that ask students to apply and integrate knowledge. With the goals of assessment in mind, teachers are in a better position to design their own tests or evaluate the tests provided by textbook publishers.

**Describe two kinds of traditional testing.** Two traditional formats for testing are the objective test and the essay test. Objective tests, which can include multiple-choice, true/false, fill-in, and matching items, should be written with specific guidelines in mind. Writing and scoring essay questions requires careful planning, in addition to criteria to discourage bias in scoring.

## Authentic Classroom Assessments (pp. 522–529)

**What is authentic assessment?** Critics of traditional testing believe that teachers should use authentic tests and other authentic assessment procedures. Authentic assessment requires students to perform tasks and solve problems that are similar to the real-life performances that will be expected of them outside of school.

**Describe portfolios and exhibitions.** Portfolios and exhibitions are two examples of authentic assessment. A portfolio is a collection of the student's work, sometimes chosen to represent growth or improvement or sometimes featuring "best work." Exhibitions are public performances of the student's understandings. With portfolios and exhibitions, there is an emphasis on performing real-life tasks in meaningful contexts.

**What are the issues of reliability, validity, and equity with portfolios and performance assessment?** Using authentic assessments does not guarantee reliability, validity, and equity (absence of bias). Using rubrics is one way to make assessment more reliable and valid. But the results from assessment based on rubrics may not predict performance on related tasks. Also, rater bias based on the appearance, speech, or behaviour of minority-group students or a lack of resources may place minority-group students at a disadvantage in performance assessments or projects.

**How can teachers use informal assessments?** Informal assessments are ungraded (formative) assessments that gather information from multiple sources to help teachers make decisions. Some examples of informal assessment are student observations and checklists, questioning, and student self-assessment. Journals are very flexible and widely used informal assessments. Students usually have personal or group journals and write in them on a regular basis.

## Grading (pp. 529–534)

**Describe two kinds of grading.** Grading can be either norm-referenced or criterion-referenced. One popular norm-referenced system is grading on the curve, based on a ranking of students in relation to the average performance level. This is not recommended. Criterion-referenced report cards usually indicate how well the individual student has met each of several objectives.

**How can failure support learning?** Students need experience in coping with failure, so standards must be high enough to encourage effort. Occasional failure can be positive if appropriate feedback is provided. Students who never learn how to cope with failure and still persist in learning may give up quickly when their first efforts are unsuccessful.

**Which is better, "social promotion" or being "held back"?** Simply retaining or promoting a student who is having difficulty will not guarantee that the student will learn. Unless the student is very young or emotionally immature compared to others in the class, the best approach may be to promote, but provide extra support such as tutoring or summer school sessions. Differentiated instruction could prevent problems.

**Can grades promote learning and motivation?** Written or oral feedback that includes specific comments on errors or faulty strategies, but that balances this criticism with suggestions about how to improve along with comments on the positive aspects of the work, increases learning. Grades can encourage students' motivation to learn if they are tied to meaningful learning.

**How can communications with families support learning?** Not every communication from the teacher needs to be tied to a grade. Communication with students and families can be important in helping a teacher understand students and present effective instruction by creating a consistent learning environment. Students and families have a legal right to see all the information in the students' records, so the contents of files must be appropriate, accurate, and supported by evidence.

## Standardized Testing (pp. 534–543)

**What are mean, median, mode, and standard deviation?** The mean (arithmetical average), median (middle score), and mode (most common score) are all measures of central tendency. The standard deviation measures how scores spread out around the mean. A normal distribution is a frequency distribution represented as a bell-shaped curve. Many scores cluster in the middle; the farther from the midpoint, the fewer the scores.

**Describe different kinds of scores.** There are several basic types of standardized test scores: percentile rankings, which indicate the percentage of others who scored at or below an individual's score; grade-equivalent scores, which indicate how closely a student's performance matches average scores for a given grade; and standard scores, which are based on the standard deviation.

**What are some current issues in testing?** Controversy over standardized testing has focused on the role and interpretation of tests, some uses of tests to evaluate schools, the problems with accountability based on test scores, and the testing of teachers. If the test matches important objectives of the curriculum, is given to students who actually studied the curriculum for a reasonable period of time, is free of bias, fits the students' language capabilities, and was administered properly, then test results provide some information about the effectiveness of the school. Teachers should use results to improve instruction, not to stereotype students or justify lowered expectations.

**Can students become better test takers? How?** Performance on standardized tests can be improved if students gain experience with this type of testing and are given training in study skills and problem solving. Many students can profit from direct instruction about how to prepare for and take tests. Involving students in designing these test preparation programs can be helpful. Students with learning challenges may benefit from intensive and ongoing preparation for taking tests, particularly if the test-taking strategies are tied to specific problems and content learned and tested.

## ▼ WHAT WOULD THEY DO?

### TEACHERS' CASEBOOK: Giving Meaningful Grades

Here is how some practising teachers responded to the grading challenge at the beginning of the chapter.

**MARCI GREEN**
H. J. Alexander Community School, Toronto, ON

The Ontario curriculum for grades 1 to 8 was introduced into my school in 1998. Previously, the teachers who worked in my Board of Education did not use letter grades for report cards. It has taken some time to adjust to this new system of grading and to ensure that the students are assessed fairly.

The provincial report card states that teachers must use letter grades from "A to R." The letter grade A represents the highest level of achievement that exceeds the provincial standard. The letter grade R represents "below 50," which means that a student has not been able to demonstrate the required knowledge and skills.

In order to implement a grading system that is fair and manageable, as a physical educator, I would initially review the Health and Physical Education curriculum for grades 1 to 8. By reviewing this curriculum, I would ensure that I was teaching the required material. Then I would determine the units I would teach for each term, ensuring I had a balanced program that incorporated the requirements from the curriculum. For each unit I would develop a grid, or rubric, which would represent the expectations for each letter grade. These expectations would reflect the skills to be taught and would be clearly stated to the students, parents, and administrators before the grading period began. Posting the rubric in the gym or classroom is helpful in reminding the students of the expectations for their report cards.

There are many ways to assess students' achievements. These consist of anecdotal records, checklists, observations, participation, and effort and tracking sheets. The students are given an appropriate amount of time to learn and practise skills before they are assessed. It is important that a variety of instructional approaches be used to ensure that students have the opportunity to learn and perform to their potential. I would make program modifications for any students with any exceptionalities. The evaluation process should be ongoing throughout the school year.

Also, reviewing the students' previous report cards may help in determining their progress or achievements throughout the school year. Once a letter grade is assigned to a student, it is important to retain any checklists, observations, etc., to help in assessing the strengths, weaknesses, and next-steps sections of the report card. It is also important to retain the information for parent–teacher interviews in case a letter grade is questioned.

**LAURA FOSTER DIGIOVANNI**
Intermediate Teacher St. Luke Catholic Elementary School, Toronto, ON

I would use open-ended projects that are authentic and inquiry-based to engage students. Providing students with real-life scenarios or problems and asking them to develop solutions allows them to participate in the entire process of knowledge construction. Detailed rubrics and assignment outlines would be important to frame the parameters of open-ended assignments and outline curriculum expectations.

I would rely heavily on long-range planning to design a school term that incorporates many high-quality assessments. Laying out the semester in chart form, mapping the curriculum expectations, and planning major and minor assessments and their grade weight have always played a vital role in ensuring a successful year with my students. It is valuable to know, at a glance, what has been covered and what is on the horizon. These plans make it easy to review and reinforce learning throughout the year, resulting in greater knowledge retention. Having long-range plans that detail your varied assessments also provides evidence to school administration and parents that you have attended to the learning strengths and needs of all children.

When teachers design assessments, major or minor, we need to ensure that a number of opportunities are created to provide feedback through formative assessments. In my assignments, formative assessments are worth 25% of the final grade. Making the formative assessments worth a significant portion of the grade ensures that the feedback is internalized and applied, and still allows for students to use feedback to achieve a high level of success in the summative assessments.

Behaviours and group participation are important components of success in the classroom and in the real world, and should be assessed in some capacity. I would include group participation as a rubric category in some assignments, but not all. Behaviours,

however, are best addressed through a variety of classroom management systems or reward programs and should not represent a significant portion of a final grade.

The wide range of criteria being used in different classrooms provides a challenge for all parties involved in education, and certainly does not always seem fair. Some teachers are more effective at planning and delivering lessons and assessments than others. Teachers are provided with a level of trust and professionalism that allow them to decide how the curriculum is delivered within their classroom. Administration is responsible for ensuring that the quality and variety of teaching strategies and assessments are acceptable. Principals are aware of concerns regarding teachers through teacher performance appraisals, contact with concerned parents, and informal observations made during day-to-day communications, activities, and events.

# Glossary

**Aboriginal or First Nations English dialects** A group of dialects of English used by Aboriginal peoples of Canada.

**Academic language** The entire range of language used in elementary, secondary, and university-level schools, including words, concepts, strategies, and processes from academic subjects.

**Academic learning time** Time when students are actually succeeding at the learning task.

**Academic tasks** The work the student must accomplish, including the content covered and the mental operations required.

**Accommodation** Altering existing schemes or creating new ones in response to new information.

**Accountable** Making teachers and schools responsible for student learning, usually by monitoring learning with high-stakes tests.

**Achievement tests** Standardized tests measuring how much students have learned in a given content area.

**Acronym** Technique for remembering by using the first letter of each word in a phrase to form a new, memorable word.

**Action research** Systematic observations or tests of methods that teachers or schools conduct to improve teaching and learning for their students.

**Action zone** Area of a classroom where the greatest amount of interaction takes place.

**Active teaching** Teaching characterized by high levels of teacher explanation, demonstration, and interaction with students.

**Adaptation** Adjustment to the environment.

**Adaptive teaching** Provides all students with challenging instruction and uses supports when needed, but removes these supports as students become able to handle more on their own.

**Adolescent egocentrism** Assumption that everyone else is interested in one's thoughts, feelings, and concerns.

**Advance organizer** Statement of inclusive concepts to introduce and sum up material that follows.

**Affective domain** Objectives focusing on attitudes and feelings.

**Algorithm** Step-by-step procedure for solving a problem; prescription for solutions.

**Allocated time** Time set aside for learning.

**Analogical thinking** Heuristic in which one limits the search for solutions to situations that are similar to the one at hand.

**Anorexia nervosa** Eating disorder characterized by very limited food intake.

**Antecedents** Events that precede an action.

**Anxiety** General uneasiness, a feeling of tension.

**Applied behaviour analysis** The application of behavioural learning principles to understand and change behaviour.

**Appropriating** Being able to internalize or take for yourself knowledge and skills developed in interaction with others or with cultural tools.

**Argumentation** The process of debating a claim with someone else.

**Arousal** Physical and psychological reactions causing a person to feel alert, excited, or tense.

**Articulation disorders** Any of a variety of pronunciation difficulties.

**Assertive discipline** Clear, firm, unhostile response style.

**Assessment bias** Qualities of an assessment instrument that offend or unfairly penalize a group of students because of the students' gender, SES, race, ethnicity, etc.

**Assessment** Procedures used to obtain information about student performance.

**Assimilation** Fitting new information into existing schemes.

**Assisted learning** Learning by having strategic help provided in the initial stages; the help gradually diminishes as students gain independence.

**Attachment** Forming an emotional bond with another person, initially a parent or family member.

**Attention** Focus on a stimulus.

**Attention-deficit/hyperactivity disorder (ADHD)** Current term for disruptive behaviour disorders marked by overactivity, excessive difficulty sustaining attention, or impulsiveness.

**Attribution theories** Descriptions of how individuals' explanations, justifications, and excuses influence their motivation and behaviour.

**Authentic assessments** Assessment procedures that test skills and abilities as they would be applied in real-life situations.

**Authentic task** Tasks that have some connection to real-life problems the students will face outside the classroom.

**Autism and autism spectrum disorders** Developmental disability significantly affecting verbal and nonverbal communication, social interaction, and imaginative creativity, generally evident before age 3 and ranging from mild to major.

**Automated basic skills** Skills that are applied without conscious thought.

**Automaticity** The result of learning to perform a behaviour or thinking process so thoroughly that the performance is automatic and does not require effort. Sometimes refers to excitement or stress.

**Autonomy** Self-control and self-confidence.

**Availability heuristic** Judging the likelihood of an event based on what is available in your memory, assuming those easily remembered events are common.

**Aversive** Irritating or unpleasant.

**Balanced bilingualism** Adding a second language capability without losing your heritage language.

**Basic skills** Clearly structured knowledge that is needed for later learning and that can be taught step by step.

**Behaviour modification** Systematic application of antecedents and consequences to change behaviour.

**Behavioural learning theories** Explanations of learning that focus on external events as the cause of changes in observable behaviours.

**Behavioural objectives** Instructional objectives stated in terms of observable behaviour.

**Being needs** Maslow's three higher-level needs, sometimes called *growth needs*.

**Belief perseverance** The tendency to hold on to beliefs, even in the face of contradictory evidence.

**Bilingual** Speaking two languages and dealing appropriately with the two different cultures.

**Bioecological model** Bronfenbrenner's theory describing the nested social and cultural contexts that shape development. Every person develops within a *microsystem*, inside a *mesosystem*, embedded in an *exosystem*, all of which are a part of the *macrosystem* of the culture.

**Blended families** Parents, children, and stepchildren merged into families through remarriages.

**Body mass index (BMI)** A measure of body fat that evaluates weight in relation to height.

**Bottom-up processing** Perceiving based on noticing separate defining features and assembling them into a recognizable pattern.

**Brainstorming** Generating ideas without stopping to evaluate them.

**Bulimia** Eating disorder characterized by overeating, then getting rid of the food by self-induced vomiting or use of laxatives.

**Canadian Charter of Rights and Freedoms** Legislation that protects the rights of all Canadians and, in particular, Canadians who are members of minority groups, including Canadians with disabilities.

**Case study** Intensive study of one person or one situation.

**Central executive** The part of working memory that is responsible for monitoring and directing attention and other mental resources.

**Central tendency** Typical score for a group of scores.

**Cerebral palsy** Condition involving a range of motor or coordination difficulties due to brain damage.

**Chain mnemonics** Memory strategies that associate one element in a series with the next element.

**Child-directed speech (CDS)** Refers to a form of language characterized by short sentences with simple constructions and delivered in higher pitched, more prosodic, and exaggerated tones.

**Chunking** Grouping individual bits of data into meaningful larger units.

**Classical conditioning** Association of automatic responses with new stimuli.

**Classification** Grouping objects into categories.

**Classroom assessments** Classroom assessments are selected and created by teachers and can take many different forms—unit tests, essays, portfolios, projects, performances, oral presentations, etc.

**Classroom management** Techniques used to maintain a healthy learning environment, relatively free of behavioural problems.

**Cloud computing** Allows computer users to access applications such as a Google document or Microsoft Web Mail, as well as computing assets such as network-accessible data storage and processing to use online applications.

**Cmaps** Tools for concept mapping developed by the Institute for Human and Machine Cognition that are connected to many knowledge maps and other resources on the internet.

**Coactions** Joint actions of individual biology and environment—each shapes and influences the other.

**Co-constructed** Constructed through a social process in which people interact and negotiate (usually verbally) to create an understanding or to solve a problem; the final product is shaped by all participants.

**Code-switching** Moving between two speech forms.

**Cognitive apprenticeship** A relationship in which a less experienced learner acquires knowledge and skills under the guidance of an expert.

**Cognitive behaviour modification** Procedures based on both behavioural and cognitive learning principles for changing your own behaviour by using self-talk and self-instruction.

**Cognitive development** Gradual, orderly changes by which mental processes become more complex and sophisticated.

**Cognitive domain** In Bloom's taxonomy, memory and reasoning objectives.

**Cognitive evaluation theory** Suggests that events affect motivation through the individual's perception of the events as controlling behaviour or providing information.

**Cognitive load** The volume of resources necessary to complete a task.

**Cognitive objectives** Instructional objectives stated in terms of higher-level thinking operations.

**Cognitive science** The interdisciplinary study of thinking, language, intelligence, knowledge creation, and the brain.

**Cognitive view of learning** A general approach that views learning as an active mental process of acquiring, remembering, and using knowledge.

**Collaboration** A philosophy about how to relate to others—how to learn and work.

**Collective monologue** Form of speech in which children in a group talk but do not really interact or communicate.

**Commitment** In Marcia's theory of identity statuses, individuals' choices concerning political and religious beliefs, for example, usually as a consequence of exploring the options.

**Community of practice** Social situation or context in which ideas are judged useful or true.

**Compensation** The principle that changes in one dimension can be offset by changes in another dimension.

**Complex learning environments** Problems and learning situations that mimic the ill-structured nature of real life.

**Concept map** A drawing that charts the relationships among ideas.

**Concept** A category used to group similar events, ideas, objects, or people.

**Concrete operations** Mental tasks tied to concrete objects and situations.

**Conditioned response (CR)** Learned response to a previously neutral stimulus.

**Conditioned stimulus (CS)** Stimulus that evokes an emotional or physiological response after conditioning.

**Confidence interval** Range of scores within which an individual's particular score is likely to fall.

**Confirmation bias** Seeking information that confirms our choices and beliefs, while disconfirming evidence.

**Consequences** Events that follow an action.

**Conservation** Principle that some characteristics of an object remain the same despite changes in appearance.

**Constructionism** How public knowledge in disciplines such as science, math, economics, or history is constructed.

**Constructivism** View that emphasizes the active role of the learner in building understanding and making sense of information.

**Constructivist approach** View that emphasizes the active role of the learner in building understanding and making sense of information.

**Context** The total setting or situation that surrounds and interacts with a person or event. It includes internal and external circumstances and situations that interact with the individual's thoughts, feelings, and actions to shape development and learning.

**Contiguity** Association of two events because of repeated pairing.

**Contingency contract** A contract between the teacher and a student specifying what the student must do to earn a particular reward or privilege.

**Continuous reinforcement schedule** Presenting a reinforcer after every appropriate response.

**Convergent questions** Questions that have a single correct answer.

**Convergent thinking** Narrowing possibilities to a single answer.

**Cooperation** Way of working with others to attain a shared goal.

**Cooperative learning** Situations in which elaboration, interpretation, explanation, and argumentation are integral to the activity of the group and where learning is supported by other individuals.

**Co-regulation** A transitional phase during which students gradually appropriate self-regulated learning and skills through modelling, direct teaching, feedback, and coaching from teachers, parents, or peers.

**Correlation** Statistical description of how closely two variables are related.

**Creativity** Imaginative, original thinking or problem solving.

**Criterion-referenced grading** Assessment of each student's mastery of course objectives.

**Criterion-referenced testing** Testing in which scores are compared to a set performance standard.

**Critical periods** If learning doesn't happen during these periods, it never will.

**Critical thinking** Evaluating conclusions by logically and systematically examining the problem, the evidence, and the solution.

**Cross-sectional studies** Studies that focus on groups of subjects at different ages rather than following the same group for many years.

**Crystallized intelligence** Ability to apply culturally approved problem-solving methods.

**Cueing** Providing a stimulus that "sets up" a desired behaviour.

**Cultural deficit model** A model that explains the school achievement problems of ethnic minority students by assuming that their culture is inadequate and does not prepare them to succeed in school.

**Cultural tools** The real tools (computers, scales, etc.) and symbol systems (numbers, language, graphs, etc.) that allow people in a society to communicate, think, solve problems, and create knowledge.

**Culturally relevant pedagogy** Excellent teaching for students from visible minorities that includes academic success and developing/maintaining cultural competence and critical consciousness to challenge the status quo.

**Culturally responsive management** Taking cultural meanings and styles into account when developing management plans and responding to students.

**Culture** The knowledge, rules, traditions, attitudes, and values that guide the behaviour of a group of people and allow them to solve the problems of living in their environment.

**Culture-fair or culture-free test** A test without cultural bias.

**Cyber aggression** Using email, Twitter, Facebook, or other social media to spread rumours, make threats, or otherwise terrorize peers.

**Decay** The weakening and fading of memories with the passage of time.

**Decentring** Focusing on more than one aspect at a time.

**Declarative knowledge** Verbal information; facts; "knowing that" something is the case.

**Deficiency needs** Maslow's four lower-level needs, which must be satisfied first.

**Defining attribute** Qualities that connect members of a group to a specific concept.

**Descriptive studies** Studies that collect detailed information about specific situations, often using observation, surveys, interviews, recordings, or a combination of these methods.

**Development** Orderly, adaptive changes that humans (or animals) go through from conception to death.

**Developmental crisis** A specific conflict whose resolution prepares the way for the next stage.

**Developmental disabilities** Significantly below-average intellectual and adaptive social behaviour evident before the age of 18.

**Deviation IQ** Score based on statistical comparison of individuals' performance with the average performance of others in that age group.

**Dialect** Any variety of a language spoken by a particular group.

**Differentiated instruction** Teaching that takes into account students' abilities, prior knowledge, and challenges so that instruction matches not only the subject being taught but also students' needs.

**Direct instruction or explicit teaching** Systematic instruction for mastery of basic skills, facts, and information.

**Disability** The inability to do something specific, such as walk or hear.

**Discrimination** Treating particular categories of people unfairly.

**Disequilibrium** In Piaget's theory, the "out-of-balance" state that occurs when a person realizes that his or her current ways of thinking are not working to solve a problem or understand a situation.

**Distractors** Wrong answers offered as choices in a multiple-choice item.

**Distributed practice** Practice in brief periods with rest intervals.

**Distributive justice** Beliefs about how to divide materials or privileges fairly among members of a group; follows a sequence of development from equality to merit to benevolence.

**Divergent questions** Questions that have no single correct answer.

**Divergent thinking** Coming up with many possible solutions.

**Domain-specific knowledge** Information that is useful in a particular situation or that applies mainly to one specific topic.

**Domain-specific strategies** Consciously applied skills to reach goals in a particular subject or problem.

**Dual coding theory** Suggests that information is stored in long-term memory as either visual images or verbal units, or both.

**Education or school act** Provincial or territorial legislation that governs education in elementary and secondary schools.

**Educational psychology** The discipline concerned with teaching and learning processes; it applies the methods and theories of psychology and has its own as well.

**Educationally blind**  Needing Braille materials in order to learn.

**Effective instruction delivery (EID)**  Instructions that are concise, clear, and specific, and that communicate an expected result. Statements work better than questions.

**Egocentric**  Assuming that others experience the world the way you do.

**Elaboration**  Adding and extending meaning by connecting new information to existing knowledge.

**Elaborative rehearsal**  Keeping information in working memory by associating it with something else you already know.

**Embodied cognition**  Theory stating that cognitive processes develop from real-time, goal-directed interactions between humans and their environment.

**Emergent literacy**  The skills and knowledge, usually developed in the preschool years, that are the foundation for the development of reading and writing.

**Emotional and behavioural disorders**  Behaviours or emotions that deviate so much from the norm that they interfere with the child's own growth and development and/or the lives of others—inappropriate behaviours, unhappiness or depression, fears and anxieties, and trouble with relationships.

**Empathetic listening**  Hearing the intent and emotions behind what another says and reflecting them back by paraphrasing.

**Empirical**  Based on systematically collected data.

**Enactive learning**  Learning by doing and experiencing the consequences of your actions.

**Engaged time/time on task**  Time spent actively engaged in the learning task at hand.

**English as a second language (ESL)**  The classes devoted to teaching ELL students English.

**English language learners (ELLs)**  Students who are learning English when their primary or heritage language is not English.

**Entity view of ability**  Belief that ability is a fixed characteristic that cannot be changed.

**Epilepsy**  Disorder marked by seizures and caused by abnormal electrical discharges in the brain.

**Episodic buffer**  The process that brings together and integrates information from the phonological loop, visuo-spatial sketchpad, and long-term memory under the supervision of the central executive.

**Episodic memory**  Long-term memory for information tied to a particular time and place, especially memory of the events in a person's life.

**Epistemological beliefs**  Beliefs about the structure, stability, and certainty of knowledge, and how knowledge is best learned.

**Equilibration**  Search for mental balance between cognitive schemes and information from the environment.

**Ethnicity**  A cultural heritage shared by a group of people.

**Ethnography**  A descriptive approach to research that focuses on life within a group and tries to understand the meaning of events to the people involved.

**Event-related potential (ERP)**  Measurements that assess electrical activity of the brain through the skull or scalp.

**Exceptional students**  Students who have unusually high abilities in particular areas or disabilities that impact learning and may require special education or other services.

**Executive control processes**  Processes such as selective attention, rehearsal, elaboration, and organization that influence encoding, storage, and retrieval of information in memory.

**Exemplar**  An actual memory of a specific object.

**Exhibition**  A performance test or demonstration of learning that is public and usually takes an extended time to prepare.

**Expectancy × value theories**  Explanations of motivation that emphasize individuals' expectations for success combined with their valuing of the goal.

**Experimentation**  Research method in which variables are manipulated and the effects recorded.

**Expert teachers**  Experienced, effective teachers who have developed solutions for classroom problems. Their knowledge of teaching process and content is extensive and well organized.

**Explicit memory**  Long-term memories that involve deliberate or conscious recall.

**Exploration**  In Marcia's theory of identity statuses, the process by which adolescents consider and try out alternative beliefs, values, and behaviours in an effort to determine which will give them the most satisfaction.

**Expressive vocabulary**  The words a person can speak.

**Extended families**  Parents, children, grandparents, aunts, uncles, and cousins living in the same household or in close proximity so they can have daily contact with one another.

**Extinction**  The disappearance of a learned response.

**Extraneous cognitive load**  The resources required to process stimuli irrelevant to the task.

**Extrinsic motivation**  Motivation created by external factors such as rewards and punishments.

**Failure-accepting students**  Students who believe their failures are due to low ability and there is little they can do about it.

**Failure-avoiding students**  Students who avoid failure by sticking to what they know, by not taking risks, or by claiming not to care about their performance.

**Finger spelling**  Communication system that "spells out" each letter with a hand position.

**First wave constructivism**  A focus on the individual and psychological sources of knowing, as in Piaget's theory.

**Flashbulb memories**  Clear, vivid memories of emotionally important events in your life.

**Flexible grouping**  Grouping and regrouping students based on learning needs.

**Fluid intelligence**  Mental efficiency that is culture-free and nonverbal and is grounded in brain development.

**Flynn effect**  A steady rise in IQ test scores because of better health, smaller families, increased complexity in the environment, and more and better schooling.

**Formal operations**  Mental tasks involving abstract thinking and coordination of a number of variables.

**Formative assessment**  Ungraded testing used before or during instruction to aid in planning and diagnosis.

**Functional behavioural assessment (FBA)**  Procedures used to obtain information about antecedents, behaviours, and consequences to determine the reason or function of the behaviour.

**Functional fixedness** Inability to use objects or tools in a new way.

**Functional magnetic resonance imaging (fMRI)** An MRI is an imaging technique that uses a magnetic field along with radio waves and a computer to create detailed pictures of the inside of the body. A functional MRI uses the MRI to measure the tiny changes that take place in the brain during brain activity.

**Funds of knowledge** Knowledge that families and community members have acquired in many areas of work, home, and religious life that can become the basis for teaching.

**Gender biases** Different views of males and females, often favouring one gender over the other.

**Gender identity** The sense of self as male or female as well as the beliefs one has about gender roles and attributes.

**Gender schemas** Organized cognitive structures that include gender-related information that influences how children think and behave.

**Genderlects** Different ways of talking for males and females.

**General intelligence (g)** A general factor in cognitive ability that is related in varying degrees to performance on all mental tests.

**General knowledge** Information that is useful in many different kinds of tasks; information that applies to many situations.

**Generalized seizure** A seizure involving a large portion of the brain.

**Generation 1.5** Children and youth, like Akahdeep, who were not born in Canada but immigrated here with their first-generation parents, typically before adolescence.

**Generativity** Sense of concern for future generations.

**Germane cognitive load** Deep processing of information related to the task, including the application of prior knowledge to a new task or problem.

**Gestalt** German for *pattern* or *whole*. Gestalt theorists hold that people organize their perceptions into coherent wholes.

**Gifted student** A very bright, creative, and talented student.

**Glial cells** The white matter of the brain. These cells greatly outnumber neurons and appear to have many functions, such as fighting infections, controlling blood flow and communication among neurons, and providing the myelin coating around axon fibres.

**Goal orientations** Patterns of beliefs about goals related to achievement in school.

**Goal structure** The way students relate to others who are also working toward a particular goal.

**Goal** What an individual strives to accomplish.

**Goal-directed actions** Deliberate actions toward a goal.

**Good behaviour game** Arrangement where a class is divided into teams and each team receives demerit points for breaking agreed-upon rules of good behaviour.

**Grade-equivalent score** Measure of grade level based on comparison with norming samples from each grade.

**Grading on the curve** Norm-referenced grading that compares students' performance to an average level.

**Group consequences** Rewards or punishments given to a class as a whole for adhering to or violating rules of conduct.

**Group discussion** Conversation in which the teacher does not have the dominant role; students pose and answer their own questions.

**Group focus** The ability to keep as many students as possible involved in activities.

**Handicap** A disadvantage in a particular situation, sometimes caused by a disability.

**Heritage language** The language spoken in the student's home or by members of the family.

**Heuristic** General strategy used in attempting to solve problems.

**Hierarchy of needs** Maslow's model of seven levels of human needs, from basic physiological requirements to the need for self-actualization.

**High-stakes testing** Standardized tests whose results have powerful influences when used by school administrators, other officials, or employers to make decisions.

**Hostile aggression** Bold, direct action that is intended to hurt someone else; unprovoked attack.

**Human agency** The capacity to coordinate learning skills, motivation, and emotions to reach your goals.

**Humanistic interpretation** Approach to motivation that emphasizes personal freedom, choice, self-determination, and striving for personal growth.

**Hyperactivity** Behaviour disorder marked by atypical, excessive restlessness and inattentiveness.

**Hypothesis** A prediction of what will happen in a research study based on theory and previous research.

**Hypothetico-deductive reasoning** A formal-operations problem-solving strategy in which an individual begins by identifying all the factors that might affect a problem and then deduces and systematically evaluates specific solutions.

**"I" message** Clear, nonaccusatory statement of how something is affecting you.

**Identity achievement** Strong sense of commitment to life choices after free consideration of alternatives.

**Identity diffusion** Uncentredness; confusion about who one is and what one wants.

**Identity foreclosure** Acceptance of parental life choices without consideration of options.

**Identity** The principle that a person or object remains the same over time.

**Images** Representations based on the physical attributes—the appearance—of information.

**Immersive virtual learning environment (IVLE)** A simulation of a real-world environment that immerses students in tasks like those required in a professional practicum.

**Immigrants** People who voluntarily leave their country to become permanent residents in a new place.

**Implicit memory** Knowledge that we are not conscious of recalling, but that influences our behaviour or thought without our awareness.

**Importance or attainment value** The importance of doing well on a task; how success on the task meets personal needs.

**Incentive** An object or event that encourages or discourages behaviour.

**Inclusion** The practice of integrating exceptional students into regular education classrooms; the emphasis is on participation rather than placement.

**Incremental view of ability** Belief that ability is a set of skills that can be changed.

**Individualized education program (IEP)** Annually revised program for an exceptional student detailing present achievement level, goals, and strategies, drawn up by teachers, family members, specialists, and (if possible) the student.

**Industry** Eagerness to engage in productive work.

**Informal assessments** Ungraded (formative) assessments that gather information from multiple sources to help teachers make decisions.

**Information processing** The human mind's activity of taking in, storing, and using information.

**Initiative** Willingness to begin new activities and explore new directions.

**Inquiry learning** Approach in which the teacher presents a puzzling situation and students solve the problem by gathering data and testing their conclusions.

**Insight** Sudden realization of a solution; the ability to deal effectively with novel situations.

**Instructional objectives** Clear statements of what students are intended to learn through instruction.

**Instrumental aggression** Strong actions aimed at claiming an object, place, or privilege—not intended to harm, but may lead to harm.

**Integration** The practice of having exceptional students participate in activities with their nonexceptional peers.

**Integrity** Sense of self-acceptance and fulfillment.

**Intelligence quotient (IQ)** Score comparing mental and chronological ages.

**Intelligence** Ability or abilities to acquire and use knowledge for solving problems and adapting to the world.

**Interest or intrinsic value** The enjoyment a person gets from a task.

**Interference** Processing new information interferes or gets confused with old information.

**Intermittent reinforcement schedule** Presenting a reinforcer after some but not all responses.

**Internalize** Process whereby children adopt external standards as their own.

**Intersubjective attitude** A commitment to build shared meaning with others by finding common ground and exchanging interpretations.

**Interval schedule** Length of time between reinforcers.

**Intimacy** Forming close, enduring relationships with others.

**Intrinsic cognitive load** The resources required by the task itself, regardless of other stimuli.

**Intrinsic motivation** Motivation associated with activities that are their own reward.

**Jigsaw classroom** A learning process in which each student is part of a group and each group member is given part of the material to be learned by the whole group. Students become "expert" on their piece and then teach it to the others in their group.

**Joint attention** Occurs when a child and caregiver, or teacher, attend to the same object or event at the same time.

**Keyword method** System of associating new words or concepts with similar-sounding cue words and images.

**KWL** A strategy to guide reading and inquiry: Before—What do I already *know*? What do I *want* to know? After—What have I *learned?*

**Lateralization** The specialization of the two hemispheres (sides) of the brain cortex.

**Learned helplessness** The expectation, based on previous experiences involving lack of control, that all of one's efforts will lead to failure.

**Learned helplessness** The expectation, based on previous experiences with a lack of control, that all one's efforts will lead to failure.

**Learning** Process through which experience causes permanent change in knowledge or behaviour.

**Learning disability** Problem with acquisition and use of language; may show up as difficulty with reading, writing, reasoning, or math.

**Learning management system (LMS)** System that delivers e-learning, provides tools and learning materials, keeps records, administers assessments, and manages learning.

**Learning preferences** Preferred ways of studying and learning, such as using pictures instead of text, working with other people versus alone, learning in structured or in unstructured situations, and so on.

**Learning sciences** An interdisciplinary science of learning, based on research in psychology, education, computer science, philosophy, sociology, anthropology, neuroscience, and other fields that study learning.

**Learning strategies** A special kind of procedural knowledge—*knowing how* to approach learning tasks.

**Learning styles** The way a person approaches learning and studying.

**Least restrictive placement** The practice of placing exceptional students in the most regular educational settings possible while ensuring that they are successful and receive support appropriate to their special needs.

**Legitimate peripheral participation** Genuine involvement in the work of the group, even if your abilities are undeveloped and contributions are small.

**Lesson study** As a group, teachers develop, test, improve, and retest lessons until they are satisfied with the final version.

**Levels of processing theory** Theory that recall of information is based on how deeply it is processed.

**LINCS vocabulary strategy** A strategy that uses stories and imagery to help students learn how to identify, organize, define, and remember words and their meanings.

**Loci method** Technique of associating items with specific places.

**Locus of causality** The location—internal or external—of the cause of behaviour.

**Longitudinal studies** Studies that document changes that occur in subjects over time, often many years.

**Long-term memory** Permanent store of knowledge.

**Low vision** Vision limited to close objects.

**Maintenance rehearsal** Keeping information in working memory by repeating it to yourself.

**Massed practice** Practice for a single extended period.

**Massive multi-player online games (MMOGs)** Interactive gaming environments constructed in virtual worlds where the learner assumes a character role of avatar.

**Mastery experiences** Our own direct experiences—the most powerful source of efficacy information.

**Mastery goal** A personal intention to improve abilities and learn, no matter how performance suffers.

**Mastery-oriented students** Students who focus on learning goals because they value achievement and see ability as improvable.

**Maturation** Genetically programmed, naturally occurring changes over time.

**Mean** Arithmetical average.

**Means-ends analysis** Heuristic in which a goal is divided into subgoals.

**Measurement** An evaluation expressed in quantitative (number) terms.

**Median** Middle score in a group of scores.

**Melting pot** A metaphor for the absorption and assimilation of immigrants into the mainstream of society so that ethnic differences vanish.

**Menarche** The first menstrual period in girls.

**Mental age** In intelligence testing, a score based on average abilities for that age group.

**Metacognition** Knowledge about our own thinking processes.

**Metalinguistic awareness** Understanding about one's own use of language.

**Microgenetic studies** Detailed observation and analysis of changes in a cognitive process as the process unfolds over several days or weeks.

**Minority group** A group of people who have been socially disadvantaged—not always a minority in actual numbers.

**Mirror systems** Areas of the brain that fire both during perception of an action by someone else and when performing the action.

**Mnemonics** Techniques for remembering; the art of memory.

**Mode** Most frequently occurring score.

**Modelling** Changes in behaviour, thinking, or emotions that happen through observing another person—a model.

**Monolingual** Speaking only one language.

**Moral dilemmas** Situations in which no choice is clearly and indisputably right.

**Moral realism** Stage of development wherein children see rules as absolute.

**Moral reasoning** The thinking process involved in judgments about questions of right and wrong.

**Morality of cooperation** Stage of development wherein children realize that people make rules and people can change them.

**Moratorium** Identity crisis; suspension of choices because of struggle.

**Motivation to learn** The tendency to find academic activities meaningful and worthwhile and to try to benefit from them.

**Motivation** An internal state that arouses, directs, and maintains behaviour.

**Movement management** Keeping lessons and the group moving at an appropriate (and flexible) pace, with smooth transitions and variety.

**Multicultural education** Education that promotes equity in the schooling of all students.

**Multiple representations of content** Considering problems using various analogies, examples, and metaphors.

**Myelination** The process by which neural fibres are coated with a fatty sheath called myelin that makes message transfer more efficient.

**Natural/logical consequences** Instead of punishing, having students redo, repair, or in some way face the consequences that naturally flow from their actions.

**Need for autonomy** The desire to have our own wishes, rather than external rewards or pressures, determine our actions.

**Negative correlation** A relationship between two variables in which a high value on one is associated with a low value on the other. Example: height and distance from top of head to the ceiling.

**Negative reinforcement** Strengthening behaviour by removing an aversive stimulus when the behaviour occurs.

**Neo-Piagetian theories** More recent theories that integrate findings about attention, memory, and strategy use with Piaget's insights about children's thinking and the construction of knowledge.

**Neurogenesis** The production of new neurons.

**Neurons** Nerve cells that store and transfer information.

**Neutral stimulus** Stimulus not connected to a response.

**Norm group** Large sample of students serving as a comparison group for scoring tests.

**Normal distribution** The most commonly occurring distribution, in which scores are distributed evenly around the mean.

**Norm-referenced grading** Assessment of students' achievement in relation to one another.

**Norm-referenced testing** Testing in which scores are compared with the average performance of others.

**Object permanence** The understanding that objects have a separate, permanent existence.

**Objective testing** Multiple-choice, matching, true/false, short-answer, and fill-in tests; scoring answers does not require interpretation.

**Observational learning** Learning by observation and imitation of others—vicarious learning.

**Operant conditioning** Learning in which voluntary behaviour is strengthened or weakened by consequences or antecedents.

**Operants** Voluntary (and generally goal-directed) behaviours emitted by a person or an animal.

**Operations** Actions that a person carries out by thinking them through instead of literally performing them.

**Organization** Ongoing process of arranging information and experience into mental systems or categories.

**Organization** Ordered and logical network of relations.

**Overlapping** Supervising several activities at once.

**Overlearning** Practising a skill past the point of mastery.

**Overregularize** To apply a rule of syntax or grammar in situations where the rule does not apply; e.g., "the bike was broked."

**Overt aggression** A form of hostile aggression that involves physical attack.

**Paraphrase rule** Policy whereby listeners must accurately summarize what a speaker has said before being allowed to respond.

**Parenting styles** The ways of interacting with and disciplining children.

**Part learning** Breaking a list of items into shorter lists.

**Partial seizure or absence seizure** A seizure involving only a small part of the brain.

**Participant observation** A method for conducting descriptive research in which the researcher becomes a participant in the situation in order to better understand life in that group.

**Participants/subjects**  People or animals being studied.

**Participation structures**  The formal and informal rules for how to take part in a given activity.

**Pedagogical content knowledge**  Teacher knowledge that combines mastery of *academic content* with knowing *how to teach* the content and how to match instruction to *student differences*.

**Peer cultures**  Groups of children or adolescents with their own rules and norms, particularly about such things as dress, appearance, music, language, social values, and behaviour.

**Percentile rank**  Percentage of those in the norming sample who scored at or below an individual's score.

**Perception**  Interpretation of sensory information.

**Performance assessments**  Any form of assessment that requires students to carry out an activity or produce a product in order to demonstrate learning.

**Performance goal**  A personal intention to seem competent or perform well in the eyes of others.

**Personal development**  Changes in personality that take place as one grows.

**Personal learning environment (PLE)**  Provides tools that support individualized learning in a variety of contexts and situations.

**Personal learning network (PLN)**  Framework in which knowledge is constructed through online peer interactions.

**Perspective-taking ability**  Understanding that others have different feelings and experiences.

**Phonological loop**  Part of working memory. A speech- and sound-related system for holding and rehearsing (refreshing) words and sounds in short-term memory for about 1.5 to 2 seconds.

**Physical development**  Changes in body structure that take place as one grows.

**Plasticity**  The brain's tendency to remain somewhat adaptable or flexible.

**Portfolio**  A collection of the student's work in an area, showing growth, self-reflection, and achievement.

**Positive behaviour supports (PBS)**  Interventions designed to replace problem behaviours with new actions that serve the same purpose for the student.

**Positive correlation**  A relationship between two variables in which the two increase or decrease together. Example: calorie intake and weight gain.

**Positive practice**  Practising correct responses immediately after errors.

**Positive reinforcement**  Strengthening behaviour by presenting a desired stimulus after the behaviour.

**Positron emission tomography (PET)**  A method of localizing and measuring brain activity using computer-assisted motion pictures of the brain.

**Pragmatics**  The rules for when and how to use language to be an effective communicator in a particular culture.

**Precorrection**  A tool for positive behaviour support that involves identifying the context for a student's misbehaviour, clearly specifying the alternative expected behaviour, modifying the situation to make the problem behaviour less likely, then rehearsing the expected positive behaviours in the new context and providing powerful reinforcers.

**prejudice**  Prejudgment, or irrational generalization about an entire category of people.

**Premack principle**  Principle stating that a more-preferred activity can serve as a reinforcer for a less-preferred activity.

**Preoperational**  The stage of development before a child masters logical mental operations.

**Presentation punishment**  Decreasing the chances that a behaviour will occur again by presenting an aversive stimulus following the behaviour; also called *Type I punishment*.

**Pretest**  Formative test for assessing students' knowledge, readiness, and abilities.

**Priming**  Activating a concept in memory or the spread of activation from one concept to another.

**Principle**  Established relationship between factors.

**Private speech**  Children's self-talk, which guides their thinking and action; eventually, these verbalizations are internalized as silent inner speech.

**Problem solving**  Creating new solutions for problems.

**Problem**  Any situation in which you are trying to reach some goal and must find a means to do so.

**Problem-based learning**  Methods that provide students with realistic problems that don't necessarily have "right" answers.

**Procedural knowledge**  Knowledge that is demonstrated when we perform a task; "knowing how."

**Procedural memory**  Long-term memory for how to do things.

**Procedures/routines**  Prescribed steps for an activity.

**Production deficiencies**  Failing to activate a learning strategy—a production—when it is appropriate and useful to use the strategy.

**Productions**  The contents of procedural memory; rules about what actions to take, given certain conditions.

**Prompt**  A reminder that follows a cue to make sure the person reacts to the cue.

**Propositional network**  Set of interconnected concepts and relationships in which long-term knowledge is held.

**Prototype**  A best example or best representative of a category.

**Psychomotor domain**  Realm of physical ability and coordination objectives.

**Psychosocial**  Describing the relation of the individual's emotional needs to the social environment.

**Puberty**  The physiological changes during adolescence that lead to the ability to reproduce.

**Punishment**  Process that weakens or suppresses behaviour.

**Pygmalion effect**  Exceptional progress by a student as a result of high teacher expectations for that student; named for the mythological king Pygmalion, who made a statue, then caused it to be brought to life.

**Quasi-experimental studies**  Studies that fit most of the criteria for true experiments, with the important exception that the participants are not assigned to groups at random. Instead, existing groups such as classes or schools participate in the experiments.

**Race**  A group of people who share common biological traits that are seen as self-defining by the people of the group.

**Racial and ethnic pride**  A positive self-concept about one's racial or ethnic heritage.

**Radical constructivism**  Knowledge is assumed to be the individual's construction; it cannot be judged right or wrong.

**Random**  Without any definite pattern; following no rule.

**Range**  Distance between the highest and the lowest scores in a group.

**Ratio schedule**  Reinforcement based on the number of responses between reinforcers.

**Receptive vocabulary**  The words a person can understand in spoken or written words.

**Reciprocal questioning**  Students work in pairs or triads to ask and answer questions about lesson material.

**Reciprocal teaching**  Designed to help students understand and think deeply about what they read.

**Reconstruction**  Recreating information by using memories, expectations, logic, and existing knowledge.

**Reflective**  Thoughtful and inventive. Reflective teachers think back over situations to analyze what they did and why, and to consider how they might improve learning for their students.

**Refugees**  A special group of immigrants who also relocate voluntarily, but who are fleeing their home country because it is not safe.

**Reinforcement**  Use of consequences to strengthen behaviour.

**Reinforcer**  Any event that follows a behaviour and increases the chances that the behaviour will occur again.

**Relational aggression**  A form of hostile aggression that involves verbal attacks and other actions meant to harm social relationships.

**Reliability**  Consistency of test results.

**Removal punishment**  Decreasing the chances that a behaviour will occur again by removing a pleasant stimulus following the behaviour; also called *Type II punishment*.

**Representativeness heuristic**  Judging the likelihood of an event based on how well the events match your prototypes—what you think is representative of the category.

**Reprimands**  Criticisms for misbehaviour; rebukes.

**Resilience**  The ability to adapt successfully in spite of difficult circumstances and threats to development.

**Resistance culture**  Group values and beliefs about refusing to adopt the behaviours and attitudes of the majority culture.

**Respondents**  Responses (generally automatic or involuntary) elicited by specific stimuli.

**Response cost**  Punishment by loss of reinforcers.

**Response set**  Rigidity; the tendency to respond in the most familiar way.

**Response to intervention (RTI)**  A process in which one of the main goals is to identify students who may have learning difficulties as early as possible so that they don't fall too far behind before their problems are recognized. A second goal is to document what works and what doesn't with each student for planning.

**Response**  Observable reaction to a stimulus.

**Restructuring**  Conceiving of a problem in a new or different way.

**Retrieval**  Process of searching for and finding information in long-term memory.

**Reversibility**  A characteristic of Piagetian logical operations—the ability to think through a series of steps, then mentally reverse the steps and return to the starting point; also called *reversible thinking*.

**Reversible thinking**  Thinking backward, from the end to the beginning.

**Reward**  An attractive object or event supplied as a consequence of a behaviour.

**Ripple effect**  "Contagious" spreading of behaviours through imitation.

**Rote memorization**  Remembering information by repetition without necessarily understanding the meaning of the information.

**Rules**  Statements specifying expected and forbidden behaviour; dos and don'ts.

**Scaffolding**  Support for learning and problem solving; the support could be clues, reminders, encouragement, breaking the problem down into steps, providing an example, or anything else that allows the student to grow in independence as a learner.

**Schema-driven problem solving**  Recognizing a problem as a "disguised" version of an old problem for which one already has a solution.

**Schemas (singular, schema)**  Basic structures for organizing information; concepts.

**Schemes**  Mental systems or categories of perception and experience.

**Scoring rubrics**  Rules that are used to determine the quality of a student's performance.

**Script**  Schema or expected plan for the sequence of steps in a common event such as buying groceries or ordering pizza.

**Scripted cooperation**  Learning strategy in which two students take turns summarizing material and criticizing the summaries.

**Seatwork**  Independent classroom work.

**Second wave constructivism**  A focus on the social and cultural sources of knowing, as in Vygotsky's theory.

**Self-actualization**  Fulfilling one's potential.

**Self-concept**  Individuals' knowledge and beliefs about themselves—their ideas, feelings, attitudes, and expectations.

**Self-efficacy**  A person's sense of being able to deal effectively with a particular task.

**Self-esteem**  The value each of us places on our own characteristics, abilities, and behaviours.

**Self-fulfilling prophecy**  A groundless expectation that is confirmed because it has been expected.

**Self-handicapping**  Students may engage in behaviour that blocks their own success in order to avoid testing their true ability.

**Self-instruction**  Talking oneself through the steps of a task.

**Self-management**  Management of your own behaviour and acceptance of responsibility for your own actions; use of behavioural learning principles to change your own behaviour.

**Self-regulated learning**  A view of learning as skills and will applied to analyzing learning tasks, setting goals and planning how to do the task, applying skills, and especially making adjustments about how learning is carried out.

**Self-regulation**  Process of activating and sustaining thoughts, behaviours, and emotions in order to reach goals.

**Self-regulatory knowledge**  Knowing how to manage your learning, or knowing how and when to use your declarative and procedural knowledge.

**Self-reinforcement**  Controlling (selecting and administering) your own reinforcers.

**Semantic memory** Memory for meaning.

**Semilingual** A lack of proficiency in any language; speaking one or more languages inadequately.

**Semiotic function** The ability to use symbols—language, pictures, signs, or gestures—to represent actions or objects mentally.

**Sensitive periods** Times when a person is especially ready for or responsive to certain experiences.

**Sensorimotor** Involving the senses and motor activity.

**Sensory memory** System that holds sensory information very briefly.

**Serial-position effect** The tendency to remember the beginning and the end, but not the middle, of a list.

**Seriation** Arrangement of objects in sequential order according to one aspect, such as size, weight, or volume.

**Service learning** Combines academic learning with personal and social development for secondary and college students.

**Sexual identity** A complex combination of beliefs about gender roles and sexual orientation.

**Shaping** Reinforcing each small step of progress toward a desired goal or behaviour.

**Shared regulation** Students working together to regulate each other through reminders, prompts, and other guidance.

**Sheltered instruction observation protocol or SIOP** An observational system to check that each element of sheltered instruction is present for a teacher.

**Sheltered instruction** Approach to teaching that improves English language skills while teaching content to ELL students by putting the words and concepts of the content into context to make the content more understandable.

**Short-term memory** Component of memory system that holds information for about 20 seconds.

**Sign language** Communication system of hand movements that symbolize words and concepts.

**Single-subject experimental studies** Systematic interventions to study effects with one person, often by applying and then withdrawing a treatment.

**Situated learning** The idea that skills and knowledge are tied to the situation in which they were learned and that they are difficult to apply in new settings.

**Social and emotional learning (SEL)** Refers to the development of competencies for recognizing and managing emotions, developing care and concern for others, establishing positive relationships, making responsible decisions, and handling challenging situations effectively.

**Social cognitive theory** Theory that adds concern with cognitive factors such as beliefs, self-perceptions, and expectations to social learning theory.

**Social conventions** Agreed-upon rules and ways of doing things in a particular situation.

**Social development** Changes over time in the ways in which one relates to others.

**Social goals** A wide variety of needs and motives to be connected to others or part of a group.

**Social isolation** Removal of a disruptive student for five to 10 minutes.

**Social learning theory** Theory that emphasizes learning through observation of others.

**Social learning theory** Theory that emphasizes learning through observation of others.

**Social negotiation** Aspect of learning process that relies on collaboration with others and respect for different perspectives.

**Social persuasion** A "pep talk" or specific performance feedback—one source of self-efficacy.

**Sociocultural theory** Theory that emphasizes the role in development of cooperative dialogues between children and more knowledgeable members of society; children learn the culture of their community (ways of thinking and behaving) through these interactions.

**Sociocultural views of motivation** Perspectives that emphasize participation, identities, and interpersonal relations within communities of practice.

**Socioeconomic status (SES)** Relative standing in the society based on income, power, background, and prestige.

**Sociolinguistics** The study of the formal and informal rules for how, when, about what, to whom, and how long to speak in conversations within cultural groups.

**Spasticity** Overly tight or tense muscles, characteristic of some forms of cerebral palsy.

**Speech impairment** Inability to produce sounds effectively for speaking.

**Speech reading** Using visual cues to understand language.

**Spermarche** The first sperm ejaculation for boys.

**Spiral curriculum** Bruner's design for teaching that introduces the fundamental structure of all subjects early in the school years, then revisits the subjects in more and more complex forms over time.

**Spreading activation** Retrieval of pieces of information based on their relatedness to one another. Remembering one bit of information activates (stimulates) recall of associated information.

**Standard deviation** Measure of how widely scores vary from the mean.

**Standard error of measurement** Hypothetical estimate of variation in scores if testing were repeated.

**Standard scores** Scores based on the standard deviation.

**Standardized tests** Tests given, usually nationwide, under uniform conditions and scored according to uniform procedures.

**Statistically significant** Not likely to be a chance occurrence.

**Stem** The question part of a multiple-choice item.

**Stereotype** Schema that organizes knowledge or perceptions of a category.

**Stereotype threat** The extra emotional and cognitive burden that one's performance in an academic situation might confirm a stereotype that others hold.

**Stimulus** Event that activates behaviour.

**Stimulus control** Capacity for the presence or absence of antecedents to cause behaviours.

**Story grammar** Typical structure or organization for a category of stories.

**Structured controversy** Students work in pairs within their four-person cooperative groups to research a particular controversy.

**Structured English immersion (SEI)** An environment that teaches English rapidly by maximizing instruction in English and using English at a level appropriate to the abilities of the ELLs in the class.

**Stuttering** Repetitions, prolongations, and hesitations that block flow of speech.

**Successive approximations** Small components that make up a complex behaviour.

**Summative assessment** Testing that follows instruction and assesses achievement.

**Sustaining expectation effect** Student performance maintained at a certain level because teachers don't recognize improvements.

**Synapses** The tiny space between neurons; chemical messages are sent across these gaps.

**Syntax** The order of words in phrases or sentences.

*T* **score** Standard score with a mean of 50 and a standard deviation of 10.

**Task analysis** System for breaking down a task hierarchically into basic skills and subskills.

**Taxonomy** Classification system.

**Teachers' sense of efficacy** A teacher's belief that he or she can reach even difficult students to help them learn.

**Theory** Integrated statement of principles that attempts to explain a phenomenon and make predictions.

**Theory-based** An explanation for concept formation that suggests our classifications are based on ideas about the world that we create to make sense of things.

**Theory of mind** An understanding that other people are people, too, with their own minds, thoughts, feelings, beliefs, desires, and perceptions.

**Theory of multiple intelligences** In Gardner's theory of intelligence, a person's eight separate abilities: linguistic, musical, spatial, logical-mathematical, bodily-kinesthetic, interpersonal, intrapersonal, and naturalist.

**Time out** Technically, the removal of all reinforcement. In practice, isolation of a student from the rest of the class for a brief time.

**Token reinforcement system** System in which tokens earned for academic work and positive classroom behaviour can be exchanged for some desired reward.

**Top down** Making sense of information by using context and what we already know about the situation; sometimes called *conceptually drivien perception*.

**Tracking** Assignment to different classes and academic experiences based on achievement.

**Transfer** Influence of previously learned material on new material; the productive (not reproductive) uses of cognitive tools and motivations.

**Transition programming** Gradual preparation of exceptional students to move from high school into further education or training, employment, or community involvement.

**Triarchic reciprocal causality** An explanation of behaviour that emphasizes the mutual effects of the individual and the environment on each other.

**Triarchic theory of intelligence** A three-part description of the mental abilities (thinking processes, coping with new experiences, and adapting to context) that lead to more or less intelligent behaviour.

**True score** The score the student would get if the measurement were completely accurate and error-free.

**Unconditioned response (UR)** Naturally occurring emotional or physiological response.

**Unconditioned stimulus (US)** Stimulus that automatically produces an emotional or physiological response.

**Universal designs for learning** Considering the needs of all users in the design of new tools, learning programs, or websites.

**Utility value** The contribution of a task to meeting one's goals.

**Validity** Degree to which a test measures what it is intended to measure.

**Variability** Degree of difference or deviation from mean.

**Verbalization** Putting your problem-solving plan and its logic into words.

**Vicarious experiences** Accomplishments that are modelled by someone else.

**Vicarious reinforcement** Increasing the chances that we will repeat a behaviour by observing another person being reinforced for that behaviour.

**Virtual learning environment (VLE)** A broad term that describes many ways of learning in virtual or online systems.

**Visuospatial sketchpad** Part of working memory. A holding system for visual and spatial information.

**Voicing problems** Speech impairments involving inappropriate pitch, quality, loudness, or intonation.

**Volition** Willpower; self-discipline; work styles that protect opportunities to reach goals by applying self-regulated learning.

**Warm demanders** Effective teachers who show both high expectations and great caring for their students.

**Within-class ability grouping** System of grouping in which students in a class are divided into two or three groups based on ability in an attempt to accommodate student differences.

**Withitness** According to Kounin, awareness of everything happening in a classroom.

**Work-avoidant learners** Students who don't want to learn or to look smart, but just want to avoid work.

**Working memory** The information that you are focusing on at a given moment.

**Working-backward strategy** Heuristic in which one starts with the goal and moves backward to solve the problem.

*z* **score** Standard score indicating the number of standard deviations above or below the mean.

**Zone of proximal development (ZPD)** Phase at which a child can master a task if given appropriate help and support.

# References

Aber, J. L., Brown, J. L., & Jones, S. M. (2003). Developmental trajectories toward violence in middle childhood: Course, demographic differences, and response to school-based intervention. *Developmental Psychology, 39*, 324–348.

Abi-Nader, J. (1991). Creating a vision of the future: Strategies for motivating minority students. *Phi Delta Kappan, 72*, 546–549.

Aboud, F. E. (2003). The formation of in-group favoritism and out-group prejudice in young children: Are they distinct attitudes? *Developmental Psychology, 39*, 48–60.

Acker, S., & Oatley, K. (1993). Gender issues in education for science and technology: Current situation and prospects for change. *Canadian Journal of Education, 18*, 255–272.

Ackerman, B. P., Brown, E. D., & Izard, C. E. (2004). The relations between contextual risk, earned income, and the school adjustment of children from economically disadvantaged families. *Developmental Psychology, 40*, 204–216.

Ackerman, P. L., Beier, M. E., & Boyle, M. O. (2005). Working memory and intelligence: The same or different constructs? *Psychological Bulletin, 131*, 30–60.

Adams, G. R., Berzonsky, M. D., & Keating, L. (2006). Psychosocial resources in first-year university students: The role of identity processes and social relationships. *Journal of Youth and Adolescence, 35*, 81–91.

Ainley, M., Hidi, S., & Berndorf, D. (2002). Interest, learning, and the psychological processes that mediate their relationship. *Journal of Educational Psychology, 94*, 545–561.

Airasian, P. W. (2005). *Classroom assessment: Concepts and applications* (5th ed.). New York, NY: McGraw-Hill.

Airasian, P. W., Engemann, J. F., & Gallagher, T. L. (2007). *Classroom assessment: Concepts and applications* (1st Cdn ed.). Toronto, ON: McGraw-Hill Ryerson.

Albanese, M. A., & Mitchell, S. A. (1993). Problem-based learning: A review of literature on its outcomes and implementation issues. *Academic Medicine, 68*, 52–81.

Alber, S. R., & Heward, W. L. (1997). Recruit it or lose it! Training students to recruit positive teacher attention. *Intervention in School and Clinic, 32*, 275–282.

Alber, S. R., & Heward, W. L. (2000). Teaching students to recruit positive attention: A review and recommendations. *Journal of Behavioral Education, 10*, 177–204.

Alberto, P., & Troutman, A. C. (2006). *Applied behavior analysis for teachers: Influencing student performance* (7th ed.). Upper Saddle River, NJ: Prentice-Hall/Merrill.

Alberto, P. A., & Troutman, A. C. (2009). *Applied Behavior Analysis for Teachers*. Upper Saddle River, NJ: Pearson.

Alderman, M. K. (2004). *Motivation for achievement: Possibilities for teaching and learning*. Mahwah, NJ: Erlbaum.

Alexander, P. A. (1992). Domain knowledge: Evolving themes and emerging concerns. *Educational Psychologist, 27*, 33–51.

Alexander, P. A. (1996). The past, present, and future of knowledge research: A reexamination of the role of knowledge in learning and instruction. *Educational Psychologist, 31*, 89–92.

Alexander, P. A. (1997). Mapping the multidimensional nature of domain learning: The interplay of cognitive, motivational, and strategic forces. *Advances in Motivation and Achievement, 10*, 213–250.

Alexander, P. A. (2006a). *Psychology in learning and instruction*. Upper Saddle River, NJ: Merrill/Prentice-Hall.

Alexander, P. A. (2006b). Evolution of a learning theory. *Educational Psychologist, 41*, 257–264.

Alexander, P. A., Kulikowich, J. M., & Schulze, S. K. (1994). How subject-matter knowledge affects recall and interest. *American Educational Research Journal, 31*, 313–337.

Alexander, P. A., & Murphy, P. K. (1998). The research base for APA's Learner-Centered Psychological Principles. In N. Lambert & B. McCombs (Eds.), *How students learn: Reforming schools through learner-centered education* (pp. 25–60). Washington, DC: American Psychological Association.

Alexander, P. A., Schallert, D. L., & Reynolds, R. E. (2009). What is learning anyway? A topographical perspective considered. *Educational Psychologist 44*(3): 176–192.

Alexander, P. A., & Winne, P. H. (2006). *Handbook of educational psychology* (2nd ed.). Mahwah, NJ: Erlbaum.

Alferink, L. A., & Farmer-Dougan, V. (2010). Brain-(not) based eduction: Dangers of misunderstanding and misapplication of neuroscience research. *Exceptionality, 18*: 42.

Alfieri, L., Brooks, P. J., Aldrich, N. J., & Tenenbaum, H. R. (2011). Does discovery-based instruction enhance learning? *Journal of Educational Psychology, 103*, 1–18.

Alliance for a Healthier Generation. [Website]. Retrieved from www.healthiergeneration.org/default.aspx

Alliance for Children. (2000, September 12). *Children and computers: A call for action.* Retrieved from www.allianceforchildhood.net/projects/computers/computers_articles_call_for_action.htm

Allington, R. L., & McGill-Frazen, A. (2003). The impact of summer setback on the reading achievement gap. *Phi Delta Kappan, 85*(1), 68–75.

Allington, R. L., & McGill-Frazen, A. (2008). *Got books? Educational Leadership, 65*(7), 20–23.

Alloway, N. (1984). *Teacher expectations.* Paper presented at the meetings of the Australian Association for Research in Education, Perth, Australia.

Alloway, T. P., Banner, G., & Smith, P. (2010). Working memory and cognitive styles in adolescents' attainment. British Journal of Educational Psychology, 80, 567–581.

Alloway, T. P., Gathercole, S. E., & Pickering, S. J. (2006). Verbal and visuo-spatial short-term and working memory in children: Are they separable? *Child Development, 77*, 1698–1716.

Alloy, L. B., & Seligman, M. E. P. (1979). On the cognitive component of learned helplessness and depression. *The Journal of Learning and Motivation, 13*, 219–276.

Aloe, A. M., Becker, B. J. (2009). Teacher verbal ability and school outcomes. *Educational Researcher, 38*(8): 612–624.

Alter, A., Aronson, J., Darley, J., Rodriguez, C., & Ruble, D. N. (2010). Rising to the threat: Reducing stereotype threat by reframing the threat as a challenge. *Journal of Experimental Social Psychology, 46*: 166–171.

Altermatt, E. R., Pomerantz, E. M., Ruble, D. N., Frey, K. S., & Greulich, F. K. (2002). Predicting changes in children's self-perceptions of academic competence: A naturalistic examination of evaluative discourse among classmates. *Developmental Psychology, 38*, 903–917.

Alton-Lee, A., Diggins, C., Klenner, L., Vine, E., & Dalton, N. (2001). Teacher management of the learning environment during a social studies discussion in a new-entrant classroom in New Zealand. *The Elementary School Journal, 101*, 549–566.

Alvidrez, J., & Weinstein, R. S. (1999). Early teacher perceptions and later student academic achievement. *Journal of Educational Psychology, 91*, 731–746.

Amabile, T. M. (1996). *Creativity in context*. Boulder, CO: Westview Press.

Amabile, T. M. (2001). Beyond talent: John Irving and the passionate craft of creativity. *American Psychologist, 56*, 333–336.

Amato, L. F., Loomis, L. S., & Booth, A. (1995). Parental divorce, marital conflict, and offspring well-being during early adulthood. *Social Forces, 73*, 895–915.

Amato, P. R. (2006). Marital discord, divorce, and children's well-being. In A. Clarke-Stewart & J. Dunn (Eds.), *Families count: Effects on child and adolescent development* (pp. 179–202). New York, NY: Cambridge University Press.

American Academy of Family Physicians. (2009). Cerebral palsy in children. Retrieved from http://familydoctor.org/online/famdocen/home/children/parents/special/birth/901.html

American Printing House for the Blind. (2009). Distribution of eligible students. Retrieved from www.aph.org/fedquotpgm/dist09.html

American Psychiatric Association. (2000). *The diagnostic and statistical manual of mental disorders* (DSM-IV-TR). Washington, DC: Author.

American Psychological Association Zero Tolerance Task Force. (2008). Are zero tolerance policies effective in schools? An evidentiary review and recommendations. *American Psychologist, 63*, 852–862.

Ames, C. (1990). Motivation: What teachers need to know. *Teachers College Record, 91*, 409–421.

Ames, C. (1992). Classrooms: Goals, structures, and student motivation. *Journal of Educational Psychology, 84*, 261–271.

Anderman, E. M., & Anderman, L. H. (2009). Motivating children and adolescents in schools. Columbus, OH: Merrill/Prentice Hall.

Anderman, E. M., & Anderman, L. H. (2010). *Motivating children and adolescents in schools.* Columbus, OH: Merrill/Prentice Hall.

Anderman, E. M., Cupp, P. K., & Lane, D. (2009). Impulsivity and academic cheating. *Journal of Experimental Education, 78*(1): 135–150.

Anderman, E. M., & Maehr, M. L. (1994). Motivation and schooling in the middle grades. *Review of Educational Research, 64*, 287–310.

Anderman, E. M., & Midgley, C. (2004). Changes in self-reported academic cheating across the transition from middle school to high school. *Contemporary Educational Psychology, 29*, 499–517.

Anderman, E. M., & Patrick, H. (2012). Achievement goal theory, conceptualization of ability/intelligence, and classroom climate. In S. L. Christenson, A. L. Reschly, & C. Wylie (Eds.), *Handbook of Research on Student Engagement*, (pp. 173–191). New York: Springer.

Anderson, C. A., Shibuya, Al, Ihori, N., Swing, E. L., Bushman, B. J., Sakamoto, A., … Saleem, M. (2010). Violent video game effects on aggression, empathy, and prosocial behavior in eastern and western countries: A meta-analytic review. *Psychological Bulletin, 136*, 151–173.

Anderson, C. W., Holland, J. D., & Palincsar, A. S. (1997). Canonical and sociocultural approaches to research and reform in science education: The story of Juan and his group. *The Elementary School Journal, 97*, 359–384.

Anderson, C. W., & Roth, K. J. (1989). Teaching for meaningful and self-regulated learning of science. In J. Brophy (Ed.), *Advances in research on teaching*, (Vol. I, pp. 265–306). Greenwich, CT: JAI Press.

Anderson, J. (1995). Listening to parents' voices: Cross cultural perceptions of learning to read and write. *Reading Horizons, 35*, 394–413.

Anderson, J., & Gunderson, L. (1997). Literacy learning from a multicultural perspective. *The Reading Teacher, 50*, 514–516.

Anderson, J. R. (1993). Problem solving and learning. *American Psychologist, 48*, 35–44.

Anderson, J. R. (2010). *Cognitive psychology and its implications*. (7th ed.). New York, NY: Worth.

Anderson, J. R., Reder, L. M., & Simon, H. A. (1995). *Applications and misapplication of cognitive psychology to mathematics education*. Unpublished manuscript. Retrieved from www.psy.cmu.edu/~mm4b/misapplied.html

Anderson, J. R., Reder, L. M., & Simon, H. A. (1996). Situated learning and education. *Educational Researcher, 25*, 5–11.

Anderson, L. M. (1985). What are students doing when they do all that seatwork? In C. Fisher & D. Berliner (Eds.), *Perspectives on instructional time* (pp. 189–202). New York, NY: Longman.

Anderson, L. M., Brubaker, N. L., Alleman-Brooks, J., & Duffy, G. G. (1985). A qualitative study of seatwork in first-grade classrooms. *Elementary School Journal, 86*, 123–140.

Anderson, L. W., & Krathwohl, D. R. (Eds.). (2001). *A taxonomy for learning, teaching, and assessing: A revision of Bloom's taxonomy of educational objectives*. New York, NY: Longman.

Anderson, L. W., & Sosniak, L. A. (Eds.). (1994). *Bloom's taxonomy: A forty-year retrospective*. Ninety-third yearbook for the National Society for the Study of Education: Part II. Chicago, IL: University of Chicago Press.

Anderson, P. J., & Graham, S. M. (1994). Issues in second-language phonological acquisition among children and adults. *Topics in Language Disorders, 14*, 84–100.

Anderson, R. C., Nguyen-Jahiel, K., McNurlen, B., Archodidou, A., Kim, S-Y., Reznitskaya, A., . . . Gilbert, L. (2001). The snowball phenomenon: Spread of ways of talking and ways of thinking across groups of children. *Cognition and Instruction, 19*, 1–46.

Anderson, S. M., Klatzky, R. L., & Murray, J. (1990). Traits and social stereotypes: Efficiency differences in social information processing. *Journal of Personality and Social Psychology, 59*, 192–201.

Angier, N., & Chang, K. (2005, January 24). Gray matter and the sexes: Still a scientific gray area. *The New York Times*, A1+.

Antonenko, P., Paas, F., Grabner, R., & Van Gog, T. (2010). Using electroencephalography (EEG) to measure cognitive load. *Educational Psychology Review, 22*, 425–438.

Anyon, J. (1980). Social class and the hidden curriculum of work. *Journal of Education, 162*, 67–92.

Archer, S. L., & Waterman, A. S. (1990). Varieties of identity diffusions and foreclosures: An exploration of the subcategories of the identity statuses. *Journal of Adolescent Research, 5*, 96–111.

Arends, R. I. (2001). *Learning to teach* (5th ed.). New York, NY: McGraw-Hill.

Arends, R. I. (2004). *Learning to teach* (6th ed.). New York, NY: McGraw-Hill.

Arends, R. I. (2007). *Learning to teach* (7th ed.). New York, NY: McGraw-Hill.

Arends, R., & Kilcher, A. (2010). *Teaching for Student Learning: Becoming an Accomplished Teacher* New York: Routledge.

Armbruster, B. B. (2000). Taking notes from lectures. In R. F. Flippo & D. C. Caverly (Eds.), *Handbook of college reading and study strategy research* (pp. 175–200). Mahwah, NJ: Lawrence Erlbaum.

Arnold, M. L. (2000). Stage, sequence, and sequels: Changing conceptions of morality, post-Kohlberg. *Educational Psychology Review, 12*, 365–383.

Aronson, E. (2000). *Nobody left to hate: Teaching compassion after Columbine*. New York, NY: Worth.

Aronson, J. (2002). Stereotype threat: Contending and coping with unnerving expectations. In J. Aronson & D. Cordova (Eds.), *Improving education: Classic and contemporary lessons from psychology* (pp. 279–301). New York, NY: Academic Press.

Aronson, J., Fried, C. B., & Good, C. (2002). Reducing the effects of stereotype threat on African American college students: The role of theories of intelligence. *Journal of Experimental Social Psychology, 33*, 113–125.

Aronson, J., & Inzlicht, M. (2004). The ups and downs of attributional ambiguity: Stereotype vulnerability and the academic self-knowledge of African American college students. *Psychological Science, 15*, 829–836.

Aronson, J., Lustina, M. J., Good, C., Keough, K., Steele, C. M., & Brown, J. (1999). When White men can't do math: Necessary and sufficient factors in stereotype threat. *Journal of Experimental Social Psychology, 35*, 29–46.

Aronson, J., & Steele, C. M. (2005). Stereotypes and the fragility of human competence, motivation, and self-concept. In C. Dweck & E. Elliot (Eds.), *Handbook of competence and motivation*. New York, NY: Guilford.

Aronson, J., Steele, C. M., Salinas, M. F., & Lustina, M. J. (1999). The effect of stereotype threat on the standardized test performance of college students. In E. Aronson (Ed.), *Readings about the social animal* (8th ed.). New York, NY: Freeman.

Arsenio, W. F. & Lemerise, E. A. (2004). Agression and moral development: Integrating social information processing and moral domain models. *Child Development, 75*, 987–1002.

Asbridge, M., Brubacher, J. R., & Chan, H. (2013). Cell phone use and traffic crash risk: A culpability analysis. *International Journal of Epidemiology, 42*(1): 259–267.

Ashcraft, M. H. (2006). *Cognition* (4th ed.). Upper Saddle River, NJ: Prentice-Hall.

Ashcraft, M. H., & Radvansky, G. A. (2010). *Cognition*, 5th edition. Pearson.

Ashton, P. T. (1978). Cross-cultural Piagetian research: An experimental perspective. *Harvard Educational Review* (Reprint Series No. 13), 475–506.

Association for the Gifted. (2001). *Diversity and developing gifts and talents: A national action plan*. Arlington, VA: Author.

Asthma Society of Canada. (2009). Asthma at school. Retrieved from www.asthma.ca/adults/community/asthmaatschool.php

Asthma Society of Canada. (2014). Retrieved February 4, 2015 from http://www.asthma.ca.

Astington, J. W., & Dack, L. A. (2008). Theory of mind. In M. M. Haith & J. B. Benson (Eds.), *Encyclopedia of Infant and Early Childhood Development*, Vol. 3, (pp. 343–356). San Diego, CA: Academic Press.

Atkinson, R. C., & Shiffrin, R. M. (1968). Human memory: A proposed system and its control processes. In K. Spence & J. Spence (Eds.), *The psychology of learning and motivation* (Vol. 2, pp. 89–195). New York, NY: Academic Press.

Atkinson, R. K., Levin, J. R., Kiewra, K. A., Meyers, T., Atkinson, L. A., Renandya, W. A., & Hwang, Y. (1999). Matrix and mnemonic text-processing adjuncts: Comparing and combining their components. *Journal of Educational Psychology, 91*, 242–257.

Atkinson, R. K., & Renkl, A. (2007). Interactive example-based learning environments: Using interactive elements to encourage effective processing of worked examples. *Educational Psychology Review, 19*, 375–386.

Atkinson, R. K., Renkl, A., & Merrill, M. M. (2003). Transitioning from studying examples to solving problems: Combining fading with prompting fosters learning. *Journal of Educational Psychology, 95*, 774–783.

Atwell, P. (2000). *Beyond the digital divide* [Working paper No. 164]. New York, NY: Russell Sage Foundation.

Au, K. H. (1980). Participation structures in a reading lesson with Hawaiian children: Analysis of a culturally appropriate instructional event. *Anthropology and Education Quarterly, 11*, 91–115.

Au, K. T., Knightly, L. M., Jun, S., & Oh, J. S. (2002). Overhearing a language during childhood. *Psychological Science, 13*, 238–243.

Au, T. K., Oh, J. S., Knightly, L. M., Jun. S-A., & Romo, L. F. (2008). Salvaging a childhood language. *Journal of Memory and Language, 58*(4): 998–1011.

Aufderheide, P., & Firestone, C. (1993). *Media literacy: A report of the national leadership conference on media literacy*. Queenstown, MD: Aspen Institute.

Ausubel, D. P. (1963). *The psychology of meaningful verbal learning*. New York, NY: Grune and Stratton.

Ausubel, D. P. (1977). The facilitation of meaningful verbal learning in the classroom. *Educational Psychologist, 12*, 162–178.

Ausubel, D. P. (1982). Schemata, advance organizers, and anchoring ideas: A reply to Anderson, Spiro, and Anderson. *Journal of Structural Learning, 7*, 63–73.

Avramidis, E., Bayliss, P., & Burden, R. (2000). Student teachers' attitudes toward the inclusion of children with special education needs in the ordinary school. Teaching and *Teacher Education, 16*, 277–293.

Azevedo, R. (2005). Using hypermedia as a metacognitive tool for enhancing student learning? The role of self-regulated learning. *Educational Psychologist, 40*, 199–209.

Azevedo, R., Cromley, J. G., & Seibert, D. (2004). Does adaptive scaffolding facilitate students' ability to regulate their learning with hypermedia? *Contemporary Educational Psychology, 29*, 344–370.

Azevedo, R., Johnson, A., Chauncey, A., & Graesser, A. (2011). Use of hypermedia to assess and convey self-regulated learning. *Handbook of self-regulation of learning and performance*: 102–121.

Azzam, A. M. (2006, April). A generation immersed in media. *Educational Leadership*, 92–93.

Babad, E. Y. (1995). The "Teachers' Pet" phenomenon, students' perceptions of differential behavior, and students' morale. *Journal of Educational Psychology, 87*, 361–374.

Babad, E. Y., Inbar, J., & Rosenthal, R. (1982). Pygmalion, Galatea, and the Golem: Investigations of biased and unbiased teachers. *Journal of Educational Psychology, 74*, 459–474.

Baddeley, A. D. (1986). *Working memory*. Oxford, England: Clarendon Books.

Baddeley, A. D. (2001). Is working memory still working? *American Psychologist, 56*, 851–864.

Baddeley, A. D. (2007). *Working memory, thought, and action*. New York, NY: Oxford University Press.

Baddeley, A. D., Hitch, G. J., & Allen, R. J. (2009). Working memory and binding in sentence recall. *Journal of Memory and Language, 61*: 438–456.

Baer, J. (1997). *Creative teachers, creative students*. Boston, MA: Allyn & Bacon.

Bagley, E., & Shaffer, D. W. (2009). When people get in the way: Promoting civic thinking through epistemic gameplay. *International Journal of Gaming and Computer-Mediated Simulations, 1* (1): 36–52.

Bailey, S. M. (1993). The current status of gender equity research in American Schools. *Educational Psychologist, 28*, 321–339.

Baillargeon, R. (1999). Yong infants' expectations about hidden objects: A reply to three challenges. *Developmental Psychology, 2*, 115–132.

Baker, K. (1998). Structured English immersion breakthrough in teaching limited-English-proficient students. *Phi Delta Kappan, 80* (3), 199–204. Available online at: http://pdkintl.org/kappan/kbak9811.htm

Bakerman, R., Adamson, L. B., Koner, M., & Barr, R. G. (1990). !Kung infancy: The social context of object exploration. *Child Development, 61*, 794–809.

Balass, M., Nelson, J. R., & Perfetti, C. A. (2010). Word learning: An ERP investigation of word experience effects on recognition and word processing. *Contemporary Educational Psychology, 35*.

Baldwin, J. M. (1895). *Mental development in the child and the race: Methods and processes*. New York, NY: Macmillan.

Ball, D. L. (1997). What do students know? Facing challenges of distance, context, and desire in trying to hear children. In B. J. Biddle, T. L. Good, & I. F. Goodson (Eds.), *The international handbook of teachers and teaching* (pp. 769–818). Dordrecht, the Netherlands: Kluwer.

Ball, J. (2008). Promoting equity and dignity for Aboriginal children in Canada. *Choices, 14*(7), 3–27.

Ball, J., & Bernhardt, B. M. (2008). First Nations English dialects in Canada: Implications for speech-language pathology. *Clinical Linguistics & Phonetics, 22*(8): 570–588.

Ball, J., Bernhardt, B., & Deby, J. (2006). First Nations English dialects in young children: Forum proceedings. University of Victoria, School of Child and Youth Care, & University of British Columbia, School of Audiology and Speech Sciences.

Bandura, A. (1965). Influence of models' reinforcement contingencies on the acquisition of imitative responses. *Journal of Personality and Social Psychology, 1*, 589–595.

Bandura, A. (1977). *Social learning theory*. Englewood Cliffs, NJ: Prentice-Hall.

Bandura, A. (1982). Self-efficacy mechanisms in human agency. *American Psychologist, 37*, 122–147.

Bandura, A. (1986). *Social foundations of thought and action*. Englewood Cliffs, NJ: Prentice-Hall.

Bandura, A. (1993). Perceived self-efficacy in cognitive development and functioning. *Educational Psychologist, 28*, 117–148.

Bandura, A. (1994). Self-efficacy. In V. S. Ramachaudran (Ed.), *Encyclopedia of human behavior* (Vol. 4, pp. 71–81). New York, NY: Academic Press.

Bandura, A. (1997). *Self-efficacy: The exercise of control*. New York, NY: Freeman.

Bandura, A. (2001). Social cognitive theory: An agentic perspective. *Annual review of psychology* (Vol. 52, pp. 1–26). Palo Alto, CA: Annual Reviews, Inc.

Bandura, A. (2002). Social cognitive theory in cultural context. *Applied Psychology: An International Review, 51*(2) 269–290.

Bandura, A. (2006). Adolescent development from an agentic perspective. In F. Pajares & T. Urdan (Eds.), *Self-efficacy beliefs of adolescents*. Greenwich, CT: Information Age.

Bandura, A. (2007). Albert Bandura. In L. Gardner & W. M. Runyan (Eds.), *A history of psychology in autobiography* (Vol. IX, pp. 43–75). Washington, DC: American Psychological Association.

Bandura, A., & Locke, E. (2003). Negative self-efficacy and goal effects revisited. *Journal of Applied Psychology, 88*, 87–99.

Bandura, A., Ross, D., & Ross, S. A. (1963). Vicarious reinforcement and imitative learning. *Journal of Abnormal and Social Psychology, 67*, 601–607.

Banks, J. A. (1997). *Teaching strategies for ethnic studies* (6th ed.). Boston, MA: Allyn & Bacon.

Banks, J. A. (1999). *An introduction to multicultural education* (2nd ed.). Boston, MA: Allyn & Bacon.

Banks, J. A. (2002). *An introduction to multicultural education* (3rd ed.). Boston, MA: Allyn & Bacon.

Banks, J. A. (2006). *Cultural diversity and education: Foundations, curriculum, and teaching* (5th ed.). Boston, MA: Allyn & Bacon.

Banks, S. R. (2005). *Classroom assessment: Issues and practice*. Boston, MA: Allyn & Bacon.

Barakett, J. M. (1986). Teachers' theories and methods in structuring routine activities in an inner city school. *Canadian Journal of Education, 11*(2), 91–108.

Barden, L. M. (1995). Effective questioning and the ever-elusive higher-order question. *American Biology Teacher, 57*, 423–426.

Bargh, J. A., McKenna, K. Y. A., & Fitzsimons, G. M. (2002). Can you see the real me? Activation and expression of the "true self" on the Internet. *Journal of Social Issues, 58*(1), 33–48.

Barkley, R. A. (Ed.). (2006). *Attention-deficit hyperactivity disorder: A handbook for diagnosis and treatment* (3rd ed., pp. 547–588). New York, NY: Guilford.

Barnett, M. S., & Ceci, S. J. (2002). When and where do we apply what we learn? A taxonomy for far transfer. *Psychological Bulletin, 128*, 612–637.

Barnhill, G. P. (2005). Functional behavioral assessment in schools. *Intervention in School and Clinic, 40*, 131–143.

Baron, R. A. (1998). *Psychology* (4th ed.). Boston, MA: Allyn & Bacon.

Baron, R. A., & Byrne, D. (2003). *Social psychology* (10th ed.). Boston, MA: Allyn & Bacon.

Baroody, A. R., & Ginsburg, H. P. (1990). Children's learning: A cognitive view. In R. Davis, C. Maher, & N. Noddings (Eds.), *Constructivist views on the teaching and learning of mathematics* (pp. 51–64). Monograph 4 of the National Council of Teachers of Mathematics, Reston, VA.

Barr, R. (2001). Research on the teaching of reading. In V. Richardson (Ed.), *Handbook of research on teaching* (4th ed., pp. 390–415). Washington, DC: American Educational Research Association.

Barros, R. M., Silver, E., & Stein, R. E. K. (2009). School recess and group classroom behavior. *Pediatrics 123*(2), 431–436.

Bartholomew, B. (2008). Sustaining the fire. *Educational Leadership, 65*(6), 55–60.

Bartlett, S. M., Rapp, J. T., Krueger, T. K., & Henrickson, M. L. (2011). The use of response cost to treat spitting by a child with autism. *Behavioral Intentions 26*(1): 76–83.

Basow, S. A., & Rubin, L. R. (1999). Gender influences on adolescent development. In N. G. Johnson, M. C. Roberts, & J. Worell (Eds.), *Beyond appearance: A new look at adolescent girls* (pp. 25–52). Washington, DC: American Psychological Association.

Batschaw, M. L. (1997). *Children with disabilities* (4th ed.). Baltimore, ML: Brookes.

Bauer, P. J. (2006). Event memory. In D. Kuhn & R. S. Siegler (Eds.), *Cognition, perception, and language* (6th ed., Vol. 2, pp. 373–425). New York, NY: Wiley.

Baumeister, R. F., Campbell, J. D., Krueger, J. L., & Vohs, K. D. (2003). Does high self-esteem cause better performance, interpersonal success, happiness, or healthier lifestyles? *Psychological Science in the Public Interest, 4*, 1–44.

Baumeister, R. F., & Leary, M. R. (1995). The need to belong: Desire for interpersonal attachments as a fundamental human motivation. Psychological Bulletin, 117, 497–529.

Baumert, J., Kunter, M., Blum, W., Brunner, M., Voss, T., Jordan, A., Klusmann, U., Krauss, S., Neubrand, M., & Tsai, Y.-M. (2010). Teachers' mathematical knowledge, cognitive activation in the classroom, and student progress. *American Educational Research Journal, 47* (1), 133–180.

Baumrind, D. (1971). Current patterns of parental authority. *Developmental Psychology, 4*, 1–103.

Baumrind, D. (1991). Effective parenting during early adolescent transitions. In P. A. Cowan & M. Hetherington (Eds.), *Family transitions* (pp. 111–165). Hillsdale, NJ: Erlbaum.

Bayliss, D. M., Jarrold, C., Baddeley, A., Gunn, D. M., & Leigh, E. (2005). Mapping the developmental constraints on working memory span performance. *Developmental Psychology, 41*(4): 579–597.

BC College of Teachers. (2008). *Standards for the competence, professional conduct and ethical behaviour of educators in British Columbia* (3rd ed.). Retrieved from www.bcct.ca/documents/AboutUs/Standards/edu_stds.pdf

BC Ministry for Children and Families, 2013. Reporting child abuse. Retrieved June 12, 2014, from www.mcf.gov.bc.ca/child_protection/reportabuse.htm

BC Ministry of Education. (n.d.). Full day kindergarten: Program guide. Retrieved from www.bced.gov.bc.ca/early_learning/fdk/pdfs/fdk_program_guide.pdf

BCTF. (2003). Summary analysis of the BC College of Teachers' standards for the education competence and professional conduct of educators in BC. Retrieved from www.bctf.ca

Beane, J. A. (1991). Sorting out the self-esteem controversy. *Educational Leadership, 49*(1), 25–30.

Bear, G. G. (with Cavalier, A. R., & Manning, M. A.). (2005). *Developing self-discipline and preventing and correcting misbehavior*. Boston, MA: Allyn & Bacon.

Beauchamp, C. & Beauchamp, M. (2013). Boundary as bridge: An analysis of the educational neuroscience literature from a boundary perspective. *Educational Psychology Review, 25*(1).

Beck, C., Hart, D., & Kosnik, C. (2002). The teaching standards movement and current teaching practices. *Canadian Journal of Education, 27*, 175–194.

Beck, I. L., McKeown, M. G., Worthy, J., Sandora, C. A., & Kucan, L. (1996). Questioning the author: A yearlong classroom implementation to engage students with text. *The Elementary School Journal, 96*, 385–414.

Bee, H. (1981). *The developing child* (3rd ed.). New York, NY: Harper & Row.

Beebe-Frankenberger, M., Bocian, K. L., MacMillan, D. L., & Gresham, F. M. (2004). Sorting second grade students with academic deficiencies: Characteristics differentiating those retained in grade from those promoted to third grade. *Journal of Educational Psychology, 96*, 204–215.

Beeth, M. E. (1998). Teaching science in fifth grade: Instructional goals that support conceptual change. *Journal of Research in Science Teaching, 35*, 1091–1101.

Beghetto, R. A. (2008). Prospective teachers' beliefs about imaginative thinking in K-12 schooling. *Thinking Skills and Creativity, 3*, 134–142.

Begley, S. (2007, October). The case for chutes and ladders. *Newsweek.* Available online at: http://www.newsweek.com/2007/10/13/the-case-for-chutes-and-ladders.html

Benenson, J. F. (1993). Greater preference among females than males for dyadic interaction in early childhood. *Child Development, 64*, 544–555.

Benjafield, J. G. (1992). *Cognition.* Englewood Cliffs, NJ: Prentice-Hall.

Bennett, C. I. (1995). *Comprehensive multicultural education: Theory and practice* (3rd ed.). Boston, MA: Allyn & Bacon.

Bennett, C. I. (1999). *Comprehensive multicultural education: Theory and practice* (4th ed.). Boston, MA: Allyn & Bacon.

Bennett, C. I. (2011). Comprehensive multicultural education: Theory and practice (7th ed.). Boston, MA: Allyn & Bacon.

Bereiter, C. (1995). A dispositional view of transfer. In A. McKeough, J. Lupart, & A. Marini (Eds.), *Teaching for mastery: Fostering generalization in learning* (pp. 21–34). Mahwah, NJ: Erlbaum.

Bereiter, C. (1997). Situated cognition and how I overcome it. In D. Kirshner & J. A. Whitson (Eds.), *Situated cognition: Social, semiotic, and psychological perspectives* (pp. 281–300). Mahwah, NJ: Erlbaum.

Berg, C. A., & Clough, M. (1991). Hunter lesson design: The wrong one for science teaching. *Educational Leadership, 48*(4), 73–78.

Berger, K. S. (2003). *The developing person through childhood and adolescence* (6th ed.). New York, NY: Worth Publishers.

Berger, K. S. (2006). *The developing person through childhood and adolescence* (7th ed.). New York, NY: Worth.

Berger, K. S. (2012). The developing person through the life span (8th ed.). New York, NY: Worth.

Berger, K. S., & Thompson, R. A. (1995). *The developing person through childhood and adolescence.* New York, NY: Worth.

Bergin, D. (1999). Influences on classroom interest. *Educational Psychologist, 34*, 87–98.

Berk, L. E. (2001). *Awakening children's minds: How parents and teachers can make a difference.* New York, NY: Oxford University Press.

Berk, L. E. (2002). *Infants, children, and adolescents* (4th ed.). Boston, MA: Allyn & Bacon.

Berk, L. E. (2005). *Infants, children, and adolescents* (5th ed.). Boston, MA: Allyn & Bacon.

Berk, L. E., & Spuhl, S. T. (1995). Maternal interaction, private speech, and task performance in preschool children. *Early Childhood Research Quarterly, 10*, 145–169.

Berko, J. (1958). The child's learning of English morphology. *Word, 14*, 150–177.

Berliner, D. C. (1983). Developing concepts of classroom environments: Some light on the T in studies of ATI. *Educational Psychologist, 18*, 1–13.

Berliner, D. C. (1987). But do they understand? In V. Richardson-Koehler (Ed.), *Educators' handbook: A research perspective* (pp. 259–293). New York, NY: Longman.

Berliner, D. C. (1988). Simple views of effective teaching and a simple theory of classroom instruction. In D. Berliner & B. Rosenshine (Eds.), *Talks to teachers* (pp. 93–110). New York, NY: Random House.

Berliner, D. C. (2002). Educational research: The hardest science of all. *Educational Researcher, 31*(8), 18–20.

Berliner, D. C. (2005). Our impoverished view of educational reform. *The Teachers College Record, 108*, 949–995.

Berliner, D. C. (2006). Educational psychology: Searching for essence throughout a century of influence. In P. A. Alexander & P. H. Winne (Eds.), *Handbook of educational psychology* (2nd ed., pp. 3–27). Mahwah, NJ: Erlbaum.

Berlyne, D. (1966). Curiosity and exploration. *Science, 153*, 25–33.

Berndt, T. J. (2004). Children's friendships: Shifts over a half-century in perspectives on their development and their effects. Merrill-Palmer Quarterly: *Journal of Development Sciences, 50*, 206–223.

Berndt, T. J., & Keefe, K. (1995). Friends' influence on adolescents' adjustment to school. *Child Development, 66*, 1312–1329.

Bernstein, D. A., & Nash, P. W. (2008). *Essentials of psychology* (4th ed.). Boston, MA: Houghton-Mifflin.

Berry, R. Q., III. (2005). Voices of success: Descriptive portraits of two successful African American male middle school mathematics students. *Journal of AfricanAmerican Studies, 8* (4), 46–62.

Berthold, K., & Renkl, A. (2009). Instructional aids to support a conceptual understanding of multiple representations. *Journal of Educational Psychology, 101*, 70–87.

Betancourt, H., & Lopez, S. R. (1993). The study of culture, ethnicity, and race in American psychology. *American Psychologist, 48*, 629–637.

Bialystok, E. (2001). *Bilingualism in development: Language, literacy, and cognition.* New York, NY: Cambridge University Press.

Bialystok, E., Majumder, S., & Martin, M. M. (2003). Developing phonological awareness: Is there a bilingual advantage? *Applied Linguistics, 24*, 27–44.

Biggs, J. (2001). Enhancing learning: A matter of style of approach. In R. Sternberg & L. Zhang (Eds.), *Perspectives on cognitive, learning, and thinking styles* (pp. 73–102). Mahwah, NJ: Erlbaum.

Blair, C. (2002). School readiness: Integrating cognition and emotion in a neurobiological conceptualization of children's functioning at school entry. *American Psychologist, 57*, 111–127.

Blair, C. (2006). How similar are fluid cognition and general intelligence? A developmental neuroscience perspective on fluid cognition as an aspect of human cognition [Main article with commentaries]. *Behavioral and Brain Sciences, 29*, 109–160.

Blakeburn Elementary & Laidlaw, L. (2001). "I can be happy at this school": Creating a socially responsible learning community. *Teacher: Newsmagazine of the British Columbia Teachers Federation, 13*(5), 1–4.

Blakemore, S. K., & Frith, U. (2005). The learning brain: Lessons for education: a precis. Developmental Science, 8, 459–461.

Blatchford, P., Baines, E., Rubie-Davis, C., Bassett, P., & Chowne, A. (2006). The effect of a new approach to group work on pupil-pupil and teacher-interactions. *Journal of Educational Psychology, 98*, 750–765.

Bloom, B. S. (1981). *All our children learning: A primer for parents, teachers, and other educators.* New York, NY: McGraw-Hill.

Bloom, B. S. (1982). The role of gifts and markers in the development of talent. *Exceptional Children, 48*, 510–522.

Bloom, B. S., Engelhart, M. D., Frost, E. J., Hill, W. H., & Krathwohl, D. R. (1956). *Taxonomy of educational objectives. Handbook I: Cognitive domain.* New York, NY: David McKay.

Bloom, P. (2002). *How children learn the meanings of words.* Cambridge, MA: MIT Press.

Blumenfeld, P. C., Puro, P., & Mergendoller, J. R. (1992). Translating motivation into thoughtfulness. In H. Marshall (Ed.), *Redefining student learning: Roots of educational change* (pp. 207–240). Norwood, NJ: Ablex.

Bolick, C. M., & Cooper, J. M. (2006). Classroom management and technology. In C. Evertson & C. S. Weinstein (Eds.), *Handbook for classroom management: Research, practice, and contemporary issues.* Mahwah, NJ: Erlbaum.

Bong, M. (2009). Age-related differences in achievement goal differentiation. *Journal of Educational Psychology, 101*, 879–896.

Bonnano, R. A. & Hymel, S. (2010). Beyond hurt feelings: Investigating why some victims of bullying are at greater risk for suicidal ideation. *Merrill-Palmer Quarterly, 56*, 420–440.

Boom, J., Brugman, D., & van der Heijden, P. G. (2001). Hierarchical structure of moral stages assessed by a sorting task. *Child Development, 72*, 535–548.

Borich, G. D. (2011). *Effective teaching methods: Research-based practice* (7th ed.). Columbus, OH: Pearson.

Borko, H., & Livingston, C. (1989). Cognition and improvisation: Differences in mathematics instruction by expert and novice teachers. *American Educational Research Journal, 26*, 473–498.

Borman, G. D., & Overman, L. T. (2004). Academic resilience in mathematics among poor and minority students. *The Elementary School Journal, 104*, 177–195.

Borrero, N. E., & Yeh, C. J. (2010). Ecological language learning among ethnic minority youth. *Educational Researcher, 39*(8): 571–581.

Bos, C. S., & Reyes, E. I. (1996). Conversations with a Latina teacher about education for language-minority students with special needs. *The Elementary School Journal, 96*, 344–351.

Bowlby, J. (1969). *Attachment and loss: Attachment.* New York, NY: Basic Books.

Boyd, D., Goldhaber, D., Lankford, H., & Wyckoff, J., (2008). The effect of certification and preparation on teacher quality. *The Future of Children, 17* (1), 45.

Boyle, J. R. (2010a). Note-taking skills of middle school students with and without learning disabilities. *Journal of Learning Disabilities, 43*, 530–540.

Boyle, J. R. (2010b). Strategic note-taking for middle school students with learning disabilities in science classes. *Learning Disabilities Quarterly, 33,* 93–109.

Boyle, J. R., & Weishaar, M. (2001). The effects of strategic notetaking on the recall and comprehension of lecture information for high school students with learning disabilities. *Learning Disabilities Research & Practice,16*(3): 133–141.

Bradshaw, C. P., Zmuda, J. H., Kellam, S. G., & Ialongo, N. S. (2009). Longitudinal impact of two universal preventive interventions in first grade on educational outcomes in high school. *Journal of Educational Psychology, 101*(4): 926–937.

Brainerd, C. J. (2003). Jean Piaget, learning research, and American education. In B. J. Zimmerman & D. H. Schunk (Eds.), *Educational psychology: A century of contributions* (pp. 251–287). Mahwah, NJ: Erlbaum.

Brannon, L. (2002). *Gender: Psychological perspectives* (3rd ed.). Boston, MA: Allyn & Bacon.

Bransford, J. D., Brown, A. L., & Cocking, R. R. (2000). *How people learn: Brain, mind, experience, and school.* Washington, DC: National Academy Press.

Bransford, J. D., & Schwartz, D. (1999). Rethinking transfer: A simple proposal with multiple implications. In A. Iran-Nejad & P. D. Pearson (Eds.), *Review of research in education* (Vol. 24, pp. 61–100). Washington, DC: American Educational Research Association.

Bransford, J. D., & Stein, B. S. (1993). *The IDEAL problem solver: A guide for improving thinking, learning, and creativity* (2nd ed.). New York, NY: Freeman.

Brantlinger, E. (2004). Who wins and who loses? Social class and students' identities. In M. Sadowski (Ed.), *Adolescents at school: Perspectives on youth, identity, and education* (pp. 107–126). Cambridge, MA: Harvard University Press.

Branum-Martin, L., Foorman, B. R., Francis, D. J., & Mehta, P. D. (2010). Contextual effects of bilingual programs on beginning reading. *Journal of Educational Psychology, 102,* 341–355.

Brault, M. C. & Lacourse, E. (2012). Prevalence of prescribed attention-deficit hyperactivity disorder medications and diagnosiss among Canadian preschoolers and school-aged children: 1994–2007. *Canadian Journal of Psychiatry, 57,* 93–101.

Bredekamp, S., & Copple, C. (1997). *Developmentally appropriate practice in early childhood programs.* Washington, DC: National Association for the Education of Young Children.

Briesch, A. M., & Chafouleas, S. M. (2009). Review and analysis of literature on self-management interventions to promote appropriate classroom behaviors (1988–2008). *School Psychology Quarterly, 24,* 106–118.

British Columbia College of Teachers. (2004, Winter). Aboriginal education initiatives: From parents clubs to teacher education. *Connected,* 9–11.

British Columbia Ministry for Children and Families. (1998). *The BC handbook for action on child abuse and neglect.* Victoria, BC: Crown Publications.

British Columbia Special Education Branch. (1995). *Special education services: A manual of policies, procedures, and guidelines.* Victoria, BC: Author.

British Columbia Special Education Branch. 2013. Retrieved June 21 from http://www.bced.gov.bc.ca/specialed/special_ed_policy_manual.pdf

Broidy, L. M., Nagin, D. S., Tremblay, R. E., Bates, J. E., Brame, B., Dodge, K., . . . Vitaro, F. (2003). Developmental trajectories of childhood disruptive behaviors and adolescent delinquency: A six site, cross-national study. *Developmental Psychology, 39,* 222–245.

Bronfenbrenner, U. (1989). Ecological systems theory. In R. Vasta (Ed.), *Annals of child development* (Vol. 6, pp. 187–249). Boston, MA: JAI Press, Inc.

Bronfenbrenner, U., & Evans, G. W. (2000). Developmental science in the 21st century: Emerging theoretical models, research designs, and empirical findings. *Social Development, 9,* 115–125.

Bronfenbrenner, U., McClelland, P., Wethington, E., Moen, P., & Ceci, S. (1996). *The state of Americans: This generation and the next.* New York, NY: Free Press.

Bronfenbrenner, U., & Morris, P. A. (2006). The bioecological model of human development. In W. Damon & R. M. Lerner (Eds.), *Handbook of child psychology: Vol. 1. Theoretical models of human development* (6th ed., pp. 793–827). Hoboken, NJ: Wiley.

Brooks-Gunn, J. (1988). Antecedents and consequences of variations in girls' maturational timing. In M. D. Levin & E. R. McAnarney (Eds.), *Early adolescent transitions* (pp. 101–121). Lexington, MA: Lexington Books.

Brophy, J. E. (1981). Teacher praise: A functional analysis. *Review of Educational Research, 51,* 5–21.

Brophy, J. E. (1985). Teacher–student interaction. In J. Dusek (Ed.), *Teacher expectancies* (pp. 303–328). Hillsdale, NJ: Erlbaum.

Brophy, J. E. (1988). On motivating students. In D. Berliner & B. Rosenshine (Eds.), *Talks to teachers* (pp. 201–245). New York, NY: Random House.

Brophy, J. E. (1998). *Motivating students to learn.* New York, NY: McGraw-Hill.

Brophy, J. E. (2003). An interview with Jere Brophy by B. Gaedke, & M. Shaughnessy. *Educational Psychology Review, 15,* 199–211.

Brophy, J. E. (2005). Goal theorists should move on from performance goals. *Educational Psychologist, 40,* 167–176.

Brophy, J. E. (2008). Developing students' appreciation for what is taught in school, *Educational Psychologist, 43,* 132–141.

Brophy, J. E., & Evertson, C. (1978). Context variables in teaching. *Educational Psychologist, 12,* 310–316.

Brophy, J. E., & Good, T. (1986). Teacher behavior and student achievement. In M. Wittrock (Ed.), *Handbook of research on teaching* (3rd ed.) (pp. 328–375). New York, NY: Macmillan.

Brophy, J. E., & Kher, N. (1986). Teacher socialization as a mechanism for developing student motivation to learn. In R. Feldman (Ed.), *Social psychology applied to education* (pp. 256–288). New York, NY: Cambridge University Press.

Brown, A. (1987). Metacognition, executive control, self-regulation, and other more mysterious mechanisms. In F. Weinert & R. Kluwe (Eds.), *Metacognition, motivation, and understanding* (pp. 65–116). Hillside, NJ: Erlbaum.

Brown, A. (1997). Transforming schools into communities of thinking and learning about serious matters. *American Psychologist, 52,* 399–413.

Brown, A. L. (1992). Design experiments: Theoretical and methodological challenges in creating complex interventions in classroom settings. *Journal of the Learning Sciences, 2,* 141–178.

Brown, A. L., Bransford, J., Ferrara, R., & Campione, J. (1983). Learning, remembering, and understanding. In P. Mussen (Ed.), *Handbook of child psychology* (Vol. 3, pp. 515–629). New York, NY: Wiley.

Brown, A. L., & Campione, J. C. (1996). Psychological theory and the design of innovative learning environments: On procedures, principles, and systems. In L. Schauble & R. Glaser (Eds.), *Innovations in learning: New environments for education* (pp. 289–325). Mahwah, NJ: Erlbaum.

Bruer, J. T. (1999). In search of . . . brain-based education. *Phi Delta Kappan, 80,* 648–657.

Bruer, J. T. (2002). Avoiding the pediatrician's error: How neuroscientists can help educators (and themselves). *Nature Neuroscience, 5,* 1031–1033.

Bruner, J. S. (1966). *Toward a theory of instruction.* New York, NY: Norton.

Bruner, J. S. (1973). *Beyond the information given: Studies in the psychology of knowing.* New York, NY: Norton.

Bruning, R. H., Schraw, G. J., Norby, M. M., & Ronning, R. R. (2004). *Cognitive psychology and instruction* (4th ed.). Columbus, OH: Merrill.

Brunner, M., Keller, U., Dierendinck, C., Reichert, M., Ugen, S., Fischbach, A., & Martin, R. (2010). The structure of academic self-concepts revisited: The nested Marsh/Shavelson model. *Journal of Educational Psychology, 102,* 964–981.

Buehler, R., Griffin, D., & Ross, M. (1994). Exploring the "planning fallacy": Why people underestimate their task completion times. *Journal of Personality and Social Psychology, 67*(3): 366–381.

Buhs, E. S., Ladd, G. W., & Herald, S. L. (2006). Peer exclusion and victimization: Processes that mediate the relation between peer group rejection and children's classroom engagement. *Journal of Educational Psychology, 98,* 1–13.

Burbules, N. C., & Bruce, B. C. (2001). Theory and research on teaching as dialogue. In V. Richardson (Ed.), *Handbook of research on teaching* (4th ed., pp. 1102–1121). Washington, DC: American Educational Research Association.

Burden, P. R. (1995). *Classroom management and discipline: Methods to facilitate cooperation and instruction.* White Plains, NY: Longman.

Burgess, S. R., Hecht, S. A., & Lonigan, C. J. (2002). Relations of the home literacy environment (HLE) to the development of reading-related abilities: A one-year longitudinal study. *Reading Research Quarterly, 37,* 408–426.

Burke-Spero, R., & Woolfolk Hoy, A. (2002). *The need for thick description: A qualitative investigation of developing teacher efficacy.* Unpublished manuscript, University of Miami.

Buss, D. M. (1995). Psychological sex differences: Origin through sexual selection. *American Psychologist, 50,* 164–168.

Butcher, K. R. (2006). Learning from text with diagrams: Promoting mental model development and inference generation. *Journal of Educational Psychology, 98,* 182–197.

Butler, D. L. (1998). A strategic content learning approach to promoting self-regulated learning by students with learning disabilities. In D. H. Schunk & B. J. Zimmerman (Eds.), *Self-regulated learning: From teaching to self-reflective practice* (pp. 160–183). New York, NY: Guilford Press.

Butler, D. L., Novak Lauscher, H. J., & Beckingham, B. (2005). Co-constructing strategies for math problem-solving: A report of three case studies. *Learning Disabilities Research and Practice, 20*, 156–174.

Butler, R. (1987). Task-involving and ego-involving properties of evaluation: Effects of different feedback conditions on motivational perceptions, interest, and performance. *Journal of Educational Psychology, 79*, 474–482.

Byers-Heinlein, K., Burns, T. F., & Werker, J. F. (2010). The roots of bilingualism in newborns. *Psychological Science, 21*, 343–348.

Byrne, B. M. (2002). Validating the measurement and structure of self-concept: Snapshots of past, present, and future research. *American Psychologist, 57*, 897–909.

Byrnes, J. P. (1996). *Cognitive development and learning in instructional contexts*. Boston, MA: Allyn & Bacon.

Byrnes, J. P. (2003). Factors predictive of mathematics achievement in White, Black, and Hispanic 12th graders. *Journal of Educational Psychology, 95*, 316–326.

Byrnes, J. P., & Fox, N. A. (1998). The educational relevance of research in cognitive neuroscience. *Educational Psychology Review, 10*, 297–342.

Cairns, R. B., & Cairns, B. D. (2006). The making of developmental psychology. In R. M. Lerner (Ed.), *Handbook of child psychology: Vol. 1. Theoretical models of human development* (6th ed., pp. 89–165). New York, NY: Wiley.

Calderhead, J. (1996). Teacher: Beliefs and knowledge. In D. Berliner & R. Calfee (Eds.), *Handbook of educational psychology* (pp. 709–725). New York, NY: Macmillan.

Callahan, C. M., Tomlinson, C. A., & Plucker, J. (1997). *Project START using a multiple intelligences model in identifying and promoting talent in high-risk students*. Storrs, CT: National Research Center for Gifted and Talented. University of Connecticut Technical Report.

Cameron-Faulkner, T., Lieven, E. & Tomasello, M. (2003). A construction based analysis of child directed speech. *Cognitive Science, 27*: 843–873. doi: 10.1207/s15516709cog2706_2

Cameron, J., & Pierce, W. D. (1994). Reinforcement, reward, and intrinsic motivation: A meta-analysis. *Review of Educational Research, 64*, 363–423.

Cameron, J., & Pierce, W. D. (1996). The debate about rewards and intrinsic motivation: Protests and accusations do not alter the results. *Review of Educational Research, 66*, 39–52.

Campaign 2000. (2009). *2009 Report card on child and family poverty: 1989–2009*. Retrieved from www.campaign2000.ca

Campaign 2000. (2013). Canada's real economic action plan begins with poverty: 2013 report card on child and family poverty in Canada. Retrieved June 2, 2014, from www.campaign2000.ca/reportCards/national/2013C2000NATIONALREPORTCARDNOV26.pdf

Canadian Cancer Society. (2008). Childhood cancer in Canada: Fast facts. Retrieved from www.quebec.cancer.ca/quebec/communiques/Stats08_FicheCancerPediatrique_en.pdf

Canadian Centre on Substance Abuse. (2007). *Substance abuse in Canada: Youth in focus*. Retrieved from www.ccsa.ca/NR/rdonlyres/5D418288-5147-4CAC-A6E4-6D09EC-6CBE13/0/ccsa0115212007e.pdf

Canadian Council on Learning (CCL). (2009). Lessons in learning: Homework helps, but not always. Retrieved from http://ccl-cca.ca/pdfs/LessonsinLearning/50-05_04_09-Lil-Homework-REV-E-meta.pdf

Canadian Fitness and Lifestyle Research Institute (CFLRI). (2008). Kids can play! Encouraging children to be active at home, at school, and in their communities. Retrieved from www.cflri.ca/eng/provincial_data/canplay_bulletins/canplay_canada.php

Canadian Institutes of Health Research (CIHR). (2006). Youth suicide: It's time to get involved. Retrieved from www.cihr-irsc.gc.ca/e/32154.html

Canadian Obesity Foundation. (2014). Childhood healthy weights intervention initiative: Our journey. Retrieved June 10, 2014, from http://childhoodobesityfoundation.ca/admin/files/files/COF_CHWII_Our_Journey_Mar_2014_FINAL.pdf

Canadian Resource Centre for Victims of Crime. (2011). Restorative justice in Canada: What victims should know. Retrieved August 1, 2014, from www.rjlillooet.ca/documents/restjust.pdf

Canadian Teachers Federation. (2009). Supporting education . . . building schools: Child poverty and schools. Retrieved from www.ctf-fce.ca/publications/Briefs/FINAL_Hilldayleavebehind_eng.pdf

Cangelosi, J. S. (1990). *Designing tests for evaluating student achievement*. New York, NY: Longman.

Canter, L. (1996). First the rapport—then the rules. *Learning, 24*(5), 12+.

Canter, L., & Canter, M. (1992). *Lee Canter's Assertive Discipline: Positive behavior management for today's classroom*. Santa Monica, CA: Lee Canter and Associates.

Cantrell, S. C., Almasi, J. F., Carter, J. C., Rintamaa, M., & Madden, A. (2010). The impact of a strategy-based intervention on the comprehension and strategy use of struggling adolescent readers. *Journal of Educational Psychology, 102*(2): 257–280.

Capa, Y. (2005). *Novice teachers' sense of efficacy* (Doctoral dissertation). The Ohio State University, Columbus, OH.

Capon, N., & Kuhn, D. (2004). What's so good about problem-based learning? *Cognition and Instruction, 22*, 61–79.

Cariglia-Bull, T., & Pressley, M. (1990). Short-term memory differences between children predict imagery effects when sentences are read. *Journal of Experimental Child Psychology, 49*, 384–398.

Carlisle, J. F., Stahl, S. A., & Birdyshaw, D. (Eds.). (2004, November). Lessons from research at the Center for the Improvement of Early Reading Achievement [Special Issue]. *The Elementary School Journal, 105*(2).

Carney, R. N., & Levin, J. R. (2000). Mnemonic instruction, with a focus on transfer. *Journal of Educational Psychology, 92*, 783–790.

Carney, R. N., & Levin, J. R. (2002). Pictorial illustrations still improve students' learning from text. *Educational Psychology Review, 14*, 5–26.

Carpendale, J. I. M. (2000). Kohlberg and Piaget on stages and moral reasoning. *Developmental Review, 20*, 181–205.

Carpenter, S. (2000). In the digital age experts pause to examine the effects on kids. *Monitor on Psychology, 31*(11), 48–49.

Carroll, J. B. (1997). The three-stratum theory of cognitive abilities. In D. P. Flanagan, J. L. Genshaft, & P. L. Harrison (Eds.), *Contemporary intellectual assessment: Theories, tests, and issues* (pp. 122–130). New York, NY: Guilford.

Carter, E. W., Wehby, J., Hughes, C., Johnson, S. M., Plank, D. R., Barton-Arwood, S. M., & Lunsford, L. B. (2005). Preparing adolescents with high-incidence disabilities for high-stakes testing with strategy instruction. *Preventing School Failure, 49* (2), 55–62.

Casanova, U. (1987). Ethnic and cultural differences. In V. Richardson-Koehler (Ed.), *Educators' handbook: A research perspective* (pp. 370–393). New York, NY: Longman.

Case, R. (1985a). *Intellectual development: Birth to adulthood*. New York, NY: Academic Press.

Case, R. (1985b). A developmentally-based approach to the problem of instructional design. In R. Glaser, S. Chipman, & J. Segal (Eds.), *Teaching thinking skills* (Vol. 2, pp. 545–562). Hillsdale, NJ: Erlbaum.

Case, R. (1992). *The mind's staircase: Exploring the conceptual underpinnings of children's thought and knowledge*. Mahwah, NJ: Erlbaum.

Case, R. (1998). The development of conceptual structures. In D. Kuhn & R. S. Siegler (Eds.), *Handbook of child psychology: Vol. 2. Cognition, perception, and language* (pp. 745–800). New York, NY: Wiley.

Casey, B. J., Getz, S., & Galvan, A. (2008). The adolescent brain. *Developmental Review, 28*(1).

Cassady, J. C., & Johnson, R. E. (2002). Cognitive anxiety and academic performance. *Contemporary Educational Psychology, 27*, 270–295.

Castellano, J. A., & Diaz, E. I. (Eds.). (2002). *Reaching new horizons. Gifted and talented education for culturally and linguistically diverse students*. Boston, MA: Allyn & Bacon.

Castle, S., Deniz, C. B., & Tortora, M. (2005). Flexible grouping and student learning in a high-needs school. *Education and Urban Society, 37*, 139–150.

Cattell, R. B. (1963). Theory of fluid and crystallized intelligence: A critical experiment. *Journal of Educational Psychology, 54*, 1–22.

Cattell, R. B. (1998). Where is intelligence? Some answers from the triadic theory. In J. J. McArdle & R. W. Woodcock (Eds.), *Human cognitive abilities in theory and practice*. Mahwah, NJ: Lawrence Erlbaum Assoc.

Cazden, C. (2001). *Classroom discourse: The language of teaching and learning* (2nd ed.). Portsmouth, NH: Heinemann.

CBC. (2007). Bullied student tickled pink by schoolmates' t-shirt campaign. Retrieved August 2, 2014, from www.cbc.ca/news/canada/bullied-student-tickled-pink-by-schoolmates-t-shirt-campaign-1.682221

CBC. (2014). Torrence Collier, 11, says he faces racism, extreme bullying in Westport. Retrieved June 12, 2014, from www.cbc.ca/news/canada/newfoundland-labrador/torrence-collier-11-says-he-faces-racism-extreme-bullying-in-westport-1.2671343

Ceci, S. J., & Roazzi, A. (1994). The effects of context on cognition: Postcards from Brazil. In R. J. Sternberg (Ed.), *Mind in context* (pp. 74–101). New York, NY: Cambridge University Press.

Ceci, S. J., & Williams, W. M. (1997). Schooling, intelligence, and income. *American Psychologist, 52*, 1051–1058.

Center for Applied Special Technology. (2012). *About UDL*. Retrieved February 4, 2015 from http://www.cast.org/udl/index.html.

Center for Parent Information and Resources. (2014). NICHCY Disability Fact Sheet 5: Emotional Disturbance:. Retreieved June 28, 2014, from www.parentcenterhub.org/repository/emotionaldisturbance

Chambers, B., & Abrami, P. C. (1991). The relationship between student team learning outcomes and achievement, causal attributions, and affect. *Journal of Educational Psychology, 83*, 140–146.

Chamot, A. U., & O'Malley, J. M. (1996). The Cognitive Academic Language Learning Approach: A model for linguistically diverse classrooms. *The Elementary School Journal, 96*, 259–274.

Chan, C. K., & Sachs, J. (2001). Beliefs about learning in children's understanding of science texts. *Contemporary Educational Psychology, 26*, 192–210.

Chance, P. (1992). The rewards of learning. *Phi Delta Kappan, 73*, 200–207.

Chance, P. (1993). Sticking up for rewards. *Phi Delta Kappan, 74*, 787–790.

Chang, L., Mak, M. C. K., Li, T., Wu, B. P., Chen, B. B., & Lu, H. J. (2011). Cultural adaptations to environmental variability: An evolutionary account of East-West differences. *Educational Psychology Review, 23*(1), 99–129.

Chao, R. (2001). Extending research on the consequences of parenting style for Chinese Americans and European Americans. *Child Development, 72*, 1832–1843.

Chao, R., & Tseng, V. (2002). Parenting of Asians. In M. H. Bornstein (Ed.), *Handbook of parenting: Social conditions and applied parenting* (2nd ed., Vol. 4, pp. 59–93). Mahwah, NJ: Erlbaum.

Chapman, J. W., Tunmer, W. E., & Prochnow, J. E. (2000). Early reading-related skills and performance, reading self-concept, and the development of academic self-concept: A longitudinal study. *Journal of Educational Psychology, 92*, 703–708.

Chapman, M. L. (1997). *Weaving webs of meaning: Writing in the elementary school.* Toronto, ON: ITP Nelson.

Charach, A., Pepler, D. J., & Ziegler, S. (1995). Bullying at school: A Canadian perspective. *Education Canada, 35*, 12–18.

Charles, C. M. (2002a). *Essential elements of effective discipline.* Boston, MA: Allyn & Bacon.

Charles, C. M. (2002b). *Building classroom discipline* (7th ed.). Boston, MA: Allyn & Bacon.

Charles, C. M. (2011). *Building classroom discipline* (10th ed.). Boston, MA: Allyn & Bacon.

Charmaraman, L., & Grossman, J. M. (2010). Importance of race and ethnicity: An exploration of Asian, Black, Latino, and multiracial adolescent identity. *Cultural Diversity and Ethnic Minority Psychology, 16*(2), 144–151.

Cheeseman Day, J., & Newburger, E. C. (2002). The big payoff: Educational attainment and synthetic estimates of work-life earnings. Washington DC: U.S. Bureau of the Census. Available online at: http://usgovinfo.about.com/od/moneymatters/a/edandearnings.htm

Chen, J. Q. (2004). Theory of multiple intelligences: Is it a scientific theory? Teachers *College Record, 106*, 17–23.

Chen, Z., & Mo, L. (2004). Schema induction in problem solving: A multidimensional analysis. *Journal of Experimental Psychology: Learning, Memory, and Cognition, 30*, 583–600.

Chen, Z., Mo, L., & Honomichl, R. (2004). Having the memory of an elephant: long-term retrieval and the use of analogues in problem solving. *Journal of Experimental Psychology: General, 133*, 415–433.

Chen, J. A., & Pajares, F. (2010). Implicit theories of ability of Grade 6 science students: Relation to epistemological beliefs and academic motivation and achievement in science. *Contemporary Educational Psychology, 35*, 75–87.

Chen, L. H., Wu, C.-H., Kee, Y. H., Lin, M.-S., & Shui, S.-H. (2009). Fear of failure, 2x2 achievement goal and self-handicapping: An examination of the hierarchical model of achievement motivation in physical education. *Contemporary Educational Psychology, 34*(4): 298–305.

Cheremshynski, C., Lucyshyn, J. M., & Olson, D. L. (2013). Implementation of a culturally appropriate positive behavior support plan with a Japanese mother of a child with autism: An experimental and qualitative analysis. *Journal of Positive Behavior Interventions, 15*, 242–253.

Chi, M. T. H. (1978). Knowledge structures and memory development. In R. Siegler (Ed.), *Children's thinking: What develops?* (pp. 73–96). Hillsdale, NJ: Erlbaum.

Chi, M. T. H., Glaser, R., & Farr, M. (Eds.). (1988). *The nature of expertise.* Hillsdale, NJ: Erlbaum.

Child and Youth Officer for British Columbia. (2007). *Health and well-being of children in care in British Columbia: Educational experience and outcomes.* Victoria, BC: Author.

Chorzempa, B. F., & Graham, S. (2006). Primary-grade teachers' use of within-class ability grouping in reading. *Journal of Educational Psychology, 98*, 529–541.

Chronicle of Higher Education, April, 28, 1995, p. A-71.

Chugani, H. T., Behen, M. E., Muzik, O., Juhasz, C. Nagy, F., & Chugani, D. C. (2001). Local brain functional activity following early deprivation: A study of postinstitutionalized orphans. *NeuroImage, 14*, 1290–1301.

Citizenship and Immigration Canada. (2007). Refugees in Canada's refugee system. Retrieved from www.cic.gc.ca/english/department/media/backgrounders/2007/2007-06-20.asp

Clark, C. M., & Peterson, P. L. (1986). Teachers' thought processes. In M. Wittrock (Ed.), *Handbook of research on teaching* (3rd ed., pp. 255–296). New York, NY: Macmillan.

Clark, C. M., & Yinger, R. (1988). Teacher planning. In D. Berliner & B. Rosenshine (Eds.), *Talks to teachers* (pp. 342–365). New York, NY: Random House.

Clark, J. M., & Paivio, A. (1991). Dual coding theory and education. *Educational Psychology Review, 3*, 149–210.

Clark, K. (2009). The case for Structured English Immersion. *Educational Leadership, 66* (7), 42–46.

Clarke, J. H., & Agne, R. M. (1997). *Interdisciplinary high school teaching.* Boston, MA: Allyn & Bacon.

Clement, S. L. (1978). Dual marking system: Simple and effective. *American Secondary Education, 8*, 49–52.

Clifford, M. M. (1990). Students need challenge, not easy success. *Educational Leadership, 48*(1), 22–26.

Clifford, M. M. (1991). Risk taking: Empirical and educational considerations. *Educational Psychologist, 26*, 263–298.

Cobb, P., & Bowers, J. (1999). Cognitive and situated learning: Perspectives in theory and practice. *Educational Researcher, 28*(2), 4–15.

Cobley, S., McKenna, J., Baker, J., & Wattie, N. (2009). How pervasive are relative age effects in secondary school education? *Journal of Educational Psychology, 101*, 520–528.

Codell, E. R. (2001). *Educating Esme: Diary of a teacher's first year.* Chapel Hill, NC: Algonquin Books.

Coffield, F. J., Moseley, D. V., Hall, E., & Ecclestone, K. (2004). *Learning styles and pedagogy in post–16 learning: A systematic and critical review.* London, England: Learning and Skills Research Centre/University of Newcastle upon Tyne.

Cognition and Technology Group at Vanderbilt. (1993). Anchored instruction and situated learning revisited. *Educational Technology, 33*(3), 52–70.

Cognition and Technology Group at Vanderbilt. (1996). Looking at technology in context: A framework for understanding technology and educational research. In D. Berliner & R. Calfee (Eds.), *Handbook of educational psychology* (pp. 807–840). New York, NY: Macmillan.

Cohen, A. B. (2009). Many forms of culture. *American Psychologist, 64*, 194–204.

Cohen, A. B. (2010). Just how many different forms of culture are there? *American Psychologist, 65*, 59–61.

Cohen, E. G. (1986). *Designing group work: Strategies for the heterogeneous classroom.* New York, NY: Teachers College Press.

Cohen, E. G. (1994). *Designing group work* (2nd ed.). New York, NY: Teachers College Press.

Cohen, E. G. (1994). Restructuring the classroom: Conditions for productive small groups. *Review of Educational Research, 64*, 1–35.

Coie, J. K., & Dodge, K. A. (1998). Aggression and antisocial behavior. In W. Damon & N. Eisenberg (Eds). *Handbook of child psychology*, 5th edition. Volume 3: Social, emotional, and personality development. NY: John Wiley & Sons.

Cokley, K. O. (2002). Ethnicity, gender, and academic self-concept: A preliminary examination of academic disidentification and implications for psychologists. *Cultural Diversity and Ethnic Minority Psychology, 8*, 378–388.

Colangelo, N., Assouline, S. G., & Gross, M. U. M. (2004). *A nation deceived: How schools hold back America's brightest students.* Iowa City, IA: The University of Iowa.

Cole, D. A., Martin, J. M., Peeke, L. A., Seroczynski, A. D., & Fier, J. (1999). Children's over- and underestimation of academic competence: A longitudinal study of gender differences, depression, and anxiety. *Child Development, 70*, 459–473.

Cole, G. A., Montgomery, R. W., Wilson, K. M., & Milan, M. A. (2000). Parametric analysis of overcorrection duration effects: Is longer really better than shorter? *Behavior Modification, 24*, 359–378.

Cole, M. (1985). The zone of proximal development: Where culture and cognition create each other. In J. V. Wertsch (Ed.), *Culture, communication, and cognition: Vygotskian perspectives* (pp. 146–161). New York, NY: Cambridge University Press.

Coleman, J. S. (1966). *Equality of educational opportunity.* Washington, DC: U.S. Government Printing Office.

Colledge, E., Bishop, D. V. M., Koeppen-Schomerus, G., Price, T. S., Happe, F., Eley, T., . . . Plomin, R. (2002). The structure of language abilities at 4 Years: A twin study. *Developmental Psychology, 38*, 749–757.

Collins, A. (2006). Cognitive apprenticeship. In R. K. Sawyer (Ed.), *The Cambridge handbook of the learning sciences* (pp. 47–77). New York, NY: Cambridge University Press.

Collins, A., Brown, J. S., & Newman, S. E. (1989). Cognitive apprenticeship: Teaching the crafts of reading, writing, and mathematics. In L. B. Resnick (Ed.), *Knowing, learning, and instruction: Essays in honor of Robert Galser* (pp. 453–494). Hillsdale, NJ: Erlbaum.

Colliver, J. A. (2000). Effectiveness of problem-based learning curricula: Research and theory. *Academic Medicine, 75*, 259–266.

Comadena, M. E., Hunt, S. K., & Simonds, C. J. (2007). The effects of teacher clarity, nonverbal immediacy, and caring on student motivation, affective and cognitive learning. *Communication Research Reports, 24*, 241–248.

Comer, J. P., Haynes, N. M., & Joyner, E. T. (1996). The School Development Program. In J. P. Comer, N. M. Haynes, E. T. Joyner, & M.

Ben-Avie (Eds.), *Rallying the whole village: The Comer process for reforming education* (pp. 1–26). New York, NY: Teachers College Press.

Committee on Increasing High School Students' Engagement and Motivation to Learn. (2004). *Engaging schools: Fostering high school students' motivation to learn.* Washington, DC: The National Academies Press.

Confrey, J. (1990a). A review of the research on students' conceptions in mathematics, science, and programming. *Review of Research in Education, 16,* 3–56.

Confrey, J. (1990b). What constructivism implies for teaching. In R. Davis, C. Maher, & N. Noddings (Eds.), *Constructivist views on the teaching and learning of mathematics* (pp. 107–122). Monograph 4 of the National Council of Teachers of Mathematics, Reston, VA.

Connell, R. W. (1996). Teaching the boys: New research on masculinity, and gender strategies for schools. *Teachers College Record, 98,* 206–235.

Conway, P. F., & Clark, C. M. (2003). The journey inward and outward: A re-examination of Fuller's concerns-based model of teacher development. *Teaching and Teacher Education, 19,* 465–482.

Cook, C. R., Williams, K. R., Guerra, N. G., Kim, T. E., & Sadek, S. (2010). Predictors of bullying and victimization in childhood and adolescence: A meta-analytic investigation. *School Psychology Quarterly, 25,* 65–83.

Cook, J. L., & Cook, G. (2009). *Child development: Principles and perspectives* (2nd ed.). Boston, MA: Allyn & Bacon.

Cooper, C. R. (1998). *The weaving of maturity: Cultural perspectives on adolescent development.* New York, NY: Oxford University Press.

Cooper, H. M. (1979). Pygmalion grows up: A model for teacher expectation communication and performance influence. *Review of Educational Research, 49,* 389–410.

Cooper, H. M. (2004). Homework [Special issue]. *Theory Into Practice, 43*(3).

Cooper, H., & Valentine, J. C. (Eds.). (2001). Homework [Special issue]. *Educational Psychologist, 36*(3).

Cooper, H. M., Robinson, J. C., Patall, E. A. (2006). Does homework improve academic achievement? A synthesis of research, 1987–2003. *Review of Educational Research, 76,* 1–62.

Cooper, H. M., Valentine, J. C., Nye, B., & Kindsay, J. J. (1999). Relationships between five after-school activities and academic achievement. *Journal of Educational Psychology, 91,* 369–378.

Copi, I. M. (1961). Introduction to logic. New York, NY: Macmillan.

Coplan, R. J., Prakash, K., O'Neil, K., & Armer, M. (2004). Do you "want" to play? Distinguishing between conflicted shyness and social disinterest in early childhood. *Developmental Psychology, 40,* 244–258.

Cordova, D. I., & Lepper, M. R. (1996). Intrinsic motivation and the process of learning: Beneficial effects of contextualization, personalization, and choice. *Journal of Educational Psychology, 88,* 715–730.

Corkill, A. J. (1992). Advance organizers: Facilitators of recall. *Educational Psychology Review, 4,* 33–67.

Cornelius-White, J. (2007). Learner-centered teacher–student relationships are effective: A meta-analysis. *Review of Educational Research, 77,* 113–143.

Corno, L. (1992). Encouraging students to take responsibility for learning and performance. *The Elementary School Journal, 93,* 69–84.

Corno, L. (1995). The principles of adaptive teaching. In A. Ornstein (Ed.), *Teaching: Theory into practice.* (pp. 98–115). Boston, MA: Allyn & Bacon.

Corno, L. (2000). Looking at homework differently. *Elementary School Journal, 100,* 529–548.

Corno, L. (2008). On teaching adaptively. *Educational Psychologist, 43,* 161–173.

Corno, L. (2011). Studying self-regulation habits. In B. Zimmerman & D. Schunk (Eds.), *Handbook of self-regulation of learning and performance* (pp. 361–375) New York, NY: Routledge.

Corpus, J. H., McClintic-Gilbert, M. S., & Hayenga, A. O. (2009). Within-year changes in children's intrinsic and extrinsic motivational orientations: Contextual predictors and academic outcomes. *Contemporary Educational Psychology, 34,* 154–166.

Cota-Robles, S., Neiss, M., & Rowe, D. C. (2002). The role of puberty in violent and nonviolent delinquency among Anglo American, Mexican American and African American boys. *Journal of Adolescent Research, 17,* 364–376.

Cote, S. Vaillancourt, T., LeBlanc, J. C., Nagin, D. C., & Tremblay, R. E. (2006). The development of physical aggression from toddlerhood to preadolescence: A nation wide longitudinal study of Canadian children. *Journal of Abnormal Child Psychology, 34,* 71–85.

Cothran, D. J., & Ennis, C. D. (2000). Building bridges to student engagement: Communicating respect and care for students in urban high school. *Journal of Research and Development in Education, 33*(2), 106–117.

Covaleskie, J. F. (1992). Discipline and morality: Beyond rules and consequences. *The Educational Forum, 56*(2), 56–60.

Covington, M. V. (1992). *Making the grade: A self-worth perspective on motivation and school reform.* New York, NY: Holt, Rinehart, & Winston.

Covington, M. V., & Mueller, K. J. (2001). Intrinsic versus extrinsic motivation: An approach/avoidance reformulation. *Education Psychology Review, 13,* 157–176.

Covington, M. V., & Omelich, C. (1987). "I knew it cold before the exam": A test of the anxiety-blockage hypothesis. *Journal of Educational Psychology, 79,* 393–400.

Cowley, G., & Underwood, A. (1998, June 15). Memory. *Newsweek, 131*(24), 48–54.

Craig, W. M., & Pepler, D. J. (1997). Observations of bullying and victimization in the school yard. *Canadian Journal of School Psychology, 13,* 41–60.

Craig, W. M., & Pepler, D. J. (1998). Observations of aggressive and nonaggressive children on the school playground. *Merrill-Palmer Quarterly, 44,* 55–76.

Craig, W. M., Peters, R. D., & Konarski, R. (1998, October). *Bullying and victimization among Canadian school children* (Working Paper Series W-98-28E). Hull, QC: Applied Research Branch of Strategic Policy, Human Resources and Development Canada.

Craik, F. I. M., & Lockhart, R. S. (1972). Levels of processing: A framework for memory research. *Journal of Verbal Learning and Verbal Behavior, 11,* 671–684.

Crawford, J. (1997). *Best evidence: Research foundations of the Bilingual Education Act.* Washington, DC: National Clearinghouse for Bilingual Education.

Crealock, C., & Bachor, D. G. (1995). *Instructional strategies for students with special needs* (2nd ed.). Scarborough, ON: Allyn & Bacon Canada.

Creese, A. (2009). Building on young people's linguistic and cultural continuity: Complementary schools in the United Kingdom. *Theory Into Practice, 48,* 267–273.

Cremin, L. (1961). *The transformation of the school: Progressivism in American education, 1876–1957.* New York, NY: Vintage.

Crick, N. R., Casas, J. F., & Mosher M. (1997). Relational and overt aggression in preschool. *Developmental Psychology, 33,* 579–588.

Crick, N. R. & Zahn-Waxler, C. (2003). The development of psychopathology in females and males: Current progress and future challenges. *Development and Psychopathology, 15,* 719–742.

Crisci, P. E. (1986). The Quest National Center: A focus on prevention of alienation. *Phi Delta Kappan, 67,* 440–442.

Crocker, J., & Park, L. E. (2004). Reaping the benefits of pursuing self-esteem without the costs. *Psychological Bulletin, 130,* 392–414.

Cromley. J. G., & Azevedo, R. (2007). Testing and refining the direct and inferential mediation model of reading comprehension. *Journal of Educational Psychology, 99,* 311–325.

Crone, D. A., & Horner, R. H. (2003). *Building positive behavior support systems in schools: Functional behavioral assessment.* New York, NY: Guilford.

Crosnoe, R., Morrison, F., Burchinal, M., Pianta, R., Keating, D., Friedman, S. L., & Clarke-Stewart, K. A. (2010). Instruction, teacher–student relations, and math achievement trajectories in elementary school. *Journal of Educational Psychology, 102,* 407–417.

Crul, M., & Holdaway, J. (2009). Children of immigrants in schools in New York and Amsterdam: The factors shaping attainment. In M. Crul, J. Holdaway, & C. Roberts (Eds.), *Educating Immigrant Youth: Pathways to Employment in International Perspectives.* Special Issue Teachers College Records.

CTV. (2013). BC school bans kindergarteners from touching each other. Retrieved August 2, 2014, from http://bc.ctvnews.ca/b-c-school-bans-kindergarteners-from-touching-each-other-1.1528348

Cummins, D. D. (1991). Children's interpretation of arithmetic word problems. *Cognition and Instruction, 8,* 261–289.

Cummins, J. (1989). A theoretical framework for bilingual special education. *Exceptional Children, 56,* 111–119.

Cummins, J. (1994). The acquisition of English as a second language. In K. Spangenberg-Urbschat & R. Prichard (Eds.), *Kids come in all languages: Reading instruction for ESL students* (pp. 36–62). Newark, DE: International Reading Association.

Cunningham, D. J. (1992). Beyond educational psychology: Steps toward an educational semiotic. *Educational Psychology Review, 4,* 165–194.

Daley, T. C., Whaley, S. E., Sigman, M. D., Espinosa, M. P., & Neumann, C. (2003). IQ on the rise: The Flynn Effect in rural Kenyan children. *Psychological Science, 14*(3), 215–219.

Daly, B. P., Kral, M. C., & Brown, R. T. (2008). Cognitive and academic problems associated with childhood cancers and sickle cell disease. *School Psychology Quarterly, 23,* 230–242.

Daly, L. A. & Perez, L. M. (2009). Exposure to media violence and other correlates of aggressive behavior in preschool children. *Early Childhood Research & Practice, 11*(2). Retrieved June 16, 2014, from http://ecrp.uiuc.edu/v11n2/daly.html

D'Amico, A., & Guarnera, M. (2005). Exploring working memory in children with low arithmetical achievement. *Learning and Individual Differences, 15*: 189–202.

Damon, W. (1994). Fair distribution and sharing: The development of positive justice. In B. Puka (Ed.), Fundamental research in moral development (pp. 189–254). *Moral development: A compendium, Vol. 2.* New York, NY: Garland Publishing.

Darcey, J. S., & Travers, J. F. (2006). *Human development across the lifespan* (6th ed.). New York, NY: McGraw-Hill.

Dark, V. J., & Benbow, C. P. (1991). Differential enhancement of working memory with mathematical versus verbal precocity. *Journal of Educational Psychology, 83,* 48–60.

Darling-Hammond, L. (2000). Teacher quality and student achievement: A review of state policy evidence. *Educational Policy Analysis Archives, 8,* 1–48. Retrieved from http://epaa.asu.edu/epaa/v8n1

Darling-Hammond, L., & Youngs, P. (2002). Defining "highly qualified teachers": What does "scientifically-based research" actually tell us? *Educational Researcher, 31*(9): 13–25.

Darnon, C., Dompnier, B., Gilliéron, O., & Butera, F. (2010). The interplay of mastery and performance goals in social comparison: A multiple goal perspective. *Journal of Educational Psychology, 102,* 212–222.

Das, J. P. (1995). Some thoughts on two aspects of Vygotsky's work. *Educational Psychologist, 30,* 93–97.

DaSilva Idings, A. C. (2009). Bridging home and school literacy practices: Empowering families of recent immigrant children. *Theory Into Practice, 48,* 304–311.

Daunic, A. P., Smith. S. W., Brank, E. M., & Penfield, R. D. (2006). Classroom based cognitive-behavioral intervention to prevent aggression: Efficacy and social validity. *Journal of School Psychology, 44,* 123–139.

Davies, D. (2004*). Child development: A practitioner's guide.* New York, NY: Guilford Press.

Davies, S. & Guppy, N. (2006). *The schooled society.* Don Mills, ON: Oxford University Press.

Davis, G. A., Rimm, S. B., & Siegle, D. (2011). *Education of the Gifted and Talented,* 6th edition.

Davis, H. A. (2003). Conceptualizing the role and influence of student–teacher relationships on children's social and cognitive development. *Educational Psychologist, 38,* 207–234.

Davis-Kean, P. E., & Sandler, H. M. (2001). A meta-analysis of measures of self-esteem for young children: A framework for future measures. *Child Development, 72,* 887–906.

Dawson-Tunik, T. L., Fischer, K. W., Stein, Z. (2004). Do stages belong at the center of developmental theory? A commentary on Piaget's stages. *New Ideas in Psychology, 22.*

de Boer, H., Bosker, R. J., & van der Werf, M. P. C. (2010). Sustainability of teacher expectation bias effects on long-term student performance. *Journal of Educational Psychology, 102*(1): 168–179.

De Corte, E. (2003). Transfer as the productive use of acquired knowledge, skills, and motivations. *Current Directions in Psychological Research, 12,* 142–146.

De Corte, E., Greer, B., & Verschaffel, L. (1996). Mathematics learning and teaching. In D. Berliner & R. Calfee (Eds.), *Handbook of educational psychology* (pp. 491–549). New York, NY: Macmillan.

De Corte, E., & Verschaffel, L. (1985). Beginning first graders' initial representation of arithmetic word problems. *Journal of Mathematical Behavior, 4,* 3021.

De George, G. (2008). Is it language or is it special needs? Appropriately diagnosing English language learners having achievement difficulties. In L. S. Verplaetse & N. Migliacci (Eds.), *Inclusive pedagogy for English language learners: A handbook of research-informed practices* (pp. 277–303). New York, NY: Erlbaum.

de Kock, A., Sleegers, P., & Voeten, M. J. M. (2004). New learning and the classification of learning environments in secondary education. *Review of Educational Research, 74*(2), 141–170.

Dearing, E., Kreider, H., Simpkins, S., & Weiss, H. B. (2006). Family involvement in school and low-income children's literacy: Longitudinal associations between and within families. *Journal of Educational Psychology, 98,* 653–664.

Deaux, K. (1993). Commentary: Sorry, wrong number: A reply to Gentile's call. *Psychological Science, 4,* 125–126.

DeCecco, J., & Richards, A. (1974). *Growing pains: Uses of school conflicts.* New York, NY: Aberdeen.

deCharms, R. (1983). Intrinsic motivation, peer tutoring, and cooperative learning: Practical maxims. In J. Levine & M. Wang (Eds.), *Teacher and student perceptions: Implications for learning* (pp. 391–398). Hillsdale, NJ: Erlbaum.

Deci, E. L. (1975). *Intrinsic motivation.* New York, NY: Plenum.

Deci, E. L., Koestner, R., & Ryan, R. M. (1999). A meta-analytic review of experiments examining the effects of extrinsic rewards on intrinsic motivation. *Psychological Bulletin, 125,* 627–668.

Deci, E. L., & Ryan, R. M. (1985). *Intrinsic motivation and self-determination in human behavior.* New York, NY: Plenum.

Deci, E. L., & Ryan, R. M. (Eds.). (2002). *Handbook of self-determination research.* Rochester, NY: University of Rochester Press.

Deci, E. L., Vallerand, R. J., Pelletier, L. G., & Ryan, R. M. (1991). Motivation and education: The self-determination perspective. *Educational Psychologist, 26,* 325–346.

Dee, J. R., & Henkin, A. B. (2002). Assessing dispositions toward cultural diversity among preservice teachers. *Urban Education, 37*(1), 22–40.

Delazer, M., Ischebeck, A., Domahs, F., Zamarian, L., Koppelstaetter, F., Siednetoph, C. M., . . . Felber, S. (2005). Learning by strategies and learning by drill: Evidence from an fMRI study. *NeuroImage, 25,* 838–849.

Delpit, L. (1995). *Other people's children: Cultural conflict in the classroom.* New York, NY: The New York Press.

Delpit, L. (2003). Educators as "Seed People": Growing a new future. *Educational Researcher, 7*(32), 14–21.

Demetriou, A., Christou, C., Spanoudis, G., & Platsidou, M. (2002). The development of mental processing: Efficiency, working memory and thinking. *Monographs of the Society for Research in Child Development, 67*(1).

Dempster, F. N. (1991). Synthesis of research on reviews and tests. *Educational Leadership, 48*(7), 71–76.

Dempster, F. N. (1993). Exposing our students to less should help them learn more. *Phi Delta Kappan, 74,* 432–437.

Demuth, K. (1990). Subject, topic, and Sesotho passive. *Journal of Child Language, 17,* 67–84.

Derry, S. J. (1989). Putting learning strategies to work. *Educational Leadership, 47*(5), 4–10.

Derry, S. J. (1991). Strategy and expertise in solving word problems. In C. McCormick, G. Miller, & M. Pressley (Eds.), *Cognitive strategies research: From basic research to educational applications.* New York, NY: Springer-Verlag.

Derry, S. J. (1992). Beyond symbolic processing: Expanding horizons for educational psychology. *Journal of Educational Psychology, 84,* 413–419.

Derry, S. J., Hmelo-Silver, C. E., Nagarajan, A., Chernobilsky, E., & Beitzel, B. (2006). Cognitive transfer revisited: Can we exploit new media to solve old problems on a large scale? *Journal of Educational Computing Research, 35,* 145–162.

Desautel, D, (2009). Becoming a thinking thinker: Metacognition, self-reflection, and classroom practice. *Teachers College Record, 111,* 1997–2020. http://www.tcrecord.org ID Number: 15504.

Deshler, D., Ellis, E. S., & Lenz, B. K. (1996). *Teaching adolescents with learning disabilities: Strategies and methods* (2nd ed.). Denver, CO: Love Publishing.

Deshler, D. D., & Schumaker, J. B. (2005). *Teaching Adolescents with Disabilities: Accessing the General Education Curriculum.* Corwin Press.

Dettmers, S., Trautwein, U., Lüdtke, O., Kunter, M., & Baumert, J. (2010). Homework works if homework quality is high: Using multilevel modeling to predict the development of achievement in mathematics. *Journal of Educational Psychology, 102*(2): 467–482.

Dewey, J. (1913). *Interest and effort in education.* Cambridge, MA: Houghton-Mifflin.

Diamond, A. & Lee, K. (2011). Interventions shown to aid executive function development in children 4 to 12 years old. *Science, 333,* 959–963.

Diaz-Rico, L. T., & Weed, K. Z. (2002). *The cross-cultural, language, and academic development handbook* (2nd ed.). Boston, MA: Allyn & Bacon.

Dickinson, D., McCabe, A., Anastopoulos, L., Peisner-Feinberg, E., & Poe, M. (2003). The comprehensive language approach to early literacy: The interrelationships among vocabulary, phonological sensitivity, and print knowledge among preschool-aged children. *Journal of Educational Psychology, 95,* 465–481.

Dinnel, D., & Glover, J. A. (1985). Advance organizers: Encoding manipulations. *Journal of Educational Psychology, 77,* 514–522.

Dinsmore, D. L., Alexander, P. A., & Loughlin, S. M. (2008). Focusing the conceptual lens on metacognition, self-regulation, and self-regulated learning. *Educational Psychology Review, 20,* 391–409.

Di Vesta, F. J., & Di Cintio, M. J. (1997). Interactive effects of working memory span and text comprehension on reading comprehension and retrieval. *Learning and Individual Differences, 9,* 215–231.

Doctorow, M., Wittrock, M. C., & Marks, C. (1978). Generative processes in reading comprehension. *Journal of Educational Psychology, 70,* 109–118.

Dodge, K. A. (2011). Context matters in child and family policy. *Child Development, 82,* 433–442.

Dodge, K. A., Coie, J. D., & Lynam, D. (2006). Aggression and antisocial behaviour in youth. In N. Eisenberg, W. Dammon, & R. M. Lerner (Eds.), *Handbook of child psychology: Vol. 3. Social, emotional, and personality development* (6th ed., pp. 719–788). Hoboken, NJ: John Wiley & Sons.

Dodge, K. A., & Pettit, G. S. (2003). A biopsychosocial model of the development of chronic conduct problems in adolescence. *Developmental Psychology, 39,* 349–371.

Dodge, K. A., & Somberg, D. R. (1987). Hostile attributional biases among aggressive boys are exacerbated under conditions of threats to the self. *Child Development, 58*, 213–224.

Dolezal, S. E., Welsh, L. M., Pressley, M., & Vincent, M. (2003). How do nine third-grade teachers motivate their students? *Elementary School Journal, 103*, 239–267.

Doll, B., Zucker, S., & Brehm, K. (2005). *Resilient classrooms: Creating healthy environments for learning*. New York, NY: Guilford.

Dotterer, A. M., McHale, S. M., & Crouter, A .C. (2009). The development and correlates of academic interests from childhood through adolescence. *Journal of Educational Psychology, 101*, 509–519.

Dorrell, O. (2009, November). *Schools' zero-tolerance policies tested. USA Today*. Retrieved February 8, 2015 from http://usatoday30. usatoday.com/news/nation/2009-11-01-zero-tolerance_N.htm.

Doyle, A., & Aboud, F. (1995). A longitudinal study of White children's racial prejudice as a social cognitive development. *Merrill-Palmer Quarterly, 41*, 213–223.

Doyle, W. (1977). The uses of nonverbal behaviors: Toward an ecological model of classrooms. *Merrill-Palmer Quarterly, 23*, 179–192.

Doyle, W. (1986). Classroom organization and management. In M. C. Wittrock (Ed.), *Handbook of research on teaching* (3rd ed., pp. 392–431). New York, NY: Macmillan.

Doyle, W. (2006). Ecological approaches to classroom management. In C. Evertson & C. S. Weinstein (Eds.), *Handbook for classroom management: Research, practice, and contemporary issues*. Mahwah, NJ: Erlbaum.

Driscoll, M. P. (2005). *Psychology of learning for instruction* (3rd ed.). Boston, MA: Allyn & Bacon.

Dubinsky, J. M., Roehrig, G., & Varma, S. (2013). Infusing neuroscience into teacher professional development. *Educational Researcher, 42*, 317–329.

Duell, O. K. (1994). Extended wait time and university student achievement. *American Educational Research Journal, 31*, 397–414.

Dufrene, B. A., Doggett, R. A., Henington, C., & Watson, T. S. (2007). Functional assessment and intervention for disruptive classroom behaviors in preschool and head start classrooms. *Journal of Behavioral Education, 16*, 368–388.

Duncan, G. J., & Brooks-Gunn, J. (2000). Family poverty, welfare reform, and child development. *Child Development, 71*, 188–196.

Duncan, R. M., & Cheyne, J. A. (1999). Incidence and functions of self-reported private speech in young adults: A self-verbalization questionnaire. *Canadian Journal of Behavioural Sciences, 31*, 133–136.

Duncker, K. (1945). On solving problems. *Psychological Monographs, 58*(5, Whole No. 270).

Dunn, K., & Dunn, R. (1978). *Teaching students through their individual learning styles*. Reston, VA: National Council of Principals.

Dunn, K., & Dunn, R. (1987). Dispelling outmoded beliefs about student learning. *Educational Leadership, 44*(6), 55–63.

Dunn, R., Dunn, K., & Price, G. E. (1989). *Learning style inventory*, Lawrence, KS: Price Systems. Pearson.

Dunn, R., & Griggs, S. (2003). *Synthesis of the Dunn and Dunn Learning-Style Model Research: Who, what, when, where, and so what?* New York, NY: St. John's University.

Durik, A. M., & Harackiewicz, J. M. (2007). Different strokes for different folks: How individual interest moderates the effects of situational factors on task interest. *Journal of Educational Psychology, 99*, 597–610.

Durik, A. M., Vida, M., & Eccles, J. S. (2006). Task values and ability beliefs as predictors of high school literacy choices: A developmental analysis. *Journal of Educational Psychology, 98*(2), 382–393.

Dusenbury, L., & Falco, M. (1995). Eleven components of effective drug abuse prevention curricula. *Journal of School Health, 65*(10): 420–425.

Dweck, C. S. (2000). *Self-theories: Their role in motivation, personality, and development*. Philadelphia, PA: Routledge Press.

Dweck, C. S. (2006). *Mindset: The new psychology of success*. New York, NY: Random House.

Dweck, C. S., & Bempechat, J. (1983). Children's theories on intelligence: Consequences for learning. In S. Paris, G. Olson, & W. Stevenson (Eds.), *Learning and motivation in the classroom* (pp. 239–256). Hillsdale, NJ: Erlbaum.

Dymond, S. K., Renzaglia, A., & Chun, E. (2007). Elements of effective high school service learning programs that include students with and without disabilities. *Remedial and Special Education, 28*, 227–243.

Dyson, A. H. (1997). *Writing superheroes: Contemporary childhood, popular culture, and classroom literacy*. New York, NY: Teachers College Press.

Ebbinghaus, H. (1964). *Memory* (H. A. Ruger & C. E. Bussenius, Trans.). New York, NY: Dover. (Original work published 1885)

Ebersbach, M. (2009). Achieving a new dimension: Children integrate three stimulus dimensions in volume estimations. *Developmental Psychology, 45*, 877–833.

Eccles, J. (2009) Who am I and what am I going to do with my life? Personal and collective identities as motivators of action. *Educational Psychologist, 44*, 78–89.

Eccles, J., & Wigfield, A. (1985). Teacher expectations and student motivation. In J. Dusek (Ed.), *Teacher expectancies* (pp. 185–226). Hillsdale, NJ: Erlbaum.

Eccles, J. S., & Wigfield, A. (2002). Motivational beliefs, values, and goals. *Annual Review of Psychology, 53*, 109–132.

Eccles, J., Wigfield, A., & Schiefele, U. (1998). Motivation to succeed. In W. Damon (Series Ed.) & N. Eisenberg (Volume Ed.), *Handbook of child psychology: Vol. 3. Social, emotional, and personality development* (5th ed., pp. 1017–1095). New York, NY: Wiley.

Echevarria, M. (2003). Anomalies as a catalyst for middle school students' knowledge construction and scientific reasoning during science inquiry. *Journal of Educational Psychology, 95*, 357–374.

Echevarria, J. J., & Graves, A. (2011). *Sheltered Content Instruction: Teaching English Language Learners with Diverse Abilities*, 4th edition. Pearson.

Echevarria, J. J., Vogt, M. E., & Short, D. J. (2014). *Making content comprehensible for secondary English learners: The SIOP model* (2nd ed.). Boston: Pearson.

Edelman, G. M. (1992). *Bright air, brilliant fire: On the matter of the mind*. New York, NY: Basic Books.

Egan, S. K., Monson, T. C., & Perry, D. G. (1998). Social-cognitive influences on change in aggression over time. *Developmental Psychology, 34*, 996–1006.

Ehrenfeld, T. (2001). Reflections on mirror neurons. *Observer: Association for Psychological Science, 24* (3), 11–13.

Eisenberg, N., & Fabes, R. A. (1998). Prosocial development. In W. Damon (Series Ed.) & N. Eisenberg (Vol. Ed.), *Handbook of child psychology: Vol. 3. Social, emotional, and personality development* (5th ed., pp. 701–778). New York, NY: Wiley.

Eisenberg, N., Martin, C. L., & Fabes, R. A. (1996). Gender development and gender effects. In D. Berliner & R. Calfee (Eds.), *Handbook of educational psychology* (pp. 358–396). New York, NY: Macmillan.

Eisenberg, N., Shell, R., Pasernack, J., Lennon, R., Beller, R., & Mathy, R. M. (1987). Prosocial development in middle childhood: A longitudinal study. *Developmental Psychology, 23*, 712–718.

Eisenberg, R., Pierce, W. D., & Cameron, J. (1999). Effects of rewards on intrinsic motivation—Negative, neutral, and positive: Comment on Deci, Koestner, and Ryan (1999) *Psychological Bulletin, 125*, 677–691.

Eisner, E. W. (1999). The uses and limits of performance assessments. *Phi Delta Kappan, 80*, 658–660.

Elementary Teachers' Federation of Ontario. (2008). *Full-day kindergarten: Moving Ontario forward*. Author.

Elias, M. J., & Schwab, Y. (2006). From compliance to responsibility: Social and emotional learning and classroom management. In C. Evertson & C. S. Weinstein (Eds.), *Handbook for classroom management: Research, practice, and contemporary issues*. Mahwah, NJ: Erlbaum.

Elias, S. M., & MacDonald, S. (2007). Using past performance, proxy efficacy, and academic self-efficacy to predict college performance. *Journal of Applied Social Psychology, 37*, 2518–2531.

Elkind, D. (1981). Obituary—Jean Piaget (1896–1980). *American Psychologist, 36*, 911–913.

Elkind, D. (1991). Formal education and early childhood education: An essential difference. In K. M. Cauley, F. Linder, & J. H. MacMillan (Eds.), *Annual Editions: Educational Psychology, 91/92* (pp. 27–37). Guilford, CT: Duskin.

Ellerbrock, C. R., & Kiefer, S. M. (2010). Creating a ninth-grade community of care. *The Journal of Educational Research, 103*(6): 393–406.

Elrich, M. (1994). The stereotype within. *Educational Leadership, 51*(8), 12–15.

Else-Quest, N. M., Hyde, J. S., & Linn, M. C. (2010). Cross-national patterns of gender differences in mathematics: A meta-analysis. *Psychological Bulletin, 136*(1), 103–127.

Embry, D. D. (2002). The Good Behavior Game: A best practice candidate as a universal behavior vaccine. *Clinical Child and Family Psychology Review, 5*, 273–297.

Emerson, M. J., & Miyake, A. (2003). The role of inner speech in task switching: A dual-task investigation. *Journal of Memory and Language, 48*, 148–168.

Emmer, E. T., & Aussiker, A. (1990). School and classroom discipline problems: How well do they work? In O. Moles (Ed.), *Student discipline strategies: Research and practice*. Albany, NY: SUNY Press.

Emmer, E. T., & Evertson, C. M. (1981). Synthesis of research on classroom management. *Educational Leadership, 38*, 342–345.

Emmer, E. T., & Evertson, C. M. (1982). Effective classroom management at the beginning of the school year in junior high school classes. *Journal of Educational Psychology, 74*, 485–498.

Emmer, E. T., & Evertson, C. M. (2009). *Classroom management for middle and high school teachers* (8th ed.). Boston, MA: Allyn & Bacon.

Emmer, E. T., & Evertson, C. M., (2013). *Classroom management for middle and high school teachers* (9th ed.). Boston, MA: Allyn & Bacon.

Emmer, E. T., Evertson, C. M., & Anderson, L. M. (1980). Effective classroom management at the beginning of the school year. *Elementary School Journal, 80,* 219–231.

Emmer, E. T., & Gerwels, M. C. (2006). Classroom management in middle school and high school classrooms. In C. Evertson & C. S. Weinstein (Eds.), *Handbook for classroom management: Research, practice, and contemporary issues.* Mahwah, NJ: Erlbaum.

Emmer, E., & Hickman, J. (1991). Teacher efficacy in classroom management. *Educational and Psychological Measurement, 51,* 755–765.

Emmer, E. T., & Stough, L. M. (2001). Classroom management: A critical part of educational psychology with implications for teacher education. *Educational Psychologist, 36,* 103–112.

Engelmann, S., & Engelmann, T. (1981). *Give your child a superior mind.* New York, NY: Cornerstone.

Engle, R. W. (2001). What is working memory capacity? In H. Roediger, J. Nairne, I. Neath, & A. Suprenant (Eds.), *The nature of remembering: Essays in honor of Robert G. Crowder* (pp. 297–314). Washington, DC: American Psychological Association.

Entenman, J., Murnen, T. J., & Hendricks, C. (2006). Victims, bullies, and bystanders in K-3 literature. *The Reading Teacher, 59,* 352–364.

Entwisle, D. R., & Alexander, K. L. (1998). Facilitating the transition to first grade: The nature of transition and research on factors affecting it. *The Elementary School Journal, 98,* 351–364.

Epstein, J. L. (1989). Family structure and student motivation. In R. E. Ames & C. Ames (Eds.), *Research on motivation in education: Vol. 3. Goals and cognitions* (pp. 259–295). New York, NY: Academic Press.

Epstein, J. L. (1995). School/Family/Community partnerships: Caring for the children we share. *Phi Delta Kappan, 76,* 701–712.

Epstein, J. L., & MacIver, D. J. (1992). *Opportunities to learn: Effects on eighth graders of curriculum offerings and instructional approaches.* Baltimore, MD: Johns Hopkins University Center for Research on Effective Schooling for Disadvantaged Children.

Epstein, J. L., & Van Voorhis, F. L. (2001). More than minutes: Teachers' roles in designing homework. *Educational Psychologist, 36,* 181–193.

Erdelyi, M. H. (2010). The ups and downs of memory. *American Psychologist, 65,* 623–633.

Ericsson, A. (2011, August). *Deliberate practice and the future of education and professional training.* Keynote address at the European Association for Research on Learning and Instruction, University of Exeter, UK.

Ericsson, K. A. (1999). Expertise. In R. Wilson & F. Keil (Eds.), *The MIT encyclopedia of the cognitive sciences* (pp. 298–300). Cambridge, MA: MIT Press.

Ericsson, K. A., & Charness, N. (1994). Expert performance: Its structure and acquisition. *American Psychologist, 49*(8), 725–747.

Ericsson, K. A., & Charness, N. (1999). Expert performance: Its structure and acquisition. In S. Ceci & W. Williams (Eds.), The nature-nurture debate: The essential readings. *Essential readings in developmental psychology.* Malden, MA: Blackwell.

Erikson, E. H. (1963). *Childhood and society* (2nd ed.). New York, NY: Norton.

Erikson, E. H. (1980). *Identity and the life cycle* (2nd ed.). New York, NY: Norton.

Espe, C., Worner, C., & Hotkevich, M. (1990). Whole language—What a bargain. *Educational Leadership, 47*(6), 45.

Evans, G. W. (2004). The environment of childhood poverty. *American Psychologist, 59,* 77–92.

Evans, L., & Davies, K. (2000). No sissy boys here: A content analysis of the representation of masculinity in elementary school reading texts. *Sex Roles, 42,* 255–270.

Evensen, D. H., Salisbury-Glennon, J. D., & Glenn, J. (2001). A qualitative study of six medical students in a problem-based curriculum: Toward a situated model of self-regulation. *Journal of Educational Psychology, 93,* 659–676.

Evertson, C. M., & Emmer, E. T. (2009). *Classroom management for elementary school teachers* (8th ed.). Boston, MA: Allyn & Bacon.

Evertson, C. M., & Emmer, E. T. (2013). *Classroom management for elementary school teachers* (9th ed.). Boston, MA: Allyn & Bacon.

Evertson, C. M., & Weinstein, C. S. (Eds.). (2006). *Handbook of classroom management: Research, practice, and contemporary issues.* Mahwah, NJ: Erlbaum.

Ezeife, A. N. (2011). A cultural and environmental spin to mathematics education: Research implementation experience in a Canadian Aboriginal community. *First Nations Perspective, 4,* 2–39.

Ezeife, A. N. (2013). Culture sensitive mathematics: The Walpole Island experience. In J. P. White, S. Wingert, D. Beavon, & P. Maxim (Eds.), *Aboriginal Policy Research* (Vol. III, pp. 53–68). Toronto, ON: Thompson Educational Publishing.

Fabiano, G. A., Pelham, W. E., Coles, E. K., Gnagy, E. M., Chronis-Tuscano, A., & O'Connor, B. C. (2009). A meta-analysis of behavioral treatments for attention-deficit/hyperactivity disorder. *Clinical PsychologyReview, 29,* 129–140.

Facione, P. A. (2011). *Think critically.* Boston, MA: Pearson.

Farnham-Diggory, S. (1994). Paradigms of knowledge and instruction. *Review of Educational Research, 64,* 463–477.

Farver, J. A. M. (2007). *Family environments and Latino preschoolers' emergent literacy skills.* Paper presented at the biennial meeting of the Society for Research in Child Development, Boston, MA.

Fast, L., Lewis, J., Bryant, M., Bocian, K., Cardullo, R., Rettig, M., & Hammond, K. (2010). Does math self-efficacy mediate the effect of the perceived classroom environment on standardized math test performance? *Journal of Educational Psychology, 102*(3), 729–740.

Feather, N. T. (1982). *Expectations and actions: Expectancy-value models in psychology.* Hillsdale, NJ: Erlbaum.

Feldman. J. (2003). The simplicity principle in human concept learning. *Current Directions in Psychological Science, 12,* 227–232.

Feldman, R. S. (2004). *Child development* (3rd ed.). Upper Saddle River, NJ: Prentice-Hall.

Fenton, D. F. (2007). The implications of research on expertise for curriculum and pedagogy. *Educational Psychology Review, 19,* 91–110.

Ferguson, A. A. (2000). *Bad boys: Public schools and the making of Black masculinity.* Ann Arbor, MI: University of Michigan Press.

Ferrer, E., & McArdle, J. J. (2004). An experimental analysis of dynamic hypotheses about cognitive abilities and achievement from childhood to early adulthood. *Developmental Psychology, 40,* 935–952.

Ferretti, R. P., Lewis, W. E., Andrews-Weckerly, S. (2009). Do goals affect the structure of students' argumentative writing strategies? *Journal of Educational Psychology, 101*(3): 577–589.

Fillmore, L.W., & Snow, C. (2000). What teachers need to know about language. [On-line]. Retrieved from www.cal.org/ericcll/teachers.pdf

Finkel, D., Reynolds, C. A., McArdle, J. J., Gatz, M., & Pedersen, N. L. (2003). Latent growth curve analyses of accelerating decline in cognitive abilities in adulthood. Developmental Psychology, 39, 535–550.

Fischer, M. A., & Gillespie, C. S. (2003). Computers and young children's development. Young Children, 58(4), 85–91.

Fisher, D., Roach, V., & Frey, N. (2002). Examining the general programmatic benefits of inclusive schools. *International Journal of Inclusive Education, 6,* 63–78.

Fiske, E. B. (1981, October 27). Teachers reward muddy prose, study finds. *The New York Times,* p. C1.

Fiske, S. T. (1993). Social cognition and social perception. *Annual Review of Psychology, 44,* 155–194.

Fitts, P. M., & Posner, M. I. (1967). *Human performance.* Belmont, CA: Brooks Cole.

Fitzgerald, J. (1995). English-as-a-second-language learners' cognitive reading process: A review of the research in the United States. *Review of Educational Research, 62,* 145–190.

Fitzgerald, M. (2005). *The genesis of artistic creativity: Asperger's syndrome and the arts.* London, England: Jessica Kingsley Publishers.

Fives, H. R., Hamman, D., & Olivarez, A. (2005, April). *Does burnout begin with student teaching? Analyzing efficacy, burnout, and support during the student-teaching semester.* Paper presented at the Annual Meeting of the American Educational Research Association, Montreal, QC.

Fivush, R., & Nelson, K. (2004). Culture and language in the emergence of autobiographical memory. *Psychological Science, 15,* 573–577.

Flammer, A. (1995). Developmental analysis of control beliefs. In A. Bandura (Ed.), *Self-efficacy in changing societies* (pp. 69–113). New York, NY: Cambridge University Press.

Flanagan, C. A., Cumsille, P., Gill, S., & Gallay, L. S. (2007). School and community climates and civic commitments: Patterns for ethnic minority and majority students. *Journal of Educational Psychology, 99,* 421–431.

Flavell, J. H., Friedrichs, A. G., & Hoyt, J. D. (1970). Developmental changes in memorization processes. *Cognitive Psychology, 1,* 324–340.

Flavell, J. H., Green, F. L., & Flavell, E. R. (1995). Young children's knowledge about thinking. *Monographs of the Society for Research in Child Development, 60*(1) (Serial No. 243).

Flavell, J. H., Miller, P. H., & Miller, S. A. (2002). *Cognitive development* (4th ed.). Upper Saddle River, NJ: Prentice-Hall.

Fleith, D. (2000). Teacher and student perceptions of creativity in the classroom environment. *Roeper Review, 22,* 148–153.

Fletcher, A., Bonell, C., & Hargreaves, J. (2008). School effects on young people's drug use: A systematic review of intervention and observational studies. *Journal of Adolescent Health, 42*(3): 209–220.

Fletcher, J. M. (2012). Classification and identification of learning disabilities. In B. Y. L. Wong & D. L. Butler (Eds.), *Learning about learning disabilities* (4th Ed., pp. 1–25). Amsterdam: Elsevier Academic Press.

Flink, C. F., Boggiano, A. K., & Barrett, M. (1990). Controlling teaching strategies: Undermining children's self-determination and performance. *Journal of Personality and Social Psychology, 59,* 916–924.

Floden, R. E. (2001). Research on effects of teaching: A continuing model for research on teaching. In V. Richardson (Ed.), *Handbook of research on teaching* (4th ed., pp. 3–16). Washington, DC: American Educational Research Association.

Floden, R. E., & Klinzing, H. G. (1990). What can research on teacher thinking contribute to teacher preparation? A second opinion. *Educational Researcher, 19*(4), 15–20.

Flom, R., & Pick, A.D. (2003). Verbal encouragement and joint attention in 18-month-olds *Infant Behavior and Development, 26,* 121–134.

Flum, H., & Kaplan, A. (2006). Exploratory orientation as an educational goal. *Educational Psychologist, 41,* 99–110.

Ford, D. Y. (2000). *Infusing multicultural content into the curriculum for gifted students.* (ERIC EC Digest #E601). Arlington, VA: The ERIC Clearinghouse on Disabilities and Gifted Education.

Forness, S. R., & Knitzer, J. (1992). A new proposed definition and terminology to replace "Serious Emotional Disturbance" in Individuals with Disabilities Education Act. *School Psychology Review, 21,* 12–20.

Foster, W. (1981, August). *Social and emotional development in gifted individuals.* Paper presented at the Fourth World Conference on Gifted and Talented Children, Montreal, QC.

Fox, L. H. (1981). Identification of the academically gifted. *American Psychologist, 36,* 1103–1111.

Francis, D., Lesaux, N. K., & August, D. (2006). Language of instruction. In D. L. August & T. Shanahan (Eds.), *Developing literacy in a second language: Report of the National Literacy Panel* (pp. 365–410). Mahwah, NJ: Erlbaum.

Frank, S. J., Pirsch, L. A., & Wright, V. C. (1990). Late adolescents' perceptions of their parents: Relationships among deidealization, autonomy, relatedness, and insecurity and implications for adolescent adjustment and ego identity status. *Journal of Youth and Adolescence, 19,* 571–588.

Franklin, J. (2007). Achieving with autism: Dispelling common misconceptions is essential for success. *Education Update, 49* (7), 1–9.

Frattura, E. & Capper, C. A. (2006). Segregated programs versus integrated comprehensive service delivery for all learners. *Remedial and Special Education, 27,* 355–364.

Fredricks, J. A., Blumenfeld, P. C., & Paris, A. H. (2004). School engagement: Potential of the concept, state of the evidence. *Review of Educational Research, 74,* 59–109.

Free the Children. (2005). Child poverty. Retrieved from www.freethechildren.com/get-involved/geteducated/childpoverty.htm

Freiberg, H. J. (1999). Sustaining the paradigm. In H. J. Freiberg (Ed.), *Beyond behaviorism: Changing the classroom management paradigm* (pp. 164–173). Boston, MA: Allyn & Bacon.

Freiberg, H. J. (Ed.). (1999). *Beyond behaviorism: Changing the classroom management.* Boston, MA: Allyn & Bacon.

Freiberg, H. J., & Driscoll, A. (2005). *Universal teaching strategies* (4th ed.). Boston, MA: Allyn & Bacon.

Freiberg, J. (2006). Research-based programs for preventing and solving discipline problems. In C. Evertson & C. S. Weinstein (Eds.), *Handbook for classroom management: Research,*

*practice, and contemporary issues.* Mahwah, NJ: Erlbaum.

Frenzel, A. C., Goetz, T., Ludtke, O., Pekrun, R., & Sutton, R. E. (2009). Emotional transmission in the classroom: Exploring the relationship between teacher and student enjoyment. *Journal of Educational Psychology, 101*(3): 705–716.

Frey, N., & Fisher, D. (2010). Reading and the brain: What early childhood educators need to know. *Early Childhood Education Journal, 38,* 103–110.

Frick, T. W. (1990). Analysis of patterns in time: A method of recording and quantifying temporal relations in education. *American Educational Research Journal, 27,* 180–204.

Friedman-Weieneth, J. L., Harvey, E. A., Youngswirth, S. D., & Goldstein, L. H. (2007). The relation between 3-year-old-children's skills and their hyperactivity, inattention, and aggression. *Journal of Educational Psychology, 99,* 671–681.

Friend, M. (2006). *Special education: Contemporary perspectives for school professionals.* Boston, MA: Allyn & Bacon.

Friend, M. (2008). *Special education: Contemporary perspectives for school professionals* (2nd ed.). Boston, MA: Pearson/Allyn & Bacon.

Friend, M. (2011). *Special education: Contemporary perspectives for school professionals* (3rd ed.). Boston, MA: Allyn & Bacon/Pearson.

Friend, M., & Bursuck, W. D. (2002). *Including students with special needs* (3rd ed.). Boston, MA: Allyn & Bacon.

Friend, M., & Bursuck, W. D. (2009). *Including students with special needs: A practical guide for classroom teachers* (5th ed.). Boston, MA: Allyn & Bacon/Pearson.

Friend, M., & Bursuck, W. D. (2012). *Including students with special needs: A practical guide for classroom teachers* (6th ed.). Boston, MA: Allyn & Bacon/Pearson.

Friend, M., Bursuck, W., & Hutchinson, N. (1998). *Including exceptional students: A practical guide for classroom teachers.* Scarborough, ON: Allyn & Bacon Canada.

Frisbie, D. A. (2005). Measurement 101: Some fundamentals revisited. *Educational Measurement: Issues and Practices, 24* (2), 21–28.

Frost, J. L., Wortham, S. C., & Reifel, S. (2005). *Play and child development* (2nd ed.). Upper Saddle River, NJ: Prentice-Hall.

Fuchs, L. S. & Fuchs, D. (2007, May/June). A model for implementing responsiveness to intervention. *Teaching Exceptional Children, 39*(5), 14–20.

Fuchs, L. S., Fuchs, D., Compton, D. L., Rowell, S. R., Seethaler, P. M., Capizzi, A. M, Schatschneider, C., & Fletcher, J. M. (2006). The cognitive correlates of third-grade skill in arithmetic, algorithmic, computation, and arithmetic work problems. *Journal of Educational Psychology, 98,* 29–43.

Fuchs, L. S., Fuchs, D., Hamlett, C. L., & Karns, K. (1998). High-achieving students' interactions and performance on complex mathematical tasks as a function of homogeneous and heterogeneous pairings. *American Educational Research Journal, 35,* 227–268.

Fuchs, L. S., Fuchs, D., Prentice, K., Burch, M., Hamlett, C. L., Owen, R., & Schroeter, K. (2003). Enhancing third-grade students' mathematical problem solving with self-regulated learning strategies. *Journal of Educational Psychology, 95*(2), 306–315.

Fulk, C. L., & Smith, P. J. (1995). Students' perceptions of teachers' instructional and manage-

ment adaptations for students with learning or behavior problems. *The Elementary School Journal, 95,* 409–419.

Fuller, F. G. (1969). Concerns of teachers: A developmental conceptualization. *American Educational Research Journal, 6,* 207–226.

Fuller-Thomson, E., & Dalton, A. D. (2011). Suicidal ideation among individuals whose parents have divorced: Findings from a representative Canadian community survey. *Psychiatric Research, 187,* 150–155.

Furrer, C., & Skinner, E. (2003). Sense of relatedness as a factor in children's academic engagement and performance. *Journal of Educational Psychology, 95*(11), 148–161.

Gage, N. L. (1991). The obviousness of social and educational research results. *Educational Researcher, 20*(A), 10–16.

Gagné, E. D. (1985). *The cognitive psychology of school learning.* Boston, MA: Little, Brown.

Gagné, E. D., Yekovich, C. W., & Yekovich, F. R. (1993). *The cognitive psychology of school learning* (2nd ed.). New York, NY: Harper-Collins.

Gagné, R. M. (1985). *The conditions of learning and theory of instruction* (4th ed.). New York, NY: Holt, Rinehart & Winston.

Galambos, S. J., & Goldin-Meadow, S. (1990). The effects of learning two languages on metalinguistic development. *Cognition, 34,* 1–56.

Galliher, R. V., Rostosky, S. S., & Hughes, H. K. (2004). School belonging, self-esteem, and depressive symptoms in adolescents: An examination of sex, sexual attraction status, and urbanicity. *Journal of Youth and Adolescence, 33*(3), 235–245.

Gallimore, R., & Goldenberg, C. (2001). Analyzing cultural models and settings to connect minority achievement and school improvement research. *Educational Psychologist, 36,* 45–56.

Gallini, J. K. (1991). Schema-based strategies and implications for instructional design in strategy training. In C. McCormick, G. Miller, & M. Pressley (Eds.), *Cognitive strategies research: From basic research to educational applications.* New York, NY: Springer-Verlag.

Galton, M., Hargreaves, L. & Pell, T. (2009). Groupwork and whole class teaching with 11–14-year-olds, *compared. Cambridge Journal of Education, 39*(1): 119–114.

Gamoran, A. (1987). The stratification of high school learning opportunities. *Sociology of Education, 60,* 135–155.

Ganis, G., Thompson, W. L., and Kosslyn, S. M. (2004). Brain areas underlying visual mental imagery and visual perception: An fMRI study. *Cognitive Brain Research, 20,* 226–241.

Garbarino, J., & deLara, E. (2002). *And words can hurt forever: How to protect adolescents from bullying, harassment, and emotional violence.* New York, NY: Free Press.

Garcia, E. E. (2002). *Student cultural diversity: Understanding the meaning and meeting the challenge.* Boston, MA: Houghton Mifflin.

Garcia, R. L. (1991). *Teaching in a pluralistic society: Concepts, models, and strategies.* New York, NY: HarperCollins.

Gardner, H. (1983). *Frames of mind: The theory of multiple intelligences.* New York, NY: Basic Books.

Gardner, H. (1991). *The unschooled mind: How children think and how schools should teach.* New York, NY: Basic Books.

Gardner, H. (1993). *Creating minds: An anatomy of creativity seen through the lives of Freud, Einstein, Picasso, Stravinsky, Elliot, Graham, and Gandhi.* New York, NY: Basic Books.

Gardner, H. (1998). Reflections on multiple intelligences: Myths and messages. In A. Woolfolk (Ed.), *Readings in educational psychology* (2nd ed., pp. 61–67). Boston, MA: Allyn & Bacon.

Gardner, H. (2003, April 21). *Multiple intelligence after twenty years*. Paper presented at the American Educational Research Association, Chicago, Illinois.

Gardner, H. (2009). Birth and the spreading of a meme. In J-Q Chen, S. Moran, & H. Gardner (Eds.), *Multiple intelligences around the world* (pp. 3–16). San Francisco, CA: Wiley.

Gardner, H., & Moran, S. (2006). The science of multiple intelligences theory: A response to Lynn Waterhouse. *Educational Psychologist, 41*, 227–232.

Gardner, R., Brown, R., Sanders, S., & Menke, D. J. (1992). "Seductive details" in learning from text. In K. A. Renninger, S. Hidi, & A. Krapp (Eds.), *The role of interest in learning and development* (pp. 239–254). Hillsdale, NJ: Erlbaum.

Garmon, L. C., Basinger, K. S., Gregg, V. R., & Gibbs, J. C. (1996). Gender differences in stage and expression of moral judgment. *Merrill-Palmer Quarterly, 42*(3), 418–437.

Garner, P. W., & Spears, F. M. (2000). Emotion regulation in low-income preschool children. *Social Development, 9*, 246–264.

Garner, R. (1990). When children and adults do not use learning strategies: Toward a theory of settings. *Review of Educational Psychology, 60*, 517–530.

Garner, R. (1998). Choosing to learn and not-learn in school. *Educational Psychology Review, 10*, 227–238.

Garnets, L. (2002). Sexual orientations in perspective. *Cultural Diversity and Ethnic Minority Psychology, 8*, 115–129.

Garrison, J. (1995). Deweyan pragmatism and the epistemology of contemporary social constructivism. *American Educational Research Journal, 32*, 716–741.

Garrod, A., Beal, C., & Shin, P. (1990). The development of moral orientation in elementary school children. *Sex Roles, 22*, 13–27.

Gathercole, S. E., Pickering, S. J., Ambridge, B., & Wearing, H. (2004). The structure of working memory from 4 to 15 years of age. *Developmental Psychology, 40*, 177–190.

Gay, G. (2000). *Culturally responsive teaching: Theory, research, and practice.* New York, NY: Teachers College Press.

Gay, G. (2006). Connections between classroom management and culturally responsive teaching. In C. Evertson & C. S. Weinstein (Eds.), *Handbook for classroom management: Research, practice, and contemporary issues.* Mahwah, NJ: Erlbaum.

Geary, D. C. (1995). Sexual selection and sex differences in spatial cognition. *Learning and Individual Differences, 7*, 289–303.

Geary, D. C. (1999). Evolution and developmental sex differences. *Current Directions in Psychological Science, 8*, 115–120.

Geary, D. C. (2004). Mathematics and learning disabilities. *Journal of Learning Disabilities, 37*, 4–15.

Geary, D. C., & Bjorklund, D. F. (2000). Evolutionary developmental psychology. *Child Development, 7*, 57–65.

Gee, J. P. (2003). *What Video Games Have to Teach Us about Learning and Literacy.* New York: Palgrave MacMillan.

Gee, J. P., (2008). Learning and games. In K. Salen (Ed.), *The ecology of games: Connecting youth, games, and learning* (pp. 21–40). Cambridge, MA: The MIT Press, The John D. and

Catherine T. MacArthur Foundation Series on Digital Media and Learning. doi:10.1162/dmal. 9780262693646.021

Gehlbach, H. (2004). A new perspective on perspective taking: A multidimensional approach to conceptualizing an aptitude. *Educational Psychology Review, 16*, 207–234.

Geier, R., Blumenfeld, P., Marx, R., Krajcik, J., Fishman, B., & Soloway, E. (2008). Standardized test outcomes for students engaged in inquiry-based science curriculum in the context of urban reform. *Journal of Research in Science Teaching, 45*, 922–939.

Gelman, R. (2000). The epigenesis of mathematical thinking. *Journal of Applied Developmental Psychology, 21*, 27–37.

Gelman, R., & Cordes, S. A. (2001). Counting in animals and humans. In E. Dupoux (Ed.), *Essay in honor of Jacques Mehler.* Cambridge, MA: MIT Press.

Gentner, D., Loewenstein, J., & Thompson, L. (2003). Learning and transfer: A general role for analogical encoding. *Journal of Educational Psychology, 95*, 393–408.

George, P. S. (2005). A rationale for differentiated instruction in the regular classroom. *Theory Into Practice, 44*, 185–193.

Gergen, K. J. (1997). Constructing constructivism: Pedagogical potentials. *Issues in Education: Contributions from Educational Psychology, 3*, 195–202.

Gersten, R. (1996a). The language-minority students in transition: Contemporary instructional research. *The Elementary School Journal, 96*, 217–220.

Gersten, R. (1996b). Literacy instruction for language-minority students: The transition years. *The Elementary School Journal, 96*, 217–220.

Gersten, R., Baker, S. K., Shanahan, T., Linan-Thompson, S., Collins, P., & Scarcella, R. (2007). *Effective literacy and English language instruction for English learners in the elementary grades.* IES Practice Guide. Princeton, NJ: What Works Clearinghouse.

Gess-Newsome, J. (2012). Pedagogical content knowledge. In J. Hattie & E. Anderman (Eds.), *International handbook of student achievement.* New York, NY: Routledge.

Gibbs, J. W., & Luyben, P. D. (1985). Treatment of self-injurious behavior: Contingent versus noncontingent positive practice overcorrection. *Behavior Modification, 9*, 3–21.

Gibson, D., Aldrich, C., & Prensky, M. (Eds.). (2006). *Games and simulations in online learning: Research and development frameworks.* Hershey, PA: Information Science Publishing.

Gick, M. L. (1986). Problem-solving strategies. *Educational Psychologist, 21*, 99–120.

Gillett, M., & Gall, M. (1982, March). *The effects of teacher enthusiasm on the at-task behavior of students in the elementary grades.* Paper presented at the annual meeting of the American Educational Research Association, New York, NY.

Gillies, R. (2003). The behaviors, interactions, and perceptions of junior high school students during small-group learning. *Journal of Educational Psychology, 96*, 15–22.

Gillies, R. (2004). The effects of cooperative learning on junior high school students during small group learning. *Learning and Instruction, 14*, 197–213.

Gillies R. M., & Boyle M. (2011). Teachers' reflections on cooperative learning (CL): A two-year follow-up. *Teaching Education, 1*: 63–78.

Gilligan, C. (1982). *In a different voice: Psychological theory and women's development.* Cambridge, MA: Harvard University Press.

Gilligan, C., & Attanucci, J. (1988). Two moral orientations: Gender differences and similarities. *Merrill-Palmer Quarterly, 34*, 223–237.

Gini, G. (2008). Italian elementary and middle school students' blaming the victim of bullying and perception of school moral atmosphere. *The Elementary School Journal, 108*, 335–354.

Ginott, H. G. (1972). *Teacher and child: A book for parents and teachers.* New York, NY: Collier Books.

Ginsburg, H., & Opper, S. (1988). *Piaget's theory of intellectual development* (3rd ed.). Englewood Cliffs, NJ: Prentice-Hall.

Ginsburg, K. R. (2007). The importance of play in promoting healthy child development and maintaining strong parent-child bonds. *Pediatrics, 119*, 182–191.

Glasser, W. (1969). *Schools without failure.* New York, NY: Harper & Row.

Glasser, W. (1990). *The quality school: Managing students without coercion.* New York, NY: Harper & Row.

Glassman, M. (2001). Dewey and Vygotsky: Society, experience, and inquiry in educational practice. *Educational Researcher, 30*(4), 3–14.

Gleitman, H., Fridlund, A. J., & Reisberg, D. (1999). *Psychology* (5th ed.). New York, NY: Norton.

Gluck, M. A., Mercado, E., & Myers, C. E. (2008). *Learning and memory: From brain to behavior.* New York, NY: Worth.

Godden, D. R., & Baddeley, A. D. (1975). Context-dependent memory in two natural environments: On land and underwater. *British Journal of Psychology, 66*(3): 325–331.

Goetz, T., Cronjaeger, H., Frenzel, A. C., Ludtke, O., & Hall, N. C. (2010). Academic self-concept and emotion relations: Domain specificity and age effects. *Contemporary Educational Psychology, 35*, 44–58.

Goetz, T., Frenzel, A. C., Hall, N. C., & Pekrun, R. (2008). Antecedents of academic emotions: Testing the internal/external frame of reference model for academic enjoyment. *Contemporary Educational Psychology, 33*, 9–33.

Goldenberg, C. (1996). The education of language-minority students: Where are we, and where do we need to go? *The Elementary School Journal, 96*, 353–361.

Goldman, S. R., Lawless, K., Pellegrino, J. W., & Plants, R. (2006). Technology for teaching and learning with understanding. In J. Cooper (Ed.), *Classroom teaching skills* (8th ed., pp. 104–150). Boston, MA: Houghton-Mifflin.

Goleman, D. (1988, April 10). An emerging theory on blacks' I.Q. scores. *New York Times* (Education Life Section), pp. 22–24.

Goleman, D. (1995). *Emotional intelligence.* New York, NY: Bantam.

Golombok, S., Rust, J., Zervoulis, K., Croudace, T., Golding, J., & Hines, M. (2008). Developmental trajectories of sex-typed behavior in boys and girls: A longitudinal general population study of children aged 2.5–8 years. *Child Development, 79*(5): 1583–1593.

Gonzalez, V. (1999). *Language and cognitive development in second language learning: Educational implications for children and adults.* Boston, MA: Allyn & Bacon.

Gonzalez, N., Moll, L. C., Floyd-Tenery, M., Rivera, A., Rendon, P., Gonzales, R., & Amanti, C. (1993). *Teacher research on funds of knowledge: Learning from households.* Washington, DC: The Georgetown University National Center for Research on Cultural Diversity and Second Language Learning. Available online at: http://www.ncela.gwu.edu/pubs/ncrcdsll/epr6.htm

Gonzalez, N., Moll, L. C., and Amanti, C. (2005). *Funds of knowledge: Theorizing practices in households and classrooms*. Mahwah, NJ: Erlbaum.

Good, C., Aronson, J., & Inzlicht, M. (2003). Improving adolescents' standardized test performance: An intervention to reduce the effects of stereotype threat. *Journal of Applied Developmental Psychology, 24*, 645–662.

Good, T. L. (1983a). Classroom research: A decade of progress. *Educational Psychologist, 18*, 127–144.

Good, T. L. (1983b). Research on classroom teaching. In L. Shulman & G. Sykes (Eds.), *Handbook of teaching and policy* (pp. 42–80). New York, NY: Longman.

Good, T. L. (1988). Teacher expectations. In D. Berliner & B. Rosenshine (Eds.), *Talks to teachers* (pp. 159–200). New York, NY: Random House.

Good, T. L. (1996). Teaching effects and teacher evaluation. In J. Sikula (Ed.), *Handbook of research on teacher education* (pp. 617–665). New York, NY: Macmillan.

Good, T. L., & Brophy, J. (2003). *Looking in classrooms* (9th ed.). Boston, MA: Allyn & Bacon.

Good, T. L., & Brophy, J. E. (2008). *Looking in classrooms* (10th ed.). New York, NY: Allyn & Bacon/Longman.

Goodman, Y. M., & Goodman, K. S. (1990). Vygotsky in a whole-language perspective. In L. Moll (Ed.), *Vygotsky and education: Instructional implications and applications of sociohistorical psychology* (pp. 223–250). New York, NY: Cambridge University Press.

Goodrich, H. (1997). Understanding rubrics. *Educational Leadership, 54*(4), 14–17.

Gordon, D. (2001, June, 18). The dominator. *Newsweek*, 42–47.

Gordon, E. W. (1991). Human diversity and pluralism. *Educational Psychologist, 26*, 99–108.

Gordon, J. A. (1998). Caring through control: Reading urban African American youth. *Journal for a Just and Caring Education, 4*, 418–440.

Gordon, T. (1981). Crippling our children with discipline. *Journal of Education, 163*, 228–243.

Goswami, U. (2004). Neuroscience, education, and special education. *British Journal of Special Education, 31*, 175–183.

Gottlieb, G., Wahlsten, D., & Lickliter, R. (2006). The significance of biology for human development: A developmental psychobiological systems view. In R. M. Lerner (Ed.), *Handbook of child psychology: Vol. 1. Theoretical models of human development* (6th ed., pp. 210–257). New York, NY: Wiley.

Government of Canada (2006). *Child maltreatment in Canada: Overview paper*. Prepared by Susan Jack et al. Ottawa: Public Health Agency of Canada.

Graham, S. (1991). A review of attribution theory in achievement contexts. *Educational Psychology Review, 3*, 5–39.

Graham, S. (1994). Motivation in African Americans. *Review of Educational Research, 64*, 55–117.

Graham, S. (1995). Narrative versus meta-analytic reviews of race differences in motivation. *Review of Educational Research, 65*, 509–514.

Graham, S. (1996). How causal beliefs influence the academic and social motivation of African-American children. In G. G. Brannigan (Ed.), *The enlightened educator: Research adventures in the schools* (pp. 111–126). New York, NY: McGraw-Hill.

Graham, S. (1998). Self-blame and peer victimization in middle school: An attributional analysis. *Developmental Psychology, 34*, 587–599.

Graham, S., & Barker, G. (1990). The downside of help: An attributional developmental analysis of helping behavior as a low ability cue. *Journal of Educational Psychology, 82*, 7–14.

Graham, S., & Perin, D. (2007). A meta-analysis of writing instruction for adolescent students. *Journal of Educational Psychology, 99*, 445–476.

Graham, S., & Weiner, B. (1996). Theories and principles of motivation. In D. Berliner & R. C. Calfee (Eds.), *Handbook of educational psychology* (pp. 63–84). New York, NY: Macmillan.

Gray, P. (2002). *Psychology* (4th ed.). New York, NY: Worth.

Gray, P. (2011). *Psychology* (6th ed.). New York, NY: Worth.

Gredler, M. E. (2005). *Learning and instruction: Theory into practice* (5th ed.). Boston, MA: Allyn & Bacon.

Gredler, M. E. (2007). Of Cabbages and Kings: Concepts and inferences curiously attributed to Lev Vygotsky (Commentary on McVee, Dunsmore, and Gavelek, 2005). *Review of Educational Research, 77*, 233–238.

Gredler, M. E. (2009). *Learning and instruction: Theory into practice* (6th ed.). Columbus, OH: Merrill.

Gredler, M. E. (2009). Hiding in plain sight: The stages of mastery/self-regulation in Vygotsky's cultural-historical theory. *Educational Psychologist, 44*, 1–19.

Green, M., & Piel, J. A. (2010). *Theories of human development: A comparative approach*. Boston, MA: Allyn & Bacon.

Greene, J., Muis, K. R., & Pieschl, S. (2010). Modeling, measuring, and fostering interactions between epistemic beliefs and self-regulated learning in computer-based learning environments. *Educational Psychologist, 45*, 245–257.

Greeno, J. G., Collins, A. M., & Resnick, L. B. (1996). Cognition and learning. In D. Berliner & R. Calfee (Eds.), *Handbook of educational psychology* (pp. 15–46). New York, NY: Macmillan.

Gregorc, A. F. (1982). *Gregorc Style Delineator: Development, technical, and administrative manual*. Maynard, MA: Gabriel Systems.

Gresham, F. (1981). Social skills training with handicapped children. *Review of Educational Research, 51*, 139–176.

Griffins, P. E., & Gray, R. D. (2005). Discussion: Three ways to misunderstand developmental systems theory. *Biology and Philosophy, 20*, 417–425.

Grigorenko, E. L., Jarvin, L., Diffley, R., Goodyear, J., Shanahan, E. J., & Sternberg, R. J. (2009). Are SSATs and GPA enough? A theory-based approach to predicting academic success in high school. *Journal of Educational Psychology, 101*, 964–981.

Grigorenko, E. L., & Sternberg, R. J. (1998). Dynamic testing. *Psychological Bulletin, 124*, 75–111.

Grissom, J. B., & Shepard, L. A. (1989). Repeating and dropping out of school. In L. A. Shepard & M. L. Smith (Eds.), *Flunking grades: Research and policies on retention* (pp. 34–63). New York, NY: Falmer.

Grolnick, W. S., Gurland, S.T., Jacob, K.F., & DeCourcey, W. (2002). The development of self-determination in middle childhood and adolescence. In A. Wigfield & J. Eccles (Eds.), *Development of achievement motivation* (pp. 147–171). New York, NY: Academic Press.

Grolnick, W. S., Ryan, R. M., & Deci, E. L. (1991). Inner resources for school achievement: Motivational mediators of children's perceptions of their parents. *Journal of Educational Psychology, 83*, 508–517.

Gronlund, N. E., & Brookhart, S. M. (2009). *Gronlund's writing instructional objectives* (8th ed.). Columbus, OH: Pearson.

Gronlund, N. E., & Waugh, C. K. (2009). *Assessment of student achievement* (9th ed.). Columbus, OH: Pearson.

Gröschner, A., Seidel, T., & Shavelson, R. S. (2012). Methods for studying teacher and teaching effectiveness. In J. Hattie & E. Anderman (Eds.), *International handbook of student achievement*. New York, NY: Routledge.

Gross, E. F., Juvonen, J., & Gable, S. L. (2002). Internet use and well-being in adolescence. *Journal of Social Issues, 58*(1), 75–90.

Gross, M. (2005). *Studying Children's Questions: Imposed and Self-Generated Information Seeking at School*. Lanham, MD: The Scarecrow Press.

Grossman, H., & Grossman, S. H. (1994). *Gender issues in education*. Boston, MA: Allyn & Bacon.

Grotevant, H. D. (1998). Adolescent development in family contexts. In N. Eisenberg (Ed.), *Handbook of child psychology: Vol 3. Social, emotional, and personality development* (5th ed., pp. 1097–1149). New York, NY: Wiley.

Guay, F., Larose, S., & Boivin, M. (2004). Academic self-concept and educational attainment level: A ten-year longitudinal study. *Self and Identity, 3*, 53–68.

Guerra, N. G., Williams, K. R., & Sadek, S. (2011). Understanding bullying and victimization during childhood and adolescence: A mixed methods study. *Child Development, 82*(1): 295–310.

Guèvremont, A., Roos, N. P., & Brownell, M. (2007). Predictors and consequences of grade retention. Examining data from Manitoba, Canada. *Canadian Journal of School Psychology, 22*, 50–67.

Guglielmi, R. S. (2008). Native language proficiency, English literacy, academic achievement, and occupational attainment in limited-English-proficient students: A latent growth modeling perspective. *Journal of Educational Psychology, 100*, 322–342.

Guilford, J. P. (1988). Some changes in the Structure-of-Intellect model. *Educational and Psychological Measurement, 48*, 1–4.

Guo, Y. (2012). Exploring linguistic, cultural, and religious diversity in Canadian schools: Pre-service teachers' learning from immigrant parents. *Journal of Contemporary Issues in Education, 7*, 4–23.

Gurian, M., & Henley, P. (2001). *Boys and girls learn differently: A guide for teachers and parents*. San Francisco, CA: Jossey-Bass.

Guskey, T. R. (1994). Making the grade: What benefits students? *Educational Leadership, 52*(2), 14–21.

Guskey, T. R. (2011). Five obstacles to grading reform. *Educational Leadership, 69*(3), 17–21.

Guskey, T. R., & Bailey, J. M. (2001*). Developing grading and reporting systems for student learning*. Thousand Oaks, CA: Corwin Press.

Gustafsson, J-E., & Undheim, J. O. (1996). Individual differences in cognitive functioning. In D. Berliner & R. Calfee (Eds.), *Handbook of educational psychology* (pp. 186–242). New York, NY: Macmillan.

Guthrie, J. T., & Alao, S. (1997). Designing contexts to increase motivations of reading. *Educational Psychologist, 32*, 95–105.

Guthrie, J. T., Cox, K. E., Anderson, E., Harris, K., Mazzoni, S., & Rach, L. (1998). Principles of integrated instruction for engagement in reading. *Educational Psychology Review, 10,* 227–238.

Guthrie, J. T., Wigfield, A., Humenick, N. M., Perencivich, K. C., Taboada, A., Barbosa, P. (2006). Influences of stimulating tasks on reading motivation and comprehension. *Journal of Educational Research, 99*(4), 232–245.

Gutman, L. M., Sameroff, A. J., & Cole, R. (2003). Academic growth curve trajectories from 1st grade to 12th grade: Effects of multiple social risk factors and preschool child factors. *Developmental Psychology, 39*(4): 777–790.

Hacker, D. J., & Tenent, A. (2002). Implementing reciprocal teaching in the classroom: Overcoming obstacles and making modifications. *Journal of Educational Psychology, 94,* 699–718.

Hadwin, A. F., Jäevelä, S., & Miller, M. (2011). Self-regulated, co-regulated, and socially shared regulation of learning. In B. J. Zimmerman & D. H. Schunk (Eds.), *Handbook of Self-Regulation of Learning and Performance* (pp. 65–84). New York, NY: Routledge.

Haertel, E. H. (1999). Performance assessment and educational reform. *Phi Delta Kappan, 80,* 662–666.

Hagborg, W. J. (1993). Rosenberg Self-Esteem Scale and Harter's Self-Perception Profile for Adolescents: A concurrent validity study. *Psychology in Schools, 30,* 132–136.

Hakuta, K. (1986). *Mirror of language: The debate on bilingualism.* New York, NY: Basic Books.

Hakuta, K., & Garcia, E. E. (1989). Bilingualism and education. *American Psychologist, 44,* 374–379.

Hakuta, K., & Gould, L. J. (1987). Synthesis of research on bilingual education. *Educational Leadership, 44*(6), 38–45.

Haladyna, T. H. (2002). *Essentials of standardized achievement testing: Validity and accountability.* Boston, MA: Allyn & Bacon.

Hall, V. C., Bailey, J. & Tillman, C. (1997). Can student-generated illustrations be worth ten thousand words? *Journal of Educational Psychology, 89* (4), 677–681.

Hall, L. J., Grundon, G. S., Pope, C., & Romero, A. B. (2010). Training paraprofessionals to use behavioral strategies when educating learners with autism spectrum disorders across environments. *Behavioral Intentions, 25*(1): 37–51.

Hallahan, D. P., & Kauffman, J. M. (2006). *Exceptional learners: Introduction to special education* (10th ed.). Boston, MA: Allyn & Bacon.

Hallahan, D. P., Kauffman, J. M., & Pullen, P. C. (2009). *Exceptional learners: Introduction to special education* (11th ed.). Boston, MA: Allyn & Bacon.

Hallahan, D. P., Lloyd, J. W., Kauffman, J. M., Weiss, M. P., & Martinez, E. A. (2005). *Introduction to learning disabilities* (5th ed.). Boston, MA: Allyn & Bacon.

Hallowell, E. M., & Ratey, J. J. (1994). *Driven to distraction.* New York, NY: Pantheon Books.

Halpern, D. F., Benbow, C. P., Geary. D. C., Gur, R. C., Hyde, J. S., & Gernsbacher, M. A. (2007). The science of sex differences in science and mathematics. Psychological Science in the Public Interest, 8, 1–51.

Hamann, D. L., Baker, D. S., McAllister, P. A., & Bauer, W. I. (2000). Factors affecting university music students' perceptions of lesson quality and teaching effectiveness. *Journal of Research in Music Education, 48,* 102–113.

Hambrick, D. Z., Kane, M. J., & Engle, R. W. (2005). The role of working memory in higher-level cognition. In R. Sternberg & J. E. Pretz (Eds.), *Cognition and intelligence: Identifying the mechanisms of the mind* (pp. 104–121). New York, NY: Cambridge University Press.

Hamers, J. F., & Blanc, M. H. A. (2000). *Bilinguality and bilingualism* (2nd ed.). Cambridge, England: Cambridge University Press.

Hamilton, J. (2009). Multitasking teens may be muddling their brains. Available online at: http://www.npr.org/templates/story/story.php?storyId_95524385

Hamilton, R. J. (1985). A framework for the evaluation of the effectiveness of adjunct questions and objectives. *Review of Educational Research, 55,* 47–86.

Hamman, D., Berthelot, J., Saia, J., & Crowley, E. (2000). Teachers' coaching of learning and its relation to students' strategic learning. *Journal of Educational Psychology, 92,* 342–348.

Hammer, C. S., Farkas, G., & Maczuga, S. (2010). The language and literacy development of Head Start children: A study using the Family and Child Experiences Survey Database. *Language, Speech and Hearing Services in Schools, 41,* 70–83.

Hammer, C. S., Lawrence, F. R., & Miccio, A. W. (2007). Bilingual children's language abilities and early reading outcomes in Head Start and Kindergarten. *Language, Speech, and Hearing Services in Schools, 38,* 237–248.

Hamre, B. K., & Pianta, R. C. (2001). Early teacher–child relationships and the trajectory of children's school outcomes through eighth grade. *Child Development, 72,* 625–638.

Hanushek, E. A., Rivkin, S. G., & Kain, J. J. (2005). Teachers, schools and academic achievement. *Econometrica 73,* 417–458.

Hapgood, S., Magnusson, S. J., and Palincsar, A. S. (2004). Teacher, text, and experience mediating children's learning of scientific inquiry. *Journal of the Learning Sciences, 13*(4), 455–506.

Harackiewicz, J. M., Barron, K. E., Pintrich, P. R., Elliot, A. J., & Thrash, T. M. (2002). Revision of achievement goal theory: Necessary and illuminating. *Journal of Educational Psychology, 94,* 562–575.

Harackiewicz, J. M., & Linnenbrink, E. A. (2005). Multiple achievement goals and multiple pathways for learning: The agenda and impact of Paul R. Pintrich. *Educational Psychologist, 40,* 75–84.

Hardiman, P. T., Dufresne, R., & Mestre, J. P. (1989). The relation between problem categorization and problem solving among experts and novices. *Memory & Cognition, 17,* 627–638.

Hardin, C. J. (2008). *Effective classroom management: Models and strategies for today's classrooms* (2nd ed.). Columbus, OH: Merrill/Prentice-Hall.

Hardman, M. L., Drew, C. J., & Egan, M. W. (2005). *Human exceptionality: Society, school, and family* (8th ed.). Boston, MA: Allyn & Bacon.

Harklau, L., Losey, K. M., & Seigal, M. (1999). Linguistically diverse students and college writing: What is equitable and appropriate? In L. Harklau, K. Losey, & M. Seigal (Eds.), *Generation 1.5 meets college composition: Issues in teaching of writing to U.S.-educated learners of ESL* (pp. 1–16). Mahwah, NJ: Lawrence Erlbaum.

Harp, S. F., & Mayer, R. E. (1998). How seductive details do their damage: A theory of cognitive interest in science learning. *Journal of Educational Psychology, 90,* 414–434.

Harris, M. A., Prior, J. C., & Koehoom, M. (2008). Age at menarche in the Canadian population: Secular Trends and Relationship to Adulthood BMI. *Journal of Adolescent Health, 43*(6).

Harris, J. R. (1998). *The nurture assumption: Why children turn out the way they do; parents matter less than you think and peers matter more.* New York, NY: Free Press.

Harris, K. R. (1990). Developing self-regulated learners: The role of private speech and self-instruction. *Educational Psychologist, 25,* 35–50.

Harris, K. R., Alexander, P., & Graham, S. (2008). Michael Pressley's contributions to the history and future of strategies research. *Educational Psychologist, 43,* 86–96.

Harris, K. R., & Graham, S. (1996). Memo to constructivist: Skills count too. *Educational Leadership, 53*(5), 26–29.

Harris, K. R., Graham, S., & Pressley, M. (1992). Cognitive-behavioral approaches in reading and written language: Developing self-regulated learners. In N. N. Singh & I. L. Beale (Eds.), *Learning disabilities: Nature, theory, and treatment* (pp. 415–451). New York, NY: Springer-Verlag.

Harris, K. R., & Pressley, M. (1991). The nature of cognitive strategy instruction: Interactive strategy construction. *Exceptional Children, 57,* 392–404.

Harris, P. L. (2006). Social cognition. In D. Kuhn & R. Siegler (Eds.), *Handbook of child psychology* (6th ed., Vol. 2). New York, NY: Wiley.

Harrow, A. J. (1972). *A taxonomy of the psychomotor domain: A guide for developing behavior objectives.* New York, NY: David McKay.

Harrower, J. K., & Dunlap, G. (2001). Including children with autism in general education classrooms: A review of effective strategies. *Behavior Modification, 25:* 762–784.

Harter, S. (1990). Issues in the assessment of self-concept of children and adolescents. In A. LaGreca (Ed.), *Through the eyes of a child* (pp. 292–325). Boston, MA: Allyn & Bacon.

Harter, S. (1998). The development of self-representations. In N. Eisenberg (Ed.), *Handbook of child psychology: Vol. 3. Social, emotional, and personality development* (5th ed., pp. 553–618). New York, NY: Wiley.

Harter, S. (2003). The development of self-representation during childhood and adolescence. In M. R. Leary & J. P. Tangney (Eds.), *Handbook of self and identity* (pp. 610–642). New York, NY: Guilford.

Harter, S. (2006). The self. In W. Damon & R. M. Lerner (Series Eds.) *Social, emotional and personality development* (6th ed., pp. 646–718). New York, NY: Wiley.

Hartshore, J. K., & Ullman, M. T. (2006). Why girls say "holded" more than boys. *Developmental Science, 9,* 21–32.

Hartup, W. W., & Stevens, N. (1999). Friendships and adaptation across the lifespan. *Current Directions in Psychological Science, 8,* 76–79.

Hattie, J., & Timperley, H. (2007). The power of feedback. *Review of Educational Research, 77,* 81–112.

Haugland, S. W., & Wright, J. L. (1997). *Young children and technology: A world of discovery.* Needham Heights, MA: Allyn and Bacon.

Hawkins, M. R. (2004). Researching English language and literacy development in schools. *Educational Researcher, 33* (3), 14–25.

Hayes, S. C., Rosenfarb, I., Wulfert, E., Munt, E. D., Korn, Z., & Zettle, R. D. (1985). Self-reinforcement effects: An artifact of social standard setting? *Journal of Applied Behavior Analysis, 18,* 201–214.

Health Canada. (2004/05). *Summary of results of the 2004–05 Youth Smoking Survey.* Retrieved from www.hc-sc.gc.ca/hl-vs/tobac-tabac/research-recherche/stat/survey-sond-age/2004-2005/result_e.html

Health Canada. (2006). First Nations, Inuit and Aboriginal Health: Suicide prevention. Retrieved from www.hc-sc.gc.ca/fniah-spnia/promotion/suicide/index-eng.php

Health Canada. (2014). Summary of results of the Youth Smoking Survey, 2012–2013. Retrieved June 14, 2014, from www.hc-sc.gc.ca/hc-ps/tobac-tabac/research-recherche/stat/_survey-sondage_2012-2013/result-eng.php

Heath, N. (1996). The emotional domain: Self-concept and depression in children with learning disabilities. *Advances in Learning and Behavioural Disabilities, 10,* 47–75.

Heath, N. L., & Ross, S. (2000). The prevalence and expression of depressive symptomatology in children with and without learning disabilities. *Learning Disability Quarterly, 23,* 24–36.

Heath, S. B. (1983). *Ways with words: Language, life and work in communities and classrooms.* Cambridge University Press.

Heath, S. B. (1989). Oral and literate traditions among black Americans living in poverty. *American Psychologist, 44,* 367–373.

Heath, S. B. (1983). *Ways with words: Language, life and work in communities and classrooms.* NY: Cambridge University Press.

Hecht, S. A., & Vagi, K. J. (2010). Sources of group and individual differences in emerging fraction skills. *Journal of Educational Psychology, 102*(4): 843–859.

Helms, J. E. (1995). An update of Helms's White and People of Color racial identity models. In J. G. Ponterotto, J. M. Casas, L. A. Suzuki & C. M. Alexander (Eds.), *Handbook of multicultural counseling* (pp. 181–198). Thousand Oaks, CA: Sage.

Helwig, C. C., Arnold, M. L., Tan, D., & Boyd, D.(2003). Chinese adolescents' reasoning about democratic and authority-based decision making in peer, family, and school contexts. *Child Development, 74,* 783–800.

Henry, B. (2011, May 2). Personal communication.

Herbert, E. A. (1998). Design matters: How school environment affects children. *Educational Leadership, 56*(1), 69–71.

Herman, J. (1997). Assessing new assessments: How do they measure up? *Theory Into Practice, 36,* 197–204.

Herman, J., & Winters. L. (1994). Portfolio research: A slim collection. *Educational Leadership, 52*(2), 48–55.

Herman, M. (2004). Forced to choose: Some determinants of racial identification in multiracial adolescents. *Child Development, 75,* 730–748.

Herzig, A. H. (2004). Becoming mathematicians: Women and students of color choosing and leaving doctoral mathematics. *Review of Educational Research, 74,* 171–214.

Hetherington, E. M. (2006). The influence of conflict, marital problem solving and parenting on children's adjustment in nondivorced, divorced and remarried families. In A. Clarke-Stewart & J. Dunn (Eds.), *Families count: Effects on child and adolescent development* (pp. 203–237). New York, NY: Cambridge University Press.

Hetherington, E. M., & Kelly, J. (2002). *For better or for worse: Divorce reconsidered.* New York, NY: W. W. Norton.

Hewson, P. W., Beeth, M. E., & Thorley, N. R. (1998). Teaching for conceptual change. In B. J. Fraserr & K. G. Tobin (Eds.), *International handbook of science education* (pp. 199–218). New York, NY: Kluwer.

Hewstone, M. (1989). Changing stereotypes with disconfirming information. In D. Bar-Tal, C. Graumann, A. Kruglanski, & W. Stroebe (Eds.), *Stereotyping and prejudice: Changing conceptions* (pp. 207–223). New York, NY: Springer-Verlag.

Hickey, D. T. (2003). Engaged participation vs. marginal non-participation: A stridently sociocultural model of achievement motivation. *Elementary School Journal, 103*(4), 401–429.

Hickey, D. T., Kindfield, A. C. H., Horwitz, P., & Christie, M. A. (1999). Advancing educational theory by enhancing practice in a technology supported genetics learning environment. *Journal of Education, 181,* 25–55.

Hickey, D. T., Wolfe, E. W., & Kindfield, A. C. H. (2000). Assessing learning in a technology-supported genetics environment: Evidential and consequential validity issues. *Educational Assessment, 6,* 155–196.

Hidi, S., & Renninger, K. A. (2006). The four-phase model of interest development. *Educational Psychologist, 41,* 111–127.

Hidi, S., Renninger, K. A., & Krapp, A. (2004). Interest, a motivational variable that combines affective and cognitive functioning. In D. Y. Dai & R. J. Sternberg (Eds.), *Motivation, emotion, and cognition: Integrative perspectives on intellectual functioning and development* (pp. 89–115). Mahwah, NJ: Erlbaum.

Hilgard, E. R. (1996). History of educational psychology. In R. Calfee & D. Berliner (Eds.), *Handbook of educational psychology* (pp. 990–1004). New York, NY: Macmillan.

Hill, H.C., Rowan, B., & Ball, D.L. (2005) Effects of teachers' mathematical knowledge for teaching on student achievement. *American Educational Research Journal, 42,* 371–406.

Hill, W. F. (2002). *Learning: A survey of psychological interpretations* (7th ed.). Boston, MA: Allyn & Bacon.

Hindi, E. R., & Perry, N. (2007). Elementary teachers' application of Jean Piaget's theories of cognitive development during social studies curriculum debates in Arizona. *The Elementary School Journal, 108,* 64–79.

Hines, C. V., Cruickshank, D. R., & Kennedy, J. J. (1985). Teacher clarity and its relation to student achievement and satisfaction. *American Educational Research Journal, 22,* 87–99.

Hines, M. (2004) *Brain gender.* New York, NY: Oxford University Press.

Hinnant, J. B., O'Brien, M., & Ghazarian, S. R. (2009). The longitudinal relations of teacher expectations to achievement in the early school years. *Journal of Educational Psychology, 101*(3): 662–670.

Hinton, C., Miyamoto, K., & Della-Chiesa, B. (2008). Brain research, learning and emotions: Implications for education research, policy and practice. *European Journal of Education, 43,* No. 1.

Hipsky, S. (2011). *Differentiated literacy and language arts strategies for the elementary classroom.* Columbus, OH: Merrill.

Hiroto, D. S., & Seligman, M. E. P. (1975). Generality of learned helplessness in man. *Journal of Personality and Social Psychology, 31,* 311–327.

Hirvikoski, T., Waaler, E., Alfredsson, J., Pihlgren, C., et al. (2011). Reduced ADHD symptoms in adults with ADHD after structured skills training group: Results from a randomized controlled trial. *Behaviour Research and Therapy, 49*(3): 175–185.

Hirsch, E. D., Jr. (1996). *The schools we need: Why we don't have them.* New York, NY: Doubleday.

Hmelo, C. E. (1998). Problem-based learning: Effects on the early acquisition of cognitive skill in medicine. *Journal of the Learning Sciences, 7,* 173–208.

Hmelo-Silver, C. E. (2004). Problem-based learning: What and how do students learn? *Educational Psychology Review, 16,* 235–266.

Hmelo-Silver, C. E., Ravit, G. D., & Chinn, C. A. (2007). Scaffolding and achievement in problem-based and inquiry learning: A response to Kirschner, Sweller, and Clark (2006). *Educational Psychologist, 42,* 99–107.

Hobbs, R. (2004). A review of school-based initiatives in media literacy education. *American Behavioral Scientist, 48,* 42–59.

Hodges, E. V. E., & Perry, D. G. (1999). Personal and interpersonal consequences of victimization by peers. *Journal of Personality and Social Psychology, 76,* 677–685.

Hofer, B. K., & Pintrich, P. R. (1997). The development of epistemological theories: Beliefs about knowledge and knowing and their relation to learning. *Review of Educational Research, 67,* 88–140.

Hofer, M. (2010). Adolescents' development of individual interests: A product of multiple goal regulation? *Educational Psychologist, 45* (3), 149–166.

Hoff, E. (2006). How social contexts support and shape language development. *Developmental Review, 26,* 55–88.

Hofferth, S. L., & Sandberg, J. F. (2000). *Changes in American children's time, 1981–1997.* Ann Arbor, MI: University of Michigan Population Studies Center.

Hoffler, T. N., & Leutner, D. (2011). The role of spatial ability in learning from instructional animations—evidence for an ability-as-compensator-hypothesis. *Computers in Human Behavior, 27,* 209–216.

Hoffman, M. L. (2000). *Empathy and moral development.* New York, NY: Cambridge University Press.

Hoffman, M. L. (2001). A comprehensive theory of prosocial moral development. In A. Bohart & D. Stipek & (Eds.), *Constructive and destructive behavior* (pp. 61–86). Washington, DC: American Psychological Association.

Hogan, T., Rabinowitz, M., & Craven, J. A. III. (2003). Representation in teaching: Inferences from research of expert and novice teachers. *Educational Psychologist, 38,* 235–247.

Hoge, D. R., Smit, E. K., & Hanson, S. L. (1990). School experiences predicting changes in self-esteem of sixth- and seventh-grade students. *Journal of Educational Psychology, 82,* 117–126.

Hohman, C. (1998). Evaluating and selecting software for children. *Child Care Information Exchange, 123,* 60–62.

Holahan, C. K., & Sears, R. R. (1995). *The gifted group in later maturity.* Stanford, CA: Stanford University Press.

Hong, G., & Raudenbush, S. W. (2005). Effects of kindergarten retention policy on children's cognitive growth in reading and mathematics. *Educational Evaluation and Policy Analysis, 27*(3): 205–224.

Hoover-Dempsey, K. V., Bassler, O. C., & Burow, R. (1995). Parents' reported involvement in students' homework: Strategies and practices. *The Elementary School Journal, 95,* 435–450.

Hoover-Dempsey, K. V., Battiato, A. C., Walker, J. M. T., Reed, R. P., DeJong, J. M., & Jones, K. P. (2001). Parental involvement in homework. *Educational Psychologist, 36,* 195–209.

Horn, J. L. (1998). A basis for research on age differences in cognitive capabilities. In J. J. McArdle & R. W. Woodcock (Eds.), *Human cognitive theories in theory and practice* (pp. 57–87). Mahwah, NJ: Erlbaum.

Horovitz, B. (2002, April 22). Gen Y: A tough crowd to sell. *USA Today*, pp. B1–2.

Howe, M. J. A., Davidson, J. W., & Sloboda, J. A. (1998). Innate talents: Reality or myth? *Behavioral and Brain Sciences, 21*, 399–406.

Hoy, W. K., & Woolfolk, A. E. (1993). Teachers' sense of efficacy and the organizational health of schools. *Elementary School Journal, 93*, 355–372.

Hudley, C., Graham, S., & Taylor, A. (2007). Reducing aggressive behavior and increasing motivation in school: The evolution of an intervention to strengthen school adjustment. *Educational Psychologist, 42*, 251–260.

Hudley, C., & Novak, A. (2007). Environmental influences, the developing brain, and aggressive behavior. *Theory Into Practice, 46*, 121–129.

Huesmann, L. R., Moise-Titus, J., Podolski, C.-L., & Eron, L. D. Longitudinal relations between children's exposure to TV violence and their aggressive and violent behavior in young adulthood: 1977–1992. *Developmental Psychology, 39*(2), 201–221.

Huff, C. R. (1989). Youth gangs and public policy. *Crime & Delinquency, 35*, 524–537.

Hughes, D. R. (1998). *Kids online: Protecting your children in cyberspace*. Grand Rapids, MI: Fleming H. Revell.

Huguet, P., & Régner, I. (2007). Stereotype threat among schoolgirls in quasi-ordinary classroom circumstances. *Journal of Educational Psychology, 99*, 345–360.

Hulit, L., & Howard, M. (2006). *Born to talk: An introduction to speech and language development* (4th ed.). Boston, MA: Allyn & Bacon.

Hulleman, C. S., Godes, O., Hendricks, B. L., & Harackiewicz, J. M. (2010). Enhancing interest and performance with a utility value intervention. *Journal of Educational Psychology*. Advance online publication.

Human Resources and Social Development Canada. (2004). Advancing the Inclusion of Persons with Disabilities. Retrieved from www.hrsdc.gc.ca/en/hip/odi/documents/advancingInclusion04/index.shtml

Hung, D. W. L. (1999). Activity, apprenticeship, and epistemological appropriation: Implications from the writings of Michael Polanyi. *Educational Psychologist, 34*, 193–205.

Hunt, E. (2000). Let's hear it for crystallized intelligence. *Learning and Individual Differences, 12*, 123–129.

Hunt, J. M. (1961). *Intelligence and experience*. New York, NY: Ronald.

Hunt, N., & Marshall, K. (2002). *Exceptional children and youth: An introduction to special education* (3rd ed.). Boston, MA: Houghton Mifflin.

Hunt, R. R., & Ellis, H. C. (1999). *Fundamentals of cognitive psychology* (6th ed.). New York, NY: McGraw-Hill College.

Hunter, M. (1982). *Mastery teaching*. El Segundo, CA: TIP Publications.

Hurry, J., Nunes, T., Bryant, P., Pretzlik, U., Parker, M., Curno, C., & Midgley, L. (2005) Transforming research on morphology into teacher practice *Research Papers In Education, 20* (2), 187–206.

Hutchinson, N. L. (2007). *Inclusion of exceptional learners in Canadian schools*. (2nd ed.). Toronto, ON: Prentice-Hall.

Hutchinson, N. L. (2013). *Inclusion of exceptional learners in Canadian schools: A practical handbook for teachers* (4th ed.). Toronto, ON: Pearson Education Canada.

Hutchinson, N. L., Versnel, J., Poth, C., Berg, D., deLugt, J., Dalton, C. J., Chin, P., & Munby, H. (2011). They want to come to school: Work-based education programs to prevent social exclusion of vulnerable youth. *Journal of Prevention, Assessment, & Rehabilitation, 40*, 195–209.

Hutchinson, N. L., Wintermute, J., Munby, H., Versnel, J., Chin, P., & Dalgarno, N. (2005, April). *Negotiating accommodations so that work-based education facilitates career development for youth with disabilities*. Paper presented at the annual meeting of the American Educational Research Association, Montreal, QC.

Hyman, I., Kay, B., Tabori, A., Weber, M., Mahon, M., & Cohen, I. (2006). Bullying: Theory, research, and interventions. In C. M. Evertson & C. S. Weinstein (Eds.), *Handbook of classroom management: Research, practice, and contemporary issues* (pp. 855–884). Mahwah, NJ: Erlbaum.

Institute of Marriage and Family Canada. (2010). Canadian Divorce Statistics. Retrieved from www.imfcanada.org/article_files/Canadian%20Divorce%20Statistics.pdf

International Reading Association & National Association for the Education of Young Children. (1998). Learning to read and write: Developmentally appropriate practices for young children. *The Reading Teacher, 52*, 193–216.

Ipsos Reid Interactive Group. (2010) Weekly internet usage overtakes television watching. Retrieved from www.ipsos-na.com/news-polls/pressrelease.aspx?id=4720

Iran-Nejad, A. (1990). Active and dynamic self-regulation of learning processes. *Review of Educational Research, 60*, 573–602.

Irvine, J. J. (1990). *Black students and school failure: Policies, practices, and prescriptions*. New York, NY: Praeger.

Irvine, J. J., & Armento, B. J. (2001). *Culturally responsive teaching: Lesson planning for elementary and middle grades*. New York, NY: McGraw-Hill.

Irvine, J. J. & Fraser, J. W. (1998, May). Warm demanders. *Education Week*. Retrieved from www.edweek.org/ew/ewstory.cfm?slug=35irvine.h17& keywords=Irvine

Irving, O., & Martin, J. (1982). Withitness: The confusing variable. *American Educational Research Journal, 19*, 313–319.

Irwin, J. W. (1991). *Teaching reading comprehension* (2nd ed.). Boston, MA: Allyn & Bacon.

Isabella, R., & Belsky, J. (1991). Interactional synchrony and the origins of infant–mother attachment: A replication study. *Child Development, 62*, 373–384.

Jackson, A., & Davis, G. (2000). *Turning points 2000: Educating adolescents in the 21st century*. New York, NY: Teachers College Press.

Jackson, L. A., von Eye, A., Biocca, F. A., Barbatsis, G., Zhao, Y., & Fitzgerald, H. E. (2006). Does home Internet use influence the academic performance of low-income children? *Developmental Psychology, 42*, 429–435.

Jacobs, J. E., Lanza, S., Osgood, D. W., Eccles, J. S., & Wigfield, A. (2002). Changes in children's self-competence and values: Gender and domain differences across grades one through twelve. *Child Development, 73*, 509–527.

Jain, S., & Dowson, M. (2009). Mathematics anxiety as a function of multidimensional self-regulation and self-efficacy. *Contemporary Educational Psychology, 34*(3): 240–249.

Jaffee, S. & Hyde, J. S. (2000). Gender differences in moral orientation: A meta-analysis. *Psychological Bulletin, 126*(5): 703.

James, W. (1890). *The principles of psychology* (Vol. 2). New York, NY: Holt.

James, W. (1912). *Talks to teachers on psychology: And to students on some of life's ideals*. New York, NY: Holt.

Jang, H., Reeve, J., & Deci, E. L. (2010). Engaging students in learning activities: It's not autonomy support or structure, but autonomy support and structure. *Journal of Educational Psychology, 102*, 588–600.

Jarrett, R. (1995). Growing up poor: The family experiences of socially mobile youth in low-income African American neighborhoods. *Journal of Adolescent Research, 10*, 111–135.

Jarrold, C., Tam, H., Baddeley, A. D., & Harvey, C. E. (2011). How does processing affect storage in working memory tasks? Evidence for both domain-general and domain-specific effects. *Journal of Experimental Psychology: Learning, Memory, and Cognition, 37*(3): 688–705.

Jaswal, V. K., & Markman, E. M. (2001). Learning proper and common names in inferential versus ostensive contexts. *Child Development, 72*, 787–802.

Jensen, E. (2009). *Teaching with poverty in mind: What being poor does to kids' brains and what schools can do about it*. Alexandria, VA: Association for Supervision and Curriculum Development.

Jensen, L. A., Arnett, J. J., Feldman, S. S., & Cauffman, E. (2002). It's wrong but everybody does it: Academic dishonesty among high school and college students. *Contemporary Educational Psychology, 27*, 209–228.

Jerome, E. M., Hamre, B. K., & Pianta, R. C. (2009). Teacher—child relationships from kindergarten to sixth grade: Early childhood predictors of teacher-perceived conflict and closeness. *Social Development, 18* (4), 915–945.

Jia, Y., Way, N., Ling, G., Yoshikawa, H., Chen, X., & Hughes, D. (2009). The influence of student perceptions of school climate on socioemotional and academic adjustment: A comparison of Chinese and American adolescents. *Child Development, 80*, 1514–1530.

Jimenez, R. (2000). Literacy and identity development of Latina/o students who are successful English readers: Opportunities and obstacles. *American Educational Research Journal, 37*, 971–1000.

Jimerson, S. R. (1999). On the failure of failure: Examining the association between early grade retention and education and employment outcomes during late adolescence. *Journal of School Psychology, 37*, 243–272.

Jimerson, S. R., Anderson, G. E., & Whipple, A. D. (2002). Winning the battle and losing the war: Examining the relation between grade retention and dropping out of high school. *Psychology in the Schools, 39*, 441–457.

Jimerson, S. R., & Ferguson, P. (2007). A longitudinal study of grade retention: Academic and behavioral outcomes of retained students through adolescence. *School Psychology Quarterly, 22*(3): 314–339.

Jitendra, A. K., Star, J. R., Starosta, K., Leh J. M., Sood, S., Caskie, G., … Mack, T. R. (2009). Improving seventh grade students' learning of ratio and proportion: The role of schema-based instruction. *Contemporary Educational Psychology, 34*, 250–264.

Johnson, A. (2003). Procedural memory and skill acquisition. In A. F. Healy & R. W. Proctor (Eds.), *Experimental psychology* (Vol. 4, pp. 499–523). New York, NY: Wiley.

Johnson, A. M., & Notah, D. J. (1999). Service learning: History, literature, review, and a pilot study of eighth graders. *The Elementary School Journal, 99*, 453–467.

Johnson, D. W., & Johnson, R. T. (1999a). *Learning together and alone: Cooperation, competition, and individualization* (5th ed.). Boston, MA: Allyn & Bacon.

Johnson, D. W., & Johnson, R. T. (1999b). The three Cs of school and classroom management. In H. J. Freiberg (Ed.), *Beyond behaviorism: Changing the classroom management paradigm* (pp. 119–144). Boston, MA: Allyn & Bacon.

Johnson, D. W., & Johnson, R. T. (2002). *Meaningful assessment: A meaningful and cooperative process*. Boston, MA: Allyn & Bacon.

Johnson, D. W., & Johnson, R. T. (2009a). An educational psychology success story: Social interdependence theory and cooperative learning. *Educational Researcher, 38*, 365–379.

Johnson, D. W., & Johnson, R. T. (2009b). Energizing learning: The instructional power of conflict. *Educational Researcher, 38*, 37–51.

Johnson, D. W., Johnson, R. T., Dudley, B., Ward, M., & Magnuson, D. (1995). The impact of peer mediation training on the management of school and home conflicts. *American Educational Research Journal, 32*, 829–844.

Johnson, S. (2008, January 14). A childhood in poverty informs her teaching. *USA Today*, p. 7D.

John-Steiner, V., & Mahn, H. (1996). Sociocultural approaches to learning and development: A Vygotskian framework. *Educational Psychologist, 31*, 191–206.

Johnston, L. D., O'Malley, P. M., Bachman, J. G., & Schulenberg, J. E. (2004, December 21). *Overall teen drug use continues gradual decline; but use of inhalants rises*. [Online]. Ann Arbor, MI: University of Michigan News and Information Services. Retrieved from www.monitoringthefuture.org

Jonassen, D. H. (2003). Designing research-based instruction for story problems. *Educational Psychology Review, 15*, 267–296.

Jonassen, D. H. (2011). Ask systems: Interrrogative access to multiple ways of thinking. *Education Technology Research and Development, 59*, 159–175.

Jones, D. C. (2004). Body image among adolescent girls and boys: A longitudinal study. *Developmental Psychology, 40*, 823–835.

Jones, E. D., & Southern, W. T. (1991). Conclusions about acceleration: Echoes of a debate. In W. Southern & E. Jones (Eds.), *The academic acceleration of gifted children* (pp. 223–228). New York, NY: Teachers College Press.

Jones, M. G., & Gerig, T. M. (1994). Silent sixth-grade students: Characteristics, achievement, and teacher expectations. *Elementary School Journal, 95*, 169–182.

Jones, M. S., Levin, M. E., Levin, J. R., & Beitzel, B. D. (2000). Can vocabulary-learning strategies and pair-learning formats be profitably combined? *Journal of Educational Psychology, 92*, 256–262.

Jones, S. M., & Dindia, K. (2004). A meta-analytic perspective on sex equity in the classroom. *Review of Educational Research, 74*, 443–471.

Jurbergs, N., Palcic, J., & Kelly, M. L. (2007). School-home notes with and without response cost: Increasing attention and academic performance in low-income children with attention deficit/hyperactivity disorder. *School Psychology Quarterly, 22*, 358–379.

Jurden, F. H. (1995). Individual differences in working memory and complex cognition. *Journal of Educational Psychology, 87*, 93–102.

Jussim, L. (2012). *Social perception and social reality: Why accuracy dominates bias and self-fulfilling prophecy*. New York: Oxford University Press.

Jussim, L., & Harber, K. D. (2005). Teacher expectations and self-fulfilling prophecies: Knowns and unknowns, resolved and unresolved controversies. *Personality and Social Psychology Review, 9*, 131–155.

Jussim, L., Robustelli, S. & Cain, T. (2009). Teacher expectations and self-fulfilling prophecies. In A. Wigfield & K. Wentzel (Eds.), *Handbook of Motivation at School* (pp. 249–380). Erlbaum: Mahwah, NJ.

Kagan, J. (1976). Commentary on reflective and impulsive children: Strategies of information processing underlying differences in problem solving. *Monograph of the Society for Research in Child Development, 41*(5) (Ser. No. 168).

Kagan, J., & Herschkowitz, N. (2005). *A young mind in a growing brain*. Mahwah, NJ: Erlbaum.

Kagan, S. (1994). *Cooperative learning*. San Juan Capistrano, CA: Kagan Cooperative Learning.

Kail, R. (2000). Speed of processing: Developmental change and links to intelligence. *Journal of School Psychology, 38*, 51–61.

Kail, R., & Hall, L. K. (1999). Sources of developmental change in children's word-problem performance. *Journal of Educational Psychology, 91*, 600–668.

Kail, R., & Park, Y. (1994). Processing time, articulation time, and memory span. *Journal of Experimental Child Psychology, 57*, 281–291.

Kalyuga, S. (2011). Cognitive load theory: How many types of load does it really need? *Educational Psychology Review, 23*, 1–19.

Kalyuga, S., Chandler, P., Tuovinen, J., & Sweller, J. (2001). When problem solving is superior to studying worked examples. *Journal of Educational Psychology, 93*, 579–588.

Kalyuga, S., & Renkl A. (2010). Expertise reversal effect and its instructional implications: introduction to the special issue. *Instructional Science, 38*(3): 209–215.

Kanaya, T., Scullin, M.H., & Ceci, S. J. (2003). The Flynn effect and U.S. policies: The impact of rising IQ scores on American society via mental retardation diagnoses. *American Psychologist, 58*, 1–13.

Kanazawa, S. (2010). Evolutionary psychology and intelligence research. *American Psychologist, 65*(4), 279–289.

Kaplan, A., & Maehr, M. L. (2007). The contributions and prospects of goal orientation theory. *Educational Psychology Review, 19*, 141–184.

Kaplan, J. S. (1991). *Beyond behavior modification* (2nd ed.). Austin, TX: Pro-Ed.

Kardash, C. M., & Howell, K. L. (2000). Effects of epistemological beliefs and topic-specific beliefs on undergraduates' cognitive and strategic processing of dual-positional text. *Journal of Educational Psychology, 92*, 524–535.

Karpov, Y. V., & Bransford, J. D. (1995). L. S. Vygotsky and the doctrine of empirical and theoretical learning. *Educational Psychologist, 30*, 61–66.

Karpov, Y. V., & Haywood, H. C. (1998). Two ways to elaborate Vygotsky's concept of mediation implications for instruction. *American Psychologist, 53*, 27–36.

Karweitt, N. (1989). Time and learning: A review. In R. E. Slavin (Ed.), *School and classroom organization* (pp. 69–95). Hillsdale, NJ: Erlbaum.

Karweitt, N., & Slavin, R. (1981). Measurement and modeling choices in studies of time and learning. *American Educational Research Journal, 18*, 157–171.

Katz, I., & Assor, A. (2007). When choice motivates and when it does not. *Educational Psychology Review, 19*, 429–442.

Katz, J. (2012). *Teaching to diversity: The three-block model of universal design for learning*. Winnipeg, MB: Portage & Main Press.

Katz, J., & Mirenda, P. (2002). Including students with developmental disabilities in general education classrooms: Educational benefits. *International Journal of Special Education, 17*, 86–96.

Katz, P. A. (2003). Racists or tolerant multiculturalists? How do they begin? *American Psychologist, 58*, 897–909.

Katz, S. R. (1999). Teaching in tensions: Latino immigrant youth, their teachers, and the structures of schooling. *Teachers College Record, 100*(4), 809–840.

Katzir, T., & Paré-Blagoev, J. (2006). Applying cognitive neuroscience research to education: The case of literacy. *Educational Psychologist, 4*, 53–74.

Kazdin, A. E. (1984). *Behavior modification in applied settings*. Homewood, IL: Dorsey Press.

Kazdin, A. E. (2001). *Behavior modification in applied settings* (6th ed.). Belmont, CA: Wadsworth.

Kazdin, A. E. (2008). *The Kazdin method for parenting the defiant child*. Boston, MA: Houghton-Mifflin.

Keating, D. P. (1991). Curriculum options for the developmentally advanced: A developmental alternative for gifted education. *Exceptionality Education Canada, 1*, 53–83.

Keefe, J. W. (1982). Assessing student learning styles: An overview. In *Student learning styles and brain behavior*. Reston, VA: National Association of Secondary School Principals.

Keefe, J. W., & Monk, J. S. (1986). *Learning style profile: Examiner's manual*. Reston, VA: National Association of Secondary School Principals.

Keller, M., Neumann, K., & Fischer, H. E. (2012). Teacher enthusiasm and student learning. In J. Hattie & E. Anderman (Eds.), *International handbook of student achievement*. New York, NY: Routledge.

Kelly, K. (1999). Retention vs. social promotion: Schools search for alternatives. *Harvard Education Letter, 15*(1), 1–3.

Kenney-Benson, G. A., Pomerantz, E. M., Ryan, A. M., & Patrick, H. (2006). Sex differences in math performance: The role of children's approach to school work. *Developmental Psychology, 42*, 11–26.

Kerckhoff, A. C. (1986). Effects of ability grouping in British secondary schools. *American Sociological Review, 51*, 842–858.

Keyser, V., & Barling, J. (1981). Determinants of children's self-efficacy beliefs in an academic environment. *Cognitive Therapy and Research, 5*, 29–40.

KidsHealth. (2009). Cerebral Palsy. Retrieved from http://kidshealth.org/parent/medical/brain/cerebral_palsy.html#

Kiewra, K. A. (1985). Investigating notetaking and review: A depth of processing alternative. *Educational Psychologist, 20*, 23–32.

Kiewra, K. A. (1988). Cognitive aspects of autonomous note taking: Control processes, learning strategies, and prior knowledge. *Educational Psychologist, 23*, 39–56.

Kiewra, K. A. (1989). A review of note-taking: The encoding storage paradigm and beyond. *Educational Psychology Review, 1*, 147–172.

Kiewra, K. A. (2002). How classroom teachers can help students learn and teach them how to learn. *Theory Into Practice, 41*, 71–80.

Kim, K. M. (1998). Korean children's perceptions of adult and peer authority and moral reasoning. *Developmental Psychology, 5*, 310–329.

Kim, J. & Duff, P. A. (2012). The language socialization and identity negotiations of Generation 1.5 Korean-Canadian university students. *TESL Canada Journal, 29*, 81–102.

Kim, J. S., & Guryan, J. (2010). The efficacy of a voluntary summer book reading intervention for low-income Latino children from language minority families. *Journal of Educational Psychology, 102*(1): 20–31.

Kindsvatter, R., Wilen, W., & Ishler, M. (1992). *Dynamics of effective teaching* (2nd ed.). New York, NY: Longman.

King, A. (1990). Enhancing peer interaction and learning in the classroom through reciprocal questioning. *American Educational Research Journal, 27*, 664–687.

King, A. (1994). Guiding knowledge construction in the classroom: Effects of teaching children how to question and how to explain. *American Educational Research Journal, 31*, 338–368.

King, A. (2002). Structuring peer interactions to promote high-level cognitive processing. *Theory Into Practice, 41*, 31–39.

King, G. (1979, June). [Personal communication]. University of Texas at Austin.

Kirk, S., Gallagher, J. J., & Anastasiow, N. J. (1993). *Educating exceptional children* (7th ed.). Boston, MA: Houghton Mifflin.

Kirk, S. A., Gallagher, J. J., Anastasiow, N. J., & Coleman, M. R. (2006). *Educating exceptional children* (11th ed.). Boston, MA: Houghton Mifflin.

Kirschner, P. A., Sweller, J., & Clark, R. E. (2006). Why minimal guidance during instruction does not work: An analysis of the failure of constructivist, discovery, problem-based, experiential, and inquiry-based teaching. *Educational Psychologist, 41*(2): 75–86.

Kirst, M. (1991). Interview on assessment issues with James Popham. *Educational Researcher, 20*(2), 24–27.

Klahr, D., & Nigam, M. (2004). The equivalence of learning paths in early science instruction: Effects of direct instruction and discovery learning. *Psychological Science, 15*(10): 661–667.

Klass, P. (2011, October). Hearing bilingual: How babies sort out language. *New York Times.* Retrieved July 26, 2013, from www.nytimes.com/2011/10/11/health/views/11klass.html?_r=0

Klassen, R. M. (2004). A cross-cultural investigation of the efficacy beliefs of South Asian immigrant and Anglo Canadian nonimmigrant early adolescents. *Journal of Educational Psychology, 96*, 731–742.

Klein, S. S., & Harris, A. H. (2007). A users guide to the Legacy Cycle. *Journal of Education and Human Development, 1.* Retrieved from www.scientificjournals.org/journals2007/articles/1088.pdf

Kleinfeld, J. (2005, May 20). *Culture fuels boys' learning problems.* Alaska Daily News, p. B6.

Kling, K. C., Hyde, J. S., Showers, C. J., & Buswell, B. N. (1999). Gender differences in self-esteem: A meta-analysis. *Psychological Bulletin, 125*, 470–500.

Knapp, M., Turnbull, B. J., & Shields, P. M. (1990). New directions for educating children of poverty. *Educational Leadership, 48*(1), 4–9.

Knapp, M. S., & Woolverton, S. (2003). Social class and schooling. In J. A. Banks & C. A. Banks (Eds.), *Handbook of research on multicultural education.* San Francisco, CA: Jossey-Bass.

Kneedler, R. (1984). *Special education for today.* Englewood Cliffs, NJ: Prentice-Hall.

Knoblauch, D., & Woolfolk Hoy, A. (2008). "Maybe I can teach those kids." The influence of contextual factors on student teachers' sense of efficacy. *Teaching and Teacher Education, 24*, 166–179.

Kohlberg, L. (1963). The development of children's orientations toward moral order: Sequence in the development of moral thought. *Vita Humana, 6*, 11–33.

Kohlberg, L. (1975). The cognitive-developmental approach to moral education. *Phi Delta Kappan, 56*, 670–677.

Kohlberg, L. (1981). *The philosophy of moral development.* New York, NY: Harper & Row.

Kohn, A. (1993). Rewards versus learning: A response to Paul Chance. *Phi Delta Kappan, 74*, 783–787.

Kohn, A. (1996a). *Beyond discipline: From compliance to community.* Alexandria, VA: Association for Supervision and Curriculum Development.

Kohn, A. (1996b). By all available means: Cameron and Pierce's defense of extrinsic motivators. *Review of Educational Research, 66*, 1–4.

Kohn, A. (2005). Unconditional teaching. *Educational Leadership, 62*, 12–17.

Kohn. A. (2006). *The homework myth: Why our kids get too much of a bad thing.* Cambridge, MA: Da Capo Press.

Kokko, K., & Pulkkinen, L. (2000). Aggression in childhood and long-term unemployment in adulthood: A cycle of maladaptation and some protective factors. Printed originally *Developmental Psychology, 36*, 463–472.

Kolb, A. Y. & Kolb, D. A. (2005). *The Kolb learning style inventory—Version 3.1 2005 specifications.* Retrieved February 4, 2015 from http://learningfromexperience.com/media/2010/08/tech_spec_lsi.pdf.

Kolb, G., & Whishaw, I. Q. (1998). Brain plasticity and behavior. In J. T. Spence, J. M. Darley, & D. J. Foss (Eds.), Annual review of psychology (pp. 43–64). Palo Alto, CA: Annual Reviews.

Koppelman, K. (2008). *Understanding human differences: Multicultural education for a diverse America* (2nd ed.). Boston, MA: Pearson/Allyn & Bacon.

Koppleman, K. L. (2011). *Understanding human differences: Multicultural education for a diverse America* (3rd ed.). Boston, MA: Pearson.

Korenman, S., Miller, J., & Sjaastad, J. (1995). Long-term poverty and child development in the United States: Results from the NLSY. *Children and Youth Services Review, 17*, 127–155.

Korf, R. (1999). Heuristic search. In R. Wilson & F. Keil (Eds.), *The MIT encyclopedia of the cognitive sciences* (pp. 372–373). Cambridge, MA: MIT Press.

Koriat, A., Goldsmith, M., & Pansky, A. (2000). Toward a psychology of memory accuracy. In S. Fiske (Ed.), *Annual review of psychology* (pp. 481–537). Palo Alto, CA: Annual Reviews.

Kornhaber, M., Fierros, E., & Veenema, S. (2004). *Multiple intelligences: Best ideas for research and practice.* Boston, MA: Allyn & Bacon.

Kosslyn, S. M., & Koenig, O. (1992). *Wet mind: The new cognitive neuroscience.* New York, NY: Free Press.

Kounin, J. S. (1970). *Discipline and group management in classrooms.* New York, NY: Holt, Rinehart & Winston.

Kozulin, A. (1990). *Vygotsky's psychology: A biography of ideas.* Cambridge, MA: Harvard University Press.

Kozulin, A., (2003). Psychological tools and mediated learning. In A. Kouzlin, B. Gindis, V. Ageyev, & S. M. Miller (Eds.), *Vygotsky's educational theory in cultural context* (pp. 15–38). Cambridge, England: Cambridge University Press.

Kozulin, A. (Ed.). (2003). *Vygotsky's educational theory in cultural context.* Cambridge, England: Cambridge University Press.

Kozulin, A., & Presseisen, B. Z. (1995). Mediated learning experience and psychological tools: Vygotsky's and Feuerstein's perspectives in a study of student learning. *Educational Psychologist, 30*, 67–75.

Krahn, H. & Taylor, A. (2008). "Streaming" in the 10th grade in four Canadian provinces in 2000. *Statistics Canada.* Retrieved from www.statcan.gc.ca/pub/81-004-x/2007002/9994-eng.htm

Krajcik, J., & Czerniak, C. (2007). *Teaching science in elementary and middle school classrooms: A project-based approach* (3rd ed.). Mahwah, NJ: Erlbaum.

Krathwohl, D. R., Bloom, B. S., & Masia, B. B. (1964). *Taxonomy of educational objectives. Handbook II: Affective domain.* New York, NY: David McKay.

Krätzig, G. P., & Arbuthnott, K. D. (2006). Perceptual learning style and learning proficiency: A test of the hypothesis. *Journal of Educational Psychology, 98*, 238–246.

Kreitzer, A. E., & Madaus, G. F. (1994). Empirical investigations of the hierarchical structure of the taxonomy. In L. W. Anderson & L. A. Sosniak (Eds.), *Bloom's taxonomy: A forty-year retrospective.* Ninety-third yearbook for the National Society for the Study of Education: Part II (pp. 64–81). Chicago, IL: University of Chicago Press.

Kroesbergen, E. H., Van Luit, J. E. H., & Maas, C. J. M. (2004). Effectiveness of explicit and constructivist mathematics for low-achieving students in the Netherlands. *The Elementary School Journal, 104*, 233–251.

Kroger, J. (2000). *Identity development: Adolescence through adulthood.* Thousand Oaks, CA: Sage.

Kronholz, J. (2011), Challenging the gifted: Nuclear chemistry and Sartre draw the best and brightest to Reno. *Education Next, 11* (2), 1–8. Available online at: http://educationnext.org/challenging-the-gifted/

Krumboltz, J. D., & Yeh, C. J. (1996). Competitive grading sabotages good teaching. *Phi Delta Kappan, 78*, 324–326.

Kuhl, P. K., Stevens, E., Hayashi, A., Deguchi, T., Kiritani, S., & Iverson, P. (2006). Infants show facilitation for native language phonetic perception between 6 and 12 months. *Developmental Science, 9*, 13–21.

Kuhn, D. (2007). Is direct instruction an answer to the right question? *Educational Psychologist, 42*, 109–113.

Kuhn, D., & Dean, D. (2004). Metacognition: A bridge between cognitive psychology and educational practice. *Theory Into Practice, 43*(4): 268–273.

Kuhn, D., Goh, W., Iordanou, K., & Shaenfield, D. (2008). Arguing on the computer: A microgenetic study of developing argument skills in a computer-supported environment. *Child Development, 79*(5), 1310–28.

Kuhn, D., & Franklin, S. (2006). The second decade: What develops (and how). In D. Kuhn & R. S. Siegler (Eds.), *Cognition, perception, and language* (6th ed., Vol. 2, pp. 953–993). New York, NY: Wiley.

Kuklinski, M. R., & Weinstein, R. S. (2001). Classroom and developmental differences in a path model of teacher expectancy effects. *Child Development, 72*, 1554–1578.

Kulik, J. A., & Kulik, C. C. (1984). Effects of accelerated instruction on students. *Review of Educational Research, 54*, 409–425.

Kulik, J. A., & Kulik, C. L. (1997). Ability grouping. In N. Colangelo & G. Davis (Eds.), *Handbook of gifted education* (2nd ed., pp. 230–242). Boston, MA: Allyn & Bacon.

Kumar, D. D., & Sherwood, R. D. (2007). Effect of problem-based simulation on the conceptual understanding of undergraduate science educational majors. *Journal of Science Education and Technology, 16*, 239–246.

Kuo, L., & Anderson, R. C. (2006). Morphological awareness and learning to read: A cross-language perspective. *Educational Psychologist, 41*, 161–180.

Lachter, J., Forster, K. I., & Ruthruff, K. I. (2004). Forty-five years after Broadbent (1958): Still no identification without attention. *Psychological Review, 111*, 880–913.

Ladson-Billings, G. (1990). Like lightning in a bottle: Attempting to capture the pedagogical excellence of successful teachers of Black students. *Qualitative Studies in Education, 3*, 335–344.

Ladson-Billings, G. (1992). Culturally relevant teaching: The key to making multicultural education work. In C. A. Grant (Ed.), *Research and multicultural education* (pp. 106–121). London, England: Falmer Press.

Ladson-Billings, G. (1994). *The dream keepers.* San Francisco, CA: Jossey-Bass.

Ladson-Billings, G. (1995). But that is just good teaching! The case for culturally relevant pedagogy. *Theory Into Practice, 34*, 161–165.

Ladson-Billings, G. (2004). Landing on the wrong note: The price we paid for Brown. *Educational Researcher, 33*(7), 3–13.

Laidlaw, L. (2004). The importance of little details: Complexity, emergence, and pedagogy. Retrieved from www.ccfi.educ.ubc.ca/publication/insights/v09n01/articles/laidlaw.html

Lajoie, S. P., & Azevedo, R. (2006). Teaching and learning in technology-rich environments. In A. Alexander & P. H. Winne (Eds.), *Handbook of educational psychology* (2nd ed., pp. 803–823). Mahwah, NJ: Erlbaum.

Lamb, M. E., & Lewis, C. (2005). The role of parent-child relationships in child development. In M. H. Bornstein & M. E. Lamb (Eds.), *Developmental science: An advanced textbook* (5th ed., pp. 429–468). Mahwah, NJ: Erlbaum.

Lambert, A. J. (1995). Stereotypes and social judgment: The consequences of group variability. *Journal of Personality and Social Psychology, 68*, 388–403.

Lambert, N. M. (1994). Seating arrangement in classrooms. In *International encyclopedia of education* (2nd ed., Vol. 9, pp. 5355–5359). Oxford, England: Pergamon.

Lamborn, S. D., Mounts, N. S., Steinberg, L., & Dornbusch, S. M. (1991). Patterns of competence and adjustment among adolescents from authoritative, authoritarian, indulgent, and neglectful families. *Child Development, 63*, 1049–1065.

Landrum, T. J., & Kauffman, J. M. (2006). Behavioral approaches to classroom management. In C. M. Evertson & C. S. Weinstein (Eds.), *Handbook of classroom management: Research, practice, and contemporary issues.* Mahwah, NJ: Erlbaum.

Lane, K., Falk, K., & Wehby, J. (2006). Classroom management in special education classrooms and resource rooms. In C. M. Evertson & C. S. Weinstein (Eds.), *Handbook of classroom management: Research, practice, and contemporary issues.* Mahwah, NJ: Erlbaum.

Langan-Fox, J., Waycott, J. L., & Albert, K. (2000). Linear and graphic organizers: Properties and processing. *International Journal of Cognitive Ergonomics, 4*(1), 19–34.

Language Development and Hypermedia Group. (1992). "Open" software design: A case study. *Educational Technology, 32*, 43–55.

Lashley, T. J., II, Matczynski, T. J., & Rowley, J. B. (2002). *Instructional models: Strategies for teaching in a diverse society* (2nd ed.). Belmont, CA: Wadsworth/ Thomson Learning.

Lave, J. (1988). *Cognition in practice: Mind, mathematics, and culture in everyday life.* New York, NY: Cambridge University Press.

Lave, J. (1997). The culture of acquisition and the practice of understanding. In D. Kirshner & J. A. Whitson (Eds.), *Situated cognition: Social, semiotic, and psychological perspectives* (pp. 17–35). Mahwah, NJ: Erlbaum.

Lave, J., & Wenger, E. (1991). *Situated learning: Legitimate peripheral participation.* Cambridge, MA: Cambridge University Press.

Leaper, C. (2002). Parenting girls and boys. In M. H. Bornstein (Ed.), *Handbook of parenting, Vol. 1: Children and parenting* (2nd ed., pp. 127–152). Mahwah, NJ: Erlbaum.

Leaper, C., & Smith, T. E. (2004). A meta-analytic review of gender variations in children's talk: Talkativeness, affiliative speech, and assertive speech. *Developmental Psychology, 40*, 993–1027.

Lee, A. Y., & Hutchinson, L. (1998). Improving learning from examples through reflection. *Journal of Experimental Psychology: Applied, 4*, 187–210.

Lee, K., Ng, E. L., & Ng, S. F. (2009). The contributions of working memory and executive functioning to problem representation and solution generation in algebraic word problems. *Journal of Educational Psychology, 101*, 373–387.

Lee, R. M. (2005). Resilience against discrimination: Ethnic identity and other-group orientation as protective factors for Korean Americans. *Journal of Counseling Psychology, 52*, 36–44.

Lee, S. J. (2004). Model minorities and perpetual foreigners: The impact of stereotyping on Asian American students. In M. Sadowski (Ed.), *Adolescents at school: Perspectives on youth, identity, and education* (pp. 41–49). Cambridge, MA: Harvard University Press.

Lee, S. J., Wong, N. W., & Alvarez, A. N. (2009). The model minority and the perpetual foreigner: Stereotypes of Asian Americans. In N. Tewari & A. N. Alvarez (Eds.), *Asian American psychology: Current perspectives* (pp. 69-84). New York, NY: Routledge/Taylor & Francis Group.

Leets, L. & Sunwolf. (2005). Adolescent rules for social exclusion: When is it fair to exclude someone else? *Journal of Moral Education, 34*, 343–362.

Lehman, D. R., & Nisbett, R. E. (1990). A longitudinal study of the effects of undergraduate training on reasoning. *Developmental Psychology, 26*, 952–960.

Leinhardt, G. (2001). Instructional explanations: A commonplace for teaching and location for contrasts. In V. Richardson (Ed.), *Handbook of research on teaching* (4th ed., pp. 333–357). Washington, DC: American Educational Research Association.

LeMahieu, P., Gitomer, D. H., & Eresh, J. T. (1993). *Portfolios in large-scale assessment: Difficult but not impossible.* Unpublished manuscript, University of Delaware.

Lemelson, R. (2003). Obsessive-compulsive disorder in Bali. *Transcultural Psychiatry, 40*, 377–408.

Leming, J. S. (1981). Curriculum effectiveness in value/moral education. *Journal of Moral Education, 10*, 147–164.

Lepper, M. R., & Greene, D. (1978). *The hidden costs of rewards: New perspectives on the psychology of human motivation.* Hillsdale, NJ: Erlbaum.

Lepper, M. R., Keavney, M., & Drake, M. (1996). Intrinsic motivation and extrinsic reward: A commentary on Cameron and Pierce's meta-analysis. *Review of Educational Research, 66*, 5–32.

Lerner, R. M., Theokas, C., & Bobek, D. L. (2005). Concepts and theories of human development: Historical and contemporary dimensions. In M. H. Bornstein & M. E. Lamb (Eds.), *Developmental science: An advanced textbook* (5th ed., pp. 3–43). Mahwah, NJ: Erlbaum.

Leung, A. K-Y., & Chiu, C-Y. (2008). Interactive effects of multicultural experiences and openness to experience on creativity. *Creativity Research Journal, 20*: 376–382.

Leung, A. K., Maddux, W. W., Galinsky, A. D., & Chiu, C. (2008). Multicultural experience enhances creativity: The when and how. *American Psychologist, 63*, 169–181.

Leung, K., Lau, S., & Lam, W. (1998). Parenting styles and academic achievement: A cross-cultural study. *Merrill-Palmer, 44*, 157–167.

Levin, J. R. (1994). Mnemonic strategies and classroom learning: A twenty-year report card. *Elementary School Journal, 94*, 235–254.

Levin, J. R., & Nolan, J. F. (2000). *Principles of classroom management: A professional decision-making model.* Boston, MA: Allyn & Bacon.

Lewinsohn, P. M., Rohde, P., & Seeley, J. R. (1994). Psychological risk factors for future attempts. *Journal of Consulting and Clinical Psychology, 62*, 297–305.

Lewis, R. (2001). Classroom discipline and student responsibility: The students' view. *Teaching and Teacher Education, 17*, 307–319.

Lewis, T. J., Sugai, G., & Colvin, G. (1998). Reducing problem behavior through a school-wide system of effective behavioral support: Investigation of a school-wide social skills training program and contextual interventions. *School Psychology Review, 27*, 446–459.

Liben, L. S., & Bigler, R. S. (2002). The developmental course of gender differentiation. Conceptualizing, measuring, and evaluating constructs and pathways. *Monographs of the Society for Research in Child Development, 67*(2).

Liben, L. S., & Signorella, M. L. (1993). Gender-schematic processing in children: The role of initial interpretations of stimuli. *Developmental Psychology, 29*, 141–149.

Lim, S. (2013). Diversity begins in the classroom for students. *Canadian Immigrant.* Retrieved March 8, 2014, from http://canadianimmigrant.ca/guides/moving-to-canada/diversity-begins-in-the-classroom-for-students

Lindberg, S. M., Hyde, J. S., Petersen, J. L., & Linn, M. C. (2010). New trends in gender and mathematics performance: A meta-analysis. *Psychological Bulletin, 136*(6): 1123–1135.

Lindsay, P. H., & Norman, D. A. (1977). *Human information processing: An introduction to psychology* (2nd ed.). New York, NY: Academic Press.

Linebarger, D. L., Kosanic, A. Z., Greenwood, C. R., & Doku, N. S. (2004). Effects of viewing the television program Between the Lions on the emergent literacy skills of young children. *Journal of Educational Psychology, 96*, 297–308.

Linn, M. C., & Eylon, B. S. (2006). Science education: Integrating views of learning and instruction. In P. A. Alexander & P. H. Winne (Eds.), *Handbook of educational psychology* (2nd ed., pp. 511–544). Mahwah, NJ: Erlbaum.

Linn, M. C., & Hyde, J. S. (1989). Gender, mathematics, and science. *Educational Researcher, 18*, 17–27.

Linn, R. L., & Miller, M. D. (2005). *Measurement and assessment in teaching* (9th ed.). Upper Saddle River, NJ: Prentice-Hall/ Merrill.

Linnenbrink-Garcia, L., & Pekrun, R. (2011). Students' emotions and academic engagement: Introduction to the special issue. *Contemporary Educational Psychology, 36*, 13–24.

Lipman, P. (1997). Restructuring in context: A case study of teacher participation and the dynamics of ideology, race, and power. *American Educational Research Journal, 34*, 3–37.

Liu, W. M., Ali, S. R., Soleck, G., Hopps, J., Dunston, K., & Pickett, T., Jr. (2004). Using social class in counseling psychology research. *Journal of Counseling Psychology, 51*, 3–18.

Lochman, J. E., & Wells, K. C. (2003a). The Coping Power program for preadolescent aggressive boys and their parents: Effects at the one-year follow-up. *Journal of Consulting and Clinical Psychology, 72*, 571–578.

Lochman, J. E., & Wells, K. C. (2003b). Effectiveness of the Coping Power program and of classroom intervention with aggressive children: Outcomes at a 1-year follow-up. *Behavior Therapy, 34*, 403–515.

Locke, E. A., & Latham, G. P. (2002). Building a practically useful theory of goal setting and task motivation: A 35-year odyssey. *American Psychologist, 57*, 705–717.

Loftus, E., & Palmer, J. C. (1974). Reconstruction of automobile destruction: An example of the interaction between language and memory. *Journal of Verbal Learning and Verbal Behavior, 13*, 585–589.

Lorch, R. F., Lorch, E. P., Ritchey, K., McGovern, L., & Coleman, D. (2001). Effects of headings on text summarization. *Contemporary Educational Psychology, 26*, 171–191.

Loveless, T. (1998). The tracking and ability grouping debate. *Fordham Report, 2*(88), 1–27.

Loveless, T. (1999). Will tracking reform promote social equity? *Educational Leadership, 56*(7), 28–32.

Lovett, M. W., Lacerenza, L., Borden, S. L., Frijters, J. C., Steinbach, K. A., & De Palma, M. (2000). Components of effective remediation for developmental disabilities: Combining phonological and strategy-based instruction to improve outcomes. *Journal of Educational Psychology, 92*, 263–283.

Lowenstein, G. (1994). The psychology of curiosity: A review and reinterpretation. *Psychological Bulletin, 117*, 75–98.

Luckner, A. E., & Pianta, R. C. (2011). Teacher-student interactions in fifth grade classrooms: Relations with children's peer behavior. *Journal of Applied Developmental Psychology, 32*(5), 257–266.

Lucyshyn, J. M., Horner, R. H., Dunlap, G., Albin, R. W., & Ben, K. R. (2002). Positive behavior support with families. In J. M. Lucyshyn, G. Dunlap, & R. W. Albin (Eds.), *Families and positive behavior support: Addressing problem behavior in family contexts* (pp. 3–43). Baltimore, MD: Paul H. Brookes.

Luiten, J., Ames, W., & Ackerson, G. (1980). A meta-analysis of the effects of advance organizers on learning and retention. *American Educational Research Journal, 17*, 211–218.

Lupart, J., & Barva, C. (1998). Promoting female achievement in the sciences: Research and implications. *International Journal for the Advancement of Counselling, 20*, 319–338.

Lupart, J. L., & Timmons, V. (2003). Preamble. *Exceptionality Education Canada, 13*, 5–7.

Lupart, J. L., & Pyryt, M. C. (1996). "Hidden gifted" students: Underachiever prevalence and profile. *Journal for the Education of the Gifted, 20*(1), 36–53.

Lyon, G. R., Shaywitz, S. E., & Shaywitz, B. A. (2003). A definition of dyslexia. *Annals of Dyslexia, 53*, 1–14.

Ma, X. (2012). The relation of teacher characteristics to student achievement. In J. Hattie & E. Anderman (Eds.), *International handbook of student achievement*. New York, NY: Routledge.

Maag, J. W., & Kemp, S. E. (2003). Behavioral intent of power and affiliation: Implications for functional analysis. *Remedial and Special Education, 24*, 57–64.

Mabry, L. (1999). Writing to the rubrics: Lingering effects of traditional standardized testing on direct writing assessment. *Phi Delta Kappan, 80*, 673–679.

Maccoby, E. E. (1998). *The two sexes: Growing up apart, coming together.* Cambridge, MA: Belknap/Harvard University Press.

Maccoby, E. E. & Martin, J. A. (1983). Socialization in the context of the family. In E. M. Heatherington (Ed.), *Handbook of Child Psychology: Vol. 4. Socialization, personality, and social development* (pp. 1–101). New York, NY: Wiley.

Mace, F. C., Belfiore, P. J., & Hutchinson, J. M. (2001). Operant theory and research on self-regulation. In B. Zimmerman & D. Schunk (Eds.), *Self- regulated learning and academic achievement: Theoretical perspectives* (2nd ed.). Mahwah, NJ: Erlbaum.

Macionis, J. J. (2003). *Sociology* (9th ed.). Upper Saddle River, NJ: Prentice-Hall.

MacKay, A. W. (1986). The Charter's equality provisions and education: A structural analysis. *Canadian Journal of Education, 11*, 293–312.

MacKinnon McQuarrie, M. A., Siegel, L. S., Perry, N. E., & Weinberg, J. (2012). Reactivity to stress and the cognitive components of math disability in grade 1 children. *Journal of Learning Disabilities, 47*(4): 349–365.

Macrae, C. N., Milne, A. B., & Bodenhausen, C. V. (1994). Stereotypes as energy-saving devices: A peek inside the cognitive toolbox. *Journal of Personality and Social Psychology, 66*, 37–47.

Maczewski, M. (2002). Exploring identities through the Internet: Youth Experiences Online. *Child and Youth Care Forum, 31*(2), pp. 111–129.

Maddux, W. W., & Galinsky, A. D. (2009). Cultural borders and mental barriers: The relationship between living abroad and creativity. *Journal of Personality and Social Psychology, 96*, 1047–1061.

Maddux, W. W., Leung, K. Y., Chiu, C. Y., & Galinsky, A. D. (2009). Toward a more complete understanding of the link between multicultural experience and creativity. *American Psychologist, 64*(2), 156–158.

Madsen, C. H., Becker, W. C., Thomas, D. R., Koser, L., & Plager, E. (1968). An analysis of the reinforcing function of "sit down" commands. In R. K. Parker (Ed.), *Readings in educational psychology*. Boston, MA: Allyn & Bacon.

Madsen, K. (2003). The effect of accuracy of instruction, teacher delivery, and student attentiveness on musicians' evaluation of teacher effectiveness. *Journal of Research in Music Education, 51*, 38–51.

Mager, R. (1975). *Preparing instructional objectives* (2nd ed.). Palo Alto, CA: Fearon.

Magnusson, S. J., & Palincsar, A. S. (1995). The learning environment as a site of science reform. *Theory Into Practice, 34*, 43–50.

Maguire, E. A., Gadian, D.G., Johnsrude, I. S., Good, C. D., Ashburner, J., Frackowiak, R. S., & Frith, C. D. (2000). Navigation-related structural change in the hippocampi of taxi drivers. *Proceedings of the National Academy of Science, USA, 97*(8), 4398–4403.

Maier, N. R. F. (1933). An aspect of human reasoning. *British Journal of Psychology, 24*, 144–155.

Major, B., & Schmader, T. (1998). Coping with stigma through psychological disengagement. In J. Swim & C. Stangor (Eds.), *Stigma: The target's perspective* (pp. 219–241). New York, NY: Academic Press.

Maker, C. J. (1987). Gifted and talented. In V. Richardson-Koehler (Ed.), *Educators' handbook: A research perspective* (pp. 420–455). New York, NY: Longman.

Manning, B. H., & Payne, B. D. (1996). Self-talk for teachers and students: *Metacognitive strategies for personal and classroom use*. Boston, MA: Allyn & Bacon.

Manning, M. L., & Baruth, L. G. (1996). *Multicultural education of children and adolescents*, 2nd edition. Needham Heights, MA: Allyn & Bacon.

Mantzicopolos, P., & Morrison, D. (1992). Kindergarten retention: Academic and behavioral outcomes through the end of second grade. *American Educational Research Journal, 29*, 182–198.

Marchland, G., & Skinner, E. A. (2007). Motivational dynamics of children's academic help-seeking and concealment. *Journal of Educational Psychology, 99*, 65–82.

Marcia, J. E. (1987). The identity status approach to the study of ego identity development. In T. Honess & K. Yardley (Eds.), *Self and identity: Perspectives across the life span* (pp. 161–171). London, England: Routledge & Kegan Paul.

Marcia, J. E. (1991). Identity and self development. In R. Lerner, A. Peterson, & J. Brooks-Gunn (Eds.), *Encyclopedia of adolescence* (Vol. 1). New York, NY: Garland.

Marcia, J. E. (1994). The empirical study of ego identity. In H. Bosma, T. Graafsma, H. Grotebanc, & D. DeLivita (Eds.), *The identity and development*. Newbury Park, CA: Sage.

Marcia, J. E. (1999). Representational thought in ego identity, psychotherapy, and psychosocial development. In I. E. Sigel (Ed.), Development of mental representation: *Theories and applications*. Mahwah, NJ: Erlbaum.

Marcus, N., Cooper, M., & Sweller, J. (1996). Understanding instructions. *Journal of Educational Psychology, 88*, 49–63.

Marinova-Todd, S., Marshall, D., & Snow, C. (2000). Three misconceptions about age and L2 learning. *TESOL Quarterly, 34*(1), 9–34.

Markman, E. M. (1977). Realizing that you don't understand: A preliminary investigation. *Child Development, 48,* 986–992.

Markman, E. M. (1979). Realizing that you don't understand: Elementary school children's awareness of inconsistencies. *Child Development, 50,* 643–655.

Markman, E. M. (1992). Constraints on word learning: Speculations about their nature, origins, and domain specificity. In M. Gunnar & M. Maratsos (Eds.), *Minnesota symposium on child psychology* (Vol. 25, pp. 59–101). Hillsdale, NJ: Erlbaum.

Marks, A. K, Patton, F., & Coll, C. G. (2011). Being bicultural: A mixed - methods study of adolescents' implicitly and explicitly measured multiethnic identities. *Developmental Psychology, 47,* 270–288.

Markstrom-Adams, C. (1992). A consideration of intervening factors in adolescent identity formation. In G. R. Adams, R. Montemayor, & T. Gullotta (Eds.), *Advances in adolescent development: Vol. 4. Adolescent identity f ormation* (pp. 173–192). Newbury Park, CA: Sage.

Marsh, H. W. (1990). Influences of internal and external frames of reference on the formation of math and English self-concepts. *Journal of Educational Psychology, 82,* 107–116.

Marsh, H. W., & Ayotte, V. (2003). Do multiple dimensions of self-concept become more differentiated with age? The differential distinctiveness hypothesis. *Journal of Educational Psychology, 95,* 687–706.

Marsh, H. W., & Craven, R. (2002). The pivotal role of frames of reference in academic self-concept formation: The Big Fish Little Pond Effect. In F. Pajares & T. Urdan (Eds.), *Adolescence and Education* (Vol. II, pp. 83–123). Greenwich, CT: Information Age.

Marsh, H. W., & Hau, K-T. (2003). Big-Fish-Little-Pond effect on academic self-concept. *American Psychologist, 58,* 364–376.

Marsh, H. W., Craven, R. G., & Martin, A. (2006). What is the nature of self-esteem: Unidimensional and multidimensional perspectives. In M. Kernis (Ed.), *Self-esteem: Issues and Answers* (pp. 16–24). Psychology Press.

Marsh, H. W., Seaton M., Trautwein, U., Lüdtke, O., Hau, K. T., O'Mara, A. J., & Craven, R. G. (2008). The Big-fish -little-pond-effect stands up to critical scrutiny: Implications for theory, methodology, and future research. *Educational Psychology Review, 20,* 319–350.

Marsh, H. W., Trautwein, U., Lüdtke, O., Köller, O., & Baumert, J. (2006). Integration of multidimensional self-concept and core personality constructs: Construct validation and relations to well-being and achievement. *Journal of Personality, 74,* 403–456.

Marsh, H. W., & Yeung, A. S. (1997). Coursework selection: Relation to academic self-concept and achievement. *American Educational Research Journal, 34,* 691–720.

Marshall, H. H. (Ed.). (1992). *Redefining student learning: Roots of educational change.* Norwood, NJ: Ablex.

Marshall, H. H. (1996). Implications of differentiating and understanding constructivist approaches. *Journal of Educational Psychology, 31,* 235–240.

Martin, J. (2006). Social cultural perspectives in educational psychology. In P. A. Alexander & P. H. Winne (Eds.), *Handbook of educational psychology* (2nd ed., pp. 595–614). Mahwah, NJ: Erlbaum.

Martin, J., & Sugarman, J. (1993). *Models of classroom management: Principles, applications and critical perspectives* (2nd ed.). Calgary, AB: Detselig.

Martinez-Pons, M. (2002). A social cognitive view of parental influence on student academic self-regulation. *Theory Into Practice, 61,* 126–131.

Marvin, K. L., Rapp, J. T., Stenske, M. T., Rojas, N. R., Swanson, G. J., & Bartlett, S. M. (2010). Response repetition as an error-correction procedure for sight-word reading: A replication and extension. *Behavioral Intentions, 25*(2): 109–127.

Marzano, R. J., & Marzano, J. S. (2003, September). The key to classroom management. *Educational Leadership, 61*(1), 6–13.

Mascolo, M. F., & Fischer, K. W. (2005). Constructivist theories. In B. Hopkins (Ed.), *The Cambridge encyclopedia of child development.* New York, NY: Cambridge University Press.

Maslow, A. H. (1968). *Toward a psychology of being* (2nd ed.). New York, NY: Van Nostrand.

Maslow, A. H. (1970). *Motivation and personality* (2nd ed.). New York, NY: Harper and Row.

Mason, D. A., & Good, T. L. (1993). Effects of two-group and whole-class teaching on regrouped elementary students' mathematics achievement. *American Educational Research Journal, 30,* 328–360.

Mason, L. (2007). Introduction: Bridging the cognitive and sociocultural approaches in research on conceptual change: Is it possible? *Educational Psychologist, 42,* 1–7.

Matlin, M. W., & Foley, H. J. (1997). *Sensation and perception* (4th ed.). Boston, MA: Allyn & Bacon.

Matson, J. L., Matson, M. L., & Rivet, T. T. (2007). Social-skills treatments for children with autism spectrum disorders: An overview. *Behavior Modification, 31*(5): 682–707.

Matsumura, L. C., & Crosson, A. (2008). Classroom climate, rigorous instruction and curriculum, and students' interactions in urban middle schools. *The Elementary School Journal, 108,* 293–312.

Matthews, D. (1996). Giftedness at adolescence: Diverse educational options required. *Exceptionality Education Canada, 6,* 25–49.

Matthews, J. S., Kizzie, K. T., Rowley, S. J., & Cortina, K. (2010). African American boys: Understanding the literacy gap predicting academic trajectories and evaluating learning-related skills. *Journal of Educational Psychology, 102*(3): 757–771.

Matthews, J. S., Ponitz, C. C., & Morrison, F. J. (2009). Early gender differences in self-regulation and academic achievement. *Journal of Educational Psychology, 101*(3): 689–704.

Mautone, P. D., & Mayer, R. E. (2001). Signaling as a cognitive guide in multimedia learning. *Journal of Educational Psychology, 93,* 377–389.

Mayer, M. J. & Furlong, M. J. (2010). How safe are our schools? *Educational Researcher, 39,* 16–26.

Mayer, R. E. (1983a). Can you repeat that? Qualitative and quantitative effects of repetition and advance organizers on learning from science prose. *Journal of Educational Psychology, 75,* 40–49.

Mayer, R. E. (1983b). *Thinking, problem solving, cognition.* San Francisco, CA: Freeman.

Mayer, R. E. (1984). Twenty-five years of research on advance organizers. *Instructional Science, 8,* 133–169.

Mayer, R. E. (1992). *Thinking, problem solving, cognition* (2nd ed.). New York, NY: Freeman.

Mayer, R. E. (1996). Learners as information processors: Legacies and limitations of educational psychology's second metaphor. *Journal of Educational Psychology, 31,* 151–161.

Mayer, R. E. (1999a). Multimedia aids to problem-solving transfer. *International Journal of Educational Research, 31,* 611–623.

Mayer, R. E. (1999b). *The promise of educational psychology: Learning in the content areas.* Upper Saddle River, NJ: Prentice-Hall.

Mayer, R. E. (2001). *Multimedia learning.* New York, NY: Cambridge University Press.

Mayer, R. E. (2004). Should there be a three-strikes rule against discovery learning? A case for guided methods of instruction. *American Psychologist, 59,* 14–19.

Mayer, R. E. (2005). Cognitive theory of multimedia learning. In R. E. Mayer (Ed.), *The Cambridge handbook of multimedia learning* (pp. 31–48). New York, NY: Cambridge University Press.

Mayer, R. E. (2008). *Learning and instruction* (2nd ed.). Columbus, OH: Merrill/Prentice-Hall.

Mayer, R. E. (2011). *Applying the science of learning.* Boston, MA: Pearson.

Mayer, R. E., & Gallini, J. K. (1990). When is an illustration worth ten thousand words? *Journal of Educational Psychology, 82,* 715–726.

Mayer, R. E., & Massa, L. J. (2003). Three facets of visual and verbal learners: Cognitive ability, cognitive style and learning preference. *Journal of Educational Psychology, 95*(4), 833–846.

Mayer, R. E., & Sims, V. K. (1994). For whom is a picture worth a thousand words? Extensions of a dual-coding theory of multimedia learning. *Journal of Educational Psychology, 86,* 389–401.

Mayer, R. E., & Wittrock, M. C. (1996). Problem-solving transfer. In D. Berliner & R. Calfee (Eds.), *Handbook of educational psychology* (pp. 47–62). New York, NY: Macmillan.

Mayer, R. E., & Wittrock, M. C. (2006). Problem solving. In P. A. Alexander & P. H. Winne (Eds.), *Handbook of educational psychology* (2nd ed., pp. 287–303). Mahwah, NJ: Erlbaum.

Mayo Clinic. (2009). *Type 2 diabetes: Complications.* Available online at: http://www.mayoclinic.com/health/type-2-diabetes/DS00585/DSECTION_complications

Mayo Clinic Staff. (2013). Teen sleep: Why is your teen so tired? Retrieved June 8, 2014 from www.mayoclinic.org/healthy-living/tween-and-teen-health/in-depth/teens-health/art-20046157?pg=1

McAnarney, E. R. (2008). Adolescent brain development: Forging new links. *Journal of Adolescent Health, 42,* 321–323.

McCafferty, S. G. (2004). Introduction. *International Journal of Applied Linguistics, 14*(1), 1–6.

McCaslin, M., & Good, T. (1996). The informal curriculum. In D. Berliner & R. Calfee (Eds.), *Handbook of educational psychology* (pp. 622–670). New York, NY: Macmillan.

McCaslin, M., & Good, T. L. (1998). Moving beyond management as sheer compliance: Helping students to develop goal coordination strategies. *Educational Horizons, 76,* 169–176.

McCaslin, M., & Hickey, D. T. (2001). Self-regulated learning and academic achievement: A Vygotskian view. In B. Zimmerman & D. Schunk (Eds.), *Self-regulated learning and academic achievement: Theoretical perspectives* (2nd ed., pp. 227–252). Mahwah, NJ: Erlbaum.

McClelland, D. (1985). *Human motivation.* Glenview, IL: Scott, Foresman.

McCoach, D. B., Kehle, T. J., Bray, M. L., & Siegle, D. (2001). Best practices in the identification of gifted students with learning disabilities. *Psychology in the Schools, 38,* 403–411.

McCoy, A. R., & Reynolds, A. J. (1999). Grade retention and school performance: An extended investigation. *Journal of School Psychology, 37,* 273–298.

McDonald, J. P. (1993). Three pictures of an exhibition: Warm, cool, and hard. *Phi Delta Kappan, 6,* 480–485.

McGoey, K. E., & DuPaul, G. J. (2000). Token reinforcement and response cost procedures: Reducing disruptive behavior of children with attention-deficit/hyperactivity disorder. *School Psychology Quarterly, 15,* 330–343.

McKenzie, T. L., & Rushall, B. S. (1974). Effects of self-recording on attendance and performance in a competitive swimming training environment. *Journal of Applied Behavior Analysis, 7,* 199–206.

McKinley, J. C. (2011, January 24). Shot in the head, but getting back on his feet and on with his life. *New York Times,* A-16. Available online at: http://www.nytimes.com/2011/01/24/us/24rehab.html?scp=7&sq=Houston%20rehabilition&st=cse.

McKown, C. (2005). Applying ecological theory to advance the science and practice of school-based prejudice reduction interventions. *Educational Psychologist, 40,* 177–189.

McLoyd, V. C. (1998). Economic disadvantage and child development. *American Psychologist, 53,* 185–204.

McMillan, J. H. (2004). *Classroom assessment: Principles and practice for effective instruction* (3rd ed.). Boston, MA: Allyn & Bacon.

McNeely, C. A., Nonnemaker, J. M., & Blum, R. W. (2002). Promoting school connectedness: Evidence from the National Longitudinal Study of Adolescent Health. *Journal of School Health, 72*(4), 138–146.

McTigue, E. M. (2009). Does multimedia learning theory extend to middle-school students? *Contemporary Educational Psychology, 34,* 143–153.

Mears, T. (1998). Saying 'Si' to Spanish. *Boston Globe,* April 12. Mediascope. (1996). *National television violence study: Executive summary 1994–1995.* Studio City, CA: Author.

Media Awareness Network (2005). Young Canadians in a wired world, phase 2: Student survey report. Retrieved from: www.media-awareness.ca/english/research/YCWW/phaseII/upload/YCWWII_Student_Survey.pdf

Meece, J. L. (2002). *Child and adolescent development for educators* (2nd ed.). New York, NY: McGraw-Hill.

Meece, J. L., & Daniels, D. H. (2008). *Child and adolescent development for educators* (3rd ed.). New York, NY: McGraw-Hill.

Meichenbaum, D. (1977). *Cognitive behavior modification: An integrative approach.* New York, NY: Plenum.

Meichenbaum, D., Burland, S., Gruson, L., & Cameron, R. (1985). Metacognitive assessment. In S. Yussen (Ed.), *The growth of reflection in children* (pp. 1–30). Orlando, FL: Academic Press.

Meijer, A. M., & van den Wittenboer, G. L. H. (2004). The joint contribution of sleep, intelligence and motivation to school performance. *Personality and Individual Differences, 37,* 95–106.

Melnick, S. A., & Meister, D. G. (2008). A comparison of beginning and experienced teacher concerns. *Education Research Quarterly, 31*(3), 39–56.

Meltzer, L. (2007). *Executive function in education: From theory to practice.* New York: Guilford Press.

Mendle, J., Turkheimer, E., & Emery, R. E. (2007). Detrimental psychological outcomes associated with early pubertal timing in adolescent girls. *Developmental Review, 27.*

Mendoza, E. M., & Johnson, K. O. (2000). Land of Plenty: Diversity as America's competitive edge in science, engineering, and technology. Washington DC: Congressional Commission on the Advancement of Women and Minorities in Science, Engineering and Technology Development.

Mercer, N. (2007). Commentary on the reconciliation of cognitive and sociocultural accounts of conceptual change. *Educational Psychologist, 42,* 75–78.

Merrell, K. W., Isava, D. M., Gueldner, B. A., & Ross, S. W. (2008). How effective are school bullying intervention programs? A meta-analysis of intervention research. *School Psychology Quarterly, 23,* 26–42.

Mertler, C. A., & Charles, C. M. (2005). *Introduction to Educational Research.* 5th edtion. Allyn & Bacon.

Merton, R. K. (1948). The self-fulfilling prophecy. *Antioch Review, 8,* 193–210.

Messick, S. (1975). The standard problem: Meaning and values in measurement and evaluation. *American Psychologist, 35,* 1012–1027.

Metcalfe, J., & Shimamura, A. P. (Eds.). (1994). *Metacognition: Knowledge about knowing.* Cambridge, MA: MIT Press.

Metzler, C. W., Biglan, A., Rusby, J. C., & Sprague, J. R. (2001). Evaluation of a comprehensive behavior management program to improve school-wide positive behavior support. *Education and Treatment of Children, 24*(4), 448–470.

Midgley, C. (2001). A goal theory perspective on the current status of middle level schools. In T. Urdan & F. Pajares (Eds.), *Adolescence and education* (Vol. I, pp. 33–59). Greenwich, CT: Information Age Publishing.

Midgley, C., Kaplan, A., & Middleton, M. (2001). Performance-approach goals: Good for what, for whom, under what circumstances, and at what cost? *Journal of Educational Psychology, 93,* 77–86.

Midgley, C., Kaplan, A., Middleton, M., Maehr, M. L., Urdan, T., Anderman, L. H., Anderman, E., & Roser, R. (1998). The development and validation of scales assessing students' achievement goal orientations. *Contemporary Educational Psychology, 23,* 113–131.

Mifflin, M. (1999, December 13). *Singing the pink blues. Mothers who think.* Retrieved from www.salon.com/mwt/feature/1999/12/13/toys

Miller, D. M., Linn, R. L., & Gronlund, N. E. (2009). *Measurement and assessment in teaching* (10th ed.). Boston, MA: Allyn & Bacon.

Miller, G. A. (1956). The magical number seven, plus or minus two: Some limits on our capacity for processing information. *Psychological Review, 63,* 81–97.

Miller, G. A., Galanter, E., & Pribram, K. H. (1960). *Plans and the structure of behavior.* New York, NY: Holt, Rinehart & Winston.

Miller, N., & Harrington, H. J. (1993). Social categorization and intergroup acceptance: Principles for the development an design of cooperative learning teams. In R. Hertz-Lasarowitz & N. Miller (Eds.), *Interaction in cooperative groups: The theoretical anatomy of group learning* (pp. 203–227). New York, NY: Cambridge University Press.

Miller, P. H. (2002). *Theories of developmental psychology* (4th ed.). New York, NY: Worth.

Miller, P. H. (2011). *Theories of developmental psychology* (5th ed.). New York, NY: Worth.

Miller, R. B. (1962). Analysis and specification of behavior for training. In R. Glaser (Ed.), *Training research and education: Science edition.* New York, NY: Wiley.

Miller, S. A. (2005). Tips for getting children's attention. *Early Childhood Today, 19.*

Miller, S. A. (2009). Children's understanding of second-order mental statuses. *Psychological Bulletin, 135,* 749–773.

Mills, J. R., & Jackson, N. E. (1990). Predictive significance of early giftedness: The case of precocious reading. *Journal of Educational Psychology, 82,* 410–419.

Milner, H. R. (2003). Teacher reflection and race in cultural contexts: History, meaning, and methods in teaching. *Theory into Practice 42*(3), 173–180.

Milner, H. R. (2006). Classroom management in urban classrooms. In C. M. Evertson & C. S. Weinstein, (Eds.), *Handbook of classroom management: Research, practice, and contemporary issues* (pp. 491–522). Mahwah, NJ: Erlbaum.

Milner, H. R. IV. (2010). *Start where you are but don't stay there: Understanding diversity, opportunity gaps, and teaching in today's schools.* Cambridge, MA: Harvard Education Press.

Miranda, T. Z. (2008). Bilingual education for all students: Still standing after all these years. In L. S. Verplaetse & N. Migliacci (Eds.), *Inclusive pedagogy for English language learners: A handbook of research-informed practices* (pp. 257–275). New York, NY: Erlbaum.

Mitchell, M. (1993). Situational interest: Its multifaceted structure in the secondary school mathematics classroom. *Journal of Educational Psychology, 85,* 424–436.

Moll, L. C., Amanti, C., Neff, D., & Gonzales, N. (1992). Funds of knowledge for teaching: Using a qualitative approach to connect homes and classrooms. *Theory into Practice, 31,* 132–141.

Moller, A. C., Deci, E. L., & Ryan, R. M. (2006). Choice and ego-depletion: The moderating role of autonomy. *Personality and Social Psychology Bulletin, 32*(8), 1024–1036.

Möller, J., & Pohlmann, B. (2010). Achievement differences and self-concept differences: Stronger associations for above or below average students? *British Journal of Educational Psychology, 80*(3): 435–50.

Monroe, C. R., & Obidah, J. E. (2002, April). *The impact of cultural synchronization on a teacher's perceptions of disruption: A case study of an African American middle school classroom.* Paper presented at the American Educational Research Association, New Orleans, LA.

Monteleone, J. A. (1998). *Child abuse.* St. Louis, MO: G. W. Medical Publisher.

Montrul, S. (2010). Dominant language transfer in adult second language learners and heritage speakers. *Second Language Research, 26,* 293–327.

Moore, M. K., & Meltzoff, A. N. (2004). Object permanence after a 24-hr delay and leaving the locale of disappearance: the role of memory, space, and identity. *Developmental Psychology, 40,* 606–620.

Moreno, R., Ozogul, G., & Reisslein, M. (2011). Teaching with concrete and abstract visual representations: Effects on students' problem solving, problem representations, and learning perceptions. *Journal of Educational Psychology, 103*(1): 32–47.

Morin, V. A., & Miller, S. P. (1998). Teaching multiplication to middle school students with mental retardation. *Education & Treatment of Children, 21*, 22–36.

Morine-Dershimer, G. (2006). Instructional planning. In J. Cooper (Ed.), *Classroom teaching skills* (7th ed., pp. 20–54). Boston, MA: Houghton-Mifflin.

Morris, P. F. (1990). Metacognition. In M. W. Eysenck, (Ed.), *The Blackwell dictionary of cognitive psychology* (pp. 225–229). Oxford, England: Basil Blackwell.

Morrow, L. M. (1983). Home and school correlates of early interest in literature. *Journal of Educational Research, 76*, 221–230.

Morrow, L. M., & Weinstein, C. (1986). Encouraging voluntary reading: The impact of a literature program on children's use of library centers. *Reading Research Quarterly, 21*, 330–346.

Moshman, D. (1982). Exogenous, endogenous, and dialectical constructivism. *Developmental Review, 2*, 371–384.

Moshman, D. (1997). Pluralist rational constructivism. *Issues in Education: Contributions from Educational Psychology, 3*, 229–234.

Moskowitz, G., & Hayman, M. L. (1976). Successful strategies of inner-city teachers: A year-long study. *Journal of Educational Research, 69*, 283–289.

Moss, P. A. (1992). Shifting conceptions of validity in educational measurement: Implications for performance assessment. *Review of Educational Research, 62*, 229–258.

Mueller, C. M., & Dweck, C. S. (1998). Praise for intelligence can undermine children's motivation and performance. *Journal of Personality and Social Psychology, 75*, 33–52.

Muis, K. R., & Franco, G. (2009). Epistemic beliefs: Setting the standards in self-regulated learning. *Contemporary Educational Psychology, 34*, 306–318.

Mullis, I. V. S., Martin, M. O., Gonzalez, E., & Kennedy, A. M. (2003). *PIRLS 2001 International report: IEA's study of reading literacy achievement in primary schools.* Chestnut Hill, MA: Boston College. Retrieved from http://timss.bc.edu/pirls2001i/PIRLS2001_Pubs_IR.html

Mumford, M. D., Costanza, D. P., Baughman, W. A., Threlfall, V., & Fleishman, E. A. (1994). Influence of abilities on performance during practice: Effects of massed and distributed practice. *Journal of Educational Psychology, 86*, 134–144.

Murayama, K., & Elliot, A.J. (2009). The joint influence of personal achievement goals and classroom goal structures on achievement-related outcomes. *Journal of Educational Psychology, 101*, 432–447.

Murdock, S. G., O'Neill, R. E., & Cunningham, E. (2005). A comparison of results and acceptability of functional behavioral assessment procedures with a group of middle school students with emotional/behavioral disorders (E/BD). *Journal of Behavioral Education, 14*, 5–18.

Murdock, T. A., & Anderman, E. M. (2006). Motivational perspectives on student cheating: Toward an integrated model of academic dishonesty. *Educational Psychologist, 42*, 129–145.

Murdock, T. B., Hale, N. M., & Weber, M. J. (2001). Predictors of cheating among early adolescents: Academic and social motivations. *Contemporary Educational Psychology, 26*, 96–115.

Murdock, T. B., & Miller, A. (2003). Teachers as sources of middle school students' motivational identity: Variable-centered and person-centered analytic approaches. *Elementary School Journal, 103*, 383–399.

Murphy, P. K., & Alexander, P. A. (2000). A motivated exploration of motivation terminology. *Contemporary Educational Psychology, 25*, 3–53.

Murphy, P. K., & Benton, S. L. (2010). The new frontier of educational neuropsychology: Unknown opportunities and unfulfilled hopes. *Contemporary Educational Psychology, 35*, 153–155.

Murphy, P. K., Wilkinson, I. A. G., Soter, A. O., Hennessey, M. N., & Alexander, J. F. (2009). Examining the effects of classroom discussion on students' comprehension of text: A meta-analysis. *Journal of Educational Psychology, 101*, 740–764.

Mussen, P., Conger, J. J., & Kagan, J. (1984). *Child development and personality* (6th ed.). New York, NY: Harper & Row.

Muter, V., Hulme, C., Snowling, M. J., & Stevenson, J. (2004). Phonemes, rimes, vocabulary, and grammatical skills as foundation of early reading development: Evidence from a longitudinal study. *Developmental Psychology, 40*, 665–681.

Myers, D. G. (2005). *Exploring psychology* (6th ed. in modules). New York, NY: Worth.

Myers, D. G. (2010). *Psychology* (9th ed.). New York, NY: Worth.

Myers, I. B., & McCaulley, M. H. (1988). *Manual: A guide to the development and use of the Myers-Briggs Type Indicator.* Palo Alto, CA: Consulting Psychologists.

Nakamura, J., & Csikszentmihalyi, M. (2001). Catalytic creativity: The case of Linus Pauling. *American Psychologist, 56*, 337–341.

Nathan, M. J., & Knuth, E. J. (2003). A study of whole class mathematical discourse and teacher change. *Cognition and Instruction, 21*, 175–207.

National Association for the Education of Young Children. (2006). *The value of recess and outdoor play.* Retrieved from www.naeyc.org/ece/1998/08.asp

National Cancer Institute (NCI). (2009). Cancer in children and adolescents. Retrieved February 4, 2015 from http://www.cancer.gov/cancertopics/factsheet/Sites-Types/childhood.

National Center for Educational Statistics. (2003). *Indicators of school crime and safety2002.* Available online at: http://nces.ed.gov/pubs2003/schoolcrime/6.asp?nav=1

National Center for Education Statistics. (2009). *The nation's report card: Mathematics 2009 (NCES 2010–451).* Institute of Education Sciences, U.S. Department of Education, Washington, DC.

National Center for Education Statistics. (2010). *Condition of education 2010, indicator 23 (NCES 2010–028).* Institute of Education Sciences, U.S. Department of Education, Washington, DC.

National Commission on Teaching and America's Future. (2003). *No dream denied: A pledge to America's children.* Washington, DC: Author.

National Science Foundation. (1996, December 31). *Women and underrepresented minority scientists and engineers have lower levels of employment in business and industry, 1996* (14). Available from www.nsf.gov/sbe/srs/data-brf/sdb96331.htm

National Science Foundation, Division of Science Resources Statistics. (2011). *Women, minorities, and persons with disabilities in science and engineering: 2011.* Special Report NSF 11-309. Arlington, VA. Available online at: http://www.nsf.gov/statistics/wmpd/

National Service Learning Clearinghouse. (n.d.). *Service learning is. . . .* Retrieved from www.servicelearning.org/welcome_to_service-learning/service-learning_is/index.php

Navarro, R. L., Flores, L. Y., & Worthington, R. L. (2007). Mexican American middle school students' goal intentions in mathematics and science: A test of social cognitive career theory. *Journal of Counseling Psychology, 54*, 320–335.

Naveh-Benjamin, M. (1991). A comparison of training programs intended for different types of test-anxious students: Further support for an information-processing model. *Journal of Educational Psychology, 83*, 134–139.

Naveh-Benjamin, M., McKeachie, W. J., & Lin, Y. (1987). Two types of test-anxious students: Support for an information processing model. *Journal of Educational Psychology, 79*, 131–136.

Needles, M., & Knapp, M. (1994). Teaching writing to children who are undeserved. *Journal of Educational Psychology, 86*, 339–349.

Neisser, U. (1976). *Cognition and reality.* San Francisco, CA: Freeman.

Neisser, U., Boodoo, G., Bouchard, A., Boykin, W., Brody, N., Ceci, S. J., . . . Urbina, S. (1996). Intelligence: Knowns and unknowns. *American Psychologist, 51*, 77–101.

Nelson, C.A. (2001). The development and neural bases of face recognition. *Infant and Child Development, 10*, 3–18.

Nelson, C. A., Zeanah, C. H., Fox, N. A., Marshall, P. J., Smyke, A. T., & Guthrie, D. (2007). Cognitive recovery in socially deprived young children: The Bucharest Early Intervention Project. *Science, 318,* 1937–1940.

Nelson, J. R., & Roberts, M. L. (2000). Ongoing reciprocal teacher-student interactions involving disruptive behaviors in general education classrooms. *Journal of Emotional and Behavioral Disorders, 4*, 147–161.

Nelson, K. (2004). Evolution and the development of human memory systems. In B. J. Ellis & D. Bjorklund (Eds.), *Origins of the social mind: Evolutionary psychology and child development* (pp. 354–382). New York, NY: Guilford.

Nelson, K., & Fivush, R. (2004). The emergence of autobiographical memory: A social cultural developmental theory. *Psychological Review, 111*, 486–511.

Nelson, T. O. (1996). Consciousness and metacognition. *American Psychologist, 51*, 102–116.

Nesbit, J. C., & Adesope, O. O. (2006). Learning with concept and knowledge maps: A meta-analysis. *Review of Educational Research, 76*, 413–448.

Nesbit, J. C., & Hadwin, A. F. (2006). Methodological issues in educational psychology. In P. A Alexander & P. H. Winne (Eds.), *Handbook of educational psychology* (2nd ed., pp. 825–847). Mahwah, NJ: Erlbaum.

Neuman, S. B., & Roskos, K. A. (1997). Literacy knowledge in practice: Contexts of participation for young writers and readers. *Reading Research Quarterly, 32*, 10–32.

Neumeister, K. L. S., & Cramond, B. (2004). E. Paul Torrance (1915–2003). American *Psychologist, 59*, 179.

Neville, H. (2007, March). *Experience shapes human brain development and function.* Paper presented at the biennial meeting of the Society for Research in Child Development, Boston, MA.

Newcombe, N., & Baenninger, M. (1990). The role of expectations in spatial test performance: A meta-analysis. *Sex Roles, 16*, 25–37.

Nguyen, H. H., & Ryan, A. M. (2008). Does stereotype threat affect test performance of minorities and women? A meta-analysis of experimental evidence. *Journal of Applied Psychology, 93*(6): 1314–1334.

NICHD Early Child Care Research Network. (2005a). *Child care and child development.* New York, NY: Guilford Press.

NICHD Early Child Care Research Network. (2005b). Pathways to reading: The role of oral language in the transition to reading. *Developmental Psychology, 41*(2), 428–442.

Nicholls, J., Cobb, P., Wood, T., Yackel, E., & Patashnick, M. (1990). Assessing student's theories of success in mathematics: Individual and classroom differences. *Journal for Research in Mathematics Education, 21*, 109–122.

Nicholls, J. G., & Miller, A. (1984). Conceptions of ability and achievement motivation. In R. Ames & C. Ames (Eds.), *Research on motivation in education: Vol. 1.Student Motivation* (pp. 39–73). New York, NY: Academic Press.

Nie, Y., & Lau, S. (2009). Complementary roles of care and behavioral control in classroom management: The self-determination theory perspective. *Contemporary Educational Psychology, 34*, 185–194.

Nielsen. (2010). *U.S. teen mobile report: Calling yesterday, texting today, using apps tomorrow.* New York, NY: The Nielsen Company. Available online at: http://blog.nielsen.com/nielsenwire/online_mobile/u-s-teen-mobile-report-calling-yesterday-texting-today-using-apps-tomorrow/

Nieto, S. (2004). *Affirming diversity: The sociopolitical context of multicultural education* (4th ed.). Boston, MA: Allyn & Bacon.

Nieto, S., & Bode, P. (2008). *Affirming diversity: The sociopolitical context of multicultural education* (5th ed.). Boston, MA: Allyn & Bacon.

Nissani, M., & Hoefler-Nissani, D. M. (1992). Experimental studies of belief dependence of observations and of resistance to conceptual change. *Cognition and Instruction, 9*, 97–111.

Nitko, A. J., & Brookhart, S. M. (2011). *Educational Assessment of Students.* Pearson/Allyn & Bacon.

Noddings, N. (1990). Constructivism in mathematics education. In R. Davis, C. Maher, & N. Noddings (Eds.), *Constructivist views on the teaching and learning of mathematics* (pp. 7–18). Monograph 4 of the National Council of Teachers of Mathematics, Reston, VA.

Noddings, N. (1992). *The challenge to care in schools: An alternative approach to education.* New York, NY: Teachers College Press.

Noddings, N. (1995). Teaching themes of care. *Phi Delta Kappan, 76*, 675–679.

Noguera, P. (2005). The racial achievement gap: How can we assume an equity of outcomes. In L. Johnson, M. E. Finn, & R. Lewis (Eds.), *Urban education with an attitude.* Albany, NY: SUNY Press.

Nokes, J. D., Dole, J. A., & Hacker, D. J. (2007). Teaching high school students to use heuristics while reading historical texts. *Journal of Educational Psychology, 99*, 492–504.

Noland, H., Price, J. H., Dake, J., & Telljohann, S. K. (2009). Adolescents' sleep behaviours and perceptions of sleep. *Journal of School Health, 79*, 224–230.

Norbert, F. (2005). Research findings on early first language attrition: Implications for the discussion of critical periods in language acquisition. *Language Learning, 55*(3), 491–531.

Nucci, L. P. (2001). Education in the moral domain. New York, NY: Cambridge Press.

Nungester, R. J., & Duchastel, P. C. (1982). Testing versus review: Effects on retention. *Journal of Educational Psychology, 74*, 18–22.

Nurmi, J. (2004). Socialization and self-development: Channeling, selection, adjustment, and reflection. In R. Lerner & L. Steinberg (Eds.), *Handbook of adolescent psychology.* New York, NY: Wiley.

Nylund, D. (2000). *Treating Huckleberry Finn: A new narrative approach to working with kids diagnosed ADD/ADHD.* San Francisco, CA: Jossey-Bass.

O'Boyle, M. W., & Gill, H. S. (1998). On the relevance of research findings in cognitive neuroscience to educational practice. *Educational Psychology Review, 10*, 397–410.

O'Donnell, A. M. (Ed.). (2002, Winter). Promoting thinking through peer learning [Special issue]. *Theory Into Practice, 61*(1).

O'Donnell, A. M. (2006). The role of peers and group learning. In P. A. Alexander & P. H. Winne (Eds.), *Handbook of educational psychology* (2nd ed., pp. 781–802). Mahwah, NJ: Erlbaum.

O'Donnell, A. M., & O'Kelly, J. (1994). Learning from peers: Beyond the rhetoric of positive results. *Educational Psychology Review, 6*, 321–350.

O'Leary, K. D., & O'Leary, S. (Eds.). (1977). *Classroom management: The successful use of behavior modification* (2nd ed.). Elmsford, NY: Pergamon.

O'Leary, S. (1995). Parental discipline mistakes. *Current Directions in Psychological Science, 4*, 11–13.

O'Mara, A. J., Marsh, H. W., Craven, R. G., & Debus, R. L. (2006). Do self-concept interventions make a difference? A synergistic blend of construct validation and meta-analysis. *Educational Psychologist, 41*, 181–206.

Oakes, J. (1990a). Opportunities, achievement, and choice: Women and minority students in science and math. *Review of Research in Education, 16*, 153–222.

Oakes, J. (1990b). *Multiplying inequities: The effects of race, social class, and tracking on opportunities to learn mathematics and science.* Santa Monica, CA: Rand.

Oakes, J. (1999). Promotion or retention: Which one is social? *Harvard Education Letter, 15*(1), 8.

Oakes, J., & Wells, A. S. (2002). Detracking for high student achievement. In L. Abbeduto (Ed.), *Taking sides: Clashing views and controversial issues in educational psychology* (2nd ed., pp. 26–30). Guilford, CT: McGraw-Hill Duskin.

Ogbu, J. U. (1987). Variability in minority school performance: A problem in search of an explanation. *Anthropology and Education Quarterly, 18*, 312–334.

Ogbu, J. U. (1997). Understanding the school performance of urban blacks: Some essential background knowledge. In H. Walberg, O. Reyes, & R. P. Weissberg (Eds.), *Children and youth: Interdisciplinary perspectives* (pp. 190–240). Norwood, NJ: Ablex.

Ogden, J. E., Brophy, J. E., & Evertson, C. M. (1977, April). *An experimental investigation of organization and management techniques in first-grade reading groups.* Paper presented at the annual meeting of the American Educational Research Association, New York, NY.

Okagaki, L. (2001). Triarchic model of minority children's school achievement. *Educational Psychologist, 36*, 9–20.

Okagaki, L. (2006). Ethnicity, learning. In P. Alexander & P. Winne (Eds.), *Handbook of educational psychology* (2nd ed., pp. 615–634). Mahwah, NJ: Erlbaum.

Ollendick, T. H., Dailey, D., & Shapiro, E. S. (1983). Vicarious reinforcement: Expected and unexpected effects. *Journal of Applied Behavior Analysis, 16*, 485–491.

Olsen, L. (1988). *Crossing the schoolhouse border: Immigrant students and the California public schools.* San Francisco, CA: California Tomorrow.

Olson, D. R. (2004). The triumph of hope over experience in the search for "what works": A response to Slavin. *Educational Researcher, 33*(1), 24–26.

Olson, K. (2008). The wounded student. *Educational Leadership, 65*(6), 46–48.

Omi, M., & Winant, H. (1994). *Racial formation in the United States: From the 1960s to the 1990s* (2nd ed.). New York, NY: Routledge.

Ontario Ministry of Education (2006). *Language: The Ontario curriculum, grades 1–8.* Retrieved from www.edu.gov.on.ca/eng/curriculum/elementary/language18currb.pdf

Oosterhof, A. (2009). *Developing and using classroom assessments* (4th ed.). Columbus, OH: Pearson/Merrill.

Orange, C. (2000). *25 biggest mistakes teachers make and how to avoid them.* Thousand Oaks, CA: Corwin.

Orange, C. (2005). *44 smart strategies for avoiding classroom mistakes.* Thousand Oaks, CA: Corwin Press.

Organization for Economic Cooperation and Development. (2007). *Understanding the brain: The birth of a learning science.* Paris: Author OECD.

Orlando L., & Machado, A. (1996). In defense of Piaget's theory: A reply to 10 common criticisms. *Psychological Review, 103*, 143–164.

Ormrod, J. E. (2004). *Human learning* (4th ed.). Columbus, OH: Merrill/Prentice-Hall.

Ormrod, J. E. (2012). *Human learning* (6th ed.). Boston, MA: Pearson.

Ortony, A., Clore, G. L., & Collins, A. (1988). *The cognitive structure of emotions.* Cambridge, MA: Cambridge University Press.

Osborn, A. F. (1963). *Applied imagination* (3rd ed.). New York, NY: Scribner's.

Osborne, J. W. (2001). Testing stereotype threat: Does anxiety explain race and sex differences in achievement. *Contemporary Educational Psychology, 26*, 291–310.

Osher, D., Bear, G. G., Sprague, J. R., & Doyle, W. (2010). How can we improve school discipline? *Educational Researcher, 39*(1), 48–58.

Osterman, K. F. (2000). Students' need for belonging in the school community. *Review of Educational Research, 70*, 323–367.

Ostrov, J. M., & Godleski, S. A. (2010). Toward an integrated gender-linked model of aggression subtypes in early and middle childhood. *Psychological Review, 117*, 233–242.

Otto, B. (2010). *Language development in early childhood* (5th ed.). Columbus, OH: Merrill.

Overton, W. F. (2006). Developmental psychology: Philosophy, concepts, and methodology. In R. M. Lerner (Ed.), *Handbook of child psychology: Vol. 1: Theoretical models of human development* (6th ed., pp. 18–88). New York, NY: Wiley.

Owens, R. (1999). *Language disorders: A functional approach to assessment and intervention* (3rd ed.). Boston, MA: Allyn & Bacon.

Owens, R. E. (2012). *Language development: An introduction* (8th ed.). Boston, MA: Allyn & Bacon.

Owens, R. E. J. (2005). *Language development: An introduction* (6th ed.). Boston, MA: Allyn & Bacon.

Owens, R. E. (2012). *Language development: An introduction* (8th ed.). Boston, MA: Allyn & Bacon.

Padilla, F. M. (1992). *The gang as an American enterprise.* New Brunswick, NJ: Rutgers University Press.

Pai, Y., & Adler, S. A. (2001). *Cultural foundations of education* (3rd ed.). Upper Saddle River, NJ: Merrill.

Paivio, A. (1986). *Mental representations: A dual-coding approach.* New York, NY: Oxford University Press.

Paivio, A. (2006). *Mind and its evolution; A dual coding theoretical interpretation.* Mahwah, NJ: Lawrence Erlbaum Associates, Inc.

Pajares, F. (1997). Current directions in self-efficacy research. In M. L. Maehr & P. R. Pintrich (Eds.), *Advances in motivation and achievement* (Vol. 10, pp. 1–49). Greenwich, CT: JAI Press.

Pajares, F. (2000, April). *Seeking a culturally attentive educational psychology.* Paper presented at the annual meeting of the American Educational Research Association, New Orleans, LA. Retrieved from www.emory.edu/EDUCATION/mfp/AERA2000Discussant.html

Pajares, F. (2002). *Self-efficacy beliefs in academic contexts: An outline.* Retrieved from http://des.emory.edu/mfp/efftalk.html

Pajares, F. (2003). William James: Our father who begot us. In B. J. Zimmerman & D. H. Schunk (Eds.), *Educational psychology: A century of contributions* (pp. 41–64). Mahwah, NJ: Erlbaum.

Pajares, F. (2008). Self-efficacy information. Retrieved from: http://www.des.emory.edu/mfp/banconversion.html

Pajares, F., & Schunk, D. H. (2001). Self-beliefs and school success: Self-efficacy, self-concept, and school achievement. In R. Riding & S. Rayner (Eds.), *Perception* (pp. 239–266). Westport, CT: Ablex Publishing.

Pajares, F., & Schunk, D. H. (2002). Self and self-belief in psychology and education: An historical perspective. In J. Aronson & D. Cordova (Eds.), *Psychology of education: Personal and interpersonal forces* (pp. 1–19). New York, NY: Academic Press.

Palincsar, A. S. (1986). The role of dialogue in providing scaffolded instruction. *Educational Psychologist, 26,* 73–98.

Palincsar, A. S. (1996). Language-minority students: Instructional issues in school cultures and classroom social systems. *Elementary School Journal, 96,* 221–226.

Palincsar, A. S. (1998). Social constructivist perspectives on teaching and learning. In J. T. Spence, J. M. Darley, & D. J. Foss (Eds.), *Annual Review of Psychology* (pp. 345–375). Palo Alto, CA: Annual Reviews.

Palincsar, A. S., & Brown, A. L. (1984). Reciprocal teaching of comprehension-fostering and monitoring activities. *Cognition and Instruction, 1,* 117–175.

Palincsar, A. S., & Brown, A. L. (1989). Classroom dialogues to promote self-regulated comprehension. In J. Brophy (Ed.), *Advances in research on teaching* (Vol. 1, pp. 35–67). Greenwich, CT: JAI Press.

Palincsar, A. S., & Herrenkohl, L. R. (2002). Designing collaborative learning contexts. *Theory Into Practice, 61,* 26–32.

Palincsar, A. S., Magnusson, S. J., Collins, K. M., and Cutter, J. (2001). Promoting deep understanding of science in students with disabilities in inclusion classrooms. *Learning Disabilities Quarterly, 24*(1), 15–32.

Palincsar, A. S., Magnuson, S. J., Marano, N., Ford, D., & Brown, N. (1998). Designing a community of practice: Principles and practices of the GIsML community. *Teaching and Teacher Education, 14,* 5–19.

Panitz, T. (1996). *A definition of collaborative vs cooperative learning.* Retrieved from www.city. londonmet.ac.uk/deliberations/collab.learning/panitz2.html

Papanikolaou, K., & Boubouka, M. (2011). Promoting collaboration in a project-based e-learning context. *Journal of Research on Technology in Education, 43*(2): 135–155.

Papert, S. (1980). *Mindstorms; Children, computers, and powerful ideas.* New York, NY: Basic Books.

Paris, S. G. & Ayres, L. R. (1994). *Becoming reflective students and teachers: With portfolios and authentic assessment.* Washington, DC: American Psychological Association.

Paris, S. G., Byrnes, J. P., & Paris, A. H. (2001). Constructing theories, identities, and actions of self-regulated learners. In B. J. Zimmerman & D. H. Schunk (Eds.), *Self-regulated learning and academic achievement: Theoretical perspectives* (2nd ed., pp. 253–287). Mahwah, NJ: Erlbaum.

Paris, S. G., & Cunningham, A. E. (1996). Children becoming students. In D. Berliner & R. Calfee, (Eds.), *Handbook of educational psychology* (pp. 117–146). New York, NY: Macmillan.

Paris, S. G., Lipson, M. Y., & Wixson, K. K. (1983). Becoming a strategic reader. *Contemporary Educational Psychology, 8,* 293–316.

Paris, S. G., Morrison, F. J., & Miller, K. F. (2006). Academic pathways from preschool through elementary school. In P. A. Alexander & P. H. Winne (Eds.), *Handbook of educational psychology* (2nd ed., pp. 61–85). Mahwah, NJ: Erlbaum.

Parke, R. D. & Buriel, R. (2006). Socialization in the family: Ethnic and ecological perspectives. In W. Damon & N. Eisenberg (Eds.), *Handbook of child psychology: Vol. 3. Social, emotional, and personality development* (6th ed., pp. 429–504). New York, NY: Wiley.

Parker, W. C., & Hess, D. (2001). Teaching with and for discussion. *Teaching and Teacher Education, 17,* 273–289.

Parks, C. P. (1995). Gang behavior in the schools: Myth or reality? *Educational Psychology Review, 7,* 41–68.

Pashler, H., McDaniel, M., Rohrer, D., & Bjork, R. (2008). Learning styles: Concepts and evidence. *Psychological Science in the Public Interest, 9*(3): 105119.

Passolunghi, M. C. & Siegel, L. S. (2004). Working memory and access to numerical information in children with disability in mathematics. *Journal of Experimental Child Psychology, 88,* 348–367.

Pate, P. E., McGinnis, K., & Homestead, E. (1995). Creating coherence through curriculum integration. In M. Harmin (1994), *Inspiring active learning: A handbook for teachers* (pp. 62–70). Alexandria, VA: Association for Supervision and Curriculum Development.

Patterson, C. (1995). *Lesbian and gay parents and their children: Summary of research findings.* Retreived from www.apa.org/pi/parent.html

Pauk, W., Owens, R. J. Q. (2010) [1962]. *How to Study in College* (10th ed.). Florence, KY: Cengage Learning; http://academic.cuesta.edu/acasupp/as/618.htm; and www.ldonline.org/article/6210.

Paul, A. M. (2011, September 10). The trouble with homework. *New York Times,* Sunday Review Section, p. 6.

Paulman, R. G., & Kennelly, K. J. (1984). Test anxiety and ineffective test taking: Different names, same construct? *Journal of Educational Psychology, 76,* 279–288.

Paulos, L. (2007). Multitasking madness. *Scholastic Choices, 23* (1), 10–13.

Pea, R. D., & Maldonado, H. (2006). WILD for learning: Interacting through new computing devices anywhere, anytime. In R. K. Sawyer (Ed.), *The Cambridge handbook of the learning sciences* (pp. 427–441). New York, NY: Cambridge University Press.

Pearl, R., Leung, M. C., Acker, R. V., Farmer, T. W., & Rodkin, P. C. (2007). Fourth- and fifth-grade teachers' awareness of their classrooms' social networks. *The Elementary School Journal, 108,* 25–39.

Pearson, B. Z., Fernandez, S. C., Lewedeg, V., & Oller, D. K. (1997). The relation of input factors to lexical learning by bilingual infants. *Applied Linguistics, 18,* 41–58.

Pekrun, R., Elliot, A. J., & Maier, M. A. (2006). Achievement goals and discrete achievement emotions: A theoretical model and prospective test. *Journal of Educational Psychology, 98,* 583–597.

Pekrun, R., Elliot, A. J., & Maier, M. A. (2009). Achievement goals and achievement emotions: Testing a model of their joint relations with academic performance. *Journal of Educational Psychology, 101,* 115–135.

Pekrun, R., Goetz, T., Daniels, L. M., Stupinsky, R. H., & Perry, R. P. (2010). Boredom in achievement settings: Exploring control–value antecedents and performance outcomes of a neglected emotion. *Journal of Educational Psychology, 102*(3).

Pekrun, R., Goetz, T., Titz, W., & Perry, R. P. (2002). Academic emotions in students' self-regulated learning and achievement. A program of qualitative and quantitative research. *Educational Psychologist, 37,* 91–105.

Pelham, W. E. (1981). Attention deficits in hyperactive and learning-disabled children. *Exceptional Education Quarterly, 2,* 13–23.

Pelligrini, A. D., Bartini, M., & Brooks, F. (1999). School bullies, victims, and aggressive victims: Factors relating to group affiliation and victimization in early adolescence. *Journal of Educational Psychology, 91*(2): 216–224.

Pellegrini, A. D., & Bohn, C. M. (2005). The role of recess in children's cognitive performance and school adjustment. *Educational Researcher, 34,* 13–19.

Pellegrini, A. D., Dupuis, D., & Smith, P. K. (2007). Play in evolution and development. *Developmental Review, 27,* 261–276.

Pellis, S. (2006). The effects of orbital frontal cortex damage on the modulation of defensive responses by rats in playful and nonplayful social contexts. *Behavioral Neuroscience, 120,* 72–84.

Peng, S., & Lee, R. (1992, April). *Home variables, parent–child activities, and academic achievement: A study of 1988 eighth graders.* Paper presented at the annual meeting of the American Educational Research Association, San Francisco, CA.

Penuel, W. R., & Wertsch, J. V. (1995). Vygotsky and identity formation: A sociocultural approach. *Educational Psychologist, 30,* 83–92.

Pepler, D., Craig, W., Jiang, D., & Connolly, J. (2008). Developmental trajectories of bullying and associated factors. *Child Development, 79,* 325–338.

Peregoy, S. F., & Boyle, O. F. (2009). *Reading, writing, and learning in ESL: A resource book for teaching K -12 English learners* (5th ed.). Boston, MA: Allyn & Bacon/Pearson.

Perkins, D. N., Jay, E., & Tishman, S. (1993). New conceptions of thinking: From ontology to education. *Educational Psychologist, 28,* 67–85.

Perkins, D. N., & Salomon, G. (1989). Are cognitive skills context-bound? *Educational Researcher, 18,* 16–25.

Perner, J. (2000). Memory and theory of mind. In E. Tulving & F. I. M. Craik (Eds.), *The Oxford handbook of memory* (pp. 297–312). New York, NY: Oxford.

Perry, N. E. (1998). Young children's self-regulated learning and contexts that support it. *Journal of Educational Psychology, 90,* 715–729.

Perry, N. E., & Collie, R. J. (2011, April). Can teaching students to self-regulate learning enhance motivation for teaching and well-being in student teachers? In R. Klassen & N. Perry (Co-chairs), *Teachers' motivation and well-being from a career stage perspective.* Symposium presented at the annual meeting of the American Educational Research Association, New Orleans, LA.

Perry, N. E., & Drummond, L. (2002). Helping young students become self-regulated researchers and writers. *The Reading Teacher, 56,* 298–310.

Perry, N. E., McNamara, J. K., & Mercer, K. L. (2001). Principles, policies, and practices in special education in British Columbia. *Exceptionality Education Canada, 11,* 63–89.

Perry, N., Mirenda, P., and Siegel, L. (2007, October). Beyond placement: Supporting effective inclusion education. *Educational Leadership Centre at UBC, 1,* 6–9, 12.

Perry, N. E., Phillips, L., & Dowler, J. (2004). Examining features of tasks and their potential to promote self-regulated learning. Teachers College Record, 106, 1854–1878.

Perry, N. E. & Rahim, A. (2011). Studying self-regulated learning in classrooms. In B. J. Zimmerman & D. H. Schunk (Eds.), *Handbook of self-regulation of learning and performance* (pp. 122–136). New York: Routledge.

Perry, N. E., VandeKamp, K. O., & Mercer, L. K. (2000, April). *Investigating teacher-student interactions that foster self-regulated learning.* In N. E. Perry (Chair), Symposium conducted at the meeting of the American Educational Research Association, New Orleans, LA.

Perry, N. E., VandeKamp, K. O., Mercer, L. K., & Nordby, C. J. (2002). Investigating teacher-student interactions that foster self-regulated learning. *Educational Psychologist, 37,* 5–15.

Peterson, P. L. (1992). Revising their thinking: Keisha Coleman and her third-grade mathematics class. In H. Marshall (Ed.), *Redefining student learning: Roots of educational change* (pp. 151–176). Norwood, NJ: Ablex.

Petitclearc, A., Boivin, M., Dionne, G., Zoccolillo, M., & Tremblay, R. E. (2009). Disregard for rules: The early development and predictors of a specific dimension of disruptive behavior disorders. *Journal of Child Psychology and Psychiatry, 50*(12), 1477–1484.

Petitto, L. A., & Kovelman, I. (2003). The bilingual paradox: How signing-speaking bilingual children help us resolve bilingual issues and teach us about the brain's mechanisms underlying all language acquisition. *Language Learning, 8*(3), 5–18.

Petitto, L. A. (2009). New discoveries from the bilingual brain and mind across the life span: Implications for education. *Brain, Mind, and Education, 3,* 185–197.

Petrill, S. A., & Wilkerson, B. (2000). Intelligence and achievement: A behavioral genetic perspective. *Educational Psychology Review, 12,* 185–199.

Pettigrew, T. (1998). Intergroup contact theory. In J. T. Spence, J. M. Darley, & D. J. Foss (Eds.), *Annual review of psychology* (pp. 65–85). Palo Alto, CA: Annual Reviews.

Peverly, S. T., Ramaswamy, V., Garner, J., Brown, Sumowowski, J., & Alidoost, M. (2007). What predicts skill in lecture note taking? *Journal of Educational Psychology, 99,* 167–180.

Peverly, S., Brobst, K., Graham, M., & Shaw, R. (2003). College adults are not good at self-regulation: A study on the relationship of self-regulation, note-taking, and test-taking. *Journal of Educational Psychology, 95,* 335–346.

Pfiffner, L., Barkley, R. A., & DuPaul, G. J. (2006). Treatment of ADHD in school settings. In R. A. Barkley (Ed.), *Attention deficit hyperactivity disorder: A handbook for diagnosis and treatment,* 3rd edition. New York: Guilford.

Pfiffner, L. J., & O'Leary, S. G. (1987). The efficacy of all positive management as a function of the prior use of negative consequences. *Journal of Applied Behavior Analysis, 20,* 265–271.

Phillips, D. (1997). How, why, what, when, and where: Perspectives on constructivism and education. *Issues in Education: Contributions from Educational Psychology, 3,* 151–194.

Phillips, D. A., & Zimmerman, M. (1990). The developmental course of perceived competence and incompetence among competent children. In R. J. Steinberg & J. Kolligan, Jr. (Eds.), *Competence Considered.* New Haven: Yale University Press.

Phinney, J. (2003). Ethnic identity and acculturation. In K. Chun, P. Ball, & Marin, G. (Eds.), *Acculturation: Advances in theory, measurement, and applied research* (pp. 63–81). Washington, DC: American Psychological Association.

Phinney, J. S. (1990). Ethnic identity in adolescents and adults: Review of research. *Psychological Bulletin, 108*(3), 499–514.

Phinney, J. S., & Devich-Navarro, M. (1997). Variations in bicultural identification among African American and Mexican American adolescents. *Journal of Research on Adolescence, 7,* 3–32.

Phye, G. D. (1992). Strategic transfer: A tool for academic problem solving. *Educational Psychology Review, 4,* 393–421.

Phye, G. D. (2001). Problem-solving instruction and problem-solving transfer: The correspondence issue. *Journal of Educational Psychology, 93,* 571–578.

Phye, G. D., & Sanders, C. E. (1994). Advice and feedback: Elements of practice for problem solving. *Contemporary Educational Psychology, 17,* 211–223.

Piaget, J. (1954). *The construction of reality in the child* (M. Cook, Trans.). New York, NY: Basic Books.

Piaget, J. (1962). *Comments on Vygotsky's critical remarks concerning "The language and thought of the child" and "Judgment and reasoning in the child."* Cambridge, MA: MIT Press.

Piaget, J. (1963). *Origins of intelligence in children.* New York, NY: Norton.

Piaget, J. (1964). Development and learning. In R. Ripple & V. Rockcastle (Eds.), *Piaget rediscovered* (pp. 7–20). Ithaca, NY: Cornell University Press.

Piaget, J. (1965). *The moral judgment of the child.* New York, NY: Free Press.

Piaget, J. (1965/1995). *Sociological studies.* New York, NY: Routledge. (Original work published in 1965.)

Piaget, J. (1969). *Science of education and the psychology of the child.* New York, NY: Viking.

Piaget, J. (1970a). Piaget's theory. In P. Mussen (Ed.), *Handbook of child psychology* (3rd ed., Vol. 1, pp. 703–732). New York, NY: Wiley.

Piaget, J. (1970b). *The science of education and the psychology of the child.* New York, NY: Orion Press.

Piaget, J. (1971). *Biology and knowledge.* Edinburgh, Scotland: Edinburgh Press.

Piaget, J. (1974). *Understanding causality* (D. Miles and M. Miles, Trans.). New York, NY: Norton.

Piaget, J. (1985). *The equilibrium of cognitive structures: The central problem of intellectual development* (T. Brown & K. L. Thampy, Trans.). Chicago, IL: University of Chicago Press.

Pianta, R. C., Belsky, J., Vandergrift, N., Houts, R., & Morrison, F. J. (2008). Classroom effects on children's achievement trajectories in elementary school. *American Educational Research Journal, 45,* 365–397.

Pianta, R. C., Howes, C., Burchinal, M., Bryant, D. M., Clifford, R. M., Early, D. M., & Barbarin, O. (2005). Features of pre-kindergarten programs, classrooms, and teachers: Do they predict observed classroom quality and child-teacher interactions? *Applied Developmental Science, 9* (3), 144–159.

Pierson, L. H., & Connell, J. P. (1992). Effect of grade retention on self-system processes, school engagement, and academic performance. *Journal of Educational Psychology, 84,* 300–307.

Pigge, F. L., & Marso, R. N. (1997). A seven-year longitudinal multi-factor assessment of teaching concerns development through preparation and early teaching. *Teaching and Teacher Education, 13,* 225–235.

Pinker, S. (2002). *The blank slate: The modern denial of human nature.* New York, NY: Penguin.

Pintrich, P. R. (2000). Educational psychology at the millennium: A look back and a look forward. *Educational Psychologist, 35,* 221–226.

Pintrich, P. R. (2003). A motivational science perspective on the role of student motivation in learning and teaching. *Journal of Educational Psychology, 95,* 667–686.

Pintrich, R. R., & De Groot, E. V. (1990). Motivational and self-regulated learning components of classroom academic performance. *Journal of Educational Psychology, 82,* 33–40.

Pintrich, P. R., Marx, R. W., & Boyle, R. A. (1993). Beyond cold conceptual change: The role of motivational beliefs and classroom contextual factors in the process of conceptual change. *Review of Educational Research, 63,* 167–199.

Pintrich, P. R., & Schrauben, B. (1992). Students' motivational beliefs and their cognitive engagement in academic tasks. In D. Schunk & J. Meece (Eds.), *Students' perceptions in the classroom: Causes and consequences* (pp. 149–183). Hillsdale, NJ: Erlbaum.

Pintrich, R. R., & Sinatra, G. M. (2003). Future direction for theory and research on intentional conceptual change. In G. M. Sinatra & P. R. Pintrich (Eds.), *Intentional conceptual change* (pp. 429–441). Mahwah, NJ: Erlbaum.

Pintrich, P. R., & Zusho, A. (2002). The development of academic self-regulation: The role of cognitive and motivational factors. In A. Wigfield & J. Eccles (Eds.), *Development of achievement motivation* (pp. 249–284). San Diego, CA: Academic Press.

Pinxten, M., De Fraine, B., Van Damme, J., & D'Haenens, E. (2010). Causal ordering of academic self-concept and achievement: Effects of type of achievement measure. *British Journal of Educational Psychology, 80*(4), 689–709.

Pisha, B., & Coyne, P. (2001). Smart for the start: The promise of universal design for learning. *Remedial and Special Education, 22,* 197–203.

Pitts, J. M. (1992). Constructivism: Learning rethought. In J. B. Smith & J. C. Coleman, Jr. (Eds.), *School Library Media Annual* (Vol. 10, pp. 14–25). Englewood, CO: Libraries Unlimited.

Plucker, J. A., Beghetto, R. A., & Dow, G. T. (2004). Why isn't creativity more important to educational psychologists? Potential pitfalls and future directions in creativity research. *Educational Psychology, 39*(2), 83–96.

Polk, J. A. (2006). Traits of effective teachers. *Arts Education Policy Review, 107*(4), 23–29.

Polson, P. G., & Jeffries, R. (1985). Instruction in general problem-solving skills: An analysis of four approaches. In J. Segal, S. Chipman, & R. Glaser (Eds.), *Thinking and learning skills* (Vol. 1, pp. 417–455). Mahwah, NJ: Erlbaum.

Ponitz, C. C., Rimm-Kaufman, S. E., Grimm, K. J., & Curby, T. W. (2009). Kindergarten classroom quality, behavioral engagement, and reading achievement. *School Psychology Review, 38*(1).

Popham, W. J. (2005a). *Classroom assessment : What teachers need to know* (4th ed.). Boston, MA: Allyn & Bacon.

Popham, W. J. (2005b). Instructional quality: Collecting credible evidence. *Educational Leadership, 62*(6), 80–81.

Popham, W. J. (2008). *Classroom assessment: What teachers need to know* (5th ed.). Boston, MA: Allyn & Bacon.

Popham, W. J. (2011). *Classroom assessment: What teachers need to know* (6th ed.). Boston, MA: Allyn & Bacon.

Porac, C., Coren, S., & Searleman, A. (1986). Environmental factors in hand preference formation: Evidence from attempts to switch the preferred hand. *Behavioral Genetics, 16*, 250–261.

Porath, M. (1996). Narrative performance in verbally gifted children. *Journal for the Education of the Gifted, 19*, 276–292.

Porath, M. (2001). Young girls' social understanding: Emergent interpersonal expertise. *High Ability Studies, 12*, 113–126.

Porath, M. (2003). Social understanding in the first years of school. *Early Childhood Research Quarterly, 18*(4), 468–484.

Portes, A., & Hao, L. (1998). E pluribus unum: Bilingualism and loss of language in the second generation. *Sociology of Education, 71*: 269–294.

Posada, G., Jacobs, A., Richmond, M., Carbonell, O. A., Alzate, G., Bustamante, M. R., & Quiceno, J. (2002). Maternal care giving and infant security in two cultures. *Developmental Psychology, 38*, 67–78.

Posner, M. I. (1973). Cognition: An introduction. Glenview, IL: Scott, Foresman.

Prat-Sala, M., & Redford, P. (2010). The interplay between motivation, self-efficacy, and approaches to studying. *British Journal of Educational Psychology, 80*(2): 283–305.

Prawat, R. S. (1991). The value of ideas: The immersion approach to the development of thinking. *Educational Researcher, 20*, 3–10.

Prawat, R. S. (1992). Teachers beliefs about teaching and learning: A constructivist perspective. *American Journal of Education, 100*, 354–395.

Prawat, R. S. (1996). Constructivism, modern and postmodern. *Issues in Education: Contributions from Educational Psychology, 3*, 215–226.

Preckel, F. Götz, T., & Frenzel, A. (2010). Ability of gifted students: Effects on academic self-concept and boredom. *British Journal of Educational Psychology, 80*(3): 451–472.

Premack, D. (1965). Reinforcement theory. In D. Levine (Ed.), *Nebraska symposium on motivation* (Vol. 13, pp. 123–180). Lincoln, NE: University of Nebraska Press.

Pressley, M. (1995). More about the development of self-regulation: complex, long-term, and thoroughly social. *Educational Psychologist, 30*, 207–212.

Pressley, M. (1996, August). *Getting beyond whole language: Elementary reading instruction that makes sense in light of recent psychological research.* Paper presented at the annual meeting of the American Psychological Association, Toronto, ON.

Pressley, M., Allington, R. L., Wharton-McDonald, R., Collins, C. B., & Morrow, L. M. (2001). *Learning to read: Lessons from exemplary first-grade classrooms.* New York, NY: Guilford Press.

Pressley, M., Barkowski, J. G., & Schneider, W. (1987). Cognitive strategies: Good strategy users coordinate metacognition and knowledge. In R. Vasta & G. Whitehurst (Eds.), *Annals of Child Development* (Vol. 5, pp. 89–129). Greenwich, CT: JAI Press.

Pressley, M., & Harris, K. A. (2006). Cognitive strategies instruction: From basic research to classroom instruction. In P. A. Alexander & P. H. Winne (Eds.), *Handbook of educational psychology* (2nd ed., pp. 265–286). Mahwah, NJ: Erlbaum.

Pressley, M., Levin, J., & Delaney, H. D. (1982). The mnemonic keyword method. *Review of Research in Education, 52*, 61–91.

Pressley, M., Mohan, L., Raphael, L. M., & Fingeret, L. (2007). How does Bennett Woods Elementary School produce such high reading and writing achievement? *Journal of Educational Psychology, 99*, 221–240.

Pressley, M., Rahael, L., Gallagher, J. D. & DiBella, J. (2004). Providence St. Mel School: How a school that works for African American students works. *Journal of Educational Psychology, 96*(2), 216–235.

Pressley, M., & Roehrig, A. (2003). Educational psychology in the modern era: 1960 to the present. In B. J. Zimmerman & D. H. Schunk (Eds.), *Educational psychology: A century of contributions* (pp. 333–366). [A Project of Division 15 (Educational Psychology) of the American Psychological Association]. Mahwah, NJ: Erlbaum.

Pressley, M., & Woloshyn, V.E. (Eds.), (1995). *Cognitive strategy instruction that really improves children's academic performance.* Cambridge MA: Brookline Books.

PREVNet. (2010). *Promoting relationships and eliminating violence.* [Website]. Retrieved from http://prevnet.ca/Home/tabid/36/Default.aspx

Price, L. F. (2005). The biology of risk taking. *Educational Leadership, 62*(7), 22–27.

Price, W. F., & Crapo, R. H. (2002). *Cross-cultural perspectives in introductory psychology* (4th ed.). Pacific Grove, CA: Wadsworth.

Proctor, C. P., August, D., Carlo, M. S., & Snow, C. (2006). The intriguing role of Spanish language vocabulary knowledge in predicting English reading comprehension. *Journal of Educational Psychology, 98*, 159–169.

Public Health Agency of Canada. (2008). Canadian incidence study of reported child abuse and neglect. Retrieved June 12, 2014, from www.phac-aspc.gc.ca/cm-vee/csca-ecve/2008/fs-am/index-eng.php

Pugh, K. J., & Bergin, D. A. (2006). Motivational influences on transfer. *Educational Psychologist, 41*, 147–160.

Pugh, K. J., & Phillips, M. M. (2011). Content appreciation: Why it matters and how you can foster it. *Theory Into Practice, 50.*

Puncochar, J., & Fox, P. W. (2004). Confidence in individual and group decision-making: When "Two Heads" are worse than one. *Journal of Educational Psychology, 96*, 582–591.

Puntambekar, S., & Hubscher, R. (2005). Tools for scaffolding students in a complex learning environment: What have we gained and what have we missed? *Educational Psychologist, 40*, 1–12.

Purdie, N., Hattie, J., & Carroll, A. (2002). A review of the research on interventions for Attention Deficit Hyperactivity Disorder: What works best? *Review of Educational Research, 72*(1): 61–99.

Puustinen, M., & Pulkkinen, L. (2001). Models of self-regulated learning: A review. *Scandinavian Journal of Educational Research, 45*, 269–286.

Rachlin, H. (1991). *Introduction to modern behaviorism* (3rd ed.), New York, NY: W. H. Freeman.

Rachlin, H. (2004). *The science of self-control.* Cambridge, MA: Harvard University Press.

Ramirez, J. D., Yuen, S. D., & Ramey, D. R. (1991). *Longitudinal study of structured English immersion strategy, early-exit and late-exit transitional bilingual education programs for language-minority children. Final report to the U.S. Department of Education.* Executive Summary and Vols. I and II. San Mateo, CA: Aguirre International.

Range, L. M. (1993). Suicide prevention: Guidelines for schools. *Educational Psychology Review, 5*, 135–154.

Raudenbush, S. (1984). Magnitude of teacher expectancy effects on pupil IQ as a function of the credibility of expectancy induction: A synthesis of findings from 18 experiments. *Journal of Educational Psychology, 76*, 85–97.

Raudenbush, S.W. (2009). The *Brown* Legacy and the O'Connor Challenge: Transforming schools in the images of children's potential. *Educational Researcher, 38*, 169–180.

Raudsepp, E., & Haugh, G. P. (1977). *Creative growth games.* New York, NY: Harcourt Brace Jovanovich.

Rauscher, F. H., & Shaw, G. L. (1998). Key components of the Mozart effect. *Perceptual and Motor Skills, 86*, 835–841.

Recht, D. R., & Leslie, L. (1988). Effect of prior knowledge on good and poor readers' memory of text. *Journal of Educational Psychology, 80*, 16–20.

Reder, L. M. (1996). Different research programs on metacognition: Are the boundaries imaginary? *Learning and Individual Differences, 8*, 383–390.

Reder, L. M., Park, H., & Kieffaber, P. D. (2009). Memory systems do not divide on consciousness: Reinterpreting memory in terms of activation and binding. *Psychological Bulletin, 135*(1): 23–49.

Reed, S., & Sautter, R. C. (1990). Children of poverty: The status of 12 million Americans. *Phi Delta Kappan, 71*(10), K1–K12.

Reed, S. K. (2006). Cognitive architecture for multimedia learning. *Educational Psychologist, 41*, 87–98.

Reeve, J. (1996). *Motivating others: Nurturing inner motivational resources.* Boston, MA: Allyn & Bacon.

Reeve, J. (2002). Self-determination theory applied to educational settings. In E. L. Deci & R. M. Ryan (Eds.), *Handbook of self-determination research* (pp. 183–203). Rochester, NY: University of Rochester Press.

Reeve, J. (2009). Why teachers adopt a controlling motivating style toward students and how they can become more autonomy supportive. *Educational Psychologist, 44*, 159–175.

Reeve, J., Deci, E. L., & Ryan, R. M. (2004). *Self-determination theory: A dialectical framework for understanding the sociocultural influences on motivation and learning: Big theories revisited* (Vol. 4, pp. 31–59). Greenwich, CT: Information Age Press.

Reeve, J., & Jang, H. (2006a). Teachers as facilitators: What autonomy-supportive teachers do and why their students benefit. *Elementary School Journal, 106,* 225–236.

Reeve, J., & Jang, H. (2006b). What teachers say and do to support students' autonomy during a learning activity. *Journal of Educational Psychology, 98,* 209–218.

Reeve, J., Nix, G., & Hamm, D. (2003). The experience of self-determination in intrinsic motivation and the conundrum of choice. *Journal of Educational Psychology, 95,* 347–392.

Reid, J. M., & Byrd, P. (1998). *Grammar in the composition classroom.* New York, NY: Heinle & Heinle Publisher.

Reimann, P., & Chi, M. T. H. (1989). Human expertise. In K. J. Gilhooly (Ed.), *Human and machine problem solving* (pp. 161–191). New York, NY: Plenum Press.

Reinke, W. M., & Herman, K. C. (2002a). A research agenda for school violence prevention. *American Psychologist, 57,* 796–797.

Reinke, W. M., & Herman, K. C. (2002b). Creating school environments that deter antisocial behaviors in youth. *Psychology in the Schools, 39,* 549–560.

Reis, S. M., Kaplan, S. N., Tomlinson, C. A., Westberg, K. L., Callahan, C. M., & Cooper, C. R. (2002). Equal does not mean identical. In L. Abbeduto (Ed.), *Taking sides: Clashing on controversial issues in educational psychology* (pp. 31–35). Guilford, CT: McGraw-Hill/Duskin.

Reis, S. M., McCoach, D. B., Coyne, M., Schreiber, F. J., Eckert, R. D., & Gubbins, E. J. (2007). Using planned enrichment strategies with direct instruction to improve reading fluency, comprehension, and attitude toward reading: An evidence-based study. *The Elementary School Journal, 108,* 3–23.

Reis, S. M., & Renzulli, J. S. (2004). Current research on the social and emotional development of gifted and talented students: Good news and future possibilities. *Psychology in the Schools, 41.* Published online in Wiley InterScience (www.interscience.wiley.com).

Reisberg, D., & Heuer, F. (1992). Remembering the details of emotional events. In E. Winograd & U. Neisser (Eds.), *Affect and accuracy in recall: Studies of "flashbulb" memories.* Cambridge, England: Cambridge University Press.

Reiss, S. (2004). Multifaceted nature of intrinsic motivation: The theory of 16 basic desires. *Review of General Psychology, 8,* 179–193.

Render, G. F., Padilla, J. N. M., & Krank, H. M. (1989). What research really shows about assertive discipline. *Educational Leadership, 46*(6), 72–75.

Renninger, K. A. (2009). Interest and identity development in instruction: An inductive model. *Educational Psychologist, 44,* 105–118.

Renzulli, J. S., & Reis, S. M. (2003). The schoolwide enrichment model: Developing creative and productive giftedness. In N. Colangelo & G. A. Davis (Eds.), *Handbook of gifted education* (pp. 184–203). Boston, MA: Allyn & Bacon.

Resnick, L. B. (1981). Instructional psychology. *Annual Review of Psychology, 32,* 659–704.

Reynolds, A. (1992). Grade retention and school adjustment: An explanatory analysis. *Educational Evaluation and Policy Analysis, 14*(2), 101–121.

Rhodes, R. A. (1997). *Community service and higher learning: Explorations of the caring self.* Albany, NY: State University of New York Press.

Rice, F. P., & Dolgin, K. G. (2002). *The adolescent: Development, relationships, and culture* (10th ed.). Boston, MA: Allyn & Bacon.

Rice, M. L. (1989). Children's language acquisition. *American Psychologist, 44,* 149–156.

Richards, J. (2011). School Dropouts: Who are they and what can be done? C.D. Howe Institute. Retrieved July 25, 2014, from www.cdhowe.org/pdf/ebrief_109.pdf

Richardson, T. M., & Benbow, C. P. (1990). Long-term effects of acceleration on the social-emotional adjustment of mathematically precocious youths. *Journal of Educational Psychology, 82,* 464–470.

Richell, R., Deakin, J., & Anderson, I. (2005). Effect of acute tryptophan depletion on the response to controllable and uncontrollable noise stress. *Biological Psychiatry, 57,* 295–300.

Richtel, M. (2011, September 3). In classroom of the future, stagnant score. *New York Times,* A1.

Rideout, V. J., Foehr, U. G., & Roberts, D. F. (2010, January). Generation M2: Media in the lives of 8–18-year-olds. Kaiser Family Foundation. Available at http://www.kff.org/entmedia/upload/8010.pdf

Rideout, V., Roberts, D. F., Foehr, U. G. (2005). *Generation M: Media in the Lives of 8–18 year-olds: Executive Summary.* Menlo Park, CA: Kaiser Family Foundation.

Rittle-Johnson, B., & Star, J. R. (2007). Does comparing solution methods facilitate conceptual and procedural knowledge? An experimental study on learning to solve equations. *Journal of Educational Psychology, 99,* 561–574.

Rivers, I., Voret, V. P., Pote, N., & Ashurst, N. (2009). Observing bullying at school: The mental health implications of witness status. *School Psychology Quarterly, 24,* 211–223.

Rizzolatti, G., Fadiga, L., Gallese, V., & Fogassi, L. (1996). Premotor cortex and the recognition of motor actions. *Brain Research: Cognitive Brain Research, 3*(2), 131–141.

Robbins, S. B., Lauver, K., Davis, H. L., Davis, D., Langley, R., & Carlstrom, A. (2004). Psychosocial and study skill factors predict college outcomes? *A meta-analysis. Psychological Bulletin, 130,* 261–288.

Robbins, S. B., Le, L., & Lauver, K. (2005). Promoting successful college outcomes for all students: Reply to Weissberg and Owen (2005). *Psychological Bulletin, 131,* 410–411.

Roberge, M. M. (2002). California's Generation 1.5 immigrants: What experiences, characterisitcs, and needs do they bring to our English classes? *The CATESOL Journal, 14* (1), 107–129.

Roberson, D., Davidoff, J., Davies, I. R. L., & Shapiro, L. R. (2004). The development of color categories in two languages: A longitudinal study. *Journal of Experimental Psychology: General, 133,* 554–571.

Roberts, D. F., Foehr, U. G., & Rideout, V. (2005). *Generation M: Media in the lives of 8–18 year-olds.* Technical Reports 7250/7251. Menlo Park, CA: Kaiser Family foundation. Retrieved from www.kff.org/entmedia/7251.cfm

Roberts, D. S., Tingstrom, D. H., Olmi, D. J., & Bellipanni, K. D. (2008). Positive antecedent and consequent components in child compliance training. *Behavior Modification, 32,* 21–38.

Roberts, G., Mohammed, S. S., & Vaughn, S. (2010). Reading achievement across three language groups: Growth estimates for overall reading and reading subskills obtained with the early childhood longitudinal survey. *Journal of Educational Psychology, 102*(3): 668–686.

Robinson, A., & Clinkenbeard, P. R. (1998). Giftedness: An exceptionality examined. In J. T. Spence, J. M. Darley, & D. J. Foss (Eds.), *Annual review of psychology* (pp. 117–139). Palo Alto, CA: Annual Reviews.

Robinson, D. H. (1998). Graphic organizers as aids to test learning. *Reading Research and Instruction, 37,* 85–105.

Robinson, D. H., & Kiewra, K. A. (1995). Visual argument: Graphic outlines are superior to outlines in improving learning from text. *Journal of Educational Psychology, 87,* 455–467.

Roediger, H. L., & Karpicke, J. D. (2006). Test-enhanced learning: Taking memory tests improves long-term retention. *Psychological Science, 17*(3): 249–255.

Roeser, R. W., Peck, S. C., & Nasir, N. S. (2006). Self and identity processes in school motivation, learning, and achievement. In P. A. Alexander & P. H, Winne (Eds.), *Handbook of educational psychology* (2nd ed., pp. 391–424). Mahwah, NJ: Erlbaum.

Rogers, C. R., & Freiberg, H. J. (1994). *Freedom to learn* (3rd ed.). Columbus, OH: Charles E. Merrill.

Rogoff, B. (1990). *Apprenticeship in thinking: Cognitive development in social context.* New York, NY: Oxford University Press.

Rogoff, B. (1995). Observing sociocultural activity on three planes: Participatory appropriation, guided participation, and apprenticeship. In J. Wertsch, P. del Rio, & A. Alverez (Eds.), *Sociocultural studies of mind* (pp. 139–164). Cambridge, England: Cambridge University Press.

Rogoff, B. (1998). Cognition as a collaborative process. In W. Damon (Series Ed.) and D. Kuhn & R. S. Siegler (Vol. Eds.), *Handbook of child psychology* (5th ed., Vol. 2, pp. 679–744). New York, NY: Wiley.

Rogoff, B. (2003). *The cultural nature of human development.* New York, NY: Oxford University Press.

Rogoff, B., & Morelii, G. (1989). Perspectives on children's development from cultural psychology. *American Psychologist, 44,* 343–348.

Rogoff, B., Turkanis, C. G., & Bartlett, L. (2001). *Learning together: Children and adults in a school community.* New York, NY: Oxford.

Rohrkemper, M., & Corno, L. (1988). Success and failure on classroom tasks: Adaptive learning and classroom teaching. *Elementary School Journal, 88,* 297–312.

Roid, G. H. (2003). *Stanford-Binet Intelligence Scales, Fifth Edition.* Itasca, IL: Riverside Publishing.

Rosch, E. H. (1973). On the internal structure of perceptual and semantic categories. In T. Moore (Ed.), *Cognitive development and the acquisition of language* (pp. 111–144). New York, NY: Academic Press.

Roschelle, J. M., Pea, R. D., Hoadley, C. M., Gordon, D. N., & Means, B. M. (2000, Fall/Winter). Changing how and what children learn in school with computer-based technologies. *Children and Computer Technology, 10*(2), 76–101.

Rose, D. H., & Gravel, J. W. (2010). Universal design for learning. In P. Peterson, E. Baker, & B. McGraw (Eds.), *International Encyclopedia of Education* (pp. 199–124). Oxford: Elsevier.

Rose, L. C., & Gallup, A. M. (1999). The 31st annual Phi Delta Kappa/Gallup Poll of the public's attitude toward the public schools. *Phi Delta Kappan, 81*(1), 41–58.

Rose, L. C., & Gallup, A. M. (2001). The 33rd annual Phi Delta Kappa/Gallup Poll of the public's attitude toward the public schools. *Phi Delta Kappan, 83*(1), 41–58.

Rose, L. C., & Gallup, A. M. (2007). The 39th annual Phi Delta Kappa/Gallup Poll of the public's attitude toward the public schools. *Phi Delta Kappan, 89*(1), 33–45.

Rosen, N. (2004). *Background report and recommendations for setting up adult Michif language classes.* Unpublished Technical Report.

Rosenberg, M. (1979). *Conceiving the self.* New York, NY: Basic Books.

Rosenberg, M. S., Westling, D. L., & McLeskey, J. (2008). *Special education for today's teachers: An introduction.* Boston, MA: Pearson/Allyn & Bacon.

Rosenfeld, M., & Rosenfeld, S. (2004). Developing teacher sensitivities to individual learning differences. *Educational Psychology, 24,* 465–486.

Rosenshine, B. (1979). Content, time, and direct instruction. In P. Peterson & H. Walberg (Eds.), *Research on teaching: Concepts, findings, and implications* (pp. 28–56). Berkeley, CA: McCutchan.

Rosenshine, B. (1988). Explicit teaching. In D. Berliner & B. Rosenshine (Eds.), *Talks to teachers* (pp. 75–92). New York, NY: Random House.

Rosenshine, B., & Furst, N. (1973). The use of direct observation to study teaching. In R. Travers (Ed.), *Second handbook of research on teaching.* Chicago, IL: Rand McNally.

Rosenshine, B., & Meister, C. (1992, April). *The uses of scaffolds for teaching less structured academic tasks.* Paper presented at the annual meeting of the American Educational Research Association, San Francisco, CA.

Rosenshine, B., & Meister, C. (1994). Reciprocal teaching: A review of the research. *Review of Educational Research, 64,* 479–530.

Rosenshine, B., & Stevens, R. (1986). Teaching functions. In M. Wittrock (Ed.), *Handbook of research on teaching* (3rd ed., pp. 376–391). New York, NY: Macmillan.

Rosenthal, R. (1987). Pygmalion effects: Existence, magnitude and social importance. A reply to Wineburg. *Educational Researcher, 16,* 37–41.

Rosenthal, R. (1995). Critiquing Pygmalion: A 25-year perspective. *Current Directions in Psychological Science, 4,* 171–172.

Rosenthal, R., & Jacobson, L. (1968). *Pygmalion in the classroom.* New York, NY: Holt, Rinehart, Winston.

Roskos, K., & Neuman, S. B. (1998). Play as an opportunity for literacy. In O. N. Saracho & B. Spodek (Eds.), *Multiple perspectives on play in early childhood education* (pp. 100–115). Albany, NY: State University of New York Press.

Ross, J. A., & Raphael, D. (1990). Communication and problem solving achievement in cooperative learning groups. *Journal of Curriculum Studies, 22,* 149–164.

Roth, W-M., & Bowen, G. M. (1995). Knowing and interacting: A study of culture, practices, and resources in a grade 8 open-inquiry science guided by an apprenticeship metaphor. *Cognition and Instruction, 13,* 73–128.

Roth, W.-M., & McGinn, M. K. (1997). Toward a new perspective on problem solving. *Canadian Journal of Education, 22,* 18–32.

Roth, W.-M., & Roychoudhury, A. (1993). The development of science process skills in authentic contexts. *Journal of Research on Science Teaching, 30,* 127–152.

Rotherham-Borus, M. J. (1994). Bicultural reference group orientations and adjustment. In M. Bernal & G. Knight (Eds.), *Ethnic identity.* Albany, NY: State University of New York Press.

Rowe, E. W., Kingsley, J. M., & Thompson, D. F. (2010). Predictive ability of the General Ability Index (GAI) versus the Full Scale IQ among gifted referrals. *School Psychology Quarterly, 25*(2): 119–128.

Rowe, M. B. (1974). Wait-time and rewards as instructional variables: Their influence on language, logic, and fate control. Part 1: Wait-time. *Journal of Research in Science Teaching, 11,* 81–94.

Rubin, K. H., Bukowski, W. M., Parker, J. G. (2006). Peer interactions, relationships, and groups. In N. Eisenberg, W. Dammon, & R. M. Lerner (Eds.), *Handbook of child psychology: Vol. 3. Social, emotional, and personality development* (6th ed., pp. 571–645). Hoboken, NJ: John Wiley & Sons.

Rubin, K. H., Coplan, R., Chen, X, & Buskirk, A. A., & Wojslawowicz, J. C. (2005). Peer relationships in childhood. In M. H. Borstein & Lamb, M. E. (Eds.), *Developmental science: An advanced textbook* (pp. 469–512). Mahwah, NJ: Lawrence Erlbaum.

Ruble, D. N., Martin, C. L., & Berenbaum, S. A. (2006). Gender development. In W. Damon (Series Ed.) & N. Eisenberg (Vol. Ed.), *Handbook of Child Psychology* (6th ed., Vol. 3, pp. 858-932). New York: Wiley.

Rudolph, K. D., Lambert, S. F., Clark, A. G., & Kurlakowsky, K. D. (2001). Negotiating the transition to middle school: The role of self-regulatory processes. *Child Development, 72,* 926–946.

Rubie-Davies, C. M. (2010). Teacher expectations and perceptions of student attributes: Is there a relationship? *British Journal of Educational Psychology, 80,* 121–135.

Rueda, R., & Moll, L. C. (1994) A sociocultural perspective on motivation. In F. O'Neil Jr. & M. Drillings (Eds.), *Motivation: Theory and research* (pp. 117–137). Hillsdale, NJ: Erlbaum.

Rumelhart, D., & Ortony, A. (1977). The representation of knowledge in memory. In R. Anderson, R. Spiro & W. Montague (Eds.), *Schooling and the acquisition of knowledge* (pp. 99–135). Hillsdale, NJ: Erlbaum.

Rummel, N., Levin, J. R., & Woodward, M. M. (2003). Do pictorial mnemonic text-learning aids give students something worth writing about? *Journal of Educational Psychology, 95,* 327–334.

Ryan, A. (2001). The peer group as a context for development of young adolescents' motivation and achievement. *Child Development, 72,* 1135–1150.

Ryan, K. E., & Ryan, A. M. (2005). Psychological processes underlying stereotype threat and standardized math test performance. *Educational Psychologist, 40,* 53–63.

Ryan, R. M., & Deci, E. L. (1996). When paradigms clash: Comments on Cameron and Pierce's claim that rewards do not undermine intrinsic motivation. *Review of Educational Research, 66,* 33–38.

Ryan, R. M., & Deci, E. L. (2000). Intrinsic and extrinsic motivation: Classic definitions and new directions. *Contemporary Educational Psychology, 25,* 54–67.

Sackett, P. R., Hardison, C. M., & Cullen, M. J. (2004). On the value of correcting mischaracterizations of stereotype threat. *American Psychologist, 59,* 48–49.

Sackett, P. R., Kuncel, N. R., Arneson, J. J., Cooper, S. R., & Waters, S. D. (2009). Does socioeconomic status explain the relationship between admissions tests and post-secondary academic performance? *Psychological Bulletin, 135*(1): 1–22.

Sadker, M., & Sadker, D. (1994). *Failing at fairness: How America's schools cheat girls.* New York, NY: Scribner.

Sadker, M., & Sadker, D. (2006). Questioning skills. In J. Cooper (Ed.), *Classroom teaching skills* (8th ed., pp. 104–150). Boston, MA: Houghton-Mifflin.

Sadker, M., Sadker, D., & Klein, S. (1991). The issue of gender in elementary and secondary education. *Review of Research in Education, 17,* 269–334.

Sagor, R. (2003). *Motivating students and teachers in an era of standards.* Alexandria, VA: Association for Supervision and Curriculum Development.

Sakiz, G., Pape, S., & Woolfolk Hoy, A. (2008, March). *Does teacher affective support matter? The role of affective support in middle school mathematics classrooms.* Paper presented at the annual meeting of the American Educational Research Association, New York, NY.

Salomon, G., & Perkins, D. N. (1989). Rocky roads to transfer: Re-thinking mechanisms of a neglected phenomenon. *Educational Psychologist, 24,* 113–142.

Sanchez, F., & Anderson, M. L. (1990, May). Gang mediation: A process that works. *Principal, 54*–56.

Sattler, J. M. (1992). *Assessment of children* (3rd ed. rev.). San Diego, CA: Jerome M. Sattler.

Sattler, J. M. (2001). *Assessment of children: Cognitive applications* (4th ed.). San Diego, CA: Jerome M. Sattler.

Sattler, J. M., & Hoge, R. D. (2006). *Assessment of Children: Behavioral, Social, and Clinical Foundations,* 5th edition. San Diego: Jerome M. Sattler, Publisher, Inc.

Savage, T. V. (1999). *Teaching self-control through management and discipline.* Boston, MA: Allyn & Bacon.

Savin-Williams, R. C., & Diamond, L. M. (2004). Sex. In R. M. Lerner & L. Steinberg (Eds.), *Handbook of adolescent psychology* (2nd ed., pp. 189–231). New York, NY: John Wiley & Sons.

Sawyer, R. J., Graham, S., & Harris, K. R. (1992). Direct teaching, strategy instruction, and strategy instruction with explicit self-regulation: Effects on the composition skills and self-efficacy of learning disabled students. *Journal of Educational Psychology, 84,* 340–352.

Sawyer, R. K. (2006a). *Explaining creativity: The science of human motivation.* New York, NY: Oxford University Press.

Sawyer, R. K. (2006b). Introduction: The new science of learning. In R. K. Sawyer (Ed.), *The Cambridge handbook of the learning sciences* (pp. 1–16). New York, NY: Cambridge.

Saxe, G. B. (1999). Source of concepts: A cross cultural-developmental perspective. In E. K. Scholnick, K. Nelson, S. A. Gelman, & P. H. Miller (Eds.), *Conceptual development: Piaget's legacy* (pp. 253–267). Mahwah, NJ: Erlbaum.

Scardamalia, M., & Bereiter, C. (1996). Adaptation and understanding: A case for new cultures of schooling. In S. Vosniado, E. De Corte, R. Glasse, & H. Mandl (Eds.), *International perspectives on the design of technology-supported learning environments* (pp. 149–163). Hillsdale, NJ: Erlbaum.

Schacter, D. L., Gilbert, D. T., & Wenger, D. M. (2009). *Psychology,* New York, NY: Worth.

Scheibe, C., & Rogow, F. (2004). *12 basic principles for incorporating media literacy and criticalthinking into any curriculum* (2nd ed.). Ithaca, NY: Project Look Sharp—Ithaca College.

Scherer, M. (1993). On savage inequalities: A conversation with Jonathan Kozol. *Educational Leadership, 50*(4), 4–9.

Scherer, M. (1999). The discipline of hope: A conversation with Herb Kohl. *Educational Leadership, 56*(1), 8–13.

Schiefele, U. (1991). Interest, learning, and motivation. *Educational Psychologist, 26*, 299–324.

Schmidt, H. G., van der Molen, H. T., te Winkel, W. W. R., & Wijnen, W. H. F. W. (2009). Constructivist, problem-based learning does work: A meta-analysis of curricular comparisons involving a single medical school. *Educational Psychologist, 44*: 1–23.

Schneider, W., & Bjorklund, D. F. (1992). Expertise, aptitude, and strategic remembering. *Child Development, 63*, 416–473.

Schoenfeld, A. H. (1989). Teaching mathematical thinking and problem solving. In L. B. Resnick & L. E. Klopfer (Eds.), *Toward the thinking curriculum: Current cognitive research* (pp. 83–103). Alexandria, VA: ASCD.

Schoenfeld, A. H. (1994). Mathematics thinking and problem solving. Hillsdale, NJ: Erlbaum.

Schoenfeld, A. H. (2011). *How we think: The theory of goal-oriented decision making and its educational applications*. New York, NY: Routledge.

Schommer, M. (1997). The development of epistemological beliefs among secondary students: A longitudinal study. Journal of Educational Psychology, 89, 37–40.

Schommer-Aikins, M. (2002). An evolving theoretical framework for an epistemological belief system. In B. K. Hofer & P. R. Pintrich (Eds.), Personal epistemology: The psychology of beliefs about knowledge and knowing (pp. 103–118). Mahwah, NJ: Erlbaum.

Schonert-Reichl, K. A. (1994). Gender differences in depressive symptomatology and egocentrism in adolescence. *Journal of Early Adolescence, 14*, 49–65.

Schonert-Reichl, K. A. & Hymel, S. (2007). Educating the heart as well as the mind: Social and emotional learning for school and life success. *Education Canada, 42 (2)*, 20–25.

Schraw, G. (2006). In P. A Alexander & P. H. Winne (Eds.), *Handbook of educational psychology* (2nd ed., pp. 825–847). Mahwah, NJ: Erlbaum.

Schraw, G., & Olafson, L. (2002). Teachers epistemological world views and educational practices. *Issues in Education, 8*, 99–148.

Schunk, D. H. (2000). *Learning theories: An educational perspective* (3rd ed.). Columbus, OH: Merrill/Prentice-Hall.

Schunk, D. H. (2004). *Learning theories: An educational perspective* (4th ed.). Columbus, OH: Merrill/Prentice-Hall.

Schunk, D. H. (2005). Self-regulated learning: The educational legacy of Paul R. Pintrich. *Educational Psychologist, 40*, 85–94.

Schunk, D. H. (2008). *Learning theories: An educational perspective* (5th ed.). Columbus, OH: Merrill/Prentice-Hall.

Schunk, D. H. (2012). *Learning theories: An educational perspective* (6th ed.). Boston, MA: Allyn & Bacon/Pearson.

Schunk, D. H., & Hanson, A. R. (1985). Peer models: Influence on children's self-efficacy and achievement. *Journal of Educational Psychology, 77*, 313–322.

Schunk, D. H., Pintrich, P. R., & Meece, J. L. (2008). *Motivation in education: Theory, research, and applications* (3rd ed.). Columbus, OH: Merrill/Prentice-Hall.

Schutz, P. A., & Davis, H. A. (2000). Emotions and self-regulations during test-taking. *Educational Psychologist, 35*, 243–256.

Schwab, J. J. (1973). The Practical 3: Translation into curriculum. *School Review, 81*, 501–522.

Schwartz, B., & Reisberg, D. (1991). *Learning and memory*. New York, NY: Norton.

Schwartz, B., Wasserman, E. A., & Robbins, S. J. (2002). *Psychology of learning and behavior* (5th ed.). New York, NY: W. W. Norton.

Schwarz, B. B., Neuman, Y., & Biezuner, S. (2000). Two wrongs may make a right . . . if they argue together! *Cognition and Instruction, 18*, 461–494.

Schworm, S., & Renkl, A. (2007). Learning argumentation skills through the use of prompts for self-explaining examples. *Journal of Educational Psychology, 99*, 285–295.

Scott, C. L. (1999). Teachers' biases toward creative children. *Creativity Research Journal, 12*, 321–337.

Seaton, M., Marsh, H. W., & Craven, R. G. (2009). Big-fish-little-pond effect: Generalizability and Moderation—Two sides of the same coin. *American Educational Research Journal, 47*(2): 390–433.

Seligman, M. E. P. (1975). *Helplessness: On depression, development, and death*. San Francisco, CA: Freeman.

Seligman, M. E. P. (2006). *Learned optimism: How to change your mind and your life* (2nd ed.). New York, NY: Pocket Books.

Selman, R. L. (1980). *The growth of interpersonal understanding*. New York, NY: Academic Press.

Semb, G. B., & Ellis, J. A. (1994). Knowledge taught in school: What is remembered? *Review of Educational Research, 64*, 253–286.

Sénéchal, M., & LeFevre, J. A. (2002). Parental involvement in the development of children's reading skills: A five-year longitudinal study. *Child Development, 73*, 445–460.

Senghas, A., & Coppola, M. (2001). Children creating language: How Nicaraguan sign language acquired a spatial grammar. *Psychological Science, 12*(4): 323–328.

Serpell, R. (1993). Interface between sociocultural and psychological aspects of cognition. In E. Forman, N. Minick, & C. A. Stone (Eds.), *Contexts for learning: Sociocultural dynamics in children's development* (pp. 357–368). New York, NY: Oxford University Press.

Sesma, H. W., Mahone, E. M., Levine, T., Eason, S. H., & Cutting, L. E. (2009). The contribution of executive function skills to reading comprehension. *Child Neuropsychology, 3*, 232–46.

Shaffer, D. W. (2010). *The Bicycle Helmets of "Amsterdam": Computer games and the problem of transfer* (Epistemic Games Group Working Paper No. 2010-01). Madison, WI: University of Wisconsin-Madison.

Shaffer, D. W., Hatfield, D., Svarovsky, G. N., Nash, P., Nulty, A., Bagley, E., . . . Mislevy, R. J. (2009). Epistemic network analysis: A prototype for 21st century assessment of learning. *International Journal of Learning Media, 1* (2), 33–53.

Shapka, J. D., & Keating, D.P. (2003). Effects of a girls-only curriculum during adolescence: Performance, persistence, and engagement in mathematics and science. *American Education Research Journal, 40*, 929–960.

Shapka, J. D., & Keating, D. P. (2005). Structure and change in self-concept during adolescence. *Canadian Journal of Behavioural Sciences, 37*, 83–96.

Shavelson, R. J. (1987). Planning. In M. Dunkin (Ed.), *The international encyclopedia of teaching and teacher education* (pp. 483–486). New York, NY: Pergamon Press.

Shaywitz, B. A., Shaywitz, S.E., Blachman, B. A., Pugh, K. R., Fulbright, R. K., Skudlarski, P., . . . Gore, J.C. (2004). Development of left occipitotemporal systems for skilled reading in children after a phonologically-based intervention. *Biological Psychiatry, 55*, 926–933.

Sheets, R. H. (2005). *Diversity pedagogy: Examining the role of culture in the teaching-learning process*. Boston, MA: Allyn & Bacon.

Shepard, L. A., & Smith, M. L. (1989). Academic and emotional effects of kindergarten retention. In L. Shepard & M. Smith (Eds.), *Flunking grades: Research and policies on retention* (pp. 79–107). Philadelphia, PA: Falmer Press.

Sherwood, R. D. (2002). Problem-based multimedia software for middle grades science: Development issues and an initial field study. *Journal of Computers in Mathematics and Science Teaching, 21*, 147–165.

Shields, P., Gordon, J., & Dupree, D. (1983). Influence of parent practices upon the reading achievement of good and poor readers. *Journal of Negro Education, 52*, 436–445.

Shih, S. S. (2008). The relation of self-determination and achievement goals to Taiwanese eighth graders' behavioral and emotional engagement in schoolwork. *The Elementary School Journal, 108*, 313–334.

Shonkoff, J. P. (2006). A promising opportunity for developmental and behavioral pediatrics at the interface of neuroscience, psychology, and social policy: remarks on receiving the 2005 C. Anderson Aldrich Award. *Pediatrics, 118*, 2187–2191.

Shu, H., McBride-Chang, C., Wu, S., & Liu, H. (2006). Understanding Chinese developmental dyslexia: Morphological awareness as a core cognitive construct. *Journal of Educational Psychology, 98*, 122–133.

Shuell, T. J. (1986). Cognitive conceptions of learning. *Review of Educational Research, 56*, 411–436.

Shuell, T. J. (1990). Phases of meaningful learning. *Review of Educational Psychology, 60*, 531–548.

Shuell, T. J. (1996). Teaching and learning in a classroom context. In D. Berliner & R. Calfee (Eds.), *Handbook of educational psychology* (pp. 726–764). New York, NY: Macmillan.

Shulman, L. S. (1987). Knowledge and teaching: Foundations of the new reform. *Harvard Educational Review, 19*(2), 4–14.

Shultz, J., & Florio, S. (1979). Stop and freeze: The negotiation of social and physical space in a kindergarten/first grade classroom. *Anthropology and Education Quarterly, 10*, 166–181.

Shute, V. J. (2008). Focus on formative feedback. *Review of Educational Research, 78*, 153–189.

Siddle Walker, V. (2001). African American teaching in the South: 1940–1960. *Review of Educational Research, 38*, 751–779.

Siegel, J., & Shaughnessy, M. F. (1994). Educating for understanding: An interview with Howard Gardner. *Phi Delta Kappan, 75*, 536–566.

Siegel, L. S. (1989). IQ is irrelevant to the definition of learning disabilities. *Journal of Learning Disabilities, 22*, 469–479.

Siegel, L. S. (1999). Issues in the definition and diagnosis of learning disabilities. *Journal of Learning Disabilities, 32*, 304–319.

Siegel, L. S. (2003). Basic cognitive processes and reading disabilities. In H. L. Swanson, K. R.

Harris, & S. Graham (Eds.), *Handbook of learning disabilities* (pp. 158–181). New York, NY: Guilford Press.

Siegler, R. S. (1993). Adaptive and non-adaptive characteristics of low-income children's mathematical strategy use. In B. Penner (Ed.), *The challenge in mathematics and science education: Psychology's response* (pp. 341–366). Washington, DC: American Psychological Association.

Siegler, R. S. (1998). *Children's thinking* (3rd ed.). Upper Saddle River, NJ: Prentice-Hall.

Siegler, R. S. (2000). The rebirth of children's learning. *Child Development, 71*, 26–35.

Siegler, R. S. (2004). Turning memory development inside out. *Developmental Review, 24*, 469–475.

Siegler, R. S., & Alibali, M. W. (2005). *Children's thinking* (4th ed.). Upper Saddle River, NJ: Prentice-Hall.

Siegler, R. S., & Crowley, K. (1991). The microgenetic method: A direct means for studying cognitive development. *American Psychologist, 56*, 606–620.

Sillars, L. (1995). Studying crime in school. *Alberta Report, 22*(25), 37.

Silvén, M. (2001). Attention in very young infants predicts learning of first words. *Infant Behavior & Development, 24*, 229–237.

Silven, M., Poskiparata, E., Niemi, P., & Voeten, M. (2007). Precursors of reading skill from infancy to first grade in Finnish: Continuity and change in a highly inflected language. *Journal of Educational Psychology, 99*, 516–531.

Silverman, S. K. (2008, April, 11). Personal communication, Columbus, Ohio.

Simon, D. P., & Chase, W. G. (1973). Skill in chess. *American Scientist, 61*, 394–403.

Simon, H. A. (1995). The information-processing view of mind. *American Psychologist, 50*, 507–508.

Simon, T. (2010). Rewards and challenges of cognitive neuroscience studies of persons with intellectual and developmental disabilities. Special Issue for the *American Journal on Intellectual and Developmental Disabilities, 115*, 79-82. doi: 10.1352/1944-7558-115.2.79.

Simonton, D. K. (1999). Creativity from a historiometric perspective. In R. J. Sternberg (Ed.), *Handbook of creativity* (pp. 116–133). New York, NY: Cambridge University Press.

Simonton, D. K. (2000). Creativity: Cognitive, personal, developmental, and social aspects. *American Psychologist, 55*, 151–158.

Simpson, E. J. (1972). *The classification of educational objectives in the psychomotor domain: The psychomotor domain* (Vol. 3). Washington, DC: Gryphon House.

Sinatra, G. M. (2005). The "Warming Trend" in conceptual change research: The legacy of Paul R. Pintrich. *Educational Psychologist, 40*, 107–115.

Sinatra, G. M., & Mason, L. (2008). Beyond knowledge: Learner characteristics influencing conceptual change. In S. Vosniadou (Ed.), *International handbook of research on conceptual change*. Mahwah, NJ: Erlbaum.

Sinatra, G. M., & Taasoobshirazi, G. (2011). Intentional conceptual change: The self-regulation of sciene learning. In B. Zimmerman & D. Schunk (Eds.), *Handbook of self-regulation of learning and performance* (pp. 203–216). New York, NY: Routledge.

Singley, K., & Anderson, J. R. (1989). *The transfer of cognitive skill*. Cambridge, MA: Harvard University Press.

Sio, U. N., & Ormerod, T. C. (2009). Does incubation enhance problem solving? A meta-analytic review. *Psychological Bulletin, 135*(1): 94–120.

Sirin, S. R. (2005). Socioeconomic status and academic achievement: A meta-analytic review of research. *Review of Educational Research, 75*, 417–453.

Sisk, D. A. (1988). Children at risk: The identification of the gifted among the minority. *Gifted Education International, 5*, 138–141.

Skiba, R. J., Michael, R. S., Nardo, A. C., & Peterson, R. (2000). *The color of discipline: Sources of racial and gender disproportionality in school punishment* (Report #SRS1). Bloomington, IN: Indiana Education Policy Center.

Skinner, B. F. (1950). Are theories of learning necessary? *Psychological Review, 57*, 193–216.

Skinner, B. F. (1953). Science and human behavior. New York, NY: Macmillan.

Skinner, B. F. (1989). The origins of cognitive thought. *American Psychologist, 44*, 13–18.

Skoe, E. E. A. (1998). The ethic of care: Issues in moral development. In E. E. A. Skoe & A. L. von der Lippe (Eds.), *Personality development in adolescence* (pp. 143–171). London, England: Routledge.

Slaby, R. G., Roedell, W. C., Arezzo, D., & Hendrix, K. (1995). *Early violence prevention*. Washington, DC: National Association for the Education of Young Children.

Slater, L. (2002, February 3). The trouble with self-esteem. *The New York Times Magazine*, pp. 44–47.

Slavin, R. E. (1995). *Cooperative learning* (2nd ed.). Boston, MA: Allyn & Bacon.

Slavin, R. E. (2002). Evidence-based education policies: Transforming education practice and research. *Educational Researcher, 31*(7), 15–21.

Slavin, R. E., Lake, C., Chambers, B., Cheung, A., & Davis, S. (2009). Effective reading programs for the elementary grades: A best-evidence synthesis. *Review of Educational Research, 79*(4), 1391–1465.

Smetana, J. G. (2000). Middle-class African American adolescents' and parents' conceptions of parental authority and parenting practices: A longitudinal investigation. *Child Development, 71*, 1672–1686.

Smith, C. B. (Moderator). (1994). *Whole language: The debate*. Bloomington, IN: EDINFO Press.

Smith, C. R. (2004). *Learning disabilities: The interaction of learner, task, and setting* (5th ed.). Boston, MA: Allyn & Bacon.

Smith, C. S., & Hung, L-C. (2008). Stereotype threat: Effects on education. *Social Psychology of Education, 11*, 243–257.

Smith, D. D. (1998). *Introduction to special education: Teaching in an age of challenge* (3rd ed.). Boston, MA: Allyn & Bacon.

Smith, D. D. (2006). *Introduction to special education: Teaching in an age of opportunity* (5th ed.). Boston, MA: Allyn & Bacon.

Smith, E. E., & Kosslyn, S. M. *Cognitive Psychology: Mind and Brain*. Pearson.

Smith, F. (1975). *Comprehension and learning: A conceptual framework for teachers*. New York, NY: Holt, Rinehart & Winston.

Smith, J. K., Smith, L. F., & De Lisi, R. (2001). *Natural classroom assessment: Designing seamless instruction and assessment*. Thousand Oaks, CA: Corwin Press.

Smith, J. L., Sansone, C., & White, P. H. (2007). The stereotyped task process: The role of interest and achievement motivation. *Journal of Educational Psychology, 88*, 99–114.

Smith, S. M., Glenberg, A., & Bjork, R. A. (1978). Environmental context and human memory. *Memory and Cognition, 6*, 342–353.

Smyke, A. T., Zeanah, C. H., Fox, N. A., Nelson, C. A. & Guthrie, D. (2010). Placement in foster care enhances quality of attachment among young institutionalized children. *Child Development, 81*, 212–223.

Snapp, M., & Woolfolk, A. E. (1973, March). An examination of children in special education over a thirteen-year period. Paper presented at the National Association of School Psychologists, 5th Annual Meeting, New York.

Snider, V. E. (1990). What we know about learning styles from research in special education. *Educational Leadership, 48*(2), 53.

Snow, C. E. (1977). The development of conversation between mothers and babies. *Journal of Child Language, 4*, l–22.

Snow, C. E. (1993). Families as social contexts for literacy development. In C. Daiute (Ed.), *New directions for child development* (No. 61, pp. 11–24). San Francisco, CA: Josey-Bass.

Snow, R. E. (1995). Pygmalion and intelligence. *Current Directions in Psychological Science, 4*, 169–171.

Snow, R. E., Corno, L., & Jackson, D. (1996). Individual differences in affective and cognitive functions. In D. Berliner & R. Calfee (Eds.), *Handbook of educational psychology* (pp. 243–310). New York, NY: Macmillan.

Snowman, J. (1984). Learning tactics and strategies. In G. Phye & T. Andre (Eds.), *Cognitive instructional psychology* (pp. 243–275). Orlando, FL: Academic Press.

Soar, R. S., & Soar, R. M. (1979). Emotional climate and management. In P. Peterson & H. Walberg (Eds.), *Research on teaching: Concepts, findings, and implications* (pp. 97–119). Berkeley, CA: McCutchan.

Soares, D. A., Vannest, K. J., & Harrison, J. R. (2009). Computer aided self-monitoring to increase academic production and reduce self-injurious behavior in a child with autism. *Behavioral Interventions, 24*(3): 171–183.

Sobesky, W. E. (1983). The effects of situational factors on moral judgment. *Child Development, 54*, 575–584.

Society for Research in Child Development (SRCD). (2009). Young Hispanic children: Boosting opportunities for learning. *Society for Research in Child Development: Social Policy Report Briefs, 23* (2), 1–2.

Sokolove, S., Garrett, J., Sadker, D., & Sadker, M. (1986). Interpersonal communications skills. In J. Cooper (Ed.), *Classroom teaching skills: A handbook* (pp. 233–278). Lexington, MA: D. C. Heath.

Solomon, D., Watson, M. S., & Battistich, V. A. (2001). Teaching and schooling effects on moral/prosocial development. In V. Richardson (Ed.), *Handbook of research on teaching* (4th ed., pp. 566–603). Washington, DC: American Educational Research Association.

Soodak, L. C., & McCarthy, M. R. (2006). Classroom management in inclusive settings. In C. M. Evertson & C. S. Weinstein (Eds.), *Handbook of classroom management: Research, practice, and contemporary issues*. Mahwah, NJ: Erlbaum.

Sotillo, S. M. (2002). Finding our voices, finding ourselves: Becoming bilingual and bicultural. In G. S. Boutte (Ed.), *Resounding voices: School experiences of people from diverse ethnic backgrounds* (pp. 275–307). Boston, MA: Allyn & Bacon.

Spearman, C. (1927). *The abilities of man: Their nature and measurement*. New York, NY: Macmillan.

Spencer, M. B., & Markstrom-Adams, C. (1990). Identity processes among racial and ethnic-minority children in America. *Child Development, 61*, 290–310.

Spencer, M. B., Noll, E., Stoltzfus, J., & Harpalani, V. (2001). Identity and school adjustment: Questioning the "Acting White" assumption. *Educational Psychologist, 36*(1), 21–30.

Spera, C. (2005). A review of the relationship among parenting practices, parenting styles, and adolescent school achievement. *Educational Psychology Review, 17*, 125–146.

Sperling, G. (1960). The information available in brief visual presentations. *Psychological Monographs, 74* (11, Whole No. 498).

Spinelli, C. G. (2002). *Classroom assessment for students with special needs in inclusive classrooms.* Upper Saddle River, NJ: Merrill/Prentice-Hall.

Spiro, R. J., Feltovich, P. J., Jacobson, M. L., & Coulson, R. L. (1991). Cognitive flexibility, constructivism, and hypertext: Random access instruction for advanced knowledge acquisition in ill-structured domains. *Educational Technology, 31*(5), 24–33.

Sprague, J., & Walker, H. (2000). Early identification and intervention for youth with antisocial and violent behavior. *Exceptional Children, 66*, 367–379.

Sprenger, M. (2005). In side Amy's brain. *Educational Leadership, 62*(7), 28–32.

Sprenger, M. (2010). *Brain-based teaching in the digital age.* Alexandria, VA: Association for Supervision and Curriculum Development.

Stage, S. A., Jackson, H. G., Erickson M. J., Moscovitz, K. K., Bush, J. W., Violette, H. D., . . . Pious, C. (2008). A validity study of functionally-based behavioral consultation with students with emotional/behavioral disabilities. *School Psychology Quarterly, 23*, 327–353.

Stahl, S. A. (2002). Different strokes for different folks? In L. Abbeduto (Ed.), *Taking sides: Clashing on controversial issues in educational psychology* (pp. 98–107). Guilford, CT: McGraw-Hill/Duskin.

Stahl, S. A., & Miller, P. D. (1989). Whole language and language experience approaches for beginning reading: A quantitative research synthesis. *Review of Educational Research, 59*, 87–116.

Stahl, S. A., & Yaden, D. B. Jr. (2004). The development of literacy in preschool and primary grades: Work by the Center for the Improvement of Early Reading Achievement. *The Elementary School Journal, 82*, 141–166.

Stanovich, K. E. (1992). *How to think straight about psychology* (3rd ed.). Glenview, IL: Scott, Foresman.

Stanovich, P. J., & Jordan, A. (1998). Canadian teachers' and principals' beliefs about inclusive education as predictors of effective teaching in heterogeneous classrooms. *Elementary School Journal, 98*, 221–238.

Star, J. R., & Rittle-Johnson, B. (2009). It pays to compare: An experimental study on computational estimation. *Journal of Experimental Child Psychology, 102*, 408–426.

STAR Legacy Cycle. Retreived from https://repo.vanth.org/portal/public-content/star-legacy-cycle/star-legacy-cycle

Starch, D., & Elliot, E. C. (1913a). Reliability of grading work in history. *Scholastic Review, 21*, 676–681.

Starch, D., & Elliot, E. C. (1913b). Reliability of grading work in mathematics. *Scholastic Review, 21*, 254–259.

Statistics Canada. (2006, March 31). Television viewing. *The Daily.* Retrieved from www.statcan.gc.ca/daily-quotidien/060331/dq060331b-eng.htm

Statistics Canada. (2008). Socioeconomic status (SES). Retrieved from www.statcan.gc.ca/pub/81-004-x/def/4068719-eng.htm#tphp

Statistics Canada. (2010a). Characteristics of individuals using the Internet. Retrieved from www40.statcan.gc.ca/l01/cst01/comm35a-eng.htm

Statistics Canada. (2010b). Father's day . . . by the numbers. Retrieved from www42.statcan.ca/smr08/2010/smr08_143_2010-eng.htm

Statistics Canada. (2010c). Internet use by individuals, by selected characteristics. Detailed tables from CANSIM. Retrieved from http://cansim2.statcan.gc.ca/cgi-win/cnsmcgi.exe?Lang=E&ResultTemplate=CST&CORCmd=GetCRel&CORId=COMM35A&CORRel=4

Statistics Canada. (2010d). Study: Projections of the diversity of the Canadian population. Retrieved from www.statcan.gc.ca/daily-quotidien/100309/dq100309a-eng.htm

Statistics Canada. (2011). Aboriginal peoples and language. Retrieved March 8, 2014, from www12.statcan.gc.ca/nhs-enm/2011/as-sa/99-011-x/99-011-x2011003_1-eng.cfm

Statistics Canada. (2012). Body mass index of Canadian children and youth, 2009–2011. Retrieved June 10, 2014, from www.statcan.gc.ca/pub/82-625-x/2012001/article/11712-eng.htm

Statistics Canada. (2013). Immigration and ethnocultural diversity in Canada: National Household Survey, 2011. Retrieved June 2, 2014, from www12.statcan.gc.ca/nhs-enm/2011/as-sa/99-010-x/99-010-x2011001-eng.cfm

Statistics Canada. (2014). Linguistic Characteristics of Canadians. Retrieved March 8, 2014, from www12.statcan.gc.ca/census-recensement/2011/as-sa/98-314-x/98-314-x2011001-eng.cfm

Steele, C. (1992). *Race and the schooling of African-Americans.* Atlantic Monthly, 269(4), 68–78.

Steele, K. M., Bass, K. E., & Crook, M. D. (1999). The mystery of the Mozart effect: Failure to replicate. *Psychological Science, 10*, 366–368.

Stefanou, C. R., Perencevich, K. C., DiCintio, M., & Turner, J. C. (2004). Supporting autonomy in the classroom: Ways teachers encourage student decision making and ownership. *Educational Psychologist, 39*, 97–110.

Steinberg, L. (1996). *Beyond the classroom: Why schools are failing and what parents need to do.* New York, NY: Simon & Schuster.

Steinberg, L. (1998). Standards outside the classroom. In D. Ravitch (Ed.), *Brookings papers on educational policy* (pp. 319–358). Washington, DC: Brookings Institute.

Steinberg, L. (2005). *Adolescence* (7th ed.). New York, NY: McGraw-Hill.

Steinberg, L. (2008). A social neuroscience perspective on adolescent risk-taking. *Developmental Review, 28*, 78–106.

Stemler, S. E., Sternberg, R. J., Grigorenko, E. L., Jarvin, L., & Sharpes, K. (2009). Using the theory of successful intelligence as a framework for developing assessments in AP physics. *Contemporary Educational Psychology, 34*(3): 195–209.

Sternberg, R. J. (1985). *Beyond IQ: A triarchic theory of human intelligence.* New York, NY: Cambridge University Press.

Sternberg, R. J. (1997). *Successful intelligence.* New York, NY: Plume.

Sternberg, R. J. (1999). *Cognitive psychology* (2nd ed.). Fort Worth, TX: Harcourt Brace.

Sternberg, R. J. (2000). *Handbook of human intelligence.* New York, NY: Cambridge University Press.

Sternberg, R. J. (2004). Culture and intelligence. *American Psychologist, 59*, 325–338.

Sternberg, R. J., & Davidson, J. (1982, June). The mind of the puzzler. *Psychology Today*, 37–44.

Sternberg, R. J., & Detterman, D. L. (Eds.). (1986). *What is intelligence? Contemporary viewpoints on its nature and definition.* Norwood, NJ: Ablex.

Sternberg, R. J., & Sternberg, K. (2012). *Cognitive psychology* (6th ed.). Belmont, CA: Wadsworth.

Sternberg, R. J., & Wagner, R. K. (1993). The geocentric view of intelligence and job performance is wrong. *Current Directions in Psychological Science, 2*, 1–5.

Sternberg, R. J., Wagner, R. K., Williams, W. M., & Horvath, J. A. (1995). Testing common sense. *American Psychologist, 50*, 912–927.

Stevens, R. J. & Slavin, R. E. (1995). The cooperative elementary school: Effects on students' achievement, attitudes, and social relations. *American Educational Research Journal, 32*, 321–351.

Stevenson, H. W., & Stigler, J. (1992). *The learning gap.* New York, NY: Summit Books.

Stewart, L., Henson, R., Kampe, K., Walsh, V., Turner, R., & Frith, U. (2003). Brain changes after learning to read and play music. *NeuroImage, 20*(1), 71–83.

Stice, E., & Shaw, H. (2004). Eating disorder prevention programs: A meta-analytic review. *Psychological Bulletin, 130*, 206–227.

Stiggins, R. J., & Chappuis, J. (2005). Using student-involved classroom assessment to close achievement gaps. *Theory Into Practice, 44*, 11–18.

Stigler, J. W., Lee, S., & Stevenson, H. W. (1987). Mathematics classrooms in Japan, Taiwan, and the United States. *Child Development, 58*, 1272–1285.

Stinson, D. W. (2006). African American male adolescents, schooling, (an mathematics): Deficiency, rejection, and achievement. *Review of Educational Research, 76*, 477–506.

Stipek, D. J. (1981). Children's perceptions of their own and their peers' academic competence. *Journal of Educational Psychology, 73*, 404–410.

Stipek, D. J. (1993). *Motivation to learn* (2nd ed.). Boston, MA: Allyn & Bacon.

Stipek, D. J. (2002). *Motivation to learn: Integrating theory and practice* (4th ed.). Boston, MA: Allyn & Bacon.

Stipek, D. (2006). Relationships matter. *Educational Leadership, 64*(1), 46–49.

Stipek, D., de la Sota, A., & Weishaupt, L. (1999). Life lessons: An embedded classroom approach to preventing high-risk behaviors among preadolescents. *The Elementary School Journal, 99*, 433–451.

Stodolsky, S. S. (1988). *The subject matters: Classroom activity in math and social studies.* Chicago, IL: University of Chicago Press.

Stoeger, H. & Ziegler, A. (2011). Self-regulatory training through elementary students' homework completion. In B. Zimmerman & D. Schunk (Eds.), *Handbook of self-regulation of learning and performance* (pp. 87–101). New York: Routledge.

Storch, S., & Whitehurst, G. (2002). Oral language and code-related precursors to reading: Evidence from a longitudinal structural model. *Developmental Psychology, 38*, 934–947.

Stormont, M., Stebbins, M. S., & Holliday, G. (2001). Characteristics and educational support needs of underrepresented gifted adolescents. *Psychology in the Schools, 38*, 413–423.

Stormshak, E. A., Bierman, K. L., Bruschi, C., Dodge, K. A., & Coie, J. D. (1999). The relation between behavior problems and peer preference in different classroom contexts. *Child Development, 70*, 169–182.

Strom, P. S., & Strom, R. D. (2005). Cyberbullying by adolescents: A preliminary assessment. *The Educational Forum, 70*(1), 21–36.

Stumpf, H. (1995). Gender differences on test of cognitive abilities: Experimental design issues and empirical results. *Learning and Individual Differences, 7*, 275–288.

Subrahmanyam, K., Greenfield, P., Kraut, R., & Gross, E. (2001). The impact of computer use on children's and adolescents' development. *Applied Developmental Psychology, 22*, 7–30.

Suldo, S. M., Friedrich, A. A., White, T., Farmer, J., Minch, D., & Michalowski, J. (2009). Teacher support and adolescents' subjective well-being: A mixed-methods investigation. *School Psychology Review, 38*(1), 67–85.

Sullivan, K. (2000). *The anti-bullying handbook.* New York, NY: Oxford University Press.

Sullivan, M. A., & O'Leary, S. G. (1990). Maintenance following reward and cost token programs. *Behavior Therapy, 21*, 139–149.

Suzuki, B. H. (1983). The education of Asian and Pacific Americans: An introductory overview. In D. Nakanishi & M. HiranoNakanishi (Eds.), *The education of Asian and Pacific Americans: Historical perspectives and prescriptions for the future* (pp. 1–14). Phoenix, AZ: Oryx Press.

Svoboda, J. S. (2001). Review of *Boys and girls learn differently.*The Men's Resource Network. Retrieved from www.themenscenter.com/mensight/reviews/Svoboda/boys and girls.htm

Swanson, H. L. (1990). The influence of metacognitive knowledge and aptitude on problem solving. *Journal of Educational Psychology, 82*, 306–314.

Swanson, H. L. (2001). Research on interventions for adolescents with learning disabilities: A meta-analysis of outcomes related to higher-order processing. *The Elementary School Journal, 101*, 332–348.

Swanson, H.L., & Saez, L. (2003). Memory difficulties in children and adults with learning disabilities. In H. L. Swanson, S. Graham, & K. R. Harris (Eds.), *Handbook of learning disabilities*, pp. 182–198. New York: Guildford Press.

Swearer, S. M., Espelage, D. L., Vaillancourt, T. & Hymel, S. (2010). What can be done about school bullying? Linking research to educational practice. *Educational Researcher, 39*(1), 38–47.

Sweeney, W. J., Salva, E., Cooper, J. O., & Talbert-Johnson, C. (1993). Using self-evaluation to improve difficult to read handwriting for secondary students. *Journal of Behavioral Education, 3*, 427–443.

Sweller, J., Kirschner, P. A., & Clark, R. E. (2007). Why minimally guided teaching techniques do not work: A reply to commentaries. *Educational Psychologist, 42*, 115–121.

Sweller, J., van Merriënboer, J. J. G., & Paas, F. G. W. C. (1998). Cognitive architecture and instructional design. *Educational Psychology Review, 10*, 251–296.

Sylvester, R. (2003). *A biological brain in a cultural classroom* (2nd ed.). Thousand Oaks, CA: Sage.

Symons, S., Woloshyn, V., & Pressley, M. (1994). The scientific evaluation of the whole language approach to literacy development [Special issue]. *Educational Psychologist, 29*(4).

Syvertsen, A. K., Flanagan, C. A., & Stout, M. (2009). Code of Silence: Students' perceptions of school climate and willingness to intervene in a peer's dangerous plan. *Journal of Educational Psychology, 101*(1), 219–232.

Tait, H., & Entwistle, N. J. (1998). Identifying students at risk through ineffective study strategies. *Higher Education, 31*, 97–116.

Talbot, M. (2002, February 24). Girls just want to be mean. *The New York Times Magazine*, pp. 24–29+.

Tallal, P., & Miller, S. L. (2003). How the brain learns to read. *Middle Matters, 12*(1), 7.

Tang, Y., Zhang, W., Chen, K., Feng, S., Ji, Y. Shen, J, . . . Liu, Y. (2006). Arithmetic processing in the brain shaped by cultures. *Proceedings of the National Academy of Sciences USA, 103*, 10775–10780.

Taylor, E. (1998). Clinical foundation of hyperactivity research. *Behavioural Brain Research, 94*, 11–24.

Taylor, R. L., Richards, S. B., & Brady, M. (2005). *Mental retardation: Historical perspectives, current practices, and future trends.* Boston: Pearson/Allyn & Bacon.

TenBrink, T. D. (2003). Assessment. In J. Cooper (Ed.), *Classroom teaching skills* (7th ed., pp. 311–353). Boston, MA: Houghton-Mifflin.

TenBrink, T. D. (2006). Assessment. In J. Cooper (Ed.), *Classroom teaching skills* (8th ed., pp. 55–78). Boston, MA: Houghton-Mifflin.

Tenenbaum, H. R., & Ruck, M.D. (2007). Are teachers' expectations different for racial minority than for European American students? A meta-analysis. *Journal of Educational Psychology, 99*, 253–273.

Terman, L. M., Baldwin, B. T., & Bronson, E. (1925). Mental and physical traits of a thousand gifted children. In L. M. Terman (Ed.), *Genetic studies of genius* (Vol. 1). Stanford, CA: Stanford University Press.

Terman, L. M., & Oden, M. H. (1947). The gifted child grows up. In L. M. Terman (Ed.), *Genetic studies of genius* (Vol. 4). Stanford, CA: Stanford University Press.

Terman, L. M., & Oden, M. H. (1959). The gifted group in mid-life. In L. M. Terman (Ed.), *Genetic studies of genius* (Vol. 5). Stanford, CA: Stanford University Press.

Tesser, A., Stapel, D. A., & Wood, J. V. (2002). *Self and motivation: Emerging psychological perspectives.* Washington, DC: American Psychological Association.

Tharp, R. G. (1989). Psychocultural variables and constants: Effects on teaching and learning in schools. *American Psychologist, 44*, 349–359.

Tharp, R. G., & Gallimore, R. (1988). *Rousing minds to life: Teaching, learning, and schooling in social context.* New York, NY: Cambridge University Press.

Theodore, L. A., Bray, M. A., Kehle, T. J., & Jenson, W. R. (2001). Randomization of group contingencies and reinforcers for reduce classroom disruptive behavior. *Journal of School Psychology, 39*, 267–277.

Thomas, K. T., & Thomas, J. R. (2008). Principles of motor development for elementary school physical education. *The Elementary School Journal, 108*, 181–195.

Thompson, A., Hollis, C., & Richards, D. (2003). Authoritarian parenting attitudes as a risk for conduct problems. *European Child & Adolescent Psychiatry, 12*, 84.

Thompson, G. (2008). Beneath the apathy. *Educational Leadership, 65*(6), 50–54.

Thompson, R. A., & Raikes, H. A. (2003). Toward the next quarter-century: Conceptual and methodological challenges for attachment theory. *Development and Psychopathology, 15*, 691–718.

Tierney, R. J., Readence, J. E., & Dishner, E. K. (1990). *Reading strategies and practices: A compendium* (3rd ed.). Boston, MA: Allyn & Bacon.

Tierney, W. G. (1993). *Building communities of difference: Higher education in the twenty-first century.* Westport, CT: Bergin and Garvey.

TIMSS. (1998). *Third International Mathematics and Science Study.* Washington, DC: National Center for Educational Statistics. Available online at: http://nces.ed.gov/timss/

Tingstrom, D. H., Sterling-Turner, H. E., & Wilczynski, S. M. (2006). The Good Behavior Game: 1962–2002. *Behavior Modification, 30*, 225–253.

Tishman, S., Perkins, D., & Jay, E. (1995). *The thinking classroom: Creating a culture of thinking.* Boston, MA: Allyn & Bacon.

Tobias, S. (2010). Generative learning theory, paradigm shifts, and constructivism in educational psychology: A tribute to Merl Wittrock. *Educational Psychologist, 45*, 51–54.

Tobler, N., & Stratton, H. (1997). Effectiveness of school based drug prevention programs: A meta-analysis of the research. *Journal of Primary Prevention, 18*: 71–128.

Tollefson, N. (2000). Classroom applications of cognitive theories of motivation. *Education Psychology Review, 12*, 63–83.

Tomasello, M. (2006). Acquiring linguistic constructions. In D. Kuhn & R. S. Siegler (Eds.), *Handbook of child psychology: Vol. 2. Cognition, language, and perception* (6th ed., pp. 255–298). New York, NY: Wiley.

Tomasello, M., Kruger, A. C., & Ratner, H. H. (1993). Cultural learning. *Behavioral and Brain Sciences, 16*, 495–552.

Tomlinson, C. A. (2003). *Fulfilling the promise of the differentiated classroom.* Alexandria, VA: Association for Supervision and Curriculum Development.

Tomlinson, C. A. (2005a). Grading and differentiation: Paradox or good practice? *Theory Into Practice, 44*, 262–269.

Tomlinson, C. A. (2005b, Summer). Differentiating instruction. *Theory Into Practice, 44*(3).

Tomporowski, P. D., Davis, C. L., Miller, P. H., & Naglieri, J. A. (2008). Exercise and children's intelligence, cognition, and academic achievement. *Educational Psychology Review, 20*(2), 111–131.

Toppo, G. (2003, January 13). School violence hits lower grades: Experts who see violent behavior in younger kids blame parents, prenatal medical problems and an angry society; educators search for ways to cope. *USAToday.* Retrieved from www.usatoday.com/educate/college/education/articles/20030119.htm

Torrance, E. P. (1972). Predictive validity of the Torrance tests of creative thinking. Journal of Creative Behavior, 6, 236–262. Torrance, E. P. (1986). Teaching creative and gifted learners. In M. Wittrock (Ed.), *Handbook of research on teaching* (3rd ed., pp. 630–647). New York, NY: Macmillan.

Torrance, E. P. (1986). Teaching creative and gifted learners. In M. Wittrock (Ed.), *Handbook of research on teaching* (3rd ed., pp. 630–647). New York, NY: Macmillan.

Torrance, E. P., & Hall, L. K. (1980). Assessing the future reaches of creative potential. *Journal of Creative Behavior, 14*, 1–19.

Toth, E., Klahr, D., & Chen, Z. (2000). Bridging research and practice: A cognitively based classroom intervention for teaching experimentation to elementary school children. *Cognition and Instruction, 18*, 423–459.

Trautwein, U. (2007). The homework–achievement relation reconsidered: Differentiating homework time, homework frequency, and homework effort. *Learning and Instruction, 17*, 372–388.

Trautwein, U., & Lüdtke, O. (2007). Students' self-reported effort and time on homework in six school subjects: Between-students differences and within-student variation. *Journal of Educational Psychology, 99,* 232–234.

Trautwein, U., Schnyder, I., Niggli, A., Neumann, M. & Lüdtke, O. (2009). Chameleon effects in homework research: The homework-achievement association depends on the measures used and the level of analysis chosen. *Contemporary Educational Psychology, 34,* 77–88.

Tremblay, R. E., Boulerice, B., Harden, P. W., McDuff, P., Perusse, D., Pihl, R. O., & Zoccolillo, M. (1996). Do children in Canada become more aggressive as they approach adolescence? In *Growing up in Canada: National Longitudinal Survey of Children and Youth.* Ottawa, ON: Statistics Canada, Human Resources Development.

Trouilloud, D., Sarrazin, P., Bressoux, P., & Bois, J. (2006). Relation between teachers' early expectations and students' later perceived competence in physical education classes: autonomy-supportive climate as a moderator. *Journal of Educational Psychology, 98,* 75–86.

Tsantis, L. A., Bewick, C. J., & Thouvenelle, S. (2003). Examining some common myths about computer use in the early years [Electronic version]. *Beyond the Journal: Young Children on the Web, 1–9.* Retrieved from www.journal.naeyc.org/btj/200311/CommonTechnoMyths.pdf

Tschannen-Moran, M., & Woolfolk Hoy, A. (2001). Teacher efficacy: Capturing an elusive construct. *Teaching and Teacher Education, 17,* 783–805.

Tschannen-Moran, M., & Woolfolk Hoy, A. (2007). The differential antecedents of self-efficacy beliefs of novice and experienced teachers. *Teaching and Teacher Education, 23,* 944–956.

Tschannen-Moran, M., Woolfolk Hoy, A., & Hoy, W. K. (1998). Teacher efficacy: Its meaning and measure. *Review of Educational Research, 68,* 202–248.

Turiel, E. (1998). The development of morality. In W. Damon (Series Ed.) & N. Eisenberg (Vol. Ed.), *Handbook of child psychology: Vol. 3. Social, emotional, and personality development* (5th ed., pp. 863–932). New York, NY: Wiley.

Turkle, S. (2011). *Alone together: Why we expect more from technology and less from ourselves.* New York, NY: Basic Books.

Turner, J., Patrick, H., & Meyer, D. (2011). Engaging students in learning: A Special Issue dedicated to Jere Brophy. *Theory Into Practice, 50.*

Turner, J. C. (1997). Starting right: Strategies for engaging young literacy learners. In J. T. Guthrie & A. Wigfield (Eds.), *Reading engagement: Motivating readers through integrated instruction* (pp. 183–204). Newark, DE: International Reading Association.

Turner, J. C., & Paris, S. G. (1995). How literacy tasks influence students' motivation for literacy. *The Reading Teacher, 48,* 662–673.

Twardosz, S. (2012). Effects of experience on the brain: The role of neuroscience in early development and education. *Early Education and Development, 23,* 96–119.

Twenge, J. M., & Campbell, W. K. (2001). Age and birth cohort differences in self-esteem: A cross temporal meta-analysis. *Journal of Personality and Social Psychology Review, 5,* 321–344.

Udell, W. (2007). Enhancing adolescent girls' argument skills in reasoning about personal and non-personal decisions. *Cognitive Development, 22,* 341–352.

Uline, C. L., & Johnson, J. F. (2005, Winter). Closing the achievement gap: What will it take? Special Issue of *Theory Into Practice, 44*(1).

Umbreit, J. (1995). Functional analysis of disruptive behavior in an inclusive classroom. *Journal of Early Intervention, 20*(1), 18–29.

Underwood, M. K. (2003). *Social aggression among girls.* New York, NY: Guilford.

UNICEF. (2012). Measuring child poverty: New league tables of child poverty in the world's rich countries. Retrieved July 14, 2014, from www.unicef.ca/sites/default/files/imce_uploads/TAKE%20ACTION/ADVOCATE/DOCS/canadian_companion_updated.pdf

Unsworth, N., & Engle, R. W. (2005). Working memory capacity and fluid abilities: Examining the correlation between Operation Span and Raven. *Intelligence, 33,* 67–81.

Urdan, T. C., & Maehr, M. L. (1995). Beyond a two-goal theory of motivation and achievement: A case for social goals. *Review of Educational Research, 65,* 213–243.

U.S. Department of Education. (2004). *26th Annual report to Congress on the implementation of the Individuals with Disabilities Act, 2005.* Washington DC: Office of Special Education and Rehabilitative Services.

U.S. Department of Education. (2010). OSEP center on positive behavioral interventions and supports. [Website]. *Office of Special Education Programs.* Retrieved from http://pbis.org/school/default.aspx

Usher, E. L., & Pajares, F. (2009). Sources of self-efficacy in mathematics: A validation study. *Contemporary Educational Psychology, 34,* 89–101.

Uttal, D. H., Hand, L. L., & Newcombe, N. S. (2009, April). *Malleability of spatial cognition: Results of a meta-analysis.* Paper presented at the biennial meeting of the Society for Research in Child Development, Denver, CO.

Valentine, J. C., DuBois, D. L., & Cooper, H. (2004). The relations between self-beliefs and academic achievement: A systematic review. *Educational Psychologist, 39,* 111–133.

Valenzuela, A. (1999). *Subtractive schooling: U.S.-Mexican youth and the politics of caring.* Albany, NY: SUNY Press.

Valiente, C., Lemery-Chalfant, K., & Swanson, J. (2010). Predication of kindergarteners' academic achievement from their effortful control and emotionality: Evidence for direct and moderated relations. *Journal of Educational Psychology, 102*(3): 550–560.

Valkenburg, P. M., Schouten, A. P., & Peter, J. (2005). Adolescents' identity experiments on the internet. *New Media & Society, 7*(3), 383–402.

van de Pol, J., Volman, M., & Beishuizen, J. (2010). Scaffolding in Teacher–Student Interaction: A Decade of Research. *Educational Psychology Review, 22*(3): 271–296.

van den Broek, P., Lorch, E. P., & Thurlow, R. (1996). Children's and adult's memory for television stories: The role of causal factors, story-grammar categories, and hierarchical level. *Child Development, 67,* 3010–3028.

van der Maas, H. L. J., Dolan, C. V., Grasman, R. P., Wicherts, J. M., Huizenga, H. M., & Raijmakers, M. E. J. (2006). A dynamic model of general intelligence: The positive manifold of intelligence by mutualism. *Psychological Review, 113,* 842–861.

Van de Walle, J. A., Karp, K. S., & Bay-Williams, J. M. (2010). *Elementary and Middle School Mathematics: Teaching Developmentally,* 7th edition. Pearson.

Van Der Veer, R. (2007). Vygotsky in context: 1900–1935. In H. Daniels, M. Cole, & J. V. Wertsch (Eds.), *The Cambridge companion to Vygotsky* (pp. 21–49). New York, NY: Cambridge University Press.

van Gog, T., Paas, F., & Sweller, J. (Eds.) (2010). Cognitive load theory: Advances in research on worked examples, animations, and cognitive load measurement [special issue]. *Educational Psychology Review, 22*(4).

van Gelderen, A., Schoonen, R., Stoel, R., De Glopper, K., & Hulstijn, J. (2007). Development of adolescent reading comprehension in language 1 and language 2: A longitudinal analysis of constituent components. *Journal of Educational Psychology, 99*(3): 477.

Van Houten, R., & Doleys, D. M. (1983). Are social reprimands effective? In S. Axelrod & J. Apsche (Eds.), *The effects of punishment on human behavior.* San Diego, CA: Academic Press.

van Kraayenoord, C. E., Rice, D., Carroll, A., Fritz, E., Dillon, L., & Hill, A. (2001). *Attention deficit hyperactivity disorder: Impact and implications for Queensland.* Queensland, Australia: Queensland Disability Services. Available online at: www.families.qld.gov.au.

van Laar, C. (2000). The paradox of low academic achievement but high self-esteem in African American students: An attributional account. *Educational Psychology Review, 12,* 33–61.

Van Matre, J. C., Valentine, J. C., & Cooper, H. (2000). Effect of students' after-school activities on teachers' academic expectations. *Contemporary Educational Psychology, 25,* 167–183.

van Merriënboer, J. J. G., & Sweller, J. (2005). Cognitive load and complex learning: Recent developments and future directions. *Educational Psychology Review, 17,* 147–177.

Van Meter, P. (2001). Drawing construction as a strategy for learning from text. *Journal of Educational Psychology, 93,* 129–140.

Van Meter, P., Yokoi, L., & Pressley, M. (1994). College students' theory of note-taking derived from their perceptions of note-taking. *Journal of Educational Psychology, 86,* 323–338.

Vandell, D. L. (2004). Early child care: The known and the unknown. *Merrill-Palmer Quarterly, 50,* 387–414.

Vandewater, E. A., Bickham, D. S., Lee, J. H., Cummings, H. M., Wartella, E. A., & Rideout, V. J. (2005). When the television is always on: Heavy television exposure and young children's development. *American Behavioral Scientist, 48,* 562–567.

Vansteenkiste, M., Lens, W., & Deci, E. L. (2006). Intrinsic versus extrinsic goal contents in self-determination theory: Another look at the quality of academic motivation. *Educational Psychologist, 41,* 19–31.

Vansteenkiste, M., Simons, J., Lens, W., Sheldon, K. M., & Deci, E. L. (2004). Motivating learning, performance, and persistence: The synergistic role of intrinsic goals and autonomy-support. *Journal of Personality and Social Psychology, 87,* 246–260.

Varma, S., McCandliss, B. D., & Schwartz, D. L. (2008). Scientific and pragmatic challenges for bridging education and neuroscience. *Educational Researcher, 37,* 140–152.

Vaughn, S., Levy, S., Coleman, M., & Bos, C. S. (2002). Reading instruction for students with LD and EBD: A synthesis of observation studies. *Journal of Special Education, 36*(1), 2–13.

Vecchio, G. M., Gerbino, M., Pastorelli, C., Del Bove, G., & Caprara, G. V. (2007). Multi-faceted self-efficacy beliefs as predictors of life satisfaction in late adolescence. *Personality and Individual Differences, 43*, 1807–1818.

Veenman, S. (1984). Perceived problems of beginning teachers. *Review of Educational Research, 54*, 143–178.

Veenman, S. (1997). Combination classes revisited. *Educational Research and Evaluation, 65*(4), 319–381.

Vera, A. H., & Simon, H. A. (1993). Situated action: A symbolic interpretation. *Cognitive Science, 17*, 7–48.

Verhallen, M. J. A. J., Bus, A. G., de Jong, M. T. (2006). The promise of multimedia stories for kindergarten children at risk. *Journal of Educational Psychology, 98*(2): 410–419.

Verplaetse, L. S., & Migliacci, N. (2008). Making mainstream content comprehensible through sheltered instruction. In L. S. Verplaetse & N. Migliacci (Eds.), *Inclusive Pedagogy for English Language Learners: A Handbook of Research-Informed Practices* (pp. 127–165). New York: Lawrence Erlbaum.

Vispoel, W. P., & Austin, J. R. (1995). Success and failure in junior high school: A critical incident approach to understanding students' attributional beliefs. *American Educational Research Journal, 32*, 377–412.

Vogt, M. E., Echevarria, J., & Short, D. (2010). *The SIOP Model for Teaching English-Language Arts to English Learners*. Boston: Allyn & Bacon.

Volet, S. (1999). Learning across cultures: Appropriateness of knowledge transfer. *International Journal of Educational Research, 31*, 625–643.

von Glasersfeld, E. (1997). Amplification of a constructivist perspective. *Issues in Education: Contributions from Educational Psychology, 3*, 203–210.

Vroom, V. (1964). *Work and motivation*. New York, NY: Wiley.

Vygotsky, L. S. (1978). *Mind in society: The development of higher mental process*. Cambridge, MA: Harvard University Press.

Vygotsky, L. S. (1986). *Thought and language*. Cambridge, MA: MIT Press.

Vygotsky, L. S. (1987a). The genetic roots of thinking and speech. In R. W. Rieber & A. S. Carton (Eds.), *Problems of general psychology: Vol. 1. Collected works* (pp. 101–120). New York, NY: Plenum. (Work originally published in 1934.)

Vygotsky, L. S. (1987b). *Problems of general psychology*. New York, NY: Plenum.

Vygotsky, L. S. (1987c). Thought and word. In R.W. Rieber & A. S. Carton (Eds.), *Collected works of L. S. Vygotsky: Vol. 1. Problems of general psychology* (pp. 243–285). New York, NY: Plenum. (Work originally published in 1934.)

Vygotsky, L. S. (1993). *The collected works of L. S. Vygotsky: Vol. 2* (J. Knox & C. Stevens, Trans.). New York, NY: Plenum.

Vygotsky, L. S. (1997). *Educational psychology* (R. Silverman, Trans.). Boca Raton, FL: St. Lucie.

Wade, S. E., Schraw, G., Buxton, W. M., & Hayes, M. T. (1993). Seduction of the strategic reader: Effects of interest on strategies and recall. *Reading Research Quarterly, 28*, 3–24.

Waddell, C. (2007). Improving the mental health of young children: A discussion paper prepared for the British Columbia Healthy Child Alliance. Retrieved June 28, 2014, from www.firstcallbc.org/pdfs/Communities/4-alliance.pdf

Wadsworth, B. J. (1978). *Piaget for the classroom teacher*. Oxford, England: Longman.

Waits, B. K., & Demana, F. (2000). Calculators in mathematics teaching and learning: Past, present, future. In M. J. Burke & F. R. Curcio (Eds.), *Learning mathematics for a new century: NCTM 2000 Yearbook* (pp. 51–66). Reston, VA: National Council of Teachers of Mathematics.

Walberg, H. J. (1990). Productive teaching and instruction: Assessing the knowledge base. *Phi Delta Kappan, 72*, 470–478.

Wald, J. (2001, August 29). The failure of zero tolerance. *Salon Magazine*. Retrieved from www.salon.com/mwt/feature/2001/08/29/zero_tolerance/index.html?sid=1046257

Walker, J. E., Shea, T. M., & Bauer, A. M. (2004). *Behavior management: A practical approach for educators*. Upper Saddle River, NJ: Merrill/Prentice Hall.

Walker, L. J. (1991). Sex differences in moral reasoning. In W. M. Kurtines & J. L. Gewirtz (Eds.), *Handbook of moral behavior and development* (Vol. 2, pp. 333–362). Hillsdale, NJ: Erlbaum.

Walker, L. J., & Pitts, R. C. (1998). Naturalistic conceptions of moral maturity. *Developmental Psychology, 34*, 403–419.

Walker, L. J., Pitts, R. C., Hennig, K. H., & Matsuba, M. K. (1995). Reasoning about morality and real-life moral problems. In M. Killen & D. Hart (Eds.), *Morality in everyday life: Developmental perspectives* (pp. 371–407). Cambridge, England: Cambridge University Press.

Walker, V. S. (1996). *Their highest potential*. Chapel Hill, NC: University of North Carolina Press.

Walqui, A. (2008). The development of teacher expertise to work with adolescent English learners: A model and a few priorities. In L. S. Verplaetse & N. Migliacci (Eds.), *Inclusive pedagogy for English language learners: A handbook of research-informed practices* (pp. 103–125). New York, NY: Lawrence Erlbaum.

Wang, A. Y., & Thomas, M. H. (1995). Effects of keywords on long-term retention: Help or hindrance? *Journal of Educational Psychology, 87*, 468–475.

Wang, A. Y., Thomas, M. H., & Ouellette, J. A. (1992). Keyword mnemonic and retention of second-language vocabulary words. *Journal of Educational Psychology, 84*, 520–528.

Wang, M. C., & Palincsar, A. S. (1989). Teaching students to assume an active role in their learning. In M. Reynolds (Ed.), *Knowledge base for the beginning teacher* (pp. 71–84). New York, NY: Pergamon.

Ward, L. M. (2004). Wading through the stereotypes: Positive and negative associations between media use and Black adolescents' conception of self. *Developmental Psychology, 40*, 284–294.

Warren, J. S., Bohanon-Edmonson, H. M., Turnbull, A. P., Sailor, W., Wickham, D., Griggs, P., & Beech, S. E. (2006). School-wide positive behavior support: Addressing behavior problems that impede student learning. *Educational Psychology Review, 18*, 187–198.

Waterhouse, L. (2006). Multiple intelligences, the Mozart effect, and emotional intelligence: A critical review. *Educational Psychologist, 41*, 207–225.

Waxman, S. R., & Lidz, J. L. (2006). Early word learning. In D. Kuhn & R. S. Siegler (Eds.), *Handbook of child psychology: Vol. 2. Cognition, perception, and language* (6th ed., pp. 299–335). New York, NY: Wiley.

Wayne, A. J., & Youngs, P. (2003). Teacher characteristics and student achievement gains: A review. *Review of Educational Research, 73*, 89–122.

Webb, N. M., Farivar, S. H., & Mastergeorge, A. M. (2002). Productive helping in cooperative groups. *Theory Into Practice, 41*, 13–20.

Webb, N. M., & Mastergeorge, A. M. (2003). The development of students' helping behavior and learning in peer-directed small groups. *Cognition and Instruction, 21*, 361–428.

Webb, N. M., & Palincsar, A. (1996). Group processes in the classroom. In D. C. Berliner & R. C. Calfee (Eds.), *Handbook of educational psychology* (pp. 841–876). New York, NY: Macmillan.

Weil, E. (2008, March 2). Should boys and girls be taught separately? *The New York Times Magazine*, pp. 33–45+.

Weiner, B. (1979). A theory of motivation for some classroom experiences. *Journal of Educational Psychology, 71*, 3–25.

Weiner, B. (1986). *An attributional theory of motivation and emotion*. New York, NY: Springer.

Weiner, B. (1994a). Ability versus effort revisited: The moral determinants of achievement evaluation an achievement as a moral system. *Educational Psychologist, 29*, 163–172.

Weiner, B. (1994b). Integrating social and persons theories of achievement striving. *Review of Educational Research, 64*, 557–575.

Weiner, B. (2000). Interpersonal and intrapersonal theories of motivation from an attributional perspective. *Educational Psychology Review, 12*, 1–14.

Weiner, B. (2010). The development of an attribution-based theory of motivation: A history of ideas. *Educational Psychologist, 45*, 28–36.

Weiner, B., & Graham, S. (1989). Understanding the motivational role of affect: Lifespan research from an attributional perspective. *Cognition and Emotion, 4*, 401–419.

Weinert, F. E., & Helmke, A. (1995). Learning from wise mother nature or big brother instructor: The wrong choice as seen from an educational perspective. *Educational Psychologist, 30*, 135–143.

Weinstein, C. (1988). Preservice teachers' expectations about the first year of teaching. *Teaching and Teacher Education, 4*, 31–41.

Weinstein, C. E. (1994). Learning strategies and learning to learn. In *International encyclopedia of education*. New York, NY: Pergamon.

Weinstein, C. S. (1977). Modifying student behavior in an open classroom through changes in the physical design. *American Educational Research Journal, 14*, 249–262.

Weinstein, C. S. (1999). Reflections on best practices and promising programs: Beyond assertive classroom discipline. In H. J. Freiberg (Ed.), *Beyond behaviorism: Changing the classroom management paradigm* (pp. 147–163). Boston, MA: Allyn & Bacon.

Weinstein, C. S. (2007). *Middle and secondary classroom management: Lessons from research and practice* (3rd ed.). New York, NY: McGraw-Hill.

Weinstein, C. S., & Mignano, A. (2007). *Elementary classroom management: Lessons from research and practice* (4th ed.). New York, NY: McGraw-Hill.

Weinstein, C. S., Romano, M. E., & Mignano, A. J. (2011). Elementary classroom management: *Lessons from research and practice* (5th ed.). New York, NY: McGraw-Hill.

Weinstein, R. S., Madison, S. M., & Kuklinski, M. R. (1995). Raising expectations in schools: Obstacles and opportunities for change. *American Educational Research Journal, 32*, 121–159.

Weinstein, C. S., & Novodvorsky, I. (2011). *Middle and Secondary Classroom Management* (4th edition). New York, NY: McGraw-Hill.

Weisberg, R. W. (1993). *Creativity: Beyond the myth of genius*. New York, NY: W. H. Freeman.

Wellman, H. M., Baron-Cohen, S., Caswell, R., Gomez, J.C., Swettenham, J., Toye, E., & Lagattuta, K. (2002). Thought bubbles help children with autism acquire an alternative to a theory of mind. *Autism, 6*, 343–363.

Welsh, J. A., Nix, R. L., Blair, C., Bierman, K. L., & Nelson, K. E. (2010). The development of cognitive skills and gains in academic school readiness for children from low-income families. *Journal of Educational Psychology, 102*(1): 43–53.

Wenger, E. (1998). *Communities of practice: learning, meaning, and identity.* New York, NY: Cambridge University Press.

Wentzel, K. R. (1999). Social-motivational processes and interpersonal relations: Implications for understanding motivation in school. *Journal of Educational Psychology, 91,* 76–97.

Wentzel, K. R. (2002). Are effective teachers like good parents? Teaching styles and student adjustment in early adolescence. *Child Development, 73,* 287–301.

Wentzel, K. R., Barry, C. M., & Caldwell, K. A. (2004). Friendships in middle school: Influences on motivation and school adjustment. *Journal of Educational Psychology, 96,* 195–203.

Werker, J. F. Becoming a native listener. *American Science, 77,* 54–59.

Werts, M. G., Culatta, A., & Tompkins, J. R. (2007). *Fundamentals of special education: What every teacher should know* (3rd ed.). Columbus, OH: Pearson/Allyn & Bacon-Merrill.

Wertsch, J. V. (1991). *Voices of the mind: A sociocultural approach to mediated action.* Cambridge, MA: Harvard University Press.

Wertsch, J. V. (2007). Mediation. In H. Daniels, M. Cole, & J. V. Wertsch (Eds.), *The Cambridge companion to Vygotsky* (pp. 178–192). New York, NY: Cambridge University Press.

Wertsch, J. V., & Tulviste, P. (1992). L. S. Vygotsky and contemporary developmental psychology. *Developmental Psychology, 28,* 548–557.

Westberg, K. L., Archambault, F. X., Dodyns, S. M., & Slavin, T. J. (1993). The classroom practices observation study. *Journal of the Education of the Gifted, 16*(2), 120–146.

Westling, E., Andrews, J. A., Hampson, S. E., & Peterson, M. Pubertal timing and substance abuse: The effects of gender, parental monitoring and deviant peers. *Journal of Adolescent Health, 42*(6).

Wharton-McDonald, R., Pressley, M., Rankin, J., Mistretta, J., Yokoi, L., & Ettenberger, S. (1997). Effective primary-grades literacy instruction = Balanced literacy instruction. *The Reading Teacher, 50,* 518–521.

Wheatley, K. F. (2002). The potential benefits of teacher efficacy doubts for educational reform. *Teaching and Teacher Education, 18,* 5–22.

Wheatley, K. F. (2005). The case for reconceptualizing teacher efficacy research. *Teaching and Teacher Education, 21,* 747–766.

White, S., & Tharp, R. G. (1988, April). *Questioning and wait-time: A cross cultural analysis.* Paper presented at the annual meeting of the American Educational Research Association, New Orleans, LA.

Whitehead, A. N. (1929). *The aims of education.* New York, NY: Macmillan.

Whitehurst, G. J. (2003, April). *The Institute of Educational Sciences: New wine, new bottles.* Paper presented at the annual meeting of the American Educational Research Association, Chicago, IL.

Whitehurst, G. J., Epstein, J. N., Angell, A. L., Payne, A. C., Crone, D. A., & Fischel, J. E. (1994). Outcomes of an emergent literacy program in headstart. *Journal of Educational Psychology, 86,* 542–555.

Wigfield, A., Byrnes, J. P., & Eccles, J. S. (2006). Development during early and middle adolescence. In P. A. Alexander & P. H. Winne (Eds.), *Handbook of educational psychology* (2nd ed., pp. 87–113). Mahwah, NJ: Erlbaum.

Wigfield, A., & Eccles, J. (1989). Test anxiety in elementary and secondary school students. *Educational Psychologist, 24,* 159–183.

Wigfield, A., & Eccles, J. S. (2002a). Students' motivation during the middle school years. In J. Aronson (Ed.), *Improving academic development: Impact of psychological factors in education* (pp. 159–184). New York, NY: Academic Press.

Wigfield, A., & Eccles, J. S. (2002b). The development of competence beliefs, expectancies of success, and achievement values from childhood through adolescence. In A. Wigfield & J. Eccles (Eds.), *Development of achievement motivation* (pp. 91–120). San Diego, CA: Academic Press.

Wigfield, A., Eccles, J. S., MacIver, D., Rueman, D., & Midgley, C. (1991). Transitions during early adolescence: Changes in children's domain-specific self-perceptions and general self-esteem across the transition to junior high school. *Developmental Psychology, 27,* 552–565.

Wigfield, A., Eccles, J. S., & Pintrich, P. R. (1996). Development between the ages of 11 and 25. In D. Berliner & R. Calfee (Eds.), *Handbook of educational psychology* (pp. 148–185). New York, NY: Macmillan.

Wigfield, A., & Wentzel, K. R. (2007). Introduction to motivation at school: Interventions that work. *Educational Psychologist, 42,* 191–196.

Wiggins, G. (1989). Teaching to the authentic test. *Educational Leadership, 46*(7), 41–47.

Wiggins, G. (1991). Standards, not standardization: Evoking quality student work. *Educational Leadership, 48*(5), 18–25.

Wiggins, G. (1993). Assessment, authenticity, context, and validity. *Phi Delta Kappan, 75,* 200–214.

Wikipedia. (2014, June). The suicide of Amanda Todd. Retrieved August 2, 2014, from http://en.wikipedia.org/wiki/Suicide_of_Amanda_Todd

Wikipedia. (2014, July). Anti-bullying day. Retrieved August 2, 2014, from http://en.wikipedia.org/wiki/Anti-Bullying_Day

Wikipedia. (2014, July). Suicide of Rehtaeh Parsons. Retrieved August 2, 2014, from http://en.wikipedia.org/wiki/Suicide_of_Rehtaeh_Parsons

Willcutt, E. G., Pennington, B. F., Boada, R., Ogline, J. S., Tunick, R. A., Chhabidas, N. A., & Olson, R. K. (2001). A comparison of the cognitive deficits in reading disability and attention-deficit/hyperactivity disorder. *Journal of Abnormal Psychology, 110,* 157–172.

Williams, C., & Bybee J. (1994). What do children feel guilty about? Developmental and gender differences. *Developmental Psychology, 30,* 617–623.

Williams, J. (2002). Using the Theme Scheme to improve story comprehension. In C. C. Block & M. Pressley (Eds.), *Comprehension instruction: Research-based best practices* (pp. 126–139). New York, NY: Guilford.

Williams, T., & Williams, K. (2010). Self-efficacy and performance in mathematics: Reciprocal determinism in 33 nations. *Journal of Educational Psychology, 102*(2): 453–466.

Willingham, D. T. (2004). Reframing the mind. *Education Next, 4*(3), 19–24.

Willingham, W. W., & Cole, N. S. (1997). *Gender and fair assessment.* Mahwah, NJ: Erlbaum.

Willis, J. (2009). What brain research suggests for teaching reading strategies. *Educational Forum, 73,* 333–346.

Willis, P. (1977). *Learning to labor.* Lexington, MA: D.C. Heath.

Willoughby, T., Porter, L., Belsito, L., & Yearsley, T. (1999). Use of elaboration strategies by grades two, four, and six. *Elementary School Journal, 99,* 221–231.

Wilson, A. M., Armstrong, C. D., Furrie, A. & Walcot, E. (2009). The mental health of Canadians with self-reported learning disabilities. *Journal of Learning Disabilities, 42,* 24–40.

Wilson, M. (2001). The case for sensorimotor coding in working memory. *Psychonomic Bulletin and Review, 8,* 44–57.

Wilson, M. (2002). Six views of embodied cognition. *Psychonomic Bulletin and Review, 9,* 625–636.

Wilson M., & Trainin, G. (2007). First-grade students' motivation and achievement for reading, writing, and spelling. *Reading Psychology, 28,* 257–282.

Windschitl, M. (2002). Framing constructivism in practice as the negotiation of dilemmas; An analysis of the conceptual, pedagogical, cultural, and political challenges facing teachers. *Review of Educational Research, 72,* 131–175.

Windsor, J., Glaze, L. E., Koga, S. F., & BEIP Core Group. (2007). Language acquisition with limited input: Romanian institution and foster care. *Journal of Speech, Language, and Hearing Research, 50,* 1365–1381.

Winett, R. A., & Winkler, R. C. (1972). Current behavior modification in the classroom: Be still, be quiet, be docile. *Journal of Applied Behavior Analysis, 15,* 499–504.

Wink, J., & Putney, L. (2002). *A vision of Vygotsky.* Boston, MA: Allyn & Bacon.

Winne, P. H. (1995). Inherent details in self-regulated learning. *Educational Psychologist, 30,* 173–188.

Winne, P. H. (2001). Self-regulated learning viewed from models of information processing. In B. J. Zimmerman & D. H. Schunk (Eds.), *Self-regulated learning and academic achievement: Theoretical perspectives* (2nd ed., pp. 153–189). Mahwah, NJ: Erlbaum.

Winne, P. H. (2011). A cognitive and metacognitive analysis of self-regulated learning. In B. J. Zimmerman and D. H. Schunk (Eds.), *Handbook of self-regulation of learning and performance* (pp. 15–32). New York, NY: Routledge.

Winne, P. H. (2013). Learning strategies, study skills and self-regulated learning in postsecondary education. In M. B. Paulsen (Ed.), *Higher education: Handbook of theory and research. Volume 28* (pp. 377–403). Dordrecht: Springer.

Winne, P. H., & Hadwin, A. F. (1998). Studying as self-regulated learning. In D. J. Hacker, J. Dunlosky, & A. C. Graesser (Eds.), *Metacognition in educational theory and practice* (pp. 277–304). Mahwah, NJ: Erlbaum.

Winne, P. H., & Hadwin, A. F. (2010). Self-regulated learning and sociocognitive theory. In P. Peterson, E. Baker & B. McGaw (Eds.), *International encyclopedia of education* (Vol. 5, pp. 503–508). Amsterdam, the Netherlands: Elsevier.

Winne, P. H., & Perry, N. E. (2000). Measuring self-regulated learning. In P. Pintrich, M. Boekaerts, & M. Zeidner (Eds.), *Handbook of self-regulation* (pp. 531–566). Orlando, FL: Academic Press.

Winner, E. (2000). The origins and ends of giftedness. *American Psychologist, 55,* 159–169.

Winner, E. (2003). Musical giftedness. *Bulletin of Psychology and the Arts, 4,* 1, 2–5.

Winsler, A., Carlton, M. P., & Barry, M. J. (2000). Age-related changes in preschool children's systematic use of private speech in a natural setting. *Journal of Child Language, 27,* 665–687.

Winsler, A., & Naglieri, J. A. (2003). Overt and covert verbal problem-solving strategies: Developmental trends in use, awareness, and relations with task performance in children age 5 to 17. *Child Development, 74*, 659–678.

Winzer, M. A. (2006). *Children with exceptionalities in Canadian classrooms* (6th ed.). Toronto, ON: Prentice-Hall.

Wittrock, M. C. (1982, March). *Educational implications of recent research on learning and memory*. Paper presented at the annual meeting of the American Educational Research Association, New York, NY.

Wittrock, M. C. (Ed.). (1986). *Handbook of research on teaching* (3rd ed.). New York, NY: Macmillan.

Wittrock, M. C. (1992). An empowering conception of educational psychology. *Educational Psychologist, 27*, 129–142.

Wittwer, J., & Renkl, A. (2010). How effective are instructional explanations in example-based learning? A meta-analytic review. *Educational Psychology Review, 22*, 393–409.

Wolf, D., Bixby, J., Glenn, J., III, & Gardner, H. (1991). To use their minds well: New forms of student assessment. *Review of Research in Education, 17*, 31–74.

Wolf, M., Barzillai, M., Gottwald, S., Miller, L., Spencer, K., Norton, E., . . . Morris, R. (2009). The RAVE-O intervention: Connecting neuroscience to the classroom. *Mind, Brain, and Education, 3*, 84–93.

Wolfe, P. (2010). *Brain matters: Translating research into classroom practice* (2nd ed.). Alexandria, VA: Association for Supervision and Curriculum Development.

Wolters, C. A., Yu, S. L., & Pintrich, P. R. (1996). The relation between goal orientation and students' motivational beliefs and self-regulated learning. *Learning and Individual Differences, 8*, 211–238.

Wong, B. Y. L. (1996). *The ABCs of learning disabilities*. San Diego, CA: Academic Press.

Wong, B. Y. L., Harris, K. R., Graham, S., & Butler, D. L. (2003). Cognitive strategies instruction research in learning disabilities. In H. L. Swanson, K. R. Harris, & S. Graham (Eds.), *Handbook of learning disabilities* (pp. 383–402). New York, NY: Guilford Press.

Wong, L. (1987). Reaction to research findings: Is the feeling of obviousness warranted? *Dissertation Abstracts International, 48/12*, 3709B. (University Microfilms #DA 8801059)

Wood, D., Bruner, J., & Ross, S. (1976). The role of tutoring in problem solving. *British Journal of Psychology, 66*, 181–191.

Woods, B. S., & Murphy, P. K. (2002). Thickening the discussion: What can William James tell us about constructivism? *Educational Theory, 52*, 443–449.

Woodward, A., & Needham, A. (Eds.) (2009). *Learning and the infant mind*. New York, NY: Oxford University Press.

Woolfolk, A. E., & Brooks, D. (1983). Nonverbal communication in teaching. In E. Gordon (Ed.), *Review of research in education* (Vol. 10, pp. 103–150). Washington, DC: American Educational Research Association.

Woolfolk, A. E., & Brooks, D. (1985). The influence of teachers' nonverbal behaviors on students' perceptions and performance. *Elementary School Journal, 85*, 514–528.

Woolfolk, A. E., & Hoy, W. K. (1990). Prospective teachers' sense of efficacy and beliefs about control. *Journal of Educational Psychology, 82*, 81–91.

Woolfolk, A., E. & Perry, N. E. (2012). *Child development*. Boston Allyn & Bacon/Pearson.

Woolfolk, A. & Perry, N. E. (2015). *Child and adolescent development* (2nd Ed.). Boston: Pearson Education.

Woolfolk, A. E., Perry, N., & Winne, P. (2006). *Educational psychology: Third Canadian edition* (3rd ed.). Toronto, ON: Pearson.

Woolfolk Hoy, A., & Burke-Spero, R. (2005). Changes in teacher efficacy during the early years of teaching: A comparison of four measures. *Teaching and Teacher Education, 21*, 343–356.

Woolfolk Hoy, A., Demerath, P., & Pape, S. (2002). Teaching adolescents: Engaging developing selves. In T. Urdan & F. Pajares (Eds.), *Adolescence and education* (Vol. I, pp. 119–169). Greenwich, CT: Information Age Publishing.

Woolfolk Hoy, A., Hoy, W. K., & Davis, H. (2009). Teachers' self-efficacy beliefs. In K. Wentzel & A. Wigfield (Eds.), *Handbook of motivation in school*. Mahwah, NJ: Erlbaum.

Woolfolk Hoy, A., & Murphy, P. K. (2001). Teaching educational psychology to the implicit mind. In R. Sternberg & B. Torff (Eds.), *Understanding and teaching the implicit mind* (pp. 145–185). Mahwah, NJ: Erlbaum.

Woolfolk Hoy, A., Pape, S., & Davis, H. (2006). Teachers' knowledge, beliefs, and thinking. In P. A. Alexander & P. H, Winne (Eds.), *Handbook of educational psychology* (2nd ed.). Mahwah, NJ: Erlbaum.

Woolfolk Hoy, A., & Tschannen-Moran. M. (1999). Implications of cognitive approaches to peer learning for teacher education. In A. O'Donnell & A. King (Eds.), *Cognitive perspectives on peer learning* (pp. 257–284). Mahwah, NJ: Erlbaum.

Woolfolk Hoy, A., & Weinstein, C. S. (2006). Students' and teachers' perspectives about classroom management. In C. Evertson & C. S. Weinstein (Eds.), *Handbook for classroom management: Research, practice, and contemporary issues*. Mahwah, NJ: Erlbaum.

Wout, D., Dasco, H., Jackson, J., & Spencer, S. (2008). The many faces of stereotype threat: Group- and self-threat. *Journal of Experimental Social Psychology, 44*, 792–799.

Wright, S. C., & Taylor, D. M. (1995). Identity and the language of the classroom: Investigating the impact of heritage versus second language instruction on personal and collective self-esteem. *Journal of Educational Psychology, 87*, 241–252.

Wu, W., West, S. G., & Hughes, J. N. (2010). Effect of grade retention in first grade on psychosocial outcomes. *Journal of Educational Psychology, 102*(1): 135–152.

Wyler, R. S. (1988). Social memory and social judgment. In P. Solomon, G. Goethals, C. Kelly, & B. Stephans (Eds.), *Perspectives on memory research*. New York, NY: Springer-Verlag.

Yarhouse, M. A. (2001). Sexual identity development: The influence of valuative frameworks on identity synthesis. *Psychotherapy, 38*(3), 331–341.

Yates, M., & Youniss, J. (1999). Promoting identity development: Ten ideas for school-based service-learning programs. In J. Claus & C. Ogden (Eds.), *Service learning for youth empowerment and social change* (pp. 43–67). New York, NY: Peter Lang.

Ybarra, M. L., & Mitchell, K. J. (2004). Youth engaging in online harassment: associations with caregiver-child relationships, Internet use, and personal characteristics. *Journal of Adolescence, 27*, 319–336.

Yee, A. H. (1992). Asians as stereotypes and students: Misperceptions that persist. *Educational Psychology Review, 4*, 95–132.

Yerkes, R. M., & Dodson, J. D. (1908). The relation of strength of stimulus to rapidity of habit formation. *Journal of Comparative Neurology, 18*, 459–482.

Yont, K.M., Snow, C.E., & Vernon-Feagans, L. (2003). The role of context in mother-child interactions: An analysis of communicative intents expressed during toy play and book reading with 12-month-olds. *Journal of Pragmatics, 35*, 436–454.

Yough, M. (2010, August). *An intervention: Teaching candidates' beliefs and linguistic minority students*. Paper presented at the American Psychological Association Annual Convention, San Diego, CA.

Young, A. J. (1997). I think, therefore I'm motivated: The relations among cognitive strategy use, motivational orientation, and classroom perceptions over time. *Learning and Individual Differences, 9*, 249–283.

Younger, M. R., & Warrington, M. (2006). Would Harry and Hermione have done better in single-sex teaching in coeducational secondary schools in the United Kingdom? *American Educational Research Journal, 43*, 579–620.

Youniss, J., & Yates, M. (1997). *Community service and social responsibility in youth*. Chicago, IL: University of Chicago Press.

Zeidner, M. (1995). Adaptive coping with test situations. *Educational Psychologist, 30*, 123–134.

Zeidner, M. (1998). *Test anxiety: The state of the art*. New York, NY: Plenum.

Zentall, S. S. (1993). Research on the educational implications of attention deficit hyperactivity disorder. *Exceptional Children, 60*, 143–153.

Zhang, L., & Sternberg, R. J. (2005). The threefold model of intellectual styles. *Educational Psychology Review, 17*, 1–53.

Zhou, Z., Peverly, S. T., Beohm, A. E., & Chongde, L. (2001). American and Chinese children's understanding of distance, time, and speed interrelations. *Cognitive Development, 15*, 215–240.

Zimmerman, B. (2011). Motivational sources and outcomes of self-regulated learning and performance. In B. Zimmerman & D. Schunk, (Eds.), *Handbook of self-regulation of learning and performance* (pp. 49–64). New York, NY: Routledge.

Zimmerman, B., & Schunk, D. (Eds.). (2011). *Handbook of self-regulation of learning and performance*. New York, NY: Routledge.

Zimmerman, B. J. (2002). Becoming a self-regulated learner: An overview. *Theory Into Practice, 41*, 64–70.

Zimmerman, B. J., & Schunk, D. H. (Eds.). (2001). *Self-regulated learning and academic achievement: Theoretical perspectives* (2nd ed.). Mahwah, NJ: Erlbaum.

Zimmerman, B. J., & Schunk, D. H. (Eds) (2003). *Educational psychology: A century of contributions* [A Project of Division 15 (Educational Psychology) of the American Psychological Association]. Mahwah, NJ: Erlbaum.

Zimmerman, B. J., & Schunk, D. H. (2004). Self-regulating intellectual processes and outcomes: A social cognitive perspective. In D. Y. Dao & R. J. Sternberg (Eds.), *Motivation, emotion, and cognition: Integrative perspectives on intellectual functioning and development* (pp. 323–350). Mahwah, NJ: Erlbaum.

Zimmerman, D. W. (1981). On the perennial argument about grading "on the curve" in college courses. *Educational Psychologist, 16*, 175–178.

# Name Index

Page numbers followed by italic *f* indicate figures, those followed by italic *t* indicate tables, and those followed by italic *n* indicate notes.

# Subject Index

Page numbers followed by italic *f* indicate figures, and those followed by italic *t* indicate tables.